Derivatives

Derivatives

The theory and practice of financial engineering

Paul Wilmott

www.wilmott.com

JOHN WILEY & SONS
Chichester • New York • Weinheim • Brisbane • Singapore • Toronto

Published by John Wiley & Sons Ltd,
Baffins Lane, Chichester,
West Sussex PO19 IUD, England

National 01243 779777
International (+44) 1243 779777
e-mail (for orders and customer service enquiries): cs-books@wiley.co.uk
Visit our Home Page on http://www.wiley.co.uk
or http://www.wiley.com

Other Wiley Editorial Offices

John Wiley & Sons, Inc., 605 Third Avenue,
New York, NY 10158-0012, USA

WILEY-VCH Verlag GmbH, Pappelallee 3,
D-69469 Weinheim, Germany

Jacaranda Wiley Ltd, 33 Park Road, Milton,
Queensland 4064, Australia

John Wiley & Sons (Canada) Ltd, 22 Worcester Road,
Rexdale, Ontario M9W 1L1, Canada

John Wiley & Sons (Asia) Pte Ltd, 2 Clementi Loop #02-01,
Jin Xing Distripark, Singapore 129809

British Library Cataloguing in Publication Data

A catalogue record for this book is available from the British Library

ISBN 0-471-983 89-6 (HB) 0-471-983 66-7 (PB)

Typeset in 10/12pt Times by Laser Words, Madras, India
Printed and bound in Great Britain by Bookcraft, Midsomer Norton, Somerset
This book is printed on acid-free paper responsibly manufactured from sustainable forestry, in which at least two trees are planted for each one used for paper production.

To all of my students, past and present, with affection

contents

Icon	Meaning
	Points to chapter(s) with a significant amount of related material or more details.
	Example of how something works. This may be a made-up illustration, a real-life practical example or code.
	Definition or description of an important financial or mathematical concept.
	Take a moment to ponder on the topic, answer a question yourself, or consider the validity of an assumption.
	Places marked with this icon are crucially important. Remember the concept, technique or even formulae. These parts make up an 'executive summary' of the book.

prolog

My other books on derivatives were such a success that I decided to write another. This time I have given myself the freedom to write from a more personal perspective. I have also tried to keep to a minimum the previous knowledge needed to get started, giving plenty of details about the things that really matter and few details about things that don't. If I use jargon I hope it makes communication faster and simpler, and does not obscure. Even though my other books were a great success, there were some people who didn't like them, can you believe it? The books received some criticism for their lack of rigor. I'm afraid those people won't like this book either; if anything this book is even worse. I cannot make rigor consistent with readability.

Like many quantitative researchers working in finance, my background is in the physical sciences. My research was, for many years, in various aspects of fluid mechanics. Originally I worked in the very 'classical' area of free surface flows; my doctorate was on the motion of submarines. Later I moved on to work on 'real-world' problems originating in industry. As a general 'mathematical modeler' I worked on the manufacture of fibers (glass and fabric), the design of aircraft wings and the cooling of turbine blades, the distribution of rubble after an explosion, and many, many more problems. Many of these problems were presented at industrial workshops and week-long 'study groups' at Oxford University. I was thus trained in mathematical techniques, mathematical modeling and, most importantly, open-mindedness. This Oxford style of working in teams to solve real-world problems, since exported worldwide, was created by John Ockendon and Alan Tayler CBE. Then, in the late 'eighties, I became aware that there were interesting math problems in the subject of finance.

The classical subject of fluid mechanics is centered around the Navier–Stokes equation, which is based on Newtonian principles, and conservation of mass. Experiments in fluids are predictable, using the classical model, with repeatable results. Finance is not fluid mechanics. Having worked on both classical and non-classical problems, I can see the potential of quantitative models and their limitations.

Financial modeling is both an art and a science. Some researchers take an axiomatic approach to the subject. One of the reasons for this is to make the subject respectable. (Anything having to do with money in academia is suspect.) I believe this approach to be inappropriate when it comes to practice; every financial axiom I've ever seen is demonstrably wrong. Most of the sophisticated finance theory is based on incorrect assumptions. The real question is *how* wrong is the theory, and how useful is it regardless of its validity. As I work more and more in this area, so I question more and more the accepted core of the subject. Even finance has its classical side, and because of my background I can distinguish between the pseudo-classical of finance and the real thing of the physical sciences. Everything that you read in any theoretical finance book, including this one, you must take with a generous pinch of salt.

The book contains the tried and tested ideas that have become popular over the years. But they have not gone without criticism here. There are also plenty of new and untried techniques and models, some of them my own personal favorites. Math finance is a relatively young subject and there is plenty of room for people to experiment.

The book is laid out as follows. Part One contains the basics of the subject of finance, introduced in the equity world. Fundamental concepts such as hedging and no arbitrage are introduced. Part Two describes some complex contracts and explains path dependency. Part Three takes us beyond the classical Black–Scholes world, introducing new models, some of which are unpublished. Part Four is about models for interest rates and fixed-income products. Part Five describes and models some problems in risk management, including credit risk. Part Six describes several numerical methods for solving the financial problems. At the beginning of each part is a more-detailed description of the contents of the chapters in that part. Most chapters are quite short. This is deliberate, the book is long and to make it manageable I have divided it up into easily-digested chunks.

There are Visual Basic programs throughout the book. These programs show how to implement most of the methods I describe. I have chosen VB rather than C++ because everyone has Excel, and thus VB, on their PCs. Everyone who knows how to start a 'module' can start to program. In several of the chapters are real-life contract term sheets. These show the details of specific contracts, and together with the analysis of data and several case studies ensure that the theory and the practice go hand in hand. At the end of each chapter there are suggestions for further reading, with a few pertinent comments. Finally there are exercises. These were mostly written by my student, David Epstein. He has also produced an Instructor's Manual which provides worked solutions to all these exercises. A copy of the Manual (ISBN 0471 986 704) is available, free of charge, to instructors who intend to adopt *Derivatives: The theory and practice of financial engineering* for their course. Requests should be directed to College Publishing, John Wiley & Sons Ltd, Baffins Lane, Chichester, West Sussex, PO19 1UD, UK (Fax: +44 1243 779777).

I hope that the book will have a wide readership, and I have 'road tested' it on many different types of people who might be interested: students; academics; practitioners; programmers and laymen. I would like to thank the following for their advice and help (some of them helped *a lot*): Hyungsok Ahn, Mohammed Apabhai, Richard Arkell, Colin Atkinson F.R.S., David Bakstein, Bafkam Bim, Ingrid Blauer, Mauricio Bouabci, Daniel Bruno, Russel Caflisch, Keesup Choe, Elsa Cortina, Grace Davies, Sam Ehrlichman, David Epstein, Rich Haber, Einar Holstad, Philip Hua, Arefin Huq, Jesse Jones, Varqa Khadem, Fouad Khennach, Christine Kirton, Ohad Kondor, Mariano Kruskevitch, Eli Lilly, Nick Mayor, Rob McComb, Asli Oztukel, Howard Roark, Aram Schlosberg, Philipp Schönbucher, Samantha Shore, Richard Skora, Elizabeth Whalley, Oscar Wilmott, Zachary Wilmott and David Wilson. Many of these commented on the manuscript. In the main, I have incorporated their suggestions. Undoubtedly some errors remain; for these I naturally blame my parents.

My contribution to the 'he/she' debate is to use 'he' throughout. Although, of course, believing in the natural superiority of females in every way, shape and form, I was reluctantly persuaded to use the masculine form. Should conventions change, I will ensure that future editions of the book are kept fully up-to-date in this important matter. I would hate to offend anyone.

On to business. For information about training courses on which I teach, either open or in-house, see www.wilmott.com. To download research papers and to find out about our part-time Postgraduate Diploma in Mathematical Finance visit Oxford's Mathematical Finance

Group website at www.maths.ox.ac.uk/mfg. If you want to employ me as a consultant, talk about my research, offer me a job or tell me how great this book is, please email me on paul@wilmott.com. In fact, whether you like the book or not, email me just for a chat.

ABOUT THE AUTHOR

Paul Wilmott is the immensely talented author of several books and many research articles on finance. He is a Royal Society University Research Fellow at Oxford University and Imperial College, London (the second best academic job in the UK), Director of software companies, Partner in this-and-that, and consultant. He is a founding editor-in-chief of the journal *Applied Mathematical Finance* and an editor of others. He owns patents, trademarks and, until he crashes them, beautiful cars. His ambition is to continue to irritate his colleagues in academia by earning far too much money. He has two children, Oscar and Zachary and is married to Ingrid. He is a typical Scorpio.

Two acid-free trees were planted for every student pulped in the making of this book.

PART ONE
basic theory of derivatives

The first part of the book contains the fundamentals of derivatives theory and practice. It only deals with the equity, currency and commodity worlds since these are simpler than the fixed-income world, for technical reasons. I introduce the important concepts of hedging and no arbitrage, on which most sophisticated finance theory is based.

The assumptions, key concepts and results in Part One make up what is loosely known as the 'Black–Scholes world,' named for Fisher Black and Myron Scholes who, together with Robert Merton, first conceived them. Their original work was published in 1973, after some resistance (the famous equation was first written down in 1969). In October 1997 Myron Scholes and Robert Merton were awarded the Nobel Prize for Economics for their work, Fisher Black having died in August 1995. The *New York Times* of Wednesday, October 15th 1997 wrote: 'Two North American scholars won the Nobel Memorial Prize in Economic Science yesterday for work that enables investors to price accurately their bets on the future, a breakthrough that has helped power the explosive growth in financial markets since the 1970s and plays a profound role in the economics of everyday life.'

Part One is self contained, requiring little knowledge of finance or any more than elementary calculus.

Chapter 1: Products and Markets An overview of the workings of the financial markets and their products. A chapter such as this is obligatory. However, my readers will fall into one of two groups. Either they will know everything in this chapter and much, much more besides. Or they will know little, in which case what I write will not be enough.

Chapter 2: Derivatives An introduction to options, options markets, market conventions. Definitions of the common terms, simple no arbitrage, put–call parity and elementary trading strategies.

Chapter 3: The Random Behavior of Assets An examination of data for various financial quantities, leading to a model for the random behaviour of prices. Almost all of sophisticated finance theory assumes that prices are random, the question is how to model that randomness.

Chapter 4: Elementary Stochastic Calculus We'll need a little bit of theory for manipulating our random variables. I keep the requirements down to the bare minimum. The key concept is Itô's lemma which I will try to introduce in as accessible a manner as possible.

Chapter 5: The Black–Scholes Model I present the classical model for the fair value of options on stock, currencies and commodities. This is the chapter in which I describe delta hedging and no arbitrage and show how they lead to a unique price for an option. This is the foundation for most quantitative finance theory and I will be building on this foundation for much, but by no means all, of the book.

Chapter 6: Partial Differential Equations Partial differential equations play an important role in most physical applied mathematics. They also play a role in finance. Most of my readers trained in the physical sciences, engineering and applied mathematics will be comfortable with the idea that a partial differential equation is almost the same as 'the answer,' the two being separated by at most some computer code. If you are not sure of this connection I hope that you will persevere with the book. This requires some faith on your part, you may have to read the book through twice: I have necessarily had to relegate the numerics, the real 'answer,' to the last few chapters.

Chapter 7: The Black–Scholes Formulae and the 'Greeks' From the Black–Scholes partial differential equation we can find formulae for the prices of some options. Derivatives of option prices with respect to variables or parameters are important for hedging. I will explain some of the most important such derivatives and how they are used.

Chapter 8: Simple Generalizations of the Black–Scholes World Some of the assumptions of the Black–Scholes world can be dropped or stretched with ease. I will describe several of these. Later chapters are devoted to more extensive generalizations.

Chapter 9: Early Exercise and American Options Early exercise is of particular importance financially. It is also of great mathematical interest. I will explain both of these aspects.

Chapter 10: Probability Density Functions and First Exit Times The random nature of financial quantities means that we cannot say with certainty what the future holds in store. For that reason we need to be able to describe that future in a probabilistic sense.

Chapter 11: Multi-asset Options Another conceptually simple generalization of the basic Black–Scholes world is to options on more than one underlying asset. Theoretically simple, this extension has its own particular problems in practice.

Chapter 12: The Binomial Model One of the reasons that option theory has been so successful is that the ideas can be explained and implemented very easily with no complicated mathematics. This chapter is a slight digression, but it's hard not to include it.

CHAPTER 1
products and markets

In this Chapter...

- the time value of money
- an introduction to equities, commodities, currencies and indices
- fixed and floating interest rates
- futures and forwards
- no arbitrage, one of the main building blocks of finance theory

1.1 INTRODUCTION

This first chapter is a very gentle introduction to the subject of finance, and is mainly just a collection of definitions and specifications concerning the financial markets in general. There is little technical material here, and the one technical issue, the 'time value of money,' is extremely simple. I will give the first example of 'no arbitrage.' This is important, being one part of the foundation of derivatives theory. Whether you read this chapter thoroughly or just skim it will depend on your background: mathematicians new to finance may want to spend more time on it than practitioners, say.

1.2 THE TIME VALUE OF MONEY

The simplest concept in finance is that of the **time value of money**; $1 today is worth more than $1 in a year's time. This is because of all the things we can do with $1 over the next year. At the very least, we can put it under the mattress and take it out in one year. But instead of putting it under the mattress we could invest it in a gold mine, or a new company. If those are too risky, then lend the money to someone who is willing to take the risks and give you back the dollar with a little bit extra, the **interest**. That is what banks do, they borrow your money and invest it in various risky ways, but by spreading their risk over many investments they reduce their overall risk. And by borrowing money from many people they can invest in ways that the average individual cannot. The banks compete for your money by offering high interest rates. Free markets and the ability to quickly and cheaply change banks ensure that interest rates are fairly consistent from one bank to another.

I am going to denote interest rates by r. Although rates vary with time I am going to assume for the moment that they are constant. We can talk about several types of interest. First of all there is **simple** and **compound interest**. Simple interest is when the interest you receive is based only on the amount you initially invest, whereas compound interest is when you also get interest on your interest. Compound interest is the only case of relevance. And compound interest comes in two forms, **discretely compounded** and **continuously compounded**. Let me illustrate how they both work.

Suppose I invest \$1 in a bank at a discrete interest rate of r paid once *p.a.*. At the end of one year my bank account will contain

$$1 \times (1 + r).$$

If the interest rate is 10% I will have one dollar and ten cents. After two years I will have

$$1 \times (1 + r) \times (1 + r) = (1 + r)^2,$$

or one dollar and twenty-one cents. After n years I will have $(1 + r)^n$. That is an example of discrete compounding.

Now suppose I receive m interest payments at a rate of r/m *p.a.*. After one year I will have

$$\left(1 + \frac{r}{m}\right)^m. \tag{1.1}$$

Now I am going to imagine that these interest payments come at increasingly frequent intervals, but at an increasingly smaller interest rate: I am going to take the limit $m \to \infty$. This will lead to a rate of interest that is paid continuously. Expression (1.1) becomes

$$\left(1 + \frac{r}{m}\right)^m = e^{m \log(1+(r/m))} \sim e^r.$$

That is how much money I will have in the bank after one year if the interest is continuously compounded. And similarly, after a time t I will have an amount

$$e^{rt} \tag{1.2}$$

in the bank. Almost everything in this book assumes that interest is compounded continuously.

Another way of deriving the result (1.2) is via a differential equation. Suppose I have an amount $M(t)$ in the bank at time t. How much does this increase in value from one day to the next? If I look at my bank account at time t and then again a short while later, time $t + dt$, the amount will have increased by

$$M(t + dt) - M(t) \approx \frac{dM}{dt}\,dt + \cdots,$$

where the right-hand side comes from a Taylor series expansion. But I also know that the interest I receive must be proportional to the amount I have, M, the interest rate, r, and the timestep, dt. Thus

$$\frac{dM}{dt}\,dt = rM(t)\,dt.$$

Dividing by dt gives the ordinary differential equation

$$\boxed{\frac{dM}{dt} = rM(t)}$$

the solution of which is

$$M(t) = M(0)e^{rt}.$$

If the initial amount at $t = 0$ was \$1 then I get (1.2) again.

This equation relates the value of the money I have now to the value in the future. Conversely, if I know I will get one dollar at time T in the future, its value at an earlier time t is simply

$$e^{-r(T-t)}.$$

I can relate cashflows in the future to their **present value** by multiplying by this factor. As an example, suppose that r is 5% i.e. $r = 0.05$, then the present value of \$1,000,000 to be received in two years is

$$\$1{,}000{,}000 \times e^{-0.05\times 2} = \$904{,}837.$$

The present value is clearly less than the future value.

Interest rates are a very important factor determining the present value of future cashflows. For the moment I will only talk about one interest rate, and that will be constant. In later chapters I will generalize.

1.3 EQUITIES

The most basic of financial instruments is the **equity**, **stock** or **share**. This is the ownership of a small piece of a company. If you have a bright idea for a new product or service then you could raise capital to realise this idea by selling off future profits in the form of a stake in your new company. The investors may be friends, your Aunt Joan, a bank, or a venture capitalist. The investor in the company gives you some cash, and in return you give him a contract stating how much of the company he owns. The **shareholders** who own the company between them then have some say in the running of the business, and technically the directors of the company are meant to act in the best interests of the shareholders. Once your business is up and running, you could raise further capital for expansion by issuing new shares.

This is how small businesses begin. Once the small business has become a large business, your Aunt Joan may not have enough money hidden under the mattress to invest in the next expansion. At this point shares in the company may be sold to a wider audience or even the general public. The investors in the business may have no link with the founders. The final point in the growth of the company is with the quotation of shares on a regulated stock exchange so that shares can be bought and sold freely, and capital can be raised efficiently and at the lowest cost.

In Figure 1.1 I show an excerpt from The *Wall Street Journal* of 23rd December 1997. This shows a small selection of the many stocks traded on the New York Stock Exchange. The listed information includes highs and lows for the day as well as the change since the previous day's close.

The behavior of the quoted prices of stocks is far from being predictable. In Figure 1.2 I show the Dow Jones Industrial Average over the period May 1979 to October 1995. If we could predict the behavior of stock prices in the future then we could become very rich. Although many people have claimed to be able to predict prices with varying degrees of accuracy, no one has yet made a completely convincing case. In this book I am going to take the point of view that prices have a large element of randomness. This does *not* mean that we cannot model stock prices, but it does mean that the modeling must be done in a probabilistic sense. No doubt the

THE WALL STREET JOURNAL TUESDAY, DECEMBER 23, 1997

NEW YORK STOCK EXCHANGE COMPOSITE TRANSACTIONS

Quotations as of 5 p.m. Eastern Time
Monday, December 22, 1997

-A-A-A-

52 Weeks Hi	52 Weeks Lo	Stock	Sym	Div	Yld %	PE	Vol 100s	Hi	Lo	Close	Net Chg
40 1/2	24 1/4	AAR	AIR	.48	1.2	24	411	39 5/8	38 13/16	38 13/16	...
▲30 11/16	16 1/8	ABM Indus	ABM	.48f	1.6	25	173	31 1/4	30 9/16	30 11/16	+ 3/8
n 24 7/16	18 1/4	ABN AMRO ADR	AAN	.25p	...	...	678	19 1/2	19 1/4	19 1/2	− 1/8
11 1/4	10	ACM Gvt Fd	ACG	.90	8.2	...	805	11	10 15/16	11	+ 1/8
8 1/4	7	ACM OppFd	AOF	.63	7.7	...	471	8 1/4	8 1/8	8 3/16	+ 1/16
10 1/4	8 7/8	ACM SecFd	GSF	.90	8.9	...	1671	10 1/8	10	10 1/8	+ 1/16
7	6 1/4	ACM SpctmFd	SI	.57	8.5	...	2443	6 11/16	6 1/2	6 11/16	+ 1/8
15	12 1/16	ACM MgmdInc	ADF	1.35	9.6	...	584	14 1/4	13 15/16	14 1/16	+ 3/16
10 1/2	9 1/4	ACM MgdIncFd	AMF	.90	9.0	...	288	10 1/16	10	10	...
▲14 9/16	12 1/2	ACM MuniSec	AMU	.90	6.2	...	176	14 5/8	14 1/2	14 5/8	+ 1/16
27 1/2	17 5/8	♣ACX Tch A	ACX		...	dd	736	24 15/16	24 1/2	24 1/2	− 7/16
s 49 5/8	21 7/8	♣AES Cp	AES		...	40	4146	41 13/16	40 5/16	40 1/2	− 1 1/2
57 7/8	37 1/2	♣AFLAC	AFL	.46	.9	11	5507	50 3/8	49 7/8	50	...
36 5/16	25	AGCO Cp	AG	.04	.1	11	1101	29 7/16	28 13/16	28 7/8	− 1/2
21 5/8	17 3/4	AGL Res	ATG	1.08	5.4	14	2720	20 3/16	19 7/16	19 7/8	+ 11/16
20 1/4	13 5/8	AgSvcAm	ASV		...	19	25	18	17 7/8	17 7/8	...
n 25 13/16	25	AICI CapTr pf		2.25	8.9	...	180	25 1/2	25 5/16	25 3/8	− 1/8
n 26	19 1/4	AIPC	PLB		...	...	179	24 1/8	23	23 1/8	− 1 1/8
19 1/4	10 7/16	AJL PepsTr	AJP	1.44	13.3	...	701	11	10 3/4	10 13/16	− 3/16
n 24 1/4	22 1/4	AMB Prop	AMB	.13p	...	...	344	24 1/8	23 7/8	24	+ 1/8
n 25 3/16	20	AMF Bowlng	PIN		...	...	780	24 3/16	24	24 1/8	...
24 3/4	21 1/2	♣AMLI Resdntl	AML	1.76f	8.0	17	629	21 15/16	21 7/8	21 7/8	...
56 11/16	33 1/8	♣AMP	AMP	1.04	2.6	30	10317	40 3/4	39 7/16	39 9/16	− 9/16
132 9/16	78 1/4	AMR	AMR		...	10	6783	126 1/8	123 1/8	123 5/8	− 1 1/4
51 1/4	40 7/8	♣ARCO Chm	RCM	2.80	6.1	40	517	45 13/16	44 15/16	45 5/8	+ 11/16
37 5/8	19	ASA	ASA	1.20	5.7	...	698	21 5/16	21 1/16	21 3/16	+ 3/8
▲61 5/8	30 3/4	AT&T	T	1.32	2.1	21	54934	63 15/16	61 3/8	63 15/16	+ 2 5/8
39 7/8	29 1/4	AXA-UAP ADR	AXA	.65p	...	...	538	39 1/4	38 3/4	39 1/4	+ 1/4
s 32 3/8	9 5/8	AamesFnl	AAM	.13	1.1	11	4936	12 5/8	12 3/16	12 5/8	+ 3/16
26 15/16	24 1/2	AbbeyNtl		2.19	8.4	...	4	26 3/16	26 3/16	26 3/16	− 1/8
69 1/4	49 3/4	AbbotLab	ABT	1.08	1.6	25	10830	66 3/8	64 11/16	66 1/16	+ 1 7/16
36 1/8	12 1/2	Abercrombie A	ANF		...	...	774	28 11/16	27 3/8	28 1/4	− 7/16
21	12 1/2	Abitibi g	ABY	.40	...	...	2223	12 7/8	12 3/4	12 13/16	+ 1/16
28 5/8	17 3/4	♣AcceptIns	AIF		...	11	395	24 23/32	23 3/4	23 3/4	− 15/16
32	15 3/4	AccuStaff	ASI		...	37	3716	26 3/8	25 1/2	25 5/8	− 5/8
101 1/16	55 3/4	ACE Ltd	ACL	.96f	1.0	12	1022	94 1/8	93 1/16	93 13/16	+ 1/4
18 1/2	10	AckrlyGrp	AK	.02	.1	27	169	17 1/8	16 11/16	16 11/16	− 7/16
10 3/8	4 7/8	AcmeElec	ACE		...	83	246	5 1/4	5	5	− 1/16
19 3/4	8 1/2	AcmeMetals	AMI		...	dd	377	9 1/8	8 5/8	8 13/16	+ 1/4
24 5/8	14	ACNielsen	ART		...	42	470	23	22 5/8	22 7/8	+ 3/16
29 3/4	15 1/16	Acuson	ACN		...	38	1781	16 11/16	15 15/16	16 1/2	+ 9/16
25 1/2	19 3/8	♣AdamsExp	ADX	1.96e	8.4	...	500	23 5/16	22 7/8	23 1/4	+ 5/16
n 26 1/2	13 3/4	Administaff	ASF		...	...	82	24	23 1/4	24	+ 9/16
48 1/2	17 1/2	♣AdvMicro	AMD		...	dd	13557	19 5/16	18 3/8	18 9/16	− 1/4
27 1/2	10 1/8	Advest	ADV	.16f	.6	16	186	25	24 3/4	24 15/16	+ 1/16
23 5/8	11 3/8	Advo	AD		...	19	543	20 9/16	20 3/8	20 7/16	+ 1/8
12 15/16	7	♣Advocat	AVC		...	9	421	7 15/16	7 1/2	7 1/2	− 3/8
89 11/16	54 5/8	♣AEGON	AEG	1.52e	1.7	23	116	87 5/8	87 1/4	87 3/8	− 1/8
12 1/2	**3 1/8**	**♣Aeroflex**	**ARX**		**...**	**20**	**1342**	**7 1/2**	**7 1/4**	**7 1/2**	**+ 3/8**
57 1/2	32 5/8	AeroVick	ANV	.80	1.6	15	1742	50	48 3/8	49 1/16	− 13/16
n 73 5/8	48	AES Tr pfA		2.69	4.2	...	1	64 3/4	64 3/4	64 3/4	+ 1
27 1/2	26 1/4	AetnaMIPS pfA		2.37	8.9	...	172	26 3/4	26 5/8	26 11/16	...
▼118 1/8	67 1/16	Aetna	AET	.80	1.2	21	8072	68 1/4	66 5/16	67 5/8	− 9/16
104	67 3/4	Aetna pfC		4.76	6.9	...	671	69 1/2	68	68 9/16	− 5/8
30 1/4	19 1/2	AffilCptrSvc	AFA		...	23	2309	25 7/8	25 1/16	25 7/16	+ 5/16
n 29 9/16	23 7/8	AffilMangr	AMG		...	...	782	29 7/16	28 3/8	29	− 9/16
14 3/4	4 5/16	♣AgnicoEgl	AEM	.02m	.4	...	1172	5 9/16	5 1/8	5 3/8	− 1/8
22 3/8	18 3/4	AgreeRlty	ADC	1.84	8.7	14	81	22 1/8	21	21 3/16	...
15 7/8	9 7/8	♣Agrium g	AGU	.11	...	...	1322	11 7/16	11 1/4	11 5/16	− 1/8
▲67 1/4	31 7/8	Ahmanson	AHM	.88	1.3	18	5545	67 13/16	65 1/4	65 3/4	− 7/16
26 3/8	25 3/16	Ahmanson pfC		2.10	8.3	...	26	25 5/16	25 5/16	25 5/16	...
136 15/16	67 3/4	Ahmanson pfD		3.00	2.2	...	37	136	134 5/8	134 5/8	+ 2 5/8
s 31 15/16	19 11/16	Ahold	AHO		...	11	171	26	25 3/4	25 7/8	+ 3/8
27 1/16	13 3/4	AirNetSys	ANS		...	19	141	19 15/16	19 1/4	19 1/4	− 7/8
89 5/8	66 3/8	AirProduct	APD	1.20	1.6	20	3105	77 5/8	76 7/8	77 3/8	+ 3/8
74 7/16	21 1/2	AirbornFrght	ABF	.30	.5	13	1954	61 13/16	60 3/8	60 3/4	+ 3/4
24 3/8	13 3/8	♣Airgas	ARG		...	28	2339	14 5/16	14	14 1/16	− 1/16
17 5/8	9 7/8	Airlease	FLY	1.80a	13.6	8	95	13 1/4	13 1/8	13 3/16	− 1/16
42	22	♣AirTouch	ATI		...	63	8433	39 1/16	38 11/16	39	+ 7/16
37 1/8	25 1/4	♣AirTouch pfB		1.74	5.1	...	90	34 1/2	34 1/4	34 7/16	− 1/16
63	42 1/2	♣AirTouch pfC		2.13	3.6	...	520	60	59 1/8	59 3/4	+ 1 1/8
s 24 1/32	16 1/8	♣AK Steel	AKS	.50	3.0	7	2794	17 1/8	16 3/4	16 15/16	+ 1/16
n 26 5/8	23 3/8	ALr TOPRS		1.90	7.5	...	119	25 7/16	25 5/16	25 7/16	+ 1/16
25 7/16	23 1/8	AL PwrCap TOPrS		1.84	7.3	...	148	25 3/8	25	25 3/8	+ 1/4
n 25 1/8	24 3/4	AL Pwr notesA	ALZ		...	...	1112	24 7/8	24 13/16	24 7/8	...
25 3/4	23 5/16	AlaPwr pfC		1.60	6.4	...	1	25 3/16	25 3/16	25 3/16	+ 1/16
25 3/8	22 1/8	AlaPwr pfB		1.70	6.9	...	1	24 11/16	24 11/16	24 11/16	− 3/16
25 3/8	21 3/4	AlaPwr pfD		1.69e	6.9	...	60	24 105/256	24 105/256	24 105/256	+ 1/16
23 3/4	13 1/2	AlamoGp	ALG	.40	1.8	19	13	21 15/16	21 5/8	21 15/16	+ 3/8
20 5/8	12 3/4	ApriaHlthcr	AHG		...	dd	2198	13 7/8	13 1/4	13 5/8	− 1/4
19 3/8	9 7/8	APT Satelt	ATS		...	...	564	11	10	10 5/8	− 3/8
59 1/8	32 3/4	♣AptarGp	ATR	.32	.6	21	777	54	53 7/16	53 9/16	− 1/4
▲33 1/2	24 3/8	Aquarion	WTR	1.64	4.7	22	300	34 9/16	33 7/16	34 9/16	+ 1 3/8
16 1/2	9 5/16	♣AquilaGasPip	AQP	.05	.4	13	48	13	12 7/8	12 15/16	− 1/16
s 22 9/16	13	Aracruz	ARA	.19e	1.4	...	915	13 5/16	13 1/8	13 1/8	...
19 3/8	6 1/4	♣ArcadiaFnl	AAC		...	dd	6927	6 11/16	6 1/4	6 5/8	+ 1/16
n 30 1/2	24 3/8	ArchCoal	ACI	.46	1.5	...	331	30 1/16	29 3/8	29 7/8	− 7/16
24 5/8	16 3/16	ArcherDan	ADM	.20b	.9	24	7718	21 11/16	21 3/8	21 1/2	− 1/16
32 3/8	23 3/8	ArdenRlty	ARI	1.60	5.5	21	1092	29 1/16	28 5/8	29	+ 3/8
32 1/4	20	Argentaria	AGR	.99e	3.3	...	44	30 3/8	30	30 5/16	− 5/16
n 25 3/4	24	ArgnCapTr pfA		1.96	7.9	...	387	25	24 115/128	24 115/128	+ 1/16
16 3/4	10 15/16	ArgntnaFd	AF		...	...	407	12 1/2	12 1/8	12 1/2	+ 1/8
5 3/4	2 3/4	ArgosyGaming	AGY		...	dd	443	3 1/2	3 3/8	3 3/8	...
27 15/16	26 1/4	ArizPubSvc un	AZD	2.50	9.3	...	31	26 15/16	26 7/8	26 15/16	+ 1/16
6 3/8	3 3/8	Armco	AS		...	9	1724	4 13/16	4 5/8	4 11/16	+ 1/16
51 3/4	46 1/4	Armco pfA		4.50	9.0	...	6	50 1/8	49 15/16	50	+ 1/16
52 1/8	39	Armco pfB		3.63	7.8	...	8	47	46 3/4	46 3/4	− 1/4
75 3/8	61 1/2	ArmstrngWld	ACK	1.76	2.4	14	805	74 15/16	73 5/8	74 3/4	+ 1/2
s 36	25 1/8	♣ArrowElec	ARW		...	21	5127	33	32	32 13/16	+ 5/8
6 3/8	**2 1/2**	**ArtraGp**	**ATA**		**...**	**35**	**122**	**3 1/16**	**2 13/16**	**2 13/16**	**− 1/4**
41 5/8	21	♣ArvinInd	ARV	.80f	2.5	11	659	32 3/8	31 1/4	31 7/16	+ 3/16
▼34 1/4	21 15/16	Asarco	AR	.80	3.7	6	6727	22 3/16	21 3/4	21 3/4	− 5/16
15 5/8	6 1/2	AshntGldfld	ASL	.38e	4.3	...	599	9 1/8	8 13/16	8 15/16	− 1/16
55	39 1/4	Ashland	ASH	1.10	2.1	14	5667	51 7/8	50 1/4	51 3/4	+ 1 9/16
▼13 5/8	7 1/2	AsiaPacFd	APB	.44e	6.0	...	2340	7 11/16	7 1/4	7 5/16	− 5/16
6	2	AsiaPacif A	ARH		...	...	250	2 3/16	2	2 1/16	+ 1/16
n 14 1/16	7 3/4	AsiaPacWre	AWC		...	...	66	7 13/16	7 3/4	7 3/4	− 1/8
▼17 1/8	9 1/16	AsiaPulp	PAP	.05e	.5	...	3397	10 1/16	9 1/2	10	− 3/16
31 5/8	19 3/8	AsiaSatTelcm	SAT	.20e	1.0	...	85	20 13/16	20 3/8	20 3/8	− 9/16
11 11/16	6 3/4	AsiaTigers	GRR	.01j	...	...	4252	7 3/16	7	7	− 1/4
s 22 1/2	**15 5/8**	**AssetInvest**	**AIC**	**1.40f**	**6.7**	**40**	**602**	**21 1/8**	**19 5/8**	**20 7/8**	**+ 1 1/4**
24 3/4	21	♣AssocEstate	AEC	1.86	7.8	22	653	24 1/16	23 3/4	23 7/8	+ 1/16
27 1/4	24 1/2	♣AssocEstate pf		2.44	9.2	...	15	26 7/16	26 7/16	26 7/16	...
70 1/2	42 1/8	AssocFstCap A	AFS	.40	.6	24	1416	69	68 5/16	68 3/8	...
s 20 15/16	13 7/8	Astra A	A		...	...	2448	16 7/8	16 1/8	16 3/8	− 1/2
s 19 3/8	13 13/16	Astra B	AAB		...	...	90	16 5/16	15 13/16	15 15/16	− 9/16
22 1/4	15 11/16	♣AtchisnCstg	FDY		...	9	223	16 1/4	16	16	− 7/16
26 1/2	24 1/8	AtlaCap QUIPS		2.06	7.9	...	17	26 1/4	26 1/8	26 1/8	...
21 7/16	16	AtlEngy	ATE	1.54	7.4	13	1480	21 1/16	20 7/8	20 7/8	...
s 87 1/4	62 9/16	AtlanRich	ARC	2.85	3.7	13	5032	77 3/4	76 11/16	77	+ 1
47 3/4	19 7/8	AtlasAir	CGO		...	13	267	24 1/8	23 3/8	23 9/16	− 11/16
▲28 9/16	22 1/8	♣ATMOS Eng	ATO	1.06f	3.6	40	388	29 3/8	28 1/2	29 3/8	+ 7/8
s 61 5/8	25 3/8	♣AtwdOcn	ATW		...	35	278	42 9/16	41 1/16	41 1/16	− 7/8
41 5/8	29 7/8	Aus&NZ Bk	ANZ	1.74e	5.6	...	64	31 5/8	31 5/16	31 5/16	− 3/8
28 1/8	26 1/2	Aus&NZ Bk pf		2.28	8.3	...	36	27 7/16	27 5/16	27 3/8	− 1/16
11 1/8	8 11/16	♣AustriaFd	OST		...	...	177	10 5/16	10 1/4	10 5/16	+ 1/16
8 1/2	5 7/8	AztarCp	AZR		...	11	2217	6 15/16	6 3/4	6 15/16	+ 3/16
24 9/16	8	AztecMfg	AZZ	.06f	.4	14	162	14	13 3/4	13 7/8	− 1/8

-B-B-B-

52 Weeks Hi	52 Weeks Lo	Stock	Sym	Div	Yld %	PE	Vol 100s	Hi	Lo	Close	Net Chg
n 22 1/4	12	BA MerchSvc	BPI		...	...	382	16 5/8	16 1/2	16 1/2	...
65	34 5/8	BB&T Cp	BBK	1.24	2.0	23	2017	63 7/8	62 7/8	63 1/16	− 1/2
s 33 13/16	**22**	**BCE Inc g**	**BCE**	**1.36**	**...**	**...**	**4068**	**33 1/2**	**32 3/8**	**33 7/16**	**+ 1 1/16**
37	25 1/8	BCE MblComm	BCX		...	...	2	25 1/8	25 1/8	25 1/8	...
80 7/8	51	BCP IntBk pfA		4.00	5.6	...	50	71 3/4	71 11/16	71 3/4	+ 1 1/4
8 3/4	7 3/8	♣BEA IncoFd	FBF	.72a	8.3	...	341	8 11/16	8 9/16	8 5/8	...
10 5/16	9	♣BEA StrgGlbl	FBI	.87	8.6	...	329	10 5/16	10 1/16	10 1/16	− 1/8
6 1/8	4	BEC Gp	EYE		...	26	538	5 15/16	5 13/16	5 13/16	...
55 5/8	24 7/8	BET Hldg	BTV		...	36	38	54 1/16	53 7/8	54	+ 3/8
s 24 3/8	12 3/4	BG	BRG	2.43e	10.6	...	32	23	22 13/16	23	+ 1/8
n 32	26	♣BJs WhslClb	BJ		...	...	930	30 1/16	29 11/16	29 15/16	...
90 3/4	38 1/4	♣BJ Svc	BJS		...	25	11663	69 11/16	66 1/4	66 5/16	− 2 1/16
64 1/2	**15 1/4**	**BJ Svc wt**			**...**	**...**	**60**	**42 5/8**	**40 1/4**	**40 1/4**	**− 2 3/8**
35 5/8	16 1/4	BMC	BMC	.06	.4	12	952	16 7/8	16 1/2	16 5/8	− 1/16
n 26 1/2	24 11/16	BNY Cap2 pfC		1.95	7.5	...	84	26 1/8	26	26 1/8	+ 1/8
18 3/4	15	BP Prudhoe	BPT	2.04e	12.7	...	408	16 3/16	15 5/8	16 1/16	+ 1/16
30	22 7/8	♣BRE Prop	BRE	1.38	5.1	11	481	27 5/16	27 1/16	27 1/8	+ 1/16
9 1/4	6	BRT RltyTr	BRT		...	9	206	7 7/8	7 11/16	7 7/8	+ 1/16
13	6 11/16	BT OffPdt	BTF		...	16	1375	8 5/16	7 13/16	7 13/16	+ 5/16
11 3/8	6 1/4	Bairnco	BZ	.20	2.0	11	55	10	10	10	...
49 5/8	32 5/8	♣BakrHughs	BHI	.46	1.1	49	10636	42	40	40 1/4	− 7/8
s 19 1/16	14 1/2	♣BakrFentrs	BKF	2.77e	15.3	...	686	18 1/16	17 3/4	18 1/16	− 1/16
s 23 13/16	17 11/16	♣BaldorElec	BEZ	.40	1.8	22	315	23	22 3/4	22 13/16	...
39	23 3/4	Ball Cp	BLL	.60	1.7	31	586	35 15/16	35 1/16	35 3/16	− 3/4
s 22 1/2	12	Ballantyne	BTN		...	22	54	17 1/2	17	17 3/8	+ 3/8
25	17 7/8	♣BallrdMed	BMP	.10	.4	22	472	23 11/16	23 1/4	23 1/2	+ 7/16
▲32 5/16	24 3/4	BaltGE	BGE	1.64	5.0	22	3494	33 1/4	32 13/16	32 15/16	+ 11/16
59 7/8	39 1/4	♣BancOne	ONE	1.52	2.8	22	16112	54 15/16	54	54 1/2	+ 1/2
22 3/8	15 7/8	BcoBHIF	BB	.80p	...	...	22	16	15 15/16	15 15/16	− 1/8
29	27 1/8	BcoBilV pf		2.44	8.7	...	75	28 1/8	28 1/8	28 1/8	+ 1/16
n 26 5/8	24 3/16	BcoBilV pfE		2.00	7.7	...	45	25 7/8	25 7/8	25 7/8	...
s 32 1/4	16 7/8	BcoBilViz	BBV	.68e	2.2	...	64	31 1/8	30 1/2	30 1/2	− 3/16
29 9/16	26	BcoBilV pfB		2.25	7.9	...	10	28 7/16	28 7/16	28 7/16	+ 1/8
▲23	11 7/8	BancoCntrl	BCH	.41e	1.8	...	15	23 1/8	22 7/8	22 15/16	+ 9/16
22 3/4	15 1/4	BcoEdwards	AED	.67e	4.2	...	941	16 1/8	15 15/16	16 1/16	...
38 1/8	21	BcoFran	BFR	.60e	2.3	...	1295	26 1/2	25 15/16	26 1/8	+ 5/16
▲43 7/16	25 3/8	BcoGandr	BGA	.99e	2.3	...	50	43 1/2	43 1/2	43 1/2	+ 1/16
x 20 3/4	13 5/16	BcoIndColm	CIB	.99e	7.4	...	150	13 3/8	13 3/8	13 3/8	+ 3/16
55 1/2	38	BancoLatin	BLX	.96f	2.4	12	70	40 1/2	40 3/16	40 3/8	...
n 16 3/4	9 3/4	BncoRioPlta ADS	BRS		...	...	2220	12 7/16	12 1/8	12 7/16	+ 3/16
18 1/2	11 5/8	BcoSntdrChl	BSB	.42e	3.2	...	260	13 1/4	13 1/8	13 1/4	...
s 33 1/2	18 1/2	BcoSantdr	STD	.39e	1.3	...	167	30 1/8	29 9/16	29 5/8	− 1/4
n 28 5/8	20 1/4	BcoSantiago	SAN	1.31p	...	...	247	21 1/4	21	21 1/4	+ 1/4

The Dow Jones Averages Hour by Hour

Following are the Dow Jones averages of INDUSTRIAL, TRANSPORTATION and UTILITY stocks with the total sales of each group for the period included in the chart.

DATE	OPEN	10 AM	11 AM	12 NOON	1 PM	2 PM	3 PM	CLOSE	CHG	%	HIGH*	LOW*	HIGH[q]	LOW[q]
30 INDUSTRIALS: (divisor: 0.25089315)											(THEORETICAL)		(ACTUAL)	
Dec 22	7758.97	7838.75	7816.57	7777.71	7750.56	7768.75	7790.42	7819.31	+ 63.02	+ 0.81	7892.05	7710.45	7844.72	7743.34
Dec 19	7846.50	7742.84	7636.22	7676.33	7734.62	7731.38	7734.62	7756.29	− 90.21	− 1.15	7878.60	7563.23	7846.50	7576.93
Dec 18	7953.63	7937.76	7909.91	7918.86	7893.75	7866.64	7859.68	7846.50	− 110.91	− 1.39	7991.48	7781.35	7955.87	7810.45
Dec 17	7978.53	8006.89	7954.42	7985.51	7991.97	7998.19	8001.42	7957.41	− 18.90	− 0.24	8068.81	7879.08	8034.00	7932.04
Dec 16	7924.83	7962.63	7992.72	7999.43	8014.35	7996.70	7984.26	7976.31	+ 53.72	+ 0.68	8069.06	7889.52	8019.82	7924.34
20 TRANSPORTATION COS.: (divisor: 0.34598082)											(THEORETICAL)		(ACTUAL)	
Dec 22	3142.33	3155.88	3149.20	3144.86	3145.22	3144.14	3145.95	3149.38	+ 6.14	+ 0.20	3199.42	3110.54	3163.29	3140.53
Dec 19	3173.04	3124.63	3092.12	3087.42	3107.11	3108.19	3118.49	3143.24	− 30.53	− 0.96	3177.38	3055.62	3173.41	3074.05
Dec 18	3234.10	3224.89	3202.67	3213.33	3200.14	3189.12	3174.49	3173.77	− 61.42	− 1.90	3257.04	3148.12	3237.53	3162.57
Dec 17	3254.21	3273.30	3262.10	3258.13	3255.42	3260.48	3251.99	3235.19	− 20.23	− 0.62	3304.55	3214.05	3276.55	3229.59
Dec 16	3274.75	3278.00	3281.61	3280.89	3277.28	3267.70	3253.61	3255.42	− 16.98	− 0.52	3314.31	3232.48	3288.48	3247.65
15 UTILITIES: (divisor: 2.2811277)											(THEORETICAL)		(ACTUAL)	
Dec 22	264.62	265.22	264.89	265.44	265.58	266.67	267.36	267.71	+ 2.96	+ 1.12	268.92	263.27	268.21	264.51
Dec 19	265.16	263.25	262.07	262.37	263.66	263.60	264.34	264.75	− 0.44	− 0.17	266.32	260.62	265.22	261.33
Dec 18	265.80	264.48	265.16	265.55	265.36	264.89	265.03	265.19	− 0.69	− 0.26	267.06	262.81	265.93	264.01
Dec 17	264.04	265.22	264.70	265.36	265.47	265.52	265.77	265.88	+ 1.84	+ 0.70	266.89	263.36	265.99	264.04
Dec 16	263.85	264.29	264.59	264.32	264.34	264.10	263.85	264.04	+ 0.19	+ 0.07	266.10	261.96	264.86	263.41
65 STOCKS COMPOSITE AVERAGE: (divisor: 1.4321074)											(THEORETICAL)		(ACTUAL)	
Dec 22	2539.60	2558.16	2552.14	2545.16	2540.71	2545.37	2550.87	2557.16	+ 17.24	+ 0.68	2583.91	2521.63	2561.43	2538.26
Dec 19	2563.62	2530.67	2502.26	2508.63	2525.65	2525.26	2529.49	2539.92	− 23.88	− 0.93	2572.08	2478.34	2563.71	2486.85
Dec 18	2598.23	2591.00	2581.85	2586.60	2578.71	2570.56	2566.02	2563.80	− 35.36	− 1.36	2612.28	2542.39	2599.24	2553.55
Dec 17	2604.10	2615.99	2603.26	2608.79	2609.45	2611.85	2610.76	2599.16	− 5.27	− 0.20	2637.05	2576.31	2620.83	2592.70
Dec 16	2599.38	2607.83	2614.68	2615.12	2617.08	2610.97	2605.09	2604.43	+ 5.62	+ 0.22	2638.18	2580.37	2618.34	2598.55

*a-Actual high or low exceeds theoretical value due to computational method. q-Actual. r-Revised.

Figure 1.1 The *Wall Street Journal*, 23rd December 1997. Reproduced by permission of *Dow Jones & Company, Inc.*

reality of the situation lies somewhere between complete predictability and perfect randomness, not least because there have been many cases of market manipulation where large trades have moved stock prices in a direction that was favorable to the person doing the moving.

To whet your appetite for the mathematical modeling later, I want to show you a simple way to simulate a random walk that looks something like a stock price. One of the simplest random

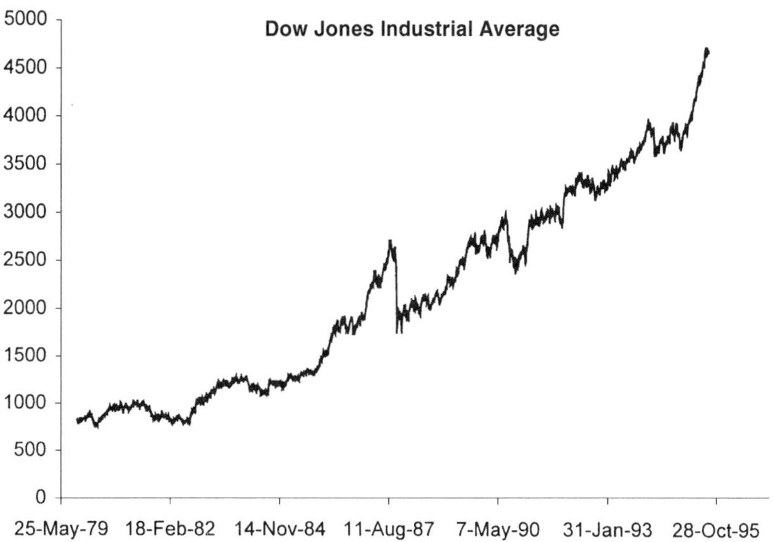

Figure 1.2 A time series of the Dow Jones Industrial Average from May 1979 to October 1995.

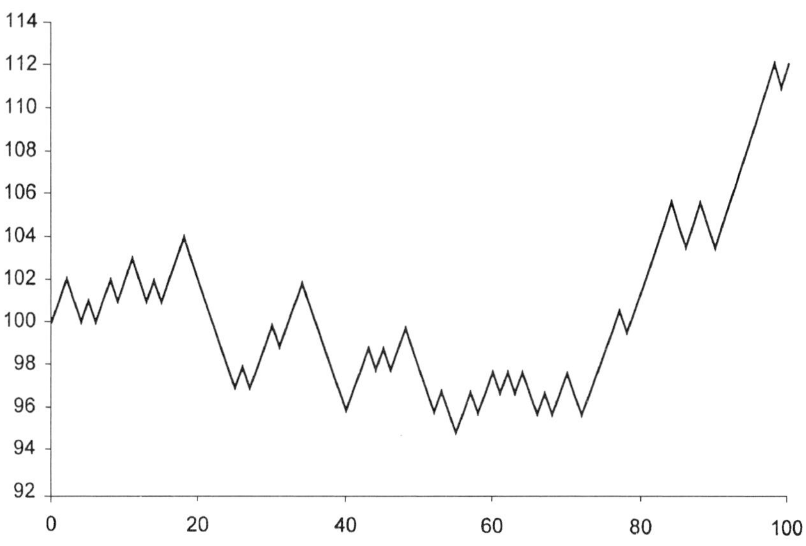

Figure 1.3 A simulation of an asset price path?

processes is the tossing of a coin. I am going to use ideas related to coin tossing as a model for the behavior of a stock price. As a simple experiment start with the number 100 which you should think of as the price of your stock, and toss a coin. If you throw a head multiply the number by 1.01, if you throw a tail multiply by 0.99. After one toss your number will be either 99 or 101. Toss again. If you get a head multiply your *new* number by 1.01 or by 0.99 if you throw a tail. You will now have either $1.01^2 \times 100$, $1.01 \times 0.99 \times 100 = 0.99 \times 1.01 \times 100$ or $0.99^2 \times 100$. Continue this process and plot your value on a graph each time you throw the coin. Results of one particular experiment are shown in Figure 1.3. Instead of physically tossing a coin, the

	A	B	C	D	E
1	**Initial stock price**	**100**		**Stock**	
2	**Up move**	**1.01**		100	
3	**Down move**	**0.99**		99	
4	**Probability of up**	**0.5**		99.99	
5				100.9899	
6				99.98	
7				98.9802	
8				97.9904	
9				[illegible]03	
10				99.98001	
11				100.9596	
12				99.95001	
13				98.95051	
14				99.94001	
15				100.9394	
16				99.93002	
17				98.93072	
18				97.94141	
19				98.92083	
20				99.91004	
21				100.9091	
22				101.9182	
23				102.9374	
24				103.9668	
25				105.0065	
26				106.0565	
27				107.1171	
28				106.0459	

=B1

=D6*If(RAND()>1-$B$4,$B$2,$B$3)

Figure 1.4 Simple spreadsheet to simulate the coin-tossing experiment.

series used in this plot was generated on a spreadsheet like that in Figure 1.4. This uses the Excel spreadsheet function `RAND()` to generate a uniformly distributed random number between 0 and 1. If this number is greater than one half it counts as a 'head,' otherwise a 'tail.'

1.3.1 Dividends

The owner of the stock theoretically owns a piece of the company. This ownership can only be turned into cash if he owns so much of the stock that he can take over the company and keep all the profits for himself. This is unrealistic for most of us. To the average investor the value in holding the stock comes from the **dividends** and any growth in the stock's value. Dividends are lump sum payments, paid out every quarter or every six months, to the holder of the stock.

The amount of the dividend varies from year to year depending on the profitability of the company. As a general rule companies like to try to keep the level of dividends about the same each time. The amount of the dividend is decided by the board of directors of the company and is usually set a month or so before the dividend is actually paid.

When the stock is bought it either comes with its entitlement to the next dividend (**cum**) or not (**ex**). There is a date at around the time of the dividend payment when the stock goes from cum to ex. The original holder of the stock gets the dividend but the person who buys it obviously does not. All things being equal a stock that is cum dividend is better than one that is ex dividend. Thus at the time that the dividend is paid and the stock goes ex dividend there will be a drop in the value of the stock. The size of this drop in stock value offsets the disadvantage of not getting the dividend.

This jump in stock price is in practice more complex than I have just made out. Often capital gains due to the rise in a stock price are taxed differently from a dividend, which is often treated as income. Some people can make a lot of risk-free money by exploiting tax 'inconsistencies.'

FOOTPATH

I discuss dividends in depth in Chapter 8.

1.3.2 Stock Splits

Stock prices in the US are usually of the order of magnitude of $100. In the UK they are typically around £1. There is no real reason for the popularity of the number of digits. After all, if I buy a stock I want to know what percentage growth I will get: the absolute level of the stock is irrelevant to me, it just determines whether I have to buy tens or thousands of the stock to invest a given amount. Nevertheless there is some psychological element to the stock size. Every now and then a company will announce a **stock split**. For example, the company with a stock price of $900 announces a two-for-one stock split. This simply means that instead of holding one stock valued at $900, I hold three valued at $300 each.[1]

1.4 COMMODITIES

Commodities are usually raw products such as precious metals, oil, food products etc. The prices of these products are unpredictable but often show seasonal effects. Scarcity of the product results in higher prices. Commodities are usually traded by people who have no need of the raw material. For example they may just be speculating on the direction of gold without wanting to stockpile it or make jewellery. Most trading is done on the futures market, making deals to buy or sell the commodity at some time in the future. The deal is then closed out before the commodity is due to be delivered. Futures contracts are discussed below.

1.5 CURRENCIES

Another financial quantity we shall discuss is the **exchange rate**, the rate at which one currency can be exchanged for another. This is the world of **foreign exchange** or **FX** for short. Some currencies are pegged to one another, and others are allowed to float freely. Whatever the exchange rates from one currency to another, there must be consistency throughout. If it is possible to exchange dollars for pounds and then the pounds for yen, this implies a relationship between the dollar/pound, pound/yen and dollar/yen exchange rates. If this relationship moves out of line it is possible to make **arbitrage profits** by exploiting the mispricing.

Figure 1.5 is an excerpt from The *Wall Street Journal* of 23rd December 1997. At the bottom of this excerpt is a matrix of exchange rates.

Although the fluctuation in exchange rates is unpredictable, there is a link between exchange rates and the interest rates in the two countries. If the interest rate on dollars is higher than the

[1] In the UK this would be called a three-for-one split.

CURRENCY TRADING

Monday, December 22, 1997

EXCHANGE RATES

The New York foreign exchange selling rates below apply to trading among banks in amounts of $1 million and more, as quoted at 4 p.m. Eastern time by Dow Jones and other sources. Retail transactions provide fewer units of foreign currency per dollar.

Country	U.S. $ equiv. Mon	U.S. $ equiv. Fri	Currency per U.S. $ Mon	Currency per U.S. $ Fri
Argentina (Peso)	1.0001	1.0001	.9999	.9999
Australia (Dollar)	.6520	.6530	1.5337	1.5314
Austria (Schilling)	.07981	.08024	12.529	12.462
Bahrain (Dinar)	2.6518	2.6525	.3771	.3770
Belgium (Franc)	.02723	.02736	36.727	36.550
Brazil (Real)	.8986	.8980	1.1129	1.1136
Britain (Pound)	1.6635	1.6700	.6011	.5988
1-month forward	1.6615	1.6679	.6019	.5996
3-months forward	1.6566	1.6630	.6036	.6013
6-months forward	1.6794	1.6560	.5955	.6039
Canada (Dollar)	.6971	.6988	1.4345	1.4311
1-month forward	.6979	.6995	1.4329	1.4295
3-months forward	.6988	.7005	1.4311	1.4276
6-months forward	.6995	.7013	1.4295	1.4259
Chile (Peso)	.002286	.002277	437.35	439.15
China (Renminbi)	.1203	.1203	8.3100	8.3100
Colombia (Peso)	.0007767	.0007704	1287.51	1298.00
Czech. Rep. (Koruna)	....	....	....	....
Commercial rate	.02891	.02936	34.586	34.057
Denmark (Krone)	.1474	.1480	6.7850	6.7555
Ecuador (Sucre)	....	....	....	....
Floating rate	.0002283	.0002283	4380.00	4380.00
Finland (Markka)	.1857	.1870	5.3842	5.3462
France (Franc)	.1678	.1681	5.9585	5.9485
1-month forward	.1682	.1684	5.9457	5.9365
3-months forward	.1687	.1690	5.9267	5.9168
6-months forward	.1696	.1699	5.8965	5.8868
Germany (Mark)	.5615	.5632	1.7808	1.7755
1-month forward	.5626	.5643	1.7774	1.7721
3-months forward	.5646	.5662	1.7713	1.7662
6-months forward	.5674	.5691	1.7625	1.7573
Greece (Drachma)	.003560	.003577	280.87	279.60
Hong Kong (Dollar)	.1290	.1290	7.7500	7.7500
Hungary (Forint)	.004945	.004976	202.21	200.97
India (Rupee)	.02552	.02544	39.185	39.310
Indonesia (Rupiah)	.0001907	.0001961	5245.00	5100.00
Ireland (Punt)	1.4505	1.4579	.6894	.6859
Israel (Shekel)	.2827	.2827	3.5369	3.5371
Italy (Lira)	.0005727	.0005741	1746.00	1742.00
Japan (Yen)	.007685	.007732	130.12	129.33
1-month forward	.007722	.007771	129.50	128.68
3-months forward	.007790	.007838	128.37	127.59
6-months forward	.007900	.007947	126.58	125.83
Jordan (Dinar)	1.4134	1.4134	.7075	.7075
Kuwait (Dinar)	3.2798	3.2830	.3049	.3046
Lebanon (Pound)	.0006547	.0006547	1527.50	1527.50
Malaysia (Ringgit)	.2621	.2621	3.8147	3.8153
Malta (Lira)	2.5478	2.5608	.3925	.3905
Mexico (Peso)	....	....	....	....
Floating rate	.1234	.1233	8.1030	8.1130
Netherland (Guilder)	.4980	.4994	2.0079	2.0026
New Zealand (Dollar)	.5762	.5820	1.7355	1.7182
Norway (Krone)	.1370	.1373	7.2988	7.2843
Pakistan (Rupee)	.02296	.02296	43.560	43.560
Peru (new Sol)	.3709	.3710	2.6964	2.6955
Philippines (Peso)	.02522	.02522	39.650	39.650
Poland (Zloty)	.2869	.2855	3.4860	3.5030
Portugal (Escudo)	.005488	.005503	182.20	181.72
Russia (Ruble) (a)	.0001682	.0001682	5947.00	5945.00
Saudi Arabia (Riyal)	.2666	.2666	3.7505	3.7505
Singapore (Dollar)	.5979	.5979	1.6725	1.6725
Slovak Rep. (Koruna)	.02897	.02916	34.515	34.294
South Africa (Rand)	.2058	.2058	4.8590	4.8600
South Korea (Won)	.0005839	.0006452	1712.50	1550.00
Spain (Peseta)	.006629	.006645	150.85	150.48
Sweden (Krona)	.1287	.1289	7.7685	7.7575
Switzerland (Franc)	.6949	.6969	1.4390	1.4350
1-month forward	.6978	.6995	1.4331	1.4295
3-months forward	.7023	.7043	1.4239	1.4199
6-months forward	.7095	.7116	1.4095	1.4053
Taiwan (Dollar)	.03067	.03095	32.603	32.311
Thailand (Baht)	.02235	.02230	44.750	44.850
Turkey (Lira)	.00000495	.00000498	202175.00	200725.00
United Arab (Dirham)	.2723	.2723	3.6725	3.6725
Uruguay (New Peso)	....	....	....	....
Financial	.1002	.1002	9.9800	9.9800
Venezuela (Bolivar)	.001988	.001988	503.05	502.92
SDR	1.3518	1.3586	.7398	.7360
ECU	1.1102	1.1133	....	....

Special Drawing Rights (SDR) are based on exchange rates for the U.S., German, British, French, and Japanese currencies. Source: International Monetary Fund.

European Currency Unit (ECU) is based on a basket of community currencies.

a-fixing, Moscow Interbank Currency Exchange.

The Wall Street Journal daily foreign exchange data for 1996 and 1997 may be purchased through the Readers' Reference Service (413) 592-3600.

OPTIONS

PHILADELPHIA EXCHANGE

		Calls Vol.	Calls Last	Puts Vol.	Puts Last
British Pound					**166.52**
31,250 Brit. Pounds-cents per unit.					
165	Feb	4	2.96	...	...
165	Mar	1	3.40	...	...
170	Mar	13	1.53	...	...
British Pound-GMark					**296.33**
31,250 British Pound-German Mark cross.					
292	Mar	7	6.76	...	...
Canadian Dollar					**69.72**
50,000 Canadian Dollars-cents per unit.					
69	Feb	...	...	9	0.28
70	Feb	5	0.49	...	...
70½	Jan	...	...	20	0.83
71	Mar	20	0.30	...	...
72	Mar	...	...	83	2.23
German Mark					**56.16**
62,500 German Mark EOM-European style.					
56	Jan	...	...	25	0.63
62,500 German Marks EOM-European style.					
55½	Jan	...	...	50	0.46
62,500 German Marks-cents per unit.					
56	Mar	1	1.33	...	...
57	Mar	...	...	1	1.46
60	Mar	...	...	1	3.80
Japanese Yen					**76.75**
6,250,000J.Yen EOM 100ths of a cent per unit.					
77	Dec	2	0.44	...	...
6,250,000J.Yen-100ths of a cent per unit.					
72	Mar	...	...	500	0.41
77	Jan	2	1.10	3	1.26
77½	Mar	...	...	2	2.04
80	Jan	5	0.40	...	...
80½	Mar	291	1.05	...	...
81	Mar	34	0.91	...	...
82	Mar	...	..	400	5.41
6,250,000J.Yen-EuropeanStyle.					
74	Jan	...	...	10	0.34
77	Feb	45	1.79	...	...
Swiss Franc					**69.53**
62,500 Swiss Francs-European Style.					
67	Jan	4	2.85	...	...
70	Mar	4	1.55	...	...
71	Jan	...	...	12	1.33
71	Mar	...	...	4	1.80
72	Jan	...	...	5	2.36
73	Jan	...	...	12	3.08
62,500 Swiss Francs-cents per unit.					
69½	Feb	...	...	64	1.01

Call Vol ...... 1,486 Open Int ... 89,727
Put Vol .... 2,734 Open Int ... 98,777

Key Currency Cross Rates Late New York Trading Dec 22, 1997

	Dollar	Pound	SFranc	Guilder	Peso	Yen	Lira	D-Mark	FFranc	CdnDlr
Canada	1.4345	2.3863	.99687	.71443	.17703	.01102	.00082	.80554	.24075	....
France	5.9585	9.9120	4.1407	2.9675	.73534	.04579	.00341	3.3460	....	4.1537
Germany	1.7808	2.9624	1.2375	.88690	.21977	.01369	.00102	....	.29887	1.2414
Italy	1746.0	2904.5	1213.3	869.57	215.48	13.418	....	980.46	293.03	1217.1
Japan	130.12	216.45	90.424	64.804	16.058	....	.07452	73.068	21.838	90.708
Mexico	8.1030	13.479	5.6310	4.0356	....	.06227	.00464	4.5502	1.3599	5.6487
Netherlands	2.0079	3.3401	1.3953	....	.24780	.01543	.00115	1.1275	.33698	1.3997
Switzerland	1.4390	2.3938	....	.71667	.17759	.01106	.00082	.80806	.24150	1.0031
U.K.	.60114	....	.41775	.29939	.07419	.00462	.00034	.33757	.10089	.41906
U.S.	....	1.6635	.69493	.49803	.12341	.00769	.00057	.56155	.16783	.69711

Source: Dow Jones

Figure 1.5 The *Wall Street Journal* of 23rd December 1997, currency exchange rates. Reproduced by permission of *Dow Jones & Company, Inc.*

interest rate on pounds sterling we would expect to see sterling depreciating against the dollar. Central banks can use interest rates as a tool for manipulating exchange rates, but only to a degree.

1.6 INDICES

For measuring how the stock market/economy is doing as a whole, there have been developed the stock market **indices**. A typical index is made up from the weighted sum of a selection or **basket** of representative stocks. The selection may be designed to represent the whole market, such as the Standard & Poor's 500 (S&P500) in the US or the Financial Times Stock Exchange index (FTSE100) in the UK, or a very special part of a market. In Figure 1.2 we saw the DJIA, representing major US stocks. In Figure 1.6 is shown JP Morgan's Emerging Market Bond Index. The EMBI+ is an index of emerging market debt instruments, including external-currency-denominated Brady bonds, Eurobonds and US dollar local markets instruments. The main components of the index are the three major Latin American countries, Argentina, Brazil and Mexico. Bulgaria, Morocco, Nigeria, the Philippines, Poland, Russia and South Africa are also represented.

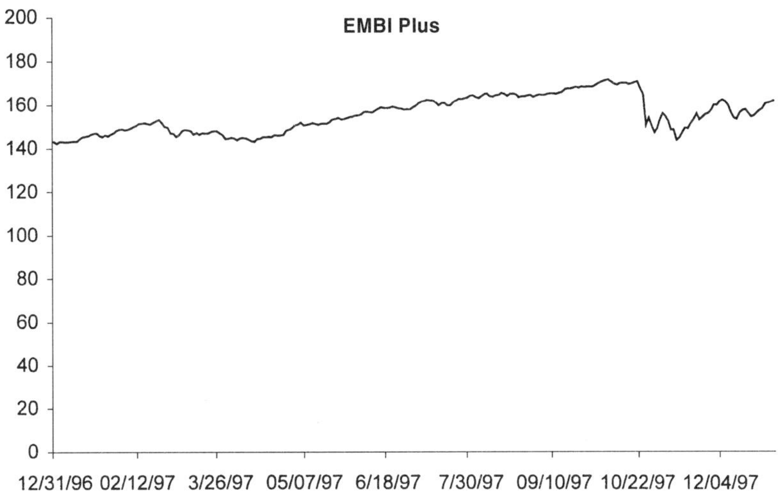

Figure 1.6 JP Morgan's EMBI Plus.

1.7 FIXED-INCOME SECURITIES

In lending money to a bank you may get to choose for how long you tie your money up and what kind of interest rate you receive. If you decide on a fixed-term deposit the bank will offer to lock in a fixed rate of interest for the period of the deposit, a month, six months, a year, say. The rate of interest will not necessarily be the same for each period, and generally the longer the time that the money is tied up the higher the rate of interest, although this is not always the case. Often, if you want to have immediate access to your money then you will be exposed to interest rates that will change from time to time, interest rates are not constant.

These two types of interest payments, **fixed** and **floating**, are seen in many financial instruments. **Coupon-bearing bonds** pay out a known amount every six months or year. This is the **coupon** and would often be a fixed rate of interest. At the end of your fixed term you get a final coupon and the return of the **principal**, the amount on which the interest was calculated. **Interest rate swaps** are an exchange of a fixed rate of interest for a floating rate of interest. Governments and companies issue bonds as a form of borrowing. The less creditworthy the issuer, the higher the interest that they will have to pay out. Bonds are actively traded, with prices that continually fluctuate.

Fixed-income modeling and products are the subject of the whole of Part Four.

1.8 INFLATION-PROOF BONDS

A very recent addition to the list of bonds issued by the US government is the **index-linked bond**. These have been around in the UK since 1981, and have provided a very successful way of ensuring that income is not eroded by inflation.

In the UK inflation is measured by the **Retail Price Index** or **RPI**. This index is a measure of year-on-year inflation, using a 'basket' of goods and services, including mortgage interest payments. The index is published monthly. The coupons and principal of the index-linked bonds are related to the level of the RPI. Roughly speaking, the amounts of the coupon and principal are scaled with the increase in the RPI over the period from the issue of the bond to the time of the payment. There is one slight complication in that the actual RPI level used in these calculations is set back *eight months*. Thus the base measurement is eight months before issue and the scaling of any coupon is with respect to the increase in the RPI from this base measurement to the level of the RPI eight months before the coupon is paid. One of the reasons for this complexity is that the initial estimate of the RPI is usually corrected at a later date.

Figure 1.7 shows the UK gilts prices published in The *Financial Times* of 10th November 1997. The index-linked bonds are on the right. The figures in parentheses give the base for the index, the RPI eight months prior to the issue of the gilt.

I will not pursue the modeling of inflation or index-linked bonds in this book. I would just like to say that the dynamics of the relationship between inflation and short-term interest rates is particularly interesting. Clearly the level of interest rates will affect the rate of inflation directly through mortgage repayments, but also interest rates are often used by central banks as a tool for keeping inflation down.

1.9 FORWARDS AND FUTURES

A **forward contract** is an agreement where one party promises to buy an asset from another party at some specified time in the future and at some specified price. No money changes hands until the **delivery date** or **maturity** of the contract. The terms of the contract make it an obligation to buy the asset at the delivery date, there is no choice in the matter. The asset could be a stock, a commodity or a currency.

A **futures contract** is very similar to a forward contract. Futures contracts are usually traded through an exchange, which standardizes the terms of the contracts. The profit or loss from the futures position is calculated every day and the change in this value is paid from one party to the other. Thus with futures contracts there is a gradual payment of funds from initiation until maturity.

Forwards and futures have two main uses, in speculation and in hedging. If you believe that the market will rise you can benefit from this by entering into a forward or futures contract. If your market view is right then a lot of money will change hands (at maturity or every day)

UK GILTS PRICES

	Notes	Price £	W'k % +/–	Amnt £m	Interest due	Last xd	City line
Shorts" (Lives up to Five Years)							
Treas $4\frac{5}{8}$pc 1998‡‡		116	0.1	800	Ap27 Oc27	20.10	1753
Exch $9\frac{3}{4}$pc 1998		$100\frac{7}{16}$	–.1	3,550	Jy19 Ja19	10.7	1273
Treas $7\frac{1}{4}$pc 1998‡‡		$100\frac{1}{32}$	–.1	8,150	Se30 Mr30	22.9	1788
Treas $15\frac{1}{2}$pc '98‡‡		$106\frac{31}{32}$	–.4	935	Mr30 Se30	22.9	1308
Exch 12pc 1998		$104\frac{9}{16}$	–.3	3,909	My20 Nv20	9.5	1259
Treas $9\frac{1}{2}$pc 1999‡‡		$102\frac{1}{2}$	–.3	1,900	Jy15 Ja15	4.7	1347
Treas Fltg Rate 1999‡‡		$100\frac{1}{4}$	....	5,700	9MrJeSeDe	2.9	4945
Exch $12\frac{1}{4}$pc 1999		$106\frac{9}{16}$	–.4	3,050	Se26 Mr26	22.9	1264
Treas $10\frac{1}{2}$pc 1999		$104\frac{3}{4}$	–.3	1,252	Nv19 My19	8.5	1288
Treas 6pc 1999 ‡‡		$98\frac{5}{16}$	–.3	6,950	Fe10 Au10	31.7	3635
Conv $10\frac{1}{4}$pc 1999		$105\frac{25}{32}$	–.4	1,798	My22 Nv22	13.5	1242
Treas $8\frac{1}{2}$pc 2000	✠	$102\frac{25}{32}$	–.4	109	Jy28 Ja28	17.7	–
Conv 9pc 2000‡‡		$104\frac{1}{32}$	–.4	5,358	Se3 Mr3	22.8	1244
Treas 13pc 2000		$114\frac{7}{32}$	–.5	3,171	Ja14 Jy14	3.7	1299
Treas 14pc 1998–1		$103\frac{15}{32}$	–.2	970	Nv22 My22	13.5	1306
Treas 8pc 2000‡‡		$102\frac{13}{16}$	–.5	9,800	Je7 De7	29.5	4948
Treas Fltg Rate 2001		$100\frac{3}{8}$	....	3,000	8OcJaApJy	7.7	–
Treas 10pc 2001		$108\frac{5}{8}$	–.5	4,406	Au26 Fe26	14.8	1280
Conv $9\frac{1}{2}$pc 2001‡‡	✠	108	–.5	3	Ja12 Jy12	3.7	–
Conv $9\frac{3}{4}$pc 2001	✠	$108\frac{31}{32}$	–.5	35	Fe10 Au10	31.7	–
Treas 7pc 2001 ‡‡		$100\frac{13}{32}$	–.5	12,750	My6 Nv6	24.4	3031
Exch 12pc 1999–2	✠	$105\frac{5}{16}$	–.3	105	Jy22 Ja22	11.7	–
Conv 10pc 2002	✠	$111\frac{3}{4}$	–.5	21	Oc11 Ap11	6.10	–
Treas 7pc 2002‡‡		$100\frac{15}{16}$	–.5	9,000	De7 Je7	29.5	–
Five to Fifteen Years							
Conv $9\frac{1}{2}$pc 2002	✠	$110\frac{7}{32}$	–.5	2	De14 Je14	5.6	–
Treas $9\frac{3}{4}$pc 2002		$111\frac{5}{8}$	–.5	6,527	Fe27 Au27	15.8	1349
Exch 9pc 2002	✠	$108\frac{15}{16}$	–.5	83	My19 Nv19	8.5	–
Conv $9\frac{3}{4}$pc 2003‡‡	✠	$113\frac{5}{32}$	–.5	11	Nv7 My7	25.4	–
Treas 8pc 2003‡‡		$105\frac{21}{32}$	–.6	8,600	Je10 De10	30.5	2010
Treas $13\frac{3}{4}$pc 2000–3	✠	$116\frac{3}{16}$	–.6	53	Ja25 Jy25	16.7	–
Treas 10pc 2003		$115\frac{1}{4}$	–.6	2,503	Mr8 Se8	28.8	1281
Treas $11\frac{1}{2}$pc 2001–4		$113\frac{7}{32}$	–.5	1,620	Se19 Mr19	10.9	1290
Treas 10pc 2004	✠	$116\frac{23}{32}$	–.6	23	Nv18 My18	8.5	–
Funding $3\frac{1}{2}$pc 1999–4		$88\frac{13}{16}$	–.5	543	Ja14 Jy14	3.7	1274
Conv $9\frac{1}{2}$pc 2004		$115\frac{5}{16}$	–.6	3,412	Ap25 Oc25	20.10	1246
Treas $6\frac{3}{4}$pc 2004‡‡		$100\frac{3}{8}$	–.6	6,500	My26 Nv26	15.5	3541
Conv $9\frac{1}{2}$pc 2005		$116\frac{1}{16}$	–.5	4,842	Oc18 Ap18	13.10	1247
Exch $10\frac{1}{2}$pc 2005	✠	$122\frac{27}{32}$	–.6	23	Mr20 Se20	11.9	–
Treas $12\frac{1}{2}$pc 2003–5		$127\frac{27}{32}$	–.5	2,200	My21 Nv21	12.5	1295
Treas $8\frac{1}{2}$pc 2005‡‡		$111\frac{7}{32}$	–.5	10,373	Je7 De7	29.5	4946
Conv $9\frac{3}{4}$pc 2006	✠	$120\frac{11}{16}$	–.4	6	My15 Nv15	6.5	–
Treas $7\frac{1}{2}$pc 2006‡‡		$105\frac{7}{8}$	–.4	11,700	Je7 De7	29.5	1148
Treas $7\frac{3}{4}$pc 2006‡‡		$107\frac{5}{32}$	–.4	4,000	Mr8 Se8	28.8	2300
Treas 8pc 2002–6‡‡		$104\frac{7}{16}$	–.5	2,050	Ap5 Oc5	25.9	1334
Treas $11\frac{3}{4}$pc 2003–7		$121\frac{5}{32}$	–.6	3,150	Jy22 Ja22	11.7	1293
Treas $8\frac{1}{2}$pc 2007 ‡‡		$112\frac{31}{32}$	–.4	7,397	Ja16 Jy16	7.7	1339
Treas $7\frac{1}{4}$pc 2007‡‡		$104\frac{13}{16}$	–.4	9,000	Je7 De7	29.5	–
Treas $13\frac{1}{2}$pc 2004–8	✠	$134\frac{3}{16}$	–.7	95	Se26 Mr26	22.9	–
Treas 9pc 2008 ‡‡		$118\frac{31}{32}$	–.2	5,621	Ap13 Oc13	6.10	1343
Treas 8pc 2009		$111\frac{9}{16}$	–.3	3,450	Mr25 Se25	16.9	1336
Treas $6\frac{1}{4}$pc 2010‡‡		$96\frac{27}{32}$	–.2	4,750	Mr25 Nv25	15.5	4632
Conv 9pc Ln 2011 ‡‡		$121\frac{3}{16}$	–.2	5,273	Jy12 Ja12	3.7	1245
Treas 9pc 2012‡‡		$122\frac{5}{32}$xd	–.2	5,360	Fe6 Au6	6.10	1701
Treas $5\frac{1}{2}$pc 2008–12‡‡		$91\frac{3}{8}$	....	1,000	Mr10 Se10	1.9	1330
Treas $7\frac{3}{4}$pc 2012–15‡‡		$110\frac{1}{8}$	–.2	800	Jy26 Ja26	17.7	1332
Over Fifteen Years							
Treas 8pc 2013‡‡		$113\frac{11}{16}$	–.2	6,100	Mr27 Se27	22.9	2229
Treas 8pc 2015‡‡		$115\frac{23}{32}$	–.1	13,787	Je7 De7	29.5	4992
Treas $8\frac{3}{4}$pc 2017‡‡		$124\frac{7}{32}$	–.1	7,550	Fe25 Au25	14.8	1982
Exch 12pc 2013–17	✠	$152\frac{27}{32}$	–.2	57	Je12 De12	3.6	–
Treas 8pc 2021‡‡		$118\frac{3}{8}$	–.1	16,500	Je7 De7	29.5	–
Undated							
Consols 4pc		59	–.1	359	Au1 Fe1	23.7	1239
War Loan $3\frac{1}{2}$pc‡‡		$53\frac{11}{32}$	–.2	1,909	Je1 De1	16.5	1352
Conv $3\frac{1}{2}$pc '61 Aft.		$70\frac{1}{2}$	–.1	115	Ap1 Oc1	22.9	1243
Treas 3pc '66 Aft.		$42\frac{7}{8}$	–.1	56	Ap5 Oc5	29.9	1324
Consols $2\frac{1}{2}$pc		$37\frac{7}{8}$	–.2	276	5JaApJyOc	29.9	1238
Treas. $2\frac{1}{2}$pc		$37\frac{5}{16}$	0.2	475	Ap1 Oc1	22.9	1315
Index-Linked	(b)						
$2\frac{1}{2}$pc '99	✠	$186\frac{13}{32}$	–.4	2	My22 Nv22	13.5	–
$2\frac{1}{2}$pc '01	(78.3)	$193\frac{1}{8}$	–.2	2,150	Mr24 Se24	15.9	1316
$2\frac{1}{2}$pc '03	(78.8)	$190\frac{7}{16}$	–.2	2,400	My20 Nv20	9.5	1317
$4\frac{3}{8}$pc '04‡‡	(135.6)	$123\frac{5}{16}$	–.2	1,150	Ap21 Oc21	13.10	1255
2pc '06	(69.5)	$203\frac{3}{4}$	–.2	2,500	Ja19 Jy19	10.7	1314
$2\frac{1}{2}$pc '09	(78.8)	$185\frac{3}{8}$	–.3	2,625	My20 Nv20	9.5	1318
$2\frac{1}{2}$pc '11	(74.6)	$193\frac{13}{16}$	–.2	3,100	Fe23 Au23	14.8	1319
$2\frac{1}{2}$pc '13	(89.2)	$160\frac{13}{16}$	–.3	3,750	Fe16 Au16	7.8	1320
$2\frac{1}{2}$pc '16	(81.6)	$173\frac{23}{32}$	–.3	3,825	Ja26 Jy26	17.7	1321
$2\frac{1}{2}$pc '20	(83.0)	$168\frac{11}{32}$	–.2	3,700	Ap16 Oc16	13.10	1322
$2\frac{1}{2}$pc '24‡‡	(97.7)	$141\frac{3}{16}$	–.3	3,850	Ja17 Jy17	8.7	1323
$4\frac{1}{8}$pc '30‡‡	(135.1)	$138\frac{9}{16}$	–.3	1,300	Ja16 Jy22	11.7	1134

(b) Figures in parentheses show RPI base for indexing, (ie 8 months prior to issue) and have been adjusted to reflect rebasing of RPI to 100 in February 1987. Conversion factor 3.945. RPI for February 1997: 155.0 and for September 1997: 159.3.

Other Fixed Interest

	Price £	W'k % +/–	Amnt £m	Interest due	Last xd	City line
Asian Dev $10\frac{1}{4}$pc 2009	$126\frac{1}{16}$	–.5	100	Mr24 Se24	24.3	–
B'ham $11\frac{1}{2}$pc 2012	$139\frac{1}{2}$xd	....	45	My15 Nv15	20.10	1837
Leeds $13\frac{1}{2}$pc 2006	$143\frac{1}{2}$	....	40	Ap1 Oc1	10.9	3146
Liverpool $3\frac{1}{2}$pc Irred.	50	....	5	1ApJyOcJa	1.9	–
LCC 3pc '20 Aft.	43	....	26	1MrJeSeDe	1.8	–
Manchester $11\frac{1}{2}$pc 2007	$130\frac{1}{2}$	....	6	Ap25 Oc25	29.9	3275
Met. Wtr. 3pc 'B'	84	–1.2	25	Mr1 Se1	1.8	3361
N'wide Anglia $3\frac{7}{8}$pc 2021	$163\frac{7}{16}$	–.3	60	Ja30 Jy30	16.6	3465
$4\frac{1}{4}$pc IL 2024	$154\frac{7}{8}$	–.3	50	Au23 Fe23	14.7	–

● 'Tap' stock. ‡‡ Tax-free to non-residents on application. E Auction basis. xd Ex dividend. Closing mid-prices are shown in pounds per £100 nominal of stock. Weekly percentage changes are calculated on a Friday to Friday basis. ✠ Indicative price.

Figure 1.7 UK gilts prices from The *Financial Times* of 10th November 1997. Reproduced by permission of The *Financial Times*.

in your favor. That is speculation and is very risky. Hedging is the opposite, it is avoidance of risk. For example, if you are expecting to get paid in yen in six months' time, but you live in America and your expenses are all in dollars, then you could enter into a futures contract to lock in a guaranteed exchange rate for the amount of your yen income. Once this exchange rate is locked in you are no longer exposed to fluctuations in the dollar/yen exchange rate. But then you won't benefit if the yen appreciates.

1.9.1 A First Example of no Arbitrage

Although I won't be discussing futures and forwards very much they do provide us with our first example of the **no-arbitrage** principle. I am going to introduce mathematical notation now for the first time in the book, it will be fairly consistent throughout. Consider a forward contract that obliges us to hand over an amount $\$F$ at time T to receive the underlying asset. Today's date is t and the price of the asset is currently $\$S(t)$; this is the **spot price**, the amount for which we could get immediate delivery of the asset. When we get to maturity we will hand over the amount $\$F$ and receive the asset, then worth $\$S(T)$. How much profit we make cannot be known until we know the value $\$S(T)$, and we can't know this until time T. From now on I am going to drop the '\$' sign from in front of monetary amounts.

We know all of F, $S(t)$, t and T: is there any relationship between them? You might think not, since the forward contract entitles us to receive an amount $S(T) - F$ at expiry and this is unknown. However, by entering into a special portfolio of trades *now* we can eliminate all randomness in the future. This is done as follows.

Enter into the forward contract. This costs us nothing up front but exposes us to the uncertainty in the value of the asset at maturity. Simultaneously sell the asset. It is called **going short** when you sell something you don't own. This is possible in many markets, but with some timing restrictions. We now have an amount $S(t)$ in cash due to the sale of the asset, a forward contract, and a short asset position. But our net position is zero. Put the cash in the bank, to receive interest.

When we get to maturity we hand over the amount F and receive the asset. This cancels our short asset position regardless of the value of $S(T)$. At maturity we are left with a guaranteed $-F$ in cash as well as the bank account. The word 'guaranteed' is important because it emphasizes that it is independent of the value of the asset. The bank account contains the initial investment of an amount $S(t)$ with added interest, this has a value at maturity of

$$S(t)e^{r(T-t)}.$$

Our net position at maturity is therefore

$$S(t)e^{r(T-t)} - F.$$

Since we began with a portfolio worth zero and we end up with a predictable amount, that predictable amount should also be zero. We can conclude that

$$F = S(t)e^{r(T-t)}. \tag{1.3}$$

This is the relationship between the spot price and the forward price. It is a linear relationship, the forward price is proportional to the spot price.

Table 1.1 Cashflows in a hedged portfolio of asset and forward.

Holding	Worth today (t)	Worth at maturity (T)
Forward	0	$S(T) - F$
$-$ Stock	$-S(t)$	$-S(T)$
Cash	$S(t)$	$S(t)e^{r(T-t)}$
Total	0	$S(t)e^{r(T-t)} - F$

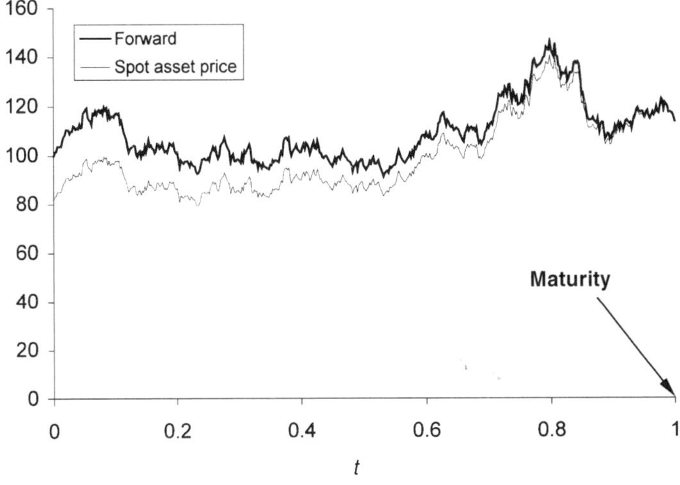

Figure 1.8 A time series of a spot asset price and its forward price.

The cashflows in this special hedged portfolio are shown in Table 1.1.

In Figure 1.8 is a path taken by the spot asset price and its forward price. As long as interest rates are constant, these two are related by (1.3).

If this relationship is violated then there will be an arbitrage opportunity. To see what is meant by this, imagine that F is less than $S(t)e^{r(T-t)}$. To exploit this and make a riskless arbitrage profit, enter into the deals as explained above. At maturity you will have $S(t)e^{r(T-t)}$ in the bank, a short asset and a long forward. The asset position cancels when you hand over the amount F, leaving you with a profit of $S(t)e^{r(T-t)} - F$. If F is greater than that given by (1.3) then you enter into the opposite positions, going short the forward. Again you make a riskless profit. The standard economic argument then says that investors will act quickly to exploit the opportunity, and in the process prices will adjust to eliminate it.

1.10 SUMMARY

The above descriptions of financial markets are enough for this introductory chapter. Perhaps the most important point to take away with you is the idea of no arbitrage. In the example here, relating spot prices to futures prices, we saw how we could set up a very simple portfolio which completely eliminated any dependence on the future value of the stock. When we come to value derivatives, in the way we just valued a future, we will see that the same principle can be applied albeit in a far more sophisticated way.

FURTHER READING

- For general financial news visit www.bloomberg.com and www.reuters.com. CNN has online financial news at www.cnnfn.com. There are also online editions of The *Wall Street Journal*, www.wsj.com, The *Financial Times*, www.ft.com and *Futures and Options World*, www.fow.com.
- For more information about futures see the Chicago Board of Trade website www.cbot.com.
- Many, many financial links can be found at Wahoo!, www.io.com/˜gibbonsb/wahoo.html.
- See Bloch (1995) for an empirical analysis of inflation data and a theoretical discussion of pricing index-linked bonds.
- In the main, we'll be assuming that markets are random. For insight about alternative hypotheses see Schwager (1990, 1992).
- See Brooks (1967) for how the raising of capital for a business might work in practice.
- Cox, Ingersoll & Ross (1981) discuss the relationship between forward and future prices.

EXERCISES

1. A company makes a 3-for-1 stock split. What effect does this have on the share price?
2. A company whose stock price is currently S, pays out a dividend DS, where $0 \leq D \leq 1$. What is the price of the stock just after the dividend date?
3. A particular forward contract costs nothing to enter into at time t and obligates the holder to buy the asset for an amount F at expiry, T. The asset pays a dividend DS at time t_d, where $0 \leq D \leq 1$ and $t \leq t_d \leq T$. Use an arbitrage argument to find the forward price, $F(t)$.

   Hint: Consider the point of view of the writer of the contract when the dividend is re-invested immediately in the asset.

CHAPTER 2

derivatives

In this Chapter...

- the definitions of basic derivative instruments
- option jargon
- no arbitrage and put–call parity
- how to draw payoff diagrams
- simple option strategies

2.1 INTRODUCTION

The previous chapter dealt with some of the basics of financial markets. I didn't go into any detail, just giving the barest outline and setting the scene for this chapter. Here I introduce the theme that is central to the book, the subject of options, a.k.a. derivatives or contingent claims. This chapter is non-technical, being a description of some of the most common option contracts, and explaining the market-standard jargon. It is in later chapters that I start to get technical.

Options have been around for many years, but it was only on 26th April 1973 that they were first traded on an exchange. It was then that The Chicago Board Options Exchange (CBOE) first created standardized, listed options. Initially there were just calls on 16 stocks. Puts weren't even introduced until 1977. In the US options are traded on CBOE, the American Stock Exchange, the Pacific Stock Exchange and the Philadelphia Stock Exchange. Worldwide, there are over 50 exchanges on which options are traded.

2.2 OPTIONS

If you are reading the book in a linear fashion, from start to finish, then the last topics you read about will have been futures and forwards. The holder of future or forward contracts is *obliged* to trade at the maturity of the contract. Unless the position is closed before maturity the holder must take possession of the commodity, currency or whatever is the subject of the contract, regardless of whether the asset has risen or fallen. Wouldn't it be nice if we only had to take possession of the asset if it had risen?

The simplest **option** gives the holder the *right* to trade in the future at a previously agreed price but takes away the obligation. So if the stock falls, we don't have to buy it after all.

> A **call option** is the right to buy a particular asset for an agreed amount at a specified time in the future

As an example, consider the following call option on Iomega stock. It gives the holder the right to buy one of Iomega stock for an amount \$25 in one month's time. Today's stock price is \$24.5. The amount '25' which we can pay for the stock is called the **exercise price** or **strike price**. The date on which we must **exercise** our option, if we decide to, is called the **expiry** or **expiration date**. The stock on which the option is based is known as the **underlying asset**.

Let's consider what may happen over the next month, up until expiry. Suppose that nothing happens, that the stock price remains at \$24.5. What do we do at expiry? We could exercise the option, handing over \$25 to receive the stock. Would that be sensible? No, because the stock is only worth \$24.5. Either we wouldn't exercise the option or if we really wanted the stock we would buy it in the stock market for the \$24.5. But what if the stock price rises to \$29? Then we'd be laughing; we would exercise the option, paying \$25 for a stock that's worth \$29, a profit of \$4.

We would exercise the option at expiry if the stock is above the strike and not if it is below. If we use S to mean the stock price and E the strike then at expiry the option is worth

$$\max(S - E, 0).$$

This function of the underlying asset is called the **payoff function**. The 'max' function represents the optionality.

Why would we buy such an option? Clearly, if you own a call option you want the stock to rise as much as possible. The higher the stock price the greater will be your profit. I will discuss this below, but our decision whether to buy it will depend on how much it costs. The option is valuable: there is no downside to it, unlike a future. In our example the option was valued at \$1.875. Where did this number come from? The valuation of options is the subject of this book, and I'll be showing you how to find this value later on.

What if you believe that the stock is going to fall; is there a contract that you can buy to benefit from the fall in a stock price?

> A **put option** is the right to *sell* a particular asset for an agreed amount at a specified time in the future

The holder of a put option wants the stock price to fall so that he can sell the asset for more than it is worth. The payoff function for a put option is

$$\max(E - S, 0).$$

Now the option is only exercised if the stock falls below the strike price.

LISTED OPTIONS QUOTATIONS

Monday, December 22, 1997

Composite volume and close for actively traded equity and LEAPS, or long-term options, with results for the corresponding put or call contract. Volume figures are unofficial. Open interest is total outstanding for all exchanges and reflects previous trading day. Close when possible is shown for the underlying stock on primary market. **CB**-Chicago Board Options Exchange. **AM**-American Stock Exchange. **PB**-Philadelphia Stock Exchange. **PC**-Pacific Stock Exchange. **NY**-New York Stock Exchange. **XC**-Composite. **p**-Put.

MOST ACTIVE CONTRACTS

Option/Strike				Vol	Exch	Last	Net Chg	a-Close	Open Int
Netscpe	Jan	30		8,727	XC	⅝	– ⅞	25½	14,759
Netscpe	Jan	25	p	8,391	XC	1¾	+ ½	25½	12,660
Coke	Feb	60	p	7,181	XC	1¼	+ 1/16	66 1/16	3,723
Intel	Jan	70	p	5,714	AM	2¼	– 1¼	71 7/16	43,100
Intel	Jan	70		5,338	AM	4⅛	+ ⅝	71 7/16	19,245
UUnlao	Jan	30		4,850	XC	1 3/16	– ⅛	27⅜	1,878
TelBrasl	Jan	115		4,729	XC	3½	+ ½	107 11/16	10,962
Intel	Jan	75		4,070	AM	1½	– ¼	71 7/16	29,162
Coke	Jan	60	p	3,970	XC	½	– ⅛	66 1/16	8,413
Ph Mor	Jan	45		3,700	AM	1¼	– 1/16	45	24,092
CompAssoc	Jan	45		3,611	CB	7¼	+ 1⅜	51⅝	4,271
MicrTc	Jan	30	p	3,560	XC	4⅛	+ ¾	26¼	6,924
Intel	Jan	75	p	3,507	AM	4⅞	– 1⅜	71 7/16	39,629
Coke	Jan	65	p	3,333	XC	1 9/16	– 1/16	66 1/16	7,776
Micsft	Jan	120	p	3,271	PC	1¾	+ ¼	127 1/16	12,603
I B M	Jan	105		3,154	XC	2 15/16	– 3/16	102 9/16	15,522
I B M	Jan	110		3,124	XC	1 5/16	– ¼	102 9/16	17,372
Intel	Jan	80		3,110	AM	11/16	...	71 7/16	31,598
AscendC	Jan	30		3,037	XC	13/16	– 11/16	25⅝	18,193
TelBrasl	Apr	115		2,987	XC	10⅝	+ 1⅝	107 11/16	4,164
I B M	Jan	95	p	2,787	XC	1 7/16	– 5/16	102 9/16	10,319
Merril	Jan	65		2,550	XC	5¾	– ⅜	70 7/16	1,397
Merril	Jan	65	p	2,522	XC	1	– ⅜	70 7/16	1,611
MicrTc	Jan	37½	p	2,515	XC	11	– 1⅛	26¼	2,767
M C I	Jan	42½		2,510	CB	1⅞	– ⅛	43⅝	18,063
AmExpr	Jan	75	p	2,469	XC	5/16	...	87½	1,784
K-III	Jun	12½	p	2,400	XC	⅝	– ⅛	12 13/16	100
DellCptr	Jan	85		2,350	PB	3¼	+ ⅜	81⅝	6,255
MedPart	Jan	22½		2,330	XC	2¼	– ¾	22⅜	4,450
M C I	Jan	40		2,284	CB	3⅞	– ½	43⅝	18,423
AT&T o	Jan	60		2,250	CB	4¾	+ 1 15/16	63 15/16	6,685
DellCptr	Jan	80		2,247	PB	5½	+ ⅞	81⅝	4,717
Motorola	Jan	60		2,223	AM	1 15/16	– 5/16	57¾	12,152
CUC Intl	Feb	35		2,186	XC	13/16	– 5/16	32¼	5,510
Compaq	Jan	65		2,119	PC	11/16	– 3/16	54½	23,993
Starbcks	Jan	45		2,110	CB	⅜	+ ⅛	40 1/16	1,241
Ph Mor	Feb	50		2,045	AM	½	...	45	...
I B M	Jan	100		2,043	XC	5⅞	...	102 9/16	15,024
I B M	Jan	95		2,015	XC	9¼	– ¾	102 9/16	9,093
Intel	Jan	72½		1,982	AM	2⅝	+ ⅛	71 7/16	4,257

WSJ.com Complete equity option listings and data are available in The Wall Street Journal Interactive Edition at **http://wsj.com** on the Internet's World Wide Web.

Figure 2.1 The *Wall Street Journal* of 23rd December 1997, Stock Options. Reproduced by permission of *Dow Jones & Company, Inc.*

Figure 2.1 is an excerpt from The *Wall Street Journal* of 23rd December 1997 showing options on various stocks. The table lists closing prices of the underlying stocks and the last traded prices of the options on the stocks. To understand how to read this let us examine the prices of options on Gateway 2000. Go to 'Gtwy2000' in the list. The closing price on 22nd December was $\$32\frac{5}{16}$, or \$32.3125 in decimal, and is written beneath 'Gtwy2000' several times.

INDEX OPTIONS TRADING

Monday, December 22, 1997

Volume, last, net change and open interest for all contracts. Volume figures are unofficial. Open interest reflects previous trading day. p-Put c-Call

CHICAGO

Strike		Vol.	Last	Net Chg.	Open Int.
CB MEXICO INDEX(MEX)					
Jan	110p	7	1¼	− 1½	58
Mar	110c	10	17⅜	+ ¼	48
Jan	115c	10	9¾	− 2¼	...
Jan	120p	10	4	− 2⅞	48
Mar	120p	10	7¾	− 4⅜	46
Mar	130c	10	6¾	+ 1½	50
Call Vol.		**40**	**Open Int.**		**415**
Put Vol.		**27**	**Open Int.**		**468**
CB TECHNOLOGY(TXX)					
Jan	200p	5	3⅜	− 2⅞	52
Jan	210c	2	9⅝	− ⅛	2
Feb	210c	5	14⅞	...	...
Feb	215c	1	14⅛	...	...
Call Vol.		**8**	**Open Int.**		**1,126**
Put Vol.		**5**	**Open Int.**		**157**
DJ INDUS AVG(DJX)					
Jan	64p	101	⅛	− ⅛	4,357
Jan	68p	30	⅜	− ¼	525
Mar	68p	220	1	− ¼	1,268
Jan	72c	32	7	+ ⅝	295
Jan	72p	10	9/16	− ¼	2,249
Feb	72p	228	1 5/16	− ⅛	883
Mar	72p	50	1⅞	+ 1/16	2,612
Jun	72p	6	2 13/16	− 1/16	1,029
Jan	73p	30	13/16	− 7/16	209
Jan	74c	5	5¼	+ ⅛	612
Jan	74p	2,491	15/16	− 1/16	1,399
Jan	75p	222	1⅛	− ¼	1,760
Jan	76c	86	3⅝	+ ⅛	1,576
Jan	76p	252	1¼	− 5/16	2,647
Mar	76c	3	5½	+ ½	5,130
Mar	76p	25	2 13/16	− 5/16	6,408
Jun	76c	2	7	+ ⅛	110
Jan	77c	125	2 15/16	+ 3/16	520
Jan	77p	305	1½	− ¼	1,985
Jan	78c	324	2¼	+ ⅛	2,487
Jan	78p	193	1⅞	− 3/16	6,977
Feb	78c	15	3⅜	+ ⅛	202
Feb	78p	25	2⅞	− ¾	2,790
Mar	78c	308	4¼	+ ½	1,485
Mar	78p	382	3⅜	− ½	1,495
Jan	79c	109	1¾	+ ¼	5,688
Jan	79p	326	2 5/16	− ⅜	5,618
Feb	79p	3	3½	...	5
Jan	80c	869	1 3/16	+ 1/16	20,816
Jan	80p	207	2⅞	− ⅜	19,686
Feb	80c	6	2 5/16	+ 7/16	116
Feb	80p	2	4	+ ¼	214
Mar	80c	248	2⅞	...	8,133
Mar	80p	937	4¼	− ⅜	11,436
Jun	80c	35	4⅞	+ ¼	3,695
Jan	81c	130	¾	− 1/16	512
Feb	81p	4	4⅜	...	...
Jan	82c	172	⅜	− ⅛	1,553
Jan	82p	66	4⅛	− ½	489
Mar	82c	10	2 3/16	+ ¼	19,707
Mar	82p	3	5¼	− 1	1,047
Jan	83c	550	⅜	...	...
Feb	83c	2	1	...	...
Jan	84c	220	3/16	...	1,304
Jan	84p	50	5½	− 1⅞	196
Mar	84c	75	1 5/16	− 11/16	2,647
Jan	86c	50	3/16	+ 1/16	385
Call Vol.		**3,376**	**Open Int.**		**116,693**
Put Vol.		**6,168**	**Open Int.**		**153,717**
DJ TRANP AVG(DTX)					
Jan	310p	2	4⅛	− 2¾	23
Jan	315p	6	5½	+ 2⅝	60
Jan	320p	3	9⅜	− 2	3
Jan	325c	14	2 15/16	+ 3/16	22
Call Vol.		**14**	**Open Int.**		**872**
Put Vol.		**11**	**Open Int.**		**1,259**

RANGES FOR UNDERLYING INDEXES

Monday, December 22, 1997

	High	Low	Close	Net Chg.	From Dec. 31	% Chg.
DJ Indus (DJX)	78.45	77.43	78.19	+ 0.63	+ 13.71	+ 21.3
DJ Trans (DTX)	316.33	314.05	314.94	+ 0.62	+ 89.37	+ 39.6
DJ Util (DUX)	268.21	264.51	267.71	+ 2.96	+ 35.18	+ 15.1
S&P 100 (OEX)	456.24	449.61	453.81	+ 3.28	+ 93.82	+ 26.1
S&P 500 -A.M.(SPX)	956.73	946.25	953.70	+ 6.92	+ 212.96	+ 28.8
CB-Tech (TXX)	215.91	210.90	212.92	+ 1.99	+ 13.04	+ 6.5
CB-Mexico (MEX)	122.79	121.23	122.69	+ 0.47	+ 40.73	+ 49.7
CB-Lps Mex (VEX)	12.28	12.12	12.27	+ 0.05	+ 4.07	+ 49.6
MS Multintl (NFT)	529.05	521.10	526.87	+ 4.90	+ 128.42	+ 32.2
GSTI Comp (GTC)	142.13	138.74	140.38	+ 1.61	+ 23.93	+ 20.6
Nasdaq 100 (NDX)	990.81	969.49	975.69	+ 5.79	+ 154.33	+ 18.8
NYSE (NYA)	501.61	497.18	500.48	+ 3.09	+ 108.18	+ 27.6
Russell 2000 (RUT)	423.75	420.03	422.88	+ 2.85	+ 60.27	+ 16.6
Lps S&P 100 (OEX)	90.90	87.94	90.11	0.00	+ 18.11	+ 25.2
Lps S&P 500 (SPX)	95.67	94.63	95.37	+ 0.69	+ 21.30	+ 28.8
S&P Midcap (MID)	322.60	320.26	321.41	+ 1.15	+ 65.83	+ 25.8
Major Mkt (XMI)	827.05	816.71	825.96	+ 8.85	+ 158.17	+ 23.7
Leaps MMkt (XLT)	82.71	81.67	82.60	+ 0.89	+ 15.82	+ 23.7
HK Fltg (HKO)	203.62	203.62	203.62	− 4.52	− 69.63	− 25.5
HK Fixed (HKD)	....	....	204.12	− 4.53	− 69.13	− 25.3
Leaps HK (DKL)	....	....	20.41	− 0.45	− 6.92	− 25.3
IW Internet (IIX)	257.44	250.14	254.58	+ 4.24	+ 10.50	+ 4.3
AM-Mexico (MXY)	136.14	134.06	136.14	+ 1.18	+ 46.42	+ 51.7
Institut'l -A.M.(XII)	1042.00	1027.81	1037.52	+ 8.52	+ 244.84	+ 30.9
Japan (JPN)	....	....	152.74	− 5.08	− 44.35	− 22.5
MS Cyclical (CYC)	466.11	460.65	463.32	+ 1.92	+ 74.76	+ 19.2
MS Consumr (CMR)	438.19	433.75	436.99	+ 2.06	+ 101.04	+ 30.1
MS Hi Tech (MSH)	441.16	429.35	434.08	+ 4.73	+ 51.04	+ 13.3
Pharma (DRG)	527.71	519.77	527.27	+ 6.32	+ 167.81	+ 46.7
Biotech (BTK)	162.53	159.40	159.53	− 0.73	+ 15.23	+ 10.6
Comp Tech (XCI)	440.58	429.33	433.77	+ 4.44	+ 93.85	+ 27.6
Gold/Silver (XAU)	72.42	71.40	71.75	+ 0.53	− 45.00	− 38.5
OTC (XOC)	735.35	721.45	725.42	+ 3.67	+ 142.55	+ 24.5
Utility (UTY)	303.90	298.96	303.81	+ 5.42	+ 47.25	+ 18.4
Value Line (VLE)	854.16	847.24	853.17	+ 5.93	+ 170.55	+ 25.0
Bank (BKX)	912.21	744.36	749.07	− 0.20	+ 211.39	+ 39.3
Semicond (SOX)	273.48	265.60	269.77	+ 2.85	+ 29.47	+ 12.3
Top 100 (TPX)	901.53	889.56	897.57	+ 6.75	+ 218.49	+ 32.2
Oil Service (OSX)	107.95	102.60	103.40	− 3.19	+ 31.45	+ 43.7
PSE Tech (PSE)	286.15	281.47	283.79	+ 2.91	+ 41.60	+ 17.2

Strike		Vol.	Last	Net Chg.	Open Int.
Jan	430p	10	12	+ 4¾	10
Feb	430c	5	14⅞	...	16
Jan	435c	166	6¾	+ 1⅞	722
Feb	435c	1	13⅜	+ 1⅞	9
Feb	435p	35	20½	...	...
Jan	440c	37	4⅜	+ 2 9/16	1,530
Jan	445p	25	19⅞	− 12⅜	55
Jan	450p	4	26¾	− 7⅜	34
Jan	480c	25	¼	− 1 5/16	4
Call Vol.		**895**	**Open Int.**		**16,028**
Put Vol.		**725**	**Open Int.**		**12,451**
S & P 100 INDEX(OEX)					
Jan	380p	2,090	1⅜	− ⅜	8,232
Feb	380p	20	3⅝	− ⅞	2,239
Jan	390c	45	65¾	...	136
Jan	390p	281	1¾	− ¾	2,670
Feb	390p	3	4½	− 1⅜	262
Jan	400p	2,374	2¼	− ⅞	3,973

Strike		Vol.	Last	Net Chg.	Open Int.
Feb	470p	1	24⅝	− 1⅞	578
Mar	470c	11	14⅞	...	3,436
Mar	470p	34	27⅝	− 1⅜	6,314
Apr	470p	32	30¼	...	...
Jan	475c	2,099	3	+ ⅛	6,206
Jan	475p	359	23	− 1½	1,784
Feb	475c	4	8¾	+ ¾	1,236
Mar	475c	5	12	...	...
Jan	480c	3,146	1⅞	− ⅛	8,389
Jan	480p	45	29¼	− 5¾	170
Feb	480c	3	6¾	− ½	3,310
Feb	480p	13	32	− 9	69
Mar	480c	519	10	+ 2	1,636
Mar	480p	31	33¾	− 1¼	526
Apr	480p	20	35¾	...	...
Jan	485c	2,240	1 1/16	− 3/16	5,151
Jan	485p	6	31½	− 9	145
Feb	485c	501	4⅞	+ ⅜	5,462
Jan	490c	1,285	11/16	...	6,487

Strike		Vol.	Last	Net Chg.	Open Int.
Mar	915p	400	27	− 3	4,528
Jan	920c	33	47¾	+ 6¼	3,430
Jan	920p	562	12¾	− 4¼	8,706
Feb	920p	16	23	− 3	310
Jan	925c	11	42¼	+ 3¼	984
Jan	925p	433	13½	− 4	16,189
Mar	925c	274	66⅞	+ 8⅞	11,687
Mar	925p	1,817	30¼	− 3¼	23,989
Jan	930c	22	43	+ 5⅞	805
Jan	930p	791	16⅛	− 3⅜	7,596
Feb	930c	1	57	− 12⅞	21
Feb	930p	10	25	− 10½	1,048
Mar	930c	21	63	+ 1½	7,022
Jan	935c	6	35	...	56
Jan	935p	231	17½	− 9	278
Jan	940c	64	35¼	+ 3¼	9,868
Jan	940p	3,527	18¾	− 3¼	11,483
Feb	940c	1	50½	+ 8½	222
Feb	940p	65	30	− 3½	582
Jan	945c	66	32	+ 1½	932
Jan	945p	75	22½	− 2⅜	95
Mar	945c	50	52	+ 6½	230
Mar	945p	1,325	37½	− 5	222
Jan	950c	158	28¾	+ 3	11,786
Jan	950p	2,275	21	− 5	19,195
Feb	950c	26	40	+ 4	72
Feb	950p	218	35	− 2½	2,478
Mar	950c	63	51¾	+ 4¼	20,965
Mar	950p	2,058	40	+ ¼	33,248
Jan	955c	93	25	+ 2½	3,085
Jan	955p	34	24	− 3⅜	3,973
Jan	960c	124	22½	+ 2	13,386
Jan	960p	291	29	− 2½	15,161
Feb	960c	30	34½	− 13⅛	284
Feb	960p	10	36½	− 4	907
Mar	960c	282	44½	+ 2½	4,400
Mar	960p	236	41⅜	− 4⅛	5,716
Jan	965c	136	19¼	+ 3	422
Jan	965p	1	28	− 11	150
Mar	965c	105	42	+ 7	651
Mar	965p	99	43	− 5	607
Jan	970c	186	16½	+ 1½	11,694
Jan	970p	43	30¼	− 5¾	8,352
Feb	970c	25	28	+ 2	44
Mar	970c	10	38	+ ½	6,725
Mar	970p	30	46¾	+ 3¾	3,645
Jan	975c	1,634	14½	+ 2½	4,089
Jan	975p	31	33	− 17	3,568
Feb	975c	320	27⅞	− 8	695
Mar	975c	2	36	+ 7	18,963
Mar	975p	1	47	− 9	6,343
Jan	980c	3,820	12	+ 1¾	9,799
Jan	980p	5	38	− 1	5,760
Feb	980c	54	25¾	+ 3¼	1,484
Feb	980p	1	46	− 5½	820
Mar	980p	100	49½	− 9	6,376
Jan	990c	471	9	+ 1⅛	6,198
Jan	990p	57	43	− 5	873
Feb	990c	255	19	+ 1½	1,047
Mar	990c	100	27	...	...
Jan	995c	799	7	+ 1½	1,384
Jan	995p	250	43¼	− 22¾	341
Mar	995c	4	26	+ 2	7,179
Jan	1005c	1,945	3½	− ¼	2,113
Jan	1010c	495	3	− ½	3,395
Jan	1010p	1	60	− 9	1,433
Feb	1010c	57	12¼	+ 1	2,356
Mar	1010c	20	18¾	+ 2¾	839
Mar	1010p	10	67	+ 1	37
Jan	1025c	608	1½	− 1/16	6,951
Feb	1025c	5	8½	+ 1½	63
Mar	1025c	250	15	+ 4	4,876
Mar	1025p	2	75	− 12½	3,559
Jan	1030c	65	1	...	988
Jan	1050c	459	½	...	4,635
Feb	1050c	170	3	− ¼	1,189
Mar	1050c	204	8¼	+ 1	4,971
Mar	1050p	29	94	...	7,088
Jan	1055c	10	⅜	...	206
Jan	1075c	50	½	+ 5/16	882
Jan	1075p	155	117½	− 9½	641
Mar	1075c	650	4	...	3,583
Mar	1100c	100	2	− 1	2,503
Call Vol.		**17,963**	**Open Int.**		**508,984**
Put Vol.		**41,820**	**Open Int.**		**719,783**

Figure 2.2 The *Wall Street Journal* of 23rd December 1997, Index Options. Reproduced by permission of *Dow Jones & Company, Inc.*

Calls and puts are quoted here with strikes of \$30, \$35 and \$40, others may exist but are not mentioned in the newspaper for want of space. The available expiries are January, March and June. Part of the information included here is the volume of the transactions in each series, we won't worry about that but some people use option volume as a trading indicator. From the data, we can see that the January calls with a strike of \$30 were worth \$4. The puts with same strike and expiry were worth \$1. The January calls with a strike of \$35 were worth $\$1\frac{3}{16}$ and the puts with same strike and expiry were worth $\$3\frac{1}{8}$. Note that the higher the strike, the lower the value of the calls but the higher the value of the puts. This makes sense when you remember that the call allows you to buy the underlying for the strike, so that the lower the strike price the more this right is worth to you. The opposite is true for a put since it allows you to sell the underlying for the strike price.

There are more strikes and expiries available for options on indices, so let's now look at the Index Options section of The *Wall Street Journal* of 23rd December 1997, this is shown in Figure 2.2.

In Figure 2.3 are the quoted prices of the January and March DJIA calls against the strike price. Also plotted is the payoff function *if the underlying were to finish at its current value at expiry*, the current closing price of the DJIA was 7819.

This plot reinforces the fact that the higher the strike the lower the value of a call option. It also appears that the longer time to maturity the higher the value of the call. Is it obvious that this should be so? As the time to expiry decreases what would we see happen? As there is less and less time for the underlying to move, so the option value must converge to the payoff function.

One of the most interesting feature of calls and puts is that they have a nonlinear dependence on the underlying asset. This contrasts with futures which have a linear dependence on the

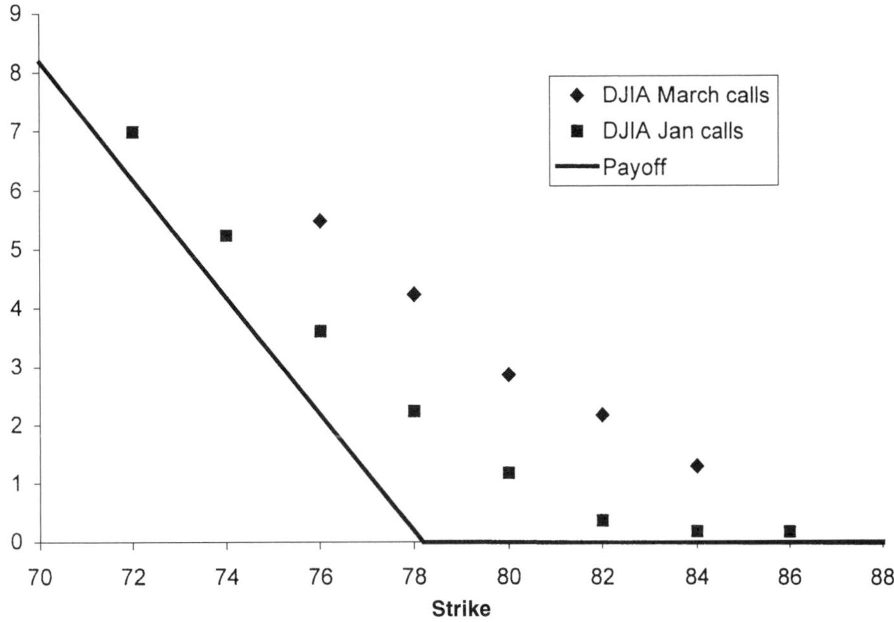

Figure 2.3 Option prices versus strike, January and March series of DJIA.

underlying. This nonlinearity is very important in the pricing of options, the randomness in the underlying asset and the curvature of the option value with respect to the asset are intimately related.

Calls and puts are the two simplest forms of option. For this reason they are often referred to as **vanilla** because of the ubiquity of that flavor. There are many, many more kinds of options, some of which will be described and examined later on. Other terms used to describe contracts with some dependence on a more fundamental asset are **derivatives** or **contingent claims**.

2.3 DEFINITION OF COMMON TERMS

The subjects of mathematical finance and derivatives theory are filled with jargon. The jargon comes from both the mathematical world and the financial world. Generally speaking the jargon from finance is aimed at simplifying communication, and to put everyone on the same footing.[1] Here are a few loose definitions to be going on with; some you have already seen and there will be many more throughout the book.

- **Premium**: The amount paid for the contract initially. How to find this value is the subject of much of this book.
- **Underlying (asset)**: The financial instrument on which the option value depends. Stocks, commodities, currencies and indices are going to be denoted by S. The option payoff is defined as some function of the underlying asset at expiry.
- **Strike (price)** or **exercise price**: The amount for which the underlying can be bought (call) or sold (put). This will be denoted by E. This definition only really applies to the simple calls and puts. We will see more complicated contracts in later chapters and the definition of strike or exercise price will be extended.
- **Expiration (date)** or **expiry (date)**: Date on which the option can be exercised or date on which the option ceases to exist or give the holder any rights. This will be denoted by T.
- **Intrinsic value**: The payoff that would be received if the underlying is at its current level when the option expires.
- **Time value**: Any value that the option has above its intrinsic value. The uncertainty surrounding the future value of the underlying asset means that the option value is generally different from the intrinsic value.
- **In the money**: An option with positive intrinsic value. A call option when the asset price is above the strike, a put option when the asset price is below the strike.
- **Out of the money**: An option with no intrinsic value, only time value. A call option when the asset price is below the strike, a put option when the asset price is above the strike.
- **At the money**: A call or put with a strike that is close to the current asset level.
- **Long position**: A positive amount of a quantity, or a positive exposure to a quantity.
- **Short position**: A negative amount of a quantity, or a negative exposure to a quantity. Many assets can be sold short, with some constraints on the length of time before they must be bought back.

[1] I have serious doubts about the purpose of most of the math jargon.

2.4 PAYOFF DIAGRAMS

The understanding of options is helped by the visual interpretation of an option's value at expiry. We can plot the value of an option at expiry as a function of the underlying in what is known as a **payoff diagram**. At expiry the option is worth a known amount. In the case of a call option the contract is worth $\max(S - E, 0)$. This function is the bold line in Figure 2.4.

The payoff for a put option is $\max(E - S, 0)$. This is the bold line plotted in Figure 2.5

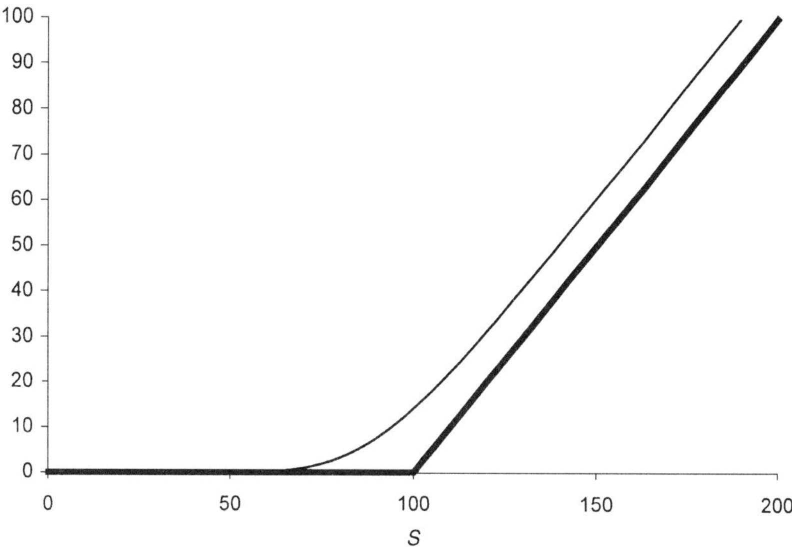

Figure 2.4 Payoff diagram for a call option.

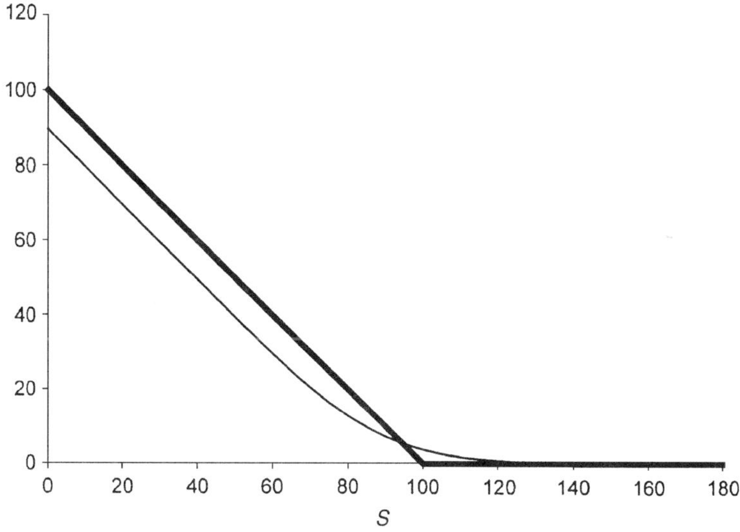

Figure 2.5 Payoff diagram for a put option.

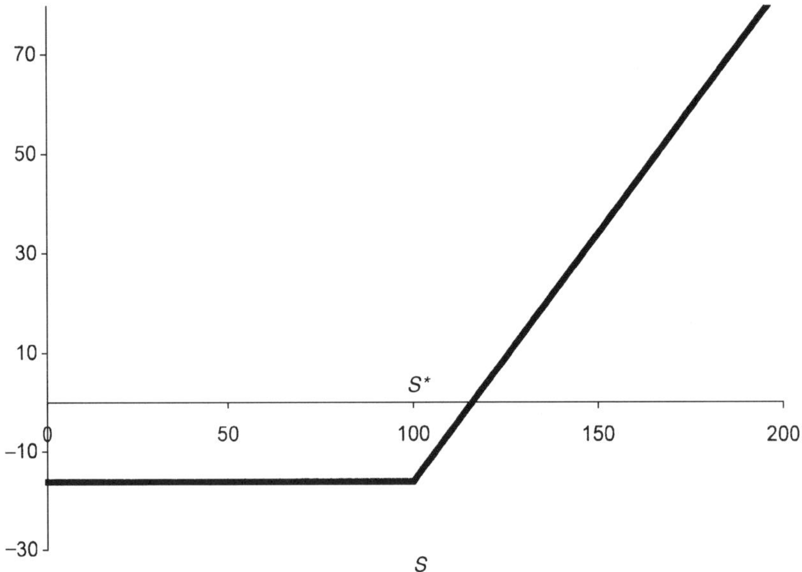

Figure 2.6 Profit diagram for a call option.

These payoff diagrams are useful since they simplify the analysis of complex strategies involving more than one option.

Make a note of the thin lines in these two figures. The meaning of these will be explained very shortly.

2.4.1 Other Representations of Value

The payoff diagrams shown only tell you about what happens at expiry, how much money your option contract is worth at that time. It makes no allowance for how much premium you had to pay for the option. To adjust for the original cost of the option, sometimes one plots a diagram such as that shown in Figure 2.6. In this **profit diagram** for a call option I have subtracted off from the payoff the premium originally paid for the call option. This figure is helpful because it shows how far into the money the asset must be at expiry before the option becomes profitable. The asset value marked S^* is the point which divides profit from loss; if the asset at expiry is above this value then the contract has made a profit, if below the contract has made a loss.

As it stands, this profit diagram takes no account of the time value of money. The premium is paid up front but the payoff, if any, is only received at expiry. To be consistent one should either discount the payoff by multiplying by $e^{-r(T-t)}$ to value everything at the present, or multiply the premium by $e^{r(T-t)}$ to value all cashflows at expiry.

2.5 WRITING OPTIONS

I have talked above about the rights of the purchaser of the option. But for every option that is sold, someone somewhere must be liable if the option is exercised. If I hold a call option entitling me to buy a stock some time in the future, who do I buy this stock from? Ultimately, the stock must be delivered by the person who **wrote** the option. The **writer** of an option is the person who promises to deliver the underlying asset, if the option is a call, or buy it, if the option is a put. The writer is the person who receives the premium.

In practice, most option contracts are handled through an exchange so that the purchaser of an option does not know who the writer is. The holder of the option can even sell the option on to someone else via the exchange to close his position. However, regardless of who holds the option, or who has handled it, the writer is the person who has the obligation to deliver or buy the underlying.

The asymmetry between owning and writing options is now clear. The purchaser of the option hands over a premium in return for special rights, and an uncertain outcome. The writer receives a guaranteed payment up front, but then has obligations in the future.

2.6 MARGIN

Writing options is very risky. The downside of buying an option is just the initial premium, the upside may be unlimited. The upside of writing an option is limited, but the downside could be huge. For this reason, to cover the risk of default in the event of an unfavorable outcome, the **clearing houses** that register and settle options insist on the deposit of a **margin** by the writers of options. Clearing houses act as counterparty to each transaction.

Margin comes in two forms, the **initial margin** and the **maintenance margin**. The initial margin is the amount deposited at the initiation of the contract. The total amount held as margin must stay above a prescribed maintenance margin. If it ever falls below this level then more money (or equivalent in bonds, stocks etc.) must be deposited. The levels of these margins vary from market to market.

2.7 MARKET CONVENTIONS

Most of the simpler options contracts are bought and sold through exchanges. These exchanges make it simpler and more efficient to match buyers with sellers. Part of this simplification involves the conventions about such features of the contracts as the available strikes and expiries. For example, simple calls and puts come in **series**. This refers to the strike and expiry dates. Typically a stock has three choices of expiries trading at any time. Having standardized contracts traded through an exchange promotes liquidity of the instruments.

Some options are an agreement between two parties, often brought together by an intermediary. These agreements can be very flexible and the contract details do not need to satisfy any conventions. Such contracts are known as **over the counter** or **OTC** contracts. I give an example at the end of this chapter.

2.8 THE VALUE OF THE OPTION BEFORE EXPIRY

We have seen how much calls and puts are worth at expiry, and drawn these values in payoff diagrams. The question that we can ask, and the question that is central to this book, is 'How much is the contract worth *now*, before expiry?' How much would you pay for a contract, a piece of paper, giving you rights in the future? You may have no idea what the stock price will do between now and expiry in six months, say, but clearly the contract has value. At the very least you know that there is no downside to owning the option. The contract gives you specific rights but no *obligations*. Two things are clear about the contract value before expiry: the value will depend on how high the asset price is today and how long there is before expiry.

The higher the underlying asset today, the higher we might expect the asset to be at expiry of the option and therefore the more valuable we might expect a call option to be. On the other hand a put option might be cheaper by the same reasoning.

The dependence on time to expiry is more subtle. The longer the time to expiry, the more time there is for the asset to rise or fall. Is that good or bad if we own a call option? Furthermore, the longer we have to wait until we get any payoff, the less valuable will that payoff be simply because of the time value of money.

I will ask you to suspend disbelief for the moment (it won't be the last time in the book) and trust me that we will be finding a 'fair value' for these options contracts. The aspect of finding the 'fair value' that I want to focus on now is the dependence on the asset price and time. I am going to use V to mean the value of the option, and it will be a function of the value of the underlying asset S at time t. Thus we can write $V(S,t)$ for the value of the contract.

We know the value of the contract *at expiry*. If I use T to denote the expiry date then at $t = T$ the function V is known, it is just the payoff function. For example if we have a call option then

$$V(S,T) = \max(S - E, 0).$$

This is the function of S that I plotted in the earlier payoff diagrams. Now I can tell you what the fine lines are in Figures 2.4 and 2.5. They are the values of the contracts $V(S,t)$ *at some time before expiry*, plotted against S. I have not specified how long before expiry, since the plot is for explanatory purposes only. I will spend a lot of time showing you how to find these values for a wide variety of contracts.

2.9 FACTORS AFFECTING DERIVATIVE PRICES

The two most important factors affecting the prices of options are the value of the underlying asset S and the time to expiry t. These quantities are **variables**, meaning that they inevitably change during the life of the contract; if the underlying did not change then the pricing would be trivial. This contrasts with the **parameters** that affect the price of options.

Examples of parameters are the interest rate and strike price. The interest rate will have an effect on the option value via the time value of money since the payoff is received in the future. The interest rate also plays another role which we will see later. Clearly the strike price is important: the higher the strike in a call, the lower the value of the call.

If we have an equity option then its value will depend on any dividends that are paid on the asset during the option's life. If we have an FX option then its value will depend on the interest rate received by the foreign currency.

There is one important parameter that I have not mentioned, and which has a major impact on the option value. That parameter is the **volatility**. Volatility is a measure of the amount of fluctuation in the asset price, a measure of the randomness. Figure 2.7 shows two asset price paths; the more jagged of the two has the higher volatility. The technical definition of volatility is the 'annualized standard deviation of the asset returns.' I will show how to measure this parameter in Chapter 3.

Volatility is a particularly interesting parameter because it is so hard to estimate. And having estimated it, one finds that it never stays constant and is unpredictable. Once you start to think

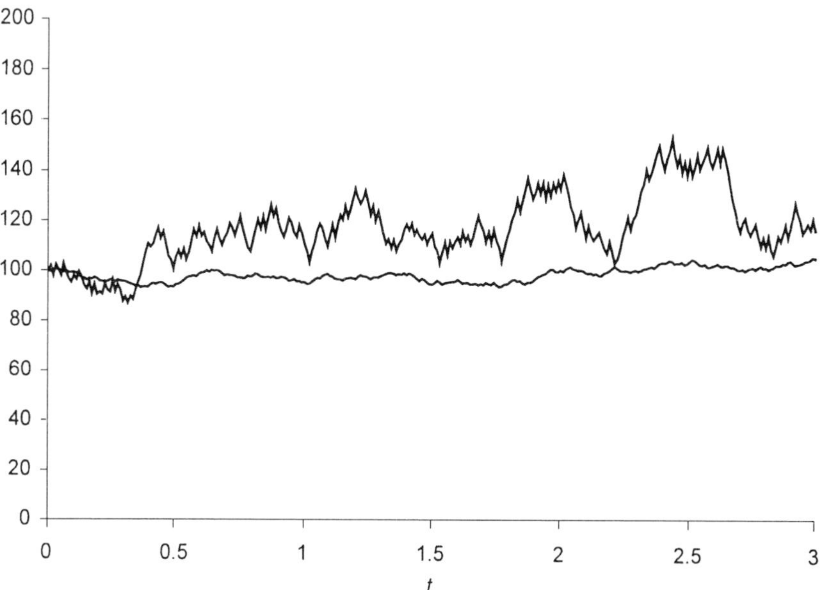

Figure 2.7 Two asset price paths, one much more volatile than the other.

of the volatility as varying in a random fashion then it becomes natural to treat it as a variable also. We will see examples of this later in the book.

The distinction between parameters and variables is very important. I shall be deriving equations for the value of options, partial differential equations. These equations will involve differentiation with respect to the variables, but the parameters, as their name suggests, remain as parameters in the equations.

2.10 SPECULATION AND GEARING

If you buy a far out-of-the-money option it may not cost very much, especially if there is not very long until expiry. If the option expires worthless, then you also haven't lost very much. However, if there is a dramatic move in the underlying, so that the option expires in the money, you may make a large profit relative to the amount of the investment. Let me give an example.

Example

Today's date is 14th April and the price of Wilmott Inc. stock is \$666. The cost of a 680 call option with expiry 22nd August is \$39. I expect the stock to rise significantly between now and August. How can I profit if I am right?

Buy the Stock

Suppose I buy the stock for \$666. And suppose that by the middle of August the stock has risen to \$730. I will have made a profit of \$64 per stock. More importantly my investment will have risen by

$$\frac{730 - 666}{666} \times 100 = 9.6\%.$$

Buy the Call

If I buy the call option for \$39, then at expiry I can exercise the call, paying \$680 to receive something worth \$730. I have paid \$39 and I get back \$50. This is a profit of \$11 per option, but in percentage terms I have made

$$\frac{\text{value of asset at expiry} - \text{strike} - \text{cost of call}}{\text{cost of call}} \times 100 = \frac{730 - 680 - 39}{39} \times 100 = 28\%.$$

This is an example of **gearing** or **leverage**. The out-of-the-money option has a high gearing, a possible high payoff for a small investment. The downside of this leverage is that the call option is more likely than not to expire completely worthless and you will lose all of your investment. If Wilmott Inc. remains at \$666 then the stock investment has the same value but the call option experiences a 100% loss.

Highly-leveraged contracts are very risky for the writer of the option. The buyer is only risking a small amount; although he is very likely to lose, his downside is limited to his initial premium. But the writer is risking a large loss in order to make a probable small profit. The writer is likely to think twice about such a deal unless he can offset his risk by buying other contracts. This offsetting of risk by buying other related contracts is called **hedging**.

Gearing explains one of the reasons for buying options. If you have a strong view about the direction of the market then you can exploit derivatives to make a better return, if you are right, than buying or selling the underlying.

2.11 EARLY EXERCISE

The simple options described above are examples of **European options** because exercise is only permitted *at expiry*. Some contracts allow the holder to exercise *at any time* before expiry, and these are called **American options**. American options give the holder more rights than their European equivalent and can therefore be more valuable, and they can never be less valuable. The main point of interest with American-style contracts is deciding *when* to exercise. In Chapter 9 I will discuss American options in depth, and show how to determine when it is *optimal* to exercise, so as to give the contract the highest value.

Note that the terms 'European' and 'American' do not in any way refer to the continents on which the contracts are traded.

Finally, there are **Bermudan options**. These allow exercise on specified dates, or in specified periods. In a sense they are half way between European and American since exercise is allowed on some days and not on others.

2.12 PUT-CALL PARITY

Imagine that you buy one European call option with a strike of E and an expiry of T and that you write a European put option with the same strike and expiry. Today's date is t. The payoff you receive at T for the call will look like the line in the first plot of Figure 2.8. The payoff for the put is the line in the second plot in the figure. Note that the sign of the payoff is negative; you *wrote* the option and are liable for the payoff. The payoff for the portfolio of the two options is the sum

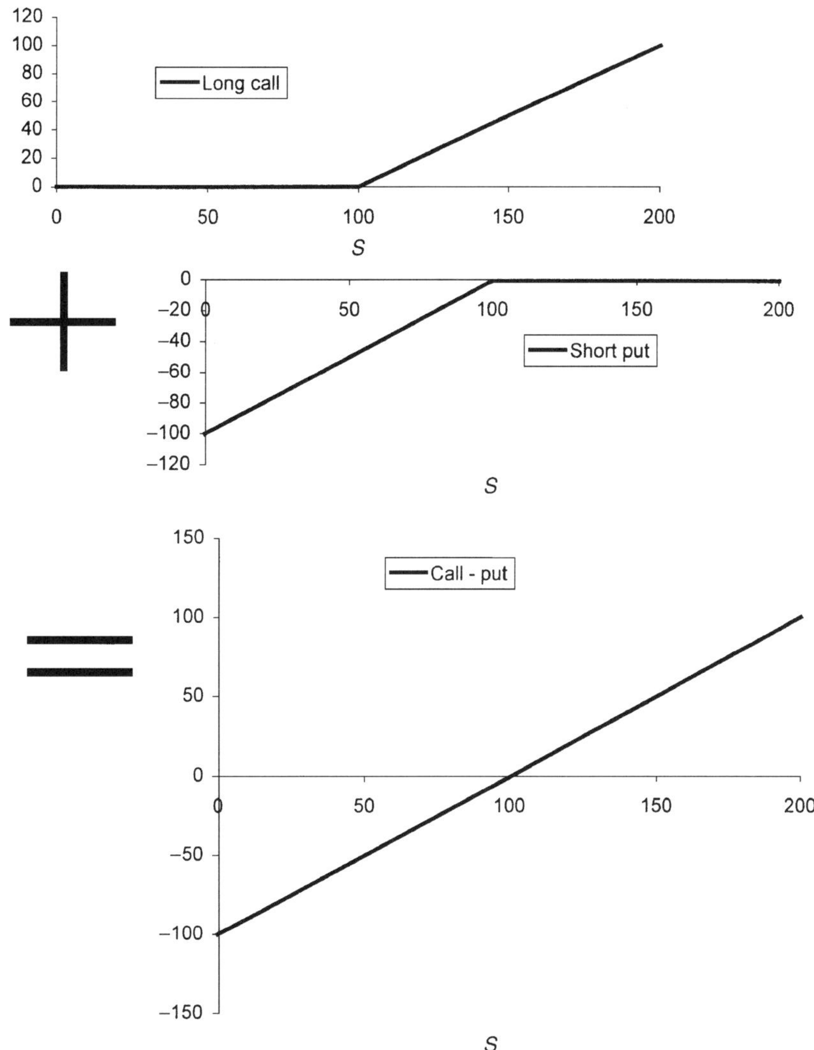

Figure 2.8 Schematic diagram showing put–call parity.

of the individual payoffs, shown in the third plot. The payoff for this portfolio of options is

$$\max(S(T) - E, 0) - \max(E - S(T), 0) = S(T) - E,$$

where $S(T)$ is the value of the underlying asset at time T.

The right-hand side of this expression consists of two parts, the asset and a fixed sum E. Is there another way to get exactly this payoff? If I buy the asset today it will cost me $S(t)$ and be worth $S(T)$ at expiry. I don't know what the value $S(T)$ will be but I do know how to guarantee to get that amount, and that is to buy the asset. What about the E term? To lock in a payment of E at time T involves a cash flow of $Ee^{-r(T-t)}$ at time t. The conclusion is that the portfolio of a long call and a short put gives me exactly the same payoff as a long asset,

Table 2.1 Cashflows in a hedged portfolio of options and asset.

Holding	Worth today (t)	Worth at expiry (T)
Call	C	$\max(S(T) - E, 0)$
Put	$-P$	$-\max(E - S(T), 0)$
Stock	$-S(t)$	$-S(T)$
Cash	$Ee^{-r(T-t)}$	E
Total	$C - P - S(t) + Ee^{-r(T-t)}$	0

short cash position. The equality of these cashflows is independent of the future behavior of the stock and is model independent:

$$C - P = S - Ee^{-r(T-t)},$$

where C and P are today's values of the call and the put respectively. This relationship holds at any time up to expiry and is known as **put–call parity**. If this relationship did not hold then there would be riskless arbitrage opportunities.

In Table 2.1 I show the cashflows in the perfectly hedged portfolio. In this table I have set up the cashflows to have a guaranteed value of zero at expiry.

2.13 BINARIES OR DIGITALS

The original and still most common contracts are the vanilla calls and puts. Increasingly important are the **binary** or **digital options**. These contracts have a payoff at expiry that is discontinuous in the underlying asset price. An example of the payoff diagram for one of these options, a **binary call**, is shown in Figure 2.9. This contract pays \$1 at expiry, time T, if the asset price is then greater than the exercise price E. Again, and as with the rest of the figures in this chapter, the bold line is the payoff and the fine line is the contract value some time before expiry.

Why would you invest in a binary call? If you think that the asset price will rise by expiry, to finish above the strike price, then you might choose to buy either a vanilla call or a binary call. The vanilla call has the best upside potential, growing linearly with S beyond the strike. The binary call, however, can never pay off more than the \$1. If you expect the underlying to rise dramatically then it may be best to buy the vanilla call. If you believe that the asset rise will be less dramatic then buy the binary call. The gearing of the vanilla call is greater than that for a binary call if the move in the underlying is large.

Figure 2.10 shows the payoff diagram for a **binary put**, the holder of which receives \$1 if the asset is *below* E at expiry. The binary put would be bought by someone expecting a modest fall in the asset price.

There is a particularly simple binary put–call parity relationship. What do you get at expiry if you hold both a binary call and a binary put with the same strikes and expiries? The answer is that you will always get \$1 regardless of the level of the underlying at expiry. Thus

$$\text{Binary call} + \text{Binary put} = e^{-r(T-t)}.$$

What would the table of cashflows look like for the perfectly hedged digital portfolio?

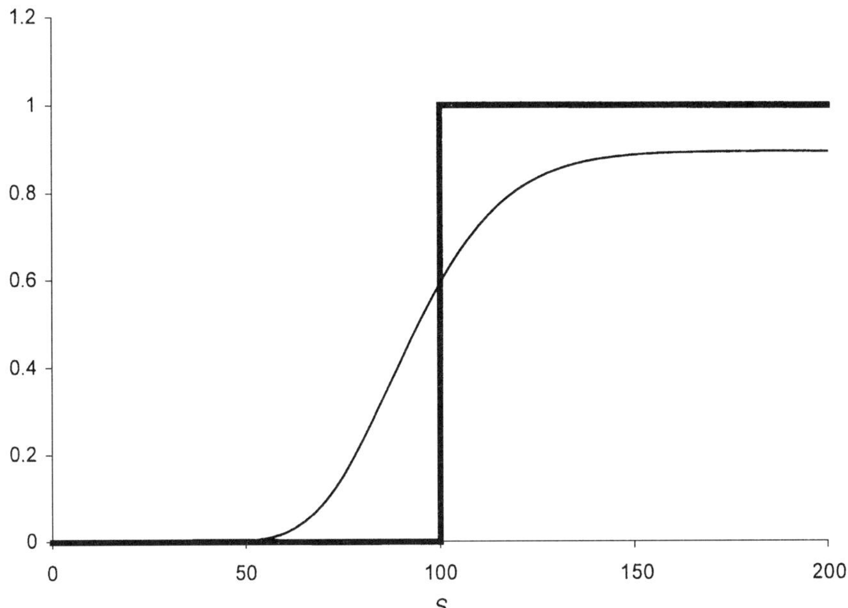

Figure 2.9 Payoff diagram for a binary call option.

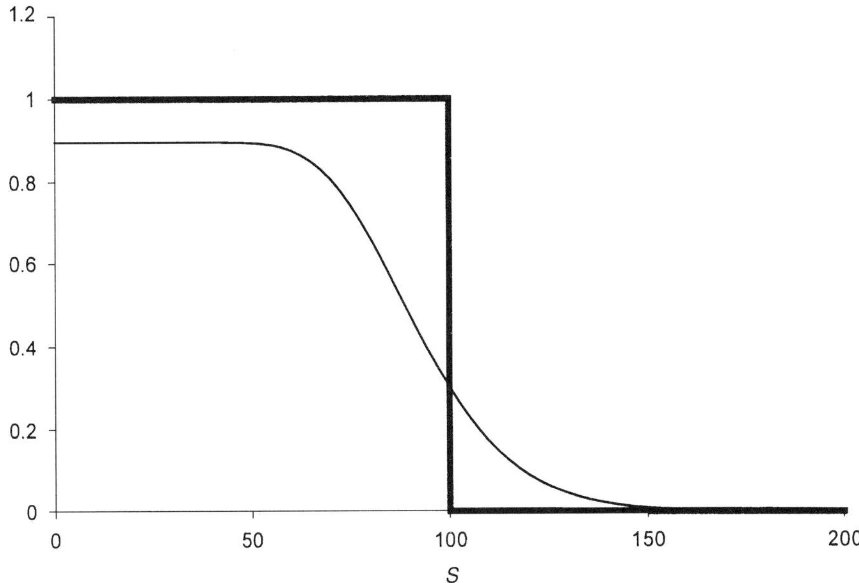

Figure 2.10 Payoff diagram for a binary put option.

2.14 BULL AND BEAR SPREADS

A payoff that is similar to a binary option can be made up with vanilla calls. This is our first example of a **portfolio of options** or an **option strategy**.

Suppose I buy one call option with a strike of 100 and write another with a strike of 120 and with the same expiration as the first, then my resulting portfolio has a payoff that is shown in Figure 2.11. This payoff is zero below 100, 20 above 120 and linear in between. The payoff

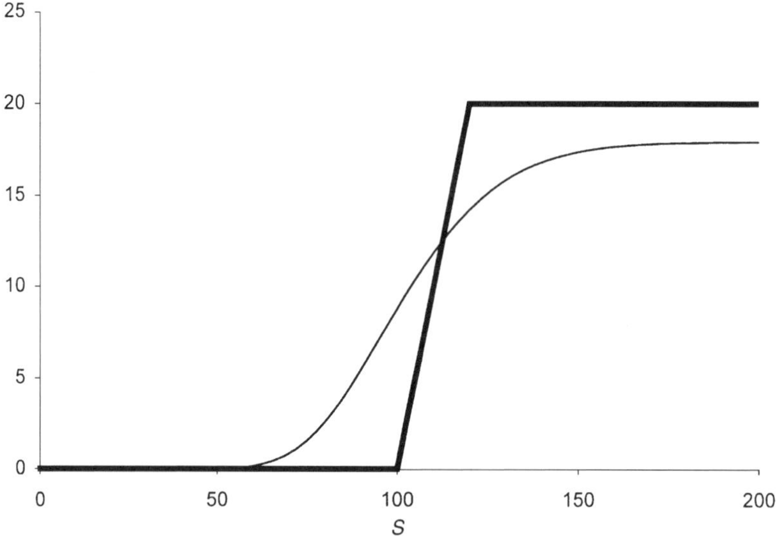

Figure 2.11 Payoff diagram for a bull spread.

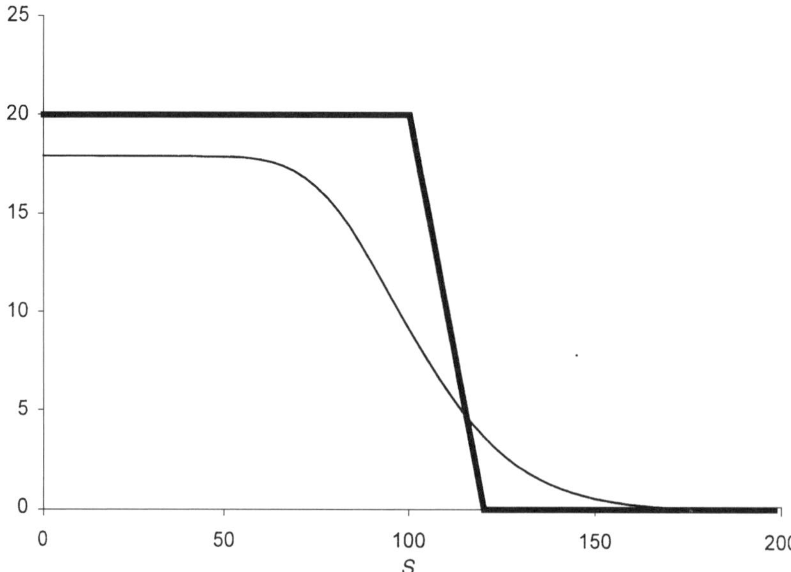

Figure 2.12 Payoff diagram for a bear spread.

is continuous, unlike the binary call, but has a payoff that is superficially similar. This strategy is called a **bull spread** because it benefits from a bull, i.e. rising, market.

The payoff for a general bull spread, made up of calls with strikes E_1 and E_2, is given by

$$\frac{1}{E_2 - E_1}(\max(S - E_1, 0) - \max(S - E_2, 0)),$$

where $E_2 > E_1$. Here I have bought/sold $(E_2 - E_1)^{-1}$ of each of the options so that the maximum payoff is scaled to 1.

If I write a put option with strike 100 and buy a put with strike 120 I get the payoff shown in Figure 2.12. This is called a **bear spread**, benefitting from a bear, i.e. falling, market. Again, it is very similar to a binary put except that the payoff is continuous.

Because of put–call parity it is possible to build up these payoffs using other contracts.

A strategy involving options of the same type (i.e. calls or puts) is called a **spread**.

2.15 STRADDLES AND STRANGLES

If you have a precise view on the behavior of the underlying asset you may want to precise in your choice of option. Simple calls, puts, and binaries may be too crude.

The **straddle** consists of a call and a put with the same strike. The payoff diagram is shown in Figure 2.13. Such a position is usually bought at the money by someone who expects the underlying to either rise or fall, but not to remain at the same level. For example, just before an anticipated major news item stocks often show a 'calm before the storm.' On the announcement the stocks suddenly moves either up or down, depending on whether or not the news was favorable to the company.

They may also be bought by technical traders who see the stock at a key support or resistance level and expect the stock to either break through dramatically or bounce back.

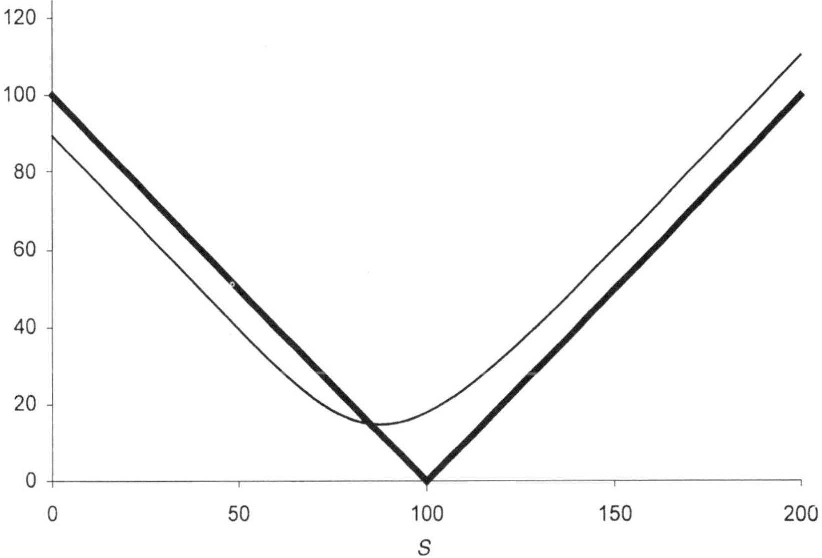

Figure 2.13 Payoff diagram for a straddle.

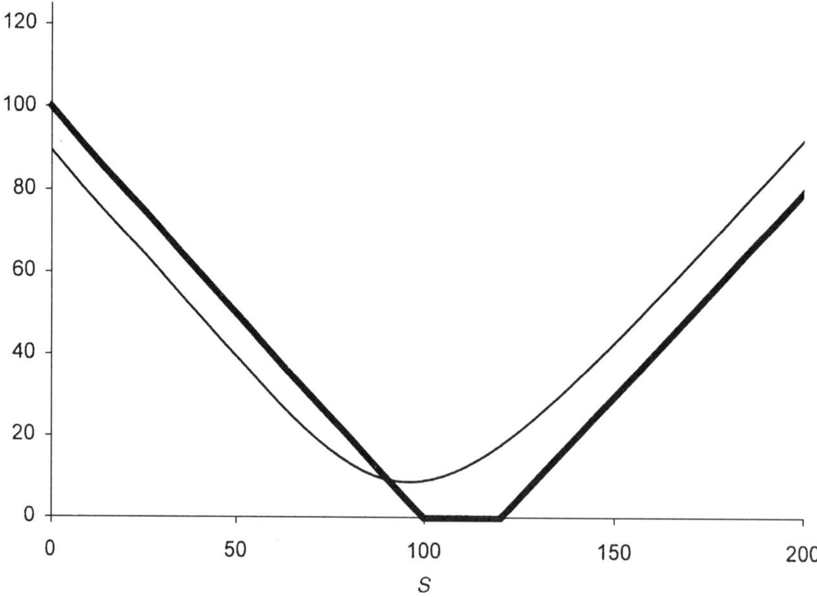

Figure 2.14 Payoff diagram for a strangle.

The straddle would be sold by someone with the opposite view, someone who expects the underlying price to remain stable.

The **strangle** is similar to the straddle except that the strikes of the put and the call are different. The contract can be either an **out-of-the-money strangle** or an **in-the-money strangle**. The payoff for an out-of-the money strangle is shown in Figure 2.14. The motivation behind the purchase of this position is similar to that for the purchase of a straddle. The difference is that the buyer expects an even larger move in the underlying one way or the other. The contract is usually bought when the asset is around the middle of the two strikes and is cheaper than a straddle. This cheapness means that the gearing for the out-of-the-money strangle is higher than that for the straddle. The downside is that there is a much greater range over which the strangle has no payoff at expiry; for the straddle there is only the one point at which there is no payoff.

There is another reason for a straddle or strangle trade that does not involve a view on the direction of the underlying. These contracts are bought or sold by those with a view on the direction of volatility. They are one of the simplest **volatility trades**. Because of the relationship between the price of an option and the volatility of the asset one can speculate on the direction of volatility. Do you expect the volatility to rise? If so, how can you benefit from this? Until we know more about this relationship, we cannot go into this in more detail.

Straddles and strangles are rarely held until expiry.

A strategy involving options of different types (i.e. both calls and puts) is called a **combination**.

2.16 BUTTERFLIES AND CONDORS

A more complicated strategy involving the purchase and sale of options with *three* different expiries is a **butterfly spread**. Buying a call with a strike of 90, writing two calls struck at 100 and buying a 110 call gives the payoff in Figure 2.15. This is the kind of position you might enter if you believe that the asset is not going anywhere, either up or down. Because it has no large upside potential (in this case the maximum payoff is 10) the position will be relatively cheap. With options, cheap is good.

The **condor** is like a butterfly except that four strikes, and four call options, are used. The payoff is shown in Figure 2.16.

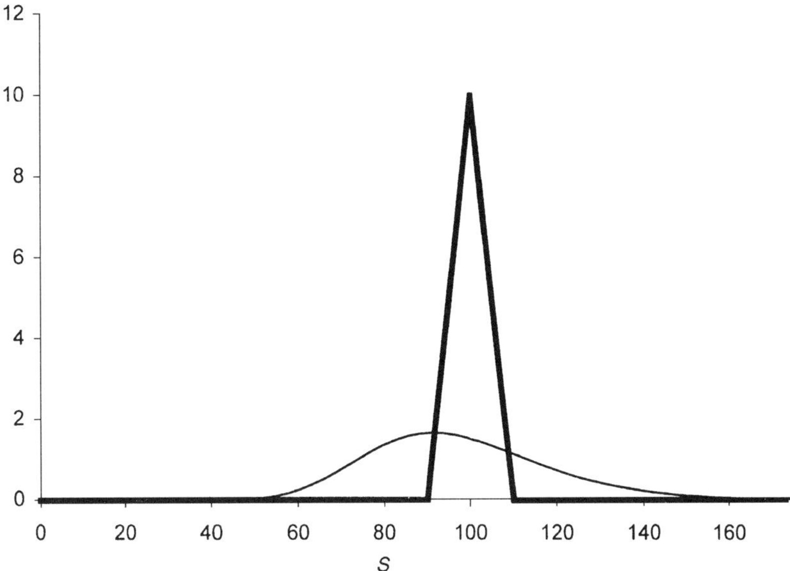

Figure 2.15 Payoff diagram for a butterfly spread.

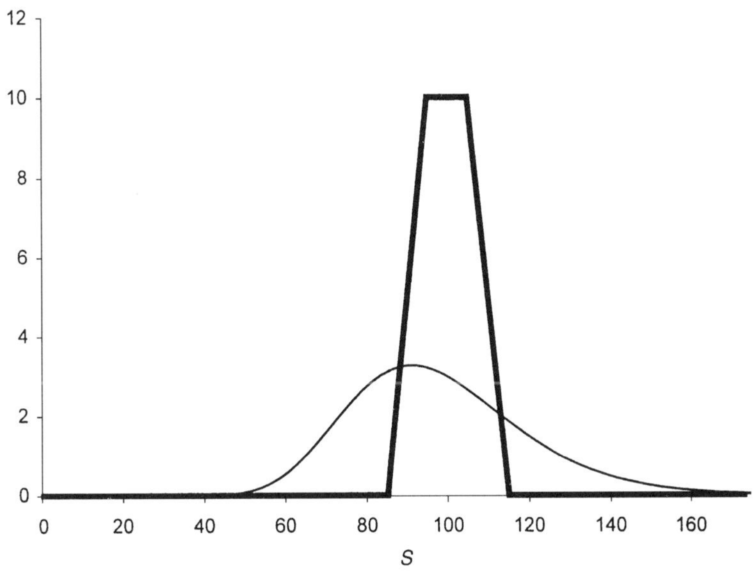

Figure 2.16 Payoff diagram for a condor.

2.17 CALENDAR SPREADS

All of the strategies I have described above have involved buying or writing calls and puts with different strikes *but all with the same expiration.* A strategy involving options with different expiry dates is called a **calendar spread**. You may enter into such a position if you have a precise view on the timing of a market move as well as the direction of the move. As always the motive behind such a strategy is to reduce the payoff at asset values and times which you believe are irrelevant, while increasing the payoff where you think it will matter. Any reduction in payoff will reduce the overall value of the option position.

2.18 LEAPS AND FLEX

LEAPS or **long-term equity anticipation securities** are longer-dated exchange-traded calls and puts. They began trading on the CBOE in the late nineteen-eighties. They are standardized so that they expire in January each year and are available with expiries up to three years. They come with three strikes, corresponding to at the money and 20% in and out of the money with respect to the underlying asset price when issued.

Figure 2.17 shows LEAPS quoted in The *Wall Street Journal.*

In 1993 the CBOE created **FLEX** or **flexible exchange-traded options** on several indices. These allow a degree of customization, in the expiry date (up to five years), the strike price and the exercise style.

LEAPS — LONG TERM OPTIONS

Option/Strike		Exp.	Call Vol.	Call Last	Put Vol.	Put Last
AT&T	50	Jan 99	135	16 3/4	50	2
AbtLab	65	Jan 00	1005	11 1/4	5	7
AMD	50	Jan 99	304	5/8	...	...
Altera	55	Jan 00	109	7 7/8	...	...
Amgen	60	Jan 00	250	10 3/8	30	10 5/8
AppleC	15	Jan 99	83	3	171	3 7/8
13 5/16	35	Jan 00	171	1 3/16	...	...
ApldMatl	30	Jan 00	152	11 7/8	20	7 5/8
30 1/2	30	Jan 99	123	8 3/8	...	...
Ascend	40	Jan 99	116	2 11/16	...	...
25 5/8	60	Jan 99	80	9/16	150	34 5/8
Boeing	55	Jan 99	1015	4 3/4	...	...
WstingEl	35	Jan 00	110	4	...	...
Cabletrn	25	Jan 00	...	...	500	11 1/4
14 3/16	35	Jan 99	15	13/16	263	21 1/8
ChaseM	30	Jan 99	111	5 5/8	...	...
Chevron	85	Jan 99	125	4 5/8	...	...
Chiron	30	Jan 00	150	1 1/2	30	12 7/8
16 15/16	32 1/2	Jan 99	420	7/16	...	...
CocaCola	40	Jan 99	110	27 7/8	...	...
66 1/16	70	Jan 99	327	7 1/4	60	8 5/8
66 1/16	80	Jan 99	766	3 7/8	...	...
66 1/16	90	Jan 99	443	1 3/4	...	...
Compaq	40	Jan 00	2	25	110	5 3/4
54 1/2	50	Jan 99	28	15	500	7 5/8
54 1/2	80	Jan 99	606	6 1/2	...	...
CypSemi	10	Jan 99	118	2	...	...
D S C	25	Jan 99	110	4 1/8	...	...
FedNM	60	Jan 99	175	6 3/8	...	...
Hilton	30	Jan 99	6	3 1/4	300	4 1/2
Hmstke	7 1/2	Jan 99	155	3 1/8	30	7/16
9 1/2	12 1/2	Jan 99	204	1 1/16	...	...
9 1/2	20	Jan 99	251	1/4	...	...

Option/Strike		Exp.	Call Vol.	Call Last	Put Vol.	Put Last
ITT Cp	85	Jan 99	300	8	...	...
Informix	5	Jan 99	171	1 1/2	80	1 3/4
4 1/4	5	Jan 00	171	2	...	...
4 1/4	10	Jan 00	10	1	230	5 7/8
4 1/4	10	Jan 99	82	9/16	435	5 7/8
Intel	60	Jan 00	30	25	220	6 7/8
71 7/16	70	Jan 99	195	13 5/8	25	8 3/4
71 7/16	75	Jan 00	227	18 5/8	12	14 1/8
71 7/16	75	Jan 99	123	11 3/8	1510	10 7/8
71 7/16	80	Jan 00	163	15 7/8	9	16 5/8
71 7/16	80	Jan 99	1675	9 3/4	742	14 1/8
71 7/16	100	Jan 00	146	10	4	29 1/4
71 7/16	120	Jan 99	234	2 1/4	12	49 1/8
IBM	110	Jan 99	168	12	...	...
K mart	15	Jan 99	160	1 3/16	...	...
MBNA o	26 5/8	Jan 99	360	5 1/8	...	...
MadgeNtw	5	Jan 99	190	1 1/2	...	...
McDnlds	55	Jan 99	909	2 1/2	...	...
MicrnT	25	Jan 00	121	10	...	...
26 1/4	40	Jan 00	132	5 7/8	3	15 3/4
26 1/4	50	Jan 99	121	1 7/8	...	...
26 1/4	80	Jan 00	...	...	110	53 5/8
Microsft	150	Jan 99	226	11 7/8	...	...
127 1/16	170	Jan 99	353	6 1/2	2	42 5/8
127 1/16	200	Jan 99	185	2 1/4	...	...
MoblTel	20	Jan 99	250	5 3/4	...	...
Oracle	20	Jan 00	45	8 1/2	120	4
21 3/4	30	Jan 99	140	2 3/4	...	...
PepsiCo	37 1/2	Jan 99	11	5 1/4	174	3 5/8
PlacerD	17 1/2	Jan 99	150	1	...	...
SaraLee	45	Jan 99	110	14 1/4	...	...
SeagateT	25	Jan 99	115	3 1/2	8	7
Sears	40	Jan 99	11	7 3/4	600	4 1/2

Option/Strike		Exp.	Call Vol.	Call Last	Put Vol.	Put Last
SunMic	40	Jan 99	241	8 1/2	...	
TelMex	50	Jan 99	...	...	169	6 3/8
TexInst	50	Jan 99	134	8 3/8	5	10 1/2
TWA	7 1/2	Jan 99	130	4	...	...
10 3/8	10	Jan 00	242	3 5/8	...	...
TycoInt	30	Jan 99	...	...	200	1 1/4
Unisys	12 1/2	Jan 99	5	2 3/4	200	2 1/4
WalMart	40	Jan 99	172	4 7/8	...	...
WorldCm	25	Jan 00	314	12 1/4	...	...

VOLUME & OPEN INTEREST SUMMARIES

	Vol.		Open Int.
CHICAGO BOARD			
Call Vol:	14,092	**Open Int:**	1,494,796
Put Vol:	4,995	**Open Int:**	1,312,746
AMERICAN			
Call Vol:	9,982	**Open Int:**	1,009,896
Put Vol:	5,362	**Open Int:**	446,487
PACIFIC			
Call Vol:	5,263	**Open Int:**	553,191
Put Vol:	1,673	**Open Int:**	287,769
PHILADELPHIA			
Call Vol:	2,468	**Open Int:**	413,430
Put Vol:	630	**Open Int:**	255,345
TOTAL			
Call Vol:	31,805	**Open Int:**	3,471,313
Put Vol:	12,660	**Open Int:**	2,302,347

Figure 2.17 The *Wall Street Journal* of 23rd December 1997, LEAPS. Reproduced by permission of *Dow Jones & Company, Inc.*

2.19 WARRANTS

A contract that is very similar to an option is a **warrant**. Warrants are call options issued by a company on its own equity. The main differences between traded options and warrants are the

timescales involved (warrants usually have a longer lifespan) and on exercise the company issues new stock to the warrant holder. On exercise, the holder of a *traded* option receives stock that has already been issued. Exercise is usually allowed any time before expiry, but after an initial waiting period.

The typical lifespan of a warrant is five or more years. Occasionally **perpetual warrants** are issued; these have no maturity.

2.20 CONVERTIBLE BONDS

Convertible bonds or **CB**s have features of both bonds and warrants. They pay a stream of coupons with a final repayment of principal at maturity, but they can be converted into the underlying stock before expiry. On conversion rights to future coupons are lost. If the stock price is low then there is little incentive to convert to the stock; the coupon stream is more valuable. In this case the CB behaves like a bond. If the stock price is high then conversion is likely and the CB responds to the movement in the asset. Because the CB can be converted into the asset, its value has to be at least the value of the asset. This makes CBs similar to American options; early exercise and conversion are mathematically the same.

There are other interesting features of convertible bonds, callback, resetting, etc. and the whole of Chapter 36 is devoted to their description and analysis.

2.21 OVER THE COUNTER OPTIONS

Not all options are traded on an exchange. Some, known as over the counter or OTC options, are sold privately from one counterparty to another. In Figure 2.18 is the term sheet for an OTC put option, having some special features. A **term sheet** specifies the precise details of an OTC contract. In this OTC put the holder gets a put option on S&P500, but more cheaply than a vanilla put option. This contract is cheap because part of the premium does not have to be paid until and unless the underlying index trades above a specified level. Each time that a new level is reached an extra payment is triggered. This feature means that the contract is not vanilla, and makes the pricing more complicated. We will be discussing special features like the ones in this contract in later chapters. Quantities in square brackets will be set at the time that the deal is struck.

2.22 SUMMARY

We now know the basics of options and markets, and a few of the simplest trading strategies. We know some of the jargon and the reasons why people might want to buy an option. We've also seen another example of no arbitrage in put–call parity. This is just the beginning. We don't know how much these instruments are worth, how they are affected by the price of the underlying, how much risk is involved in the buying or writing of options. And we have only seen the very simplest of contracts. There are many, many more complex products to examine. All of these issues are going to be addressed in later chapters.

Over-the-counter Option linked to the S&P500 Index

Option Type	European put option, with contingent premium feature
Option Seller	XXXX
Option Buyer	[dealing name to be advised]
Notional Amount	USD 20MM
Trade Date	[12 August 1998]
Expiration Date	[11 August 1999]
Underlying Index	S&P500
Settlement	Cash settlement
Cash Settlement Date	5 business days after the Expiration Date
Cash Settlement Amount	Calculated as per the following formula: #Contracts * max[0,S&Pstrike − S&Pfinal] where #Contracts = Notional Amount/ S&Pinitial This is the same as a conventional put option: **S&Pstrike** will be equal **to 95% of the closing price on the Trade Date** **S&Pfinal** will be the level of the Underlying Index at the valuation time on the Expiration Date **S&Pinitial** is the level of the Underlying Index at the time of execution
Initial Premium Amount	[2%] of Notional Amount
Initial Premium Payment Date	5 business days after Trade Date
Additional Premium Amounts	[1.43%] of Notional Amount per Trigger Level
Additional Premium Payment Dates	The Additional Premium Amounts shall be due only if the Underlying Index at any time from and including the Trade Date and to and including the Expiration Date is equal to or greater than any of the Trigger Levels.
Trigger Levels	103%, 106%, and 109% of **S&P500initial**
Documentation	ISDA
Governing law	New York

This indicative termsheet is neither an offer to buy or sell securities or an OTC derivative product which includes options, swaps, forwards and structured notes having similar features to OTC derivative transactions, nor a solicitation to buy or sell securities or an OTC derivative product. The proposal contained in the foregoing is not a complete description of the terms of a particular transaction and is subject to change without limitation.

Figure 2.18 Term sheet for an OTC 'Put.'

FURTHER READING

- McMillan (1996) and Options Institute (1995) describe many option strategies used in practice.
- Most exchanges have websites. The London International Financial Futures Exchange website contains information about the money markets, bonds, equities, indices and

commodities. See www.liffe.com. For information about options and derivatives generally, see www.cboe.com, the Chicago Board Options Exchange website. The American Stock Exchange is on www.amex.com and the New York Stock Exchange on www.nyse.com.

- Derivatives have often had bad press. See Miller (1997) for a refreshing discussion of the pros and cons of derivatives.
- The best books on options are Hull (1997) and Cox & Rubinstein (1985); modesty forbids me mentioning others.

EXERCISES

1. Consider a put option to buy 200 shares of the company for \$25 per share. How should the option contract be adjusted after a three-for-one stock split? How is the option price affected?
2. Find the value of the following portfolios of options at expiry, as a function of the share price:

   (a) Long one share, long one put with exercise price E.

   (b) Long one call and one put, both with exercise price E.

   (c) Long one call, exercise price E_1, short one call, exercise price E_2, where $E_1 < E_2$.

   (d) Long one call, exercise price E_1, long one put, exercise price E_2. There are three cases to consider.

   (e) Long two calls, one with exercise price E_1 and one with exercise price E_2, short two calls, both with exercise price E, where $E_1 < E < E_2$.

3. What is the difference between a payoff diagram and a profit diagram? Illustrate with a portfolio of short one share, long two calls with exercise price E.
4. A share currently trades at \$60. A European call with exercise price \$58 and expiry in three months trades at \$3. The three month default-free discount rate is 5%. A put is offered on the market, with exercise price \$58 and expiry in three months, for \$1.50. Do any arbitrage opportunities now exist? If there is a possible arbitrage, then construct a portfolio that will take advantage of it. (This is an application of put–call parity.)

CHAPTER 3
the random behavior of assets

In this Chapter...

- more notation commonly used in mathematical finance
- how to examine time-series data to model returns
- the Wiener process, a mathematical model of randomness
- a simple model for equities, currencies, commodities and indices

3.1 INTRODUCTION

In this chapter I describe a simple continuous-time model for equities and other financial instruments, inspired by our earlier coin-tossing experiment. This takes us into the world of stochastic calculus and Wiener processes. Although there is a great deal of theory behind the ideas I describe, I am going to explain everything in as simple and accessible manner as possible. We will be modeling the behavior of equities, currencies and commodities, but the ideas are applicable to the fixed-income world as we shall see in Part Four.

3.2 SIMILARITIES BETWEEN EQUITIES, CURRENCIES, COMMODITIES AND INDICES

When you invest in something, whether it is a stock, commodity, work of art or a racehorse, your main concern is that you will make a comfortable return on your investment. By **return** we tend to mean the percentage growth in the value of an asset, together with accumulated dividends, over some period:

$$\text{Return} = \frac{\text{Change in value of the asset + accumulated cashflows}}{\text{Original value of the asset}}.$$

I want to distinguish here between the percentage or relative growth and the absolute growth. Suppose we could invest in either of two stocks, both of which grow on average by \$10 p.a. Stock A has a value of \$100 and stock B is currently worth \$1000. Clearly the former is a better investment: at the end of the year stock A will probably be worth around \$110 (if the past is anything to go by) and stock B \$1010. Both have gone up by \$10, but A has risen by 10% and B by only 1%. If we have \$1000 to invest we would be better off investing in ten of asset A than one of asset B. This illustrates that when we come to model assets, it is the return that we should concentrate on. In this respect, all of equities, currencies, commodities and stock market indices can be treated similarly. What return do we expect to get from them?

Part of the business of estimating returns for each asset is to estimate how much unpredictability there is in the asset value. In the next section I am going to show that randomness plays a large part in financial markets, and start to build up a model for asset returns incorporating this randomness.

3.3 EXAMINING RETURNS

In Figure 3.1 I show the quoted price of Perez Companc, an Argentinean conglomerate, over the period February 1995 to November 1996. This is a very typical plot of a financial asset. The asset shows a general upward trend over the period but this is far from guaranteed. If you bought and sold at the wrong times you would lose a lot of money. The unpredictability that is seen in this figure is the main feature of financial modeling. Because there is so much randomness, any mathematical model of a financial asset must acknowledge the randomness and have a probabilistic foundation.

Remembering that the returns are more important to us than the absolute level of the asset price, I show in Figure 3.2 how to calculate returns on a spreadsheet. Denoting the asset value on the ith day by S_i, then the return from day i to day $i+1$ is given by

$$\frac{S_{i+1} - S_i}{S_i} = R_i.$$

(I've ignored dividends here. They are easily allowed for, especially since they only get paid two or four times a year typically.) Of course, I didn't need to use data spaced at intervals of a day; I will comment on this later.

Figure 3.1 Perez Companc from February 1995 to November 1996.

	A	B	C	D	E	F	G
1	**Date**	**Perez**	**Return**				
2	01-Mar-95	2.11			**Average return**	0.002916	
3	02-Mar-95	1.90	-0.1		**Standard deviation**	0.024521	
4	03-Mar-95	2.18	0.149906				
5	06-Mar-95	2.16	-0.010809				
6	07-Mar-95	1.91	-0.112583	= AVERAGE(C3:C463)			
7	08-Mar-95	1.86	-0.029851				
8	09-Mar-95	1.97	0.061538				
9	10-Mar-95	2.27	0.15		= STDEVP(C3:C463)		
10	13-Mar-95	2.49	0.099874				
11	14-Mar-95	2.76	0.108565				
12	15-Mar-95	2.61	-0.054264				
13	16-Mar-95	2.67	0.021858				
14	17-Mar-95	2.64	-0.010695				
15	20-Mar-95	2.60	-0.016216	=(B13-B12)/B12			
16	21-Mar-95	2.59	-0.002747				
17	22-Mar-95	2.59	-0.002755				
18	23-Mar-95	2.55	-0.012321				
19	24-Mar-95	2.73	0.069307				
20	27-Mar-95	2.91	0.064815				
21	28-Mar-95	2.92	0.002899				
22	29-Mar-95	2.92	0				
23	30-Mar-95	3.12	0.069364				
24	31-Mar-95	3.14	0.005405				
25	03-Apr-95	3.13	-0.002688				
26	04-Apr-95	3.24	0.037736				
27	05-Apr-95	3.25	0.002597				
28	06-Apr-95	3.28	0.007772				
29	07-Apr-95	3.21	-0.020566				
30	10-Apr-95	3.02	-0.060367				
31	11-Apr-95	3.08	0.019553				
32	12-Apr-95	3.19	0.035616				
33	17-Apr-95	3.21	0.007936				
34	18-Apr-95	3.17	-0.013123				
35	19-Apr-95	3.24	0.021277				

Figure 3.2 Spreadsheet for calculating asset returns.

In Figure 3.3 I show the daily returns for Perez Companc. This looks very much like 'noise,' and that is exactly how we are going to model it. The mean of the returns distribution is

$$\overline{R} = \frac{1}{M}\sum_{i=1}^{M} R_i \tag{3.1}$$

and the sample standard deviation is

$$\sqrt{\frac{1}{M-1}\sum_{i=1}^{M}(R_i - \overline{R})^2}, \tag{3.2}$$

where M is the number of returns in the sample (one fewer than the number of asset prices). From the data in this example we find that the mean is 0.002916 and the standard deviation is 0.024521.

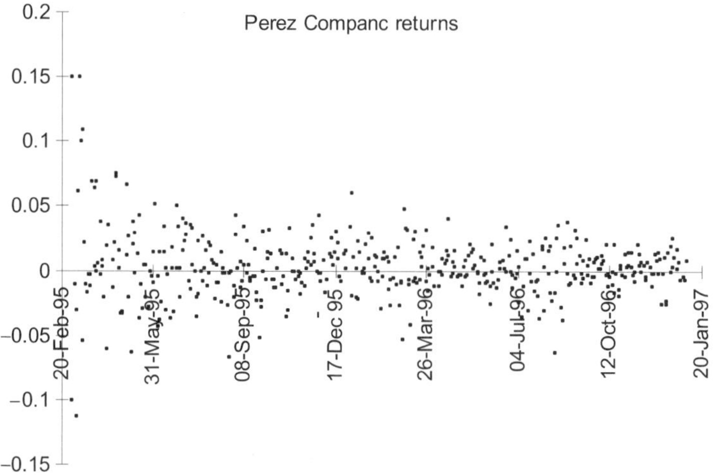

Figure 3.3 Daily returns of Perez Companc.

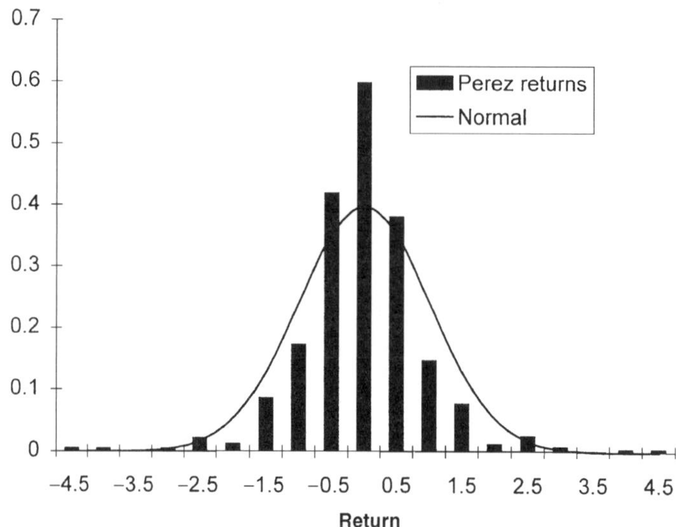

Figure 3.4 Normalized frequency distribution of Perez Companc and the standardized Normal distribution.

The frequency distribution of this time series of daily returns is easily calculated, and very instructive to plot. In Excel use Tools | Data Analysis | Histogram. In Figure 3.4 is shown the frequency distribution of daily returns for Perez Companc. This distribution has been scaled and translated to give it a mean of zero, a standard deviation of one and an area under the curve of one. On the same plot is drawn the probability density function for the standardized Normal distribution function

$$\frac{1}{\sqrt{2\pi}}e^{-1/2\phi^2},$$

where ϕ is a standardized Normal variable. The two curves are not identical but are fairly close.

Supposing that we believe that the empirical returns are close enough to Normal for this to be a good approximation, then we have come a long way towards a model. I am going to write the returns as a random variable, drawn from a Normal distribution with a known, constant, non-zero mean and a known, constant, non-zero standard deviation:

$$R_i = \frac{S_{i+1} - S_i}{S_i} = \text{mean} + \text{standard deviation} \times \phi.$$

3.4 TIMESCALES

How do the mean and standard deviation of the returns' time series, as estimated by (3.1) and (3.2), scale with the timestep between asset price measurements? In the example the timestep is one day, but suppose I sampled at hourly intervals or weekly, how would this affect the distribution?

Call the timestep δt. The mean of the return scales with the size of the timestep. That is, the larger the time between sampling the more the asset will have moved in the meantime, *on average*. I can write

$$\text{mean} = \mu\, \delta t,$$

for some μ which we will assume to be constant.

Ignoring randomness for the moment, our model is simply

$$\frac{S_{i+1} - S_i}{S_i} = \mu\, \delta t.$$

Rearranging, we get

$$S_{i+1} = S_i(1 + \mu\, \delta t).$$

If the asset begins at S_0 at time $t = 0$ then after one timestep $t = \delta t$ and

$$S_1 = S_0(1 + \mu\, \delta t).$$

After two timesteps $t = 2\, \delta t$ and

$$S_2 = S_1(1 + \mu\, \delta t) = S_0(1 + \mu\, \delta t)^2,$$

and after M timesteps $t = M\, \delta t = T$ and

$$S_M = S_0(1 + \mu\, \delta t)^M.$$

This is just

$$S_M = S_0(1 + \mu\, \delta t)^M = S_0 e^{M \log(1+\mu\, \delta t)} \approx S_0 e^{\mu M\, \delta t} = S_0 e^{\mu T}.$$

In the limit as the timestep tends to zero with the total time T fixed, this approximation becomes exact. This result is important for two reasons.

First, in the absence of any randomness the asset exhibits exponential growth, just like cash in the bank.

Second, the model is meaningful in the limit as the timestep tends to zero. If I had chosen to scale the mean of the returns distribution with any other power of δt it would have resulted in either a trivial model ($S_T = S_0$) or infinite values for the asset.

The second point can guide us in the choice of scaling for the random component of the return. How does the standard deviation of the return scale with the timestep δt? Again, consider what happens after $T/\delta t$ timesteps each of size δt (i.e. after a total time of T). Inside the square root in expression (3.2) there are a large number of terms, $T/\delta t$ of them. In order for the standard deviation to remain finite as we let δt tend to zero, the individual terms in the expression must each be of $O(\delta t)$. Since each term is a square of a return, the standard deviation of the asset return over a timestep δt must be $O(\delta t^{1/2})$:

$$\text{standard deviation} = \sigma\, \delta t^{1/2},$$

where σ is some parameter measuring the amount of randomness. The larger this parameter the more uncertain is the return. For the moment let's assume that it is constant.

Putting these scalings explicitly into our asset return model

$$R_i = \frac{S_{i+1} - S_i}{S_i} = \mu\, \delta t + \sigma\phi\, \delta t^{1/2}. \tag{3.3}$$

I can rewrite Equation (3.3) as

$$S_{i+1} - S_i = \mu S_i\, \delta t + \sigma S_i \phi\, \delta t^{1/2}. \tag{3.4}$$

The left-hand side of this equation is the change in the asset price from timestep i to timestep $i+1$. The right-hand side is the 'model.' We can think of this equation as a model for a **random walk** of the asset price. This is shown schematically in Figure 3.5. We know exactly where the asset price is today but tomorrow's value is unknown. It is distributed about today's value according to (3.4).

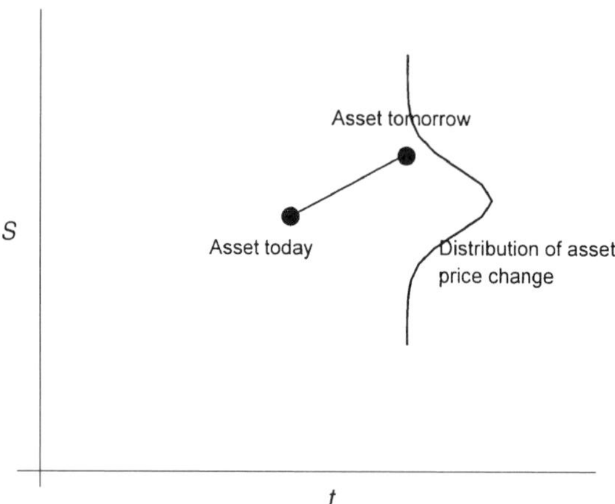

Figure 3.5 A representation of the random walk.

3.4.1 The Drift

The parameter μ is called the **drift rate**, the **expected return** or the **growth rate** of the asset. Statistically it is very hard to measure since the mean scales with the usually small parameter δt. It can be estimated by

$$\mu = \frac{1}{M\, \delta t} \sum_{i=1}^{M} R_i.$$

The unit of time that is usually used is the year, in which case μ is quoted as an *annualized* growth rate.

3.4.2 The Volatility

The parameter σ is called the **volatility** of the asset. It can be estimated by

$$\sqrt{\frac{1}{(M-1)\,\delta t}\sum_{i=1}^{M}(R_i-\overline{R})^2}.$$

Again, this is almost always quoted in annualized terms.

The volatility is the most important and elusive quantity in the theory of derivatives. I will come back again and again to its estimation and modeling.

Because of their scaling with time, the drift and volatility have different effects on the asset path. The drift is not apparent over short timescales for which the volatility dominates. Over long timescales, for instance decades, the drift becomes important. Figure 3.6 is a realized path of the logarithm of an asset, together with its expected path and a 'confidence interval.' In this example the confidence interval represents one standard deviation. With the assumption of Normality this means that 68% of the time the asset should be within this range. The mean path is growing linearly in time and the confidence interval grows like the square root of time. Thus over short timescales the volatility dominates.[1]

Figure 3.6 Path of the logarithm of an asset, its expected path and one standard deviation above and below.

[1] Why did I take the logarithm? Because changes in the logarithm are related to the return on the asset.

3.5 THE RANDOM WALK ON A SPREADSHEET

The random walk (3.4) can be written as a 'recipe' for generating S_{i+1} from S_i:

$$S_{i+1} = S_i(1 + \mu\,\delta t + \sigma\phi\,\delta t^{1/2}). \tag{3.5}$$

We can easily simulate the model using a spreadsheet. In this simulation we must input several parameters, a starting value for the asset, a timestep δt, the drift rate μ, the volatility σ and the total number of timesteps. Then, at each timestep, we must choose a random number ϕ from a Normal distribution. I will talk about simulations in depth in Chapter 49, but for the moment let me just say that an approximation to a Normal variable that is fast in a spreadsheet, and quite accurate, is simply to add up twelve random variables drawn from a uniform distribution over zero to one, and subtract six:

$$\left(\sum_{i=1}^{12} \texttt{RAND()}\right) - 6.$$

The Excel spreadsheet function `RAND()` gives a uniformly-distributed random variable.

	A	B	C	D	E	F	G	H
1	**Asset**	**100**		**Time**	**Asset**			
2	**Drift**	**0.15**		0	100			
3	**Volatility**	**0.25**		0.01	101.2378			
4	**Timestep**	**0.01**		0.02	103.8329			
5				0.03	106.5909			
6				0.04	110.993			
7		=D4+$B$4		0.05	115.9425			
8				0.06	117.1478			
9				0.07	115.9868			
10				0.08	114.921			
11	=E7*(1+$B$2*$B$4+$B$3*SQRT($B$4)*(RAND()+RAND()+RAND()							
12	+RAND()+RAND()+RAND()+RAND()+RAND()+RAND()+RAND()+RAND()-6))							
13				0.11	113.3875			
14				0.12	108.5439			
15				0.13	107.4318			
16				0.14	109.092			
17				0.15	110.8794			
18				0.16	113.5328			
19				0.17	116.099			
20				0.18	116.2446			
21				0.19	119.315			
22				0.2	120.0332			
23				0.21	124.337			
24				0.22	128.3446			
25				0.23	125.5112			
26				0.24	128.2683			
27				0.25	124.0548			
28				0.26	125.9068			
29				0.27	122.4632			
30				0.28	122.4472			
31				0.29	121.3325			
32				0.3	124.593			
33				0.31	121.9263			

Figure 3.7 Simulating the random walk on a spreadsheet.

In Figure 3.7 I show the details of a spreadsheet used for simulating the asset price random walk.

3.6 THE WIENER PROCESS

So far we have a model that allows the asset to take any value after a timestep. This is a step forward but we have still not reached our goal of continuous time. We still have a discrete timestep. This section is a brief introduction to the continuous-time limit of equations like (3.3). I will start to introduce ideas from the world of stochastic modeling and Wiener processes, delving more deeply in Chapter 4.

I am now going to use the notation $d\cdot$ to mean 'the change in' some quantity. Thus dS is the 'change in the asset price.' But this change will be in *continuous time*. Thus we will go to the limit $\delta t = 0$. The first δt on the right-hand side of (3.4) becomes dt but the second term is more complicated.

I cannot straightforwardly write $dt^{1/2}$ instead of $\delta t^{1/2}$. If I do go to the zero-timestep limit then any random $dt^{1/2}$ term will dominate any deterministic dt term. Yet in our problem the factor in front of $dt^{1/2}$ has a mean of zero, so maybe it does not outweigh the drift after all. Clearly something subtle is happening in the limit.

It turns out, and we will see this in Chapter 4, that because the *variance* of the random term is $O(\delta t)$ we *can* make a sensible continuous-time limit of our discrete-time model. This brings us into the world of Wiener processes.

I am going to write the term $\phi\,\delta t^{1/2}$ as

$$dX.$$

You can think of dX as being a random variable, drawn from a Normal distribution with mean zero and variance dt:

$$E[dX] = 0 \quad \text{and} \quad E[dX^2] = dt.$$

This is not exactly what it is, but it is close enough to give the right idea. This is called a **Wiener process**. The important point is that we can build up a continuous-time theory using Wiener processes instead of Normal distributions and discrete time.

3.7 THE WIDELY-ACCEPTED MODEL FOR EQUITIES, CURRENCIES, COMMODITIES AND INDICES

Our asset price model in the continuous-time limit, using the Wiener process notation, can be written as

$$dS = \mu S\,dt + \sigma S\,dX. \tag{3.6}$$

This is our first **stochastic differential equation**. It is a continuous-time model of an asset price. It is the most widely-accepted model for equities, currencies, commodities and indices, and the foundation of so much finance theory.

3.8 SUMMARY

In this chapter I introduced a simple model for the random walk of an asset. Initially I built the model up in discrete time, showing what the various terms mean, how they scale with the timestep and showing how to implement the model on a spreadsheet.

Most of this book is about continuous-time models for assets. The continuous-time version of the random walk involves concepts such as stochastic calculus and Wiener processes. I introduced these briefly in this chapter and will now go on to explain the underlying theory of stochastic calculus to give the necessary background for the rest of the book.

FURTHER READING

- Mandelbrot (1963) and Fama (1965) did some of the early work on the analysis of financial data.
- For an introduction to random walks and Wiener processes see Øksendal (1992) and Schuss (1980).
- Some high frequency data can be ordered through Olsen Associates, www.olsen.ch. It's not free, but nor is it expensive.
- The famous book by Malkiel (1990) is well worth reading for its insights into the behavior of the stock market. Read what he has to say about chimpanzees, blindfolds and darts. In fact, if you haven't already read Malkiel's book make sure it is the next book you read after finishing mine.

EXERCISES

1. A share has an expected return of 12% per annum (with continuous compounding) and a volatility of 20% per annum. Changes in the share price satisfy $dS = \mu S\,dt + \sigma S\,dX$. Simulate the movement of the share price, currently \$100, over a year, using a time interval of one week.
2. What is the distribution of the price increase for the share movement described in Question 1?
3. Using daily share price data, find and plot returns for the asset. What are the mean and standard deviation for the sample you have chosen?
4. Compare interest rate data to your share price data. Are there any major differences? Is the asset price model

$$dS = \mu S\,dt + \sigma S\,dX$$

also suitable for modeling interest rates?

CHAPTER 4
elementary stochastic calculus

In this Chapter...

- all the stochastic calculus you need to know, and no more
- the meaning of Markov and martingale
- Brownian motion
- stochastic integration
- stochastic differential equations
- Itô's lemma in one and more dimensions

4.1 INTRODUCTION

Stochastic calculus is very important in the mathematical modeling of financial processes. This is because of the underlying random nature of financial markets. Because stochastic calculus is such an important tool I want to ensure that it can be used by everyone. To that end, I am going to try to make this chapter as accessible and intuitive as possible. By the end, I hope that the reader will know what various technical terms mean (and rarely are they very complicated), but, more importantly, will also know how to use the techniques with the minimum of fuss.

Most academic articles in finance have a 'pure' mathematical theme. The mathematical rigor in these works is occasionally justified, but more often than not it only succeeds in obscuring the content. When a subject is young, as is mathematical finance (young*ish*), there is a tendency for technical rigor to feature very prominently in research. This is due to lack of confidence in the methods and results. As the subject ages, researchers will become more cavalier in their attitudes and we will see much more rapid progress.

4.2 A MOTIVATING EXAMPLE

Toss a coin. Every time you throw a head I give you \$1; every time you throw a tail you give me \$1. Figure 4.1 shows how much money you have after six tosses. In this experiment the sequence was THHTHT, and we finished even.

If I use R_i to mean the random amount, either \$1 or −\$1, you make on the ith toss then we have

$$E[R_i] = 0, \quad E[R_i^2] = 1 \quad \text{and} \quad E[R_iR_j] = 0.$$

In this example it doesn't matter whether or not these expectations are conditional on the past. In other words, if I threw five heads in a row it does not affect the outcome of the sixth toss.

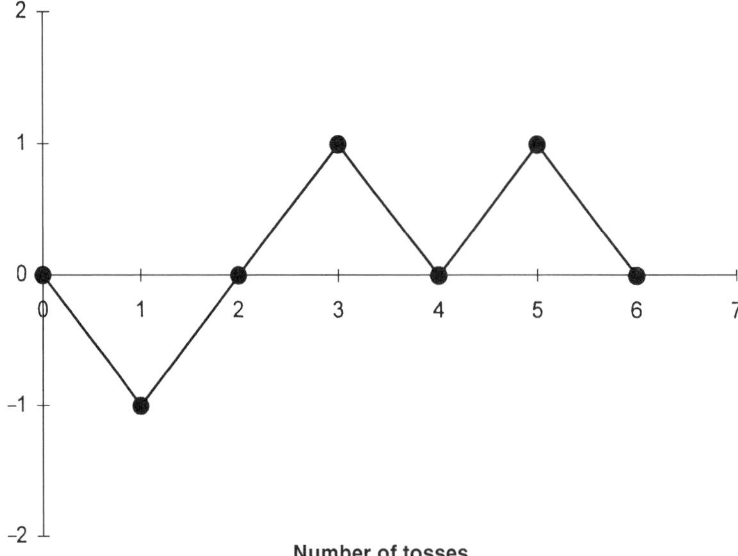

Figure 4.1 The outcome of a coin tossing experiment.

To the gamblers out there, this property is also shared by a fair die, a balanced roulette wheel, but not by the deck of cards in Blackjack. In Blackjack the same deck is used for game after game, the odds during one game depending on what cards were dealt out from the same deck in previous games. That is why you can in the long run beat the house at Blackjack but not roulette.

Introduce S_i to mean the total amount of money you have won up to and including the ith toss so that

$$S_i = \sum_{j=1}^{i} R_j.$$

Later on it will be useful if we have $S_0 = 0$, i.e., you start with no money.

If we now calculate expectations of S_i it *does* matter what information we have. If we calculate expectations of future events before the experiment has even begun then

$$E[S_i] = 0 \quad \text{and} \quad E[S_i^2] = E[R_1^2 + 2R_1R_2 + \cdots] = i.$$

On the other hand, suppose there have been five tosses already. Can I use this information and what can we say about expectations for the sixth toss? This is the **conditional expectation**. The expectation of S_6 conditional upon the previous five tosses gives

$$E[S_6|R_1, \ldots, R_5] = S_5.$$

4.3 THE MARKOV PROPERTY

This result is special, the expected value of the random variable S_i conditional upon all of the past events *only depends on the previous value* S_{i-1}. This is the **Markov property**. We say that the random walk has no memory beyond where it is now. Note that it doesn't have to be the case that the expected value of the random variable S_i is the same as the previous value.

This can be generalized to say that given information about S_j for some values of $1 \le j < i$ then the only information that is of use to us in estimating S_i is the value of S_j for the largest j for which we have information.

Almost all of the financial models that I will show you have the Markov property. This is of fundamental importance in modeling in finance. I will also show you examples where the system has a small amount of memory, meaning that one or two other pieces of information are important. And I will also give a couple of examples where *all* of the random walk path contains relevant information.

4.4 THE MARTINGALE PROPERTY

The coin tossing experiment possesses another property that can be important in finance. You know how much money you have won after the fifth toss. Your expected winnings after the sixth toss, and indeed after any number of tosses if we keep playing, is just the amount you already hold. That is, the conditional expectation of your winnings at any time in the future is just the amount you already hold:

$$E[S_i|S_j,\, j < i] = S_j.$$

This is called the **martingale property**.

4.5 QUADRATIC VARIATION

I am now going to define the **quadratic variation** of the random walk. This is defined by

$$\sum_{j=1}^{i} (S_j - S_{j-1})^2.$$

Because you either win or lose an amount \$1 after each toss, $|S_j - S_{j-1}| = 1$. Thus the quadratic variation is always i:

$$\sum_{j=1}^{i} (S_j - S_{j-1})^2 = i.$$

I want to use the coin-tossing experiment for one more demonstration, and that will lead us to a continuous-time random walk.

4.6 BROWNIAN MOTION

I am going to change the rules of my coin-tossing experiment. First of all I am going to restrict the time allowed for the six tosses to a period t, so each toss will take a time $t/6$. Second, the size of the bet will not be \$1 but $\sqrt{t/6}$.

This new experiment clearly still possesses both the Markov and martingale properties, and its quadratic variation measured over the whole experiment is

$$\sum_{j=1}^{6} (S_j - S_{j-1})^2 = 6 \times \left(\sqrt{\frac{t}{6}}\right)^2 = t.$$

I have set up my experiment so that the quadratic variation is just the time taken for the experiment.

I will change the rules again, to speed up the game. We will have n tosses in the allowed time t, with an amount $\sqrt{t/n}$ riding on each throw. Again, the Markov and martingale properties are retained and the quadratic variation is still

$$\sum_{j=1}^{n}(S_j - S_{j-1})^2 = n \times \left(\sqrt{\frac{t}{n}}\right)^2 = t.$$

I am now going to make n larger and larger. All I am doing with my rule changes is to speed up the game, decreasing the time between tosses, with a smaller amount for each bet. But I have chosen my new scalings very carefully. The timestep is decreasing like n^{-1} but the bet size only decreases by $n^{-1/2}$.

In Figure 4.2 I show a series of experiments, each lasting for a time 1, with increasing number of tosses per experiment.

As I go to the limit $n = \infty$, the resulting random walk stays finite. It has an expectation, conditional on a starting value of zero, of

$$E[S(t)] = 0$$

and a variance

$$E[S(t)^2] = t.$$

I use $S(t)$ to denote the amount you have won or the value of the random variable after a time t. The limiting process for this random walk as the timesteps go to zero is called **Brownian motion**, and I will denote it by $X(t)$.

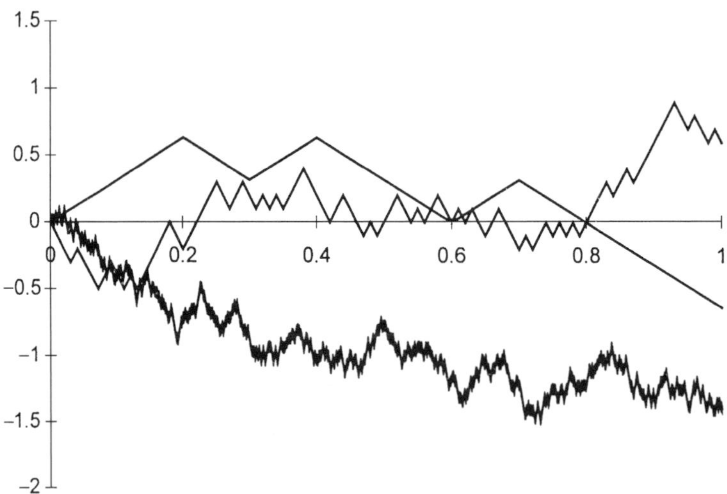

Figure 4.2 A series of coin-tossing experiments, the limit of which is Brownian motion.

The important properties of Brownian motion are as follows.

- *Finiteness*: Any other scaling of the bet size or 'increments' with timestep would have resulted in either a random walk going to infinity in a finite time, or a limit in which there was no motion at all. It is important that the increment scales with the square root of the timestep.

- *Continuity*: The paths are continuous, there are no discontinuities. Brownian motion is the continuous-time limit of our discrete time random walk.
- *Markov*: The conditional distribution of $X(t)$ given information up until $\tau < t$ depends only on $X(\tau)$.
- *Martingale*: Given information up until $\tau < t$ the conditional expectation of $X(t)$ is $X(\tau)$.
- *Quadratic variation*: If we divide up the time 0 to t in a partition with $n+1$ partition points $t_i = i\,t/n$ then

$$\sum_{j=1}^{n}(X(t_j) - X(t_{j-1}))^2 \to t. \quad \text{(Technically 'almost surely.')}$$

- *Normality*: Over finite time increments t_{i-1} to t_i, $X(t_i) - X(t_{i-1})$ is Normally distributed with mean zero and variance $t_i - t_{i-1}$.

Having built up the idea and properties of Brownian motion from a series of experiments, we can discard the experiments, to leave the Brownian motion that is defined by its properties. These properties will be very important for our financial models.

4.7 STOCHASTIC INTEGRATION

I am going to define a **stochastic integral** by

$$W(t) = \int_0^t f(\tau)\,dX(\tau) = \lim_{n\to\infty}\sum_{j=1}^{n} f(t_{j-1})(X(t_j) - X(t_{j-1}))$$

with

$$t_j = \frac{jt}{n}.$$

Before I manipulate this is any way or discuss its properties, I want to stress that the function $f(t)$ which I am integrating is evaluated in the summation at the *left-hand point* t_{j-1}. It will be crucially important that each function evaluation does not know about the random increment that multiplies it, i.e. the integration is **non-anticipatory**. In financial terms, we will see that we take some action such as choosing a portfolio and only then does the stock price move. This choice of integration is natural in finance, ensuring that we use no information about the future in our current actions.

4.8 STOCHASTIC DIFFERENTIAL EQUATIONS

Stochastic integrals are important for any theory of stochastic calculus since they can be meaningfully defined. (And in the next section I show how the definition leads to some important properties.) However, it is very common to use a shorthand notation for expressions such as

$$W(t) = \int_0^t f(\tau)\,dX(\tau). \tag{4.1}$$

That shorthand comes from 'differentiating' (4.1) and is

$$dW = f(t)\,dX. \tag{4.2}$$

Think of dX as being an increment in X, i.e. a Normal random variable with mean zero and standard deviation $dt^{1/2}$.

Equations (4.1) and (4.2) are meant to be equivalent. One of the reasons for this shorthand is that the equation (4.2) looks a lot like an ordinary differential equation. We *do not* go the further step of dividing by dt to make it look exactly like an ordinary differential equation because then we would have the difficult task of defining dX/dt.

Pursuing this idea further, imagine what might be meant by

$$dW = g(t)\,dt + f(t)\,dX. \tag{4.3}$$

This is simply shorthand for

$$W(t) = \int_0^t g(\tau)\,d\tau + \int_0^t f(\tau)\,dX(\tau).$$

Equations like (4.3) are called **stochastic differential equations**. Their precise meaning comes, however, from the technically more accurate equivalent stochastic integral. In this book I will use the shorthand versions almost everywhere and no confusion should arise.

4.9 THE MEAN SQUARE LIMIT

I am going to describe the technical term **mean square limit**. This is useful in the precise definition of stochastic integration. I will explain the idea by way of the simplest example.

Examine the quantity

$$E\left[\left(\sum_{j=1}^{n}(X(t_j) - X(t_{j-1}))^2 - t\right)^2\right] \tag{4.4}$$

where

$$t_j = \frac{jt}{n}.$$

This can be expanded as

$$E\left[\sum_{j=1}^{n}(X(t_j) - X(t_{j-1}))^4 + 2\sum_{i=1}^{n}\sum_{j<i}(X(t_i) - X(t_{i-1}))^2(X(t_j) - X(t_{j-1}))^2 \right.$$
$$\left. - 2t\sum_{j=1}^{n}(X(t_j) - X(t_{j-1}))^2 + t^2\right].$$

Since $X(t_j) - X(t_{j-1})$ is Normally distributed with mean zero and variance t/n we have

$$E[(X(t_j) - X(t_{j-1}))^2] = \frac{t}{n}$$

and

$$E[(X(t_j) - X(t_{j-1}))^4] = \frac{3t^2}{n^2}.$$

Thus (4.4) becomes

$$n\frac{3t^2}{n^2} + n(n-1)\frac{t^2}{n^2} - 2tn\frac{t}{n} + t^2 = O\left(\frac{1}{n}\right).$$

As $n \to \infty$ this tends to zero. We therefore say that

$$\sum_{j=1}^{n} (X(t_j) - X(t_{j-1}))^2 = t$$

in the 'mean square limit.' This is often written, for obvious reasons, as

$$\int_0^t (dX)^2 = t.$$

I am not going to use this result, nor will I use the mean square limit technique. However, when I talk about 'equality' in the following 'proof' I mean equality in the mean square sense.

4.10 FUNCTIONS OF STOCHASTIC VARIABLES AND ITÔ'S LEMMA

I am now going to introduce the idea of a function of a stochastic variable. In Figure 4.3 is shown a realization of a Brownian motion $X(t)$ and the function $F(X) = X^2$.

If $F = X^2$ is it true that $dF = 2X\,dX$? No. The ordinary rules of calculus do not generally hold in a stochastic environment. Then what are the rules of calculus?

I am going to 'derive' the most important rule of stochastic calculus, **Itô's lemma**. My derivation is more heuristic than rigorous, but at least it is transparent. I will do this for an arbitrary function $F(X)$.

In this derivation I will need to introduce various timescales. The first timescale is very, very small. I will denote it by

$$\frac{\delta t}{n} = h.$$

This timescale is so small that the function $F(X(t+h))$ can be approximated by a Taylor series:

$$F(X(t+h)) - F(X(t)) = (X(t+h) - X(t))\frac{dF}{dX}(X(t)) + \tfrac{1}{2}(X(t+h) - X(t))^2\frac{d^2F}{dX^2}(X(t)) + \cdots.$$

From this it follows that

$$\begin{aligned}
&(F(X(t+h)) - F(X(t))) + (F(X(t+2h)) - F(X(t+h))) + \cdots + (F(X(t+nh)) \\
&\qquad - F(X(t+(n-1)h))) \\
&\qquad = \sum_{j=1}^{n} (X(t+jh) - X(t+(j-1)h))\frac{dF}{dX}(X(t+(j-1)h)) \\
&\qquad + \tfrac{1}{2}\frac{d^2F}{dX^2}(X(t))\sum_{j=1}^{n} (X(t+jh) - X(t+(j-1)h))^2 + \cdots.
\end{aligned}$$

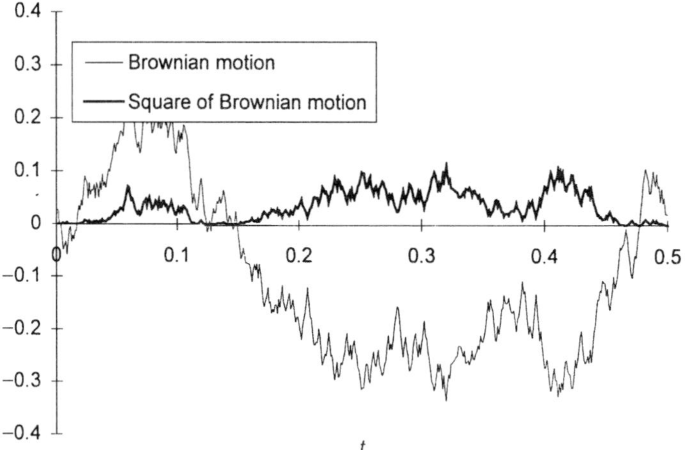

Figure 4.3 A realization of a Brownian motion and its square.

In this I have used the approximation

$$\frac{d^2F}{dX^2}(X(t+(j-1)h)) = \frac{d^2F}{dX^2}(X(t)).$$

This is consistent with the order of accuracy I require.

The first line in this becomes simply

$$F(X(t+nh)) - F(X(t)) = F(X(t+\delta t)) - F(X(t)).$$

The second is just the definition of

$$\int_t^{t+\delta t} \frac{dF}{dX}\,dX$$

and the last is

$$\tfrac{1}{2}\frac{d^2F}{dX^2}(X(t))\,\delta t,$$

in the *mean square sense*. Thus we have

$$F(X(t+\delta t)) - F(X(t)) = \int_t^{t+\delta t} \frac{dF}{dX}(X(\tau))\,dX(\tau) + \tfrac{1}{2}\int_t^{t+\delta t} \frac{d^2F}{dX^2}(X(\tau))\,d\tau.$$

I can now extend this result over longer timescales, from zero up to t, over which F *does* vary substantially to get

$$F(X(t)) = F(X(0)) + \int_0^t \frac{dF}{dX}(X(\tau))\,dX(\tau) + \tfrac{1}{2}\int_0^t \frac{d^2F}{dX^2}(X(\tau))\,d\tau.$$

This is the integral version of **Itô's lemma**, which is usually written as

$$dF = \frac{dF}{dX}\,dX + \tfrac{1}{2}\frac{d^2F}{dX^2}\,dt. \tag{4.5}$$

We can now answer the question, if $F = X^2$ what stochastic differential equation does F satisfy? In this example

$$\frac{dF}{dX} = 2X \quad \text{and} \quad \frac{d^2F}{dX^2} = 2.$$

Therefore Itô's lemma tells us that

$$dF = 2X\,dX + dt.$$

This is *not* what we would get if X were a deterministic variable. In integrated form

$$X^2 = F(X) = F(0) + \int_0^t 2X\,dX + \int_0^t 1\,d\tau = \int_0^t 2X\,dX + t.$$

Therefore

$$\int_0^t X\,dX = \tfrac{1}{2}X^2 - \tfrac{1}{2}t.$$

Having derived Itô's lemma, I am going to give some intuition behind the result and then slightly generalize it.

If we were to do a naive Taylor series expansion of F, completely disregarding the nature of X, and treating dX as a small increment in X, we would get

$$F(X + dX) = F(X) + \frac{dF}{dX}\,dX + \tfrac{1}{2}\frac{d^2F}{dX^2}\,dX^2,$$

ignoring higher-order terms. We could argue that $F(X + dX) - F(X)$ was just the 'change in' F and so

$$dF = \frac{dF}{dX}\,dX + \tfrac{1}{2}\frac{d^2F}{dX^2}\,dX^2.$$

This is very similar to (4.5) (and Taylor series *is* very similar to Itô), with the only difference being that there is a dX^2 instead of a dt. However, since in a sense

$$\int_0^t (dX)^2 = t$$

I could perhaps write

$$dX^2 = dt. \tag{4.6}$$

Although this lacks any rigor (because it's wrong) it does give the correct result. However, on a positive note you can, with little risk of error, use Taylor series with the 'rule of thumb' (4.6) and in practice you will get the right result. Although this is technically incorrect, you almost certainly[1] won't get the wrong result. I will use this rule of thumb almost every time I want to differentiate a function of a random variable. In Chapter 21 I will show when it *is* correct, and better, to use Taylor series.

To end this section I will generalize slightly. Suppose my stochastic differential equation is

$$dS = a(S)\,dt + b(S)\,dX, \tag{4.7}$$

say, for some functions $a(S)$ and $b(S)$. Here dX is the usual Brownian increment. Now if I have a function of S, $V(S)$, what stochastic differential equation does it satisfy? The answer is

$$dV = \frac{dV}{dS}\,dS + \tfrac{1}{2}b^2\frac{d^2V}{dS^2}\,dt.$$

We could derive this properly or just cheat by using Taylor series with $dX^2 = dt$. I could, if I wanted, substitute for dS from (4.7) to get an equation for dV in terms of the pure Brownian motion X:

$$dV = \left(a(S)\frac{dV}{dS} + \tfrac{1}{2}b(S)^2\frac{d^2V}{dS^2}\right)dt + b(S)\,dX.$$

4.11 ITÔ IN HIGHER DIMENSIONS

In financial problems we often have functions of one stochastic variable S and a determinisic variable t, time: $V(S, t)$. If

$$dS = a(S, t)\,dt + b(S, t)\,dX,$$

then the increment dV is given by

$$dV = \frac{\partial V}{\partial t}\,dt + \frac{\partial V}{\partial S}\,dS + \tfrac{1}{2}b^2\frac{\partial^2 V}{\partial S^2}\,dt. \tag{4.8}$$

Again, this is shorthand notation for the correct integrated form. This result is obvious, as is the use of partial instead of ordinary derivatives.

Occasionally, we have a function of two, or more, random variables, and time as well: $V(S_1, S_2, t)$. An example would be the value of an option to buy the more valuable out of Nike and Reebok. I will write the behaviour of S_1 and S_2 in the general form

$$dS_1 = a_1(S_1, S_2, t)\,dt + b_1(S_1, S_2, t)\,dX_1$$

and

$$dS_2 = a_2(S_1, S_2, t)\,dt + b_2(S_1, S_2, t)\,dX_2.$$

Note that I have *two* Brownian increments dX_1 and dX_2. We can think of these as being Normally distributed with variance dt, but *they are correlated*. The correlation between these two random variables I will call ρ. This can also be a function of S_1, S_2 and t but must satisfy

$$-1 \le \rho \le 1.$$

[1] Or should that be 'almost surely'?

The 'rules of thumb' can readily be imagined:

$$dX_1^2 = dt, \quad dX_2^2 = dt \quad \text{and} \quad dX_1\,dX_2 = \rho\,dt.$$

Itô's lemma becomes

$$dV = \frac{\partial V}{\partial t}\,dt + \frac{\partial V}{\partial S_1}\,dS_1 + \frac{\partial V}{\partial S_2}\,dS_2 + \tfrac{1}{2}b_1^2\frac{\partial^2 V}{\partial S_1^2}\,dt + \rho b_1 b_2\frac{\partial^2 V}{\partial S_1 \partial S_2}\,dt + \tfrac{1}{2}b_2^2\frac{\partial^2 V}{\partial S_2^2}\,dt. \tag{4.9}$$

4.12 SOME PERTINENT EXAMPLES

In this section I am going to introduce a few common random walks and talk about their properties.

The first example is like the simple Brownian motion but with a drift:

$$dS = \mu\,dt + \sigma\,dX.$$

A realization of this is shown in Figure 4.4. The point to note about this realization is that S has gone negative. This random walk would therefore not be a good model for many financial quantities, such as interest rates or equity prices. This stochastic differential equation can be integrated exactly to get

$$S(t) = S(0) + \mu t + \sigma(X(t) - X(0)).$$

My second example is similar to the above but the drift and randomness scale with S:

$$dS = \mu S\,dt + \sigma S\,dX. \tag{4.10}$$

A realization of this is shown in Figure 4.5. If S starts out positive it can never go negative; the closer that S gets to zero the smaller the increments dS. For this reason I have had to start the simulation with a non-zero value for S. The property of this random walk is clearly seen if

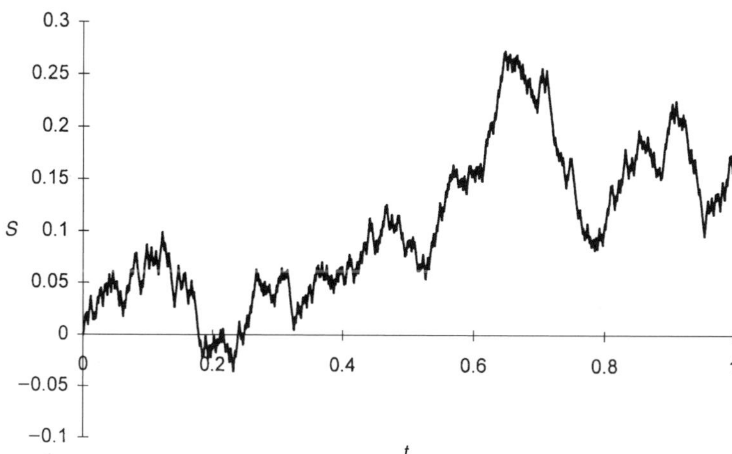

Figure 4.4 A realization of $dS = \mu\,dt + \sigma\,dX$.

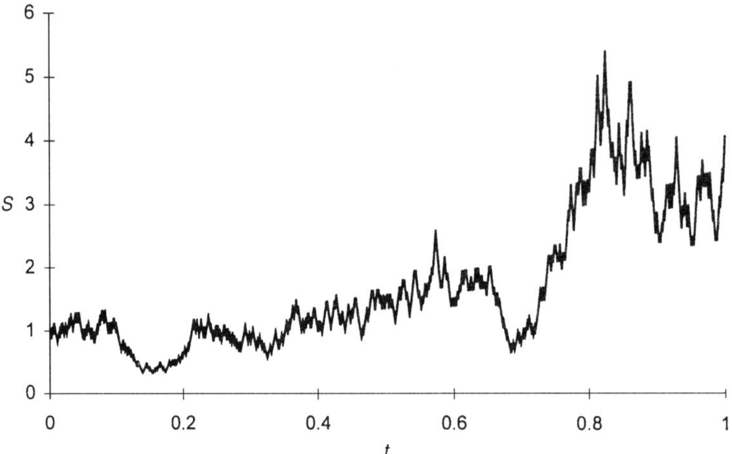

Figure 4.5 A realization of $dS = \mu S\,dt + \sigma S\,dX$.

we examine the function $F(S) = \log S$ using Itô's lemma. From Itô we have

$$dF = \frac{dF}{dS}\,dS + \tfrac{1}{2}\sigma^2 S^2 \frac{d^2F}{dS^2}\,dt = \frac{1}{S}(\mu S\,dt + \sigma S\,dX) - \tfrac{1}{2}\sigma^2\,dt$$
$$= \left(\mu - \tfrac{1}{2}\sigma^2\right)dt + \sigma\,dX.$$

This shows us that $\log S$ can range between minus and plus infinity but cannot reach these limits in a finite time, therefore S cannot reach zero or infinity in a finite time.

The integral form of this stochastic differential equation follows simply from the stochastic differential equation for $\log S$:

$$S(t) = S(0)e^{(\mu-(1/2)\sigma^2)t+\sigma(X(t)-X(0))}.$$

The stochastic differential equation (4.10) will be particularly important in the modeling of many asset classes. And if we have some function $V(S, t)$ then from Itô it follows that

$$dV = \frac{\partial V}{\partial t}\,dt + \frac{\partial V}{\partial S}\,dS + \tfrac{1}{2}\sigma^2 S^2 \frac{\partial^2 F}{\partial S^2}\,dt. \qquad (4.11)$$

The third example is

$$dS = (\nu - \mu S)\,dt + \sigma\,dX.$$

A realization of this is shown in Figure 4.6.

This random walk is an example of a **mean-reverting** random walk. If S is large, the negative coefficient in front of dt means that S will move down on average; if S is small it rises on average. There is still no incentive for S to stay positive in this random walk. With r instead of S this random walk is the Vasicek model for the short-term interest rate.

The final example is similar to the third but I am going to adjust the random term slightly:

$$dS = (\nu - \mu S)\,dt + \sigma S^{1/2}\,dX.$$

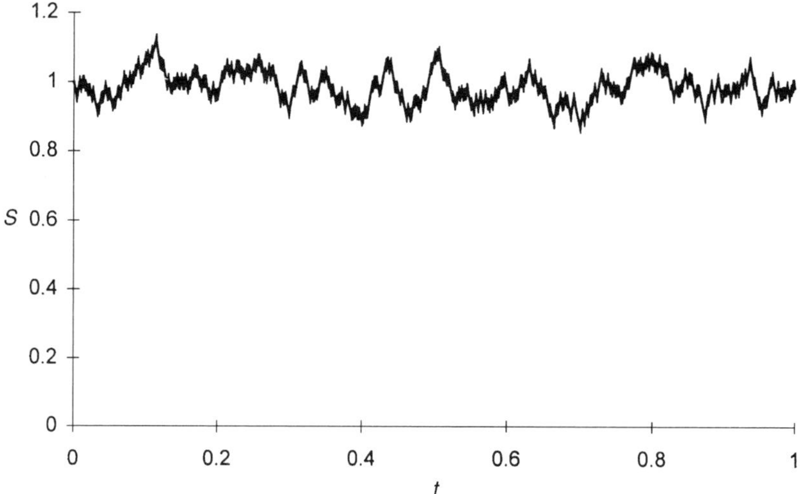

Figure 4.6 A realization of $dS = (\nu - \mu S)\,dt + \sigma\,dX$.

Now if S ever gets close to zero the randomness decreases. Perhaps this will stop S from going negative? Let's play around with this example for a while and we'll see Itô in practice.

Write $F = S^{1/2}$. What stochastic differential equation does F satisfy? Since

$$\frac{dF}{dS} = \tfrac{1}{2}S^{-1/2} \quad \text{and} \quad \frac{d^2F}{dS^2} = -\frac{1}{4}S^{-3/2}$$

we have

$$dF = \left(\frac{4\nu - \sigma^2}{2F} - \tfrac{1}{2}\mu F\right)dt + \tfrac{1}{2}\sigma\,dX.$$

I have just turned the original stochastic differential equation with a variable coefficient in front of the random term into a stochastic differential equation with a constant random term. In so doing I have made the drift term nastier. In particular, the drift is now singular at $F = S = 0$.

Continuing with this example, can I find a function $F(S)$ such that its stochastic differential equation has a zero drift term? For this I will need

$$(\nu - \mu S)\frac{dF}{dS} + \tfrac{1}{2}\sigma^2 S\frac{d^2F}{dS^2} = 0.$$

This is easily integrated once to give

$$\frac{dF}{dS} = AS^{-2\nu/\sigma^2}e^{2\mu S/\sigma^2} \tag{4.12}$$

for any constant A. I won't take this any further but just make one observation. If

$$\frac{2\nu}{\sigma^2} \geq 1$$

we cannot integrate (4.12) at $S = 0$. This makes the origin **non-attainable**. In other words, if the parameter ν is sufficiently large it forces the random walk to stay away from zero.

This particular stochastic differential equation for S will be important later on. It is the Cox, Ingersoll & Ross model for the short-term interest rate.

These are just four of the many random walks we will be seeing.

4.13 SUMMARY

This chapter introduced the most important tool of the trade, Itô's lemma. Itô's lemma allows us to manipulate functions of a random variable. If we think of S as the value of an asset for which we have a stochastic differential equation, a 'model,' then we can handle functions of the asset, and ultimately value contracts such as options.

If we use Itô as a tool we do not need to know why or how it works, only how to use it. Essentially all we require to successfully use the lemma is a rule of thumb, as explained in the text. Unless we are using Itô in highly unusual situations, then we are unlikely to make any errors.

FURTHER READING

- Neftci (1996) is the only readable book on stochastic calculus for beginners. It does not assume any knowledge about anything. It takes the reader very slowly through the basics as applied to finance.
- Once you have got beyond the basics, move on to Øksendal (1992) and Schuss (1980).

EXERCISES

In all of these $X(t)$ is Brownian motion.

1. By considering $X^2(t)$, show that
$$\int_0^t X(\tau)\,dX(\tau) = \tfrac{1}{2}X^2(t) - \tfrac{1}{2}t.$$
2. Show that
$$\int_0^t \tau\,dX(\tau) = tX(t) - \int_0^t X(\tau)\,d\tau.$$
3. Show that
$$\int_0^t X^2(\tau)\,dX(\tau) = \tfrac{1}{3}X^3(t) - \int_0^t X(\tau)\,d\tau.$$
4. Consider a function $f(t)$ which is continuous and bounded on $[0, t]$. Prove integration by parts, i.e.
$$\int_0^t f(\tau)\,dX(\tau) = f(t)X(t) - \int_0^t X(\tau)\,df(\tau).$$
5. Find $u(W, t)$ and $v(W, t)$ where
$$dW(t) = u\,dt + v\,dX(t)$$

and

(a) $W(t) = X^2(t)$,
(b) $W(t) = 1 + t + e^{X(t)}$,
(c) $W(t) = f(t)X(t)$,

where f is a bounded, continuous function.

6. If S follows a lognormal random walk, use Itô's lemma to find the differential equations satisfied by

   (a) $f(S) = AS + B$,
   (b) $g(S) = S^n$,

   where A, B and n are constants.

7. The change in a share price satisfies

$$dS = A(S,t)\,dX + B(S,t)\,dt,$$

   for some functions A, B What is the stochastic differential equation satisfied by $f(S,t)$? Can A, B be chosen so that a function $g(S)$ has a zero drift, but non-zero variance?

8. Two shares follow geometric Brownian motions, i.e.

$$dS_1 = \mu_1 S_1\,dt + \sigma_1 S_1\,dX_1,$$
$$dS_2 = \mu_2 S_2\,dt + \sigma_2 S_2\,dX_2,$$

   The share price changes are correlated with correlation coefficient ρ. Find the stochastic differential equation satisfied by a function $f(S_1, S_2)$.

9. If $dS = \mu S\,dt + \sigma S\,dX$, use Itô's lemma to find the stochastic differential equation satisfied by $f(S) = \log(S)$.

CHAPTER 5
the Black–Scholes model

In this Chapter...

- the foundations of derivatives theory: delta hedging and no arbitrage
- the derivation of the Black–Scholes partial differential equation
- the assumptions that go into the Black–Scholes equation
- how to modify the equation for commodity and currency options

5.1 INTRODUCTION

This is, without doubt, the most important chapter in the book. In it I describe and explain the basic building blocks of derivatives theory. These building blocks are delta hedging and no arbitrage. They form a moderately sturdy foundation to the subject and have performed well since 1973 when the ideas became public.

In this chapter I begin with the stochastic differential equation model for equities and exploit the correlation between this asset and an option on this asset to make a perfectly risk-free portfolio. I then appeal to no arbitrage to equate returns on all risk-free portfolios to the risk-free interest rate, the so called 'no free lunch' argument.

The arguments are trivially modified to incorporate dividends on the underlying and also to price commodity and currency options and options on futures.

This chapter is quite theoretical, yet all of the ideas contained here are regularly used in practice. Even though all of the assumptions can be shown to be wrong to a greater or lesser extent, the Black–Scholes model is profoundly important both in theory and in practice.

5.2 A VERY SPECIAL PORTFOLIO

In Chapter 2 I described some of the characteristics of options and options markets. I introduced the idea of call and put options, amongst others. The value of a call option is clearly going to be a function of various parameters in the contract, such as the strike price E and the time to expiry $T - t$, where T is the date of expiry, and t is the current time. The value will also depend on properties of the asset itself, such as its price, its drift and its volatility, as well as the risk-free rate of interest.[1] We can write the option value as

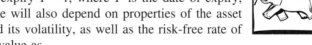

$$V(S, t; \sigma, \mu; E, T; r).$$

---

[1] Actually, I'm lying. One of these parameters does not affect the option value.

Notice that the semi-colons separate different types of variables and parameters:

- S and t are variables;
- σ and μ are parameters associated with the asset price;
- E and T are parameters associated with the details of the particular contract;
- r is a parameter associated with the currency in which the asset is quoted.

I'm not going to carry all the parameters around, except when it is important. For the moment I'll just use $V(S, t)$ to denote the option value.

One simple observation is that a call option will rise in value if the underlying asset rises, and will fall if the asset falls. This is clear since a call has a larger payoff the greater the value of the underlying at expiry. This is an example of **correlation** between two financial instruments. In this case the correlation is positive. A put and the underlying have a negative correlation. We can exploit these correlations to construct a very special portfolio.

Use Π to denote the value of a portfolio of one long option position and a short position in some quantity Δ, **delta**, of the underlying:

$$\Pi = V(S, t) - \Delta S. \tag{5.1}$$

The first term on the right is the option and the second term is the short asset position. Notice the minus sign in front of the second term. The quantity Δ will for the moment be some constant quantity of our choosing. We will assume that the underlying follows a lognormal random walk

$$dS = \mu S\,dt + \sigma S\,dX.$$

It is natural to ask how the value of the portfolio changes from time t to $t + dt$. The change in the portfolio value is due partly to the change in the option value and partly to the change in the underlying:

$$d\Pi = dV - \Delta\,dS.$$

Notice that Δ has not changed during the timestep; we have not anticipated the change in S. From Itô we have

$$dV = \frac{\partial V}{\partial t}\,dt + \frac{\partial V}{\partial S}\,dS + \tfrac{1}{2}\sigma^2 S^2 \frac{\partial^2 V}{\partial S^2}\,dt.$$

Thus the portfolio changes by

$$d\Pi = \frac{\partial V}{\partial t}\,dt + \frac{\partial V}{\partial S}\,dS + \tfrac{1}{2}\sigma^2 S^2 \frac{\partial^2 V}{\partial S^2}\,dt - \Delta\,dS. \tag{5.2}$$

5.3 ELIMINATION OF RISK: DELTA HEDGING

The right-hand side of (5.2) contains two types of terms, the deterministic and the random. The deterministic terms are those with the dt, and the random terms are those with the dS. Pretending for the moment that we know V and its derivatives then we know everything about the right-hand side of (5.2) *except for the value of* dS. And this quantity we can never know in advance.

IMPORTANT

These random terms are the risk in our portfolio. Is there any way to reduce or even eliminate this risk? This can be done in theory (and *almost* in practice) by carefully choosing Δ. The random terms in (5.2) are

$$\left(\frac{\partial V}{\partial S} - \Delta\right) dS.$$

If we choose

$$\Delta = \frac{\partial V}{\partial S} \tag{5.3}$$

then the randomness is reduced to zero.

Any reduction in randomness is generally termed **hedging**, whether that randomness is due to fluctuations in the stock market or the outcome of a horse race. The perfect elimination of risk, by exploiting correlation between two instruments (in this case an option and its underlying) is generally called **delta hedging**.

Delta hedging is an example of a **dynamic hedging** strategy. From one timestep to the next the quantity $\partial V/\partial S$ changes, since it is, like V, a function of the ever-changing variables S and t. This means that the perfect hedge must be continually rebalanced. In later chapters we will see examples of static hedging, where a hedging position is *not* changed as the variables evolve.

Delta hedging was effectively first described by Thorp & Kassouf (1967) but they missed the crucial (Nobel prize winning) next step. (We will see more of Thorp when we look at casino Blackjack as an investment in Chapter 41.)

5.4 NO ARBITRAGE

After choosing the quantity Δ as suggested above, we hold a portfolio whose value changes by the amount

$$d\Pi = \left(\frac{\partial V}{\partial t} + \tfrac{1}{2}\sigma^2 S^2 \frac{\partial^2 V}{\partial S^2}\right) dt. \tag{5.4}$$

This change is completely *riskless*. If we have a completely risk-free change $d\Pi$ in the portfolio value Π then it must be the same as the growth we would get if we put the equivalent amount of cash in a risk-free interest-bearing account:

$$d\Pi = r\Pi\, dt. \tag{5.5}$$

This is an example of the **no arbitrage** principle.

To see why this should be so, consider in turn what might happen if the return on the portfolio were, first, greater and, second, less than the risk-free rate. If we were guaranteed to get a return of greater than r from the delta-hedged portfolio then what we could do is borrow from the bank, paying interest at the rate r, invest in the risk-free option/stock portfolio and make a profit. If, on the other hand the return were less than the risk-free rate we should go short the option, delta hedge it, and invest the cash in the bank. Either way, we make a riskless profit in excess of the risk-free rate of interest. At this point we say that, all things being equal, the action of investors buying and selling to exploit the arbitrage opportunity will cause the market price of the option to move in the direction that eliminates the arbitrage.

5.5 THE BLACK–SCHOLES EQUATION

Substituting (5.1), (5.3) and (5.4) into (5.5) we find that

$$\left(\frac{\partial V}{\partial t}+\tfrac{1}{2}\sigma^2S^2\frac{\partial^2V}{\partial S^2}\right)dt=r\left(V-S\frac{\partial V}{\partial S}\right)dt.$$

On dividing by dt and rearranging we get

$$\frac{\partial V}{\partial t}+\tfrac{1}{2}\sigma^2S^2\frac{\partial^2V}{\partial S^2}+rS\frac{\partial V}{\partial S}-rV=0. \tag{5.6}$$

This is the **Black–Scholes equation**. The equation was first written down in 1969, but a few years passed, with Fisher Black and Myron Scholes justifying the model, before it was published. The derivation of the equation was finally published in 1973, although the call and put formulae had been published a year earlier.

The Black–Scholes equation is a **linear parabolic partial differential equation**. In fact, almost all partial differential equations in finance are of a similar form. They are almost always linear, meaning that if you have two solutions of the equation then the sum of these is itself also a solution. Or at least they tended to be linear until recently. In Part Three I will show you some examples of recent models which lead to nonlinear equations. Financial equations are also usually parabolic, meaning that they are related to the heat or diffusion equation of mechanics. One of the good things about this is that such equations are relatively easy to solve numerically.

The Black–Scholes equation contains all the obvious variables and parameters such as the underlying, time, and volatility, but there is no mention of the drift rate μ. Why is this? Any dependence on the drift dropped out at the same time as we eliminated the dS component of the portfolio. The economic argument for this is that since we can perfectly hedge the option with the underlying we should not be rewarded for taking unnecessary risk; only the risk-free rate of return is in the equation. This means that if you and I agree on the volatility of an asset we will agree on the value of its derivatives *even if we have differing estimates of the drift.*

Another way of looking at the hedging argument is to ask what happens if we hold a portfolio consisting of just the stock, in a quantity Δ, and cash. If Δ is the partial derivative of some option value then such a portfolio will yield an amount at expiry that is simply that option's payoff. In other words, we can use the same Black–Scholes argument to **replicate** an option just by buying and selling the underlying asset. This leads to the idea of a **complete market**. In a complete market an option can be replicated with the underlying, thus making options redundant. Why buy an option when you can get the same payoff by trading in the asset? Many things conspire to make markets incomplete and we will discuss some of these, such as transaction costs and stochastic volatility, in later chapters.

Since the Black–Scholes equation is of such importance I'm going to spend a moment relating the equation to ideas and models in other parts of the book.

For the rest of this part of the book I'm going to explain what the Black–Scholes equation means as a differential equation and show how to solve it in a few special cases. I will generalize the model slightly but not too much. I will also show what happens to the equation when early exercise is allowed. Superficially, early exercise does not make much difference, but on a closer inspection it changes the whole nature of the problem.

The second part of the book is devoted to more serious generalizations to accommodate the pricing of exotic derivative contracts. Still the extensions are what might be termed 'classical,' there is nothing too outrageous here and there is nothing outside the 'Black–Scholes world.'

Part Three is devoted to more serious generalizations and some advanced topics. Some of the generalizations are minor modifications to the Black–Scholes world and can still be thought of as classical. These are just attempts to broaden the Black–Scholes world, to relax some of the assumptions. Other models take us a long way from the Black–Scholes world into fairly new and uncharted waters. Delta hedging and no arbitrage are seen to be not quite as straightforward as I had led you to understand. You are free to believe or disbelieve any of these models, but I do ask that you appreciate them.

Many of the Black–Scholes ideas, plus a few new ones, will be found in Part Four on the pricing of interest rate products. There are some technical reasons that make the fixed-income world harder than the equity, currency, commodity world. Nevertheless delta hedging and no arbitrage play the same role.

Risk management is the subject of Part Five. Delta hedging is supposed to eliminate risk. Not only is this not quite true but also there are times when you might not want to hedge at all. We also discuss credit risk issues here.

In Part Six I show how to solve the Black–Scholes equation, and related equations, numerically. I describe the two main numerical methods: finite-difference methods and Monte Carlo simulations. I include Visual Basic code to illustrate many of the methods. None of these methods are hard; we are lucky in this subject that the governing equation, usually being parabolic, is simple to solve numerically.

5.6 THE BLACK–SCHOLES ASSUMPTIONS

What are the 'assumptions' that I've just been referring to? Here is a partial list, together with some discussion.

- *The underlying follows a lognormal random walk.* This is not entirely necessary. To find explicit solutions we will need the random term in the stochastic differential equation for S to be proportional to S. The 'factor' σ does not need to be constant to find solutions, but it must only be time dependent (see Chapter 7). As far as the validity of the equation is concerned it doesn't matter if the volatility is also asset-price dependent, but then the equation will either have very messy explicit solutions, if it has any at all, or have to be solved numerically. Then there is the question of the drift term μS. Do we need this term to take this form. After all it doesn't even appear in the equation? There is a technicality here that whatever the stochastic differential equation for the asset S, the domain over which the asset can range must be zero to infinity. This is a technicality I am not going into, but it amounts to another elimination of arbitrage. It is possible to choose the drift so that the asset is restricted to lie within a range; such a drift would not be allowed. 
- *The risk-free interest rate is a known function of time.* This restriction is just to help us find explicit solutions again. If r were constant this job would be even easier. In practice, the interest rate is often taken to be time dependent but known in advance. Explicit formulae still exist for the prices of simple contracts and I discuss this issue in Chapter 8. In reality the rate r is not known in advance and is itself stochastic, or so it seems from data. I will discuss stochastic

interest rates in Part Four. We've also assumed that lending and borrowing rates are the same. It is not difficult to relax this assumption, and it is related to ideas in Chapter 24.

- *There are no dividends on the underlying.* I will drop this restriction in a moment, and discuss the subject more generally in Chapter 8.
- *Delta hedging is done continuously.* This is definitely impossible. Hedging must be done in discrete time. Often the time between rehedges will depend on the level of transaction costs in the market for the underlying; the lower the costs, the more frequent the rehedging. This subject is covered in depth in Chapter 20.
- *There are no transaction costs on the underlying.* The dynamic business of delta hedging is in reality expensive since there is a bid-offer spread on most underlyings. In some markets this matters and in some it doesn't. Chapter 21 is devoted to a discussion of these issues.
- *There are no arbitrage opportunities.* This is a beauty. Of course there are arbitrage opportunities; a lot of people make a lot of money finding them. It is extremely important to stress that we are ruling out model-dependent arbitrage. This is highly dubious since it depends on us having the correct model in the first place, and that is unlikely. I am happier ruling out model-independent arbitrage, i.e. arbitrage arising when two identical cashflows have different values. But even that can be criticized.

There are many more assumptions but the above are the most important. In other parts of the book I will drop these assumptions or, if I don't drop them, I will at least loosen them a bit.

5.7 FINAL CONDITIONS

The Black–Scholes equation (27.7) knows nothing about what kind of option we are valuing, whether it is a call or a put, nor what is the strike and the expiry. These points are dealt with by the **final condition**. We must specify the option value V as a function of the underlying at the expiry date T. That is, we must prescribe $V(S, T)$, the payoff.

For example, if we have a call option then we know that

$$V(S, T) = \max(S - E, 0).$$

For a put we have

$$V(S, T) = \max(E - S, 0),$$

for a binary call

$$V(S, T) = \mathcal{H}(S - E)$$

and for a binary put

$$V(S, T) = \mathcal{H}(E - S),$$

where $\mathcal{H}(\cdot)$ is the **Heaviside function**, which is zero when its argument is negative and one when it is positive.

The imposition of the final condition will be explained in Chapters 6 and 7, and implemented numerically in Part Six.

As an aside, observe that both the asset, S, and 'money in the bank,' e^{rt} satisfy the Black–Scholes equation.

5.8 OPTIONS ON DIVIDEND-PAYING EQUITIES

The first generalization we discuss is how to value options on stocks paying dividends. This is just about the simplest generalization of the Black–Scholes model. To keep things simple (I will complicate matters in Chapter 8) let's assume that the asset receives a continuous and constant dividend yield, D. Thus in a time dt each asset receives an amount $DS\,dt$. This must be factored into the derivation of the Black–Scholes equation. I take up the Black–Scholes argument at the point where we are looking at the change in the value of the portfolio:

$$d\Pi = \frac{\partial V}{\partial t}\,dt + \frac{\partial V}{\partial S}\,dS + \tfrac{1}{2}\sigma^2 S^2 \frac{\partial^2 V}{\partial S^2}\,dt - \Delta\,dS - D\Delta S\,dt.$$

The last term on the right-hand side is simply the amount of the dividend per asset, $DS\,dt$, multiplied by the number of the asset held, $-\Delta$. The Δ is still given by the rate of change of the option value with respect to the underlying, but after some simple substitutions we now get

$$\frac{\partial V}{\partial t} + \tfrac{1}{2}\sigma^2 S^2 \frac{\partial^2 V}{\partial S^2} + (r - D)S\frac{\partial V}{\partial S} - rV = 0. \tag{5.7}$$

5.9 CURRENCY OPTIONS

Options on currencies are handled in exactly the same way. In holding the foreign currency we receive interest at the foreign rate of interest r_f. This is just like receiving a continuous dividend. I will skip the derivation but we readily find that

$$\frac{\partial V}{\partial t} + \tfrac{1}{2}\sigma^2 S^2 \frac{\partial^2 V}{\partial S^2} + (r - r_f)S\frac{\partial V}{\partial S} - rV = 0. \tag{5.8}$$

5.10 COMMODITY OPTIONS

The relevant feature of commodities requiring that we adjust the Black–Scholes equation is that they have a **cost of carry**. That is, the storage of commodities is not without cost. Let us introduce q as the fraction of the value of a commodity that goes towards paying the cost of carry. This means that just holding the commodity will result in a gradual loss of wealth even if the commodity price remains fixed. To be precise, for each unit of the commodity held an amount $qS\,dt$ will be required during short time dt to finance the holding. This is just like having a negative dividend and so we get

$$\frac{\partial V}{\partial t} + \tfrac{1}{2}\sigma^2 S^2 \frac{\partial^2 V}{\partial S^2} + (r + q)S\frac{\partial V}{\partial S} - rV = 0. \tag{5.9}$$

5.11 OPTIONS ON FUTURES

The final modification to the Black–Scholes model in this chapter is to value options on futures. Recall that the future price of a non-dividend paying equity F is related to the spot price by

$$F = e^{r(T_F - t)}S$$

where T_F is the maturity date of the futures contract. We can easily change variables, and look for a solution $V(S,t) = \mathcal{V}(F,t)$. We find that

$$\frac{\partial \mathcal{V}}{\partial t} + \tfrac{1}{2}\sigma^2 F^2 \frac{\partial^2 \mathcal{V}}{\partial F^2} - r\mathcal{V} = 0. \tag{5.10}$$

The equation for an option on a future is actually simpler than the Black–Scholes equation.

5.12 SUMMARY

This was an important but not too difficult chapter. In it I introduced some very powerful and beautiful concepts such as delta hedging and no arbitrage. These two fundamental principles led to the Black–Scholes option pricing equation. Everything from this point on is based on, or is inspired by, these ideas.

FURTHER READING

- The history of option theory, leading up to Black–Scholes is described in Briys, Mai, Bellalah & de Varenne (1998).
- The story of the derivation of the Black–Scholes equation, written by Bob Whaley, can be found in the 10th anniversary issue of *Risk* Magazine, published in December 1997.
- Of course, you must read the original work, Black & Scholes (1973) and Merton (1973).
- See Black (1976) for the details of the pricing of options on futures, and Garman & Kohlhagen (1983) for the pricing of FX options.

EXERCISES

1. Check that the following are solutions of the Black–Scholes equation:

   (a) $V(S,t) = S$,
   (b) $V(S,t) = e^{rt}$.

   Why are these solutions of particular note?

2. What is the most general solution of the Black–Scholes equation with each of the following forms?

   (a) $V(S,t) = A(S)$,
   (b) $V(S,t) = B(S)C(t)$.

3. Prove the following bounds on European call options $C(S,t)$, with expiry at time T, on an underlying share price S, with no dividends:

   (a)
   $$C \le S,$$

   (b)
   $$C \ge \max(S - Ee^{-r(T-t)}, 0),$$

   (c)
   $$0 \le C_1 - C_2 \le (E_2 - E_1)e^{-r(T-t)},$$

   where C_1 and C_2 are calls with exercise prices E_1 and E_2 respectively, and $E_1 < E_2$.

4. Prove the following bounds on European put options $P(S, t)$, with expiry at time T, on an underlying share price S, with no dividends:

   (a)
$$P \leq Ee^{-r(T-t)},$$

   (b)
$$P \geq Ee^{-r(T-t)} - S,$$

   (c)
$$0 \leq P_2 - P_1 \leq (E_2 - E_1)e^{-r(T-t)},$$

   where P_1 and P_2 are calls with exercise prices E_1 and E_2 respectively, and $E_1 < E_2$.

5. Prove the following bounds on European call options $C(S, t)$, on an underlying share price S, with no dividends:

   (a)
$$C_A \geq C_B,$$

   where C_A and C_B are calls with the same exercise price, E, and expiry dates T_A and T_B respectively, and $T_A > T_B$.

   (b)
$$C_2 \leq \frac{E_3 - E_2}{E_3 - E_1} C_1 + \frac{E_2 - E_1}{E_3 - E_1} C_3,$$

   where C_1, C_2 and C_3 are calls with the same expiry, T, and have exercise prices E_1, E_2 and E_3 respectively, where $E_1 < E_2 < E_3$.

   Hint: Consider $E_2 = \lambda E_1 + (1 - \lambda)E_3$.

6. $C(S, t)$ and $P(S, t)$ are the values of European call and put options, with exercise price E and expiry at time T. Show that a portfolio of long the call and short the put satisfies the Black–Scholes equation. What boundary and final conditions hold for this portfolio?

7. Consider an option which expires at time T. The current value of the option is $V(S, t)$. It is possible to synthesize the option using vanilla European calls, all with expiry at time T. We assume that calls with all exercise prices are available and buy $f(E)$ of the call with exercise price E, which has value $C(S, t; E)$.The value of the synthesized option is then

$$V(S, t) = \int_0^\infty f(E')C(S, t; E')\,dE'.$$

   Find the density of call options, $f(E)$, that we must use to synthesize the option.

   Hint: Synthesize the option payoff to find $f(E)$.

8. Find the random walk followed by a European option, $V(S, t)$. Use Black–Scholes to simplify the equation for dV.

9. Compare the equation for futures to Black–Scholes with a constant, continuous dividend yield. How might we price options on futures if we know the value of an option with the same payoff with the asset as underlying?

   Hint: Consider Black–Scholes with a constant, continous dividend yield $D = r$.

CHAPTER 6
partial differential equations

In this Chapter...

- properties of the parabolic partial differential equation
- the meaning of terms in the Black–Scholes equation
- some solution techniques

6.1 INTRODUCTION

The analysis and solution of partial differential equations is a BIG subject. We can only skim the surface in this book. If you don't feel comfortable with the subject, then the list of books at the end should be of help. However, to understand finance, and even to solve partial differential equations numerically, does not require any great depth of understanding. The aim of this chapter is to give just enough background to the subject to permit any reasonably numerate person to follow the rest of the book; I want to keep the entry requirements to the subject as low as possible.

6.2 PUTTING THE BLACK–SCHOLES EQUATION INTO HISTORICAL PERSPECTIVE

The Black–Scholes partial differential equation is in two dimensions, S and t. It is a parabolic equation, meaning that it has a second derivative with respect to one variable, S, and a first derivative with respect to the other, t. Equations of this form are more colloquially known as **heat** or **diffusion equations**.

The equation, in its simplest form, goes back to almost the beginning of the 19th century. Diffusion equations have been successfully used to model:

- diffusion of one material within another, smoke particles in air
- flow of heat from one part of an object to another
- chemical reactions, such as the Belousov–Zhabotinsky reaction which exhibits fascinating wave structure
- electrical activity in the membranes of living organisms, the Hodgkin–Huxley model
- dispersion of populations; individuals move both randomly and to avoid overcrowding
- pursuit and evasion in predator–prey systems

- pattern formation in animal coats, the formation of zebra stripes
- dispersion of pollutants in a running stream

In most of these cases the resulting equations are more complicated than the Black–Scholes equation.

The simplest heat equation for the temperature in a bar is usually written in the form

$$\frac{\partial u}{\partial t} = \frac{\partial^2 u}{\partial x^2}$$

where u is the temperature, x is a spatial coordinate and t is time. This equation comes from a heat balance. Consider the flow into and out of a small section of the bar. The flow of heat along the bar is proportional to the spatial gradient of the temperature

$$\frac{\partial u}{\partial x}$$

and thus the derivative of this, the *second* derivative of the temperature, is the heat retained by the small section. This retained heat is seen as a rise in the temperature, represented mathematically by

$$\frac{\partial u}{\partial t}.$$

The balance of the second x-derivative and the first t-derivative results in the heat equation. (There would be a coefficient in the equation, depending on the properties of the bar, but I have set this to one.)

6.3 THE MEANING OF THE TERMS IN THE BLACK–SCHOLES EQUATION

The Black–Scholes equation can be accurately interpreted as a reaction-convection-diffusion equation. The basic diffusion equation is a balance of a first-order t derivative and a second-order S derivative:

$$\frac{\partial V}{\partial t} + \tfrac{1}{2}\sigma^2 S^2 \frac{\partial^2 V}{\partial S^2}.$$

If these were the only terms in the Black–Scholes equation it would still exhibit the smoothing-out effect, that any discontinuities in the payoff would be instantly diffused away. The only difference between these terms and the terms as they appear in the basic heat or diffusion equation, is that the diffusion coefficient is a function of one of the variables S. Thus we really have diffusion in a non-homogeneous medium.

The first-order S-derivative term

$$rS\frac{\partial V}{\partial S}$$

can be thought of as a convection term. If this equation represented some physical system, such as the diffusion of smoke particles in the atmosphere, then the convective term would be due to a breeze, blowing the smoke in a preferred direction.

The final term

$$-rV$$

is a reaction term. Balancing this term and the time derivative would give a model for decay of a radioactive body, with the half-life being related to r.

Put these terms together and we get a reaction-convection-diffusion equation. An almost identical equation would be arrived at for the dispersion of pollutant along a flowing river with absorption by the sand. In this, the dispersion is the diffusion, the flow is the convection, and the absorption is the reaction.

6.4 BOUNDARY AND INITIAL/FINAL CONDITIONS

To uniquely specify a problem we must prescribe **boundary conditions** and an **initial** or **final condition**. Boundary conditions tell us how the solution must behave for all time at certain values of the asset. In financial problems we usually specify the behavior of the solution at $S = 0$ and as $S \to \infty$. We must also tell the problem how the solution begins. The Black–Scholes equation is a backward equation, meaning that the signs of the t derivative and the second S derivative in the equation are the same when written on the same side of the equals sign. We therefore have to impose a final condition. This is usually the payoff function at expiry.

The Black–Scholes equation in its basic form is linear; add together two solutions of the equation and you will get a third. This is not true of nonlinear equations. Linear diffusion equations have some very nice properties. Even if we start out with a discontinuity in the final data, due to a discontinuity in the payoff, this *immediately* gets smoothed out, due to the diffusive nature of the equation. Another nice property is the uniqueness of the solution. Provided that the solution is not allowed to grow too fast as S tends to infinity the solution will be unique. This precise definition of 'too fast' need not worry us, we will not have to worry about uniqueness for any problems we encounter.

6.5 SOME SOLUTION METHODS

We are not going to spend much time on the exact solution of the Black–Scholes equation. Such solution is important, but current market practice is such that models have features which preclude the exact solution. The few explicit, closed-form solutions that are used by practitioners will be covered in the next two chapters.

6.5.1 Transformation to Constant Coefficient Diffusion Equation

It can sometimes be useful to transform the basic Black–Scholes equation into something a little bit simpler by a change of variables. If we write

$$V(S, t) = e^{\alpha x + \beta \tau} U(x, \tau),$$

where

$$\alpha = -\tfrac{1}{2}\left(\frac{2r}{\sigma^2} - 1\right), \quad \beta = -\tfrac{1}{4}\left(\frac{2r}{\sigma^2} + 1\right)^2, \quad S = e^x \quad \text{and} \quad t = T - \frac{2\tau}{\sigma^2},$$

then $U(x, \tau)$ satisfies the basic diffusion equation

$$\frac{\partial U}{\partial \tau} = \frac{\partial^2 U}{\partial x^2}. \tag{6.1}$$

This simpler equation is easier to handle than the Black–Scholes equation. Sometimes that can be important, for example when seeking closed-form solutions, or in some simple numerical schemes. We shall not pursue this any further.

6.5.2 Green's Functions

One solution of the Black–Scholes equation is

$$V'(S,t) = \frac{e^{-r(T-t)}}{\sigma S'\sqrt{2\pi(T-t)}} e^{-(\log(S/S')+(r-(1/2)\sigma^2)(T-t))^2/2\sigma^2(T-t)} \tag{6.2}$$

for any S'. (You can verify this by substituting back into the equation, but we'll also be seeing it derived in the next chapter.) This solution is special because as $t \to T$ it becomes zero everywhere, except at $S = S'$. In this limit the function becomes what is known as a **Dirac delta function**. Think of this as a function that is zero everywhere except at one point where it is infinite, in such a way that its integral is one. How is this of help to us?

Expression (6.2) is a solution of the Black–Scholes equation for any S'. Because of the linearity of the equation we can multiply (6.2) by any constant, and we get another solution. But then we can also get another solution by adding together expressions of the form (6.2) but with different values for S'. Putting this together, and thinking of an integral as just a way of adding together many solutions, we find that

$$\frac{e^{-r(T-t)}}{\sigma\sqrt{2\pi(T-t)}} \int_0^\infty e^{-(\log(S/S')+(r-(1/2)\sigma^2)(T-t))^2/2\sigma^2(T-t)} f(S') \frac{dS'}{S'}$$

is also a solution of the Black–Scholes equation for any function $f(S')$. (If you don't believe me, substitute it into the Black–Scholes equation.)

Because of the nature of the integrand as $t \to T$ (i.e. that it is zero everywhere except at S' and has integral one), if we choose the arbitrary function $f(S')$ to be the payoff function then this expression becomes the solution of the problem:

$$V(S,t) = \frac{e^{-r(T-t)}}{\sigma\sqrt{2\pi(T-t)}} \int_0^\infty e^{-(\log(S/S')+(r-(1/2)\sigma^2)(T-t))^2/2\sigma^2(T-t)} \,\text{Payoff}(S') \frac{dS'}{S'}.$$

The function $V'(S,t)$ given by (6.2) is called the **Green's function**.

6.5.3 Series Solution

Sometimes we have boundary conditions at two finite (and non-zero) values of S, S_u and S_d, say (we see examples in Chapter 14). For this type of problem, we postulate that the required solution of the Black–Scholes equation can be written as an infinite sum of special functions. First of all, transform to the nicer basic diffusion equation in x and τ. Now write the solution as

$$e^{\alpha x+\beta\tau} \sum_{i=0}^{\infty} a_i(\tau)\sin(i\omega x) + b_i(\tau)\cos(i\omega x),$$

for some ω and some functions a and b to be found. The linearity of the equation suggests that a sum of solutions might be appropriate. If this is to satisfy the Black–Scholes equation then we must have

$$\frac{da_i}{d\tau} = -i^2\omega^2 a_i(\tau) \quad \text{and} \quad \frac{db_i}{d\tau} = -i^2\omega^2 b_i(\tau).$$

You can easily show this by substitution. The solutions are thus

$$a_i(\tau) = A_i e^{-i^2\omega^2\tau} \quad \text{and} \quad b_i(\tau) = B_i e^{-i^2\omega^2\tau}.$$

The solution of the Black–Scholes equation is therefore

$$e^{\alpha x + \beta\tau} \sum_{i=0}^{\infty} e^{-i^2\omega^2\tau}(A_i \sin(i\omega x) + B_i \cos(i\omega x)). \tag{6.3}$$

We have solved the equation; all that we need to do now is to satisfy boundary and initial conditions.

Consider the example where the payoff at time $\tau = 0$ is $f(x)$ (although it would be expressed in the original variables, of course) but the contract becomes worthless if ever $x = x_d$ or $x = x_u$.[1]

Rewrite the term in brackets in (6.3) as

$$C_i \sin\left(i\omega' \frac{x - x_d}{x_u - x_d}\right) + D_i \cos\left(i\omega' \frac{x - x_d}{x_u - x_d}\right).$$

To ensure that the option is worthless on these two x values, choose $D_i = 0$ and $\omega' = \pi$. The boundary conditions are thereby satisfied. All that remains is to choose the C_i to satisfy the final condition:

$$e^{\alpha x} \sum_{i=0}^{\infty} C_i \sin\left(i\omega' \frac{x - x_d}{x_u - x_d}\right) = f(x).$$

This also is simple. Multiplying both sides by

$$\sin\left(j\omega' \frac{x - x_d}{x_u - x_d}\right),$$

and integrating between x_d and x_u we find that

$$C_j = \frac{2}{x_u - x_d} \int_{x_d}^{x_u} f(x) e^{-\alpha x} \sin\left(j\omega' \frac{x - x_d}{x_u - x_d}\right) dX.$$

This technique, which can be generalized, is the **Fourier series method**. There are some problems with the method if you are trying to represent a discontinuous function with a sum of trigonometrical functions. The oscillatory nature of an approximate solution with a finite number of terms is known as **Gibbs phenomenon**.

6.6 SIMILARITY REDUCTIONS

We're not going to use any of the above techniques in this book, and rarely will we even find explicit solutions. But the one technique that we will find useful is the **similarity reduction**. I will demonstrate the idea using the simple diffusion equation. We will later use it in many other, more complicated problems.

[1] This is an example of a double knock-out option (see Chapter 14).

The basic diffusion equation

$$\frac{\partial u}{\partial t} = \frac{\partial^2 u}{\partial x^2} \tag{6.4}$$

is an equation for the function u which depends on the two variables x and t. Sometimes, in very, very special cases we can write the solution as a function of just one variable. Let me give an example. Verify that the function

$$u(x, t) = \int_0^{x/t^{1/2}} e^{-(1/4)\xi^2}\, d\xi$$

satisfies (6.4). But in this function x and t only appear in the combination

$$\frac{x}{t^{1/2}}.$$

Thus, in a sense, u is a function of only one variable.

A slight generalization, but also demonstrating the idea of similarity solutions, is to look for a solution of the form

$$u = t^{-1/2} f(\xi) \tag{6.5}$$

where

$$\xi = \frac{x}{t^{1/2}}.$$

Substitute (6.5) into (6.4) to find that a solution for f is

$$f = e^{-(1/4)\xi^2},$$

so that

$$t^{-1/2} e^{-(1/4)(x^2/t)}$$

is also a special solution of the diffusion equation.

Be warned, though. You can't always find similarity solutions. Not only must the equation have a particularly nice structure but also the similarity form must be consistent with any initial condition or boundary conditions.

6.7 OTHER ANALYTICAL TECHNIQUES

The other two main solution techniques for linear partial differential equations are Fourier and Laplace transforms. These are such large and highly technical subjects that I really cannot begin to give an idea of how they work; space is far too short. But be reassured that it is probably not worth your while learning the techniques, as in finance they can be used to solve only a very small number of problems. If you want to learn something useful then move on to the next section.

6.8 NUMERICAL SOLUTION

Even though there are several techniques that we can use for finding solutions, in the vast majority of cases we must solve the Black–Scholes equation numerically. But we are lucky.

Parabolic differential equations are just about the easiest equations to solve numerically. Obviously, there are any number of really sophisticated techniques, but if you stick with the simplest then you can't go far wrong. In Chapters 12, 46 and 47 we discuss these methods in detail. I want to stress that I am going to derive many partial differential equations from now on, and I am going to assume you trust me that we will at the end of the book see how to solve them.

6.9 SUMMARY

This short chapter is only intended as a primer on partial differential equations. If you want to study this subject in depth, see the books and articles mentioned below.

FURTHER READING

- Grindrod (1991) is all about reaction-diffusion equations, where they come from and their analysis. The book includes many of the physical models described above.
- Murray (1989) also contains a great deal on reaction-diffusion equations, but concentrating on models of biological systems.
- Wilmott & Wilmott (1990) describe the diffusion of pollutant along a river with convection and absorption by the river bed.
- The classical reference works for diffusion equations are Crank (1989) and Carslaw & Jaeger (1989). But also see the book on partial differential equations by Sneddon (1957) and the book on general applied mathematical methods by Strang (1986).

EXERCISES

1. Consider an option with value $V(S, t)$, which has payoff at time T. Reduce the Black–Scholes equation, with final and boundary conditions, to the diffusion equation, using the following transformations:

   (a) $S = Ee^x, \quad t = T - \frac{2\tau}{\sigma^2}, \quad V(S, t) = Ev(x, \tau),$

   (b) $v = e^{\alpha x + \beta\tau}u(x, \tau),$

   for some α and β. What is the transformed payoff? What are the new initial and boundary conditions? Illustrate with a vanilla European call option.

2. The solution to the initial value problem for the diffusion equation is unique (given certain constraints on the behavior, it must be sufficiently smooth and decay sufficiently fast at infinity). This can be shown as follows.

   Suppose that there are two solutions $u_1(x, \tau)$ and $u_2(x, \tau)$ to the problem

$$\frac{\partial u}{\partial \tau} = \frac{\partial^2 u}{\partial x^2}, \quad \text{on } -\infty < x < \infty,$$

   with

$$u(x, 0) = u_0(x).$$

Set $v(x, \tau) = u_1 - u_2$. This is a solution of the equation with $v(x, 0) = 0$. Consider

$$E(\tau) = \int_{-\infty}^{\infty} v^2(x, \tau)\, dx.$$

Show that

$$E(\tau) \geq 0, \quad E(0) = 0,$$

and integrate by parts to find that

$$\frac{dE}{d\tau} \leq 0.$$

Hence show that $E(\tau) \equiv 0$ and, consequently, $u_1(x, \tau) \equiv u_2(x, \tau)$.

3. Suppose that $u(x, \tau)$ satisfies the following initial value problem:

$$\frac{\partial u}{\partial \tau} = \frac{\partial^2 u}{\partial x^2}, \quad \text{on} \quad -\pi < x < \pi, \quad \tau > 0,$$

with

$$u(-\pi, \tau) = u(\pi, \tau) = 0, \quad u(x, 0) = u_0(x).$$

Solve for u using a Fourier Sine series in x, with coefficients depending on τ.

4. Check that u_δ satisfies the diffusion equation, where

$$u_\delta = \frac{1}{2\sqrt{\pi\tau}} e^{-(x^2/4\tau)}.$$

5. Solve the following initial value problem for $u(x, \tau)$ on a semi-infinite interval, using a Green's function:

$$\frac{\partial u}{\partial \tau} = \frac{\partial^2 u}{\partial x^2}, \quad \text{on} \quad x > 0, \quad \tau > 0,$$

with

$$u(x, 0) = u_0(x) \quad \text{for} \quad x > 0, \quad u(0, \tau) = 0 \quad \text{for} \quad \tau > 0.$$

Hint: Define $v(x, \tau)$ as

$$v(x, \tau) = u(x, \tau) \quad \text{if} \quad x > 0,$$
$$v(x, \tau) = -u(-x, \tau) \quad \text{if} \quad x < 0.$$

Then we can show that $v(0, \tau) = 0$ and

$$u(x, \tau) = \frac{1}{2\sqrt{\pi\tau}} \int_0^{\infty} u_0(s)(e^{-(x-s)^2/4\tau} - e^{-(x+s)^2/4\tau})ds.$$

6. Reduce the following parabolic equation to the diffusion equation.

$$\frac{\partial u}{\partial \tau} = \frac{\partial^2 u}{\partial x^2} + a\frac{\partial u}{\partial x} + b,$$

where a and b are constants.

7. Using a change of time variable, reduce

$$c(\tau)\frac{\partial u}{\partial \tau} = \frac{\partial^2 u}{\partial x^2},$$

to the diffusion equation when $c(\tau) > 0$.

Consider the Black–Scholes equation, when σ and r can be functions of time, but $k = 2r/\sigma^2$ is still a constant. Reduce the Black–Scholes equation to the diffusion equation in this case.

8. Show that if

$$\frac{\partial u}{\partial \tau} = \frac{\partial^2 u}{\partial x^2}, \quad \text{on} \quad -\infty < x < \infty, \quad \tau > 0,$$

with

$$u(x, 0) = u_0(x) > 0,$$

then $u(x, \tau) > 0$ for all τ.

Use this result to show that an option with positive payoff will always have a positive value.

9. If $f(x, \tau) \geq 0$ in the initial value problem

$$\frac{\partial u}{\partial \tau} = \frac{\partial^2 u}{\partial x^2} + f(x, \tau), \quad \text{on} \quad -\infty < x < \infty, \quad \tau > 0,$$

with

$$u(x, 0) = 0, \quad \text{and} \quad u \to 0 \quad \text{as} \quad |x| \to \infty,$$

then $u(x, \tau) \geq 0$. Hence show that if C_1 and C_2 are European calls with volatilities σ_1 and σ_2 respectively, but are otherwise identical, then $C_1 > C_2$ if $\sigma_1 > \sigma_2$.

Use put–call parity to show that the same is true for European puts.

CHAPTER 7

the Black–Scholes formulae and the 'greeks'

In this Chapter...

- the derivation of the Black–Scholes formulae for calls, puts and simple digitals
- the meaning and importance of the 'greeks,' delta, gamma, theta, vega and rho
- the difference between differentiation with respect to variables and to parameters
- formulae for the greeks for calls, puts and simple digitals

7.1 INTRODUCTION

The Black–Scholes equation has simple solutions for calls, puts and some other contracts. In this chapter I'm going to walk you through the derivation of these formulae step by step. This is one of the few places in the book where I do derive formulae. The reason that I don't often derive formulae is that the majority of contracts do not have explicit solutions. Instead much of my emphasis will be placed on finding numerical solutions of the Black–Scholes equation.

We've seen how the quantity 'delta,' the first derivative of the option value with respect to the underlying, occurs as an important quantity in the derivation of the Black–Scholes equation. In this chapter I describe the importance of other derivatives of the option price, with respect to the variables (the underlying asset and time) and with respect to some of the parameters. These derivatives are important in the hedging of an option position, playing key roles in risk management. It can be argued that it is more important to get the hedging correct than to be precise in the pricing of a contract. The reason for this is that if you are accurate in your hedging you will have reduced or eliminated future uncertainty. This leaves you with a profit (or loss) that is set the moment that you buy or sell the contract. But if your hedging is inaccurate, then it doesn't matter, within reason, what you sold the contract for initially, future uncertainty could easily dominate any initial profit. Of course, life is not so simple. In reality we are exposed to model error, which can make a mockery of anything we do. However, this illustrates the importance of good hedging, and that's where the 'greeks' come in.

7.2 DERIVATION OF THE FORMULAE FOR CALLS, PUTS AND SIMPLE DIGITALS

The Black–Scholes equation is

$$\frac{\partial V}{\partial t} + \tfrac{1}{2}\sigma^2 S^2 \frac{\partial^2 V}{\partial S^2} + rS\frac{\partial V}{\partial S} - rV = 0. \tag{7.1}$$

This equation must be solved with final condition depending on the payoff: each contract will have a different functional form prescribed at expiry $t = T$, depending on whether it is a call, a put or something more fancy. This is the final condition that must be imposed to make the solution unique. We'll worry about final conditions later. For the moment concentrate on manipulating (7.1) into something we can easily solve.

The first step in the manipulation is to change from present value to future value terms. Recalling that the payoff is received at time T but that we are valuing the option at time t this suggests that we write

$$V(S, t) = e^{-r(T-t)}U(S, t).$$

This takes our differential equation to

$$\frac{\partial U}{\partial t} + \tfrac{1}{2}\sigma^2 S^2 \frac{\partial^2 U}{\partial S^2} + rS\frac{\partial U}{\partial S} = 0.$$

The second step is really trivial. Because we are solving a backward equation, discussed in Chapter 6, we'll write

$$\tau = T - t.$$

This now takes our equation to

$$\frac{\partial U}{\partial \tau} = \tfrac{1}{2}\sigma^2 S^2 \frac{\partial^2 U}{\partial S^2} + rS\frac{\partial U}{\partial S}.$$

When we first started modeling equity prices we used intuition about the asset price *return* to build up the stochastic differential equation model. Let's go back to examine the return and write

$$\xi = \log S.$$

With this as the new variable, we find that

$$\frac{\partial}{\partial S} = e^{-\xi}\frac{\partial}{\partial \xi} \quad \text{and} \quad \frac{\partial^2}{\partial S^2} = e^{-2\xi}\frac{\partial^2}{\partial \xi^2} - e^{-\xi}\frac{\partial}{\partial \xi}.$$

Now the Black–Scholes equation becomes

$$\frac{\partial U}{\partial \tau} = \tfrac{1}{2}\sigma^2 \frac{\partial^2 U}{\partial \xi^2} + \left(r - \tfrac{1}{2}\sigma^2\right)\frac{\partial U}{\partial \xi}.$$

What has this done for us? It has taken the problem defined for $0 \le S < \infty$ to one defined for $-\infty < \xi < \infty$. But more importantly, the coefficients in the equation are now all constant, independent of the underlying. This is a big step forward, made possible by the lognormality of the underlying asset. We are nearly there.

The last step is simple, but the motivation is not so obvious. Write

$$x = \xi + \left(r - \tfrac{1}{2}\sigma^2\right)\tau,$$

and $U = W(x, \tau)$. This is just a 'translation' of the coordinate system. It's a bit like using the forward price of the asset instead of the spot price as a variable. After this change of variables the Black–Scholes becomes the simpler

$$\frac{\partial W}{\partial \tau} = \tfrac{1}{2}\sigma^2 \frac{\partial^2 W}{\partial x^2}. \tag{7.2}$$

To summarize,

$$\begin{aligned} V(S,t) &= e^{-r(T-t)}U(S,t) = e^{-r\tau}U(S, T-\tau) = e^{-r\tau}U(e^{\xi}, T-\tau) \\ &= e^{-r\tau}U(e^{x-(r-(1/2)\sigma^2)\tau}, T-\tau) = e^{-r\tau}W(x,\tau). \end{aligned}$$

To those of you who already know the Black–Scholes formulae for calls and puts the variable x will ring a bell:

$$x = \xi + \left(r - \tfrac{1}{2}\sigma^2\right)\tau = \log S + \left(r - \tfrac{1}{2}\sigma^2\right)(T-t).$$

Having turned the original Black–Scholes equation into something much simpler, let's take a break for a moment while I explain where we are headed.

I'm going to derive an expression for the value of any option whose payoff is a known function of the asset price at expiry. This includes calls, puts and digitals. This expression will be in the form of an integral. For special cases, I'll show how to rewrite this integral in terms of the cumulative distribution function for the Normal distribution. This is particularly useful since the function can be found on spreadsheets, calculators and in the backs of books. But there are two steps before I can write down this integral.

The first step is to find a special solution of (7.2), called the fundamental solution. This solution has useful properties. The second step is to use the linearity of the equation and the useful properties of the special solution to find the *general solution* of the equation. Here we go.

I'm going to look for a special solution of (7.2) of the following form

$$W(x,\tau) = \tau^{\alpha} f\left(\frac{(x-x')}{\tau^{\beta}}\right), \tag{7.3}$$

where x' is an arbitrary constant. And I'll call this special solution $W_f(x, \tau; x')$. Note that the unknown function depends on only *one* variable $(x - x')/\tau^{\beta}$. As well as finding the function f we must find the constant parameters α and β. We can expect that if this approach works, the equation for f will be an ordinary differential equation since the function only has one variable. This reduction of dimension is an example of a similarity reduction, discussed in Chapter 6

Substituting expression (7.3) into (7.2) we get

$$\tau^{\alpha-1}\left(\alpha f - \beta\eta\frac{df}{d\eta}\right) = \tfrac{1}{2}\sigma^2\tau^{\alpha-2\beta}\frac{d^2 f}{d\eta^2}, \tag{7.4}$$

where

$$\eta = \frac{x-x'}{\tau^{\beta}}.$$

Examining the dependence of the two terms in (7.4) on both τ and η we see that we can only have a solution if

$$\alpha - 1 = \alpha - 2\beta \quad \text{i.e.} \quad \beta = \tfrac{1}{2}.$$

I want to ensure that my 'special solution' has the property that its integral over all ξ is independent of τ, for reasons that will become apparent. To ensure this, I require

$$\int_{-\infty}^{\infty} \tau^{\alpha} f((x - x')/\tau^{\beta})\, dx$$

to be constant. I can write this as

$$\int_{-\infty}^{\infty} \tau^{\alpha+\beta} f(\eta)\, d\eta$$

and so I need

$$\alpha = -\beta = \tfrac{1}{2}.$$

The function f now satisfies

$$-f - \eta \frac{df}{d\eta} = \sigma^2 \frac{d^2 f}{d\eta^2}.$$

This can be written

$$\sigma^2 \frac{d^2 f}{d\eta^2} + \frac{d(\eta f)}{d\eta} = 0,$$

which can be integrated once to give

$$\sigma^2 \frac{df}{d\eta} + \eta f = a,$$

where a is a constant. For my special solution I'm going to choose $a = 0$. This equation can be integrated again to give

$$f(\eta) = b e^{-\frac{\eta^2}{2\sigma^2}}.$$

I will choose the constant b such that the integral of f from minus infinity to plus infinity is one:

$$f(\eta) = \frac{1}{\sqrt{2\pi}\sigma} e^{-\frac{\eta^2}{2\sigma^2}}.$$

This is the special solution I have been seeking:[1]

$$W(x, \tau) = \frac{1}{\sqrt{2\pi\tau}\sigma} e^{-\frac{(x-x')^2}{2\sigma^2\tau}}.$$

Now I will explain why it is useful in our quest for the Black–Scholes formulae.

In Figure 7.1 is plotted W as a function of x' for several values of τ. Observe how the function rises in the middle but decays at the sides. As $\tau \to 0$ this becomes more pronounced. The 'middle' is the point $x' = x$. At this point the function grows unboundedly and away from this point the function decays to zero as $\tau \to 0$. Although the function is increasingly confined to a narrower and narrower region its area remains fixed at one. These properties of decay away from one point, unbounded growth at that point and constant area, result in a **Dirac delta function** $\delta(x' - x)$ as $\tau \to 0$. The delta function has one important property, namely

$$\int \delta(x' - x) g(x')\, dx' = g(x)$$

---

[1] It is just the probability density function for a Normal random variable with mean zero and standard deviation σ.

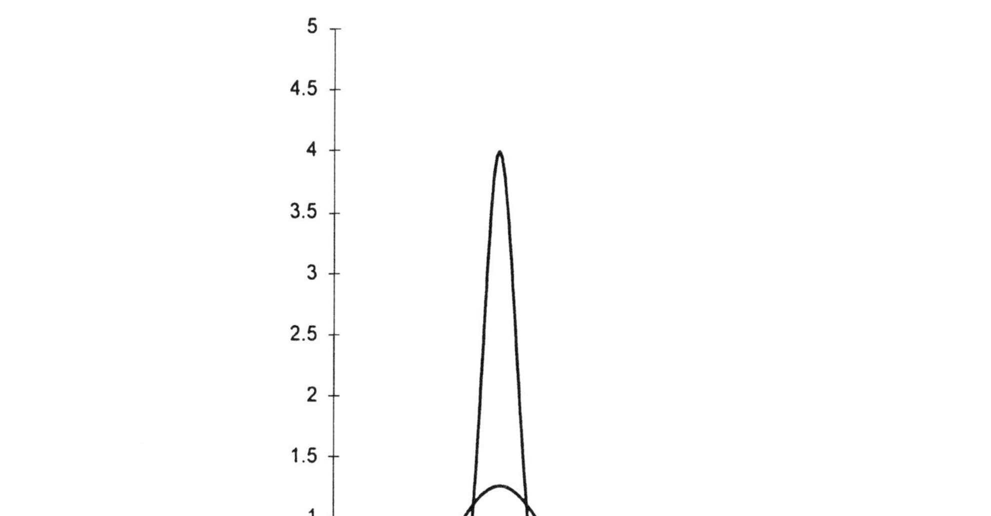

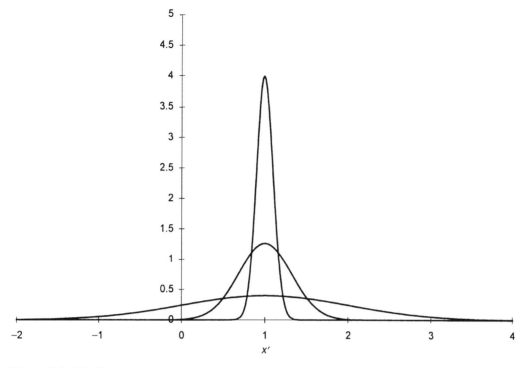

Figure 7.1 The fundamental solution.

where the integration is from any point below x to any point above x. Thus the delta function 'picks out' the value of g at the point where the delta function is singular, i.e. at $x' = x$. In the limit as $\tau \to 0$ the function W becomes a delta function at $x = x'$. This means that

$$\lim_{\tau\to 0} \frac{1}{\sqrt{2\pi\tau}\sigma} \int_{-\infty}^{\infty} e^{-\frac{(x'-x)^2}{2\sigma^2\tau}} g(x')\, dx' = g(x).$$

This property of the special solution, together with the linearity of the Black–Scholes equation are all that are needed to find some explicit solutions.

Now is the time to consider the payoff. Let's call it

$$\text{Payoff}\,(S).$$

This is the value of the option at time $t = T$. It is the final condition for the function V, satisfying the Black–Scholes equation:

$$V(S, T) = \text{Payoff}\,(S).$$

In our new variables, this final condition is

$$W(x, 0) = \text{Payoff}(e^x). \tag{7.5}$$

I claim that the solution of this for $\tau > 0$ is

$$W(x, \tau) = \int_{-\infty}^{\infty} W_f(x, \tau; x')\, \text{Payoff}(e^{x'})\, dx'. \tag{7.6}$$

To show this, I just have to demonstrate that the expression satisfies the equation (7.2) and the final condition (7.5). Both of these are straightforward. The integration with respect to x' is similar to a summation, and since each individual component satisfies the equation so does the sum/integral. Alternatively, differentiate (7.6) under the integral sign to see that it satisfies the partial differential equation. That it satisfies the condition (7.5) follows from the special properties of the fundamental solution W_f.

Retracing our steps to write our solution in terms of the original variables, we get

$$V(S,t) = \frac{e^{-r(T-t)}}{\sigma\sqrt{2\pi(T-t)}}\int_0^\infty e^{-(\log(S/S')+(r-(1/2)\sigma^2)(T-t))^2/2\sigma^2(T-t)}\,\mathrm{Payoff}\,(S')\frac{dS'}{S'}, \qquad (7.7)$$

where I have written $x' = \log S'$.

This is the exact solution for the option value in terms of the arbitrary payoff function. In the next sections I will manipulate this expression for special payoff functions.

7.2.1 Formula for a Call

The call option has the payoff function

$$\mathrm{Payoff}\,(S) = \max(S-E, 0).$$

Expression (7.7) can then be written as

$$\frac{e^{-r(T-t)}}{\sigma\sqrt{2\pi(T-t)}}\int_E^\infty e^{-(\log(S/S')+(r-(1/2)\sigma^2)(T-t))^2/2\sigma^2(T-t)}(S'-E)\frac{dS'}{S'}.$$

Return to the variable $x' = \log S'$, to write this as

$$\frac{e^{-r(T-t)}}{\sigma\sqrt{2\pi(T-t)}}\int_{\log E}^\infty e^{-(-x'+\log S+(r-(1/2)\sigma^2)(T-t))^2/2\sigma^2(T-t)}(e^{x'}-E)\,dx'$$

$$= \frac{e^{-r(T-t)}}{\sigma\sqrt{2\pi(T-t)}}\int_{\log E}^\infty e^{-(-x'+\log S+(r-(1/2)\sigma^2)(T-t))^2/2\sigma^2(T-t)}e^{x'}\,dx'$$

$$- E\frac{e^{-r(T-t)}}{\sigma\sqrt{2\pi(T-t)}}\int_{\log E}^\infty e^{-(-x'+\log S+(r-(1/2)\sigma^2)(T-t))^2/2\sigma^2(T-t)}\,dx'.$$

Both integrals in this expression can be written in the form

$$\int_d^\infty e^{-(1/2)x'^2}\,dx'$$

for some d (the second is just about in this form already, and the first just needs a completion of the square).

Thus the option price can be written as two separate terms involving the cumulative distribution function for a Normal distribution:

$$\text{Call option value } = SN(d_1) - Ee^{-r(T-t)}N(d_2)$$

where

$$d_1 = \frac{\log(S/E) + \left(r + \frac{1}{2}\sigma^2\right)(T-t)}{\sigma\sqrt{T-t}}$$

and

$$d_2 = \frac{\log(S/E) + \left(r - \frac{1}{2}\sigma^2\right)(T-t)}{\sigma\sqrt{T-t}}.$$

When there is continuous dividend yield on the underlying, or it is a currency, then

Call option value

$$Se^{-D(T-t)}N(d_1) - Ee^{-r(T-t)}N(d_2)$$

$$\text{where } d_1 = \frac{\log(S/E) + \left(r - D + \frac{1}{2}\sigma^2\right)(T-t)}{\sigma\sqrt{T-t}}$$

$$d_2 = \frac{\log(S/E) + \left(r - D - \frac{1}{2}\sigma^2\right)(T-t)}{\sigma\sqrt{T-t}} = d_1 - \sigma\sqrt{T-t}$$

The option value is shown in Figure 7.2 as a function of the underlying asset at a fixed time to expiry. In Figure 7.3 the value of the at-the-money option is shown as a function of time; expiry is $t = 1$. In Figure 7.4 is the call value as a function of both the underlying and time.

When the asset is 'at-the-money forward,' i.e. $S = E^{-(r-D)(T-t)}$, then there is a simple approximation for the call value (Brenner & Subrahmanyam, 1994):

$$\text{Call} \approx 0.4\, Se^{-D(T-t)}\sigma\sqrt{T-t}.$$

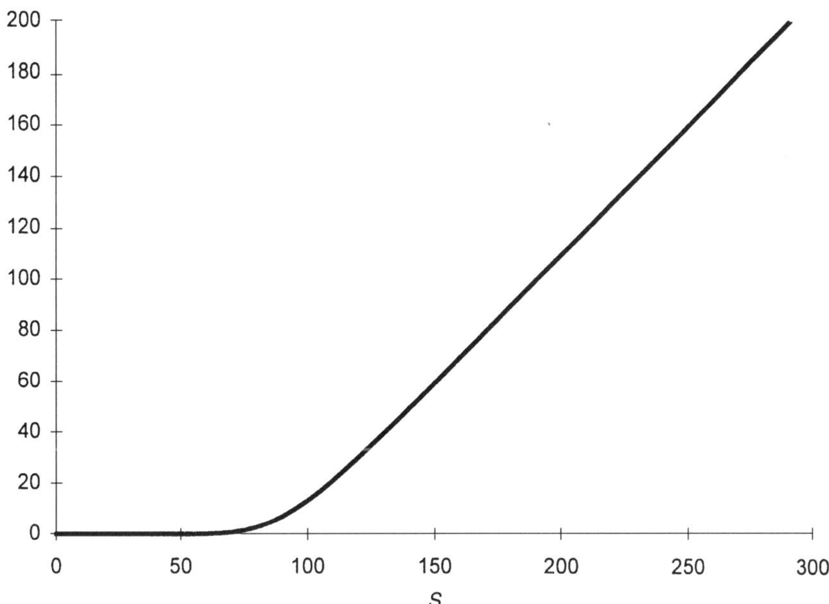

Figure 7.2 The value of a call option as a function of the underlying asset price at a fixed time to expiry.

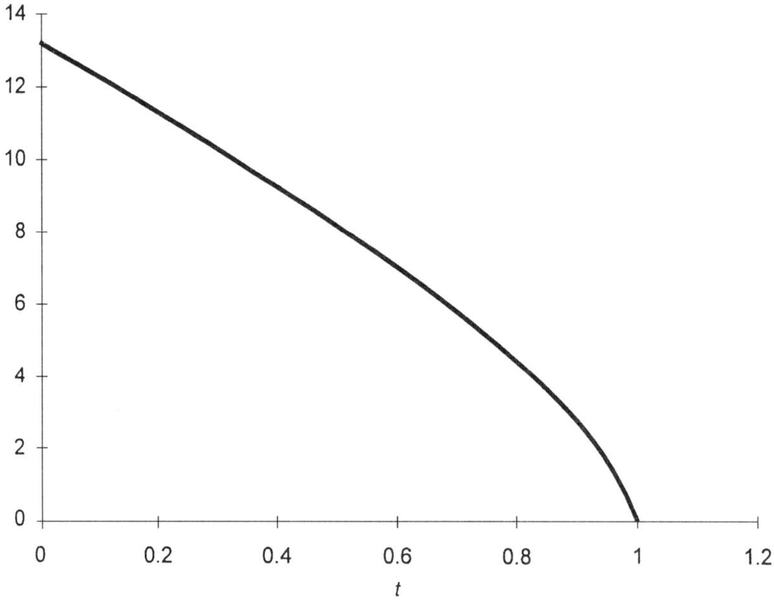

Figure 7.3 The value of an at-the-money call option as a function of time.

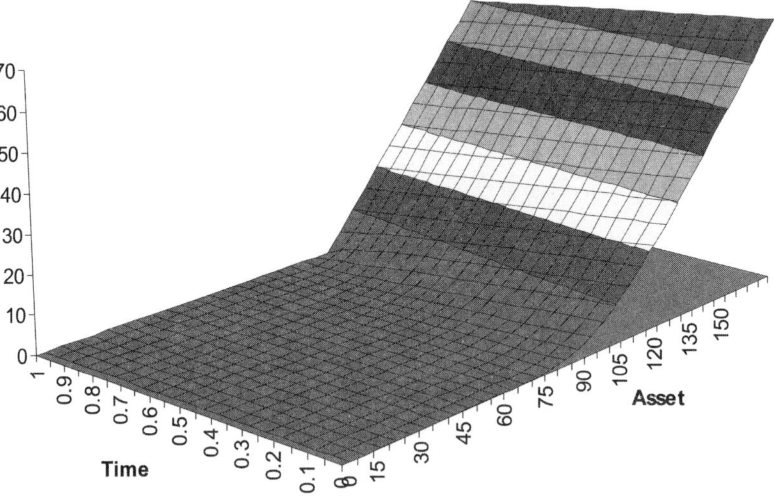

Figure 7.4 The value of a call option as a function of asset and time.

7.2.2 Formula for a Put

The put option has payoff

$$\text{Payoff}(S) = \max(E - S, 0).$$

The value of a put option can be found in the same way as above, or using put–call parity

$$\text{Put option value} = -SN(-d_1) + Ee^{-r(T-t)}N(-d_2),$$

with the same d_1 and d_2.

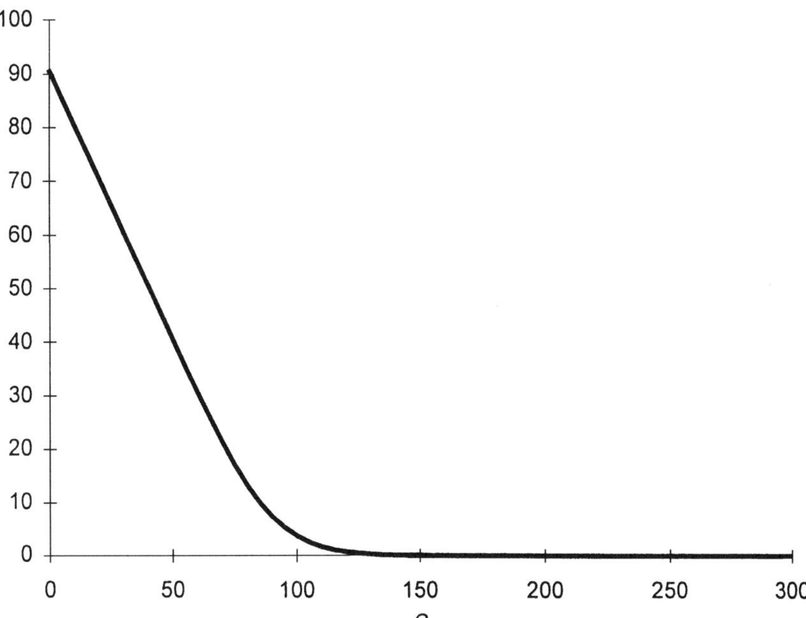

Figure 7.5 The value of a put option as a function of the underlying asset at a fixed time to expiry.

When there is continuous dividend yield on the underlying, or it is a currency, then

Put option value

$$-Se^{-D(T-t)}N(-d_1) + Ee^{-r(T-t)}N(-d_2)$$

The option value is shown in Figure 7.5 against the underlying asset and in Figure 7.6 against time. In Figure 7.7 is the option value as a function of both the underlying asset and time.

When the asset is at-the-money forward the simple approximation for the put value (Brenner & Subrahmanyam, 1994) is

$$\text{Put } \approx 0.4Se^{-D(T-t)}\sigma\sqrt{T-t}.$$

7.2.3 Formula for a Binary Call

The binary call has payoff

$$\text{Payoff}\,(S) = \mathcal{H}(S-E),$$

where $\mathcal{H}$ is the Heaviside function taking the value one when its argument is positive and zero otherwise.

Incorporating a dividend yield, we can write the option value as

$$\frac{e^{-r(T-t)}}{\sigma\sqrt{2\pi(T-t)}}\int_{\log E}^{\infty} e^{-(x'-\log S-(r-D-(1/2)\sigma^2)(T-t))^2/2\sigma^2(T-t)}\,dx'.$$

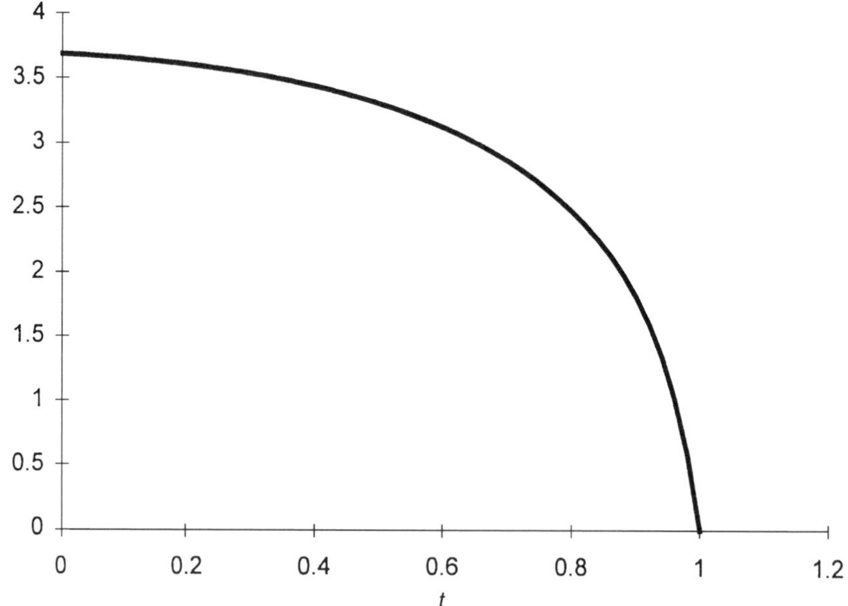

Figure 7.6 The value of an at-the-money put option as a function of time.

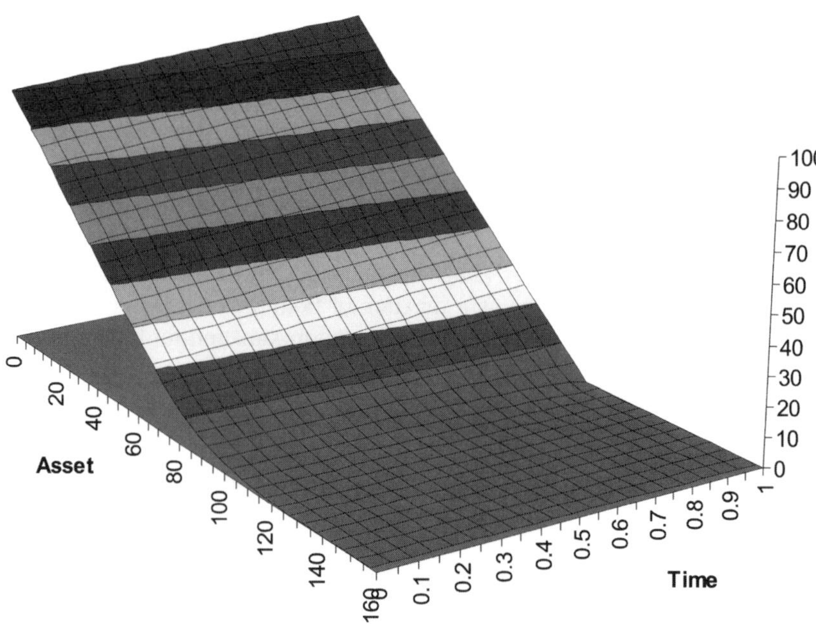

Figure 7.7 The value of a put option as a function of asset and time.

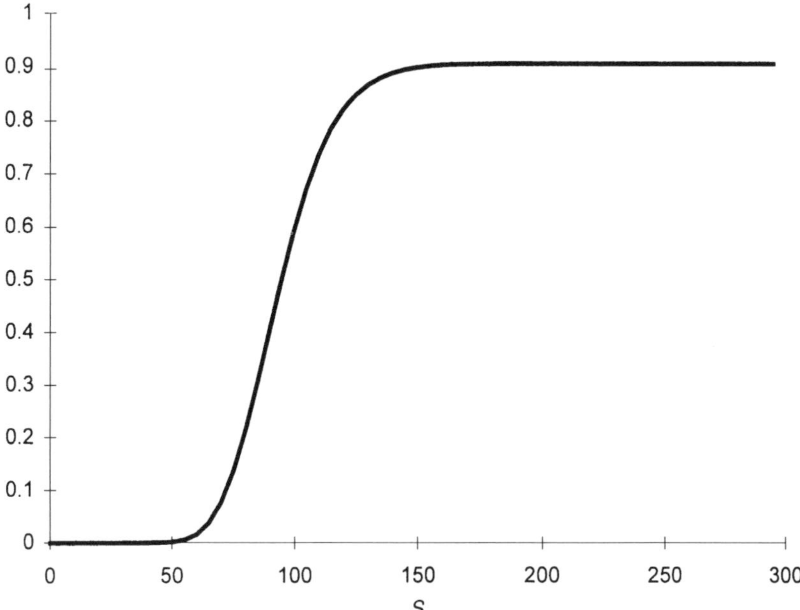

Figure 7.8 The value of a binary call option.

This term is just like the second term in the call option equation and so

Binary call option value

$$e^{-r(T-t)}N(d_2)$$

The option value is shown in Figure 7.8.

7.2.4 Formula for a Binary Put

The binary put has a payoff of one if $S < E$ at expiry. It has a value of

Binary put option value

$$e^{-r(T-t)}(1 - N(d_2))$$

since a binary call and a binary put must add up to the present value of \$1 received at time T. The option value is shown in Figure 7.9.

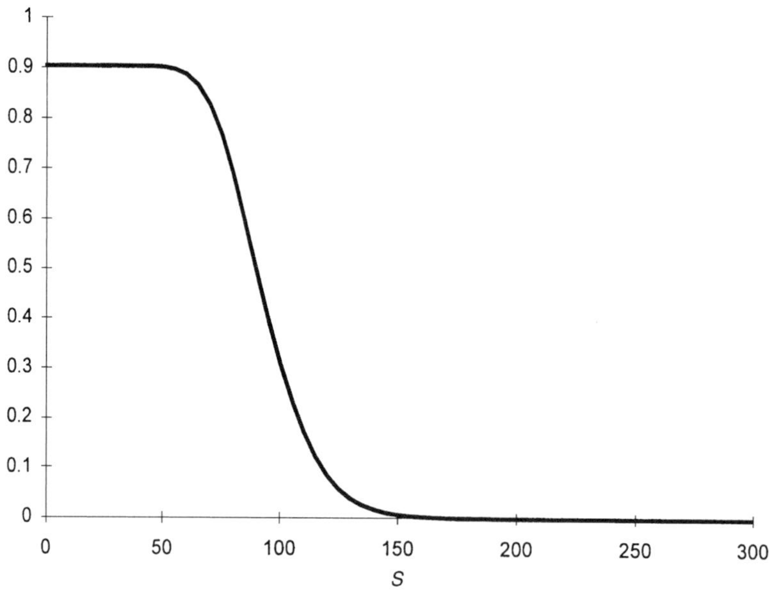

Figure 7.9 The value of a binary put option.

7.3 DELTA

The **delta** of an option or a portfolio of options is the sensitivity of the option or portfolio to the underlying. It is the rate of change of value with respect to the asset:

$$\Delta = \frac{\partial V}{\partial S}$$

Here V can be the value of a single contract or of a whole portfolio of contracts. The delta of a portfolio of options is just the sum of the deltas of all the individual positions.

The theoretical device of delta hedging, introduced in Chapter 5, for eliminating risk is, far more than that, a very important practical technique.

Roughly speaking, the financial world is divided up into speculators and hedgers. The speculators take a view on the direction of some quantity such as the asset price (or more abstract quantities such as volatility) and implement a strategy to take advantage of their view. Such people may not hedge at all.

Then there are the hedgers. There are two kinds of hedger: the ones who hold a position already and want to eliminate some very specific risk (usually using options) and the ones selling (or buying) the options because they believe they have a better price and can make money by hedging away *all* risk. It is the latter type of hedger that is delta hedging. They can only guarantee to make a profit by selling a contract for a high value if they can eliminate all of the risk due to the random fluctuation in the underlying.

Delta hedging means holding one of the option and short a quantity Δ of the underlying. Delta can be expressed as a function of S and t; I'll give some formulae later in this section. This function varies as S and t vary. This means that the number of assets held must be continuously changed to maintain a **delta neutral** position. This procedure is called **dynamic hedging**. Changing the number of assets held requires the continual purchase and/or sale of the stock. This is called **rehedging** or **rebalancing** the portfolio.

This delta hedging may take place very frequently in highly liquid markets where it is relatively costless to buy and sell. Thus the Black–Scholes assumption of continuous hedging may be quite accurate. In less liquid markets, you lose a lot on bid-offer spread and will therefore hedge less frequently. Moreover, you may not even be able to buy or sell in the quantities you want. Even in the absence of costs, you cannot be sure that your model for the underlying is accurate. There will certainly be some risk associated with the model. These issues make delta hedging less than perfect and in practice the risk in the underlying cannot be hedged away perfectly. Issues of discrete hedging and transaction costs are covered in depth in Chapters 20 and 21.

Some contracts (see especially Chapter 14) have a delta that becomes very large at special times or asset values. The size of the delta makes delta hedging impossible; what can you do if you find yourself with a theoretical delta requiring you to buy more stock than exists? In such a situation the basic foundation of the Black–Scholes world has collapsed and you would be right to question the validity of any pricing formula. This happens at expiry close to the strike for binary options. Although I've given a formula for their price above and a formula for their delta below, I'd be careful using them if I were you.

Here are some formulae for the deltas of common contracts (all formulae assume that the underlying pays dividends or is a currency):

Deltas of common contracts

Call	$e^{-D(T-t)}N(d_1)$
Put	$e^{-D(T-t)}(N(d_1)-1)$
Binary call	$\dfrac{e^{-r(T-t)}N'(d_2)}{\sigma S\sqrt{T-t}}$
Binary put	$-\dfrac{e^{-r(T-t)}N'(d_2)}{\sigma S\sqrt{T-t}}$

$$N'(x)=\frac{1}{\sqrt{2\pi}}e^{-(1/2)x^2}$$

Examples of these functions are plotted in Figure 7.10, with some scaling of the binaries.

7.4 GAMMA

The **gamma**, Γ, of an option or a portfolio of options is the second derivative of the position with respect to the underlying:

$$\Gamma=\frac{\partial^2 V}{\partial S^2}$$

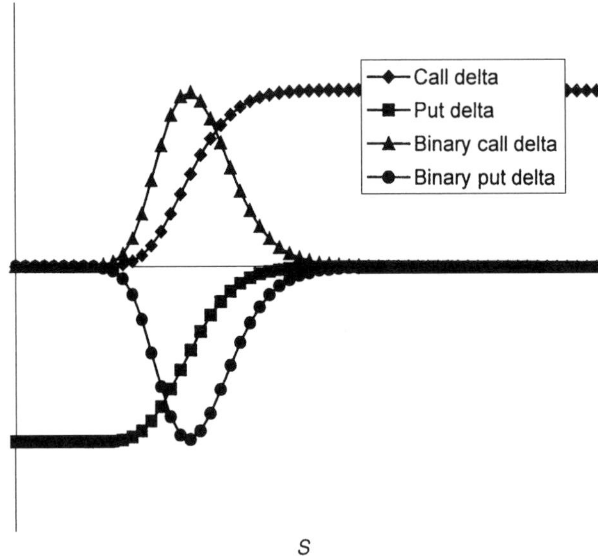

Figure 7.10 The deltas of a call, a put, a binary call and a binary put option. (Binary values scaled to a maximum value of one.)

Since gamma is the sensitivity of the delta to the underlying it is a measure of by how much or how often a position must be rehedged in order to maintain a delta-neutral position. Although the delta also varies with time this effect is dominated by the Brownian nature of the movement in the underlying.

In a delta-neutral position the gamma is partly responsible for making the return on the portfolio equal to the risk-free rate, the no-arbitrage condition of Chapter 5. The rest of this task falls to the time-derivative of the option value, discussed below. Actually, the situation is far more complicated than this because of the necessary discreteness in the hedging; there is a finite time between rehedges. In any delta-hedged position you make money on some hedges and lose some on others. In a long gamma position ($\Gamma > 0$) you make money on the large moves in the underlying and lose it on the small moves. To be precise, you make money 32% of the time and lose it 68%. But when you make it, you make more. The net effect is to get the risk-free rate of return on the portfolio. You won't have a clue where this fact came from, but all will be made clear in Chapter 20.

Gamma also plays an important role when there is a mismatch between the market's view of volatility and the actual volatility of the underlying. Again this is discussed in Chapter 20.

Because costs can be large and because one wants to reduce exposure to model error it is natural to try to minimize the need to rebalance the portfolio too frequently. Since gamma is a measure of sensitivity of the hedge ratio Δ to the movement in the underlying, the hedging requirement can be decreased by a gamma-neutral strategy. This means buying or selling more *options*, not just the underlying. Because the gamma of the underlying (its second derivative) is zero, we cannot add gamma to our position just with the underlying. We can have as many options in our position as we want; we choose the quantities of each such that both delta and gamma are zero. The minimal requirement is to hold two different types of option and the underlying. In practice, the option position is not readjusted too often because, if the cost of transacting in the underlying is large, then the cost of transacting in its derivatives is even larger.

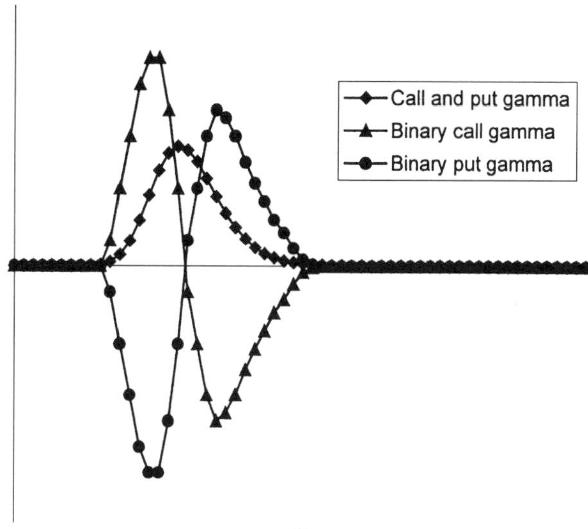

Figure 7.11 The gammas of a call, a put, a binary call and a binary put option.

Here are some formulae for the gammas of common contracts:

Gammas of common contracts

Call	$\dfrac{e^{-D(T-t)}N'(d_1)}{\sigma S\sqrt{T-t}}$
Put	$\dfrac{e^{-D(T-t)}N'(d_1)}{\sigma S\sqrt{T-t}}$
Binary call	$-\dfrac{e^{-r(T-t)}d_1N'(d_2)}{\sigma^2S^2(T-t)}$
Binary put	$\dfrac{e^{-r(T-t)}d_1N'(d_2)}{\sigma^2S^2(T-t)}$

Examples of these functions are plotted in Figure 7.11, with some scaling for the binaries.

7.5 THETA

Theta, Θ, is the rate of change of the option price with time.

$$\Theta = \frac{\partial V}{\partial t}$$

The theta is related to the option value, the delta and the gamma by the Black–Scholes equation. In a delta-hedged portfolio the theta contributes to ensuring that the portfolio earns the risk-free

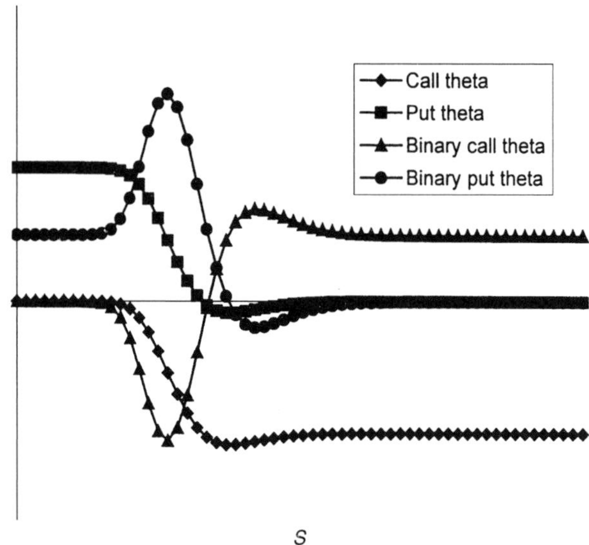

Figure 7.12 The thetas of a call, a put, a binary call and a binary put option.

rate. But it contributes in a completely certain way, unlike the gamma which contributes the right amount *on average*.

Here are some formulae for the thetas of common contracts:

Thetas of common contracts

Call	$-\dfrac{\sigma S e^{-D(T-t)} N'(d_1)}{2\sqrt{T-t}} + DSN(d_1)e^{-D(T-t)} - rEe^{-r(T-t)}N(d_2)$
Put	$-\dfrac{\sigma S e^{-D(T-t)} N'(-d_1)}{2\sqrt{T-t}} - DSN(-d_1)e^{-D(T-t)} + rEe^{-r(T-t)}N(-d_2)$
Binary call	$re^{-r(T-t)}N(d_2) + e^{-r(T-t)}N'(d_2)\left(\dfrac{d_1}{2(T-t)} - \dfrac{r-D}{\sigma\sqrt{T-t}}\right)$
Binary put	$re^{-r(T-t)}(1-N(d_2)) - e^{-r(T-t)}N'(d_2)\left(\dfrac{d_1}{2(T-t)} - \dfrac{r-D}{\sigma\sqrt{T-t}}\right)$

These functions are plotted in Figure 7.12.

7.6 VEGA

Vega, a.k.a. zeta and kappa, is a very important but confusing quantity. It is the sensitivity of the option price to volatility.

$$\text{Vega} = \frac{\partial V}{\partial \sigma}$$

IMPORTANT

This is completely different from the other greeks[2] since it is a derivative with respect to a parameter and not a variable. This makes something of a difference when we come to finding numerical solutions for such quantities.

In practice, the volatility of the underlying is not known with certainty. Not only is it very difficult to measure at any time, it is even harder to predict what it will do in the future. Suppose that we put a volatility of 20% into an option pricing formula; how sensitive is the price to that number? That's the vega.

As with gamma hedging, one can vega hedge to reduce sensitivity to the volatility. This is a major step towards eliminating some model risk, since it reduces dependence on a quantity that, to be honest, is not known very accurately.

There is a downside to the measurement of vega. It is only really meaningful for options having single-signed gamma everywhere. For example it makes sense to measure vega for calls and puts but not binary calls and binary puts. I have included the formulae for the vega of such contracts below, but they should be used with care, if at all. The reason for this is that call and put values (and options with single-signed gamma) have values that are monotonic in the volatility: increase the volatility in a call and its value increases everywhere. Contracts with a gamma that changes sign may have a vega measured at zero because as we increase the volatility the price may rise somewhere and fall somewhere else. Such a contract is very exposed to volatility risk but that risk is not measured by the vega. See Chapter 24 for more details.

Here are formulae for the vegas of common contracts:

Vegas of common contracts

Call	$S\sqrt{T-t}e^{-D(T-t)}N'(d_1)$
Put	$S\sqrt{T-t}e^{-D(T-t)}N'(d_1)$
Binary call	$-e^{-r(T-t)}N'(d_2)\left(\sqrt{T-t}+\frac{d_2}{\sigma}\right)$
Binary put	$e^{-r(T-t)}N'(d_2)\left(\sqrt{T-t}+\frac{d_2}{\sigma}\right)$

In Figure 7.13 is shown the value of an at-the-money call option as a function of the volatility. There is one year to expiry, the strike is 100, the interest rate is 10% and there are no dividends. No matter how far in or out of the money this curve is always monotonically increasing for call options and put options. Uncertainty adds value to the contract. The slope of this curve is the vega.

In Figure 7.14 is shown the value of an out-of-the-money binary call option as a function of the volatility. There is one year to expiry, the asset value is 88, strike is 100, the interest rate is 10% and there are no dividends. Observe that there is maximum at a volatility of about 24%. The value of the option is not monotonic in the volatility. We will see later why this makes the meaning of vega somewhat suspect.

[2] It's not even greek. Among other things it is an American car, a star (Alpha Lyrae), there are a couple of 16th century Spanish authors called Vega, an Op art painting by Vasarely and a character in the computer game 'Street Fighter.' And who could forget Vincent?

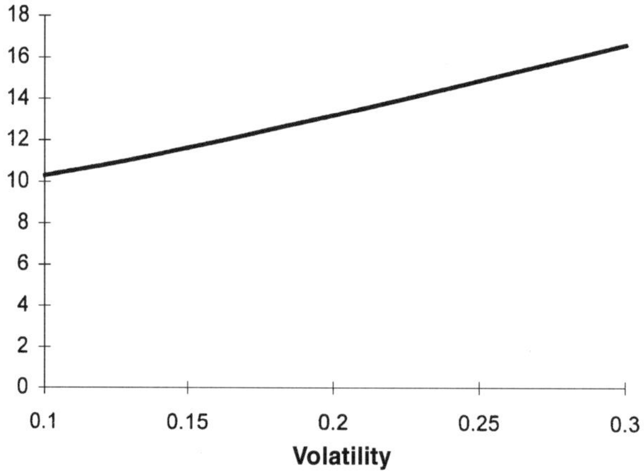

Figure 7.13 The value of an at-the-money call option as a function of volatility.

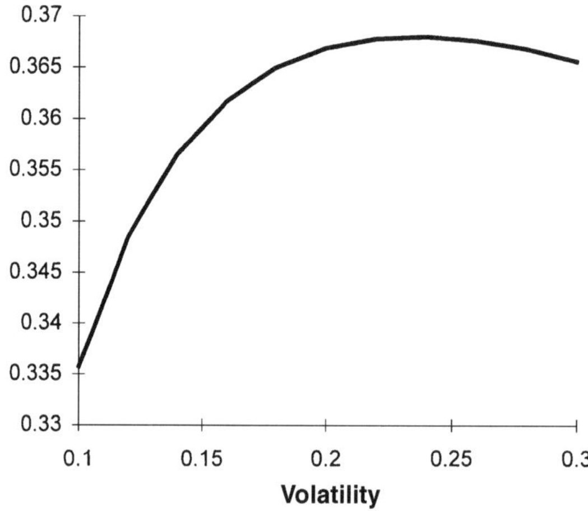

Figure 7.14 The value of an out-of-the-money binary call option as a function of volatility.

7.7 RHO

Rho, ρ, is the sensitivity of the option value to the interest rate used in the Black–Scholes formulae:

$$\rho = \frac{\partial V}{\partial r}$$

In practice one often uses a whole term structure of interest rates, meaning a time-dependent rate $r(t)$. Rho would then be the sensitivity to the level of the rates assuming a parallel shift in rates at all times. Again, you must be careful for which contracts you measure rho (see Chapter 24 for more details).

Here are some formulae for the rhos of common contracts:

Rhos of common contracts

Call	$E(T-t)e^{-r(T-t)}N(d_2)$
Put	$-E(T-t)e^{-r(T-t)}N(-d_2)$
Binary call	$-(T-t)e^{-r(T-t)}N(d_2)+\dfrac{\sqrt{T-t}}{\sigma}e^{-r(T-t)}N'(d_2)$
Binary put	$-(T-t)e^{-r(T-t)}(1-N(d_2))-\dfrac{\sqrt{T-t}}{\sigma}e^{-r(T-t)}N'(d_2)$

The sensitivities of common contract to the dividend yield or foreign interest rate are given by the following formulae:

Sensitivity to dividend for common contracts

Call	$-(T-t)Se^{-D(T-t)}N(d_1)$
Put	$(T-t)Se^{-D(T-t)}N(-d_1)$
Binary call	$-\dfrac{\sqrt{T-t}}{\sigma}e^{-r(T-t)}N'(d_2)$
Binary put	$\dfrac{\sqrt{T-t}}{\sigma}e^{-r(T-t)}N'(d_2)$

7.8 IMPLIED VOLATILITY

The Black–Scholes formula for a call option takes as input the expiry, the strike, the underlying and the interest rate *together with the volatility* to output the price. All but the volatility are easily measured. How do we know what volatility to put into the formulae? A trader can see on his screen that a certain call option with four months until expiry and a strike of 100 is trading at 6.51 with the underlying at 101.5 and a short-term interest rate of 8%. Can we use this information in some way?

Turn the relationship between volatility and an option price on its head. If we can see the price at which the option is trading, we can ask 'What volatility must I use to get the correct market price?' This is called the **implied volatility**. The implied volatility is the volatility of the underlying which when substituted into the Black–Scholes formula gives a theoretical price equal to the market price. In a sense it is the market's view of volatility over the life of the option. Assuming that we are using call prices to estimate the implied volatility then provided the option price is less than the asset and greater than zero then we can find a unique value for the implied volatility. (If the option price is outside these bounds then there's a very extreme arbitrage opportunity.) Because there is no simple formula for the implied volatility as a function of the option value we must solve the equation

$$V_{BS}(S_0, t_0; \sigma, r; E, T) = \text{known value}$$

for σ, where V_{BS} is the Black–Scholes formula. Today's asset price is S_0, the date is t_0 and everything is known in this equation except for σ. Below is an algorithm for finding the implied volatility from the market price of a call option to any required degree of accuracy. The method used is **Newton–Raphson** which uses the derivative of the option price with respect to the volatility (the vega) in the calculation. This method is particularly good for such a well-behaved function as a call value.

```
Function ImpVolCall(MktPrice As Double, Strike As Double,  _
                     Expiry As Double, Asset As Double, _
                     IntRate As Double, error As Double)
Volatility = 0.2
dv = error + 1
While Abs(dv) > error
    d1 = Log(Asset / Strike) + (IntRate + 0.5 * Volatility
    * Volatility) * Expiry
    d1 = d1 / (Volatility * Sqr(Expiry))
    d2 = d1 - Volatility * Sqr(Expiry)
    PriceError = Asset * cdf(d1) - Strike * Exp(-IntRate * Expiry)
    * cdf(d2) - MktPrice
    Vega = Asset * Sqr(Expiry / 3.1415926 / 2) * _
               Exp(-0.5 * d1 * d1)
    dv = PriceError / Vega
    Volatility = Volatility - dv
Wend
ImpVolCall = Volatility
End Function
```

In this we need the cumulative distribution function for the Normal distribution. The following is a simple algorithm which gives an accurate, and fast, approximation to the cumulative distribution function of the standardized Normal:

$$\text{For } x \geq 0 \, N(x) \approx 1 - \frac{1}{\sqrt{2\pi}} e^{-(1/2)x^2}(ad + bd^2 + cd^3)$$

where

$$d = \frac{1}{1 + 0.33267x}, \quad a = 0.4361836 \quad b = -0.1201676 \quad \text{and} \quad c = 0.937298.$$

For $x < 0$ use the fact that $N(x) + N(-x) = 1$.

```
Function cdf(x)
d = 1 / (1 + 0.33267 * Abs(x))
a = 0.4361836
b = -0.1201676
c = 0.937298
cdf = 1 - 1 / Sqr(2 * 3.1415926) * Exp(-0.5 * x * x) * _
                                    (a * d + b * d * d + _
                                     c * d * d * d)
If x < 0 Then cdf = 1 - cdf
End Function
```

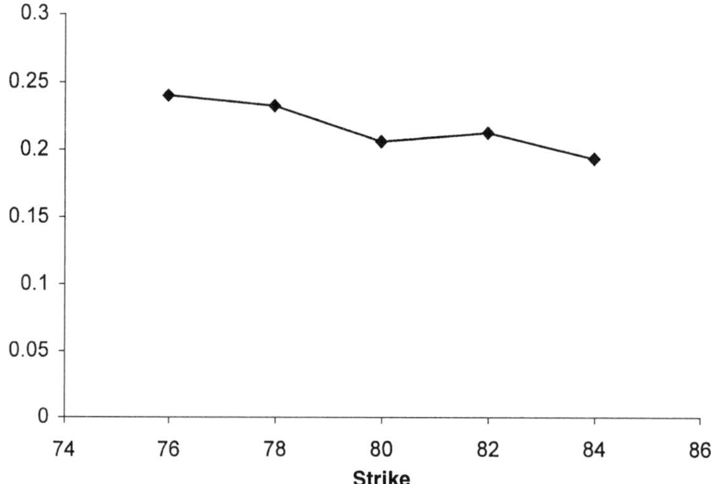

Figure 7.15 Implied volatilities for Dow Jones Industrial Average, 23rd December 1997.

In practice if we calculate the implied volatility for many different strikes and expiries on the same underlying then we find that *the volatility is not constant.* A typical result is that of Figure 7.15 which shows the implied volatilities for Dow Jones Industrial Average on 23rd December 1997.

This shape is commonly referred to as the **smile**, but it could also be in the shape of a **frown**. In this example it's a rather lopsided wry grin. Whatever the shape, it tends to persist with time, with certain shapes being characteristic of certain markets.

The dependence of the implied volatility on strike and expiry can be interpreted in many ways. The easiest interpretation is that it represents the market's view of future volatility in some complex way. This issue is covered in depth in Chapter 22. Another possibility is that it reflects the uncertainty in volatility, perhaps volatility is also a stochastic variable (see Chapter 23).

7.9 SUMMARY

In this chapter we went through the derivation of some of the most important formulae. We also saw the definitions and descriptions of the hedge ratios. Trading in derivatives would be no more than gambling if you took away the ability to hedge. Hedging is all about managing risk and reducing uncertainty.

FURTHER READING

- See Taleb (1997) for a lot of detailed analysis of vega.
- See Press et al. (1992) for more routines for finding roots, i.e. for finding implied volatilities.
- There are many 'virtual' option pricers on the internet. See, for example, www.cboe.com.
- I'm not going to spend much time on deriving or even presenting formulae. There are 1001 books that contain option formulae, there is even one book with 1001 formulae (Haug, 1997).

EXERCISES

1. Find the explicit solution for the value of a European option with payoff $\Lambda(S)$ and expiry at time T, where

$$\Lambda(S) = \begin{cases} S & \text{if } S > E \\ 0 & \text{if } S < E. \end{cases}$$

2. Find the explicit solution for the value of a European supershare option, with expiry at time T and payoff

$$\Lambda(S) = \mathcal{H}(S - E_1) - \mathcal{H}(S - E_2),$$

where $E_1 < E_2$.

3. Consider the pay-later call option. This has payoff $\Lambda(S) = \max(S - E, 0)$ at time T. The holder of the option does not pay a premium when the contract is set up, but must pay Q to the writer at expiry, only if $S \geq E$. What is the value of Q?

4. Find the implied volatility of the following European call. The call has four months until expiry and an exercise price of \$100. The call is worth \$6.51 and the underlying trades at \$101.5, discount using a short-term risk-free continuously compounding interest rate of 8% per annum.

5. Consider a European call, currently at the money. Why is delta-hedging self financing in the following situations?
(a) The share price rises until expiry.
(b) The share price falls until expiry.

6. Using the explicit solutions for the European call and put–options, check that put–call parity holds.

7. Consider an asset with zero volatility. We can explicitly calculate the future value of the asset and hence that of a call option with the asset as the underlying. The value of the call option will then depend on the growth rate of the asset, μ. On the other hand, we can use the explicit formula for the call option, in which μ does not appear. Explain this apparent contradiction.

8. The range forward contract is specified as follows: at expiry, the holder must buy the asset for E_1 if $S < E_1$, for S if $E_1 \leq S \leq E_2$ and for E_2 if $S > E_2$. Find the relationship between E_1 and E_2 when the initial value of the contract is zero and $E_1 < E_2$.

9. A forward start call option is specified as follows: at time T_1, the holder is given a European call option with exercise price $S(T_1)$ and expiry at time $T_1 + T_2$. What is the value of the option for $0 \leq t \leq T_1$?

10. Consider a delta-neutral portfolio of derivatives, Π. For a small change in the price of the underlying asset, δS, over a short time interval, δt, show that the change in the portfolio value, $\delta\Pi$, satisfies

$$\delta\Pi = \Theta\delta t + \tfrac{1}{2}\Gamma\delta S^2,$$

where $\Theta = \dfrac{\partial\Pi}{\partial t}$ and $\Gamma = \dfrac{\partial^2\Pi}{\partial S^2}$.

11. Show that for a delta-neutral portfolio of options on a non-dividend paying stock, Π,

$$\Theta + \tfrac{1}{2}\sigma^2 S^2\Gamma = r\Pi.$$

12. Show that the vega of an option, v, satisfies the differential equation

$$\frac{\partial v}{\partial t} + \tfrac{1}{2}\sigma^2 S^2 \frac{\partial^2 v}{\partial S^2} + rS\frac{\partial v}{\partial S} - rv + \sigma S^2 \Gamma = 0,$$

where $\Gamma = \dfrac{\partial^2 V}{\partial S^2}$. What is the final condition?

13. Find the partial differential equation satisfied by ρ the sensitivity of the option value to the interest rate.

14. Use put–call parity to find the relationships between the deltas, gammas, vegas, thetas and rhos of European call and put options.

15. The fundamental solution, u_δ, is the solution of the diffusion equation on $-\infty < x < \infty$ and $\tau > 0$ with $u(x, 0) = \delta(x)$. Use this solution to solve the more general problem:

$$\frac{\partial u}{\partial \tau} = \frac{\partial^2 u}{\partial x^2}, \quad \text{on} \quad -\infty < x < \infty, \tau > 0,$$

with $u(x, 0) = u_0(x)$.

CHAPTER 8

simple generalizations of the Black–Scholes world

In this Chapter...

- complex dividend structures
- jump conditions
- time-dependent volatility, interest rate and dividend yield

8.1 INTRODUCTION

This chapter is an introduction to some of the possible generalizations of the 'Black–Scholes world.' In particular, I will discuss the effect of dividend payments on the underlying asset and how to incorporate time-dependent parameters into the framework. These subjects lead to some interesting and important mathematical and financial conclusions.

The generalizations are very straightforward. However, later, in Part Three, I describe other models of the financial world that take us a long way from Black–Scholes.

8.2 DIVIDENDS, FOREIGN INTEREST AND COST OF CARRY

In Chapter 5 I showed how to incorporate certain types of dividend structures into the Black–Scholes option pricing framework, and then in Chapter 7 I gave some formulae for the values of some common vanilla contracts, again with dividends on the underlying. The dividend structure that I dealt with was the very simplest from a mathematical point of view. I assumed that an amount was paid to the holder of the asset that was proportional to the value of the asset and that it was paid continuously. In other words, the owner of one asset received a dividend of $DS\,dt$ in a timestep dt. This dividend structure is realistic if the underlying is an index on a large number of individual assets each receiving a lump sum dividend but with all these dividends spread out through the year. It is also a good model if the underlying is a currency, in which case we simply take the 'dividend yield' to be the foreign interest rate. Similarly, if the underlying is a commodity with a cost of carry that is proportional to its value, then the 'dividend yield' is just the cost of carry (with a minus sign, we benefit from dividends but must pay out the cost of carry).

To recap, if the underlying receives a dividend of $DS\,dt$ in a timestep dt when the asset price is S then

$$\frac{\partial V}{\partial t} + \tfrac{1}{2}\sigma^2 S^2 \frac{\partial^2 V}{\partial S^2} + (r - D)S\frac{\partial V}{\partial S} - rV = 0.$$

However, if the underlying is a stock, then the assumption of constant and continuously-paid dividend yield is not a good one.

8.3 DIVIDEND STRUCTURES

Typically, dividends are paid out quarterly in the US and semi-annually or quarterly in the UK. The dividend is set by the board of directors of the company some time before it is paid out and the amount of the payment is made public. The amount is often chosen to be similar to previous payments, but will obviously reflect the success or otherwise of the company. The amount specified is a dollar amount, it is *not* a percentage of the stock price on the day that the payment is made. So reality differs from the above simple model in three respects:

- the amount of the dividend is not known until shortly before it is paid
- the payment is a given dollar amount, independent of the stock price
- the dividend is paid discretely, and not continuously throughout the year.

In what follows I am going to make some assumptions about the dividend. I will assume that

- the amount of the dividend is a known amount, possibly with some functional dependence on the asset value *at the payment date*
- the dividend is paid discretely on a known date.

Other assumptions that I could, but won't, make because of the subsequent complexity of the modeling are that the dividend amount and/or date are random, that the dividend amount is a function of the stock price on the day that the dividend is set, that the dividend depends on how well the stock has done in the previous quarter...

8.4 DIVIDEND PAYMENTS AND NO ARBITRAGE

How does the stock react to the payment of a dividend? To put the question another way, if you have a choice whether to buy a stock just before or just after it goes ex dividend, which should you choose?

Let me introduce some notation. The dates of dividends will be t_i and the amount of the dividend paid on that day will be D_i. This may be a function of the underlying asset, but it then must be a deterministic function. The moment just before the stock goes ex dividend will be denoted by t_i^- and the moment just after will be t_i^+.

The person who buys the stock on or before t_i^- will also get the rights to the dividend. The person who buys it at t_i^+ or later will not receive the dividend. It looks like there is an advantage in buying the stock just before the dividend date. Of course, this advantage is balanced by *a fall in the stock price as it goes ex dividend.* Across a dividend date the stock falls by the amount

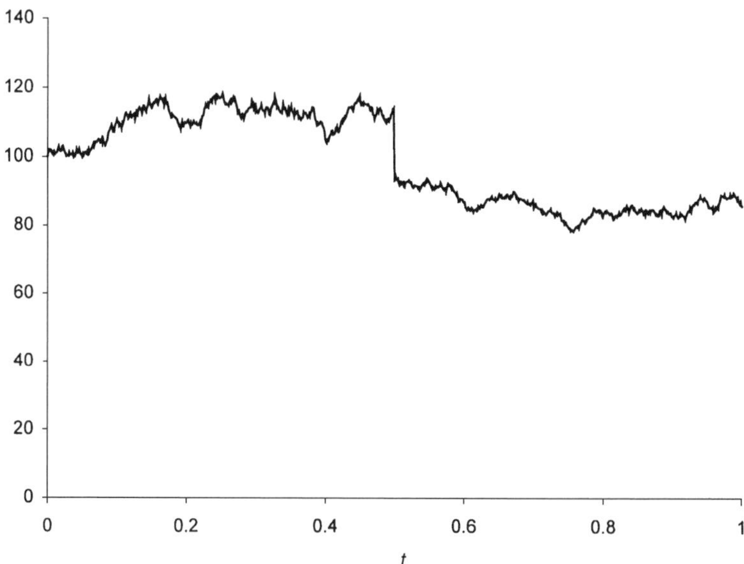

Figure 8.1 A stock price path across a dividend date.

of the dividend. If it did not, then there would be arbitrage opportunities. We can write

$$S(t_i^+) = S(t_i^-) - D_i. \tag{8.1}$$

In Figure 8.1 is shown an asset price path showing the fall in the asset price as it goes ex dividend. The drop has been exaggerated.

This jump in the stock price will presumably have some effect on the value of an option. We will discuss this next.

8.5 THE BEHAVIOR OF AN OPTION VALUE ACROSS A DIVIDEND DATE

We have just seen how the underlying asset jumps in value, in a completely predictable way, across a dividend date.

Jump conditions tell us about the value of a dependent variable, an option price, when there is a discontinuous change in one of the independent variables. In the present case, there is a discontinuous change in the asset price due to the payment of a dividend but how does this affect the option price? Does the option price also jump? The jump condition relates the values of the option across the jump, from times t_i^- to t_i^+. The jump condition will be derived by a simple no-arbitrage argument.

To see what the jump condition should be, ask the question, 'By how much do I profit or lose when the stock price jumps?' If you hold the option then you do not see any of the dividend, that goes to the holder of the stock not you, the holder of the option. If the dividend amount and date are known in advance then there is no surprise in the fall in the stock price. The conclusion must be that the option does not change in value across the dividend date,

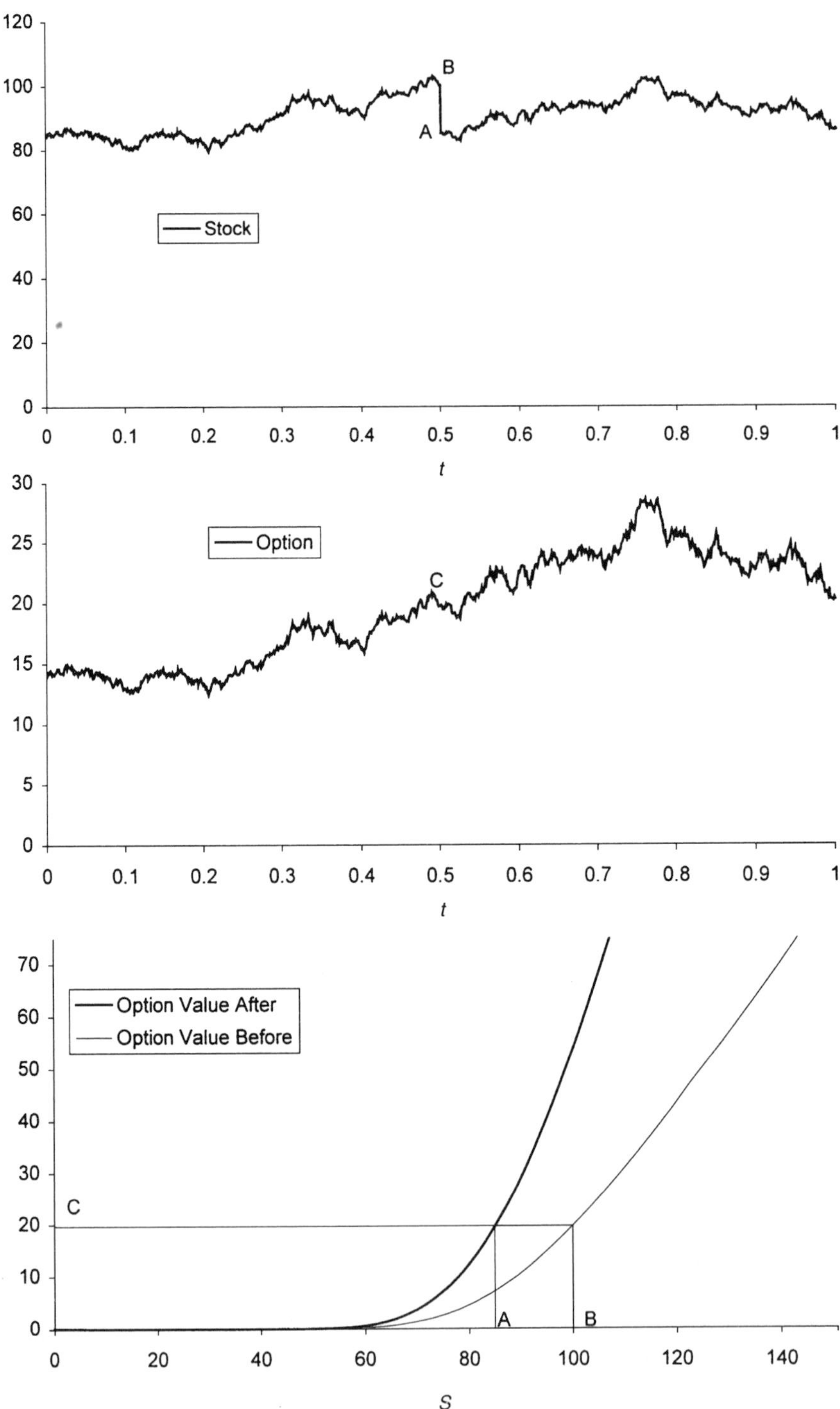

Figure 8.2 Top picture: a realization of the stock price showing a fall across the dividend date. Middle picture: the corresponding realization of the option price (in this example a call). Bottom picture: the option value as a function of the stock price just before and just after the dividend date.

its path is continuous. Continuity of the option value across a dividend date can be written as

$$V(S(t_i^-), t_i^-) = V(S(t_i^+), t_i^+) \tag{8.2}$$

or, in terms of the amount of the dividend,

$$V(S, t_i^-) = V(S - D_i, t_i^+). \tag{8.3}$$

The jump condition and its effect on the option value can be explained by reference to Figure 8.2. In this figure, the top picture shows a realization of the stock price with a fall across the dividend date. The middle picture shows the corresponding realization of a call option price. The bottom picture shows the option value as a function of the stock price just before and just after the dividend date. Observe the points 'A' and 'B' on these pictures. 'A' is the stock price after the dividend has been paid and 'B' is the price before. On the bottom picture we see the values of the option associated with these before and after asset prices. *These option values are the same* and are denoted by 'C.' Even though there is a fall in the asset value, the option value is unchanged because the whole V *versus* S plot changes. The relationship between the before and after values of the option are related by (8.3). I will give two examples.

Suppose that the dividend paid out is proportional to the asset value, $D_i = DS$. In this case

$$S(t_i^+) = (1 - D)S(t_i^-).$$

Equation (8.3) is then just

$$V(S, t_i^-) = V((1 - D)S, t_i^+).$$

The two option price curves are identical if one stretches the after curve by a factor of $(1 - D)^{-1}$ in the horizontal direction. Thus, even though the option value is continuous across a dividend date, the delta changes discontinuously.

If the dividend is independent of the stock price then

$$S(t_i^+) = S(t_i^-) - D_i,$$

where D_i is independent of the asset value. The before curve is then identical to the after curve, but shifted by an amount D_i.

8.6 TIME-DEPENDENT PARAMETERS

The next generalization concerns the term structure of parameters. In this section I show how to derive formulae for options when the interest rate, volatility and dividend yield/foreign interest rate are time dependent.

The Black–Scholes partial differential equation is valid as long as the parameters r, D and σ are known functions of time; in practice one often has a view on the future behavior of these parameters. For instance, you may want to incorporate the market's view on the direction of interest rates. Assume that you want to price options knowing $r(t)$, $D(t)$ and $\sigma(t)$. Note that when I write '$D(t)$' I am specifically assuming a time-dependent dividend yield, that is, the amount of the dividend is $D(t)S\,dt$ in a timestep dt.

The equation that we must solve is now

$$\frac{\partial V}{\partial t} + \tfrac{1}{2}\sigma^2(t)S^2\frac{\partial^2 V}{\partial S^2} + (r(t) - D(t))S\frac{\partial V}{\partial S} - r(t)V = 0, \tag{8.4}$$

where the dependence on t is shown explicitly.

Introduce new variables as follows.

$$\overline{S} = Se^{\alpha(t)}, \quad \overline{V} = Ve^{\beta(t)}, \quad \bar{t} = \gamma(t).$$

We are free to choose the functions α, β and γ and so we will choose them so as to eliminate all time-dependent coefficients from (8.4). After changing variables (8.4) becomes

$$\dot{\gamma}(t)\frac{\partial \overline{V}}{\partial \bar{t}} + \tfrac{1}{2}\sigma(t)^2\overline{S}^2\frac{\partial^2 \overline{V}}{\partial \overline{S}^2} + (r(t) - D(t) + \dot{\alpha}(t))\overline{S}\frac{\partial \overline{V}}{\partial \overline{S}} - (r(t) + \dot{\beta}(t))\overline{V} = 0, \tag{8.5}$$

where $\dot{} = d/dt$. By choosing

$$\beta(t) = \int_t^T r(\tau)\,d\tau$$

we make the coefficient of $\overline{V}$ zero and then by choosing

$$\alpha(t) = \int_t^T (r(\tau) - D(\tau))\,d\tau,$$

we make the coefficient of $\partial\overline{V}/\partial\overline{S}$ also zero. Finally, the remaining time dependence, in the volatility term, can be eliminated by choosing

$$\gamma(t) = \int_t^T \sigma^2(\tau)\,d\tau.$$

Now (8.5) becomes the much simpler equation

$$\frac{\partial \overline{V}}{\partial \bar{t}} = \tfrac{1}{2}\overline{S}^2\frac{\partial^2 \overline{V}}{\partial \overline{S}^2}. \tag{8.6}$$

The important point about this equation is that it has coefficients which are *independent of time*, and there is no mention of r, D or σ. If we use $\overline{V}(\overline{S}, \bar{t})$ to denote any solution of (8.6), then the corresponding solution of (8.5), in the original variables, is

$$V = e^{-\beta(t)}\overline{V}(Se^{\alpha(t)}, \gamma(t)). \tag{8.7}$$

Now use V_{BS} to mean any solution of the Black–Scholes equation for *constant* interest rate r_c, dividend yield D_c and volatility σ_c. This solution can be written in the form

$$V_{BS} = e^{-r_c(T-t)}\overline{V}_{BS}(Se^{-(r_c+D_c)(T-t)}, \sigma_c^2(T-t)) \tag{8.8}$$

for some function $\overline{V}_{BS}$. By comparing (8.7) and (8.8) it follows that the solution of the time-dependent parameter problem is the same as the solution of the constant parameter problem if we use the following substitutions:

$$r_c = \frac{1}{T-t}\int_t^T r(\tau)\,d\tau$$

$$D_c = \frac{1}{T-t}\int_t^T D(\tau)\,d\tau$$

$$\sigma_c^2 = \frac{1}{T-t}\int_t^T \sigma^2(\tau)\,d\tau$$

These formulae give the average, over the remaining lifetime of the option, of the interest rate, the dividend yield and the squared volatility.

Just to make things absolutely clear, here is the formula for a European call option with time-dependent parameters:

$$Se^{-\int_t^T D(\tau)\,d\tau}N(d_1) - Ee^{-\int_t^T r(\tau)\,d\tau}N(d_2)$$

where

$$d_1 = \frac{\log(S/E) + \displaystyle\int_t^T (r(\tau) - D(\tau))\,d\tau + \tfrac{1}{2}\int_t^T \sigma^2(\tau)\,d\tau}{\sqrt{\displaystyle\int_t^T \sigma^2(\tau)\,d\tau}}$$

and

$$d_2 = \frac{\log(S/E) + \displaystyle\int_t^T (r(\tau) - D(\tau))\,d\tau - \tfrac{1}{2}\int_t^T \sigma^2(\tau)\,d\tau}{\sqrt{\displaystyle\int_t^T \sigma^2(\tau)\,d\tau}}.$$

There are some conditions that I must attach to the use of these formulae. They are generally not correct if there is early exercise, or for certain types of exotic option. The question to ask to decide whether they are correct is 'Are all the conditions, final and boundary, preserved by the transformations?'

8.7 FORMULAE FOR POWER OPTIONS

An option with a payoff that depends on the asset price at expiry raised to some power is called a **power option**. Suppose that it has a payoff

$$\text{Payoff}\,(S^\alpha)$$

we can find a simple formula for the value of the option if we have a simple formula for an option with payoff given by

$$\text{Payoff}\,(S). \tag{8.9}$$

This is because of the lognormality of the underlying asset.

Writing

$$\mathcal{S} = S^\alpha$$

the Black–Scholes equation becomes, in the new variable $\mathcal{S}$

$$\frac{\partial V}{\partial t} + \tfrac{1}{2}\alpha^2\sigma^2\mathcal{S}^2\frac{\partial^2 V}{\partial \mathcal{S}^2} + \alpha\left(\tfrac{1}{2}\sigma^2(\alpha-1)+r\right)\mathcal{S}\frac{\partial V}{\partial \mathcal{S}} - rV = 0.$$

Thus whatever the formula for the option value with simple payoff (8.9), the formula for the power version has S^α instead of S and adjustment made to σ, r and D.

8.8 SUMMARY

In this chapter I made some very simple generalizations to the Black–Scholes world. I showed the effect of discretely-paid dividends on the value of an option, deriving a jump condition by a no-arbitrage argument. Generally, this condition would be applied numerically and its implementation is discussed in Chapter 47. I also showed how time-dependent parameters can be incorporated into the pricing of simple vanilla options.

FURTHER READING

- See Merton (1973) for the original derivation of the Black–Scholes formulae with time-dependent parameters.
- For a model with stochastic dividends see Geske (1978).
- The practical implications of discrete dividend payments are discussed by Gemmill (1992).

EXERCISES

1. Consider the Black–Scholes equation for a European call option on an asset with a constant, continuous dividend yield, DS. Transform the problem to a diffusion equation problem. How many dimensionless parameters are there?
2. What is the value of a European call option on an asset paying a constant, continuous dividend yield, DS?
3. What is the value of a European call option on an asset paying a single, discrete dividend, DS, at time t_d?
4. An asset pays a continuous dividend yield, DS. Find the put–call parity relationship for European options on this underlying.
5. An asset pays a single, discrete dividend, DS, at time t_d. Find the put–call parity relationship for European options on this underlying.
6. What is the value of a European call on an asset that pays out discrete dividends $D_1S(t_1)$ at time t_1 and $D_2S(t_2)$ at time t_2?
7. Is there a difference between the following portfolios?
   (a) long a forward contract,
   (b) long a call option and short a put option.

   where both options are European and all the contracts have the same expiry.
8. An asset pays a single, discrete dividend, DS, at time t_d. By solving the Black–Scholes equation with an appropriate jump condition, find the forward price for $t < t_d$.

CHAPTER 9

early exercise and American options

In this Chapter...

- the meaning of 'early exercise'
- the difference between European, American and Bermudan options
- how to value American options in the partial differential equation framework
- how to decide when to exercise early
- early exercise and dividends

9.1 INTRODUCTION

American options are contracts that may be exercised early, *prior* to expiry. For example, if the option is a call, we may hand over the exercise price and receive the asset whenever we wish. These options must be contrasted with European options for which exercise is only permitted *at* expiry. Most traded stock and futures options are American style, but most index options are European.

The right to exercise at any time at will is clearly valuable. The value of an American option cannot be less than an equivalent European option. But as well as giving the holder more rights, they also give him more headaches; when should he exercise? Part of the valuation problem is deciding when is the best time to exercise. This is what makes American options much more interesting than their European cousins. Moreover, the issues I am about to raise have repercussions in many other financial problems.

9.2 THE PERPETUAL AMERICAN PUT

There is a very simple example of an American option that we can examine for the insight that it gives us in the general case. This simple example is the **perpetual American put**. This contract can be exercised for a put payoff at *any* time. There is no expiry; that's why it is called a 'perpetual' option. So we can, at any time of *our* choosing, sell the underlying and receive an amount E. That is, the payoff is

$$\max(E - S, 0).$$

We want to find the value of this option before exercise.

The first point to note is that the solution is independent of time, $V(S)$. It depends only on the level of the underlying. This is a property of perpetual options when the contract details are time-homogeneous, provided that there is a finite solution. When we come to the general, non-perpetual, American option, we unfortunately lose this property. ('Unfortunately,' since it makes it easy for us to find the solution in this special case.)

The second point to note, which is important for all American options, is that the option value can never go below the early-exercise payoff. In the case under consideration

$$V \geq \max(E - S, 0). \tag{9.1}$$

Consider what would happen if this 'constraint' were violated. Suppose that the option value is less than $\max(E - S, 0)$. I could buy the option for $\max(E - S, 0)$, immediately exercise it by handing over the asset (worth S) and receive an amount E. I thus make

$$-\text{ cost of put} - \text{cost of asset} + \text{strike price} = -V - S + E > 0.$$

This is a riskless profit. If we believe that there are no arbitrage opportunities then we must believe (9.1).

While the option value is strictly greater than the payoff, it must satisfy the Black–Scholes equation; I return to this point in the next section. Recalling that the option is perpetual and therefore that the value is independent of t, it must satisfy

$$\tfrac{1}{2}\sigma^2 S^2 \frac{d^2V}{dS^2} + rS\frac{dV}{dS} - rV = 0.$$

This is the ordinary differential equation you get when the option value is a function of S only. The general solution of this second-order ordinary differential equation is

$$V(S) = AS + BS^{-2r/\sigma^2},$$

where A and B are arbitrary constants.

The first part of this solution (that with coefficient A) is simply the asset: the asset itself satisfies the Black–Scholes equation. If we can find A and B we have found the solution for the perpetual American put.

Clearly, for the perpetual American put the coefficient A must be zero; as $S \to \infty$ the value of the option must tend to zero. What about B?

Let us postulate that while the asset value is 'high' we won't exercise the option. But if it falls too low we immediately exercise the option, receiving $E - S$. (Common sense tells us we don't exercise when $S > E$.) Suppose that we decide that $S = S^*$ is the value at which we exercise, i.e. as soon as S reaches this value from above we exercise. How do we choose S^*?

When $S = S^*$ the option value must be the same as the exercise payoff:

$$V(S^*) = E - S^*.$$

It cannot be less as that would result in an arbitrage opportunity, and it cannot be more or we wouldn't exercise. Continuity of the option value with the payoff gives us one equation:

$$V(S^*) = B(S^*)^{-2r/\sigma^2} = E - S^*.$$

But since both B and S^* are unknown, we need one more equation. Let's look at the value of the option as a function of S^*, eliminating B using the above. We find that for $S > S^*$

$$V(S) = (E - S^*)\left(\frac{S}{S^*}\right)^{-2r/\sigma^2}. \tag{9.2}$$

We are going to choose S^* to *maximize the option's value at any time before exercise*. In other words, what choice of S^* makes V given by (9.2) as large as possible? The reason for this is obvious: if we can exercise whenever we like then we do so in such a way to maximize our worth. We find this value by differentiating (9.2) with respect to S^* and setting the resulting expression equal to zero:

$$\frac{\partial}{\partial S^*}(E-S^*)\left(\frac{S}{S^*}\right)^{-2r/\sigma^2} = \frac{1}{S^*}\left(\frac{S}{S^*}\right)^{-2r/\sigma^2}\left(-S^* + \frac{2r}{\sigma^2}(E-S^*)\right) = 0.$$

We find that

$$S^* = \frac{E}{1+\sigma^2/2r}.$$

This choice maximizes $V(S)$ for *all* $S \geq S^*$. The solution with this choice for S^* and with the corresponding B given by

$$\frac{\sigma^2}{2r}\left(\frac{E}{1+\sigma^2/2r}\right)^{1+2r/\sigma^2}$$

is shown in Figure 9.1.

The observant reader will notice something special about this function: the slope of the option value and the slope of the payoff function are the same at $S = S^*$. To see that this follows from the choice of S^* let us examine the difference between the option value and the payoff function:

$$(E-S^*)\left(\frac{S}{S^*}\right)^{-2r/\sigma^2} - (E-S).$$

Differentiate this with respect to S and you will find that the expression is zero at $S = S^*$.

This demonstrates, in a completely non-rigorous way, that if we want to maximize our option's value by a careful choice of exercise strategy, then this is equivalent to solving the Black–Scholes equation with continuity of option *value* and option *delta*, the slope. This is

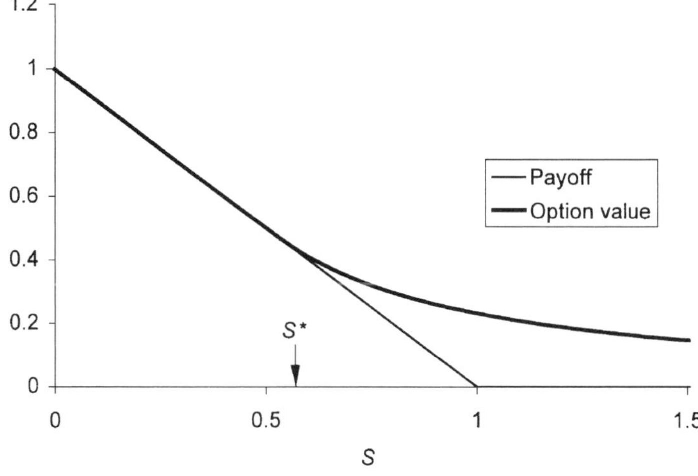

Figure 9.1 The solution for the perpetual American put.

called the **high-contact** or **smooth-pasting condition**.

> The American option value is maximized by an exercise strategy that makes the option value and option delta continuous

We exercise the option as soon as the asset price reaches the level at which the option price and the payoff meet. This position, S^*, is called the **optimal exercise point**.

Another way of looking at the condition of continuity of delta is to consider what happens if the delta is not continuous at the exercise point. The two possibilities are shown in Figure 9.2. In this figure the curve (a) corresponds to exercise that is not optimal because it is premature, the option value is lower than it could be. In case (b) there is clearly an arbitrage opportunity. If we take case (a) but progressively delay exercise by lowering the exercise point, we will maximize the option value everywhere when the delta is continuous.

When there is a continuously paid and constant dividend yield on the asset, or the asset is a foreign currency, the relevant ordinary differential equation for the perpetual option is

$$\tfrac{1}{2}\sigma^2 S^2 \frac{d^2V}{dS^2} + (r-D)S\frac{dV}{dS} - rV = 0.$$

The general solution is now

$$AS^{\alpha^+} + BS^{\alpha^-},$$

where

$$\alpha^{\pm} = \tfrac{1}{2}\left(-\frac{2r}{\sigma^2}\left(r - D - \tfrac{1}{2}\sigma^2\right) \pm \sqrt{\frac{4r^2}{\sigma^4}\left(r - D - \tfrac{1}{2}\sigma^2\right)^2 + \frac{8r}{\sigma^2}}\right),$$

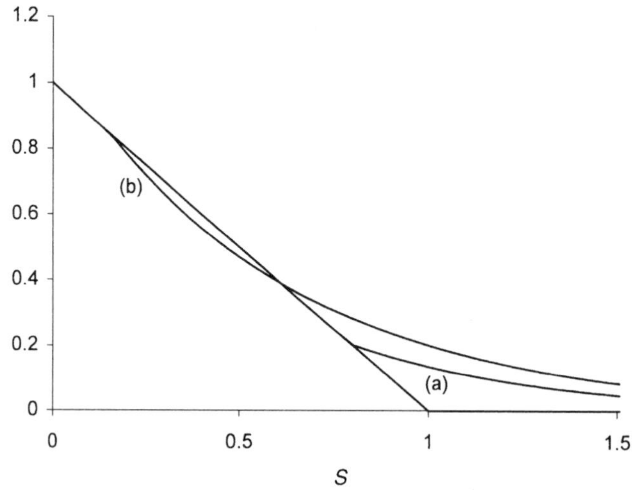

Figure 9.2 Option price when exercise is (a) too soon or (b) too late.

with $\alpha^- < 0 < \alpha^+$. The perpetual American put now has value

$$BS^{\alpha^-},$$

where

$$B = -\frac{1}{\alpha^-}\left(\frac{E}{1 - 1/\alpha^-}\right)^{1+\alpha^-}.$$

It is optimal to exercise when S reaches the value

$$\frac{E}{1 - 1/\alpha^-}.$$

Before considering the formulation of the general American option problem, we consider one more special case.

9.3 PERPETUAL AMERICAN CALL WITH DIVIDENDS

The solution for the American perpetual call is

$$AS^{\alpha^+},$$

where

$$A = \frac{1}{\alpha^+}\left(\frac{E}{1 - 1/\alpha^+}\right)^{1+\alpha^+}$$

and it is optimal to exercise as soon as S reaches

$$S^* = \frac{E}{1 - 1/\alpha^+}$$

from below.

An interesting special case is when $D = 0$. Then the solution is $V = S$ and S^* becomes infinite. Thus it is never optimal to exercise the American perpetual call when there are no dividends on the underlying; its value is the same as the underlying. As we see in a moment, this result also holds for the ordinary non-perpetual American call in the absence of dividends.

9.4 MATHEMATICAL FORMULATION FOR GENERAL PAYOFF

Now I build up the theory for American-style contracts with arbitrary payoff and expiry, following the standard Black–Scholes argument with minor modifications. The contract will no longer be perpetual and the option value will now be a function of both S and t.

Construct a portfolio of one American option with value $V(S, t)$ and short a number Δ of the underlying:

$$\Pi = V - \Delta S.$$

The change in value of this portfolio in excess of the risk-free rate is given by

$$d\Pi - r\Pi\,dt = \left(\frac{\partial V}{\partial t} + \tfrac{1}{2}\sigma^2 S^2 \frac{\partial^2 V}{\partial S^2} - r(V - \Delta S)\right) dt + \left(\frac{\partial V}{\partial S} - \Delta\right) dS.$$

With the choice

$$\Delta = \frac{\partial V}{\partial S}$$

this becomes

$$\left(\frac{\partial V}{\partial t} + \tfrac{1}{2}\sigma^2 S^2 \frac{\partial^2 V}{\partial S^2} + rS\frac{\partial V}{\partial S} - rV\right) dt.$$

In the Black–Scholes argument for European options we set this expression equal to zero, since this precludes arbitrage. But it precludes arbitrage whether we are buying or selling the contract. When the contract is American the long/short relationship is asymmetrical; it is the holder of the exercise rights who controls the early-exercise feature. The writer of the option can do no more than sit back and enjoy the view. If V is the value of a long position in an American option then all we can say is that we can earn *no more* than the risk-free rate on our portfolio. Thus we arrive at the *inequality*

$$\frac{\partial V}{\partial t} + \tfrac{1}{2}\sigma^2 S^2 \frac{\partial^2 V}{\partial S^2} + rS\frac{\partial V}{\partial S} - rV \le 0. \qquad (9.3)$$

The writer of the American option *can* make more than the risk-free rate if the holder does not exercise *optimally*. He also makes more profit if the holder of the option has a poor estimate of the volatility of the underlying and exercises in accordance with that estimate.

Equation (9.3) can easily be modified to accommodate dividends on the underlying.

If the payoff for early exercise is $P(S, t)$, possibly time-dependent, then the no-arbitrage constraint

$$V(S, t) \ge P(S, t), \qquad (9.4)$$

must apply everywhere. At expiry we have the final condition

$$V(S, T) = P(S, T). \qquad (9.5)$$

> The option value is maximized if the owner of the option exercises such that
>
> $$\Delta = \frac{\partial V}{\partial S} \text{ is continuous} \qquad (9.6)$$

The American option valuation problem consists of (9.3), (9.4), (9.5) and (9.6).

If we substitute the Black–Scholes European call solution, in the absence of dividends, into the inequality (9.3) then it is clearly satisfied; it actually satisfies the *equality*. If we substitute the expression into the constraint (9.4) with $P(S, t) = \max(S - E, 0)$ then this too is satisfied. The conclusion is that the value of an American call option is the same as the value of a

European call option when the underlying pays no dividends. Compare this with our above result that the perpetual call option should not be exercised—the American call option with a finite time to expiry should also not be exercised before expiry. To exercise before expiry would be 'sub-optimal.'

None of this is true if there are dividends on the underlying. Again, to see this simply substitute the expressions from Chapter 8 into the constraint. Since the call option has a value which approaches $Se^{-D(T-t)}$ as $S \to \infty$ there is clearly a point at which the European value fails to satisfy the constraint (9.4). *If the constraint is not satisfied somewhere then the problem has not been solved anywhere.* This is very important; our 'solution' must satisfy the inequalities everywhere or the 'solution' is invalid. This is due to the diffusive nature of the differential equation; an error in the solution at any point is immediately propagated *everywhere*.

The problem for the American option is what is known as a **free boundary problem**. In the European option problem we know that we must solve for all values of S from zero to infinity. When the option is American we do not know *a priori* where the Black–Scholes equation is to be satisfied; this must be found as part of the solution. This means that we do not know the position of the early exercise boundary. Moreover, except in special and trivial cases, this position is time-dependent. For example, we should exercise the American put if the asset value falls below $S^*(t)$, but how do we find $S^*(t)$?

Not only is this problem much harder than the fixed boundary problem (for example, where we know that we solve for S between zero and infinity), but this also makes the problem nonlinear. That is, if we have two solutions of the problem we do not get another solution if we add them together. This is easily shown by considering the perpetual American straddle on a dividend-paying stock. If this is defined as a *single* contract that may at any time be exercised for an amount $\max(S-E,0)+\max(E-S,0)=|S-E|$ then its value is not the same as the sum of a perpetual American put and a perpetual American call. Its solution is again of the form

$$V(S) = AS^{\alpha^+} + BS^{\alpha^-},$$

and I suggest that the reader find the solution for himself. The reason that this contract is not the sum of two other American options is that there is only one exercise opportunity. The two-option contract has one exercise opportunity per contract. If the contracts were both European then the sum of the two separate solutions would give the correct answer; the European valuation problem is linear. This contract can also be used to demonstrate that there can easily be more than one optimal exercise boundary. With the perpetual American straddle, as defined here, one should exercise either if the asset gets too low or too high. The exact positions of the boundaries can be determined by making the option and its delta everywhere continuous. One can imagine that if a contract has a really strange payoff, that there could be any number of free boundaries. Since we don't know *a priori* how many free boundaries there are going to be (although common sense gives us a clue) it is useful to have a numerical method that can find these boundaries without having to be told how many to look for. I discuss these issues in Chapter 47.

In Figure 9.3 are shown the values of a European and an American put with strike 100, volatility 20%, interest rate 5% and with one year to expiry. The position of the free boundary, the optimal exercise point is marked. Remember that this point moves in time.

In Figure 9.4 are shown the values of a European and an American call with strike 100, volatility 20%, interest rate 5% and with one year to expiry. There is a constant dividend yield of 5% on the underlying. (If there were no dividend payment then the two curves would be identical.) The position of the free boundary, the optimal exercise point is marked.

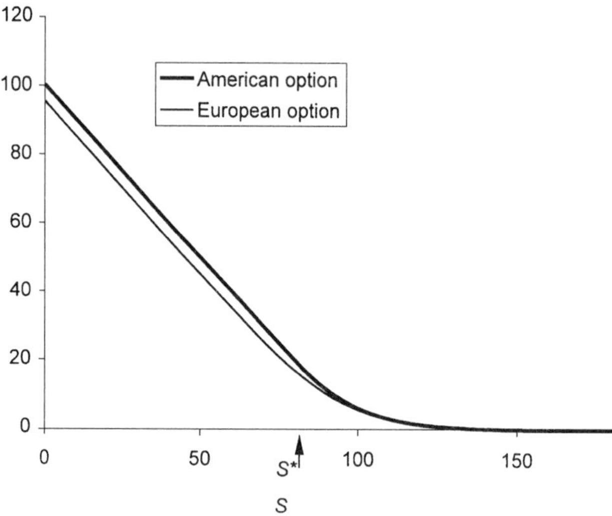

Figure 9.3 Values of a European and an American put. See text for parameter values. The optimal exercise point is marked.

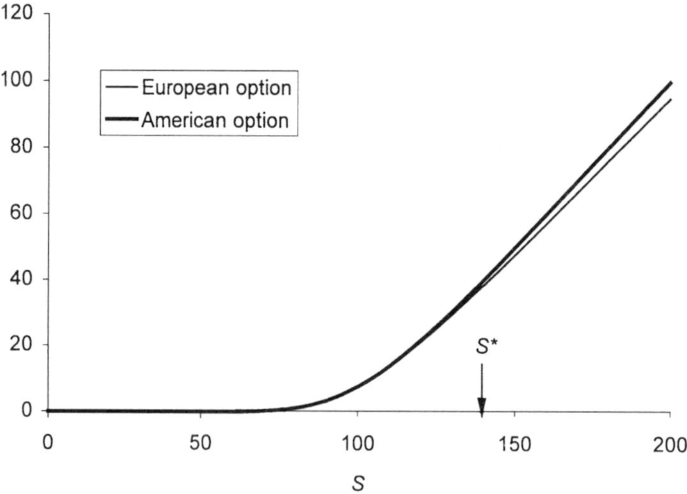

Figure 9.4 Values of a European and an American call. See text for parameter values. The optimal exercise point is marked.

9.5 LOCAL SOLUTION FOR CALL WITH CONSTANT DIVIDEND YIELD

If we cannot find full solutions to non-trivial problems, we can at least find local solutions, solutions that are good approximations for some values of the asset at some times. We have seen the solution for the American call with dividends when there is a long time to expiry; what about close to expiry? I will state the results without any proof. The proofs are simple but tedious, and the relevant literature is cited at the end of the chapter.

First let's consider the case $r > D$. This is usually true for options on equities, for which the dividend is small. Close to expiry the optimal exercise boundary is

$$S^*(t) \sim \frac{rE}{D}\left(1 + 0.9034\ldots\sigma\sqrt{\tfrac{1}{2}(T-t)} + \cdots\right).$$

The call should be exercised if the asset rises above this value. Note that as $T - t \to -\infty$ we have from the perpetual call analysis that the free boundary tends to

$$\frac{E}{1 - 1/\alpha^+}.$$

If the asset value rises above the free boundary it is better to exercise the option to receive the dividends than to continue holding it.

Near the point $t = T$, $S = Er/D$ the option price is approximately

$$V \sim S - E + E(T-t)^{3/2} f\left(\frac{\log(SD/Er)}{\sqrt{T-t}}\right),$$

where

$$f(x) = -\frac{2r}{\sigma^2}x + 0.075\ldots\left((x^2+4)e^{-\frac{1}{4}x^2} + 1/2(x^2+6x)\int_{-\infty}^{x} e^{-\frac{1}{4}s^2}\,ds\right).$$

When $D = 0$ there is no free boundary, it is never optimal to exercise early.

When $r < D$ the free boundary 'starts' from $S = E$ at time $t = T$. The local analysis is more subtle. (There is a nasty $\sqrt{(T-t)\log(T-t)}$ term.)

9.6 OTHER DIVIDEND STRUCTURES

Other dividend structures present no difficulties. The discretely-paid dividend does have an interesting effect on the option value, and on the jump condition across the dividend date.

In Chapter 8 I showed that if there is a discretely paid dividend then the asset falls by the amount of the dividend:

$$S(t_d^+) = S(t_d^-) - D.$$

If the dividend takes the asset value from $S(t_d^-)$ to $S(t_d^+)$ then we must apply the jump condition

$$V(S(t_d^-), t_d^-) = V(S(t_d^+), t_d^+),$$

across the dividend date T_d. Thus

$$V(S, t_d^-) = V(S - D, t_d^+).$$

This ensures that the realized option value is continuous. When the option is American it is possible that such a jump condition takes the option value below the payoff just before the dividend date. This is not allowed. If we find that this happens, we must impose the no-arbitrage constraint that the option value is at least the payoff function. Thus the jump condition becomes

$$V(S, t_d^-) = \max(V(S - D, t_d^+), P(S, t_d^-))$$

But this means that the realized option value may no longer be continuous. Is this correct? Yes, this does not matter because continuity is only lost *if one should have already optimally exercised before the dividend is paid.*

9.7 ONE-TOUCH OPTIONS

We saw the European binary option in Chapters 2 and 7. The payoff for that option is \$1 if the asset is above, for a binary call, a specified level at expiry. The **one-touch option** is an American version of this. This contract can be exercised at any time for a fixed amount, \$1 if the asset is above some specified level. There is no benefit in holding the option once the level has been reached, therefore it should be exercised immediately the level is reached for the first time, hence the name 'one touch.' These contracts fall into the class of 'once exotic now vanilla,' due to their popularity. They are particularly useful for hedging other contracts that also have a payoff that depends on whether or not the specified level is reached.

Since they are American-style options we must decide as part of the solution when to optimally exercise. As I have said, they would clearly be exercised as soon as the level is reached. This makes an otherwise complicated free boundary problem into a rather simple *fixed* boundary problem. For a one-touch call, we must solve the Black–Scholes equation with $V(S_u, t) = 1$, where S_u is the strike price of the contract, and $V(S, T) = 0$. We only need solve for S less than S_u. The solution of this problem is

$$V(S, t) = \left(\frac{S_u}{S}\right)^{2r/\sigma^2} N(d_5) + \frac{S}{S_u} N(d_1),$$

with the usual d_1, and

$$d_5 = \frac{\log(S/S_u) - \left(r + \frac{1}{2}\sigma^2\right)(T - t)}{\sigma\sqrt{T - t}}.$$

(The subscript '5' is to make the notation consistent with that in a later chapter.) The option value is shown in Figure 9.5 and the delta in Figure 9.6.

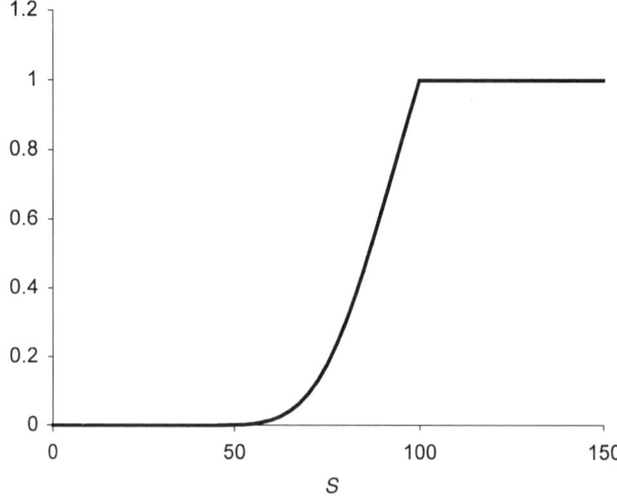

Figure 9.5 The value of a one-touch call option.

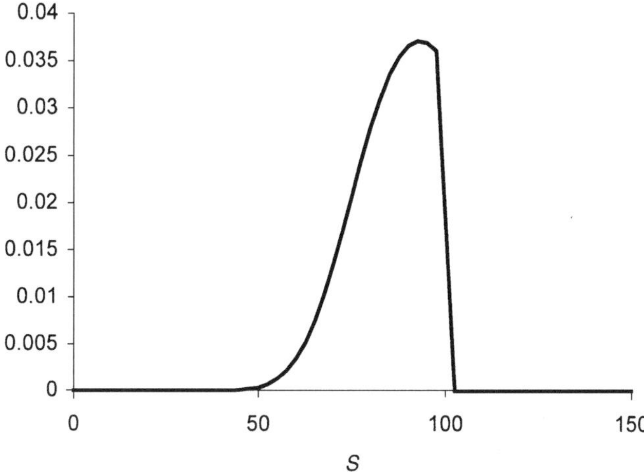

Figure 9.6 The delta of a one-touch call option.

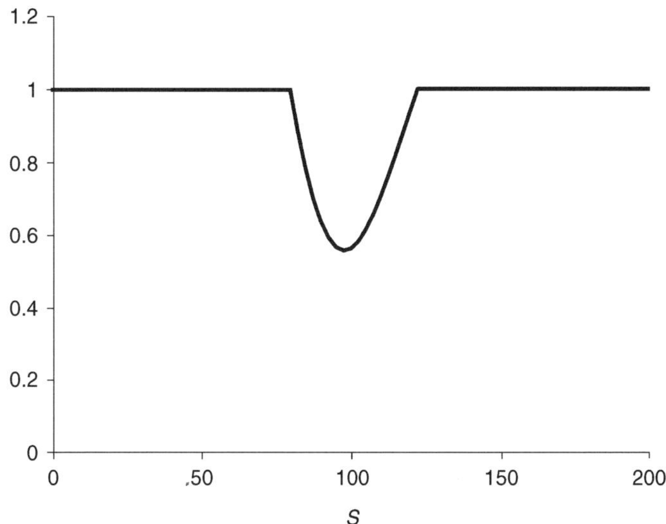

Figure 9.7 The value of a double one-touch option.

The problem for the one-touch put is obvious and the solution is

$$V(S,t) = \left(\frac{S_l}{S}\right)^{2r/\sigma^2} N(-d_5) + \frac{S}{S_l} N(-d_1),$$

with

$$d_5 = \frac{\log(S/S_l) - \left(r + \frac{1}{2}\sigma^2\right)(T-t)}{\sigma\sqrt{T-t}}.$$

The double one-touch option has both an upper and a lower level on which the payoff of \$1 is received. Thus $V(S_l, t) = V(S_u, t) = 1$. The solution, shown in Figure 9.7, can be found by Fourier series (see Chapter 6). Note that the value is not the sum of a one-touch call and a one-touch put.

9.8 OTHER FEATURES IN AMERICAN-STYLE CONTRACTS

The American option can be made even more interesting in many ways. Two possibilities are described in this section. These are the intermittent exercise opportunities of the Bermudan option, and the make-your-mind-up feature where the decision to exercise and the actual exercise occur at different times.

9.8.1 Bermudan Options

It is common for contracts that allow early exercise to permit the exercise only at certain specified times, and not at *all* times before expiry. For example, exercise may only be allowed on Thursdays between certain times. An option with such intermittent exercise opportunities is called a **Bermudan option**. All that this means mathematically is that the constraint (9.4) is only 'switched on' at these early exercise dates. The pricing of a such a contract numerically is, as we shall see, no harder than the pricing of American options when exercise is permitted at all times.

This situation can be made more complicated by the dependence of the exercise dates on a second asset. For example, early exercise is permitted only when a second asset is above a certain level. This makes the contract a multi-asset contract (see Chapter 11).

9.8.2 Make Your Mind Up

In some contracts the decision to exercise must be made before exercise takes place. For example, we must give two weeks' warning before we exercise, and we cannot change our mind. This contract is not hard to value theoretically. Suppose that we must give a warning of time τ. If at time t we decide to exercise at time $t+\tau$ then on exercise we receive a certain deterministic amount. To make the analysis easier to explain, assume that there is no time dependence in this payoff, so that on exercise we receive $P(S)$. The value of this payoff at a time τ earlier is $V_\tau(S, \tau)$ where $V_\tau(S, t)$ is the solution of

$$\frac{\partial V_\tau}{\partial t} + \tfrac{1}{2}\sigma^2 S^2 \frac{\partial^2 V_\tau}{\partial S^2} + rS\frac{\partial V_\tau}{\partial S} - rV_\tau = 0$$

with

$$V_\tau(S, 0) = P(S).$$

Because $V_\tau(S, 0)$ is the value of the contract at decision time if we have decided to exercise then our early-exercise constraint becomes

$$V(S, t) \geq V_\tau(S, \tau).$$

As an example, suppose that we get a payoff of $S - E$, this is $P(S)$. Note that there is no $\max(\cdot)$ function in this; we have said we will exercise and exercise we must, even if the asset is out of the money. The function $V_\tau(S, \tau)$ is clearly $S - Ee^{-r\tau}$ so that our **make-your-mind-up option** satisfies the constraint

$$V(S, t) \geq S - Ee^{-r\tau}.$$

Thus it is like an ordinary American option with an adjusted strike price.

A further complication is to allow one change of mind. That is, we say we will exercise in two weeks' time, but when that date comes we change our mind, and do not exercise. But the next time we say we will exercise, we must. This is also not too difficult to price theoretically. The trick is to introduce two functions for the option value, $V_0(S, t)$ and $V_1(S, t)$. The former is the value before making the first decision to exercise; the latter is the value having made that decision but having changed your mind. The problem for V_1 is exactly the same as for the basic make-your-mind-up option. The function V_0 satisfies the Black–Scholes equation with the constraint

$$V_0(S, t) \geq \max(P(S), V_1(S, t)),$$

representing the potential to exercise ($V_0 = P(S)$) or to change your mind ($V_0 = V_1$). Obviously, we can introduce more levels if we are permitted to change our minds a specified number of times.

In Part Three we will see many problems where we must introduce more than one function to value a single contract.

9.9 OTHER ISSUES

The pricing of American options and all the issues that this raises are important for many reasons. Some of these we describe here, but we will come back to the ideas again and again.

9.9.1 Nonlinearity

The pricing of American options is a nonlinear problem because of the free boundary. There are other nonlinear problems in finance, some nonlinear because of the free boundary and some because the governing differential equation is itself nonlinear. Nonlinearity can be important for several reasons. Most obviously, nonlinear problems are harder to solve than linear problems, usually requiring numerical solution.

Nonlinear governing equations are found in Chapter 21 for models of pricing with transaction costs, Chapter 24 for uncertain parameter models, Chapter 27 for models of market crashes, and Chapter 28 for models of options used for speculative purposes.

9.9.2 Free Boundary Problems

Free boundary problems, in other contexts, will be found scattered throughout the book. Again, the solution must almost always be found numerically. As an example of a free boundary problem that is not quite an American option (but is similar), consider the **instalment option**. In this contract the owner must keep paying a premium, on prescribed dates, to keep the contract alive. If the premium is not paid then the contract lapses. Consider two cases: the first is when the premium is paid out continuously day by day, and the second, more realistic case, is when the premium is paid at discrete intervals. Part of the valuation is to decide whether or not it is worth paying the premium, or whether the contract should be allowed to lapse.

First, consider the case of continuous payment of a premium. If we pay out a constant rate $L\,dt$ in a timestep dt to keep the contract alive then we must solve

$$\frac{\partial V}{\partial t} + \tfrac{1}{2}\sigma^2 S^2 \frac{\partial^2 V}{\partial S^2} + rS\frac{\partial V}{\partial S} - rV + L \leq 0.$$

The term L represents the continual input of cash. But we would only pay the premium if it is, in some sense, 'worth it.' As long as the contract value is positive, we should maintain the payments. If the contract value ever goes negative, we should let the contract lapse. However, we can do better than this. If we impose the constraint

$$V(S,t) \geq 0,$$

with continuity of the delta, and let the contract lapse if ever $V = 0$ then we give our contract the *highest value possible*. This is very much like the American option problem, but now we must optimally cease to pay the premium (instead of optimally exercising).

Now let us consider the more realistic discrete payment case. Suppose that payments of L (not $L\,dt$) are made discretely at time t_i. The value of the contract must increase in value from before the premium is paid to just after it is paid. The reason for this is clear. Once we have paid the premium on date t_i we do not have to worry about handing over any more money until time t_{i+1}. The rise in value exactly balances the premium, L:

$$V(S,t_i^-) = V(S,t_i^+) - L,$$

where the superscripts $+$ and $-$ refer to times just after and just before the premium is paid. But we would only hand over L if the contract would be worth more than L at time t_i^+. Thus we arrive at the jump condition

$$V(S,t_i^-) = \max(V(S,t_i^+) - L, 0).$$

If $V(S,t_i^+) \leq L$ then it is optimal to discontinue payment of the premia.

In practice, the premium L is chosen so that the value of the contract at initiation is exactly equal to L. This means that the start date is just like any other payment date.

9.9.3 Numerical Solution

Although free boundary problems must usually be solved numerically, this is not difficult as we shall see in later chapters. We solve the relevant equation by either a finite-difference method or the binomial method.

The other numerical method that I describe is the Monte Carlo simulation. If there is any early-exercise feature in a contract this makes solution by Monte Carlo very complicated indeed. I discuss this issue in Chapter 49.

9.10 SUMMARY

This chapter raised a lot of issues that will be important for much of the rest of the book. The reader should familiarize himself with these concepts. Most importantly, free boundary problems and optimal strategies occur in many guises. So, even if a contract is not explicitly called 'American,' these modeling issues could well be present.

FURTHER READING

- See Merton (1992) and Duffie (1992) for further discussion of the 'high contact' condition.
- Approximate solutions for American option problems, and exact solutions as infinite sums, can be found in Roll (1977), Whaley (1981), Johnson (1983) and Barone-Adesi & Whaley (1987).

- See Rupf, Dewynne, Howison & Wilmott (1993) for the local solution of the American call problem and Barles, Burdeau, Romano & Samsen (1995) for the put. Kruske & Keller (1998) also study the local solution of the put problem and go to a higher order of accuracy.
- The exercise strategy of the holder of an American option and its effect on the profit of both the holder and the writer are discussed in Ahn & Wilmott (1998).

EXERCISES

1. Find the value of the perpetual American straddle with dividends. The straddle has payoff

$$\Lambda(S) = |S - E|.$$

The solution is of the form

$$V(S) = AS^{\alpha^+} + BS^{\alpha^-}.$$

Compare the solution to the sum of the values of the perpetual American put and the perpetual American call.

2. Solve the one-touch call option. This is an American option with payoff

$$\Lambda(S) = \begin{cases} 1 & \text{if } S > E \\ 0 & \text{if } S < E. \end{cases}$$

Transform the problem to a diffusion equation problem, where the free boundary is always at $x = 0$, and use the method of images to find a solution.

Hint: Set

$$u(x, \tau) = \frac{1}{E} e^{\frac{1}{4}(k+1)^2\tau} F(x) + w(x, \tau),$$

and choose $F(x)$ so that $w(0, \tau) = 0$. Then extend the initial data to the whole of the x-axis and use the fundamental solution of the diffusion equation.

3. By creating a suitable portfolio and using your answer for the value of the one-touch call option, or otherwise, find the value of the one-touch put option.

4. How would we value a Bermudan option with the following properties?
   (a) The option has payoff $\Lambda(S) = \max(E - S, 0)$,
   (b) The option expires at time T,
   (c) At time $\frac{1}{2}T$, the option may be exercised early.

5. Prove the following inequality for an American call option:

$$C \geq S - Ee^{-r(T-t)}.$$

Show that it is never optimal to exercise the American call option before expiry when the asset pays no dividends.

6. Prove the following put–call parity relations for American options:

$$S - E \leq C - P \leq S - Ee^{-r(T-t)}.$$

CHAPTER 10
probability density functions and first exit times

In this Chapter...

- the transition probability density function
- how to derive the forward and backward equations for the transition probability density function
- how to use the transition probability density function to solve a variety of problems
- first exit times and their relevance to American options

10.1 INTRODUCTION

Modern financial theory, especially derivative theory, is based on the random movement of financial quantities. In the main, the building block is the Wiener process and Normal distributions. I have shown how to derive deterministic equations for the values of options in this random world, but I have said little about the way that the future may actually evolve, which direction is a stock expected to move, or what is the probability of the option expiring in the money. This may seem perverse, but the majority of derivative theory uses ideas of hedging and no arbitrage so as to avoid dealing with the issue of randomness; uncertainty is bad. Nevertheless, it is important to acknowledge the underlying randomness, to study it, to determine properties about possible future outcomes, if one is to have a thorough understanding of financial markets.

10.2 THE TRANSITION PROBABILITY DENSITY FUNCTION

The results of this chapter will be useful for equities, currencies, interest rates or anything that evolves according to a stochastic differential equation. For that reason, I will describe the theories in terms of the general stochastic differential equation

$$dy = A(y,t)\,dt + B(y,t)\,dX \tag{10.1}$$

for the variable y. In our lognormal equity world we would have $A = \mu y$ and $B = \sigma y$, and then we would write S in place of y.

To analyze the probabilistic properties of the random walk, I will introduce the **transition probability density function** $p(y, t; y', t')$ defined by

$$\text{Prob } (a < y < b \text{ at time } t' | y \text{ at time } t) = \int_a^b p(y, t; y', t')\,dy'.$$

In words this is 'the probability that the random variable y lies between a and b at time t' in the future, given that it started out with value y at time t.'

Think of y and t as being current values with y' and t' being future values. The transition probability density function can be used to answer the question, 'What is the probability of the variable y being in a certain range at time t' given that it started out with value y at time t?'

The transition probability density function $p(y, t; y', t')$ satisfies two equations, one involving derivatives with respect to the future state and time (y' and t') and called the forward equation, and the other involving derivatives with respect to the current state and time (y and t) and called the backward equation. These two equations are parabolic partial differential equations not dissimilar to the Black–Scholes equation.[1]

I derive these two equations in the next few sections, using a simple trinomial approximation to the random walk for y.

10.3 A TRINOMIAL MODEL FOR THE RANDOM WALK

By far the easiest and most straightforward way to derive the forward and backward equations is via a trinomial approximation to the continuous-time random walk. This approximation is shown in Figure 10.1.

The variable y can either rise, fall or take the same value after a timestep δt. These movements have certain probabilities associated with them. I am going to choose the size of the rise and the fall to be the same, with probabilities such that the mean and standard deviation of the discrete-time approximation are the same as the mean and standard deviation of the continuous-time model over the same timestep. I have three quantities to play with here, the jump size δy, the probability of a rise and the probability of a fall, but only two quantities to fix, the mean and standard deviation. The probability of not moving is such that the three probabilities sum to one. I will thus carry around the quantity δy which will drop out from the final equation.

I will use $\phi^+(y, t)$ and $\phi^-(y, t)$ to be the probabilities of a rise and fall respectively. The *mean* of the change in y after the timestep is thus

$$(\phi^+ - \phi^-)\delta y,$$

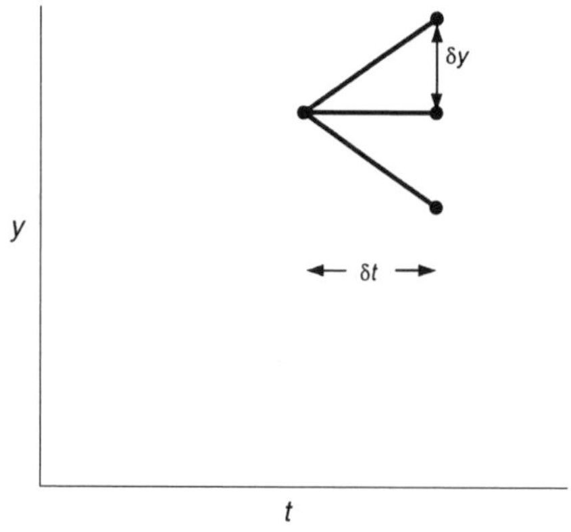

Figure 10.1 The trinomial approximation to the random walk for y.

[1] One of them, the backward equation, is *very* similar to the Black–Scholes equation.

and the variance is

$$(\phi^+(1-\phi^+ +\phi^-)^2 + (1-\phi^+ -\phi^-)(\phi^+ -\phi^-)^2 + \phi^-(1+\phi^+ -\phi^-)^2)\delta y^2.$$

In both of these the arguments of ϕ^+ and ϕ^- are y and t.

The mean of the change in the continuous-time version of the random walk is, from Equation (10.1),

$$A(y,t)\delta t$$

and the variance is

$$B(y,t)^2\delta t.$$

(These are correct only to leading order; the discrete versions are exact.)

To match the mean and standard deviation we choose

$$\phi^+(y,t) = \tfrac{1}{2}\frac{\delta t}{\delta y^2}(B(y,t)^2 + A(y,t)\delta y)$$

and

$$\phi^-(y,t) = \tfrac{1}{2}\frac{\delta t}{\delta y^2}(B(y,t)^2 - A(y,t)\delta y).$$

Although I said that we have two equations for three unknowns, we must have

$$\delta y = O(\sqrt{\delta t}),$$

otherwise the diffusive properties of the problem are lost.

Now we are set to find the equations for the transition probability density function.

10.4 THE FORWARD EQUATION

In Figure 10.2 is shown a trinomial representation of the random walk. The variable y takes the value y' at time t', but how did it get there?

In our trinomial walk we can only get to the point y' from the three values $y'+\delta y$, y' and $y'-\delta y$. The probability of being at y' at time t' is related to the

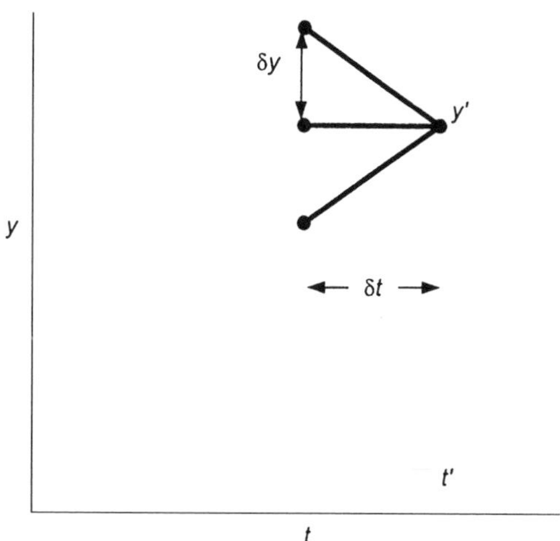

Figure 10.2 The trinomial approximation to the random walk used in finding the forward equation.

probabilities of being at the previous three values and *moving in the right direction*:

$$p(y,t;y',t') = \phi^-(y'+\delta y, t'-\delta t)p(y,t;y'+\delta y,t'-\delta t) + (1-\phi^-(y't'-\delta t)$$
$$-\phi^+(y',t'-\delta t))p(y,t;y',t'-\delta t)$$
$$+\phi^+(y'-\delta y,t'-\delta t)p(y,t;y'-\delta y,t'-\delta t).$$

We can easily expand each of the terms in Taylor series about the point y', t'. For example,

$$p(y,t;y'+\delta y,t'-\delta t) \approx p(y,t;y',t') + \delta y\frac{\partial p}{\partial y'} + \tfrac{1}{2}\delta y^2\frac{\partial^2 p}{\partial y'^2} - \delta t\frac{\partial p}{\partial t'} + \cdots.$$

I will omit the rest of the details, but the result is

$$\frac{\partial p}{\partial t'} = \tfrac{1}{2}\frac{\partial^2}{\partial y'^2}(B(y',t')^2 p) - \frac{\partial}{\partial y'}(A(y',t')p). \tag{10.2}$$

This is the **Fokker-Planck** or **forward Kolmogorov equation**. It is a forward parabolic partial differential equation, requiring initial conditions at time t and to be solved for $t' > t$.

This equation is to be used if there is some special state now and you want to know what could happen later. For example, you know the current value of y and want to know the distribution of values at some later date.

Example

The most important example to us is that of the distribution of equity prices in the future. If we have the random walk

$$dS = \mu S\,dt + \sigma S\,dX$$

then the forward equation becomes

$$\frac{\partial p}{\partial t'} = \tfrac{1}{2}\frac{\partial^2}{\partial S'^2}(\sigma^2 S'^2 p) - \frac{\partial}{\partial S'}(\mu S' p).$$

A special solution of this is the one having a delta function initial condition

$$p(S,t;S',t) = \delta(S'-S),$$

representing a variable that begins with certainty with value S at time t. The solution of this problem is

$$p(S,t;S',t') = \frac{1}{\sigma S'\sqrt{2\pi(t'-t)}}e^{-\left(\log(S/S')+(\mu-1/2\sigma^2)(t'-t)\right)^2/2\sigma^2(t'-t)}. \tag{10.3}$$

This is plotted as a function of S' in Figure 10.3 and as a function of both S' and t' in Figure 10.4.

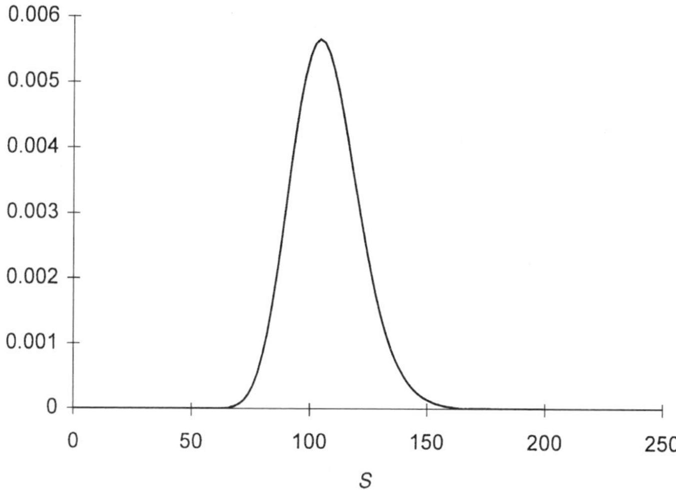

Figure 10.3 The probability density function for the lognormal random walk.

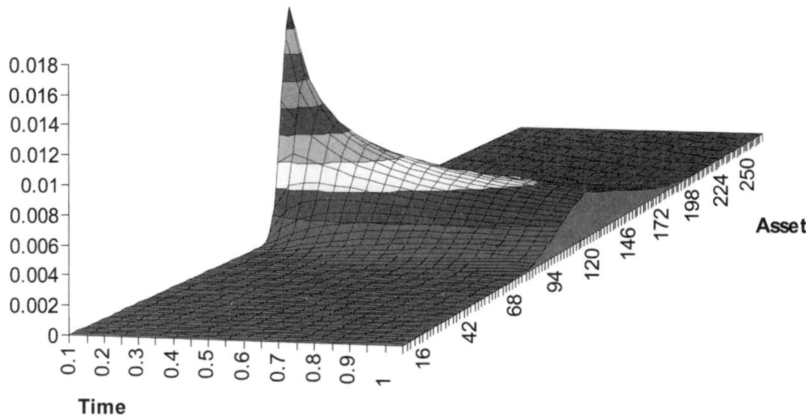

Figure 10.4 The probability density function for the lognormal random walk evolving through time.

10.5 THE STEADY-STATE DISTRIBUTION

Some random walks have a steady-state distribution. That is, in the long run as $t' \to \infty$ the distribution $p(y, t; y', t')$ as a function of y' settles down to be independent of the starting state y and time t. Loosely speaking, this requires at least that the random walk is time homogeneous, i.e. that A and B are independent of t, asymptotically. Some random walks have no such steady state even though they have a time-independent equation; the lognormal random walk either grows without bound or decays to zero.

If there is a steady-state distribution $p_\infty(y')$ then it satisfies

$$\frac{1}{2}\frac{d^2}{dy'^2}(B_\infty^2 p_\infty) - \frac{d}{dy'}(A_\infty p_\infty) = 0.$$

In this equation A_∞ and B_∞ are the functions in the limit $t \to \infty$. We'll see this equation used several times in later chapters, sometimes to calculate $p_\infty(y')$ knowing A and B and sometimes to calculate A knowing $p_\infty(y')$ and B.

10.6 THE BACKWARD EQUATION

Now we come to find the backward equation. This will be useful if we want to calculate probabilities of reaching a specified final state from various initial states. It will be a backward parabolic partial differential equation requiring conditions imposed in the future, and solved backwards in time. The equation I am about to derive is very similar to the Black–Scholes equation for the fair value of an option, indeed, the value of an option can be interpreted as an expectation over possible future states (much more of this later). Here is the derivation.

The backward equation is easier to derive than the forward equation. The derivation uses the trinomial random walk directly as drawn in Figure 10.1. We can relate the probability of being at y at time t to the probability of being at the three states at time $t + \delta t$ by

$$p(y, t; y', t') = \phi^-(y, t)p(y + \delta y, t + \delta t; y', t') + (1 - \phi^-(y, t) - \phi^+(y, t))p(y, t + \delta t; y', t')$$
$$+ \phi^+(y, t)p(y - \delta y, t + \delta t; y', t').$$

The Taylor series expansion leads to the **backward Kolmogorov equation**

$$\frac{\partial p}{\partial t} + \tfrac{1}{2}B(y, t)^2\frac{\partial^2 p}{\partial y^2} + A(y, t)\frac{\partial p}{\partial y} = 0. \qquad (10.4)$$

Example

The transition probability density function (10.3) for the lognormal random walk satisfies this equation, but note the different independent variables.

10.7 FIRST EXIT TIMES

The **first exit time** is the time at which the random variable reaches a given boundary. Perhaps we want to know how long before a certain level is reached or perhaps we want to know how long before an American option should be optimally exercised. An example of a first exit time is given in Figure 10.5.

Questions to ask about first exit times are 'What is the probability of an asset level being reached before a certain time?', 'How long do we expect it to take for an interest rate to fall to a given level?' I will address these problems now.

10.8 CUMULATIVE DISTRIBUTION FUNCTIONS FOR FIRST EXIT TIMES

What is the probability of your favourite asset doubling or halving in value in the next year? This is a question that can be answered by the solution of a simple diffusion equation. It is an example of the more general question, 'What is the probability of a random variable leaving a given range before a given time?' This question is illustrated in Figure 10.6.

Figure 10.5 An example of a first exit time.

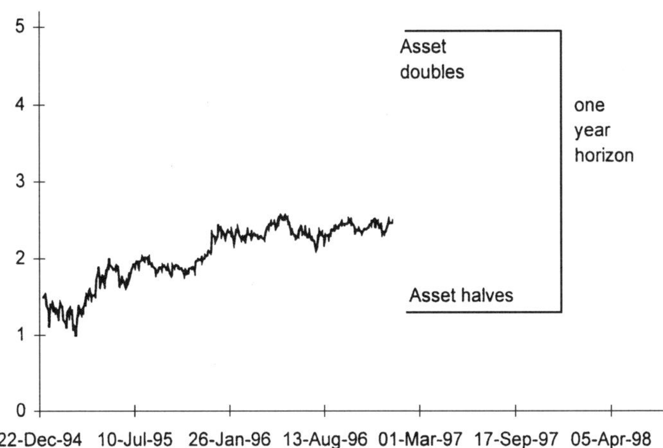

Figure 10.6 What is the probability of the asset leaving the region before the given time?.

Let me introduce the function $C(y, t; t')$ as the probability of the variable y leaving the region Ω before time t'. This function can be thought of as a cumulative distribution function. This function also satisfies the backward equation

$$\frac{\partial C}{\partial t} + \tfrac{1}{2}B(y, t)^2 \frac{\partial^2 C}{\partial y^2} + A(y, t)\frac{\partial C}{\partial y} = 0.$$

What makes the problem different from that for the transition probability density function are the boundary and final conditions. If the variable y is actually *on* the boundary of the region Ω then clearly the probability of exiting is one. On the other hand if we are inside the region Ω at time t' then there is no time left for the variable to leave the region and so the probability is zero. Thus we have

$$C(y, t', t') = 0$$

and

$$C(y, t, t') = 1 \quad \text{on the edge of } \Omega.$$

10.9 EXPECTED FIRST EXIT TIMES

In the previous section I showed how to calculate the probability of leaving a given region. We can use this function to find the *expected* time to exit. Once we have found C then it is simple to find the **expected first exit time**. Let me call the expected first exit time $u(y, t)$. It is a function of where we start out, y and t.

Because C is a cumulative distribution function the expected first exit time can be written as

$$u(y, t) = \int_t^\infty (t' - t)\frac{\partial C}{\partial t'}\, dt'.$$

After an integration by parts we get

$$u(y, t) = \int_t^\infty 1 - C(y, t; t')\, dt'.$$

The function C satisfies the backward equation in y and t so that, after differentiating under the integral sign, we find that u satisfies the equation

$$\frac{\partial u}{\partial t} + \tfrac{1}{2}B(y, t)^2\frac{\partial^2 u}{\partial y^2} + A(y, t)\frac{\partial u}{\partial y} = -1. \tag{10.5}$$

Since C is one on the boundary of Ω, u must be zero around the boundary of the region. What about the final condition? Typically one solves over a region Ω that is bounded in time, for example as shown in Figure 10.7.

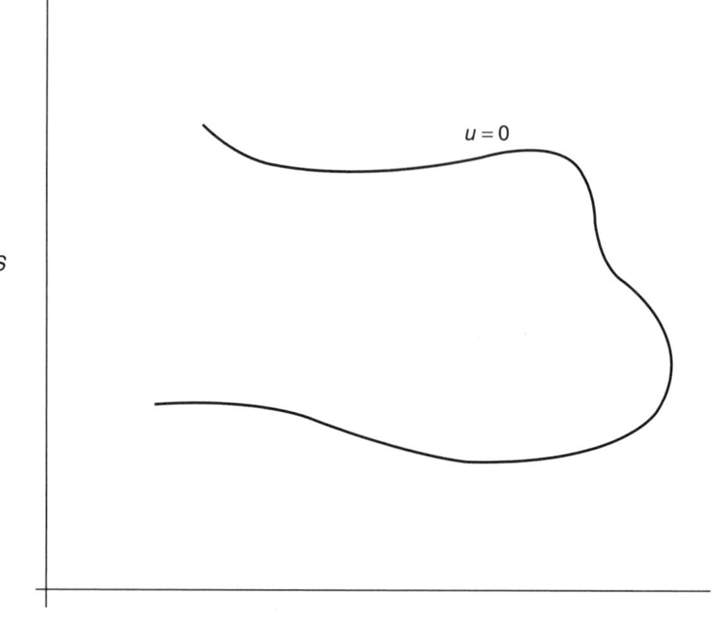

Figure 10.7 The first exit time problem.

Example

When the stochastic differential equation is independent of time, that is, both A and B are functions of y only, and the region Ω is also time homogeneous, then there may be a steady-state solution of (10.5). Returning to the logarithmic asset problem, what is the expected time for the asset to leave the range (S_0, S_1)? The answer to this question is the solution of

$$\mu S \frac{du}{dS} + \tfrac{1}{2}\sigma^2 S^2 \frac{d^2u}{dS^2} = -1,$$

with

$$u(S_0) = u(S_1) = 0,$$

and is

$$u(S) = \frac{1}{\frac{1}{2}\sigma^2 - \mu}\left(\log(S/S_0) - \frac{1 - (S/S_0)^{1-2\mu/\sigma^2}}{1 - (S_1/S_0)^{1-\mu/(1/2)\sigma^2}}\log(S_1/S_0)\right).$$

10.10 EXPECTATIONS AND BLACK–SCHOLES

The transition probability density $p(S, t; S', t')$ for S following the random walk

$$dS = \mu S\, dt + \sigma S\, dX$$

satisfies

$$\frac{\partial p}{\partial t} + \tfrac{1}{2}\sigma^2 S^2 \frac{\partial^2 p}{\partial S^2} + \mu S \frac{\partial p}{\partial S} = 0. \tag{10.6}$$

This is the backward Kolmogorov equation.

To calculate the expected value of some function $F(S)$ at time T we must solve (10.6) for the function $p_F(S, t)$ with

$$p_F(S, T) = F(S).$$

If the function $F(S)$ represents an amount of money received at time T then it is natural to ask what is the present value of the expected amount received. In other words, what is the expected amount of an option's payoff? To calculate this present value we simply multiply by the discount factor. This gives

$$e^{-r(T-t)} p_F(S, t), \tag{10.7}$$

when interest rates are constant. In this we have calculated the present value today of the expected payoff received at time T, given that today, time t, the asset value is S. Call the function (10.7) $V(S, t)$; what equation does it satisfy? Substituting

$$p_F(S, t) = e^{r(T-t)} V(S, t)$$

into (10.6) we find that $V(S, t)$ satisfies

$$\frac{\partial V}{\partial t} + \tfrac{1}{2}\sigma^2 S^2 \frac{\partial^2 V}{\partial S^2} + \mu S \frac{\partial V}{\partial S} - rV = 0.$$

This looks very like the Black–Scholes equation, with one small difference. In the Black–Scholes equation there is no μ.

Now forget that there is such a quantity as μ and replace it in this equation with r. The resulting equation is *exactly* the Black–Scholes equation. There must be something special about the random walk in which μ is replaced by r:

$$dS = rS\,dt + \sigma S\,dX. \tag{10.8}$$

This is called the **risk-neutral random walk**. It has the same drift as money in the bank.

Our conclusion is that

> The fair value of an option is the present value of the expected payoff at expiry under a risk-neutral random walk for the underlying

We can write

$$\text{option value} = e^{-r(T-t)}E\ [\text{payoff}\,(S)]$$

provided that the expectation is with respect to the risk-neutral random walk, not the *real* one.

In this expression we see the short-term interest rate playing two distinct roles. First, it is used for discounting the payoff to the present. This is the term $e^{-r(T-t)}$ outside the expectation. Second, the return on the asset in the risk-neutral world is expected to be $rS\,dt$ in a timestep dt.

10.11 SUMMARY

Although probability theory underpins most finance theory, it is possible to go a long way without even knowing what a transition probability density function is. But it is important in many circumstances to remember the foundation of uncertainty and to examine the future in a probabilistic sense. A couple of obvious examples spring to mind. First, if you own an American option when do you expect to exercise it? The value depends theoretically on the parameter σ in the asset price random walk but the expected time to exercise also depends on μ; the payoff may be certain because of hedging but you cannot be certain whether you will still hold the option at expiry. The second example concerns speculation with options. What if you *don't* hedge? In that case your final payoff is at the mercy of the markets, it is uncertain and can only be described probabilistically. Both of these problems can be addressed via transition probability density functions. In Chapter 28 we explore the random behaviour of unhedged option positions.

FURTHER READING

- A very good book on probability theory that carefully explains the derivation, meaning and use of transition probability density functions is Cox & Miller (1965).
- The two key references that rigorously relate option values and results from probability theory are by Harrison & Kreps (1979) and Harrison & Pliska (1981).
- Atkinson & Wilmott (1993) discuss transition densities for moving averages of asset prices.

EXERCISES

1. Check that to match the mean and standard deviation of the trinomial model to the continuous-time random walk, we must choose

$$\phi^{+}(y,t)=\tfrac{1}{2}\frac{\delta t}{\delta y^{2}}(B(y,t)^{2}+A(y,t)\delta y),$$

and

$$\phi^{-}(y,t)=\tfrac{1}{2}\frac{\delta t}{\delta y^{2}}(B(y,t)^{2}-A(y,t)\delta y).$$

2. Expand the probability terms in Section 10.4 as Taylor series to find the Fokker-Planck equation:

$$\frac{\partial p}{\partial t'}=\tfrac{1}{2}\frac{\partial^{2}}{\partial y'^{2}}(B(y',t')^{2}p)-\frac{\partial}{\partial y'}(A(y',t')p).$$

3. Solve the example problem in Section 10.4: derive the probability density function for the future distribution of S by solving the Fokker-Planck equation in the form:

$$\frac{\partial p}{\partial t'}=\tfrac{1}{2}\frac{\partial^{2}}{\partial S'^{2}}(\sigma^{2}S'^{2}p)-\frac{\partial}{\partial S'}(\mu S'p),$$

with the initial condition

$$p(S,t;S',t)=\delta(S'-S),$$

to find

$$p(S,t;S',t')=\frac{1}{\sigma S'\sqrt{2\pi(t'-t)}}e^{-\left(\log(S/S')+(\mu-1/2\sigma^{2})(t'-t)\right)^{2}/2\sigma^{2}(t'-t)}.$$

4. Solve the example problem:

$$\mu S\frac{du}{dS}+\tfrac{1}{2}\sigma^{2}S^{2}\frac{d^{2}u}{dS^{2}}=-1,$$

with boundary conditions

$$u(S_{0})=u(S_{1})=0,$$

to find that

$$u(S)=\frac{1}{\frac{1}{2}\sigma^{2}-\mu}\left(\log(S/S_{0})-\frac{1-(S/S_{0})^{1-2\mu/\sigma^{2}}}{1-(S_{1}/S_{0})^{1-2\mu/\sigma^{2}}}\log(S_{1}/S_{0})\right).$$

5. What is the probability that $S(T)>E$ given $S(t)$, for $t<T$? i.e. the probability that a European call expires in the money. How could we use this to find the value of a European cash-or-nothing call?

6. In the text we saw the problem for the expected first exit time from a region. What equation does the *variance* of the first exit time satisfy?

CHAPTER 11

multi-asset options

In this Chapter...

- how to model the behavior of many assets simultaneously
- estimating correlation between asset price movements
- how to value and hedge options on many underlying assets in the Black–Scholes framework
- the pricing formula for European non-path-dependent options on dividend-paying assets
- how to price and hedge quantos and the role of correlation

11.1 INTRODUCTION

In this chapter I introduce the idea of higher dimensionality by describing the Black–Scholes theory for options on more than one underlying asset. This theory is perfectly straightforward; the only new idea is that of correlated random walks and the corresponding multifactor version of Itô's lemma.

Although the modeling and mathematics is easy, the final step of the pricing and hedging, the 'solution,' can be extremely hard indeed. I explain what makes a problem easy, and what makes it hard, from the numerical analysis point of view.

11.2 MULTI-DIMENSIONAL LOGNORMAL RANDOM WALKS

The basic building block for option pricing with one underlying is the lognormal random walk

$$dS = \mu S\,dt + \sigma S\,dX.$$

This is readily extended to a world containing many assets via models for each underlying

$$dS_i = \mu_i S_i\,dt + \sigma_i S_i\,dX.$$

Here S_i is the price of the ith asset, $i = 1, \ldots, d$, and μ_i and σ_i are the drift and volatility of that asset respectively and dX_i is the increment of a Wiener process. We can still continue to think of dX_i as a random number drawn from a Normal distribution with mean zero and standard deviation $dt^{1/2}$ so that

$$E[dX_i] = 0 \quad \text{and} \quad E[dX_i^2] = dt$$

but the random numbers dX_i and dX_j are **correlated**:

$$E[dX_i\,dX_j] = \rho_{ij}\,dt.$$

here ρ_{ij} is the correlation coefficient between the ith and jth random walks. The symmetric matrix with ρ_{ij} as the entry in the ith row and jth column is called the **correlation matrix**. For example, if we have seven underlyings $d = 7$ and the correlation matrix will look like this:

$$\Sigma = \begin{pmatrix} 1 & \rho_{12} & \rho_{13} & \rho_{14} & \rho_{15} & \rho_{16} & \rho_{17} \\ \rho_{21} & 1 & \rho_{23} & \rho_{24} & \rho_{25} & \rho_{26} & \rho_{27} \\ \rho_{31} & \rho_{32} & 1 & \rho_{34} & \rho_{35} & \rho_{36} & \rho_{37} \\ \rho_{41} & \rho_{42} & \rho_{43} & 1 & \rho_{45} & \rho_{46} & \rho_{47} \\ \rho_{51} & \rho_{52} & \rho_{53} & \rho_{54} & 1 & \rho_{56} & \rho_{57} \\ \rho_{61} & \rho_{62} & \rho_{63} & \rho_{64} & \rho_{65} & 1 & \rho_{67} \\ \rho_{71} & \rho_{72} & \rho_{73} & \rho_{74} & \rho_{75} & \rho_{76} & 1 \end{pmatrix}$$

Note that $\rho_{ii} = 1$ and $\rho_{ij} = \rho_{ji}$. The correlation matrix is positive definite, so that $y^T \Sigma y \geq 0$. The **covariance matrix** is simply

$$\mathbf{M}\Sigma\mathbf{M},$$

where $\mathbf{M}$ is the matrix with the σ_i along the diagonal and zeros everywhere else.

To be able to manipulate functions of many random variables we need a multidimensional version of Itô's lemma. If we have a function of the variables $S_1, \ldots, S_d$ and t, $V(S_1, \ldots, S_d, t)$, then

$$dV = \left(\frac{\partial V}{\partial t} + \frac{1}{2} \sum_{i=1}^{d} \sum_{j=1}^{d} \sigma_i \sigma_j \rho_{ij} S_i S_j \frac{\partial^2 V}{\partial S_i \partial S_j} \right) dt + \sum_{i=1}^{d} \frac{\partial V}{\partial S_i} dS_i.$$

We can get to this same result by using Taylor series and the rules of thumb:

$$dX_i^2 = dt \quad \text{and} \quad dX_i \, dX_j = \rho_{ij} \, dt.$$

11.3 MEASURING CORRELATIONS

If you have time series data at intervals of δt for all d assets you can calculate the correlation between the returns as follows. First, take the price series for each asset and calculate the return over each period. The return on the ith asset at the kth data point in the time series is simply

$$R_i(t_k) = \frac{S_i(t_k + \delta t) - S_i(t_k)}{S_i(t_k)}.$$

The historical volatility of the ith asset is

$$\sigma_i = \sqrt{\frac{1}{\delta t(M-1)} \sum_{k=1}^{M} (R_i(t_k) - \overline{R}_i)^2}$$

where M is the number of data points in the return series and $\overline{R}_i$ is the mean of all the returns in the series.

The covariance between the returns on assets i and j is given by

$$\frac{1}{\delta t(M-1)} \sum_{k=1}^{M} (R_i(t_k) - \overline{R}_i)(R_j(t_k) - \overline{R}_j).$$

The correlation is then

$$\frac{1}{\delta t(M-1)\sigma_i\sigma_j}\sum_{k=1}^{M}(R_i(t_k)-\overline{R}_i)(R_j(t_k)-\overline{R}_j).$$

In Excel correlation between two time series can be found using the CORREL worksheet function, or Tools | Data Analysis | Correlation.

Correlations measured from financial time series data are notoriously unstable. If you split your data into two equal groups, up to one date and beyond that date, and calculate the correlations for each group you may find that they differ quite markedly. You could calculate a 60-day correlation, say, from several years' data and the result would look something like Figure 11.1. You might want to use a historical 60-day correlation if you have a contract of that maturity. But, as can be seen from the figure, such a historical correlation should be used with care; correlations are even more unstable than volatilities.

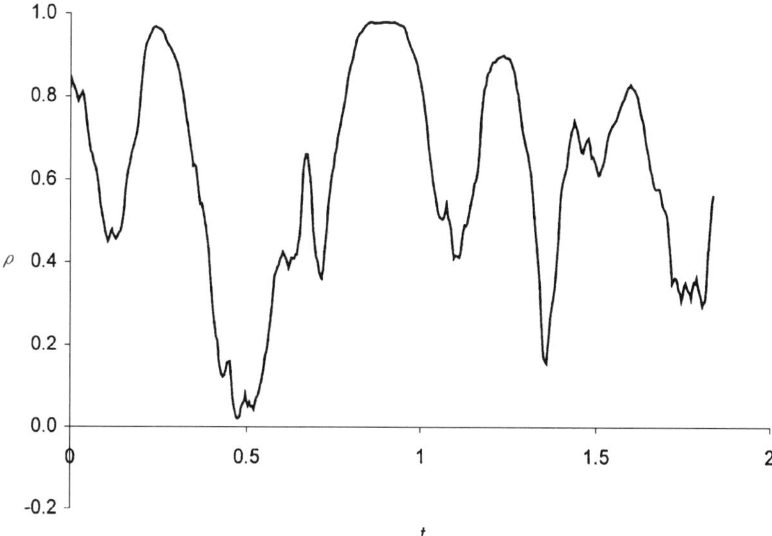

Figure 11.1 A correlation time series.

The other possibility is to back out an **implied correlation** from the quoted price of an instrument. The idea behind that approach is the same as with implied volatility, it gives an estimate of the market's perception of correlation.

11.4 OPTIONS ON MANY UNDERLYINGS

Options with many underlyings are called **basket options**, **options on baskets** or **rainbow options**. The theoretical side of pricing and hedging is straightforward, following the Black–Scholes arguments but now in higher dimensions.

Set up a portfolio consisting of one basket option and short a number Δ_i of each of the assets S_i:

$$\Pi = V(S_1,\ldots,S_d,t)-\sum_{i=1}^{d}\Delta_i S_i.$$

The change in this portfolio is given by

$$d\Pi = \left(\frac{\partial V}{\partial t} + \frac{1}{2}\sum_{i=1}^{d}\sum_{j=1}^{d}\sigma_i\sigma_j\rho_{ij}S_iS_j\frac{\partial^2 V}{\partial S_i \partial S_j}\right)dt + \sum_{i=1}^{d}\left(\frac{\partial V}{\partial S_i} - \Delta_i\right)dS_i.$$

If we choose

$$\Delta_i = \frac{\partial V}{\partial S_i}$$

for each i, then the portfolio is hedged, is risk-free. Setting the return equal to the risk-free rate we arrive at

$$\frac{\partial V}{\partial t} + \frac{1}{2}\sum_{i=1}^{d}\sum_{j=1}^{d}\sigma_i\sigma_j\rho_{ij}S_iS_j\frac{\partial^2 V}{\partial S_i \partial S_j} + r\sum_{i=1}^{d}S_i\frac{\partial V}{\partial S_i} - rV = 0. \tag{11.1}$$

This is the multidimensional version of the Black–Scholes equation. The modifications that need to be made for dividends are obvious. When there is a dividend yield of D_i on the ith asset we have

$$\frac{\partial V}{\partial t} + \frac{1}{2}\sum_{i=1}^{d}\sum_{j=1}^{d}\sigma_i\sigma_j\rho_{ij}S_iS_j\frac{\partial^2 V}{\partial S_i \partial S_j} + \sum_{i=1}^{d}(r - D_i)S_i\frac{\partial V}{\partial S_i} - rV = 0$$

11.5 THE PRICING FORMULA FOR EUROPEAN NON-PATH-DEPENDENT OPTIONS ON DIVIDEND-PAYING ASSETS

Because there is a Green's function for this problem (see Chapter 6) we can write down the value of a European non-path-dependent option with payoff of Payoff $(S_1, \ldots, S_d)$ at time T:

$$\begin{gathered} V = e^{-r(T-t)}(2\pi(T-t))^{-d/2}(\text{Det }\boldsymbol{\Sigma})^{-1/2}(\sigma_1\ldots\sigma_d)^{-1} \\ \int_0^\infty \cdots \int_0^\infty \frac{\text{Payoff}\,(S_1'\ldots S_d')}{S_1'\ldots S_d'}\exp\left(-\tfrac{1}{2}\boldsymbol{\alpha}^T\,\boldsymbol{\Sigma}^{-1}\boldsymbol{\alpha}\right)dS_1'\ldots dS_d'. \\ \alpha_i = \frac{1}{\sigma_i(T-t)^{1/2}}\left(\log\left(\frac{S_i}{S_i'}\right) + \left(r - D_i - \frac{\sigma_i^2}{2}\right)(T-t)\right) \end{gathered} \tag{11.2}$$

This has included a constant continuous dividend yield of D_i on each asset.

11.6 EXCHANGING ONE ASSET FOR ANOTHER: A SIMILARITY SOLUTION

An **exchange option** gives the holder the right to exchange one asset for another, in some ratio. The payoff for this contract at expiry is

$$\max(q_1S_1 - q_2S_2, 0),$$

where q_1 and q_2 are constants.

The partial differential equation satisfied by this option in a Black–Scholes world is

$$\frac{\partial V}{\partial t} + \tfrac{1}{2}\sum_{i=1}^{2}\sum_{j=1}^{2}\sigma_i\sigma_j\rho_{ij}S_iS_j\frac{\partial^2 V}{\partial S_i \partial S_j} + \sum_{i=1}^{2}(r - D_i)S_i\frac{\partial V}{\partial S_i} - rV = 0.$$

A dividend yield has been included for both assets. Since there are only two underlyings the summations in these only go up to two.

This contract is special in that there is a similarity reduction. Let's postulate that the solution takes the form

$$V(S_1, S_2, t) = q_1S_2H(\xi, t),$$

where the new variable is

$$\xi = \frac{S_1}{S_2}.$$

If this is the case, then instead of finding a function V of three variables, we only need find a function H of two variables, a much easier task.

Changing variables from S_1, S_2 to ξ we must use the following for the derivatives.

$$\frac{\partial}{\partial S_1} = \frac{1}{S_2}\frac{\partial}{\partial \xi}, \quad \frac{\partial}{\partial S_2} = -\frac{\xi}{S_2}\frac{\partial}{\partial \xi},$$

$$\frac{\partial^2}{\partial S_1^2} = \frac{1}{S_2^2}\frac{\partial^2}{\partial \xi^2}, \quad \frac{\partial^2}{\partial S_2^2} = \frac{\xi^2}{S_2^2}\frac{\partial^2}{\partial \xi^2} + \frac{2\xi}{S_2^2}\frac{\partial}{\partial \xi}, \quad \frac{\partial^2}{\partial S_1 \partial S_2} = -\frac{\xi}{S_2^2}\frac{\partial^2}{\partial \xi^2} - \frac{1}{S_2^2}\frac{\partial}{\partial \xi}.$$

The time derivative is unchanged. The partial differential equation now becomes

$$\frac{\partial H}{\partial t} + \tfrac{1}{2}\sigma'^2\xi^2\frac{\partial^2 H}{\partial \xi^2} + (D_2 - D_1)\xi\frac{\partial H}{\partial \xi} - D_2H = 0.$$

where

$$\sigma' = \sqrt{\sigma_1^2 - 2\rho_{12}\sigma_1\sigma_2 + \sigma_2^2}.$$

You will recognise this equation as being the Black–Scholes equation for a single stock with D_2 in place of r, D_1 in place of the dividend yield on the single stock and with a volatility of σ'.

From this it follows, retracing our steps and writing the result in the original variables, that

$$V(S_1, S_2, t) = q_1S_1e^{-D_1(T-t)}N(d_1') - q_2S_2e^{-D_2(T-t)}N(d_2')$$

where

$$d_1' = \frac{\log(q_1S_1/q_2S_2) + (D_2 - D_1 + \tfrac{1}{2}\sigma'^2)(T - t)}{\sigma'\sqrt{T - t}} \quad \text{and} \quad d_2' = d_1' - \sigma'\sqrt{T - t}.$$

11.7 QUANTOS

There is one special, and very important type of multi-asset option. This is the cross-currency contract called a **quanto**. The quanto has a payoff defined with respect to an asset or an index (or an interest rate) in one country, but then the payoff is converted to another currency for payment. An example of such a contract would be a call on the Nikkei Dow index but paid in US dollars. This contract is exposed to the dollar–yen exchange rate and the Nikkei Dow index. We could write down the differential equation directly assuming that the underlyings satisfy lognormal random walks with correlation ρ. But we will build up the problem from first principles to demonstrate what hedging must take place.

Define $S_\$$ to be the yen–dollar exchange rate (number of dollars per yen[1]) and S_N is the level of the Nikkei Dow index. We assume that they satisfy

$$dS_\$ = \mu_\$ S_\$\,dt + \sigma_\$ S_\$\,dX_\$ \quad \text{and} \quad dS_N = \mu_N S_N\,dt + \sigma_N S_N\,dX_N,$$

with a correlation coefficient ρ between them.

Construct a portfolio consisting of the quanto in question, hedged with yen and the Nikkei Dow index:

$$\Pi = V(S_\$, S_N, t) - \Delta_\$ S_\$ - \Delta_N S_N S_\$.$$

Note that every term in this equation is measured in dollars. $\Delta_\$$ is the number of yen we hold short, so $-\Delta_\$ S_\$$ is the dollar value of that yen. Similarly, with the term $-\Delta_N S_N S_\$$ we have converted the yen-denominated index S_N into dollars, Δ_N is the amount of the index held short.

The change in the value of the portfolio is due to the change in the value of its components and the interest received on the yen:

$$d\Pi = \left(\frac{\partial V}{\partial t} + \tfrac{1}{2}\sigma_\$^2 S_\$^2 \frac{\partial^2 V}{\partial S_\$^2} + \rho\sigma_\$\sigma_N S_\$ S_N \frac{\partial^2 V}{\partial S_\$ \partial S_N} + \tfrac{1}{2}\sigma_N^2 S_N^2 \frac{\partial^2 V}{\partial S_N^2} - \rho\sigma_\$\sigma_N \Delta_N S_\$ S_N - r_f \Delta_\$ S_\$\right) dt$$

$$+ \left(\frac{\partial V}{\partial S_\$} - \Delta_\$ - \Delta_N S_N\right) dS_\$ + \left(\frac{\partial V}{\partial S_N} - \Delta_N S_\$\right) dS_N.$$

There is a term in the above that we have not seen before, the $-\rho\sigma_\$\sigma_N S_\$ S_N$. This is due to the increment of the product $-\Delta_N S_N S_\$$. There is also the interest received by the yen holding; we *have* seen such a term before. We now choose

$$\Delta_\$ = \frac{\partial V}{\partial S_\$} - \frac{S_N}{S_\$}\frac{\partial V}{\partial S_N} \quad \text{and} \quad \Delta_N = \frac{1}{S_\$}\frac{\partial V}{\partial S_N}$$

to eliminate the risk in the portfolio. Setting the return on this riskless portfolio equal to the *US risk-free rate of interest* $r_\$$, since Π is measured entirely in dollars, yields

$$\frac{\partial V}{\partial t} + \tfrac{1}{2}\sigma_\$^2 S_\$^2 \frac{\partial^2 V}{\partial S_\$^2} + \rho\sigma_\$\sigma_N S_\$ S_N \frac{\partial^2 V}{\partial S_\$ \partial S_N} + \tfrac{1}{2}\sigma_N^2 S_N^2 \frac{\partial^2 V}{\partial S_N^2}$$

$$+ S_\$ \frac{\partial V}{\partial S_\$}(r_\$ - r_f) + S_N \frac{\partial V}{\partial S_N}(r_f - \rho\sigma_\$\sigma_N) - r_\$ V = 0.$$

This completes the formulation of the pricing equation. The equation is valid for any contract with underlying measured in one currency but paid in another. To fully specify our particular quanto we must give the final conditions on $t = T$:

$$V(S_\$, S_N, T) = \max(S_N - E, 0).$$

Note that as far as the payoff is concerned we don't much care what $S_\$$ is (only that we can hedge with it somehow). We do *not* multiply this by the exchange rate. Because of the simple

[1] This is the opposite of market convention. Currencies are usually quoted against the dollar with pound sterling being an exception. I use this way around for this problem just to simplify the algebra.

form of the payoff we can look for a solution that is independent of the exchange rate. Trying

$$V(S_\$, S_N, t) = W(S_N, t)$$

we find that

$$\frac{\partial W}{\partial t} + \tfrac{1}{2}\sigma_N^2 S_N^2 \frac{\partial^2 W}{\partial S_N^2} + S_N \frac{\partial W}{\partial S_N}(r_f - \rho\sigma_\$\sigma_N) - r_\$ V = 0.$$

This is the simple one-factor Black–Scholes equation. If we compare this equation with the Black–Scholes equation with a constant dividend yield we see that pricing the quanto is equivalent to using a dividend yield of

$$r_\$ - r_f + \rho\sigma_\$\sigma_N.$$

The only noticeable effect of the cross-currency feature on the option value is an adjustment to a dividend yield. This yield depends on the volatility of the exchange rate and the correlation between the underlying and the exchange rate. This is a common result for the simpler quantos.

11.8 TWO EXAMPLES

In Figure 11.2 is shown the term sheet for 'La Tricolore' Capital-guaranteed Note. This contract pays off the *second* best performing of three currencies against the French Franc, but only if

'La Tricolore' Capital-guaranteed Note

Issuer	XXXX
Principal Amount	FRF 100,000,000
Issue Price	98.75%
Maturity Date	Twelve months after Issue Date
Coupon	Zero
Redemption Amount	If at least two of the following three appreciation indices, namely: $\frac{\text{USD/FRF - 6.0750}}{\text{6.0750}}, \frac{\text{GBP/FRF - 10.2000}}{\text{10.2000}}, \frac{\text{DEM/FRF - 3.3775}}{\text{3.3775}}$ are positive at Maturity, the Note will redeem in that currency whose appreciation index is the second highest of the three; in all other circumstances the Note will redeem at Par in FRF. If the Note redeems in a currency other than FRF, the amount of that currency shall be calculated by dividing the FRF Principal Amount by the spot Currency/FRF exchange rate prevailing on the Issue Date.

This indicative termsheet is neither an offer to buy or sell securities or an OTC derivative product which includes options, swaps, forwards and structured notes having similar features to OTC derivative transactions, nor a solicitation to buy or sell securities or an OTC derivative product. The proposal contained in the foregoing is not a complete description of the terms of a particular transaction and is subject to change without limitation.

Figure 11.2 Term sheet for 'La Tricolore' Capital-guaranteed Note.

the second-best performing has appreciated against the Franc, otherwise it pays off at par. This contract does not have any unusual features, and has a value that can be written as a three-dimensional integral, of the form (11.2). But what would the payoff function be? You wouldn't use a partial differential equation to price this contract. Instead you would estimate the multiple integral directly by the methods of Chapter 49.

The next example, whose term sheet is shown in Figure 11.3, is of basket equity swap. This rather complex, high-dimensional contract, is for a swap of interest payment based on three-month LIBOR and the level of an index. The index is made up of the weighted average of 20 pharmaceutical stocks. To make matters even more complex, the index uses a time averaging of the stock prices.

International Pharmaceutical Basket Equity Swap

Indicative terms	
Trade Date	[ ]
Initial Valuation Date	[ ]
Effective Date	[ ]
Final Valuation Date	26th September 2002
Averaging Dates	The monthly anniversaries of the Initial Valuation Date commencing 26th March 2002 and up to and including the Expiration Date
Notional Amount	US$25,000,000
Counterparty floating amounts (US$ LIBOR)	
Floating Rate Payer	[ ]
Floating Rate Index	USD-LIBOR
Designated Maturity	Three months
Spread	Minus 0.25%
Day Count Fraction	Actual/360
Floating Rate Payment Dates	Each quarterly anniversary of the Effective Date
Initial Floating Rate Index	[ ]
The Bank Fixed and Floating Amounts (Fee, Equity Option)	
Fixed Amount Payer	XXXX
Fixed Amount	1.30% of Notional Amount
Fixed Amount Payment Date	Effective Date
Basket	A basket comprising 20 stocks and constructed as described in attached Appendix
Initial Basket Level	Will be set at 100 on the Initial Valuation Date
Floating Equity Amount Payer	XXXX
Floating Equity Amount	Will be calculated according to the performance of the basket of stocks in the following way:

Figure 11.3 Term sheet for a basket equity swap.

	Notional Amount* max $\left[0, \left(\frac{\text{BASKET}_{\text{average}} - 100}{100}\right)\right]$ where $\text{BASKET}_{\text{average}} = 100^* \sum_{120\ \text{stocks}} \left(\text{Weight}^* \frac{\text{P}_{\text{average}}}{\text{P}_{\text{initial}}}\right)$ And for each stock the weight is given in the Appendix P_initial is the local currency price of each stock on the Initial Valuation Date P_average is the arithmetic average of the local currency price of each stock on each of the Averaging Dates
Floating Equity Amount Payment Date	Termination Date

Appendix
Each of the following stocks are equally weighted (5%):
Astra (Sweden), Glaxo Wellcome (UK), Smithkline Beecham (UK), Zeneca Group (UK), (Novartis (Switzerland), Roche Holding Genus (Switzerland), Sanofi (France), Synthelabo (France), Bayer (Germany), Abbott Labs (US), Bristol Myers Squibb (US), American Home Products (US), Amgen (US), Eli Lilly (US), Medtronic (US), Merck (US), Pfizer (US), Schering-Plough (US), Sankyo (Japan), Takeda Chemical (Japan).

This indicative termsheet is neither an offer to buy or sell securities or an OTC derivative product which includes options, swaps, forwards and structured notes having similar features to OTC derivative transactions, nor a solicitation to buy or sell securities or an OTC derivative product. The proposal contained in the foregoing is not a complete description of the terms of a particular transaction and is subject to change without limitation.

Figure 11.3 Term sheet for a basket equity swap (continued).

11.9 OTHER FEATURES

Basket options can have many of the other features that we have seen or will see. This includes early exericse and, seen later, path dependency. Sometimes the payoff is in one asset with a feature such as early exercise being dependent on another asset. This would still be a multifactor problem, in this particular case there are two sources of randomness.

Continuing with this example, suppose that the payoff is $P(S_1)$ at expiry. Also suppose that the option can be exercised early receiving this payoff, but only when $S_2 > E_2$. To price this contract we must find $V(S_1, S_2, t)$ where

$$\frac{\partial V}{\partial t} + \frac{1}{2}\sum_{i=1}^{2}\sum_{j=1}^{2}\sigma_i\sigma_j\rho_{ij}S_iS_j\frac{\partial^2 V}{\partial S_i \partial S_j} + \sum_{i=1}^{2} rS_i\frac{\partial V}{\partial S_i} - rV = 0,$$

with

$$V(S_1, S_2, T) = P(S_1)$$

subject to

$$V(S_1, S_2, t) \geq P(S_1) \quad \text{for} \quad S_2 > E_2,$$

and continuity of V and its first derivatives.

If we can price and hedge an option on a single asset with a set of characteristics, then we can price and hedge a multi-asset version also, theoretically. The practice of pricing and hedging may be much harder as I mention below.

11.10 REALITIES OF PRICING BASKET OPTIONS

The factors that determine the ease or difficulty of pricing and hedging multi-asset options are

- existence of a closed-form solution
- number of underlying assets, the dimensionality
- path dependency
- early exercise

We have seen all of these except path dependency, it is the subject of Part Two.

The solution technique that we use will generally be one of

- finite-difference solution of a partial differential equation
- numerical integration
- Monte Carlo simulation

These methods are the subjects of Part Six.

11.10.1 Easy Problems

If we have a closed-form solution then our work is done; we can easily find values and hedge ratios. This is provided that the solution is in terms of sufficiently simple functions for which there are spreadsheet functions or other libraries. If the contract is European with no path-dependency then the solution may be of the form (11.2). If this is the case, then we often have to do the integration numerically. This is not difficult. Several methods are described in Chapter 49, including Monte Carlo integration and the use of low-discrepancy sequences.

11.10.2 Medium Problems

If we have low dimensionality, less than three or four, say, the finite-difference methods are the obvious choice. They cope well with early exercise and many path-dependent features can be incorporated, though usually at the cost of an extra dimension.

For higher dimensions, Monte Carlo simulations are good. They cope with all path-dependent features. Unfortunately, they are not very efficient for American-style early exercise.

11.10.3 Hard Problems

The hardest problems to solve are those with both high dimensionality, for which we would like to use Monte Carlo simulation, and with early exercise, for which we would like to use finite-difference methods. There is currently no numerical method that copes well with such a problem.

11.11 REALITIES OF HEDGING BASKET OPTIONS

Even if we can find option values and the greeks, they are often very sensitive to the level of the correlation. But as I have said, the correlation is a very difficult quantity to measure. So the hedge ratios are very likely to be inaccurate. If we are delta hedging then we need accurate estimates of the deltas. This makes basket options very difficult to delta hedge successfully.

When we have a contract that is difficult to delta hedge we can try to reduce sensitivity to parameters, and the model, by hedging with other derivatives. This was the basis of vega hedging, mentioned in Chapter 7. We could try to use the same idea to reduce sensitivity to the correlation. Unfortunately, that is also difficult because there just aren't enough contracts traded that depend on the right correlations.

11.12 CORRELATION VERSUS COINTEGRATION

The correlations between financial quantities are notoriously unstable. One could easily argue that a theory should not be built up using parameters that are so unpredictable. I would tend to agree with this point of view. One could propose a stochastic correlation model, but that approach has its own problems.

An alternative statistical measure to correlation is **cointegration**. Very loosely speaking, two time series are cointegrated if a linear combination has constant mean and standard deviation. In other words, the two series never stray too far from one another. This is probably a more robust measure of the linkage between two financial quantities but as yet there is little derivative theory based on the concept.

11.13 SUMMARY

The new ideas in this chapter were the multifactor, correlated random walks for assets, and Itô's lemma in higher dimensions. These are both simple concepts, and we will use them often, especially in interest-rate-related topics.

FURTHER READING

- See Hamilton (1994) for further details of the measurement of correlation and cointegration.
- The first solution of the exchange option problem was by Margrabe (1978).
- For analytical results, formulae or numerical algorithm for the pricing of some other multifactor options see Stulz (1982), Johnson (1987), Boyle, Evnine & Gibbs (1989), Boyle & Tse (1990), Rubinstein (1991) and Rich & Chance (1993).
- For details of cointegration, what it means and how it works see the papers by Alexander & Johnson (1992, 1994).

EXERCISES

1. N shares follow geometric Brownian motions, i.e.

$$dS_i = \mu_i S_i\,dt + \sigma_i S_i\,dX_i,$$

   for $1 \leq i \leq N$. The share price changes are correlated with correlation coefficients ρ_{ij}. Find the stochastic differential equation satisfied by a function $f(S_1, S_2, \ldots, S_N)$.

2. Using tick-data for at least two assets, measure the correlations between the assets using the entirety of the data. Split the data in two halves and perform the same calculations on

each of the halves in turn. Are the correlation coefficients for the first half equal to those for the second? If so, do these figures match those for the whole data set?

3. Check that if we use the pricing formula for European non-path-dependent options on dividend-paying assets, but for a single asset (i.e. in one dimension), we recover the solution found in Chapter 6:

$$V(S,t) = \frac{e^{-r(T-t)}}{\sigma\sqrt{2\pi(T-t)}} \int_0^\infty e^{-(\log(S/S')+(r-(1/2)\sigma^2)(T-t))^2/2\sigma^2(T-t)}\,\text{Payoff}(S')\frac{dS'}{S'}.$$

4. Set-up the following problems mathematically (i.e. what equations do they satisfy and with what boundary and final conditions?) The assets are correlated.
   (a) An option that pays the positive difference between two share prices S_1 and S_2 and which expires at time T.
   (b) An option that has a call payoff with underlying S_1 and strike price E at time T only if $S_1 > S_2$ at time T.
   (c) An option that has a call payoff with underlying S_1 and strike price E_1 at time T if $S_1 > S_2$ at time T and a put payoff with underlying S_2 and strike price E_2 at time T if $S_2 > S_1$ at time T.

5. What is the explicit formula for the price of a quanto which has a put payoff on the Nikkei Dow index with strike at E and which is paid in yen. $S_\$$ is the yen–dollar exchange rate and S_N is the level of the Nikkei Dow index. We assume

$$dS_\$ = \mu_\$ S_\$\,dt + \sigma_\$ S_\$\,dX_\$$$

and

$$dS_N = \mu_N S_N\,dt + \sigma_N S_N\,dX_N,$$

with a correlation of ρ.

CHAPTER 12
the binomial model

In this Chapter...

- a simple model for an asset price random walk
- delta hedging
- no arbitrage
- the basics of the binomial method for valuing options
- risk neutrality

12.1 INTRODUCTION

We have seen in Chapter 3 a model for equities and other assets that is based on the mathematical theory of stochastic calculus. There is another, equally popular, approach that leads to the same partial differential equation, the Black–Scholes equation, in a way that some people find more 'accessible,' which can be made equally 'rigorous.' This approach, via the **binomial model** for equities, is the subject of this chapter.

Undoubtedly, one of the reasons for the popularity of this model is that it can be implemented without any higher mathematics (such as differential calculus) and there is actually no need to derive a partial differential equation before this implementation. This is a positive point, however the downside is that it is harder to attain greater levels of sophistication or numerical analysis in this setting.

Before I describe this model I want to stress that the binomial model may be thought of as being either a genuine *model* for the behavior of equities, or, alternatively, as a numerical method for the solution of the Black–Scholes equation.[1] Most importantly, we see the ideas of delta hedging, risk elimination and risk-neutral valuation occuring in another setting.

The binomial model is very important because it shows how to get away from a reliance on closed-form solutions. Indeed, it is extremely important to have a way of valuing options that only relies on a simple model and fast, accurate numerical methods. Often in real life a contract may contain features that make analytic solution very hard or impossible. Some of these features may be just a minor modification to some other, easily-priced, contract but even minor changes to a contract can have important effects on the value and especially on the method of solution. The classic example is of the American put. Early exercise may seem to be a small change to a contract but the difference between the values of a European and an American put can

---

[1] In this case, it is very similar to an explicit finite-difference method, of which more later.

be large and certainly there is no simple closed-form solution for the American option and its value must be found numerically.

12.2 EQUITIES CAN GO DOWN AS WELL AS UP

In the binomial model we assume that the asset, which initially has the value S, can, during a timestep δt, either rise to a value uS or fall to a value vS, with $0 < v < 1 < u$. The probability of a rise is p and so the probability of a fall is $1 - p$. This behavior is shown in Figure 12.1.

The three constants u, v and p are chosen to give the binomial walk the same drift and standard deviation as that given by the stochastic differential equation (3.6). Having only these two equations for the three parameters gives us one degree of freedom in this choice. This degree of freedom is often used to give the random walk the further property that after an up and a down movement (or a down followed by an up) the asset returns to its starting value, S.[2] This gives us the requirement that

$$uv = 1. \tag{12.1}$$

For the random walk to have the correct drift we need

$$pu + (1 - p)\, v = e^{\mu\, \delta t}.$$

Rearranging this equation we get

$$p = \frac{e^{\mu\, \delta t} - v}{u - v}. \tag{12.2}$$

Then for the random walk to have the correct standard deviation we need

$$pu^2 + (1 - p)\, v^2 = e^{(2\mu + \sigma^2)\, \delta t}. \tag{12.3}$$

Equations (12.1), (12.2) and (12.3) can be solved to give

$$u = \tfrac{1}{2}\left(e^{-\mu\, \delta t} + e^{(\mu+\sigma^2)\, \delta t}\right) + \tfrac{1}{2}\sqrt{\left(e^{-\mu\, \delta t} + e^{(\mu+\sigma^2)\, \delta t}\right)^2 - 4}. \tag{12.4}$$

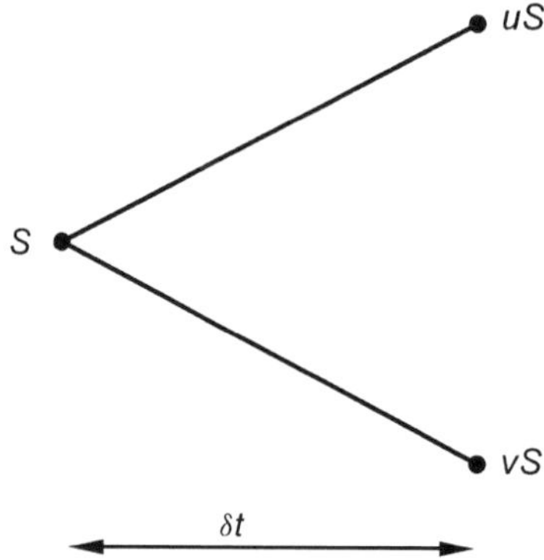

Figure 12.1 A schematic diagram of one timestep in the life of a binomial walk.

[2] Other choices are possible. For example, sometimes the probability of an up move is set equal to the probability of a down move i.e. $p = \frac{1}{2}$.

12.3 THE BINOMIAL TREE

The binomial model, just introduced, allows the stock to move up or down a prescribed amount over the next timestep. If the stock starts out with value S then it will take either the value uS or vS after the next timestep. We can extend the random walk to the next timestep. After two timesteps the asset will be at either u^2S, if there were two up moves, uvS, if an up was followed by a down or vice versa, or v^2S, if there were two consecutive down moves. After three timesteps the asset can be at u^3S, u^2vS, etc. One can imagine extending this random walk out all the way until expiry. The resulting structure looks like Figure 12.2 where the nodes represent the values taken by the asset. This structure is called the **binomial tree**. Observe how the tree bends due to the geometric nature of the asset growth. Often this tree is drawn as in Figure 12.3 because it is easier to draw, but this doesn't quite capture the correct structure.

The top and bottom branches of the tree at expiry can only be reached by one path each, either all up or all down moves. Whereas there will be several paths possible for each of the intermediate values at expiry. Therefore the intermediate values are more likely to be reached

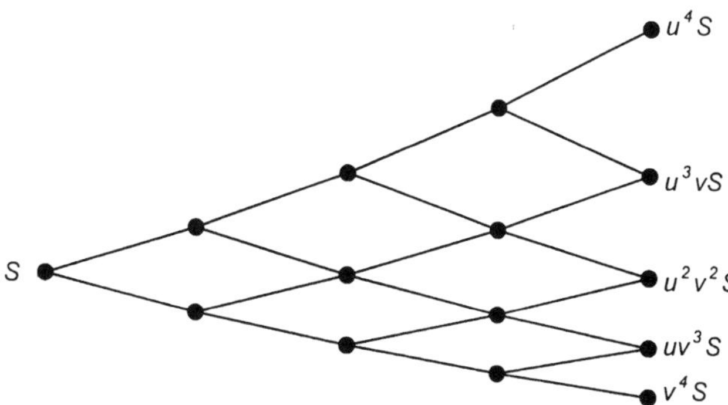

Figure 12.2 The binomial tree.

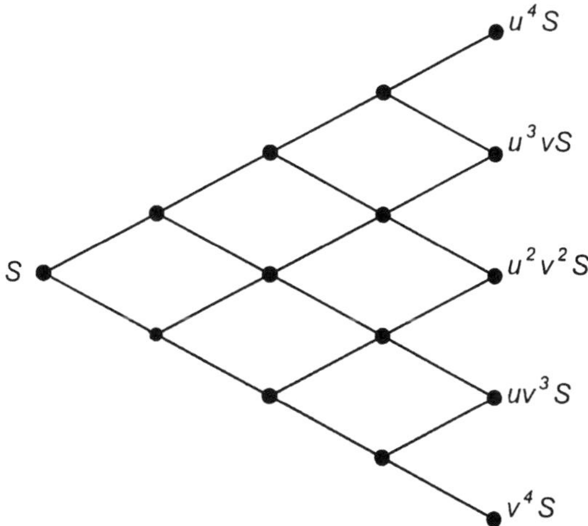

Figure 12.3 The binomial tree: a schematic version.

than the end values if one were doing a simulation. The binomial tree therefore contains within it an approximation to the probability density function for the lognormal random walk.

12.4 AN EQUATION FOR THE VALUE OF AN OPTION

Suppose, for the moment, that we know the value of the option at the time $t + \delta t$. For example, this time may be the expiry of the option, say. Now construct a portfolio at time t consisting of one option and a short position in a quantity Δ of the underlying. At time t this portfolio has value

$$\Pi = V - \Delta S,$$

where the value V is to be determined.

At time $t + \delta t$ the portfolio takes one of two values, depending on whether the asset rises or falls. These two values are

$$V^+ - \Delta u S \quad \text{and} \quad V^- - \Delta v S.$$

Since we assume that we know V^+, V^-, u, v, S and Δ, the values of both of these expressions are known, and, in particular, depend on Δ.

Having the freedom to choose Δ, we can make the value of this portfolio the same whether the asset rises or falls. This is ensured if we make

$$V^+ - \Delta u S = V^- - \Delta v S.$$

This gives us the choice

$$\Delta = \frac{V^+ - V^-}{(u - v)S}, \tag{12.5}$$

when the new portfolio value is

$$\Pi + \delta\Pi = V^+ - \frac{u(V^+ - V^-)}{(u - v)} = V^- - \frac{v(V^+ - V^-)}{(u - v)}.$$

Since the value of the portfolio has been guaranteed, we can say that its value must coincide with the value of the original portfolio plus any interest earned at the risk-free rate; this is the no-arbitrage argument. Thus

$$\delta\Pi = r\Pi\,\delta t.$$

After some manipulation this equation becomes

$$V = \frac{V^+ - V^-}{u - v} + \frac{uV^- - vV^+}{(1 + r\,\delta t)(u - v)}. \tag{12.6}$$

This, then, is an equation for V given V^+, and V^-, the option values at the next timestep, and the parameters u and v describing the random walk of the asset.

To $O(\delta t)$ we can write (12.6) as

$$e^{r\,\delta t}V = p'V^+ + (1 - p')\,V^-, \tag{12.7}$$

where

$$p' = \frac{e^{r\,\delta t} - v}{u - v}. \tag{12.8}$$

Expressions (12.2) and (12.8) differ in that where one has the interest rate r the other has the drift μ, but are otherwise the same. Interpreting p' as a probability, this is just risk neutrality again. And (12.7) is the statement that the option value at time t is the present value of the risk-neutral expected value at any later time.

Supposing that we know V^+ and V^- we can use (12.7) to find V. But do we know V^+ and V^-?

12.5 VALUING BACK DOWN THE TREE

We certainly know V^+ and V^- at expiry, time T, because we know the option value as a function of the asset then, this is the payoff function. If we know the value of the option at expiry we can use Equation (12.7) to find the option value at the time $T - \delta t$ for all values of S on the tree. But knowing these values means that we can find the option values one step further back in time. Thus we work our way back down the tree until we get to the root. This root is the current time and asset value, and thus we find the option value today.

This method is illustrated in Figure 12.4. Here we are valuing a European call option with strike price 100 and maturity in four months' time. Today's asset price is 100, and the volatility is 20%. To make things as simple as possible the interest rate is zero.

I use a timestep of one month so that there are four steps until expiry. Using these numbers we have $\delta t = 1/12 = 0.08333$, $u = 1.0604$, $v = 0.9431$ and $p' = 0.5567$. As an example, after one timestep the asset takes either the value $100 \times 1.0604 = 106.04$ or $100 \times 0.9431 = 94.31$. Working back from expiry, the option value at the timestep before expiry when $S = 119.22$ is given by

$$e^{-0.1 \times 0.0833}(0.5567 \times 26.42 + (1 - 0.5567) \times 12.44) = 20.05.$$

Working right back down the tree to the present time, the option value when the asset is 100 is 6.14. Compare this with the theoretical, continuous-time solution (given by the Black–Scholes call value) of 6.35. The difference is entirely due to the size and number of the timesteps. The larger the number of timesteps, the greater the accuracy. I come back to the issue of accuracy in later chapters.

In practice, the binomial method is programmed rather than done on a spreadsheet. Here is a function that takes inputs for the underlying and the option, using an externally-defined payoff function. Key points to note about this program concern the building up of the arrays for the asset `S()` and the option `V()`. First of all, the asset array is built up only in order to find the final values of the asset at each node at the final timestep, expiry. The asset values on other nodes are never used. Second, the argument `j` refers to how far up the asset is from the lowest node *at that timestep*.

```
Function Price(Asset As Double, Volatility As Double, _
                        IntRate As Double, Strike As Double, _
                        Expiry As Double, NoSteps As Integer)
ReDim S(0 To NoSteps)
ReDim V(0 To NoSteps)
timestep = Expiry / NoSteps
DiscountFactor = Exp(-IntRate * timestep)
temp1 = Exp((IntRate + Volatility * Volatility) * timestep)
temp2 = 0.5 * (DiscountFactor + temp1)
```

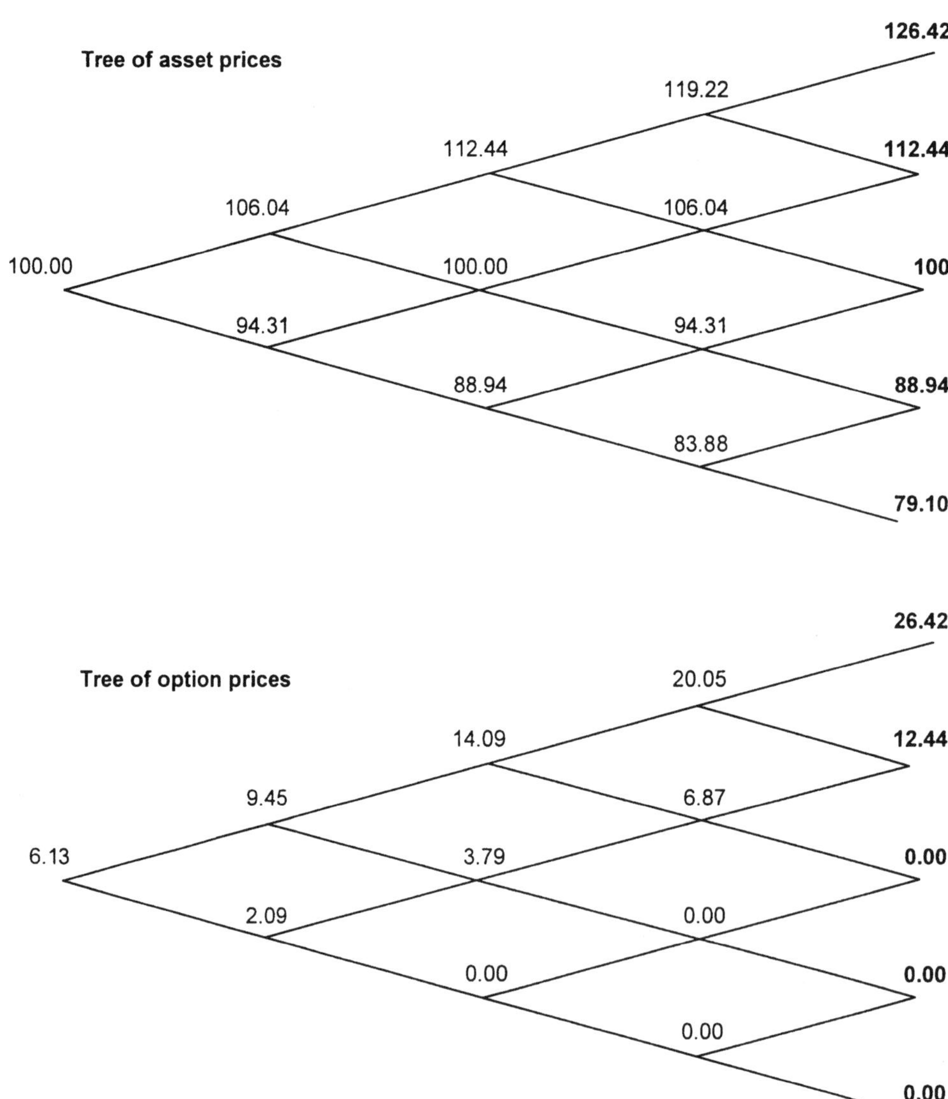

Figure 12.4 The binomial tree and corresponding option prices.

```
u = temp2 + Sqr(temp2 * temp2 - 1)
d = 1 / u
p = (Exp(IntRate * timestep) - d) / (u - d)

S(0) = Asset
For n = 1 To NoSteps
    For j = n To 1 Step -1
        S(j) = u * S(j - 1)
    Next j
        S(0) = d * S(0)
Next n
```

```
For j = 0 To NoSteps
    V(j) = Payoff(S(j), Strike)
Next j

For n = NoSteps To 1 Step -1
    For j = 0 To NoSteps - 1
        V(j) = (p * V(j + 1) + (1 - p) * V(j)) _
            * DiscountFactor
    Next j
Next n
Price = V(0)
End Function
```

Here is the externally-defined payoff function `Payoff (S, Strike)` for a call.

```
Function Payoff(S, K)
Payoff = 0
If S > K Then Payoff = S - K
End Function
```

Because I never use the asset nodes other than at expiry I could have used only the one array in the above, with the same array being used for both S and V. I have kept them separate to make the program more transparent. Also, I could have saved the values of V at all of the nodes; in the above I have only used the node at the present time. Saving all the values will be important if you want to see how the option value changes with the asset price and time, if you want to calculate greeks for example.

In Figure 12.5 I show a plot of the calculated option price against the number of timesteps using this algorithm. The inset figure is a close up. Observe the oscillation. In this example, an odd number of timesteps gives an answer that is too high and an even an answer that is too low.

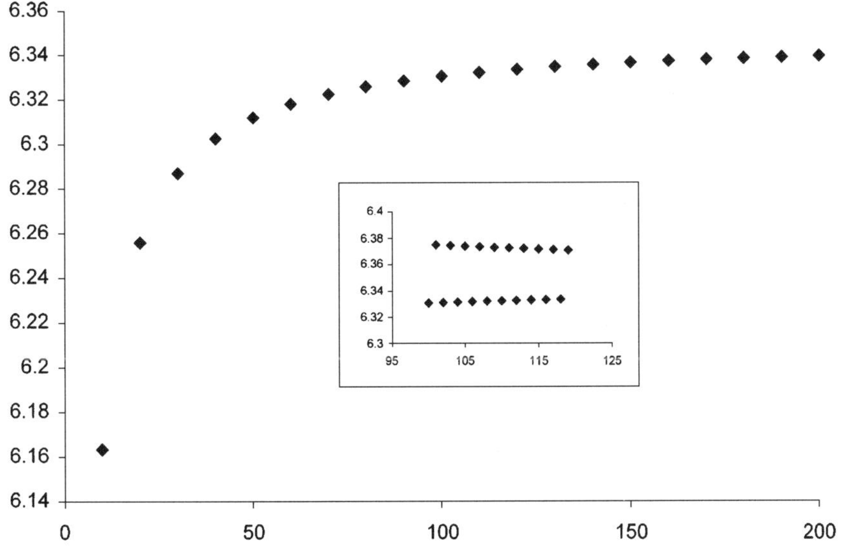

Figure 12.5 Option price as a function of number of timesteps.

12.6 THE GREEKS

The greeks are defined as derivatives of the option value with respect to various variables and parameters. It is important to distinguish whether the differentiation is with respect to a variable or a parameter (it could, of course, be with respect to both). If the differentiation is only with respect to the asset price and/or time then there is sufficient information in our binomial tree to estimate the derivative. It may not be an accurate estimate, but it will be *an* estimate. The option's delta, gamma and theta can all be estimated from the tree.

On the other hand, if you want to examine the sensitivity of the option with respect to one of the parameters, then you must perform another binomial calculation. This applies to the option's vega and rho for example.

Let me take these two cases in turn.

From the binomial model the option's delta is defined by

$$\frac{V^+ - V^-}{(u - v)S}.$$

We can calculate this quantity directly from the tree. Referring to Figure 12.6, the delta uses the option value at the two points marked 'D,' together with today's asset price and the parameters u and v. This is a simple calculation.

In the limit as the timestep approaches zero, the delta becomes

$$\frac{\partial V}{\partial S}.$$

The gamma of the option is also defined as a derivative of the option with respect to the underlying:

$$\frac{\partial^2 V}{\partial S^2}.$$

To estimate this quantity using our tree is not so clear. It will be much easier when we use a finite-difference grid. However, gamma is a measure of how much we must rehedge at the next timestep. But we can calculate the delta at points marked with a D in Figure 12.6 from the option value one timestep further in the future. The gamma is then just the change in the delta from one of these to the other divided by the distance between them. This calculation uses the points marked 'G' in Figure 12.6.

The theta of the option is the sensitivity of the option price to time, assuming that the asset price does not change. Again, this is easier to calculate from a finite-difference grid. An

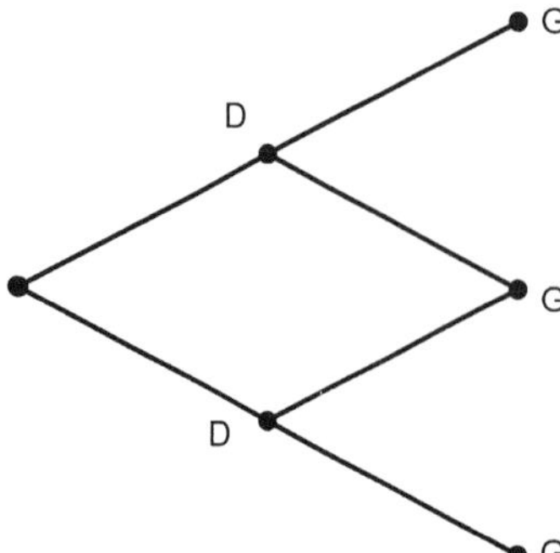

Figure 12.6 Calculating the delta and gamma.

obvious choice for the discrete-time definition of theta is interpolate between V^+ and V^- to find a theoretical option value *had the asset not changed* and use this to estimate

$$\frac{\partial V}{\partial t}.$$

This results in

$$\frac{\frac{1}{2}(V^+ + V^-) - V}{\delta t}.$$

As the timestep gets smaller and smaller these greeks approach the Black–Scholes continuous-time values.

Estimating the other type of greeks, the ones involving differentiation with respect to parameters, is slightly harder. They are harder to calculate in the sense that you must perform a second binomial calculation. I will illustrate this with the calculation of the option's vega.

The vega is the sensitivity of the option value to the volatility

$$\frac{\partial V}{\partial \sigma}.$$

Suppose we want to find the option value and vega when the volatility is 20%. The most efficient way to do this is to calculate the option price twice, using a binomial tree, with two different values of σ. Calculate the option value using a volatility of $\sigma \pm \varepsilon$, for a small number ε, call the values you find $V_\pm$. The option value is approximated by the average value

$$V = \tfrac{1}{2}(V_+ + V_-)$$

and the vega is approximated by

$$\frac{V_+ - V_-}{2\varepsilon}.$$

The idea can be applied to other greeks.

12.7 EARLY EXERCISE

American-style exercise is easy to implement in a binomial setting. The algorithm is identical to that for European exercise with one exception. We use the same binomial tree, with the same u, v and p, but there is a slight difference in the formula for V. We must ensure that there are no arbitrage opportunities at any of the nodes.

For reasons which will become apparent, I'm going to change my notation now, making it more complex but more informative. Introduce the notation S_j^n to mean the asset price at the nth timestep, at the node j from the bottom, $0 \le j \le n$. This notation is consistent with the code above. In our lognormal world we have

$$S_j^n = Su^j v^{n-j},$$

where S is the current asset price. Also introduce V_j^n as the option value at the same node. Our ultimate goal is to find V_0^0 knowing the payoff, i.e. knowing V_j^N for all $0 \le j \le M$ where M is the number of timesteps.

Returning to the American option problem, arbitrage occurs if the option value goes below the payoff at any time. If our theoretical value falls below the payoff then it is time to exercise.

If we do then exercise the option its value and the payoff must be the same. If we find that

$$\frac{V_{j+1}^{n+1} - V_j^{n+1}}{u - v} + e^{-r\,\delta t}\frac{uV_j^{n+1} - vV_{j+1}^{n+1}}{u - v} \geq \text{Payoff}\,(S_j^n)$$

then we use this as our new value. But if

$$\frac{V_{j+1}^{n+1} - V_j^{n+1}}{u - v} + e^{-r\,\delta t}\frac{uV_j^{n+1} - vV_{j+1}^{n+1}}{u - v} < \text{Payoff}\,(S_j^n)$$

we should exercise, giving us a better value of

$$V_j^n = \text{Payoff}\,(S_j^n).$$

We can put these two together to get

$$V_j^n = \max\left(\frac{V_{j+1}^{n+1} - V_j^{n+1}}{u - v} + e^{-r\,\delta t}\frac{uV_j^{n+1} - vV_{j+1}^{n+1}}{u - v}, \text{Payoff}\,(S_j^n)\right)$$

instead of (12.6). This ensures that there are no arbitrage opportunities. This modification is easy to code, but note that the payoff is a function of the asset price at the node in question. This is new, not seen in the European problem for which we did not have to keep track of the asset values on each of the nodes.

Below is a function for calculating the value of an American-style option. Note the differences between this program and the one for European-style exercise. The code is the same except that we keep track of more information and the line that updates the option value incorporates the no-arbitrage condition.

```
Function USPrice(Asset As Double, Volatility As Double, _
                    IntRate As Double, Strike As Double, _
                    Expiry As Double, NoSteps As Integer)
ReDim S(0 To NoSteps, 0 To NoSteps)
ReDim V(0 To NoSteps, 0 To NoSteps)
timestep = Expiry / NoSteps
DiscountFactor = Exp(-IntRate * timestep)
temp1 = Exp((IntRate + Volatility * Volatility) * timestep)
temp2 = 0.5 * (DiscountFactor + temp1)
u = temp2 + Sqr(temp2 * temp2 - 1)
d = 1 / u
p = (Exp(IntRate * timestep) - d) / (u - d)

S(0, 0) = Asset
For n = 1 To NoSteps
    For j = n To 1 Step -1
        S(j, n) = u * S(j - 1, n - 1)
    Next j
        S(0, n) = d * S(0, n - 1)
Next n

For j = 0 To NoSteps
    V(j, NoSteps) = Payoff(S(j, NoSteps), Strike)
```

```
Next j

For n = NoSteps To 1 Step -1
    For j = 0 To NoSteps - 1
        V(j, n - 1) = max((p * V(j + 1, n) + (1 - p) * V(j, n)) _
            * DiscountFactor, Payoff(S(j, n - 1), Strike))
    Next j
Next n
USPrice = V(0, 0)
End Function
```

12.8 THE CONTINUOUS-TIME LIMIT

Equation (12.6) and the Black–Scholes equation (27.7) are more closely related than they may at first seem. Recalling that the Black–Scholes equation is in continuous time, we examine (12.6) as $\delta t \to 0$.

First of all, from (12.4) we have that

$$u \sim 1 + \sigma\sqrt{\delta t} + \tfrac{1}{2}\sigma^2\,\delta t + \cdots$$

and

$$v \sim 1 - \sigma\sqrt{\delta t} + \tfrac{1}{2}\sigma^2\,\delta t + \cdots.$$

Next we write

$$V = V(S,t), \quad V^+ = V(uS, t+\delta t) \quad \text{and} \quad V^- = V(vS, t+\delta t).$$

Expanding these expressions in Taylor series for small δt and substituting into (12.5) we find that

$$\Delta \sim \frac{\partial V}{\partial S} \quad \text{as} \quad \delta t \to 0.$$

Thus the binomial delta becomes, in the limit, the Black–Scholes delta.

Similarly, we can substitute the expressions for V, V^+ and V^- into (12.6) to find

$$\frac{\partial V}{\partial t} + \tfrac{1}{2}\sigma^2 S^2 \frac{\partial^2 V}{\partial S^2} + r\frac{\partial V}{\partial S} - rV = 0.$$

This is the Black–Scholes equation. Again, the drift rate μ has disappeared from the equation.

12.9 NO ARBITRAGE IN THE BINOMIAL, BLACK–SCHOLES AND ‘OTHER’ WORLDS

With the binomial discrete-time model, as with the Black–Scholes continuous-time model, we have been able to eliminate uncertainty in the value of a portfolio by a judicious choice of a hedge. In both cases we find that it does not matter how the underlying asset moves, the resulting value of the portfolio is the same. This is especially clear in the above binomial model. This hedging is only possible in these two simple, popular models. For consider a trivial generalization: the trinomial random walk.

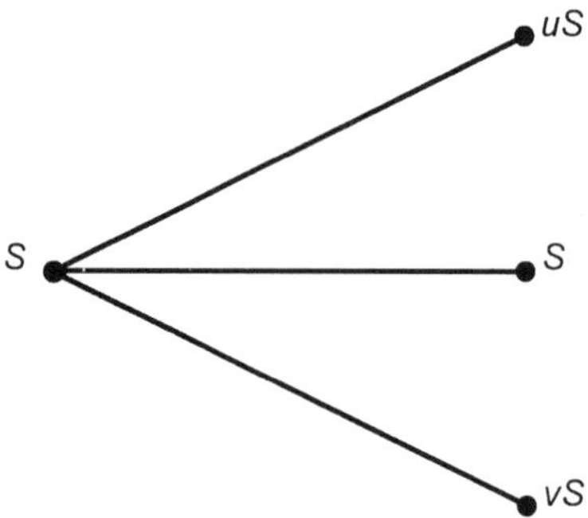

Figure 12.7 The trinomial tree. Perfect risk-free hedging is not possible under this scenario.

In Figure 12.7 we see a representation of a trinomial random walk. After a timestep δt the asset could have risen to uS, fallen to vS or not moved from S.

What happens if we try to hedge an option under this scenario? As before, we can 'hedge' with $-\Delta$ of the underlying but this time we would like to choose Δ so that the value of the portfolio (of one option and $-\Delta$ of the asset) is the same at time $t + \delta t$ no matter to which value the asset moves. In other words, we want the portfolio to have the same value for all *three* possible outcomes. Unfortunately, we cannot choose a value for Δ that ensures this to be the case: this amounts to solving two equations (first portfolio value = second portfolio value = third portfolio value) with just one unknown (the delta). Hedging is not possible in the trinomial world. Indeed, perfect hedging, and thus the application of the 'no-arbitrage principle' is only possible in the two special cases: the Black–Scholes continuous time/continuous asset world, and the binomial world. And in the far more complex 'real' world, delta hedging is *not* possible.[3]

12.10 SUMMARY

In this chapter I described the basics of the binomial model, deriving pricing equations and algorithms for both European- and American-style exercise. The method can be extended in many ways, to incorporate dividends, to allow Bermudan exercise, to value path-dependent contracts and to price contracts depending on other stochastic variables such as interest rates. I have not gone into the method in any detail for the simple reason that the binomial method is just a simple version of an explicit finite-difference scheme. As such it will be discussed in depth in Part Six. Finite-difference methods have an obvious advantage over the binomial method: they are far more flexible.

FURTHER READING

- The original binomial concept is due to Cox, Ross & Rubinstein (1979).
- Almost every book on options describes the binomial method in more depth than I do. One of the best is Hull (1997) who also describes its use in the fixed-income world.

[3] Is it good for the popular models to have such an unrealistic property? These models are at least a good *starting* point.

EXERCISES

1. Solve the three equations for u, v and p to find

$$u = \tfrac{1}{2}(e^{-\mu\,\delta t} + e^{(\mu+\sigma^2)=,\delta t}) + \tfrac{1}{2}\sqrt{(e^{-\mu\,\delta t} + e^{(\mu+\sigma^2)\,\delta t})^2 - 4}.$$

2. Repeat the analysis of Question 1, using the alternative condition $p = \frac{1}{2}$. (This replaces the condition that the tree reconnects, i.e. $uv = 1$.)
3. Starting from the approximations for u and v, check that in the limit $\delta t \to 0$ we recover the Black–Scholes equation.
4. A share price is currently \$80. At the end of three months, it will be either \$84 or \$76. Ignoring interest rates, calculate the value of a three month European call option with exercise price \$79. (In this and the following questions, you will need to set up a Black–Scholes hedged portfolio.)
5. A share price is currently \$92. At the end of one year, it will be either \$86 or \$98. Calculate the value of a one year European call option with exercise price \$90 using a single-step binomial tree. The risk-free interest rate is 2% p.a. with continuous compounding.
6. A share price is currently \$45. At the end of each of the next two months, it will change by going up \$2 or going down \$2. Calculate the value of a two month European call option with exercise price \$44. The risk-free interest rate is 6% p.a. with continuous compounding.
7. A share price is currently \$63. At the end of each three month period, it will change by going up \$3 or going down \$3. Calculate the value of a six month American put option with exercise price \$61. The risk-free interest rate is 4% p.a. with continuous compounding.
8. A share price is currently \$15. At the end of three months, it will be either \$13 or \$17. Ignoring interest rates, calculate the value of a three month European option with payoff $\max(S^2 - 159, 0)$, where S is the share price at the end of three months.
9. A share price is currently \$180. At the end of one year, it will be either \$203 or \$152. The risk-free interest rate is 3% p.a. with continuous compounding. Consider an American put on this underlying. Find the exercise price for which holding the option for the year is equivalent to exercising immediately. This is the break-even exercise price. What effect would a decrease in the interest rate have on this break-even price?
10. A share price is currently \$75. At the end of three months, it will be either \$59 or \$92. What is the risk-neutral probability that the share price increases? The risk-free interest rate is 4% p.a. with continuous compounding.
11. The movements of the underlying for a particular European option can be expressed as a two-step binomial tree (the above examples can be thought of as single-step binomial tree movements). Is it possible to create a Black–Scholes hedged portfolio in this case?

PART TWO
path dependency

The second part of the book builds upon both the mathematics and the finance of Part One. The mathematical tools are extended to examine and model path dependency. The financial contracts that we look at now include path-dependent contracts such as barriers, Asians and lookbacks.

Chapter 13: An Introduction to Exotic and Path-dependent Options This is just an overview of exotic options in which I unsuccessfully try to classify various kinds of exotics. I describe several important features to look out for.

Chapter 14: Barrier Options The commonest type of path-dependent option is the barrier option. It is only weakly path dependent (a concept I will explain) and slots very easily into the Black–Scholes framework.

Chapter 15: Strongly Path-dependent Options Some options are harder to price for technical reasons, they are strongly path dependent. However, with a little bit of ingenuity, not much, we can price these contracts quite easily.

Chapter 16: Asian Options Asian options depend on the realized average of an asset price path. They are considered in some depth.

Chapter 17: Lookback Options Lookback options depend on the realized maximum or minimum of the asset price path. They are explained in depth.

Chapter 18: Miscellaneous Exotics My failure to classify all exotic option means that I am left with a chapter of miscellaneous contracts. I describe some more tricks of the trade for their valuation.

CHAPTER 13

an introduction to exotic and path-dependent options

In this Chapter...

- how to classify options according to important features
- how to think about derivatives in a way that makes it easy to compare and contrast different contracts
- the names and contract details for many basic types of exotic options

13.1 INTRODUCTION

The contracts we have seen so far are the most basic, and most important, derivative contracts but they only hint at the features that can be found in the more interesting products. In this chapter I prepare the way for the complex products I will be discussing in the next few chapters.

It is an impossible task to classify all options. The best that we can reasonably achieve is a rough characterization of the most popular of the features to be found in derivative products. I list some of these features in this chapter and give several examples. In the following few chapters I go into more detail in the description of the options and their pricing and hedging. The features that I describe now are discrete cashflows, early exercise, weak path dependence and strong path dependence, time dependence and dimensionality. Finally, I comment on the 'order' of an option.

Exotic options are interesting for several reasons. They are harder to price, sometimes being very model dependent. The risks inherent in the contracts are usually more obscure and can lead to unexpected losses. Careful hedging becomes important, whether delta hedging or some form of static hedging to minimize cashflows. Actually, how to hedge exotics is all that really matters. A trader may have a good idea of a reasonable price for an instrument, either from experience or by looking at the prices of similar instruments. But he may not be so sure about the risks in the contract or how to hedge them away successfuly.

We are going to continue with the Black–Scholes theme for the moment and show how to price and hedge exotics in their framework. Their assumptions will be relaxed in later chapters.

13.2 DISCRETE CASHFLOWS

Imagine a contract that pays the holder an amount q at time t_q. The contract could be a bond and the payment a coupon. If we use $V(t)$ to denote the contract value (ignoring any dependence

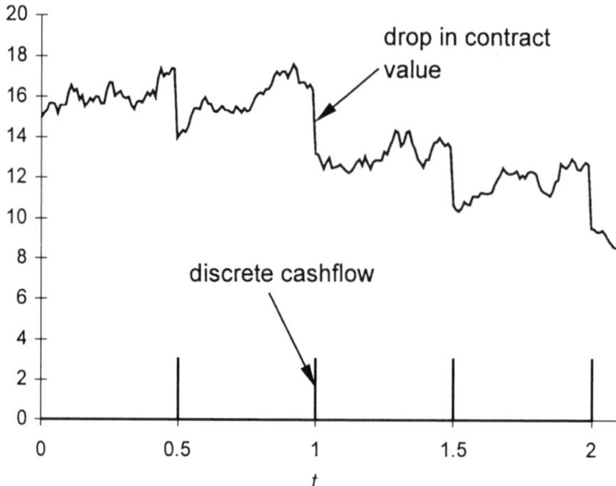

Figure 13.1 A discrete cashflow and its effect on a contract value.

on any underlying asset) and t_q^- and t_q^+ to denote just before and just after the cashflow date then simple arbitrage considerations lead to

$$V(t_q^-) = V(t_q^+) + q.$$

This is a jump condition. The value of the contract jumps by the amount of the cashflow. If this were not the case then there would be an arbitrage opportunity. The behavior of the contract value across the payment date is shown in Figure 13.1.

If the contract is contingent on an underlying variable so that we have $V(S, t)$ then we can accommodate cashflows that depend on the level of the asset S, i.e. we could have $q(S)$. Furthermore, this also allows us to lump all our options on the same underlying into one large portfolio. Then, across the expiry of each option, there will be a jump in the value of our whole portfolio of the amount of the payoff for that option.

There is one small technical requirement here, the cashflow must be a deterministic function of time and the underlying asset. For example, the contract holder could receive a payment of S^2, for some asset with price S. The above argument would not be valid if, for example, the cashflow depended on the toss of a coin; one dollar is received if heads is thrown and nothing otherwise. The jump condition does not necessarily apply, because the cashflow is not deterministic.

If the cashflow is not deterministic the modeling is not so straightforward. There is no 'no arbitrage' argument to appeal to, and the result could easily depend on an individual's risk preferences. Nevertheless, we could say, for example, that the jump condition would be that the change in value of the contract would be the *expected* value of the cashflow:

$$V(t_q^-) = V(t_q^+) + E[q].$$

Such a condition would not, however, allow for the risk inherent in the uncertain cashflow.

13.3 EARLY EXERCISE

We have seen early exercise in the American option problem. Early exercise is a common feature of other contracts, perhaps going by other names. For example, the conversion of convertible bonds (Chapter 36) is mathematically identical to the early exercise of an American option. The key point about early exercise is that the holder of this valuable right should ideally act *optimally*, i.e. they must decide *when* to exercise or convert. In the partial differential equation framework that has been set up, this optimality is achieved by solving a free boundary problem, with a constraint on the option value, together with a smoothness condition. It is this smoothness condition, that the derivative of the option value with respect to the underlying is continuous, that ensures optimality, i.e. maximization of the option value with respect to the exercise or conversion strategy. It is perfectly possible for there to be more than one early-exercise region.

One rarely-mentioned aspect of American options, and, generally speaking, contracts with early exercise-type characteristics, is that they are path dependent. Whether the owner of the option still holds the option at expiry depends on whether or not he has exercised the option, and thus on the path taken by the underlying. For American-type options this path dependence is weak, in the sense that the partial differential equation to be solved has no more independent variables than a similar, but European, contract.

13.4 WEAK PATH DEPENDENCE

The next most common reason for weak path dependence in a contract is a **barrier**. Barrier (or knock-in, or knock-out) options are triggered by the action of the underlying hitting a prescribed value at some time before expiry. For example, as long as the asset remains below 150, the contract will have a call payoff at expiry. However, should the asset reach this level before expiry then the option becomes worthless; the option has 'knocked out.' This contract is clearly path dependent, for consider the two paths in Figure 13.2; one has a payoff at expiry because the barrier was not triggered, the other is worthless, yet both have the same value of the underlying at expiry.

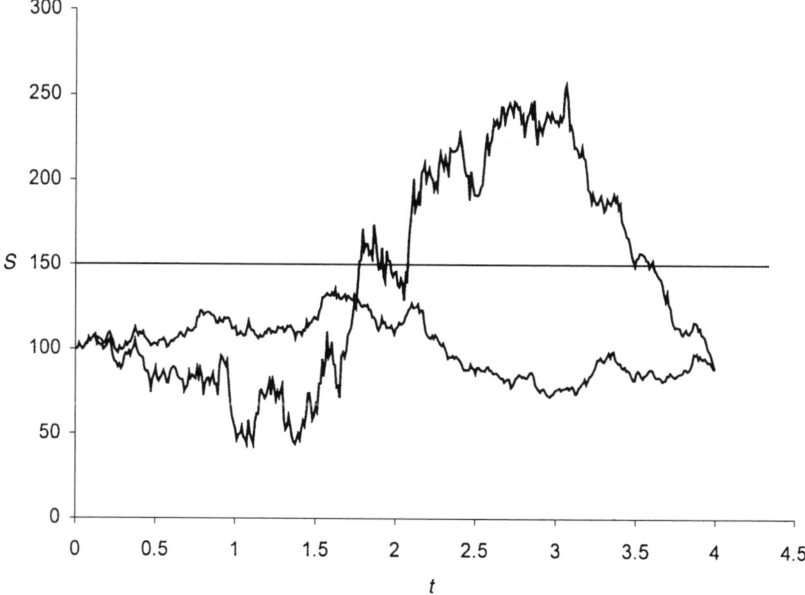

Figure 13.2 Two paths, having the same value at expiry, but with completely different payoffs.

We shall see in Chapter 14 that such a contract is only weakly path dependent: we still solve a partial differential equation in the two variables, the underlying and time.

13.5 STRONG PATH DEPENDENCE

Of particular interest, mathematical and practical, are the strongly path-dependent contracts. These have payoffs that depend on some property of the asset price path in addition to the value of the underlying at the present moment in time; in the equity option language, we cannot write the value as $V(S, t)$. The contract value is a function of at least one more independent variable. This is best illustrated by an example.

The Asian option has a payoff that depends on the average value of the underlying asset from inception to expiry. We must keep track of more information about the asset price path than simply its present position. The extra information that we need is contained in the 'running average.' This is the average of the asset price from inception until the present, when we are valuing the option. No other information is needed. This running average is then used as a new independent variable, the option value is a function of this as well as the usual underlying and time, and a derivative of the option value with respect to the running average appears in the governing equation.

There are many such contracts in existence, and I show how to put many of them into the same general framework.

13.6 TIME DEPENDENCE

We have seen time dependence in parameters, and have shown how to apply the Black–Scholes formulae when interest rates, dividends and volatility vary in time (in a known, deterministic, way). Here we are concerned with time dependence in the option contract. We can add such time dependence to any of the features described above. For example, early exercise might only be permitted on certain dates or during certain periods. This intermittent early exercise is a characteristic of **Bermudan options**. Similarly, the position of the barrier in a knock-out option may change with time. Every month it may be reset at a higher level than the month before. Or we can readily imagine a knock-out option in which the barrier is only active (i.e. can be triggered) during the last week of every month. These contracts are referred to as time-inhomogeneous.

13.7 DIMENSIONALITY

Dimensionality refers to the number of underlying independent variables. The vanilla option has two independent variables, S and t, and is thus two dimensional. The weakly path-dependent contracts have the same number of dimensions as their non-path-dependent cousins, i.e. a barrier call option has the same two dimensions as a vanilla call. For these contracts the roles of the asset dimension and the time dimension are quite different from each other, as discussed in Chapter 6 on the diffusion equation. This is because the governing equation, the Black–Scholes equation, contains a second asset-price derivative but only a first time derivative.

We can have two types of three-dimensional problem. The first occurs when we have a second source of randomness, such as a second underlying asset. We might, for example, have an option on the maximum of two equities. Both of these underlyings are stochastic, each with a volatility, and there will be a correlation between them. In the governing equation we will see a second derivative of the option value with respect to each asset. We say that there is diffusion in both S_1 and S_2.

The other type of problem that is also three dimensional is the strongly path-dependent contract. We will see examples of these in later chapters. Typically, the new independent variable is a measure of the path-dependent quantity on which the option is contingent. The new variable may be the average of the asset price to date, say. In this case, derivatives of the option value with respect to this new variable are only of the first order. Thus the new variable acts more like another time-like variable.

13.8 THE ORDER OF AN OPTION

The final classification that we make is the **order** of an option. Not only is this a classification but the idea also introduces fundamental modeling issues.

The basic, vanilla options are of first order. Their payoffs depend only on the underlying asset, the quantity that we are *directly* modeling. Other, path-dependent, contracts can still be of first order if the payoff only depends only on properties of the asset price path. 'Higher order' refers to options whose payoff, and hence value, is contingent on the value of *another* option. The obvious first-order options are compound options, for example, a call option giving the holder the right to buy a put option. The compound option expires at some date T_1 and the option on which it is contingent, expires at a later time T_2. Technically speaking, such an option is weakly path dependent. The *theoretical* pricing of such a contract is straightforward as we shall see.

From a practical point of view, the compound option raises some important modeling issues: the payoff for the compound option depends on the *market* value of the underlying option, and not on the theoretical price. If you hold a compound option, and want to exercise the first option then you must take possession of the underlying option. If that option is worth less than you think it should (because your model says so) then there is not much you can do about it. High order option values are very sensitive to the basic pricing model and should be handled with care. This issue of not only modeling the underlying, but also modeling what the market does (regardless of whether it is 'correct' or not) will be seen in other parts of this book.

13.9 COMPOUNDS AND CHOOSERS

Compound and **chooser options** are simply options on options. The compound option gives the holder the right to buy (call) or sell (put) another option. Thus we can imagine owning a call on a put, for example. This gives us the right to buy a put option for a specified amount on a specified date. If we exercise the option then we will own a put option which gives us the right to sell the underlying. This compound option is second order because the compound option gives us rights over another derivative. Although the Black–Scholes model can theoretically cope with second-order contracts it is not so clear that the model is completely satisfactory in practice; when we exercise the contract we get an option at the market price, not at our theoretical price.

In the Black–Scholes framework the compound option is priced as follows. There are two steps: first price the underlying option and then price the compound option. Suppose that the underlying option has a payoff of $F(S)$ at time T, and that the compound option can be exercised at time $T_{Co} < T$ to get $G(V(S, T_{Co}))$ where $V(S, t)$ is the value of the underlying option. Step one is to price the underlying option, i.e. to find $V(S, t)$. This satisfies

$$\frac{\partial V}{\partial t} + \tfrac{1}{2}\sigma^2 S^2 \frac{\partial^2 V}{\partial S^2} + rS\frac{\partial V}{\partial S} - rV = 0 \quad \text{with} \quad V(S, T) = F(S).$$

Solve this problem so that you have found $V(S, T_{Co})$. This is the (theoretical) value of the underlying option at time T_{Co}, which is the time at which you can exercise your compound option. Now comes the second step, to value the compound option. The value of this is $Co(S, t)$ which satisfies

$$\frac{\partial Co}{\partial t} + \tfrac{1}{2}\sigma^2 S^2 \frac{\partial^2 Co}{\partial S^2} + rS\frac{\partial Co}{\partial S} - rCo = 0 \quad \text{with} \quad Co(S, T_{Co}) = G(V(S, T_{Co})).$$

As an example, if we have a call on a call with exercise prices E for the underlying and E_{Co} for the compound option, then we have

$$F(S) = \max(S - E, 0) \quad \text{and} \quad G(V) = \max(V - E_{Co}, 0).$$

In Figure 13.3 is shown the value of a vanilla call option at the time of expiry of a put option on this call. This is obviously some time before the expiry of the underlying call. In the same figure is the payoff for the put on this option. This is the final condition for the Black–Scholes partial differential equation.

It is possible to find analytical formulae for the price of basic compound options in the Black–Scholes framework when volatility is constant. These formulae involve the cumulative distribution function for a bivariate Normal variable. However, because of the second-order nature of compound options and thus their sensitivity to the precise nature of the asset price random walk, these formulae are dangerous to use in practice. Practitioners use either a stochastic volatility model or an implied volatility surface, two subjects I cover in later chapters.

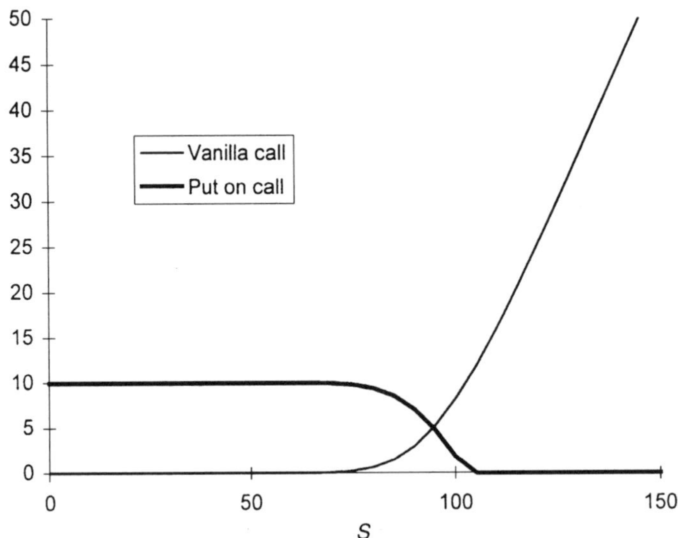

Figure 13.3 The value of a vanilla call option some time before expiry and the payoff for a put on this option.

Chooser options are similar to compounds in that they give the holder the right to buy a further option. With the chooser option the holder can choose whether to receive a call or a put, for example. Generally, we can write the value of the chooser option as $Ch(S,t)$ and the value of the underlying options as $V_1(S,t)$ and $V_2(S,t)$ (or more). Now

$$\frac{\partial Ch}{\partial t}+\tfrac{1}{2}\sigma^2S^2\frac{\partial^2 Ch}{\partial S^2}+rS\frac{\partial Ch}{\partial S}-rCh=0,$$

$$\frac{\partial V_1}{\partial t}+\tfrac{1}{2}\sigma^2S^2\frac{\partial^2 V_1}{\partial S^2}+rS\frac{\partial V_1}{\partial S}-rV_1=0.$$

and

$$\frac{\partial V_2}{\partial t}+\tfrac{1}{2}\sigma^2S^2\frac{\partial^2 V_2}{\partial S^2}+rS\frac{\partial V_2}{\partial S}-rV_2=0$$

Final conditions are the usual payoffs for the underlying options at their expiry dates and

$$Ch(S,T_{Ch})=\max(V_1(S,T_{Ch})-E_1,V_2(S,T_{Ch})-E_2,0),$$

with the obvious notation.

The practical problems with pricing choosers are the same as for compounds.

In Figure 13.4 are shown the values of a vanilla call and a vanilla put some time before expiry. In the same figure is the payoff for a call on the best of these two options (less an exercise price). This is the final condition for the Black–Scholes partial differential equation.

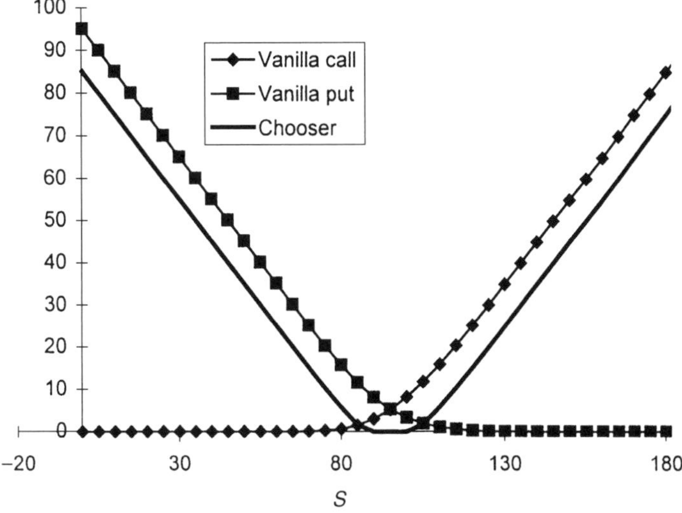

Figure 13.4 The value of a vanilla call option some time before expiry and the payoff for a put on this option.

13.10 RANGE NOTES

Range notes are very popular contracts, existing on the 'lognormal' assets such as equities and currencies, and as fixed-income products. In its basic, equity derivative, form the

6 Month In-Out Range Accrual Option on MXN/USD FX Rate

Settlement Date	One week from Trade Date
Maturity Date	6 months from Trade Date
Option Premium	USD 50,000+
Option Type	In MINUS Out Range Accrual on MXN/USD FX rate
Option Payment Date	2 business days after Maturity Date
Option Payout	USD 125,000* Index
Where Index	
	$\frac{\text{FX daily In MINUS FX daily Out}}{\text{Total Business Days}}$ (subject to a minimum of zero)
FX daily In	The number of business days Spot MXN/USD Exchange Rate is within Range
FX daily Out	The number of business days Spot MXN/USD Exchange Rate is outside Range
Range	MXN/USD 7.7200-8.1300
Spot MXN/USD Exchange Rate	Official spot exchange rate as determined by the Bank of mexico as appearing on Reuters page "BNMX" at approximately 3:00 p.m. New York time.
Current Spot MXN/USD	7.7800

This indicative termsheet is neither an offer to buy or sell securities or an OTC derivative product which includes options, swaps, forwards and structured notes having similar features to OTC derivative transactions, nor a solicitation to buy or sell securities or an OTC derivative product. The proposal contained in the foregoing is not a complete description of the terms of a particular transaction and is subject to change without limitation.

Figure 13.5 Term sheet for an In-out Range Accrual Note on MXN/USD.

range note pays at a rate of L all the time that the underlying lies within a given range, $S_l \le S \le S_u$. That is, for every dt that the asset is in the range you receive $L\,dt$. Introducing $\mathcal{I}(S)$ as the function taking the value 1 when $S_l \le S \le S_u$ and zero otherwise, the range note satisfies

$$\frac{\partial V}{\partial t} + \tfrac{1}{2}\sigma^2 S^2 \frac{\partial^2 V}{\partial S^2} + rS\frac{\partial V}{\partial S} - rV + L\mathcal{I}(S) = 0.$$

In Figure 13.5 is shown the term sheet for a range note on the Mexican peso, US dollar exchange rate. This contract pays out the positive part of the difference between number of days the exchange rate is inside the range less the number of days outside the range. This payment is received at expiry. (This contract is subtly different, and more complicated than the basic range note described above. Why? When you have finished Part Two you should be able to price this contract.)

13.11 BARRIER OPTIONS

Barrier options have a payoff that is contingent on the underlying asset reaching some specified level before expiry. The critical level is called the barrier; there may be more than one. Barrier options are weakly path dependent. Barrier options are discussed in depth in Chapter 14.

Barrier options come in two main varieties, the 'in' barrier option (or **knock-in**) and the 'out' barrier option (or **knock-out**). The former only have a payoff if the barrier level is reached before expiry and the latter only have a payoff if the barrier is *not* reached before expiry. These contracts are weakly path dependent, meaning that the price depends only on the current level of the asset and the time to expiry. They satisfy the Black–Scholes equation, with special boundary conditions as we shall see.

13.12 ASIAN OPTIONS

Asian options have a payoff that depends on the average value of the underlying asset over some period before expiry. They are the first strongly path-dependent contract we examine. They are strongly path dependent because their value prior to expiry depends on the path taken and not just on where they have reached. Their value depends on the *average to date* of the asset. This average to date will be very important to us; we introduce something like it as a new state variable. We shall see how to derive a partial differential equation for the value of this Asian contract, but now the differential equation will have *three* independent variables.

The average used in the calculation of the option's payoff can be defined in many different ways. It can be an arithmetic average or a geometric average, for example. The data could be continuously sampled, so that every realized asset price over the given period is used. More commonly, for practical and legal reasons, the data is usually sampled discretely; the calculated average may only use every Friday's closing price, for example. We shall see in Chapter 16 how to price contracts with a wide range of definitions for the average and with either continuous or discrete sampling.

13.13 LOOKBACK OPTIONS

Lookback options have a payoff that depends on the realized maximum or minimum of the underlying asset over some period prior to expiry. An extreme example that captures the flavour of these contracts is the option that pays off the difference between that maximum realized value of the asset and the minimum value over the next year. Thus it enables the holder to buy at the lowest price and sell at the highest, every trader's dream. Of course, this payoff comes at a price. And for such a contract that price would be very high.

Again the maximum or minimum can be calculated continuously or discretely, using every realized asset price or just a subset. In practice the maximum or minimum is measured discretely.

13.14 SUMMARY

This chapter suggests ways to think about derivative contracts that make their analysis simpler. To be able to make comparisons between different contracts is a big step forward in understanding them. After digesting this, and the next few, chapters, you will be able to tell very quickly whether a particular contract is easy or difficult to price and hedge. And you will know whether the Black–Scholes framework is suitable, or whether it may be dangerous to apply it directly.

In this chapter we also began to look at some rather more complicated contracts than we have seen so far. We examine some of these contracts in depth in the next few chapters, considering them from both a theoretical and a practical viewpoint.

FURTHER READING

- Geske (1979) discusses the valuation of compound options.
- See Taleb (1997) for more details of classifications of the type I have described. This book is an excellent, and entertaining read.
- The book by Zhang (1997) is a discussion of many types of exotic options, with many fomulae. There are, however, so many typos in this book as to make it almost useless. Maybe these errors will be corrected in future printings.[1]

EXERCISES

1. A chooser option has the following properties:

   At time $T_C < T$, the option gives the holder the right to buy a European call or put option with exercise price E and expiry at time T, for an amount E_C. What is the value of this option when $E_C = 0$?

   Hint: Write down the payoff of the option and then use put–call parity to simplify the result.
2. How would we value the chooser option in the above question if E_C was non-zero?
3. Prove put–call parity for European compound options:

$$C_C + P_P - C_P - P_C = S - E_2 e^{-r(T_2-t)},$$

   where C_C is a call on a call, C_P is a call on a put, P_C is a put on a call and P_P is a put on a put. The compound options have exercise price E_1 and expiry at time T_1 and the underlying calls and puts have exercise price E_2 and expiry at time T_2.
4. Find the value of the power European call option. This is an option with exercise price E, expiry at time T, when it has a payoff:

$$\Lambda(S) = \max(S^2 - E, 0).$$

   Hint: Note that if the underlying asset price is assumed to be lognormally distributed then the square of the price is also lognormally distributed.

---

[1] Corrections to errors in my book will be posted on www.wilmott.com.

CHAPTER 14
barrier options

In this Chapter

- the different types of barrier options
- how to price many barrier contracts in the partial differential equation framework
- some of the practical problems with the pricing and hedging of barriers

14.1 INTRODUCTION

I mentioned barrier options briefly in the previous chapter. In this chapter we study them in detail, from both a theoretical and a practical perspective. **Barrier options** are path-dependent options. They have a payoff that is dependent on the realized asset path via its level; certain aspects of the contract are triggered if the asset price becomes too high or too low. For example, an up-and-out call option pays off the usual $\max(S - E, 0)$ at expiry unless at any time previously the underlying asset has traded at a value S_u or higher. In this example, if the asset reaches this level (from below, obviously) then it is said to 'knock out,' becoming worthless. Apart from 'out' options like this, there are also 'in' options which only receive a payoff if a level is reached, otherwise they expire worthless.

Barrier options are popular for a number of reasons. Perhaps the purchaser uses them to hedge very specific cashflows with similar properties. Usually, the purchaser has very precise views about the direction of the market. If he wants the payoff from a call option but does not want to pay for all the upside potential, believing that the upward movement of the underlying will be limited prior to expiry, then he may choose to buy an up-and-out call. It will be cheaper than a similar vanilla call, since the upside is severely limited. If he is right and the barrier is not triggered he gets the payoff he wanted. The closer that the barrier is to the current asset price then the greater the likelihood of the option being knocked out, and thus the cheaper the contract.

Conversely, an 'in' option will be bought by someone who believes that the barrier level will be realized. Again, the option is cheaper than the equivalent vanilla option.

14.2 DIFFERENT TYPES OF BARRIER OPTIONS

There are two main types of barrier option:

- The **out option**, that only pays off if a level is *not* reached. If the barrier is reached then the option is said to have **knocked out**.

- The **in option**, that pays off as long as a level is reached before expiry. If the barrier is reached then the option is said to have **knocked in**.

Then we further characterize the barrier option by the position of the barrier relative to the initial value of the underlying:

- If the barrier is above the initial asset value, we have an **up** option.
- If the barrier is below the initial asset value, we have a **down** option.

Finally, we describe the payoff received at expiry:

- The payoffs are all the usual suspects, call, put, binary, etc.

The above classifies the commonest barrier options. In all of these contracts the position of the barrier could be time dependent. The level may begin at one level and then rise, say. Usually the level is a piecewise-constant function of time.

Another style of barrier option is the **double barrier**. Here there is both an upper and a lower barrier, the first above and the second below the current asset price. In a double 'out' option the contract becomes worthless if *either* of the barriers is reached. In a double 'in' option one of the barriers must be reached before expiry, otherwise the option expires worthless. Other possibilities can be imagined: one barrier is an 'in' and the other an 'out,' at expiry the contract could have either an 'in' or an 'out' payoff.

Sometimes a **rebate** is paid if the barrier level is reached. This is often the case for 'out' barriers in which case the rebate can be thought of as cushioning the blow of losing the rest of the payoff. The rebate may be paid as soon as the barrier is triggered or not until expiry.

USD/MXN Double Knock-Out Note

Principal Amount	USD 10,000,000
Issuer	XXXX
Maturity	6 months from Trade Date
Issue Price	100%
Coupon	If the USD/MXN spot exchange rate trades above the Upper Barrier or below the Lower Barrier at any time during the term of the Note: Zero Otherwise: $400\% \times \max\left(0, \frac{8.2500 - FX}{FX}\right)$ where FX is the USD/MXN spot exchange rate at Maturity
Redemption Amount	100%
Upper Barrier Level	8.2500
Lower Barrier Level	7.4500

This indicative termsheet is neither an offer to buy or sell securities or an OTC derivative product which includes options, swaps, forwards and structured notes having similar features to OTC derivative transactions, nor a solicitation to buy or sell securities or an OTC derivative product. The proposal contained in the foregoing is not a complete description of the terms of a particular transaction and is subject to change without limitation.

Figure 14.1 Term sheet for a USD/MXN Double Knock-out Note.

In Figure 14.1 is shown the term sheet for a double knock-out option on the Mexican peso, US dollar exchange rate. The upper barrier is set at 8.25 and the lower barrier at 7.45. If the exchange rate trades inside this range until expiry then there is a payment. This is a very vanilla example of a barrier contract.

14.3 PRICING BARRIERS IN THE PARTIAL DIFFERENTIAL EQUATION FRAMEWORK

Barrier options are path dependent. Their payoff, and therefore value, depends on the path taken by the asset up to expiry. Yet that dependence is weak. We only have to know whether or not the barrier has been triggered, we do not need any other information about the path. This is in contrast to some of the contracts we will be seeing shortly, such as the Asian option, that are strongly path dependent. I use $V(S, t)$ to denote the value of the barrier contract *before the barrier has been triggered.* This value still satisfies the Black–Scholes equation

$$\frac{\partial V}{\partial t} + \tfrac{1}{2}\sigma^2 S^2 \frac{\partial^2 V}{\partial S^2} + r\frac{\partial V}{\partial S} - rV = 0.$$

The details of the barrier feature come in through the specification of the boundary conditions.

14.3.1 'Out' Barriers

If the underlying asset reaches the barrier in an 'out' barrier option then the contract becomes worthless. This leads to the boundary condition

$$V(S_u, t) = 0 \quad \text{for } t < T,$$

for an up-barrier option with the barrier level at $S = S_u$. We must solve the Black–Scholes equation for $0 \le S \le S_u$ with this condition on $S = S_u$ and a final condition corresponding to the payoff received if the barrier is not triggered. For a call option we would have

$$V(S, T) = \max(S - E, 0).$$

If we have a down-and-out option with a barrier at S_d then we solve for $S_d \le S < \infty$ with

$$V(S_d, t) = 0,$$

and the relevant final condition at expiry.

The boundary conditions are easily changed to accommodate rebates. If a rebate of R is paid when the barrier is hit then

$$V(S_d, t) = R.$$

14.3.2 'In' Barriers

An 'in' option only has a payoff if the barrier is triggered. If the barrier is not triggered then the option expires worthless

$$V(S, T) = 0.$$

The value in the option is in the potential to hit the barrier. If the option is an up-and-in contract then on the upper barrier the contract must have the same value as a vanilla contract:

$$V(S_u, t) = \text{ value of vanilla contract, a function of } t.$$

Using the notation $V_v(S, t)$ for value of the equivalent vanilla contract (a vanilla call, if we have an up-and-in call option) then we must have

$$V(S_u, t) = V_v(S_u, t) \quad \text{for } t < T.$$

A similar boundary condition holds for a down-and-in option.

The contract we receive when the barrier is triggered is a derivative itself, and therefore the 'in' option is a second-order contract.

In solving for the value of an 'in' option completely numerically we must solve for the value of the vanilla option first, before solving for the value of the barrier option. The solution therefore takes roughly twice as long as the solution of the 'out' option.[1]

14.3.3 Some Formulae When Volatility is Constant

When volatility is constant we can solve for the theoretical price of many types of barrier contract. Some examples are given here and lots more can be found at the end of the chapter. (However, such formulae are rarely used in practice for reasons to be discussed below.)

I continue to use $V_v(S, t)$ for the value of the equivalent vanilla contract.

Down-and-out Call Option

As the first example, consider the down-and-out call option with barrier level S_d below the strike price E. The function $V_v(S, t)$ is the Black–Scholes value of a vanilla option with the same maturity and payoff as our barrier option. The value of the down-and-out option is then given by

$$V(S, t) = V_v(S, t) - \left(\frac{S}{S_d}\right)^{1-2r/\sigma^2} V_v(S_d^2/S, t).$$

Let us confirm that this is indeed the solution. First, does it satisfy the Black–Scholes equation? Clearly, the first term on the right-hand side does. The second term does also. Actually, if we have any solution, V_{BS}, of the Black–Scholes equation it is easy to show that

$$S^{1-2r/\sigma^2} V_{BS}(X/S, t)$$

is also a solution for any X.

What about the condition that the option value must be zero on $S = S_d$? Substitute $S = S_d$ in the above to confirm that this is the case. And the final condition? Since $S_d^2/S < E$ for $S > S_d$ the value of $V_v(S_d^2/S, T)$ is zero. Thus the final condition is satisfied.

The value of this option is shown as a function of S in Figure 14.2.

Down-and-in Call Option

In the absence of any rebates the relationship between an 'in' barrier option and an 'out' barrier option (with same payoff and same barrier level) is very simple:

$$\text{in} + \text{out} = \text{vanilla}.$$

If the 'in' barrier is triggered then so is the 'out' barrier, so whether or not the barrier is triggered we still get the vanilla payoff at expiry.

---

[1] And, of course, the vanilla option must be solved for $0 \le S < \infty$.

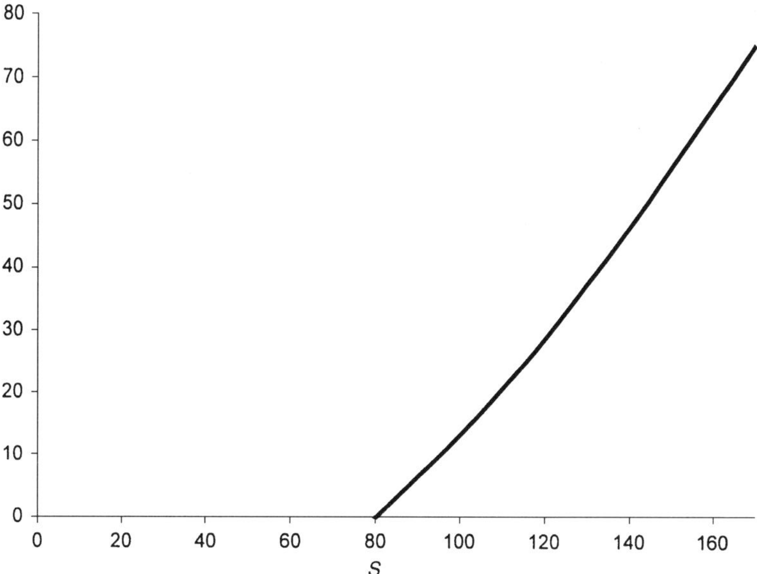

Figure 14.2 Value of a down-and-out call option.

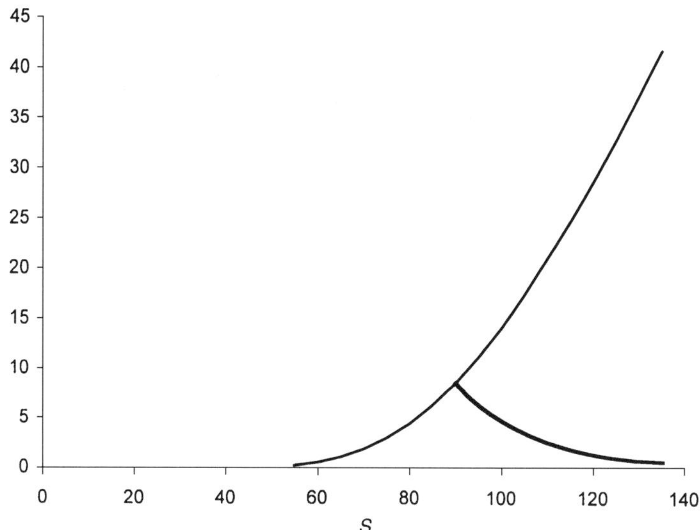

Figure 14.3 Value of a down-and-in call option.

Thus, the value of a down-and-in call option is

$$V(S,t) = \left(\frac{S}{S_d}\right)^{1-2r/\sigma^2} V_v(S_d^2/S, t).$$

The value of this option is shown as a function of S in Figure 14.3. Also shown is the value of the vanilla call. Note that the two values coincide at the barrier.

Up-and-out Call Option

The barrier S_u for an up-and-out call option must be above the strike price E (otherwise the option would be valueless). This makes the solution for the price more complicated, and I just quote it here. The value of an up-and-in call option is

$$S\left(N(d_1) - N(d_3) - b(N(d_6) - N(d_8))\right) - Ee^{-r(T-t)}\left(N(d_2) - N(d_4) - a(N(d_5) - N(d_7))\right),$$

where $N(\cdot)$ is the cumulative distribution function for a standardized Normal variable and a, b and the ds are given at the end of the chapter.

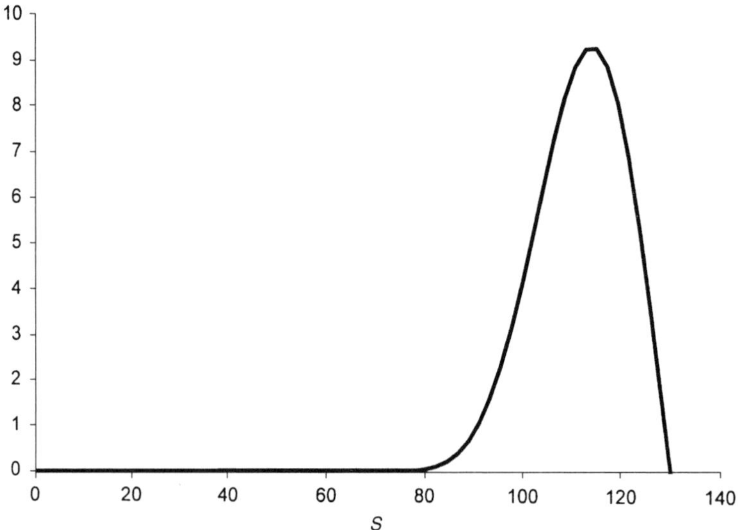

Figure 14.4 Value of an up-and-out call option.

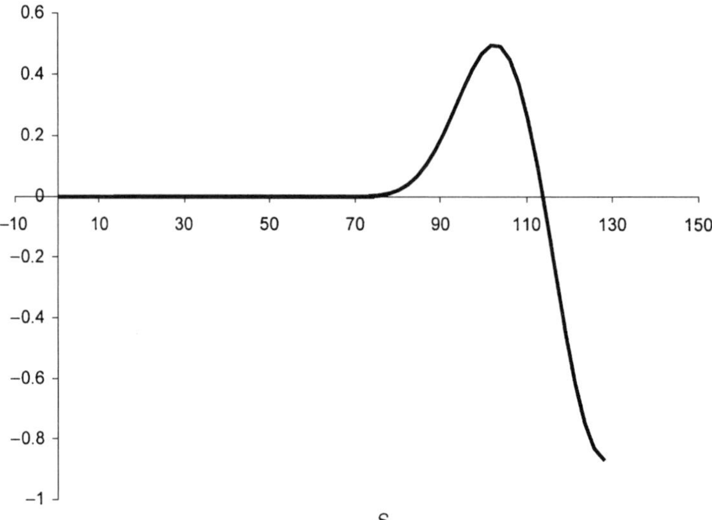

Figure 14.5 Delta of an up-and-out call option.

The value of this option is shown as a function of S in Figure 14.4. In Figure 14.5 is shown the delta.

Formulae can be found for many barrier options (assuming volatility is constant). When there are two barriers the solution can often be found by Fourier series (see Chapter 6).

14.4 OTHER FEATURES IN BARRIER-STYLE OPTIONS

Not so long ago barrier options were exotic, the market for them was small and few people were comfortable pricing them. Nowadays they are heavily traded and it is only the contracts with more unusual features that can rightly be called exotic. Some of these features are described below.

14.4.1 Early Exercise

It is possible to have American-style early exercise. The contract must specify what the payoff is if the contract is exercised before expiry. As always, early exercise is a simple constraint on the value of the option.

In Figure 14.6 is the term sheet for a Knock-out Instalment Premium Option on the US dollar, Japanese yen exchange rate. This knocks out if the exchange rate ever goes above 140. If the option expires without ever hitting this level there is a vanilla call payoff. I mention this contract in the section on early exercise because it has a similar feature. To keep the contract alive the

USD/JPY KO Instalment-Premium Option

Notional Amount	USD 50,000,000
Option Type	133.25 (ATMS) USD Put/JPY Call with KO and Instalment Premium
Maturity	6 months from Trade Date
Knockout Mechanism	If, at any time from Trade Date to Maturity, the USD/JPY spot rate trades in the interbank market at or above JPY 140.00 per USD, the option will automatically be cancelled, with no further rights or obligations arising for the parties thereto.
Upfront Premium	JPY 1.50 per USD
Instalments	JPY 1.50 per USD, payable monthly from Trade Date (5 instalments)
Instalment Mechanism	As long as the instalments continue to be paid, the option will be kept alive, but the Counterparty has the right to cease paying the instalments and to thereby let the option be cancelled at any time.
Spot Reference	JPY 133.25 per USD

This indicative termsheet is neither an offer to buy or sell securities or an OTC derivative product which includes options, swaps, forwards and structured notes having similar features to OTC derivative transactions, nor a solicitation to buy or sell securities or an OTC derivative product. The proposal contained in the foregoing is not a complete description of the terms of a particular transaction and is subject to change without limitation.

Figure 14.6 Terms sheet for a USD/JPY Knock-out Instalment Premium Option.

holder must pay in instalments, every month another payment is due. We saw this instalment feature in Chapter 9 where it was likened to American exercise. The question is when to stop paying the instalments? This can be done optimally.

14.4.2 The Intermittent Barrier

The position of the barrier(s) can be time-dependent. A more extreme version of a time-dependent barrier is to have a barrier that disappears altogether for specified time periods. These options are called **protected** or **partial** barrier options. An example is shown in Figure 14.7.

There are two types of such contract. In one the barrier is triggered as long as the asset price is beyond the barrier on days on which the barrier is active. The solution of this problem is shown schematically in Figure 14.8.

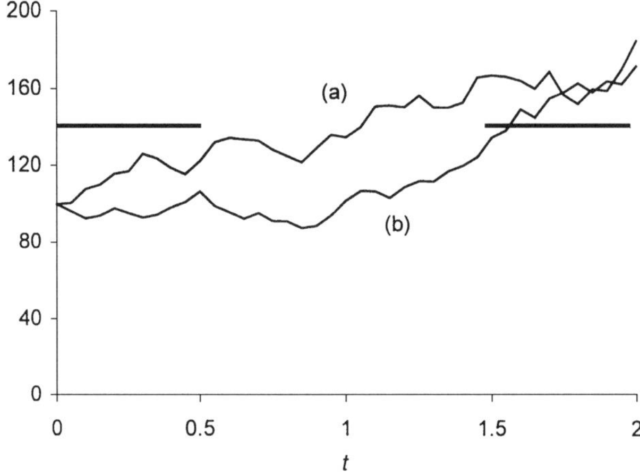

Figure 14.7 The intermittent barrier. Two varieties: barrier triggered if asset outside barrier on active days; barrier only triggered by asset price crossing barrier.

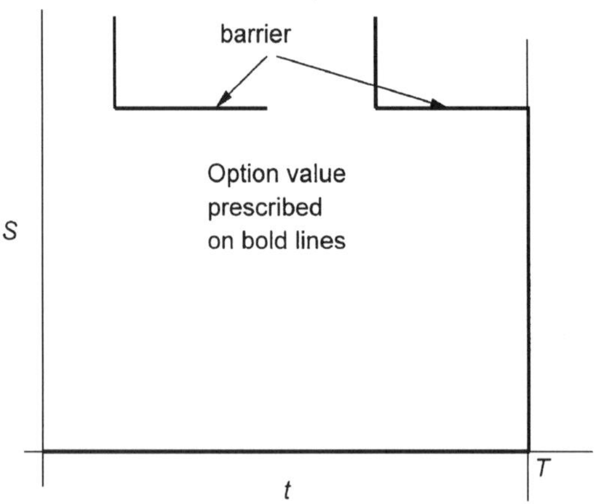

Figure 14.8 The intermittent barrier: barrier triggered if asset outside barrier on active days. Solution procedure.

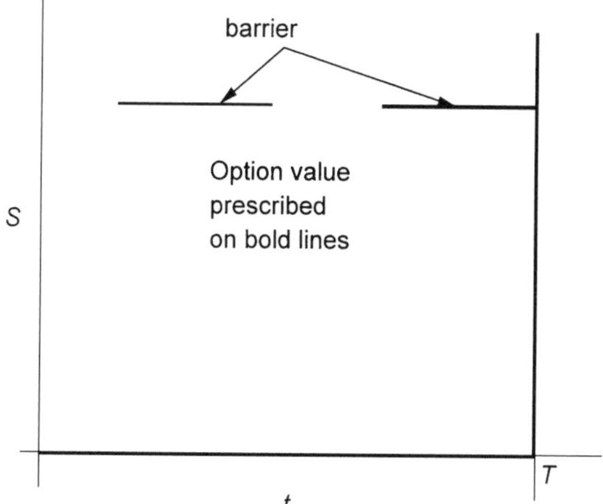

Figure 14.9 The intermittent barrier: barrier only triggered by asset price crossing barrier. Solution procedure.

The second type of intermittent barrier is only triggered if the asset path crosses the barrier on an active day. The barrier will not be triggered if the asset weaves its way through the barriers. The solution of this problem is shown schematically in Figure 14.9.

14.4.3 Repeated Hitting of the Barrier

The double barrier that we have seen above can be made more complicated. Instead of only requiring one hit of either barrier we could insist that *both* barriers are hit before the barrier is triggered.

This contract is easy to value. Observe that the first time that one of the barriers is hit the contract becomes a vanilla barrier option. Thus on the two barriers we solve the Black–Scholes equation with boundary conditions that our double barrier value is equal to an up-barrier option on the lower barrier and a down-barrier option on the upper barrier.

In Chapter 18 we will see the related Parisian option, the payoff of which depends on the time that the asset has been beyond the barrier.

14.4.4 Resetting of Barrier

Another type of barrier contract that can be priced by the same two- (or more) step procedure as 'in' barriers is the reset barrier. When the barrier is hit the contract turns into another barrier option with a different barrier level. The contract may be time dependent in the sense that if the barrier is hit before a certain time we get a new barrier option, if it is hit after a certain time we get the vanilla payoff.

Related to these contracts are the **roll-up** and **roll-down options**. These begin life as vanilla options, but if the asset reaches some predefined level they become a barrier option. For example, with a roll-up put, if the roll-up strike level is reached the contract becomes an up-and-out put with the roll-up strike being the strike of the barrier put. The barrier level will then be at a prespecified level.

14.4.5 Outside Barrier Options

Outside or **rainbow barrier options** have payoffs or a trigger feature that depends on a second underlying. Thus the barrier might be triggered by one asset, with the payoff depending on the other. These products are clearly multi-factor contracts.

14.5 FIRST EXIT TIME

The path dependency in a barrier option arises because the option payoff depends on whether or not the barrier has been triggered. The *value* can be interpreted as the present value of the risk-neutral expected payoff but the likelihood of the barrier being triggered before expiry only has meaning if we calculate the probability using the *real* random walk for the asset. For an up-and-in barrier option, the probability of the barrier being triggered before expiry, $Q(S, t)$, is given by the solution of

$$\frac{\partial Q}{\partial t} + \tfrac{1}{2}\sigma^2 S^2 \frac{\partial^2 Q}{\partial S^2} + \mu S \frac{\partial Q}{\partial S} = 0$$

with

$$Q(S, T) = 0 \quad \text{and} \quad Q(S_u, t) = 1,$$

as discussed in Chapter 10. Because we are using the real process for S this problem contains the real drift rate μ. The expected time $u(S)$ before the level S_u is hit from below is the solution of

$$\tfrac{1}{2}\sigma^2 S^2 \frac{d^2 u}{dS^2} + \mu S \frac{du}{dS} = -1$$

i.e.

$$\frac{1}{\tfrac{1}{2}\sigma^2 - \mu} \log\left(\frac{S}{S_u}\right),$$

but only for $2\mu > \sigma^2$. If $2\mu < \sigma^2$ then the expected first exit time is infinite.

Calculations like these can be used by the speculator who has a view on the direction of the underlying, believing that the barrier will or will not be triggered. His view can be quantified as a probability, for example. Or he can determine whether the first exit time is greater or less than the remaining time to maturity.

The hedger will also find such calculations useful. As we discuss below, delta hedging barrier options is notoriously difficult and usually they are statically hedged as well to some extent. The choice of the static hedge may be influenced by the *real* time at which the barrier is expected to be triggered.

14.6 MARKET PRACTICE: WHAT VOLATILITY SHOULD I USE?

Practitioners do not price contracts using a single, constant volatility. Let us see some of the pitfalls with this, and then see what practitioners do.

In Figure 14.10 we see a plot of the value of an up-and-out call option using three different volatilities, 15%, 20% and 25%. I have chosen three very different values to make a point. If we are unsure about the value of the volatility (as we

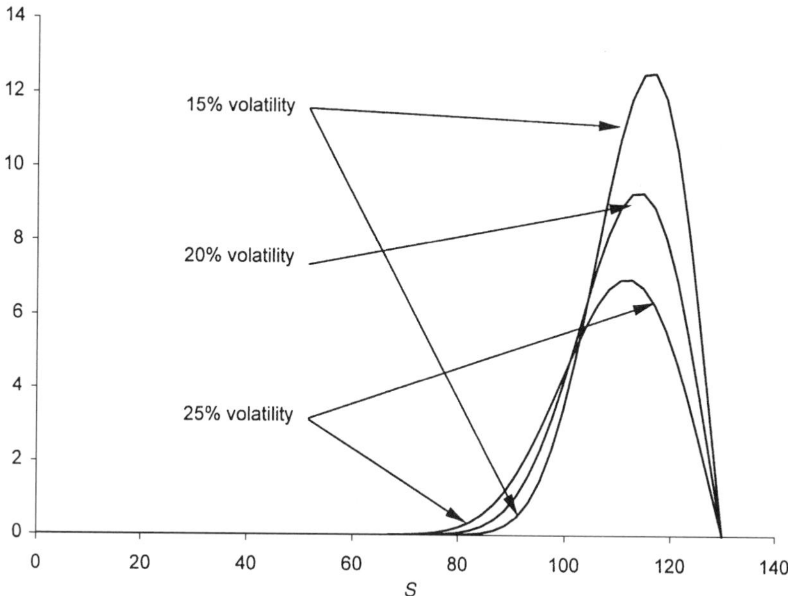

Figure 14.10 Theoretical up-and-out call price with three different volatilities.

surely are) then which value do we use to price the contract? Observe that at approximately $S = 100$ the option value seems to be insensitive to the volatility, the vega is zero. If S is greater than this value perhaps we should only sell the contract for a volatility of 15% to be on the safe side. If S is less than this, perhaps we should sell the contract for 25%, again to play it safe. Now ask the question, do I believe that volatility will be one of 15%, 20% or 25%, and will be fixed at that level? Or do I believe that volatility could move around between 15% and 25%? Clearly the latter is closer to the truth. But the measurement of vega, and the plots in Figure 14.10 assume that volatility is fixed until expiry. If we are concerned with playing it safe we should assume that the behavior of volatility will be that which gives us the lowest value if we are buying the contract. The worst outcome for volatility is for it to be low around the strike price, and high around the barrier. Financially, this means that if we are near the strike we get a small payoff, but if we are near the barrier we are likely to hit it. Mathematically, the 'worst' choice of volatility path depends on the sign of the gamma at each point. If gamma is positive then low volatility is bad; if gamma is negative then high volatility is bad. A better way to price options when the volatility is uncertain is described in Chapter 24. When the gamma is not single signed, the measurement of vega can be meaningless. Barrier options with non-single-signed gamma include the up-and-out call, down-and-out put and many double-barrier options.

To accommodate problems like this, practitioners have invented a number of 'patches.' One is to use two different volatilities in the option price. For example, one can calculate implied volatilities from vanilla options with the same strike, expiry and payoff as the barrier option and also from American-style one-touch options with the strike at the barrier level. The implied volatility from the vanilla option contains the market's estimate of the value of the payoff, but including all the upside potential that the call has but which is irrelevant for the up-and-out option. The one-touch volatility, however, contains the market's view of the likelihood of the barrier level being reached. These two volatilities can be used to price an up-and-out call by observing that an 'out' option is the same as a vanilla minus an 'in' option. Use the vanilla volatility to price the vanilla call and the one-touch volatility to price the 'in' call.

The other practitioner approach to the pricing is to use a volatility surface, implied from market prices of all traded vanilla contracts. This is then employed in a binomial tree or finite-difference scheme to price the barrier option *consistently* across instruments. This is the subject of Chapter 22.

14.7 HEDGING BARRIER OPTIONS

Barrier options have discontinuous delta at the barrier. For a knock-out, the option value is continuous, decreasing approximately linearly towards the barrier then being zero beyond the barrier. This discontinuity in the delta means that the gamma is instantaneously infinite at the barrier. Delta hedging through the barrier is virtually impossible, and certainly very costly. This raises the issue of whether there are improvements on delta hedging for barrier options.

There have been a number of suggestions made for ways to *statically* hedge barrier options. These methods try to mimic as closely as possible the value of a barrier option with vanilla calls and puts, or with binary options. In Chapter 30 I describe a couple of ways of statically hedging barrier options with traded vanilla options. A very common practice for hedging a short up-and-out call is to buy a long call with the same strike and expiry. If the option does knock out then you are fortunate in being left with a long call position.

I now describe another simple but useful technique, based on the **reflection principle** and **put–call symmetry**. This technique only really works if the barrier and strike lie in the correct order, as we shall see. The method gives an approximate hedge only.

The simplest example of put–call symmetry is actually put–call parity. At all asset levels we have

$$V_C - V_P = S - Ee^{-r(T-t)},$$

where E is the strike of the two options, and C and P refer to call and put. Suppose we have a down-and-in call, how can we use this result? To make things simple for the moment, let's have the barrier and the strike at the same level. Now hedge our down-and-in call with a short position in a vanilla put with the same strike. If the barrier is reached we have a position worth

$$V_C - V_P.$$

The first term is from the down-and-in call and the second from the vanilla put. This is exactly the same as

$$S - Ee^{-r(T-t)} = E(1 - e^{-r(T-t)}),$$

because of put–call parity and since the barrier and the strike are the same. If the barrier is not touched then both options expire worthless. If the interest rate were zero then we would have a perfect hedge. If rates are non-zero what we are left with is a one-touch option with small and time-dependent value on the barrier. Although this leftover cashflow is non-zero, it is small, bounded and more manageable than the original cashflows.

Now suppose that the strike and the barrier are distinct. Let us continue with the down-and-in call, now with barrier below the strike. The static hedge is not much more complicated than the previous example. All we need to know is the relationship between the value of a call option with strike E when $S = S_d$ and a put option with strike S_d^2/E. It is easy to show from the formulae for calls and puts that if interest rates are zero, the value of this call at $S = S_d$ is equal to a number E/S_d of the puts, valued at S_d. We would therefore hedge our down-and-in call with E/S_d puts struck at S_d^2/E. Note that the geometric average of the strike of the call and the strike of the put is the same as the barrier level. This is where the idea of 'reflection' comes in. The strike of the hedging put is at the reflection in the barrier of the call's strike. When rates are non-zero there is some error in this hedge, but again it is small and manageable, decreasing as we get closer to expiry. If the barrier is not touched then both options expire worthless (the strike of the put is below the barrier remember).

If the barrier level is above the strike, matters are more complicated since if the barrier is touched we get an in-the-money call. The reflection principle does not work because the put would also be in the money at expiry if the barrier is not touched.

14.8 SUMMARY

In this chapter we have seen a description of many types of barrier option. We have seen how to put these contracts into the partial differential equation framework. Many of these contracts have simple pricing formulae. Unfortunately, the extreme nature of these contracts make them very difficult to hedge in practice and in particular, they can be very sensitive to the volatility of the underlying. Worse still, if the gamma of the contract changes sign we cannot play safe by adding a spread to the volatility. Practitioners seem to be most comfortable statically hedging as much of the barrier contract as possible using traded vanilla options and pricing the residual using a full implied volatility surface. The combination of these two principles is crucial. If one were to use a volatility surface without statically hedging then one could make matters worse, the volatility surface implied from vanillas may turn out to give the barrier option an inaccurate value. Less dangerous, but still not ideal, is the static hedging of the barrier option with vanillas and then using a single volatility to price the barrier. If both of these concepts are used together there is an element of consistency across the pricing.

MORE FORMULAE

In the following I use $N(\cdot)$ to denote the cumulative distribution function for a standardized Normal variable. Also

$$a = \left(\frac{S_b}{S}\right)^{-1+2r/\sigma^2},$$

$$b = \left(\frac{S_b}{S}\right)^{1+2r/\sigma^2},$$

where S_b is the barrier position (whether S_u or S_d should be obvious from the example),

$$d_1 = \frac{\log(S/E) + \left(r + \frac{1}{2}\sigma^2\right)(T-t)}{\sigma\sqrt{T-t}},$$

$$d_2 = \frac{\log(S/E) + \left(r - \frac{1}{2}\sigma^2\right)(T-t)}{\sigma\sqrt{T-t}},$$

$$d_3 = \frac{\log(S/S_b) + \left(r - \frac{1}{2}\sigma^2\right)(T-t)}{\sigma\sqrt{T-t}},$$

$$d_4 = \frac{\log(S/S_b) + \left(r + \frac{1}{2}\sigma^2\right)(T-t)}{\sigma\sqrt{T-t}},$$

$$d_5 = \frac{\log(S/S_b) - \left(r + \frac{1}{2}\sigma^2\right)(T-t)}{\sigma\sqrt{T-t}},$$

$$d_6 = \frac{\log(S/S_b) - \left(r - \frac{1}{2}\sigma^2\right)(T-t)}{\sigma\sqrt{T-t}},$$

$$d_7 = \frac{\log(SE/S_b^2) - \left(r - \frac{1}{2}\sigma^2\right)(T-t)}{\sigma\sqrt{T-t}},$$

$$d_8 = \frac{\log(SE/S_b^2) - \left(r + \frac{1}{2}\sigma^2\right)(T-t)}{\sigma\sqrt{T-t}}.$$

Up-and-out Call

$$S\left(N(d_1) - N(d_3) - b(N(d_6) - N(d_8))\right) - Ee^{-r(T-t)}\left(N(d_2) - N(d_4) - a(N(d_5) - N(d_7))\right).$$

Up-and-in Call

$$S\left(N(d_3) + b(N(d_6) - N(d_8))\right) - Ee^{-r(T-t)}\left(N(d_4) + a(N(d_5) - N(d_7))\right).$$

Down-and-out Call

1. $E > S_b$:

$$S\left(N(d_1) - b(1 - N(d_8))\right) - Ee^{-r(T-t)}\left(N(d_2) - a(1 - N(d_7))\right).$$

2. $E < S_b$:

$$S\left(N(d_3) - b(1 - N(d_6))\right) - Ee^{-r(T-t)}\left(N(d_4) - a(1 - N(d_5))\right).$$

Down-and-in Call

1. $E > S_b$:

$$Sb(1 - N(d_8)) - Ee^{-r(T-t)}a(1 - N(d_7)).$$

2. $E < S_b$:

$$S\left(N(d_1) - N(d_3) + b(1 - N(d_6))\right) - Ee^{-r(T-t)}\left(N(d_2) - N(d_4) + a(1 - N(d_5))\right).$$

Down-and-out Put

$$Ee^{-r(T-t)}\left(N(d_4) - N(d_2) - a(N(d_7) - N(d_5))\right) - S\left(N(d_3) - N(d_1) - b(N(d_8) - N(d_6))\right).$$

Down-and-in Put

$$Ee^{-r(T-t)}\left(1 - N(d_4) + a(N(d_7) - N(d_5))\right) - S\left(1 - N(d_3) + b(N(d_8) - N(d_6))\right).$$

Up-and-out Put

1. $E > S_b$:

$$Ee^{-r(T-t)}\left(1 - N(d_2) - a(N(d_7) - N(d_5))\right) - S\left(1 - N(d_1) - bN(d_8)\right).$$

2. $E < S_b$:

$$Ee^{-r(T-t)}\left(1 - N(d_4) - aN(d_7)\right) - S\left(1 - N(d_3) - bN(d_6)\right).$$

Up-and-in Put

1. $E > S_b$:

$$Ee^{-r(T-t)}\left(N(d_4) - N(d_2) + aN(d_5)\right) - S\left(N(d_3) - N(d_1) + bN(d_6)\right).$$

2. $E < S_b$:

$$Ee^{-r(T-t)}\left(1 - N(d_4) - aN(d_5)\right) - S\left(1 - N(d_3) - bN(d_6)\right).$$

FURTHER READING

- The formulae above are explained in Taleb (1997). He discusses barrier options in great detail, including the reality of hedging that I have only touched upon.
- The article by Carr (1995) contains an extensive literature review as well as a detailed discussion of protected barrier options and rainbow barrier options.
- See Derman, Ergener & Kani (1997) for a full description of the static replication of barrier options with vanilla options.
- See Carr (1994) for more details of put–call symmetry.

EXERCISES

1. Check that the solution for the down-and-out call option, $V_{D/O}$, satisfies Black–Scholes, where

$$V_{D/O}(S,t) = C(S,t) - \left(\frac{S}{S_d}\right)^{1-2r/\sigma^2} C(S_d^2/S, t),$$

and $C(S,t)$ is the value of a vanilla call option with the same maturity and payoff as the barrier option.

Hint: Show that $S^{1-2r/\sigma^2}V(X^2/S,t)$ satisfies Black–Scholes for any X, when $V(S,t)$ satisfies Black–Scholes.

2. Why do we need the condition $S_d < E$ to be able to value a down-and-out call by adding together known solutions of Black–Scholes equation (as in Question 1)? How would we value the option in the case that $S_d > E$?
3. Check the value for the down-and-in call option using the explicit solutions for the down-and-out call and the vanilla call option.
4. Formulate the following problem for the accrual barrier option as a Black–Scholes partial differential equation with appropriate final and boundary conditions:

The option has barriers at levels S_u and S_d, above and below the initial asset price, respectively. If the asset touches either barrier before expiry then the option knocks out with an immediate payoff of $\Phi(T - t)$. Otherwise, at expiry the option has a payoff of $\max(S - E, 0)$.

5. Formulate the following barrier option pricing problems as partial differential equations with suitable boundary and final conditions:

   (a) The option has barriers at levels S_u and S_d, above and below the initial asset price, respectively. If the asset touches both barriers before expiry, then the option has payoff $\max(S - E, 0)$. Otherwise the option does not pay out.

   (b) The option has barriers at levels S_u and S_d, above and below the initial asset price, respectively. If the asset price first rises to S_u and then falls to S_d before expiry, then the option pays out \$1 at expiry.

6. Price the following double-knockout option. The option has barriers at levels S_u and S_d, above and below the initial asset price, respectively. The option has payoff \$1, unless the asset touches either barrier before expiry, in which case the option knocks out and has no payoff.

7. Prove put–call parity for simple barrier options:

$$C_{D/O} + C_{D/I} - P_{D/O} - P_{D/I} = S - Ee^{-r(T-t)},$$

   where $C_{D/O}$ is a European down-and-out call, $C_{D/I}$ is a European down-and-in call, $P_{D/O}$ is a European down-and-out put and $P_{D/I}$ is a European down-and-in put, all with expiry at time T and exercise price E.

8. Why might we prefer to treat a European up-and-out call option as a portfolio of a vanilla European call option and a European up-and-in call option?

CHAPTER 15

strongly path-dependent options

In this Chapter...

- strong path dependence
- pricing many strongly path-dependent contracts in the Black–Scholes partial differential equation framework
- how to handle both continuously-sampled and discretely-sampled paths
- jump conditions for differential equations

15.1 INTRODUCTION

To be able to turn the valuation of a derivative contract into the solution of a partial differential equation is a big step forward. The partial differential equation approach is one of the best ways to price a contract because of its flexibility and because of the large body of knowledge that has grown up around the fast and accurate numerical solution of these problems. This body of knowledge was, in the main, based around the solution of differential equations arising in physical applied mathematics but is starting to be used in the financial world.

In this chapter I show how to generalize the Black–Scholes analysis, delta hedging and no arbitrage, to the pricing of many more derivative contracts, specifically contracts that are strongly path dependent. I will describe the theory in the abstract, giving brief examples occasionally, but saving the detailed application to specific contracts until later chapters.

15.2 PATH-DEPENDENT QUANTITIES REPRESENTED BY AN INTEGRAL

We start by assuming that the underlying asset follows the lognormal random walk

$$dS = \mu S\,dt + \sigma S\,dX$$

IMPORTANT

Imagine a contract that pays off at expiry, T, an amount that is a function of the path taken by the asset between time zero and expiry. Let us suppose that this path-dependent quantity can be represented by an integral of some function of the asset over the period zero to T:

$$I(T) = \int_0^T f(S, \tau)\,d\tau.$$

This is not such a strong assumption; in particular most of the path-dependent quantities in exotic derivative contracts, such as averages, can be written in this form with a suitable choice of $f(S, t)$.

We are thus assuming that the payoff is given by

$$P(S, I)$$

at time $t = T$.

Prior to expiry we have information about the possible final value of S (at time T) in the present value of S (at time t). For example, the higher S is today, the higher it will probably end up at expiry. Similarly, we have information about the possible final value of I in the value of the integral to date:

$$I(t) = \int_0^t f(S, \tau)\, d\tau \tag{15.1}$$

As we get closer to expiry, so we become more confident about the final value of I.

One can imagine that the value of the option is therefore not only a function of S and t, but also a function of I; I will be our new independent variable, called a **state variable**. We see in the next section how this observation leads to a pricing equation. In anticipation of an argument that will use Itô's lemma, we need to know the stochastic differential equation satisfied by I. This could not be simpler. Incrementing t by dt in (15.1) we find that

$$dI = f(S, t)\, dt. \tag{15.2}$$

Observe that I is a smooth function (except at discontinuities of f) and from (15.2) we can see that its stochastic differential equation contains no stochastic terms.

Examples

An Asian option has a payoff that depends on the average of the asset price over some period. If that period is from time zero to expiry and the average is arithmetic then we write

$$I = \int_0^t S\, d\tau.$$

The payoff may then be, for example,

$$\max\left(\frac{I}{T} - S, 0\right).$$

This would be an average strike put, of which more later.

If the average is geometric then we write

$$I = \int_0^t \log(S)\, d\tau.$$

As another example, imagine a contract that pays off a function of the square of the underlying asset, but only counts those times for which the asset is below S_u. We write

$$I = \int_0^t S^2 \mathcal{H}(S_u - S)\, d\tau,$$

where $\mathcal{H}(\cdot)$ is the Heaviside function.

We are now ready to price some options.

15.3 CONTINUOUS SAMPLING: THE PRICING EQUATION

I will derive the pricing partial differential equation for a contract that pays some function of our new variable I. The value of the contract is now a function of the three variables, $V(S, I, t)$. Set up a portfolio containing one of the path-dependent option and short a number Δ of the underlying asset:

$$\Pi = V(S, I, t) - \Delta S.$$

The change in the value of this portfolio is given by

$$d\Pi = \left(\frac{\partial V}{\partial t} + \tfrac{1}{2}\sigma^2 S^2 \frac{\partial^2 V}{\partial S^2} \right) dt + \frac{\partial V}{\partial I} dI + \left(\frac{\partial V}{\partial S} - \Delta \right) dS.$$

Choosing

$$\Delta = \frac{\partial V}{\partial S}$$

to hedge the risk, and using (15.2), we find that

$$d\Pi = \left(\frac{\partial V}{\partial t} + \tfrac{1}{2}\sigma^2 S^2 \frac{\partial^2 V}{\partial S^2} + f(S, t) \frac{\partial V}{\partial I} \right) dt.$$

This change is risk free, thus earns the risk-free rate of interest r, leading to the pricing equation

$$\frac{\partial V}{\partial t} + \tfrac{1}{2}\sigma^2 S^2 \frac{\partial^2 V}{\partial S^2} + f(S, t) \frac{\partial V}{\partial I} + rS \frac{\partial V}{\partial S} - rV = 0 \qquad (15.3)$$

This is to be solved subject to

$$V(S, I, T) = P(S, I).$$

The obvious changes can be made to accommodate dividends on the underlying. This completes the formulation of the valuation problem.

Example

Continuing with the arithmetic Asian example, we have

$$I = \int_0^t S \, d\tau,$$

so that the equation to be solved is

$$\frac{\partial V}{\partial t} + \tfrac{1}{2}\sigma^2 S^2 \frac{\partial^2 V}{\partial S^2} + S \frac{\partial V}{\partial I} + rS \frac{\partial V}{\partial S} - rV = 0.$$

15.4 PATH-DEPENDENT QUANTITIES REPRESENTED BY AN UPDATING RULE

For practical and legal reasons path-dependent quantities are never measured continuously. There is minimum timestep between sampling of the path-dependent quantity. This timestep may be small, one day, say, or much longer. From a practical viewpoint it is difficult to incorporate every single traded price into an average, for example. Data can be unreliable and the exact time of a trade may not be known accurately. From a legal point of view, to avoid disagreements over the value of the path-dependent quantity, it is usual to only use key prices, such as closing prices, that are, in a sense, guaranteed to be a genuine traded price. If the time between samples is small we can confidently use a continuous-sampling model, the error will be small. If the time between samples is long, or the time to expiry itself is short we must build this into our model. This is the goal of this section.

I introduce the idea of an **updating rule**, an algorithm for defining the path-dependent quantity in terms of the current 'state of the world.' The path-dependent quantity is measured on the **sampling dates** t_i, and takes the value I_i for $t_i \leq t < t_{i+1}$. At the sampling date t_i the quantity I_{i-1} is updated according to a rule such as

$$I_i = F(S(t_i), I_{i-1}, i).$$

Note how, in this simplest example (which can be generalized), the new value of I is determined by only the old value of I and the value of the underlying on the sampling date, and the sampling date.

When we come to concrete examples, as next, I shall change notation and use names for variables that are meaningful. I hope this does not cause any confusion.

Examples

We saw how to use the continuous running integral in the valuation of Asian options. But what if that integral is replaced by a discrete sum? In practice, the payoff for an Asian option depends on the quantity

$$I_M = \sum_{k=1}^{M} S(t_k),$$

where M is the total number of sampling dates. This is the discretely sampled sum. A more natural quantity to consider is

$$A_M = \frac{I_M}{M} = \frac{1}{M} \sum_{k=1}^{M} S(t_k), \tag{15.4}$$

because then the payoff for the discretely-sampled arithmetic average strike put is

$$\max(A_M - S, 0).$$

Can we write (15.4) in terms of an updating rule? Yes, easily: if we write

$$A_i = \frac{1}{i} \sum_{k=1}^{i} S(t_k)$$

then we have

$$A_1 = S(t_1), \quad A_2 = \frac{S(t_1) + S(t_2)}{2} = \tfrac{1}{2}A_1 + \tfrac{1}{2}S(t_2),$$

$$A_3 = \frac{S(t_1) + S(t_2) + S(t_3)}{3} = \frac{2}{3}A_2 + \frac{1}{3}S(t_3), \ldots$$

or generally

$$A_i = \frac{1}{i}S(t_i) + \frac{i-1}{i}A_{i-1}.$$

We will see how to use this for pricing in the next section. But first, another example.

The lookback option has a payoff that depends on the maximum or minimum of the realized asset price. If the payoff depends on the maximum sampled at times t_i then we have

$$I_1 = S(t_1), \quad I_2 = \max(S(t_2), I_1), \quad I_3 = \max(S(t_3), I_2) \ldots.$$

The updating rule is therefore simply

$$I_i = \max(S(t_i), I_{i-1}).$$

In Chapter 17, where we consider lookbacks in detail, we use the notation M_i for minimum or maximum.

How do we use these updating rules in the pricing of derivatives?

15.5 DISCRETE SAMPLING: THE PRICING EQUATION

Following the continuous-sampling case we can anticipate that the option value will be a function of three variables, $V(S, I, t)$. We derive the pricing equation in a heuristic fashion. The derivation can be made more rigorous, but there is little point since the conclusion is correct and so obvious.

The first step in the derivation is the observation that the stochastic differential equation for I is degenerate:

$$dI = 0.$$

This is because the variable I can only change at the discrete set of dates t_i. This is true if $t \neq t_i$ for any i. So provided we are not *on* a sampling date the quantity I is constant, the stochastic differential equation for I reflects this, and the pricing equation is simply the basic Black–Scholes equation:

$$\frac{\partial V}{\partial t} + \tfrac{1}{2}\sigma^2 S^2 \frac{\partial^2 V}{\partial S^2} + rS\frac{\partial V}{\partial S} - rV = 0.$$

Remember, though, that V is still a function of *three* variables; I is effectively treated as a parameter.

How does the equation know about the path dependency? What happens *at* a sampling date?

The answer to the latter question gives us the answer to the former. Across a sampling date nothing much happens. Across a sampling date the option value stays the same. As we get closer and closer to the sampling date we become more and more sure about the value that I will take according to the updating rule. Since the outcome on the sampling date is known and since *no money changes hands* there cannot be any jump in the value of the option. This is a simple application of the no arbitrage principle.

Across a sampling date the option value is continuous. If we introduce the notation t_i^- to mean the time infinitesimally before the sampling date t_i and t_i^+ to mean infinitesimally just after the sampling date, then continuity of the option value is represented mathematically by

$$V(S, I_{i-1}, t_i^-) = V(S, I_i, t_i^+).$$

In terms of the updating rule, we have

$$V(S, I, t_i^-) = V(S, F(S, I, i), t_i^+)$$

This is called a **jump condition**.

We call this a jump condition even though there is no jump in this case. When money does change hands on a special date there will be a sudden change in the value of the option at that time, as discussed in Chapter 13. If we follow the path of S in time we see that it is continuous. However, the path for I is discontinuous. There is a deterministic jump in I across the sampling date. If we were to plot V as a function of S and I just before and just after the sampling date we would see that *for fixed S and I* the option price would be discontinuous. But this plot would have to be interpreted correctly; $V(S, I, t)$ may be discontinuous as a function of S and I but V is continuous along each *realized* path of S and I.

Examples

To price an arithmetic Asian option with the average sampled at times t_i solve the Black–Scholes equation for $V(S, A, t)$ with

$$V(S, A, t_i^-) = V\left(S, \frac{i-1}{i}A + \frac{1}{i}S, t_i^+\right),$$

and a suitable final condition representing the payoff.

To price a lookback depending on the maximum sampled at times t_i solve the Black–Scholes equation for $V(S, M, t)$ with

$$V(S, M, t_i^-) = V(S, \max(S, M), t_i^+). \tag{15.5}$$

How this particular jump condition works is shown in Figure 15.1. The top right-hand plot is the S, M plane just after the sample of the maximum has been taken. Because the sample has just been taken the region $S > M$ cannot be reached, it is the region labelled 'Unattainable.' When we come to solve the Black–Scholes equation numerically in Part Six we will see how we work backwards in time, so that we will find the option value for time t_i^+ *before* the value for time t_i^-. So we will have found the option value $V(S, M, t_i^+)$ for all $S < M$. To find the option value just before the sampling we must apply the jump condition (15.5). Pictorially, this means that the option value at time t_i^- for $S < M$ is the same as the t_i^+ value, just follow the left-hand arrow in the figure. *However*, for $S > M$ (which is attainable before the sample is taken) the option value comes from the $S = M$ line at time t_i^+ for the same S value, after all, S is continuous. Now, just follow the right-hand arrow.

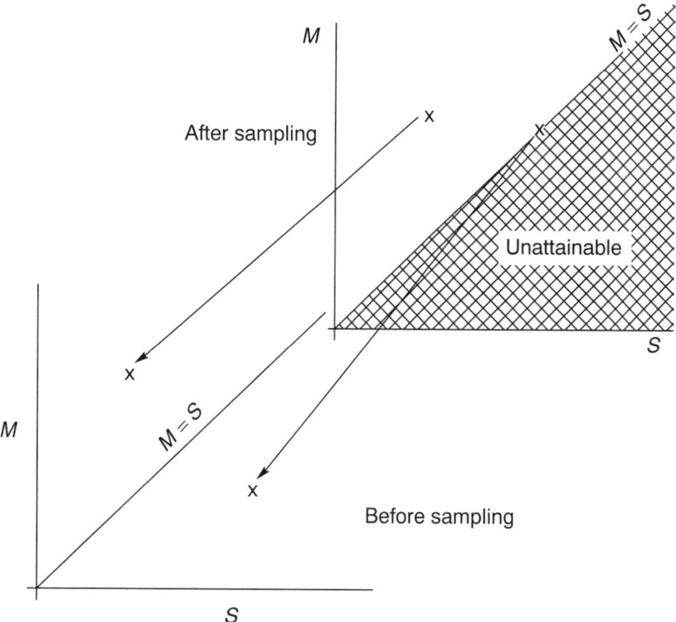

Figure 15.1 The jump condition for a lookback option.

15.5.2 The Algorithm for Discrete Sampling

Because the path-dependent quantity, I, is updated discretely and is therefore constant between sampling dates, the partial differential equation for the option value between sampling dates is the Black–Scholes equation with I treated as a parameter. The algorithm for valuing an option on a discretely-sampled quantity is as follows:

- Working backwards from expiry, solve

$$\frac{\partial V}{\partial t} + \tfrac{1}{2}\sigma^2 S^2 \frac{\partial^2 V}{\partial S^2} + rS\frac{\partial V}{\partial S} - rV = 0$$

  between sampling dates. (How to do this is the subject of Part Six.) Stop when you get to the timestep on which the sampling takes place.
- Then apply the appropriate jump condition across the current sampling date to deduce the option value immediately before the present sampling date using the calculated value of the option just after. Use this as your final condition for further timestepping of the Black–Scholes equation.
- Repeat this process as necessary to arrive at the current value of the option.

15.6 HIGHER DIMENSIONS

The methods outlined above are not restricted to a single path-dependent quantity. Any finite number of path-dependent variables can be accommodated, theoretically. Imagine a contract that pays off the difference between a continuous geometric and a continuous arithmetic average.

To price this one would need to introduce I_g and I_a, defined by

$$I_g = \int_0^t \log(S)\,d\tau \quad \text{and} \quad I_a = \int_0^t S\,d\tau.$$

The solution would then be a function of four variables, $V(S, I_g, I_a, t)$. However, this is at the limit of practicality for a numerical solution of a partial differential equation. Unless there is a similarity solution, reducing the dimensionality of the problem, it may be better to consider Monte Carlo simulation.

The same thoughts apply to discrete sampling or a combination of discrete and continuous.

15.7 PRICING VIA EXPECTATIONS

In Chapter 10 I showed how we can value options in the Black–Scholes world by taking the present value of the expected payoff under a risk-neutral random walk. This approach applies perfectly well to all of the path-dependent options we have described or are going to describe. Simply simulate the random walk

$$dS = rS\,dt + \sigma S\,dX,$$

as will be discussed in Chapter 49, for many paths, calculate the payoff for each path—and this means calculating the value of the path-dependent quantity, which is usually very simple to do—take the average payoff over all the paths and then take the present value of that average. That is the option fair value. Note that there is no μ in this, it is the risk-neutral random walk that must be simulated.

This is a very general and powerful technique, useful for path-dependent contracts for which either a partial differential equation approach is impossible or too high dimensional. The only disadvantage, and it's a big one, is that it is hard to value American options in this framework.

15.8 EARLY EXERCISE

If you have found a partial different equation formulation of the option problem then it is simple to incorporate the early exercise feature of American and Bermudan options. Simply apply the constraint

$$V(S, I, t) \geq P(S, I),$$

together with continuity of the delta of the option, where $P(S, I)$ is the payoff function (and it can also be time dependent). This condition is to be applied at any time that early exercise is allowed. If you have found a partial different equation formulation of the problem and it is in sufficiently low dimension then incorporating early exercise in the numerical scheme is a matter of adding a couple of lines of code (see Chapter 47).

15.9 SUMMARY

The basic theory has been explained above for the pricing of many path-dependent contracts in the partial differential equation framework. We have examined both continuously-sampled and discretely-sampled path-dependent quantities. In the next three chapters we discuss these matters in more detail, first with Asian and lookback options and then for a wider range of exotic contracts. The practical implementation of these models is described in Chapter 47.

FURTHER READING

- See Bergman (1985) for the early work on a unified partial differential equation framework for path-dependent contracts.
- The excellent book by Ingersoll (1987) also discusses the partial differential equation approach to pricing exotics.
- The general framework for exotics is described in a *Risk* magazine article by Dewynne & Wilmott (1993) and also in Dewynne & Wilmott (1996).

EXERCISES

1. If we represent our path dependent quantity by

$$I(t) = \int_0^t f(S,\tau)\,d\tau,$$

then show that over a small time step dt, we find

$$dI = f(S,t)\,dt.$$

2. Find the updating rules and jump conditions for the following discretely-sampled options:
   (a) an Asian option with payoff dependent on the arithmetic average of the sampled asset prices,
   (b) an Asian option with payoff dependent on the geometric average of the sampled asset prices,
   (c) an Asian option with payoff dependent on an exponentially-weighted arithmetic average of the sampled asset prices,
   (d) a lookback option with payoff dependent on the maximum of the sampled asset prices.
3. An asian option depends on the path-dependent quantity:

$$I = \left(\int_0^t (S(\tau))^n\,d\tau\right)^{1/n}$$

When the option is continuously sampled, what form does the partial differential equation for the price of this option take? How would we represent this option using discrete sampling?

4. Consider the average strike foreign exchange Asian option. The option has payoff

$$\max\left(1 - \frac{1}{ST}\int_0^T S(\tau)\,d\tau, 0\right).$$

What is the partial differential equation for the price of this option?

Hint: Assume that the foreign currency receives interest continuously at a constant rate r_f. You can include this in the same way that you would normally include dividend payments from an asset.

5. How would you define the path-dependent quantity as an integral for the range note whose term sheet is shown in Chapter 13? What partial different equation does the product satisfy?

CHAPTER 16

Asian options

In this Chapter...

- many types of Asian option with a payoff that depends on an average
- the different types of averaging of asset prices that are used in defining the payoff
- how to price these contracts in the partial differential equation framework

16.1 INTRODUCTION

Asian options give the holder a payoff that depends on the average price of the underlying over some prescribed period. This averaging of the underlying can significantly reduce the price of an Asian option compared with a similar vanilla contract. Anything that reduces the up-front premium in an option contract tends to make them more popular.

Asian options might be bought by someone with a stream of cashflows in a foreign currency, due to sales abroad for example, and who wants to hedge against fluctuations in the exchange rate. The Asian tail that we see later is designed to reduce exposure to sudden movements in the underlying just before expiry. Some pension payments have such a feature.

In this chapter we find differential equations for the value of a wide variety of such Asian options. There are many ways to define an 'average' of the price, and we begin with a discussion of the obvious possibilities. We will see how to write the price as the solution of a partial differential equation in *three* variables: the underlying asset, time, and a new state variable representing the evolution of the average.

16.2 PAYOFF TYPES

Assuming for the moment that we have defined our average A, what sort of payoffs are common? As well as calls, puts etc. there is also the classification of **strike** and **rate**. These classifications work as follows. Take the payoff for a vanilla option, a vanilla call, say,

$$\max(S - E, 0).$$

Replace the strike price E with an average and you have an **average strike call**. This has payoff

$$\max(S - A, 0).$$

An **average strike put** thus has payoff

$$\max(A - S, 0).$$

Now take the vanilla payoff and instead replace the asset with its average; what you get is a rate option. For example, an **average rate call** has payoff

$$\max(A - E, 0)$$

and an **average rate put** has payoff

$$\max(E - A, 0).$$

The average rate options can be used to lock in the price of a commodity or an exchange rate for those who have a continual and fairly predictable exposure to one of these over extended periods.

The difference between calls and puts is simple from a pricing point of view, but the strike/rate distinction can make a big difference. Strike options are easier to value numerically.

16.3 TYPES OF AVERAGING

The precise definition of the average used in an Asian contract depends on two elements: how the data points are combined to form an average and which data points are used. The former means whether we have an arithmetic or geometric average or something more complicated. The latter means how many data points do we use in the average: all quoted prices, or just a subset, and over what time period?

16.3.1 Arithmetic or Geometric

The two simplest and obvious types of average are the **arithmetic average** and the **geometric average**. The arithmetic average of the price is the sum of all the constituent prices, equally weighted, divided by the total number of prices used. The geometric average is the *exponential* of the sum of all the *logarithms* of the constituent prices, equally weighted, divided by the total number of prices used. Another popular choice is the exponentially weighted average, meaning instead of having an equal weighting to each price in the average, the recent prices are weighted more than past prices in an exponentially decreasing fashion.

16.3.2 Discrete or Continuous

How much data do we use in the calculation of the average? Do we take every traded price or just a subset? If we take closely-spaced prices over a finite time then the sums that we calculate in the average become integrals of the asset (or some function of it) over the averaging period. This would give us a **continuously-sampled average**. More commonly, we only take data points that are reliable, using closing prices, a smaller set of data. This is called **discrete sampling**. This issue of continuous or discrete sampling was discussed in the previous chapter.

16.4 EXTENDING THE BLACK–SCHOLES EQUATION

16.4.1 Continuously-Sampled Averages

Figure 16.1 shows a realization of the random walk followed by an asset, in this case YPF, an Argentine oil company, together with a continuously-sampled running arithmetic average.

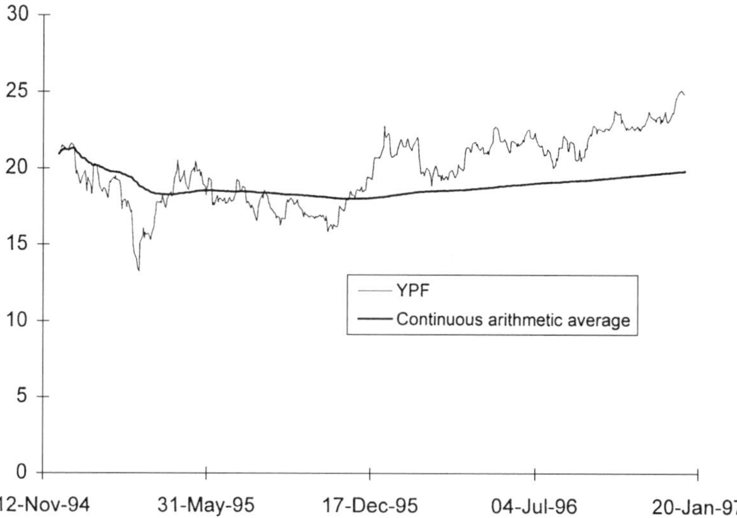

Figure 16.1 An asset price random walk and its continuously measured arithmetic running average.

This average is defined as

$$\frac{1}{t}\int_0^t S(\tau)\,d\tau.$$

If we introduce the new state variable

$$I = \int_0^t S(\tau)\,d\tau$$

then, following the analysis of Chapter 15, the partial differential equation for the value of an option contingent on this average is

$$\frac{\partial V}{\partial t} + S\frac{\partial V}{\partial I} + \tfrac{1}{2}\sigma^2 S^2 \frac{\partial^2 V}{\partial S^2} + rS\frac{\partial V}{\partial S} - rV = 0.$$

Figure 16.2 shows a realization of an asset price random walk with the continuously-sampled geometric running average.

The continuously-sampled geometric average is defined to be

$$\exp\left(\frac{1}{t}\int_0^t \log S(\tau)\,d\tau\right).$$

To value an option contingent on this average we define

$$I = \int_0^t \log S(\tau)\,d\tau$$

and, following again the analysis of Chapter 15, the partial differential equation for the value of the option is

$$\frac{\partial V}{\partial t} + \log S\frac{\partial V}{\partial I} + \tfrac{1}{2}\sigma^2 S^2 \frac{\partial^2 V}{\partial S^2} + rS\frac{\partial V}{\partial S} - rV = 0.$$

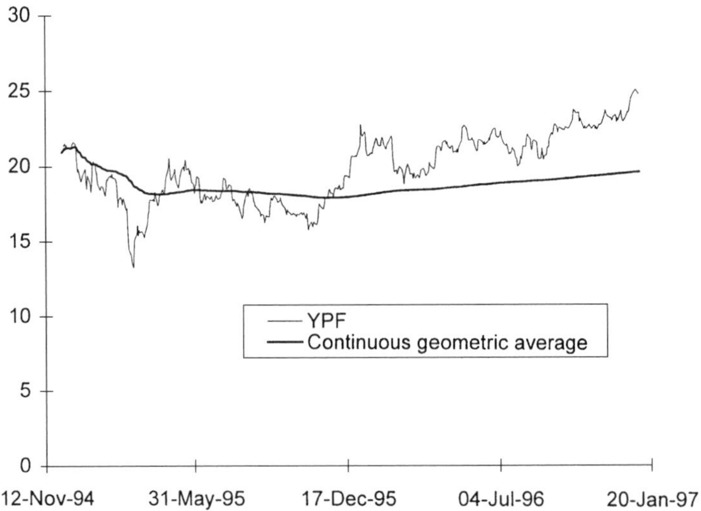

Figure 16.2 An asset price random walk and its continuous geometric running average.

16.4.2 Discretely-sampled Averages

Discretely-sampled averages, whether arithmetic or geometric, fit easily into the framework established in Chapter 15. In Figures 16.3 and 16.4 are shown examples of a realized asset price and discretely-sampled arithmetic and geometric averages respectively.

Above, we modeled the continuously-sampled average as an integral. By a discretely-sampled average we mean the sum, rather than the integral, of a finite number of values of the asset during the life of the option. Such a definition of average is easily included within the framework of our model.

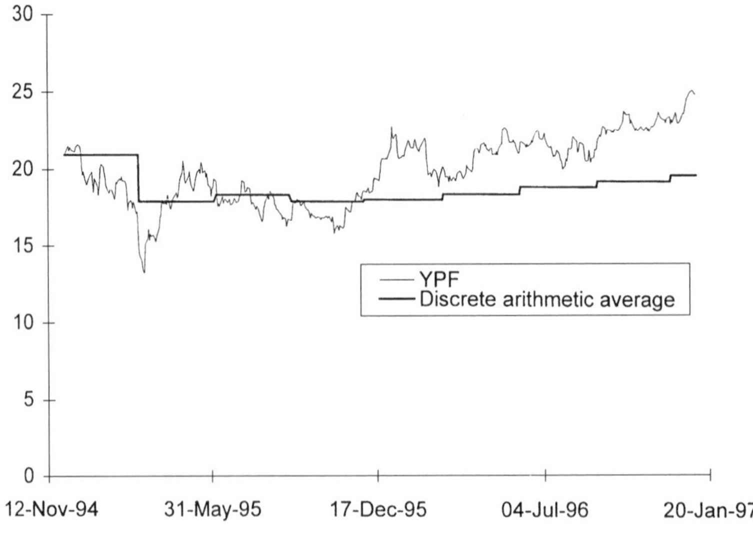

Figure 16.3 An asset price random walk and its discretely-sampled arithmetic running average.

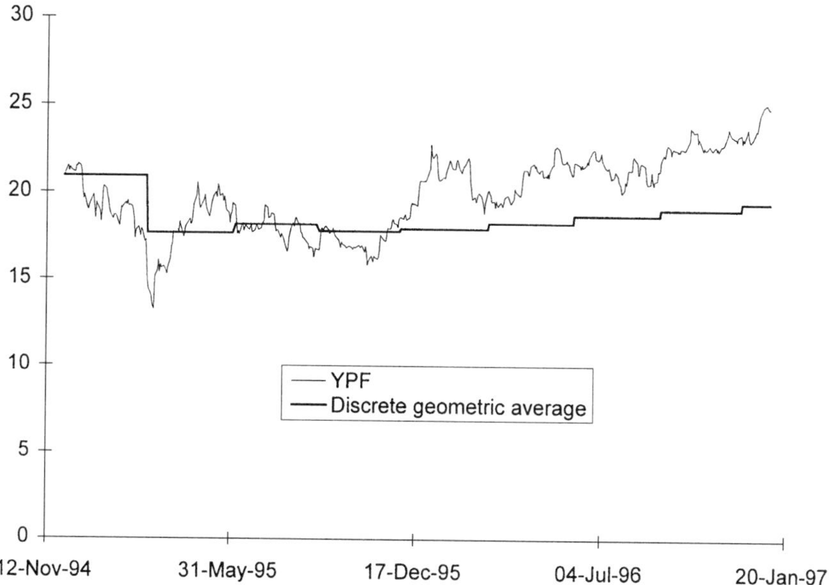

Figure 16.4 An asset price random walk and its discretely-sampled geometric running average.

If the sampling dates are t_i, $i = 1, \dots$ then the discretely-sampled arithmetic averages are defined by

$$A_i = \frac{1}{i}\sum_{k=1}^{i} S(t_k).$$

In particular

$$A_1 = S(t_1), \quad A_2 = \frac{S(t_1) + S(t_2)}{2} = \tfrac{1}{2}A_1 + \tfrac{1}{2}S(t_2),$$

$$A_3 = \frac{S(t_1) + S(t_2) + S(t_3)}{3} = \frac{2}{3}A_2 + \frac{1}{3}S(t_3), \dots .$$

It is easy to see that these are equivalent to

$$A_i = \frac{i-1}{i}A_{i-1} + \frac{1}{i}S(t_i).$$

At the top of Figure 16.5 is shown a realized asset price path. Below that is the discretely-sampled average. This is necessarily piecewise constant. At the bottom of the figure is the value of some option (it doesn't matter which). The option value must be continuous to eliminate arbitrage opportunities.

Using the results of Chapter 15, the jump condition for an Asian option with discrete arithmetic averaging is then simply

$$V(S, A, t_i^-) = V\left(S, \frac{i-1}{i}A + \frac{1}{i}S, t_i^+\right).$$

This is a result of the continuity of the option price across a sampling date, i.e. no arbitrage.

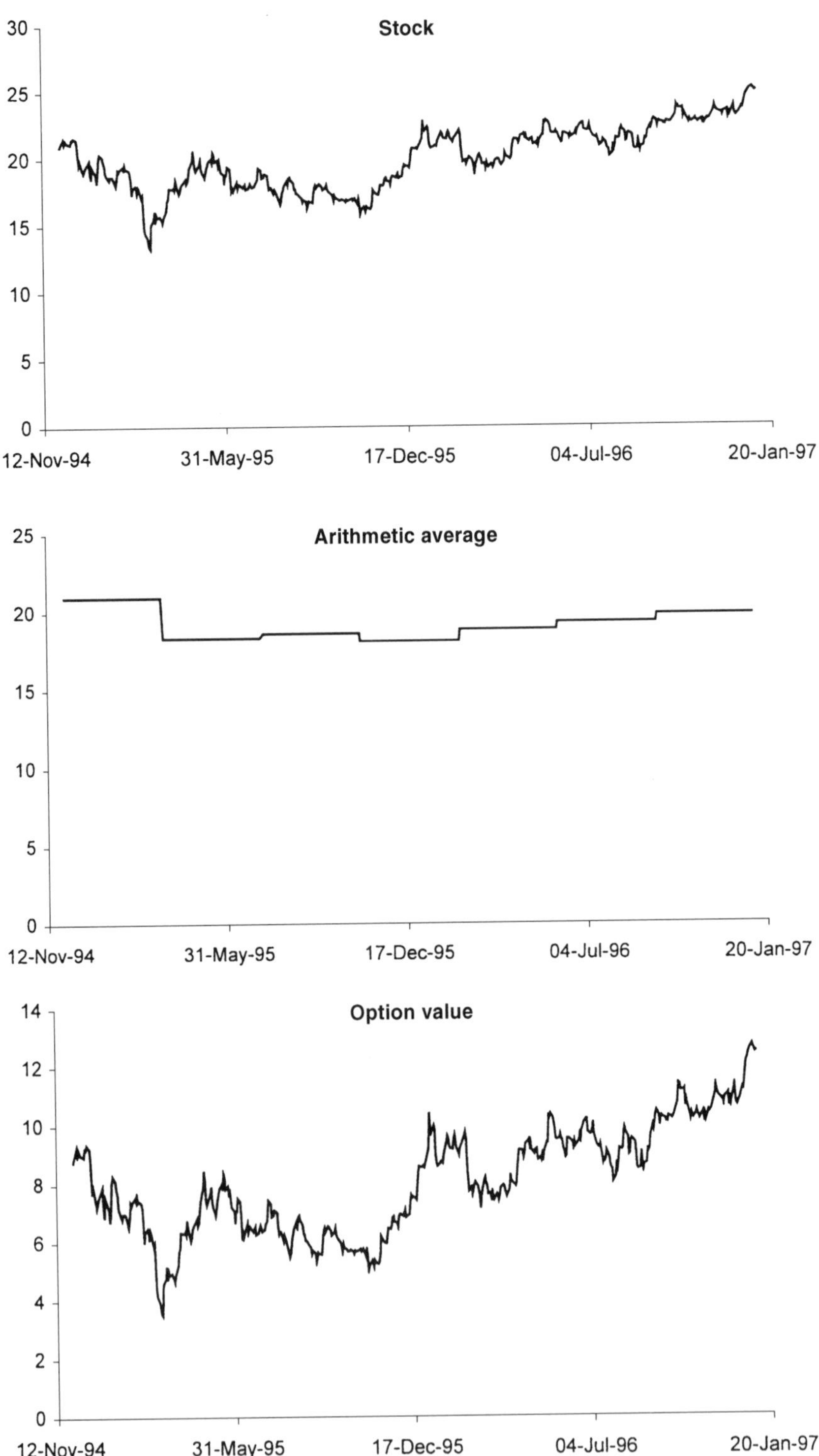

Figure 16.5 Top: An asset price random walk. Middle: Its discretely-sampled arithmetic running average. Bottom: The option value.

Similarly the discretely-sampled geometric average has the jump condition

$$V(S, A, t_i^-) = V\left(S, \exp\left(\frac{i-1}{i}\log(A) + \frac{1}{i}\log(S)\right), t_i^+\right)$$

where

$$A_i = \exp\left(\frac{i-1}{i}\log(A_{i-1}) + \frac{1}{i}\log(S(t_i))\right).$$

16.4.3 Exponentially-weighted and Other Averages

Simple modifications that are easily handled in the partial differential equation framework are the exponential average and the average up to a fixed time.

In the exponential continuously-sampled arithmetic average just introduce the new variable

$$I = \lambda \int_{-\infty}^{t} e^{-\lambda(t-\tau)} S(\tau)\, d\tau$$

which satisfies

$$dI = \lambda(S - I)\, dt.$$

From this, the governing partial differential equation is obvious. The geometric equivalent is dealt with similarly.

The reader can determine for himself the jump condition when the average is a discretely-sampled exponential average.

When the average is only taken up to a fixed point, so that, for example, the payoff depends on

$$I = \int_0^{T_0} S(\tau)\, d\tau \quad \text{with} \quad T_0 < T,$$

then the new term in the partial differential equation (the derivative with respect to I) disappears for times greater that T_0. That is,

$$\frac{\partial V}{\partial t} + S\mathcal{H}(T_0 - t)\frac{\partial V}{\partial I} + \tfrac{1}{2}\sigma^2 S^2 \frac{\partial^2 V}{\partial S^2} + rS\frac{\partial V}{\partial S} - rV = 0,$$

where $\mathcal{H}$ is the Heaviside function.

One type of contract that is *not* easily put into a partial differential equation framework with a finite number of underlyings is the moving window option. In this option, the holder can exercise early for an amount that depends on the average over the previous three months, say. The key point about this contract that makes it difficult is that the starting point of the averaging period is not fixed in time. As a result the stochastic differential equation for the path-dependent quantity cannot be written in terms of *local* values of the independent variables: all details of the path need to be known and recorded.

16.4.4 The Asian Tail

Often the averaging is confined to only a part of the life of the option. For example, if the averaging of the underlying is only over the final part of the option's life it is referred to as an **Asian tail**. Such a contract would reduce the exposure of the option to sudden moves in the underlying just before the payoff is received. A feature like this is also common in pension awards.

16.5 EARLY EXERCISE

There is not much to be said about early exercise that has not already been said elsewhere in this book. The only point to mention is that the details of the payoff on early exercise have to be well defined. The payoff at expiry depends on the value of the average up to expiry; this will, of course, not be known until expiry. Typically, on early exercise it is the average to date that is used. For example, in an American arithmetic average strike put the early payoff would be

$$\max\left(\frac{1}{t}\int_0^t S(\tau)\,d\tau - S, 0\right).$$

16.6 SIMILARITY REDUCTIONS

As long as the stochastic differential equation or updating rule for the path-dependent quantity only contains references to S, t and the path-dependent quantity itself then the value of the option depends on three variables. Unless we are very lucky, the value of the option must be calculated numerically. Some options have a particular structure that permits a reduction in the dimensionality of the problem by use of a similarity variable. I will illustrate the idea with an example. The dimensionality of the continuously-sampled arithmetic average strike option can be reduced from three to two.

The payoff for the call option is

$$\max\left(S - \frac{1}{T}\int_0^T S(\tau)\,d\tau, 0\right).$$

We can write the running payoff for the call option as

$$I\max\left(R - \frac{1}{t}, 0\right),$$

where

$$I = \int_0^t S(\tau)\,d\tau$$

and

$$R = \frac{S}{\int_0^t S(\tau)\,d\tau}. \tag{16.1}$$

The payoff at expiry may then be written as

$$I\max\left(R - \frac{1}{T}, 0\right).$$

In view of the form of the payoff function, it seems plausible that the option value takes the form

$$V(S, R, t) = IW(R, t), \quad \text{with } R = \frac{S}{I}.$$

We find that W satisfies

$$\frac{\partial W}{\partial t} + \tfrac{1}{2}\sigma^2 R^2 \frac{\partial^2 W}{\partial R^2} + R(r-R)\frac{\partial W}{\partial R} - (r-R)W \leq 0. \qquad (16.2)$$

If the option is European we have strict equality in (16.2). If it is American we may have inequality in (16.2) but the constraint

$$W(R,t) \geq \max\left(R - \frac{1}{t}, 0\right)$$

must be satisfied. Moreover, if the option price ever meets the early exercise payoff it must do so smoothly. That is, the function $W(R,t)$ and its first R-derivative must be continuous everywhere.

For the European option we must impose boundary conditions at both $R = 0$ and as $R \to \infty$:

$$W(0,t) = 0,$$

and

$$W(R,t) \sim R \quad \text{as} \quad R \to \infty.$$

The solution of the European problem can be written as an infinite sum of confluent hypergeometric functions. I do not give this exact solution because it is easier (and certainly a more flexible approach) to obtain values by applying numerical methods directly to the partial differential equation.

In Figure 16.6 we see W against R at three months before expiry and with three months' averaging completed; $\sigma = 0.4$ and $r = 0.1$.

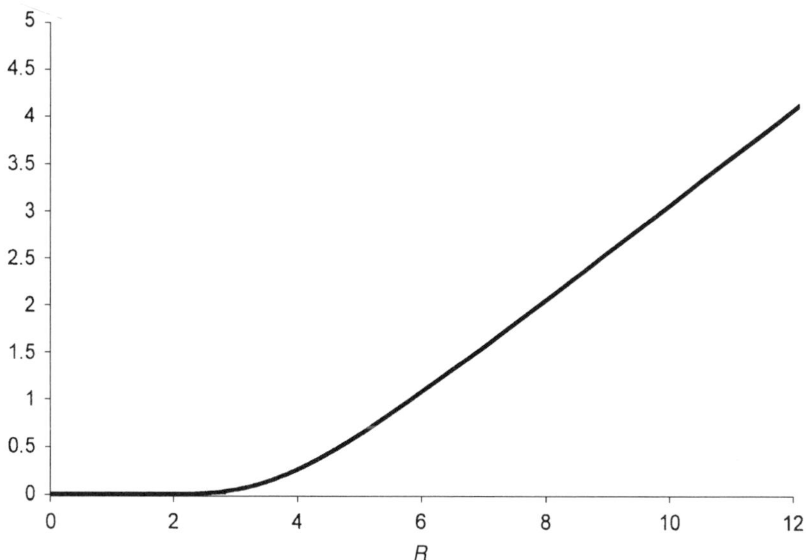

Figure 16.6 The European average strike call option; similarity variable W versus similarity variable R with $\sigma = 0.4$ and $r = 0.1$ at three months before expiry; there has already been three months' averaging.

In the case of an American option, we have to solve the partial differential inequality (16.2) subject to the constraint, the final condition and the boundary conditions. We cannot do this analytically and we must find the solution numerically.

16.6.1 Put–Call Parity for the European Average Strike

The payoff at expiry for a portfolio of one European average strike call held long and one put held short is

$$I\max(R - 1/T, 0) - I\max(1/T - R, 0).$$

Whether R is greater or less than T at expiry, this payoff is simply

$$S - \frac{I}{T}.$$

The value of this portfolio is identical to one consisting of one asset and a financial product whose payoff is

$$-\frac{I}{T}.$$

In order to value this product find a solution of the average strike equation of the form

$$W(R, t) = b(t) + a(t)R \tag{16.3}$$

and with $a(T) = 0$ and $b(T) = -1/T$; such a solution would have the required payoff of $-I/T$. Substituting (16.3) into (16.2) and satisfying the boundary conditions, we find that

$$a(t) = -\frac{1}{rT}\left(1 - e^{-r(T-t)}\right), \quad b(t) = -\frac{1}{T}e^{-r(T-t)}.$$

We conclude that

$$V_C - V_P = S - \frac{S}{rT}\left(1 - e^{-r(T-t)}\right) - \frac{1}{T}e^{-r(T-t)}\int_0^t S(\tau)\,d\tau,$$

where V_C and V_P are the values of the European arithmetic average strike call and put. This is put–call parity for the European average strike option.

16.7 SOME FORMULAE

There are very few nice formulae for the values of Asian options. The most well known are for average rate calls and puts when the average is a continuously-sampled, geometrical average.

The Geometric Average Rate Call

This option has payoff

$$\max(A - E, 0),$$

where A is the continuously-sampled geometric average. This option has a Black–Scholes value of

$$Se^{(a-r)(T-t)}N(d_1) - Ee^{-r(T-t)}N(d_2),$$

where

$$d_1 = \frac{\log(S/E) + (a + \frac{1}{2}\sigma_A^2)(T-t)}{\sigma_A\sqrt{T-t}}$$

and

$$d_2 = d_1 - \sigma_A\sqrt{T-t}.$$

Here

$$a = \tfrac{1}{2}(r - D + \tfrac{1}{6}\sigma^2)$$

and

$$\sigma_A = \frac{\sigma}{\sqrt{3}}.$$

The geometric average of a lognormal random walk is itself lognormally distributed, but with a reduced volatility.

The Geometric Average Rate Put

This option has payoff

$$\max(E - A, 0),$$

where A is the continuously-sampled geometric average. This option has a Black–Scholes value of

$$Ee^{-r(T-t)}N(-d_2) - Se^{(a-r)(T-t)}N(-d_1),$$

where

$$d_1 = \frac{\log(S/E) + (a + \frac{1}{2}\sigma_A^2)(T-t)}{\sigma_A\sqrt{T-t}}$$

and

$$d_2 = d_1 - \sigma_A\sqrt{T-t}.$$

Here

$$a = \tfrac{1}{2}(r - D + \tfrac{1}{6}\sigma^2)$$

and

$$\sigma_A = \frac{\sigma}{\sqrt{3}}.$$

16.8 SUMMARY

I applied the general theory of Chapter 15 to the problem of pricing Asian options, options with a payoff depending on an average. The partial differential equation approach is very powerful for these types of options, and hard to beat if your option has a similarity reduction or is American style. The approach can be generalized much further. We will see this in Chapter 18.

FURTHER READING

- Some exact solutions can be found in Boyle (1991).
- Bergman (1985) and Ingersoll (1987) present the partial differential equation formulation of some average strike options and demonstrate the similarity reduction.

- For another, rather abstract, method for valuing Asian options see Geman & Yor (1993).
- The application of the numerical Monte Carlo method is described by Kemna & Vorst (1990). They also derive some exact formulae.
- More examples of the methods described here can be found in Dewynne & Wilmott (1995 b, c).
- For an approximate valuation of arithmetic Asian options see Levy (1990) who replaces the density function for the distribution of the average by a lognormal function.

EXERCISES

1. Using the method suggested in the text, or otherwise, prove put–call parity for arithmetic average strike Asian options:

$$V_C - V_P = S(1 - (1 - e^{-r(T-t)})/rT) - \frac{1}{T}e^{-r(T-t)}\int_0^t S(\tau)\,d\tau.$$

2. Consider the arithmetic average strike call option. This has payoff

$$\max\left(S - \frac{1}{T}\int_0^T S(\tau)\,d\tau, 0\right).$$

What partial differential equation does the value of this option satisfy? By writing the value of the option, $C(S, I, t)$ in the form

$$C(S, I, t) = SW(R, t),$$

where $R = I/S$, find a similarity reduction. What is the payoff in the similarity variables?

3. How would we write the jump condition for a discretely sampled arithmetic average strike call option in terms of the similarity variables, when we write

$$C(S, I, t) = IW(S/I, t),$$

4. Find a similarity reduction for the geometric average rate call option, with payoff

$$\max\left(S - \exp\left(\frac{1}{T}\int_0^T \log S(\tau)\,d\tau\right) - E, 0\right).$$

What partial differential equation do you find for the continuously sampled option?

5. What jump condition does the discretely sampled version of the geometric average rate call option satisfy when we use a similarity reduction?

CHAPTER 17
lookback options

In this Chapter...

- the features that make up a lookback option
- how to put the lookback option into the Black–Scholes framework for both the continuous- and discrete-sampling cases

17.1 INTRODUCTION

The dream contract has to be one that pays the difference between the highest and the lowest asset prices realized by an asset over some period. Any speculator is trying to achieve such a trade. The contract that pays this is an example of a **lookback option**, an option that pays off some function of the realized maximum and/or minimum of the underlying asset over some prescribed period. Since lookback options have such an extreme payoff they tend to be expensive.

We can price these contracts in the Black–Scholes environment quite easily, theoretically. There are two cases to consider, whether the maximum/minimum is measured continuously or discretely. Here I will always talk about the 'maximum' of the asset. The treatment of the 'minimum' should be obvious.

17.2 TYPES OF PAYOFF

For the basic lookback contracts, the payoff comes in two varieties, like the Asian option: the *rate* and the *strike* option, also called the **fixed strike** and the **floating strike** respectively. These have payoffs that are the same as vanilla options except that in the strike option the vanilla exercise price is replaced by the maximum. In the rate option it is the asset value in the vanilla option that is replaced by the maximum.

17.3 CONTINUOUS MEASUREMENT OF THE MAXIMUM

In Figure 17.1 is shown the term sheet for a foreign exchange lookback swap. One counterparty pays a floating interest rate every six months, while the other counterparty pays on maturity a linear function of the maximum realized level of the exchange rate. The floating interest payments of six-month LIBOR can be represented as a much simpler cashflow, to be explained in Chapter 32. Then this contract becomes a very straightforward lookback option.

USD/DEM Lookback Swap

Counterparties	Counterparty A The Customer
Notional Amount	USD 50 Millions
Settlement Date	Two days after Trade Date
Maturity Date	Two years after Trade Date
Payments made by Customer	**USD 6m LIBOR** + **190** bps paid semiannually, A/360
Payments made by Counterparty A	In USD on Maturity Date $\text{Notional}^* \left(\frac{\text{FX}_{\text{max}} - \text{Strike}}{\text{FX}_{\text{maturity}}} - 1\right)$
FX_max	The highest daily official USD/DEM Fixing from Settlement Date until Maturity Date
FX_maturity	The USD/DEM Fixing on Maturity Date
Strike	1.7180
Fixing	The daily USD/DEM FX exchange rate as seen on Telerate page SAFE1 at noon, New York time
USD 6m LIBOR	The USD 6m LIBOR rate as seen on Telerate page 3750 at noon, London time, on each Fixing Date
Documentation	ISDA
Governing Law	English

This indicative termsheet is neither an offer to buy or sell securities or an OTC derivative product which includes options, swaps, forwards and structured notes having similar features to OTC derivative transaction, nor a solicitation to buy or sell securities or an OTC derivative product. The proposal contained in the foregoing is not a complete description of the terms of a particular transaction and is subject to change without limitation.

Figure 17.1 Term sheet for USD/DEM lookback swap.

Introduce the new variable M as the realized maximum of the asset from the start of the sampling period $t = 0$, say, until the current time t:

$$M = \max_{0 \le \tau \le t} S(\tau).$$

In Figure 17.2 is shown a realization of an asset price path and the continuously-sampled maximum. An obvious point about this plot, but one that is worth mentioning, is that the asset price is always below the maximum. (This will not be the case when we come to examine the discretely-sampled case.) The value of our lookback option is a function of three variables, $V(S, M, t)$ but now we have the restriction

$$0 \le S \le M.$$

This observation will also lead us to the correct partial differential equation for the option's value, and the boundary conditions. We derive the equation in a heuristic fashion that can be made rigorous.

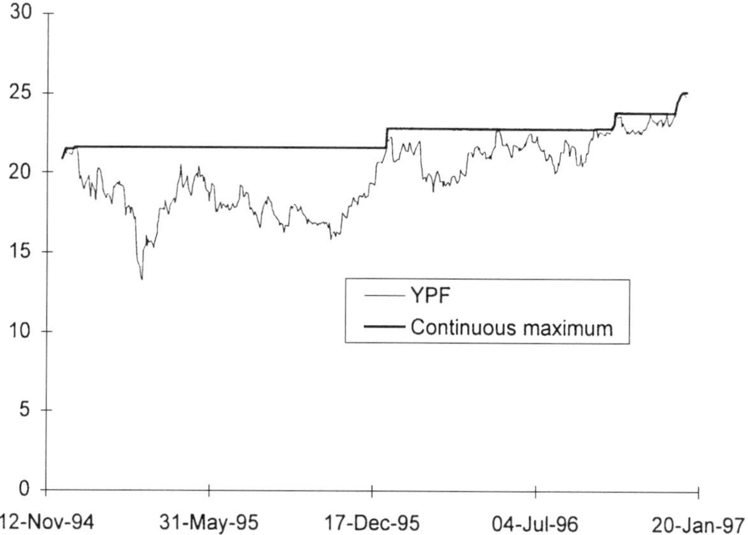

Figure 17.2 An asset price path and the continuously-sampled maximum.

From Figure 17.2 we can see that for most of the time the asset price is below the maximum. But there are times when they coincide. When $S < M$ the maximum cannot change and so the variable M satisfies the stochastic differential equation

$$dM = 0.$$

Hold that thought. While $0 \leq S < M$ the governing equation must be Black–Scholes

$$\frac{\partial V}{\partial t} + \tfrac{1}{2}\sigma^2 S^2 \frac{\partial^2 V}{\partial S^2} + rS\frac{\partial V}{\partial S} - rV = 0,$$

with M as a 'parameter' and only for $S < M$.

The behavior of the option value when $S = M$ tells us the *boundary condition* to apply there. The boundary condition is

$$\frac{\partial V}{\partial M} = 0 \quad \text{on} \quad S = M.$$

The reason for this boundary condition is that the option value is insensitive to the level of the maximum when the asset price is *at* the maximum. This is because the probability of the present maximum still being the maximum at expiry is zero. The rigorous derivation of this boundary condition is rather messy; see the original paper by Goldman, Sosin & Gatto (1979) for the details.

Finally, we must impose a condition at expiry to reflect the payoff. As an example, consider the lookback rate call option. This has a payoff given by

$$\max(M - E, 0).$$

The lookback strike put has a payoff given by

$$\max(M - S, 0).$$

17.4 DISCRETE MEASUREMENT OF THE MAXIMUM

The discretely-sampled maximum is shown in Figure 17.3. Not only can the asset price go above the maximum, but in this figure we see that the maximum has very rarely been increased. Discrete sampling, as well as being more practical than continuous sampling, is used to decrease the value of a contract.

When the maximum is measured at discrete times we must first define the updating rule, from which follows the jump condition to apply across the sampling dates.

If the maximum is measured at times t_i then the updating rule is simply

$$M_i = \max(S(t_i), M_{i-1}).$$

The jump condition is then simply

$$V(S, M, t_i^-) = V(S, \max(S, M), t_i^+).$$

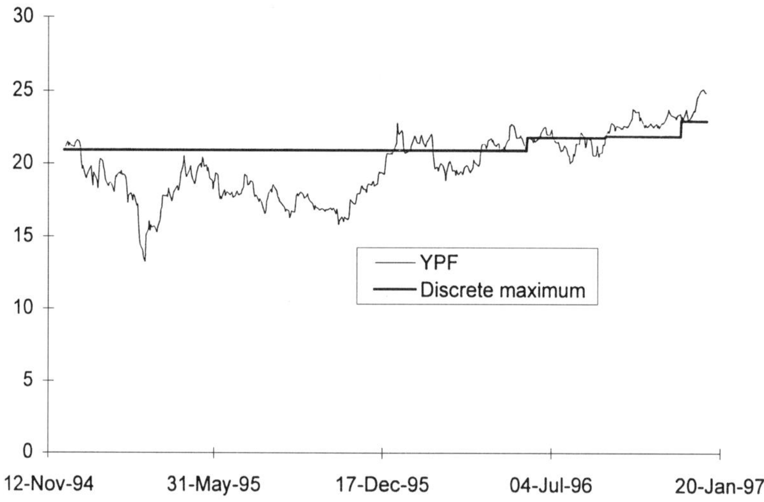

Figure 17.3 An asset price path and the discretely-sampled maximum.

Note that the Black–Scholes equation is to be solved for all S, it is no longer constrained to be less than the maximum.

17.5 SIMILARITY REDUCTION

The general lookback option with a payoff depending on one path-dependent quantity is a three-dimensional problem. The three dimensions are asset price, the maximum and time. The numerical solution of this problem is more time consuming than a two-dimensional problem. However, there are some special, and important, cases when the dimensionality of the problem can be reduced.

This reduction relies on some symmetry properties in the equation and is not something that can be applied to all, or, indeed, many, lookback contracts. It is certainly possible if the payoff takes the form

$$M^{\alpha}P(S/M). \tag{17.1}$$

For example, this is true for the lookback strike put which has payoff

$$\max(M-S,0)=M\max\left(1-\frac{S}{M},0\right).$$

Generally, if the payoff takes the form (17.1), then the substitution

$$\xi=\frac{S}{M}$$

leads to a problem for $W(\xi,t)$ where

$$V(S,M,t)=M^{\alpha}W(\xi,t)$$

where W satisfies the governing equation

$$\frac{\partial W}{\partial t}+\tfrac{1}{2}\sigma^2\xi^2\frac{\partial^2 W}{\partial \xi^2}+r\xi\frac{\partial W}{\partial \xi}-rW=0,$$

the final condition

$$W(\xi,T)=P(\xi)$$

and the boundary condition

$$\frac{\partial W}{\partial \xi}-\alpha W=0 \quad \text{on} \quad \xi=1.$$

17.6 SOME FORMULAE

Floating Strike Lookback Call

The continuously-sampled version of this option has a payoff

$$\max(S-M,0)=S-M,$$

where M is the realized minimum of the asset price. In the Black–Scholes world the value is

$$Se^{-D(T-t)}N(d_1)-Me^{-r(T-t)}N(d_2)$$
$$+\,Se^{-r(T-t)}\frac{\sigma^2}{2b}\left(\left(\frac{S}{M}\right)^{-2(r-D)/\sigma^2}N\left(-d_1+\frac{2(r-D)\sqrt{T-t}}{\sigma}\right)-e^{(r-D)(T-t)}N(-d_1)\right),$$

where

$$d_1=\frac{\log(S/M)+\left(r-D+\frac{1}{2}\sigma^2\right)(T-t)}{\sqrt{T-t}}$$

and

$$d_2=d_1-\sigma\sqrt{T-t}.$$

Floating Strike Lookback Put

The continuously-sampled version of this option has a payoff

$$\max(M - S, 0) = M - S,$$

where M is the realized maximum of the asset price. The value is

$$Me^{-r(T-t)}N(-d_2) - Se^{-D(T-t)}N(-d_1)$$

$$+ Se^{-r(T-t)}\frac{\sigma^2}{2b}\left(-\left(\frac{S}{M}\right)^{-2(r-D)/\sigma^2} N\left(d_1 - \frac{2(r-D)\sqrt{T-t}}{\sigma}\right) + e^{(r-D)(T-t)}N(d_1)\right),$$

where

$$d_1 = \frac{\log(S/M) + \left(r - D + \frac{1}{2}\sigma^2\right)(T-t)}{\sqrt{T-t}}$$

and

$$d_2 = d_1 - \sigma\sqrt{T-t}.$$

Fixed Strike Lookback Call

This option has a payoff given by

$$\max(M - E, 0)$$

where M is the realized maximum. For $E > M$ the fair value is

$$Se^{-D(T-t)}N(d_1) - Ee^{-r(T-t)}N(d_2)$$

$$+ Se^{-r(T-t)}\frac{\sigma^2}{2b}\left(-\left(\frac{S}{E}\right)^{-2(r-D)/\sigma^2} N\left(d_1 - \frac{2(r-D)\sqrt{T-t}}{\sigma}\right) + e^{(r-D)(T-t)}N(d_1)\right),$$

where

$$d_1 = \frac{\log(S/E) + \left(r - D + \frac{1}{2}\sigma^2\right)(T-t)}{\sqrt{T-t}}$$

and

$$d_2 = d_1 - \sigma\sqrt{T-t}.$$

When $E < M$ the value is

$$(M - E)e^{-r(T-t)} + Se^{-D(T-t)}N(d_1) - Me^{-r(T-t)}N(d_2)$$

$$+ Se^{-r(T-t)}\frac{\sigma^2}{2b}\left(-\left(\frac{S}{M}\right)^{-2(r-D)/\sigma^2} N\left(d_1 - \frac{2(r-D)\sqrt{T-t}}{\sigma}\right) + e^{(r-D)(T-t)}N(d_1)\right),$$

where

$$d_1 = \frac{\log(S/M) + \left(r - D + \frac{1}{2}\sigma^2\right)(T-t)}{\sqrt{T-t}}$$

and

$$d_2 = d_1 - \sigma\sqrt{T-t}.$$

Fixed Strike Lookback Put

This option has a payoff given by

$$\max(E - M, 0)$$

where M is the realized minimum. For $E < M$ the fair value is

$$Ee^{-r(T-t)}N(-d_2) - Se^{-D(T-t)}N(-d_1)$$
$$+ Se^{-r(T-t)}\frac{\sigma^2}{2b}\left(\left(\frac{S}{E}\right)^{-2(r-D)/\sigma^2} N\left(-d_1 + \frac{2(r-D)\sqrt{T-t}}{\sigma}\right) - e^{(r-D)(T-t)}N(-d_1)\right),$$

where

$$d_1 = \frac{\log(S/E) + \left(r - D + \frac{1}{2}\sigma^2\right)(T-t)}{\sqrt{T-t}}$$

and

$$d_2 = d_1 - \sigma\sqrt{T-t}.$$

When $E > M$ the value is

$$(E - M)e^{-r(T-t)} - Se^{-D(T-t)}N(-d_1) + Me^{-r(T-t)}N(-d_2)$$
$$+ Se^{-r(T-t)}\frac{\sigma^2}{2b}\left(-\left(\frac{S}{M}\right)^{-2(r-D)/\sigma^2} N\left(-d_1 + \frac{2(r-D)\sqrt{T-t}}{\sigma}\right) - e^{(r-D)(T-t)}N(-d_1)\right),$$

where

$$d_1 = \frac{\log(S/M) + \left(r - D + \frac{1}{2}\sigma^2\right)(T-t)}{\sqrt{T-t}}$$

and

$$d_2 = d_1 - \sigma\sqrt{T-t}.$$

17.7 SUMMARY

Lookback options, and lookback features generally, are seen in many types of contract. They are quite common in fixed-income products where an interest payment may depend on the maximum level that rates have reached over some previous period. The same partial differential equation framework that we have seen in the equity world, carries over in principle to the more complicated stochastic interest rate world.

FURTHER READING

- See Goldman, Sosin & Gatto (1979) for the first academic description of lookback options. They show how to rigorously derive the crucial boundary condition.
- Conze & Viswanathan (1991) give the derivation of formulae for several types of lookback option.
- Babbs (1992) puts the lookback option into a binomial setting.

- See Dewynne & Wilmott (1994 b) for a derivation of the governing equation and boundary conditions.
- Heynen & Kat (1995) discuss the discrete and partial monitoring of the maximum.
- Two contracts that are related to lookback options are the stop-loss option, described by Fitt, Dewynne & Wilmott (1994), and the Russian option, see Duffie & Harrison (1992).

EXERCISES

1. Consider the continuously-sampled lookback strike put, with payoff

$$\max(M - S, 0) = M \max\left(1 - \frac{S}{M}, 0\right),$$

where

$$M = \max_{0 \le \tau \le t} S(\tau).$$

Use the substitution $\xi = \dfrac{S}{M}$ to find a similarity reduction of the form

$$V(S, M, t) = M^{\alpha} W(\xi, t).$$

What differential equation does W satisfy?

2. The stop-loss is a perpetual barrier lookback with a rebate that is a fixed proportion of the maximum realized value of the asset price. A particular stop-loss option has the following specification:
   (a) The option is set-up at time 0,
   (b) The option has no expiry,
   (c) If S falls to λM then the option immediately pays out S, where

$$M(t) = \max_{0 \le \tau \le t} S(\tau) \quad \text{and} \quad \lambda < 1.$$

When the asset pays a continuous dividend yield, D, what equation does the value of the option, $V(S, M, t)$ satisfy? What are the boundary conditions? By writing

$$V(S, M, t) = MW(\xi),$$

where $\xi = S/M$, solve the equation. What happens when $D = 0$?

Hint: Try a solution of the form $W = \xi^{\alpha}$ and solve the resulting quadratic for α.

3. The Russian option is a perpetual lookback that pays out the maximum realized value of the asset price. A particular Russian option has the following specification:
   (a) The option is set-up at time 0,
   (b) The option has no expiry,
   (c) At any time, the option may be exercised for a payoff of M, where

$$M(t) = \max_{0 \le \tau \le t} S(\tau).$$

When the asset pays a continuous dividend yield, D, what equation does the value of the option, $V(S, M, t)$ satisfy? What are the boundary conditions? By writing

$$V(S, M, t) = MW(\xi),$$

where $\xi = S/M$, solve the equation.

CHAPTER 18
miscellaneous exotics

In this Chapter...

- contract specifications for many more exotic derivatives
- more 'tricks of the trade' for valuing exotic contracts in the partial differential equation framework

18.1 INTRODUCTION

The universe of exotic derivatives is large, becoming larger all the time. I have tried to bring together, and even classify, many of these contracts. For example, a whole chapter was devoted entirely to Asian options, options depending on an average of the realized asset path. Nevertheless, because of the complexity of the instruments available and the increase in their number, the classification exercise can become a labor of Sisyphus. In this chapter I give up on this exercise and introduce a miscellany of exotics, with the aim of expanding the techniques available to the reader for pricing new contracts. Typically, I introduce the pricing and hedging concepts in an equity framework, but by the end of the book the astute reader will appreciate their applicability to other worlds, such as fixed income.

18.2 FORWARD START OPTIONS

As its name suggests, a **forward start** is an option that comes into being some time in the future. Let us consider an example: a forward start call option is bought now, at time $t = 0$, but with a strike price that is not known until time T_1, when the strike is set at the asset price on that date, say. The option expires later at time T. There are two ways to solve this problem in a Black–Scholes world, the simple and the complicated. We begin with the former.

The simple way to price this contract is to ask what happens at time T_1. At that time we get an at-the-money option with a time $T - T_1$ left to expiry. If the stock price at time T_1 is S_1 then the value of the contract is simply the Black–Scholes value with $S = S_1$, $t = T - T_1$, $E = S_1$ and with given values for r and σ. For a call option this value, as a function of S_1, is

$$S_1 N(d_1) - S_1 e^{-r(T-T_1)} N(d_2),$$

where

$$d_1 = \frac{r + \frac{1}{2}\sigma^2}{\sigma}\sqrt{T - T_1}$$

and

$$d_2 = \frac{r - \frac{1}{2}\sigma^2}{\sigma}\sqrt{T - T_1}.$$

The value is proportional to S. Thus, at time T_1 we will hold an asset worth

$$S_1 f(T - T_1).$$

Since this is a constant multiplied by the asset price at time T_1 the value today must be

$$S f(T - T_1)$$

where S is today's asset price.

The other way of valuing this option, within our general path-dependent framework, is to introduce a new state variable $\mathcal{S}$ which is defined for $t \geq T_1$ as being the asset price at time T_1,

$$\mathcal{S} = S(T_1). \tag{18.1}$$

For times before that, we set $\mathcal{S} = 0$, although it does not actually matter what it is. The result of this pricing method is, as we now see, identical to the above simple method but the technique of introducing a new variable has a very wide applicability.

The option has a value that depends on three variables: $V(S, \mathcal{S}, t)$. This function satisfies the Black–Scholes equation in S and t since $\mathcal{S}$ is not stochastic and is constant after the date T_1. At expiry we have

$$V(S, \mathcal{S}, T) = \max(S - \mathcal{S}, 0).$$

At the start date, T_1, the strike price is set to the current asset price; this is Equation (18.1). The jump condition across T_1 is simply

$$V(S, \mathcal{S}, T_1^-) = V(S, S, T_1^+).$$

And that's all there is to it.

For this, the simplest of forward start options, we can take the analysis considerably further. We can either observe that the option value after time T_1 is that of a vanilla call, and therefore we have a formula for it as above, or we can use the similarity variable, $\xi = S/\mathcal{S}$ to transform the problem to

$$\frac{\partial H}{\partial t} + \frac{1}{2}\sigma^2\xi^2\frac{\partial^2 H}{\partial \xi^2} + r\frac{\partial H}{\partial \xi} - rH = 0$$

with

$$H(\xi, T) = \max(\xi - 1, 0)$$

and where $V(S, \mathcal{S}, t) = \mathcal{S}H(\xi, t)$.

Across time T_1 we have

$$V(S, \mathcal{S}, T_1^-) = V(S, S, T_1^+) = SH(1, T_1^+).$$

If we use this as the final condition (at time T_1) for the value for the option up to time T_1 then we see that for such times the option value is simply proportional to S. The unique solution is therefore

$$V(S, \mathcal{S}, t) = SH(1, T_1) \quad \text{for} \quad t < T_1.$$

Of course, $H(1, T_1)$ is just the value of an at-the-money call option with a strike of 1 at a time $T - T_1$ before expiry. This takes us back to the result of the simple approach.

I have stressed the path-dependent approach, although unnecessarily complicated for the simple forward start option, because of its applicability to many other contracts.

18.3 SHOUT OPTIONS

A **shout call** option is a vanilla call option but with the extra feature that the holder can at any time reset the strike price of the option to the current level of the asset (if it is higher than the original strike). There is simultaneously a payment, usually of the difference between the old and the new strike prices. The action of resetting is called 'shouting.'

Since there is clearly an element of optimization in the matter of shouting, one would expect to see a free boundary problem occur quite naturally as with American options.

To value this contract introduce the two functions: $V_a(S, X, t)$ and $V_b(S, X, t)$. The former is the value of the option after shouting and the latter, before. S is the underlying asset value, X the strike level. Because the variable X is updated discretely, the relevant equation to solve is the basic Black–Scholes equation. The final conditions are

$$V_a(S, X, T) = V_b(S, X, T) = \max(S - X, 0).$$

The function $V_b(S, X, t)$ must satisfy the constraint

$$V_b(S, X, t) \geq V_a(S, \max(S, X), t) - R(S, X),$$

with gradient continuity. Here $R(S, X)$ is the amount of money that must be paid on shouting. This represents the optimization of the shouting policy; when the two sides of this expression are equal it is optimal to shout.

This problem must be solved numerically; depending on the form of R there may be a similarity reduction to two dimensions. The option value is then $V(S_0, X_0, t_0)$ where the subscripts denote the initial values of the variables.

The definition of this simple shout option can be easily extended to allow for other rules about how the strike is reset, what the payment is on shouting, and to allow for multiple shouts.

18.4 CAPPED LOOKBACKS AND ASIANS

In **capped lookbacks** and **capped Asians** there is some limit or guarantee placed on the size of the maximum, minimum or average. A typical example of a capped Asian would have the path-dependent quantity being the average of the lesser of the underlying asset and some other prescribed level. This is represented by

$$A = \frac{I}{t}$$

with

$$I = \int_0^t \min(S, S_u)\, d\tau.$$

The stochastic differential equation for I from which follows the governing partial differential equation is

$$dI = \min(S, S_u)\, dt.$$

18.5 COMBINING PATH-DEPENDENT QUANTITIES: THE LOOKBACK-ASIAN ETC.

We have seen in Chapters 15–17 how to value options whose payoff, and therefore value, depend on various path-dependent quantities. There is no reason why we cannot price a contract that depends on more than one path-dependent quantity. Often, all that this requires is the use of one state-variable for each quantity.

As an example, let us consider the pricing of an option that we could call a **lookback-Asian**. By this, we mean a contract that depends on both a maximum (or minimum) and an average. But what do we mean by the 'maximum,' is it the realized maximum of the underlying asset or, perhaps, the maximum of the average? Clearly, there are a great many possible meanings for such a contract. We consider three of them here, although the reader can doubtless think of many more (and should).

18.5.1 The Maximum of the Asset and the Average of the Asset

The simplest example, and the one closest to the problems we have encountered so far, is that of a contract depending on both the realized maximum of the asset and the realized average of the asset. Suppose that the average is arithmetic and that both path-dependent quantities are sampled discretely, and on the same dates. These assumptions can easily be generalized.

First of all, we observe that the option value is a function of *four* variables, S, t, M, the maximum, and A, the average. The variables M and A are measured discretely according to the definitions

$$M_i = \max(S(t_1), S(t_2), \ldots, S(t_i))$$

and

$$A_i = \frac{1}{i}\sum_{i}^{i} S(t_j).$$

Now we need to find the jump condition across a sampling date. This follows directly from the updating rule across sampling dates. The updating rule across a sampling date for the maximum is, as we have seen,

$$M_i = \max(M_{i-1}, S(t_i)).$$

The updating rule for the average is

$$A_i = \frac{(i-1)A_{i-1} + S(t_i)}{i}.$$

Thus the jump condition across a sampling date for this type of lookback-Asian is therefore given by

$$V(S, M, A, t_i^-) = V\left(S, \max(M, S), \frac{(i-1)A + S}{i}, t_i^+\right).$$

This together with the Black–Scholes equation and a suitable final condition, is the full specification of this lookback-Asian.

18.5.2 The Average of the Asset and the Maximum of the Average

In this contract, the payoff depends on the average of the underlying asset and on the maximum *of that average*. We still have an option value that is a function of the four variables but now the updating rules are

$$A_i = \frac{(i-1)A_{i-1} + S(t_i)}{i},$$

and

$$M_i = \max(M_{i-1}, A_i).$$

Observe how we have taken the average first and then used that new average in the definition of the maximum. Again, there is plenty of scope for generalization.

Thus the jump condition across a sampling date for this type of lookback-Asian is given by

$$V(S, M, A, t_i^-) = V\left(S, \max\left(M, \frac{(i-1)A + S}{i}\right), \frac{(i-1)A + S}{i}, t_i^+\right).$$

18.5.3 The Maximum of the Asset and the Average of the Maximum

In this final example, we just swap the role of maximum and average in the previous case. We take the maximum of the asset first and then the average of that maximum, thus we have the following updating rules

$$M_i = \max(M_{i-1}, S(t_i))$$

and

$$A_i = \frac{(i-1)A_{i-1} + M_i}{i},$$

and consequently we have the jump condition

$$V(S, M, A, t_i^-) = V\left(S, \max(M, S), \frac{(i-1)A + \max(M, S)}{i}, t_i^+\right).$$

Finally, let us comment that for many of the obvious and natural payoffs, there is a similarity reduction, so that we need only solve a three-dimensional problem. I leave this issue to the reader to follow up.

18.6 THE VOLATILITY OPTION

A particularly interesting path-dependent quantity that can be the payoff for an exotic option is the realized historical volatility. By this, I mean a statistical quantity such as

$$\sqrt{\frac{1}{\delta t}\frac{1}{M-1}\sum_{j=1}^{M}\log(S(t_j)/S(t_{j-1}))^2},$$

where δt is the time interval between samples of the asset price. (Note that I have not taken off the drift of the asset. This becomes increasingly less significant as we let δt tend to zero.) The data points used in this expression are shown in Figure 18.1.

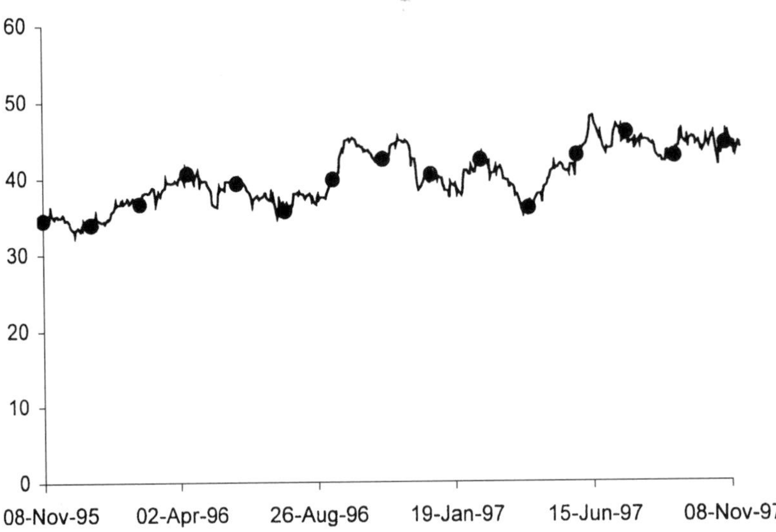

Figure 18.1 A schematic representation of the calculation of the historical volatility.

The reader might ask 'Won't this quantity simply be the volatility that we put into the model?' If so, what is the point of having a model for the historical volatility at all? The answer is that either we do not take δt sufficiently small for the above quantity to be necessarily close to the input volatility, or we assume a more complicated model for the volatility (such as stochastic or uncertain volatility (see Chapters 23 and 24) or assume an implied volatility surface (see Chapter 22)).

Let us begin by valuing a contract with the above payoff in a Black–Scholes, constant volatility world, and then briefly discuss improvements.

The trick is to introduce *two* path-dependent quantities, the running volatility and the last sampled asset price:

$$I_i = \sqrt{\frac{1}{\delta t(i-1)} \sum_{j=1}^{i} \log(S(t_j)/S(t_{j-1}))^2};$$

$$\mathcal{S}_i = S(t_{i-1}).$$

The option value is a function of four variables: $V(S, \mathcal{S}, I, t)$. The updating rules at time t_i for the two path-dependent quantities are

$$\mathcal{S}_i = S(t_{i-1})$$

and

$$I_i = \sqrt{\frac{1}{\delta t(i-1)} \sum_{j=1}^{i} \log(S(t_j)/S(t_{j-1}))^2}$$

$$= \sqrt{\frac{i}{i-1} I_{i-1}^2 + \frac{1}{\delta t(i-1)} (\log(S_i) - \log(\mathcal{S}_i))^2}.$$

We can see from the second updating rule why we had to keep track of the old sampled asset price: it is used in the updating rule for the running volatility.

The jump condition across a sampling date is

$$V(S, \mathcal{S}, I, t_i^-) = V\left(S, \mathcal{S}, \sqrt{\frac{i}{i-1}I^2 + \frac{1}{\delta t(i-1)}(\log(S) - \log(\mathcal{S}))^2}, t_i^+\right).$$

If the option pays off the realized volatility at expiry, T, then

$$V(S, \mathcal{S}, I, T) = I.$$

The dimensionality of this problem can be reduced to three by the use of the similarity variable $S/\mathcal{S}$.

If we do not believe in constant volatility then we could introduce a stochastic volatility model. This does not change the specification of our model in any way other than to introduce a new variable σ which satisfies some stochastic differential equation. The problem to solve is then in five dimensions, becoming four with the use of a similarity reduction, with the same path-dependent quantities and the same updating rules and jump condition. The high (four) dimensionality makes this problem computationally intensive and it may well be a candidate for a Monte Carlo simulation (see Chapter 49).

18.7 LADDERS

The **ladder option** is a lookback option that is discretely sampled, but this time discretely sampled in asset price rather than time. Thus the option receives a payoff that is a function of the highest asset price achieved out of a given set. For example, the ladder is set at multiples of \$5: ..., 50, 55, 60, 65, ... If during the life of the contract the asset reached a maximum of 58, then the maximum registered would be 55. Such an option would clearly be cheaper than the continuous version.

This contract can be decomposed into a series of barrier-type options triggered at each of the rungs of the ladder. Alternatively, using the framework of Chapter 17, we simply have a payoff that is a step function of the maximum, M; see Figure 18.2.

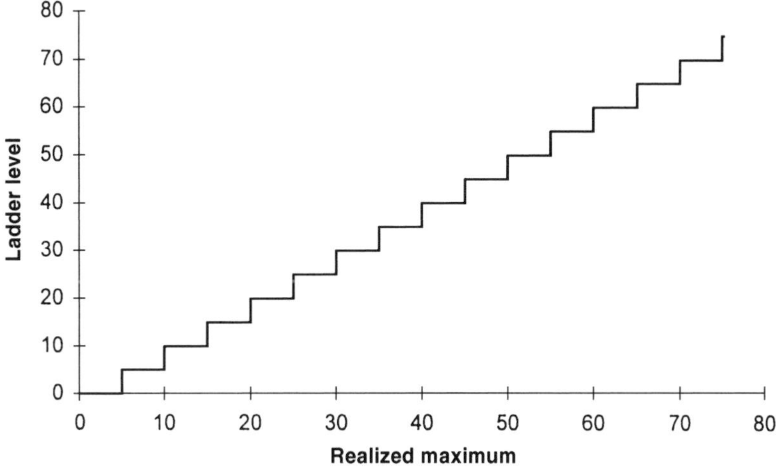

Figure 18.2 The payoff for a ladder option as a function of the realized maximum.

18.8 PARISIAN OPTIONS

Parisian options are barrier options for which the barrier feature (knock in or knock out) is only triggered after the underlying has spent a certain prescribed time beyond the barrier. The effect of this more rigorous triggering criterion is to 'smooth' the option value (and delta and gamma) near the barrier to make hedging somewhat easier. It also makes manipulation of the triggering, by manipulation of the underlying asset, much harder. In the classical Parisian contract the 'clock' measuring the time outside the barrier is reset when the asset returns to within the barrier. In the Par*asian* contract the clock is not reset. We only consider the former here, the latter is a simple modification.

In Figure 18.3 is shown a representation of a Parisian contract. The bottom curve is the (scaled) time that the stock price has been above the barrier level. Once it has reached ten days (here scaled to one) the barrier is triggered.

Parisian options are clearly strongly path dependent, but in a way that is perfectly manageable in the differential equation framework. We do not need all the details of the path taken, the only extra information we need to know is the value of the variable τ, defined as the length of time the asset has been beyond the barrier:

$$\tau = t - \sup\{t' \leq t | S(t') \leq S_u\}$$

for an up barrier at S_u, and there is a similar expression for a down barrier. The stochastic differential equation for τ is given by

$$d\tau = \begin{cases} d\tau & S > S_u \\ -\tau^- & S = S_u \\ 0 & S < S_u \end{cases}$$

where τ^- is the value of τ before it jumps to zero on resetting. We use this equation to derive the partial differential equation for the option value. Notice how, outside the barrier, real time t and the trigger time τ are increasing at the same rate. The barrier is triggered when τ reaches the value ω.

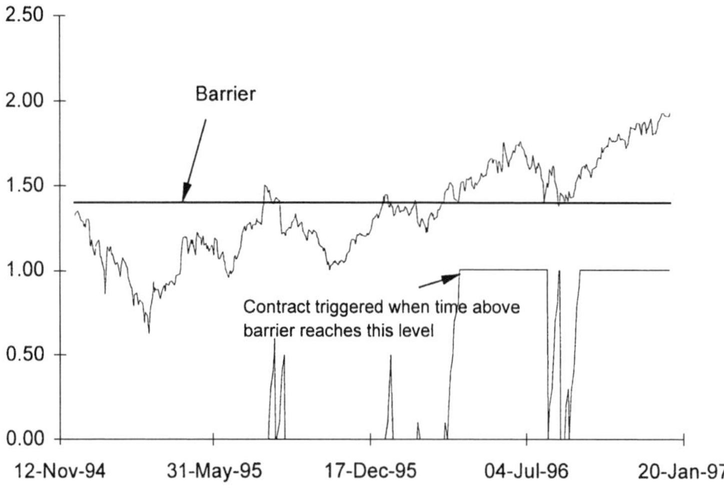

Figure 18.3 Representation of a Parisian contract.

We must solve for V as a function of three variables S, t and τ, $V(S, t, \tau)$. We solve for V in two regions: inside the barrier and outside. Inside the barrier the clock is switched off and we solve

$$\frac{\partial V}{\partial t} + \tfrac{1}{2}\sigma^2 S^2 \frac{\partial^2 V}{\partial S^2} + rS\frac{\partial V}{\partial S} - rV = 0.$$

In this region there is no τ dependence (this is not true for Par*asians*). Outside the barrier the clock is ticking and we have

$$\frac{\partial V}{\partial t} + \frac{\partial V}{\partial \tau} + \tfrac{1}{2}\sigma^2 S^2 \frac{\partial^2 V}{\partial S^2} + rS\frac{\partial V}{\partial S} - rV = 0.$$

At $S = S_u$, where τ is reset, we must impose continuity of the option value:

$$V(S_u, t, \tau) = V(S_u, t, 0).$$

Now we come to the exact specification of the payoff in the event of triggering (or the event of not-triggering). If the barrier has not been triggered by expiry T then the option has the payoff $F(S, \tau)$. If the barrier has been triggered before expiry the option pays off $G(S)$ at expiry. For example an up-and-in Parisian put would have $F = 0$ and $G = \max(E - S, 0)$. An up-and-out call would have $F = \max(S - E, 0)$ and $G = 0$. In this framework ins and outs are treated the same. The boundary conditions are applied as follows:

$$V(S, T, \omega) = G(S)$$

and

$$V(S, T, \tau) = F(S, \tau).$$

American-style Parisians (Henry Miller options?) have the additional constraint that

$$V(S, t, \tau) \geq A(S, t, \tau),$$

with continuity of the delta, where the function A defines the payoff in the event of early exercise.

18.9 PERFECT TRADER AND PASSPORT OPTIONS

For my last example in this chapter I want to describe an option that sits outside the framework we have developed so far. It is not too difficult to analyze but it introduces some new ideas, and in particular it is a gentle introduction to the subject of **stochastic control**.

Suppose that you invest in a particular stock, keeping track of its movements and buying or selling according to your view of its future direction. The amount of money that you accumulate due to trading in this stock is called the **trading account**. If you are a good trader or lucky then the amount in the account will grow; if you are a bad trader or unlucky then the amount will be negative. How much would you pay to be insured against losing money over a given time horizon? A **perfect trader** or **passport option** is a call option on the trading account, giving the holder the amount in his account at the end of the horizon if it is positive, or zero if it is negative.

To value this contract we must introduce a new variable π which is the value of the trading account, meaning the value of the stocks held together with any cash accumulated. This quantity satisfies the following stochastic differential equation

$$d\pi = r(\pi - qS)\,dt + q\,dS, \tag{18.2}$$

where S is still the lognormally distributed stock price and q is the amount of stock held at time t. The quantity q is of our choosing, will vary as time and the stock price change, and is called the **strategy**; it will be a function of S, π and t. I will restrict the size of the position in the stock by insisting that $|q| \leq 1$. Equation (18.2) contains a deterministic and a random term. The first term says that there is growth in the cash holding, $\pi - qS$, due to the addition of interest at a rate r, and the second term is due to the change in value of the stock holding.

The contract will pay off an amount

$$\max(\pi, 0)$$

at time T. This will be the final condition for our option value $V(S, \pi, t)$. Note that the option value is a function of three variables.

Now let us hedge this option:

$$\Pi = V - \Delta S.$$

We find that

$$d\Pi = \left(\frac{\partial V}{\partial t} + \tfrac{1}{2}\sigma^2 S^2 \frac{\partial^2 V}{\partial S^2} + q\sigma^2 S^2 \frac{\partial^2 V}{\partial S\,\partial \pi} + \tfrac{1}{2}q^2\sigma^2 S^2 \frac{\partial^2 V}{\partial \pi^2} \right) + \frac{\partial V}{\partial S}\,dS + \frac{\partial V}{\partial \pi}\,d\pi - \Delta\,dS.$$

Since $d\pi$ contains a dS term the correct hedge ratio is

$$\Delta = \frac{\partial V}{\partial S} + q\frac{\partial V}{\partial \pi}.$$

From the no-arbitrage principle follows the pricing equation

$$\frac{\partial V}{\partial t} + \tfrac{1}{2}\sigma^2 S^2 \frac{\partial^2 V}{\partial S^2} + q\sigma^2 S^2 \frac{\partial^2 V}{\partial S\,\partial \pi} + \tfrac{1}{2}q^2\sigma^2 S^2 \frac{\partial^2 V}{\partial \pi^2} + rS\frac{\partial V}{\partial S} + r\pi\frac{\partial V}{\partial \pi} - rV = 0. \qquad (18.3)$$

This is not a diffusion equation in two space-like variables because S and π are perfectly correlated, the equation really has one space-like and two time-like variables.

We come to the stochastic control part of the problem in choosing q. If we are selling this contract then we should assume that the holder acts optimally, making the contracts value as high as possible. That doesn't mean the holder will follow such a strategy since he will have other priorities, he will have a view on the market and will not be hedging. The highest value for the contract occurs when q is chosen to maximize the terms in (18.3):

$$\max_{|q|\leq 1} \left(q\sigma^2 S^2 \frac{\partial^2 V}{\partial S\,\partial \pi} + \tfrac{1}{2}q^2\sigma^2 S^2 \frac{\partial^2 V}{\partial \pi^2} \right).$$

This is the only term containing q.

18.9.1 Similarity Solution

If the payoff is simply

$$V(S, \pi, T) = \max(\pi, 0)$$

then we can find a similarity solution of the form

$$V(S, \pi, t) = SH(\xi, t), \quad \xi = \frac{\pi}{S}.$$

In this case Equation (18.3) becomes

$$\frac{\partial H}{\partial t} + \tfrac{1}{2}\sigma^2(\xi - q)^2\frac{\partial^2 H}{\partial \xi^2} = 0,$$

the payoff is

$$H(\xi, T) = \max(\xi, 0)$$

and the optimal strategy is

$$\max_{|q|\le 1}\left((\xi - q)^2\frac{\partial^2 H}{\partial \xi^2}\right).$$

Assuming that $\partial^2 H/\partial\xi^2 > 0$ (and this can be verified *a posteriori*) because of the nature of the equation and its final condition, the optimal strategy is

$$q = \begin{cases} -1 & \text{when } \xi > 0 \\ 1 & \text{when } \xi < 0. \end{cases}$$

For a more general payoff the strategy would depend on the sign of $\partial^2 H/\partial\xi^2$.

The option value, assuming the optimal strategy, thus satisfies

$$\frac{\partial H}{\partial t} + \tfrac{1}{2}\sigma^2(|\xi| + 1)^2\frac{\partial^2 H}{\partial \xi^2} = 0.$$

A term sheet for perfect trader option is shown in Figure 18.4. The holder of the option is allowed to make a series of hypothetical trades on the USD/DEM exchange rate. Two trades are allowed per day with a maximum allowed position long and short. The holder then receives the positive part of his transactions. If his trades result in a negative net balance this is written off.

USD/DEM 'Perfect Trader' Option

Notional Amount	USD 25,000,000+
Option Maturity	Three months from Trade Date
Allowed Position	Long or short up to Notional Amount
Transaction Frequency	Up to two times daily
Settlement Amount	Max (0, sum total in DEM of the gains + losses on each of the trades)
Upfront Premium	3.35% of Notional Amount

This indicative termsheet is neither an offer to buy or sell securities or an OTC derivative product which includes options, swaps, forwards and structured notes having similar features to OTC derivative transactions, nor a solicitation to buy or sell securities or an OTC derivative product. The proposal contained in the foregoing is not a complete description of the terms of a particular transaction and is subject to change without limitation.

Figure 18.4 Term sheet for a Perfect Trader option.

18.10 SUMMARY

I hope that after reading the chapters in this part of the book the reader will feel confident to find partial differential equation formulations for many other types of derivative contract. In

Part Four, on interest rates and products, it is assumed that the reader can transfer ideas from the lognormal asset world to the more complicated world of fixed income.

FURTHER READING

- See Dewynne & Wilmott (1994 c) for a mixed bag of exotics and their modeling.
- Chesney, Cornwall, Jeanblanc-Picqué, Kentwell & Yor (1997) price Parisians via Laplace transforms.
- See Haber, Schönbucher & Wilmott (1997) for a more detailed description of partial differential equation approach to pricing Parisian options. A fully-functional stand-alone Parisian option pricer may be downloaded from www.wilmott.com.
- Hyer, Lipton–Lifschitz & Pugachevsky (1997) describe the passport option.
- Ahn, Penaud & Wilmott (1998) and Penaud, Wilmott & Ahn (1998) discuss many, many extensions to the passport option concept.
- See Whaley (1993) for a description of his implied volatility index.

EXERCISES

1. Consider the 10% European rebate put. It has the following features:
   If the share price falls by more than 10% before expiry, then the option pays out $\max(E - S, 0)$ at expiry. Otherwise the option pays out 20% of the initial cost of the option at expiry.

   By decomposing the option into contracts with known values, or otherwise, find the fair price for this option.
2. A particular wedge option compensates the holder for falls in the asset price of up to 20%, paying out the difference between the initial and current prices at expiry. What contract, of known value, is this equivalent to?
3. A shout option has payoff $\max(S - E, 0)$ at expiry. Only one shout is allowed before expiry. By considering the payoff at expiry with and without shouting, show that if the share price rises above E before expiry, then it will be optimal to shout at some point.
4. Consider the capped lookback strike put, with payoff dependent on the capped maximum asset price over the time to expiry. What differential equation would we find in the case of the continuously sampled option? What jump condition would the discretely sampled version satisfy?
5. What updating rule and jump condition would we find for a discretely-sampled capped Asian option with payoff dependent on the arithmetic average of the asset prices?
6. Find the updating rules and jump conditions for discretely-sampled, geometric average lookback-Asians dependent on the following path-dependent quantities:
   (a) The maximum of the asset and the average of the asset,
   (b) The average of the asset and the maximum of the average,
   (c) The maximum of the asset and the average of the maximum.
7. A ladder option has rungs set at multiples of \$10 and has payoff $\max(M - E, 0)$, where the maximum, M, is only registered at the rungs. The initial asset price is \$50. Show how we could value this option by decomposing it into a set of barrier options (with known values).

8. The ratchet option is a variant of the shout option. The holder has no choice over the occurrence of a shout. A particular ratchet has the following features:

   Initially, the option is a European call. At set times T_1, T_2, ..., T_n before expiry, the exercise price of the option is reset to the current asset price. The option also pays out any positive value of the asset price minus the old exercise price.

   By considering forward start options, show how could we decompose this option to make its valuation simpler.

PART THREE
extending Black–Scholes

The third part of the book concerns extensions to the Black–Scholes world. All of the assumptions in the Black–Scholes model are incorrect to a greater or lesser degree. I will show how to incorporate ideas aimed at improving the modeling of the underlying asset. Some of these ideas are relatively standard, fitting easily into a classical Black–Scholes-type framework. Others take us far from the well-trodden path into new and uncharted territories. One of the most important points to watch out for is whether or not a model is linear or nonlinear; is the value of a portfolio of options the same as the sum of the values of the individual components? I believe that nonlinear models capture some important features that are neglected by the more common linear models. I will expand on this point at various times throughout the rest of the book.

Chapter 19: Defects in the Black–Scholes Model Many deficiencies in the simple Black–Scholes model are brought together in this chapter for a general discussion. The issues raised here will be expanded upon in later chapters.

Chapter 20: Discrete Hedging Even if all of the other assumptions that go into the Black–Scholes model were correct, the impossibility of delta hedging continuously in time would have an enormous effect on the actual profit and loss experienced during the business of hedging.

Chapter 21: Transaction Costs This was one of the first areas of research for me when I discovered mathematical finance. Unfortunately, most of of the advanced work in this subject cannot easily be condensed into a chapter of a book. For that reason I will summarize many of the ideas and results, giving details only for the Leland model for vanilla options and its Hoggard–Whalley–Wilmott extension to arbitrary contracts.

Chapter 22: Volatility Smiles and Surfaces Volatility is the most important parameter in the valuation of options. It is difficult to measure statistically from time series data; however, we can tell from the prices of traded instruments what the market thinks is the correct value or structure for volatility.

Chapter 23: Stochastic Volatility It is natural to model volatility as a stochastic variable because it is so clearly not constant and not predictable.

Chapter 24: Uncertain Parameters The difficulties associated with observing, estimating and predicting important parameters mean that we should try to reduce the dependence of a price on such quantities. One way of doing this is to allow parameters to lie in a prescribed range. We don't even need to know their value at any point in time if we price in a worst-case scenario. This is the Avellaneda, Levy, Parás and Lyons model for uncertain volatility.

Chapter 25: Empirical Analysis of Volatility It is not too difficult to find a decent stochastic model for volatility if one knows how to examine the data. I make a few suggestions in that direction.

Chapter 26: Jump Diffusion One of the real-life features not captured by the Black–Scholes world is that of discontinuous asset price paths. I describe the Merton model for jump-diffusive random walks.

Chapter 27: Crash Modeling The Merton model for jumps requires quite a few parameters to be input, as well as an estimate of the distribution of jump sizes. This, together with the impossibility of hedging in the Merton world, makes the model somewhat unsatisfactory. If we price assuming the worst-case scenario then most of these difficulties vanish.

Chapter 28: Speculating with Options Option theory is built on the idea of hedging. But what about those people who use options for speculation? Very little is ever said about how they can make investment decisions. I will try to remedy that in this chapter.

Chapter 29: The Feedback Effect of Hedging in Illiquid Markets This chapter describes a highly non-classical detour away from the Black–Scholes world. What if there is so much trade in the underlying asset for the hedging of derivatives that the normal causal link between the underlying and the option gets confused?

Chapter 30: Static Hedging The nonlinearity in many of the preceeding models means that the value of a portfolio of contracts is not the same as the sum of the values of the individual components. Thus the value of a contract depends on what you hedge it with. The beautiful consequences of this are discussed in the final chapter of Part Three.

CHAPTER 19
defects in the Black–Scholes model

In this Chapter...

- why the Black–Scholes assumptions are wrong
- how to improve the Black–Scholes model

19.1 INTRODUCTION

Before pointing out some of the flaws in the assumptions of the Black–Scholes world, I must emphasize how well the model has done in practice, how widespread is its use and how much impact it has had on financial markets, not to mention a Nobel Prize for two of its three creators. The model is used by everyone working in derivatives, whether they are salesmen, traders or quants. It is used confidently in situations for which it was not designed, usually successfully. The value of vanilla options are often not quoted in monetary terms, but in volatility terms with the understanding that the price of a contract is its Black–Scholes value using the quoted volatility. You use a model other than Black–Scholes only with extreme caution, and you will have to be pretty convincing to persuade your colleagues that you know what you are doing. The ideas of delta hedging and risk-neutral pricing have taken a formidable grip on the minds of academics and practitioners alike. In many ways, especially with regards to commercial success, the Black–Scholes model is remarkably robust.

Nevertheless, there is room for improvement. Certainly, we can find models that better describe the underlying, what is not clear is whether these models make us more money. In the next few sections I introduce the ideas and models that will be expanded upon in the rest of the book. Some of these ideas are classical, in the sense that they are academically respectable, require no great leaps of imagination and are thoroughly harmless. Other ideas are too new to say what the future has in store for them. Yet there is at least a grain of truth in all that follows.

Each section corresponds to a chapter. First I give the relevant Black–Scholes assumption, and then I say why it is wrong and how, later, I try to relax the assumption. All the details will be found in the relevant chapters.

19.2 DISCRETE HEDGING

Black–Scholes assumes

- Delta hedging is continuous

Consider first the continuous-time world of stochastic calculus. When we derived the Black–Scholes equation we used the continuous-time Itô's lemma. The delta hedging that was necessary for risk elimination also had to take place continuously. If there is a finite time between rehedges then there is risk that has not been eliminated.

In Chapter 20 we consider the effect of hedging at discrete intervals of time, taking real expectations over finite time periods rather than applying continuous-time calculus.

19.3 TRANSACTION COSTS

Black–Scholes assumes

- Delta hedging is continuous
- There are no costs in delta hedging

But not only must we worry about hedging discretely, we must also worry about how much it costs us to rehedge. The buying and selling of assets exposes us to bid-offer spreads. In some markets this is insignificant, then we rehedge as often as we can. In other markets, the cost can be so great that we cannot afford to hedge as often as we would like. These issues, and several models, are described in Chapter 21.

19.4 VOLATILITY SMILES AND SURFACES

Black–Scholes assumes

- Volatility is a known constant (or a known deterministic function)

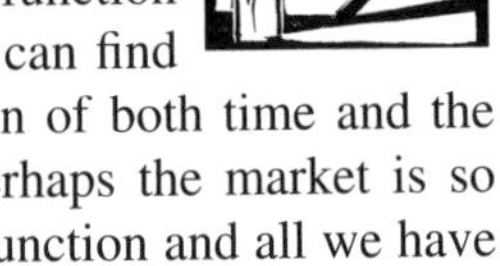

If volatility is not a simple constant then perhaps it is a more complicated function of time and/or the underlying. If it is a function of time alone then we can find explicit solutions as described in Chapter 8. But what if it is a function of both time and the underlying? Perhaps the market even knows what this function is. Perhaps the market is so clever that it prices all traded contracts consistently with this volatility function and all we have to do is deduce from these traded prices what the volatility function is.

The link between the prices of vanilla options in the market and a deterministic volatility is the subject of Chapter 22. We see how to back out from market prices the 'implied volatility surface.'

This technique is popular for pricing exotic options, yielding prices that are 'consistent' with traded prices of similar contracts.

19.5 STOCHASTIC VOLATILITY

Black–Scholes assumes

- Volatility is a known constant (or a known deterministic function)

The Black–Scholes *formulae* require the volatility of the underlying to be a known deterministic function of time. The Black–Scholes *equation* requires the volatility to be a known function of time and the asset value. Neither of these is true. All volatility time series show volatility to be a highly unstable quantity. It is very variable and unpredictable. It is therefore natural to represent volatility itself as a random variable. I show the theory behind this in Chapter 23.

Stochastic volatility models are currently popular for the pricing of contracts that are very sensitive to the behavior of volatility. Barrier options are the most obvious example.

19.6 UNCERTAIN PARAMETERS

Black–Scholes assumes

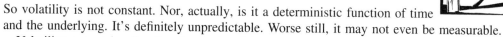

- Volatility, interest rates, dividends are known constants (or known deterministic functions)

So volatility is not constant. Nor, actually, is it a deterministic function of time and the underlying. It's definitely unpredictable. Worse still, it may not even be measurable.

Volatility cannot be directly observed and its measurement is very difficult. How then can we hope to model it? Maybe we should not attempt to model something we can't even observe. What we should do is to make as few statements about its behavior as possible. We will not say what volatility currently is or even what probability distribution it has. We shall content ourselves with placing a bound on its value, restricting it to lie within a given range. The probability distribution of the volatility within this range will not be prescribed. If it so desires, the volatility can jump from one extreme to the other as often as it wishes. This 'model' is then used to price contracts in a 'worst-case scenario.'

The idea of ranges for parameters is extended to allow the short-term interest rate and dividends to be uncertain, and to lie within specified ranges.

19.7 EMPIRICAL ANALYSIS OF VOLATILITY

Black–Scholes assumes

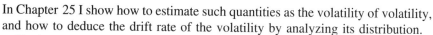

- Volatility is a known constant (or a known deterministic function)

In Chapter 25 I show how to estimate such quantities as the volatility of volatility, and how to deduce the drift rate of the volatility by analyzing its distribution.

Having determined a plausible stochastic differential equation model for the volatility from data, I suggest ways in which it can be used. It can be used directly in a stochastic volatility model, or indirectly in an uncertain volatility model to determine the likelihood of volatility ranges being breached.

19.8 JUMP DIFFUSION

Black–Scholes assumes

- The underlying asset path is continuous

It is common experience that markets are discontinuous; from time to time they 'jump,' usually downwards. This is not incorporated in the lognormal asset price model, for which all paths are continuous.

When I say 'jump' I mean two things. First, that the sudden moves are not contained in the lognormal model; they are too large, occuring too frequently, to be from a Normally distributed returns model. Second, they are unhedgeable; the moves are too sudden for continuous hedging through to the bottom of the jump.

The jump-diffusion model described in Chapter 26 is an attempt to incorporate discontinuities into the price path. These discontinuities are not modeled by the lognormal random walk that we have been using so far. Jump-diffusion is an improvement on the model of the underlying but introduces some unsatisfactory elements: risk elimination is no longer possible and we must price in an 'expected' sense.

19.9 CRASH MODELING

Black–Scholes assumes

- The underlying asset path is continuous

If risk elimination is not possible can we consider worst-case scenarios? That is, assume that the worst does happen and then allow for it in the pricing. But what exactly is 'the worst'? The worst outcome will be different for different portfolios.

In Chapter 27 I show how to model the worst-case scenario and price options accordingly.

19.10 SPECULATING WITH OPTIONS

Black–Scholes assumes

- Options are delta hedged

In Chapter 28 I show how to 'value' options when one is *not* hedging, rather one is speculating with derivatives because one has a good idea where the underlying is going. If one has a view on the underlying, then it is natural to invest in options because of their gearing. But how can this view be quantified? One way is to estimate real expected returns from an unhedged position. This together with an estimate of the risk in a position enables one to choose which option gives the best risk/reward profile for the given market view.

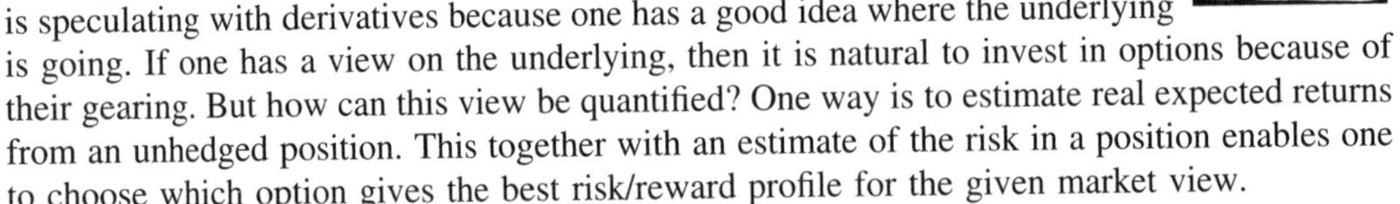

This idea can be extended to consider many types of model for the underlying, each one representing a different view of the behavior of the market. Furthermore, many trading strategies can be modeled. For example, how can one model the optimal closure of an option position? When should one sell back an option? Should you at times hedge, and at others speculate? Is there a best way to choose between the two?

19.11 THE FEEDBACK EFFECT OF HEDGING IN ILLIQUID MARKETS

Black–Scholes assumes

- The underlying asset is unaffected by trade in the option

The buying and selling of assets move their prices. A large trade will move prices more than a small trade. In the Black–Scholes model it is assumed that moves in the underlying are exogenous, that some cosmic random number generator tells us the prices of all 'underlyings.' In reality, a large trade in the underlying will move the price in a fairly predictable fashion. For example, it is not unheard of for unscrupulous people to deliberately move prices to ensure that a barrier option is triggered. In that case, a small move in the underlying could have a very big effect on the payoff of an option.

In Chapter 29 I will try to quantify this effect, introducing the idea that a trade in the underlying initiated by the need to delta hedge can move the price of the underlying. Thus it is no longer the case that the underlying moves and the option price follows, now it is more of a chicken-and-egg scenario. We will see that close to expiry of an option, when the gamma is large, the underlying can move in a very dramatic way.

19.12 OPTIMAL STATIC HEDGING

Many of the non-Black–Scholes models of this part of the book are nonlinear. This includes the models of Chapters 21, 24, 27 and 28 (and 40). If the governing equation for pricing is nonlinear then the value of a portfolio of contracts is *not* the same as the sum of the values of each component on its own. One aspect of this is that the value of a contract depends on what it is hedged with. As an extreme example, consider the contract whose cashflows can be hedged exactly with traded instruments; to price this contract we do not even need a model. In fact, to use a model would be suicidal.

The beauty of the nonlinear equation is that fitting parameters to traded prices (as in the implied volatility surfaces in Chapter 22 or in 'yield curve fitting' of Chapter 34) becomes redundant. Traded prices may be right or wrong, we don't much care which. All we care about is that if we want to put them into our portfolio then we know how much they will cost.

Imagine that we have a contract called 'contract,' which has a value that we can write as

$$V_{NL}(\text{contract}),$$

where V_{NL} means the value of the contract using whatever is our nonlinear pricing equation (together with relevant boundary and final conditions). Now imagine we want to hedge 'contract' with another contract called 'hedge.' And suppose that it costs 'cost' to buy or sell this second contract in the market. Suppose that we buy λ of these hedging contracts and put them in our portfolio, then the *marginal value* of our original 'contract' is

$$V_{NL}(\text{contract} + \lambda\ \text{hedge}) - \lambda\ \text{cost}. \tag{19.1}$$

In this expression 'contract $+\lambda$ hedge' should be read as the portfolio made up of the 'union' of the original contract and λ of the hedging contract. Since V_{NL} is nonlinear, this marginal value is not the value of the contract on its own. We have hedged 'contract' statically, and we may hold 'hedge' until expiry of 'contract.' We can go one step further and hedge *optimally*. Since the quantity λ can be chosen, let us choose it to maximize the marginal value of 'contract.' That is, choose λ to maximize (19.1). This is optimal static hedging. We can, of course, have as many traded contracts for hedging as we want, and we can easily incorporate bid-offer spread.

In the event that 'contract' can have all its cashflows hedged away by one or more 'hedge' contracts, we find that we are using our nonlinear equation to value an empty portfolio and that the contract value is model independent.

19.13 SUMMARY

There are many faults with the Black–Scholes assumptions. Some of these are addressed in the next few chapters. Although it is easy to come up with any number of models that improve on Black–Scholes from a technical and mathematical point of view, it is nearly impossible to improve on its commercial success.

FURTHER READING

- For a discussion of some real-world modeling issues see the collection of papers edited by Kelly, Howison & Wilmott (1995).
- There are many other ways to improve on the lognormal model for the underlying. One which I don't have space for is a model of asset returns using hyperbolic, instead of Normal, distributions; see Eberlain & Keller (1995).

EXERCISES

1. Are there any other defects in the Black–Scholes model, not mentioned in this chapter? (You may wish to re-read the list of assumptions made in the Black–Scholes model, in Chapter 5.) How might we counteract them?
2. Why is there no point in using an optimal static hedging strategy in the Black–Scholes model (assuming that the results it gives are accurate)?

CHAPTER 20
discrete hedging

In this Chapter...

- the effect of hedging at discrete times
- hedging error
- the real distribution of profit and loss

20.1 INTRODUCTION

In this chapter we concentrate on one of the erroneous assumptions in the Black–Scholes model, that of continuous hedging. The Black–Scholes analysis requires the continuous rebalancing of a hedged portfolio according to a delta neutral strategy. This strategy is, in practice, impossible.

The structure of this chapter is as follows. We begin by examining the concept of delta hedging in a discrete-time framework. We will see that taking expectations leads to the Black–Scholes equation without any need for stochastic calculus. I then show how this can be extended to a higher-order approximation, valid when the hedging period is not infinitesimal. We then discuss the nature of the hedging error, the error between the expected change in portfolio and the actual. This quantity is commonly ignored (perhaps because it averages out to zero) but is important, especially when one examines the real distribution of returns.

20.2 A MODEL FOR A DISCRETELY-HEDGED POSITION

The Black–Scholes analysis requires *continuous* hedging, which is possible in theory but impossible, and even undesirable, in practice. Hence one hedges in some discrete way.

Our first step in analyzing the discrete hedging problem is to choose a hedging strategy. If there are no transaction costs then there is no penalty for continuous rehedging and so the 'optimal' strategy is simply the Black–Scholes strategy, and the option value is the Black–Scholes value. This is the 'mathematical solution.' However, this strategy is clearly impractical. Unfortunately, it may be difficult to associate a 'cost' to the inconvenience of continuous rehedging. (This contrasts with the later problems when we do include transaction costs and optimal strategies are found.) For this reason a common assumption is that rehedging takes place regularly at times separated by a constant interval, the hedging period, here denoted by δt. This is a strategy commonly used in practice with δt ranging from half a day to a couple of weeks. Note the use of $\delta\cdot$ to denote a discrete change in a quantity; this is to make a distinction with $d\cdot$, the earlier continuous changes.

The first work in this area was by Boyle and Emanuel who examined the discrepancy, the hedging error, between the Black–Scholes strategy of continuous rehedging and discrete hedging. They find that in each interval the hedging error is a random variable, from a chi-squared distribution, and proportional to the option gamma. We will see why this is shortly.

The spreadsheet below shows how to simulate delta hedging in the Black–Scholes fashion, but in discrete time. In this example the option is a call, there are no dividends on the underlying and there are no transaction costs. All of these can easily be incorporated. The spreadsheet uses a simple approximation to the Normal distribution. Note that the real drift of the asset is used in the simulation.

Results of this simulation are shown in Figures 20.2 and 20.3. In the first figure is the time series of the running **total hedging error** for a single realization of the underlying asset. This is the difference between the actual and theoretical values of the net option position as time evolves from the start to the end of the contract's life. The final value of -0.282 means that if you sold the option for the Black–Scholes value and hedged in the Black–Scholes manner until expiry to eliminate risk, you would have lost 0.282.

In Figure 20.3 are the results of option replication over many realizations of the underlying asset. Each dot represents the final asset price and accumulated profit and loss after hedging for the life of the contract. If hedging had been perfect each dot would lie on the payoff function, in this case $\max(S-60, 0)$.

Now we take this analysis one stage further. We use simple Taylor series expansions first to find a *better* hedge than the Black–Scholes and second to find an adjusted value for the option. The better hedge comes from hedging the option with the underlying using the number of shares that minimizes the variance of the hedged portfolio over the next timestep.

	A	B	C	D	E	F	G	H	I	J	K
1	Spot price	100		Strike	100		Total H.E	0.022329575			
2	Volatility	0.2		Expiry	1						
3	Return	0.12									
4	Int. rate	0.05		Timestep	0.01						
5											
6		Time	Asset	d1	Delta	Option	Cashflow	Balance			
7		0	100	0.35	0.63683059	10.45057563		53.23248337			
8		0.01	99.61783186	0.329004141	0.628923656	10.14458595	−0.787671583	52.47143468			
9		0.02	100.9003074	0.24062161	0.595075752	9.045311898	−3.314585674	49.18309128			
10		0.03	98.61440614	0.27387527	0.607909702	9.396104961	1.265612274	50.47330125			
11		0.04	97.63401867	0.220738823	0.587352063	8.746710443	−2.007124829	48.49141938			
12		0.05	100.2836075	0.355665969	0.638954573	10.30762805	5.174885854	53.69[illegible]			
13		0.06	102.2358172	0.453370966	0.674859161	11.52425209	3.670734851	57.38[illegible]			
14		0.07	102.9157654	0.486541139	0.686708226	11.92020972	1.219455624	58.63630072			
15		0.08	102.1571498	0.446961728	0.672548631	11.33742592	−1.446503906	57.2191223			
16		0.09	104.7837003	[illegible]	[illegible]805	13.09756132	4.829419842	62.07715885			
17		0.1	108.3185339	[illegible]	[illegible]956	15.67013801	6.032422715	68.14062791			
18		0.11	111.4842283	0.906366796	0.81762916	18.12345493	4.827222581	73.00192932			
19		0.12	110.3979786	0.855583205	0.803885868	17.17462507	−1.517231735	71.52120768			
20		0.13	109.9044232	0.83271[illegible]	[illegible]	[illegible]	[illegible]	70.85483919			
21		[illegible]	[illegible]	[illegible]392	[illegible]	[illegible]	[illegible]	71.23666615			
22		[illegible]	[illegible]	[illegible]3282066	0.848091401	19.86118963	5.404123809	76.6764172			
23		[illegible]	[illegible]	[illegible]0494218	0.846252921	19.6156665	−0.209007248	76.50575775			
24		0.17	115.8582115	1.126713352	0.870068105	21.41414525	2.75918453	79.30320472			
25		0.18	120.5238063	1.347690388	0.911120947	25.50896674	4.947844843	84.29071108			
26		0.19	123.0967478	1.469446821	0.929144146	27.81441555	2.2185972	86.55146417			
27		0.2	123.0428919	1.47224294	0.929522322	27.70250621	0.046531842	86.64128257			
28		0.21	128.1052385	1.704406438	0.955847441	32.41892175	3.372385664	90.05699971			
29		0.22	129.3637088	1.766678833	0.961359032	33.56728645	0.712999817	90.81503928			

=-F107+C107*E107-H107

=B7+$E$4

=C8*(1+$B$3*$E$4+$B$2*SQRT($E$4)*(RAND()+RAND()+RAND()+RAND()+RAND()+RAND()+RAND()+RAND()+RAND()+RAND()+RAND()+RAND()-6))

=H9*EXP($B$4*$E$4)+G10

=NORMSDIST(D13)

=(E13-E12)*C13

=C14*NORMSDIST(D14)-$E$1*EXP(-$B$4*($E$2-B14))*NORMSDIST(D14-$B$2*SQRT($E$2-B14))

=(LN(C13/$E$1)+($B$4+0.5*$B$2*$B$2)*($E$2-B13))/$B$2/SQRT($E$2-B13)

Figure 20.1 Spreadsheet for simulating hedging during the life of an option.

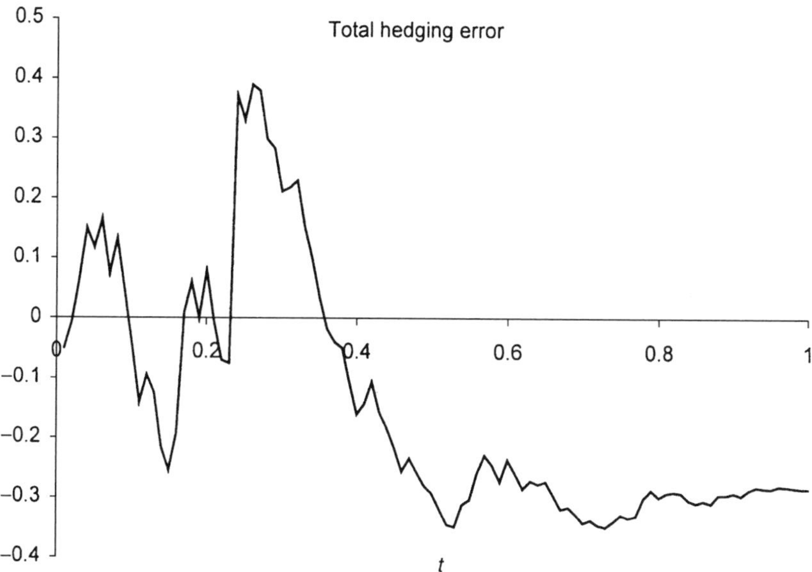

Figure 20.2 The running total hedging error.

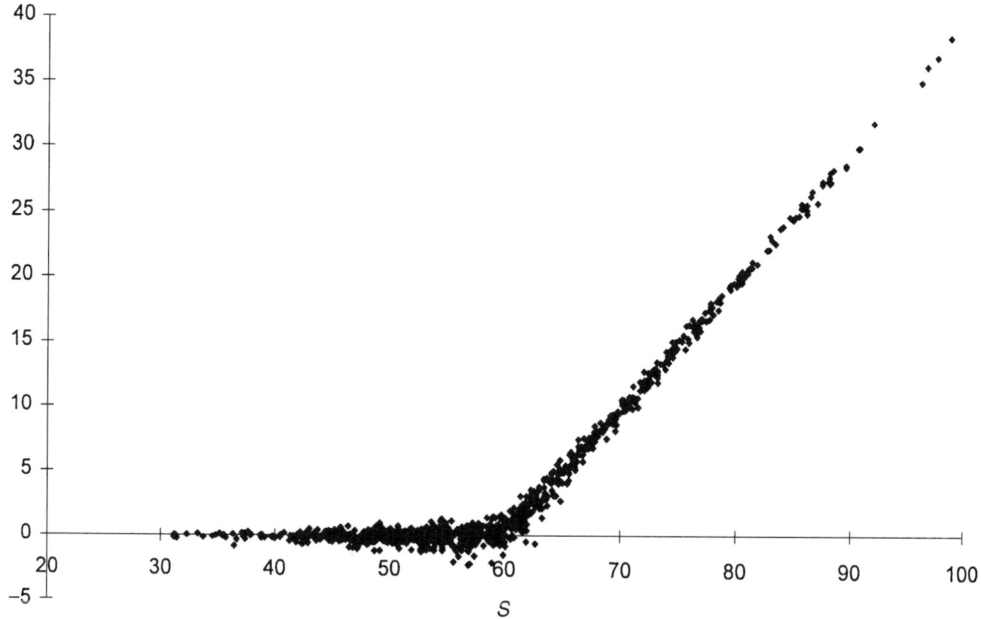

Figure 20.3 The results of discrete hedging.

The first step towards valuing an option is to choose a good model for the underlying in discrete time. A sensible choice is

$$S = e^x \tag{20.1}$$

where

$$\delta x = \left(\mu - \frac{\sigma^2}{2}\right)\delta t + \sigma\phi\,\delta t^{1/2}. \tag{20.2}$$

This is a discrete-time version of the earlier continuous-time stochastic differential equation for S.[1] Here ϕ is a random variable drawn from a standardized normal distribution and the term $\phi\,\delta t^{1/2}$ replaces the earlier Wiener process. In principle, the ideas that we describe do not depend on the random walk being lognormal and many models for S could be examined. In particular, ϕ need not be Normal but could even be measured empirically. If historic volatility is to be used then it should be measured at the same frequency as the rehedging takes place, i.e., using data at intervals of δt.

As in the Black–Scholes analysis we construct a hedged portfolio

$$\Pi = V - \Delta S, \tag{20.3}$$

with Δ to be chosen. As in Black–Scholes we first choose the hedge and then use it to derive an equation for the option value. (I have called this a 'hedged portfolio' but we will see that it is not perfectly hedged.)

We no longer have Itô's lemma, since we are in discrete time, but we still have the Taylor series expansion. Thus, it is a very simple matter to derive $\delta\Pi$ as a power series in δt and δx. On substituting for δx from (20.2) this expression becomes

$$\delta\Pi = \delta t^{1/2} A_1(\phi, \Delta) + \delta t\, A_2(\phi, \Delta) + \delta t^{3/2} A_3(\phi, \Delta) + \delta t^2 A_4(\phi, \Delta) + \cdots. \tag{20.4}$$

Actually, V and its derivatives appear in each A_i, but only the dependence on ϕ and Δ is shown. For example, the first term A_1 is given by

$$A_1(\phi, \Delta) = \sigma\phi S\left(\frac{\partial V}{\partial S} - \Delta\right),$$

and the second term by

$$A_2(\phi, \Delta) = \frac{\partial V}{\partial t} + S\left(\frac{\partial V}{\partial S} - \Delta\right)\left(\mu + \tfrac{1}{2}\sigma^2(\phi^2 - 1)\right) + \tfrac{1}{2}\sigma^2\phi^2 S^2\frac{\partial^2 V}{\partial S^2}.$$

This expansion in powers of $\delta t^{1/2}$ can be continued indefinitely; we stop at the order shown above because it is at this order that we find results that differ from Black–Scholes. Since time is measured in units of a year, δt is small but not zero. I have not put all of the algebraic details here, this is definitely big-picture time. They are not hard to derive, just take up a lot of space. Treat the derivation of A_1, A_2, A_3 and A_4 as an exercise.

Now I can state the very simple hedging strategy and valuation policy.

[1] Why have I not chosen $\delta S = \mu S\,\delta t + \sigma S\phi\,\delta t^{1/2}$? Because that would only be an approximation to the continuous-time stochastic differential equation. We are going to look at high order terms in the Taylor series expansion of V and the above is exact.

- Choose Δ to minimize the variance of $\delta\Pi$
- Value the option by setting the *expected* return on Π equal to the risk-free rate

The first of these, the hedging strategy, is easy to justify: the portfolio is, after all, hedged so as to reduce risk. But how can we justify the second, the valuation policy, since the portfolio is not riskless? The argument for the latter is that since options are in practice valued according to Black–Scholes yet necessarily discretely hedged, the second assumption is already being used by the market, but with an inferior choice for Δ.

Because we cannot totally eliminate risk I could also argue for a pricing equation that depends on risk preferences. I won't pursue that here, just note that even though we'll get an option 'value' that is different from the Black–Scholes value this does not mean that there is an arbitrage opportunity.

20.2.1 Choosing the Best Δ

The variance of $\delta\Pi$ is easily calculated from (20.4) since

$$\mathrm{var}[\delta\Pi] = E[\delta\Pi^2] - (E[\delta\Pi])^2. \tag{20.5}$$

In taking the expectations of $\delta\Pi$ and $\delta\Pi^2$ to calculate (20.5), all of the ϕ terms are integrated out leaving the variance of $\delta\Pi$ as a function of V, its derivatives, and, most importantly, Δ. Then, to minimize the variance we find the value of Δ for which

$$\frac{\partial}{\partial \Delta}\mathrm{var}[\delta\Pi] = 0.$$

The result is that the optimal Δ is given by

$$\Delta = \frac{\partial V}{\partial S} + \delta t(\cdots). \tag{20.6}$$

The first term will be recognized as the Black–Scholes delta. The second term, which I give explicitly in a moment, is the correction to the Black–Scholes delta that gives a better reduction in the variance of $\delta\Pi$, and thus a reduction in risk. This term contains V and its derivatives.

20.2.2 The Hedging Error

The leading-order random term in the 'hedged' portfolio is, with this choice for Δ,

$$\tfrac{1}{2}\sigma^2\phi^2 S^2\frac{\partial^2 V}{\partial S^2}.$$

We can write this as

$$\tfrac{1}{2}\sigma^2 S^2\frac{\partial^2 V}{\partial S^2} + \tfrac{1}{2}(\phi^2 - 1)\sigma^2 S^2\frac{\partial^2 V}{\partial S^2}.$$

The first term will, in the next section, be part of our pricing equation (and is part of the Black–Scholes equation). The second, which has a mean value of zero because ϕ is drawn from a standardized Normal distribution, is the **hedging error**. This term is random. The distribution of the square of a standardized Normal variable is called the **chi-squared distribution** (with

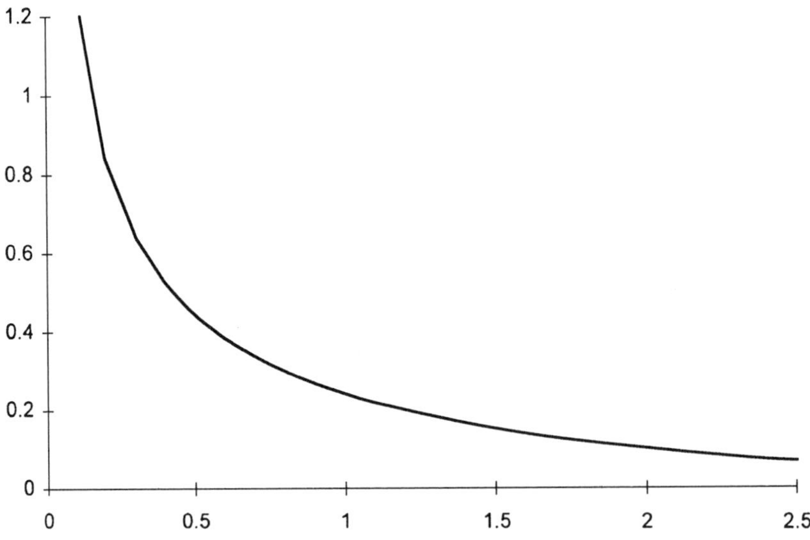

Figure 20.4 The chi-squared distribution.

a single degree of freedom). This chi-squared distribution is plotted in Figure 20.4. It has a mean of 1.

This distribution is asymmetrical about its mean, to say the least. The average value is 1 but 68% of the time the variable is less than this, and only 32% above. If one is long gamma, most of the time one loses money on the hedge (these are the small moves in the underlying), but 32% of the time you gain (and the size of that gain is on average larger than the small losses). The net position is zero. This result demonstrates the path dependency of hedging errors: ideally, if long gamma, one would like large moves when gamma is large and small moves when gamma is small.

During the life of the hedged option the hedging errors at each rehedge add up to give the total hedging error. This is the final discrepancy between the theoretical profit and loss on

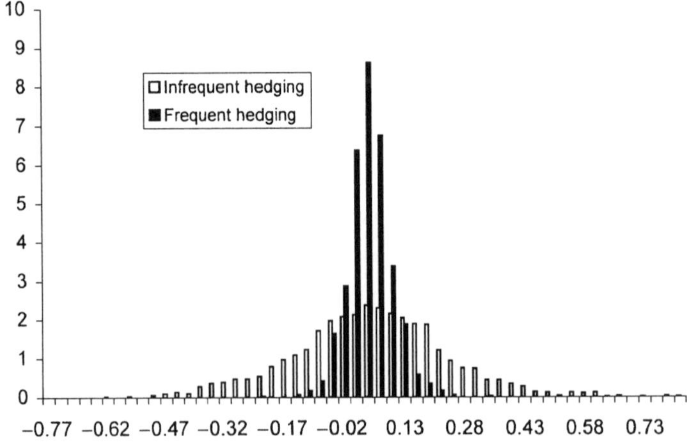

Figure 20.5 The distribution of the total hedging error for a call hedged frequently and infrequently.

the position and the actual. The total hedging error also has a mean of zero, and a standard deviation of $O(\delta t^{1/2})$. The actual outcome for the total hedging error is highly path dependent. In Figure 20.5 is shown the distribution of the *total* hedging error for a call option hedged at different intervals. Note how the spread of the hedging error is much greater for the more infrequently hedged option.

In passing we note that the commonly-held belief that 'time decay is the expected profit and loss (P&L) from a position' is wrong. The expected P&L from a self-financed and delta-hedged option position is zero.

20.2.3 Pricing the Option

Having chosen the best Δ, we now derive the pricing equation. The option should not be valued at the Black–Scholes value since that assumes perfect hedging and no risk: the fair value to an imperfectly hedged investor may be different. We find that the option value to the investor is equal to the Black–Scholes value plus a correction which prices the hedging risk.

The pricing policy that we have adopted has been stated as equating the expected return on the discretely hedged portfolio with the risk-free rate. This may be written as

$$E[\delta\Pi] = \left(r\,\delta t + \tfrac{1}{2}r^2\delta t^2 + \cdots\right)\Pi. \tag{20.7}$$

This is slightly different from the usual right-hand side, but simply represents a consistent higher order correction to exponential growth: $e^{r\,\delta t} = 1 + r\,\delta t + r^2\delta t^2/2 + \cdots$. Now substitute (20.3) and (20.4) into (20.7) to get the equation

$$\frac{\partial V}{\partial t} + \tfrac{1}{2}\sigma^2 S^2\frac{\partial^2 V}{\partial S^2} + rS\frac{\partial V}{\partial S} - rV + \delta t(\cdots) = 0. \tag{20.8}$$

Again the first term is that derived by Black and Scholes and the second term is a correction to allow for the imperfect hedge; it contains V and its derivatives. I give the second term shortly.

20.2.4 The Adjusted Δ and Option Value

The as yet undisclosed terms in parentheses in (20.6) and (20.8) contain V and its derivatives, up to the second derivative with respect to t and up to the fourth with respect to S. However, since the adjusted option price is clearly close in value to the Black–Scholes price we can put the Black–Scholes value into the terms in parentheses without any reduction in accuracy. This amounts to solving (20.6) and (20.8) iteratively.

The result[2] is that the adjusted option price satisfies

$$\frac{\partial V}{\partial t} + \tfrac{1}{2}\sigma^2 S^2\frac{\partial^2 V}{\partial S^2} + rS\frac{\partial V}{\partial S} - rV + \tfrac{1}{2}\delta t(\mu - r)(r - \mu - \sigma^2)S^2\frac{\partial^2 V}{\partial S^2} = 0 \tag{20.9}$$

and the better Δ is given by

$$\Delta = \frac{\partial V}{\partial S} + \delta t\left(\mu - r + \tfrac{1}{2}\sigma^2\right)S\frac{\partial^2 V}{\partial S^2}.$$

The important point to note about the above results is that the growth rate of the asset μ appears explicitly. This is a very important contrast with the Black–Scholes result. The

[2] They were published in *Risk* magazine in 1994 but with an algebraic error. Oops!

Black–Scholes formulae do not contain μ. Thus any ideas about 'risk-neutral valuation' must be used with great care. There is no such thing as 'perfect hedging' in the real world. In practice the investor is *necessarily* exposed to risk in the underlying, and this manifests itself in the appearance of the drift of the asset price.

Notice how the second derivative terms in (20.9) are both of the form constant $\times\ S^2$. Therefore the correction to the option price can very easily be achieved by adjusting the volatility and using the value σ^* where

$$\sigma^* = \sigma\left(1 + \frac{\delta t}{2\sigma^2}(\mu - r)(r - \mu - \sigma^2)\right).$$

There is a similar volatility adjustment when there are transaction costs (see Chapter 21). The correction is symmetric for long and short positions.

Is this volatility effect important? Fortunately, in most cases it is not. With typical values for the parameters and daily rehedging there is a volatility correction of one or two percent. In trending markets, however, when large μ can be experienced, this correction can reach five or ten percent, a value that cannot be ignored.

More importantly, in trending markets the corrected Δ will give a better risk reduction since it is in effect an anticipatory hedge: the variance is minimized over the time horizon until the next rehedge. This has been called **hedging with a view**.

Since the option should be valued with a modified volatility, the difference between the adjusted option value and the Black–Scholes value is proportional to the option vega, its derivative with respect to σ.

20.3 THE REAL DISTRIBUTION OF RETURNS AND THE HEDGING ERROR

All of the above assumes that the return on the underlying is Normally distributed with a known volatility. In reality the distribution is close to, but certainly not identical to, Normal. In Figure 20.6 is shown the distribution of daily returns for the Dow Jones index from 1977 until 1996, scaled to have a mean of zero and a standard deviation of one, and the standardized Normal distribution. The empirical distribution has a higher peak, and fatter tails than the Normal. This is typical of the randomness in financial variables, whether they are stocks, commodities, currencies or even interest rates. How does this distribution affect our hedging arguments and the hedging error?

Let us assume that the return on the underlying in a time δt is given by

$$\frac{\delta S}{S} = \psi,$$

where ψ is a random variable (with distribution determined empirically). We will examine the change in the value of a hedged portfolio assuming that the option component satisfies the Black–Scholes equation with an implied volatility of σ_i. Our hedged portfolio has a random return in excess of the risk-free rate given by

$$\delta\Pi - r\Pi\,\delta t = S\left(\Delta - \frac{\partial V}{\partial S}\right)(r\,\delta t - \psi) + \tfrac{1}{2}S^2\frac{\partial^2 V}{\partial S^2}(\psi^2 - \sigma_i^2\delta t) + \cdots. \qquad (20.10)$$

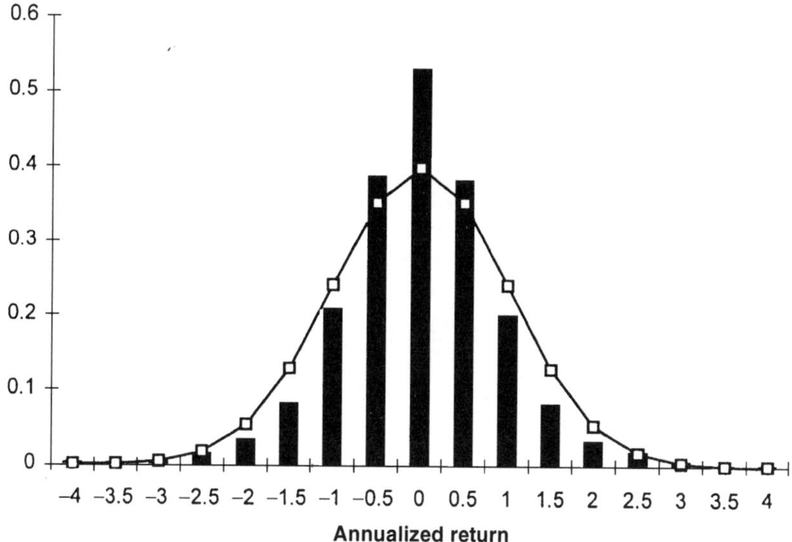

Figure 20.6 The distribution of returns on the Dow Jones index and the Normal distribution.

If we delta hedge in the Black–Scholes fashion then we are left with

$$\delta\Pi - r\Pi\,\delta t = \tfrac{1}{2}S^2\frac{\partial^2 V}{\partial S^2}(\psi^2 - \sigma_i^2\delta t),$$

to leading order. Obviously, we are interested in the distribution of ψ and in particular its variance. If the variance of ψ is different from σ_i^2 then theoretically we make money on the hedged portfolio (if our gamma is of the right sign, otherwise we lose money). This amounts to saying that the actual and implied volatilities are different. Of course, it is notoriously difficult to measure the actual volatility of the underlying. But what about the *distribution* of the returns? Is the hedging error chi-squared as the theory effectively assumes?

In Figure 20.7 is shown the normalized distribution of the square of returns and the chi-squared distribution, translated to have zero means. Both of these distributions have a mean of zero, but the empirical distribution is considerably higher at small values of the square and has a fatter tail (too far out to fit on the figure). Assuming that the standard deviation of the distribution of returns is $\sigma_i \delta t^{1/2}$ (i.e. the actual and implied volatilities are the same), then the Black–Scholes value for a discretely-hedged position will be correct in the sense of *expectations*. On *average* the portfolio earns the risk-free rate, but this is achieved via a particularly extreme distribution. Most of the time the stock price moves less than the theory would have, but makes up for this by the occasional large movement.

If the distribution were Normally distributed then 68% of the time the return would be less than the standard deviation and 32% greater. With a long gamma position you would lose a small amount 68% of the time but regain that loss on average due to the rarer but larger moves. However, this situation is exaggerated with the real distribution. From the Dow Jones data the higher peak and fatter tails mean that 78% of the time the move is less than the standard deviation and only 22% of the time is it greater. If you have a long gamma position then approximately one fifth of the asset moves will lose you money. But again this is recovered on average with the rare large asset moves.

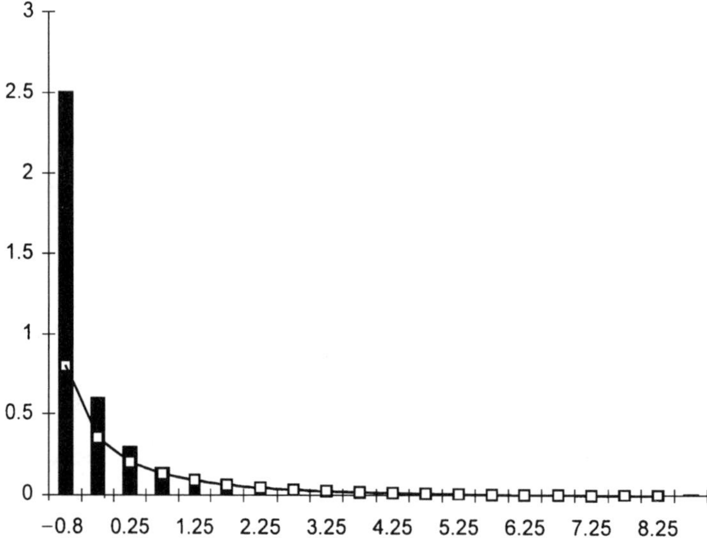

Figure 20.7 The distribution of the square of returns on the Dow Jones index and the translated chi-squared distribution.

20.4 SUMMARY

Hedging error is often overlooked in the pricing of a contract. In each timestep the order of magnitude of the change in P&L is the same order as the growth due to interest, i.e. of the order of the timestep. Just because this averages out to zero does not mean it should be ignored. In this chapter I showed some of the effects of hedging error on an option value and how real returns differ from the theoretical Normal in such a way as to make the hedging error distribution even worse than theoretical.

FURTHER READING

- Boyle & Emanuel (1980) explain some of the problems associated with the *discrete* rehedging of an option portfolio.
- Wilmott (1994) derives the 'better' hedge.
- Leland (1985), Henrotte (1993) and Lacoste (1996) derive analytical results for the statistical properties of the tracking error.
- Mercurio & Vorst (1996) discuss the implications of discrete hedging strategies.
- See Hua (1997) for more details and examples of hedging error.

EXERCISES

1. Construct a spreadsheet to simulate discrete delta hedging for a vanilla European call option. Perform 100 simulations. What is the average difference between the accumulated profit and loss and the option payoff for each simulation? Change δt, the time between hedging dates. What difference does this make to the average that you have calculated?

2. Using a discrete model for the share price,

$$\delta x = \left(\mu - \tfrac{1}{2}\sigma^2\right)\delta t + \sigma\phi\,\delta t^{1/2},$$

where $S = e^x$, and forming a hedged portfolio, find expressions for the values of:

(a) $\mathrm{E}[\delta\Pi]$,
(b) $\mathrm{E}[\delta\Pi^2]$,
(c) $\mathrm{var}[\delta\Pi]$.

Use your answer to part (c) to solve the equation

$$\frac{\partial}{\partial\Delta}\mathrm{var}[\delta\Pi] = 0.$$

(You will have to decide for yourself what accuracy you need in order to rederive the results in the text.)

3. Using the model for Question 2, and assuming that we delta hedge with the optimal delta, find the adjusted Black–Scholes equation for the value of the option, $V(S, t)$.

4. Consider a delta-hedged European call option. How do large movements in the share price affect the value of our Black–Scholes hedged portfolio in the cases when we are long and short the option?

CHAPTER 21
transaction costs

In this Chapter...

- how to allow for transaction costs in option prices
- how economies of scale work
- about a variety of hedging strategies and their effects on option prices

21.1 INTRODUCTION

Transaction costs are the costs incurred in the buying and selling of the underlying, related to the bid-offer spread. The Black–Scholes analysis requires the continuous rebalancing of a hedged portfolio, and no 'friction' such as transaction costs in such rebalancing. In practice, this assumption is incorrect. Depending on the underlying market in question, costs may be important or not. In a market with high transaction costs, stocks in emerging markets for example, it will be too costly to rehedge frequently. In more liquid markets, government bonds in first-world countries for example, costs are low and portfolios can be hedged often. If costs are important then this will be an important factor in the bid-offer spread in option prices.

The modeling of transaction costs was initiated by Hayne Leland. I will describe his model and then a simple model for transaction costs, the Hoggard–Whalley–Wilmott model for non-vanilla options and option portfolios, which is based on Leland's hedging strategy and model. These models will give us some insight into the effect of costs on the prices of option. Due to the mathematical complexity of this subject, the latter part of this chapter is necessarily just a review of key results with little of the underlying mathematical theory. The interested reader is referred to the original papers for further details.

21.2 THE EFFECT OF COSTS

In the Black–Scholes analysis we assumed that hedging took place continuously. In a sense, we take the limit as the time between rehedges goes to zero, $\delta t \to 0$. We therefore find ourselves rehedging an infinite number of times until expiry. With a bid-offer spread on the underlying the cost of rehedging leads to infinite total transaction costs. Clearly, even with discrete hedging the consequences of these costs associated with rehedging are important. Different people have different levels of transaction costs; there are economies of scale, so that the larger the amount that a person trades, the less significant are his costs. In contrast with the basic Black–Scholes model, we may expect that there is no unique option value. Instead, the value of the option depends on the investor.

Not only do we expect different investors to have different values for contracts, we also expect an investor *if they are hedging* to have different values for long and short positions in the same contract. Why is this? It is because transaction costs are always a sink of money for hedgers, they always lose out on the bid-offer spread on the underlying. Thus we expect a hedger to value a long position at less than the Black–Scholes value and a short position at more than the Black–Scholes value; whether the position is long or short, some estimate of hedging costs must be taken away from the value of the option. Since the 'sign' of the payoff is now important, it is natural to think of a long position as having a positive payoff and a short position a negative payoff.

21.3 THE MODEL OF LELAND (1985)

The groundwork of modeling the effects of transaction costs was done by Leland (1985). He adopted the hedging strategy of rehedging at *every* timestep. That is, every δt the portfolio is rebalanced, whether or not this is optimal in any sense. He assumes that the cost of trading ν assets costs an amount $\kappa\nu S$ for both buying and selling. This models bid-offer spread; the cost is proportional to the value traded.

In the main the Leland assumptions are those mentioned in Chapter 5 for the Black–Scholes model but with the following exceptions:

- The portfolio is revised every δt where δt is a finite and fixed, small timestep.
- The random walk is given in discrete time by[1]

$$\delta S = \mu S\,\delta t + \sigma S\phi\sqrt{\delta t}$$

  where ϕ is drawn from a standardized Normal distribution
- Transaction costs are proportional to the *value* of the transaction in the underlying. Thus if ν shares are bought ($\nu > 0$) or sold ($\nu < 0$) at a price S, then the cost incurred is $\kappa|\nu|S$, where κ is a constant. The value of κ will depend on the individual investor. A more complex cost structure can be incorporated into the model with only a small amount of effort, see later. We will then also see economies of scale appearing.
- The hedged portfolio has an *expected* return equal to that from a risk-free bank deposit. This is exactly the same valuation policy as earlier on discrete hedging with no transaction costs.

He allows for the cost of trading in valuing his hedged portfolio and by equating the *expected* return on the portfolio with the risk-free rate, he finds that long call and put positions should be valued with an adjusted volatility of $\breve{\sigma}$ where

$$\breve{\sigma} = \sigma\left(1 - \sqrt{\left(\frac{8}{\pi\,\delta t}\right)}\frac{\kappa}{\sigma}\right)^{1/2}.$$

Similarly short positions should be valued using $\hat{\sigma}$ where

$$\hat{\sigma} = \sigma\left(1 + \sqrt{\left(\frac{8}{\pi\,\delta t}\right)}\frac{\kappa}{\sigma}\right)^{1/2}.$$

As I have mentioned, long and short positions have different values.

---

[1] We don't need the more accurate discrete lognormal model of (20.1) and (20.2) since we are not going to high order of accuracy.

Although the Leland concept is sound it is, in this form, only applicable to vanilla calls and puts, or any contract having a gamma of the same sign for all S and t. In the next section the Leland idea is extended to arbitrary option payoffs or portfolios and the Leland result is derived along the way.

21.4 THE MODEL OF HOGGARD, WHALLEY & WILMOTT (1992)

The Leland strategy can be applied to arbitrary payoffs and to portfolios of options but the final result is not as simple as an adjustment to the volatility in a Black–Scholes formula. Instead, we will arrive at a nonlinear equation for the value of an option, derived by Hoggard, Whalley & Wilmott, and one of the first nonlinear models in derivatives theory.

Let us suppose we are going to hedge and value a portfolio of European options and allow for transaction costs. We can still follow the Black–Scholes analysis but we must allow for the cost of the transaction. If Π denotes the value of the hedged portfolio and $\delta\Pi$ the change in the portfolio over the timestep δt, then we must subtract the cost of any transaction from the equation for $\delta\Pi$ at each timestep. Note that we are not going to the limit $\delta t = 0$.

After a timestep the change in the value of the hedged portfolio is now given by

$$\delta\Pi = \sigma S\left(\frac{\partial V}{\partial S} - \Delta\right)\phi\,\delta t^{1/2} + \left(\tfrac{1}{2}\sigma^2 S^2 \frac{\partial^2 V}{\partial S^2}\phi^2 + \mu S\frac{\partial V}{\partial S} + \frac{\partial V}{\partial t} - \mu\Delta S\right)\delta t - \kappa S|\nu|. \tag{21.1}$$

This is similar to the Black–Scholes expression since but now contains a transaction cost term. Transaction costs have been subtracted from the change in the value of the portfolio. Because these costs are always positive, there is a modulus sign, $|\cdot|$, in the above.

We will follow the same hedging strategy as before, choosing $\Delta = \partial V/\partial S$. However, the portfolio is only rehedged at discrete intervals. The number of assets held short is therefore

$$\Delta = \frac{\partial V}{\partial S}(S, t)$$

where this has been evaluated at time t and asset value S. I have not given the details, but this choice minimizes the risk of the portfolio, as measured by the variance, to leading order. After a timestep δt and rehedging, the number of assets we hold is

$$\frac{\partial V}{\partial S}(S + \delta S, t + \delta t).$$

Note that this is evaluated at the new time and asset price. We can subtract the former from the latter to find the number of assets we have traded to maintain a 'hedged' position. The number of asset traded is therefore

$$\nu = \frac{\partial V}{\partial S}(S + \delta S, t + \delta t) - \frac{\partial V}{\partial S}(S, t).$$

Since the timestep and the asset move are both small we can apply Taylor's theorem to expand the first term on the right-hand side:

$$\frac{\partial V}{\partial S}(S + \delta S, t + \delta t) = \frac{\partial V}{\partial S}(S, t) + \delta S\frac{\partial^2 V}{\partial S^2}(S, t) + \delta t\frac{\partial^2 V}{\partial S\partial t}(S, t) + \cdots.$$

Since $\delta S = \sigma S\phi\delta t^{1/2} + O(\delta t)$, the dominant term is that which is proportional to δS; this term is $O(\delta t^{1/2})$ and the other terms are $O(\delta t)$. To leading order the number of assets bought (sold) is

$$\nu \approx \frac{\partial^2 V}{\partial S^2}(S, t)\,\delta S \approx \frac{\partial^2 V}{\partial S^2}\sigma S\phi\,\delta t^{1/2}.$$

We don't know beforehand how many shares will be traded, but we can calculate the *expected* number, and hence the expected transaction costs. The expected transaction cost over a timestep is

$$E[\kappa S|\nu|] = \sqrt{\frac{2}{\pi}}\kappa\sigma S^2 \left|\frac{\partial^2 V}{\partial S^2}\right| \delta t^{1/2}, \tag{21.2}$$

where the factor $\sqrt{2/\pi}$ is the expected value of $|\phi|$. We can now calculate the expected change in the value of our portfolio from (21.1), including the usual Black–Scholes terms and also the new cost term:

$$E[\delta\Pi] = \left(\frac{\partial V}{\partial t} + \tfrac{1}{2}\sigma^2 S^2\frac{\partial^2 V}{\partial S^2} - \kappa\sigma S^2\sqrt{\frac{2}{\pi\,\delta t}}\left|\frac{\partial^2 V}{\partial S^2}\right|\right)\delta t. \tag{21.3}$$

Except for the modulus sign, the new term above is of the same form as the second S derivative that has appeared before; it is a gamma term, multiplied by the square of the asset price, multiplied by a constant.

Now assuming that the holder of the option *expects* to make as much from his portfolio as if he had put the money in the bank, then we can replace the $E[\delta\Pi]$ in (21.3) with $r(V - S(\partial V/\partial S))\delta t$ as before to yield an equation for the value of the option:

$$\frac{\partial V}{\partial t} + \tfrac{1}{2}\sigma^2 S^2\frac{\partial^2 V}{\partial S^2} - \kappa\sigma S^2\sqrt{\frac{2}{\pi\,\delta t}}\left|\frac{\partial^2 V}{\partial S^2}\right| + rS\frac{\partial V}{\partial S} - rV = 0. \tag{21.4}$$

There is a nice financial interpretation of the term that is not present in the usual Black–Scholes equation. The second derivative of the option price with respect to the asset price, the gamma, $\Gamma = \partial^2 V/\partial S^2$, is a measure of the degree of mishedging of the hedged portfolio. The leading-order component of randomness is proportional to δS and this has been eliminated by delta-hedging. But this delta hedging leaves behind a small component of risk proportional to the gamma. The gamma of an option or portfolio of options is related to the amount of rehedging that is expected to take place at the next rehedge and hence to the expected transaction costs.

The equation is a *nonlinear* parabolic partial differential equation, one of the first such in finance. It is obviously also valid for a portfolio of derivative products. This is the first time in this book that we distinguish between single options and a portfolio of options. But for much of the rest of the book this distinction will be important. In the presence of transaction costs, the value of a portfolio is not the same as the sum of the values of the individual components. We can best see this by taking a very extreme example.

We have positions in two European call options with the same strike price and the same expiry date and on the same underlying asset. One of these options is held long and the other short. Our net position is therefore exactly zero because the two positions exactly cancel each other out. But suppose that we do not notice the cancellation effect of the two opposite positions and decide to hedge each of the options separately. Because of transaction costs we lose money at each rehedge on both options. At expiry the two payoffs will still cancel, but we have a negative net balance due to the accumulated costs of all the rehedges in the meantime. This contrasts greatly with our net balance at expiry if we realize beforehand that our positions cancel. In the latter case we never bother to rehedge, leaving us with no transaction costs and a net balance of zero at expiry.

Now consider the effect of costs on a single vanilla option held long. We know that

$$\frac{\partial^2 V}{\partial S^2} > 0$$

for a single call or put held long in the absence of transaction costs. Postulate that this is true for a single call or put when transaction costs are included. If this is the case then we can drop the modulus sign from (21.4). Using the notation

$$\breve{\sigma}^2 = \sigma^2 - 2\kappa\sigma\sqrt{\frac{2}{\pi\,\delta t}} \tag{21.5}$$

the equation for the value of the option is identical to the Black–Scholes value with the exception that the actual variance σ^2 is replaced by the modified variance $\breve{\sigma}^2$. Thus our assumption that $\partial^2 V/\partial S^2 > 0$ is true for a single vanilla option even in the presence of transaction costs. The modified volatility will be recognized as the Leland volatility correction mentioned at the start of this chapter.

For a short call or put option position we simply change all the signs in the above analysis with the exception of the transaction cost term, which must always be a drain on the portfolio. We then find that the call or put is valued using the new variance

$$\hat{\sigma}^2 = \sigma^2 + 2\kappa\sigma\sqrt{\frac{2}{\pi\,\delta t}}. \tag{21.6}$$

Again this is the Leland volatility correction.

The results (21.5) and (21.6) show that a long position in a single call or put with costs incorporated has an apparent volatility that is less than the actual volatility. When the asset price rises the owner of the option must sell some assets to remain delta hedged. But then the effect of the bid-offer spread on the underlying is to reduce the price at which the asset is sold. The effective increase in the asset price is therefore less than the actual increase, being seen as a reduced volatility. The converse is true for a short option position.

The above volatility adjustments are applicable when you have an option or a portfolio of options having a gamma of one sign. If the gamma is always and everywhere positive use the lower volatility value for a long position, and the higher value for a short position. If gamma is always and everywhere negative, swap these values around.

For a single vanilla call or put, we can get some idea of the total transaction costs associated with the above strategy by examining the difference between the value of an option with the cost-modified volatility and that with the usual volatility; that is, the difference between the Black–Scholes value and the value of the option taking into account the costs. Consider

$$V(S,t) - \hat{V}(S,t),$$

where the hatted function is Black–Scholes with the modified volatility. Expanding this expression for small κ we find that it becomes

$$(\sigma - \hat{\sigma})\frac{\partial V}{\partial \sigma} + \cdots.$$

This is proportional to the vega of the option. We know the formula for a European call option and therefore we find the expected spread to be

$$\frac{2\kappa SN(d_1)\sqrt{(T-t)}}{\sqrt{2\pi\,\delta t}},$$

where $N(d_1)$ has its usual meaning.

The most important quantity appearing in the model is

$$K = \frac{\kappa}{\sigma\sqrt{\delta t}}. \tag{21.7}$$

K is a non-dimensional quantity, meaning that it takes the same value whatever units are used for measuring the parameters. If this parameter is very large, we write $K \gg 1$, then the transaction costs term is much greater than the underlying volatility. This means that costs are high and that the chosen δt is too small. The portfolio is being rehedged too frequently. If the transaction costs are very large or the portfolio is rehedged very often then it is possible to have $\kappa > 2\sigma\sqrt{2\delta t/\pi}$. In this case the equation becomes forward parabolic for a long option position. Since we are still prescribing final data, the equation is ill-posed. Although the asset price may have risen, its effective value due to the addition of the costs will have actually dropped. I discuss such ill posedness later.

If the parameter K is very small, we write $K \ll 1$, then the costs have only a small effect on the option value. Hence δt could be decreased to minimize risk. The portfolio is being rehedged too infrequently.

We can see how to use this result in practice if we have data for the bid-offer spread, volatility and time between rehedges for a variety of stocks. Plot the parameter κ/σ against the quantity $1/\sqrt{\delta t}$ for each stock. An example of this for a real portfolio is shown in Figure 21.1. In this

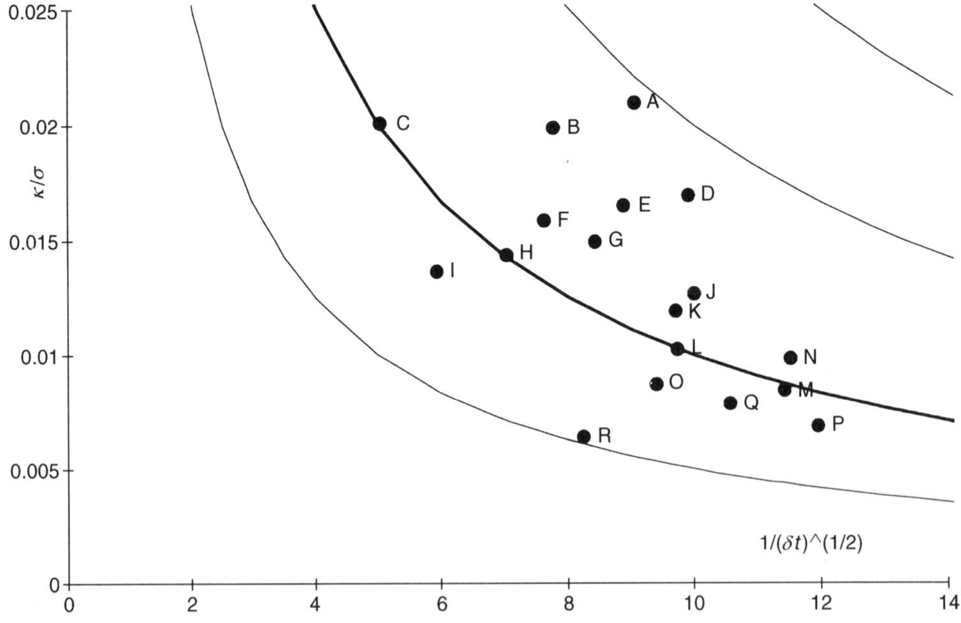

Figure 21.1 The parameter κ/σ against $1/\delta t^{1/2}$ for a selection of stocks. On each curve the transaction cost parameter K is the same.

figure are also shown lines on which K is constant. To be consistent in our attitude towards transaction costs across all stocks we might decide that a value of $K = K'$ is ideal. If this is the bold line in the figure then options on those stocks above the line, such as A, are too infrequently hedged, while those below, such as R, are hedged too often. Of course, this is a very simple approach to optimizing a hedging strategy. A more sophisticated approach would also take into account the advantage of increased hedging: the reduction of risk.

21.5 NON-SINGLE-SIGNED GAMMA

For an arbitrary portfolio of options, the gamma, $\partial^2 V/\partial S^2$, is not of one sign. If this is the case then we cannot drop the modulus sign. Since the Hoggard–Whalley–Wilmott equation is nonlinear we must in general solve it numerically.

In Figures 21.2 and 21.3 is shown the value of a long bull spread consisting of one long call with $E = 45$ and one short call with $E = 55$ and the delta at six months before expiry for the two cases, with and without transaction costs. The volatility is 20% and the interest rate 10%. In this example $K = 0.25$. The bold curve shows the values in the presence of transaction costs and the other curve in the absence of transaction costs. The latter is simply the Black–Scholes value for the combination of the two options. The bold line approaches the other line as the transaction costs decrease.

In Figures 21.4 and 21.5 is shown the value of a long butterfly spread and its delta, before and at expiry. In this example the portfolio contains one long call with $E = 45$, two short calls

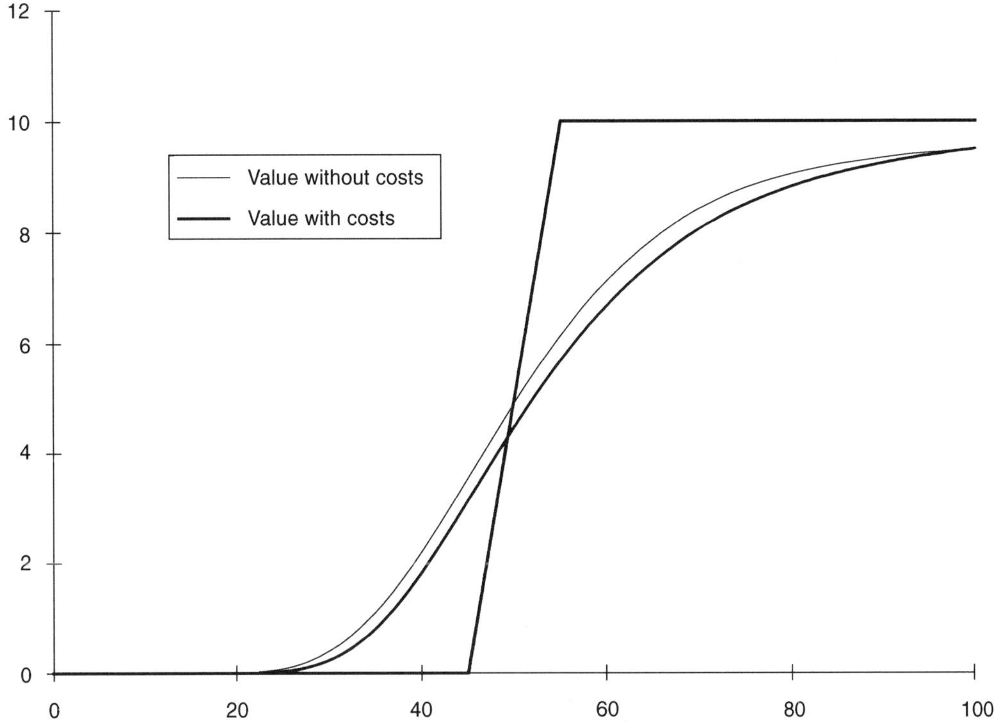

Figure 21.2 The value of a bull spread with (bold) and without transaction costs. The payoff is also shown.

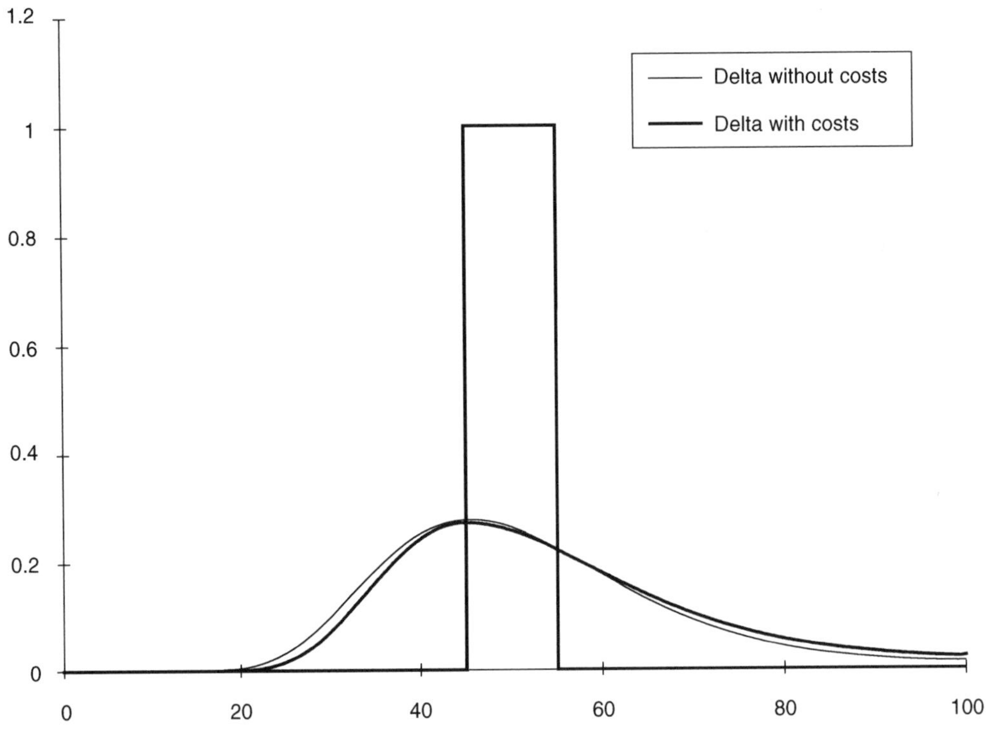

Figure 21.3 The delta for a bull spread prior to and at expiry with (bold) and without transaction costs.

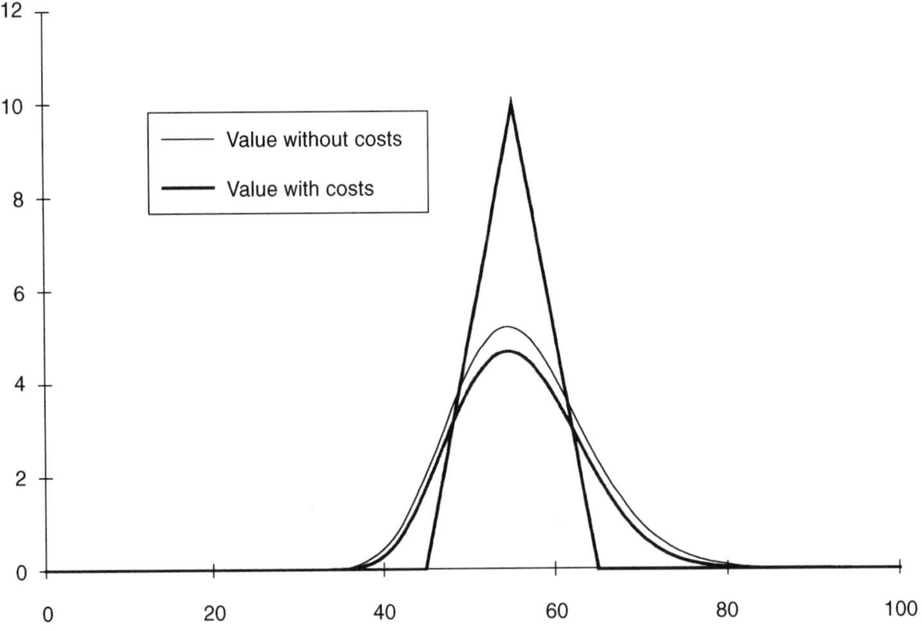

Figure 21.4 The value of a butterfly spread with (bold) and without transaction costs.

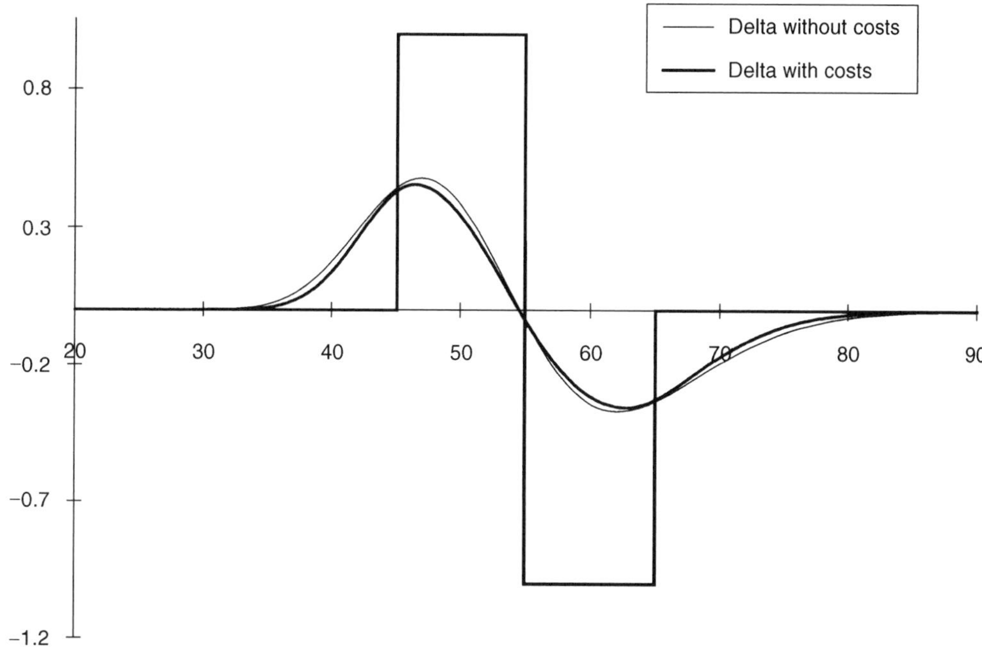

Figure 21.5 The delta for a butterfly spread with (bold) and without transaction costs.

with $E = 55$ and another long call with $E = 65$. The results are with one month until expiry for the two cases, with and without transaction costs. The volatility, the interest rate and K are as in the previous example.

21.6 THE MARGINAL EFFECT OF TRANSACTION COSTS

Suppose we hold a portfolio of options, let's call its value $P(S, t)$, and we want to add another option to this portfolio. What will be the effect of transaction costs? Call the value of the new, larger, portfolio $P + V$, what equation is satisfied by the marginal value V? This is not just the cost equation applied to V because of the nonlinearity of the problem. We can write

$$\frac{\partial P}{\partial t} + \tfrac{1}{2}\sigma^2 S^2 \frac{\partial^2 P}{\partial S^2} - \kappa\sigma S^2 \sqrt{\frac{2}{\pi\,\delta t}} \left| \frac{\partial^2 P}{\partial S^2} \right| + rS\frac{\partial P}{\partial S} - rP = 0$$

since the original portfolio must satisfy the costs equation. But now the new portfolio also satisfies this equation:

$$\frac{\partial(P+V)}{\partial t} + \tfrac{1}{2}\sigma^2 S^2 \frac{\partial^2(P+V)}{\partial S^2} - \kappa\sigma S^2 \sqrt{\frac{2}{\pi\,\delta t}} \left| \frac{\partial^2(P+V)}{\partial S^2} \right| + rS\frac{\partial(P+V)}{\partial S} - r(P+V) = 0.$$

Both of these equations are nonlinear. But if the size of the new option is much less than the original portfolio we can linearize the latter equation to examine the equation satisfied by the marginal value V. We find that

$$\frac{\partial V}{\partial t}+\tfrac{1}{2}\sigma^2S^2\frac{\partial^2 V}{\partial S^2}-\operatorname{sgn}\left(\frac{\partial^2 P}{\partial S^2}\right)\kappa\sigma S^2\sqrt{\frac{2}{\pi\,\delta t}}\frac{\partial^2 V}{\partial S^2}+rS\frac{\partial V}{\partial S}-rV=0.$$

This equation is now linear. The important point to note is that the volatility correction only depends on the sign of the gamma of the original portfolio, P. If the gamma of the original portfolio is positive then the addition of another contract with positive gamma only makes the cost situation worse. However, the addition of a new contract with negative gamma will reduce the level of transaction costs. The benefits of reducing gamma may even make it worthwhile to buy/sell a contract for more/less than the Black–Scholes value, theoretically.

21.7 OTHER COST STRUCTURES

The above model can be extended to accommodate other transaction cost structures. Suppose that the cost of buying or selling ν assets is $\kappa(\nu, S)$. We follow the analysis of Section 21.4 up to the point where we take expectations of the transaction cost of hedging. The number of assets traded is still proportional to the gamma, and the expected cost of trading is

$$E[\kappa(\sigma S\,\delta t^{1/2}\Gamma\phi, S)].$$

The option pricing equation then becomes

$$\frac{\partial V}{\partial t}+\tfrac{1}{2}\sigma^2S^2\frac{\partial^2 V}{\partial S^2}+rS\frac{\partial V}{\partial S}-rV=\frac{1}{\delta t^{1/2}}E[\kappa(\sigma S\,\delta t^{1/2}\Gamma\phi, S)].$$

For example, suppose that trading in shares costs $k_1+k_2\nu+k_3\nu S$, where k_1, k_2 and k_3 are constants. This cost structure contains fixed costs (k_1), a cost proportional to volume traded ($k_2\nu$), and a cost proportional to the value traded ($k_3\nu S$). The option value satisfies the nonlinear diffusion equation

$$\frac{\partial V}{\partial t}+\tfrac{1}{2}\sigma^2S^2\frac{\partial^2 V}{\partial S^2}+rS\frac{\partial V}{\partial S}-rV=\frac{k_1}{\delta t}+\sqrt{\frac{2}{\pi\delta t}}\sigma S(k_2+k_3S)\left|\frac{\partial^2 V}{\partial S^2}\right|. \tag{21.8}$$

21.8 HEDGING TO A BANDWIDTH: THE MODEL OF WHALLEY & WILMOTT (1993) AND HENROTTE (1993)

We have so far seen how to model option prices when hedging takes place at fixed intervals of time. Another commonly used strategy is to rehedge whenever the position becomes too far out of line with the perfect hedge position. Prices are therefore monitored continuously but hedging still has to take place discretely.

Due to the complexity of this problem and those that follow, I only give a brief sketch of the ideas and results.

With $V(S, t)$ as the option value, the perfect Black–Scholes hedge is given by

$$\Delta=\frac{\partial V}{\partial S}.$$

Suppose, however, that we are not perfectly hedged, that we hold $-D$ of the underlying asset but do not want to accept the extra cost of buying or selling to reposition our hedge. The risk, as measured by the variance over a timestep δt of this imperfectly hedged position is, to leading order,

$$\sigma^2 S^2 \left(D - \frac{\partial V}{\partial S} \right)^2 \delta t.$$

I can make two observations about this expression. The first is simply to confirm that when $D = \partial V/\partial S$ this variance is zero. The second observation is that a natural hedging strategy is to bound the variance within a given tolerance and that this strategy is equivalent to restricting D so that

$$\sigma S \left| D - \frac{\partial V}{\partial S} \right| \leq H_0. \tag{21.9}$$

The parameter H_0 is now a measure of the maximum expected risk in the portfolio. When the perfect hedge ($\partial V/\partial S$) and the current hedge (D) move out of line so that (21.9) is violated, then the position should be rebalanced. Equation (21.9) defines the **bandwidth** of the hedging position.

The model of Whalley & Wilmott (1993) and Henrotte (1993) takes this as the hedging strategy: the investor prescribes H_0 and on rehedging rebalances to $D = \partial V/\partial S$.

We find that the option value satisfies the nonlinear diffusion equation

$$\frac{\partial V}{\partial t} + \tfrac{1}{2}\sigma^2 S^2 \frac{\partial^2 V}{\partial S^2} + rS\frac{\partial V}{\partial S} - rV = \frac{\sigma^2 S^4 \Gamma^2}{H_0}\left(k_1 + (k_2 + k_3 S)\frac{H_0^{1/2}}{S} \right), \tag{21.10}$$

where Γ is the option's gamma and the parameters k_1, k_2 and k_3 are the cost parameters for the cost structure introduced in Section 21.7. Note that again there is a nonlinear correction to the Black–Scholes equation that depends on the gamma.

21.9 UTILITY-BASED MODELS

21.9.1 The Model of Hodges & Neuberger (1989)

All of the above models for transaction costs take the hedging strategy as exogenously given. That is, the investor chooses his strategy and then prices his option afterwards. Strategies like this have been called **local in time** because they only worry about the state of an option at the present moment in time. An alternative, first examined by Hodges & Neuberger (1989), is to find a strategy that is in some sense *optimal*. These have been called **global-in-time models** because they are concerned with what may happen over the rest of the life of the option.

The seminal work in this area, combining both utility theory and transaction costs, was by Hodges & Neuberger (HN), with Davis, Panas & Zariphopoulou (DPZ) making improvements to the underlying philosophy. HN explain that they assume that a financial agent holds a portfolio that is already optimal in some sense but then has the opportunity to issue an option and hedge the risk using the underlying. However, since rehedging is costly, they must define their strategy in terms of a 'loss function.' They thus aim to maximize expected utility. This entails the investor specifying a 'utility function.' The case considered in most detail by HN and DPZ is of the exponential utility function. This has the nice property of constant risk aversion. Mathematically, such a problem is one of stochastic control and the differential equations involved are very similar to the Black–Scholes equation.

21.9.2 The Model of Davis, Panas & Zariphopoulou (1993)

The ideas of HN were modified by DPZ. Instead of valuing an option on its own, they embed the option valuation problem within a more general portfolio management approach. They then consider the effect on a portfolio of adding the constraint that at a certain date, expiry, the portfolio has an element of obligation due to the option contract. They introduce the investor's utility function; in particular, they assume it to be exponential. They only consider costs proportional to the value of the transaction ($\kappa\nu S$), in which case they find that the optimal hedging strategy is not to rehedge until the position moves out of line by a certain amount. Then, the position is rehedged as little as possible to keep the delta at the edge of this hedging bandwidth. This result is shown schematically in Figure 21.6. Here we see the Black–Scholes delta position and the hedging bandwidth.

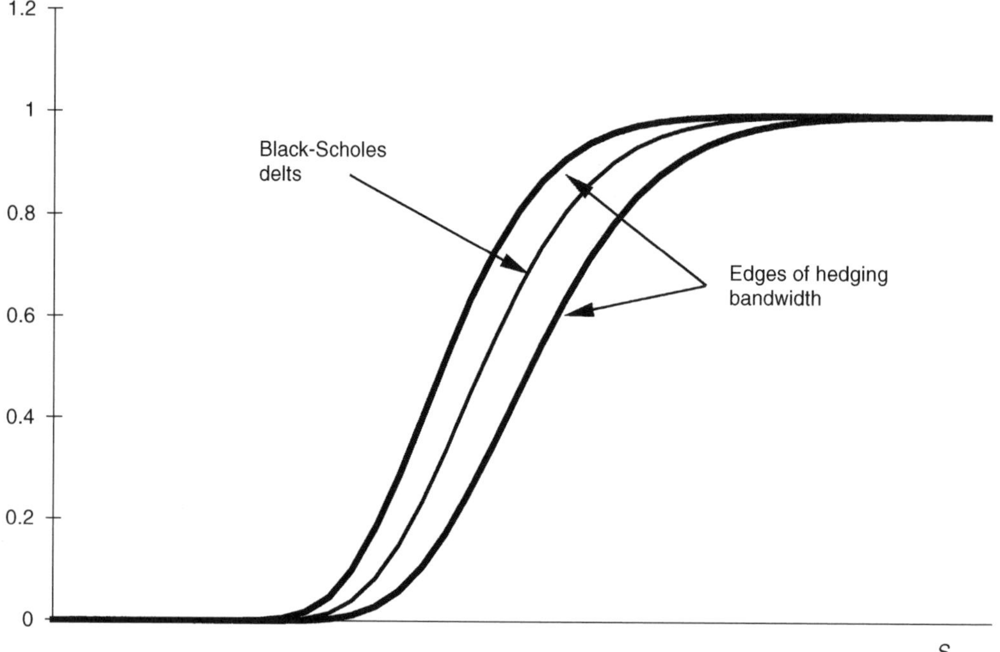

Figure 21.6 The optimal hedging strategy with proportional costs.

In HN and DPZ the value of the option and, most importantly, the hedging strategy are given in terms of the solution of a three-dimensional free boundary problem. The variables in the problem are asset price S, time t, as always, and also D, the number of shares held in the hedged portfolio.

21.9.3 The Asymptotic Analysis of Whalley & Wilmott (1993)

The models of HN and DPZ are unwieldy because they are time-consuming to compute. As such it is difficult to gain any insight into the optimal hedging strategy. Whalley & Wilmott did an asymptotic analysis of the DPZ model assuming that transaction costs are small, which is, of course, the case in practice. This analysis shows that the option price is given by the solution of an inhomogeneous diffusion equation, similar to the Black–Scholes equation.

This asymptotic analysis also shows that the HN optimal hedging bandwidth is symmetric about the Black–Scholes delta so that

$$\left|D - \frac{\partial V}{\partial S}\right| \leq \left(\frac{3k_3 S e^{-r(T-t)} F(S, t, \Gamma)^2}{2\gamma}\right)^{1/3},$$

where

$$F(S, t, \Gamma) = \left|\Gamma - \frac{e^{-r(T-t)}(\mu - r)}{\gamma S^2 \sigma^2}\right|.$$

The parameter γ is the index of risk aversion in the utility function.

These results are important in that they bring together all the local-in-time models mentioned above and the global-in-time models of HN and DPZ into the same diffusion equation framework.

This hedging bandwidth has been tested using Monte Carlo simulations by Mohamed (1994) and found to be the most successful strategy that he tested. The model has been extended by Whalley & Wilmott (1994) to an arbitrary cost structure; this is described below.

21.9.4 Arbitrary Cost Structure

The above description concentrates on the proportional cost case. If there is a fixed cost component then shares are traded to position the number of shares to be at some **optimal rebalance point**. This is illustrated schematically in Figure 21.7

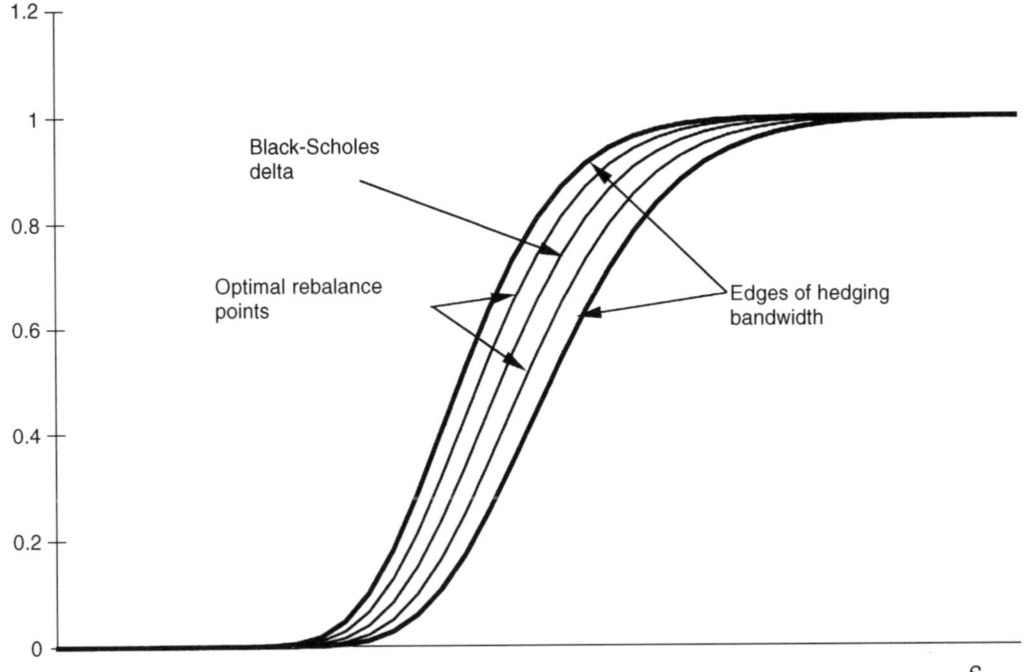

Figure 21.7 The optimal hedging strategy with arbitrary cost structure.

I do not give any of the details but note that the algorithm for finding the optimal rebalance point and the hedging bandwidth is as follows.

Assume that costs take the form $K(S, \nu)$, and that this is symmetric for buying and selling. The bandwidth is given by

$$\Delta - A(S, t) \leq D \leq \Delta + A(S, t)$$

where Δ is the Black–Scholes delta. The optimal rebalance points are given by

$$D = \Delta \pm B(S, t).$$

A and B come from solving

$$\gamma AB(A + B) = 3\delta\Gamma^2 \left.\frac{\partial K}{\partial \nu}\right|_{\nu=A-B}$$

and

$$\gamma(A + B)^3(A - B) = 12\delta\Gamma^2 K(S, A - B),$$

where

$$\delta = e^{-r(T-t)},$$

Γ is the Black–Scholes gamma and γ is the index of risk aversion.

21.10 INTERPRETATION OF THE MODELS

Nonlinear and inhomogeneous diffusion equations appear throughout the physical science literature. Thus there is a ready-made source of theoretical results and insights. I describe some of these in this section.

21.10.1 Nonlinearity

The effect of the nonlinearity on the valuation equations is that the sum of two or more solutions is not necessarily a solution itself. As I have said, a portfolio consisting of an equal number of the same options but held long and short (which has value identically zero), is not equal to the sum of the values of the two sub-portfolios of all the long and short options. This makes sense because in valuing each sub-portfolio separately we are assuming that each would be hedged separately, with attendant transaction costs to be taken into account. Upon recombining the two, the intrinsic values cancel, but the two sets of costs remain, giving a negative net value. The importance of nonlinearity extends far beyond this however.

Consider the following. Transaction cost models are nonlinear. The value of a portfolio of options is generally not the same as the sum of the values of the individual components. We can add contracts to our portfolio by paying the market prices, but the marginal value of these contracts may be greater or less than the amount that we pay for them. Is it possible to optimize the value of our portfolio by adding traded contracts until we give our portfolio its best value? This question is answered (in the affirmative) in Chapter 30. In a sense, the optimization amounts to finding the cheapest way to globally reduce the gamma of the portfolio, since the costs of hedging are directly related to the gamma.

21.10.2 Negative Option Prices

The transaction cost models above can result in negative option prices for some asset values depending on the hedging strategy implied by the model. So for example in the Hoggard–Whalley–Wilmott model with fixed transaction costs, $k_1 > 0$, option prices can become negative if they are sufficiently far out of the money. This model assumes that we rehedge at the end of *every* timestep, irrespective of the level of risk associated with our position and also irrespective of the option value. Thus there is some element of obligation in our position, and the strategy should be amended so that we do not rehedge if this would make the option value go negative. In the case of a call therefore, there may be an asset price below which we would cease to rehedge and in this case we would regard the option as worthless.

Note that this is not equivalent to discarding the option; if the asset price were subsequently to rise above the appropriate level (which will change over time), we would begin to hedge again and the option would once more have a positive value. So we introduce the additional conditions for a moving boundary:

$$V(S_s(t), t) = 0$$

and

$$\frac{\partial V}{\partial S}(S_s(t), t) = 0.$$

The value $S_s(t)$ is to be found as part of the solution. This problem is now a 'free boundary problem,' similar mathematically to the American option valuation problem. In our transaction cost problem for a call option, we must find the boundary, $S_s(t)$, below which we stop hedging. This is illustrated in Figure 21.8.

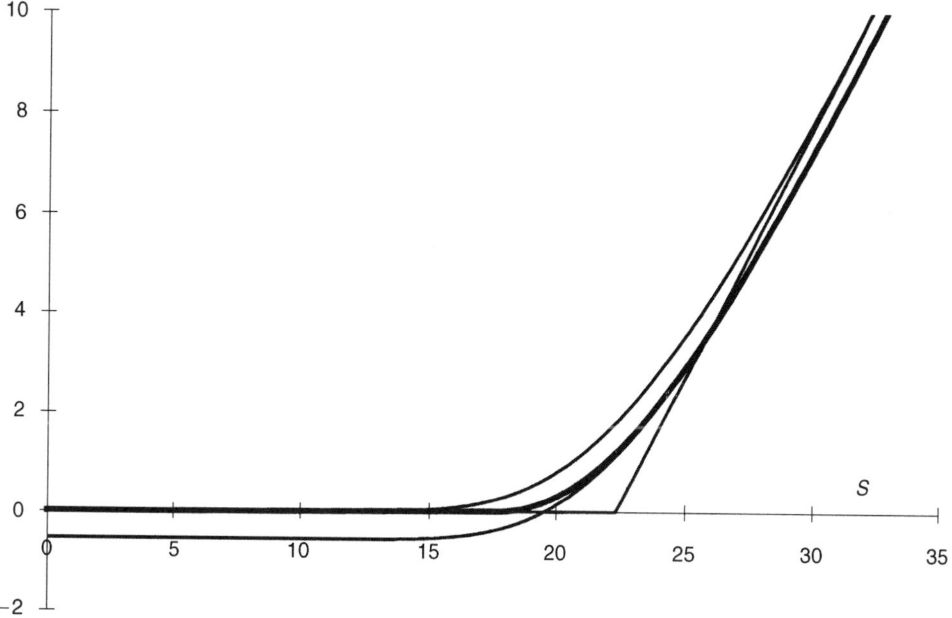

Figure 21.8 When to stop hedging if there are fixed costs.

In this figure we are valuing a long vanilla call with fixed costs at each rehedge. The top curve is the Black–Scholes option value as a function of S at some time before expiry. The bottom curve allows for the cost of rehedging but with the obligation to hedge at each timestep. The option value is thus negative far out of the money. The middle curve also incorporates costs but without the obligation to rehedge. It thus always has a positive value and is, of course, also below the Black–Scholes option value.

21.10.3 Existence of Solutions

Linear diffusion equations have many nice properties, as we discussed in Chapter 6. The solution to a 'sensible' problem exists and is unique. This need not be the case for nonlinear equations. The form of the equation and the final data $V(S,T)$ for the equation (the payoff at expiry) may result in the solution 'blowing up,' that is, becoming infinite and thus financially unrealistic.

This can occur in some models even if transaction costs are small because of the effect of the option's gamma, which in those models is raised to some power greater than one in the extra transaction cost term. So wherever the gamma is large this term can dominate. For example, near the exercise price for a vanilla call or put option, $\partial^2 V/\partial S^2(S,0)$ is infinite. We consider the case for the model of Equation (21.10).

The governing equation in this case has a transaction cost term proportional to Γ^2. Close to expiry and near the exercise price, E, we write $t = T - \tau$ and $S = E + s$ where $|s|/E \ll 1$ and then the equation can be approximated by

$$\frac{\partial V}{\partial \tau} = \beta \left(\frac{\partial^2 V}{\partial s^2} \right)^2, \tag{21.11}$$

where

$$\beta = \frac{\sigma^2 E^4}{H_0} \left(k_1 + H_0^{1/2} \left(\frac{k_2}{E} + k_3 \right) \right). \tag{21.12}$$

Taking H_0 to be a constant, which is equivalent to a fixed bandwidth for the delta, it can be shown that equation (21.11) is ill-posed, that is it has no solution, if $\Gamma(S,0) > 0$.[2]

So a long vanilla call or put hedged under this strategy has no finite value. Note that for short vanilla options, $\Gamma(S,0) < 0$ and a solution does exist, so they *can* be valued under such a strategy, and can be hedged with a constant level of risk throughout the life of the option. However, returning to the case of payoffs with positive gamma, as the option approaches expiry, the number of hedging transactions required, and hence the cost of maintaining the hedging strategy, increases unboundedly unless the level of risk allowed (H_0) is itself allowed to become unbounded.

21.11 SUMMARY

For equity derivatives and derivatives on emerging market underlyings transaction costs are large and important. In these markets pricing and hedging must take into account costs. In

[2] We can see this intuitively as follows. If $\Gamma(S,0) > 0$ then the right-hand side of (21.11) is positive. Thus V increases in time, increasing fastest where the gamma is largest. This in turn further increases the gamma, making the growth in V even faster. The result is blow up. The linear diffusion equation also behaves in this way but the increase in V does not get out of control, since the gamma is raised only to the power one.

other markets the underlying may be so liquid that costs are irrelevant, then you would hedge as often as you could. When transaction costs are important the problem of pricing and hedging is nonlinear; if you don't price and hedge contracts together then you will miss out on cancellation effects and economies of scale. This is interesting from a mathematical point of view, but cumbersome from a practical point of view.

FURTHER READING

- Some of the material of this chapter is based on the model of Leland (1985) as extended to portfolios of options by Hoggard, Whalley & Wilmott (1994) and Whalley & Wilmott (1993 a).
- Gemmill (1992) gives an example taken from practice of the effect of transaction costs on a hedged portfolio.
- The Leland model was put into a binomial setting by Boyle & Vorst (1992). They find a similar volatility adjustment to that of Leland.
- Whalley & Wilmott (1993 b, 1994 b, 1996) and Henrotte (1993) discuss various hedging strategies and derive more nonlinear equations using ideas similar to those in this chapter.
- For alternative approaches involving 'optimal strategies' see Hodges & Neuberger (1989), Davis & Norman (1990) and Davis, Panas & Zariphopoulou (1993), and the asymptotic analyses of Whalley & Wilmott (1994a,b, 1995, 1997) for small levels of transaction costs.
- Dewynne, Whalley & Wilmott (1994, 1995) discuss the pricing of exotic options in the presence of costs.
- Avellaneda & Parás (1994) discuss the fixed-timestep equation when transaction costs are large.
- Ahn, Dayal, Grannan & Swindle (1998) discuss the variance of replication error when there are transaction costs.
- For a model of a Poisson process for stocks with transaction costs see Neuberger (1994).

EXERCISES

1. Consider the case of the lookback put, with payoff $\max(M - S, 0)$, where M is the maximum. Assuming constant time between rehedges, with a cost of

   $$k_1 + k_2\nu + k_3\nu S,$$

   find the partial differential equation for the value of the option. Are there any special cases for which it is possible to find a similarity solution of the form

   $$V(S, M, t) = MH(S/M, t)?$$

2. An average strike foreign exchange option has payoff

   $$\max\left(1 - \frac{I}{ST}, 0\right),$$

   where

   $$I = \int_0^t S d\tau.$$

In the absence of transaction costs, this option price has a similarity solution. Show that the similarity solution can still be found when the model includes transaction costs of the form

$$k_1 + k_3 \nu S.$$

3. Solve the Black–Scholes equation for the price of a European call option with a transaction cost of $k\nu S$ as follows, in the case when

$$K = \frac{k}{\sigma\sqrt{\delta t}}$$

is a small parameter. The option price satisfies the equation

$$\frac{\partial V}{\partial t} + \tfrac{1}{2}\sigma^2 S^2 \frac{\partial^2 V}{\partial S^2} - K\sigma^2 S^2 \sqrt{\frac{2}{\pi}} \left| \frac{\partial^2 V}{\partial S^2} \right| + rS\frac{\partial V}{\partial S} - rV = 0.$$

Write

$$V(S,t) = V_0(S,t) + KV_1(S,t) + \cdots,$$

and solve the problem for V_0. What problem must we then solve for V_1?

CHAPTER 22
volatility smiles and surfaces

In this Chapter...

- volatility smiles and skews
- the volatility surface
- how to determine the volatility surface that gives prices of options that are consistent with the market

22.1 INTRODUCTION

One of the erroneous assumptions of the Black–Scholes world is that the volatility of the underlying is constant. This can be seen in any statistical examination of time-series data for assets, regardless of the sophistication of the analysis. This varying volatility is also observed *indirectly* through the market prices of traded contracts. In this chapter we are going to examine the relationship between the volatility of the underlying asset and the prices of derivative products. Since the volatility is not directly observable, and is certainly not predictable, we will try to exploit the relationship between prices and volatility to determine the volatility *from* the market prices. This is the exact inverse of what we have done so far. Previously we modeled the volatility and then found the price, now we take the price and deduce the volatility.

22.2 IMPLIED VOLATILITY

In the Black–Scholes world of constant volatility, the value of a European call option is simply

$$V(S, t; \sigma, r; E, T) = SN(d_1) - Ee^{-r(T-t)}N(d_2),$$

where

$$d_1 = \frac{\log(S/E) + \left(r + \frac{1}{2}\sigma^2\right)(T-t)}{\sigma\sqrt{T-t}}$$

and

$$d_2 = \frac{\log(S/E) + \left(r - \frac{1}{2}\sigma^2\right)(T-t)}{\sigma\sqrt{T-t}}.$$

I have given the function V six arguments, the first two are the independent variables, the second two are parameters of the asset and the financial world, the last two are specific to the contract in question. All but σ are easy to measure (r may be a bit inaccurate but the price is typically not too sensitive to this). If we know σ then we can calculate the option price. Conversely, if we know the option price V then we can calculate σ. We can do this because the value of a call option is monotonic in the volatility. Provided that the market value of the option is greater than $\max(S - E^{-r(T-t)}, 0)$ and less than S there is one, and only one, value for σ that makes the theoretical option value and the market price the same. This is called the **implied volatility**. One is usually taught to think of the implied volatility as the market's view of the future value of volatility. Yes and no. If the 'market' does have a view on the future of volatility then it will be seen in the implied volatility. But the market also has views on the direction of the underlying, and also responds to supply and demand. Let me give examples.

In one month's time there is to be an election, it is not clear who will win. If the right wing party are elected markets will rise, if the left wing are successful, markets will fall. Before the election the market assumes the middle ground, splitting the difference. In fact, little trading occurs and markets have a very low volatility. But option traders know that after the election there will be a lot of movement one way or the other. Prices of both calls and puts are therefore high. If we back out implied volatilities from these option prices we see very high values. Actual and implied volatilities are shown in Figure 22.1 for this scenario.

Traders may increase option prices to reflect the expected sudden moves but if we are only observing implied volatilities then we are getting the underlying story very wrong indeed. This illustrates the fact that if you want to play around with prices there is only one parameter you can fudge, the volatility. As long as it is not too out of line compared with implied volatilities of other products no-one will disbelieve it.

Regardless of a market maker's view of future events, he is at the mercy of supply and demand. If everyone wants calls, then it is only natural for him to increase their prices. As long as he doesn't violate put–call parity (either with himself or with another market maker) who's to know that it is supply and demand driving the volatility?

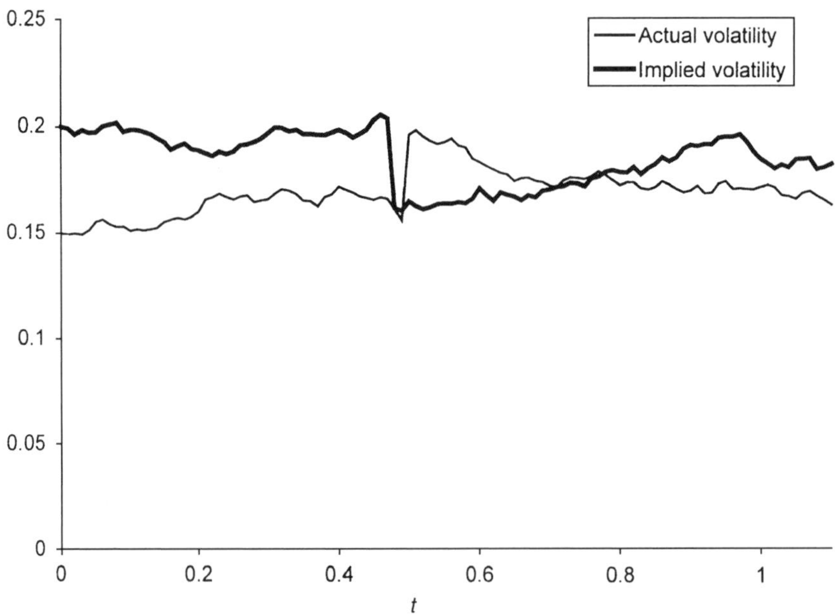

Figure 22.1 Actual and implied volatilities just before and just after an anticipated major news item.

22.3 TIME-DEPENDENT VOLATILITY

In Table 22.1 below are the market prices of European call options[1] with one, four and seven months until expiry. All have strike prices of 105 and the underlying asset is currently 106.25. The short-term interest rate over this period is about 5.6%.

As can easily be confirmed by substitution into the Black–Scholes call formula, these prices are consistent with volatilities of 21.2%, 20.5% and 19.4% for the one-, three- and seven-month options respectively. Clearly these prices cannot be correct if the volatility is constant for the whole seven months. What is to be done?

The simplest adjustment we can make to the Black–Scholes world to accommodate these prices (without any serious effect on the theoretical framework) is to assume a time-dependent, deterministic volatility. Let's assume that volatility is a function of time:

$$\sigma(t).$$

As explained in Chapter 8 the Black–Scholes formulae are still valid when volatility is time dependent provided we use

$$\sqrt{\frac{1}{T-t}\int_t^T \sigma(\tau)^2\,d\tau}$$

in place of σ, i.e. now use

$$d_1 = \frac{\log(S/E) + r(T-t) + \frac{1}{2}\int_t^T \sigma(\tau)^2\,d\tau}{\sqrt{\int_t^T \sigma(\tau)^2\,d\tau}}$$

and

$$d_2 = \frac{\log(S/E) + r(T-t) - \frac{1}{2}\int_t^T \sigma(\tau)^2\,d\tau}{\sqrt{\int_t^T \sigma(\tau)^2\,d\tau}}.$$

Table 22.1 Market prices of European call options; see text for details.

Expiry	Value
1 month	3.50
3 months	5.76
7 months	7.97

[1] I'm only using call options because put option prices should follow from the prices of the calls by put–call parity, therefore there will not be any more volatility information in the prices of puts than is already present in the prices of calls. Also the following analysis only really works if the options are European. Since most equity options are American we cannot use put prices because the values of American and European puts are different. In the absence of dividends the two call prices are the same.

In our example, all we need to do to ensure consistent pricing is to make

$$\sqrt{\frac{1}{T-t}\int_t^T \sigma(\tau)^2\,d\tau} = \text{implied volatilities.}$$

We do this 'fitting' at time t^*, and if I write $\sigma_{\text{imp}}(t^*, T)$ to mean the implied volatility measured at time t^* of a European option expiring at time T then

$$\sigma(t) = \sqrt{\sigma_{\text{imp}}(t^*, t)^2 + 2(t - t^*)\sigma_{\text{imp}}(t^*, t)\frac{\partial \sigma_{\text{imp}}(t^*, t)}{\partial t}}. \tag{22.1}$$

Practically speaking, we do not have a continuous (and differentiable) implied volatility curve. We have a discrete set of points (three in the above example). We must therefore make some assumption about the term structure of volatility between the data points. Usually one assumes that the function is piecewise constant or linear. If we have implied volatility for expiries T_i and we assume the volatility curve to be piecewise constant then

$$\sigma(t) = \sqrt{\frac{(T_i - t^*)\sigma_{\text{imp}}(t^*, T_i)^2 - (T_{i-1} - t^*)\sigma_{\text{imp}}(t^*, T_{i-1})^2}{T_i - T_{i-1}}} \quad \text{for} \quad T_{i-1} < t < T_i$$

22.4 VOLATILITY SMILES AND SKEWS

Now let me throw the cat among the pigeons. Continuing with the example above, suppose that there is also a European call option struck at 100 with an expiry of seven months and a price of 11.48. This corresponds to a volatility of 20.8% in the Black–Scholes equation. Now we have two conflicting volatilities up to the seven-month expiry, 19.4% and 20.8%. Clearly we cannot adjust the time dependence of the volatility in any way that is consistent with *both* of these values. What else can we do? Before I answer this, we'll look at a few more examples. Concentrating on the same example, suppose that there are call options traded with an expiry of seven months and strikes of 90, 92.5, 95, 97.5, 100, 102.5, 105, 107.5 and 110. In Figure 22.2 I plot the implied volatility of these options against the strike price (the actual option prices do not add anything to our insight so I haven't given them).

The shape of this implied volatility *versus* strike curve is called the **smile**. In some markets it shows considerable asymmetry, a **skew**, and sometimes it is upside down in a **frown**. The general shape tends to persist for a long time in each underlying.

If we managed to accommodate implied volatility that varied with expiry by making the volatility time dependent perhaps we can accommodate implied volatility that varies with strike by making the volatility asset-price dependent. This is exactly what we'll do. Unfortunately, it's much harder to make analytical progress except in special cases; if we have $\sigma(S)$ then rarely can we solve the Black–Scholes equation to get nice closed-form solutions for the values of derivative products. In fact, we may as well go all the way and assume that volatility is a function of *both* the asset and time, $\sigma(S, t)$.

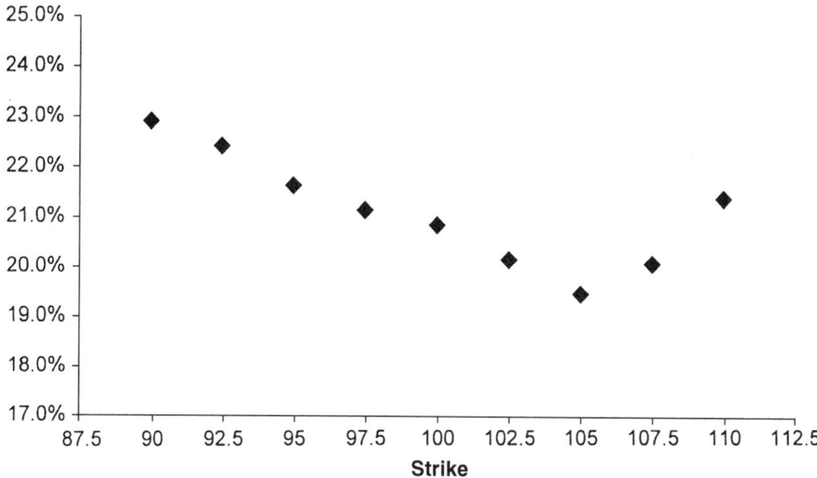

Figure 22.2 Implied volatilities against strike price.

22.5 VOLATILITY SURFACES

We can show implied volatility against both maturity and strike in a three-dimensional plot. One is shown in Figure 22.3. This implied volatility surface represents the constant value of volatility that gives each traded option a theoretical value equal to the market value.

We saw how the time dependence in implied volatility could be turned into a volatility of the underlying that was time dependent, i.e. we deduced $\sigma(t)$ from $\sigma_{\text{imp}}(t^*, T)$. Can we similarly deduce $\sigma(S, t)$ from $\sigma_{\text{imp}}(t^*, E, T)$ the implied volatility at time t^*? If we could, then we might want to call it the **local volatility surface** $\sigma(S, t)$. This local volatility surface can be thought of

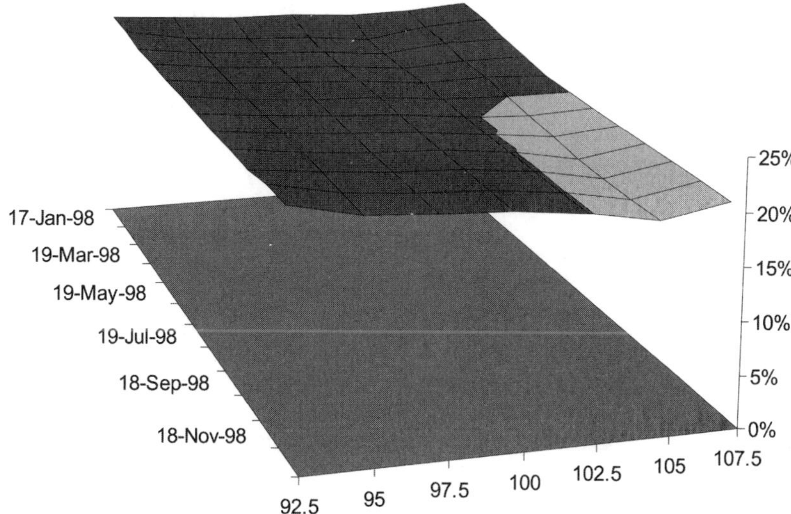

Figure 22.3 Implied volatilities against expiry and strike price.

as the market's view of the future value of volatility when the asset price is S at time t (which, of course, may not even be realized). The local volatility is also called the **forward volatility** or the **forward forward volatility**.

22.6 BACKING OUT THE LOCAL VOLATILITY SURFACE FROM EUROPEAN CALL OPTION PRICES

To back out the local volatility surface from the prices of market traded instruments I am going to assume that we have a distribution of European call prices of all strikes and maturities. This is not a realistic assumption but it gets the ball rolling. These prices will be denoted by $V(E, T)$. I could use puts but these can be converted to call prices by put–call parity. This notation is vastly different from before. Previously, we had the option value as a function of the underlying and time. Now the asset and time are fixed at S^* and t^*, today's values. I will use the dependence of the market prices on strike and expiry to calculate the volatility structure.

I will assume that the risk-neutral random walk for S is

$$dS = rS\,dt + \sigma(S, t)S\,dX.$$

This is our usual one-factor model for which all the building blocks of delta hedging and arbitrage-free pricing hold. The only novelty is that the volatility is dependent on the level of the asset and time.

In the following, I am going to rely heavily on the transition probability density function $p(S^*, t^*; S, T)$ for the risk-neutral random walk. Note that the backward variables are fixed at today's values and the forward time variable is T. Recalling that the value of an option is the present value of the expected payoff, I can write

$$\begin{aligned} V(E, T) &= e^{-r(T-t^*)} \int_0^\infty \max(S - E, 0)\,p(S^*, t^*; S, T)\,dS \\ &= e^{-r(T-t^*)} \int_E^\infty (S - E)\,p(S^*, t^*; S, T)\,dS. \end{aligned} \tag{22.2}$$

We are *very* lucky that the payoff is the maximum function so that after differentiating with respect to E we get

$$\frac{\partial V}{\partial E} = -e^{-r(T-t^*)} \int_E^\infty p(S^*, t^*; S, T)\,dS.$$

And after another differentiation, we arrive at

$$\boxed{p(S^*, t^*; E, T) = e^{r(T-t^*)} \frac{\partial^2 V}{\partial E^2}} \tag{22.3}$$

Before even calculating volatilities we can find the transition probability density function. In a sense, this is the market's view of the future distribution. But it's the market view of the risk-neutral distribution and not the real one. An example is plotted in Figure 22.4.

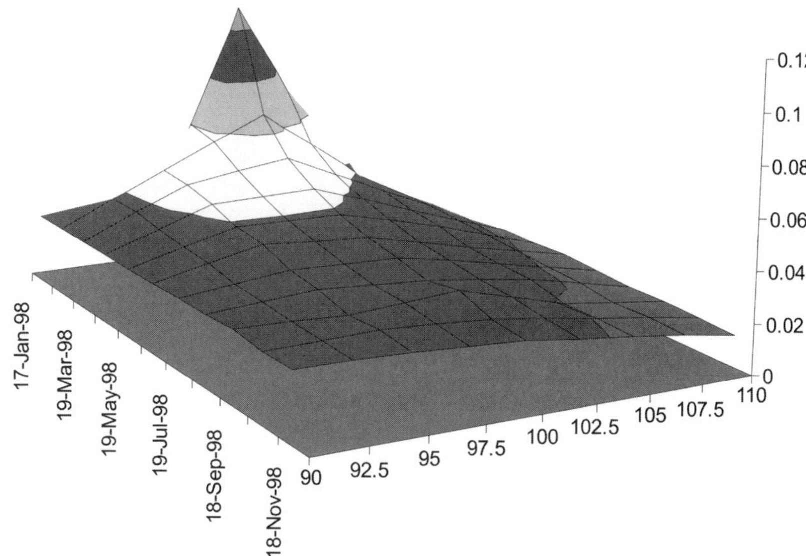

Figure 22.4 Risk-neutral transition probability density function calculated from European call prices.

The next step is to use the forward equation for the transition probability density function, the Fokker–Planck equation,

$$\frac{\partial p}{\partial T} = \tfrac{1}{2}\frac{\partial^2}{\partial S^2}(\sigma^2 S^2 p) - \frac{\partial}{\partial S}(rSp). \tag{22.4}$$

Here σ is our, still unknown, function of S and t. However, *in this equation $\sigma(S, t)$ is evaluated at $t = T$.*

From (22.2) we have

$$\frac{\partial V}{\partial T} = -rV + e^{-r(T-t^*)}\int_E^\infty (S-E)\frac{\partial p}{\partial T}\,dS.$$

This can be written as

$$\frac{\partial V}{\partial T} = -rV + e^{-r(T-t^*)}\int_E^\infty \left(\tfrac{1}{2}\frac{\partial^2(\sigma^2 S^2 p)}{\partial S^2} - \frac{\partial (rSp)}{\partial S}\right)(S-E)\,dS$$

using the forward equation (22.4). Integrating this by parts twice, assuming that p and its first S derivative tend to zero sufficiently fast as S goes to infinity we get

$$\frac{\partial V}{\partial T} = -rV + \tfrac{1}{2}e^{-r(T-t^*)}\sigma^2 E^2 p + re^{-r(T-t^*)}\int_E^\infty Sp\,dS. \tag{22.5}$$

In this expression $\sigma(S, t)$ has $S = E$ and $t = T$. Writing

$$\int_E^\infty Sp\,dS = \int_E^\infty (S-E)p\,dS + E\int_E^\infty p\,dS$$

and collecting terms, we get

$$\frac{\partial V}{\partial T} = \tfrac{1}{2}\sigma^2 E^2 \frac{\partial^2 V}{\partial E^2} - rE\frac{\partial V}{\partial E}.$$

Rearranging this we find that

$$\sigma = \sqrt{\frac{\dfrac{\partial V}{\partial T} + rE\dfrac{\partial V}{\partial E}}{\tfrac{1}{2}E^2\dfrac{\partial^2 V}{\partial E^2}}}.$$

This gives us $\sigma(E, T)$ and hence, by *relabelling the variables*, $\sigma(S, t)$.

This calculation of the volatility surface from option prices worked because of the particular form of the payoff, the call payoff, which allowed us to derive the very simple relationship between derivatives of the option price and the transition probability density function.

When there is a constant and continuous dividend yield on the underlying the relationship between call prices and the local volatility is

$$\sigma = \sqrt{\frac{\dfrac{\partial V}{\partial T} + (r-D)E\dfrac{\partial V}{\partial E} + DV}{\tfrac{1}{2}E^2\dfrac{\partial^2 V}{\partial E^2}}} \qquad (22.6)$$

There is no change in this expression when the interest rate and dividend yield are time dependent, just use the relevant forward rates.

One of the problems with this expression concerns data far in or far out of the money. Unless we are close to at the money both the numerator and denominator of (22.6) are small, leading to inaccuracies when we divide one small number by another. One way of avoiding this is to relate the local volatility surface to the implied volatility surface as I now show.

In the same way that we found a relationship between the local volatility and the implied volatility in the purely time-dependent case, Equation (22.1), we can find a relationship in the general case of asset- and time-dependent local volatility. This relationship is obviously quite complicated and I omit the details of the derivation. The result is

$$\sigma(E,T) = \sqrt{\frac{\sigma_{\text{imp}}^2 + 2(T-t^*)\sigma_{\text{imp}}\dfrac{\partial\sigma_{\text{imp}}}{\partial T} + 2(r-D)E(T-t^*)\sigma_{\text{imp}}\dfrac{\partial\sigma_{\text{imp}}}{\partial E}}{\left(1 + Ed_1\sqrt{T-t^*}\dfrac{\partial\sigma_{\text{imp}}}{\partial E}\right)^2 + E^2(T-t^*)\sigma_{\text{imp}}\left(\dfrac{\partial^2\sigma_{\text{imp}}}{\partial E^2} - d_1\left(\dfrac{\partial\sigma_{\text{imp}}}{\partial E}\right)^2\sqrt{T-t^*}\right)}} \qquad (22.7)$$

$$d_1 = \frac{\log(S^*/E) + \left(r - D + \tfrac{1}{2}\sigma_{\text{imp}}^2\right)(T-t^*)}{\sigma_{\text{imp}}\sqrt{T-t^*}}$$

In terms of the implied volatility the implied risk-neutral probability density function is

$$p(S^*, t^*; E, T) = \frac{1}{E\sigma_{\mathrm{imp}}\sqrt{2\pi(T-t^*)}} e^{-(1/2)d_1^2}$$
$$\left(\left(1 + Ed_1\sqrt{T-t^*}\frac{\partial\sigma_{\mathrm{imp}}}{\partial E}\right)^2 + E^2(T-t^*)\sigma_{\mathrm{imp}}\left(\frac{\partial^2\sigma_{\mathrm{imp}}}{\partial E^2} - d_1\left(\frac{\partial\sigma_{\mathrm{imp}}}{\partial E}\right)^2\sqrt{T-t^*}\right)\right)$$

One of the advantages of writing the local volatility and probability density function in terms of the implied volatility surface is that if you put in a flat implied volatility surface you get out a flat local surface and a lognormal distribution.

In practice there only exist a finite, discretely-spaced set of call prices. To deduce a local volatility surface from this data requires some interpolation and extrapolation. This can be done in a number of ways and there is no correct way. One of the problems with these approaches is that the final result depends sensitively on the form of the interpolation. The problem is actually 'ill-posed,' meaning that a small change in the input can lead to a large change in the output. There are many ways to get around this ill-posedness, coming under the general heading of 'regularization.' Several suggestions for further reading in this area are given at the end of the chapter.

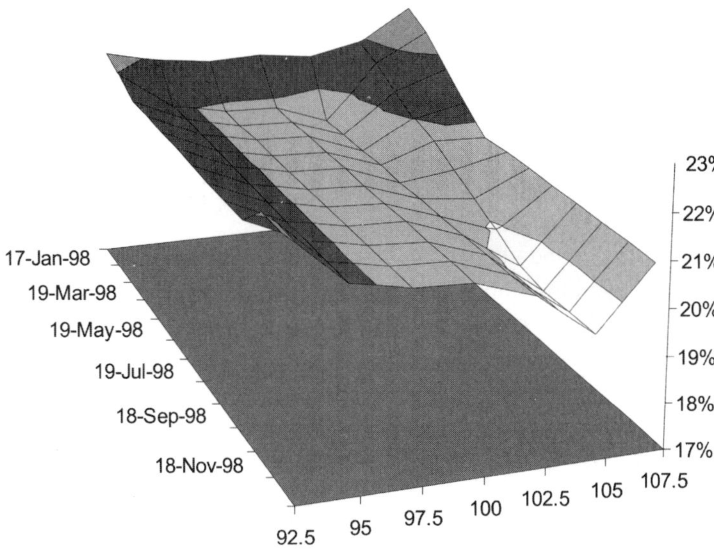

Figure 22.5 Local volatility surface calculated from European call prices.

An example of a local volatility surface is plotted in Figure 22.5.

22.7 HOW DO I USE THE LOCAL VOLATILITY SURFACE?

There are two ways to look at the local volatility surface. One is to say that it is the market's view of future volatility and that these predictions will come to pass. We then price other, more complex, products using this asset- and time-dependent volatility. This is a very naive belief. Not only do the predictions not come true but even if we come back a few days later to look at the 'prediction,' i.e. to refit the surface, we see that it has changed.

The other way of using the surface is to acknowledge that it is only a snapshot of the market's view and that tomorrow it may change. But it can be used to price non-traded contracts in a way that is consistent across all instruments. As long as we price our exotic contract consistently with the vanillas, that is, with the same volatility structure, *and simultaneously hedge with these vanillas*, then we are reducing our exposure to model error. This approach is readily justifiable, although it is a bit difficult to estimate by how much we have reduced our model exposure. However, if you price using the calibrated volatility surface but only delta hedge, then you are asking for trouble. Suppose you price, and sell, a volatility-sensitive instrument such as an up-and-out call with a fitted volatility surface which increases with stock level. If it turns out that when the volatility is realized it is a downward-sloping function of the asset then you are in big trouble.

As an example, calculate the local volatility surface using vanilla calls. Now price a barrier option using this volatility structure. This means solving the Black–Scholes partial differential equation with the asset- and time-dependent volatility and with the relevant boundary conditions. This must be done numerically, by the methods explained in Part Six, for example. Now statically hedge the barrier by buying and selling the vanilla contracts to mimic as closely as possible the payoff and boundary conditions of the barrier option. This is described more fully in Chapter 30.

22.8 SUMMARY

Whether you believe in them or not, local volatility surfaces have taken the practitioner world by storm. Now that they are commonly used for pricing and hedging exotic contracts there is no way back to the world of constant volatility.

Personally I am in two minds about this issue. But as long as you hedge as much of the cashflows using traded vanillas options then you will be reducing your model exposure anyway. Once you have done this then you have done your best to reduce dependence on volatility. The danger is always going to be there if you never bother to statically hedge, only delta hedge. This is discussed in detail in Chapter 30.

FURTHER READING

- Merton (1973) was the first to find the explicit formulae for European options with time-dependent volatility.
- See Dupire (1993, 1994) and Derman & Kani (1994) for more details of fitting the local volatility surface.
- Rubinstein (1994) constructs an implied tree using an optimization approach, and this has been generalized by Jackwerth & Rubinstein (1996).
- To get around the problem of ill-posedness, Avellaneda, Friedman, Holmes & Samperi (1997) propose calibrating the local volatility surface by entropy minimization. Their article is also a very good source of references to the volatility surface literature.
- For trading strategies involving views on the direction of volatility see Connolly (1997).

- I suspect that there is not much information about future volatility contained in the local volatility surface. This is demonstrated in Dumas, Fleming & Whaley (1998).

EXERCISES

1. Use market data for European call or put options to calculate the implied volatilities for various times to expiry and exercise prices. Now find the risk-neutral probability density function and the local volatility surface.
2. Using market data for European options with the same expiry but different exercise prices, find and plot the implied volatilities. What shape does the plotted curve have?

CHAPTER 23
stochastic volatility

In this Chapter...

- modeling volatility as a stochastic variable
- discontinuous volatility
- how to price contracts when volatility is stochastic

23.1 INTRODUCTION

Volatility does not behave how the Black–Scholes equation would like it to behave; it is not constant, it is not predictable, it's not even directly observable. This makes it a prime candidate for modeling as a random variable. There is plenty of evidence that returns on equities, currencies and commodities are not Normally distributed, they have higher peaks and fatter tails than predicted by a Normal distribution. We have seen this in several places in this book. This has also been cited as evidence for non-constant volatility.

23.2 RANDOM VOLATILITY

If we draw a number at random from a distribution with either a 10% volatility, 20% volatility or 30% volatility with equal probability, then the resulting distribution would have the higher-peak, fatter-tails properties we have seen in the data. However, as long as the standard deviation of this distribution is finite (and scales with the square root of the timestep) we can price options using the standard deviation in place of the volatility in Black–Scholes (see also Chapter 20). Pricing only becomes a problem with random volatility when the timescale of the evolution is of the same order as the evolution of the underlying. For example, if we have a stochastic differential equation model for the volatility then we must move beyond the Black–Scholes world.

23.3 A STOCHASTIC DIFFERENTIAL EQUATION FOR VOLATILITY

We continue to assume that S satisfies

$$dS = \mu S\,dt + \sigma S\,dX_1,$$

but we further assume that volatility satisfies

$$d\sigma = p(S, \sigma, t)\,dt + q(S, \sigma, t)\,dX_2. \tag{23.1}$$

The two increments dX_1 and dX_2 have a correlation of ρ. The choice of functions $p(S, \sigma, t)$ and $q(S, \sigma, t)$ is crucial to the evolution of the volatility, and thus to the pricing of derivatives. The choice of these functions is discussed later in this chapter and in Chapter 25. For the moment, I only comment that a mean-reverting process is a natural choice.

The value of an option with stochastic volatility is a function of three variables, $V(S, \sigma, t)$.

23.4 THE PRICING EQUATION

The new stochastic quantity that we are modeling, the volatility, is not a traded asset. Thus, when volatility is stochastic we are faced with the problem of having a source of randomness that cannot be easily hedged away. Because we have two sources of randomness we must hedge our option with two other contracts, one being the underlying asset as usual, but now we also need another option to hedge the volatility risk. We therefore must set up a portfolio containing one option, with value denoted by $V(S, \sigma, t)$, a quantity $-\Delta$ of the asset and a quantity $-\Delta_1$ of another option with value $V_1(S, \sigma, t)$. We have

$$\Pi = V - \Delta S - \Delta_1 V_1. \tag{23.2}$$

The change in this portfolio in a time dt is given by

$$\begin{aligned} d\Pi = &\left(\frac{\partial V}{\partial t} + \tfrac{1}{2}\sigma^2 S^2 \frac{\partial^2 V}{\partial S^2} + \rho\sigma q S \frac{\partial^2 V}{\partial S \partial \sigma} + \tfrac{1}{2} q^2 \frac{\partial^2 V}{\partial \sigma^2} \right) dt \\ &- \Delta_1 \left(\frac{\partial V_1}{\partial t} + \tfrac{1}{2}\sigma^2 S^2 \frac{\partial^2 V_1}{\partial S^2} + \rho\sigma q S \frac{\partial^2 V_1}{\partial S \partial \sigma} + \tfrac{1}{2} q^2 \frac{\partial^2 V_1}{\partial \sigma^2} \right) dt \\ &+ \left(\frac{\partial V}{\partial S} - \Delta_1 \frac{\partial V_1}{\partial S} - \Delta \right) dS \\ &+ \left(\frac{\partial V}{\partial \sigma} - \Delta_1 \frac{\partial V_1}{\partial \sigma} \right) d\sigma. \end{aligned}$$

where I have used Itô's lemma on functions of S, σ and t.

To eliminate all randomness from the portfolio we must choose

$$\frac{\partial V}{\partial S} - \Delta - \Delta_1 \frac{\partial V_1}{\partial S} = 0,$$

to eliminate dS terms, and

$$\frac{\partial V}{\partial \sigma} - \Delta_1 \frac{\partial V_1}{\partial \sigma} = 0,$$

to eliminate $d\sigma$ terms. This leaves us with

$$\begin{aligned} d\Pi = &\frac{\partial V}{\partial t} dt + \tfrac{1}{2}\sigma^2 S^2 \frac{\partial^2 V}{\partial S^2} dt + \rho\sigma S q \frac{\partial^2 V}{\partial S\, \partial \sigma} dt + \tfrac{1}{2} q^2 \frac{\partial^2 V}{\partial \sigma^2} dt \\ &- \Delta_1 \left(\frac{\partial V_1}{\partial t} dt + \tfrac{1}{2}\sigma^2 S^2 \frac{\partial^2 V_1}{\partial S^2} dt + \rho\sigma S q \frac{\partial^2 V_1}{\partial S\, \partial \sigma} dt + \tfrac{1}{2} q^2 \frac{\partial^2 V_1}{\partial \sigma^2} dt \right) \\ &= r\Pi\, dt = r(V - \Delta S - \Delta_1 V_1)\, dt, \end{aligned}$$

where I have used arbitrage arguments to set the return on the portfolio equal to the risk-free rate.

As it stands, this is *one* equation in the *two* unknowns, V and V_1. This contrast with the earlier Black–Scholes case with one equation in the one unknown.

Collecting all V terms on the left-hand side and all V_1 terms on the right-hand side we find that

$$\frac{\dfrac{\partial V}{\partial t}+\tfrac{1}{2}\sigma^2S^2\dfrac{\partial^2 V}{\partial S^2}+\rho\sigma Sq\dfrac{\partial^2 V}{\partial S\,\partial\sigma}+\tfrac{1}{2}q^2\dfrac{\partial^2 V}{\partial\sigma^2}+rS\dfrac{\partial V}{\partial S}-rV}{\dfrac{\partial V}{\partial\sigma}}$$

$$=\frac{\dfrac{\partial V_1}{\partial t}+\tfrac{1}{2}\sigma^2S^2\dfrac{\partial^2 V_1}{\partial S^2}+\rho\sigma Sq\dfrac{\partial^2 V_1}{\partial S\,\partial\sigma}+\tfrac{1}{2}q^2\dfrac{\partial^2 V_1}{\partial\sigma^2}+rS\dfrac{\partial V_1}{\partial S}-rV_1}{\dfrac{\partial V_1}{\partial\sigma}}.$$

We are lucky that the left-hand side is a function of V but not V_1 and the right-hand side is a function of V_1 but not V. Since the two options will typically have different payoffs, strikes or expiries, the only way for this to be possible is for both sides to be independent of the contract type. Both sides can only be functions of the *independent* variables, S, σ and t. Thus we have

$$\frac{\partial V}{\partial t}+\tfrac{1}{2}\sigma^2S^2\frac{\partial^2 V}{\partial S^2}+\rho\sigma Sq\frac{\partial^2 V}{\partial S\,\partial\sigma}+\tfrac{1}{2}q^2\frac{\partial^2 V}{\partial\sigma^2}+rS\frac{\partial V}{\partial S}-rV=-(p-\lambda q)\frac{\partial V}{\partial\sigma},$$

for some function $\lambda(S,\sigma,t)$.

Reordering this equation, we usually write

$$\frac{\partial V}{\partial t}+\tfrac{1}{2}\sigma^2S^2\frac{\partial^2 V}{\partial S^2}+\rho\sigma Sq\frac{\partial^2 V}{\partial S\,\partial\sigma}+\tfrac{1}{2}q^2\frac{\partial^2 V}{\partial\sigma^2}+rS\frac{\partial V}{\partial S}+(p-\lambda q)\frac{\partial V}{\partial\sigma}-rV=0 \qquad (23.3)$$

The function $\lambda(S,\sigma,t)$ is called the **market price of (volatility) risk**.

23.5 THE MARKET PRICE OF VOLATILITY RISK

If we can solve Equation (23.3) then we have found the value of the option, and the hedge ratios. Generally, this must be done numerically. But note that we find *two* hedge ratios, $\partial V/\partial S$ and $\partial V/\partial\sigma$. We have two hedge ratios because we have two sources of randomness that we must hedge away.

Because one of the modeled quantities, the volatility, is not traded we find that the pricing equation contains a market price of risk term. What does this term mean? Suppose we hold one of the option with value V, and satisfying the pricing equation (23.3), delta hedged with the underlying asset only, i.e. we have

$$\Pi=V-\Delta S.$$

The change in this portfolio value is

$$d\Pi=\left(\frac{\partial V}{\partial t}+\tfrac{1}{2}\sigma^2S^2\frac{\partial^2 V}{\partial S^2}+\rho\sigma qS\frac{\partial^2 V}{\partial S\partial\sigma}+\tfrac{1}{2}q^2\frac{\partial^2 V}{\partial\sigma^2}\right)dt$$

$$+\left(\frac{\partial V}{\partial S}-\Delta\right)dS+\frac{\partial V}{\partial\sigma}\,d\sigma.$$

Because we are delta hedging the coefficient of dS is zero. We find that

$$d\Pi - r\Pi\,dt = \left(\frac{\partial V}{\partial t} + \tfrac{1}{2}\sigma^2 S^2 \frac{\partial^2 V}{\partial S^2} + \rho\sigma q S \frac{\partial^2 V}{\partial S \partial \sigma} + \tfrac{1}{2}q^2 \frac{\partial^2 V}{\partial \sigma^2} + rS\frac{\partial V}{\partial S} - rV\right) dt + \frac{\partial V}{\partial \sigma}\,d\sigma$$
$$= q\frac{\partial V}{\partial \sigma}(\lambda\,dt + dX_2).$$

This has used both the pricing equation (23.3) and the stochastic differential equation for σ, (23.1). Observe that for every unit of volatility risk, represented by dX_2, there are λ units of extra return, represented by dt. Hence the name 'market price of risk.'

The quantity $p - \lambda q$ is called the **risk-neutral drift rate** of the volatility. Recall that the risk-neutral drift of the underlying asset is r and not μ. When it comes to pricing derivatives, it is the risk-neutral drift that matters and not the real drift, whether it is the drift of the asset or of the volatility.

23.5.1 Aside: The Market Price of Risk for Traded Assets

Let us return briefly to the Black–Scholes world of constant volatility. In Chapter 5 we derived the Black–Scholes equation for equities by constructing a portfolio consisting of one option and a number $-\Delta$ of the underlying asset. We were able to do this because the underlying asset, the equity, was traded. Suppose that instead we were to follow the analysis above and construct a portfolio of two *options* with different maturity dates (or different exercise prices, for that matter) instead of an option and the underlying. We would have

$$\Pi = V - \Delta_1 V_1.$$

Note that there are none of the underlying asset in this portfolio. The same argument as used above leads us to

$$\frac{\partial V}{\partial t} + \tfrac{1}{2}\sigma^2 S^2 \frac{\partial^2 V}{\partial S^2} + (\mu - \lambda_S\sigma)S\frac{\partial V}{\partial S} - rV = 0. \qquad (23.4)$$

What is special about the variable S? It is the value of a traded asset. This means that $V = S$ must itself be a solution of (23.4). Substituting $V = S$ into (23.4) we find that

$$(\mu - \lambda_S\sigma)S - rS = 0,$$

i.e.

$$\lambda_S = \frac{\mu - r}{\sigma};$$

this is the market price of risk for a traded asset. Now putting $\lambda_S = (\mu - r)/\sigma$ into (23.4) we arrive at

$$\frac{\partial V}{\partial t} + \tfrac{1}{2}\sigma^2 S^2 \frac{\partial^2 V}{\partial S^2} + rS\frac{\partial V}{\partial S} - rV = 0.$$

We are back at the Black–Scholes equation, which contains no mention of μ or λ_S.

23.6 NAMED MODELS

Hull & White (1987)

Hull & White considered both general and specific volatility modeling. The most important result of their analysis is that when the stock and the volatility are uncorrelated and the risk-neutral dynamics of the volatility are unaffected by the stock (i.e. $p - \lambda q$ and q are independent of S) then the fair value of an option is the average of the Black–Scholes values for the option, with the average taken over the distribution of σ^2.

One of the (risk-neutral) stochastic volatility models considered by Hull & White was

$$d(\sigma^2) = a(b - \sigma^2)\,dt + c\sigma^2\,dX_2.$$

Usually, the value of an option must be found numerically, but there are some simple approximations using Taylor series.

Heston (1993)

In Heston's model

$$d\sigma = -\gamma\sigma\,dt + \delta\,dX_2,$$

with arbitrary correlation between the underlying and its volatility.

23.7 GARCH

Generalized autoregressive conditional heteroskedasticity, or GARCH for short, is a model for an asset and its associated volatility. The simplest such model is GARCH(1,1) which takes the form

$$\sigma_{t+1}^2 = \omega + \beta\sigma_t^2 + \alpha\varepsilon_t^2,$$

where the ε_t are the asset price returns after removing the drift. That is,

$$S_{t+1} = S_t(1 + \mu + \sigma_t\varepsilon_t).$$

Note how the notation is different from, but related to, that which we are used to. This is because, historically, GARCH was developed in a econometrical and not a financial environment. There should not be any confusion as this is the only place in the book where this notation is used. It can be shown that this simplest GARCH model becomes the same as the stochastic volatility model

$$d(\sigma^2) = \phi(\theta - \sigma^2)\,dt + \nu\sigma^2\,dX_2,$$

as the timestep tends to zero. The parameters in the above are related to the parameters in the original GARCH specification and to the timestep.

There are many references to GARCH in the Further reading section.

23.8 SUMMARY

Because of the profound importance of volatility in the pricing of options, and because volatility is hard to estimate, observe or predict, it is natural to model it as a random variable. For some contracts, most notably barriers, a constant volatility model is just too inaccurate. In Chapter 26 we'll return to modeling volatility, but there we will examine jump volatility models.

FURTHER READING

- See Hull & White (1987) and Heston (1993) for more discussion of pricing derivatives when volatility is stochastic.
- GARCH is explained in Bollerslev (1986).
- Nelson (1990) shows the relationship between GARCH models and diffusion processes.
- There are many articles in *Risk* magazine, starting in 1992, covering GARCH and its extensions in detail. Recent developments are described in Engle & Mezrich (1996).
- For further work on GARCH see the papers by Engle (1982), Engle & Bollerslev (1987), Alexander (1995, 1996 b, 1997 b), Alexander & Riyait (1992), Alexander & Chibuma (1997) Alexander & Williams (1997), and the collection of papers edited by Engle (1995).
- Derman & Kani (1997) model the stochastic evolution of the whole local volatility surface.
- Ahn, Arkell, Choe, Holstad & Wilmott (1998) examine the risk involved in delta and static hedging under stochastic volatility.

EXERCISES

1. Derive the pricing equation for an option with a stochastic volatility of the form

$$d\sigma = p(S, \sigma, t)\, dt + q(S, \sigma, t)\, dX_2,$$

to find

$$\frac{\partial V}{\partial t} + \tfrac{1}{2}\sigma^2 S^2 \frac{\partial^2 V}{\partial S^2} + \rho\sigma q S \frac{\partial^2 V}{\partial S \partial \sigma} + \tfrac{1}{2}q^2 \frac{\partial^2 V}{\partial \sigma^2} + rS\frac{\partial V}{\partial S} + (p - \lambda q)\frac{\partial V}{\partial \sigma} - rV = 0.$$

2. How could we pursue the idea of stochastic volatility to a further degree? Can we make the volatility of volatility stochastic? Would this be a sensible course of action to take?

CHAPTER 24
uncertain parameters

In this Chapter...

- why the parameters in the Black–Scholes model are not reliable
- how to price contracts when volatility, interest rate and dividend are uncertain

24.1 INTRODUCTION

The Black–Scholes equation

$$\frac{\partial V}{\partial t} + \tfrac{1}{2}\sigma^2 S^2 \frac{\partial^2 V}{\partial S^2} + (r - D)S\frac{\partial V}{\partial S} - rV = 0$$

is a parabolic partial differential equation in two variables, S and t, with three parameters, σ, r and D, not to mention other parameters such as strike price, barrier levels, etc. specific to the contract. Out of these variables and parameters, which ones are easily measurable?

- *Asset price:* The asset price is quoted and therefore easy to measure in theory. In practice, two prices are quoted, the bid and the ask prices; and even these prices will differ between market makers. This issue of transaction costs and their effect on option prices was discussed in Chapter 21.
- *Time to expiry:* Today's date and the expiry date are the easiest quantities to measure. (There is some question about how to treat weekends, but this is more a question of modeling asset price movements than of parameter estimation.)
- *Volatility:* There are two traditional ways of measuring volatility: implied and historical. Whichever way is used, the result cannot be the future value of volatility; either it is the market's estimate of the future or an estimate of values in the past. The correct value of volatility to be used in an option calculation cannot be known until the option has expired. A time series plot of historical volatility, say, might look something like Figure 24.1, and it is certainly not constant as assumed in the simple Black–Scholes formulae. We can see in this figure that volatility for this stock typically ranges between 20 and 60%. The exception to this was during the October/November 1997 crash, for which jump/crash models are perhaps more relevant.
- *Risk-free interest rate:* Suppose we are valuing an option with a lifespan of six months. We can easily find the yield to maturity of a six-month bond and this could be our value for the risk-free rate. However, because the hedged portfolio earns the instantaneous spot

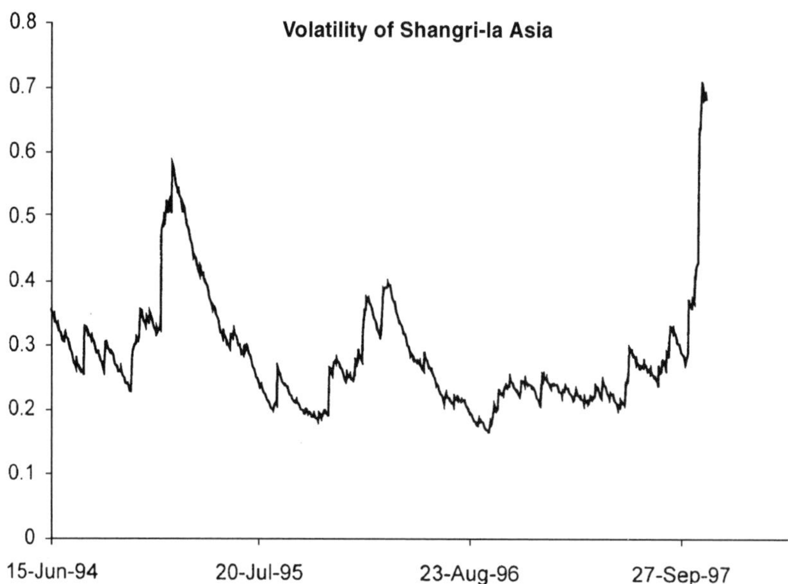

Figure 24.1 A typical time series for historical volatility; an implied volatility time series would look similar.

rate, the Black–Scholes theory requires knowledge of the future behavior of the *spot* interest rate, and this is not the same as the six-month rate. We can, of course, couple an asset price model *and* an interest rate model, as in Chapter 36, but then we have even more problems with the accuracy of our interest rate model and estimating its parameters.

- *Dividends:* Dividends are declared a few months before they are paid. However, before then what value do we use in our option value calculation? Again, we have to make a guess at the dividend value, obviously using the past as a guide. See Chapter 8 for a detailed discussion of modeling dividend structure.

In this chapter we address the problem of how to value options when parameter values are *uncertain*. Rather than assuming that we know the precise value for a parameter, we assume that all we know about the parameters is that *they lie within specified ranges*. With this assumption, we do not find a *single* value for an option, instead we find that the option's value can also lie within a range: there is no such thing as *the* value. In fact, the correct value cannot be determined until the expiry of the option when we know the path taken by the parameters. Until then, there are many possible values any of which *might* turn out to be correct.

We will see that this problem is nonlinear, and thus an option valued in isolation has a different range of values from an option valued as part of a portfolio: we find that the range of possible option values depends on what we use to hedge the contract. If we put other options into the portfolio this will change the value of the original portfolio. This leads to the idea of incorporating traded options into an OTC portfolio in such a way as to maximize its value. This is called optimal static hedging, discussed in depth in Chapter 30. In that chapter, I also show how to apply the idea to path-dependent contracts such as barrier options.

Two of the advantages of the approach we adopt in this chapter are obvious. First, we can be more certain about the correctness of a range of values than a single value: we will be happier to say that the volatility of a stock lies within the range 20–30% over the next nine months than to say that the average volatility over this period will be 24%. Another advantage concerns the crucial matter of whether to believe market prices for a contract or the value given by some model. We have seen in Chapter 22 (and will see in Chapter 34) that it is common practice to 'adjust' a model so that it gives theoretical values for liquid contracts that exactly match the market values. Since the uncertain parameter model gives ranges for option values this means that we no longer have to choose between the correctness of a prediction and of a market price. Now they can differ; all we can say is that, according to the model, arbitrage is only certain if the market value lies outside our predicted range.

24.2 BEST AND WORST CASES

The first step in valuing options with uncertain parameters is to acknowledge that we can do no better than give ranges for the future values of the parameters. For volatility, for example, this range may be the range of past historical volatility, or implied volatilities, or encompass both of these. Then again, it may just be an educated guess. The range we choose represents our estimate of the upper and lower bounds for the parameter value for the life of the option or portfolio in question. These ranges for parameters lead to ranges for the option's value. Thus it is natural to think in terms of a lowest and highest possible option value; if you are the long option, then we can also call the lowest value the *worst* value and the highest the *best*. Work in this area was started by Avellaneda, Levy, Parás and Lyons.

We begin by considering uncertain volatility and shortly address the problem of uncertain interest rate (very similar) and then uncertain discretely-paid dividends (slightly different).

24.2.1 Uncertain Volatility: the Model of Avellaneda, Levy & Parás (1995) and Lyons (1995)

Let us suppose that the volatility lies within the band

$$\sigma^- < \sigma < \sigma^+.$$

We will follow the Black–Scholes hedging and no-arbitrage argument as far as we can and see where it leads us.

Construct a portfolio of one option, with value $V(S, t)$, and hedge it with $-\Delta$ of the underlying asset. The value of this portfolio is thus

$$\Pi = V - \Delta S.$$

We still have

$$dS = \mu S\,dt + \sigma S\,dX,$$

even though σ is unknown, and so the change in the value of this portfolio is

$$d\Pi = \left(\frac{\partial V}{\partial t} + \tfrac{1}{2}\sigma^2 S^2 \frac{\partial^2 V}{\partial S^2}\right) dt + \left(\frac{\partial V}{\partial S} - \Delta\right) dS.$$

Even with the volatility unknown, the choice of $\Delta = \partial V/\partial S$ eliminates the risk:

$$d\Pi = \left(\frac{\partial V}{\partial t} + \tfrac{1}{2}\sigma^2 S^2 \frac{\partial^2 V}{\partial S^2}\right) dt.$$

At this stage we would normally say that if we know V then we know $d\Pi$. This is no longer the case since we do not know σ. The argument now deviates subtly from the vanilla Black–Scholes argument. What we will now say is that we will be pessimistic: we will assume that the volatility over the next time step is such that our portfolio increases by the least amount. If we have a long position in a call option, for example, we assume that the volatility is at the lower bound σ^-; for a short call we assume that the volatility is high. This amounts to considering the *minimum* return on the portfolio, where the minimum is taken over all possible values of the volatility within the given range. The return on this worst-case portfolio is then set equal to the risk-free rate:

$$\min_{\sigma^- < \sigma < \sigma^+} (d\Pi) = r\Pi\, dt.$$

Thus we set

$$\min_{\sigma^- < \sigma < \sigma^+} \left(\frac{\partial V}{\partial t} + \tfrac{1}{2}\sigma^2 S^2 \frac{\partial^2 V}{\partial S^2}\right) dt = \left(V - S\frac{\partial V}{\partial S}\right) dt.$$

Now observe that the volatility term in the above is multiplied by the option's gamma. Therefore the value of σ that will give this its minimum value depends on the sign of the gamma. When the gamma is positive we choose σ to be the lowest value σ^- and when it is negative we choose σ to be its highest value σ^+. We find that the worst-case value V^- satisfies

$$\frac{\partial V^-}{\partial t} + \tfrac{1}{2}\sigma(\Gamma)^2 S^2 \frac{\partial^2 V^-}{\partial S^2} + rS\frac{\partial V^-}{\partial S} - rV^- = 0 \tag{24.1}$$

where

$$\Gamma = \frac{\partial^2 V^-}{\partial S^2}$$

and

$$\sigma(\Gamma) = \begin{cases} \sigma^+ & \text{if } \Gamma < 0 \\ \sigma^- & \text{if } \Gamma > 0. \end{cases}$$

We can find the best option value V^+, and hence the range of possible values by solving

$$\frac{\partial V^+}{\partial t} + \tfrac{1}{2}\sigma(\Gamma)^2 S^2 \frac{\partial^2 V^+}{\partial S^2} + rS\frac{\partial V^+}{\partial S} - rV^+ = 0$$

where

$$\Gamma = \frac{\partial^2 V^+}{\partial S^2}$$

but this time

$$\sigma(\Gamma) = \begin{cases} \sigma^+ & \text{if } \Gamma > 0 \\ \sigma^- & \text{if } \Gamma < 0. \end{cases}$$

We won't find much use for the problem for the best case in practice since it would be financially suicidal to assume the best outcome. (Note that just by changing the signs in Equation (24.1) we go from the worst-case equation to the best. In other words, the problem for the worst price for long and short positions in a particular contract is mathematically equivalent to valuing a long position only, but in worst and best cases. This distinction between long and short positions is an important consequence of the nonlinearity of the equation and we discuss this in depth shortly.)

Equation (24.1), derived by Avellaneda, Levy & Parás and Lyons, is exactly the same as the Hoggard–Whalley–Wilmott transaction cost model that we saw in Chapter 21. The partial differential equation may be the same, but the reason for it is completely different.

Equation (24.1) must in general be solved numerically, because it is nonlinear. In Figure 24.2 are shown the best and worst prices for an up-and-out call option. As I said above, the best and worst prices could be interpreted as worst-case prices for short and long positions respectively. In the figure is a Black–Scholes value, the middle line, using a volatility of 20%. The other two bold lines give the worst-case long and short values assuming a volatility ranging over 17% to 23%.

We must solve the nonlinear equation numerically because the gamma for this contract is not single signed. The problem is genuinely nonlinear, and we cannot just substitute each of 17% and 23% into a Black–Scholes formula. If we naively priced the option using first a 17% volatility and then a 23% volatility we would get two curves looking like those in Figure 24.3. Observe that the best/worst of these two curves (the 'envelope') is not the same as the best/worst of the previous figure.

If you were to price the option using the worst out of these two Black–Scholes prices you would significantly overestimate the value of the option in the worst-case scenario. If the asset value were at around 80 you might think that the option was insensitive to the volatility. But it is around that asset value where the option is very sensitive to the volatility ranging over

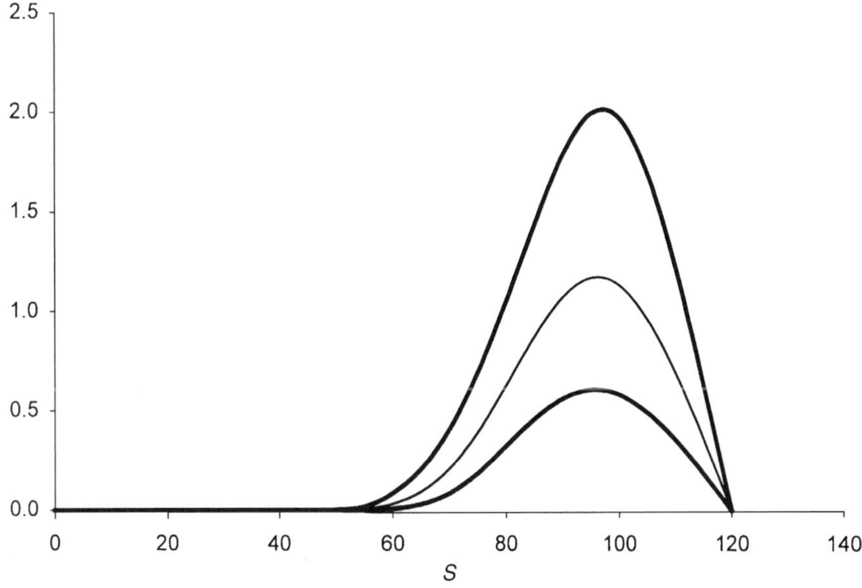

Figure 24.2 Up-and-out call value assuming a range for volatility, and the Black–Scholes price.

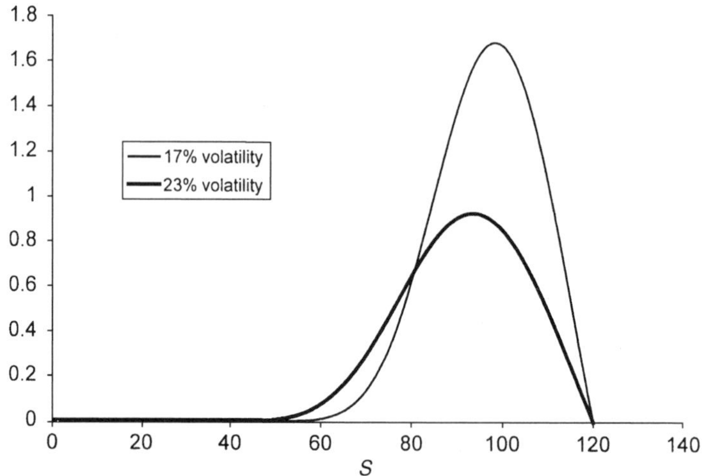

Figure 24.3 Up-and-out call values in a Black–Scholes world with volatilities of 17% and 23%.

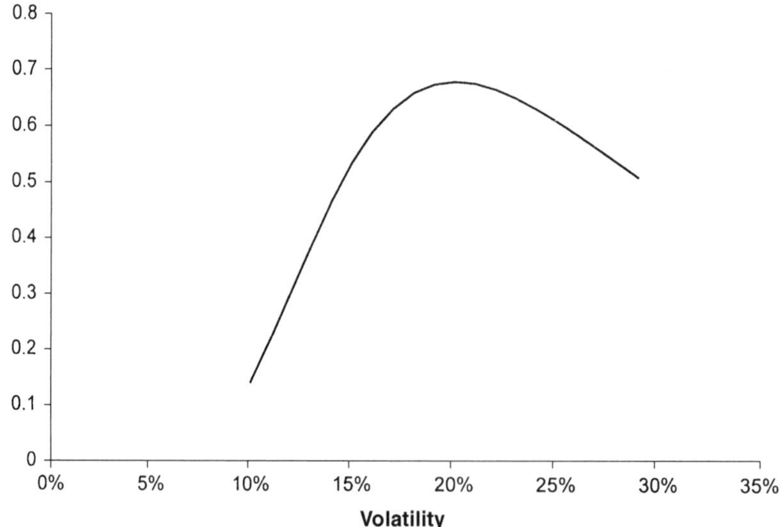

Figure 24.4 Black–Scholes values for an up-and-out call option against volatility.

17–23%. For this reason it can be extremely dangerous to calculate a contract's vega when the contract has a gamma that changes sign. Having said that, practitioners do have ways of fudging their vega calculations to make some allowance for this effect.

Continuing with this barrier option example, let us look at implied volatilities. In Figure 24.4 is shown the Black–Scholes value of an up-and-out call option as a function of the volatility. The strike is 100, the stock is at 80, the spot interest rate is 5%, the barrier is at 120 and there is one year to expiry. This contract has a gamma that changes sign, and a price that is not monotonic in the volatility. This figure shows that there is a maximum option value of 0.68 when the volatility is about

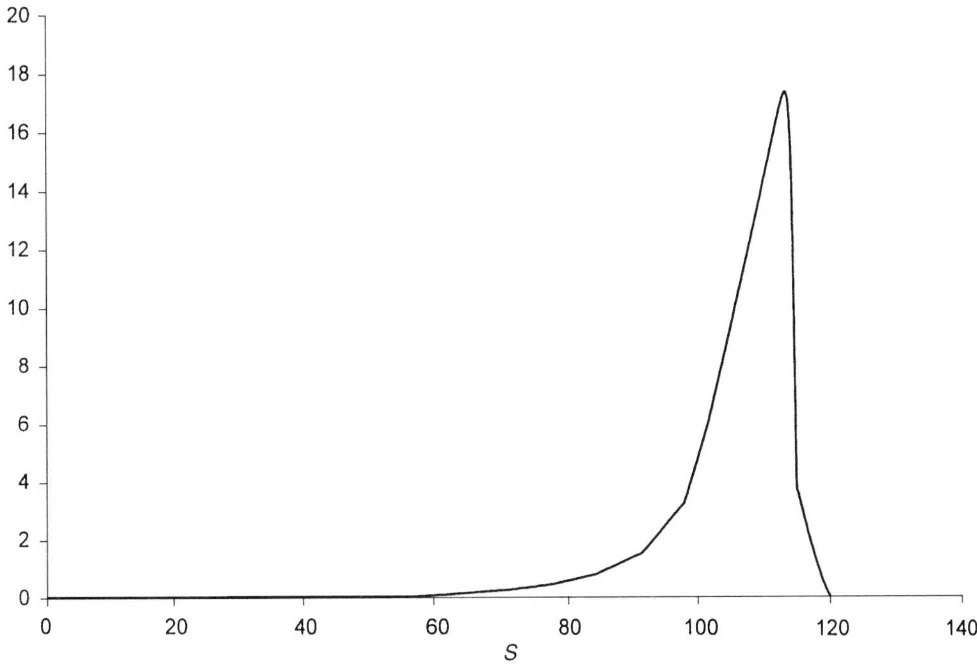

Figure 24.5 The envelope of all Black–Scholes values for an up-and-out call option.

20%. Now turn the problem around. Suppose that the market is pricing this contract at 0.55. From the figure we can see that there are *two* volatilities that correspond to this market price. Which, if either, is correct? The question is probably meaningless because of the non-single-signed gamma of this contract.

Take this example further. What if the market price is 0.72? This value cannot be reached by any single volatility. Does this mean that there are arbitrage opportunities? Not necessarily. This could be due to the market pricing with a non-constant volatility, either with a volatility surface, stochastic volatility or a volatility range. As we have seen from the best/worst prices for this contract, the uncertainty in the option value may be large enough to cover the market price of the option, and there may be no guaranteed arbitrage at all. The best value is greater than 1 for the volatility range 17–23%, as can be seen in Figure 24.2.

In Figure 24.5 is shown the envelope of all possible Black–Scholes up-and-out call option values assuming a *constant* volatility ranging from *zero to infinity*. Option values outside this envelope cannot be attained with constant volatility. With uncertain volatility, prices outside this envelope *can* easily be attained.

24.2.2 Uncertain Interest Rate

Exactly the same idea can be applied to the case of uncertain interest rate. Let us suppose that the risk-free interest rate lies within the band

$$r^- < r < r^+.$$

Continuing with the worst case, we assume that if our portfolio has a net positive value ($\Pi > 0$) then interest rates will be high, if it has a negative value then rates will be low. The reason for this is that if we have a positive amount invested in options then in the worst case we are failing to benefit from high interest rates. Thus, the interest rate we choose will depend on the sign of Π. As before, we set the return on the portfolio equal to the risk-free rate. With our special choice for this rate we arrive at the equation for the worst-case scenario:

$$\frac{\partial V^-}{\partial t} + \tfrac{1}{2}\sigma^2 S^2 \frac{\partial^2 V^-}{\partial S^2} + r(\Pi)\left(S\frac{\partial V^-}{\partial S} - V^-\right) = 0 \tag{24.2}$$

where

$$\Pi = V^- - S\frac{\partial V^-}{\partial S}$$

and

$$r(\Pi) = \begin{cases} r^+ & \text{if } \Pi > 0 \\ r^- & \text{if } \Pi < 0. \end{cases}$$

The equation for the best case is obvious.

24.2.3 Uncertain Dividends

We restrict our attention to a dividend yield that is independent of the asset price. There are two cases to consider here: continuously paid and discretely paid. In the former case (and with FX options where the dividend yield is replaced by the foreign interest rate) we assume that the dividend yield lies between two values:

$$D^- < D < D^+.$$

Now, for the option's worst value we simply solve

$$\frac{\partial V^-}{\partial t} + \tfrac{1}{2}\sigma^2 S^2 \frac{\partial^2 V^-}{\partial S^2} + r\left(S\frac{\partial V^-}{\partial S} - V^-\right) - D(\Delta)S\frac{\partial V^-}{\partial S} = 0 \tag{24.3}$$

where

$$D(\Delta) = \begin{cases} D^+ & \text{if } \Delta < 0 \\ D^- & \text{if } \Delta > 0. \end{cases}$$

The case of discretely paid dividends is slightly different. Consider what happens across a dividend date, t_i. Let us suppose that the discretely-paid dividend yield lies within the band

$$D^- < D < D^+.$$

The jump condition across a discretely-paid dividend date is

$$V(S, t_i^-) = V((1-D)S, t_i^+)$$

as shown in Chapter 8. When this dividend yield is uncertain we simply minimize over the possible values of D and this gives the following jump condition

$$V^-(S, t_i^-) = \min_{D_- < D < D_+} V^-((1-D)S, t_i^+). \tag{24.4}$$

There is a corresponding jump condition for the best case.

Of course, it is a simple matter to put together the results of the above sections to model uncertainty in all of volatility, interest rate and dividend.

I emphasize that from now on we only consider the pessimistic case. We assume the worst outcome and price contracts accordingly. By so doing we guarantee that we never lose money provided that our uncertain parameter ranges are not violated.

24.3 UNCERTAIN CORRELATION

Exactly the same idea can be applied to multi-asset instruments which have a dependence on the correlation between the underlyings. Correlation is something that is particularly difficult to calculate or predict so there is obviously a role to be played by uncertainty. The downside is that the spread on correlation is likely to be so large that the spread on the option price will be unrealistic. And since there are so few correlation instruments with which to hedge it may not be possible to reduce this spread to anything tradeable.

24.4 NONLINEARITY

All of the new partial differential equations that we have derived are nonlinear. In particular, the uncertain volatility model results in the same nonlinear equation, Equation (24.1), as the Hoggard–Whalley–Wilmott model for pricing options in the presence of transaction costs, discussed in Chapter 21. Because of this nonlinearity, we must therefore distinguish between long and short positions, for example for a long call we have

$$V^{-}(S,T) = \max(S-E,0)$$

and for a short call

$$V^{-}(S,T) = -\max(S-E,0).$$

Explicit solutions exist only in special cases, and these cases are, depending on which of the volatility, interest rate and dividend are uncertain, for options for which the gamma (for uncertain volatility), the portfolio value (for uncertain interest rate) and the delta (for uncertain dividend) are single signed. Then the formulae are simply the Black–Scholes formulae with the parameters set to the appropriate extreme values.

Because Equations (24.1) and (24.2) are nonlinear the value of a portfolio of options is not necessarily the same as the sum of the values of the individual components. Long and short positions have different values. For example, a long call position has a lower value than a short call. In both cases we are being pessimistic: if we own the call we assume that it has a low value, if we are short the call and thus may have to pay out at expiry, we assume that the value of the option to its holder is higher. Note that here we mean a long (or short) position valued *in isolation*. Obviously, if we hold one of each simultaneously then they will cancel each other regardless of the behavior of any parameters. This is a very important point to understand: the value of a contract depends on what else is in the portfolio.

Unfortunately, the model as it stands predicts very wide spreads on options. For example, suppose that we have a European call, strike price \$100, today's asset price is \$100, there are six months to expiry, no dividends but a spot interest rate that we expect to lie between 5% and 6% and a volatility between 20% and 30%. We can calculate the values for long and short calls assuming these ranges for the parameters directly from the Black–Scholes formulae. This is because the gamma and the portfolio value are single-signed for a call. A long call position is worth \$6.85 (the Black–Scholes value using a volatility of 20% and an interest rate of 5%) and a short call is worth \$9.85 (the Black–Scholes value using a volatility of 30% and an interest rate of 6%). This spread is much larger than that in the market, and in this example, is mostly due to the uncertain volatility. The market prices may, for example, be based on an interest rate of 5.5% with a volatility between 24% and 26%. Unless the model can produce narrower spreads the model will be useless in practice.

The spreads *can* be tightened by 'static hedging.' This means the purchase and sale of traded option contracts so as to improve the marginal value of our original position. This only works because we have a *nonlinear* governing equation: the price of a contract depends on what else is in the portfolio. This static hedge can be optimized so as to give the original contract its best value; we can squeeze even more value out of our contract with the best hedge.

The issues of static hedging and optimal static hedging are covered in detail in Chapter 30.

24.5 SUMMARY

Greeks such as vega and rho can be completely misleading if used carelessly and without understanding. The uncertain parameter model gives a consistent way to eliminate dependence of a price on a parameter, and to some extent reduce model dependence. Out of the three volatility models (deterministic calibrated smile, stochastic and uncertain), uncertain volatility is easily my favorite. As presented in this chapter the spreads on the best/worst prices are too large for the model to be of any practical use. Fortunately this situation will be remedied in Chapter 30.

FURTHER READING

- See Avellaneda, Levy & Parás (1995), Avellaneda & Parás (1996) and Lyons (1995) for more details about the modeling of uncertain volatility.
- See Bergman (1995) for the derivation of Equation (24.2) for a world in which there are different rates for borrowing and lending.
- See Oztukel (1996) for the uncertain parameter technique applied to correlation.
- A 'Virtual Option Pricer' for uncertain volatility can be found at home.cs.nyu.edu:8000/cgi-bin/vop.
- Ahn, Muni & Swindle (1996) explain how to modify the final payoff to reduce the effect of volatility errors in the worst-case scenario.
- See Ahn, Muni & Swindle (1998) for a stochastic control approach to utility maximization in the worst-case model.

EXERCISES

1. By substitution into the Black–Scholes equation for an option with uncertain volatility in the worst case, or otherwise, show that

$$V_{\text{worst}} = -(-V)_{\text{best}},$$

where V_{worst} is the value of the option in the worst case and V_{best} is the value of the option in the best case.

2. What is the value of a European digital call with a volatility of 10%? The call has exercise price 100 and expiry in one year. There are no dividends and the continuously-compounding risk-free interest rate is 5%. Also value the call with a volatility of 20%. Where does increased volatility give the option increased value and where does the opposite effect occur? How is this connected with the value of the gamma of the option?
3. Value a European call option using the Black–Scholes model with an uncertain volatility between 10% and 20%. How large is the spread between the worst and best case prices? How might we reduce this spread using a static hedge? Illustrate by hedging with another European call option with the same expiry, but a different exercise price.

CHAPTER 25
empirical analysis of volatility

In this Chapter...

- how to analyze volatility data to determine the most suitable time-independent stochastic model
- how to determine the probability that the volatility will stay within any specified range
- how to assign a degree of confidence to your uncertain volatility model price

25.1 INTRODUCTION

In this chapter we focus closely on real data for the behavior of volatility. Our principal aim in this is to derive a good stochastic volatility model. This volatility model can then be used in a number of ways: in a two-factor option-pricing model; to examine the time evolution of volatility from an initial known value today to, in the long run, a steady-state distribution; to estimate the probability of our uncertain volatility model price being correct. The approach we adopt must be contrasted with the traditional approach to stochastic volatility which seems to be to write down something nice and tractable and then fit the parameters.

25.2 STOCHASTIC VOLATILITY AND UNCERTAIN PARAMETERS REVISITED

The classical way of dealing with random variables is to model them stochastically. This we do here for volatility, deriving a stochastic model such that drift and variance, and the steady-state mean and dispersion of volatility are *compatible with historical data*. We can then, among other things, determine the evolution of volatility from the known value today to the steady-state distribution in the long term.

Recall also, the approach of Avellaneda, Levy, Parás and Lyons for modeling volatility. In their model they allow volatility to do just about anything as long as it doesn't move outside some given range. With this model it is natural to calculate not a single option value but a worst price and a best price for the option. This results in a nonlinear partial differential equation. This procedure yields a 'certainty interval' for the price of the option, driven by the input volatility band. Hence we know that, for example, if we could access the option in the market below our worst price then within the limits of our certainty band assumptions, we are guaranteed a profit. But what if we are not one hundred percent sure about the volatility range? Can we use our stochastic volatility model to see how likely volatility is to stay in the range?

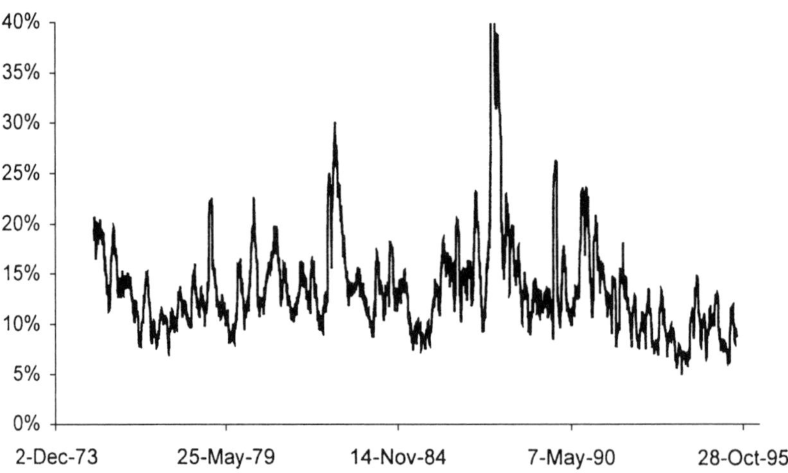

Figure 25.1 Thirty-day volatility of daily returns for the Dow Jones Industrial Average from 1975 to 1995.

25.3 DERIVING AN EMPIRICAL STOCHASTIC VOLATILITY MODEL

In this chapter we are going to work with daily Dow Jones Industrial Average spot data from January 1975 until August 1995. The method that I am going to demonstrate for determining the volatility model can be used for many financial time series, indeed later we will use the same method for modeling US short-term interest rates.

In Figure 25.1 is shown the calculated annualized 30-day volatility of daily returns for the DJIA over the period of interest. (Whether or not the volatility that has been calculated here is representative of the 'actual' volatility is debatable. Nevertheless, the techniques I describe below are applicable to whatever volatility series we have.)

Previous attempts at modeling volatility stochastically are numerous. However, since adding another stochastic variable complicates the problem of pricing options, the emphasis to date has been on deriving a tractable model. We are going to try to determine a stochastic model for volatility by fitting the drift and variance functions to empirical data, letting tractability take a secondary role. We model the volatility in isolation, assuming that it does not depend on the level of the index. Thus we assume that the stochastic process for volatility is given by

$$d\sigma = \alpha(\sigma)\,dt + \beta(\sigma)\,dX. \tag{25.1}$$

We use twenty years of daily Dow Jones closing prices (in total over 5,000 observations) to calculate daily returns and 30-day volatility of these daily returns.

25.4 ESTIMATING THE VOLATILITY OF VOLATILITY

From (25.1), the square of the day-to-day change in volatility is given by

$$(\delta\sigma)^2 = \beta(\sigma)^2\phi^2\delta t \tag{25.2}$$

to leading order, where ϕ is a standardized Normal variable.

From our time series for volatility we can easily calculate the time series for $\delta\sigma$, and thus a time series for $(\delta\sigma)^2$. Then, in order to examine the dependence of the changes in volatility

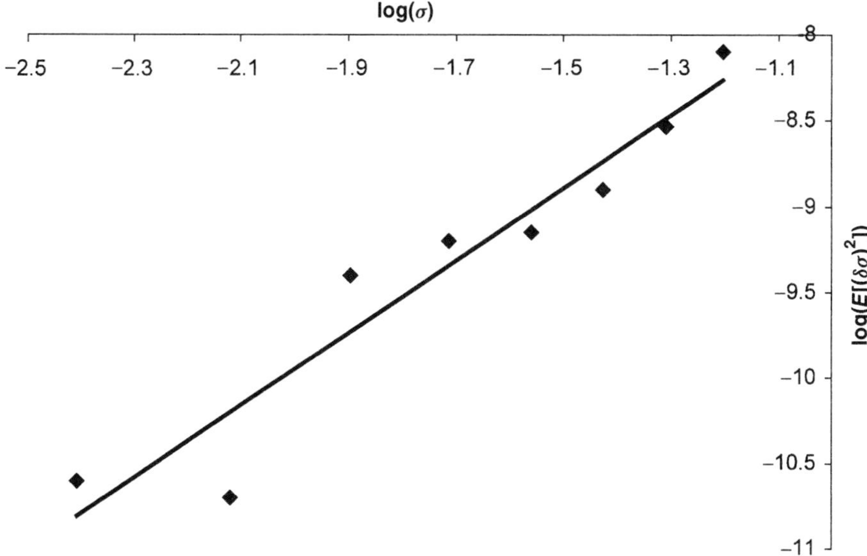

Figure 25.2 Plot of $\log(E[(\delta\sigma)^2])$ versus $\log(\sigma)$ and the fitted line.

on the level of the volatility, split σ into buckets and calculate the mean of $(\delta\sigma)^2$ for each σ falling in a particular bucket. This gives us an estimate of the dependence of $E[(\delta\sigma)^2]$ on σ.

In Figure 25.2 is plotted $\log(E[(\delta\sigma)^2])$ versus $\log(\sigma)$. Superimposed on this figure is a straight line, fitted to the dots by ordinary least squares.

The straight line suggests that

$$\log(E[(\delta\sigma)^2]) = 2\log(\beta(\sigma)) + \log \delta t = a + b\log(\sigma)$$

is a good approximation. From the data we can estimate the parameters a and b and so deduce that a good model is

$$\beta(\sigma) = \nu\sigma^\gamma \tag{25.3}$$

From the data we find that

$$\nu = 0.88 \quad \text{and} \quad \gamma = 1.05.$$

In our model we take

$$d\sigma = \alpha(\sigma)\,dt + \nu\sigma^\gamma\,dX.$$

This gives a model with volatility of volatility that is consistent with empirical data. To complete the modeling we still need to find the drift of the volatility $\alpha(\sigma)$.

25.5 ESTIMATING THE DRIFT OF VOLATILITY

To calculate $\alpha(\sigma)$ we need to examine the time series for σ in a slightly different way. In particular we are going to determine the steady-state probability density function for σ and from that deduce the drift function. The equation governing the probability density function for σ is of the form derived in Chapter 10. It is the Fokker–Planck equation (or forward Kolmogorov equation)

$$\frac{\partial p}{\partial t} = \frac{1}{2}\frac{\partial^2}{\partial \sigma^2}(\beta^2 p) - \frac{\partial}{\partial \sigma}(\alpha p) \tag{25.4}$$

where $p(\sigma, t)$ is the probability density function for σ and I am using σ and t to denote the forward variables. Suppose that somehow we know the steady-state distribution, $p_\infty(\sigma)$, for σ. This will satisfy

$$0 = \frac{1}{2}\frac{d^2}{d\sigma^2}(\beta^2 p_\infty) - \frac{d}{d\sigma}(\alpha p_\infty).$$

This is simply a steady-state version of (25.4). Integrating this once we get

$$\alpha(\sigma) = \frac{1}{2p_\infty}\frac{d}{d\sigma}(\beta^2 p_\infty). \tag{25.5}$$

The constant of integration is zero, as can be shown by examining the behavior of α for large and small σ.

From (25.5), we see that if we know p_∞ then we can find the drift term. But can we find p_∞? Yes, we can. If we assume that all parameters are independent of time, then we can determine the steady-state probability density function by using the 'ergodic property' of random walks, that is, the equivalence of ensemble and time averages.

We find p_∞ from the data by plotting the frequency distribution of σ versus buckets of σ; that is, how many observations fall into each bucket. The empirical distribution, shown in Figure 25.3, closely resembles a lognormal curve. Since we need to differentiate this function to find the drift according to (25.5) we fit a curve to the distribution. We shall assume p_∞ to be of the form of a lognormal distribution:

$$p_\infty = \frac{1}{\sqrt{2\pi}a\sigma}e^{(-1/2a^2)(\log(\sigma/\overline{\sigma}))^2}$$

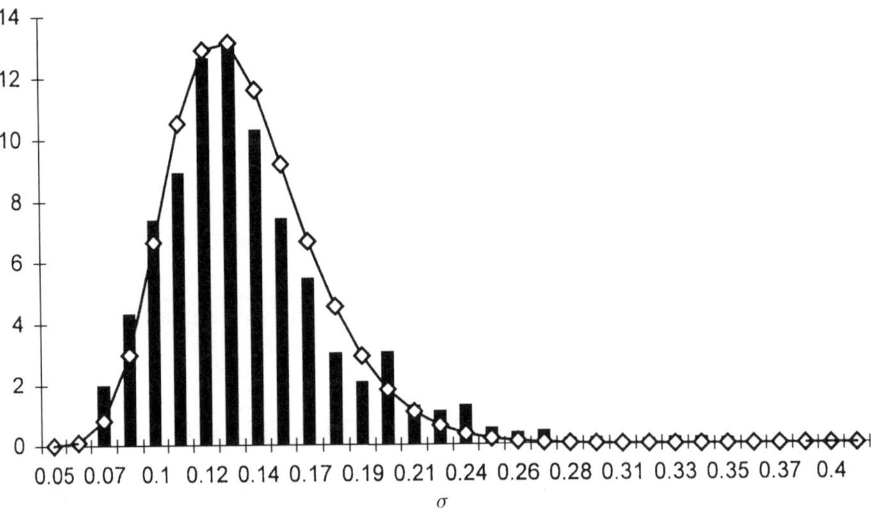

Figure 25.3 The steady-state distribution of σ and the fitted lognormal curve.

where $\log\overline{\sigma}$ represents the mean of the distribution of $\log\sigma$ and a describes the dispersion of the distribution about the mean.

This graph and fitted curve are shown in Figure 25.3.

We find from the data that,

$$a = 0.33 \quad \text{and} \quad \overline{\sigma} = 13.4\%.$$

We now have that

$$\alpha(\sigma) = \nu^2\sigma^{2\gamma-1}\left(\gamma - \tfrac{1}{2} - \frac{1}{2a^2}\log(\sigma/\overline{\sigma})\right).$$

25.6 HOW TO USE THE MODEL

We can use our model in a number of ways; here I just make a few suggestions. The three possibilities that I will describe are straightforward option pricing, determining the future distribution for volatility and estimating our confidence in volatility ranges.

25.6.1 Option Pricing with Stochastic Volatility

The first way we can use the model is in a two-factor model for pricing options. The two factors would be the underlying asset and its volatility. The only problem with this is that we have estimated from data the *real* drift rate and not the *risk-neutral* rate that we need for option pricing. Whether this matters or not is debatable.

25.6.2 The Time Evolution of Stochastic Volatility

From the stochastic volatility model we can derive the probabilistic evolution of volatility from an initial value. We turn once again to the Fokker–Planck equation, given by (25.4), which describes the evolution over time of the probability density function of a random variable defined by a stochastic differential equation. We can use the functions α and β derived above to find the probability density function of volatility over a specified time horizon. This way we can observe the evolution of the distribution of volatility.

As the initial condition for Equation (25.4) we would apply a delta function—meaning that we know the value of today's volatility with certainty—and solve for the resulting probability density function as time evolves.

What we would see would be the density function starting out with a delta function spike, and gradually smoothing out until it stabilized at the input steady-state probability density function. Because the volatility has a sensible distribution in the steady state we would not see any unreasonable behavior from the model. Other models, having nice but otherwise arbitrary drift rate and volatility of volatility might not be so well behaved.

25.6.3 Stochastic Volatility, Certainty Bands and Confidence Limits

The third way we could use the model is in conjunction with the uncertain volatility model described in Chapter 24. From our stochastic volatility model we can estimate the probability of our chosen volatility range being breached. We can therefore assign a probability to our uncertain volatility model price.

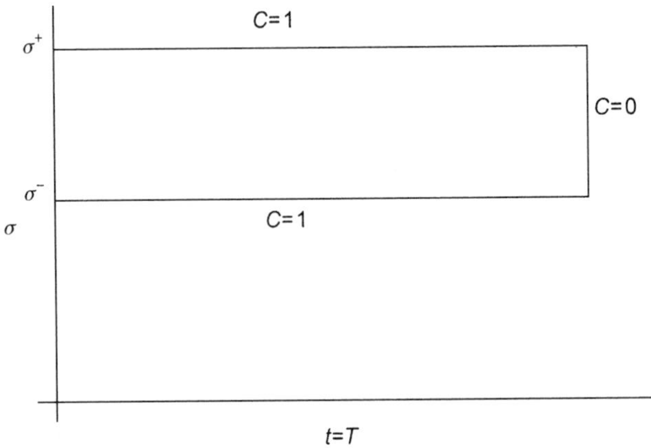

Figure 25.4 The final and boundary conditions for the exit probability.

The likelihood of the volatility staying in any range can be mathematically represented by the function $C(\sigma, t)$ satisfying

$$\frac{\partial C}{\partial t} + \tfrac{1}{2}\beta(\sigma)^2\frac{\partial^2 C}{\partial \sigma^2} + \alpha(\sigma)\frac{\partial C}{\partial \sigma} = 0,$$

see Chapter 10. The final condition is given by

$$C(\sigma, T) = 0 \quad \text{for all } \sigma$$

since at $t = T$ the likelihood of σ breaching the barriers is zero. The boundary conditions are given by

$$C(\sigma^+, t) = C(\sigma^-, t) = 1 \quad \text{for all } t.$$

Here σ^- and σ^+ are the lower and upper barriers respectively. These conditions are obvious: if $\sigma = \sigma^-$ or $\sigma = \sigma^+$ then the barrier is certain to be breached. The final and boundary conditions are shown schematically above in Figure 25.4.

This third use of the model is quite a nice compromise. One reason I like it is that it allows the volatility to be random, satisfying a given model, yet gives an option price that doesn't depend on the market price of risk.

25.7 SUMMARY

Generally speaking I don't like to accept a model because it looks nice. If at all possible I prefer to look at the data to try and find the best model. In this chapter we examined volatility data to find the best model having time-independent functions describing the drift and volatility of volatility. Crucially we modeled the volatility of volatility by examining the daily changes of volatility. After all, the randomness in the level of the volatility is seen over the shortest timescale. However, to find the best drift we looked over a longer timescale, we estimated the steady-state distribution for the volatility. The drift only really comes into its own over longer timescales. To examine the short timescale to estimate the drift would at best not make much sense and at worst result in a model with poor long-term properties.

The resulting stochastic differential equation model for the volatility can be used in several ways. One is to just accept it as the model for volatility in a two-factor option model. Of course, then you have to estimate the market price of risk, not nice. Another use for the model, which gets around the market price of risk problem, is in conjunction with an uncertain volatility model, such as described in Chapter 24. Prescribe a range for volatility and then use the stochastic differential equation to estimate the probability of the volatility staying within this range.

FURTHER READING

- The subject of bounds for option values when volatility is stochastic was first addressed by El Karoui, Jeanblanc-Picqué & Viswanathan (1991).
- See Oztukel (1996) and Oztukel & Wilmott (1998) for further details of the analysis of volatility.

EXERCISES

1. Use market data for the volatility of daily returns to calibrate your model for stochastic volatility of the form
$$d\sigma = \alpha(\sigma)\,dt + \beta(\sigma)\,dX,$$
where
$$\alpha(\sigma) = \nu^2\sigma^{2\gamma-1}\left(\gamma - \tfrac{1}{2} - \frac{1}{2a^2}\log(\sigma/\overline{\sigma})\right),$$
and
$$\beta(\sigma) = \nu\sigma^{\gamma}.$$
2. Solve the backwards Kolmogorov equation:
$$\frac{\partial C}{\partial t} + \alpha(\sigma)\frac{\partial C}{\partial \sigma} + \tfrac{1}{2}\beta(\sigma)^2\frac{\partial^2 C}{\partial \sigma^2} = 0,$$
with boundary conditions
$$C(\sigma^+, t) = C(\sigma^-, t) = 1,$$
and final condition
$$C(\sigma, T) = 0.$$
Use particular values for σ^- and σ^+ and solve numerically to find the probability that the band for volatility,
$$\sigma^- \leq \sigma \leq \sigma^+,$$
will not be breached before expiry. What happens to this probability as the time to expiry decreases or when the initial volatility nears the edges of the range?

CHAPTER 26
jump diffusion

In this Chapter...

- the Poisson process for modeling jumps
- hedging in the presence of jumps
- how to price derivatives when the path of the underlying can be discontinuous
- jump volatility

26.1 INTRODUCTION

There is plenty of evidence that financial quantities, be they equities, currencies or interest rates, for example, do not follow the lognormal random walk that has been the foundation of almost everything in this book, and almost everything in the financial literature. We look at some of this evidence in a moment. One of the striking features of real financial markets is that every now and then there is a sudden unexpected fall or crash. These sudden movements occur far more frequently than would be expected from a Normally-distributed return with a reasonable volatility. On all but the shortest timescales the move looks discontinuous, the prices of assets have jumped. This is important for the theory and practice of derivatives because *it is usually not possible to hedge through the crash.* One certainly cannot delta hedge as the stock market tumbles around one's ankles, and to offload all one's positions will lead to real instead of paper losses, and may even make the fall worse.

In this chapter I explain classical ways of pricing and hedging when the underlying follows a jump-diffusion process.

26.2 EVIDENCE FOR JUMPS

Let's look at some data to see just how far from Normal the returns really are. There are several ways to visualize the difference between two distributions, in our case the difference between the empirical distribution and the Normal distribution. One way is to overlay the two probability distributions. In Figure 26.1 we see the distribution of Xerox returns, from 1986 until 1997, normalized to unit standard deviation. The peak of the real distribution is clearly higher than the Normal distribution. Because both of these distributions have the same standard deviation then the higher peak must be balanced by fatter tails, it's just that they would be too small to see on this figure. They may be too small to see here, but they are still very important.

This difference is typical of all markets, even typical of the changes in interest rates. The empirical distribution diverges from the Normal distribution quite markedly. The peak being

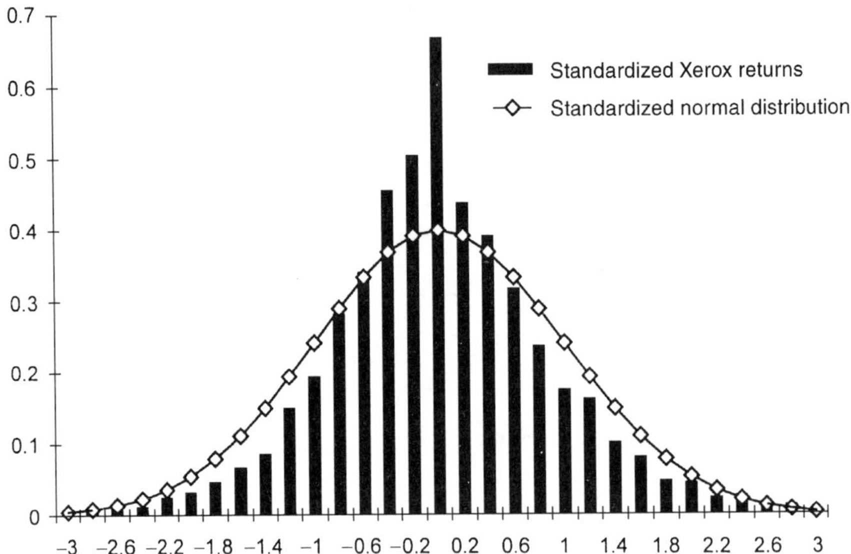

Figure 26.1 The probability density functions for Xerox daily returns, scaled to zero mean and unit standard deviation, and the standardized Normal distribution.

much higher means that there is a greater likelihood of a small move than we would expect from the lognormal random walk. More importantly, and concerning the subject of this chapter, the tails are much fatter. There is a greater chance of a large rise or fall than the Normal distribution predicts.

In Figure 26.2 is shown the difference between the cumulative distribution functions for the standardized returns of Xerox, and the Normal distribution. If you look at the figure you will see that there is more weight in the empirical distribution than the Normal distribution from about two standard deviations away from the mean. If you couple this likelihood of an extreme movement with the *importance* of an extreme movement, assuming perhaps that people are hedged against *small* movements, you begin to get a very worrying scenario.

The final picture that I plot, in Figure 26.3, is called a **Quantile-Quantile** or **Q-Q plot**. This is a common way of visualizing the difference between two distributions when you are particularly interested in the tails of the distribution. This plot is made up as follows. Rank the empirical returns in order from smallest to largest, call these y_i with an index i going from 1 to n. For the Normal distribution find the returns x_i such that the cumulative distribution function at x_i has value i/n. Now plot each point (x_i, y_i). The better the fit between the two distributions, the closer the line is to straight. In the present case the line is far from straight, due to the extra weight in the tails.

Several theories have been put forward for the non-Normality of the empirical distribution. Three of these are

- Volatility is stochastic
- Returns are drawn from another distribution, a Pareto-Levy distribution, for example
- Assets can jump in value

There is truth in all of these. The first was the subject of Chapter 23. The second is a can of worms; moving away from the Normal distribution means throwing away 99% of current

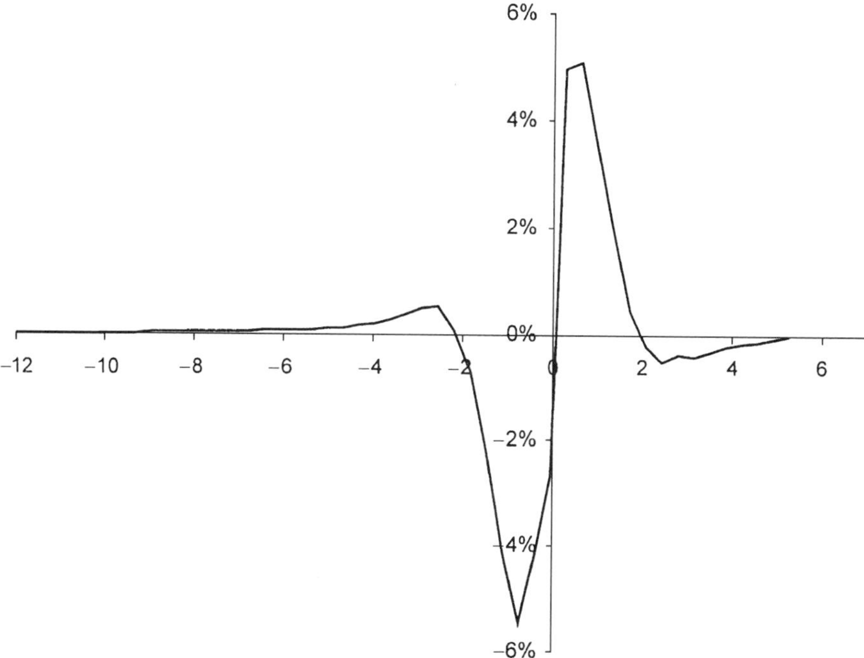

Figure 26.2 The difference between the cumulative distribution functions for Xerox daily returns, scaled to zero mean and unit standard deviation, and the standardized Normal distribution.

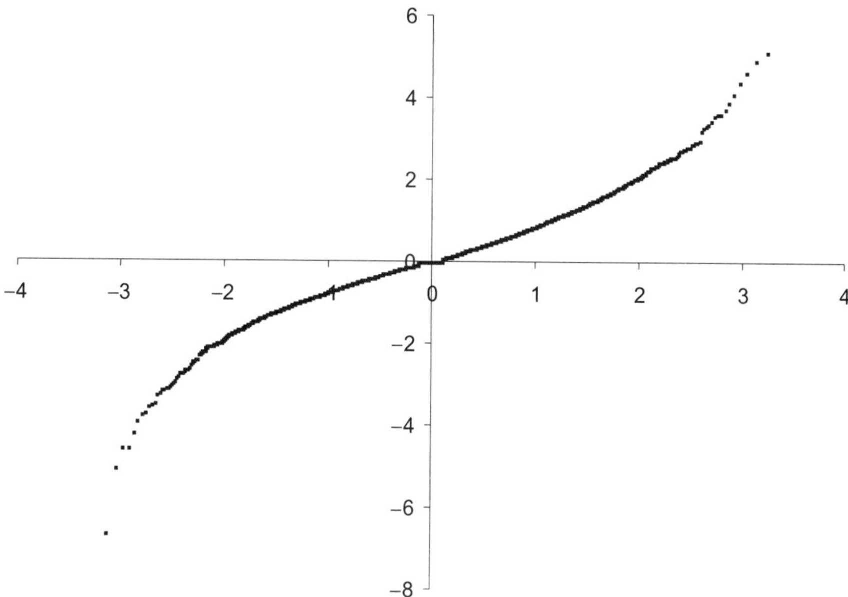

Figure 26.3 Q-Q plot for Xerox daily returns and the standardized Normal distribution.

theory and is not done lightly. But some of the issues this raises have to be addressed in jump diffusion (such as the impossibility of hedging). The third is the present subject.

26.3 POISSON PROCESSES

The basic building block for the random walks we have considered so far is continuous Brownian motion based on the Normally-distributed increment. We can think of this as adding to the return from one day to the next a Normally distributed random variable with variance proportional to timestep. The extra building block we need for the **jump-diffusion model** for an asset price is the **Poisson process**. We'll be seeing this process again in another context in Chapter 43. A Poisson process dq is defined by

$$dq = \begin{cases} 0 & \text{with probability } 1 - \lambda\, dt \\ 1 & \text{with probability } \lambda\, dt. \end{cases}$$

There is therefore a probability $\lambda\, dt$ of a jump in q in the timestep dt. The parameter λ is called the **intensity** of the Poisson process. The scaling of the probability of a jump with the size of the timestep is important in making the resulting process 'sensible,' i.e. there being a finite chance of a jump occuring in a finite time, with q not becoming infinite.

This Poisson process can be incorporated into a model for an asset in the following way:

$$dS = \mu S\, dt + \sigma S\, dX + (J - 1)S\, dq \tag{26.1}$$

We assume that there is no correlation between the Brownian motion and the Poisson process. If there is a jump ($dq = 1$) then S immediately goes to the value JS. We can model a sudden 10% fall in the asset price by $J = 0.9$.

We can generalize further by allowing J to also be a random quantity. We assume that it is drawn from a distribution with probability density function $P(J)$, again independent of the Brownian motion and Poisson process.

The random walk in $\log S$ follows from (26.1):

$$d(\log S) = \left(\mu - \tfrac{1}{2}\sigma^2\right) dt + \sigma\, dX + (\log J)\, dq.$$

This is just a jump-diffusion version of Itô.

Opposite is a spreadsheet showing how to simulate the random walk for S. In this simple example the stock jumps by 20% at random times given by a Poisson process.

26.4 HEDGING WHEN THERE ARE JUMPS

Now let us build up a theory of derivatives in the presence of jumps. Begin by holding a portfolio of the option and $-\Delta$ of the underlying:

$$\Pi = V(S, t) - \Delta S.$$

The change in the value of this portfolio is

$$d\Pi = \left(\frac{\partial V}{\partial t} + \tfrac{1}{2}\sigma^2 S^2 \frac{\partial^2 V}{\partial S^2}\right) dt + \left(\frac{\partial V}{\partial S} - \Delta\right) dS + \left(V(JS, t) - V(S, t) - \Delta(J - 1)S\right) dq. \tag{26.2}$$

Again, this is a jump-diffusion version of Itô.

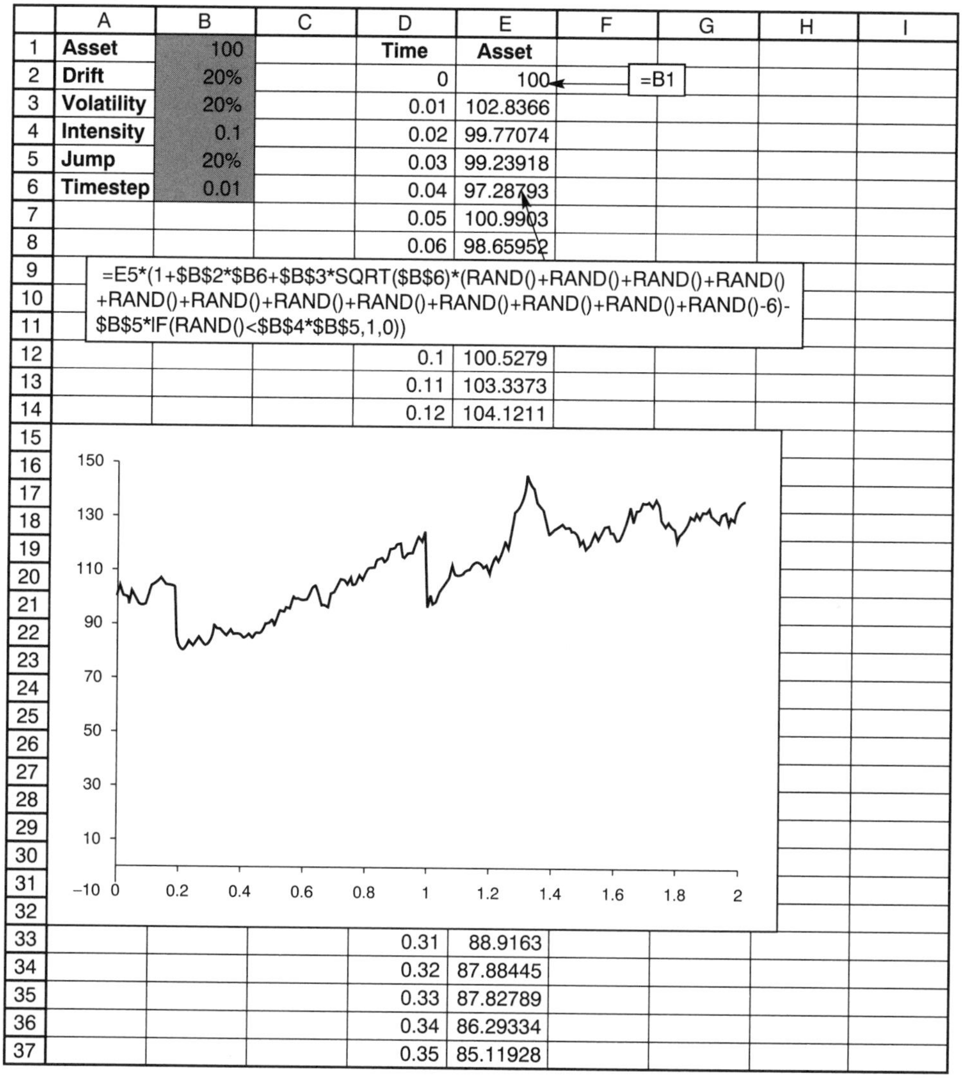

	A	B	C	D	E	F	G	H	I
1	**Asset**	100		**Time**	**Asset**				
2	**Drift**	20%		0	100		=B1		
3	**Volatility**	20%		0.01	102.8366				
4	**Intensity**	0.1		0.02	99.77074				
5	**Jump**	20%		0.03	99.23918				
6	**Timestep**	0.01		0.04	97.28793				
7				0.05	100.9903				
8				0.06	98.65952				
12				0.1	100.5279				
13				0.11	103.3373				
14				0.12	104.1211				
33				0.31	88.9163				
34				0.32	87.88445				
35				0.33	87.82789				
36				0.34	86.29334				
37				0.35	85.11928				

```
=E5*(1+$B$2*$B6+$B$3*SQRT($B$6)*(RAND()+RAND()+RAND()+RAND()
+RAND()+RAND()+RAND()+RAND()+RAND()+RAND()+RAND()+RAND()-6)-
$B$5*IF(RAND()<$B$4*$B$5,1,0))
```

Figure 26.4 Spreadsheet simulation of a jump-diffusion process.

If there is no jump at time t so that $dq = 0$, then we could have chosen $\Delta = \partial V/\partial S$ to eliminate the risk. If there is a jump and $dq = 1$ then the portfolio changes in value by an $O(1)$ amount, *that cannot be hedged away*. In that case perhaps we should choose Δ to minimize the variance of $d\Pi$. This presents us with a dilemma. We don't know whether to hedge the small(ish) diffusive changes in the underlying which are always present, or the large moves which happen rarely. Let us pursue both of these possibilities.

26.5 HEDGING THE DIFFUSION

If we choose

$$\Delta = \frac{\partial V}{\partial S}$$

we are following a Black–Scholes type of strategy, hedging the diffusive movements. The change in the portfolio value is then

$$d\Pi = \left(\frac{\partial V}{\partial t} + \tfrac{1}{2}\sigma^2 S^2 \frac{\partial^2 V}{\partial S^2} \right) dt + \left(V(JS, t) - V(S, t) - (J-1)S\frac{\partial V}{\partial S} \right) dq.$$

The portfolio now evolves in a deterministic fashion, except that every so often there is a non-deterministic jump in its value. It can be argued (see Merton, 1976) that if the jump component of the asset price process is uncorrelated with the market as a whole, then the risk in the discontinuity should not be priced into the option. Diversifiable risk should not be rewarded. In other words, we can take expectations of this expression and set that value equal to the risk-free return from the portfolio. This is not completely satisfactory, but is a common assumption whenever there is a risk that cannot be fully hedged; default risk is another example of this. If we take such an approach then we arrive at

$$\frac{\partial V}{\partial t} + \tfrac{1}{2}\sigma^2 S^2 \frac{\partial^2 V}{\partial S^2} + rS\frac{\partial V}{\partial S} - rV + \lambda E[V(JS, t) - V(S, t)] - \lambda \frac{\partial V}{\partial S} SE[(J-1)] = 0. \qquad (26.3)$$

$E[\cdot]$ is the expectation taken over the jump size J, which can also be written

$$E[x] = \int x P(J)\, dJ,$$

where $P(J)$ is the probability density function for the jump size.

This is a pricing equation for an option when there are jumps in the underlying. The important point to note about this equation, that makes it different from others we have derived, is its non-local nature. That is, the equation links together option values at distant S values, instead of just containing local derivatives. Naturally, the value of an option here and now depends on the prices to which it can instantaneously jump. When $\lambda = 0$ the equation reduces to the Black–Scholes equation.

There is a simple solution of this equation in the special case that the logarithm of J is Normally distributed. If the logarithm of J is Normally distributed with standard deviation σ' and if we write

$$k = E[J-1]$$

then the price of a European non-path-dependent option can be written as

$$\sum_{n=1}^{\infty} \frac{1}{n!} e^{-\lambda'(T-t)} (\lambda'(T-t))^n V_{BS}(S, t; \sigma_n, r_n).$$

In the above

$$\lambda' = \lambda(1+k),\ \sigma_n^2 = \sigma^2 + \frac{n\sigma'^2}{T-t} \quad \text{and} \quad r_n = r - \lambda k + \frac{n \log(1+k)}{T-t},$$

and V_{BS} is the Black–Scholes formula for the option value in the absence of jumps. This formula can be interpreted as the sum of individual Black–Scholes values, each of which assumes that there have been n jumps, and they are weighted according to the probability that there will have been n jumps before expiry.

If one does not make the assumption that jumps should not be priced in, then one has to play around with concepts such as the market price of risk.

26.6 HEDGING THE JUMPS

In the above we hedged the diffusive element of the random walk for the underlying. Another possibility is to hedge both the diffusion and jumps as much as we can. For example, we could choose Δ to minimize the variance of the hedged portfolio. After all, this is ultimately what hedging is about.

The change in the value of the portfolio with an arbitrary Δ is, to leading order,

$$d\Pi = \left(\frac{\partial V}{\partial S} - \Delta\right) dS + (-\Delta(J-1)S + V(JS,t) - V(S,t))\, dq + \cdots.$$

The variance in this change, which is a measure of the risk in the portfolio, is

$$\text{var}[d\Pi] = \left(\frac{\partial V}{\partial S} - \Delta\right)^2 \sigma^2 S^2\, dt + \lambda E[(-\Delta(J-1)S + V(JS,t) - V(S,t))^2]\, dt + \cdots. \tag{26.4}$$

This is minimized by the choice

$$\Delta = \frac{\lambda E[(J-1)(V(JS,t) - V(S,t))] + \sigma^2 S \dfrac{\partial V}{\partial S}}{\lambda S E[(J-1)^2] + \sigma^2 S}$$

(To see this, differentiate (26.4) with respect to Δ and set the resulting expression equal to zero.)

If we value the options as a pure discounted real expectation under this best-hedge strategy then we find that

$$\frac{\partial V}{\partial t} + \tfrac{1}{2}\sigma^2 S^2 \frac{\partial^2 V}{\partial s^2} + S\frac{\partial V}{\partial S}\left(\mu - \frac{\sigma^2}{d}(\mu + \lambda k - r)\right) - rV$$
$$+ \lambda E\left[(V(JS,t) - V(S,t))\left(1 - \frac{J-1}{d}(\mu + \lambda k - r)\right)\right] = 0,$$

where

$$d = \lambda E[(J-1)^2] + \sigma^2.$$

When $\lambda = 0$ this collapses to the Black–Scholes equation. At the other extreme, when there is no diffusion, so that $\sigma = 0$, we have

$$\Delta = \frac{E[(J-1)(V(JS,t) - V(S,t))]}{SE[(J-1)^2]}$$

and

$$\frac{\partial V}{\partial t} + \mu S\frac{\partial V}{\partial S} - rV + \lambda E\left[(V(JS,t) - V(S,t))\left(1 - \frac{J-1}{d}(\mu + \lambda k - r)\right)\right] = 0.$$

All of the pricing equations we have seen in this chapter are integro-differential equations. (The integral nature is due to the expectation taken over the jump size.) Because of the convolution nature of these equations they are candidates for solution by Fourier transform methods.

26.7 THE DOWNSIDE OF JUMP-DIFFUSION MODELS

Jump diffusion as described above is unsatisfying. Why bother to delta hedge at all when the portfolio will anyway be exposed to extreme movements? Hedging 'on average' is fine, after all that is being done whenever hedging is discrete, but after a crash the portfolio change is so dramatic that it makes hedging appear pointless. The other possibility is to examine the worst-case scenario. What is the worst that could happen, crashwise? Assume that this does happen and price it into the contract. This is discussed in depth in Chapter 27.

26.8 JUMP VOLATILITY

In this section I'm going to return to volatility modeling, now that we know what a Poisson process is. In Chapter 23 we saw Brownian motion models for volatility, but now let's model volatility as a jump process.

Perhaps volatility is constant for a while, then randomly jumps to another value. A bit later it jumps back. Let us model volatility as being in one of two states σ^- or $\sigma^+ > \sigma^-$. The jump from lower to higher value will be modeled by a Poisson process with intensity λ^+ and intensity λ^- going the other way. A realization of this process for σ is shown in Figure 26.5.

If we hedge the random movement in S with the underlying, then take *real* expectations, and set the return on the portfolio equal to the risk-free rate we arrive at

$$\frac{\partial V^+}{\partial t} + \tfrac{1}{2}\sigma^{+2}S^2\frac{\partial^2 V^+}{\partial S^2} + r\frac{\partial V^+}{\partial S} - rV^+ + \lambda^-(V^- - V^+) = 0,$$

for the value V^+ of the option when the volatility is σ^+. Similarly, we find that

$$\frac{\partial V^-}{\partial t} + \tfrac{1}{2}\sigma^{-2}S^2\frac{\partial^2 V^-}{\partial S^2} + r\frac{\partial V^-}{\partial S} - rV^- + \lambda^+(V^+ - V^-) = 0$$

for the value V^- when the volatility is σ^-.

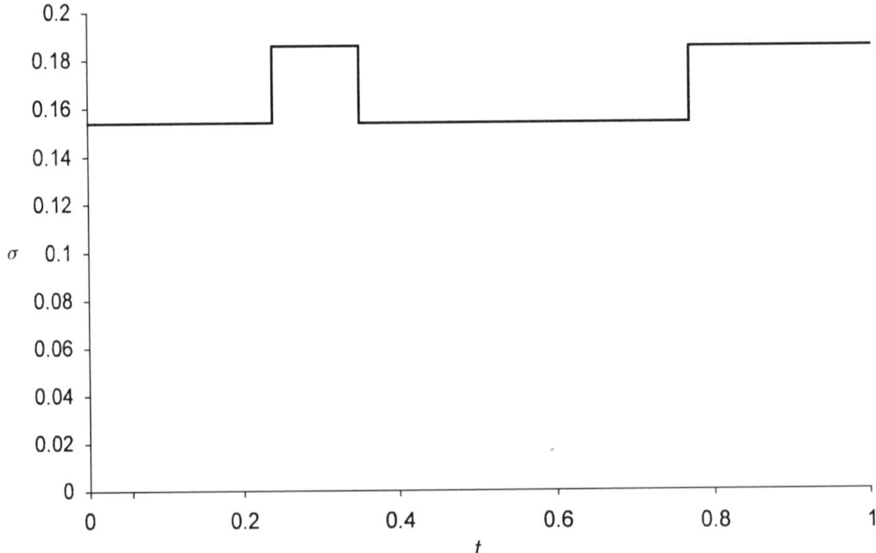

Figure 26.5 Jump volatility.

26.9 JUMP VOLATILITY WITH DETERMINISTIC DECAY

A more sophisticated jump process for the volatility, that resembles the real behavior of volatility, also contains exponential decay of the volatility after the jump. We can write

$$\sigma(\tau) = \sigma^- + (\sigma^+ - \sigma^-)e^{-\nu\tau},$$

where τ is the time since the last sudden jump in the volatility and ν is a decay parameter. It doesn't actually matter what form this function takes as long as it depends only on τ (and S and t if you want). At any time, governed by a Poisson process with intensity λ, the volatility can jump from its present level to σ^+. A realization of this process for σ is shown in Figure 26.6.

The value of an option is given by $V(S, t, \tau)$, the solution of

$$\frac{\partial V}{\partial t} + \frac{\partial V}{\partial \tau} + \tfrac{1}{2}\sigma(\tau)^2 S^2 \frac{\partial^2 V}{\partial S^2} + rS\frac{\partial V}{\partial S} - rV + \lambda(V(S, t, 0) - V(S, t, \tau)) = 0.$$

Note that the time since last jump τ is incremented at the same rate as real time t. (In this 'value' means that we have delta hedged with the underlying to eliminate risk due to the movement of the asset but we have taken real expectations with respect to the volatility jump.)

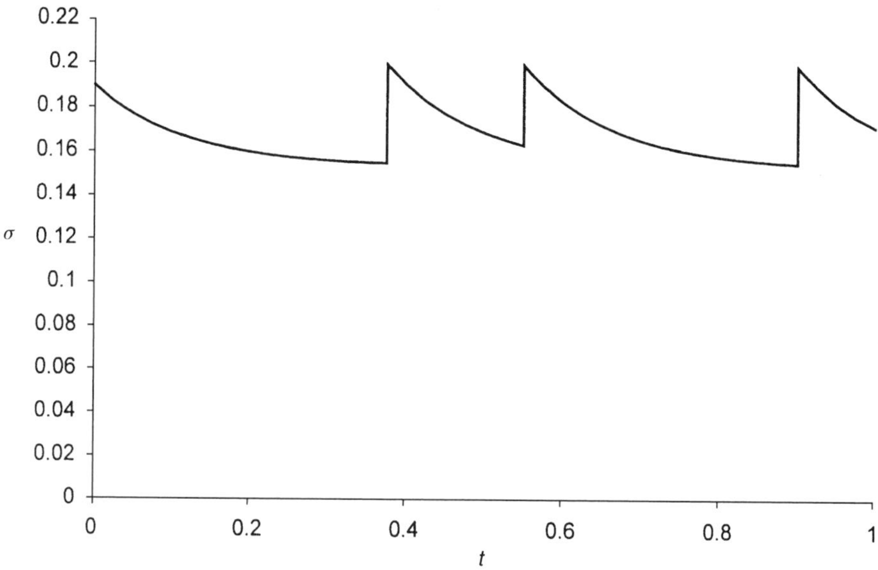

Figure 26.6 Jump volatility with exponential decay.

26.10 SUMMARY

Jump diffusion models undoubtedly capture a real phenomenon that is missing from the Black–Scholes model. Yet they are rarely used in practice. There are three main reasons for this: difficulty in parameter estimation, solution, and impossibility of perfect hedging.

In order to use any pricing model one needs to be able to estimate parameters. In the lognormal model there is just the one parameter to estimate. This is just the right number. More than one parameter is too much work, no parameters to estimate and trading could be done by machine.

The jump diffusion model in its simplest form needs an estimate of probability of a jump, measured by λ, and its size, J. This can be made more complicated by having a distribution for J.

The governing equation is no longer a diffusion equation (about the easiest problem to solve numerically), but a difference-diffusion equation. The equation does not just contain local derivatives of the value with respect to its variables, but now links option values at different asset values. The numerical solution of such an equation is certainly not impossible, but is harder than the solution of the basic Black–Scholes equation.

Finally, perfect risk-free hedging is impossible when there are jumps in the underlying. This is because of the non-local nature of the option pricing equation. We have seen two approaches to this hedging, neither of which matches the elegance of the Black–Scholes hedge. The use of a jump-diffusion model acknowledges that one's hedge is less than perfect. This bothers some people. If one sticks to the Black–Scholes model then one can pretend to be hedging perfectly. Of course, the reality of the situation is that there are many reasons why risk-free hedging is impossible, nevertheless the 'eyes wide shut' approach has become market standard.

FURTHER READING

- The original jump-diffusion model in finance was due to Merton (1976).
- An impressive tome on the modeling of extremal events is by Embrechts, Klüppelberg & Mikosch (1997).
- Jump volatility is described by Naik (1993).

EXERCISES

1. Simulate a random walk for a share price with a Poisson process representing jump diffusion. Choose suitable values for λ and J and use the model

$$dS = \mu S\,dt + \sigma S\,dX + (J-1)S\,dq.$$

Compare the results to those for $J = 1$ (the standard model).

2. Consider an asset price movement that is specified by

$$dS = \mu S\,dt + \sigma S\,dX + (J-1)S\,dq,$$

with a constant value for J. Find the equation that an option on this asset will satisfy when we hedge using $\Delta = \partial V/\partial S$. What would be the effect of setting $J = 0$ and why might we wish to do this? Solve this problem explicitly for a European call option. What conclusions can be drawn?

3. If we hedge the jump process using a strategy that will minimize the variance of the portfolio, check that our choice for Δ is

$$\Delta = \frac{\lambda E[(J-1)(V(JS,t) - V(S,t))] + \sigma^2 S \dfrac{\partial V}{\partial S}}{\lambda S E[(J-1)^2] + \sigma^2 S}.$$

4. Consider an asset price movement with jump diffusion that has a constant value for J. Find the equation that an option on this asset will satisfy when we hedge in such a way that the

portfolio variance is minimized. What effect does the value of J have on the solution of this problem?

5. Derive the pricing equations for the value of an option with a jump volatility:

$$\frac{\partial V^+}{\partial t} + \frac{1}{2}\sigma^{+2}S^2\frac{\partial^2 V^+}{\partial S^2} + rS\frac{\partial V^+}{\partial S} - rV^+ + \lambda^-(V^- - V^+) = 0,$$

and

$$\frac{\partial V^-}{\partial t} + \frac{1}{2}\sigma^{-2}S^2\frac{\partial^2 V^-}{\partial S^2} + rS\frac{\partial V^-}{\partial S} - rV^- + \lambda^+(V^+ - V^-) = 0.$$

What is the value of the option today?

CHAPTER 27

crash modeling

In this Chapter...

- how to price contracts in a worst-case scenario when there are crashes in the prices of underlyings
- how to reduce the effect of these crashes on your portfolio, the Platinum Hedge

27.1 INTRODUCTION

Jump diffusion models have two weaknesses: they don't allow you to hedge and the parameters are very hard to measure. Nobody likes a model that tells you that hedging is impossible (even though that may correspond to common sense) and in the classical jump-diffusion model of Merton the best that you can do is a kind of average hedging. It may be quite easy to estimate the impact of a rare event such as a crash, but estimating the probability of that rare event is another matter. In this chapter we discuss a model for pricing and hedging a portfolio of derivatives that takes into account the effect of an extreme movement in the underlying but we will make *no assumptions about the timing of this 'crash' or the probability distribution of its size*, except that we put an upper bound on the latter. This effectively gets around the difficulty of estimating the likelihood of the rare event. The pricing follows from the assumption that the worst scenario actually happens, i.e. the size and time of the crash are such as to give the option its worst value. And hedging, delta and static hedging, will continue to play a key role. The optimal static hedge follows from the desire to make the best of this worst value. This, latter, static hedging follows from the desire to optimize a portfolio's value. I also show how to use the model to evaluate the value at risk for a portfolio of options.

27.2 VALUE AT RISK

The true business of a financial institution is to manage risk.

The trader manages 'normal event' risk, where the world operates close to a Black–Scholes one of random walks and dynamic hedging. The institution, however, views its portfolio on a 'big picture' scale and focuses on 'tail events' where liquidity and large jumps are important (Figure 27.1).

Value at Risk (VaR) is a measure of the potential losses due to a movement in underlying markets. It usually has associated with it a timeframe and an estimate of the maximum sudden change thought likely in the markets. There is also a 'confidence interval'; for example, the daily VaR is $15 million with

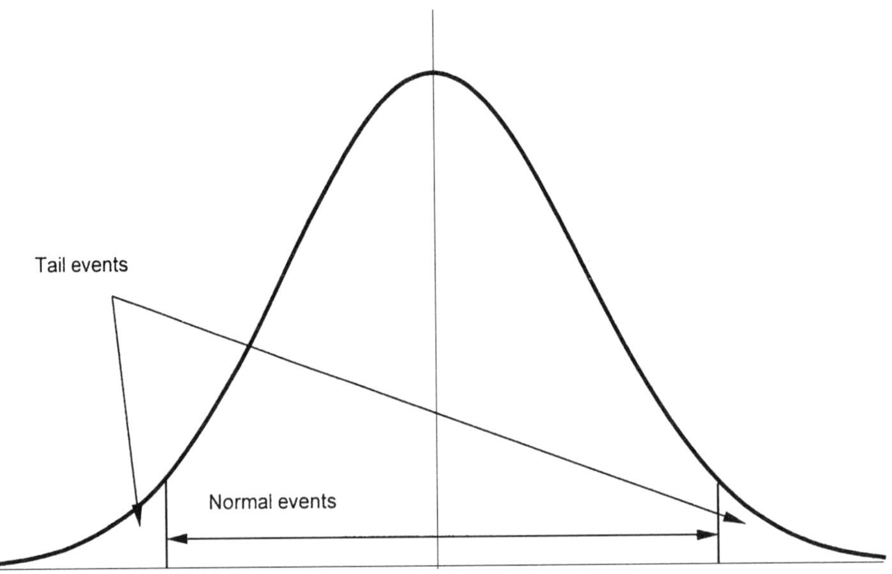

Figure 27.1 'Normal events' and 'tail events'.

a degree of confidence of 99%. The details of VaR and its measurement are discussed in Chapter 42.

A more general and more encompassing definition of VaR will give a useful tool to both book runners and senior management. A true measure of the risk in a portfolio will answer the question 'What is the value of any realistic market movement to my portfolio?'

The approach taken here in finding the value at risk for a portfolio is to model the cost to a portfolio of a crash in the underlying. I show how to value the cost of a crash in a worst-case scenario, and also how to find an optimal static hedge to minimize this cost and so reduce the value at risk.

27.3 A SIMPLE EXAMPLE: THE HEDGED CALL

To motivate the problem and model, consider this simple example. You hold a long call position, delta hedged in the Black–Scholes fashion. What is the worst that can happen, in terms of crashes, for the value of your portfolio? One might naively say that a crash is bad for the portfolio; after all, look at the Black–Scholes value for a call as a function of the underlying, the lower the underlying the lower the call value. Wrong. Remember you hold a *hedged* position; look at Figure 27.2 to see the value of the option, the short asset position and the whole portfolio. The last is the bold line in the figure. Observe that the position is currently delta neutral. Also observe that the portfolio's value is currently at its minimum; a sudden fall (or, indeed, a rise) will result in a higher portfolio value. A crash is beneficial. If we are assuming a worst-case scenario, then the worst that could happen is that there is no crash. Changing all the signs to consider a short call position we find that a crash is bad, but how do we find the worst case? If there is going to be one crash of 10% when is the worst time for this to happen? This is the motivation for the model below. Note first that, generally speaking, a positive gamma position benefits from a crash, while a negative gamma position loses.

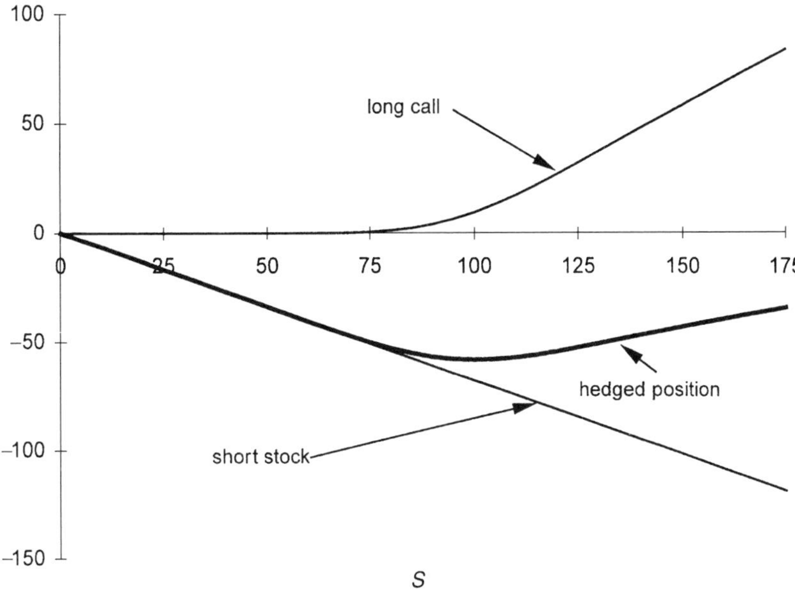

Figure 27.2 The delta-hedged long call portfolio according to Black–Scholes.

27.4 A MATHEMATICAL MODEL FOR A CRASH

The main idea in the following model is simple. We assume that the worst will happen. We value all contracts assuming this, and then, unless we are very unlucky and the worst does happen, we will be pleasantly surprised. In this context, 'pleasantly surprised' means that we make more money than we expected. We can draw an important distinction between this model and the models of Chapter 26, the jump diffusion models. In the latter we make bold statements about the frequency and distribution of jumps and finally take expectations to arrive at a value for a derivative. Here *we make no statements about the distribution of either the jump size or when it will happen*. At most the number of jumps is limited. Finally, we examine the worst-case scenario so that no expectations are taken.

I will model the underlying asset price behavior as the classical binomial tree, but with the addition of a third state, corresponding to a large movement in the asset. So, really, we have a trinomial walk but with the lowest branch being to a significantly more distant asset value. The up and down diffusive branches are modeled in the usual binomial fashion. For simplicity, assume that the crash, when it happens, is from S to $(1-k)S$ with k given; this assumption will later be dropped to allow k to cover a range of values, or even to allow a dramatic rise in the value of the underlying. Introduce the subscript 1 to denote values of the option before the crash, i.e. with one crash allowed, and 0 to denote values after. Thus V_0 is the value of the option position after the crash. This is a function of S and t and, since I am only permitting one crash, V_0 must be exactly the Black–Scholes option value.

As shown in Figure 27.3, if the underlying asset starts at value S (point O) it can go to one of three values: uS, if the asset rises; vS, if the asset falls; $(1-k)S$, if there is a crash. These three points are denoted by A, B and C respectively. The values for uS and vS are chosen in the usual manner for the traditional binomial model (see Chapter 12).

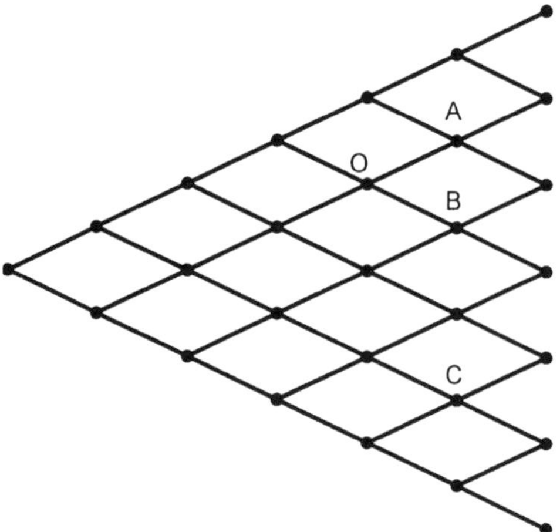

Figure 27.3 The tree structure.

Before the asset price moves, we set up a 'hedged' portfolio, consisting of our option position and $-\Delta$ of the underlying asset. At this time our option has value V_1. We must find both an optimal Δ and then V_1. The hedged portfolio is shown in Figure 27.4.

A time δt later the asset value has moved to one of the three states, A, B or C and at the same time the option value becomes either V_1^+ (for state A), V_1^- (for state B) or the Black–Scholes value V_0 (for state C).

The change in the value of the portfolio, between times t and $t + \delta t$ (denoted by $\delta\Pi$) is given by the following expressions for the three possible states:

$$\delta\Pi_A = V_1^+ - \Delta u S + \Delta S - V_1 \quad \text{(diffusive rise)}$$

$$\delta\Pi_B = V_1^- - \Delta v S + \Delta S - V_1 \quad \text{(diffusive fall)}$$

$$\delta\Pi_C = V_0 + \Delta k S - V_1 \quad \text{(crash).}$$

These three functions are plotted against Δ in Figures 27.5 and 27.6. I will explain the difference between the two figures very shortly. My aim in what follows is to choose the hedge ratio Δ so as to minimize the pessimistic, worst outcome among the three possible.

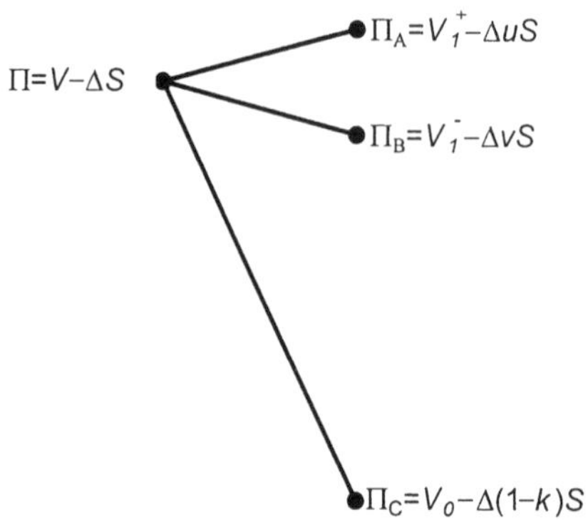

Figure 27.4 The tree and portfolio values.

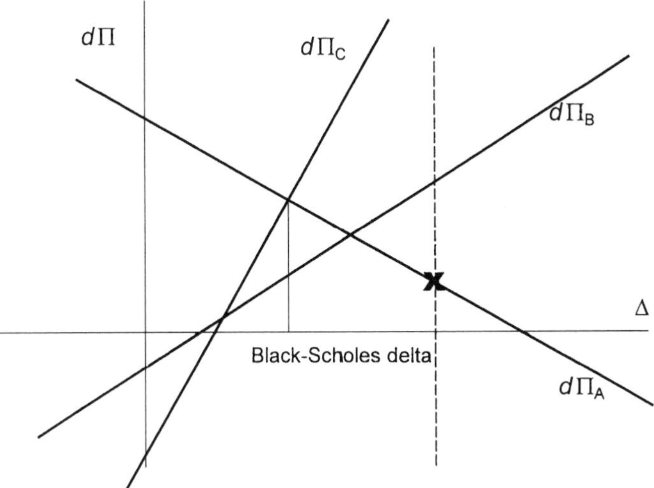

Figure 27.5 Case I: worst case is diffusive motion.

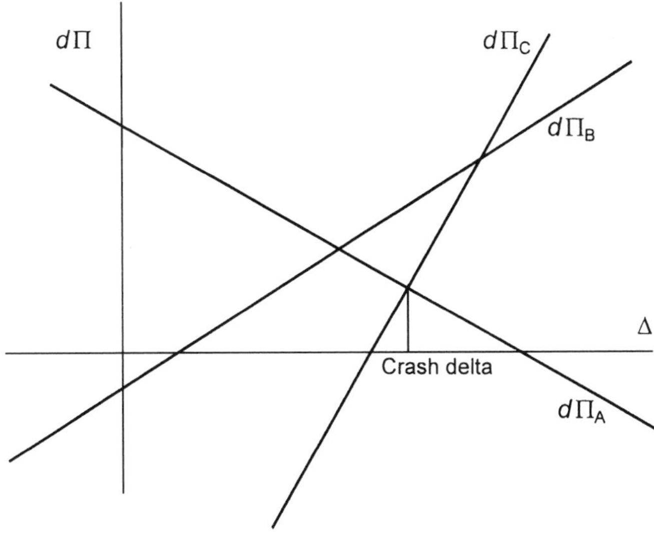

Figure 27.6 Case II: worst case is a crash.

There are two cases to consider, shown in Figures 27.5 and 27.6. The former, Case I, is when the worst-case scenario is not the crash but the simple diffusive movement of S. In this case V_0 is sufficiently large for a crash to be beneficial:

$$V_0 \geq V_1^+ + (S - uS - kS)\frac{V_1^+ - V_1^-}{uS - vS}. \tag{27.1}$$

If V_0 is smaller than this, then the worst scenario is a crash; this is Case II.

27.4.1 Case I: Black–Scholes Hedging

Refer to Figure 27.5. In this figure we see the three lines representing $\delta\Pi$ for each of the moves to A, B and C. Pick a value for the hedge ratio Δ (for example, see the dashed vertical line in Figure 27.5), and determine on which of the three lines lies the worst possible value for $\delta\Pi$ (in the example in the figure, the point is marked by a cross and lies on the A line). Change your value of Δ to maximize this worst value.

In this case the maximal-lowest value for $\delta\Pi$ occurs at the point where

$$\delta\Pi_A = \delta\Pi_B,$$

that is

$$\Delta = \frac{V_1^+ - V_1^-}{uS - vS}. \tag{27.2}$$

This will be recognized as the expression for the hedge ratio in a Black–Scholes world.

Having chosen Δ, we now determine V_1 by setting the return on the portfolio equal to the risk-free interest rate. Thus we set

$$\delta\Pi_A = r\Pi\,\delta t$$

to get

$$V_1 = \frac{1}{1 + r\,\delta t}\left(V_1^+ + (S - uS + rS\,\delta t)\frac{V_1^+ - V_1^-}{uS - vS}\right). \tag{27.3}$$

This is the equation to solve if we are in Case I. Note that it corresponds exactly to the usual binomial version of the Black–Scholes equation; there is no mention of the value of the portfolio at the point C. As δt goes to zero (27.2) becomes $\partial V/\partial S$ and Equation (27.3) becomes the Black–Scholes partial differential equation.

27.4.2 Case II: Crash Hedging

Refer to Figure 27.6. In this case the value for V_0 is low enough for a crash to give the lowest value for the jump in the portfolio. We therefore choose Δ to maximize this worst case. Thus we choose

$$\delta\Pi_A = \delta\Pi_C,$$

that is,

$$\Delta = \frac{V_0 - V_1^+}{S - uS - kS}. \tag{27.4}$$

Now set

$$\delta\Pi_A = r\Pi\,\delta t$$

to get

$$V_1 = \frac{1}{1 + r\,\delta t}\left(V_0 + S(k + r\,\delta t)\frac{V_0 - V_1^+}{S - uS - kS}\right). \tag{27.5}$$

This is the equation to solve when we are in Case II. Note that this is different from the usual binomial equation, and does not give the Black–Scholes partial differential equation as δt goes to zero (see later in the chapter). Also (27.4) is not the Black–Scholes delta. To appreciate that delta hedging is not necessarily optimal, consider the simple example of the butterfly spread. If the butterfly spread is delta hedged on the right 'wing' of the butterfly, where the delta is negative, a large fall in the underlying will result in a large loss from the hedge, whereas the loss in the butterfly spread will be relatively small. This could result in a negative value for a contract, even though its payoff is everywhere positive.

27.5 AN EXAMPLE

All that remains to be done is to solve equations (27.3) and (27.5) (which one is valid at any asset value and at any point in time depends on whether or not (27.1) is satisfied). This is easily done by working backwards down the tree from expiry in the usual binomial fashion.

As an example, examine the cost of a 15% crash on a portfolio consisting of the call options in Table 27.1.

At the moment the portfolio only contains the first two options. Later I will add some of the third option for static hedging, that is when the bid-ask prices will concern us. The volatility of the underlying is 17.5% and the risk-free interest rate is 6%.

The solution to the problem is shown in Figure 27.7. Observe how the value of the portfolio assuming the worst (21.2 when the spot is 100), is lower than the Black–Scholes value (30.5). This is especially clear where the portfolio's gamma is highly negative. This is because when the gamma is positive, a crash is beneficial to the portfolio's value. When the gamma is close to zero, the delta hedge is very accurate and the option is insensitive to a crash. If the asset price is currently 100, the difference between the before and after portfolio values is $30.5 - 21.2 = 9.3$. This is the 'Value at Risk' under the worst-case scenario.

Table 27.1 Available contracts.

Strike	Expiry	Bid	Ask	Quantity
100	75 days			−3
80	75 days			2
90	75 days	11.2	12	0

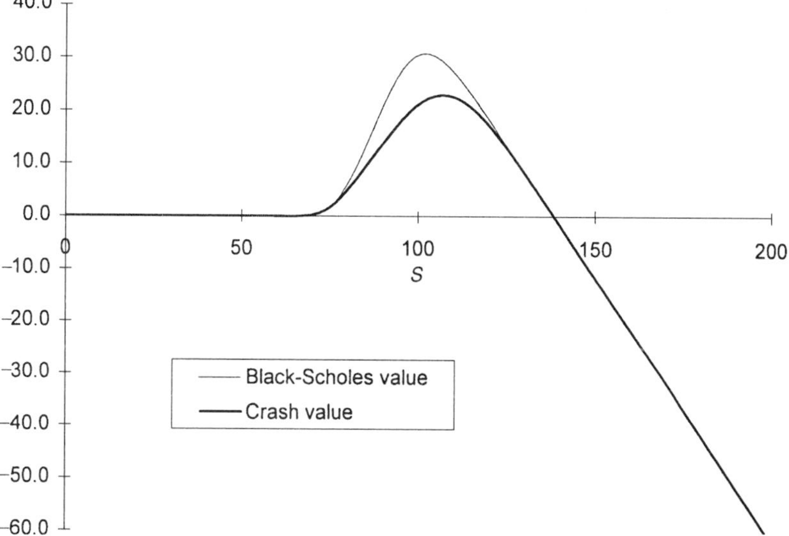

Figure 27.7 Example showing crash value and Black–Scholes value.

27.6 OPTIMAL STATIC HEDGING: VAR REDUCTION

The 9.3 value at risk is due to the negative gamma around the asset price of 100. An obvious hedging strategy that will offset some of this risk is to buy some positive gamma as a 'static' hedge. In other words, we should buy an option or options having a counterbalancing effect on the value at risk. We are willing to pay a premium for such an option. We may even pay more than the Black–Scholes fair value for such a static hedge because of the extra benefit that it gives us in reducing our exposure to a crash. Moreover, if we have a choice of contracts with which to statically hedge we should buy the most 'efficient' one. To see what this means consider the previous example in more detail.

Recall that the value of the initial portfolio under the worst-case scenario is 21.2. How many of the 90 calls should we buy (for 12) or sell (for 11.2) to make the best of this scenario? Suppose that we buy λ of these calls. We will now find the optimal value for λ.

The cost of this hedge is

$$\lambda C(\lambda)$$

where $C(\lambda)$ is 12 if λ is positive and 11.2 otherwise. Now solve Equations (27.3) and (27.5) with the final total payoffs

$$V_0(S,T) = V_1(S,T) = 2\max(S-80,0) - 3\max(S-100,0) + \lambda\max(S-90,0).$$

This is the payoff at time T for the statically hedged portfolio. The *marginal* value of the original portfolio (that is, the portfolio of the 80 and 100 calls) is therefore

$$V_1(100,0) - \lambda C(\lambda) \tag{27.6}$$

i.e. the worst-case value for the new portfolio less the cost of the static hedge. The arguments of the before-crash option value are 100 and 0 because they are today's asset value and date.

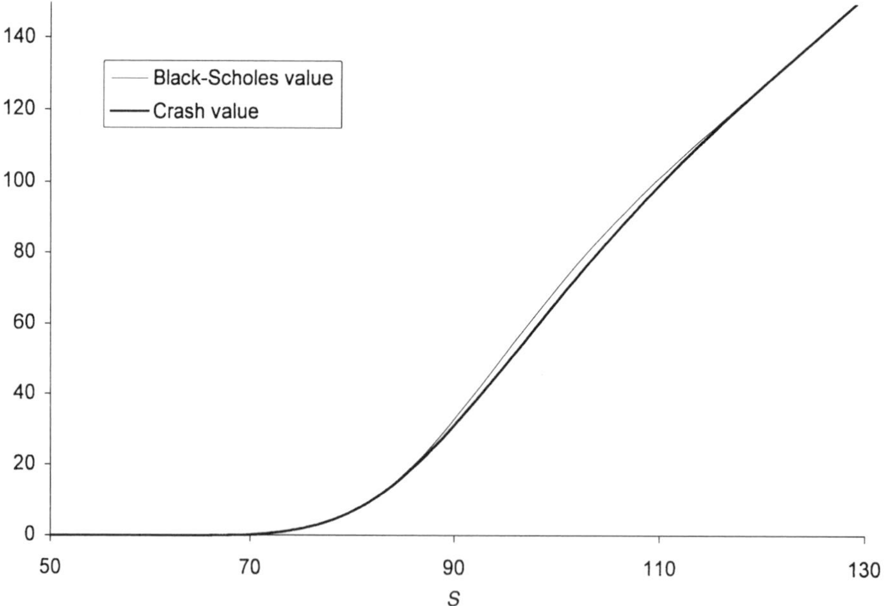

Figure 27.8 Optimally-hedged portfolio, before and after crash.

The optimality in this hedge arises when we choose the quantity λ to maximize the value, expression (27.6). With the bid-ask spread in the 90 calls being 11.2–12, we find that buying 3.5 of the calls maximizes expression (27.6). The value of the new portfolio is 70.7 in a Black–Scholes world and 65.0 under our worst-case scenario. The value at risk has been reduced from 9.3 to $70.7 - 65 = 5.7$. The optimal portfolio values before and after the crash are shown in Figure 27.8. The optimal static hedge is known as the **Platinum Hedge**.

The issues of static hedging and optimal static hedging are covered in detail in Chapter 30.

27.7 CONTINUOUS-TIME LIMIT

If we let $\delta t \to 0$ in Equations (27.1), (27.2), (27.3), (27.4) and (27.5) we find that the Black–Scholes equation is still satisfied by $V_1(S,t)$ but we also have the constraint

$$V_1(S,t) - kS\frac{\partial V_1}{\partial S}(S,t) \leq V_0(S(1-k),t)$$

Such a problem is similar in principal to the American option valuation problem, where we also saw a constraint on the derivative's value. Here the constraint is more complicated. To this we must add the condition that the first derivative of V_1 must be continuous for $t < T$.

27.8 A RANGE FOR THE CRASH

In the above model, the crash has been specified as taking a certain value. Only the timing was left to be determined for the worst-case scenario. It is simple to allow the crash to cover a range of values, so that S goes to $(1-k)S$ where

$$k^- \leq k \leq k^+.$$

A negative k^- corresponds to a rise in the asset.

In the discrete setting the worst-case option value is given by

$$V_1 = \min_{k^- \leq k \leq k^+}\left(\frac{1}{1+r\,\delta t}\left(V_0 + S(k + r\,\delta t)\frac{V_0 - V_1^+}{S - uS - kS}\right)\right).$$

This contains the min($\cdot$) because we want the worst-case crash. When a crash is beneficial we still have (27.3).

27.9 MULTIPLE CRASHES

The model described above can be extended in many ways. One of the most important is to consider the effect of multiple crashes. I describe two possibilities below. The first puts a constraint on the total number of crashes in a time period, there can be three crashes within the horizon of one year, say. The second puts a limit on the time between crashes, there cannot be another crash if there was a crash in the last six months, say.

27.9.1 Limiting the Total Number of Crashes

We will allow up to N crashes. We make no statement about the time these occur. We will assume that the crash size is given, allowing a fall of $k\%$. This can easily be extended to a range of sizes, as described above. Introduce the functions $V_i(S,t)$ with $i = 0, 1, \dots, N$, such that V_i is the value of the option with i more crashes still allowed. Thus, as before, V_0 is the Black–Scholes value.

We must now solve N coupled equations of the following form. If

$$V_{i-1} \geq V_i^+ + (S - uS - kS)\frac{V_i^+ - V_i^-}{uS - vS}$$

then we are in Case I, a crash is beneficial and is assumed not to happen. In this case we have

$$V_i = \frac{1}{1 + r\,\delta t}\left(V_i^+ + (S - uS + rS\,\delta t)\frac{V_i^+ - V_i^-}{uS - vS}\right).$$

Otherwise a crash is bad for the hedged option; this is Case II. We then have

$$V_i = \frac{1}{1 + r\,\delta t}\left(V_{i-1} + S(k + r\,\delta t)\frac{V_{i-1} - V_i^+}{S - uS - kS}\right).$$

In continuous time the equations become

$$\frac{\partial V_i}{\partial t} + \tfrac{1}{2}\sigma^2 S^2 \frac{\partial^2 V_i}{\partial S^2} + rS\frac{\partial V_i}{\partial S} - rV_i = 0$$

for $i = 0, \dots, N$, subject to

$$V_i(S,t) - kS\frac{\partial V_i}{\partial S}(S,t) \leq V_{i-1}(S(1-k), t)$$

for $i = 1, \dots, N$. Each of the V_i has the same final condition, representing the payoff at expiry.

27.9.2 Limiting the Frequency of Crashes

Finally, we model a situation where the time between crashes is limited; if there was a crash less than a time ω ago another is not allowed.

This is slightly harder than the N-crash model and we have to introduce a new variable τ measuring the time since the last crash. We now have two functions to consider $V_c(S,t)$ and $V_n(S,t,\tau)$. The former is the worst-case option value when a crash is allowed (and therefore we don't need to know how long it has been since the last crash) and the latter is the worst-case option value when a crash is not yet allowed.

The governing equations, which are derived in the same way as the original crash model, are, in continuous time, simply

$$\frac{\partial V_c}{\partial t} + \tfrac{1}{2}\sigma^2 S^2 \frac{\partial^2 V_c}{\partial S^2} + rS\frac{\partial V_c}{\partial S} - rV_c = 0$$

subject to

$$V_c(S,t) - kS\frac{\partial V_c}{\partial S}(S,t) \leq V_n(S(1-k), t, 0),$$

and for $V_n(S, t, \tau)$,

$$\frac{\partial V_n}{\partial t} + \frac{\partial V_n}{\partial \tau} + \tfrac{1}{2}\sigma^2 S^2 \frac{\partial^2 V_n}{\partial S^2} + rS\frac{\partial V_n}{\partial S} - rV_n = 0$$

with the condition

$$V_n(S, t, \omega) = V_c(S, t).$$

Observe how the time τ and real time t increase together in the equation when a crash is not allowed.

27.10 CRASHES IN A MULTI-ASSET WORLD

When we have a portfolio of options with many underlyings we can examine the worst-case scenario still, but we have two choices. Either (a) we allow a crash to happen in any underlyings completely independently of all other underlyings or (b) we assume some relationship between the assets during a crash. Clearly the latter is not as bad a worst case as the former. It is also easier to write down, so we will look at that model only. Assuming that all assets fall simultaneously by the same percentage k we have

$$V_1(S_1, \ldots, S_n, t) - k\sum_{i=1}^{n} S_i \frac{\partial V_1}{\partial S_i}(S_1, \ldots, S_n, t) \leq V_0((1-k)S_1, \ldots, (1-k)S_n, t, t).$$

We will pursue stock market crashes in CrashMetrics; see Chapter 45.

27.11 FIXED AND FLOATING EXCHANGE RATES

Many currencies are linked directly to the currency in another country. Some countries have their currency linked to the US dollar, for example the Argentine Peso is tied at a rate of one to one to the dollar. The European Monetary Union is another example of linked exchange rates.

Once an exchange rate is fixed in this way the issue of fluctuating rates becomes a credit risk issue. All being well, the exchange rate will stay constant with all the advantages of stability that this brings with it. If economic conditions in the two countries start to diverge then the exchange rate will come under pressure. In Figure 27.9 is a plot of the possible exchange rate, showing a fixed rate for a while, followed by a sudden discontinuous drop and then a random fluctuation. How can we model derivatives of the exchange rate? The models of this chapter are ideally suited to this situation.

I'm going to ignore interest rates in the following. This is because of the complex issues this would otherwise raise. For example, the pressure on the exchange rate and the decoupling of the currencies would be accompanied by changing interest rates. This can be modeled but would distract us from the application of the crash model.

While the exchange rate is fixed, before the 'crash,' the price of an option, $V_1(S, t)$, satisfies

$$\frac{\partial V_1}{\partial t} = 0,$$

since I am assuming zero interest rates. Here S is the exchange rate. After the 'crash' we have

$$\frac{\partial V_0}{\partial t} + \tfrac{1}{2}\sigma^2 S^2 \frac{\partial^2 V_0}{\partial S^2} = 0.$$

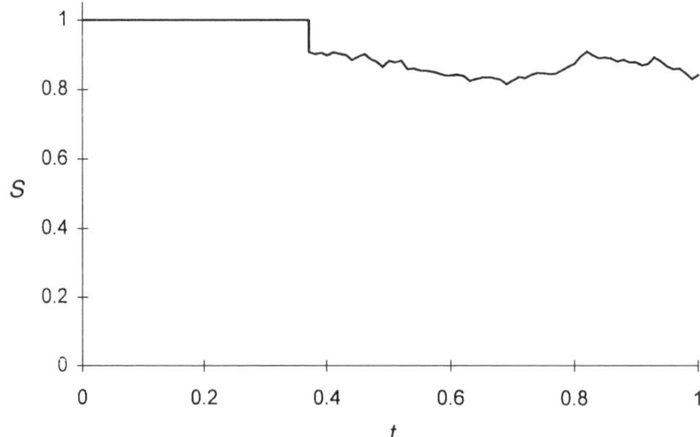

Figure 27.9 Decoupling of an exchange rate.

(But with what volatility?) This is just the Black–Scholes model, with the relevant Black–Scholes value for the particular option payoff.

The worst-case crash model is now almost directly applicable. I will leave the details to the reader.

27.12 SUMMARY

I have presented a model for the effect of an extreme market movement on the value of portfolios of derivative products. This is an alternative way of looking at value at risk. I have shown how to employ static hedging to minimize this VaR. In conclusion, note that the above is not a jump-diffusion model since I have deliberately not specified any probability distribution for the size or the timing of the jump: we model the worst-case scenario.

We have examined several possible models of crashes, of increasing complexity. One further thought is that we have not allowed for the rise in volatility that accompanies crashes. This can be done with ease. There is no reason why the after-crash model (V_0 in the simplest case above) cannot have a different volatility from the before-crash model. Of particular interest is the final model where there is a minimum time between crashes. We could easily have the volatility post crash being a decaying function of the time since the crash occured, τ. This would involve no extra computational effort.

FURTHER READING

- For further details about crash modeling see Hua & Wilmott (1997) and Hua (1997).
- Derman & Zou (1997) describe and model the behavior of implied volatility after a large move in an index.

EXERCISES

1. Examine the continuous-time limits for Equations (27.1) to (27.5): show that $V_1(S, t)$ does not satisfy the Black–Scholes equation, but instead satisfies

$$V_1(S, t) - kS\frac{\partial V_1}{\partial S}(S, t) = V_0(S(1-k), t).$$

   What is the delta for the option in this case?

2. In the continuous-time limit, if

$$V_1(S,t) - kS\frac{\partial V_1}{\partial S}(S,t) > V_0(S(1-k),t),$$

then is the value of

$$\frac{\partial V_1}{\partial t} + \tfrac{1}{2}\sigma^2 S^2 \frac{\partial^2 V_1}{\partial S^2} + rS\frac{\partial V_1}{\partial S} - rV_1$$

positive or negative?

3. We have seen two models for crashes:
   (a) There are N crashes before expiry, but no specification of at what time they occur;
   (b) Crashes can occur at any time before expiry, but they must be at least a time ω apart.

   Which model fits actual asset price data more accurately? Is it possible to combine the two models? How might we use this method to model asset price movements with lots of small jumps and occasional large crashes?

CHAPTER 28
speculating with options

In this Chapter...

- how to find the present value of the *real* expected payoff (and why you should want to know this)
- several ways to model asset price drift
- how to optimally close your option position
- when and when not to hedge

28.1 INTRODUCTION

Almost everything I have shown you so far is about finding pricing equations for derivative contracts using hedging arguments. There is a very powerful reason why such arguments should give option prices in the market regardless of whether or not investors actually hedge the option. The reason is simple: if the option is not priced at the Black–Scholes fair value and hedging is possible then either:

- the option price is too low, in which case someone will buy it, hedge away the risk and make a riskless profit or
- the option price is too high, in which case someone will artificially replicate the payoff and charge less for this contract.

Both of these are examples of market inefficiencies which would disappear quickly in practice (to a greater or lesser extent).

However, a few minutes spent on a typical trading floor will convince you that option contracts are often bought for speculation and that the value of an option to a speculator and the choice of expiry date and strike price depend strongly on his **market view**, something that is irrelevant in the Black–Scholes world. Moreover, many OTC and other contracts are used to offset risks outside the market, and if every derivative is hedged by both writer and purchaser then the whole thing is pointless, or at best a series of hedging and modeling competitions. In this chapter I show possible ways in which a speculator can choose an option contract so as to profit from his view if it turns out to be correct.

Throughout this chapter I use the word 'value' to mean the *worth of an option to a speculator* and this will not necessarily be the Black–Scholes 'fair' value. To get around the obvious criticism that what follows is nonsense in a complete market, in which delta hedging is possible, I'm going to take the point of view that the investor can value a contract at other than the Black–Scholes value because of market incompleteness, for whatever reason you like. The cause of incompleteness may be transaction costs, restrictions on sales or purchases, uncertain parameters, general model errors, etc. Thus any 'arbitrage' that you may see because values are different from Black–Scholes cannot be exploited by our investor. He is going to buy a contract as an investment, a risky investment.

One of the motivations for this chapter is the observation that in the classical Black–Scholes theory the drift of the asset plays no part. Two people will agree on the price of an option even if they differ wildly in their estimates for μ—indeed, they may not even have estimates for μ—as long as they agree on the other parameters such as the volatility.

28.2 A SIMPLE MODEL FOR THE VALUE OF AN OPTION TO A SPECULATOR

Imagine that you hold very strong views about the future behavior of a particular stock: you have an estimate of the volatility and you believe that for the next twelve months the stock will have an upwards drift of 15%, say, and that this is much greater than the risk-free rate. How can you benefit from this view if it is correct? One simple way is to follow the principles of Modern Portfolio Theory, Chapter 41, and buy a call, just out of the money, maybe, perhaps with an expiry of about one year because this may have an appealing risk/return profile (also see later in this chapter). You might choose an out of-the-money option because it is cheap, but not so far out of the money that it is likely to expire worthless. You might choose a twelve-month contract to benefit from as much of the asset price rise as possible. Now imagine it is a couple of months later, and the asset has fallen 5% instead of rising. What do you do? Maybe, the stock *did* have a drift of 15% but, since we only see one realization of the random walk, the volatility caused the drop. Alternatively, maybe you were wrong about the 15%.

This example illustrates several points.

- How do you determine the future parameters for the stock: the drift and volatility?
- How do you subsequently know whether you were right?
- And if not, what should you do about it?
- If you have a good model for the future random behavior of a stock, how can you use it to measure an option's value *to you*?
- Which option do you buy?

A thorough answer to the first of these questions is outside the scope of this book; but I have made suggestions in that direction. The other four questions fall more into the area of modeling and we discuss them here.

28.2.1 The Present Value of Expected Payoff

Speculation is the opposite side of the coin to hedging. The speculator is taking risks and hopes to profit from this risk by an amount greater than the risk-free rate. When gambling like this, it is natural to ask what is your expected profit. In option terms, this means we would ask what is the present value of the expected payoff. I say 'present value' because the payoff, if it comes, will be at expiry (assuming that we do not exercise early if the option is American, or close the position).

If the asset price random walk is

$$dS = \mu S\,dt + \sigma S\,dX$$

and the option has a payoff of

$$\max(S - E, 0)$$

at time T then the *present value of the expected payoff*[1] satisfies

$$\frac{\partial V}{\partial t} + \tfrac{1}{2}\sigma^2 S^2 \frac{\partial^2 V}{\partial S^2} + \mu S \frac{\partial V}{\partial S} - rV = 0$$

with

$$V(S, T) = \max(S - E, 0).$$

This is related to the ideas in Chapter 10 for transition density functions.

This equation differs from the Black–Scholes equation in having a μ instead of an r in front of the delta term. Seemingly trivial, this difference is of fundamental importance. The replacement of μ by r is the basis of 'risk-neutral valuation.' The absence of μ from the Black–Scholes option pricing equations means that the only asset price parameters needed are the volatility and the dividend structure. For the above equation, however, we need to know the drift rate μ in order to calculate the expected payoff.

Let us return to the earlier example, and fill in some details. Suppose we buy a call, struck at 100, with an expiry of one year, the underlying has a volatility of 20% and, we believe, a drift of 15%. The interest rate is 5%. In Figure 28.1 is shown the Black–Scholes value of the option (the lower curve) together with the present value of the *real* expected payoff (the upper curve) both plotted against S. These two curves would be identical if μ and r were equal. The lower curve is a risk-neutral expectation and the upper curve a real expectation.

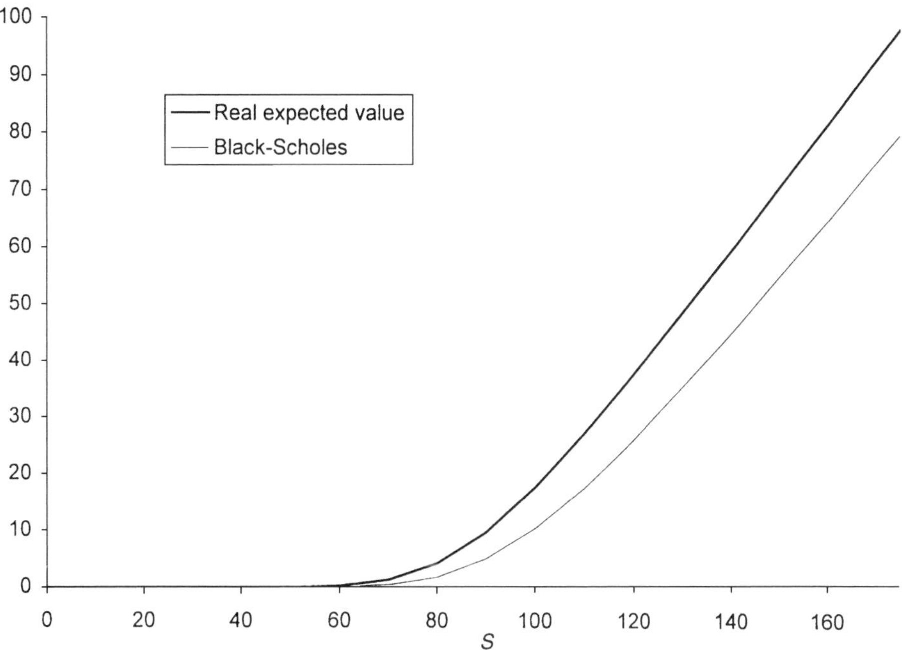

Figure 28.1 The Black–Scholes value of a call option (the lower curve) and the present value of the expected payoff (the upper curve). See text for data.

[1] This is not dissimilar to how options used to be priced in the 1960s before Black and Scholes.

It is easy to show, and financially obvious, that if $\mu > r$ then the present value of the expected payoff for a call is greater than the Black–Scholes fair value. In other words, if we expect the stock to drift upwards with a rate higher than the interest rate then we expect to make more money than if we had invested in bonds. Here the word 'expect' is of paramount importance: there is nothing certain about this investment. The greater expected return is compensation for the greater risk of speculation, absent in a hedged portfolio. Nevertheless, for the speculator the expected payoff is an important factor in deciding which option to buy. The other important factor is a measure of the risk; when we know the risk and the return for an option we are in a position to apply ideas from Modern Portfolio Theory, Chapter 41, for example.

28.2.2 Standard Deviation

As I have said, the return from an unhedged option position is uncertain. That uncertainty can be measured by the standard deviation of the return about its mean level.[2] This standard deviation can be determined as follows. Suppose that today's date is $t = 0$, and introduce the function $G(S, t)$ as the expected value of the square of the present value of the payoff. This function, being an expectation satisfies the backward Kolmogorov equation (see Chapter 10):

$$\frac{\partial G}{\partial t} + \tfrac{1}{2}\sigma^2 S^2 \frac{\partial^2 G}{\partial S^2} + \mu S \frac{\partial G}{\partial S} = 0 \tag{28.1}$$

(which, of course, is simply the Black–Scholes equation with no discounting and with μ instead of r).[3] The final condition is

$$G(S, T) = (e^{-rT} \max(S - E, 0))^2.$$

Then from its definition, the standard deviation today is given by

$$\sqrt{G(S, 0) - (V(S, 0))^2}.$$

In Figure 28.2 is shown this standard deviation plotted against S, using the same data as in Figure 28.1.

A natural way to view these results is in a risk/reward plot. In this model the reward is the logarithm of the ratio of the present value of the expected payoff to the cost of the option, divided by the time to expiry of the option. But how much will the option cost? A not unreasonable assumption is that the rest of the market is using Black–Scholes to value the option so we shall assume that the cost of the option is simply the Black–Scholes value V_{BS}. The risk is the standard deviation, again scaled with the Black–Scholes value of the option and with the square root of the time to expiry. Thus we define

$$\text{Reward} = \frac{1}{T} \log \left(\frac{V(S, 0)}{V_{BS}(S, 0)} \right)$$

and

$$\text{Risk} = \frac{\sqrt{G(S, 0) - (V(S, 0))^2}}{V_{BS}(S, 0)\sqrt{T}}.$$

[2] This is not entirely satisfactory for many products, especially those with an non-unimodal payoff distribution.

[3] The astute reader will notice that there is no $-rG$ in this 'present value' calculation; we have absorbed this into the final condition; read on.

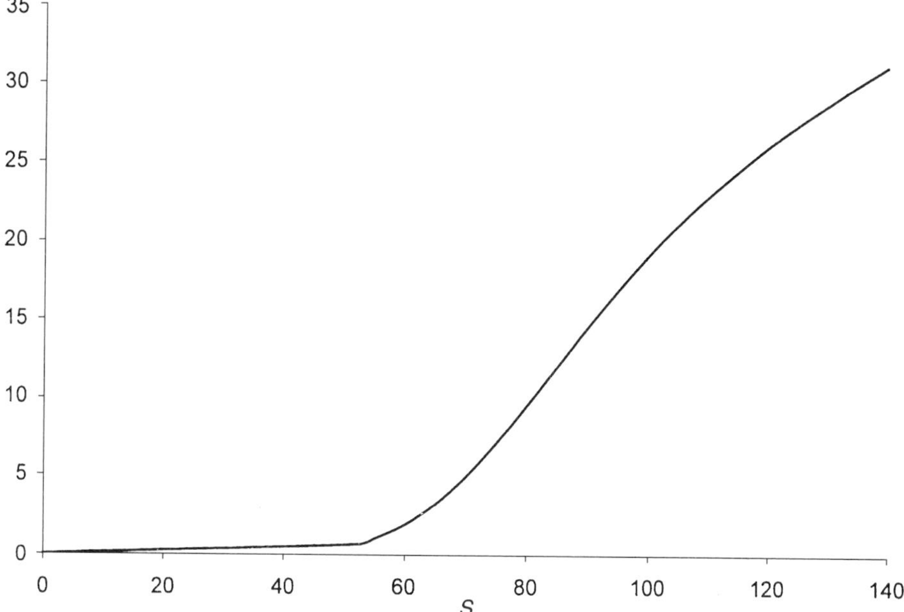

Figure 28.2 The standard deviation of the present value of the expected payoff for a call option. See text for data.

These definitions, in particular the scalings with time, have been chosen to tie in with the traditional measures of reward and risk.

In Figure 28.3 we show a plot of this reward versus the risk for a call option and the same data as the previous two figures. In Figure 28.4 we show the same plot but for a put option and with the same data. Observe how, with our data assumptions, the put option has decreasing return for increasing risk. Obviously, in this case, call options are more attractive.

(In the above we have considered only the standard deviation as a measure of risk. This measure attaches as much weight to a better outcome than average as it does to a worse outcome. A better choice as a measure of risk may be a one-sided estimate of only the downside risk; I leave the formulation of this problem as an exercise for the reader.)

28.3 MORE SOPHISTICATED MODELS FOR THE RETURN ON AN ASSET

Despite modeling the 'value' of an option to a speculator, we know from experience that as time progresses we are likely to change our view of the market and have to make a decision regarding the success, or otherwise, of our position: perhaps six months into the life of our call option we decide that we were wrong about the direction of the market and we may therefore close our position. Is there any way in which we can build into our model of the market, *a priori*, our experience that market conditions change?

I am now going to present two models for a randomly varying drift rate. The first assumes that the drift rate follows some stochastic differential equation. The second model assumes that the drift can be in one of two states: high drift or low drift. The drift jumps randomly between these two states.

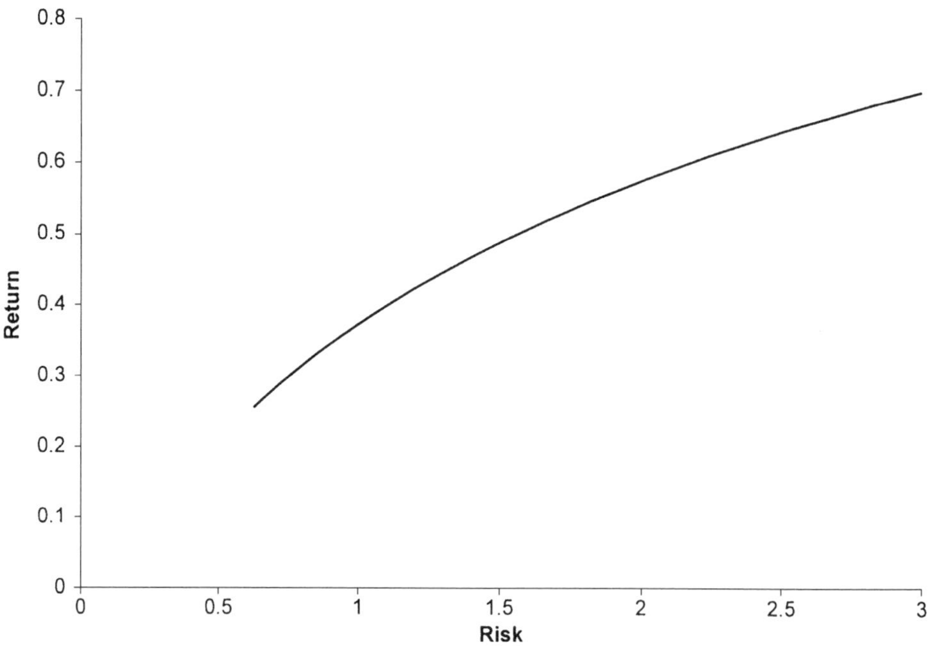

Figure 28.3 The scaled present value of expected payoff versus the scaled standard deviation for a call option. See text for details and data.

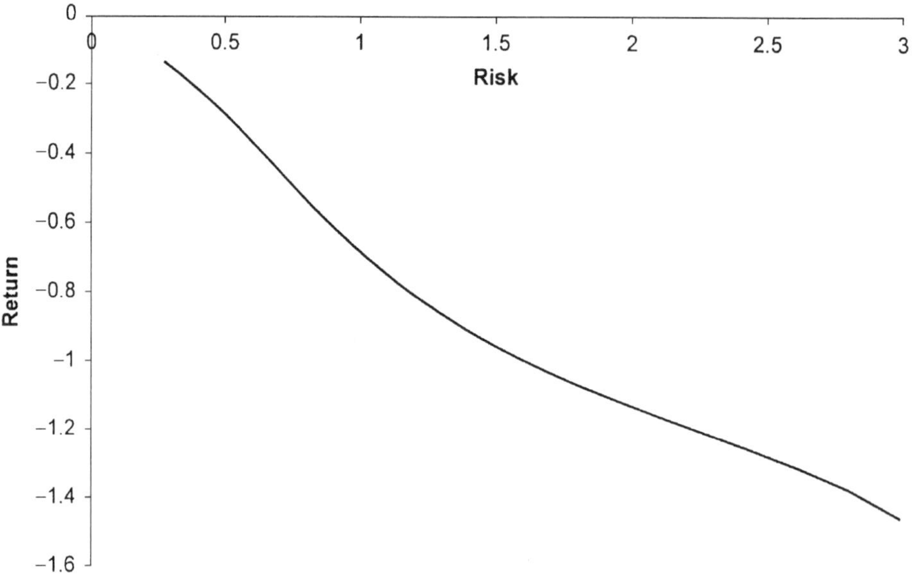

Figure 28.4 The scaled present value of expected payoff versus the scaled standard deviation for a put option. See text for details and data.

28.3.1 Diffusive Drift

The asset price still satisfies

$$dS = \mu S\,dt + \sigma S\,dX_1.$$

Now assuming that the drift rate μ satisfies

$$d\mu = \eta(S, \mu, t)\,dt + \nu(S, \mu, t)\,dX_2$$

then the present value of the expected return $V(S, \mu, t)$ satisfies the two-factor partial differential equation

$$\frac{\partial V}{\partial t} + \tfrac{1}{2}\sigma^2 S^2 \frac{\partial^2 V}{\partial S^2} + \rho\sigma\nu S \frac{\partial^2 V}{\partial S \partial \mu} + \tfrac{1}{2}\nu^2 \frac{\partial^2 V}{\partial \mu^2} + \mu S \frac{\partial V}{\partial S} + \eta \frac{\partial V}{\partial \mu} - rV = 0$$

where ρ is the correlation coefficient between the two random walks.[4]

In Figure 28.5 I show the value of a call option for the model

$$d\mu = (a - b\mu)\,dt + \beta\,dX_2.$$

In this figure I have used $a = 0.3$, $b = 3$ and $\beta = 0.1$ with $\rho = 0$. The option is a call struck at 100 with an expiry of one year and a volatility of 20%. The interest rate is 5%. When the asset is 100 and the drift is zero the option value is 11.64.

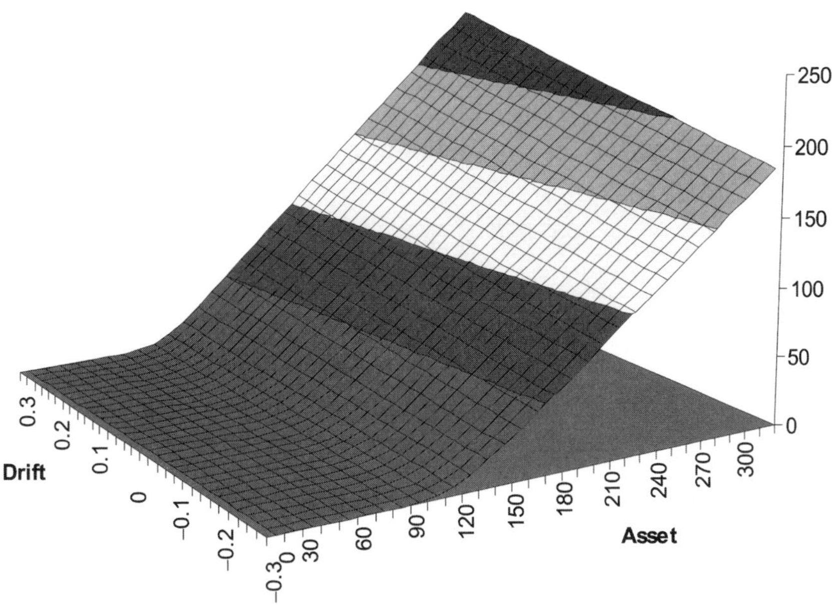

Figure 28.5 The value of a call option when the drift is diffusive. See text for details and data.

[4] At this point had we been using a Black–Scholes hedging argument we would have arrived at this equation but with r as the coefficient of the $\partial V/\partial S$ term. With final conditions independent of μ we would then find that $\partial V/\partial \mu = 0$ everywhere and thus that V satisfies the Black–Scholes equation. Thus even with stochastic drift the Black–Scholes option value is independent of μ. There are some technical details, concerning the 'support' of the real and risk-neutral random walks, that must be satisfied. Simply put, the range of values that can be attained by the two random walks must be the same.

The standard deviation of these payoffs may be found in a similar manner to that above for constant drift. The relevant equation is simply the two-factor version of (28.1).

28.3.2 Jump Drift

The above model for diffusive drift is perhaps unnecessarily complicated for describing the market view of a typical trader. A simpler model, which I describe now, allows the drift to be in one of two states, either high or low. The asset random walk is allowed to jump from one state to the other. For example, we believe that in the short term the asset in question will have a drift of 15%. However, this may only last for six months. If the drift does change then it will drop to a level of 0%. In this example, call options look appealing in the short term, but we may not want to buy longer-dated calls since we will probably suffer when the downturn arrives. We assume that the two states have constant drift and that the jump from one state to another is governed by a Poisson process. In other words, the probability of changing from a high drift to a low drift in a period dt is $\lambda^- \, dt$, and the probability of changing from a low drift to a high drift is $\lambda^+ \, dt$.

We can value options to a speculator by again looking at the present value of the expected payoff. First, we must introduce the notation. Let $V^+(S,t)$ be the option 'value' when the asset has a drift of μ^+. Similarly, the option has value $V^-(S,t)$ when the asset has a drift of $\mu^- < \mu^+$. We can easily examine expected payoffs by considering how the option value changes at each timestep.

At time t the asset value is S and we assume without loss of generality that it is in the higher drift state, with the drift of μ^+. At the later time $t + dt$ the asset price changes to $S + dS$, and at the same time the drift rate may jump to μ^- but only with a probability of $\lambda^- \, dt$.

With the real expected return equal to the risk-free rate we arrive at the following equation:

$$\frac{\partial V^+}{\partial t} + \tfrac{1}{2}\sigma^2 S^2 \frac{\partial^2 V^+}{\partial S^2} + \mu^+ S \frac{\partial V^+}{\partial S} - rV^+ + \lambda^-(V^- - V^+) = 0.$$

Similarly, we find that

$$\frac{\partial V^-}{\partial t} + \tfrac{1}{2}\sigma^2 S^2 \frac{\partial^2 V^-}{\partial S^2} + \mu^- S \frac{\partial V^-}{\partial S} - rV^- + \lambda^+(V^+ - V^-) = 0$$

when the drift starts off in the lower state. The final conditions for these equations are, for example,

$$V^+(S,T) = V^-(S,T) = \max(S - E, 0)$$

for a call option.

The standard deviation also takes two forms, depending on which state the drift is in. We must solve

$$\frac{\partial G^+}{\partial t} + \tfrac{1}{2}\sigma^2 S^2 \frac{\partial^2 G^+}{\partial S^2} + \mu^+ S \frac{\partial G^+}{\partial S} + \lambda^-(G^- - G^+) = 0$$

and

$$\frac{\partial G^-}{\partial t} + \tfrac{1}{2}\sigma^2 S^2 \frac{\partial^2 G^-}{\partial S^2} + \mu^- S \frac{\partial G^-}{\partial S} + \lambda^+(G^+ - G^-) = 0$$

with

$$G^+(S,T) = G^-(S,T) = (e^{-rT} \max(S - E, 0))^2.$$

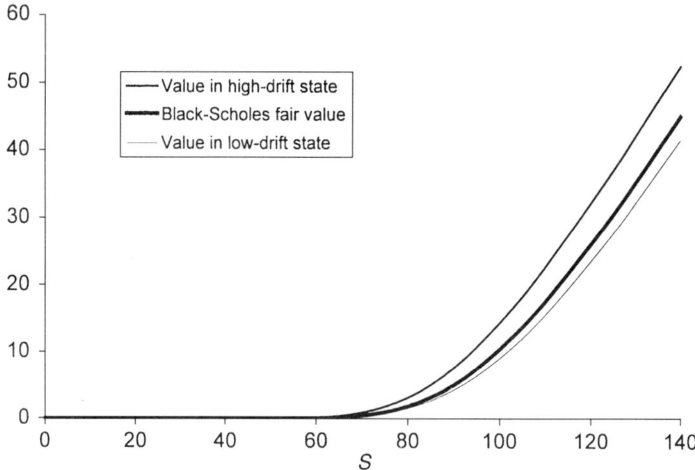

Figure 28.6 The value of a call option when the drift jumps between two levels. See text for details and data.

Then the standard deviation at time $t = 0$ is given by

$$\sqrt{G^{\pm}(S, 0) - (V^{\pm}(S, 0))^2},$$

depending on whether the drift is in the high or low drift state at that time.[5]

In Figure 28.6 we show the value of a call option against asset price. The top curve shows the option value when the asset is in the high drift state, and the bottom curve is when the asset is in the low drift state. Between the two, the bold curve, is the Black–Scholes fair value. The option is a call struck at 100 with one year to expiry. The underlying has a volatility of 20% and the interest rate is 5%. The high drift is 15% and the low drift is zero. The intensity of the Poisson process taking the asset from high to low is 1 and 0.5 going from low to high. In this example it is easier for the asset to sink to the low drift state than to recover, and this is why the expected value in the low drift case is below Black–Scholes.

28.4 EARLY CLOSING

So far we have modeled the value to a speculator of an option on which he has a strong view on the drift rate and which he will hold until expiry. The diffusive drift and the jump drift models allow for the possibility that the drift leaves its advantageous state and changes to a disadvantageous state. In our example of Section 28.2, the asset drift was initially high, but has fallen to below the risk-free rate, and our call option no longer seems like such a good bet. What can we do? Although our models price this into the option's value, they do not allow for the obvious trader reaction: sell the option and close the position.

Within the present models it is natural for the trader to close his position if the value to him falls below the market value. Why hold onto a position in which you expect to make a loss?

[5] How do we know what state we are in? That's a statistical question. Alternatively, we could say that if the underlying has fallen by a certain amount this means a change of state, this is also easy to model.

He may want to sell earlier than this but we use this very simple constraint as an example. We also assume that the market value of the option is simply the Black–Scholes value, with the same risk-free rate of interest and volatility; again, this could be generalized.

Having seen the mathematical analysis for American options in Chapter 9, it is obvious that our early-closing problem is identical in spirit: take either the diffusion model or the jump model for the drift and impose the constraint that the option value must always be greater than the Black–Scholes value and that the first derivatives must be continuous. In the diffusion model this amounts to

$$V(S,\mu,t) \geq V_{BS}(S,t) \quad \text{and} \quad \frac{\partial V}{\partial S} \text{ continuous.}$$

For the jump model we have

$$V^{+}(S,t) \geq V_{BS}(S,t), \quad V^{-}(S,t) \geq V_{BS}(S,t) \quad \text{and} \quad \frac{\partial V^{\pm}}{\partial S} \text{ continuous.}$$

In Figure 28.7 is shown the value of the option against the underlying and the drift for the diffusive drift model. The parameter values are as above. The option value at an asset value of 100 and a drift of zero is now 11.84. The extra value comes from the ability to close the position. In Figure 28.8 is plotted the difference between the option values with and without the ability to close the position.

In Figure 28.9 is shown the value of the option against the underlying in the two-state drift model. This two-state drift model is particularly interesting because the option value in the low-drift state is the same as Black–Scholes. The interpretation of this is that you should sell the option as soon as you believe that the drift is in the low state. The extra value in being able to sell the position is plotted in Figure 28.10.

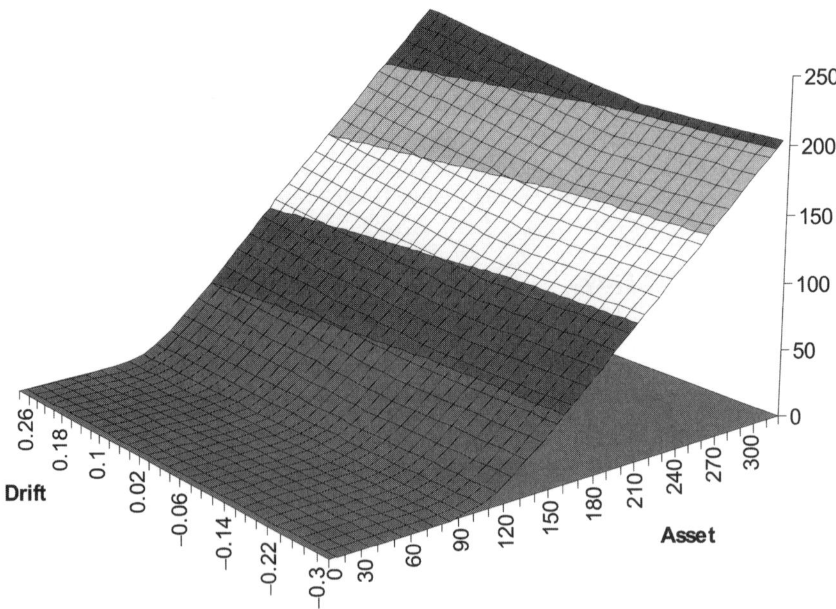

Figure 28.7 The option value to a speculator with closure of the position to ensure that it never falls below the market value: diffusive drift model.

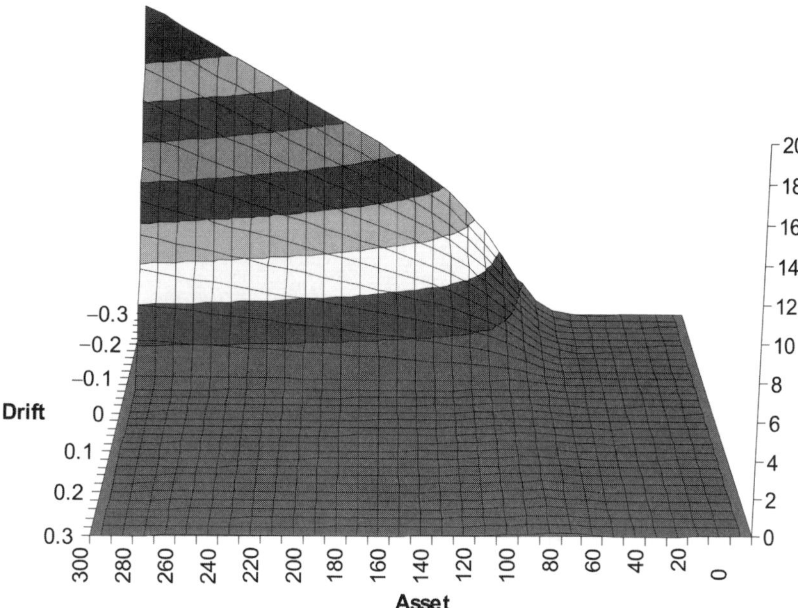

Figure 28.8 The added value of being able to close the position: diffusive-drift model.

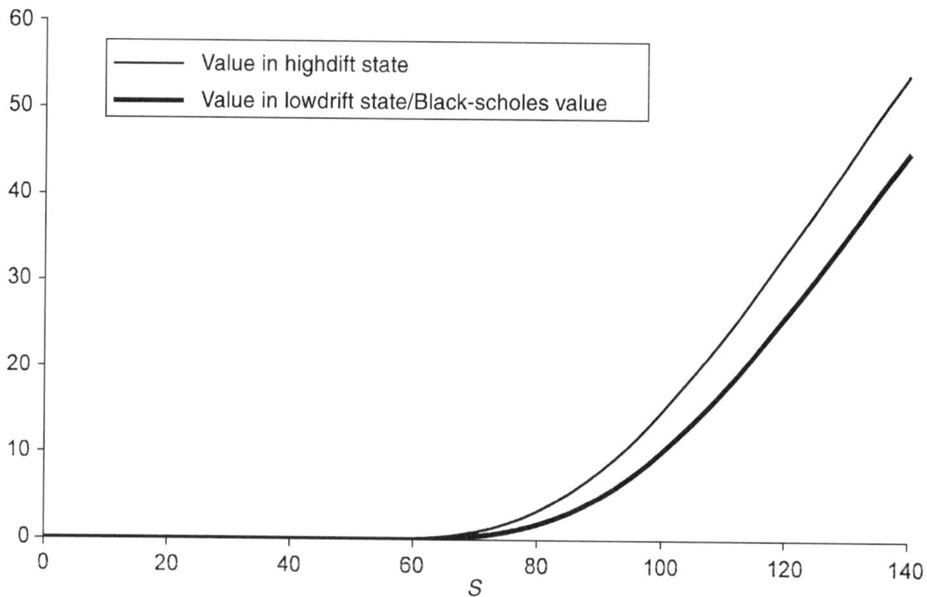

Figure 28.9 The option value to a speculator with closure of the position to ensure that it never falls below the market value: jump drift model.

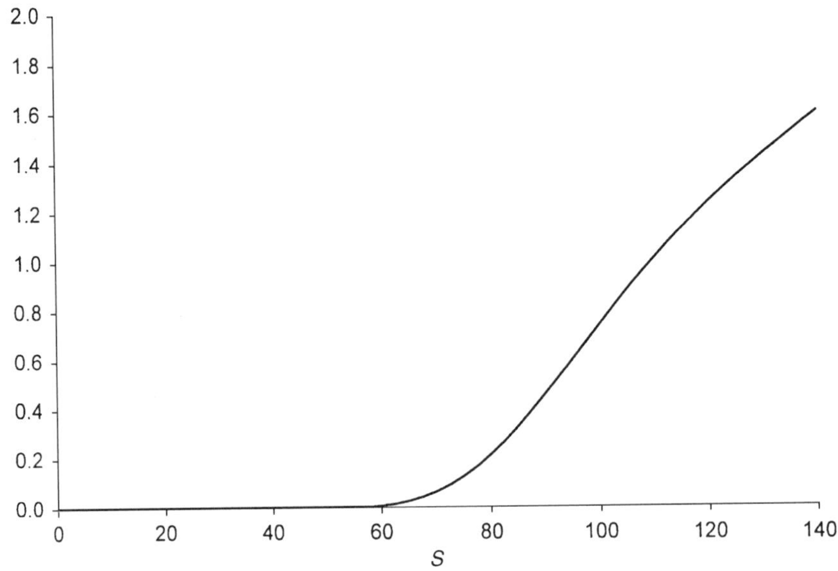

Figure 28.10 The added value of being able to close the position: two-state model.

The problem for the standard deviation is slightly more complicated when there is early closing because of the appearance of the early-closing boundary. For example, with the two-state drift model we have

$$\frac{\partial G^+}{\partial t} + \tfrac{1}{2}\sigma^2 S^2 \frac{\partial^2 G^+}{\partial S^2} + \mu^+ S \frac{\partial G^+}{\partial S} + \lambda^-(G^- - G^+) = 0$$

$$G^+(S, T) = (e^{-rT} \max(S - E, 0))^2$$

and

$$G^+(S_e(t), t) = (e^{-rt} V^+(S_e(t), t))^2.$$

Here $S_e(t)$ is the position of the early-closing boundary given by the solution of the free boundary problem for V^+ and V^-. There is a similar equation for G^-.

Again, the standard deviations are given by

$$\sqrt{G^{\pm}(S, 0) - V^{\pm}(S, 0)^2}.$$

The above illustrates the importance of not only having a model for the underlying but also, when relevant, having a model for the pricing mechanism *of the market*. This is relevant if one expects or hopes to sell the contract before its expiry, since one must sell it for its market value and not one's theoretical value. One of the benefits inherent in this is that having a model for the market value enables you to make even more money than simply having a model for the underlying. This gives you the option of either holding the contract to expiry or, if the market value rises higher than your theoretical value, closing out the position. The value of the contract to you, under this scenario, cannot be less than your theoretical value without the option to close the position. This principal can easily be extended. For example, suppose you have a model for the market's perception of volatility, you can use this to give a lower bound to the contract in question, regardless of the validity of the market's view.

In the above framework for valuing contracts it is obvious that some contracts are more appealing than others. For an asset with a drift above the risk-free rate calls would be preferred over puts for example. There are timescales associated with changes in the drift rate and these may have some bearing on the choice of expiry dates.

28.5 TO HEDGE OR NOT TO HEDGE?

So far in this chapter we have looked at 'valuing' options in the complete absence of hedging. As I have said, speculation is the opposite side of the coin to hedging. Perhaps it is possible to bring these two sides closer together.

In this section we look at the expected values of options, assuming a quite sophisticated hedging strategy, one that is intuitively highly appealing. This strategy is to speculate when we expect to make money and hedge when we would otherwise expect to lose it.

We will assume that the drift rate of the asset, μ, is constant and greater than the risk-free interest rate. This is the simplest problem that can be used to introduce the ideas. Extensions to other cases, $\mu < r$, non-constant μ etc. are obvious. With this assumption, our strategy can be modeled mathematically by a portfolio of value Π where

$$\Pi = V(S, t) - \overline{\Delta} S, \tag{28.2}$$

and V is the 'value' of our option. We choose the quantity $\overline{\Delta}$ so as to maximize the expected growth in the value of our portfolio. We also impose the constraints on the value of $\overline{\Delta}$

$$\alpha \frac{\partial V}{\partial S} \leq \overline{\Delta} \leq \beta \frac{\partial V}{\partial S}.$$

Such a constraint could be used to bound the risk in the portfolio.

Since the expected drift of the portfolio in excess of the risk-free rate is

$$\left(\mu S \frac{\partial V}{\partial S} - rV - (\mu - r) S \overline{\Delta} \right) dt,$$

it is simple to show that the choice

$$\overline{\Delta} = \begin{cases} \alpha \dfrac{\partial V}{\partial S} & \text{if} \quad \dfrac{\partial V}{\partial S} \geq 0 \\ \beta \dfrac{\partial V}{\partial S} & \text{if} \quad \dfrac{\partial V}{\partial S} \leq 0 \end{cases}$$

maximizes the expected drift of the portfolio. (These inequalities would swap for the case $\mu < r$.) The reasoning behind this choice is simple; if our option has a positive $\Delta = \partial V / \partial S$ then we *expect* to make more money by speculating than hedging since we expect the asset price to rise faster than the risk-free rate and hence we expect the portfolio value to rise faster. When Δ is negative we expect to lose out on a speculating position in comparison to a hedged position. If we now calculate the present value of the expected payoff we find that it satisfies

$$\frac{\partial V}{\partial t} + \tfrac{1}{2} \sigma^2 S^2 \frac{\partial^2 V}{\partial S^2} + rS \frac{\partial V}{\partial S} (\mu - (\mu - r) F(\Delta)) - rV = 0,$$

with

$$F(\Delta) = \begin{cases} \alpha \Delta & \text{if} \quad \Delta \geq 0 \\ \beta \Delta & \text{if} \quad \Delta \leq 0 \end{cases}$$

This is another nonlinear diffusion equation.

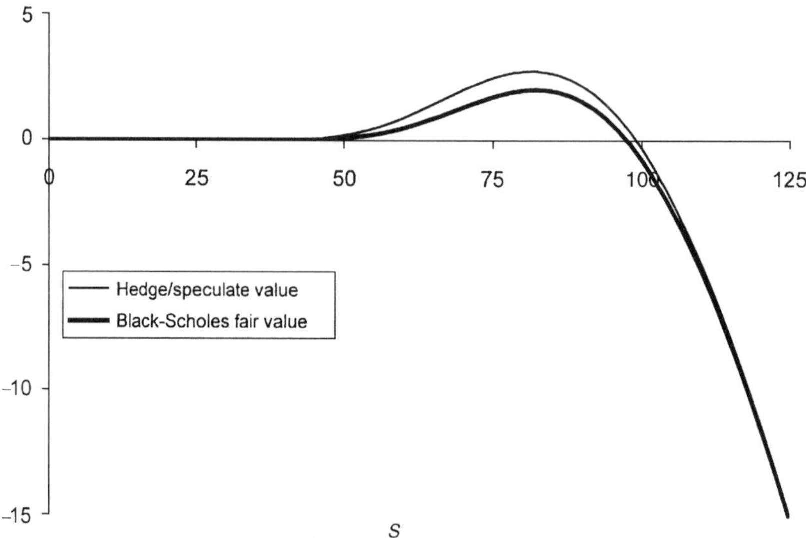

Figure 28.11 The option value to a hedger-speculator and the Black–Scholes value, see text for details.

In Figure 28.11 we see the solution of this equation for a position of two long calls at 90 and three short 100 calls. A model such as this is an obvious improvement over pure speculation.

With the parameters $\alpha = \beta = 1$ we have Black–Scholes and with $\alpha = \beta = 0$ we return to the hedging-speculating model (28.5).[6]

28.6 OTHER ISSUES

An accurate model of the drift of the underlying is especially important when speculating with barrier options or binary/digital options. Since binary options have a discontinuous payoff it is not possible in practice to follow the Black–Scholes hedging strategy no matter how frequently one hedges. Thus there is always some exposure to the drift; to some extent, one is always speculating with binary options.

We have seen how the drift rate of the underlying comes into the equation for the real expected payoff. Another simple but important calculation in a similar vein is the calculation of the real expected value of an option part way into its life. For example, we hold a five year warrant and want to know how much this will be worth in two years' time. We may want to know this so as to have some idea of the value of our portfolio at that time. We calculate the *real expected* value of the warrant in two years as follows.

First, note that the value of the option in the Black–Scholes world satisfies the Black–Scholes equation and does not depend on μ. Let us assume that this is how the market will value the contract throughout its life. However, we want to know the real expected value in two years.

[6] There are many other obvious ways to bound risk. For example by choosing α and β suitably we can overhedge if we think that this is advantageous. We could also allow α and β to depend on V or Π, we may want to take less risk with a larger portfolio.

We can do this by simply solving the equation

$$\frac{\partial V}{\partial t} + \frac{1}{2}\sigma^2 S^2 \frac{\partial^2 V}{\partial S^2} + \nu S \frac{\partial V}{\partial S} - rV = 0,$$

where

$$\nu = \begin{cases} \mu & \text{for} \quad 0 \le t \le 2 \\ r & \text{for} \quad 2 < t \le 5. \end{cases}$$

28.7 SUMMARY

One mustn't get too hung up on delta hedging, no arbitrage and risk neutrality. The concepts are extremely important but there are times when their relevance is questionable, and one of those times is when you are speculating. Sure, the price that you buy a contract for has something to do with these concepts via Black–Scholes, but from then on, if you are not hedging, there are more important things to worry about.

FURTHER READING

- See Korn & Wilmott (1996 a, b) for details about option pricing with a view.
- The best choice to make from a selection of risky investments is just asset allocation, see for example Markowitz (1959), but this is discussed in Chapter 41.

EXERCISES

1. Show that if $\mu > r$ then the present value of the expected payoff for a call is greater than the Black–Scholes fair value. What is the equivalent result for a put option? What about portfolios of options?
2. If we value an option using a jump drift model with two possible drifts, how should we decide which drift to use to determine the price of the option today?

CHAPTER 29
the feedback effect of hedging in illiquid markets

In this Chapter...

- how delta hedging an option position or replication can influence and move the market in the underlying

29.1 INTRODUCTION

I have referred constantly to the 'underlying' asset. The implication of this was that the asset price leads and the option price follows; the option value is contingent upon the value and probabilistic properties of the asset, and not the other way around. In practice in many markets, however, the trade in the options on an asset can have a nominal value that exceeds the trade in the asset itself. So, can we still think of the asset price as leading the option?

In the traditional derivation of the Black–Scholes option pricing equation it is assumed that the replication trading strategy has no influence on the price of the underlying asset itself, that the asset price moves in a random way. Sometimes the justification for this is the action of **noise traders** or the random flow of information concerning the asset or the economy. Nevertheless, a significant number of trades are for hedging or replication purposes. And, crucially, these trades are for predictable amounts. What is their impact on the market?

Usually it is assumed that the effect of individual trading on the asset price is too small to be of any importance and is neglected when the strategy is derived. This seems justifiable if the market in question has many participants and a high degree of liquidity, which is usually true for modern financial markets. On the other hand, the portfolio insurance trading strategies are very often implemented on a large scale, and the liquidity of the financial markets is sometimes very limited. In the case of the October 1987 stock market crash some empirical studies and even the official report of the investigations carried out by the Brady commission suggest that portfolio insurance trading contributed to aggravate the effects of the crash.

In this chapter we are going to address the problem of the influence of these trading strategies on the price of the underlying asset and thus, in a feedback loop, onto themselves.

29.2 THE TRADING STRATEGY FOR OPTION REPLICATION

In theory, any simple option can be replicated by following the appropriate trading strategy. These trading strategies have enjoyed tremendous popularity among portfolio managers who use them to insure themselves against large movements in the share price. This strategy is called **portfolio insurance**. One of the most popular portfolio insurance strategies is the replication of a European put option. Any simple option having a value $V(S, t)$ can be *replicated* by holding

$$\Delta(S, t) = \frac{\partial V}{\partial S}(S, t)$$

shares at time t if the share price is S. (Contrast this with *hedging* an option for which we must hold this number short.) In particular, Black and Scholes found an explicit formula for the value $V(S, t)$ of the put option. As derived in Chapter 5, this formula is

$$V(S, t) = Ee^{-r(T-t)}N(-d_2) - SN(-d_1) \tag{29.1}$$

where

$$d_1 = \frac{\log(S/E) + (r + \sigma^2/2)(T - t)}{\sigma\sqrt{T - t}}$$

$$d_2 = d_1 - \sigma\sqrt{T - t}.$$

For the European put Equation (29.1) results in

$$\Delta(S, t) = N(d_1) - 1.$$

We can now think of $\Delta(S, t)$ as corresponding to a trading *strategy*. Put replication is one of the trading strategies, corresponding to one example of portfolio insurance, that we are going to analyze in detail. Figure 29.1 shows the delta of a European put at various times before expiry; the steeper the curve, the closer the option is to expiry.

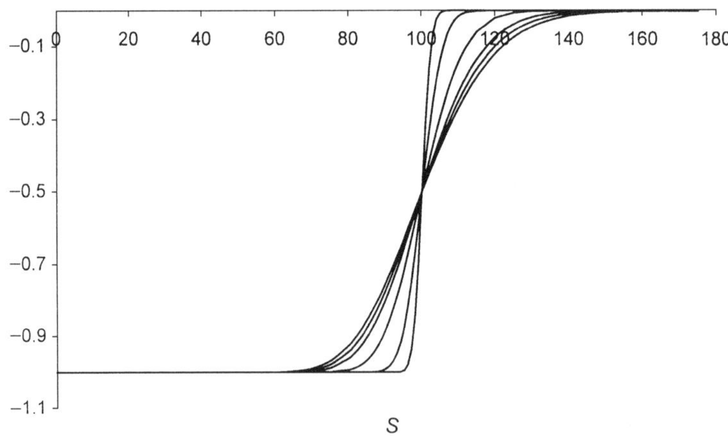

Figure 29.1 The delta for a European put at several times before expiry.

In the next Section I propose a form for the reaction of the market to a trading strategy Δ and will derive the modification of the price process that takes account of the effect of trading.

29.3 THE EXCESS DEMAND FUNCTION

In order to quantify the effects of replication on the movement of the asset we need a model describing the relationship between supply of and demand for an asset and its price. Consider the difference between demand and supply in the market. This is the **excess demand** which we assume takes the form $\mathcal{X}(S, t, x)$, i.e. it is a function of price S, time t and, importantly, a random influence x. The random influence will ensure that our model does not stray too far from the classical lognormal; this will be a limiting case of our more complex model. We will model x as a random variable shortly. Its influence can be regarded as the effect of randomly arriving new information on the value of the underlying asset or the action of noise traders. Generally $\partial\mathcal{X}/\partial S$ is negative, rising price leads to falling demand.[1]

At any given time the equilibrium price $S_{Eq}(t)$ is the price for which demand is equal to supply, or excess demand is zero;

$$\mathcal{X}(S_{Eq}(t), t, x) = 0. \tag{29.2}$$

Typically, there is a strong tendency in any market to return to the equilibrium price if it has been disturbed. Surplus demand pushes the price up, towards the equilibrium price, excess supply makes the price drop, again towards the equilibrium price. The market equilibrium is stable. Note that this argument supposes that the excess demand function is negatively sloped; for a positive slope the equilibrium would still exist but it would be unstable. We will encounter locally positively sloped excess demand functions later on.

Disequilibrium is obviously possible but given the speed of the flow of information in these markets and the large number of professionals on the stock markets a full equilibrium in stocks and flows in modern financial markets is a good approximation. This does not mean that these markets are static, in our model both demand and supply can change in time because of the stochastic parameter x.

29.4 INCORPORATING THE TRADING STRATEGY

In this section we add to the original demand the extra demand resulting from the hedging of the put option. Not only will we have the random demand due to the noise traders but also a completely deterministic demand, due to the trading strategy Δ. With this additional demand of the form $\Delta(S, t)$ the equilibrium condition (29.2) becomes

$$\mathcal{X}(S, t, x) + \Delta(S, t) = 0 \tag{29.3}$$

(dropping the subscript on the equilibrium price) and the same must hold for the changes in $\mathcal{X}$ and Δ

$$d\mathcal{X} + d\Delta = 0.$$

We could consider arbitrary excess demand function $\mathcal{X}$, but for simplicity we assume from now on that

$$\mathcal{X}(S, t, x) = \frac{1}{\varepsilon}(x - S).$$

Here ε is a positive real number and x follows the stochastic process

$$dx = \mu_x\,dt + \sigma_x\,dX;$$

μ_x and σ_x can be functions of x and t. We can now think of x as being the 'intrinsic value' of the stock.

[1] This is necessarily a simplification of the real story, but nevertheless a simplification often made in economic theory and one which holds the essence of truth.

The parameter ε shows how strongly the excess demand function reacts to changes in the price. If the price changes by dS then the excess demand changes by $-dS/\varepsilon$. It gives an indication of the liquidity of the market. Liquid markets react very strongly to changes in the price. For such markets ε is small:

> A *liquid market* is a market in which ε is *small.*
> An *illiquid market* is a market in which ε is *large.*

As mentioned before most—but not all—financial markets are liquid markets.

If the parameter ε is assumed to be zero this reduces the price process S to the random walk x. We will not take this step but merely assume ε to be small. We will see later that in certain cases no matter how small ε the individual effect on the excess demand cannot be neglected.

Now (29.3) becomes

$$(x - S) + \varepsilon\Delta(S, t) = 0. \tag{29.4}$$

In the undisturbed equilibrium, with appropriate choice of scalings, ε^{-1} is also equal to the **price elasticity of demand**.

Applying Itô's lemma to (29.4) we find that the stochastic process followed by S is

$$dS = \mu_S(S, t)\,dt + \sigma_S(S, t)\,dX \tag{29.5}$$

with μ_S and σ_S given by

$$\mu_S = \frac{\sigma_S}{\sigma_x}\left(\mu_x + \varepsilon\left(\frac{\partial\Delta}{\partial t} + \tfrac{1}{2}\sigma_S^2\frac{\partial^2\Delta}{\partial S^2}\right)\right)$$

and

$$\sigma_S = \frac{\sigma_x}{1 - \varepsilon\dfrac{\partial\Delta}{\partial S}}.$$

The details are left to the reader; the application of Itô's lemma is straightforward.

So far all analysis has been done for an arbitrary stochastic process for x. Usually the price process of share price is assumed to be lognormal, i.e.

$$dS = \mu S\,dt + \sigma S\,dX \tag{29.6}$$

with μ and σ constant. Our analysis of the model on the other hand yielded the modified price process (29.5). As the equilibrium price S is a known function of x we can choose

$$\mu_x = \mu S \quad \text{and} \quad \sigma_x = \sigma S$$

to achieve consistency between (29.5) and (29.6) in the sense that (29.5) reduces to (29.6) when $\varepsilon = 0$.

29.5 THE INFLUENCE OF REPLICATION

One of the most important portfolio insurance strategies Δ is put replication as explained in Section 29.2. Look again at Figure 29.1 to see the delta of the European put. As the expiry date of the option is approached Δ goes towards a step function with step from -1 to 0 at the exercise price.

Recalling Equation (29.4) the equilibrium condition can be written as

$$-x = -S + \varepsilon\Delta. \tag{29.7}$$

The effect of the trading strategy is a small (i.e. of order ε) perturbation added to the original demand function. Far from expiry the right-hand side of (29.7) is simply $-S$ since $\varepsilon\Delta$ is small. Close to expiry the Δ term becomes important and the shape of the demand curve alters dramatically, becoming as shown in Figure 29.2. Figure 29.2 shows the right-hand side of (29.7) for the put replication strategy. We are sufficiently close to expiry for the curve to no longer be monotonic.

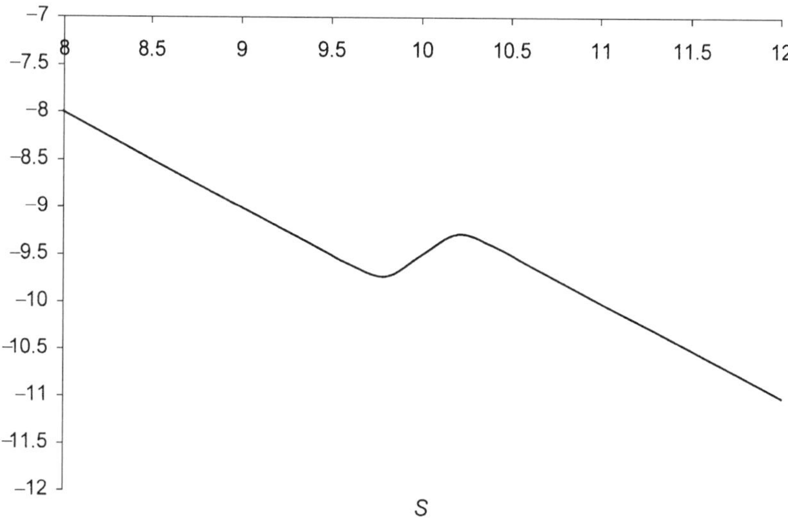

Figure 29.2 The sum of the original linear demand function and the extra demand due to put replication.

As expiry approaches the sequence of events is as follows. Far from expiry there is hardly any deviation from the normal linear function. In an interval around the expiry price the demand curve's slope becomes less and less negative until it is positively sloped. Thus there are times very close to expiry and close to the strike for which there is an unstable equilibrium.

Geometrically, Equation (29.7) can be interpreted as follows. For a given t, the market equilibria are defined as the points where the randomly moving horizontal line $-x$ intersects the function $-S + \varepsilon\Delta$. An example of this is shown in Figure 29.3. As long as $-S + \varepsilon\Delta$ is monotonically decreasing the equilibrium is unique for any value of x. But because Δ approaches a step function as expiry is approached, $-S + \varepsilon\Delta$ must become multi-valued at some point. From this time on the situation becomes more complicated.

Refer to Figure 29.3. In this figure the horizontal line denotes the left-hand side in the equilibrium condition (29.7) and the curve is the corresponding right-hand side for t close to expiry T. There are various possible situations depending on the value of x at that point in time:

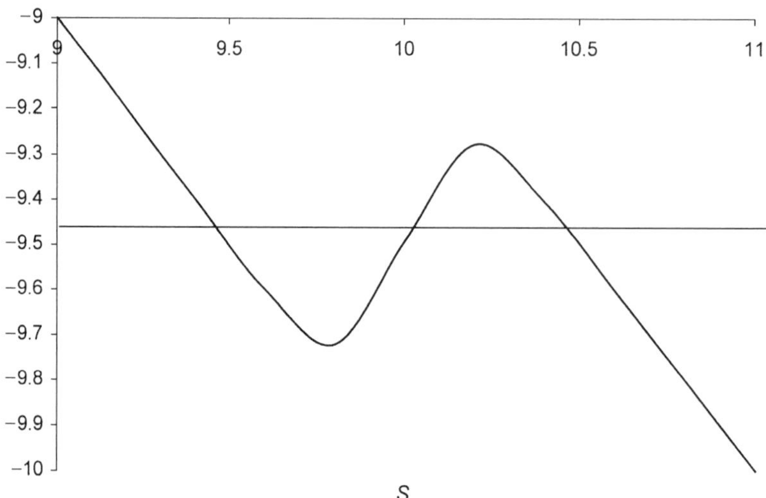

Figure 29.3 The intersection of the supply and demand curves. There are four cases depending on the relative position of the intersection and the maxima and minima.

1. x is sufficiently large or small as to be outside the critical region where there are several equilibria. The equilibrium asset price is unique, corresponding to the asset value where the horizontal line crosses the curve.
2. x is inside the critical region where there are three possible equilibria. This is the case shown in the figure. The middle equilibrium value for the asset is unstable, corresponding to a positively sloped demand function. The other two are stable.
3. The limiting case between cases 1 and 2. If the horizintal line just touches the curve, then we have two equilibria. One of these is stable, the other, corresponding to the asset value where the line just *touches* the curve, is stable only for movements in the random variable x of one sign. At this point either the equilibrium asset value will move continuously or will jump to the next equilibrium point: if a jump occurs there is a discontinuity in the price.

The third case is of particular interest. What happens to the equilibrium asset value is sketched in Figure 29.4. The points A, B, C and D are defined by

$$(A(t), -A(t) + \varepsilon\Delta(A(t), t)),$$

etc. as follows. $S = B(t)$ and $S = C(t)$ are the local extrema of the demand function, B is the local minimum and C is the local maximum. The definitions of these points are

$$-1 + \varepsilon\frac{\partial\Delta}{\partial S}(B, t) = 0 \tag{29.8}$$

$$-1 + \varepsilon\frac{\partial\Delta}{\partial S}(C, t) = 0 \tag{29.9}$$

and

$$\frac{\partial^2}{\partial S^2}\Delta(B, t) \geq 0 \geq \frac{\partial^2}{\partial S^2}\Delta(C, t). \tag{29.10}$$

$S = A(t)$ and $S = D(t)$ are defined as:

$$A \leq B \leq C \leq D \tag{29.11}$$

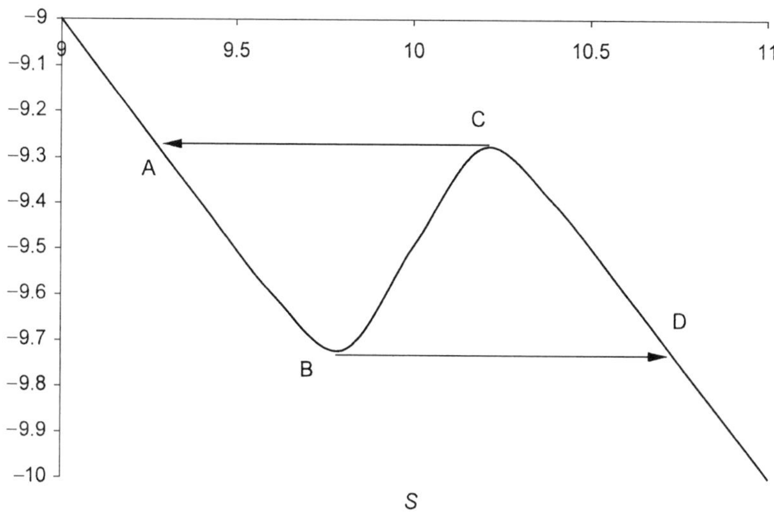

Figure 29.4 The positions of the four points A, B, C and D.

$$[-S + \varepsilon\Delta](A, t) = [-S + \varepsilon\Delta](C, t) \tag{29.12}$$

$$[-S + \varepsilon\Delta](D, t) = [-S + \varepsilon\Delta](B, t). \tag{29.13}$$

Thus there are four different points of interest: the two extrema *from* which the jumps come and the two points *to* which the price jumps.

The arrows in the figure mean that the asset can jump from one point of the curve to another, that is from B to D and from C to A. But that only happens if the increments of x are of the right sign when the asset is at B or C. If the increment is of the opposite sign then the asset price at B could fall by an infinitesimal amount, or at C rise by an infinitesimal amount. I emphasize the point that the jump is only one way.

The same result can be found by an examination of the drift μ_S and variance σ_S of the modified price process. Both have a term of the form

$$1 - \varepsilon\frac{\partial\Delta}{\partial S}$$

in the denominator. This is the negative of the derivative of the total demand function. When this becomes equal to zero the demand function has zero slope, as case 3 above. Here μ_S and σ_S approach infinity.

But even when $\partial\Delta/\partial S < \varepsilon^{-1}$, a positive $\partial\Delta/\partial S$ has the effect of increasing both σ_S and the absolute value of μ_S: the market becomes more volatile. If conversely $\partial\Delta/\partial S$ is negative, its effect is to decrease the volatility of the market. If Δ is regarded as the trading strategy to replicate a derivative security V, the relation $\Delta = \partial V/\partial S$ yields that:

- Replication of a derivative security V with positive gamma $\Gamma = \partial^2 V/\partial S^2$, i.e. with concave payoff profile, destabilizes the market of the underlying.

Long positions in put and call options have positive gamma.

29.6 THE FORWARD EQUATION

We can analyze the new stochastic process (29.5) by examining the probability density function $p(S, t)$ which gives the probability density of the share price being at S at time t subject to an initial distribution. Here S and t are the forward variables, usually written as S' and t'.

The probability density function satisfies the Kolmogorov forward equation

$$\frac{\partial p}{\partial t}(S, t) = \tfrac{1}{2}\frac{\partial^2}{\partial S^2}(p(S, t)\sigma_S^2(S, t)) - \frac{\partial}{\partial S}(p(S, t)\mu_S(S, t)).$$

We will use a delta function initial condition, meaning that we know exactly where the asset starts out.

29.6.1 The Boundaries

As pointed out in Section 29.5 there are two pairs of jump boundaries in the area close to expiry (see Figure 29.4). Jumps[2] can occur from point B to point D and from point C to point A.

The positions of these points change in time. A typical graph for a put-replicating trading strategy is shown in Figure 29.5. For any continuous time-dependent trading strategy all four boundary points have to arise at the same point. This point is characterized as a point of inflexion of the full demand function $x - S + \varepsilon\Delta$, which obviously satisfies the conditions (29.8) to (29.13). In Figure 29.5 this point is marked as I. Subsequently the points will constantly maintain the order $A < B < C < D$ and fan out as shown.

The put-replicating strategy shown in Figure 29.4 approaches a step function as expiry approaches. B and C disappear together at the exercise price and expiry date (point II). Points A

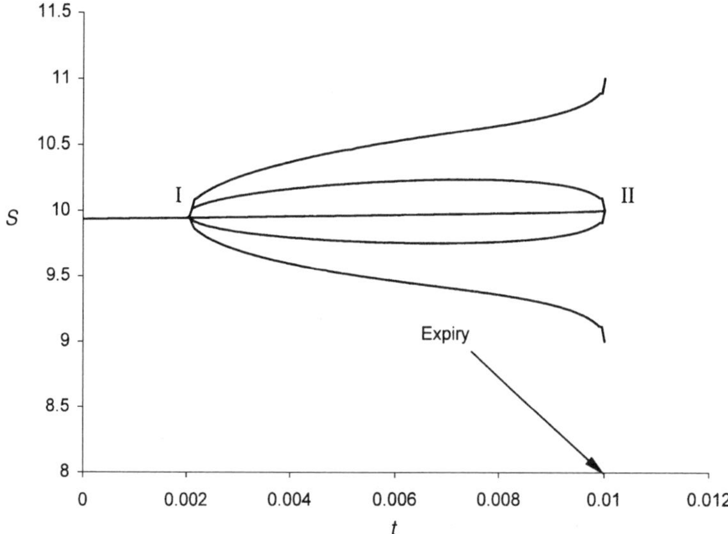

Figure 29.5 The time-dependent positions of the four points A, B, C and D for the put-replicating strategy.

---

[2] Deterministic jumps are not allowed in classical models of assets since they lead to arbitrage opportunities. We discuss this point later.

and D approach $E - \varepsilon$ and $E + \varepsilon$ respectively resulting in a curve looking like a tulip lying on its side. Note that all the boundary curves are confined to an area of order $(\varepsilon \times \varepsilon^2)$ around (E, T).

Points B and C act locally as absorbing boundaries. The appropriate boundary conditions are therefore

$$p(B, t) = 0 = p(C, t).$$

The boundary conditions for points A and D are not so obvious because μ_S and σ_S have singularities as the jump points B and C are approached. They can be derived from a conservation of probability argument (see Schönbucher (1994) for further details).

The boundary conditions at $S = 0$ and $S \to \infty$ are

$$p(0, t) = 0 \quad \text{and} \quad \lim_{S\to\infty} p(S, t) = 0.$$

29.7 NUMERICAL RESULTS

In this section I present numerical results for the solution of the forward equation in three cases. The parameters are as follows (unless otherwise stated): $E = 10$, $r = 0.1$, $\mu_x = 0.2$, $\sigma_x = 0.2$, and $\varepsilon = 1$.

The first example is the evolution of the probability density function in the absence of any feedback. Thus $\varepsilon = 0$. In Figure 29.6 is shown a three-dimensional plot of the probability density function against asset price and time. The starting condition is a delta function at $S = 10$. As time increases the curve flattens out as a lognormal density function. In Figure 29.7 is shown a contour map of this same function.

The first non-trivial case is a time-invariant trading strategy that is strong enough to give rise to the four new boundaries A, B, C and D. The time-independent addition to the demand, Δ, was taken to be that from a put-replicating trading strategy with time fixed at $t = T - 0.05$,

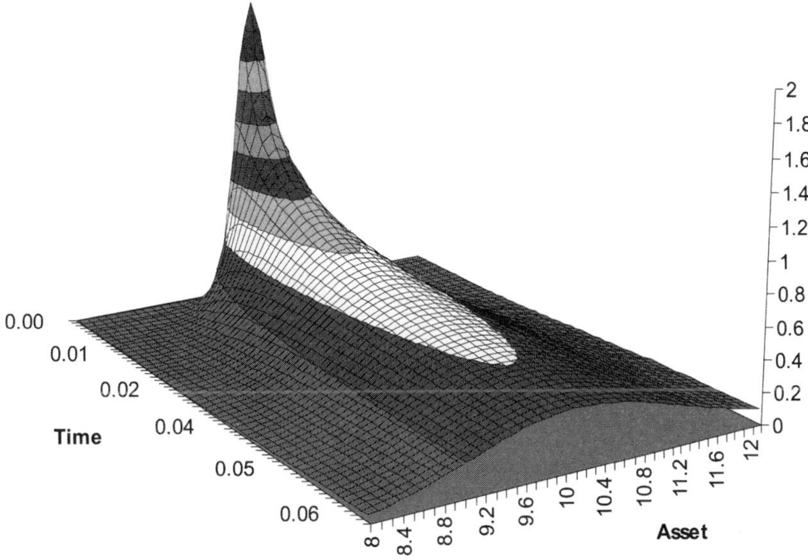

Figure 29.6 The probability density function for an asset with no feedback. The initial data is a delta function.

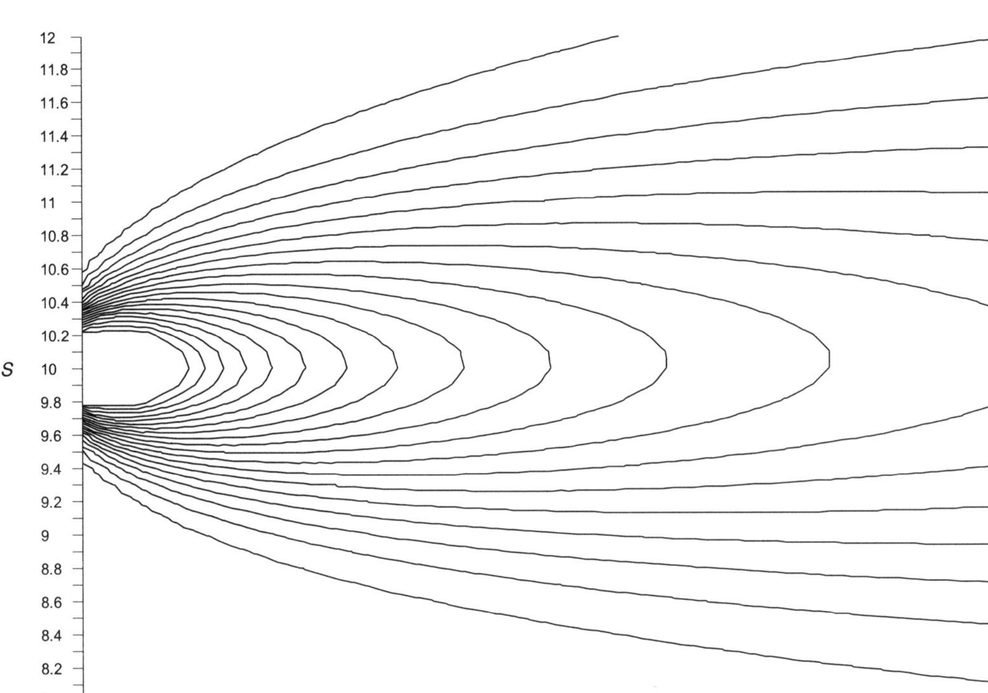

Figure 29.7 The contour plot of Figure 29.6.

shortly before expiry. The initial price is assumed to be known $S = 11$, thus the probability density function contains a delta function at $S = 11$. This case helps to visualize the effects of the boundaries. This may perhaps model the effect of a large number of investors all delta hedging using the delta of an option with the same strike but each with a different expiry date such that the overall effect of these hedgers is to add a time-independent function to the demand. This is the simplest case to consider since the coefficients in the forward equation are time independent.

The final case is simple put replication with only one investor moving the market. The trading strategy is the replication strategy for a European put option. This is one of the most popular trading strategies used by portfolio managers and of direct relevance for option pricing. The addition to the demand due to this one large investor is now time dependent.

Let's take a look at the last two examples in detail.

29.7.1 Time-independent Trading Strategy

Time-invariant hedging schemes are mainly used to maintain the general performance of the portfolio without the need to satisfy any precise conditions at fixed points in time (such as the potential liabilities from writing an option). Here we will use the delta of a European put at time 0.05 before expiry.

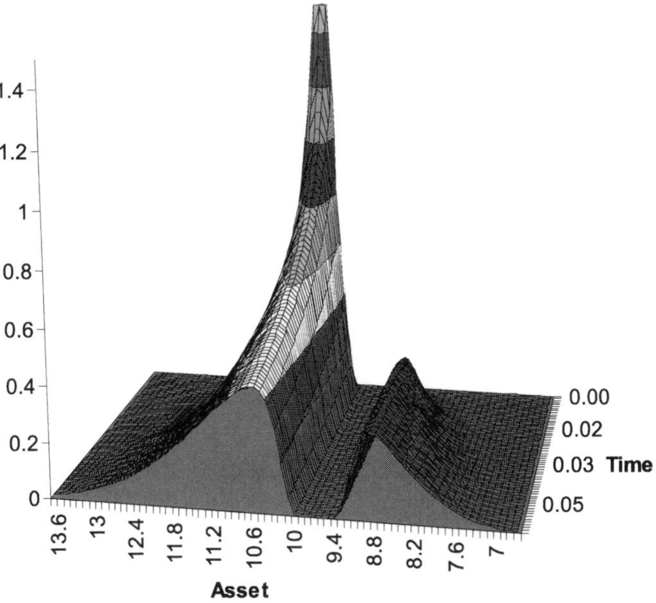

Figure 29.8 The probability density function for a time-independent trading strategy. The initial data is a delta function.

Figure 29.8 shows the full development of the probability density function according to the feedback model as time proceeds. At $t = 0$ the probability density function is a delta function at $S = 11$, meaning that the price at $t = 0$ is known to be 11. Later the probability density function spreads out. Figure 29.9 shows the contour plot for the probability density function. The contour plot shows very clearly the unattainable region, the 'corridor,' between asset values of approximately 9.6 and 10.3 which the asset price can never reach. This region is that between the two points previously labelled B and C. Since the replication strategy is time-independent this corridor does not change shape. Even though the starting value for the asset ($S = 11$) is above this region the asset can still reach values less than 9.6 by reaching the barrier C and jumping across to the point A. For more realistic values of ε this corridor is very narrow and, away from the corridor, is effectively only a small perturbation to the usual lognormal probability density function as shown in Figures 29.6 and 29.7.

29.7.2 Put Replication Trading

The more interesting case is the time-dependent put-replicating trading and the development in the area around the 'Tulip curve.'

The probability density function is shown in Figure 29.10 and the corresponding contour plot is shown in Figure 29.11. Since this replication strategy is genuinely time dependent the corridor that we saw in the above example is now the tulip shape shown in Figure 29.5 The unattainable barren region (the center of the 'Tulip curve') is most easily seen on the contour plot.

In this example, the asset price starts off at $S = 10$ and then evolves. The effect of the replication strategy is felt immediately but the tulip curve itself does not appear until about $t = 0.03$. At this time there appears the barren region around the exercise price (10) which the asset price

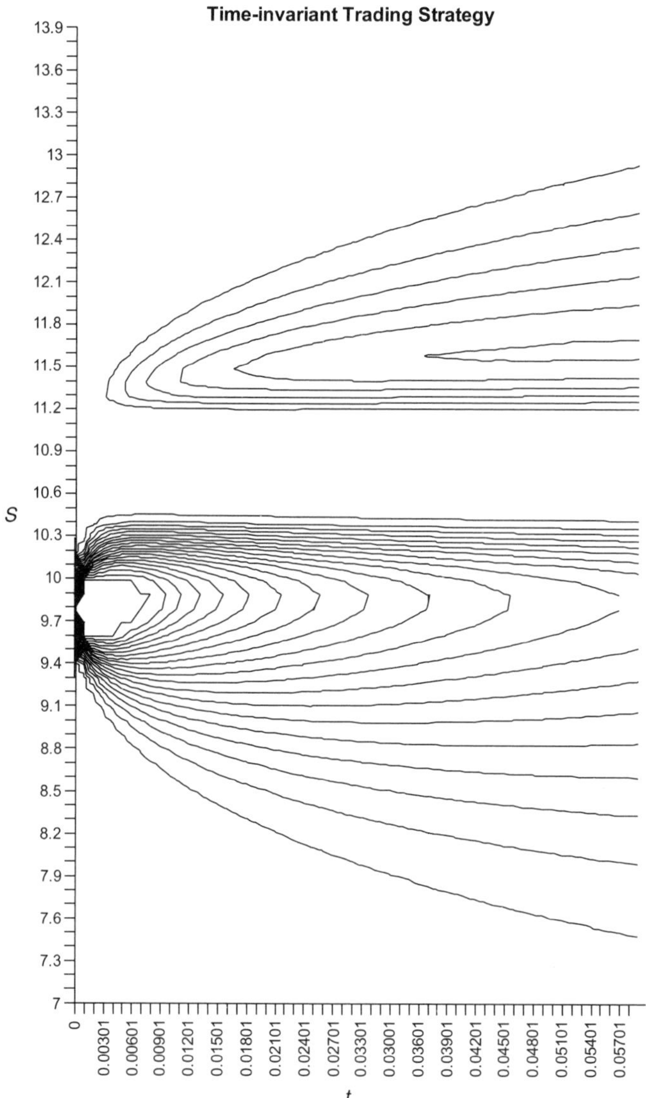

Figure 29.9 The contour plot of Figure 29.8.

avoids. This zone is shown most clearly in the contour plot of Figure 29.11. After expiry of the replicated option, $t = 0.04$, the barren zone disappears and all values of S are attainable.

29.8 SUMMARY

The influence of trading strategies has been the subject of much discussion but—apart from empirical studies—little theoretical research. In this chapter we have seen a way to formally incorporate trading strategies into the stochastic process followed by the underlying asset.

Many trading strategies that are used today are derived from replicating strategies for derivative securities. This class of trading strategies is also central to the theory of option

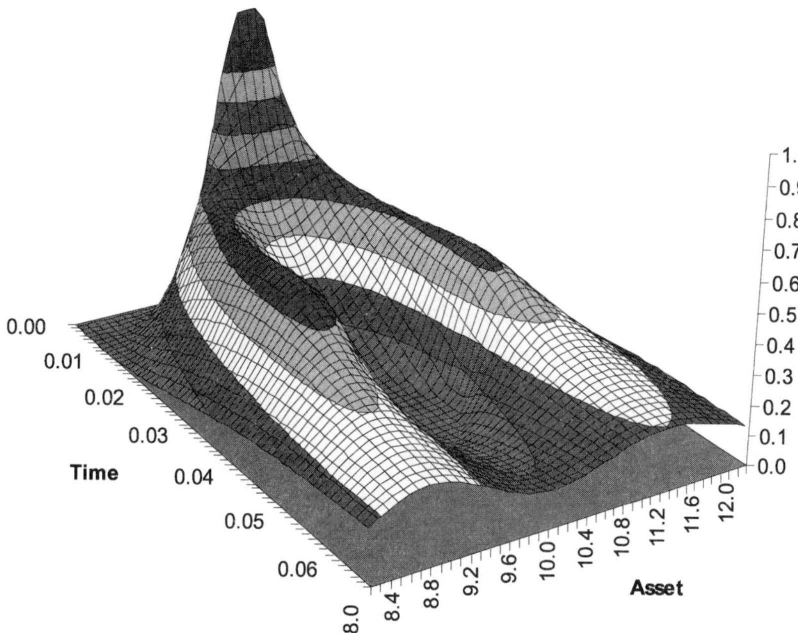

Figure 29.10 The probability density function for put replication; the initial data is a delta function.

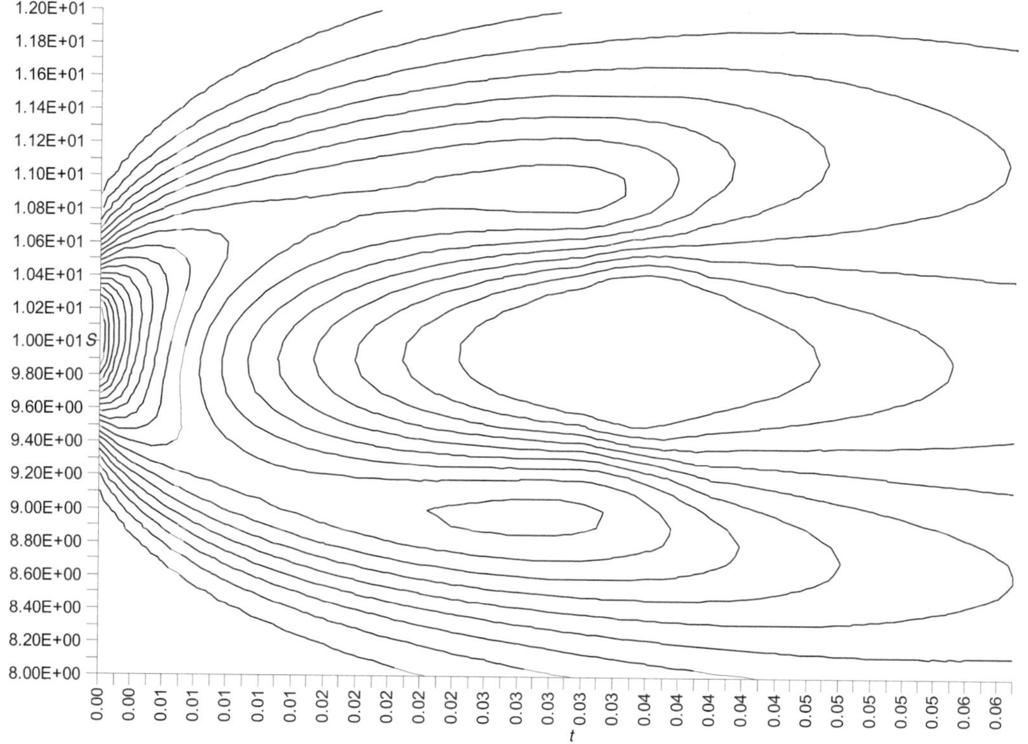

Figure 29.11 The contour plot of Figure 29.10.

pricing. We found that the securities whose replication destabilizes the market and their effects on the market can be described by their payoff profile and its gamma.

The effects are especially strong in markets with low liquidity and can even induce discontinuities in the price process. Such price discontinuities are not allowed in classical models of asset prices since they lead to arbitrage. The present model does allow such arbitrage and this can be justified in several ways. First, such effects as I describe do occur in practice and traders with a knowledge of the positions of other market players and their hedging requirements can take advantage of this knowledge. Second, this is just a simple first attempt at modeling feedback. It may be possible to remove certain arbitrage opportunites by incorporating elasticity in the response of the market price to large trades. The barren zone that we have found above may still be unstable, but no longer unattainable.

FURTHER READING

- See Schönbucher (1994), Schönbucher & Wilmott (1995 a, b), Frey & Stremme (1995) and Sircar & Papanicolaou (1996) for further examples and analysis of feedback models.
- The book by O'Hara (1995) discusses many of the issues in market microstructure.
- Taleb (1997) discusses the reality of options markets, and feedback, market manipulation and discontinuous price paths are part of that reality. A particularly interesting account of the behavior of asset prices close to the barriers of knock-out options is given there.
- Porter & Smith (1994) describe some laboratory experiments in which simulated stock market trading led to interesting bubbles and crashes.

EXERCISES

1. If x follows the stochastic process

$$dx = \mu_x\,dt + \sigma_x\,dX,$$

and

$$(x - S) + \varepsilon\Delta(S, t) = 0,$$

then show that

$$dS = \mu_S\,dt + \sigma_S\,dX,$$

where

$$\mu_S = \frac{1}{1 - \varepsilon\dfrac{\partial\Delta}{\partial S}}\left(\mu_x + \varepsilon\left(\frac{\partial\Delta}{\partial t} + \frac{1}{2}\frac{\sigma_x^2}{\left(1 - \varepsilon\dfrac{\partial\Delta}{\partial S}\right)^2}\frac{\partial^2\Delta}{\partial S^2}\right)\right),$$

and

$$\sigma_S = \frac{\sigma_x}{1 - \varepsilon\dfrac{\partial\Delta}{\partial S}}.$$

2. Set up the problem that we would have to solve to price an option in the Black–Scholes framework with a given trading strategy, when the effect of feedback is taken into account. What happens at the jump points? If the trading strategy was also, *a priori*, unknown, how would we go about solving the system?

CHAPTER 30

static hedging

In this Chapter...

- matching a contract's value at a set of points using standard contracts
- how nonlinear equations make a mockery of 'parameter fitting'
- statically hedging with traded options to improve your prices
- how to optimally statically hedge to make the most out of your contract

30.1 INTRODUCTION

Delta hedging is a wonderful concept. It leads to preference-free pricing (risk neutrality) and a risk-elimination strategy that can be used in practice. There are quite a few problems, though, on both the practical and the theoretical side. In practice, hedging must be done at discrete times and is costly. These issues were discussed in Chapters 20 and 21. Sometimes one has to buy or sell a prohibitively large number of the underlying in order to follow the theory. This is a problem with barrier options and options with discontinuous payoff.

On the theoretical side, we have to accept that the model for the underlying is not perfect, at the very least we do not know parameter values accurately. Delta hedging alone leaves us very exposed to the model. This is model risk.

Many of these problems can be reduced or eliminated if we follow a strategy of static hedging as well as delta hedging: buy or sell more liquid contracts to reduce the cashflows in the original contract. The static hedge is put into place now, and left until expiry.[1]

30.2 STATIC REPLICATING PORTFOLIO

The value of a complex derivative is usually very model dependent. Often these contracts are difficult to delta hedge, either because of transaction costs in the underlying or because of discontinuities in the payoff or the delta. Problems with delta hedging can be minimized by **static hedging** or **static replication**, a procedure which can reduce transaction costs, benefit from economies of scale and, importantly, reduce model risk.

There are two forms of static hedging that I want to discuss here. The first form of static hedging is about constructing a portfolio of traded options whose value matches the 'target' contract's value as closely as possible at a set of dates and asset values. The second form depends crucially on the governing equation being nonlinear.

[1] In practice, if conditions become favorable, one can reassess the static hedge. It is not set in stone.

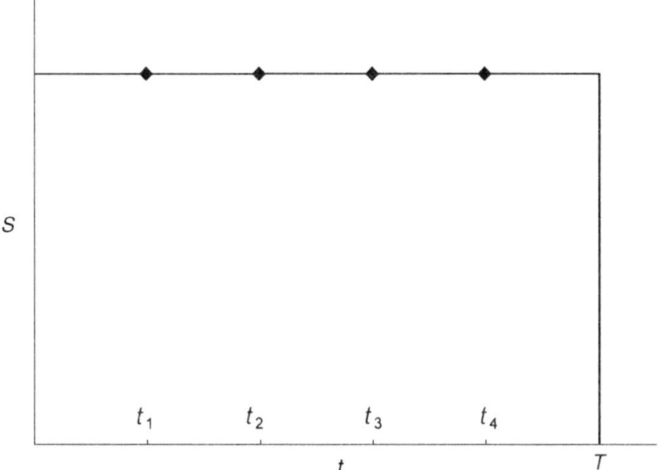

Figure 30.1 The target contract is to be replicated at the marked points.

The first idea is simple, and the implementation not much harder. Referring to Figure 30.1, the aim is to construct a portfolio of vanilla puts and calls, say, to have the same value as the target contract at expiry and at the points marked in the figure.

As a concrete example, suppose that the target contract has a call payoff at expiry T, but expires worthless on the upper boundary marked in the figure. This is an up-and-out call option. Thus on the upper boundary, our target contract has value zero. We have sold this contract and we want to statically hedge it by buying vanilla calls and puts. That is, we want to match the call payoff at T and have zero value on the boundary. This is easy. To match the payoff at expiry we buy a single call option with the same strike as the knock-out call. Ideally, we would like to have zero value on the remainder of the boundary, but this would involve us buying an infinite number of vanilla options. It is natural, therefore, since there are only a finite number of traded contracts, to match the portfolio value at the expiry dates of the traded options. In the figure, this means matching values at the four points on the upper boundary. Typically this will require us to buy four more vanilla options, in quantitities to be decided.

We have matched the payoff at expiry with a single call option. Now, working back from expiry, value until time t_4 the contract consisting of the knock-out call held short and the single long vanilla call. In this 'valuation' we use whatever model we like. We use the model to give us the theoretical value of the two-contract portfolio at time t_4 at the point marked in Figure 30.1. We want to buy or sell further vanilla contracts to make the net portfolio value zero at this point. The obvious contracts to choose for this hedging are calls with expiry at T and strikes such that they are out-of-the money for all values of S on the target-option boundary at time T. We need only one contract to achieve this, an out-of-the money call, say.

Now value this new portfolio (it now contains our original target contract and two vanillas) back until time t_3. We can find its value at the marked point at this time. To hedge this value buy or sell vanilla contracts *that expire at time* t_4, that are out-of-the money for all values of S within the target-option boundary at time t_4, and such that between them they make the portfolio value zero on the upper boundary at time t_3. We now hold three options in our static hedge (plus the target contract) and are 'hedged' from t_3 until T. In this way we work backwards until the present.

We can obviously include as many expiry dates as exist in traded contracts, and the finer their resolution the better will be our static hedge. As long as we only use a finite number of options in our static hedge, then there will be some residual risk that is not statically hedged. We can either delta hedge this, or if it is small and with bounded downside, we could leave it unhedged (assuming we have allowed for this when we sold the target contract).

I have illustrated the idea with a barrier option hedged with calls. Obviously the idea can be extended in any number of ways. One possibility is to use one-touch options; these are no longer thought of as being exotic and are actively traded.

Static hedging is obviously a useful technique. It is not perfect since there is still some exposure to the model. We had to value the portfolio using some 'model,' and the accuracy of the hedge is reflected to some degree in the accuracy of the model. However, the resulting portfolio is not as model dependent as a contract that is only delta hedged.

In the rest of this chapter we discuss static hedging when the governing equation is nonlinear. Some of these nonlinear models get a lot closer to model-independent pricing, at least they are 'parameter-insensitive' models. Note that the idea of 'optimal' static hedging that we will be seeing, can also be applied to the above replicating portfolio: it may be cheaper to statically hedge with one contract than with another.

30.3 STATIC HEDGING: NONLINEAR GOVERNING EQUATION

Many of the models described in this part of the book are nonlinear. To summarize, these models are the following.

- Transaction costs: Purchase and sale of the underlying for delta hedging when there are costs leads to nonlinear equations for the option value. There are many models, all of them nonlinear. See Chapter 21.
- Uncertain parameters: When parameters, such as volatility, dividend rate, interest rate, are permitted to lie in a range, options can be valued in a worst-case scenario, for example the model of Avellaneda, Levy & Parás and Lyons. The governing equation for uncertain volatility is mathematically identical to the Hoggard–Whalley–Wilmott transaction cost model. See Chapter 24.
- Crash modeling: Allowing the underlying to jump and valuing contracts in a worst-case scenario, with no probabilistic assumptions about the crash, leads to a nonlinear equation. This contrasts with the linear classical jump-diffusion model. See Chapter 27.

- Speculating with options: Some of the strategies for the 'valuation' of contracts when speculating lead to nonlinear equations. For example, optimal closure of an option position has a linear governing equation but the problem is nonlinear because it has a free boundary. Choosing to hedge or speculate also leads to a nonlinear governing equation. See Chapter 28.

Later, in Chapter 40, we will see a non-probabilistic interest rate model that is nonlinear. All of the ideas of this chapter can be applied to that model.

30.4 NONLINEAR EQUATIONS

Many of the new partial differential equations that we have derived are nonlinear. This nonlinearity has many important consequences. Most obviously, we must be careful when we refer to an option position, making it clear whether it is held long or short. For example, for a long call we have the final condition

$$V(S,T)=\max(S-E,0)$$

and for a short call

$$V(S,T)=-\max(S-E,0).$$

Because of the nonlinearity, the value of a portfolio of options is not necessarily the same as the sum of the values of the individual components. This is a very important point to understand: the value of a contract depends on what else is in the portfolio.

These two points are key to the importance of nonlinear pricing equations: they give us a bid-offer spread on option prices, and they allow *optimal* static hedging.

For the rest of this chapter we discuss the pricing and hedging of options when the governing equation is nonlinear. The ideas are applicable to any of the nonlinear models mentioned above. We use the notation $V_{NL}(S,t)$ to mean the solution of the model in question, whichever model it may be. So that the explanation of the issues does not get too confusing I will always refer to the concrete example of the uncertain volatility/transaction cost model, but remember *the ideas apply equally well to the other models.*

30.5 PRICING WITH A NONLINEAR EQUATION

One of the interesting points about nonlinear models is the prediction of a spread between long and short prices. If the model gives different values for long and short then this is in effect a spread on option prices. This can be seen as either a good or a bad point. It is good because it is realistic, spreads exist in practice. It only becomes bad when this spread is too large to make the model useful.

Let us consider a realistic, uncertain volatility/transaction cost model example. The reader is reminded that this model is

$$\frac{\partial V_{NL}}{\partial t}+\tfrac{1}{2}\sigma(\Gamma)^2S^2\frac{\partial^2 V_{NL}}{\partial S^2}+rS\frac{\partial V_{NL}}{\partial S}-rV_{NL}=0 \tag{30.1}$$

where

$$\Gamma=\frac{\partial^2 V_{NL}}{\partial S^2}$$

and

$$\sigma(\Gamma)=\begin{cases}\sigma^+ & \text{if } \Gamma<0\\ \sigma^- & \text{if } \Gamma>0.\end{cases}$$

(But we are using it as a proxy for any of the nonlinear equations.)

This model can predict very wide spreads on options. For example, suppose that we have a European call, strike price \$100, today's asset price is \$100, there are six months to expiry, no dividends on the underlying and a spot interest rate of 5%. We will assume that the volatility lies between 20% and 30%. We are lucky with this example. Because the gamma is single-signed for a vanilla call, we can calculate the values for long and short calls, assuming this range for volatility, directly from the Black–Scholes formulae. A long call position is worth \$6.89 (the Black–Scholes value using a volatility of 20%) and a short call is worth \$9.63 (the Black–Scholes value using a volatility of 30%). This spread is much larger than that in the market, and is due to the uncertain volatility. The market prices may, for example, be based on a volatility between 24% and 26%. The uncertain parameter model is useless unless it can produce tighter spreads. In the next section I show how the simple idea of static hedging can be used to reduce these spreads significantly. The idea was originally due to Avellaneda & Parás.

30.6 STATIC HEDGING

Suppose that we want to sell an option with some payoff that does not exist as a traded contract. (For the moment think in terms of a European contract with no path-dependent features; we will generalize later.) We want to determine how low a price we can sell it for (or how high a price we can buy it for), with the constraint that we guarantee that we will not lose money as long as our range for volatility is not breached. There are two related reasons for wanting to solve this problem. If we can sell it for more than this minimum then we are guaranteed to make money, and if our spread is tight then we will have more customers.

I motivate the idea of static hedging with a simple example. Suppose that options on a particular stock are traded with strikes of \$90 and \$110 and with six months to expiry. The stock price is currently \$100. However, we have been asked to quote prices for long and short positions in \$100 calls, again with six months before expiry. This call is *not* traded.

As above, assume that volatility lies between 20% and 30%. Remember that our pessimistic prices for the 100 call were \$9.63 to sell and \$6.85 to buy, calculated using the Black–Scholes formulae with volatilities 30% and 20% respectively. This spread is so large that we will not get the business. However, we are missing one vital point: the 90 and 110 calls are trading; can't we take advantage of them in some way?

Suppose that the market prices the 90 and 110 calls with an implied volatility of 25% (forget bid-offer spreads for the moment). The market prices, i.e. the Black–Scholes prices, are therefore 14.42 and 4.22 respectively. These numbers are shown in Table 30.1. The question marks are to emphasize that we can buy or sell as many of these contracts as we want, but in a fashion which will be made clear shortly. Shouldn't our quoted prices for the 100 call reflect the availability of contracts with which we can hedge?

Consider first the price at which we would sell the 100 call. If we sell the 100, and 'statically hedge' it by buying 0.5 of the 90 and 0.5 of the 110, then we have a residual payoff as shown in Figure 30.2. We call this a static hedge because we put it in place now and do not expect to change it. This contrasts with the delta hedge, for which we expect to hedge frequently (and would like to hedge continuously).

Table 30.1 Available contracts.

Strike	Expiry	Bid	Ask	Quantity
90	180 days	14.42	14.42	?
110	180 days	4.22	4.22	?

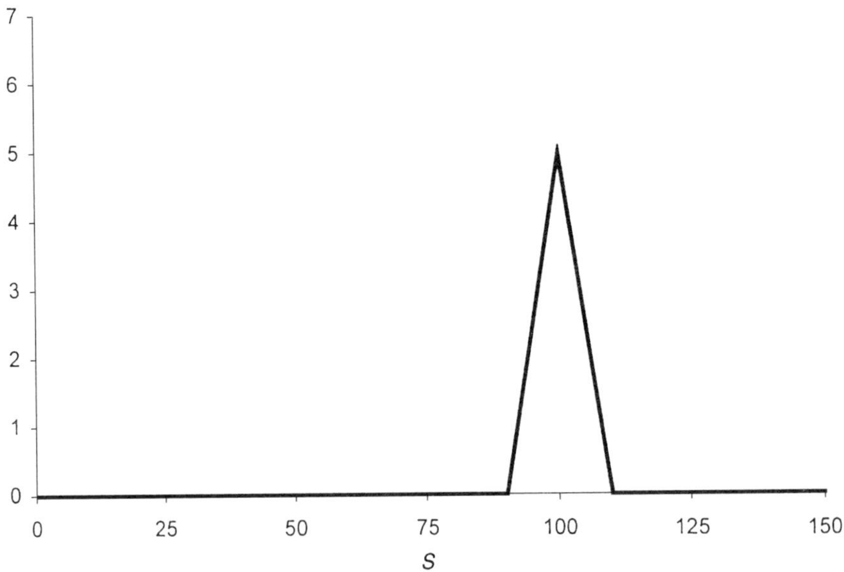

Figure 30.2 The residual risk after hedging a 100 call with 0.5 each of the 90 and 110.

The statically-hedged portfolio has a much smaller payoff than the original unhedged call, as shown in Figure 30.2. It is this *new portfolio* that we value by solving the nonlinear Equation (30.1), and that we must delta hedge; I emphasize this last point, *the residual payoff must be delta hedged*. To value the residual payoff in our uncertain parameter framework we solve Equation (30.2) with final condition

$$V_{NL}(S,T) = -\max(S-100,0) + \tfrac{1}{2}(\max(S-90,0) + \max(S-110,0)).$$

Let us see what effect this has on the price at which we would *sell* the 100 call. for the static hedge made up of 0.5 of each of the 90 and 110 calls.

First of all, observe that we have paid

$$0.5 \times \$14.42 + 0.5 \times \$4.22 = \$9.32$$

for the static hedge made up of 0.5 of each of the 90 and 110 calls.

Now, solve Equation (30.1) using the payoff shown in Figure 30.2 as the final condition. The solution gives a value for the residual contract today of \$0.58.

The net value of the call is therefore

$$\$9.32 - \$0.58 = \$8.74.$$

To determine how much we should pay to *buy* the 100 call we take as our starting point the sale of 0.5 of each of the 90 and 110 calls. This nets us \$9.32. But now we solve Equation (30.1) using the *negative* of the payoff shown in Figure 30.2 as the final condition; the effect of the nonlinearity is different from the previous case because $\sigma(\Gamma)$ takes different values in different places in S, t-space. We get a value of \$1.96 for the hedged position. Thus we find that we would pay

$$\$9.32 - \$1.96 = \$7.36.$$

Note how the use of a very simple static hedge has reduced the spread from \$6.85–9.6 to \$7.36–8.74. This is a substantial improvement, as it represents a volatility range of 22–27%; while our initial estimate for the volatility range was 20–30%. The reason for the smaller spread is that the residual portfolio has a smaller absolute spread, only \$0.58–1.96 and this is because it has a much smaller payoff than the unhedged 100 call.

In the trivial case where the option on which we are quoting is also traded then we would find that our quoted price was the same as the market price. This is because we would hedge one for one and the residual payoff, which we would normally delta hedge, would be identically zero. This means that we always match market prices, 'fitting' as described in Chapter 22 is redundant.

In the above example we decided to hedge the 100 call using 0.5 of each of the 90 and 110 calls. What prompted this choice? In this case we chose the numbers 0.5 for each option purely on the grounds of symmetry: it made the residual payoff look simple (a typical mathematician's choice). There was no reason why we should not choose other numbers. Suppose, for example, we decided to hedge with 0.4 of the 90 call and 0.7 of the 110. Would this have an effect on the value of our 100 call? Since our problem is nonlinear *the value of our OTC option depends on the combination of options with which we hedge*. So, generally speaking, we expect a different OTC option value if we choose a different static hedge portfolio. Of course, we now ask 'If we get different values for an option depending on what other contracts we hedge it with then is there a *best* static hedge?'

30.7 OPTIMAL STATIC HEDGING

Suppose that we want to find the lowest price for which we can sell a particular OTC or 'exotic' option with payoff $\Lambda(S)$. Suppose that we can hedge our exotic with a variety of traded options, of which there are n. These options will have payoffs (at the same date as our exotic to keep things simple for the moment) which we call

$$\Lambda_i(S).$$

At this point we can introduce bid and offer prices for the traded options: C_i^+ is the ask price of the ith option and C_i^- the bid, with $C_i^- < C_i^+$.

Now we set up our statically hedged portfolio: we will have λ_i of each option in our hedged portfolio. The cost of setting up this static hedge is

$$\sum_i \lambda_i C_i(\lambda_i),$$

where

$$C_i(\lambda_i) = \begin{cases} C_i^+ & \text{if } \lambda_i > 0 \\ C_i^- & \text{if } \lambda_i < 0 \end{cases}.$$

If $\lambda_i > 0$ then we have a positive quantity of option i at the offer price in the market, C_i^+; if $\lambda_i < 0$ then we have a negative quantity of option i at the bid price in the market, C_i^-.

We let $V^-(S,t)$ be the pessimistic value of our *hedged* position. The residual payoff for our statically hedged option is

$$V^-(S,T) = \Lambda(S) + \sum_i \lambda_i \Lambda_i(S).$$

Now we solve (30.1) with this as final data, to find the *net* value of our position (today, at time $t = 0$, say) as

$$V^-(S(0),0) - \sum_i \lambda_i C_i(\lambda_i) = F(\lambda_1, \ldots, \lambda_n).$$

This is a mathematical representation of the type of problem we solved in our first hedging example; $V^-(S,T)$ was the residual payoff shown in Figure 30.2.

Our goal now is to choose the λ_i to minimize $F(\cdots)$ if we are selling the exotic, and maximize if buying. (Thus the best hedge in the two cases will usually be different.) This is what we mean by 'optimal' static hedging.

Continuing with our earlier example, what are the optimal static hedges for long and short positions? Buying 0.5 of each of the two calls to hedge the short 100 call we find a marginal value of \$8.74 for the 100 call. This is actually a very good hedge. Slightly better, and optimal, is to buy 0.51 of each call, giving a marginal value of \$8.73. The optimal hedge for a long position is vastly different. We should sell 1.07 of the 90 call and sell 0.34 of the 110 call. The marginal value of the 100 call is then \$7.47.

Sometimes the results are not always immediately obvious. This is because traditionally, when we think of hedging, we tend to choose hedges so as to minimize the risky payoff. In the above algorithm the cost of the hedge plays as important a role as its effect on the residual payoff. In an extreme case, if we had an option with an implied volatility outside our best-guess range then the algorithm would tell us to buy or sell an infinite amount of that option: the optimization algorithm finds arbitrage opportunities.

There are two other aspects to this static hedging. The first is that we are not necessarily restricted to hedging with options of the same maturity as the contract in question; they can have shorter or longer maturities. The optimization procedure will still find the best choice. The second point is that the static hedge need not be fixed. We could return at any time (or even continuously in theory) to examine the choice of optimal hedge portfolio. If the optimal hedge changes then, of course, we can buy and/or sell options to improve the worst-case value. This may not happen very often if the bid-offer spread on the traded options is large, but if it is negligible then the static hedge may often be rebalanced. However, this depends on the evolution of the implied volatilities, something which we are deliberately not modeling or predicting. If we do decide to change the static hedge then this is because we can improve the worst-case option value and thus we 'lock in' more guaranteed profit.

In this section we have concentrated on hedging unusual payoffs, or non-exchange traded contracts, with vanillas having the same expiry dates. The ideas are easily extended to hedging with options having other expiry dates, either before or after the expiry of the main contract. This is simply done via jump conditions across each expiry date. As the nonlinear diffusion equation is solved backwards in time we must make the portfolio of options jump by the relevant payoff.

As a final thought in this section, observe how I never said that we 'believed' the price of market traded contracts, only that they *may possibly turn out to be correct*. This is in contrast to the less satisfying philosophy of Chapter 22 where I showed how to 'fit' the volatility structure to match traded prices.

It is a more complicated matter to extend the ideas to path-dependent options. In the following section I show how this is done for barrier options.

30.8 HEDGING PATH-DEPENDENT OPTIONS WITH VANILLA OPTIONS

Valuation with a nonlinear model and optimal static hedging are more complicated for barrier options (and other path-dependent contracts) because at the onset of the contract we do not know whether it will still exist by the final expiry date: we may start out with an excellent static hedge for a call payoff but after a few months we may find ourselves using the same hedge for a nonexistent option.

30.8.1 Barrier Options

The trick to valuing barrier options is to realize that there are two possible states for the option: untriggered and triggered. We can go from the former to the latter but not *vice versa*. Whatever static hedge we choose must take this into account. I introduce the terms 'active' and 'retired' to describe options that still exist and have been triggered, respectively.

Let $V_{NL}(S, t, 0)$ and $V_{NL}(S, t, 1)$ be the values of the portfolio of options before and after the barrier has been triggered. Both of these functions satisfy Equation (30.1), with final conditions at time T depending on the details of the option contracts. At the barrier the values of the two portfolios will be the same.

As a first example suppose that we hold a down-and-out barrier call only, i.e. there is no static hedge, and after the option is retired we hold an empty portfolio. The problem for $V_{NL}(S, t, 1)$ is simply Equation (30.1) with zero final conditions so that

$$V_{NL}(S, t, 1) = 0.$$

Of course, the solution for $V_{NL}(S, t, 1)$ is zero, since it corresponds to an empty portfolio. The problem for $V_{NL}(S, t, 0)$ is Equation (30.1) with

$$V_{NL}(S, T, 0) = \max(S - E_1, 0).$$

Finally, on the barrier

$$V_{NL}(X, t, 0) = V_{NL}(X, t, 1) = 0.$$

The problem for $V_{NL}(S, t, 1)$ only holds for $S > X$.

Now consider the slightly more complicated problem of hedging the barrier call with a vanilla call, we will hold short λ of a vanilla call, both contracts having the same expiry (although this can easily be generalized). The strike price is E_2. Thus we have hedged a barrier call with a vanilla call. The problem for $V_{NL}(S, t, 1)$ is simply Equation (30.1) with

$$V_{NL}(S, T, 1) = -\lambda \max(S - E_2, 0).$$

The problem for $V_{NL}(S, t, 0)$ is Equation (30.1) with

$$V_{NL}(S, T, 0) = \max(S - E_1, 0) - \lambda \max(S - E_2, 0).$$

Finally, on the barrier

$$V_{NL}(X, t, 0) = V_{NL}(X, t, 1).$$

The problem for $V_{NL}(S, t, 0)$ is to be solved for all S, but the problem for $V_{NL}(S, t, 1)$ only holds for $S > X$.

The ideas of optimal static hedging carry over; for example, what is the optimal choice for λ in the above?

Example

The stock price is \$100, volatility is assumed to lie between 20% and 30%, the spot interest rate is 5%. What is the optimal static hedge, using vanilla calls with strike \$110 and costing \$4.22, for a long position in a down-and-out barrier call with strike \$90? Both options expire in six months. In other words, what is the optimal number of vanilla calls to buy or sell to get as much value as possible out of the barrier option?

With no static hedge in place we simply solve the above problem with $V^-(S, t, 1) = 0$, since if the option knocks out that is the end of the story. In this case we find that the barrier option is worth \$6.32.

With a hedge of -0.47 of the vanillas the barrier is now worth \$6.6. This is the optimal static hedge.

30.8.2 Pricing and Optimally Hedging a Portfolio of Barrier Options

The pricing of a *portfolio* of barriers is a particularly interesting problem in the nonlinear equation framework. Again, this is best illustrated by an example. What is the worst value for a portfolio of one down-and-out call struck at \$100 with a barrier at \$90 and an up-and-in put struck at \$110 with a barrier at \$120? The volatility lies between 20 and 30%, the spot interest rate is 5%, there are no dividends, there are six months to expiry and the underlying asset has value \$102.

The first step is to realize that instead of there being two states for the portfolio (as in the above where the single barrier is either active or retired), now there are *four* states: each of the two barrier options can be either active or retired. In general, for n barrier options we have 2^n states; the vanilla component of the portfolio is, of course, always active. As long as the barriers are not intermittent then there is hierarchy of barrier options that can be exploited to reduce the computational time dramatically. This hierarchy exists because the triggering of one barrier means that barriers closer in are also triggered. This issue is discussed by Avellaneda & Buff (1997).

Returning to the two-option example, the four states are:

1. Both options are active; this is the initial state.
2. If the asset rises to 120 without first falling to 90 then the up barrier option is retired.
3. If the asset falls to 90 before rising to 120 then the down barrier option is retired.
4. If both barriers are triggered then both options are retired. The only active options will be any vanillas in the static hedge.

To solve this problem we must introduce the function $V_{NL}(S, t; i, j)$. The portfolio value with both options active is $V_{NL}(S, t; 0, 0)$, with the down-and-out option retired but the up-and-in still active $V_{NL}(S, t; 1, 0)$, with the down option active but the up retired $V_{NL}(S, t; 0, 1)$ and with both options retired $V_{NL}(S, t; 1, 1)$. In the absence of any static hedge, the problem to solve is Equation (30.1) for each V_{NL} with final conditions

- $V_{NL}(S, T; 0, 0) = \max(S - 90, 0)$ (since at expiry, if both options are active only the down-and-out call pays off),
- $V_{NL}(S, T; 1, 0) = 0$ (if the down-and-out has been triggered it has no pay off),
- $V_{NL}(S, T; 0, 1) = \max(S - 90, 0) + \max(120 - S, 0)$ (if the up knocks in it has the put payoff) and finally
- $V_{NL}(S, T; 1, 1) = \max(120 - S, 0)$ (if both options are triggered the payoff is that for the 'in' option).

The retirement of an option is expressed through the boundary conditions

- $V_{NL}(90, t; 0, 0) = V_{NL}(90, t; 1, 0)$ and $V_{NL}(90, t; 0, 1) = V_{NL}(90, t; 1, 1)$ (the option value just before knock-out is equal to that just after, regardless of the status of the in option),
- $V_{NL}(120, t; 0, 0) = V_{NL}(120, t; 0, 1)$ and $V_{NL}(120, t; 1, 0) = V_{NL}(120, t; 1, 1)$ (the option value just before knock-in is equal to that just after regardless of the status of the out option).

30.9 THE MATHEMATICS OF OPTIMIZATION

We have encountered several nonlinear problems, and will meet some more later on. I have explained how the nonlinearity of these models allows static hedging to be achieved in an optimal fashion. Mathematically this amounts to finding the values of parameters such that some function is maximized. This is an example of an **optimization problem**. In this section I will briefly describe some of the issues involved in optimization problems and suggest a couple of methods for the solution.

Typically we are concerned with a maximization or a minimization. And since the minimization of a function is the same as the maximization of its negative, I will only talk about maximization problems. We will have some function to maximize, over a set of variables. Let's call the variables $\lambda_1, \dots, \lambda_N$ and the function $f(\lambda_1, \dots, \lambda_N)$. Note that there are N variables so that we are trying to find the maximum over an N-dimensional space. In our financial problems we have, for example, a set of λs representing the quantities of hedging contracts and the function f is the value of our target contract.

There are two kinds of maximum, **local** and **global**. There may be many local maxima, each the highest point in its neighbourhood, but it may not be the highest point over all of the N-dimensional space. What we really want to find is the global maximum, the point having the highest function value over the whole of the space of the variables. In Figure 30.3 is shown a one-dimensional function together with a few local maxima but only one global maximum. Whatever technique we use for finding the maximum must be able to find the global maximum.

30.9.1 Downhill Simplex Method

The first method I want to describe is the **downhill simplex method**. This method is not particularly fast, but it is very robust and easy to program. If there is more than one local maximum then it may not find the global maximum, instead it might get stuck at a local high spot. I will describe a way around this weakness later. Traditionally, one talks about function minimization, and so the word 'downhill' makes sense. Because our problems are typically ones of maximization perhaps we should use the word 'uphill.'

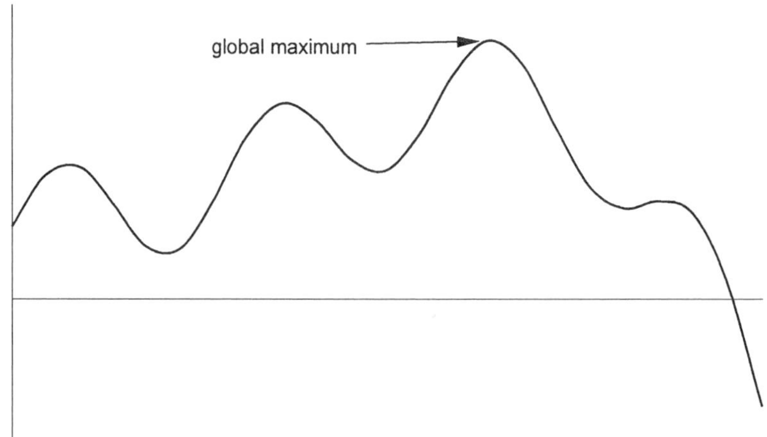

Figure 30.3 Local and global maxima.

A **simplex** in N dimensions is made up of $N + 1$ vertices. In two dimensions this gives a triangle, in three a tetrahedron. The downhill simplex method starts with an initial simplex, think of it as a ballpark guess for the position of the maximum. Suppose that the $N + 1$ vertices of this simplex are at the points given by the vectors $\boldsymbol{\lambda}_i$ for $i = 1, \dots, N + 1$. Calculate the values of the function at each of the vertices, these are $f(\boldsymbol{\lambda}_i)$. One of these values will be lower than the other N values. If this value is particularly bad, i.e., low, perhaps we should look far away from this vertex for another guess at the maximum. One systematic way of doing this is to reflect the worst point in the 'plane' made up by the remaining N points. This is easy to see for the tetrahedral simplex shown in Figure 30.4. In this figure (a) is the initial state of the simplex. The worst/lowest point is reflected in the 'base' of the tetrahedron resulting in (b). If the function evaluated at the new vertex is even better/higher than all of the values of the function at the other (old) vertices, then expand the tetrahedron a bit to exploit this. This gives (c). On the other hand, if the new vertex has a function value that is worse than the second lowest then the tetrahedron should be contracted as shown in (d), otherwise the new simplex would be worse than before. Finally, if the one-dimensional contraction doesn't make things better then the simplex is contracted about the best vertex in all dimensions simultaneously; this is (e). This algorithm sees the simplex tumbling over itself, rising to the peak of the function where it begins to contract. The process is repeated until the simplex has shrunk enough to give a sufficiently precise estimate of the maximum.

The following code finds a local maximum of the function `func` in `N` dimensions. The code is a translation of the C code in Press et al. into VB. The number of dimensions, the maximum number of iterations `MaxIts` and the tolerance `tol` must be input, as must the initial simplex. The initial guess goes in the $N + 1$ by N array `FirstGuess`, each row is a different vertex.

The subroutine `Ranking` finds the value of the function at, and the index of, the two lowest and the highest vertices. The subroutine `FindCenter` finds the center of the simplex, given by

$$\frac{1}{N+1}\sum_{i=1}^{N+1}\boldsymbol{\lambda}_i.$$

The subroutine `Deform` reflects the lowest point in the opposite face of the simplex by an amount `d`. If `d` $= 1$ there is no reflection, if `d` $= 1/N + 1$ then vertex goes to the center of the

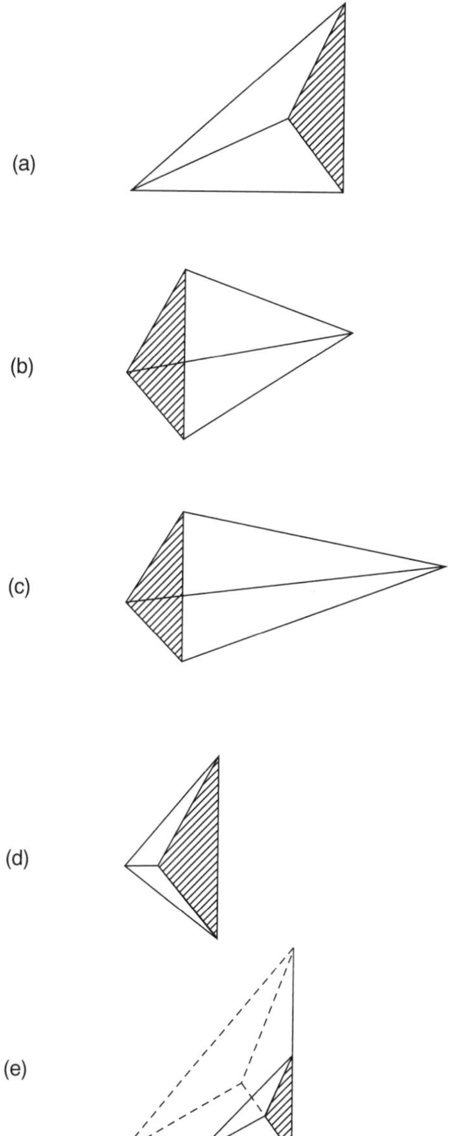

Figure 30.4 (a) Initial simplex, (b) reflection, (c) reflection and expansion, (d) contraction in one dimension and (e) multiple contractions to the highest point.

simplex and if $\text{d} = 0$ then the vertex goes into the opposite plane. Here we only use $\text{d} = -1$ for case (b), $\text{d} = 2$ for case (c) and $\text{d} = \frac{1}{2}$ for case (d).

```
Function maximize(FirstGuess As Object, N As Integer,_
                  tol As Double, MaxIts As Integer)
ReDim outputarray(1 To N + 1, 1 To N + 1) As Double
ReDim y(1 To N + 1) As Double
```

```
ReDim p(1 To N + 1, 1 To N) As Double
ReDim ptemp(1 To N) As Double
Dim ranktest(1 To 3, 1 To 2) As Double
its = 0
rtol = 1

For i = 1 To N + 1
For j = 1 To N
p(i, j) = FirstGuess(i, j)
ptemp(j) = p(i, j)
Next j
y(i) = func(ptemp)
Next i

While (rtol > tol) And (its < MaxIts)

Call Ranking(y, N, ilo, ylo, inlo, ynlo, ihi, yhi)

Call Deform(y, p, N, ilo, ylo, -1)
ytest = ylo

If ytest >= yhi Then
    Call Deform(y, p, N, ilo, ylo, 2)
    ytest = ylo
Else
    If ytest <= ynlo Then
    ysave = y(ilo)
    Call Deform(y, p, N, ilo, ylo, 0.5)
    ytest = ylo
        If ytest <= ysave Then
            For i = 1 To N + 1
            If i <> ihi Then
                For j = 1 To N
                p(i, j) = 0.5 * (p(i, j) + p(ihi, j))
                ptemp(j) = p(i, j)
                Next j
            End If
            y(i) = func(ptemp)
            Next i
        End If
   End If
End If

    its = its + 1
    rtol = 2 * Abs(yhi - ylo) / (Abs(yhi) + Abs(ylo))
Wend

For i = 1 To N + 1
For j = 1 To N
outputarray(i, j) = p(i, j)
Next j
```

```
outputarray(i, N + 1) = y(i)
Next i

maximize = outputarray

End Function

Sub FindCenter(p, N As Integer, center)
For j = 1 To N
center(j) = 0
For i = 1 To N + 1
center(j) = center(j) + p(i, j) / (N + 1)
Next i
Next j
End Sub

Sub Ranking(y, N As Integer, ilo, ylo, inlo, ynlo, ihi, yhi)
ilo = 1
inlo = 1
ihi = 1
ylo = y(ilo)
ynlo = y(inlo)
yhi = y(ihi)
For i = 2 To N + 1
    If y(i) < ynlo Then
        If y(i) < ylo Then
            inlo = ilo
            ynlo = ylo
            ilo = i
            ylo = y(i)
        Else
            inlo = i
            ynlo = y(i)
        End If
    End If
    If y(i) > yhi Then
        ihi = i
        yhi = y(i)
    End If
Next i
End Sub

Sub Deform(y, p, N As Integer, ilo, ylo, d)
ReDim ptest(1 To N) As Double
ReDim center(1 To N + 1) As Double
Call FindCenter(p, N, center)
For j = 1 To N
    ptest(j) = d * p(ilo, j) + (1 - d) * ((N + 1) / N * _
                center(j) - p(ilo, j) / N)
Next j
ytest = func(ptest)
If ytest > ylo Then
    y(ilo) = ytest
    ylo = ytest
End If
```

```
For j = 1 To N
p(ilo, j) = ptest(j)
Next j
End Sub
```

30.9.2 Simulated Annealing

The main downside of the above maximization algorithm is that it will not necessarily find the global maximum. This is a problem with many optimization techniques. Currently, one of the most popular methods for overcoming this is **simulated annealing**. This gets its name from the form of crystallization that occurs as molten metals are cooled. In the optimization algorithm there is a degree of randomness in the search for a maximum, and as the number of iterations increases, so the randomness gets smaller and smaller. The anology is with the random motion of atoms in the liquid state of the metal, as the metal cools so the motion decreases. The hope is that the random motion will find the neighbourhood of the global maximum, and as the 'temperature'/random motion decreases, the search will home in on the maximum.

One of the simplest simulated annealing techniques, related to the **Metropolis algorithm**, uses the addition or subtraction of a random number to the function value at each vertex, but is otherwise the same as the downhill simplex method. Suppose that we have a simplex and know the function values at each vertex. We now subtract a positive random number from the function value at each vertex. When we come to test a new replacement point we add a positive random number. In this way we still always accept a move to a better vertex, but occasionally we accept a move to a worse vertex. However, this worse vertex may actually be closer to the global maximum. How often we accept such a move depends on the size of the random variables. We must choose a distribution for the random variable, and importantly its scale. As the number of iterations increases, so we decrease this scale so that it tends to zero as the number of iterations increase.

The scale of the random moves must decrease slowly enough for the simplex to have a good look around before converging on the global maximum.

30.10 SUMMARY

In this chapter I showed how to statically hedge a complex product with simpler contracts. We began with the classical static hedge, by setting up a portfolio having exactly the same theoretical value as our target contract at a specified set of asset/time points. The resulting hedge then reduces the risk from delta hedging. But it is not perfect, the hedge is still sensitive to the pricing model and its parameters.

Then I described the idea of static hedging for some nonlinear models. Because some of these models are less sensitive to parameter values (such as volatility) the resulting hedged contract is also insensitive. We also saw how to optimize this static hedge by maximizing the *marginal value* of the target contract, after allowing for the real cost of setting up the hedge.

FURTHER READING

- See Bowie & Carr (1994), Carr & Chou (1997), Carr, Ellis & Gupta (1998) and Derman, Ergener & Kani (1997) for more details of static replicating portfolios.
- See Avellaneda & Parás (1996) for optimal static hedging as applied to uncertain volatility, Oztukel (1996) for uncertain correlation.
- See Epstein & Wilmott (1997, 1998) for optimal static hedging in a fixed-income world.
- For a general description of optimization, with many references, algorithms and code, see the excellent Press et al. (1992).
- Avellaneda & Buff (1997) explain how to value large portfolios of barrier options in the uncertain volatility framework.

EXERCISES

1. If we price a statically-hedged portfolio using a model which has been fitted to the hedging instruments then we find that the price of the hedged portfolio is equal to that of the unhedged portfolio. Why might it still be advisable to construct a static hedge in this case?
2. We own a statically-hedged portfolio which we value in a worst-case scenario. If we come back and re-evaluate our portfolio at a later date we may find that the optimal hedge has changed. Updating the static hedge to the new optimal hedge will lock in a profit. Why?
3. Consider pricing contracts in an uncertain world. If we attempt to statically hedge our portfolio with a hedging instrument whose market price lies outside the range of values predicted for it by our model, what optimal hedge should we find? What two possible consequences could this have?
4. Write down the specification for the down-and-out barrier option problem if we hedge with a general portfolio of options worth an amount $E(S)$ at time T, the expiry date of the barrier option.

PART FOUR
interest rates and products

The fourth part of the book introduces fixed-income products. I describe the basics of fixed-income analysis, and the commonest products. We then consider stochastic models for interest rates, and derive partial differential equation models for many products.

The mathematics of this part of the book is no different from what you have seen already. And again we apply the ideas of hedging and no arbitrage. However, the pricing and hedging of fixed-income products is technically more complicated than the pricing and hedging of equity instruments. One of the reasons for this is that the variable that we will be modeling, the short-term interest rate, is not itself a traded quantity. A consequence of this is that we must introduce the confusing quantity, the market price of risk.

Chapter 31: Fixed-Income Products and Analysis: Yield, Duration and Convexity The first chapter in this part of the book is an introduction to the simpler techniques and analyses commonly used in the market. In particular I explain the concepts of yield, duration and convexity. In this and the next chapter I assume that interest rates are known, deterministic quantities.

Chapter 32: Swaps Interest-rate swaps are very common and very liquid. I explain the basics and relate the pricing of swaps to the pricing of fixed-rate bonds.

Chapter 33: One-factor Interest Rate Modeling Interest rates are no more predictable than stock prices. I therefore show how to model them as stochastic variables. We concentrate on modeling the short-term interest rate and see how the prices of other instruments satisfy a parabolic partial differential equation. I discuss the properties of several well-known models.

Chapter 34: Yield Curve Fitting We would like an output of our simple model to be the yield curve as it is today in the market. I show how to choose parameters in the model so as to ensure that this is the case. This approach is not easy to justify, as I explain.

Chapter 35: Interest Rate Derivatives I go deeper into the pricing of interest-rate derivatives, relating the pricing equations to those from the equity world.

Chapter 36: Convertible Bonds Convertible bonds have a value that depends on a stock price. Because of their long lifespan we cannot assume that interest rates are known, and this leads us to model the value of CBs via a two-factor model with stochastic asset and stochastic interest rates.

Chapter 37: Two-factor Interest Rate Modeling If we have only the one factor, the short-term interest rate, determining the behavior of the whole yield curve then we will get unnatural results. For example, the one-factor theory says that we can hedge a ten-year instrument with a one-year bond, which is clearly not true. To better model reality we discuss two-factor modeling, where now there are two sources of randomness and hence more complicated relationships between rates of different maturities.

Chapter 38: Empirical Behavior of the Spot Interest Rate The popular models for the short-term interest rate make various assumptions about the behaviors of the volatility and drift of the rate. In this chapter I show how to examine the data to decide which, if any, of the models are close to reality.

Chapter 39: Heath, Jarrow and Morton Instead of modeling a short-term rate and then finding the full yield curve, Heath, Jarrow and Morton model the whole forward rate curve in one go. There are many advantages in this method, but also a few disadvantages.

Chapter 40: Interest Rate Modeling Without Probabilities There are many theoretical and practical problems and inconsistencies in classical stochastic interest rate models. In this chapter I describe the Epstein–Wilmott short-rate model that sidesteps many of these problems by being non-Brownian. Instead of modeling the short rate as a stochastic process, we model it in a deterministic fashion but with uncertain parameters. This is again a worst-case scenario analysis.

CHAPTER 31
fixed-income products and analysis: yield, duration and convexity

In this Chapter...

- the names and properties of the basic and most important fixed-income products
- the definitions of features commonly found in fixed-income products
- simple ways to analyze the market value of the instruments: yield, duration and convexity
- how to construct yield curves and forward rates

31.1 INTRODUCTION

This chapter is an introduction to some basic instruments and concepts in the world of fixed income, that is, the world of cashflows that are in the simplest cases independent of any stocks, commodities etc. I will describe the most elementary of fixed-income instruments, the coupon-bearing bond, and show how to determine various properties of such bonds to help in their analysis.

This chapter is self contained, and does not require any knowledge from earlier chapters. A lot of it is also not really necessary reading for anything that follows. The reason for this is that, although the concepts and techniques I describe here are used in practice and are *useful* in practice, it is difficult to present a completely coherent theory for more sophisticated products in this framework.

31.2 SIMPLE FIXED-INCOME CONTRACTS AND FEATURES

31.2.1 The Zero-coupon Bond

The **zero-coupon bond** is a contract paying a known fixed amount, the **principal**, at some given date in the future, the **maturity** date T. For example, the bond pays \$100 in 10 years' time. We're going to scale this payoff, so that in future all principals will be \$1.

This promise of future wealth is worth something now: it cannot have zero or negative value. Furthermore, except in extreme circumstances, the amount you pay initially will be smaller than the amount you receive at maturity.

We discussed the idea of time value of money in Chapter 1. This is clearly relevant here and we will return to this in a moment.

31.2.2 The Coupon-bearing Bond

A **coupon-bearing bond** is similar to the above except that as well as paying the principal at maturity, it pays smaller quantities, the coupons, at intervals up to and including the maturity date. These coupons are usually prespecified fractions of the principal. For example, the bond pays $1 in 10 years and 2%, i.e. 2 cents, every six months. This bond is clearly more valuable than the bond in the previous example because of the coupon payments. We can think of the coupon-bearing bond as a portfolio of zero-coupon bearing bonds: one zero-coupon bearing bond for each coupon date with a principal being the same as the original bond's coupon, and then a final zero-coupon bond with the same maturity as the original.

Figure 31.1 is an excerpt from The *Wall Street Journal* of 23rd December 1997 showing US Treasury Bonds, Notes and Bills. Observe that there are many different 'rates' or coupons, and different maturities. The values of the different bonds will depend on the size of the coupon, the maturity and the market's view of the future behavior of interest rates.

31.2.3 The Money Market Account

Everyone who has a bank account has a **money market account**. This is an account that accumulates interest compounded at a rate that varies from time to time. The rate at which interest accumulates is usually a short-term and unpredictable rate. In the sense that money held in a money market account will grow at an unpredictable rate, such an account is risky when compared with a one-year zero-coupon bond. On the other hand, the money market account can be closed at any time but if the bond is sold before maturity there is no guarantee how much it will be worth at the time of the sale.

31.2.4 Floating Rate Bonds

In its simplest form a **floating interest rate** is the amount that you get on your bank account. This amount varies from time to time, reflecting the state of the economy and in response to pressure from other banks for your business. This uncertainty about the interest rate you receive is compensated by the flexibility of your deposit; it can be withdrawn at any time.

The most common measure of interest is **London Interbank Offer Rate** or **LIBOR**. LIBOR comes in various maturities, one month, three month, six month, etc., and is the rate of interest offered between Eurocurrency banks for fixed-term deposits.

Sometimes the coupon payment on a bond is not a prescribed dollar amount but depends on the level of some 'index,' measured at the time of the payment or before. Typically, we cannot know at the start of the contract what the level that this index will be at when the payment is made. We will see examples of such contracts in later chapters.

31.2.5 Forward Rate Agreements

A **Forward Rate Agreement (FRA)** is an agreement between two parties that a prescribed interest rate will apply to a prescribed principal over some specified period in the future. The

TREASURY BONDS, NOTES & BILLS

Monday, December 22, 1997

Representative and Indicative Over-the-Counter quotations based on $1 million or more.

Treasury bond, note and bill quotes are as of mid-afternoon. Colons in bond and note bid-and-asked quotes represent 32nds; 101:01 means 101 1/32. Net changes in 32nds. Treasury bill quotes in hundredths, quoted in terms of a rate discount. Days to maturity calculated from settlement date. All yields are based on a one-day settlement and calculated on the offer quote. Current 13-week and 26-week bills are boldfaced. For bonds callable prior to maturity, yields are computed to the earliest call date for issues quoted above par and to the maturity date for issues quoted below par. n-Treasury note. i-Inflation-indexed. wi-When issued. iw-Inflation-indexed when issued; daily change is expressed in basis points.

Source: Dow Jones/Cantor Fitzgerald.

U.S. Treasury strips as of 3 p.m. Eastern time, also based on transactions of $1 million or more. Colons in bid-and-asked quotes represent 32nds; 99:01 means 99 1/32. Net changes in 32nds. Yields calculated on the asked quotation. ci-stripped coupon interest. bp-Treasury bond, stripped principal. np-Treasury note, stripped principal. For bonds callable prior to maturity, yields are computed to the earliest call date for issues quoted above par and to the maturity date for issues below par.

Source: Bear, Stearns & Co. via Street Software Technology Inc.

GOVT. BONDS & NOTES

Rate	Maturity Mo/Yr	Bid	Asked	Chg.	Ask Yld.
5 1/4	Dec 97n	99:30	100:00	....	5.12
6	Dec 97n	99:31	100:01	....	4.43
7 7/8	Jan 98n	100:04	100:06	....	4.70
5	Jan 98n	99:27	99:29	....	5.78
5 5/8	Jan 98n	99:29	99:31	....	5.79
7 1/4	Feb 98n	100:05	100:07	....	5.60
8 1/8	Feb 98n	100:09	100:11	....	5.60
5 1/8	Feb 98n	99:26	99:28	....	5.72
5 1/8	Mar 98n	99:26	99:28	....	5.53
6 1/8	Mar 98n	100:03	100:05	....	5.46
7 7/8	Apr 98n	100:21	100:23	....	5.44
5 1/8	Apr 98n	99:25	99:27	....	5.53
5 7/8	Apr 98n	100:01	100:03	....	5.56
6 1/8	May 98n	100:05	100:07	....	5.52
9	May 98n	101:09	101:11	....	5.47
5 3/8	May 98n	99:26	99:28	....	5.65
6	May 98n	100:03	100:05	....	5.61
5 1/8	Jun 98n	99:23	99:25	....	5.55
6 1/4	Jun 98n	100:09	100:11	....	5.57
8 1/4	Jul 98n	101:13	101:15	....	5.55
5 1/4	Jul 98n	99:23	99:25	....	5.61
6 1/4	Jul 98n	100:10	100:12	....	5.60
5 7/8	Aug 98n	100:02	100:04	....	5.66
9 1/4	Aug 98n	102:07	102:09	....	5.59
4 3/4	Aug 98n	99:10	99:12	....	5.68
6 1/8	Aug 98n	100:08	100:10	....	5.64
4 3/4	Sep 98n	99:09	99:11	....	5.62
6	Sep 98n	100:07	100:09	....	5.61
7 1/8	Oct 98n	101:03	101:05	....	5.63
4 3/4	Oct 98n	99:05	99:07	....	5.69
5 7/8	Oct 98n	100:03	100:05	....	5.67
5 1/2	Nov 98n	99:25	99:27	....	5.67
8 7/8	Nov 98n	102:23	102:25	....	5.63
5 1/8	Nov 98n	99:15	99:17	....	5.64
5 5/8	Nov 98n	99:30	100:00	....	5.62
5 1/8	Dec 98n	99:14	99:16	....	5.63
5 3/4	Dec 98n	100:02	100:04	....	5.62
6 3/8	Jan 99n	100:22	100:24	....	5.63
5	Jan 99n	99:07	99:09	....	5.67
5 7/8	Jan 99n	100:05	100:07	....	5.66
5	Feb 99n	99:06	99:08	....	5.68
8 7/8	Feb 99n	103:15	103:17	....	5.64
5 1/2	Feb 99n	99:24	99:26	....	5.66
5 7/8	Feb 99n	100:06	100:08	....	5.65
5 7/8	Mar 99n	100:07	100:09	....	5.63
6 1/4	Mar 99n	100:21	100:23	....	5.65
7	Apr 99n	101:20	101:22	....	5.64
6 3/8	Apr 99n	101:01	101:03	....	5.52
6 1/2	Apr 99n	101:01	101:03	....	5.64
6 3/8	May 99n	100:28	100:30	....	5.66

Rate	Maturity Mo./Yr.	Bid	Asked	Chg.	Ask Yld.
8 1/2	Nov 00n	107:14	107:16	....	5.65
5 5/8	Nov 00n	99:26	99:28	....	5.67
5 1/2	Dec 00n	99:14	99:16	....	5.68
5 1/4	Jan 01n	98:24	98:26	....	5.67
7 3/4	Feb 01n	105:26	105:28	....	5.68
11 3/4	Feb 01	117:12	117:16	....	5.61
5 5/8	Feb 01n	99:24	99:26	....	5.69
6 3/8	Mar 01n	101:28	101:30	....	5.71
6 1/4	Apr 01n	101:18	101:20	....	5.71
8	May 01n	106:30	107:00	....	5.70
13 1/8	May 01	122:22	122:28	....	5.62
6 1/2	May 01n	102:12	102:14	....	5.71
6 5/8	Jun 01n	102:25	102:27	....	5.72
6 5/8	Jul 01n	102:28	102:30	....	5.71
7 7/8	Aug 01n	106:31	107:01	....	5.71
13 3/8	Aug 01	124:30	125:04	....	5.65
6 1/2	Aug 01n	102:16	102:18	....	5.72
6 3/8	Sep 01n	102:04	102:06	....	5.72
6 1/4	Oct 01n	101:24	101:26	....	5.72
7 1/2	Nov 01n	106:03	106:05	....	5.71
15 3/4	Nov 01	134:19	134:25	....	5.67
5 7/8	Nov 01n	100:15	100:17	....	5.72
6 1/8	Dec 01n	101:11	101:13	....	5.73
6 1/4	Jan 02n	101:26	101:28	....	5.73
14 1/4	Feb 02	131:02	131:08	....	5.68
6 1/4	Feb 02n	101:27	101:29	....	5.73
6 5/8	Mar 02n	103:09	103:11	....	5.73
6 5/8	Apr 02n	103:18	103:20	....	5.67
7 1/2	May 02n	106:24	106:26	....	5.72
6 1/2	May 02n	103:04	103:06	....	5.68
6 1/4	Jun 02n	101:31	102:01	....	5.73
3 5/8	Jul 02i	99:26	99:27	....	3.66
6	Jul 02n	101:02	101:04	....	5.72
6 3/8	Aug 02n	102:18	102:20	....	5.72
6 1/4	Aug 02n	102:01	102:03	....	5.73
5 7/8	Sep 02n	100:17	100:19	....	5.73
5 3/4	Oct 02n	100:06	100:07	....	5.70
11 5/8	Nov 02	124:20	124:26	....	5.74
5 3/4	Nov 02n	100:05	100:06	− 2	5.70
	Dec 02wi	5:69	5:68	+ 2	....
6 1/4	Feb 03n	102:08	102:10	....	5.72
10 3/4	Feb 03	121:30	122:04	....	5.72
10 3/4	May 03	122:26	123:00	....	5.73
5 3/4	Aug 03n	100:02	100:04	....	5.72
11 1/8	Aug 03	125:16	125:22	....	5.73
11 7/8	Nov 03	130:03	130:09	....	5.74
5 7/8	Feb 04n	100:28	100:30	....	5.69
7 1/4	May 04n	108:00	108:02	....	5.73
12 3/8	May 04	134:28	135:02	....	5.74
7 1/4	Aug 04n	108:06	108:08	....	5.74
13 3/4	Aug 04	143:16	143:22	....	5.75

Rate	Maturity Mo./Yr.	Bid	Asked	Chg.	Ask Yld.
9 1/8	May 18	136:14	136:20	....	5.99
9	Nov 18	135:12	135:18	....	5.99
8 7/8	Feb 19	134:01	134:07	....	6.00
8 1/8	Aug 19	125:10	125:16	....	6.00
8 1/2	Feb 20	130:05	130:11	....	6.00
8 3/4	May 20	133:12	133:18	....	6.00
8 3/4	Aug 20	133:16	133:22	....	6.01
7 7/8	Feb 21	122:30	123:04	....	6.01
8 1/8	May 21	126:05	126:11	....	6.01
8 1/8	Aug 21	126:09	126:15	....	6.01
8	Nov 21	124:26	125:00	....	6.01
7 1/4	Aug 22	115:22	115:26	....	6.01
7 5/8	Nov 22	120:17	120:23	....	6.01
7 1/8	Feb 23	114:08	114:12	....	6.01
6 1/4	Aug 23	103:06	103:08	....	6.00
7 1/2	Nov 24	119:24	119:28	....	6.00
7 5/8	Feb 25	121:15	121:21	....	6.00
6 7/8	Aug 25	111:20	111:24	....	6.00
6	Feb 26	100:01	100:03	....	5.99
6 3/4	Aug 26	110:10	110:12	....	5.99
6 1/2	Nov 26	106:31	107:01	....	5.98
6 5/8	Feb 27	108:24	108:26	....	5.98
6 3/8	Aug 27	105:30	105:31	+ 8	5.94
6 1/8	Nov 27	103:07	103:08	+ 8	5.89

U.S. TREASURY STRIPS

Mat.	Type	Bid	Asked	Chg.	Ask Yld.
Feb 98	ci	99:06	99:06	+ 1	5.75
Feb 98	np	99:05	99:05	+ 1	5.80
May 98	ci	97:27	97:27	....	5.61
May 98	np	97:27	97:27	....	5.61
Aug 98	ci	96:14	96:14	....	5.70
Aug 98	np	96:14	96:14	....	5.71
Nov 98	ci	95:03	95:04	....	5.68
Nov 98	np	95:03	95:04	....	5.68
Feb 99	ci	93:25	93:26	− 1	5.67
Feb 99	np	93:25	93:26	− 1	5.66
May 99	ci	92:15	92:16	− 1	5.68
May 99	np	92:15	92:16	− 2	5.69
Aug 99	ci	91:06	91:07	− 1	5.68
Aug 99	np	91:05	91:06	− 1	5.69
Nov 99	ci	89:28	89:29	− 2	5.70
Nov 99	np	89:29	89:30	− 1	5.69
Feb 00	ci	88:20	88:22	− 1	5.69
Feb 00	np	88:20	88:21	− 2	5.69
May 00	ci	87:15	87:16	− 1	5.66
May 00	np	87:15	87:16	− 1	5.66
Aug 00	ci	86:05	86:06	− 2	5.70
Aug 00	np	86:05	86:06	− 3	5.70
Nov 00	ci	84:30	85:00	− 2	5.70
Nov 00	np	84:30	85:00	− 2	5.70
Feb 01	ci	83:25	83:27	− 2	5.69
Feb 01	np	83:24	83:26	− 3	5.70
May 01	ci	82:19	82:21	− 1	5.70
May 01	np	82:20	82:22	+ 1	5.68
Aug 01	ci	81:13	81:15	− 1	5.70
Aug 01	np	81:14	81:16	− 1	5.69
Nov 01	ci	80:10	80:12	− 1	5.70
Nov 01	np	80:10	80:12	....	5.70
Feb 02	ci	79:05	79:07	− 1	5.70
May 02	ci	78:02	78:04	− 1	5.70
May 02	np	78:03	78:05	....	5.69
Aug 02	ci	77:02	77:04	− 1	5.67
Aug 02	np	77:00	77:02	− 1	5.69
Nov 02	ci	76:03	76:06	− 1	5.64
Feb 03	ci	74:25	74:29	− 1	5.70
Feb 03	np	74:29	75:00	+ 3	5.67
May 03	ci	73:22	73:25	− 1	5.72
Aug 03	ci	72:20	72:23	− 1	5.72
Aug 03	np	72:26	72:30	+ 2	5.67
Nov 03	ci	71:20	71:24	− 1	5.72
Feb 04	ci	70:19	70:23	....	5.72
Feb 04	np	70:31	71:03	+ 3	5.63

Mat.	Type	Bid	Asked	Chg.	Ask Yld.
Aug 11	ci	44:22	44:28	+ 3	5.96
Nov 11	ci	44:01	44:06	+ 4	5.97
Feb 12	ci	43:11	43:17	+ 4	5.97
May 12	ci	42:22	42:27	+ 4	5.97
Aug 12	ci	42:00	42:06	+ 4	5.98
Nov 12	ci	41:12	41:18	+ 4	5.99
Feb 13	ci	40:24	40:30	+ 3	5.99
May 13	ci	40:04	40:10	+ 3	5.99
Aug 13	ci	39:17	39:23	+ 4	5.99
Nov 13	ci	38:30	39:04	+ 4	5.99
Feb 14	ci	38:12	38:18	+ 4	5.99
May 14	ci	37:25	37:31	+ 4	5.99
Aug 14	ci	37:07	37:13	+ 4	6.00
Nov 14	ci	36:22	36:27	+ 4	6.00
Feb 15	ci	36:05	36:11	+ 4	5.99
Feb 15	bp	37:00	37:06	+ 4	5.86
May 15	ci	35:20	35:25	+ 5	5.99
Aug 15	ci	35:02	35:08	+ 5	6.00
Aug 15	bp	35:12	35:18	+ 4	5.95
Nov 15	ci	34:17	34:23	+ 5	6.00
Nov 15	bp	34:21	34:27	+ 4	5.98
Feb 16	ci	34:00	34:06	+ 6	6.01
Feb 16	bp	34:06	34:12	+ 6	5.97
May 16	ci	33:15	33:21	+ 6	6.01
May 16	bp	33:24	33:30	+ 6	5.96
Aug 16	ci	32:31	33:05	+ 6	6.01
Nov 16	ci	32:16	32:21	+ 6	6.01
Nov 16	bp	32:17	32:23	+ 6	6.00
Feb 17	ci	31:31	32:05	+ 7	6.02
May 17	ci	31:16	31:22	+ 6	6.01
May 17	bp	31:17	31:23	+ 7	6.01
Aug 17	ci	31:01	31:07	+ 6	6.02
Aug 17	bp	31:02	31:08	+ 7	6.01
Nov 17	ci	30:19	30:24	+ 6	6.01
Feb 18	ci	30:01	30:07	+ 6	6.03
May 18	ci	29:19	29:25	+ 6	6.03
May 18	bp	29:20	29:25	+ 6	6.03
Aug 18	ci	29:04	29:10	+ 6	6.03
Nov 18	ci	28:22	28:28	+ 6	6.03
Nov 18	bp	28:23	28:29	+ 6	6.03
Feb 19	ci	28:08	28:13	+ 6	6.04
Feb 19	bp	28:08	28:14	+ 6	6.04
May 19	ci	27:26	28:00	+ 6	6.04
Aug 19	ci	27:14	27:19	+ 6	6.04
Aug 19	bp	27:14	27:19	+ 6	6.04
Nov 19	ci	27:00	27:05	+ 6	6.04
Feb 20	ci	26:18	26:24	+ 6	6.05
Feb 20	bp	26:19	26:24	+ 6	6.04

Mat.	Type	Bid	Asked	Chg.	Ask Yld.
May 20	ci	26:06	26:11	+ 6	6.05
May 20	bp	26:06	26:12	+ 6	6.04
Aug 20	ci	25:25	25:31	+ 6	6.05
Aug 20	bp	25:26	25:31	+ 6	6.04
Nov 20	ci	25:13	25:19	+ 6	6.05
Feb 21	ci	25:00	25:05	+ 6	6.05
Feb 21	bp	25:01	25:06	+ 6	6.05
May 21	ci	24:20	24:25	+ 6	6.05
May 21	bp	24:21	24:26	+ 5	6.05
Aug 21	ci	24:08	24:13	+ 6	6.05
Aug 21	bp	24:09	24:15	+ 5	6.05
Nov 21	ci	23:29	24:02	+ 6	6.05
Nov 21	bp	23:30	24:03	+ 6	6.05
Feb 22	ci	23:18	23:23	+ 5	6.05
May 22	ci	23:08	23:13	+ 5	6.04
Aug 22	ci	22:30	23:04	+ 5	6.03
Aug 22	bp	23:00	23:05	+ 5	6.03
Nov 22	ci	22:20	22:25	+ 5	6.03
Nov 22	bp	22:21	22:26	+ 5	6.03
Feb 23	ci	22:11	22:17	+ 5	6.02
Feb 23	bp	22:13	22:19	+ 5	6.01
May 23	ci	22:03	22:08	+ 5	6.01
Aug 23	ci	21:26	21:31	+ 5	6.00
Aug 23	bp	21:30	22:04	+ 5	5.97
Nov 23	ci	21:17	21:22	+ 5	5.99
Feb 24	ci	21:06	21:11	+ 5	5.99
May 24	ci	20:28	21:02	+ 5	5.99
Aug 24	ci	20:20	20:25	+ 5	5.99
Nov 24	ci	20:09	20:14	+ 5	5.99
Nov 24	bp	20:10	20:15	+ 5	5.99
Feb 25	ci	20:01	20:06	+ 5	5.99
Feb 25	bp	20:01	20:06	+ 5	5.98
May 25	ci	19:24	19:29	+ 5	5.98
Aug 25	ci	19:15	19:21	+ 5	5.97
Aug 25	bp	19:15	19:21	+ 5	5.97
Feb 26	ci	18:28	19:01	+ 4	5.98
Feb 26	bp	18:31	19:04	+ 4	5.96
Aug 26	ci	18:15	18:20	+ 4	5.96
Aug 26	bp	18:16	18:21	+ 4	5.95
Nov 26	ci	18:08	18:13	+ 4	5.95
Nov 26	bp	18:09	18:14	+ 4	5.94
Feb 27	ci	18:01	18:06	+ 3	5.94
Feb 27	bp	18:03	18:08	+ 3	5.92
May 27	ci	17:28	18:01	+ 3	5.92
Aug 27	ci	17:22	17:27	+ 3	5.90
Aug 27	bp	17:27	18:00	+ 4	5.87
Nov 27	ci	18:06	18:11	+ 4	5.76
Nov 27	bp	18:10	18:15	+ 5	5.73

TREASURY BILLS

Maturity	Days to Mat.	Bid	Asked	Chg.	Ask Yld.
Dec 26 '97	3	5.41	5.37	....	5.45
Jan 02 '98	10	5.26	5.22	....	5.30
Jan 08 '98	16	5.27	5.23	....	5.31
Jan 15 '98	23	5.05	5.01	....	5.10
Jan 22 '98	30	5.36	5.32	....	5.42
Jan 29 '98	37	5.29	5.25	....	5.35
Feb 05 '98	44	5.37	5.33	....	5.44
Feb 12 '98	51	5.32	5.28	....	5.39
Feb 19 '98	58	5.32	5.28	....	5.40
Feb 26 '98	65	5.33	5.31	....	5.44
Mar 05 '98	72	5.29	5.27	....	5.40
Mar 12 '98	79	5.27	5.25	....	5.38
Mar 19 '98	86	5.30	5.29	+0.11	5.43
Mar 26 '98	93	5.17	5.15	....	5.29
Mar 26 '98	**93**	**5.30**	**5.29**	**+0.14**	**5.44**
Apr 02 '98	100	5.28	5.26	....	5.41
Apr 09 '98	107	5.27	5.25	....	5.41
Apr 16 '98	114	5.27	5.25	....	5.41
Apr 23 '98	121	5.27	5.25	....	5.42
Apr 30 '98	128	5.29	5.27	....	5.45
May 07 '98	135	5.28	5.26	....	5.44
May 14 '98	142	5.29	5.27	....	5.46
May 21 '98	149	5.27	5.25	....	5.44
May 28 '98	156	5.29	5.27	....	5.47
Jun 04 '98	163	5.25	5.23	....	5.43
Jun 11 '98	170	5.24	5.22	....	5.43
Jun 18 '98	177	5.27	5.26	+0.03	5.47
Jun 25 '98	184	5.26	5.24	....	5.46
Jun 25 '98	**184**	**5.30**	**5.29**	**+0.02**	**5.51**
Jul 23 '98	212	5.26	5.24	....	5.46
Aug 20 '98	240	5.27	5.25	....	5.48
Sep 17 '98	268	5.26	5.24	....	5.48
Oct 15 '98	296	5.21	5.19	....	5.44
Nov 12 '98	324	5.24	5.22	....	5.49
Dec 10 '98	352	5.25	5.24	+0.05	5.53

INFLATION-INDEXED TREASURY SECURITIES

Rate	Mat.	Bid/Asked	Chg.	*Yld.	Accr. Prin.
3.625	07/02	99-26/27	....	3.654	1008
3.375	01/07	103-10/12	....	3.640	1019

*-Yld. to maturity on accrued principal.

GOVERNMENT AGENCY & SIMILAR ISSUES

Monday, December 22, 1997

Over-the-Counter mid-afternoon quotations based on large transactions, usually $1 million or more. Colons in bid-and-asked quotes represent 32nds; 101:01 means 101 1/32.

All yields are calculated to maturity, and based on the asked quote. * -- Callable issue, maturity date shown. For issues callable prior to maturity, yields are computed to the earliest call date for issues quoted above par, or 100, and to the maturity date for issues below par.

Source: Bear, Stearns & Co. via Street Software Technology Inc.

FNMA Issues

Rate	Mat.	Bid	Asked	Yld.
6.05	1-98	99:31	100:00	5.89
5.38	1-98	99:30	99:31	5.54
8.65	2-98	100:06	100:08	6.59
5.01	2-98	99:29	99:31	5.12
5.51	2-98	100:00	100:02	5.13
8.20	3-98	100:15	100:17	5.52

Rate	Mat.	Bid	Asked	Yld.
6.45	4-01	101:28	102:00	5.77
6.74	5-01*	100:24	100:28	6.07
7.00	5-01*	101:05	101:09	6.01
6.59	5-01	102:02	102:06	5.87
6.67	8-01	102:14	102:18	5.87
6.69	8-01	102:16	102:20	5.87
6.70	8-01*	100:30	101:02	6.00

Rate	Mat.	Bid	Asked	Yld.
6.96	4-07	107:06	107:12	5.91
6.64	7-07	104:08	104:14	6.02
6.99	7-07*	102:10	102:16	6.34
6.52	7-07	103:22	103:28	5.98
6.54	9-07	103:19	103:25	6.02
7.13	9-07*	101:27	102:01	6.29
6.59	9-07	103:30	104:04	6.02
6.39	9-07	102:06	102:12	6.06
6.87	10-07	100:20	100:26	6.75
6.83	10-07*	100:23	100:29	6.47
6.34	10-07	101:31	102:05	6.04
6.94	10-07*	100:16	100:22	6.66
6.97	10-07*	100:16	100:22	6.70
6.65	11-07*	99:28	100:02	6.64
0.00	7-14	36:10	36:18	6.18
10.35	12-15	143:00	143:08	6.30
8.20	3-16	120:11	120:19	6.28
8.95	2-18	127:11	127:19	6.48
8.10	8-19	120:10	120:18	6.34

Rate	Mat.	Bid	Asked	Yld.
6.38	12-01*	100:02	100:06	5.95
7.00	12-02	104:20	104:26	5.87
7.30	8-12	110:20	110:28	6.16
0.00	10-22	19:22	19:30	6.61

World Bank Bonds

Rate	Mat.	Bid	Asked	Yld.
8.38	10-99	104:27	104:30	5.40
8.13	3-01	107:16	107:20	5.47
6.38	5-01	102:06	102:10	5.61
6.75	1-02	102:22	102:26	5.96
12.38	10-02	124:17	124:23	6.33
5.25	9-03	97:25	97:31	5.67
6.38	7-05	103:04	103:10	5.82
6.63	8-06	104:30	105:06	5.85
8.25	9-16	120:10	120:18	6.35
8.63	10-16	124:10	124:18	6.36
9.25	7-17	131:29	132:05	6.36

Figure 31.1 The *Wall Street Journal* of 23rd December 1997, Treasury Bonds, Notes and Bills. Reproduced by permission of *Dow Jones & Company, Inc*.

cashflows in this agreement are as follows: party A pays party B the principal at time T_1 and B pays A the principal plus agreed interest at time $T_2 > T_1$. The value of this exchange at the time the contract is entered into is generally not zero and so there will be a transfer of cash from one party to the other at the start date.

31.2.6 Repos

A **repo** is a repurchase agreement. It is an agreement to sell some security to another party and buy it back at a fixed date and for a fixed amount. The price at which the security is bought back is greater than the selling price and the difference implies an interest rate called the **repo rate**. The commonest repo is the overnight repo in which the agreement is renegotiated daily.

31.2.7 Strips

STRIPS stands for 'Separate Trading of Registered Interest and Principal of Securities'. The coupons and principal of normal bonds are split up, creating artificial zero-coupon bonds of longer maturity than would otherwise be available.

31.2.8 Amortization

In all of the above products I have assumed that the principal remains fixed at its initial level. Sometimes this is not the case, the principal can **amortize** or decrease during the life of the contract. The principal is thus paid back gradually and interest is paid on the amount of the principal outstanding. Such amortization is arranged at the initiation of the contract and may be fixed, so that the rate of decrease of the principal is known beforehand, or can depend on the level of some index, if the index is high the principal amortizes faster for example. We see an example of a complex amortizing structure in Chapter 35.

31.2.9 Call Provision

Some bonds have a **call provision**. The issuer can call back the bond on certain dates or at certain periods for a prescribed, possibly time-dependent, amount. This lowers the value of the bond. The mathematical consequences of this are discussed in Chapter 33.

31.3 INTERNATIONAL BOND MARKETS

31.3.1 United States of America

In the US, bonds of maturity less than one year are called **bills** and are usually zero coupon. Bonds with maturity two–10 years are called **notes**. They are coupon bearing with coupons every six months. Bonds with maturity greater than 10 years are called **bonds**. Again they are coupon bearing. In this book I tend to call all of these 'bonds,' merely specifying whether or not they have coupons.

Bonds traded in the United States foreign bond market but which are issued by non-US institutions are called **Yankee** bonds.

Since the beginning of 1997 the US government has also issued bonds linked to the rate of inflation.

31.3.2 United Kingdom

Bonds issued by the UK government are called **gilts**. Some of these bonds are callable, some are irredeemable, meaning that they are perpetual bonds having a coupon but no repayment of principal. The government also issue convertible bonds which may be converted into another bond issue, typically of longer maturity. Finally, there are index-linked bonds having the amount of the coupon and principal payments linked to a measure of inflation, the Retail Price Index (RPI).

31.3.3 Japan

Japanese Government Bonds (**JGB**s) come as short-term treasury bills, medium-term, long-term (10 year maturity) and super long-term (20 year maturity). The long- and super long-term bonds have coupons every six months. The short-term bonds have no coupons and the medium-term bonds can be either coupon-bearing or zero-coupon bonds.

Yen denominated bonds issued by non-Japanese institutions are called **Samurai** bonds.

31.4 ACCRUED INTEREST

The market price of bonds quoted in the newspapers are **clean prices**. That is, they are quoted without any **accrued interest**. The accrued interest is the amount of interest that has built up since the last coupon payment:

$$\text{accrued interest} = \text{interest due in full period} \times \frac{\text{number of days since last coupon date}}{\text{number of days in period between coupon payments}}.$$

The actual payment is called the **dirty price** and is the sum of the quoted clean price and the accrued interest.

31.5 DAY COUNT CONVENTIONS

Because of such matters as the accrual of interest between coupon dates there naturally arises the question of how to accrue interest over shorter periods. Interest is accrued between two dates according to the formula

$$\frac{\text{number of days between the two dates}}{\text{number of days in period}} \times \text{interest earned in reference period.}$$

There are three main ways of calculating the 'number of days' in the the above expression.

- **Actual/Actual** Simply count the number of calendar days
- **30/360** Assume there are 30 days in a month and 360 days in a year
- **Actual/360** Each month has the right number of days but there are only 360 days in a year

31.6 CONTINUOUSLY- AND DISCRETELY-COMPOUNDED INTEREST

To be able to compare fixed-income products we must decide on a convention for the measurement of interest rates. So far, we have used a continuously-compounded rate, meaning that the present value of \$1 paid at time T in the future is

$$e^{-rT} \times \$1$$

for some r. We have seen how this follows from the cash-in-the-bank or money market account equation

$$dM = rM\,dt.$$

This is the convention used in the options world.

Another common convention is to use the formula

$$\frac{1}{(1+r')^T} \times \$1,$$

for present value, where r' is some interest rate. This represents discretely-compounded interest and assumes that interest is accumulated *annually* for T years. The formula is derived from calculating the present value from a single-period payment, and then compounding this for each year. This formula is commonly used for the simpler type of instruments such as coupon-bearing bonds. The two formulae are identical, of course, when

$$r = \log(1 + r').$$

This gives the relationship between the continuously-compounded interest rate r and the discrete version r'. What would the formula be if interest was discretely compounded twice per year?

Throughout the book we use the continuous definition of interest rates.

31.7 MEASURES OF YIELD

There is such a variety of fixed-income products, with different coupon structures, amortization, fixed and/or floating rates, that it is necessary to be able to consistently compare different products. One way to do this is through measures of how much each contract earns. There are several measures of this all coming under the name **yield**.

31.7.1 Current Yield

The simplest measurement of how much a contract earns is the **current yield**. This measure is defined by

$$\text{current yield} = \frac{\text{annual \$ coupon income}}{\text{bond price}}.$$

For example, consider the 10-year bond that pays 2 cents every six months and \$1 at maturity. This bond has a total income per annum of 4 cents. Suppose that the quoted market price of this bond is 88 cents. The current yield is simply

$$\frac{0.04}{0.88} = 4.5\%.$$

This measurement of the yield of the bond makes no allowance for the payment of the principal at maturity, nor for the time value of money if the coupon payment is reinvested, nor for any capital gain or loss that may be made if the bond is sold before maturity. It is a relatively unsophisticated measure, concentrating very much on short-term properties of the bond.

31.7.2 The Yield to Maturity (YTM) or Internal Rate of Return (IRR)

Suppose that we have a zero-coupon bond maturing at time T when it pays one dollar. At time t it has a value $Z(t;T)$. Applying a constant rate of return of y between t and T, then one dollar received at time T has a present value of $Z(t;T)$ at time t, where

$$Z(t;T) = e^{-y(T-t)}.$$

It follows that

$$y = -\frac{\log Z}{T-t}.$$

Let us generalize this. Suppose that we have a coupon-bearing bond. Discount all coupons and the principal to the present by using some interest rate y. The present value of the bond, at time t, is then

$$V = Pe^{-y(T-t)} + \sum_{i=1}^{N} C_i e^{-y(t_i-t)}, \tag{31.1}$$

where P is the principal, N the number of coupons, C_i the coupon paid on date t_i.

If the bond is a traded security then we know the price at which the bond can be bought. If this is the case then we can calculate the **yield to maturity** or **internal rate of return** as the value y that we must put into Equation (31.1) to make V equal to the traded price of the bond. This calculation must be performed by some trial and error/iterative procedure. For example, in the bond in Table 31.1 we have a principal of \$1 paid in five years and coupons of three cents (three percent) paid every six months.

Suppose that the market value of this bond is 96 cents. We ask 'What is the internal rate of return we must use to give these cash flows a total present value of 96 cents?' This value is

Table 31.1 An example of a coupon-bearing bond.

Time	Coupon	Principal repayment	PV (discounting at 6.8406%)
0			0
0.5	.03		0.0290
1.0	.03		0.0280
1.5	.03		0.0270
2.0	.03		0.0262
2.5	.03		0.0253
3.0	.03		0.0244
3.5	.03		0.0236
4.0	.03		0.0228
4.5	.03		0.0220
5.0	.03	1.00	0.7316
		Total	0.9600

the yield to maturity. In the fourth column in this table is the present value (PV) of each of the cashflows using a rate of 6.8406%: since the sum of these present values is 96 cents the YTM or IRR is 6.8406%.

This yield to maturity is a valid measure of the return on a bond if we intend to hold it to maturity.

To calculate the yield to maturity of a portfolio of bonds simply treat all the cashflows as if they were from the one bond and calculate the value of the whole portfolio by adding up the market values of the component bonds.

31.8 PRICE/YIELD RELATIONSHIP

From Equation (31.1) we can easily see that the relationship between the price of a bond and its yield is of the form shown in Figure 31.2 (assuming that all cash flows are positive). On this figure is marked the current market price and the current yield to maturity.

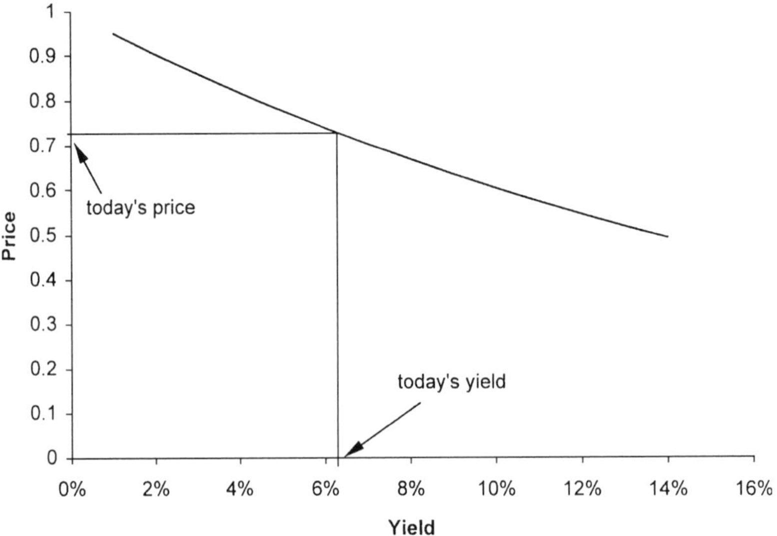

Figure 31.2 The Price/Yield relationship.

Since we are often interested in the sensitivity of instruments to the movement of certain underlying factors it is natural to ask how does the price of a bond vary with the yield, or vice versa. To a first approximation this variation can be quantified by a measure called the duration.

31.9 DURATION

From Equation (31.1) we find that

$$\frac{dV}{dy} = -(T-t)Pe^{-y(T-t)} - \sum_{i=1}^{N} C_i(t_i - t)e^{-y(t_i-t)}.$$

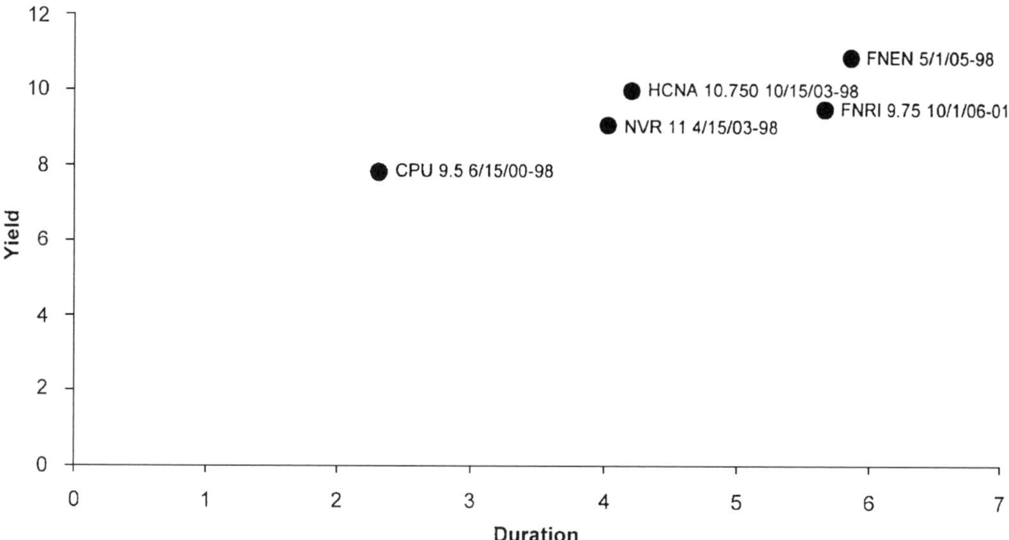

Figure 31.3 Yield *versus* duration; measuring the relative value of bonds.

This is the slope of the price/yield curve. The quantity

$$-\frac{1}{V}\frac{dV}{dy}$$

is called the **Macauley duration**. (The **modified duration** is similar but uses the discretely compounded rate.) In the expression for the duration the time of each coupon payment is weighted by its present value. The higher the value of the present value of the coupon the more it contributes to the duration. Also, since y is measured in units of inverse time, the units of the duration are time. The duration is a measure of the average life of the bond. It is easily shown that the Macauley duration for a zero-coupon bond is the same as its maturity.

For small movements in the yield, the duration gives a good measure of the change in value with a change in the yield. For larger movements we need to look at higher order terms in the Taylor series expansion of $V(y)$.

One of the most common uses of the duration is in plots of yield *versus* duration for a variety of instruments. An example is shown in Figure 31.3. Look at the bond marked 'CPU.' This bond has a coupon of 4.75% paid twice per year, callable from June 1998 and maturing in June 2000. We can use this plot to group together instruments with the same or similar durations and make comparisons between their yields. Two bonds having the same duration but with one bond having a higher yield might be suggestive of value for money in the higher-yielding bond, or of credit risk issues. However, such indicators of relative value must be used with care. It is possible for two bonds to have vastly different cashflow profiles yet have the same duration; one may have a maturity of 30 years but an average life and hence a duration of seven years, whereas another may be a seven-year zero-coupon bond. Clearly, the former has twenty-three years more risk than the latter.

31.10 CONVEXITY

The Taylor series expansion of V gives

$$\frac{dV}{V} = \frac{1}{V}\frac{dV}{dy}\,\delta y + \frac{1}{2V}\frac{d^2V}{dy^2}\,(\delta y)^2 + \cdots,$$

where δy is a change in yield. For very small movements in the yield, the change in the price of a bond can be measured by the duration. For larger movements we must take account of the curvature in the price/yield relationship.

The **dollar convexity** is defined as

$$\frac{d^2V}{dy^2} = (T-t)^2 P e^{-y(T-t)} + \sum_{i=1}^{N} C_i (t_i - t)^2 e^{-y(t_i - t)}.$$

and the **convexity** is

$$\frac{1}{V}\frac{d^2V}{dy^2}.$$

To see how these can be used, examine Figure 31.4.

In this figure we see the price/yield relationship for two bonds having the same value and duration when the yield is around 8%, but then they have different convexities. Bond A has a greater convexity than bond B. This figure suggests that bond A is better value than B because a small change in the yields results in a higher value for A. Convexity becomes particularly important in a hedged portfolio of bonds.

The calculation of yield to maturity, duration and convexity are shown in the following simple spreadsheet. Inputs are in the grey boxes.

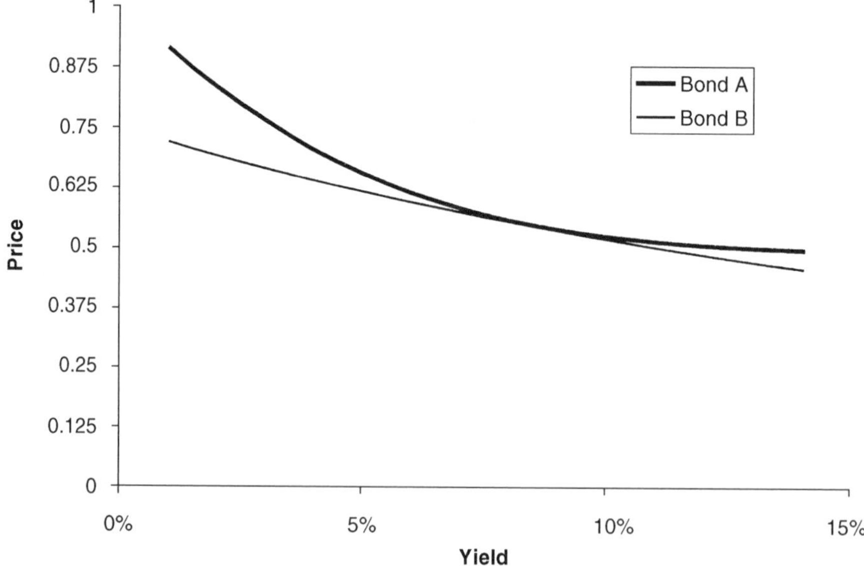

Figure 31.4 Two bonds with the same price and duration but different convexities.

31.11 HEDGING

In measuring and using yields to maturity, it must be remembered that the yield is the rate of discounting that makes the present value of a bond the same as its market value. A yield is thus identified with each individual instrument. It is perfectly possible for the yield on one instrument to rise while another falls, especially if they have significantly different maturities or durations. Nevertheless, one often wants to hedge movements in one bond with movements in another. This is commonly achieved by making one big assumption about the relative movements of yields on the two bonds. Bond A has a yield of 6.12%, bond B has a yield of 6.5%, they have different maturities and durations but we will assume that a move of $x\%$ in A's yield is accompanied by a move of $x\%$ in B's yield. This is the assumption of **parallel shifts** in the

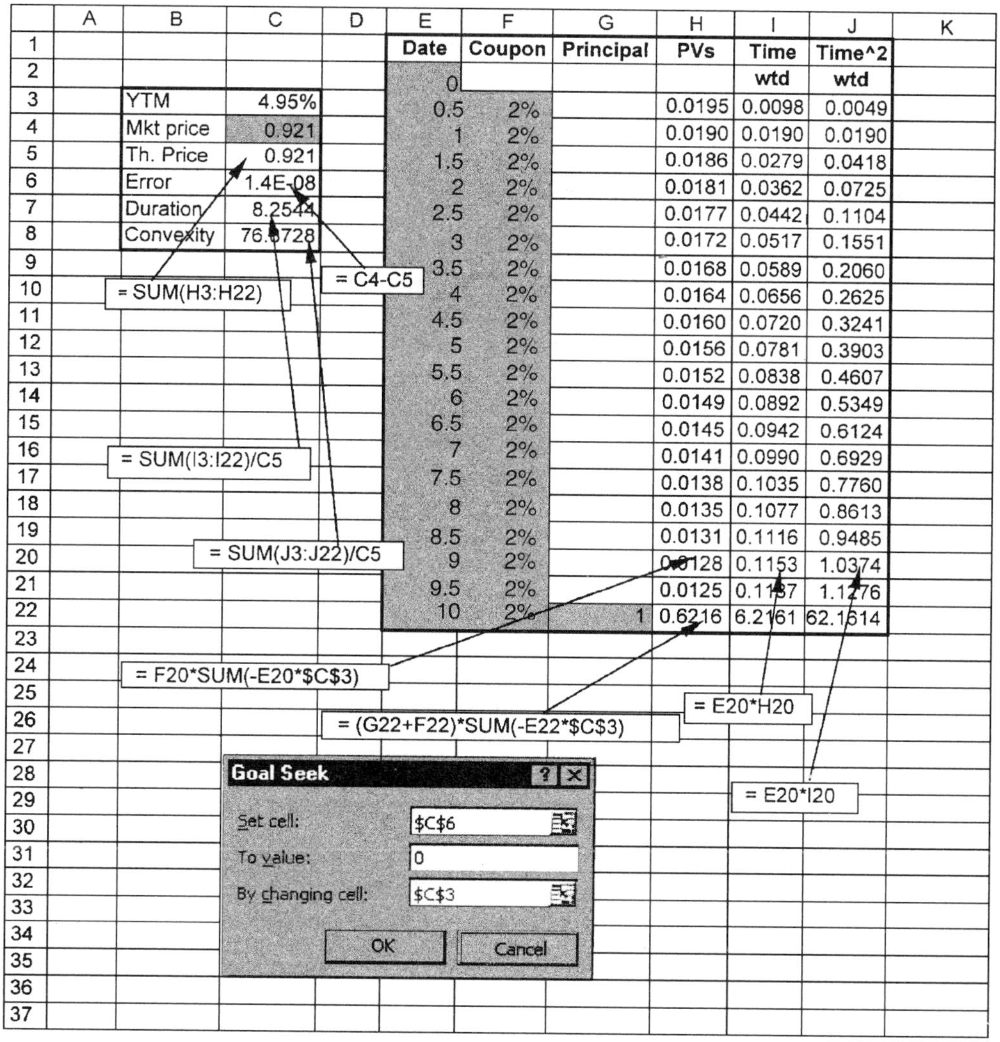

	A	B	C	D	E	F	G	H	I	J	K
1					Date	Coupon	Principal	PVs	Time	Time^2	
2					0				wtd	wtd	
3		YTM	4.95%		0.5	2%		0.0195	0.0098	0.0049	
4		Mkt price	0.921		1	2%		0.0190	0.0190	0.0190	
5		Th. Price	0.921		1.5	2%		0.0186	0.0279	0.0418	
6		Error	1.4E-08		2	2%		0.0181	0.0362	0.0725	
7		Duration	8.2544		2.5	2%		0.0177	0.0442	0.1104	
8		Convexity	76.8728		3	2%		0.0172	0.0517	0.1551	
9					3.5	2%		0.0168	0.0589	0.2060	
10					4	2%		0.0164	0.0656	0.2625	
11					4.5	2%		0.0160	0.0720	0.3241	
12					5	2%		0.0156	0.0781	0.3903	
13					5.5	2%		0.0152	0.0838	0.4607	
14					6	2%		0.0149	0.0892	0.5349	
15					6.5	2%		0.0145	0.0942	0.6124	
16					7	2%		0.0141	0.0990	0.6929	
17					7.5	2%		0.0138	0.1035	0.7760	
18					8	2%		0.0135	0.1077	0.8613	
19					8.5	2%		0.0131	0.1116	0.9485	
20					9	2%		0.0128	0.1153	1.0374	
21					9.5	2%		0.0125	0.1187	1.1276	
22					10	2%	1	0.6216	6.2161	62.1614	

= SUM(H3:H22)

= C4-C5

= SUM(I3:I22)/C5

= SUM(J3:J22)/C5

= F20*SUM(-E20*$C$3)

= (G22+F22)*SUM(-E22*$C$3)

= E20*H20

= E20*I20

Goal Seek

Set cell: $C$6

To value: 0

By changing cell: $C$3

OK Cancel

Figure 31.5 A spreadsheet showing the calculation of yield, duration and convexity.

yield curve. If this is the case, then if we hold A bonds and B bonds in the inverse ratio of their durations (with one long position and one short) we will be leading-order hedged:

$$\Pi = V_A(y_A) - \Delta V_B(y_B),$$

with the obvious notation for the value and yield of the two bonds. The change in the value of this portfolio is

$$\delta\Pi = \frac{\partial V_A}{\partial y_A}x - \Delta\frac{\partial V_B}{\partial y_B}x + \text{higher-order terms.}$$

Choose

$$\Delta = \frac{\partial V_A}{\partial y_A} \bigg/ \frac{\partial V_B}{\partial y_B}$$

to eliminate the leading-order risk. The higher-order terms depend on the convexity of the two instruments.

Of course, this is a simplification of the real situation; there may be little relationship between the yields on the two instruments, especially if the cash flows are significantly different. In this case there may be twisting or arching of the yield curve.

31.12 TIME-DEPENDENT INTEREST RATE

In this section we examine bond pricing when we have an interest rate that is a known function of time. The interest rate we consider will be what is known as a **short-term interest rate** or **spot interest rate** $r(t)$. This means that the rate $r(t)$ is to apply at time t: interest is compounded at this rate at each moment in time but *this rate may change*, generally we assume it to be time dependent.

If the spot interest rate $r(t)$ is a known function of time, then the bond price is also a function of time only: $V = V(t)$. (The bond price is, of course, also a function of maturity date T, but I suppress that dependence except when it is important.) We begin with a zero-coupon bond example. Because we receive 1 at time $t = T$ we know that $V(T) = 1$. I now derive an equation for the value of the bond at a time before maturity, $t < T$.

Suppose we hold one bond. The change in the value of that bond in a time-step dt (from t to $t + dt$) is

$$\frac{dV}{dt}dt.$$

Arbitrage considerations again lead us to equate this with the return from a bank deposit receiving interest at a rate $r(t)$:

$$\frac{dV}{dt} = r(t)V.$$

The solution of this equation is

$$V(t;T) = e^{-\int_t^T r(\tau)\,d\tau}. \tag{31.2}$$

Now let's introduce coupon payments. If during the period t to $t + dt$ we have received a coupon payment of $K(t)dt$, which may be either in the form of continuous or discrete payments or a combination, our holdings including cash change by an amount

$$\left(\frac{dV}{dt} + K(t)\right)dt.$$

Again setting this equal to the risk-free rate $r(T)$ we conclude that

$$\frac{dV}{dt} + K(t) = r(t)V. \tag{31.3}$$

The solution of this ordinary differential equation is easily found to be

$$V(t) = e^{-\int_t^T r(\tau)\,d\tau}\left(1 + \int_t^T K(t')e^{\int_{t'}^T r(\tau)\,d\tau}\,dt'\right); \tag{31.4}$$

the arbitrary constant of integration has been chosen to ensure that $V(T) = 1$.

31.13 DISCRETELY-PAID COUPONS

Equation (31.3) allows for the payment of a coupon. But what if the coupon is paid discretely, as it is in practice, for example, every six months? We can arrive at this result by a financial argument that will be useful later. Since the holder of the bond receives a coupon, call it K_c, at time t_c there must be a jump in the value of the bond across the coupon date. That is, the value before and after this date differ by K_c:

$$V(t_c^-) = V(t_c^+) + K_c.$$

This will be recognized as a jump condition. This time the realized bond price is *not* continuous. After all, there is a discrete payment at the coupon date. This jump condition will still apply when we come to consider stochastic interest rates.

Having built up a simple framework in which interest rates are time dependent I now show how to derive information about these rates from the market prices of bonds.

31.14 FORWARD RATES AND BOOTSTRAPPING

The main problem with the use of yield to maturity as a measure of interest rates is that it is not consistent across instruments. One five-year bond may have a different yield from another five-year bond if they have different coupon structures. It is therefore difficult to say that there is a single interest rate associated with a maturity.

One way of overcoming this problem is to use **forward rates**.

Forward rates are interest rates that are assumed to apply over given periods *in the future* for *all* instruments. This contrasts with yields which are assumed to apply up to maturity, with a different yield for each bond.

Let us suppose that we are in a perfect world in which we have a continuous distribution of zero-coupon bonds with all maturities T. Call the prices of these at time t $Z(t; T)$.

The **implied forward rate** is the curve of a time-dependent spot interest rate that is consistent with the market price of instruments. If this rate is $r(\tau)$ at time τ then it satisfies

$$Z(t; T) = e^{-\int_t^T r(\tau)\,d\tau}.$$

On rearranging and differentiating this gives

$$r(T) = -\frac{\partial}{\partial T}(\log Z(t;T)).$$

This is the forward rate for time T as it stands today, time t. Tomorrow the whole curve (the dependence of r on the future) may change. For that reason we usually denote the forward rate at time t applying at time T in the future as $F(t;T)$ where

$$F(t;T) = -\frac{\partial}{\partial T}(\log Z(t;T)).$$

In the less-than-perfect real world we must do with only a discrete set of data points. We continue to assume that we have zero-coupon bonds but now we will only have a discrete set of them. We can still find an implied forward rate curve as follows.

Rank the bonds according to maturity, with the shortest maturity first. The market prices of the bonds will be denoted by Z_i^M where i is the position of the bond in the ranking.

Using only the first bond, ask the question 'What interest rate is implied by the market price of the bond?' The answer is given by y_1, the solution of

$$Z_1^M = e^{-y_1(T_1-t)},$$

i.e.

$$y_1 = -\frac{\log(Z_1^M)}{T_1 - t}.$$

This rate will be the rate that we use for discounting between the present and the maturity date T_1 of the first bond. And it will be applied to *all* instruments whenever we want to discount over this period.

Now move on to the second bond having maturity date T_2. We know the rate to apply between now and time T_1, but at what interest rate must we discount between dates T_1 and T_2 to match the theoretical and market prices of the second bond? The answer is y_2 which solves the equation

$$Z_2^M = e^{-y_1(T_1-t)}e^{-y_2(T_2-T_1)},$$

i.e.

$$y_2 = -\frac{\log(Z_2^M/Z_1^M)}{T_2 - T_1}.$$

By this method of **bootstrapping** we can build up the forward rate curve. Note how the forward rates are applied between two dates, for which period we have assumed they are constant: the forward rate between 5 and 7 years is 9.85%, say. Figure 31.6 gives an example.

This method can easily be extended to accommodate coupon-bearing bonds. Again rank the bonds by their maturities, but now we have the added complexity that we may only have one market value to represent the sum of several cashflows. Thus one often has to make some assumptions to get the right number of equations for the number of unknowns.

Given the market price of zero-coupon bonds it is very easy to calculate yields and forward rates, as shown in the spreadsheet. Inputs are in the grey boxes.

There are far more swaps of different maturities than there are bonds, so that in practice swaps are used to build up the forward rates by bootstrapping. Fortunately, there is a simple

	A	B	C	D	E
1	Time to	Market	Yield to	Forward	
2	Maturity	price z-c b	maturity	rate	
3	0.25	0.9809	7.71%	7.71%	
4	0.5	0.9612	7.91%	8.12%	
5	1	0.9194	8.40%	8.89%	
6	2	0.8436	8.50%	8.60%	
7	3	0.7772	8.40%	8.20%	
8	5	0.644	8.80%	9.40%	
9	7	0.5288	9.10%	9.85%	
10	10	0.3985	9.20%	9.43%	
11					
12	= -LN(B10)/A10				
13					
14					
15		= (C10*A10-C9*A9)/(A10-A9)			
16					
17					

Figure 31.6 A spreadsheet showing the calculation of yields and forward rates from zero-coupon bonds.

decomposition of swaps prices into the prices of zero-coupon bonds so that bootstrapping is still relatively straightforward. Swaps are discussed in more detail in Chapter 32.

31.15 INTERPOLATION

We have explicitly assumed in the previous section that the forward rates are piecewise constant, jumping from one value to the next across the maturity of each bond. Other methods of 'interpolation' are also possible. For example, the forward rate curve could be made continuous, with piecewise constant gradient. Some people like to use cubic splines. The correct way of 'joining the dots' (for there are only a finite number of market prices) has been the subject of much debate. If you want to know what rate to apply to a two-and-a-half-year cashflow and the nearest bonds are at two and three years then you will have to make some assumptions; there is no 'correct' value. Perhaps the best that can be done is to bound the rate.

31.16 SUMMARY

There are good and bad points about the interest rate model of this chapter. First, I mention the advantages.

Compare the simplicity of the mathematics in this chapter with that in previous chapters on option pricing. Clearly there is benefit in having models for which the analysis is so simple. Computation of many values and hedging can be performed virtually instantaneously on even slow computers. Moreover, it may be completely unnecessary to have a more complex model. For example, if we want to compare simple cashflows it may be possible to directly value one bond by summing other bonds, if their cashflows can be made to match. Such a situation, although uncommon, is market-independent modeling. Even if exact cashflow matches are not possible, there may be sufficiently close agreement for the differences to be estimated or at least bounded; large errors are easily avoided.

On the other hand, it is common experience that interest rates are unpredictable, random, and for complex products the movement of rates in the most important factor in their pricing. To assume that interest rates follow forward rates would be financial suicide in such cases. There is therefore a need for models more closely related to the stochastic models we have seen in earlier chapters.

In this chapter we saw simple yet powerful ways to analyze simple fixed-income contracts. These methods are used very frequently in practice, far more frequently than the complex methods we later discuss for the pricing of interest rate derivatives. The assumptions underlying the techniques, such as deterministic forward rates, are only relevant to simple contracts. As we have seen in the options world, more complex products with nonlinear payoffs, require a model that incorporates the stochastic nature of variables. Stochastic interest rates will be the subject of later chapters.

FURTHER READING

- See Fabozzi (1996) for a discussion of yield, duration and convexity in greater detail. He explains how the ideas are extended to more complicated instruments.
- The argument about how to join the yield curve dots is as meaningless as the argument between the Little-Endians and Big-Endians of Swift (1726).

EXERCISES

1. A coupon bond pays out 3% every year, with a principal of \$1 and a maturity of five years. Decompose the coupon bond into a set of zero-coupon bonds.
2. Construct a spreadsheet to examine how \$1 grows when it is invested at a continuously-compounded rate of 7%. Redo the calculation for a discretely-compounded rate of 7%, paid once p.a. Which rate is more profitable?
3. A zero-coupon bond has a principal of \$100 and matures in 4 years. The market price for the bond is \$72. Calculate the yield to maturity, duration and convexity for the bond.
4. A coupon bond pays out 2% every year on a principal of \$100. The bond matures in 6 years and has market value \$92. Calculate the yield to maturity, duration and convexity for the bond.
5. Zero-coupon bonds are available with a principal of \$1 and the following maturities:

   1 year (market price \$0.93),
   2 years (market price \$0.82),
   3 years (market price \$0.74).

   Calculate the yield to maturities for the three bonds. Use a bootstrapping method to work out the forward rates that apply between 1–2 years and 2–3 years.
6. What assumption do we make when we duration hedge? Is this a reasonable assumption to make?
7. Solve the equation

$$\frac{dV}{dt} + K(t) = r(t)V,$$

PTE 6 Year Non-Call 2 Year Fixed Rate Step-up Note

Aggregate Principal Amount	PTE 10,000,000,000
Trade Date	4 November 1997
Issue Date	25 November 1997
Settlement Date	25 November 1997
Maturity Date	25 November 2003
Issue Price	100%
Coupon	Years 1-2: 5.75% Years 3-6: 6.25%
Issuer Optional Redemption	The issuer has the right, but not the obligation, to redeem the Notes at 100% of Nominal, in whole but not in part, on 25 November 1999 with 10 Business Days prior notice.
Payment Frequency	Annual
Daycount Convention	30/360
Governing Law	English

This indicative termsheet is neither an offer to buy or sell securities or an OTC derivative product which includes options, swaps, forwards and structured notes having similar features to OTC derivative transactions, nor a solicitation to buy or sell securities or an OTC derivative product. The proposal contained in the foregoing is not a complete description of the terms of a particular transaction and is subject to change without limitation.

Figure 31.7 A PTE six-year non-call two-year fixed rate step-up note.

with final data $V(T) = 1$. This is the value of a coupon bond when there is a *known* interest rate, $r(t)$. What must we do if interest rates are not known in advance?

8. The following is a term sheet for a step-up note paying a fixed rate that changes during the life of the contract.

   Plot the price/yield curve for this product today, ignoring the call feature. What effect will the call feature have on the price of this contract?

CHAPTER 32
swaps

In this Chapter...

- the specifications of basic interest rate swap contracts
- the relationship between swaps and zero-coupon bonds
- exotic swaps

32.1 INTRODUCTION

A **swap** is an agreement between two parties to exchange, or swap, future cashflows. The size of these cashflows is determined by some formulae, decided upon at the initiation of the contract. The swaps may be in a single currency or involve the exchange of cashflows in different currencies.

The swaps market is big. The total notional principal amount is, in US dollars, currently comfortably in *14* figures. This market really began in 1981 although there were a small number of swap-like structures arranged in the 1970s. Initially the most popular contracts were currency swaps, discussed below, but very quickly they were overtaken by the interest rate swap.

32.2 THE VANILLA INTEREST RATE SWAP

In the **interest rate swap** the two parties exchange cashflows that are represented by the interest on a notional principal. Typically, one side agrees to pay the other a fixed interest rate and the cashflow in the opposite direction is a **floating rate**. The parties to a swap are shown schematically in Figure 32.1. One of the commonest floating rates used in a swap agreement is LIBOR, London Interbank Offer Rate.

Commonly in a swap, the exchange of the fixed and floating interest payments occur every six months. In this case the relevant LIBOR rate would be the six-month rate. At the maturity of the contract the principal is *not* exchanged.

Let me give an example of how such a contract works.

Example

Suppose that we enter into a five-year swap on 8th July 1998, with semi-annual interest payments. We will pay to the other party a rate of interest fixed at 6% on a notional principal of \$100 million, the counterparty will pay us six-month

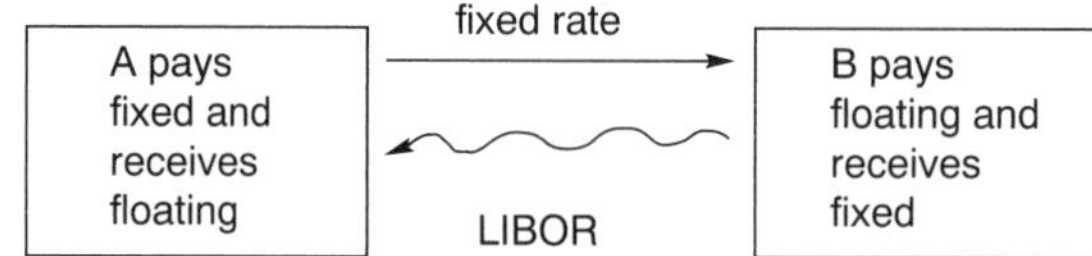

Figure 32.1 The parties to an interest rate swap.

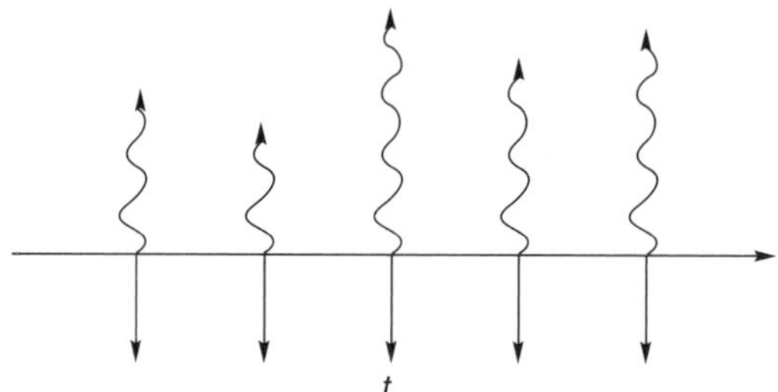

Figure 32.2 A schematic diagram of the cashflows in an interest rate swap.

LIBOR. The cashflows in this contract are shown in Figure 32.2. The straight lines denote a fixed rate of interest and thus a known amount, the curly lines are floating rate payments.

The first exchange of payments is made on 8th January 1999, six months after the deal is signed. How much money changes hands on that first date? We must pay $0.03 \times \$100{,}000{,}000 = \$3{,}000{,}000$. The cashflow in the opposite direction will be at six-month LIBOR, *as quoted six months previously*, i.e. at the initiation of the contract. This is a very important point. The LIBOR rate is set six months before it is paid, so that in the first exchange of payments the floating side is known. This makes the first exchange special.

The second exchange takes place on 8th July 1999. Again we must pay $3,000,000, but now we receive LIBOR, as quoted on 8th January 1999. Every six months there is an exchange of such payments, with the fixed leg always being known and the floating leg being known six months before it is paid. This continues until the last date, 8th July 2003.

Why is the floating leg set six months before it is paid? This 'minor' detail makes a large difference to the pricing of swaps, believe it or not. It is no coincidence that the time between payments is the same as the maturity of LIBOR that is used, six months in this example. This convention has grown up because of the meaning of LIBOR, it is the rate of interest on a fixed-term maturity, set now and paid at the end of the term. Each floating leg of the swap is like a single investment of the notional principal six months prior to the payment of the interest. Hold that thought, we return to this point in a couple of sections, to show the simple relationship between a swap and bonds.

There is also the **LIBOR in arrears swap** in which the LIBOR rate paid on the swap date is the six-month rate set that day, not the rate set six months before.

32.3 THE SWAP CURVE

When the swap is first entered into it is usual for the deal to have no value to either party. This is done by a careful choice of the fixed rate of interest. In other words, the 'present value,' let us say, of the fixed side and the floating side both have the same value, netting out to zero.

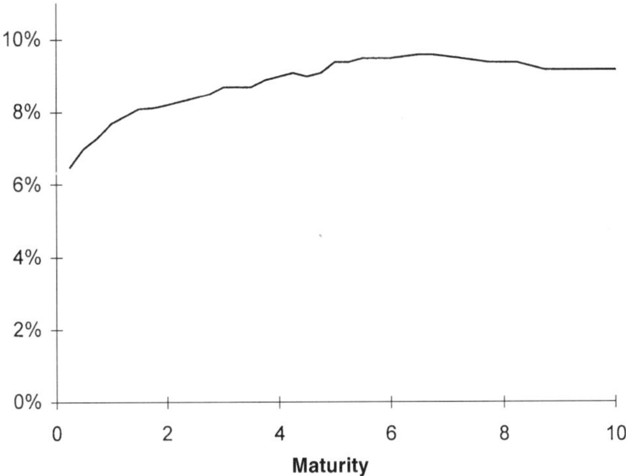

Figure 32.3 The swap curve.

Consider the two extreme scenarios, very high fixed leg and very low fixed leg. If the fixed leg is very high the receiver of fixed has a contract with a high value. If the fixed leg is low the receiver has a contract that is worth a negative amount. Somewhere in between is a value that makes the deal valueless. The fixed leg of the swap is chosen for this to be the case.

Such a statement throws up many questions: How is the fixed leg decided upon? Why should both parties agree that the deal is valueless?

There are two ways to look at this. One way is to observe that a swap can be decomposed into a portfolio of bonds (as we see shortly) and so its value is not open to question if we are given the yield curve. However, in practice the calculation goes the other way. The swaps market is so liquid, at so many maturities, that it is the prices of swaps that drive the prices of bonds. The fixed leg of a **par swap** (having no value) is determined by the market.

The rates of interest in the fixed leg of a swap are quoted at various maturities. These rates make up the **swap curve**, see Figure 32.3.

32.4 RELATIONSHIP BETWEEN SWAPS AND BONDS

There are two sides to a swap, the fixed-rate side and the floating-rate side. The fixed interest payments, since they are all known in terms of actual dollar amount, can be seen as the sum of zero-coupon bonds. If the fixed rate of interest is r_s then the fixed payments add up to

$$r_s \sum_{i=1}^{N} Z(t; T_i).$$

This is the value today, time t, of all the fixed-rate payments. Here there are N payments, one at each T_i. Of course, this is multiplied by the notional principal, but assume that we have scaled this to one.

To see the simple relationship between the floating leg and zero-coupon bonds I draw some schematic diagrams and compare the cashflows. A single floating leg payment is shown in Figure 32.4. At time T_i there is payment of r_τ of the notional principal, where r_τ is the period τ rate of LIBOR, set at time $T_i - \tau$. I add and subtract \$1 at time T_i to get the second diagram.

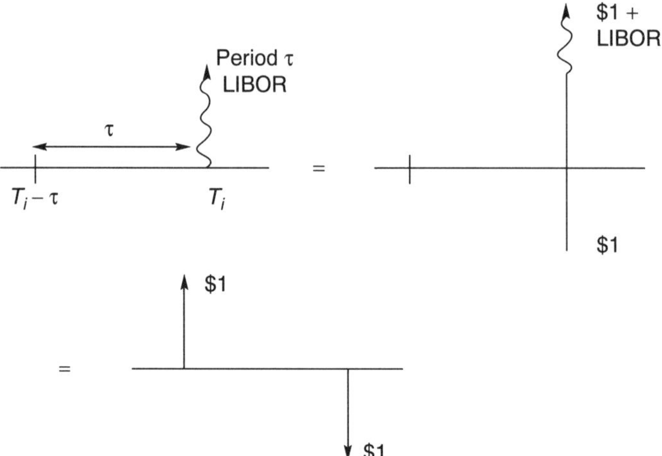

Figure 32.4 A schematic diagram of a single floating leg in an interest rate swap and equivalent portfolios.

The first and the second diagrams obviously have the same present value. Now recall the precise definition of LIBOR. It is the interest rate paid on a fixed-term deposit. Thus the $\$1 + r_\tau$ at time T_i is the same as \$1 at time $T_i - \tau$. This gives the third diagram. It follows that the single floating rate payment is equivalent to two zero-coupon bonds.

A single floating leg of a swap at time T_i is *exactly* equal to a deposit of \$1 at time $T_i - \tau$ and a withdrawal of \$1 at time τ.

Now add up all the floating legs as shown in Figure 32.5, note the cancellation of all \$1 (dashed) cashflows except for the first and last. This shows that the floating side of the swap has value

$$1 - Z(t; T_N).$$

Bring the fixed and floating sides together to find that the value of the swap, to the receiver of the fixed side, is

$$r_s \sum_{i=1}^{N} Z(t; T_i) - 1 + Z(t; T_N).$$

This result is *model independent*. This relationship is independent of any mathematical model for bonds or swaps.

At the start of the swap contract the rate r_s is usually chosen to give the contract par value, i.e. zero value initially. Thus

$$r_s = \frac{1 - Z(t; T_N)}{\sum_{i=1}^{N} Z(t; T_i)}. \tag{32.1}$$

This is the quoted swap rate.

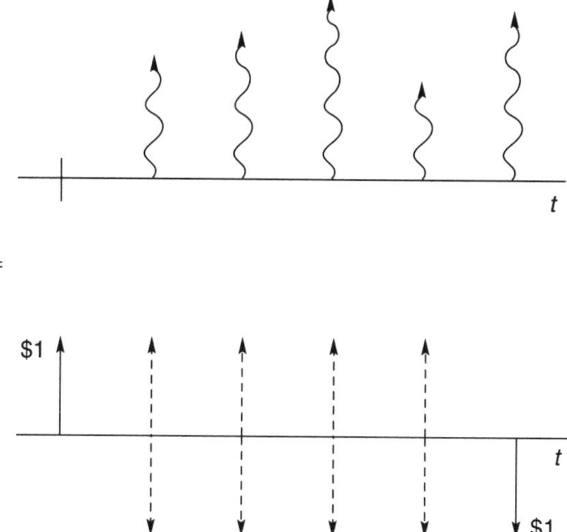

Figure 32.5 A schematic diagram of all the floating legs in a swap.

32.5 BOOTSTRAPPING

Swaps are now so liquid and exist for an enormous range of maturities that their prices determine the yield curve and not *vice versa*. In practice one is given $r_s(T_i)$ for many maturities T_i and one uses (32.1) to calculate the prices of zero-coupon bonds and thus the yield curve. For the first point on the discount-factor curve we must solve

$$r_s(T_1) = \frac{1 - Z(t; T_1)}{Z(t; T_1)},$$

i.e.

$$Z(t; T_1) = \frac{1}{1 + r_s(T_1)}.$$

After finding the first j discount factors the $j + 1$th is found from

$$Z(t : T_{j+1}) = \frac{1 - \sum_{i=1}^{j} Z(t; T_i)}{1 + r_s(T_{j+1})}$$

32.6 OTHER FEATURES OF SWAPS CONTRACTS

The above is a description of the vanilla interest rate swap. There any many features that can be added to the contract that make it more complicated, and most importantly, model dependent. A few of these features are mentioned here.

Callable and puttable swaps

A **callable** or **puttable swap** allows one side or the other to close out the swap at some time before its natural maturity. If you are receiving fixed and the floating rate rises more than you had expected you would want to close the position. Mathematically we are in the early exercise world of American-style options. The problem is model dependent and is discussed in Chapter 35.

Extendible swaps

The holder of an **extendible swap** can extend the maturity of a vanilla swap at the original swap rate.

Index amortizing rate swaps

The principal in the vanilla swap is constant. In some swaps the principal declines with time according to a prescribed schedule. The index amortizing rate swap is more complicated still with the amortization depending on the level of some index, say LIBOR, at the time of the exchange of payments. We will see this contract in detail in Chapter 35.

32.7 OTHER TYPES OF SWAP

32.7.1 Basis Rate Swap

In the **basis rate swap** the floating legs of the swap are defined in terms of two distinct interest rates. For example, the prime rate *versus* LIBOR. A bank may have outstanding loans based on this prime rate but itself may have to borrow at LIBOR. It is thus exposed to **basis risk** and can be reduced with a suitable basis rate swap.

32.7.2 Currency Swaps

A **currency swap** is an exchange of interest payments in one currency for payments in another currency. The interest rates can both be fixed, both floating or one of each. As well as the exchange of interest payments there is also an exchange of the principals (in two different currencies) at the beginning of the contract and at the end.

To value the fixed-to-fixed currency swap we need to calculate the present values of the cashflows in each currency. This is easily done, requiring the discount factors for the two currencies. Once this is done we can convert one present value to the other currency using the current *spot* exchange rate. If floating interest payments are involved we first decompose them into a portfolio of bonds (if possible) and value similarly.

32.7.3 Equity Swaps

The basic **equity swap** is an agreement to exchange two payments, one being an agreed interest rate (either fixed or floating) and the other depending on an equity index. This equity component is usually measured by the total return on an index, both capital gains and dividend are included. The principal is not exchanged.

The **equity basis swap** is an exchange of payments based on *two* different indices.

32.8 SUMMARY

The need and ability to be able to exchange one type of interest payment for another is fundamental to the running of many businesses. This has put swaps among the most liquid of financial contracts. This enormous liquidity makes swaps such an important product that one has to be very careful in their pricing. In fact, swaps are so liquid that you do not price them in any theoretical way; to do so would be highly dangerous. Instead they are almost treated like an 'underlying' asset. From the market's view of the value we can back out, for example, the yield curve. We are helped in this by the fine detail of the swaps structure, the cashflows are precisely defined in a way that makes them exactly decomposable into zero-coupon bonds. And this can be done in a completely model-independent way. To finish this chapter I want to stress the importance of not using a model when a set of cashflows can be perfectly, statically and model-independently, hedged by other cashflows. Any mispricing, via a model, no matter how small could expose you to large and risk-free losses.

FURTHER READING

- Two good technical books on swaps are by Das (1994) and Miron & Swannell (1991).
- The pocketbook by Ungar (1996) describes the purpose of the swaps market, how it works and the different types of swaps, with no mathematics.

EXERCISES

1. Consider a swap with the following specification:

   The floating payment is at the 6 month rate, and is set six months before the payment (swaplet) date. The swap expires in 5 years, and payments occur every six months on a principal of \$1. Zero-coupon bond prices are known for all maturities up to 10 years. What is the 'fair' level for the fixed rate side of the swap, so that initially the swap has no value?
2. An index amortizing rate swap has a principal which decreases at a rate dependent on the interest rate at settlement dates. Over a payment date, the principal changes from P to $g(r)P$, where $g(r)$ is a function specified in the swap contract, and $0 \le g(r) \le 1$. How will this affect the level of the fixed rate if the swap initially has no value?
3. A swap allows the side receiving floating to close out the position before maturity. How does the 'fair' value for the fixed rate side of the swap compare to that for a swap with no call/put features?

CHAPTER 33

one-factor interest rate modeling

In this Chapter...

- stochastic models for interest rates
- how to derive the bond pricing equation for many fixed-income products
- the structure of many popular interest rate models

33.1 INTRODUCTION

Until now I have assumed that interest rates are either constant or a known function of time. This may be a reasonable assumption for short-dated equity contracts. But for longer-dated contracts the interest rate must be more accurately modeled. This is not an easy task. In this chapter I introduce the ideas behind modeling interest rates using a single source of randomness. This is **one-factor interest rate modeling**. The model will allow the short-term interest rate, the spot rate, to follow a random walk. This model leads to a parabolic partial differential equation for the prices of bonds and other interest rate derivative products.

The 'spot rate' that we will be modeling is a very loosely-defined quantity, meant to represent the yield on a bond of infinitesimal maturity. In practice one should take this rate to be the yield on a liquid finite-maturity bond, say one of one month. Bonds with one *day* to expiry do exist but their price is not necessarily a guide to other short-term rates. I will continue to be vague about the precise definition of the spot interest rate. We could argue that if we are pricing a complex product that is highly model dependent then the *exact* definition of the independent variable will be relatively unimportant compared with the choice of model.

33.2 STOCHASTIC INTEREST RATES

Since we cannot realistically forecast the future course of an interest rate, it is natural to model it as a random variable. We are going to model the behavior of r, the interest rate received by the shortest possible deposit. From this we will see the development of a model for all other rates. The interest rate for the shortest possible deposit is commonly called the **spot interest rate**.

Earlier I proposed a model for the asset price as a stochastic differential equation, the lognormal random walk. Now let us suppose that the interest rate r is governed by another stochastic differential equation of the form

$$dr = u(r, t)\,dt + w(r, t)\,dX. \tag{33.1}$$

The functional forms of $u(r, t)$ and $w(r, t)$ determine the behavior of the spot rate r. For the present I will not specify any particular choices for these functions. I use this random walk to derive a partial differential equation for the price of a bond using similar arguments to those in the derivation of the Black–Scholes equation. Later I describe functional forms for u and w that have become popular with practitioners.

33.3 THE BOND PRICING EQUATION FOR THE GENERAL MODEL

When interest rates are stochastic a bond has a price of the form $V(r, t; T)$. The reader should think for the moment in terms of simple bonds, but the governing equation will be far more general and may be used to price many other contracts. That's why I'm using the notation V rather than our earlier Z, for zero-coupon bonds.

Pricing a bond presents new technical problems, and is in a sense harder than pricing an option since *there is no underlying asset with which to hedge*. We are therefore not modeling a *traded* asset; the traded asset (the bond, say) is a derivative of our independent variable r. The only way to construct a hedged portfolio is by hedging one bond with a bond of a different maturity. We set up a portfolio containing two bonds with different maturities T_1 and T_2. The bond with maturity T_1 has price $V_1(r, t; T_1)$ and the bond with maturity T_2 has price $V_2(r, t; T_2)$. We hold one of the former and a number $-\Delta$ of the latter. We have

$$\Pi = V_1 - \Delta V_2. \tag{33.2}$$

The change in this portfolio in a time dt is given by

$$d\Pi = \frac{\partial V_1}{\partial t}\,dt + \frac{\partial V_1}{\partial r}\,dr + \tfrac{1}{2}w^2\frac{\partial^2 V_1}{\partial r^2}\,dt - \Delta\left(\frac{\partial V_2}{\partial t}\,dt + \frac{\partial V_2}{\partial r}\,dr + \tfrac{1}{2}w^2\frac{\partial^2 V_2}{\partial r^2}\,dt\right), \tag{33.3}$$

where we have applied Itô's lemma to functions of r and t. Which of these terms are random? Once you've identified them you'll see that the choice

$$\Delta = \frac{\partial V_1}{\partial r}\bigg/\frac{\partial V_2}{\partial r}$$

eliminates all randomness in $d\Pi$. This is because it makes the coefficient of dr zero. We then have

$$\begin{aligned} d\Pi &= \left(\frac{\partial V_1}{\partial t} + \tfrac{1}{2}w^2\frac{\partial^2 V_1}{\partial r^2} - \left(\frac{\partial V_1}{\partial r}\bigg/\frac{\partial V_2}{\partial r}\right)\left(\frac{\partial V_2}{\partial t} + \tfrac{1}{2}w^2\frac{\partial^2 V_2}{\partial r^2}\right)\right)dt \\ &= r\Pi\,dt = r\left(V_1 - \left(\frac{\partial V_1}{\partial r}\bigg/\frac{\partial V_2}{\partial r}\right)V_2\right)dt, \end{aligned}$$

where we have used arbitrage arguments to set the return on the portfolio equal to the risk-free rate. This risk-free rate is just the spot rate.

Collecting all V_1 terms on the left-hand side and all V_2 terms on the right-hand side we find that

$$\frac{\dfrac{\partial V_1}{\partial t} + \tfrac{1}{2}w^2\dfrac{\partial^2 V_1}{\partial r^2} - rV_1}{\dfrac{\partial V_1}{\partial r}} = \frac{\dfrac{\partial V_2}{\partial t} + \tfrac{1}{2}w^2\dfrac{\partial^2 V_2}{\partial r^2} - rV_2}{\dfrac{\partial V_2}{\partial r}}.$$

At this point the distinction between the equity and interest-rate worlds starts to become apparent. This is *one* equation in *two* unknowns. Fortunately, the left-hand side is a function of T_1 but not T_2 and the right-hand side is a function of T_2 but not T_1. The only way for this to be possible is for both sides to be independent of the maturity date. Dropping the subscript from V, we have

$$\frac{\dfrac{\partial V}{\partial t}+\frac{1}{2}w^2\dfrac{\partial^2 V}{\partial r^2}-rV}{\dfrac{\partial V}{\partial r}}=a(r,t)$$

for some function $a(r, t)$. I shall find it convenient to write

$$a(r,t)=w(r,t)\,\lambda(r,t)-u(r,t);$$

for a given $u(r, t)$ and non-zero $w(r, t)$ this is always possible. The function $\lambda(r, t)$ is as yet unspecified.

The bond pricing equation is therefore

$$\frac{\partial V}{\partial t}+\frac{1}{2}w^2\frac{\partial^2 V}{\partial r^2}+(u-\lambda w)\frac{\partial V}{\partial r}-rV=0. \tag{33.4}$$

To find a unique solution of (33.4) we must impose one final and two boundary conditions. The final condition corresponds to the payoff on maturity and so for a zero-coupon bond

$$V(r,T;T)=1.$$

Boundary conditions depend on the form of $u(r, t)$ and $w(r, t)$ and are discussed later for a special model.

It is easy to incorporate coupon payments into the model. If an amount $K(r, t)\,dt$ is received in a period dt then

$$\frac{\partial V}{\partial t}+\frac{1}{2}w^2\frac{\partial^2 V}{\partial r^2}+(u-\lambda w)\frac{\partial V}{\partial r}-rV+K(r,t)=0.$$

When this coupon is paid discretely, arbitrage considerations lead to jump condition

$$V(r,t_c^-;T)=V(r,t_c^+;T)+K(r,t_c),$$

where a coupon of $K(r, t_c)$ is received at time t_c.

33.4 WHAT IS THE MARKET PRICE OF RISK?

I now give an interpretation of the function $\lambda(r, t)$. Imagine that you hold an unhedged position in one bond with maturity date T. In a time-step dt this bond changes in value by

$$dV=w\frac{\partial V}{\partial r}\,dX+\left(\frac{\partial V}{\partial t}+\frac{1}{2}w^2\frac{\partial^2 V}{\partial r^2}+u\frac{\partial V}{\partial r}\right)dt.$$

From (33.4) this may be written as

$$dV = w\frac{\partial V}{\partial r}\,dX + \left(w\lambda\frac{\partial V}{\partial r} + rV\right)dt,$$

or

$$dV - rV\,dt = w\frac{\partial V}{\partial r}(dX + \lambda\,dt). \tag{33.5}$$

The right-hand side of this expression contains two terms: a deterministic term in dt and a random term in dX. The presence of dX in (33.5) shows that this is not a riskless portfolio. The deterministic term may be interpreted as the excess return above the risk-free rate for accepting a certain level of risk. In return for taking the extra risk the portfolio profits by an extra $\lambda\,dt$ per unit of extra risk, dX. The function λ is therefore called the **market price of risk**.

33.5 INTERPRETING THE MARKET PRICE OF RISK, AND RISK NEUTRALITY

The bond pricing equation (33.4) contains references to the functions $u - \lambda w$ and w. The former is the coefficient of the first-order derivative with respect to the spot rate, and the latter appears in the coefficient of the diffusive, second-order derivative. The four terms in the equation represent, in order as written, time decay, diffusion, drift and discounting. The equation is similar to the backward equation for a probability density function (see Chapter 10) except for the final discounting term. As such we can interpret the solution of the bond pricing equation as the expected present value of all cashflows. As with equity options, this expectation is not with respect to the *real* random variable, but instead with respect to the *risk-neutral* variable. There is this difference because the drift term in the equation is not the drift of the real spot rate u, but the drift of another rate, called the **risk-neutral spot rate**. This rate has a drift of $u - \lambda w$. When pricing interest rate derivatives (including bonds of finite maturity) it is important to model, and price, using the risk-neutral rate. This rate satisfies

$$dr = (u - \lambda w)\,dt + w\,dX.$$

We need the new market-price-of-risk term because our modeled variable, r, is not traded.

If we set λ to zero then any results we find are applicable to the real world. If, for example, we want to find the distribution of the spot interest rate at some time in the future then we would solve a Fokker–Planck equation with the real, and not the risk-neutral, drift.

Because we can't observe the function λ, except possibly via the whole yield curve (see Chapter 34), I tend to think of it as a great big carpet under which we can brush all kinds of nasty, inconvenient things.

33.6 TRACTABLE MODELS AND SOLUTIONS OF THE BOND PRICING EQUATION

We have built up the bond pricing equation for an arbitrary model. That is, we have not specified the risk-neutral drift, $u - \lambda w$, or the volatility, w. How can we choose these functions to give us a good model? First of all, a simple lognormal random walk would *not* be suitable for r, since it would predict exponentially rising or falling rates. This rules out the equity price model as an interest rate model. So we must think more carefully about how to choose the drift and volatility.

Let us examine some choices for the risk-neutral drift and volatility that lead to tractable models, that is, models for which the solution of the bond pricing equation for zero-coupon bonds can be found analytically. We will discuss these models and see what properties we like or dislike.

For example, assume that $u - \lambda w$ and w take the form

$$u(r,t) - \lambda(r,t)\,w(r,t) = \eta(t) - \gamma(t)r, \tag{33.6}$$

$$w(r,t) = \sqrt{\alpha(t)r + \beta(t)}. \tag{33.7}$$

Note that we are describing a model for the risk-neutral spot rate. I will allow the functions $\alpha, \beta, \gamma, \eta$ and λ that appear in (33.7) and (33.6) to be functions of time. By suitably restricting these time-dependent functions, we can ensure that the random walk (33.1) for r has the following nice properties:

- ***Positive interest rates:*** Except for a few pathological cases, such as Switzerland in the 1960s, interest rates are positive. With the above model the spot rate can be bounded below by a positive number if $\alpha(t) > 0$ and $\beta \leq 0$. The lower bound is $-\beta/\alpha$. (In the special case $\alpha(t) = 0$ we must take $\beta(t) \geq 0$.) Note that r can still go to infinity, but with probability zero.

- ***Mean reversion:*** Examining the drift term, we see that for large r the (risk-neutral) interest rate will tend to decrease towards the mean, which may be a function of time. When the rate is small it will move up on average.

We also want the lower bound to be non-attainable. We don't want the spot interest rate to get forever stuck at the lower bound or have to impose further conditions to say how fast the spot rate moves away from this value. This requirement means that

$$\eta(t) \geq -\beta(t)\gamma(t)/\alpha(t) + \alpha(t)/2,$$

and it is discussed further below.

With the model (33.7) and (33.6) the boundary conditions for (33.4), for a zero-coupon bond, are, first, that

$$V(r,t;T) \to 0 \quad \text{as} \quad r \to \infty,$$

and, second, that on $r = -\beta/\alpha$, V remains finite. When r is bounded below by $-\beta/\alpha$, a local analysis of the partial differential equation can be carried out near $r = -\beta/\alpha$. Briefly, balancing the terms

$$\tfrac{1}{2}(\alpha r + \beta)\frac{\partial^2 V}{\partial r^2} \quad \text{and} \quad (\eta - \gamma r)\frac{\partial V}{\partial r}$$

shows that finiteness of V at $r = -\beta/\alpha$ is a sufficient boundary condition only if $\eta \geq -\beta\gamma/\alpha + \alpha/2$.

I chose u and w in the stochastic differential equation for r to take the special functional forms (33.7) and (33.6) for a very special reason. With these choices the solution of (33.4) for the zero-coupon bond is of the simple form

$$Z(r,t;T) = e^{A(t;T) - rB(t;T)}. \tag{33.8}$$

We are going to be looking at zero-coupon bonds specifically for a while, hence the change of our notation from V, meaning many interest rate products, to the very specific Z for zero coupon bonds.

The model with all of α, β, γ and η non-zero is the most general stochastic differential equation for r which leads to a solution of (33.4) of the form (33.8). This is easily shown.

Substitute (33.8) into the bond pricing equation (33.4). This gives

$$\frac{\partial A}{\partial t} - r\frac{\partial B}{\partial t} + \tfrac{1}{2}w^2B^2 - (u - \lambda w)B - r = 0. \tag{33.9}$$

Some of these terms are functions of t and T (i.e. A and B) and others are functions of r and t (i.e. u and w). Differentiating (33.9) with respect to r gives

$$-\frac{\partial B}{\partial t} + \tfrac{1}{2}B^2\frac{\partial}{\partial r}(w^2) - B\frac{\partial}{\partial r}(u - \lambda w) - 1 = 0.$$

Differentiate again with respect to r, and after dividing through by B, you get

$$\tfrac{1}{2}B\frac{\partial^2}{\partial r^2}(w^2) - \frac{\partial^2}{\partial r^2}(u - \lambda w) = 0.$$

In this, only B is a function of T, therefore we must have

$$\frac{\partial^2}{\partial r^2}(w^2) = 0 \tag{33.10}$$

and

$$\frac{\partial^2}{\partial r^2}(u - \lambda w) = 0. \tag{33.11}$$

From this follow (33.7) and (33.6).

The substitution of (33.7) and (33.6) into (33.10) and (33.11) yields the following equations for A and B:

$$\frac{\partial A}{\partial t} = \eta(t)B - \tfrac{1}{2}\beta(t)B^2 \tag{33.12}$$

and

$$\frac{\partial B}{\partial t} = \tfrac{1}{2}\alpha(t)B^2 + \gamma(t)B - 1. \tag{33.13}$$

In order to satisfy the final data that $Z(r, T; T) = 1$ we must have

$$A(T; T) = 0 \quad \text{and} \quad B(T; T) = 0.$$

33.7 SOLUTION FOR CONSTANT PARAMETERS

The solution for arbitrary α, β, γ and η is found by integrating the two ordinary differential equations (33.12) and (33.13). Generally speaking, though, when these parameters are time dependent this integration cannot be done explicitly. But in some special cases this integration *can* be done explicitly. The simplest case is when α, β, γ and η are all constant, in which case

$$\frac{\alpha}{2}A = a\psi_2 \log(a - B) + \left(\psi_2 + \tfrac{1}{2}\beta\right) b \log((B + b)/b) - \tfrac{1}{2}B\beta - a\psi_2 \log a, \tag{33.14}$$

and

$$B(t;T) = \frac{2(e^{\psi_1(T-t)} - 1)}{(\gamma + \psi_1)(e^{\psi_1(T-t)} - 1) + 2\psi_1}, \tag{33.15}$$

where

$$b, a = \frac{\pm\gamma + \sqrt{\gamma^2 + 2\alpha}}{\alpha},$$

and

$$\psi_1 = \sqrt{\gamma^2 + 2\alpha} \quad \text{and} \quad \psi_2 = \frac{\eta - a\beta/2}{a + b}.$$

When all four of the parameters are constant it is obvious that both A and B are functions of only the one variable $\tau = T - t$, and not t and T individually; this would not necessarily be the case if any of the parameters were time dependent.

A wide variety of yield curves can be predicted by the model. As $\tau \to \infty$,

$$B \to \frac{2}{\gamma + \psi_1}$$

and the yield curve Y has long term behavior given by

$$Y \to \frac{2}{(\gamma + \psi_1)^2}(\eta(\gamma + \psi_1) - \beta).$$

Thus for constant and fixed parameters the model leads to a fixed long-term interest rate, independent of the spot rate.

The probability density function, $P(r, t)$, for the risk-neutral spot rate satisfies

$$\frac{\partial P}{\partial t} = \frac{1}{2}\frac{\partial^2}{\partial r^2}(w^2 P) - \frac{\partial}{\partial r}((u - \lambda w)P).$$

In the long term this settles down to a distribution, $P_\infty(r)$, that is independent of the *initial* value of the rate. This distribution satisfies the ordinary differential equation

$$\frac{1}{2}\frac{d^2}{dr^2}(w^2 P_\infty) = \frac{d}{dr}((u - \lambda w)P_\infty).$$

The solution of this for the general affine model with constant parameters is

$$P_\infty(r) = \frac{\left(\frac{2\gamma}{\alpha}\right)^k}{\Gamma(k)}\left(r + \frac{\beta}{\alpha}\right)^{k-1} e^{\frac{-2\gamma}{\alpha}\left(r + \frac{\beta}{\alpha}\right)} \tag{33.16}$$

where

$$k = \frac{2\eta}{\alpha} + \frac{2\beta\gamma}{\alpha^2}$$

and $\Gamma(\cdot)$ is the gamma function. The boundary $r = -\beta/\alpha$ is non-attainable if $k > 1$. The mean of the steady-state distribution is

$$\frac{\alpha k}{2\gamma} - \frac{\beta}{\alpha}.$$

33.8 NAMED MODELS

There are many interest rate models, associated with the names of their inventors. The stochastic differential equation (33.1) for the risk-neutral interest rate process, with risk-neutral drift and volatility given by (33.6) and (33.7), incorporates the models of Vasicek, Cox, Ingersoll & Ross, Ho & Lee, and Hull & White.

33.8.1 Vasicek

The Vasicek model takes the form of (33.6) and (33.7) but with $\alpha = 0$, $\beta > 0$ and with all other parameters independent of time:

$$dr = (\eta - \gamma r)\,dt + \beta^{1/2}\,dX.$$

This model is so 'tractable' that there are explicit formulae for many interest rate derivatives. The value of a zero-coupon bond is given by

$$e^{A(t;T)-rB(t;T)}$$

where

$$B = \frac{1}{\gamma}(1 - e^{-\gamma(T-t)})$$

and

$$A = \frac{1}{\gamma^2}(B(t;T) - T + t)\left(\eta\gamma - \tfrac{1}{2}\beta\right) - \frac{\beta B(t;T)^2}{4\gamma}.$$

The model is mean reverting to a constant level, which is a good property, but interest rates can easily go negative, which is a very bad property.

In Figure 33.1 are shown three types of yield curves predicted by the Vasicek model. Each uses different parameters. (It is quite difficult to get the humped yield curve with reasonable numbers.)

The steady-state probability density function for the Vasicek model is a degenerate case of (33.16), since $\alpha = 0$. We find that

$$P_\infty(r) = \sqrt{\frac{\gamma}{\beta\pi}}\,e^{-\frac{\gamma}{\beta}\left(r-\frac{\eta}{\gamma}\right)^2}.$$

This is plotted in Figure 33.2. Thus, in the long run, the spot rate is Normally distributed in the Vasicek model. The mean of this distribution is

$$\frac{\eta}{\gamma}.$$

(The parameters in the figure have been deliberately chosen to give an alarming probability of a negative interest rate. For reasonable parameters the probability of negative rates is not that worrying, but then with reasonable parameters it's hard to get realistic looking yield curves.)

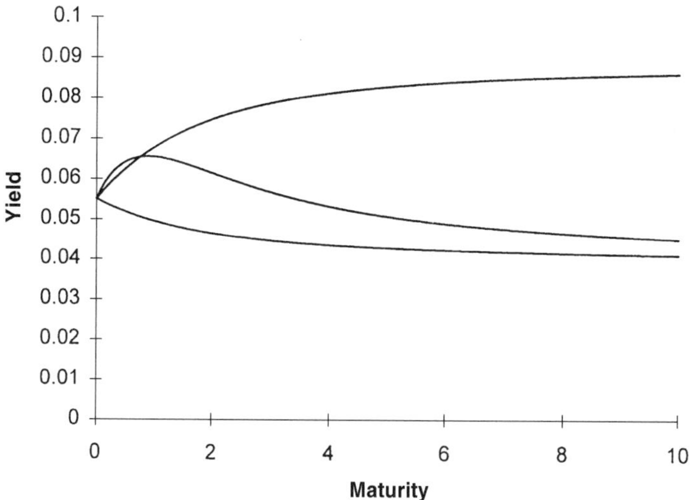

Figure 33.1 Three types of yield curve given by the Vasicek model.

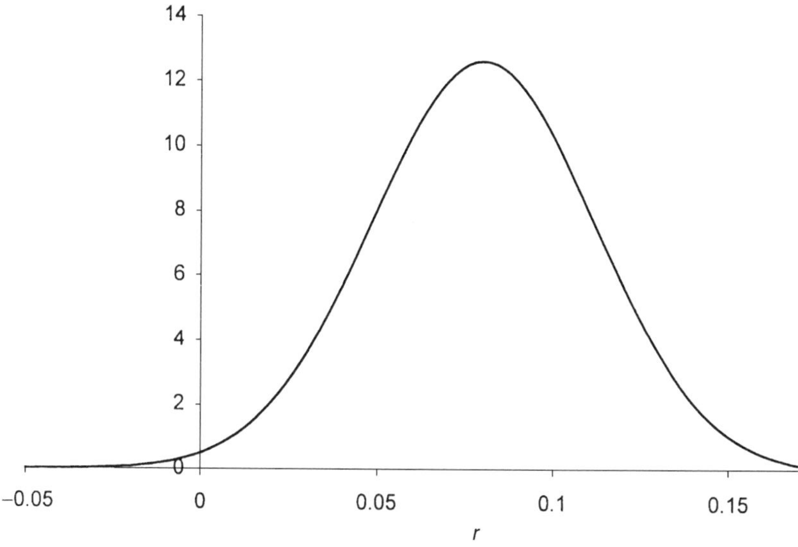

Figure 33.2 The steady-state probability density function for the risk-neutral spot rate in the Vasicek model.

33.8.2 Cox, Ingersoll & Ross

The CIR model takes (33.6) and (33.7) as the interest rate model but with $\beta = 0$, and again no time dependence in the parameters:

$$dr = (\eta - \gamma r)\,dt + \sqrt{\alpha r}\,dX.$$

The spot rate is mean reverting and if $\eta > \alpha/2$ the spot rate stays positive. There are some explicit solutions for interest rate derivatives, although typically involving integrals of the

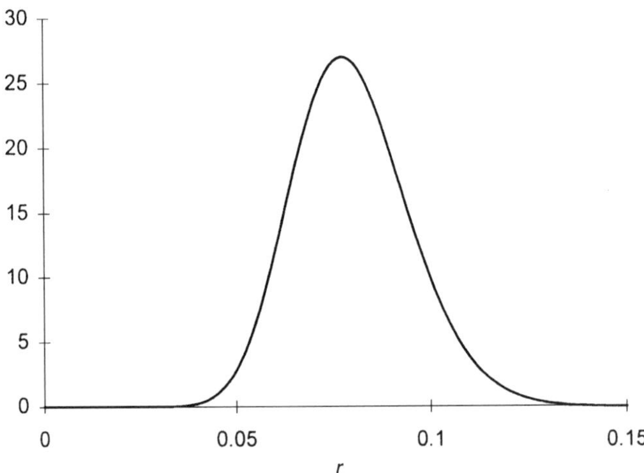

Figure 33.3 The steady-state probability density function for the risk-neutral spot rate in the CIR model.

non-central chi-squared distribution. The value of a zero-coupon bond is

$$e^{A(t;T)-rB(t;T)}$$

where A and B are given by (33.14) and (33.15) with $\beta = 0$. The resulting expression is not much simpler than in the non-zero β case.

The steady-state probability density function for the spot rate is a special case of (33.16). A plot of this function is shown in Figure 33.3. The mean of the steady-state distribution is again

$$\frac{\eta}{\gamma}.$$

In Figure 33.4 are simulations of the Vasicek and CIR models using the same random numbers. The parameters have been chosen to give similar mean and standard deviations for the two processes.

33.8.3 Ho & Lee

Ho & Lee have $\alpha = \gamma = 0$, $\beta > 0$ and constant but η can be a function of time:

$$dr = \eta(t)\,dt + \beta^{1/2}\,dX.$$

The value of zero-coupon bonds is given by

$$e^{A(t;T)-rB(t;T)}$$

where

$$B = T - t$$

and

$$A = -\int_t^T \eta(s)(T-s)\,ds + \tfrac{1}{6}\beta(T-t)^3.$$

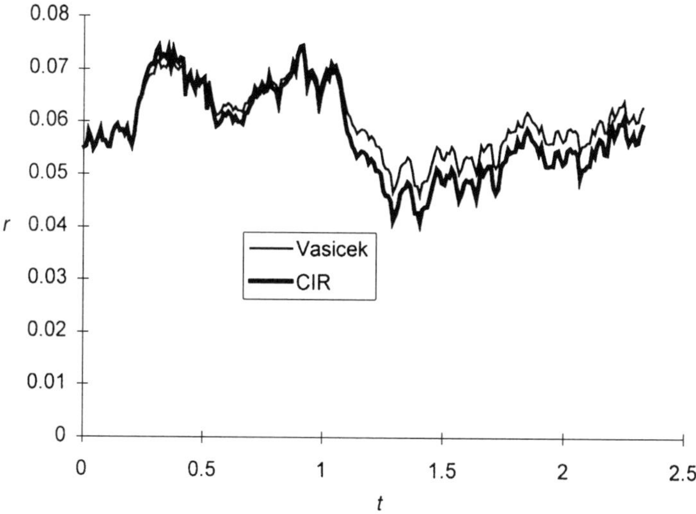

Figure 33.4 A simulation of the Vasicek and CIR models using the same random numbers.

This model was the first 'no-arbitrage model' of the term structure of interest rates. By this is meant that the careful choice of the function $\eta(t)$ will result in theoretical zero-coupon bonds prices, output by the model, which are the same as market prices. This technique is also called **yield curve fitting**. This careful choice is

$$\eta(t) = -\frac{\partial^2}{\partial t^2} \log Z_M(t^*; t) + \beta(t - t^*)$$

where today is time $t = t^*$. In this $Z_M(t^*; T)$ is the market price today of zero-coupon bonds with maturity T. Clearly this assumes that there are bonds of all maturities and that the prices are twice differentiable with respect to the maturity. We will see why this should give the 'correct' prices later. This analytically tractable model also yields simple explicit formulae for bond options. The business of 'yield curve fitting' is the subject of Chapter 34.

33.8.4 Hull & White

Hull & White have extended both the Vasicek and the CIR models to incorporate time-dependent parameters. This time dependence again allows the yield curve (and even a volatility structure) to be fitted. We will explore this model in greater depth later.

33.9 SUMMARY

In this chapter I introduced the idea of a random interest rate. The interest rate that we modeled was the 'spot rate,' a short-term interest rate. Several popular spot rate models were described. These models were chosen because simple forms of the coefficients make the solution of the basic bond pricing equation straightforward analytically.

From a model for this spot rate we can derive the whole yield curve. This is certainly unrealistic and in later chapters we will see how to make the model of more practical use.

FURTHER READING

- See the original interest rate models by Vasicek (1977), Dothan (1978), Cox, Ingersoll & Ross (1985), Ho & Lee (1986) and Black, Derman & Toy (1990).
- For details of the general affine model see the papers by Pearson & Sun (1989), Duffie (1992), Klugman (1992) and Klugman & Wilmott (1994).
- The comprehensive book by Rebonato (1996) describes all of the popular interest rate models in detail.

EXERCISES

1. Substitute
$$Z(r,t;T) = e^{A(t;T)-rB(t;T)},$$
into the bond pricing equation
$$\frac{\partial V}{\partial t} + \tfrac{1}{2}w^2\frac{\partial^2 V}{\partial r^2} + (u-\lambda w)\frac{\partial V}{\partial r} - rV = 0.$$
What are the explicit dependencies of the functions in the resulting equation?
2. Simulate random walks for the interest rate to compare the different named models suggested in this chapter.
3. What final condition (payoff) should be applied to the bond pricing equation for a swap, cap, floor, zero-coupon bond, coupon bond and a bond option?
4. What form does the bond pricing equation take when the interest rate satisfies the Vasicek model
$$dr = (\eta - \gamma r)\,dt + \beta^{1/2}\,dX?$$
Solve the resulting equations for A and B in this case, to find
$$A = \frac{1}{\gamma^2}(B - T + t)\left(\eta\gamma - \tfrac{1}{2}\beta\right) - \frac{\beta B^2}{4\gamma},$$
and
$$B = \frac{1}{\gamma}(1 - e^{-\gamma(T-t)}).$$

CHAPTER 34

yield curve fitting

In this Chapter...

- how to choose time-dependent parameters in one-factor models so that today's yield curve is an output of the model
- the advantages and disadvantages of yield curve fitting

34.1 INTRODUCTION

One-factor models for the spot rate build up an entire yield curve from a knowledge of the spot rate and the parameters in the model. In using a one-factor model we have to decide how to choose the parameters and whether to believe the output of the model. If we choose parameters using historical time series data then one of the outputs of the model will be a theoretical yield curve. Unless we are very, very lucky this theoretical curve will not be the same as the market yield curve. Which do we believe? Do we believe the theoretical yield curve or do we believe the prices trading in the market? You have to be very brave to ignore the market prices for such liquid instruments as bonds and swaps. Even if you are pricing very complex products you must still hedge with simpler, more liquid, traded contracts for which you would like to get the price right.

Because of this need to correctly price liquid instruments, the idea of **yield curve fitting** or **calibration** has become popular. When one-factor models are used in practice they are almost always fitted. This means that one or more of the parameters in the model is allowed to depend on time. This functional dependence on time is then carefully chosen to make an output of the model, the price of zero-coupon bonds, exactly match the market prices for these instruments. Yield curve fitting is the subject of this chapter.

34.2 HO & LEE

The Ho & Lee spot interest rate model is the simplest that can be used to fit the yield curve. It will be useful to examine this model in detail to see one way in which fitting is done in practice.

In the Ho & Lee model the process for the risk-neutral spot rate is

$$dr = \eta(t)\,dt + c\,dX.$$

The standard deviation of the spot rate process, c, is constant, the drift rate η is time dependent.

In this model the solution of the bond pricing equation for a zero-coupon bond is simply

$$Z(r, t; T) = e^{A(t;T)-r(T-t)},$$

where

$$A(t; T) = -\int_t^T \eta(s)(T - s)\, ds + \tfrac{1}{6}c^2(T - t)^3.$$

If we know $\eta(t)$ then the above gives us the theoretical value of zero-coupon bonds of all maturities. Now turn this relationship around and ask the question 'What functional form must we choose for $\eta(t)$ to make the theoretical value of the discount rates for all maturities equal to the market values?' Call this special choice for η, $\eta^*(t)$. The yield curve is to be fitted today, $t = t^*$, when the spot interest rate is r^* and the discount factors in the market are $Z_M(t^*; T)$. To match the market and theoretical bond prices, we must solve

$$Z_M(t^*; T) = e^{A(t^*;T)-r^*(T-t^*)}.$$

Taking logarithms of this and rearranging slightly we get

$$\int_{t^*}^T \eta^*(s)(T - s)\, ds = -\log(Z_M(t^*; T)) - r^*(T - t^*) + \tfrac{1}{6}c^2(T - t^*)^3. \tag{34.1}$$

Observe that I am carrying around in the notation today's date t^*. This is a constant but I want to emphasize that we are doing the calibration to *today's* yield curve. If we calibrate again tomorrow, the market yield curve will have changed.

Differentiate (34.1) twice with respect to T to get

$$\eta^*(t) = c^2(t - t^*) - \frac{\partial^2}{\partial t^2}\log(Z_M(t^*; t)).$$

With this choice for the time-dependent parameter $\eta(t)$ the theoretical and actual market prices of zero-coupon bonds are the same. It also follows that

$$A(t; T) = \log\left(\frac{Z_M(t^*; T)}{Z_M(t^*; t)}\right) - (T - t)\frac{\partial}{\partial t}\log(Z_M(t^*; t)) - \tfrac{1}{2}c^2(t - t^*)(T - t)^2.$$

34.3 THE EXTENDED VASICEK MODEL OF HULL & WHITE

The Ho & Lee model isn't the only one that can be calibrated, it's just the easiest. Most one-factor models have the potential for fitting, but the more tractable the model the easier the fitting. If the model is not at all tractable, having no nice explicit zero-coupon bond price formula, then we can always resort to numerical methods.

The next easiest model to fit is the Vasicek model. The Vasicek model has the following stochastic differential equation for the risk-neutral spot rate

$$dr = (\eta - \gamma r)\, dt + c\, dX.$$

Hull & White extend this to include a time-dependent parameter

$$dr = (\eta(t) - \gamma r)\, dt + c\, dX.$$

Assuming that γ and c have been estimated statistically, say, we choose $\eta = \eta^*(t)$ at time t^* so that our theoretical and the market prices of bonds coincide.

Under this risk-neutral process the value of zero-coupon bonds

$$Z(r, t; T) = e^{A(t;T) - rB(t;T)},$$

where

$$A(t; T) = -\int_t^T \eta^*(s) B(s; T) ds + \frac{c^2}{2\gamma^2}\left(T - t + \frac{2}{\gamma}e^{-\gamma(T-t)} - \frac{1}{2\gamma}e^{-2\gamma(T-t)} - \frac{3}{2\gamma}\right)$$

and

$$B(t; T) = \frac{1}{\gamma}\left(1 - e^{-\gamma(T-t)}\right).$$

To fit the yield curve at time t^* we must make $\eta^*(t)$ satisfy

$$\begin{aligned} A(t^*; T) &= -\int_{t^*}^T \eta^*(s) B(s; T)\, ds + \frac{c^2}{2\gamma^2}\left(T - t^* + \frac{2}{\gamma}e^{-\gamma(T-t^*)} - \frac{1}{2\gamma}e^{-2\gamma(T-t^*)} - \frac{3}{2\gamma}\right) \\ &= \log(Z_M(t^*; T)) + r^* B(t^*, T). \end{aligned} \tag{34.2}$$

This is an integral equation for $\eta^*(t)$ if we are given all of the other parameters and functions, such as the market prices of bonds, $Z_M(t^*; T)$.

Although (34.2) may be solved by Laplace transform methods, it is particularly easy to solve by differentiating the equation twice with respect to T. This gives

$$\eta^*(t) = -\frac{\partial^2}{\partial t^2}\log(Z_M(t^*; t)) - \gamma\frac{\partial}{\partial t}\log(Z_M(t^*; t)) + \frac{c^2}{2\gamma}\left(1 - e^{-2\gamma(t-t^*)}\right). \tag{34.3}$$

From this expression we can now find the function $A(t; T)$,

$$A(t; T) = \log\left(\frac{Z_M(t^*; T)}{Z_M(t^*; t)}\right) - B(t; T)\frac{\partial}{\partial t}\log(Z_M(t^*; t)) - \frac{c^2}{4\gamma^3}(e^{-\gamma(T-t^*)} - e^{-\gamma(t-t^*)})(e^{2\gamma(t-t^*)} - 1).$$

34.4 YIELD-CURVE FITTING: FOR AND AGAINST

34.4.1 For

The building blocks of the bond pricing equation are delta hedging and no arbitrage. If we are to use a one-factor model correctly then we must abide by the delta hedging assumptions. We must buy and sell instruments to remain delta neutral. The buying and selling of instruments must be done at the market prices. We *cannot* buy and sell at a theoretical price. But we are not modeling the bond prices directly, we model the spot rate and bond prices are then derivatives of the spot rate. This means that there is a real likelihood that our output bond prices will differ markedly from the market prices. This is useless if we are to hedge with these bonds. The model thus collapses and cannot be used for pricing other instruments, unless we can find a way to generate the correct prices for our hedging instruments from the model; this is yield curve fitting.

As an aside, suppose we are not interested in hedging but want to speculate with some fixed-income instruments. It is common knowledge that the yield curve is a poor predictor of real future interest rates. In this case it could be unnecessary or even dangerous to fit the yield curve. In this situation one could 'value' the instrument using the *real* spot rate process. This would give a 'value' for the instrument that was the expected present value of all cashflows under the *real* random walk. To do this one needs a model for the real drift u. There are ways of doing this, discussed in Chapter 38, that give satisfactory results and they don't need any fitting. This subject of valuing under speculation was the subject of Chapter 28.

34.4.2 Against

If the market prices of simple bonds were correctly given by a model, such as Ho & Lee or Hull & White, fitted at time t^* then, when we come back a week later, t^*+ one week, say, to refit the function $\eta^*(t)$, we would find that this function *had not changed* in the meantime. This *never* happens in practice. We find that the function η^* has changed out of all recognition. What does this mean? Clearly the model is wrong.[1]

By simply looking for a Taylor series solution of the bond-pricing equation for short times to expiry, we can relate the value of the risk-adjusted drift rate at the short end to the slope and curvature of the market yield curve. This is done as follows. Look for a solution of (33.4) of the form

$$Z(r, t; T) \sim 1 + a(r)(T-t) + b(r)(T-t)^2 + c(r)(T-t)^3 + \cdots.$$

Substitute this into the bond pricing equation:

$$-a - 2b(T-t) - 3c(T-t)^2 + \tfrac{1}{2}\left(w^2 - 2(T-t)w\frac{\partial w}{\partial t}\right)\left((T-t)\frac{d^2a}{dr^2} + (T-t)^2\frac{d^2b}{dr^2}\right)$$
$$+\left((u-\lambda w) - (T-t)\frac{\partial(u-\lambda w)}{\partial t}\right)(T-t)\left(\frac{da}{dr} + (T-t)^2\frac{db}{dr}\right)$$
$$-r(1 + a(T-t) + c(T-t)^2) + \cdots = 0.$$

Note how I have expanded the drift and volatility terms about $t = T$; in the above these are evaluated at r and T. By equating powers of $(T-t)$ we find that

$$a(r) = -r, \quad b(r) = \tfrac{1}{2}r^2 - \tfrac{1}{2}(u - \lambda w)$$

and

$$c(r) = \tfrac{1}{12}w^2\frac{\partial^2}{\partial r^2}(r^2 - r(u-\lambda w)) - \tfrac{1}{6}(u-\lambda w)\frac{\partial}{\partial r}(r^2 - r(u-\lambda w))$$
$$-\tfrac{1}{3}\frac{\partial}{\partial t}(u-\lambda w) + \tfrac{1}{6}r^2(r - (u-\lambda w)).$$

In all of these $u - \lambda w$ and w are evaluated at r and T.

From the Taylor series expression for Z we find that the yield to maturity is given by

$$-\frac{\log(Z(r,t;T))}{T-t} \sim -a + \left(\tfrac{1}{2}a^2 - b\right)(T-t) + (ab - c - \tfrac{1}{3}a^3)(T-t)^2 + \cdots$$

for short times to maturity.

[1] This doesn't mean that it isn't useful, or profitable. This is a much more subtle point.

The yield curve takes the value $-a(r) = r$ at maturity, obviously. The slope of the yield curve is

$$\tfrac{1}{2}a^2 - b = \tfrac{1}{2}(u - \lambda w),$$

i.e. one half of the risk-neutral drift. The curvature of the yield curve at the short end is proportional to

$$ab - c - \tfrac{1}{3}a^3,$$

which contains a term that is the derivative of the risk-neutral drift with respect to time via c. Let me stress the key points of this analysis. The slope of the yield curve at the short end depends on the risk-neutral drift, and *vice versa*. The curvature of the yield curve at the short end depends on the time derivative of the risk-neutral drift, and *vice versa*.

If we choose time-dependent parameters within the risk-adjusted drift rate such that the market prices are fitted at time t^* then we have

$$Z(r^*, t^*; T) = Z_M(t^*; T)$$

which is one equation for the time-dependent parameters.

Thus, for Ho & Lee, for example, the value of the function $\eta^*(t)$ at the short end, $t = t^*$, depends on the slope of the market yield curve. Moreover, the slope of $\eta^*(t)$ depends on the *curvature* of the yield curve at the short end. Results such as these are typical for all fitted models. These, seemingly harmless results, are actually quite profound.

It is common for the slope of the yield curve to be quite large and positive, the difference between very short and not quite so short rates is large. But then for longer maturities typically the yield curve flattens out. This means that the yield curve has a large negative curvature. If one performs the fitting procedure as outlined here for the Ho & Lee or extended Vasicek models, one typically finds the following:

- The value of $\eta^*(t)$ at $t = t^*$ is very large. This is because the yield-curve slope at the short end is often large.
- The slope of $\eta^*(t)$ at $t = t^*$ is large and negative. This is because the curvature of the yield curve is often large and negative.

A typical plot of $\eta^*(t)$ *versus* t is shown in Figure 34.1. This shows the high value for the fitted function and the large negative slope.[2] So far, so good. Maybe this is correct, maybe this is really what the fitted parameter should look like. But what happens when we come back in a few months to look at how our fitted parameter is doing? If the model is correct then we would find that the fitted curve looked like the bold part of the curve in the figure. The previous data should have just dropped off the end, the rest of the curve should remain unchanged. We would then see a corresponding dramatic flattening of the yield curve. Does this in fact happen? No. The situation looks more like that in Figure 34.2, which is really just a translation of the curve in time. Again we see the high value at the short end, the large negative slope and the oscillations. The recalibrated function in Figure 34.2 looks nothing like the bold line in Figure 34.1. This is because the yield curve has not changed that much in the meantime. It still has the high slope and curvature. In fact, we don't even have to wait for a few months for the deviation to be significant, it becomes apparent in weeks or even days.

---

[2] The strange oscillation of the function η^* beyond the short end is usually little more than numerical errors.

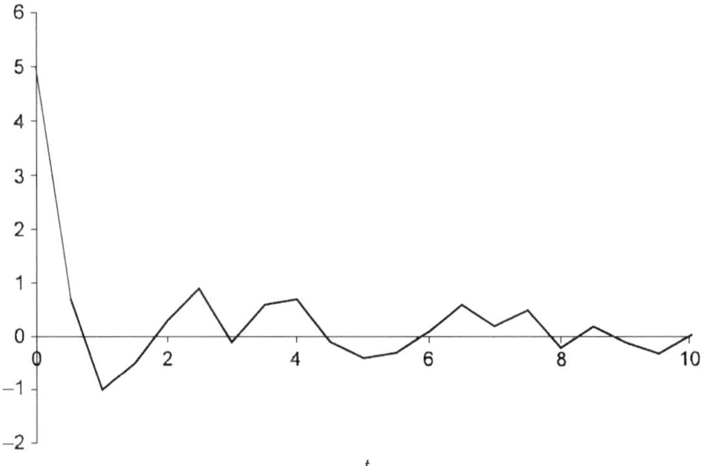

Figure 34.1 Typical fitted function $\eta^*(t)$.

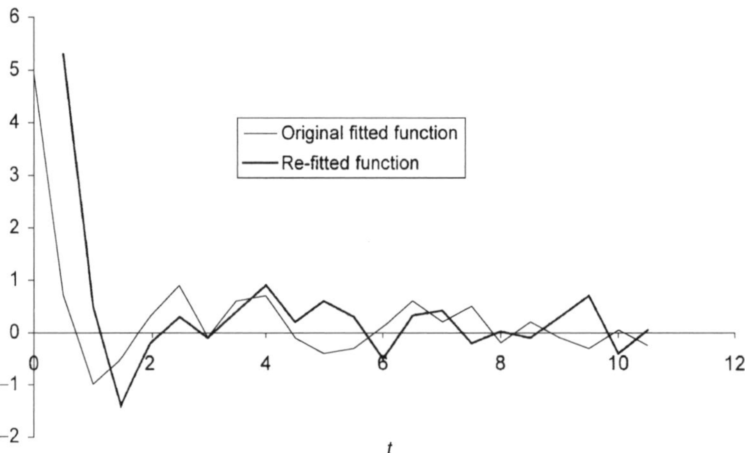

Figure 34.2 Typical *re*-fitted function $\eta^*(t)$, a short time later.

We can conclude from this that yield curve fitting is an inconsistent and dangerous business. The result presented here is by no means restricted to the models I have named; *no* one-factor model will capture the high slope and curvature that is usual for yield curves; they 'may' give reasonable results when the yield curve is fairly flat. We will discuss these criticisms of yield curve modeling in Chapter 38. In fact, very few models can accommodate the large slope and curvature that is common for yield curves. Exceptions include some HJM (see Chapter 39) and a non-probabilistic model described in Chapter 40.

34.5 OTHER MODELS

Other models for the short-term interest rate have been proposed. One of the most popular (but for which there are no explicit solutions) is the **Black, Derman & Toy** (**BDT**) model where the risk-neutral spot interest rate satisfies

$$d(\ln r) = \left(\theta(t) - \frac{\sigma'(t)}{\sigma(t)} \ln r\right) dt + \sigma(t)\, dX.$$

The two functions of time σ and θ allow both zero-coupon bonds and their volatilities to be matched. An even more general model is the **Black & Karasinski** model

$$d \ln r = (\theta(t) - a(t) \ln r)\, dt + \sigma(t)\, dX.$$

These models are popular because fitting can be done quite simply by a numerical scheme.

Any criticisms of yield curve fitting in general, of course, apply to these models. On the other hand, as we shall see in Chapter 38, the dependence of the volatility of r on r itself is, for these models, not dissimilar to that found in data for US interest rates.

34.6 SUMMARY

I have outlined why the yield curve is fitted, and how it is fitted in some simple models. From a practical perspective it is hard to argue against calibration; you cannot hedge with something if your theoretical price is very different from its traded price. But from a modeling and empirical perspective it is hard to argue in its favor, the data shows how inconsistent the concept is. This is always going to be a problem with one-factor Brownian motion models, unless yield curves suddenly decide not to be so steep. There is not a great deal that can be done theoretically. If you are concerned with consistency then avoid one-factor models, or you will end up painting yourself into a corner.

On the other hand, people seem to make money using these models and I guess that is the correct test of a model. Unless you are speculating with an interest rate derivative, you will have to delta hedge and therefore have to calibrate. Practitioners go much further than I have shown here, they fit as many market prices and properties as they can. Put in another time-dependent parameter and you can fit interest rate volatilities of different maturities, yet another parameter and you can fit the market prices of caps. By fitting more and more data, are you digging a deeper and deeper grave or are you improving and refining the accuracy of your model?

FURTHER READING

- A more sophisticated choice of time-dependent parameters is described by Hull & White (1990a).
- Klugman & Wilmott (1994) consider the fitting of the general affine model.
- Baker (1977) gives details of the numerical solution of integral equations.
- See Black, Derman & Toy (1990) for details of their popular model.
- Rebonato (1996) discusses calibration in depth for many popular models.

EXERCISES

1. Substitute the fitted function for $A(t;T)$, using the Ho & Lee model, back into the solution of the bond pricing equation for a zero-coupon bond,

$$Z(r, t; T) = e^{A(t;T) - r(T-t)}.$$

   What do you notice?

2. Differentiate Equation (34.2) twice to solve for the value of $\eta^*(t)$. What is the value of a zero-coupon bond with a fitted Vasicek model for the interest rate?
3. Use market data for the price of zero-coupon bonds to fit a Ho & Lee model. Refit the model with data for a week later in time. Compare the two curves for $\eta^*(t)$.

   Note: The second curve for η^* starts a week after the first curve. They should not be plotted starting at the same point in time.
4. Use market data for zero-coupon bond prices to fit a Vasicek model for the interest rate.

CHAPTER 35

interest rate derivatives

In this Chapter...

- common fixed-income contracts such as bond options, caps and floors
- how to price interest rate products in the consistent partial differential equation framework
- how to price contracts the market way
- path dependency in interest rate products, such as the index amortizing rate swap

35.1 INTRODUCTION

In the first part of this book I derived a theory for pricing and hedging many different types of options on equities, currencies and commodities. In Chapter 33 I presented the theory for zero-coupon bonds, boldly saying that the model may be applied to other contracts.

In the equity options world we have seen different degrees of complexity. The simple contracts have no path dependency. These include the vanilla calls and puts and contracts having different final conditions such as binaries or straddles. At the next stage of complexity we find the weakly path-dependent contracts such as American options or barriers for which, technically speaking, the path taken by the underlying is important, yet for which we only need to solve in two dimensions (S and t). Finally, we have seen strongly path-dependent contracts such as Asians or lookbacks for which we must introduce a new state variable to keep track of the key features of the path of the underlying. Many of these ideas are mirrored in the theory of interest rate derivatives.

In this chapter we delve deeper into the subject of fixed-income contracts by considering interest rate derivatives such as bond options, caps and floors, swaptions, captions and floortions, and more complicated and path-dependent contracts such as the index amortizing rate swap.

35.2 CALLABLE BONDS

As a gentle introduction to more complex fixed-income products, consider the **callable bond**. This is a simple coupon-bearing bond, but one that the issuer may call back on specified dates for a specified amount. The amount for which it may be called back may be time dependent. This feature reduces the value of the bond; if rates are low, so that the bond value is high, the issuer will call the bond back.

The callable bond satisfies

$$\frac{\partial V}{\partial t} + \tfrac{1}{2}w^2\frac{\partial^2 V}{\partial r^2} + (u - \lambda w)\frac{\partial V}{\partial r} - rV = 0,$$

with

$$V(r, T) = 1,$$

and

$$V(r, t_c^-) = V(r, t_c^+) + K_c,$$

across coupon dates. If the bond can be called back for an amount $C(t)$ then we have the constraint on the bond's value

$$V(r, t) \le C(t),$$

together with continuity of $\partial V/\partial r$.

35.3 BOND OPTIONS

The stochastic model for the spot rate presented in Chapter 33 allows us to value contingent claims such as bond options. A **bond option** is identical to an equity option except that the underlying asset is a bond. Both European and American versions exist.

As a simple example, we derive the differential equation satisfied by a call option, with exercise price E and expiry date T, on a zero-coupon bond with maturity date $T_B \ge T$. Before finding the value of the option to buy a bond we must find the value of the bond itself.

Let us write $Z(r, t; T_B)$ for the value of the bond. Thus, Z satisfies

$$\frac{\partial Z}{\partial t} + \tfrac{1}{2}w^2\frac{\partial^2 Z}{\partial r^2} + (u - \lambda w)\frac{\partial Z}{\partial r} - rZ = 0 \qquad (35.1)$$

with

$$Z(r, T_B; T_B) = 1$$

and suitable boundary conditions. Now write $V(r, t)$ for the value of the call option on this bond. Since V also depends on the random variable r, it too must satisfy equation (35.1). The

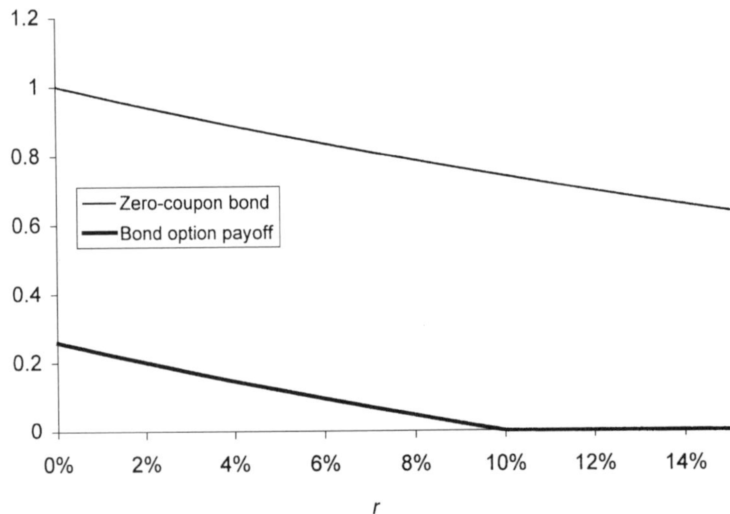

Figure 35.1 Zero-coupon bond price as a function of spot, and the payoff for a call option on the bond.

only difference is that the final value for the option is

$$V(r, T) = \max(Z(r, t; T_B) - E, 0).$$

This payoff is shown in Figure 35.1.

35.3.1 Market Practice

The above is all well and good, but suffers from the problem that any inaccuracy in the model is magnified by the process of solving once for the bond and then again for the bond option. This makes the contract second order, see Chapter 13. When the time comes to exercise the option the amount you receive will, for a call, be the difference between the *actual* bond price and the exercise price, not the difference between the *theoretical* bond price and the exercise price. So the model had better be correct for the bond price. Of course, this model can never be correct, and so we must treat the pricing of bond options with care. Practitioners tend to use an approach that is internally inconsistent but which is less likely to be very wrong. They use the Black–Scholes equity option pricing equation and formulae assuming that the underlying is the bond. That is, they assume that the bond behaves like a lognormal asset. This requires them to estimate a volatility for the bond, either measured statistically or implied from another contract, and an interest rate for the lifetime of the bond option. This will be a good model provided that the expiry of the bond is much shorter than the maturity of the underlying bond. Over short time periods, well away from maturity, the bond does behave stochastically, with a measurable volatility.

The price of a European bond call option in this model is

$$e^{-r(T-t)}(FN(d_1') - EN(d_2')),$$

and the put has value

$$e^{-r(T-t)}(EN(-d_2') + FN(-d_1')),$$

where F is the forward price of the bond at expiry of the option and

$$d_1' = \frac{\log(F/X) + \frac{1}{2}\sigma^2(T-t)}{\sigma\sqrt{T-t}} \quad \text{and} \quad d_2' = d_1' - \sigma\sqrt{T-t}.$$

This model should not be used when the life of the option is comparable to the maturity of the bond, because then there is an appreciable **pull to par**, that is, the value of the bond at maturity is the principal plus last coupon; the bond cannot behave lognormally close to maturity because we know where it must end up. This contrasts greatly with the behavior of an equity for which there is no date in the future on which we know its value for certain. This pull to par is shown in Figure 35.2.

Another approach used in practice is to model the yield to maturity of the underlying bond. The usual assumption is that this yield follows a lognormal random walk. By modeling the yield and then calculating the bond price based on this yield, we get a bond that behaves well close to its maturity; the pull to par is incorporated.

There is one technical point about the definition of the bond option concerning the meaning of 'price.' One must be careful to use whichever of the clean or dirty price is correct for the option in question. This amounts to knowing whether or not accrued interest should be included in the payoff, see Chapter 31.

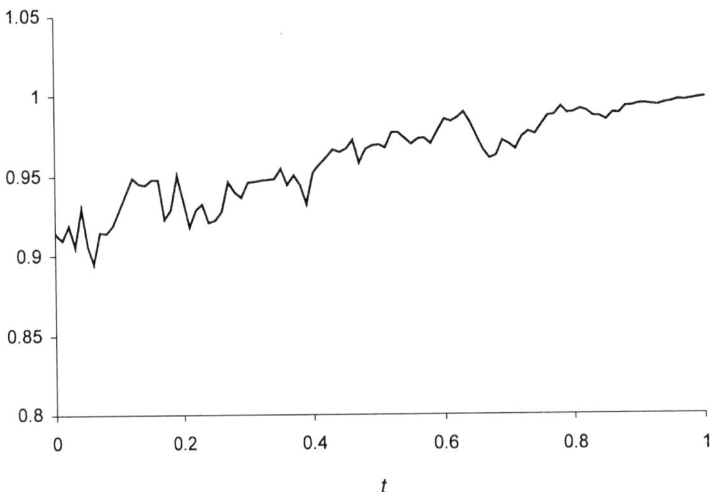

Figure 35.2 The pull to par for a zero-coupon bond.

35.4 CAPS AND FLOORS

A **cap** is a contract that guarantees to its holder that otherwise floating rates will not exceed a specified amount; the variable rate is thus capped.

A typical cap contract involves the payment at times t_i, each quarter, say, of a variable interest on a principal with the cashflow taking the form

$$\max(r_L - r_c, 0),$$

multiplied by the principal. Here r_L is the basic floating rate, for example three-month LIBOR if the payments are made quarterly, and r_c is the fixed cap rate. These payments continue for the lifetime of the cap. The rate r_L to be paid at time t_i is set at time t_{i-1}. Each of the individual cashflows is called a **caplet**, a cap is thus the sum of many caplets.

The cashflow of a caplet is shown in Figure 35.3.

If we assume that the actual floating rate is the spot rate, i.e. $r_L \approx r$ (and this approximation may not be important) then a single caplet may be priced by solving

$$\frac{\partial V}{\partial t} + \tfrac{1}{2}w^2\frac{\partial^2 V}{\partial r^2} + (u - \lambda w)\frac{\partial V}{\partial r} - rV = 0, \tag{35.2}$$

with

$$V(r, T) = \max(r - r_c, 0).$$

Mathematically, this is similar to a call option on the floating rate r.

A **floor** is similar to a cap except that the floor ensures that the interest rate is bounded below, by r_f. A floor is made up of a sum of floorlets, each of which has a cashflow of

$$\max(r_f - r_L, 0).$$

We can approximate r_L by r again, in which case the floorlet satisfies the bond pricing equation but with

$$V(r, T) = \max(r_f - r, 0).$$

A floorlet is thus a put on the spot rate.

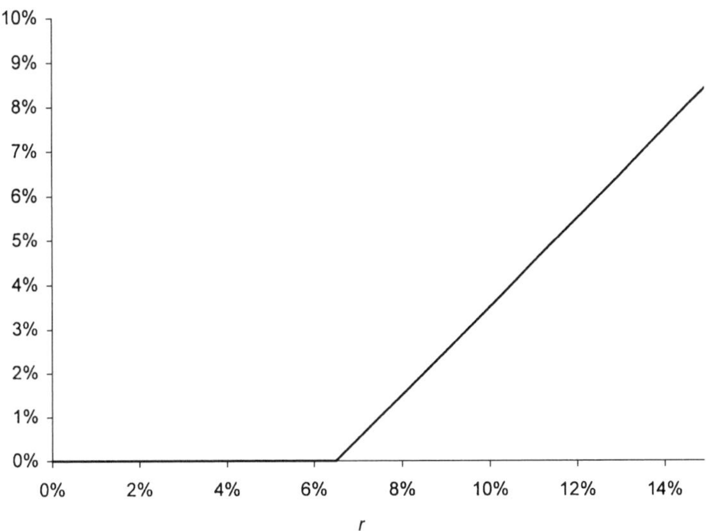

Figure 35.3 The dependence of the payment of a caplet on LIBOR.

35.4.1 Cap/Floor Parity

A portfolio of a long caplet and a short floorlet (with $r_c = r_f$) has the cashflow

$$\max(r_L - r_c, 0) - \max(r_c - r_L, 0) = r_L - r_c.$$

This is the same cashflow as one payment of a swap. Thus there is the model-independent no-arbitrage relationship

$$\text{cap} = \text{floor} + \text{swap}.$$

35.4.2 The Relationship Between a Caplet and a Bond Option

A caplet has the following cashflow

$$\max(r_L - r_c, 0).$$

This is received at time t_i but the rate r_L is set at t_{i-1}. This cashflow is *exactly* the same as the cashflow

$$\frac{1}{1 + r_L} \max(r_L - r_c, 0)$$

received at time t_{i-1}, after all, that is the definition of r_L. We can rewrite this cashflow as

$$\max\left(1 - \frac{1 + r_c}{1 + r_L}, 0\right).$$

But

$$\frac{1 + r_c}{1 + r_L}$$

is the price at time t_{i-1} of a bond paying $1 + r_c$ at time t_i. We can conclude that a caplet is equivalent to a put option expiring at time t_{i-1} on a bond maturing at time t_i.

35.4.3 Market Practice

Again, because the Black–Scholes formulae are so simple to use, it is common to use them to price caps and floors. This is done as follows. Each individual caplet (or floorlet) is priced as a call (or put) on a lognormally distributed interest rate. The inputs for this model are the volatility of the interest rate, the strike price r_c (or r_f), the time to the cashflow $t_i - t$, and *two* interest rates. One interest rate takes the place of the stock price and will be the current forward rate applying between times t_{i-1} and t_i. The other interest rate, used for discounting to the present is the yield on a bond maturing at time t_i. For a caplet the relevant formula is

$$e^{-r^*(t_i-t)}(F(t, t_{i-1}, t_i)N(d_1') - r_c N(d_2')).$$

Here $F(t, t_{i-1}, t_i)$ is the forward rate today between t_{i-1} and t_i, r^* is the yield to maturity for a maturity of t_{i-t},

$$d_1' = \frac{\log(F/r_c) + \frac{1}{2}\sigma^2(t_i - t_{i-1})}{\sigma\sqrt{t_i - t_{i-1}}} \quad \text{and} \quad d_2' = d_1' - \sigma\sqrt{t_i - t_{i-1}}.$$

σ is the volatility of the $(t_i - t_{i-1})$ interest rate. The floorlet value is

$$e^{-r^*(t_{i-t})}(-F(t, t_{i-1}, t_i)N(-d_1') + r_c N(-d_2')).$$

35.4.4 Collars

A **collar** places both an upper and a lower bound on the interest payments. It can be valued as a long cap and a short floor.

35.4.5 Step-up Swaps, Caps and Floors

Step-up swaps etc. have swap (cap etc.) rates that vary with time in a prescribed manner.

35.5 RANGE NOTES

The **range note** pays interest on a notional principal for every day that an interest rate lies between prescribed lower and upper bounds. Let us assume that the relevant interest rate is our spot rate r. In this case we must solve

$$\frac{\partial V}{\partial t} + \frac{1}{2}w^2\frac{\partial^2 V}{\partial r^2} + (u - \lambda w)\frac{\partial V}{\partial r} - rV + \mathcal{I}(r) = 0,$$

with

$$V(r, T) = 0,$$

where

$$\mathcal{I}(r) = r \quad \text{if} \quad r_l < r < r_u \quad \text{and is zero otherwise.}$$

This is only an approximation to the correct value since in practice the relevant interest rate will have a finite (not infinitesimal) maturity.

35.6 SWAPTIONS, CAPTIONS AND FLOORTIONS

A swaption has a strike rate, r_E, that is the fixed rate that will be swapped against floating if the option is exercised. In a call swaption or **payer swaption** the buyer has the right to become the fixed rate payer, in a put swaption or receiver swaption the buyer has the right to become the payer of the floating leg.

Captions and **floortions** are options on caps and floors respectively. These contracts can be put into the partial differential equation framework with little difficulty. However, these contracts are second order, meaning that their value depends on another, more basic, contract, see Chapter 13. Although the partial differential equation approach is possible, and certainly consistent across instruments, it is likely to be time consuming computationally and prone to serious mispricings because of the high order of the contracts.

35.6.1 Market Practice

With some squeezing the Black–Scholes formulae can be used to value European swaptions. Perhaps this is not entirely consistent, but it is certainly easier than solving a partial differential equation.

The underlying is assumed to be the fixed leg of a par swap with maturity T_S, call this r_f. It is assumed to follow a lognormal random walk with a measurable volatility. If at time T the par swap rate is greater than the strike rate r_E then the option is in the money. At this time the value of the swaption is

$$\max(r_f - r_E, 0) \times \text{present value of all future cashflows.}$$

It is important that we are 'modeling' the par rate because the par rate measures the rate at which the present value of the floating legs is equal to the present value of the fixed legs. Thus in this expression we only need worry about the excess of the par rate over the strike rate. This expression looks like a typical call option payoff; all we need to price the swaption in the Black–Scholes framework are the volatility of the par rate, the times to exercise and maturity and the correct discount factors. The payer swaption formula in this framework is

$$\frac{1}{F}e^{-r(T-t)}\left(1-\left(1+\tfrac{1}{2}F\right)^{-2(T_S-T)}\right)(FN(d_1')-EN(d_2'))$$

and the receiver swaption formula is

$$\frac{1}{F}e^{-r(T-t)}\left(1-\left(1+\tfrac{1}{2}F\right)^{-2(T_S-T)}\right)(EN(-d_2')+FN(-d_1'))$$

where F is the forward rate of the swap, T_S is the maturity of the swap and

$$d_1' = \frac{\log(F/X)+\frac{1}{2}\sigma^2(T-t)}{\sigma\sqrt{T-t}} \quad \text{and} \quad d_2' = d_1' - \sigma\sqrt{T-t}.$$

These formulae assume that interest payments in the swap are exchanged every six months.

35.7 SPREAD OPTIONS

Spread options have a payoff that depends on the difference between two interest rates. In the simplest case the two rates both come from the same yield curve; more generally the spread could be between rates on different but related curves (yield curve *versus* swap curve, LIBOR *versus* Treasury bills), risky and riskless curves (credit derivatives, see Chapter 44) or rates in different currencies.

Can we price this contract in the framework we have built up? No. The contract crucially depends on the tilting of the yield curve. In our one-factor world all rates are correlated and there is little room for random behavior in the spread. We will have to wait until Chapter 37 before we can price such a contract in a consistent framework.

Another method for pricing this contract is to squeeze it into the Black–Scholes-type framework. This amounts to modeling the spread directly as a lognormal (or Normal) variable and choosing suitable rates for discounting. This latter method is the market practice and although intellectually less satisfying it is also less prone to major errors.

35.8 INDEX AMORTIZING RATE SWAPS

A swap is an agreement between two parties to exchange interest payments on some principal, usually one payment at a fixed rate and the other at a floating rate. In an index amortizing rate (IAR) swap the amount of this principal decreases, or **amortizes**, according to the behavior of an 'index' over the life of the swap; typically, that index is a short-term interest rate. The easiest way to understand such a swap is by example, which I keep simple.

Example

Suppose that the principal begins at \$10,000,000 with interest payments being at 5% from one party to the other, and r%, the spot interest rate, in the other direction. These payments are to be made quarterly.[1] At each quarter, there is an exchange of $(r - 5)$% of the principal. However, at each quarter the principal may also amortize according to the level of the spot rate at that time. In the Table 35.1 we see a typical amortizing schedule.

We read this table as follows. First, on a reset date, each quarter, there is an exchange of interest payments on the principal as it then stands. What happens next depends on the level of the spot rate. If the spot interest rate (or whatever index the amortization schedule depends on) is below 3% on the date of the exchange of payments then the principal on which future interest is paid is then amortized 100%; in other words, this new level of the principal is zero and thus

Table 35.1 Typical amortizing schedule.

Spot rate	Principal reduction
less than 3%	100%
4%	60%
5%	40%
6%	20%
8%	10%
over 12%	0%

[1] In which case, r would, in practice, be a three-month rate and not the spot rate. The IAR swap is so path dependent that this difference will not be of major importance.

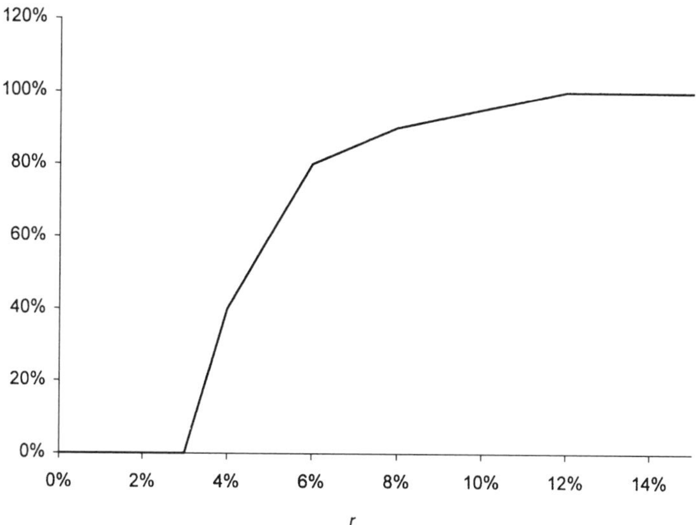

Figure 35.4 A typical amortizing schedule.

no further payments are made. If the spot rate is 4% then the amortization is 60%, i.e. the principal falls to just 40% of its level before this reset date. If the spot rate is 8% then the principal amortizes by just 10%. If the rate is over 12% there is no amortization at all and the principal remains at the same level. For levels of the rate between the values in the first column of the table the amount of amortization is a linear interpolation. This interpolation is shown in Figure 35.4 and the function of r that it represents I call $g(r)$.

So, although the principal begins at \$10,000,000, it can change after each quarter. This feature makes the index amortizing rate swap path dependent.

The party receiving the fixed rate payments will suffer if rates rise because he will pay out a rising floating rate while the principal does not decrease. If rates fall the principal amortizes and so his lower floating rate payments are unfortunately on a lower principal. Again, he suffers. Thus the receiver of the fixed rate wants rates to remain steady and is said to be selling volatility.

Valuing such an index amortizing rate swap is simple in the framework that we have set up, once we realize that we need to introduce a new state variable. This new state variable is the current level of the principal and we denote it by P. Thus the value of the swap is $V(r, P, t)$.

The variable P is *not* stochastic: it is deterministic and jumps to its new level at each resetting (every quarter in the above example). Since P is piecewise constant, the governing differential equation for the value of the swap is, in a one-factor interest rate world, simply

$$\frac{\partial V}{\partial t} + \tfrac{1}{2}w^2\frac{\partial^2 V}{\partial r^2} + (u - \lambda w)\frac{\partial V}{\partial r} - rV = 0,$$

where

$$dr = u\,dt + w\,dX$$

and λ is the market price of interest rate risk. Of course, in this, V is a function of the three variables, r, P and t.

Two things happen simultaneously at each reset date: there is an exchange of interest payments and the principal amortizes. If we use t_i to denote the reset dates and r_f for the fixed interest rate, then the swap jumps in value by an amount $(r - r_f)P$. Subsequently, the principal P becomes $g(r)P$ where the function $g(r)$ is the representation of the amortizing schedule. Thus we have the jump condition

$$V(r, P, t_i^-) = V(r, g(r)P, t_i^+) + (r - r_f)P.$$

At the maturity of the contract there is one final exchange of interest payments, thus

$$V(r, P, T) = (r - r_f)P.$$

35.8.1 Similarity Solution

Because the amortizing schedule is linear in P, the simple index amortizing rate swap described above has a similarity reduction, taking the problem from three down to two dimensions and so reducing the computational time. The solution takes the form

$$V(r, P, t) = PH(r, t).$$

The function $H(r, t)$ satisfies

$$\frac{\partial H}{\partial t} + \tfrac{1}{2}w^2\frac{\partial^2 H}{\partial r^2} + (u - \lambda w)\frac{\partial H}{\partial r} - rH = 0,$$

$$H(r, t_i^-) = g(r)H(r, t_i^+) + r - r_f$$

with

$$H(r, T) = r - r_f.$$

In Figure 35.5 is shown the term sheet for a USD IAR swap. In this contract there is an exchange every six months of a fixed rate and six-month LIBOR. This is a vanilla IAR swap with no extra features and can be priced in the way described above. Terms in square bracket would be set at the time that the deal was made.

35.8.2 Other Features in the Index Amortizing Rate Swap

Lockout Period

There is often a 'lockout' period, usually at the start of the contract's life, during which there are no reductions in the principal. During this period the interest payments are like those of a vanilla swap. Mathematically, we can model this feature by allowing the amortizing schedule, previously $g(r)$, to be time-dependent: $g(r, i)$. In this case the amount of amortizing depends on the reset date, t_i, as well as the spot interest rate. Such a model can be used for far more sophisticated structures than the simple lockout period. The similarity structure is retained.

Clean Up

Some contracts have that if the principal ever falls to a specified percentage of the original principal then it is reduced all the way to zero. Such a feature, as well as barriers, eliminates the possibility of similarity reductions.

USD Index Amortising Swap

Counterparties	XXXX The Customer
Notional Amount	USD 50 millions, subject Amortisation Schedule
Settlement Date	Two days after Trade Date
Maximum Maturity Date	Five years after Trade Date
Early Maturity Date	On any Fixing Date leading to a Notional Amount equal to 0
Payments made by Customer	**In USD 6m LIBOR** paid semiannually, A/360
Payments made by XXXX	**USD X % p.a.** paid semiannually, 30/360
Index Rate	USD 6m LIBOR
Base Rate	[]%
Amortisation Schedule (after 1st coupon period)	see table below

USD 6m LIBOR - Base Rate	Amortisation
−3%	−[]%
−2%	−[]%
−1%	−[]%
0	−[]%
1%	0%
2%	0%

NB If the observed difference falls between two entries of this schedule, the amortisation amount is interpolated

Fixing Dates	2 business days before each coupon period
USD 6m LIBOR	The USD 6m LIBOR rate as seen on Telerate page 3750 at noon, London time, on each Fixing Date
Documentation	ISDA
Governing Law	English

This indicative termsheet is neither an offer to buy or sell securities or an OTC derivative product which includes options, swaps, forwards and structured notes having similar features to OTC derivative transactions, nor a solicitation to buy or sell securities or an OTC derivative product. The proposal contained in the foregoing is not a complete description of the terms of a particular transaction and is subject to change without limitation.

Figure 35.5 Term sheet for a USD Index Amortizing Swap.

35.9 CONTRACTS WITH EMBEDDED DECISIONS

The following contract is interesting because it requires the holder to make a complex series of decisions on whether to accept or reject cashflows. The contract is path dependent.

This contract is a swap with M cashflows of floating minus fixed during its life. The catch is that the holder must choose to accept exactly $m \leq M$ of these cashflows. At each cashflow date the holder must say whether they want the cashflow or not, they cannot later change their mind. When they have taken m of them they can take no more.

Before I show how to price this contract, a few words about the representation of the cashflows. If this were a vanilla swap then we would rewrite the floating legs of the swap in terms of zero-coupon bonds and the whole contract could then be priced off the prevailing discount curve. We would certainly not solve any partial differential equations. However, since the present problem is so path dependent it is probably quite safe to make the usual assumption that each cashflow takes the form

$$r - r_f,$$

where r is the spot interest rate.

The trick to pricing this contract is to introduce $m+1$ functions of r and t: $V(r, t, i)$ with $i = 0, \ldots, m$. The index i represents how many cashflows are still left to be taken. For example, when $i = 0$ all the cashflows have been taken up already. Each function will satisfy whichever one-factor interest rate model you fancy.

Because all of its cashflows have been taken up, the function $V(r, t, 0)$ is exactly zero. But what about the other functions?

Introducing t_j as the available dates on which there are cashflows, with $j = 1, \ldots, M$, we have two things to ensure. First of all, if we have i cashflows still left to choose when there are only i cashflows left then we must accept all of them. Second, if we have a genuine choice then we must make it optimal.

The first point is guaranteed by the following conditions at cashflow dates.

$$V(r, t_{M-i}, i+1) = V(r, t_{M-i}, i) + r - r_f \quad \text{for} \quad i = 0, \ldots, m-1.$$

These equations mean that the last i cashflows are accepted if there are i left to choose.

The optimality of the remaining, earlier, choices is ensured by an American-style constraint,

$$V(r, t_j, i+1) \geq V(r, t_j, i) + r - r_f.$$

Whichever interest rate model you choose, the time taken to solve for the value of this contract will be approximately $m+1$ times the time taken to solve for a single, non-path-dependent contract of the same maturity.

35.10 WHEN THE INTEREST RATE IS *NOT* THE SPOT RATE

We have seen in the interest rate chapters the almost interchangeable use of spot interest rate, one-month rate, three-month rate and even sixth-month rate. Invariably, the contract in question would specify which interest rate is to be used. If cashflows occur each quarter then the contract almost always specifies that the interest rate is a three-month rate. We have even exploited this fact in Chapter 32 to decompose a swap into a basket of zero-coupon bonds. At other times, I have, in a cavalier fashion, replaced a real rate with the impossible-to-observe spot rate. The reason for this is that it is r, the spot rate, that we are modeling. It is nice to have cashflows written in terms of the directly modeled variable.

The following is a rough guide to when to use the theoretically useful spot rate, and when to stay with the correct rate (even though that is usually much, much harder to implement consistently).

Use the spot rate to price a contract if all of the following conditions apply:

- The real rates quoted in the contract details are sixth months or less.
- The contract has cashflows that are highly nonlinear in the rate or have early exercise or are path dependent.
- There are no more-liquid instruments available that have cashflows that match our contract.

To be on the safe side you should also statically hedge with available instruments to reduce all cashflows and then price the residual cashflows. This will reduce as much as possible any model errors. This is the real problem with making what might appear to be minor approximations: you might inadvertently introduce arbitrage.

35.10.1 The Relationship Between the Spot Interest Rate and Other Rates

The relationship between the spot rate of infinitesimal maturity and rates of finite maturity is through the zero-coupon bond pricing equation. For a general spot-rate model this relationship is complicated, unless the rates are sufficiently short.

For short maturities we can solve the zero-coupon bond pricing equation (33.4) by a Taylor series expansion. We did this at length in Chapter 34 but I will remind you of the result here. Substituting

$$Z(r, t; T) = 1 + a(r)(T - t) + \tfrac{1}{2}b(r)(T - t)^2 + \cdots$$

into (33.4) we find that

$$a(r) = -r$$

and

$$b(r) = r^2 - (u - \lambda w).$$

From this we find that the yield curve is given, for small maturities, by

$$-\frac{\log Z}{T - t} \sim r + \tfrac{1}{2}(u - \lambda w)(T - t) + \cdots \quad \text{as} \quad t \to T.$$

As part of our spot rate model we know the risk-adjusted drift $u - \lambda w$, as a function of r and t. Therefore the above gives us an approximate relationship between any short maturity interest rate and the spot rate. The use of this is demonstrated in the following example.

A caplet has a cashflow of

$$\max(r_L - r_c, 0),$$

where r_L is three month LIBOR, say. We can write this approximately as

$$\max\left(r + \tfrac{1}{8}(u - \lambda w) - r_c, 0\right).$$

The 1/8 comes from $\frac{1}{2}$ multiplied by the maturity of the three-month rate measured in years. If we believe our one-factor model then we must believe this to be a better representation of the actual cashflow than that given by simply replacing r_L with r.

35.11 A FINAL EXAMPLE

The last example of a complex interest rate derivative is given in the term sheet of Figure 35.6. This is a dual passport option, it allows the owner to trade, hypothetically, in both Bund (German government bonds) and BTP (Italian government bonds) futures. The net position of the transactions, all taken together, is paid out at expiry if this quantity is positive.

This contract can be approached at different levels of sophistication. However, given the complex nature of the contract it is probably safest to make some approximation to the random walk of the two bond futures. As ever, we would assume that they follow correlated lognormal random walks. The contract is then a two-factor version of the passport option described in Chapter 18.

35.12 SUMMARY

There are a vast number of contracts in the fixed-income world. It is an impossible task to describe and model any but a small quantity of these. In this chapter I have tried to show two of the possible approaches to the modeling in a few special cases. These two approaches to the modeling are the consistent way via a partial differential equation or the practitioner way via the Black–Scholes equity model and formulae. The former is nice because it can be made

BUND/BTP Future Linked 18 months "Dual Passport" Note

Aggregate Principal Amount	DEM 50,000,000
Trade Date	[] January 1998
Issue Date	20 January 1998
Settlement Date	20 January 1998
Maturity Date	20 July 1998
Issue Price	100%
Redemption Amount	102.5% PLUS Notional Income Where "Notional Income" is the aggregate sum of the notional profit or loss from each executed transaction.

Formula

$$\max\left(\left[\sum_{i=1}^{N1} U_{i-1}\times(\text{Price}_i-\text{Price}_{i-1})\times 25\times 100\right]+\left[\sum_{j=1}^{N2} V_{i-1}\times(\text{Price}_j-\text{Price}_{j-1})\times 20,000\times 100\right]/\text{FX}\right)$$

Where	N1 is the total number of BUND transactions during the life of the option N2 is the total number of BTP transactions during the life of the option U is the BUND position V is the BTP position FX is equal to the prevailing DEM/ITL exchange rate at Option Maturity Price means the reference price for each transaction
Coupon	Zero
Option Maturity Date	6 months and 2 business days from the Issue Date
Position	The noteholder may have a non-zero position in EITHER the BUND future Index Units or the BTP future Index Units and may switch between these. The noteholder may not hold positions in both of these simultaneously. The maximum BUND position is plus or minus 190 Index Units. The maximum BTP position is plus or minus 200 Index Units.

Figure 35.6 Term sheet for a dual passport option.

Transaction Frequency	The maximum number of transactions per day is four.
Index Units	Index Units are either LIFFE BUND futures or LIFFE BTP futures contracts. The current reference month will be Mar 98 until this becomes deliverable, at which point the noteholder must close out the position in this contract and enter transactions based on the Jun 98 contract. Once the Jun 98 contract becomes deliverable the noteholder must close out the position in this contract and enter transactions based on the Sep 98 contract.

This indicative termsheet is neither an offer to buy or sell securities or an OTC derivative product which includes options, swaps, forwards and structured notes having similar features to OTC derivative transactions, nor a solicitation to buy or sell securities or an OTC derivative product. The proposal contained in the foregoing is not a complete description of the terms of a particular transaction and is subject to change without limitation.

Figure 35.6 Term sheet for a dual passport option (continued).

consistent across all instruments, but is dangerous to use for liquid, and high-order contracts. Save this technique for the more complex, illiquid and path-dependent contracts. The alternative approach is, as everyone admits, a fudge, requiring a contract to be squeezed and bent until it looks like a call or a put on something vaguely lognormal. Although completely inconsistent across instruments it is far less likely to lead to serious mispricings.

The reader is encouraged to find out more about the pricing of products in these two distinct ways. Better still, the reader should model new contracts for himself as well.

FURTHER READING

- Black (1976) models the value of bond options assuming the bond is a lognormal asset.
- See Hull & White (1996) for more examples of pricing index amortizing rate swaps.
- Everything by Jamshidian on the pricing of interest rate derivatives is popular with practitioners. See the bibliography for some references.

EXERCISES

1. Write down the problem we must solve in order to value a puttable bond.
2. Derive a relationship between a floorlet and a call option on a zero-coupon bond.
3. How would a collar be valued practically? What is the explicit solution for a single payment?
4. When an index amortizing rate swap has a lockout period for the first year, we must solve

$$\frac{\partial V}{\partial t} + \tfrac{1}{2}w^2\frac{\partial^2 V}{\partial r^2} + (u - \lambda w)\frac{\partial V}{\partial r} - rV = 0,$$

with jump condition

$$V(r, P, t_i^-) = V(r, g(r, i)P, t_i^+) + (r - r_f)P,$$

where

$$g(r, i) = 1 \quad \text{if} \quad t_i < 1,$$

and with final condition

$$V(r, P, T) = (r - r_f)P.$$

In this case, reduce the order of the problem using a similarity reduction of the form

$$V(r, P, t) = PH(r, t).$$

5. Find the approximate value of a cashflow for a floorlet on the one month LIBOR, when we use the Vasicek model.

CHAPTER 36
convertible bonds

In this Chapter...

- the basic Convertible Bond (CB)
- market conventions for the pricing and analysis of CBs
- how to price CBs in a one-factor setting
- how to price CBs in a two-factor setting
- features that can make CBs path dependent

36.1 INTRODUCTION

The conversion feature of convertible bonds makes these contracts similar mathematically to American options. They are also particularly interesting because of their dependence on a stock price and on interest rates. I begin this chapter with some definitions used by the market in the analysis of convertible bonds. I then explain the contract terms of these bonds in a one-factor, stochastic asset price setting. Finally, I show how to price convertibles in a two-factor world of stochastic asset and stochastic interest rate.

36.2 CONVERTIBLE BOND BASICS

The **convertible bond** or **CB** on a stock pays specified coupons with return of the principal at maturity, *unless* at some previous time the owner has converted the bond into the underlying asset. A convertible bond thus has the characteristics of an ordinary bond but with the extra feature that the bond may, at a time of the holder's choosing, be exchanged for a specified asset. This exchange is called **conversion**.

The value of a CB is clearly bounded below by both:

- its **conversion value**, which is the amount received if the bond is converted immediately (regardless of whether this is optimal),

$$\text{conversion value} = \text{market price of stock} \times \text{conversion ratio}.$$

- its value as a corporate bond, with a final principal and coupons during its life. This is called its **straight value**.

The latter point shows how there are credit risk issues in the pricing of CBs. These credit risk issues are very important but we will not discuss them in any detail here. We assume that there is no risk of default. Credit risk is discussed in depth in Chapter 43.

36.3 MARKET PRACTICE

As we have just seen, the value of a CB is at least its conversion value. The bond component of the CB pushes the value up. We can thus calculate the **market conversion price**. This is the amount that the CB holder effectively pays for a stock if he exercises the option to convert immediately:

$$\text{market conversion price} = \frac{\text{market price of CB}}{\text{conversion ratio}} \geq \text{price of underlying}.$$

The purchaser of the CB pays a premium over the market price of the underlying stock. This is measured by the **market conversion premium ratio**:

$$\text{market conversion premium ratio} = \frac{\text{market conversion price} - \text{current market price of the CB}}{\text{market price of underlying stock}}.$$

By holding the underlying stock you will receive any dividends; by holding the CB you get the coupons on the bond but not the dividends on the stock. A measure of the benefit of holding the bond is the **favorable income differential**, measured by

$$\text{favorable income differential} = \frac{\text{coupon interest from bond} - (\text{conversion ratio} \times \text{dividend per share})}{\text{conversion ratio}}.$$

After calculating this we can estimate the **premium payback period**, i.e. how long it will take to recover the premium over the stock price:

$$\text{premium payback period} = \frac{\text{market conversion price} - \text{current market price of the CB}}{\text{favorable income differential}}.$$

This does not, of course, allow for the time value of money.

For small values of the underlying stock the possibility of conversion is remote and the CB trades very much like a vanilla bond. If the stock price rises high enough the CB will be converted and so begins to act like the stock.

36.4 PRICING CBS WITH KNOWN INTEREST RATE

I will continue to use S to mean the underlying asset price, the maturity date is T and the CB can be converted into n of the underlying. To introduce the ideas behind pricing convertibles I will start by assuming that interest rates are deterministic for the life of the bond. Since the bond value depends on the price of that asset we have

$$V = V(S, t);$$

the contract value depends on an asset price and on the time to maturity. Repeating the Black–Scholes analysis, with a portfolio consisting of one convertible bond and $-\Delta$ assets, we find that the change in the value of the portfolio is

$$d\Pi = \frac{\partial V}{\partial t}\,dt + \frac{\partial V}{\partial S}\,dS + \tfrac{1}{2}\sigma^2 S^2 \frac{\partial^2 V}{\partial S^2}\,dt - \Delta\,dS.$$

As before, choose

$$\Delta = \frac{\partial V}{\partial S}$$

to eliminate risk from this portfolio.

The return on this risk-free portfolio is at most that from a bank deposit and so

$$\frac{\partial V}{\partial t} + \tfrac{1}{2}\sigma^2 S^2 \frac{\partial^2 V}{\partial S^2} + (rS - D(S,t))\frac{\partial V}{\partial S} - rV \leq 0. \tag{36.1}$$

This inequality is the basic Black–Scholes inequality. Scaling the principal to \$1, the final condition is

$$V(S,T) = 1.$$

Coupons are paid discretely every quarter or half year and so we have the jump condition across each coupon date

$$V(S, t_c^-) = V(S, t_c^+) + K,$$

where K is the amount of the discrete coupon paid on date t_c.

Since the bond may be converted into n assets we have the constraint

$$V \geq nS.$$

In addition to this constraint, we require the continuity of V and $\partial V/\partial S$.

The early conversion feature makes the convertible bond similar to an American option problem; mathematically, we have another free boundary problem. It is interesting to note that the final data itself does not satisfy the pricing constraint. Thus, although the value *at* maturity may be \$1 the value *just before* is

$$\max(nS, 1).$$

In the absence of credit risk issues, boundary conditions are

$$V(S,t) \sim nS \quad \text{as} \quad S \to \infty$$

and on $S = 0$ the bond value is the present value of the principal and all the coupons:

$$V(0,t) = e^{-r(T-t)} + \sum K e^{-r(t_c - t)}.$$

Here the sum is taken over all future coupons. As said earlier, when the asset price is high the bond behaves like the underlying, but for small asset price it behaves like a non-convertible bond.

In Figures 36.1, 36.2 and 36.3 are shown the values of a convertible bond with $n = 1$, $r = 0.06$, $\sigma = 0.25$ and with two years before maturity.

In Figure 36.1 there are no coupons paid on the bond and no dividend paid on the underlying. As with the American call on a stock paying no dividends it is not optimal to exercise/convert until expiry. The fine line is the stock price, into which the CB can convert. The CB value is always above this line.

In Figure 36.2 there is a continuous dividend yield of 5%. In this case there is a free boundary, marked on the figure: for sufficiently large S the bond should be converted. The bold line is the bond value, the fine lines are the stock and the bond price without the dividends.

In Figure 36.3 there is no dividend on the underlying but a coupon of 3% paid twice a year. The value of the bond is higher than in the previous two examples. Should this ever be converted before maturity? The fine lines are the stock and the bond value with no coupons for comparison.

The number of the underlying into which the bond may be converted, n, can be time dependent. Sometimes the bond may only be converted during specified periods. This is called **intermittent conversion**. If this is the case then the constraint only needs to be satisfied during these times; at other times the contract is European.

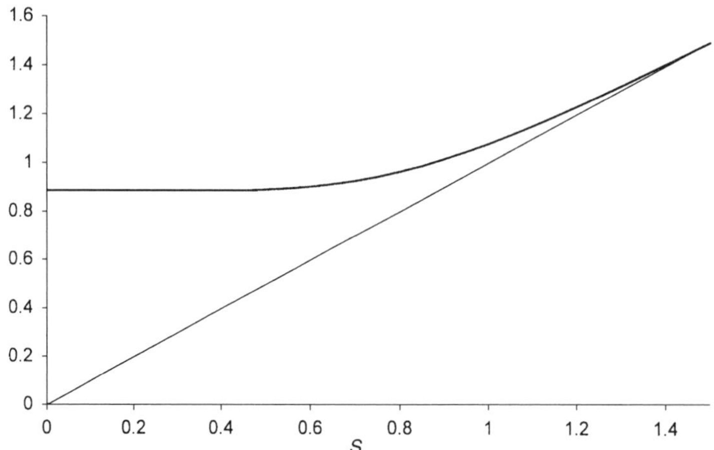

Figure 36.1 The value of a convertible bond with constant interest rate. Zero coupon and dividend. See text for details.

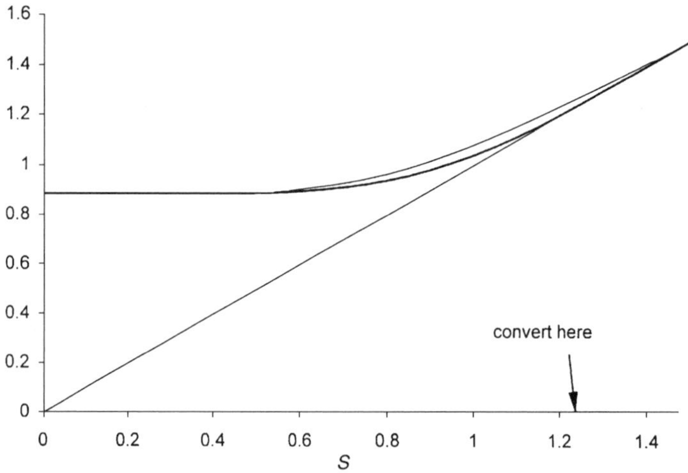

Figure 36.2 The value of a convertible bond with constant interest rate and a dividend paid on the underlying. See text for details.

36.4.1 Call and Put Features

The convertible bond permits the holder to exchange the bond for a certain number of the underlying asset at any time of their choosing. CBs often also have a **call feature** which gives the issuing company the right to purchase back the bond at any time (or during specified periods) for a specified amount. Sometimes this amount varies with time. The bond with a call feature is clearly worth less than the bond without. This is modeled exactly like US-style exercise again.

If the bond can be repurchased by the company for an amount M_1 then elimination of arbitrage opportunities leads to

$$V(S,t) \le M_C.$$

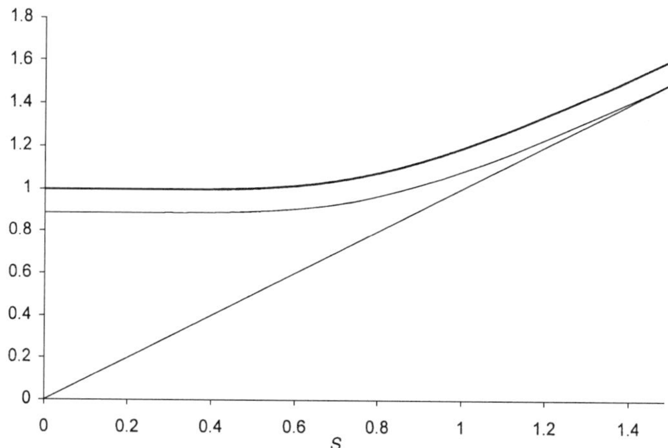

Figure 36.3 The value of a convertible bond with constant interest rate and coupons. See text for details.

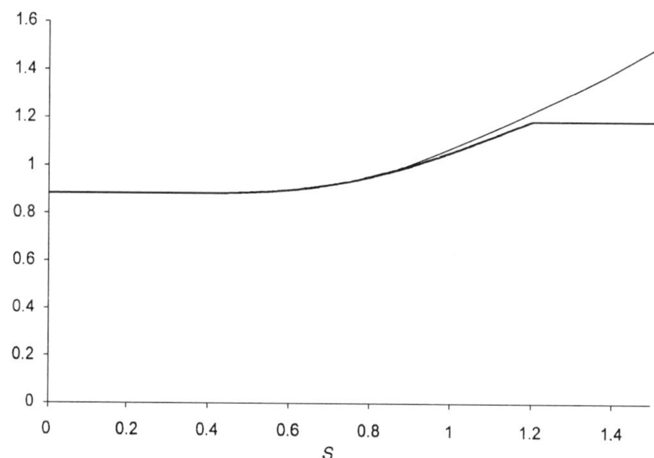

Figure 36.4 Value of a CB against the underlying when the bond is callable.

The value M_C can be time dependent. Now we must solve a constrained problem in which our bond price is bounded below by nS and above by M_C. To eliminate arbitrage and to optimize the bond's value, V and $\partial V/\partial S$ must be continuous. As with the intermittent conversion feature it is also simple to incorporate the intermittent call feature, according to which the company can only repurchase the bond during certain time periods.

In Figure 36.4 is shown an example of a CB value against the underlying where the effect of a call feature is apparent. Here the bond can be called back at any time for 1.2. The fine line is the same bond without the call feature.

Some convertible bonds incorporate a **put feature**. This right permits the holder of the bond to return it to the issuing company for an amount M_P, say. The value M_P can be time dependent. Now we must impose the constraint

$$V(S, t) \geq M_P.$$

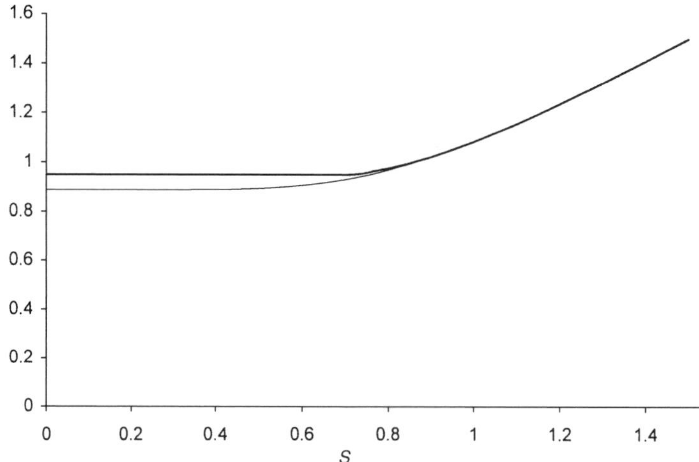

Figure 36.5 Value of a CB against the underlying when the bond is puttable.

This feature increases the value of the bond to the holder.

In Figure 36.5 is shown an example of a CB value against the underlying where the effect of the put feature is apparent. The bond is puttable for 0.95 at any time. The fine line is the bond without the put feature.

36.5 TWO-FACTOR MODELING: CONVERTIBLE BONDS WITH STOCHASTIC INTEREST RATE

The lifespan of a typical convertible is much longer than that for a traded option. It is therefore safer to price CBs using a stochastic interest rate model. When interest rates are stochastic, the convertible bond has a value of the form

$$V = V(S, r, t).$$

Before, r was just a parameter, now it is an independent variable.

We continue to assume that the asset price is governed by the lognormal model

$$dS = \mu S\, dt + \sigma S\, dX_1, \tag{36.2}$$

and the interest rate by

$$dr = u(r, t)\, dt + w(r, t)\, dX_2. \tag{36.3}$$

Eventually we are going to be finding solutions numerically, so we allow u and w to be any functions of r and t. Observe that in (36.2) and (36.3) there are two Wiener processes. This is because S and r are governed by two different random variables; this is a **two-factor model**. dX_1 and dX_2 are both still drawn from Normal distributions with zero mean and variance dt, but they are not the same random variable. They may, however, be correlated and we assume that

$$E[dX_1\, dX_2] = \rho\, dt,$$

with $-1 \leq \rho(r, S, t) \leq 1$. The subject of correlated random walks was discussed in Chapter 11. There we saw other examples of **multi-factor model**, in which there are two (or more) sources

of risk and hence two independent variables in addition to t. The theory of functions of several random variables was covered in Chapter 11; recall that Itô's lemma can be applied to functions of two or more random variables. The usual Taylor series expansion together with a few rules of thumb results in the correct expression for the small change in any function of both S and r. These rules of thumb are

- $dX_1^2 = dt$;
- $dX_2^2 = dt$;
- $dX_1\,dX_2 = \rho\,dt$.

The equation for dV is

$$dV = \frac{\partial V}{\partial t}\,dt + \frac{\partial V}{\partial S}\,dS + \frac{\partial V}{\partial r}dr + \tfrac{1}{2}\left(\sigma^2 S^2\frac{\partial^2 V}{\partial S^2} + 2\rho\sigma S w\frac{\partial^2 V}{\partial S\,\partial r} + w^2\frac{\partial^2 V}{\partial r^2}\right)dt.$$

Now we come to the pricing of the convertible bond. Construct a portfolio consisting of the convertible bond with maturity T_1, $-\Delta_2$ zero-coupon bonds with maturity date T_2 and $-\Delta_1$ of the underlying asset. We are therefore going to hedge both the interest rate risk and the underlying asset risk. Thus

$$\Pi = V - \Delta_2 Z - \Delta_1 S.$$

The analysis is much as before; the choice

$$\Delta_2 = \frac{\partial V}{\partial r}\bigg/\frac{\partial Z}{\partial r}$$

and

$$\Delta_1 = \frac{\partial V}{\partial S}$$

eliminates risk from the portfolio. Terms involving T_1 and T_2 may be grouped together separately to find that

$$\begin{aligned}\frac{\partial V}{\partial t} &+ \tfrac{1}{2}\sigma^2 S^2\frac{\partial^2 V}{\partial S^2} + \rho\sigma S w\frac{\partial^2 V}{\partial S\,\partial r} + \tfrac{1}{2}w^2\frac{\partial^2 V}{\partial r^2}\\ &+ rS\frac{\partial V}{\partial S} + (u - \lambda w)\frac{\partial V}{\partial r} - rV = 0.\end{aligned} \qquad (36.4)$$

where again $\lambda(r, S, t)$ is the market price of interest rate risk. This is exactly the same market price of risk as for ordinary bonds with no asset dependence and so we would expect it not to be a function of S, only of r and t.

This is the convertible bond pricing equation. There are two special cases of this equation that we have seen before.

- When $u = 0 = w$ we have constant interest rate r, Equation (36.4) collapses to the Black–Scholes equation.
- When there is no dependence on an asset $\partial/\partial S = 0$ we return to the basic bond pricing equation.

Dividends and coupons are incorporated in the manner discussed in Chapter 8 and earlier in this chapter. For discrete dividends and discrete coupons we have the usual jump conditions.

The condition at maturity and constraints are exactly as before; there is one constraint for each of the convertibility feature, the call feature and the put feature.

In Figure 36.6 is shown the value of a CB when the underlying asset is lognormal and interest rates evolve according to the Vasicek model fitted to a flat 7% yield curve. In Figures 36.7 and 36.8 are shown the two hedge ratios $\partial V/\partial S$ and $\partial V/\partial r$.

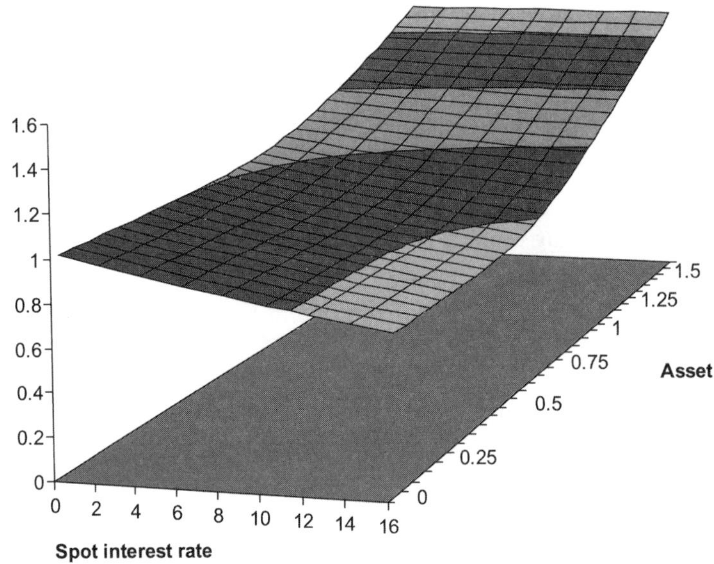

Figure 36.6 The value of a CB with stochastic asset and interest rates.

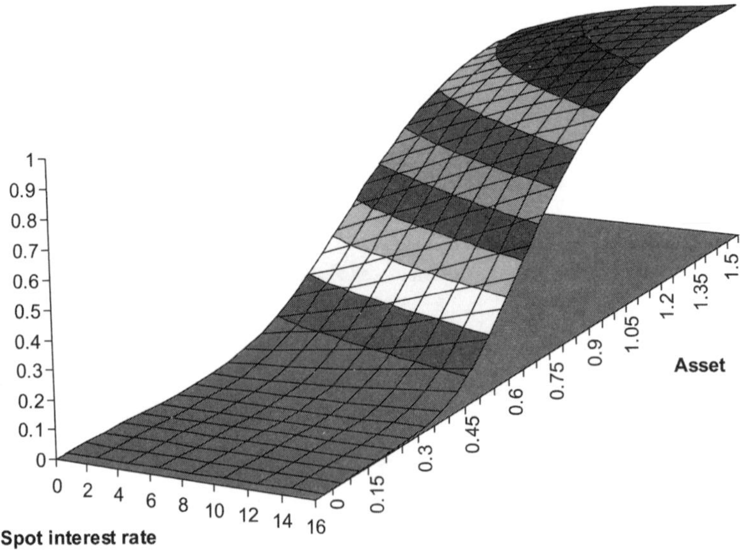

Figure 36.7 $\partial V/\partial S$ for a CB with stochastic asset and interest rates.

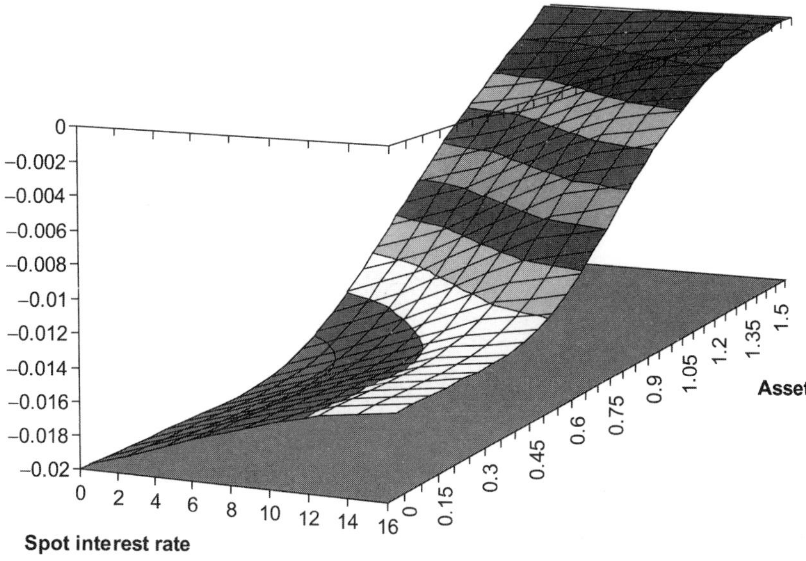

Figure 36.8 $\partial V/\partial r$ for a CB with stochastic asset and interest rates.

36.6 A SPECIAL MODEL

In some circumstances, and for a very narrow choice of interest rate model, we can find a similarity reduction. For example, if we use the Vasicek model for the risk-neutral interest rate

$$dr = (\eta - \gamma r)\,dt + \beta^{1/2}\,dX_2$$

then we can look for convertible bond prices of the form

$$V(S, r, t) = g(r, t)H\left(\frac{S}{g(r, t)}, t\right).$$

Skipping some of the details, the function $g(r, t)$ must be the value of a zero-coupon bond with the same maturity as the CB:

$$g(r, t) = Z(r, t; T) = e^{A(t;T)-rB(t;T)}$$

where

$$B(t; T) = \frac{1}{\gamma}(1 - e^{-\gamma(T-t)})$$

and

$$A(t; T) = \frac{1}{\gamma^2}\left((B(t; T) - T + t)\left(\eta\gamma - \tfrac{1}{2}\beta\right)\right) - \frac{\beta B(t; T)^2}{4\gamma}.$$

The function $H(\xi, t)$ then satisfies

$$\frac{\partial H}{\partial t} + \tfrac{1}{2}\xi^2(\sigma^2 + 2B(t; T)\rho\beta^{1/2}\sigma + B(t; T)^2\beta)\frac{\partial^2 H}{\partial \xi^2} = 0.$$

This problem must be solved subject to

$$H(\xi, T) = \max(n\xi, 1)$$

and

$$H(\xi, t) \geq n\xi.$$

Unfortunately call and put features do not fit into this similarity formulation. This is because the constraint

$$V(S, t) \leq M_C$$

becomes

$$H(\xi, t) \leq \frac{M_C}{Z(r, t; T)}$$

the right-hand side of which cannot be written in terms of just ξ and t.

36.7 PATH DEPENDENCE IN CONVERTIBLE BONDS

The above-mentioned convertible bond is the simplest of its kind; they can be far more complex. One source of complexity is, as ever, path dependency. A typical path-dependent bond would be the following.

The bond pays \$1 at maturity, time $t = T$. Before maturity, it may be converted, at any time, for n of the underlying. Initially, n is set to some constant n_b. At time T_0 the conversion ratio n is set to some function of the underlying *at that time*, $n_a(S(T_0))$. Restricting our attention to a deterministic interest rate, this three-dimensional problem (for which there is no similarity solution) satisfies

$$\frac{\partial V}{\partial t} + \tfrac{1}{2}\sigma^2 S^2 \frac{\partial^2 V}{\partial S^2} + rS\frac{\partial V}{\partial S} - rV \leq 0.$$

Where $V(S, \mathcal{S}, t)$ is the bond value with $\mathcal{S}$ being the value of S at time T_0. Dividends and coupons are to be added to this equation as necessary. The CB value satisfies the final condition

$$V(S, \mathcal{S}, T) = 1,$$

the constraint

$$V(S, \mathcal{S}, t) \geq n(S, \mathcal{S}),$$

where

$$n(S, \mathcal{S}) = \begin{cases} n_b & \text{for} \quad t \leq T_0 \\ n_a(\mathcal{S}) & \text{for} \quad t > T_0 \end{cases}$$

and the jump condition

$$V(S, \mathcal{S}, T_0^-) = V(S, S, T_0^+).$$

This problem is three dimensional, it has independent variables S, $\mathcal{S}$ and t. We could introduce stochastic interest rates with little extra theoretical work (other than choosing the interest rate model) but the computing time required for the resulting four-dimensional problem might make this unfeasible.

36.8 DILUTION

In reality, the conversion of the bond into the underlying stock requires the company to issue n new shares in the company. This contrasts with options for which exercise leaves the number of shares unchanged.

I'm going to subtly redefine S as follows. If N is the number of shares before conversion then the total worth of the company is $NS - V$ before conversion. The $-V$ in this is due to the company's obligations with respect to the CB. This means that the share price is actually

$$\frac{NS - V}{N}$$

and not S. The constraint that the CB value must be greater than the share price is

$$V \geq n\frac{NS - V}{N}$$

which can be rewritten as

$$V \geq \frac{N}{n + N} nS. \tag{36.5}$$

We must also have

$$V \leq S \tag{36.6}$$

and

$$V(S, T) = 1.$$

Constraint (36.5) bounds the bond price below by its value on conversion, which is lower than we had previously. Constraint (36.6) allows the company to declare bankruptcy if the bond becomes too valuable. The factor $N/(n + N)$ is known as the **dilution**. In the limit $n/N \to 0$ we return to $V \geq nS$.

36.9 CREDIT RISK ISSUES

The risk of default in CBs is very important. If the issuing company goes bankrupt, say, you will not receive any coupons and nor will the ability to convert into the stock have much value. We have said that in the absence of default issues, the CB trades like a bond when the stock price is low. This is true, except that the bond behaves like a risky bond, one that may default. Furthermore, if the stock price is very low it is usually indicative of a none-too-healthy company. We can expect, and this is seen in the markets, that the price of a CB *versus* the stock looks rather like the plot in Figure 36.9. Here the CB price goes to zero as $S \to 0$. We will see the model that led to this picture in Chapter 43.

36.10 SUMMARY

Convertible bonds are a very important type of contract, playing a major role in the financing of companies. From a pricing and hedging perspective they are highly complex instruments. They have the early exercise feature of American options but in *three* guises—the option to convert, call and put—sometimes behaving like a bond and sometimes like a stock. They have long lifespans, five years, say, meaning that the assumption of constant interest rates is not

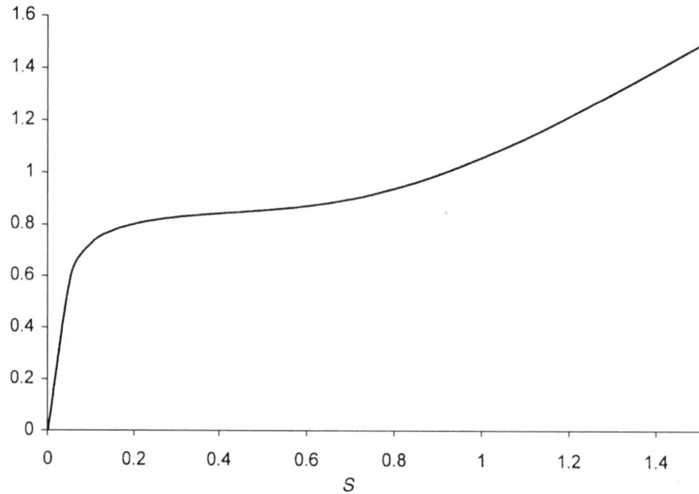

Figure 36.9 The value of a CB allowing for risk of default.

valid. In more complicated cases they can be path dependent. Finally, they are not without the risk of default. Put all these together and you have quite a sophisticated contract.

FURTHER READING

- For details of the effect of the issue of new shares on the value of convertible bonds see Brennan & Schwartz (1977), Cox & Rubinstein (1985) and Gemmill (1992).
- See Fabozzi (1996) and Nyborg (1996) for more information about the market practice of valuing CBs.
- Download stand-alone convertible bond pricing shareware from www.wilmott.com.

EXERCISES

1. If we were using convertible bonds for speculation, we may wish to use an estimated drift rate for the asset, instead of the risk-free rate. How would this change the pricing equation?
2. Incorporate uncertain volatility into the model for the share price for the convertible bond. Find the new equation for the value of the bond when the asset volatility is known to lie between values of σ^- and σ^+.
3. Adjust the model to include dividends, with both continuous and discrete versions. How do dividends affect the value of a convertible bond?

CHAPTER 37

two-factor interest rate modeling

In this Chapter...

- the theoretical framework for multi-factor interest rate modeling
- why the 'long rate' is a good second factor to use
- popular two-factor models

37.1 INTRODUCTION

The simple stochastic spot interest rate models of Chapter 33 cannot hope to capture the rich yield-curve structure found in practice: from a given spot rate at a given time they will predict the whole yield curve. Generally speaking, the one source of randomness, the spot rate, may be good at modeling the overall level of the yield curve but it will not necessarily model shifts in the yield curve that are substantially different at different maturities. For some instruments this may not be important. For example, for instruments that depend on the *level* of the yield curve it may be sufficient to have one source of randomness, i.e. one factor. More sophisticated products depend on the difference between yields of different maturities and for these products it is important to model the tilting of the yield curve. One way to do this is to invoke a second factor, a second source of randomness.

In this chapter I describe the theory behind two-factor interest rate modeling. I mention a few popular models explicitly. In these models the second factor is often, although not necessarily, a long-term interest rate. The ideas in this chapter are readily extended to more than two factors, but I leave that to the reader.

37.2 THEORETICAL FRAMEWORK

Assume that zero-coupon bonds (and all other simple interest rate instruments, for that matter) depend on two variables, r, the spot interest rate, and another independent variable l. Thus, for example, a zero-coupon bond with maturity T has a price $Z(r, l, t; T)$. The variables satisfy

IMPORTANT

$$dr = u\,dt + w\,dX_1$$

and

$$dl = p\,dt + q\,dX_2.$$

All of u, w, p and q are allowed to be functions of r, l and t. The correlation coefficient ρ between dX_1 and dX_2 may also depend on r, l and t.

Remember, as yet I have deliberately not said what l is. It could be another interest rate, a long rate, say, or the yield curve slope at the short end, or the volatility of the spot rate, for example. We set up the framework in general and look at specific models later.

Since we have two sources of randomness now, in pricing one zero-coupon bond we must hedge with *two* others to eliminate the risk:

$$\Pi = Z(r, l, t; T) - \Delta_1 Z(r, l, t; T_1) - \Delta_2 Z(r, l, t; T_2).$$

The change in the value of this portfolio is given by

$$\begin{aligned}&(\mathcal{L}(Z) - \Delta_1\mathcal{L}(Z_1) - \Delta_2\mathcal{L}(Z_2))\,dt\\ &+\left(\frac{\partial Z}{\partial r} - \Delta_1\frac{\partial Z_1}{\partial r} - \Delta_2\frac{\partial Z_2}{\partial r}\right)dr + \left(\frac{\partial Z}{\partial l} - \Delta_1\frac{\partial Z_1}{\partial l} - \Delta_2\frac{\partial Z_2}{\partial l}\right)dl,\end{aligned} \tag{37.1}$$

with the obvious notation for Z, Z_1 and Z_2. Here

$$\mathcal{L}(Z) = \frac{\partial Z}{\partial t} + \tfrac{1}{2}w^2\frac{\partial^2 Z}{\partial r^2} + \rho wq\frac{\partial^2 Z}{\partial r\partial l} + \tfrac{1}{2}q^2\frac{\partial^2 Z}{\partial l^2}.$$

Now choose Δ_1 and Δ_2 to make the coefficients of dr and dl in (37.1) equal to zero. The corresponding portfolio is risk free and should earn the risk-free rate of interest, r.

We thus have the three equations

$$\frac{\partial Z}{\partial r} - \Delta_1\frac{\partial Z_1}{\partial r} - \Delta_2\frac{\partial Z_2}{\partial r} = 0,$$
$$\frac{\partial Z}{\partial l} - \Delta_1\frac{\partial Z_1}{\partial l} - \Delta_2\frac{\partial Z_2}{\partial l} = 0$$

and

$$\mathcal{L}'(Z) - \Delta_1\mathcal{L}'(Z_1) - \Delta_2\mathcal{L}'(Z_2) = 0$$

where

$$\mathcal{L}'(Z) = \mathcal{L}(Z) - rZ.$$

These are three simultaneous equations for Δ_1 and Δ_2. As such, this system is over-prescribed and for the equations to be consistent we require

$$\det(\mathbf{M}) = 0$$

where

$$\mathbf{M} = \begin{pmatrix} \mathcal{L}'(Z) & \mathcal{L}'(Z_1) & \mathcal{L}'(Z_2) \\ \partial Z/\partial r & \partial Z_1/\partial r & \partial Z_2/\partial r \\ \partial Z/\partial l & \partial Z_1/\partial l & \partial Z_2/\partial l \end{pmatrix}.$$

The first row of the matrix $\mathbf{M}$ is a linear combination of the second and third rows. We can therefore write

$$\mathcal{L}'(Z) = (\lambda_r w - u)\frac{\partial Z}{\partial r} + (\lambda_l q - p)\frac{\partial Z}{\partial l}$$

where the two functions $\lambda_r(r, l, t)$ and $\lambda_l(r, l, t)$ are the market prices of risk for r and l respectively, and are again independent of the maturity of any bond. In full, we have

$$\frac{\partial Z}{\partial t} + \tfrac{1}{2}w^2\frac{\partial^2 Z}{\partial r^2} + \rho wq\frac{\partial^2 Z}{\partial r \partial l} + \tfrac{1}{2}q^2\frac{\partial^2 Z}{\partial l^2} + (u - \lambda_r w)\frac{\partial Z}{\partial r} + (p - \lambda_l q)\frac{\partial Z}{\partial l} - rZ = 0 \tag{37.2}$$

The model for interest rate derivatives is defined by the choices of w, q, ρ, and the risk-adjusted drift rates $u - \lambda_r w$ and $p - \lambda_l q$.

In Section 37.3 we look at popular two-factor models in more detail. First, however, we examine briefly the special case in which l is a long term interest rate.

37.2.1 Special Case: Modeling a Long-term Rate

We have not yet chosen what to model as l. There is one natural and special case that has certain advantages: a long-term interest rate. Specifically, here we examine the choice of l as the yield on a consol bond.

A simple **consol bond** is a fixed-coupon-bearing bond of infinite maturity. If C_o is the value of this bond when the coupon is \$1 p.a. then the yield is defined as

$$l = \frac{1}{C_o}.$$

This will be our definition of l. This choice for the variable l is very special because this consol bond is traded and thus its value must satisfy a pricing equation. The relevant equation is identical to (37.2) except there is an extra term:

$$\mathcal{L}'(C_o) + 1 = (\lambda_r w - u)\frac{\partial C_o}{\partial r} + (\lambda_{lq} - p)\frac{\partial C_o}{\partial l};$$

the extra term,1, is due to the coupon payment.[1] Substituting $1/l$ into this equation we find

$$p - \lambda_l q = l^2 - rl + \frac{q^2}{l^2}.$$

In other words, because we are modeling a traded quantity, we find an expression for the market price of risk for that factor. Thus the bond-pricing equation with the consol bond yield as a factor is

$$\mathcal{L}'(Z) = (\lambda_r w - u)\frac{\partial Z}{\partial r} - \left(l^2 - rl + \frac{q^2}{l^2}\right)\frac{\partial Z}{\partial l},$$

or, in full,

$$\frac{\partial Z}{\partial t} + \tfrac{1}{2}w^2\frac{\partial^2 Z}{\partial r^2} + \rho wq\frac{\partial^2 Z}{\partial r \partial l} + \tfrac{1}{2}q^2\frac{\partial^2 Z}{\partial l^2} + (u - \lambda_r w)\frac{\partial Z}{\partial r} + \left(l^2 - rl + \frac{q^2}{l^2}\right)\frac{\partial Z}{\partial l} - rZ = 0.$$

[1] Note that I have made the approximation that this coupon is paid continuously throughout the year. In practice it is paid discretely, but this has only a small effect on the following analysis.

Observe that the coefficient of $\partial Z/\partial l$ no longer contains a market price of risk term. Compare this result with options on traded stocks. In that case, since the stock is traded we do not see a market price of risk for stocks; in fact, we find a simple expression for this market price of risk in terms of the real asset drift rate. Now contrast this with the spot interest rate term; the spot rate is not traded and so we see the market price for the spot rate appear in the equation.

Because we need to model one function fewer when we use the consol yield as a factor, it is an obvious and popular choice for the second factor in two-factor interest rate modeling.

Actually, all is not as rosy as I have just made out. The long rate and the short rate are more closely linked than the above suggests, it is *not* possible to model both a short rate and a long rate completely independently. For example, in the affine one-factor world the long rate is just a simple function of the short rate. And the same applies in the two-factor world. The internal consistency requirement amounts to a restriction on the volatility of the long rate. See Duffie, Ma & Yong (1994) for more details of the restrictions.

37.2.2 Special Case: Modeling the Spread Between the Long and the Short Rate

A version of the above is to model the spread between the long and the short rate as the new variable. Call this variable s. Because

$$s = \frac{1}{C_o} - r,$$

and C_o is traded, we find a simple expression for the market price of risk of the spread. Furthermore, there is evidence that, at least in the US, the short rate and the spread are uncorrelated. This eliminates another function from the modeling, leaving us with just three terms: volatilities of short rate and spread, and the risk-adjusted spot-rate drift.

37.3 **POPULAR MODELS**

In this section I briefly describe some popular models. Most of these models are popular because the pricing equations (37.2) for these models have explicit solutions. In these models sometimes the second factor is the long rate and sometimes it is some other, usually unobservable, variable.

Brennan and Schwartz (1982)

In the Brennan & Schwartz model the risk-adjusted spot rate satisfies

$$dr = (a_1 + b_1(l - r))\,dt + \sigma_1 r\,dX_1$$

and the long rate satisfies

$$dl = l(a_2 - b_2 r + c_2 l)\,dt + \sigma_2 l\,dX_2.$$

Brennan & Schwartz choose the parameters statistically. Because of the relatively complicated functional forms of the terms in these equations there are no simple solutions of the bond pricing equation. The random terms in these two stochastic differential equations are of the lognormal form, but the drift terms are more complicated than that, having some mean reversion character.

The main problems with the Brennnan & Schwartz models are twofold. First, the long and short rates must satisfy certain internal consistency requirements. Second, as pointed out by Hogan (1993) the Brennan & Schwartz models can blow up in a finite time, meaning that rates can go to infinity. This is not a good property for an interest rate model.

Fong and Vasicek (1991)

Fong & Vasicek consider the following model for risk-adjusted variables:

$$dr = a(\overline{r} - r)\,dt + \sqrt{\xi}\,dX_1$$

and

$$d\xi = b(\overline{\xi} - \xi)\,dt + c\sqrt{\xi}\,dX_2.$$

Thus they model r, the risk-adjusted spot rate, and ξ the square root of the volatility of the spot rate. The latter cannot be observed, and this is an obvious weakness of the model. But it also makes it harder to show that the model is wrong. The simple linear mean reversion and the square roots in these equations results in explicit equations for simple interest rate products, see below.

Longstaff and Schwartz (1992)

Longstaff & Schwartz consider the following model for risk-adjusted variables:

$$dX = a(\overline{x} - x)\,dt + \sqrt{x}\,dX_1$$

and

$$dy = b(\overline{y} - y)\,dt + \sqrt{y}\,dX_2,$$

where the spot interest rate is given by

$$r = cx + dy.$$

Again, the simple nature of the terms in these equations results in explicit equations for simple interest rate products, see below.

General Affine Model

If r and l satisfy the following:

- the risk-adjusted drifts of both r and l are linear in r and l (but can have an arbitrary time dependence)
- the random terms for both r and l are both square roots of functions linear in r and l (but can have an arbitrary time dependence)
- the stochastic processes for r and l are uncorrelated

then the two-factor bond pricing equation (37.2) for a zero-coupon bond has a solution of the form

$$e^{A(t;T)-B(t;T)r-C(t;T)l}.$$

This result is a two-factor version of that found in Chapter 33 for a single factor.

The ordinary differential equations for A, B and C must in general be solved numerically.

37.4 THE PHASE PLANE IN THE ABSENCE OF RANDOMNESS

There is a very simple analysis that can be done on two-factor models to determine whether they are well behaved. This analysis is the examination of the dynamics in the *absence of randomness*. It requires the drift coefficients for the two factors to be independent of time.

I'm also going to cheat a little in the following. Ideally we would transform the stochastic differential equations into equations with constant volatilities, but I'm going to omit that step here. It will make no difference to anything I say about the singularities, but may have an effect on my description of the global behavior of rates.

To demonstrate the technique, let us consider the Fong & Vasicek model. In the absence of randomness, this model becomes

$$dr = a(\overline{r} - r)\,dt$$

and

$$d\xi = b(\overline{\xi} - \xi)\,dt.$$

Dividing one by the other we get

$$\frac{d\xi}{dr} = \frac{b(\overline{\xi} - \xi)}{a(\overline{r} - r)}. \qquad (37.3)$$

We can plot the solutions of this first-order ordinary differential equation in a **phase plane**, see Figure 37.1.

The idea behind phase planes can be described by examining this model. Each line in this plot represents a possible evolution of r and ξ. In this particular example there is a **singularity** at the point $(\overline{r}, \overline{\xi})$ where the numerator and denominator of (37.3) are both zero and so the slope $d\xi/dr$ is undefined. This singularity is, in this case called a **node**. In the Fong & Vasicek model with a and b positive this singularity is **stable**, meaning that solutions that pass close to the singular point are drawn into it. (In this case, *all* solutions are drawn to this point.) Some more types of possible singularities for other two-factor (non-random) models are shown in Figure 37.2. There are others.

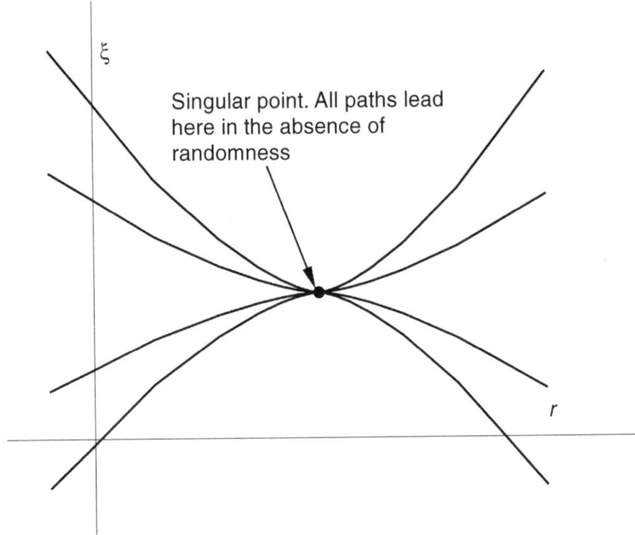

Figure 37.1 Phase plane for the Fong & Vasicek model (no randomness).

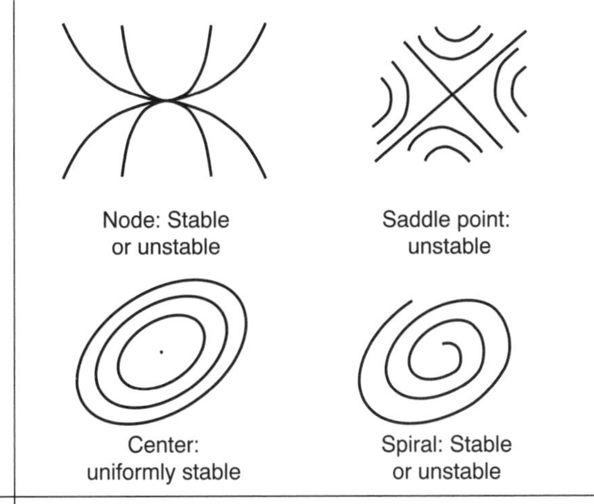

Figure 37.2 Possible phase-plane singularities.

When randomness is put back into the model the solution paths are no longer deterministic. A possible evolution of a single realization is shown in Figure 37.3 for the Fong & Vasicek model. What's wrong with this figure, and with Figure 37.2? The answer is that the phase plane only looks the way I have drawn it for points close to the singularity. Remember, I said that ideally one should transform the governing stochastic differential equations into equations with constant volatilities, and this I have not done. For the Fong & Vasicek model in particular, as

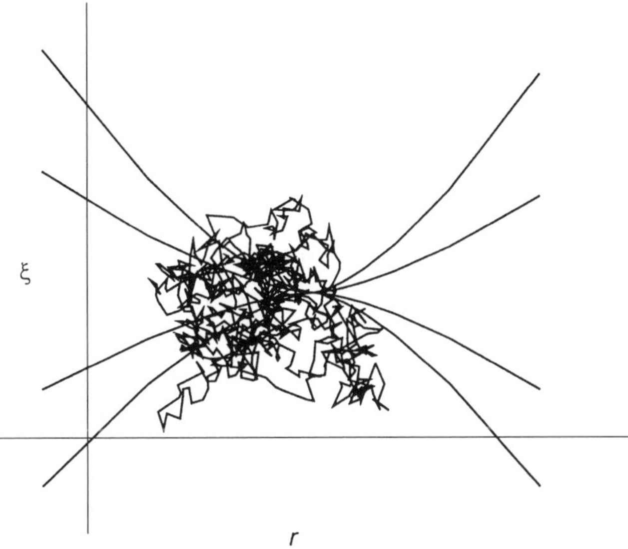

Figure 37.3 Typical realization of the Fong & Vasicek model, phase plane and time series.

long as c is not too big the variable ξ cannot go negative because of the square root in front of the random term.

We can use these phase planes to decide whether the properties of our model are realistic. A very useful example is the Brennan and Schwartz model. For certain parameter ranges the equations are so unstable that the long and short rates tend to infinity. Not a realistic property for an interest rate model.[2]

37.5 THE YIELD CURVE SWAP

One of the most important contracts for which you may need a two-factor model is the **yield curve swap**. This is a contract in which one counterparty pays a floating rate based on one part of the yield curve and the other counterparty pays a floating rate based on a different point on the curve. In Figure 37.4 is the term sheet for a yield curve swap on sterling. Every quarter one side pays three-month GBP LIBOR and the other pays the two-year swap rate plus 16 basis points. A **basis point** is one hundredth of a percent.

There are two ways to approach the pricing of this contract. One is to model the spread between these two rates as a lognormal, or more probably, Normal variable. And the other is to use a two-factor interest rate model.

Sterling Yield Curve Swap

Swap Notional	GBP []
Swap Effective Date	4 November 1997
Swap Maturity Date	4 November 1999
Counterparty A payments	
Floating Coupon	GBP 2yr Swap (Mid) plus 0.16%, as fixed on Telerate page 42279 at 11:00am London time on each period start date
Payment Frequency	Quarterly
Payment Dates	4 February, May, August, November
Calculation Basis	Act/365
Counterparty B payments	
Floating Index	GBP 3 Month LIBOR flat
Payment Frequency	Quarterly
Payment Dates	4 February, May, August, November
Calculation Basis	Act/365

This indicative termsheet is neither an offer to buy or sell securities or an OTC derivative product which includes options, swaps, forwards and structured notes having similar features to OTC derivative transactions, nor a solicitation to buy or sell securities or an OTC derivative product. The proposal contained in the foregoing is not a complete description of the terms of a particular transaction and is subject to change without limitation.

Figure 37.4 Term sheet for a Sterling Yield Curve Swap.

[2] Do not forget, of course, that in the examples given in this section, the phase plane is for the *risk-adjusted* spot interest rate, not the real rate.

If we assume that the spread is a Normal variable then we can find its volatility, from historical data, say, or implied from another contract, and price the contract in an almost Black–Scholes world. You will also need to discount using some interest rates and the natural choice would be the yield curve as it stands at the time of pricing. This is a moderately robust way to price this contract.

If we are to use a stochastic interest rate model, why must it be two factor? This is because the net cashflows depend on the spread between two rates. If you were to use a one-factor model then these two rates would be perfectly correlated, resulting in no volatility in the spread. The two-factor model is needed for there to be some volatility in the spread, and thus a non-deterministic outcome for each cashflow. The two interest payments are treated slightly differently. The three-month rate can be thought of as the spot interest rate but the two-year swap rate is more complicated; you will have to first model the swap rates using the model. Having modeled the swap rate, using the two-factor differential equation, you can then price the yield curve swap, using the same equation but with different cashflows. The contract can therefore be thought of as second order. Not only is this procedure messy and time consuming, the result may depend quite strongly on your chosen model.

37.6 SUMMARY

In this chapter we have seen the general theory for two-factor interest rate models. Two-factor models are better than one-factor in that they will allow for a richer yield curve structure. But again, as with the one-factor models, the theoretical yield curve will not be the same as the market yield curve unless the model has been calibrated. Even then, all of the problems that we saw in the one-factor fitted models are still seen here: the slope and curvature of the yield curve are in general too large to be consistently modeled by even a two-factor model.

Nevertheless, having a two-factor model does allow different parts of the yield curve to be less than one hundred percent correlated and that has to be an improvement. Indeed, for any contract that pays off the spread between two different points on the yield curve a one-factor model cannot be used.

FURTHER READING

- See the original papers by Brennan & Schwartz (1982) and Longstaff & Schwartz (1992).
- See Duffie, Ma & Yong (1994) for an explanation of the relationship between the short and the long rate and why they can't be modeled independently.
- Hogan (1993) analyses the Brennan and Schwartz models and shows that they can have some alarming features, such as rates going to infinity in a finite time.
- Rebonato (1996) discusses theoretical and practical issues concerning several two-factor models in some detail.
- Jordan & Smith (1977) is the classic reference text for phase-plane analysis.

EXERCISES

1. What is our justification for the substitution of $1/l$ into the equation for the value of the consol bond,
$$\mathcal{L}'(C_o) + 1 = (\lambda_r w - u)\frac{\partial C_o}{\partial r} + (\lambda_l q - p)\frac{\partial C_o}{\partial l}?$$

2. Find an expression for the market price of risk when we model the spread between the long and short rates, using

$$s = \frac{1}{C_o} - r.$$

3. What are the types of singularities most commonly found in phase planes? Which imply stability and which instability?

CHAPTER 38
empirical behavior of the spot interest rate

In this Chapter...

- how to analyze short-term interest rates to determine the best model for the volatility and the real drift
- how to analyze the slope of the yield curve to get information about the market price of risk
- how to build up sensible one- or two-factor spot rate models

38.1 INTRODUCTION

Earlier I described the general framework for one-factor interest rate modeling and we have seen several popular models in detail. The one-factor models that we saw in Chapter 33 for the spot interest rate were all chosen for their nice properties; for most of them we were able to find simple closed-form solutions of the bond-pricing equation. We discussed the pros and cons of these models in that chapter.

In this chapter we will see how to deduce a model for the spot rate from data. The method that we use assumes that the model is time homogeneous, and ensures that the spot rate is well behaved. The principle is the same as that in Chapter 25, used for finding a volatility model from volatility data. Here, though, we take the idea further, finding also the market price of risk from yield curve data. The downside to the resulting model is that we cannot find closed-form solutions for contract values, the risk-neutral drift and the volatility don't have a sufficiently nice structure.

I describe the analysis and modeling using empirical US spot interest rate data, making comparisons with the popular models. We use this data to determine which models seem to fit reality best and to derive a spot rate model that has certain desirable properties: it has a realistic volatility structure and a meaningful steady-state probability density function. By basing our modeling on real data we inevitably lose tractability when we come to solve the bond pricing equation. Our only concession to tractability is the assumption of time-independence of our random walk. Using this assumption, and by examining data over a long period of time, we hope to model, in a sense, the 'average' behavior of the spot rate. Such a model could, for example, be used to price long-dated instruments. I conclude with some suggestions for how to build up a two-factor model for interest rates.

38.2 POPULAR ONE-FACTOR SPOT-RATE MODELS

Because of the complexity of fixed-income instruments the most popular of the interest-rate models are chosen because they result in closed-form expressions for the prices of simple contracts. That is they are *tractable*. This reduces to a minimum the computer time required for bond calculations. Unfortunately, this also means that the the models are not necessarily a good description of reality. Let us briefly re-examine some one-factor models.

Consider the classical one-factor models of Vasicek (1977), Cox, Ingersoll & Ross (1985), Ho & Lee (1986) and the extensions of Hull & White (1990a). In these models the spot rate r satisfies the stochastic differential equation

$$dr = u(r, t)\,dt + w(r, t)\,dX. \tag{38.1}$$

Table 38.1 shows the structural forms adopted by the above authors.

Table 38.1 Popular one-factor spot interest rate models.

Model	$u(r,t) - \lambda(r,t)w(r,t)$	$w(r,t)$
Vasicek	$a - br$	c
CIR	$a - br$	$cr^{1/2}$
Ho & Lee	$a(t)$	c
HW I	$a(t) - b(t)r$	$c(t)$
HW II	$a(t) - b(t)r$	$c(t)r^{1/2}$
General affine	$a(t) - b(t)r$	$(c(t)r - d(t))^{1/2}$

Here $\lambda(r, t)$ denotes the market price of risk. The function $u - \lambda w$ is the risk-adjusted drift. The time-dependent coefficients in most of these models allow for the fitting of the yield curve and other interest-rate instruments as we have seen in Chapter 34.

If the spot rate equation is (38.1) then, as shown in Chapter 33, the zero-coupon bond pricing equation is

$$\frac{\partial Z}{\partial t} + \tfrac{1}{2}w(r,t)^2\frac{\partial^2 Z}{\partial r^2} + (u(r,t) - \lambda(r,t)w(r,t))\frac{\partial Z}{\partial r} - rZ = 0, \tag{38.2}$$

with $Z(r, T; T) = 1$. It is no coincidence that all of the models in the table give zero-coupon bond prices of the form

$$Z(r, t; T) = e^{A(t,T) - rB(t,T)}. \tag{38.3}$$

As shown independently by numerous people (Duffie (1992), Klugman (1992), Klugman & Wilmott (1994), Ritchken (1994) and others), if the solution of (38.2) for the zero-coupon bond takes the form (38.3) then the most general forms for the coefficients must be as shown at the bottom of the table; this general affine model contains four time-dependent parameters. We saw in Chapter 33 that this is the most general form which leads to explicit formulae.

Black, Derman & Toy (BDT), on the other hand, have not developed their model, given by

$$d(\log r) = \left(\theta(t) - \frac{w'(t)}{w(t)}\log r\right)dt + w(t)\,dX,$$

for reasons of tractability with respect to the solution of a partial differential equation. Their model is chosen to enable them to fit market data easily. They have a volatility structure (the coefficient of dX in the spot rate equation) that is proportional to the spot rate with a time-dependent coefficient.

This coefficient and the other time-dependent coefficient in the risk-adjusted drift rate are chosen so that the BDT model correctly fits today's yield curve and interest rate options. This data fitting is, of course, very appealing, but, as we have seen, it must be treated with care.

38.3 IMPLIED MODELING: ONE FACTOR

Now let us examine an alternative approach to the modeling of interest rates. We build up our model in stages and try not to be too sidetracked by 'tractability.' Remember, we are assuming time-independent parameters.

In Figure 38.1 is shown the US one-month LIBOR rates, daily, for the period 1977–1994, and is the data that we use in our analysis. The ideas that we introduce can be applied to any currency, but here we use US data for illustration.

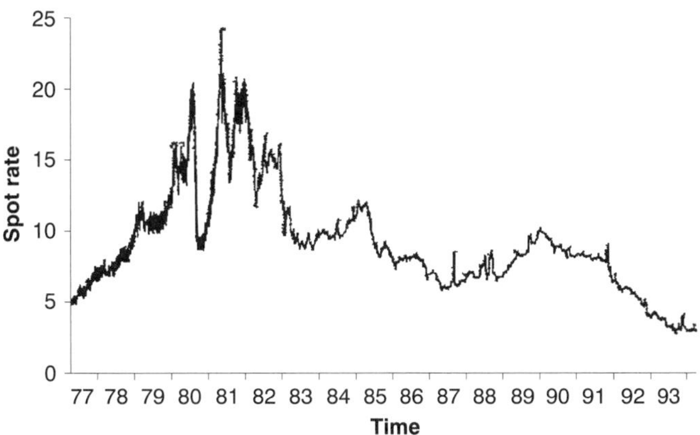

Figure 38.1 US spot rate 1977–1994.

There are three key stages:

1. By differencing spot rate time series data we determine the volatility dependence on the spot rate $w(r)$.
2. By examining the steady-state probability density function for the spot rate we determine the functional form of the drift rate $u(r)$.
3. We examine the slope of the yield curve to determine the market price of risk $\lambda(r)$.

38.4 THE VOLATILITY STRUCTURE

Our first observation is that many popular models take the form

$$dr = u(r)\,dt + \nu r^{\beta}\,dX. \tag{38.4}$$

Examples of such models are the Ho & Lee ($\beta = 0$), Vasicek ($\beta = 0$) and Cox, Ingersoll & Ross[1] ($\beta = \frac{1}{2}$) models. Because of their popularity with both practitioners and academics there

[1] In another model, Cox, Ingersoll & Ross (1980) had $\beta = 3/2$ with $u = 0$. They found analytical solutions for some perpetual instruments, but had to make some assumptions again for reasons of tractability. With these same assumptions it is possible to find explicit *similarity* solutions for zero-coupon bonds.

have been a number of empirical studies, trying to estimate the coefficient β from data. Perhaps the most cited of these works is that by Chan, Karolyi, Longstaff & Sanders (1992) on US data. They obtain the estimate $\beta = 1.36$.[2] This agrees with the experiences of many practitioners, who say that in practice the relative spot rate change dr/r is insensitive to the level of r.

We can think of models with

$$dr = \cdots + c\,dX$$

as having a Normal volatility structure and those with

$$dr = \cdots + cr\,dX$$

as having a lognormal volatility structure. In reality it seems that the spot rate is closer to the lognormal than to the Normal models. This puts the BDT model ahead of the others.

Using our US spot rate data we can estimate the best value for β. There are any number of sophisticated methods that one can use. Here I am going to describe a very simple, not at all sophisticated, method. From the time-series data divide the changes in the interest rate, δr, into buckets covering a range of r values. Then calculate the average value of $(\delta r)^2$, for each bucket. If the model (38.4) is correct we would expect

$$E[(\delta r)^2] = \nu^2 r^{2\beta}\,\delta t$$

to leading order in the timestep δt, which for our data is one day. This is the same technique as used in Chapter 25 for estimating the volatility of volatility.

In Figure 38.2 is plotted $\log(E[(\delta r)^2])$ against $\log r$ using the US data. The slope of this 'line' gives an estimate for 2β. We can see that the line is remarkably straight, especially over middle values of $\log r$, corresponding to values of r which have a large number of data points.

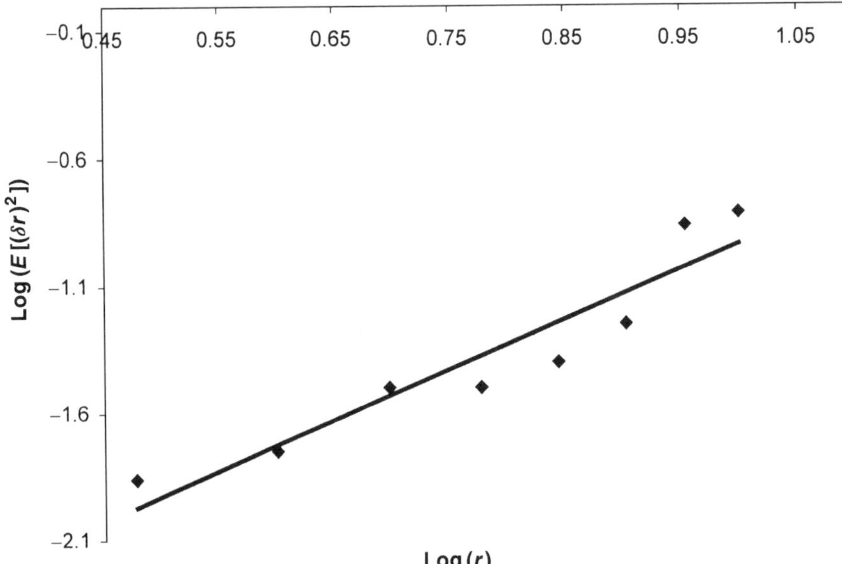

Figure 38.2 Estimation of β.

[2] Murphy (1995) finds $\beta = 0.36$ for the UK. The analysis of this chapter could equally well be applied to the UK.

From this calculation it is estimated that

$$\beta = 1.13 \quad \text{and} \quad \nu = 0.126.$$

This confirms that the spot rate volatility is close to lognormal in nature.

38.5 THE DRIFT STRUCTURE

It is statistically harder to estimate the drift term from the data; this term is smaller than the volatility term and thus subject to larger relative errors. If we were to use a naive method to determine the drift, we may find ourselves with a model that behaves well for short times but behaves poorly in the long term. We will therefore take an alternative, more stable, approach involving the empirical and analytical determination of the steady-state probability density function for r.

If r satisfies the stochastic differential equation (38.4) then the probability density function $p(r, t)$ for r satisfies the forward Fokker–Planck equation (see Chapter 10)

$$\frac{\partial p}{\partial t} = \tfrac{1}{2}\nu^2 \frac{\partial^2}{\partial r^2}(r^{2\beta} p) - \frac{\partial}{\partial r}(u(r)p). \qquad (38.5)$$

In this r and t are the forward variables, usually denoted by r' and t'. It is possible for equation (38.5) to have a steady-state distribution as a solution. This distribution is that to which the probability density function will evolve from any initial condition. We can estimate this steady state from the empirical data and thus find a solution of (38.5). Note that a steady-state distribution would clearly not exist for an equity, since equity prices generally grow (or decay) exponentially. However, a steady state probability density function is a not unreasonable property to assume for interest rates (Ramamurtie, Prezas & Ulman, 1993). This steady state $p_\infty(r)$ will satisfy

$$\tfrac{1}{2}\nu^2 \frac{d^2}{dr^2}(r^{2\beta} p_\infty) - \frac{d}{dr}(u(r)p_\infty) = 0. \qquad (38.6)$$

If this steady-state probability density function is empirically determined, then by integrating (38.6) we find that[3]

$$u(r) = \phi^2 \beta r^{2\beta-1} + \tfrac{1}{2} r^{2\beta} \frac{d}{dr}(\log p_\infty).$$

Not only is this method for finding the drift more stable in the long run, but also the steady-state probability density function is something simple to focus attention on, we will know that our model cannot behave too outrageously. This probability density function is something that it may be possible to estimate, or at least take an educated guess at. At the same time, it is harder to have an intuitive feel for the drift coefficient $u(r)$. By choosing a model with a sensible steady-state distribution, we can guarantee that the model will not allow the spot rate to do anything unrealistic such as grow unboundedly.

For special choices of β and $p_\infty(r)$ (and later $\lambda(r)$) we recover all the models mentioned in the above table.

Again, looking at US data, we can determine a plausible functional form for $p_\infty(r)$ from one-month US LIBOR rates. The steady-state distribution is determined by dividing r into buckets

[3] There are some issues to do with existence, uniqueness, and behavior at $r = 0$ and infinity that I omit for the sake of readability.

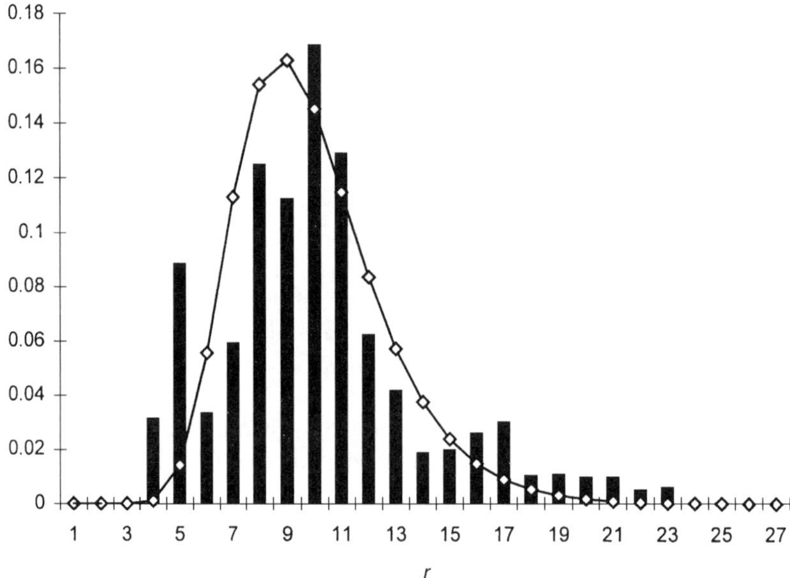

Figure 38.3 Observed and chosen probability density distributions for r.

and observing the frequency with which each bucket is reached. This is the same technique as used in Chapter 25 for estimating the drift of volatility.

The results of this analysis are shown in Figure 38.3. This figure represents our estimate for the steady-state probability density function. The shape of this graph is reminiscent of a lognormal curve. For this reason, and because it has a simple formula with just two parameters, choose $p_\infty(r)$ to be a lognormal curve that best fits the empirical data; this curve is also shown in the figure.

Our choice for $p_\infty(r)$ is

$$\frac{1}{ar\sqrt{2\pi}}\exp\left(-\frac{1}{2a^2}(\log(r/\overline{r}))^2\right)$$

where $a = 0.4$ and $\overline{r} = 0.08$. From this we find that for the US market

$$u(r) = \nu^2 r^{2\beta-1}\left(\beta - \tfrac{1}{2} - \frac{1}{2a^2}\log(r/\overline{r})\right).$$

The real spot rate is therefore mean-reverting to 8%.[4]

38.6 THE SLOPE OF THE YIELD CURVE AND THE MARKET PRICE OF RISK

Now we have found $w(r)$ and $u(r)$, it only remains for us to find $\lambda(r)$. The model will then be complete. I shall again allow λ to have a spot-rate dependence, but not a time dependence. Note that there is no information about the market price of risk in the spot-rate process, we

[4] The mean of the probability density function is *not* the same as the level at which $u = 0$ because of the volatility term in the stochastic differential equation.

must look to the yield curve to model this. In particular, we examine the short end of the curve for this information.

Let us expand $Z(r, t; T)$ in a Taylor series about $t = T$; this is the short end of the yield curve. We saw the details of this in Chapter 34. From equation (38.2) we find that

$$Z(r, t; T) \sim 1 - r(T - t) + \tfrac{1}{2}(T - t)^2(r^2 - u + \lambda w) + \cdots \quad \text{as} \quad t \to T$$

for any model $w(r)$, $u(r)$ and $\lambda(r)$. From this we have

$$-\frac{\ln Z}{T - t} \sim r + \tfrac{1}{2}(u - \lambda w)(T - t) + \cdots \quad \text{as} \quad t \to T. \tag{38.7}$$

Thus the slope of the yield curve at the short end in this one-factor model is simply $(u - \lambda w)/2$. We can use this result together with time-series data to determine the form for $u - \lambda w$ empirically.

We can calculate a time series for the yield-curve slope from one- and three-month US LIBOR data. In Figure 38.4 is plotted the yield-curve slope series against the spot rate series, with each data point connected to the following point by a straight line.

Let us continue with our strategy of finding the best fit with time-independent coefficients. The justification for this is that we are looking at data over a long period, and we choose $\lambda(r)$ to fit Figure 38.4 *on average*; by taking this approach, nothing is brushed under the carpet, we know the limitations of the model.[5]

We find that the simple choice $\lambda(r) = -40r^{\beta-1}$ is a good fit to the average, for US data.

We can now make a comparison between the tractable one-factor models and that presented here. The tractable models require the risk-adjusted drift $u - \lambda w$ to be of the form $a - br$. Our

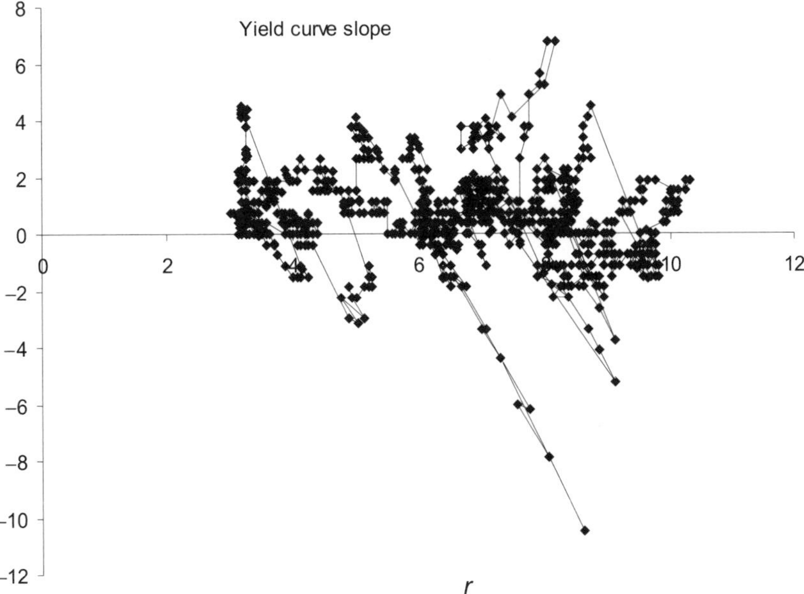

Figure 38.4 Slope of yield curve against spot rate and best fit, US LIBOR data.

[5] We could instead choose a best/worst $\lambda(r)$ to bound derivative prices. See Chapters 24 and 40 for ideas in this direction.

model requires $u - \lambda w$ to be

$$\nu^2 r^{2\beta-1}\left(\beta - \tfrac{1}{2} - \frac{1}{2a^2}\log(r/\overline{r})\right) - \lambda(r)\nu r^{\beta}.$$

We can immediately see from Figure 38.4 that the form $a - br$ for $u - \lambda w$ is not suitable if a and b are positive. Actually, the BDT risk-adjusted drift rate is much better.

Figure 38.4 is perhaps the most instructive picture. If the plot of $u - \lambda w$ showed it to be single-valued in r then we could easily find $\lambda(r)$. However, it shows no such thing. This calls into question any use of one-factor models. It also strongly suggests that naive fitting of market data gives a false sense of security; as is well known, fitted time-dependent parameters always have to be refitted.

38.7 WHAT THE SLOPE OF THE YIELD CURVE TELLS US

There are several very important points to note about this result. First, with this choice for λ the drift term u is now much smaller than the λw term. Thus, in this model the risk-adjusted spot rate is mean reverting to a much larger value of the spot rate than 8%. This is a very important observation and highlights the difference between the real and risk-neutral processes. Second, this λ is chosen to match the yield curve slope at the short end. The long rate for such a model is now far too high; the risk-neutral rate reverts to a very high level.

Because of the high yield-curve slope, the conclusion from these observations (and the validity of (38.7) for any model) is that *any* one-factor model is going to hit problems: either it will be accurate over the short end of the yield curve, with a poor long rate fit, or it will have a good long rate fit with a slope at the short end that is far too shallow. A good comparison to make is between a theoretical forward-rate curve with λ being zero, and a theoretical forward-rate curve with a λ chosen to match the slope. The former gives the *real expected* path of the spot interest rate, with no account being taken of the market price of risk. Generally speaking, empirical evidence suggests that the actual increase or decrease in rates in the short to medium term is much slower than implied by the market yield curve. In Figure 38.5 are shown a typical market forward-rate

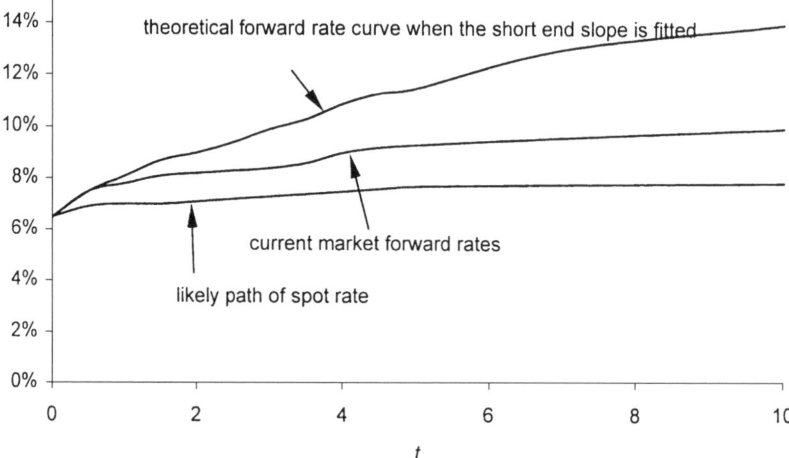

Figure 38.5 Typical market forward rates, the expected future path of the short rate using the empirical model, and the theoretical forward rates when the yield-curve slope is fitted at the short end.

curve, the expected future path of the short rate using the above model (with zero market price of risk), and the theoretical forward-rate curve when the yield-curve slope is fitted.

When $\lambda = 0$ we are in effect modeling the behavior of the real spot rate. This is are lot easier to do than model the risk-neutral spot rate and the yield curve. The model with $\lambda = 0$ is a good model of the real US spot rate.

Finally, for US data, we find that BDT is the closest popular model to the one we have derived. The BDT volatility structure is realistic and the risk-adjusted drift rate is a fair match to empirical data. The BDT model is close to ours, but the underlying philosophy is fundamentally different—the BDT model was originally chosen for its simple tree structure and to fit data, something which should be treated with care.

38.8 PROPERTIES OF THE FORWARD RATE CURVE 'ON AVERAGE'

Quite reasonably, you might say that the choice of market price of risk should not just depend on the behavior of the yield curve at the short end. What about a more global approach? Continuing with the theme of comparing time-independent models with empirical data, we can look at the behavior of the whole forward rate curve on average. First we need some theory.

From the Fokker–Planck equation we have the following relationship between the real drift, the volatility and the real steady-state probability distribution:

$$u = \frac{1}{2p_\infty}\frac{d}{dr}(w^2 p_\infty).$$

Similarly, if we denote the risk-neutral steady-state distribution by p^*_∞ then we have

$$u - \lambda w = \frac{1}{2p^*_\infty}\frac{d}{dr}(w^2 p^*_\infty).$$

Two things follow from these results. First, we can eliminate u between them to get

$$p^*_\infty = p_\infty e^{-2\int^r \frac{\lambda(s)}{w(s)}\,ds}.$$

The relationship between the real and risk-neutral steady-state distributions obviously depends on the market price of risk. Second, we can eliminate $u - \lambda w$ from the bond pricing equation to get

$$\frac{\partial Z}{\partial t} + \tfrac{1}{2}w^2\frac{\partial^2 Z}{\partial r^2} + \frac{1}{2p^*_\infty}\frac{d}{dr}(w^2 p^*_\infty)\frac{\partial Z}{\partial r} - rZ = 0.$$

This can be written as

$$p^*_\infty(r)\left(\frac{\partial Z}{\partial t} - rZ\right) = -\tfrac{1}{2}\frac{\partial}{\partial r}\left(w^2 p^*_\infty \frac{\partial Z}{\partial r}\right).$$

In terms of the real distribution we have

$$p_\infty(r)e^{-2\int^r \frac{\lambda(s)}{w(s)}\,ds}\left(\frac{\partial Z}{\partial t} - rZ\right) = -\tfrac{1}{2}\frac{\partial}{\partial r}\left(w^2 p^*_\infty \frac{\partial Z}{\partial r}\right).$$

If we integrate this over the range of permitted r then the right-hand side, being a perfect derivative with nice properties at the end of the range, is zero leaving us with

$$\int_0^\infty p_\infty(r) e^{-2\int^r \frac{\lambda(s)}{w(s)}\,ds} \left(\frac{\partial Z}{\partial t} - rZ \right) dr = 0.$$

The range need not be zero to infinity but this would be the case for our earlier choices of w and p_∞. Since there is a real probability density function in this integral it is exactly the same as the real expectation, not a risk-neutral expectation. In other words, the average value of

$$e^{-2\int^r \frac{\lambda(s)}{w(s)}\,ds} \left(\frac{\partial Z}{\partial t} - rZ \right)$$

must be zero. Because the risk-neutral spot rate model is time homogeneous we can write

$$Z(t^*; T) = Z(\tau) \quad \text{where} \quad \tau = T - t^*.$$

We can now write the integral equation as

$$E_\infty \left[g(r) \left(\frac{\partial Z}{\partial \tau} + Z(\tau) \right) \right] = 0 \quad \text{for all} \quad \tau \tag{38.8}$$

where

$$g(r) = e^{-2\int^r \frac{\lambda(s)}{w(s)}\,ds}$$

and τ is the maturity. Note that this must be true for all maturities τ. This result follows from the equivalence of time and space averages, the ergodic property. It would not be true if we had any time inhomogeneity.

This result is particularly interesting because it is a property involving both the real and risk-neutral probabilities. Previously we had properties such as the shape of an individual yield curve or its slope that depend on the risk-neutral probabilities, or the distribution of the spot interest rate that depends on the real probabilities. However, the real 'average' of the forward rate curve depends on both kinds of probabilities. Can we use this property to estimate the market price of risk?

From discount factor data we can find the forward rate curve and the spot interest rate. If we have enough data we can estimate reliable averages. Can we find a non-zero function $g(r)$ such that (38.8) is satisfied. The answer is yes. Can we find a *positive* function $g(r)$? This is much, much harder. And we need the function to be positive so that we can take its logarithm to find the market price of risk, we don't want an imaginary market price of risk. If we can't find such a function (and I haven't been able to using US data), then again we must worry about the ability of any one-factor interest rate model to give properties that bear any resemblance to reality.

38.9 IMPLIED MODELING: TWO FACTOR

In the first part of this chapter I showed one way of implying the model for the spot interest rate from empirical data for the spot rate and the slope of the yield curve. In this section I show how to apply this approach to modeling *two* factors instead of one. These are only hints at possible directions for future research. Such an approach is important, however, because it is well known that some popular two-factor models have rather unfortunate properties (such as rates reaching infinity in a finite time).

The general two-factor interest rate model is

$$dr = u\,dt + w\,dX_1$$

and

$$dl = p\,dt + q\,dX_2,$$

for the *real* rates. I am going to assume that l is a long rate, even though this has some internal consistency problems.[6] The correlation coefficient is ρ. I am going to suggest ways in which the functions u, w, p, q, ρ and λ_r can be found from empirical data. Again we assume that these functions are independent of time, but, of course, can all be functions of r and l. The following is a list of the steps to be taken to determine the functional forms of all of these six terms.

- The first two terms to be found are the volatility functions, w and q. For simplicity, assume that w and q are of the form $wr^\alpha l^\beta$ (with different values for w, α and β for each of r and l) and examine spot and long rate volatilities for the best fit. This step is identical to that in the one-factor implied model explained above.
- The next term to be modeled is the correlation ρ. At least in the US, it is a well-known empirical observation that the spot rate and the spread between long and short rates are uncorrelated. This result can be used to determine the ρ.
- Next examine the slope of the yield curve. This gives information about the risk-adjusted drift of the spot interest rate. By performing a Taylor series expansion about short maturities, we find that the risk-adjusted drift for the spot rate is still related to the slope of the yield curve even in a two-factor world. This can be used to model the function λ_r.
- Next examine the real drift rates. If we assume that we have already modeled the volatilities and the correlation, then the empirical steady-state probability density function for r and l gives one piece of information about the two functions u and p, the real drift rates. The relationship between the real drifts and the steady-state probability density function is via a steady-state two-factor forward Fokker–Planck equation.
- The sixth, and last, piece of the puzzle comes from an examination of the model dynamics in the absence of randomness. In other words, what behavior does the model exhibit when we drop the stochastic terms? The answer comes from the solution of the two ordinary differential equations

  $$dr = u(r, l)\,dt$$

  and

  $$dl = p(r, l)\,dt.$$

  From these two equations we can eliminate the time dependence to get the one ordinary differential equation

  $$\frac{dl}{dr} = \frac{p(r, l)}{u(r, l)}.$$

  The ratio of p to u is chosen to give the solution of this equation similar characteristics to that of the empirical data of l *versus* r. For example, it is at this stage that we can incorporate economic cycles into the model.

[6] These problems are only associated with risk-neutral rates and not real rates.

38.10 SUMMARY

Modeling interest rates is very hard. There are few economic rules of thumb to help us. In modeling equities we knew that the return was important, that the return should be independent of the level of the asset. This helped enormously with the modeling of equities, in fact it left us with little modeling to do. We have no such guide with interest rates. All that we know is that rates are positive (although there have been a few pathological cases where this was not true) and don't grow unboundedly. That's not much to go on.

So, in this chapter, I showed how to examine data to see for yourself what a plausible model for rates might be. The reader is encouraged to adopt the approach of modeling for himself, rather than taking some ready-made model from the literature.

The conclusion, as far as one-factor models are concerned, has to be use them with care. They don't model reality in any quantitative way, and it is not clear whether yield-curve fitting works in the long run or whether it is simply a way of putting in place a delta hedge that will work for just a short time.

FURTHER READING

- Chan, Karolyi, Longstaff & Sanders (1992) examine the US spot rate in great detail and discuss the impact of their results on the validity of popular models.
- See Apabhai, Choe, Khennach & Wilmott (1995) for further details of the approaches to the modeling in this chapter.
- Apabhai (1995) describes the two-factor implied analysis.

EXERCISES

1. Use spot rate data to find ϕ and β if we assume that interest rate movements are of the form
$$dr = \mu(r)\,dt + \phi r^{\beta}\,dX.$$
Does your estimated value of β lie close to that of any of the standard models?
2. If we construct a two-factor model of the form
$$dr = u\,dt + w\,dX_1,$$
and
$$dl = p\,dt + q\,dX_2,$$
then we must study the ordinary differential equation
$$\frac{dl}{dr} = \frac{p(r,l)}{u(r,l)}.$$
We can study this problem using phase-plane analysis. What type of singularity might create the effect of an economic cycle? Which of the possible singularities in a phase plane must we try to avoid when we construct our model?

CHAPTER 39
Heath, Jarrow and Morton

In this Chapter...

- the Heath, Jarrow & Morton forward rate model
- the relationship between HJM and spot rate models
- the advantages and disadvantages of the HJM approach
- how to decompose the random movements of the forward rate curve into its principal components

39.1 INTRODUCTION

The **Heath, Jarrow & Morton** approach to the modeling of the whole forward rate curve was a major breakthrough in the pricing of fixed-income products. They built up a framework that encompassed all of the models we have seen so far (and many that we haven't). Instead of modeling a short-term interest rate and deriving the forward rates (or, equivalently, the yield curve) from that model, they boldly start with a model for the whole forward rate curve. Since the forward rates are known today, the matter of yield-curve fitting is contained naturally within their model, it does not appear as an afterthought. Moreover, it is possible to take *real data* for the random movement of the forward rates and incorporate them into the derivative-pricing methodology.

Two things spoil this otherwise wonderful model. First, in its basic form, there is no guarantee that rates will stay positive or finite. Second, it can be slow to price derivatives.

39.2 THE FORWARD RATE EQUATION

The key concept in the HJM model is that we model the evolution of the whole forward rate curve, not just the short end. Write $F(t;T)$ for the forward rate curve at time t. Thus the price of a zero-coupon bond at time t and maturing at time T, when it pays \$1, is

$$Z(t;T) = e^{-\int_t^T F(t;s)\,ds}. \tag{39.1}$$

Let us assume that all zero-coupon bonds evolve according to

$$dZ(t;T) = \mu(t,T)Z(t;T)\,dt + \sigma(t,T)Z(t;T)\,dX. \tag{39.2}$$

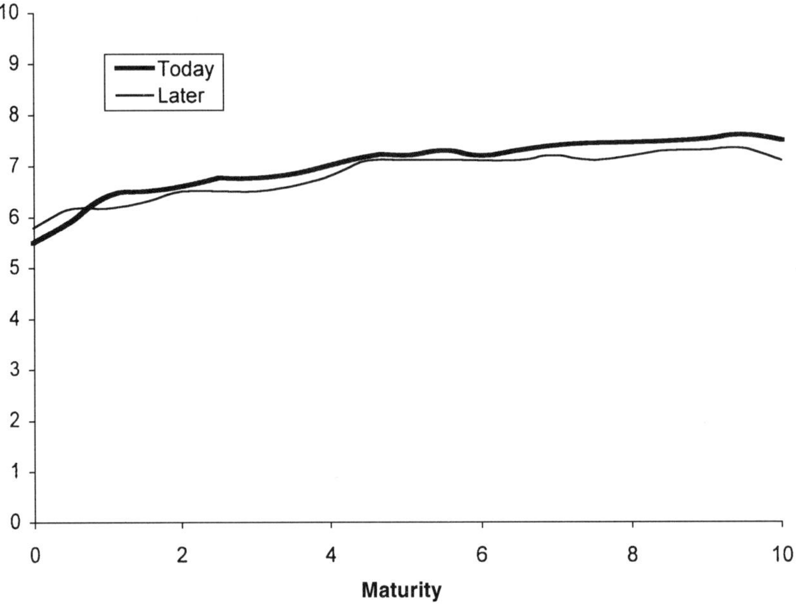

Figure 39.1 The forward rate curve today and a few days later.

This is not much of an assumption, other than to say that it is a one-factor model, and I will generalize that later. In this $d\cdot$ means that time t evolves but the maturity date T is fixed. Note that since $Z(t;t) = 1$ we must have $\sigma(t,t) = 0$. From (39.1) we have

$$F(t;T) = -\frac{\partial}{\partial T}\log Z(t;T).$$

Differentiating this with respect to t and substituting from (39.2) results in an equation for the evolution of the forward curve:

$$dF(t;T) = \frac{\partial}{\partial T}\left(\tfrac{1}{2}\sigma^2(t,T) - \mu(t,T)\right)dt - \frac{\partial}{\partial T}\sigma(t,T)\,dX. \tag{39.3}$$

In Figure 39.1 is shown the forward rate curve today, time t^*, and a few days later. The whole curve has moved according to (39.3).

Where has this got us? We have an expression for the drift of the forward rates in terms of the volatility of the forward rates. There is also a μ term, the drift of the bond. We have seen many times before how such drift terms disappear when we come to pricing derivatives, to be replaced by the risk-free interest rate r. Exactly the same will happen here.

39.3 THE SPOT RATE PROCESS

The spot interest rate is simply given by the forward rate for a maturity equal to the current date, i.e.

$$r(t) = F(t;t).$$

In this section I am going to manipulate this expression to derive the stochastic differential equation for the spot rate. In so doing we will begin to see why the HJM approach can be slow to price derivatives.

Suppose today is t^* and that we know the whole forward rate curve today, $F(t^*;T)$. We can write the spot rate for *any* time t in the future as

$$r(t) = F(t;t) = F(t^*;t) + \int_{t^*}^{t} dF(s;t).$$

From our earlier expression (39.3) for the forward rate process for F we have

$$r(t) = F(t^*;t) + \int_{t^*}^{t}\left(\sigma(s,t)\frac{\partial\sigma(s,t)}{\partial t} - \frac{\partial\mu(s,t)}{\partial t}\right)ds - \int_{t^*}^{t}\frac{\partial\sigma(s,t)}{\partial t}\,dX(s).$$

Differentiating this with respect to time t we arrive at the stochastic differential equation for r

$$\begin{aligned} dr = &\left(\frac{\partial F(t^*;t)}{\partial t} - \left.\frac{\partial\mu(t,s)}{\partial s}\right|_{s=t}\right.\\ &+\int_{t^*}^{t}\left(\sigma(s,t)\frac{\partial^2\sigma(s,t)}{\partial t^2} + \left(\frac{\partial\sigma(s,t)}{\partial t}\right)^2 - \frac{\partial^2\mu(s,t)}{\partial t^2}\right)ds\\ &\left.-\underline{\int_{t^*}^{t}\frac{\partial^2\sigma(s,t)}{\partial t^2}\,dX(s)}\right)dt - \left.\frac{\partial\sigma(t,s)}{\partial s}\right|_{s=t}dX. \end{aligned}$$

39.3.1 The Non-Markov Nature of HJM

The details of this expression are not important. I just want you to observe one point. Compare this stochastic differential equation for the spot rate with any of the models in Chapter 33. Clearly, it is more complicated, there are many more terms. All but the last one are deterministic, the last is random. The important point concerns the nature of these terms. In particular, the term underlined depends on the history of σ from the date t^* to the future date t, and *it depends on the history of the stochastic increments dX*. This term is thus highly path dependent. Moreover, for a general HJM model it makes the motion of the spot rate **non-Markov**. In a **Markov process** it is only the present state of a variable that determines the possible future (albeit random) state. Having a non-Markov model may not matter to us if we can find a small number of extra state variables that contain all the information that we need for predicting the future.[1] Unfortunately, the general HJM model requires an infinite number of such variables to define the present state; if we were to write the HJM model as a partial differential equation we would need an infinite number of independent variables.

At the moment we are in the real world. To price derivatives we need to move over to the risk-neutral world. The first step in this direction is to see what happens when we hold a hedged portfolio.

39.4 THE MARKET PRICE OF RISK

In the one-factor HJM model all stochastic movements of the forward rate curve are perfectly correlated. We can therefore hedge one bond with another of a different maturity. Such a hedged portfolio is

$$\Pi = Z(t;T_1) - \Delta Z(t;T_2).$$

[1] Remember Asian option pricing.

The change in this portfolio is given by

$$\begin{aligned} d\Pi &= dZ(t;T_1) - \Delta\, dZ(t;T_2) \\ &= Z(t;T_1)(\mu(t,T_1)\,dt + \sigma(t,T_1)\,dX) - \Delta Z(t;T_2)(\mu(t,T_2)\,dt + \sigma(t,T_2)\,dX). \end{aligned}$$

If we choose

$$\Delta = \frac{\sigma(t,T_1)Z(t;T_1)}{\sigma(t,T_2)Z(t;T_2)}$$

then our portfolio is hedged and is risk free. Setting its return equal to the risk-free rate $r(t)$ and rearranging we find that

$$\frac{\mu(t,T_1) - r(t)}{\sigma(t,T_1)} = \frac{\mu(t,T_2) - r(t)}{\sigma(t,T_2)}.$$

The left-hand side is a function of T_1 and the right-hand side is a function of T_2. This is only possible if both sides are independent of the maturity date T:

$$\mu(t,T) = r(t) + \lambda(t)\sigma(t,T).$$

As before, $\lambda(t)$ is the market price of risk (associated with the one factor).

39.5 REAL AND RISK NEUTRAL

We are almost ready to price derivatives using the HJM model. But first we must discuss the real and risk-neutral worlds, relating them to the ideas in previous chapters.

All of the variables I have introduced above have been *real* variables. But when we come to pricing derivatives we must do so in the risk-neutral world. In the present HJM context, risk-neutral 'means' $\mu(t,T) = r(t)$. This means that in the risk-neutral world the return on any traded investment is simply $r(t)$. We can see this in (39.2). The risk-neutral zero-coupon bond price satisfies

$$dZ(t;T) = r(t)Z(t;T)\,dt + \sigma(t,T)Z(t;T)\,dX.$$

The deterministic part of this equation represents exponential growth of the bond at the risk-free rate. The form of the equation is very similar to that for a risk-neutral equity, except that here the volatility will be much more complicated.

39.5.1 The Relationship Between the Risk-neutral Forward Rate Drift and Volatility

Let me write the stochastic differential equation for the *risk-neutral* forward rate curve as

$$dF(t;T) = m(t,T)\,dt + \nu(t,T)\,dX.$$

From (39.3)

$$\nu(t,T) = -\frac{\partial}{\partial T}\sigma(t,T),$$

is the forward rate volatility and, from (39.3), the drift of the forward rate is given by

$$\frac{\partial}{\partial T}\left(\tfrac{1}{2}\sigma^2(t,T) - \mu(t,T)\right) = \nu(t,T)\int_t^T \nu(t,s)\,ds - \frac{\partial}{\partial T}\mu(t,T),$$

where we have used $\sigma(t,t)=0$. In the risk-neutral world we have $\mu(t,T)=r(t)$, and so the drift of the risk-neutral forward rate curve is related to its volatility by

$$m(t,T)=\nu(t,T)\int_t^T \nu(t,s)\,ds. \tag{39.4}$$

39.6 PRICING DERIVATIVES

Pricing derivatives is all about finding the expected present value of all cashflows in a risk-neutral framework. This was discussed in Chapter 10, in terms of equity, currency and commodity derivatives. If we are lucky then this calculation can be done via a low-dimensional partial differential equation. We have seen the relevant theory in Chapter 10. The one- and two-factor models of Chapters 33 and 37 exploited this. The HJM model, however, is a very general interest rate model and in its full generality one cannot write down a finite-dimensional partial differential equation for the price of a derivative.

Because of the non-Markov nature of HJM in general a partial differential equation approach is unfeasible. This leaves us with two alternatives. One is to estimate directly the necessary expectations by simulating the random evolution of, in this case, the risk-neutral forward rates. The other is to build up a tree structure.

39.7 SIMULATIONS

If we want to use a Monte Carlo method, then we must simulate the evolution of the whole forward rate curve, calculate the value of all cashflows under each evolution and then calculate the present value of these cashflows by *discounting at the realized spot rate* $r(t)$.

To price a derivative using a Monte Carlo simulation perform the following steps. I will assume that we have chosen a model for the forward rate volatility, $\nu(t,T)$. Today is t^* when we know the forward rate curve $F(t^*;T)$.

1. Simulate a realized evolution of the whole risk-neutral forward rate curve for the necessary length of time, until T^*, say. This requires a simulation of

   $$dF(t;T)=m(t,T)\,dt+\nu(t,T)\,dX,$$

   where

   $$m(t,T)=\nu(t,T)\int_t^T \nu(t,s)\,ds.$$

   After this simulation we will have a realization of $F(t;T)$ for $t^*\le t\le T^*$ and $T\ge t$. We will have a realization of the whole forward rate path.
2. At the end of the simulation we will have the realized prices of all maturity zero-coupon bonds at every time up to T^*.
3. Using this forward rate path calculate the value of all the cashflows that would have occured.
4. Using the realized path for the spot interest rate $r(t)$ calculate the present value of these cashflows. Note that we discount at the continuously compounded risk-free rate, not at any other rate. In the risk-neutral world all assets have an expected return of $r(t)$.

5. Return to Step 1 to perform another realization, and continue until you have a sufficiently large number of realizations to calculate the expected present value as accurately as required.

The disadvantage of the HJM model is that a Monte Carlo simulation such as this can be very slow. On the plus side, because the whole forward rate curve is calculated the bond prices at all maturities are trivial to find during this simulation.

39.8 TREES

If we are to build up a tree for a non-Markov model then we find ourselves with the unfortunate result that the forward curve after an up move followed by a down is *not* the same as the curve after a down followed by an up. The equivalence of these two paths in the Markov world is what makes the binomial method so powerful and efficient. In the non-Markov world our tree structure becomes 'bushy,' and grows *exponentially* in size with the addition of new timesteps.

If the contract we are valuing is European with no early exercise then we don't need to use a tree, a Monte Carlo simulation can be immediately implemented. However, if the contract has some American feature then to correctly price in the early exercise we don't have much choice but to use a tree structure. The exponentially-large tree structure will make the pricing problem very slow.

39.9 THE MUSIELA PARAMETRIZATION

Often in practice the model for the volatility structure of the forward rate curve will be of the form

$$\nu(t, T) = \overline{\nu}(t, T - t),$$

meaning that we will model the volatility of the forward rate at each maturity, one, two, three years, and not at each maturity date, 1999, 2000, 2001. If we write τ for the maturity period $T - t$ then it is a simple matter to find that $\overline{F}(t; \tau) = F(t, t + \tau)$ satisfies

$$d\overline{F}(t; \tau) = \overline{m}(t, \tau)\, dt + \overline{\nu}(t, \tau)\, dX,$$

where

$$\overline{m}(t, \tau) = \overline{\nu}(t, \tau) \int_0^\tau \overline{\nu}(t, s)\, ds + \frac{\partial}{\partial \tau} \overline{F}(t, \tau).$$

It is much easier in practice to use this representation for the evolution of the risk-neutral forward rate curve.

39.10 MULTI-FACTOR HJM

Often a single-factor model does not capture the subtleties of the yield curve that are important for particular contracts. The obvious example is the spread option, that pays off the difference between rates at two different maturities. We then require a multi-factor model. The multi-factor theory is identical to the one-factor case, so we can simply write down the extension to many factors.

If the risk-neutral forward rate curve satisfies the N-dimensional stochastic differential equation

$$dF(t,T) = m(t,T)\,dt + \sum_{i=1}^{N} \nu_i(t,T)\,dX_i,$$

where the dX_i are uncorrelated, then

$$m(t,T) = \sum_{i=1}^{N} \nu_i(t,T) \int_t^T \nu_i(t,s)\,ds.$$

39.11 A SIMPLE ONE-FACTOR EXAMPLE: HO & LEE

In this section we make a comparison between the spot rate modeling of Chapter 33 and HJM. One of the key points about the HJM approach is that the yield curve is fitted, by default. The simplest yield-curve fitting spot rate model is Ho & Lee, so we draw a comparison between this and HJM.

In Ho & Lee the risk-neutral spot rate satisfies

$$dr = \eta(t)\,dt + c\,dX,$$

for a constant c. The prices of zero-coupon bonds, $Z(r,t;T)$, in this model satisfy

$$\frac{\partial Z}{\partial t} + \tfrac{1}{2}c^2 \frac{\partial^2 Z}{\partial r^2} + \eta(t)\frac{\partial Z}{\partial r} - rZ = 0$$

with

$$Z(r,T;T) = 1.$$

The solution is easily found to be

$$Z(r,t;T) = \exp\left(\tfrac{1}{6}c^2(T-t)^3 - \int_t^T \eta(s)(T-s)\,dS - (T-t)r\right).$$

In the Ho & Lee model $\eta(t)$ is chosen to fit the yield curve at time t^*. In forward rate terms this means that

$$F(t^*;T) = r(t^*) - \tfrac{1}{2}c^2(T-t^*)^2 + \int_{t^*}^T \eta(s)\,ds,$$

and so

$$\eta(t) = \frac{\partial F(t^*;t)}{\partial t} + c^2(t-t^*).$$

At any time later than t^*

$$F(t;T) = r(t) - \tfrac{1}{2}c^2(T-t)^2 + \int_t^T \eta(s)\,ds.$$

From this we find that

$$dF(t;T) = c^2(T-t)\,dt + c\,dX.$$

In our earlier notation, $\sigma(t, T) = -c(T - t)$ and $\nu(t, T) = c$. This is the evolution equation for the risk-neutral forward rates. It is easily confirmed for this model that Equation (39.4) holds. This is the HJM representation of the Ho & Lee model. Most of the popular models have HJM representations.

39.12 PRINCIPAL COMPONENT ANALYSIS

There are two main ways to use HJM. One is to choose the volatility structure $\nu_i(t, T)$ to be sufficiently 'nice' to make a tractable model, one that is Markov. This usually leads us back to the 'classical' popular spot-rate models. The other way is to choose the volatility structure to match data. This is where Principal Component Analysis (PCA) comes in.

In analyzing the volatility of the forward rate curve one usually assumes that the volatility structure depends only on the time to maturity, i.e.

$$\nu = \overline{\nu}(T - t).$$

I will assume this but examine a more general multi-factor model:

$$dF(t; T) = m(t, T)\,dt + \sum_{i=1}^{N} \overline{\nu}_i(T - t)\,dX_i.$$

From time series data we can determine the functions $\overline{\nu}_i$ empirically, this is **Principal Components Analysis**. I will give a loose description of how this is done.

If we have forward rate time series data going back a few years we can calculate the covariances between the *changes* in the rates of different maturities. We may have, for example, the one-, three-, six-month, one-, two, three-, five-, seven-, 10- and 30-year rates. The covariance matrix would then be a ten $\times$ ten symmetric matrix with the variances of the rates along the diagonal and the covariances between rates off the diagonal.

In Figure 39.2 is shown a spreadsheet of daily one-, three- and sixth-month rates, and the day-to-day changes. The covariance matrix for these changes is also shown.

PCA is a technique for finding common movements in the rates, for essentially finding eigenvalues and eigenvectors of the matrix. We expect to find, for example, that a large part of the movement of the forward rate curve is common between rates, that a parallel shift in the rates is the largest component of the movement of the curve in general. The next most important movement would be a twisting of the curve, followed by a bending.

Suppose that we have found the covariance matrix, $\mathbf{M}$ for the changes in the rates mentioned above. This ten by ten matrix will have ten eigenvalues, λ_i, and eigenvectors, $\mathbf{v}_i$ satisfying

$$\mathbf{M}\mathbf{v}_i = \lambda_i \mathbf{v}_i;$$

$\mathbf{v}_i$ is a column vector.

The eigenvector associated with the largest eigenvalue is the first principal component. It gives the dominant part in the movement of the forward rate curve. Its first entry represents the movement of the one-month rate, the second entry is the three-month rate, etc. Its eigenvalue is the variance of these movements. In Figure 39.3 we see the entries in this first principal component plotted against the relevant maturity. This curve is relatively flat, when compared with the other components. This indicates that, indeed, a parallel shift of the yield curve is the dominant movement. Note that the eigenvectors are orthogonal, there is no correlation between the principal components.

	A	B	C	D	E	F	G	H	I	J	K	L	M
1	**Forward rates:**				**Changes in rates:**								
2		**1 month**	**3 month**	**6 month**	**1 month**	**3 month**	**6 month**						
3	22-Sep-88	8.25000	8.31250	8.56250									
4	23-Sep-88	8.25000	8.31250	8.56250	0.00000	0.00000	0.00000						
5	26-Sep-88	8.31250	8.37500	8.62500	0.06250	0.06250	0.06250	= COVAR(E4:E1721,F4:F1721)					
6	27-Sep-88	8.31250	8.43750	8.6 [illegible] = B4-B3	[illegible]0000	0.06250	0.06250		**1 month**	**3 month**	**6 month**		
7	28-Sep-88	8.42188	8.50000	8.81250	0.10938	0.06250	0.12500	**1 month**	0.007501				
8	29-Sep-88	8.37500	8.68750	8.81250	−0.04688	0.18750	0.00000	**3 month**	0.003831	0.004225			
9	30-Sep-88	8.31250	8.62500	8.75000	−0.06250	−0.06250	−0.06250	**6 month**	0.003628	0.004020	0.004997		
10	3-Oct-88	8.31250	8.62500	8.68750	0.00000	0.00000	−0.06250						
11	4-Oct-88	8.31250	8.56250	8.68750	0.00000	−0.06250	0.00000	**Scaled covariance matrix:**					
12	5-Oct-88	8.31250	8.56250	8.68750	0.00000	0.00000	0.00000		**1 month**	**3 month**	**6 month**		
13	6-Oct-88	8.31250	8.56250	8.68750	0.00000	0.00000	0.00000	**1 month**	0.119072				
14	7-Oct-88	8.31250	8.62500	8.75000	0.00000	0.06250	0.06250	**3 month**	0.060822	0.067075			
15	10-Oct-88	8.25000	8.56250	8.56250	−0.06250	−0.06250	−0.18750	**6 month**	0.057590	0.063822	0.079320		
16	11-Oct-88	8.25000	8.56250	8.62500	0.00000	0.00000	0.06250						
17	12-Oct-88	8.31250	8.62500	8.68750	0.06250	0.06250	0.06250						
18	13-Oct-88	8.31250	8.64063	8.68750	0.00000	0.01563	0.00000		= 18*SQRT(252)				
19	14-Oct-88	8.31250	8.62500	8.62500	0.00000	−0.01563	−0.06250						
20	17-Oct-88	8.31250	8.62500	8.62500	0.00000	0.00000	0.00000						
21	18-Oct-88	8.31250	8.62500	8.62500	0.00000	0.00000	0.00000						
22	19-Oct-88	8.31250	8.62500	8.62500	0.00000	0.00000	0.00000						
23	20-Oct-88	8.37500	8.68750	8.68750	0.06250	0.06250	0.06250						
24	21-Oct-88	8.37500	8.68750	8.68750	0.00000	0.00000	0.00000						
25	24-Oct-88	8.37500	8.68750	8.75000	0.00000	0.00000	0.06250						
26	25-Oct-88	8.37500	8.68750	8.75000	0.00000	0.00000	0.00000						
27	26-Oct-88	8.37500	8.68750	8.75000	0.00000	0.00000	0.00000						
28	27-Oct-88	8.37500	8.68750	8.68750	0.00000	0.00000	−0.06250						

Figure 39.2 One-, three- and sixth-month rates and the changes.

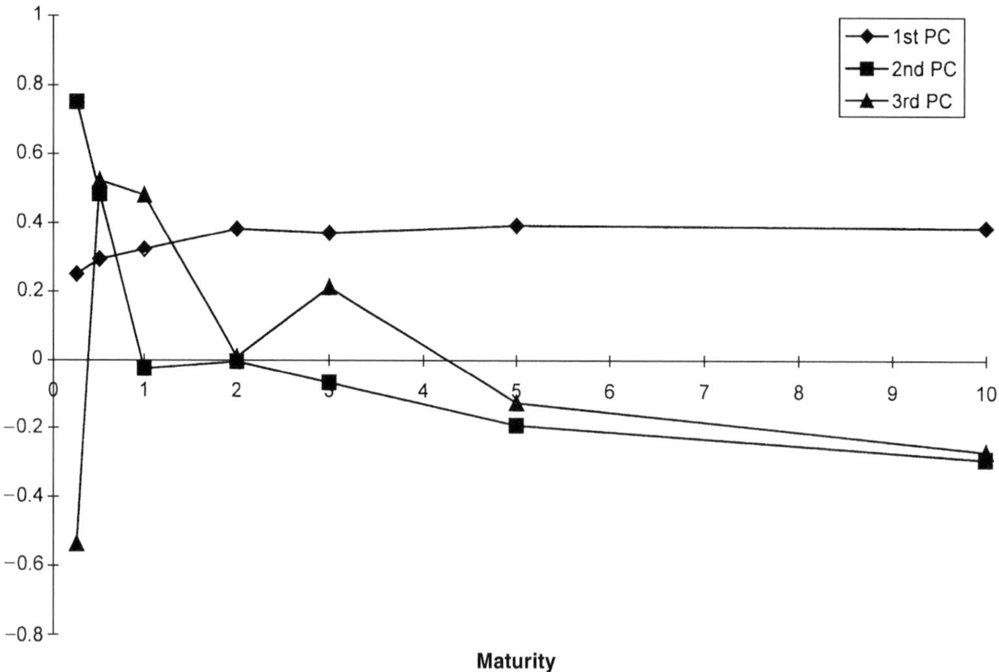

Figure 39.3 The first three principal components for the US forward rate curve. The data runs from 1988 until 1996.

In this figure are also plotted the next two principal components. Observe that one gives a twisting of the curve and the other a bending.

The result of this analysis is that the volatility factors are given by

$$\overline{\nu}_i(\tau_j) = \sqrt{\lambda_i}(\mathbf{v}_i)_j.$$

Here τ_j is the maturity, i.e. 1/12, 1/4 etc. and $(\mathbf{v}_i)_j$ is the jth entry in the vector $\mathbf{v}_i$. To get the volatility of other maturities will require some interpolation.

The calculation of the covariance matrix is simple, discussed in Chapter 11. The calculation of the eigenvalues and vectors is also simple if you use the following algorithm.

39.12.1 The Power Method

I will assume that all the eigenvalues are distinct, a reasonable assumption given the empirical nature of the matrix. Since the matrix is symmetric positive definite (it is a covariance matrix) we have all the nice properties we need. The eigenvector associated with the *largest* eigenvalue is easily found by the following iterative procedure. First make an initial guess for the eigenvector, call it $\mathbf{x}^0$. Now iterate using

$$\mathbf{y}^{k+1} = \mathbf{M}\mathbf{x}^k,$$

for $k = 0, \ldots,$ and

$$\beta^{k+1} = \text{element of } \mathbf{y}^{k+1} \text{ having largest modulus}$$

followed by

$$\mathbf{x}^{i+1} = \tfrac{1}{\beta^{k+1}}\mathbf{y}^{k+1}.$$

As $k \to \infty$, $\mathbf{x}^k$ tends to the eigenvector and β^k to the eigenvalue λ. In practice you would stop iterating once you have reached some set tolerance. Thus we have found the first principal component. It is standard to normalize the vector, and this is our $\mathbf{v}_1$.

To find the next principal component we must define a new matrix by

$$\mathbf{N} = \mathbf{M} - \lambda_1 \mathbf{v}_1 \mathbf{v}_1^T.$$

Now use the power method on this new matrix $\mathbf{N}$ to find the second principal component. This process can be repeated until all (ten) components have been found.

39.13 OPTIONS ON EQUITIES, ETC.

The pricing of options contingent on equities, currencies, commodities, indices, etc. is straightforward in the HJM framework. All that we need to know are the volatility of the asset and its correlations with the forward rate factors. The Monte Carlo simulation then uses the risk-neutral random walk for both the forward rates and the asset, i.e. zero-coupon bonds and the asset have a drift of $r(t)$. Of course, there are the usual adjustments to be made for dividends, foreign interest rate or cost of carry, amounting to a change to the drift rate for the asset.

The only fly in the ointment is that American-style exercise is difficult to accommodate. If we have early exercise then we may have to build up a bushy tree.

39.14 NON-INFINITESIMAL SHORT RATE

One of the problems with HJM is that there is no guarantee that interest rates will stay positive, nor that the money market account will stay finite. These problems are associated with the use of a continuously compounded interest rate; all rates can be deduced from the evolution of this rate, but the rate itself is not actually observable. Modeling rates with a finite accruals period, such as three-month LIBOR, for example, has two advantages: the rate is directly observable, and positivity and finiteness can be guaranteed. Let's see how this works. I use the Musiela parametrization of the forward rates.

I have said that $\overline{F}(t, \tau)$ satisfies

$$d\overline{F}(t, \tau) = \cdots + \overline{\nu}(t, \tau)\, dX.$$

A reasonable choice for the volatility structure might be

$$\overline{\nu}(t, \tau) = \gamma(t, \tau)\overline{F}(t, \tau)$$

for finite, non-zero $\gamma(t, \tau)$. At first sight, this is a good choice for the volatility, after all, lognormality is a popular choice for random walks in finance. Unfortunately, this model leads to exploding interest rates. Yet we would like to retain some form of lognormality of rates; recall that market practice is to assume lognormality of just about everything.

We can get around the explosive rates by defining an interest rate $j(t, \tau)$ that is accrued m times p.a. The relationship between the new $j(t, \tau)$ and the old $\overline{F}(t, \tau)$ is then

$$\left(1 + \frac{j(t, \tau)}{m}\right)^m = e^{\overline{F}(t, \tau)}.$$

Now what happens if we choose a lognormal model for the rates? If we choose

$$dj(t, \tau) = \cdots + \gamma(t, \tau) j(t, \tau)\, dX,$$

it can be shown that this leads to a stochastic differential equation for $\overline{F}(t,\tau)$ of the form

$$d\overline{F}(t,\tau) = \cdots + \gamma(t,\tau)m v(t,\tau)\left(1 - e^{\overline{F}(t,\tau/m)}\right)dX.$$

The volatility structure in this expression is such that all rates stay positive and no explosion occurs.

If we specify the quantity m, we can of course still do PCA to find out the best form for the function $\gamma(t,\tau) = \gamma(\tau)$.

39.15 SUMMARY

The HJM approach to modeling the whole forward rate curve in one go is very powerful. For certain types of contract it is easy to program the Monte Carlo simulations. For example, bond options can be priced in a straightforward manner. On the other hand, the market has its own way of pricing most basic contracts, such as the bond option, as we discussed in Chapter 35. It is the more complex derivatives for which a model is needed. Some of these are suitable for HJM. However, the, in a sense, trivial introduction of early exercise to a contract makes it difficult to price in the HJM setting, since Monte Carlo simulations cannot easily handle American-style exercise. If there is a partial differential equation formulation of such a contract then that is the natural way forward. Interest rate modeling and the pricing and hedging of interest rate products is still a relatively new subject. Perhaps no longer in its infancy, the subject is certainly in its troublesome teens.

FURTHER READING

- See the original paper by Heath, Jarrow & Morton (1992) for all the technical details for making their model rigorous.
- For details of the finite maturity interest rate process model see Sandmann & Sondermann (1994) and Brace, Gatarek & Musiela (1997).

EXERCISES

1. Derive the equation for the evolution of the forward rate:

$$dF(t;T) = \frac{\partial}{\partial T}\left(\tfrac{1}{2}\sigma^2(t,T) - \mu(t,T)\right)dt - \frac{\partial}{\partial T}\sigma(t,T)\,dX,$$

from

$$dZ(t;T) = \mu(t,T)Z(t;T)\,dt + \sigma(t,T)Z(t;T)\,dX,$$

and

$$F(t;T) = -\frac{\partial}{\partial T}\log Z(t;T).$$

2. Perform a simulation, using the method of Section 39.7, to value an option on a zero-coupon bond. You will need to decide upon a suitable form for $\nu(t,T)$, the forward rate volatility. Does your choice have a standard representation as a model for the spot rate?
3. Using forward rate data, perform a Principal Component Analysis. What are the three main components in the forward price movements and what are their weights?

CHAPTER 40
interest-rate modeling without probabilities

In this Chapter...

- a non-Brownian motion model for interest rates
- how to value interest-rate products in a worst-case scenario
- the Yield Envelope
- optimal static hedging

40.1 INTRODUCTION

The two main classical approaches to pricing and hedging fixed income products may be termed 'yield-based' and 'stochastic.' The former (see Chapter 31) assumes that interest rates are constant for each product, which, of course, is inconsistent across products. These ideas are used a great deal for the simpler, 'linear' products. The latter approach (see Chapters 33 and 37) assumes that interest rates are driven by a number of random factors. It is used for 'nonlinear' contracts, contracts having some form of optionality. In the stochastic models an equation for the short-term rate will give as an output the whole yield curve.

Both of these approaches can be criticized. The yield-based ideas are not suited to complex products and the popular stochastic models are inaccurate. For the latter, it is extremely difficult to estimate parameters, and after estimating them, they are prone to change, making a mockery of the underlying theory. One of the main problems is the assumption of a finite number of factors. From such an assumption it follows that you can delta hedge any contract with this same number of simpler contracts. For example, in a one-factor world you can hedge one part of the yield curve with any other part, something which is clearly not possible in practice. Is it acceptable to hedge a six-month option on a one-year bond with a ten-year bond? Although practitioners use common sense to get around this (they would hedge the option with the one-year bond); this common sense is not reflected in the modeling.

In this chapter I address the problem from a new perspective, by assuming as little as possible about the process underlying the movement of interest rates. I will model a short-term interest rate and price a portfolio of cashflows in a worst-case scenario, using the short rate as the rate for discounting. One of the key features of the model in this chapter is that delta hedging plays no important role. The resulting problem is nonlinear and thus the value of a contract then depends on what it is hedged with. This approach necessarily correctly prices traded instruments; no fitting is necessary. I also describe the Yield Envelope. This is a sophisticated version of the yield curve. We find a yield spread at maturities for which there are no traded instruments.

40.2 WHAT DO I WANT FROM AN INTEREST RATE MODEL?

Here is my list of properties of my ideal interest rate model.

- As few factors as possible, to model any realistic yield curve
- Easy to price many products quickly
- Insensitivity of results to hard-to-measure parameters, such as volatilities and correlations
- Robustness in general
- Sensible fitting to data
- Strategy for hedging

In this Chapter I describe a model that delivers all of these and more. In fact, we won't be seeing any mention of volatilities or correlations, or delta hedging. The only hedging will be entirely static.

40.3 A NON-PROBABILISTIC MODEL FOR THE BEHAVIOR OF THE SHORT-TERM INTEREST RATE

Motivated by a desire to model the behavior of the short-term interest rate, r, with as much freedom as possible, I assume only the following constraints on its movement:

$$r^- \leq r \leq r^+ \tag{40.1}$$

and

$$c^- \leq \frac{dr}{dt} \leq c^+. \tag{40.2}$$

Equation (40.1) says that the interest rate cannot move outside the range bounded below by the rate r^- and above by the rate r^+. Equation (40.2) puts similar constraints on the *speed* of movement of r. The constraints can be time dependent and, in the case of the speed constraints, functions of the spot interest rate, r.

There is an obvious difference between the classical stochastic models of the spot rate, with their Brownian motion evolution of r and locally unbounded growth and the model I am now presenting. I can justify this on several grounds: (i) we are perhaps trying to model a long-term behavior for which we are less concerned about the very short-term movements (a weak justification); (ii) the Brownian models can also be criticized, it is still an open question exactly what the stochastic process is, underlying the evolution of financial quantities, Brownian motion is often chosen for its nice mathematical properties (a slightly better justification); (iii) a combination of the model here together with bands, jumps, etc. discussed later will, in practice, be indistinguishable from the real process (excellent justification, if it's true).

The worst-case scenario that we will be addressing is hard to criticize as long as it gives decent prices. Why then don't we simply present an interest rate version of the uncertain volatility model of Chapter 24. This has been done by Lewicki & Avellaneda (1996) in a Heath, Jarrow & Morton framework. It is not entirely satisfactory because of the usual problem: what we model and what we trade are two different things. If we are going to use a delta-hedging argument, then we have to assume that what we hedge with is perfectly correlated with our contract; this can never be the case in the fixed-income world. Different points on the yield curve may be correlated but they are certainly not perfectly correlated for all time. In the model we present here *there is no delta hedging* and we do not depend on any correlation between different parts of the yield curve.

40.4 WORST-CASE SCENARIOS AND A NONLINEAR EQUATION

In this section we derive the equation governing the worst-case price of a fixed-income portfolio, first presented by Epstein & Wilmott (1997). Let $V(r, t)$ be the value of our portfolio when the short-term interest rate is r and the time is t. We consider the change in the value of this portfolio during a timestep dt.

Using Taylor's theorem to expand the value of the portfolio for small changes in its arguments, we find that

$$V(r + dr, t + dt) = V(r, t) + \frac{\partial V}{\partial r} dr + \frac{\partial V}{\partial t} dt + \cdots.$$

Note that there is no second r-derivative term because the process is not Brownian. We want to investigate this change under our worst-case assumption. This change is given by

$$\min_{dr}(dV) = \min_{dr}\left(\frac{\partial V}{\partial r} dr + \frac{\partial V}{\partial t} dt\right).$$

Since the rate of change of r is bounded according to (40.2), we find that

$$\min_{dr}(dV) = \min_{dr}\left(\frac{\partial V}{\partial r} dr + \frac{\partial V}{\partial t} dt\right) = \left(c\left(\frac{\partial V}{\partial r}\right)\frac{\partial V}{\partial r} + \frac{\partial V}{\partial t}\right) dt$$

where

$$c(x) = \begin{cases} c^+ & \text{for } x < 0 \\ c^- & \text{for } x > 0. \end{cases}$$

We shall require that, in the worst case, our portfolio always earns the risk-free rate of interest. This gives us

$$\frac{\partial V}{\partial t} + c\left(\frac{\partial V}{\partial r}\right)\frac{\partial V}{\partial r} - rV = 0. \tag{40.3}$$

This is a first-order non-linear hyperbolic partial differential equation. For an instrument having a known payoff at maturity we will know the final data $V(r, T)$. Also, if there is a cash flow K at time t_i, then we have

$$V(r, t_i^-) = V(r, t_i^+) + K.$$

Thus we solve backwards in time from T to the present, applying jump conditions when necessary.

In addition to the worst-case scenario, we can find the value of our portfolio in a best-case scenario. This is equivalent to a worst-case scenario where we are short the portfolio. We therefore have

$$-V_{\text{best}} = (-V)_{\text{worst}}.$$

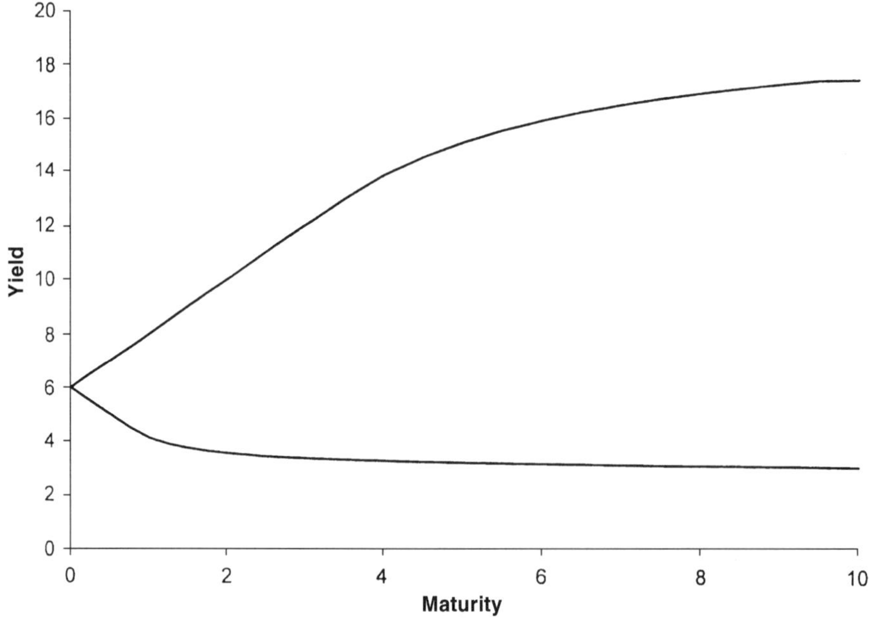

Figure 40.1 Yields in worst- and best-case scenarios for a zero-coupon bond.

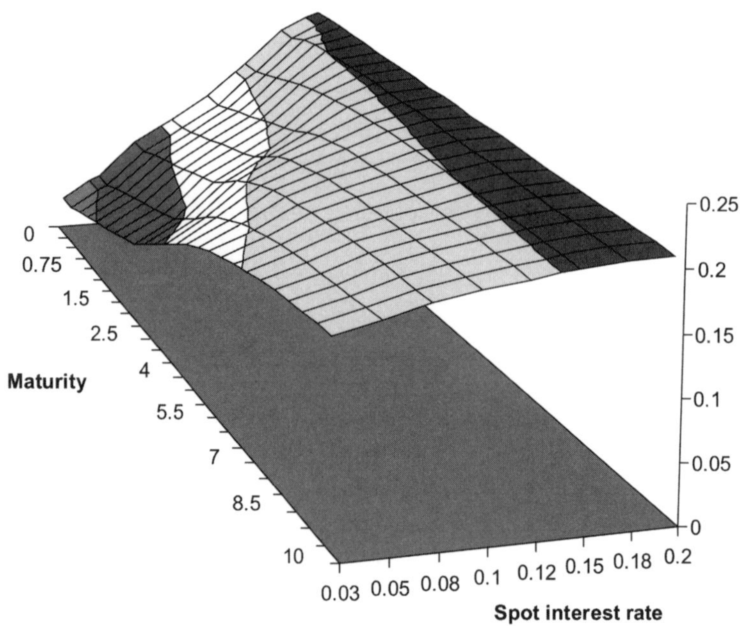

Figure 40.2 Yields in worst-case scenario for a zero-coupon bond.

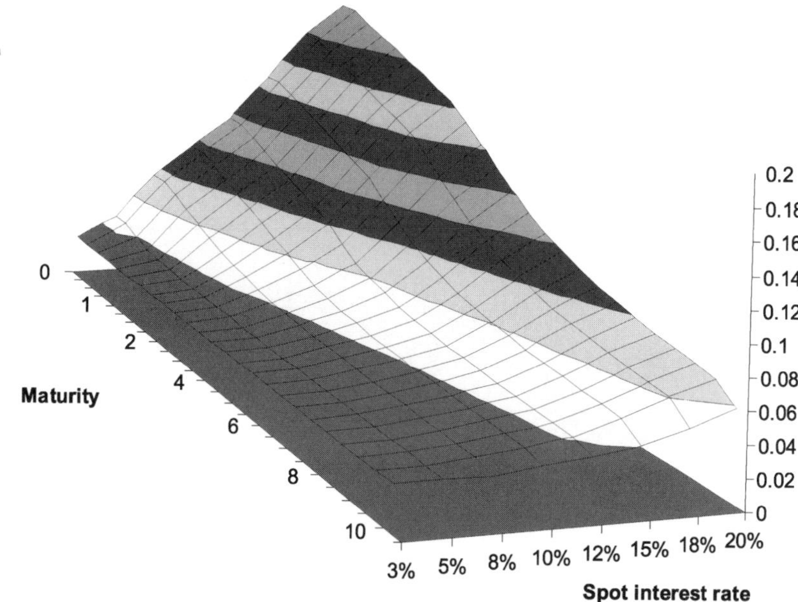

Figure 40.3 Yields in best-case scenario for a zero-coupon bond.

Example

Our first example will be the simplest possible, we will value a zero-coupon bond in the worst and best cases according to the model. Results are shown in Figure 40.1 In this example I have valued a zero-coupon bond in the two scenarios, best and worst cases, and plotted the yield for different maturities. The spot rate is initially 6%, is allowed to grow or decrease at 4% p.a. at most, and cannot go outside the range 3–20%. The important point to note about this figure is how wide the yield spread is.

If the model always gave such extreme results then it would be of no practical use. Fortunately we can reduce this dramatically by static hedging, and we will see examples of this shortly. This example is shown again in Figures 40.2 and 40.3. In these are shown the yields in the two cases but now against both the spot rate and maturity.

40.5 EXAMPLES OF HEDGING

Typically, we find that the spread between the worst- and best-case values is larger than the market spread. To reduce the spread, we hedge with market-traded instruments. Hedging is shown schematically in Figure 40.4. At the top of this figure is our original, or 'target' contract. Some of the cashflows are known amounts and some are floating. Below this are shown the contracts that are available for hedging, to keep things simple I've shown them all as zero-coupon bonds. How many of each of these available hedging bonds should we buy or sell to give our target cashflow the highest value in the worst-case scenario?

There is an optimal static hedge for which the worst-case value of the bond is as high as possible, and another for which the best-case value of the bond is as low as possible. This optimization technique was described in detail in another context in Chapter 30. To find this optimal static hedge in the worst-case scenario, we maximize the value of our zero-coupon

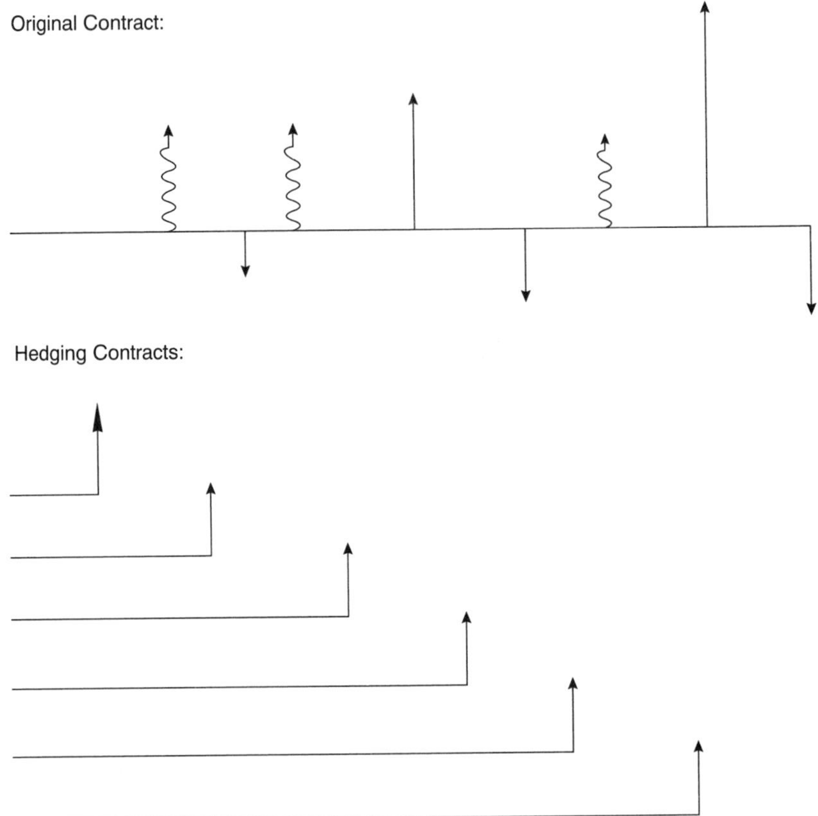

Figure 40.4 A schematic diagram of the hedging problem.

bond with respect to the hedge quantities of the hedging instruments. In the best-case scenario, we minimize with respect to the hedge quantities.

We expect that the market price of a hedging instrument is contained in the spread of values for the instrument generated by our model. If this were not the case, we could make an arbitrage profit by selling (buying) the instrument at a price above (below) its maximum (minimum) possible value, assuming that the interest rate moves within the constraints of our model.

Observe how the nonlinearity in the model means that the value of a portfolio depends on what it is hedged with. This means that the 'fitting' that we saw in Chapter 34 becomes irrelevant. In fact, we are not concerned with the market prices of traded instruments except in so far as we exploit these instruments for hedging. We never say that we 'believe' market prices are 'correct' only that they they tell us how much we must pay to get a particular cashflow.

Example I

Let's try to hedge a five-year zero-coupon bond with a one-year zero-coupon bond. The latter has a market price of \$0.90484, the spot rate is currently 10%, the interest rate range is 3–20%, and the spot rate cannot change at a rate faster than 4% p.a., either up or down. In Figure 40.5 are shown the worst- and best-case values for the five-year bond as a function of the number of one-year

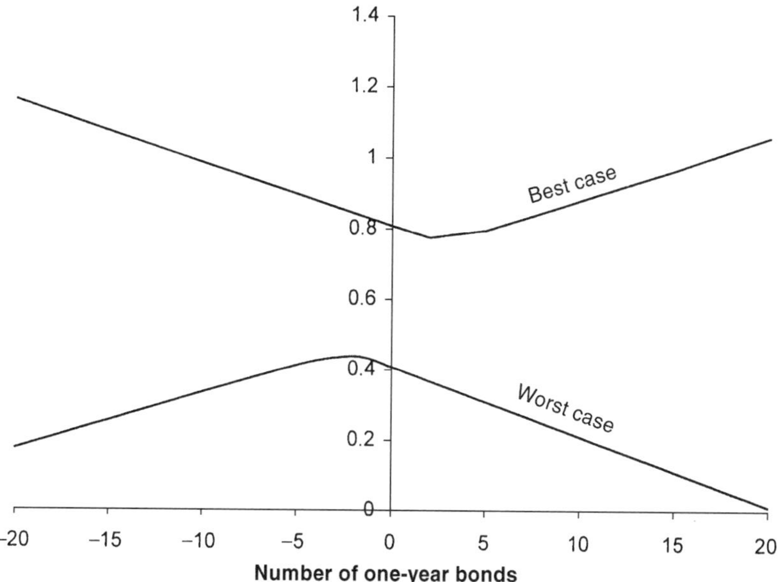

Figure 40.5 The value of the hedged five-year bond in the worst and best cases as a function of the number of one-year bonds with which it is hedged.

bonds with which it is hedged. First look at the lower curve, the worst-case value. Note that it has a maximum. To get the most from the five-year bond in the worst case it must be hedged with -2.15 of the one-year bond. If you hold the five-year bond short then to get the best out of it you must hedge it with 2.29 of the one-year bond.

Example 2

We hedge a four-year zero-coupon bond with zero-coupon bonds of maturities 0.5, 1, 2, 3, 5, 7, 10 years. These hedging bonds are shown in the Table 40.1 together with their market prices (we are assuming for the moment that the bid and ask prices are the same). The spot rate is currently 6% and we will take $r^+ = 0.2$, $r^- = 0.03$, with $c^+ = -c^- = 0.04$. Thus the spot rate is not allowed to grow or decrease faster than 4% p.a.

The results of the valuation, with and without the optimal static hedge are shown in Table 40.2.

Table 40.1 Choice of hedging instruments.

Hedging bond	Maturity (years)	Market price
A	0.5	0.970
B	1	0.933
C	2	0.868
D	3	0.805
E	5	0.687
F	7	0.579
G	10	0.449

Table 40.2 Results of the valuation, with and without the optimal static hedge.

	Worst case	Best case
No hedge	0.579	0.878
Optimally hedged	0.730	0.758

Table 40.3 The optimal static hedges for the worst- and best-case valuations of the four-year bond.

Hedging bond	Worst-case hedge quantity	Best-case hedge quantity
A	−0.051	0.204
B	0.024	−0.135
C	0.190	0.167
D	−0.734	−0.685
E	−0.466	−0.473
F	0.029	0.000
G	0.000	0.000

The optimal static hedges for the worst- and best-case valuations of the four-year bond are shown in Table 40.3.

We observe that the hedge quantities for worst- and best-case scenario valuations differ and that the optimal static hedge will not necessarily contain all of the hedging instruments; in neither case is the 10 year bond used for hedging. Most of the hedging is with the three- and five-year maturities. Hedging has reduced the spread in the value of the four-year bond from $0.878 - 0.579 = 0.299$ to $0.758 - 0.730 = 0.028$, a factor of more than ten. This is still a vast spread, but considering how few instruments we have used to hedge it, and that the hedge is *perfect*, it's very good. It will be reduced further if we are allowed to hedge with more instruments.

40.6 GENERATING THE 'YIELD ENVELOPE'

We continue with our philosophy of finding spreads for prices by generating the **Yield Envelope**. As we found in the above example of hedging a four-year bond, at a maturity for which there are no traded instruments we find a yield spread. So, we find a highest and lowest value for the yield at all maturities for which there are no traded instruments. The plot of the highest and lowest yields against maturity is called the Yield Envelope. Note that at a maturity for which there is a traded instrument, the Yield Envelope converges to the observed yield, the highest and lowest values coincide.[1]

We calculate the worst- and best-case values of a zero-coupon bond with principal 1 and maturity T. We then calculate the maximum and minimum yields possible, using

$$Y = -\frac{\log Z}{T - t}.$$

[1] This is not the case if there are distinct bid and ask prices, but this is a simple generalization of the concept.

To reduce the yield spread, we again hedge our zero-coupon bond with market-traded zero-coupon bonds.

Example

We hedge our zero-coupon bonds with the bonds in Table 40.4. This table shows the available zero-coupon bonds and their market values. The spot rate is 6%. The other parameters are as before. The results are shown in Figure 40.6 and in Table 40.5. In the table the numbers in bold represent the traded bonds. In the figure are four curves. The outer two are exactly the same as in Figure 40.1. They are the yields in the best and worst cases, without any hedging, assuming a current spot rate of 6%, a growth of ±4%, and a range of 3–20%. The inner curves (the 'string of sausages') form the Yield Envelope. These are the best and worst cases for the yields, with the same parameters, but now with optimal static hedging. Note the dramatic decrease in the yield spreads at all maturities. In particular, at maturities with traded zero-coupon bonds the spread disappears, the theoretical price becomes the market price.

Table 40.4 Available zero-coupon bonds and their market values.

Hedging bond	Maturity (years)	Market price
A	0.5	0.950
B	1	0.899
C	2	0.803
D	3	0.712
E	5	0.566
F	7	0.448
G	10	0.304

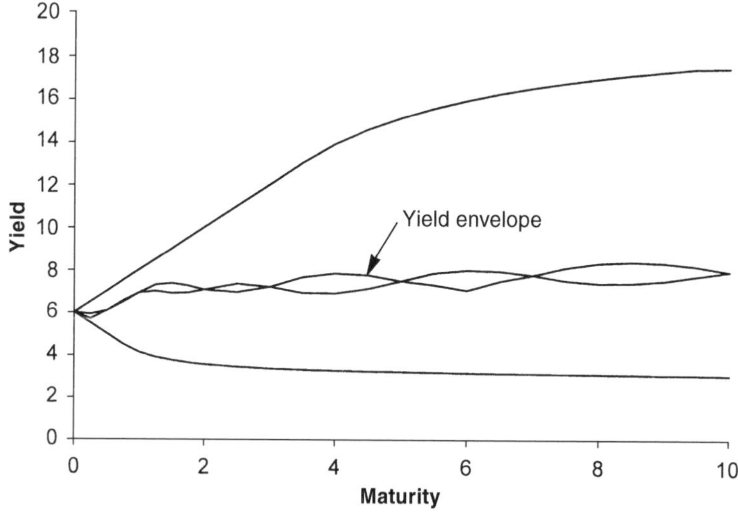

Figure 40.6 Yields in worst and best cases, with and without hedging.

Table 40.5 The optimally-hedged 'yield envelope.'.

Maturity (years)	Yield in worst case	Yield in best case
0	6.000	6.000
0.25	5.919	5.706
0.5	**6.092**	**6.092**
0.75	6.545	6.485
1.0	**6.935**	**6.935**
1.25	7.313	7.002
1.5	7.378	6.908
1.75	7.269	6.933
2.0	**7.078**	**7.078**
2.5	7.357	6.969
3.0	**7.230**	**7.230**
3.5	7.668	6.942
4.0	7.864	6.927
4.5	7.777	7.138
5.0	**7.508**	**7.508**
5.5	7.877	7.329
6.0	8.029	7.079
6.5	7.986	7.517
7.0	**7.806**	**7.806**
7.5	8.159	7.558
8.0	8.381	7.438
8.5	8.454	7.450
9.0	8.407	7.571
9.5	8.259	7.786
10.0	**8.007**	**8.007**

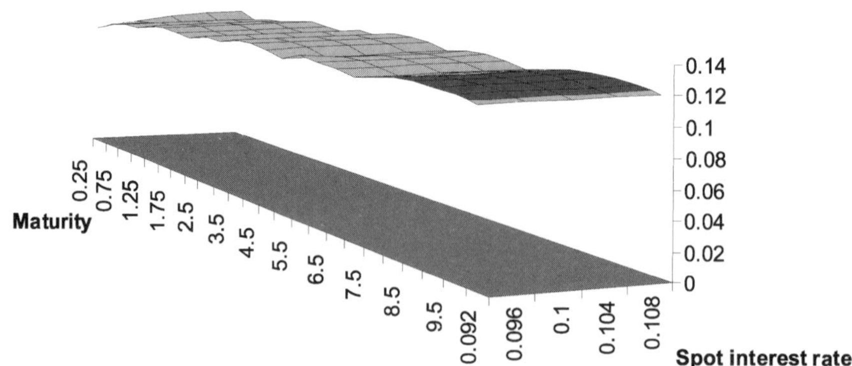

Figure 40.7 Yields in the worst-case scenario against spot rate and maturity, with optimal hedging.

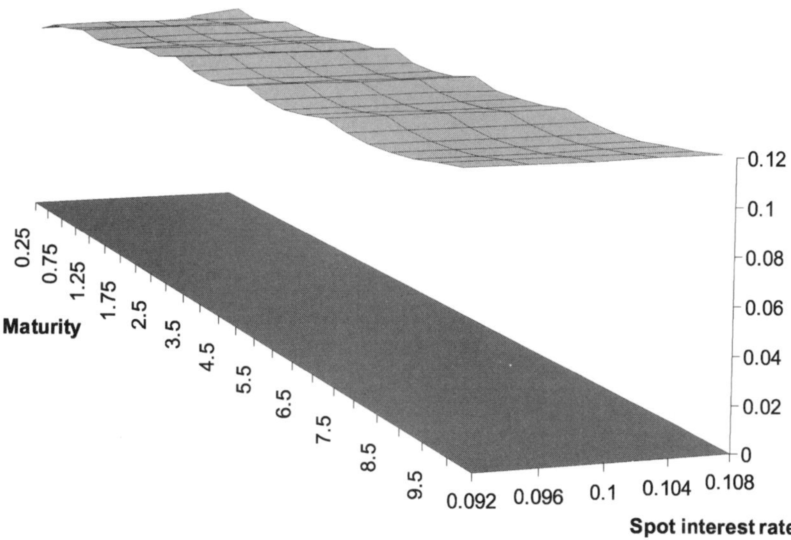

Figure 40.8 Yields in the best-case scenario against spot rate and maturity, with optimal hedging.

At maturities for which there are traded instruments, the yields in both worst- and best-case scenarios equal the market yield. This is because we can fully hedge our zero-coupon bond with the market-traded instrument and this is the optimal static hedge in both scenarios.

Figures 40.7 and 40.8 show the yields in the worst- and best-case scenarios, respectively, with varying spot rate and maturity, again when we optimally hedge with the bonds shown in the table.

40.7 A REAL PORTFOLIO

In Figure 40.9 are shown the sterling-denominated cashflows of Dresdner, Kleinwort, Benson arising from a leasing portfolio. Let's see how we might use the model to hedge this portfolio. First of all, we will calculate the present value of all the cashflows using the yield curve today, 8th January 1998. This yield curve is shown in Figure 40.10. The present value is found to be −£3,539,362. To test the sensitivity of this value to shifts in the yield curve, I show in Table 40.6 the present value of the cashflows assuming instantaneous parallel shifts in the yield curve of various magnitudes. These give a traditional way of determining whether or not a position is hedged againsts moves in the yield curve. If we are being pessimistic then a 2% downward shift in the yield curve reduces the portfolio's value to −£4,432,153.

The yield curve was estimated from the market values of benchmark bonds. These bonds are shown in Table 40.7. We are going to use these bonds, which are coupon bearing except for the first two, for hedging purposes.

Using the Epstein–Wilmott model, with the same parameters as before, we find that the worst-case value for the portfolio as it stands is −£6,135,878, and the best-case value is −£1,898,173. If we are being pessimistic then a value of −£6,135,878 is perfectly possible. This is significantly lower than the present value of −£3,539,362 calculated off the yield curve today. It is also significantly lower than the value we calculated above using a 2% parallel shift in the yield curve. Is a 2% shift in the yield curve realistic? Remember that the cashflows go out to the year 2008. The price calculated using the nonlinear model is far more robust and reliable.

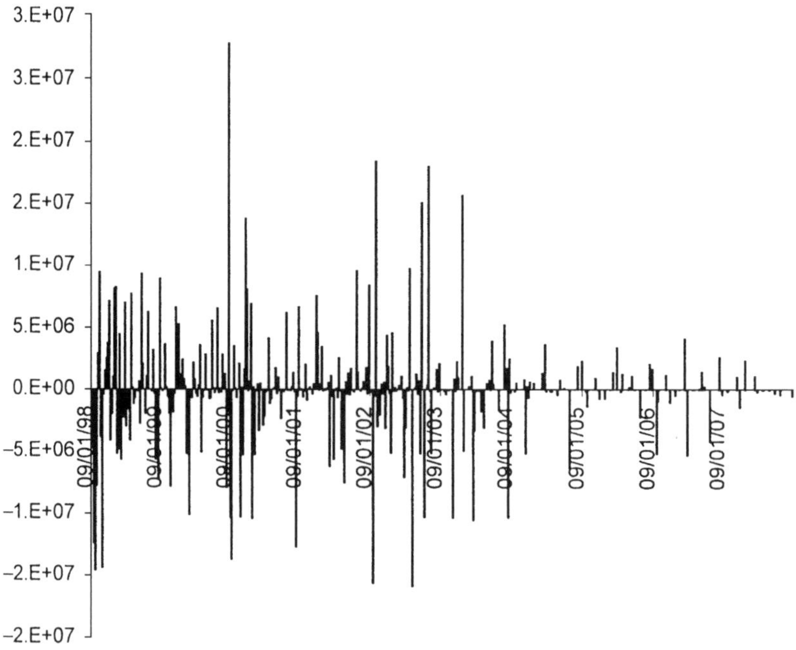

Figure 40.9 Cashflows of Dresdner, Kleinwort, Benson.

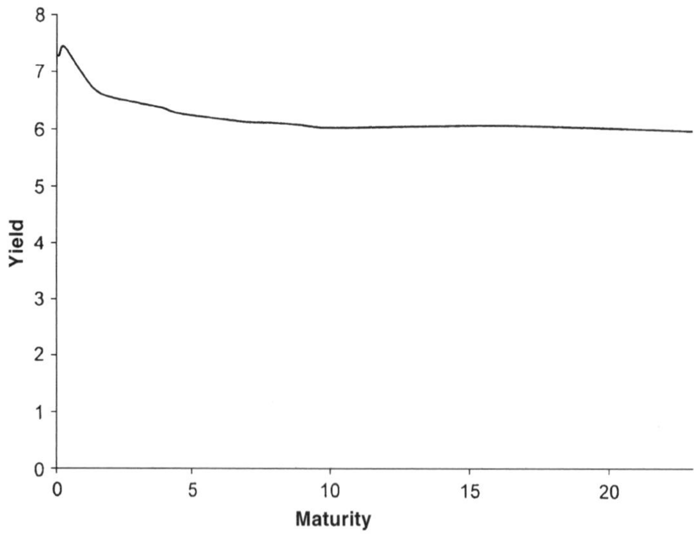

Figure 40.10 Current yield curve.

Now we will hedge the portfolio using the benchmark bonds so as to optimize the worst-case value. The quantitities of each of the hedging bonds giving the optimal hedge is shown in Table 40.8. Note the large quantity of the three-year bond sold short. The cashflows of these bonds are shown in Figure 40.11. The worst-case value for the original portfolio hedged with these bonds is now −£4,009,581. Again this is a very robust pessimistic value for the portfolio,

Table 40.6 Present value of portfolio with parallel shifts in the yield curve.

Shift in curve	Present value (£)
2%	−2,620,568
1%	−3,083,010
0%	−3,539,362
−1%	−3,989,193
−2%	−4,432,153

Table 40.7 Benchmark bonds.

	Coupon	Maturity	Market price (£)
1M T-BILL	0	04 FEB 1998	99.46
3MB T-BILL	0	08 APR 1998	98.15
1Y GILT	12	20 NOV 1998	104.125
2YB GILT	6	10 AUG 1999	99.125
3Y GILT	8	07 DEC 2000	104.03125
4Y GILT	7	06 NOV 2001	102.09375
5YB GILT	7	07 JUN 2002	102.75
6Y GILT	8	10 JUN 2003	108.09375
7Y GILT	6.75	26 NOV 2004	103.40625
8Y GILT	8.5	07 DEC 2005	114.75
9Y GILT	7.5	07 DEC 2006	109.625
10YB GILT	7.25	07 DEC 2007	108.96875
15Y GILT	8	27 SEP 2013	119.21875
20YB GILT	8.75	25 AUG 2017	130.75
25YB GILT	8	07 JUN 2021	125.03125

Table 40.8 Optimal hedge for the leasing portfolio.

Hedging bond	Hedge quantity
1M	762
3M	556
1Y	745
2Y	−7112
3Y	−123013
4Y	7064
5Y	−30844
6Y	1689
7Y	3135
8Y	−6944
9Y	−285
10Y	11674
15Y	−122
20Y	1456
25Y	−1299

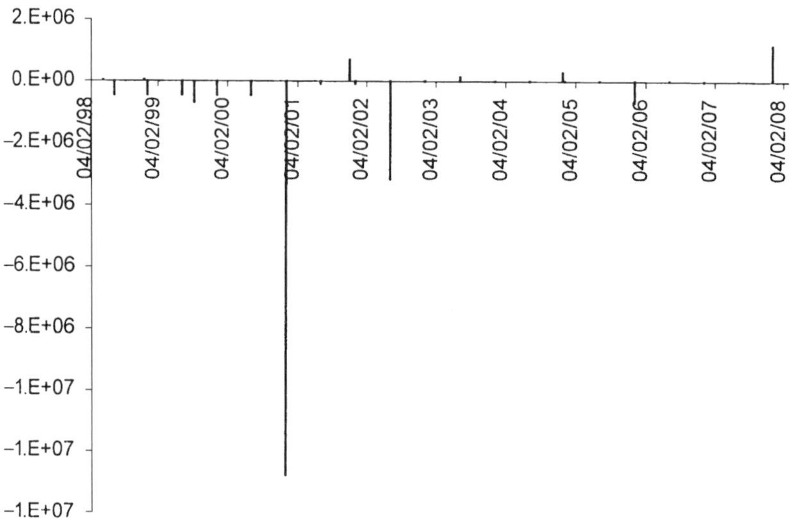

Figure 40.11 Optimal hedging portfolio cashflows.

when optimally hedged. It is hedged against a far broader set of future scenarios than a simple yield curve shift and is consequentially far more reliable. Moreover, it is only −£470,219 less than the simple present value off the yield curve. By optimally hedging the worst-case has improved from −£6,135,878 to −£4,009,581, simply by hedging with benchmark bonds. (As a matter of interest, the best-case value when hedged with these same bonds is −£3,112,337.)

40.8 PRICING AND HEDGING OTHER INSTRUMENTS

It is no harder to price and hedge other common instruments. The easiest to price and hedge all have cashflows that are simple functions of the short-term interest rate (or can be accurately approximated by this). This includes FRAs, swaps, caps and floors. It is easy to incorporate American-style features, such as callability and early exercise. Here I am going to give just two examples, the pricing of an index amortizing rate swap and a convertible bond.

40.8.1 The Index Amortizing Rate Swap

We saw the IAR swap in Chapter 35. Here we will see how to value it using the model of this chapter. This is a particularly good example of the use of this model because static hedging of the IAR swap with vanilla swaps can be done in an optimal fashion.

As before we must introduce a new state variable. This new state variable is the current level of the principal, again denoted by P. The the value of the IAR swap is $V(r, P, t)$.

The variable P is deterministic and jumps to its new level at each resetting. Since P is piecewise constant, the governing differential equation for the value of the swap is, in the present model,

$$\frac{\partial V}{\partial t} + c\left(\frac{\partial V}{\partial r}\right)\frac{\partial V}{\partial r} - rV = 0.$$

At each reset date there is an exchange of interest payments and an amortization of the principal. If we use t_i to denote the reset dates and r_f for the fixed interest rate, then the swap jumps in value by an amount $(r - r_f)P$. Subsequently, the principal P becomes $g(r)P$ where the function $g(r)$ is the representation of the amortizing schedule. This gives us the jump condition

$$V(r, P, t_i^-) = V(r, g(r)P, t_i^+) + (r - r_f)P.$$

At the maturity of the contract there is one final exchange of interest payments, thus

$$V(r, P, T) = (r - r_f)P.$$

The problem is nonlinear, and must be solved numerically. The structure of this particular IAR swap is such that there is a similarity reduction; just look for a solution of the form

$$V(r, P, t) = PH(r, t).$$

We are lucky that the similarity reduction is not affected by the nonlinearity.

Of course, this model is of little practical use unless the contract is simultaneously statically hedged with traded contracts. The natural choice of hedging contracts would be vanilla swaps.

40.8.2 Pricing Convertible Bonds

The model can easily be applied to contracts with other asset-price dependence such as convertible bonds. In this case the pricing equation is

$$\frac{\partial V}{\partial t} + \tfrac{1}{2}\sigma^2 S^2 \frac{\partial^2 V}{\partial S^2} + rS\frac{\partial V}{\partial S} + c\left(\frac{\partial V}{\partial r}\right)\frac{\partial V}{\partial r} - rV = 0,$$

where the bond value is a function of S, r and t: $V(S, r, t)$. The usual payoff condition and constraints apply as discussed in Chapter 36.

Worst-case results are shown in Figure 40.12 for a two-year CB with conversion allowed at any time. In Figure 40.13 is plotted the difference between the best and the worst cases.

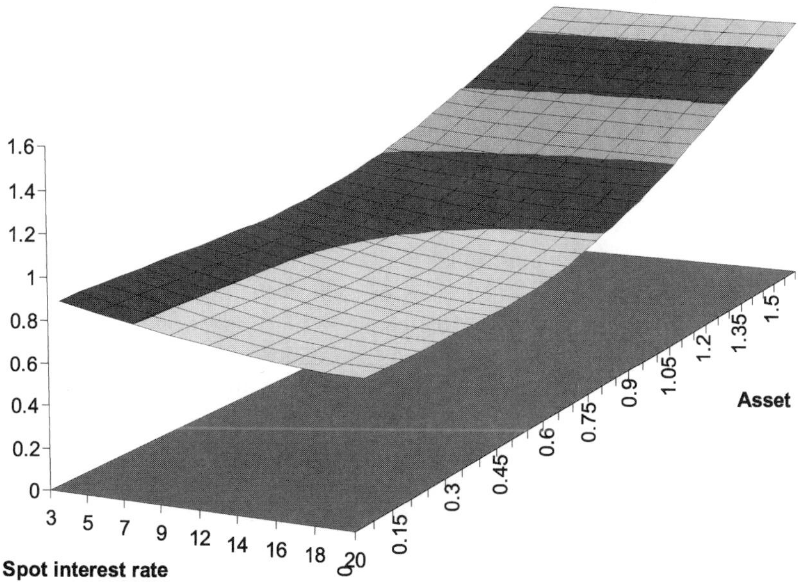

Figure 40.12 The worst-case value of a convertible bond using the Epstein–Wilmott interest rate model.

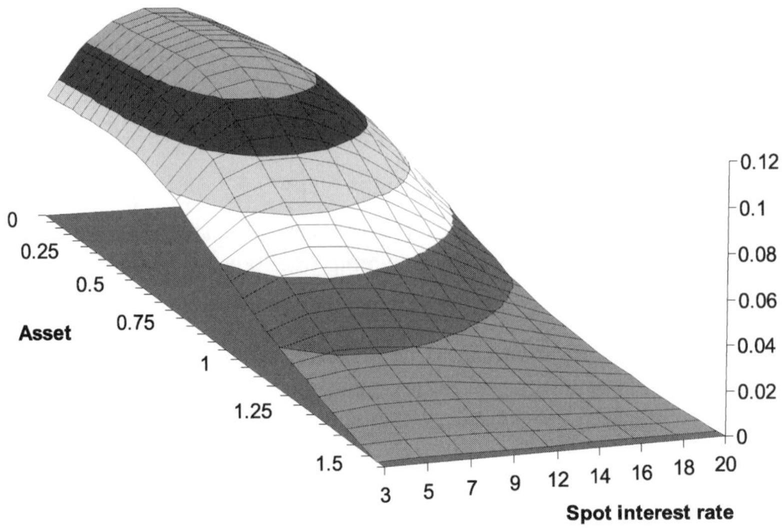

Figure 40.13 The spread in values of a convertible bond using the Epstein–Wilmott interest rate model.

Example

In this example we value a convertible bond using three different models. The convertible bond matures in 18 months, is convertible into 0.5 of the underlying at any time and there are 3% coupons paid twice p.a. The underlying asset is currently 1.5, and has a dividend yield of 3% and a volatility of 25%.

The simplest model is the stochastic asset model having a constant interest rate. With an interest rate of 7% this model gives the CB value of 1.058.

The second model is Vasicek fitted to a flat 7% yield curve. This model gives a value of 1.059. The results from these two models are very close. But are these values realistic?

The final example is of the Epstein–Wilmott model worst- and best-case analyses. In the worst case we get a value of 1.042 and in the best case 1.089. This spread is very large, yet it is a very robust estimate of the bond's range of values. Can we improve these values by static hedging?

Table 40.9 shows three zero-coupon bonds with which we can hedge and their market prices. In the third column are the optimal quantitities of each of the bonds that maximize the worst-case value of the convertible bond. With this hedge in place the worst case is improved from 1.042 to 1.052. This price is far less sensitive to the interest rate model than the other prices we have obtained with the other two models. When optimally hedged the best-case value is

Table 40.9 Universe of hedging bonds, market prices and optimal hedge quantitities.

Maturity	Market price	Hedge (worst)
0.5	0.9656	−0.7350
1	0.9323	−0.1639
2	0.8693	−0.4882

1.067. The spread has been reduced from 1.089 − 1.042 =
factor of three.

40.9 A MORE SOPHISTICATED MODEL CYCLES

There is evidence that interest rates follow economic cyc
years. Can we incorporate this observation into our mode
A starting point for such a model could be to say that an
by simple harmonic motion, i.e. by the solution of

$$\frac{d^2r}{dt^2} = a - \omega^2 r.$$

The period of this cycle is $2\pi/\omega$, with the cycle centred
Of course, we cannot be sure about either the period
been observed but they are far from being predictable.
Accordingly, we modify the above equation for the evol

$$a^- - \omega^{-2} r \leq \frac{d^2r}{dt^2} \leq a^+ - \omega^{+2} r.$$

More generally we could write

$$a^-(r, s) \leq \frac{d^2r}{dt^2} \leq a^+(r, s),$$

where

$$s = \frac{dr}{dt}.$$

The governing equation for the worst-case value, $V(r, s, t)$, of a product is then

$$\frac{\partial V}{\partial t} + s\frac{\partial V}{\partial r} + a\left(r, s, \frac{\partial V}{\partial s}\right)\frac{\partial V}{\partial s} - rV = 0,$$

where

$$a(r, s, x) = \begin{cases} a^-(r, s) & \text{for} \quad x \geq 0 \\ a^+(r, s) & \text{for} \quad x < 0. \end{cases}$$

Constraints on r and s will result in proscribed regions of r, s, t space.

40.10 OTHER MODELS

There is no end to the number of bells and whistles that can be attached to financial models. We can incorporate many of the features that we have seen in other chapters into the present model. The obvious improvement, that will not take much more computational effort, is to include jumps of some form. It is common experience that rates do jump. In some countries these jumps are orchestrated by governments. The crash models of Chapter 27 are a nice addition to the model since they are also based on a worst-case scenario analysis.

40.10.1 Interest Rate Bands

Interest rates do have a stochastic nature that is not quite captured by the present model. This stochastic nature may or may not be Brownian motion, and it may or may not matter in practice. We can easily extend the model to allow for interest rate movements that are practically indistinguishable from the real behavior of rates. This extension is the introduction of **uncertainty bands**. We subtly redefine r to be some estimate of the spot interest rate that is always within a distance ε of the *real* short-term rate. Thus

$$|\text{real spot rate } - r| \leq \varepsilon.$$

The details of the worst-case analysis are obvious, we must discount at either $r+\varepsilon$ or $r-\varepsilon$ depending on the sign of the value V:

$$\frac{\partial V}{\partial t} + c\left(\frac{\partial V}{\partial r}\right)\frac{\partial V}{\partial r} - (r+\varepsilon(V))V = 0,$$

where

$$\varepsilon(x) = \begin{cases} \varepsilon & \text{for } x > 0 \\ -\varepsilon & \text{for } x < 0. \end{cases}$$

40.10.2 Fitting Forward Rates

As a final thought, consider taking the Epstein–Wilmott model explained above and making it closer in spirit to both the classical stochastic models and the duration type of models. Suppose that we believe interest rates to be completely deterministic and governed by the equation

$$\frac{dr}{dt} = a(b(t) - r). \tag{40.4}$$

That is, the rates are mean reverting to some level $b(t)$ at a rate a. This is similar to a fitted Vasicek, but without the random element. If this is true and markets price according to this model, then the forward rate curve today $F(t^*; T)$ must satisfy

$$\frac{d}{dt}F(t^*; t) = a(b(t) - F(t^*; t)).$$

It follows that

$$b(t) = F(t^*; t) + \frac{1}{a}\frac{d}{dt}F(t^*; t). \tag{40.5}$$

So our interest rate model is just (40.4) with $b(t)$ given by (40.5). Now add a 'margin of error' to this model so that it becomes

$$a(b(t) - r) - c < \frac{dr}{dt} < a(b(t) - r) + c.$$

This puts the model firmly into the Epstein–Wilmott framework. This model combines the best of all possible model worlds. The margin of error c can be found by 'fitting' the function $b(t)$ many, many times using historical forward-rate data, and then determining by how much this function is in error.

40.11 SUMMARY

In this chapter I have presented a model for valuing and hedging interest rate securities. The framework is that of 'worst-case scenarios' and we have derived a nonlinear first-order partial differential equation for the value of a portfolio of products. Since the equation is nonlinear we find that the value of a product depends on the rest of the portfolio. This nonlinearity gives the model both advantages and disadvantages compared with other, more traditional approaches. The main disadvantage is that to obtain the full benefit of the model one must solve the equation for the entire portfolio. The principal advantage is that optimal hedges can be found, maximizing the portfolio's value. A further advantage of the model is that one can be fairly confident in the accuracy of the model parameters.

FURTHER READING

- See Epstein & Wilmott (1997, 1998) for examples of pricing other fixed-income instruments.
- See Lewicki & Avellaneda (1996) for an interest rate model in the HJM framework but assuming uncertain volatility.

EXERCISES

1. What equation must we solve to value our portfolio in the best case? By substituting into the equation for the worst case, check that
$$V_{\text{best}} = -(-V)_{\text{worst}}.$$
2. Hedge a five-year zero-coupon bond with an amount λ of a one year zero-coupon bond. What is the optimal hedge when we value the five-year bond in a worst case scenario? What do you notice about the value of the five-year bond when we hedge with a very large amount (either positive or negative) of the one-year bond? What explanation is there for this?
3. What is the advantage of this model over probabalistic models if we choose our values for c^- and c^+ so that the actual interest rate movements do in fact lie within the band predicted?
4. Derive the pricing equation for a convertible bond when we have a stochastic asset price model and an uncertain interest rate model. How does the uncertain interest rate model affect the value of convertible bonds? Compare with the Extended Vasicek model.
5. Derive the uncertain interest rate equation for the value of a portfolio in a worst case scenario when we have an uncertain second derivative, i.e. for an economic cycle. We now have:
$$r^- \leq r \leq r^+,$$
with
$$c^- \leq s \leq c^+,$$
and
$$a^-(r,s) \leq \frac{d^2r}{dt^2} \leq a^+(r,s).$$
where $s = dr/dt$.

6. The fitted Epstein–Wilmott model has

$$a(b(t) - r) - c^- < \frac{dr}{dt} < a(b(t) - r) + c^+.$$

   How does the method of fitting compare with the way in which we fitted the Vasicek model to yield data?

7. We can incorporate the crash model of Chapter 27 into the uncertain interest rate world. What equation would we have to solve if we allowed one large interest rate movement over the time to expiry? What other type of crash or jump could we include in the model?

PART FIVE
risk measurement and management

The fifth part of the book addresses the wider issues of risk, its measurement and management. Derivative theory is typically based in a Black–Scholes world where all options are delta hedged, no risk is taken, and all portfolios earn the risk-free rate of interest. This is a two-dimensional cross-section of a more interesting three-dimensional world. I will now flesh out that third dimension.

Chapter 41: Portfolio Management If you are willing to accept some risk how should you invest? I explain the classical ideas of Modern Portfolio Theory and the Capital Asset Pricing Model.

Chapter 42: Value at Risk How risky is your portfolio? How much might you conceivably lose if there is an adverse market move? These are the topics of this chapter.

Chapter 43: Credit Risk Hedging plays a minor, if any, role when there is a real risk of default. How should you price a bond when you suspect that the issuer may default? I describe popular models for risk of default, including endogenous and exogenous default and change of credit rating. The subject of credit risk is immensely important, but from a modeling viewpoint, still in its infancy.

Chapter 44: Credit Derivatives If you hold a bond which may default you can buy insurance that pays you in that event. This is the simplest of credit derivatives. More complex structures exist that pay off upon a change of credit rating for example. These and other contracts are discussed in this chapter.

Chapter 45: RiskMetrics, CreditMetrics and CrashMetrics In order to make the measurement of risk easier, and consistent from one bank to another, there have grown up several methodologies. I describe three of these here. One is for basic value at risk measurement in normal market situations, one is for credit risk and the final one is for measuring risk in the event of market crashes.

CHAPTER 41

portfolio management

In this Chapter...

- the Kelly criterion
- Modern Portfolio Theory and the Capital Asset Pricing Model
- optimizing your portfolio
- alternative methodologies such as cointegration
- how to analyze portfolio performance

41.1 INTRODUCTION

The theory of derivative pricing is a theory of deterministic returns: we hedge our derivative with the underlying to eliminate risk, and our resulting risk-free portfolio then earns the risk-free rate of interest. Banks make money from this hedging process; they sell something for a bit more than it's worth and hedge away the risk to make a guaranteed profit.

But not everyone is hedging. Fund managers buy and sell assets (including derivatives) with the aim of beating the bank's rate of return. In so doing they take risk. In this chapter I explain some of the theories behind the risk and reward of investment. Along the way I show the benefits of diversification, how the return and risk on a portfolio of assets is related to the return and risk on the individual assets, and how to optimize a portfolio to get the best value for money.

For the most part, the assumptions are as follows.

- We hold a portfolio for 'a single period,' examining the behavior after this time.
- During this period returns on assets are Normally distributed.
- The return on assets can be measured by an expected return (the drift) for each asset, a standard deviation of return (the volatility) for each asset and correlations between the asset returns.

41.2 THE KELLY CRITERION

To get us into the spirit of asset choice, consider the following real-life example. You have \$1000 to invest and the only investments available to you are in a casino playing Blackjack or roulette. We will concentrate on Blackjack. Optimal strategies at Blackjack were first described by Thorp (1962).

If you play Blackjack with no strategy you will lose your money quickly. The odds, as ever, are in favor of the house. If your strategy is to copy the dealer's rules then there is a house edge of between five and six percent. This is because when you bust you lose, even if the dealer busts later. There is, however, an optimal strategy. The best strategy involves knowing when to hit or stand, when to split, double down, take insurance (pretty much never) etc. This decision will be based on the two cards you hold and the dealer's face up card. If you play the best strategy you can cut the odds down to about evens, the exact figure depending on the rules of the particular casino. To consistently win at Blackjack takes two things: patience and the ability to count cards. The latter only means keeping track of, for example, the number of aces and ten-count cards left in the deck. Aces and tens left in the deck improve your odds of winning. If you follow the optimal strategy and simultaneously bet high when there are a lot of aces and tens left, and low otherwise, then you will in the long run do well. If there are any casino managers reading this, I'd like to reassure them that I have never mastered the technique of card counting, so its not worth them banning me. On the other hand, I always seem to win, but that may just be selective memory.

What does this have to do with investing?

Let me introduce the following notation: ϕ is the random variable denoting the outcome of a bet, μ is its mean and σ its standard deviation. In Blackjack and roulette ϕ will take discrete values. Suppose I bet a fraction f of my \$1000, how much will I have after the hand? The amount will be

$$1000(1 + f\phi_1),$$

where the subscript 1 denotes the first hand. I will consistently bet a constant fraction f of my holdings each hand, so that after two hands I have an amount

$$1000(1 + f\phi_1)(1 + f\phi_2).$$

This is not quite what one does when counting cards, since one will change the amount f. After M hands I have

$$1000\,\Pi_{i=1}^{M}(1 + f\phi_i).$$

How should I choose the amount f? I am going to choose it to maximize my expected long-term growth rate. This growth rate is

$$\frac{1}{M}\log(1000\,\Pi_{i=1}^{M}(1 + f\phi_i)) = \frac{1}{M}\sum_{i=1}^{M}\log(1 + f\phi_i) + \frac{1}{M}\log(1000).$$

Assuming that the outcome of each hand is independent, an assumption, not true for Blackjack of course, then the expected value of this is

$$E[\log(1 + f\phi_i)],$$

ignoring the scaling factor log(1000). Expanding the argument of the logarithm in Taylor series, assuming that the mean is small but that the standard deviation is not, we get approximately

$$f\mu - \tfrac{1}{2}f^2\sigma^2.$$

This is maximized by the choice

$$f^* = \frac{\mu}{\sigma^2},$$

giving an expected growth rate of

$$\frac{\mu^2}{2\sigma^2}$$

per hand. If $\mu > 0$ then $f > 0$ and we stand to make a profit, in the long term. If $\mu < 0$, as it is for roulette or if you follow a naive Blackjack strategy, then you should invest a negative amount, i.e. own the casino. If you must play roulette, put all your money you would gamble in your lifetime on a color, and play once. Not only do you stand an almost 50% chance of doubling your money, you will gain an invaluable reputation as a serious player. The long-run growth rate maximization and the optimal amount to invest is called the **Kelly criterion**.

If you can play M times in an evening you would expect to make

$$\frac{\mu^2 M}{2\sigma^2}. \tag{41.1}$$

This illustrates one possible way of choosing a portfolio, which asset to invest in (Blackjack) and how much to invest (f^*). Faced with other possible investments, then you could argue in favor of choosing the one with the highest (41.1), depending on the mean of the return, its standard deviation and how often the investment opportunity comes your way. These ideas are particularly important to the technical analyst or chartist who trades on the basis of signals such as golden crosses, saucer bottoms, and head and shoulder patterns. Not only do the risk and return of these signals matter, but so does their frequency of occurrence.

41.3 DIVERSIFICATION

In this section I introduce some more notation, and show the effects of diversification on the return of the portfolio.

We hold a portfolio of N assets. The value today of the ith asset is S_i and its random return is R_i over our time horizon T. The Rs are Normally distributed with mean $\mu_i T$ and standard deviation $\sigma_i\sqrt{T}$. The correlation between the returns on the ith and jth assets is ρ_{ij} (with $\rho_{ii} = 1$). The parameters μ, σ and ρ correspond to the drift, volatility and correlation that we are used to. Note the scaling with the time horizon.

If we hold w_i of the ith asset, then our portfolio has value

$$\Pi = \sum_{i=1}^{N} w_i S_i.$$

At the end of our time horizon the value is

$$\Pi + \delta\Pi = \sum_{i=1}^{N} w_i S_i (1 + R_i).$$

We can write the relative change in portfolio value as

$$\frac{\delta\Pi}{\Pi} = \sum_{i=1}^{N} W_i R_i, \tag{41.2}$$

where

$$W_i = \frac{w_i S_i}{\Sigma_{i=1}^{N} w_i S_i}.$$

The weights W_i sum to one.

From (41.2) it is simple to calculate the expected return on the portfolio

$$\mu_\Pi = \frac{1}{T} E\left[\frac{\delta\Pi}{\Pi}\right] = \sum_{i=1}^{N} W_i \mu_i \tag{41.3}$$

and the standard deviation of the return

$$\sigma_\Pi = \frac{1}{\sqrt{T}} \sqrt{\text{var}\left[\frac{\delta\Pi}{\Pi}\right]} = \sqrt{\sum_{i=1}^{N}\sum_{j=1}^{N} W_i W_j \rho_{ij} \sigma_i \sigma_j}. \tag{41.4}$$

In these, we have related the parameters for the individual assets to the expected return and the standard deviation of the entire portfolio.

41.3.1 Uncorrelated Assets

Suppose that we have assets in our portfolio that are uncorrelated, $\rho_{ij} = 0$, $i \neq j$. To make things simple assume that they are equally weighted so that $W_i = 1/N$. The expected return on the portfolio is represented by

$$\mu_\Pi = \frac{1}{N} \sum_{i=1}^{N} \mu_i,$$

the average of the expected returns on all the assets, and the volatility becomes

$$\sigma_\Pi = \sqrt{\frac{1}{N^2} \sum_{i=1}^{N} \sigma_i^2}.$$

This volatility is $O(N^{-1/2})$ since there are N terms in the sum. As we increase the number of assets in the portfolio, the standard deviation of the returns tends to zero. It is rather extreme to assume that all assets are uncorrelated but we will see something similar when I describe the Capital Asset Pricing Model below, diversification reduces volatility without hurting expected return.

I am now going to refer to volatility or standard deviation as **risk**, a bad thing to be avoided (within reason), and the expected return as **reward**, a good thing that we want as much of as possible.

41.4 MODERN PORTFOLIO THEORY

We can use the above framework to discuss the 'best' portfolio. The definition of 'best' was addressed very successfully by Nobel laureate Harry Markowitz. His model provides a way of defining portfolios that are **efficient**. An efficient portfolio is one that has the highest reward for a given level of risk, or the lowest risk for a given reward. To see how this works imagine that there are five assets in the world, A, B, C, D and E with reward and risk as shown in Figure 41.2. If you could buy any one of these (but as yet you are not allowed more than one), which would you buy? Would you choose D? No, because it has the same risk as B but less reward. It has the same reward as C but for a higher risk. We can rule out D. What about B or C? They are

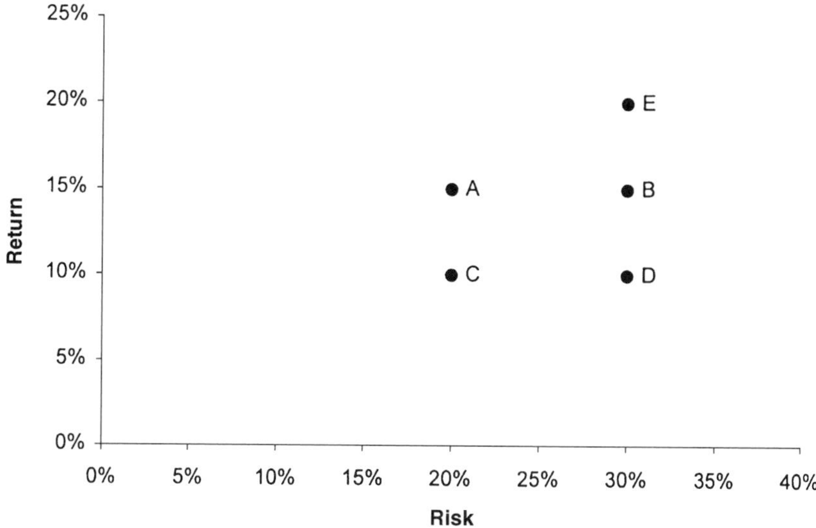

Figure 41.1 Risk and reward for five assets.

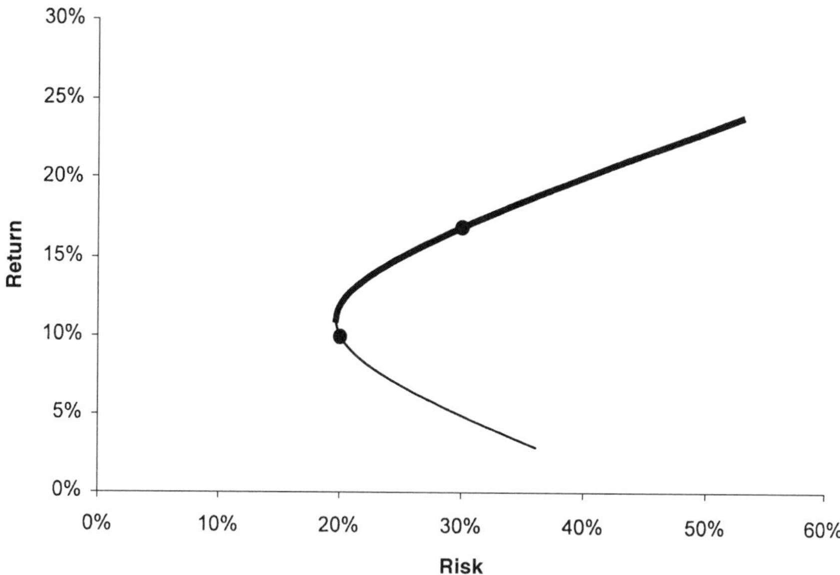

Figure 41.2 Two assets and any combination.

both appealing when set against D, but against each other it is not so clear. B has a higher risk, but gets a higher reward. However, comparing them both with A we see that there is no contest. A is the preferred choice. B, C and D cannot be efficient portfolios. If we introduce asset E with the same risk as B and a higher reward than A, then we cannot objectively say which out of A and E is the better, this is a subjective choice and depends on an investor's **risk preferences**.

Now suppose that I have the two assets A and E of Figure 41.2, and I am now allowed to combine them in my portfolio, what effect does this have on my risk/reward?

From (41.3) and (41.4) we have

$$\mu_\Pi = W\mu_A + (1 - W)\mu_E$$

and

$$\sigma_\Pi^2 = W^2\sigma_A^2 + 2W(1 - W)\rho\sigma_A\sigma_E + (1 - W)^2\sigma_E^2.$$

Here W is the weight of asset A, and, remembering that the weights must add up to one, the weight of asset E is $1 - W$.

As we vary W, so the risk and the reward change. The line in risk/reward space that is parametrized by W is a hyperbola, as shown in Figure 41.2. The part of this curve in bold is efficient, and is preferable to the rest of the curve. Again, an individual's risk preferences will say where he wants to be on the bold curve. When one of the volatilities is zero the line becomes straight. Anywhere on the curve between the two dots requires a long position in each asset. Outside this region, one of the assets is sold short to finance the purchase of the other. Everything that follows assumes that we can sell short as much of an asset as we want. The results change slightly when there are restrictions.

If we have many assets in our portfolio we no longer have a simple hyperbola for our possible risk/reward profiles, instead we get something like that shown in Figure 41.3. In this figure we can see the **efficient frontier** marked in bold. Given any choice of portfolio we would choose to hold one that lies on this efficient frontier.

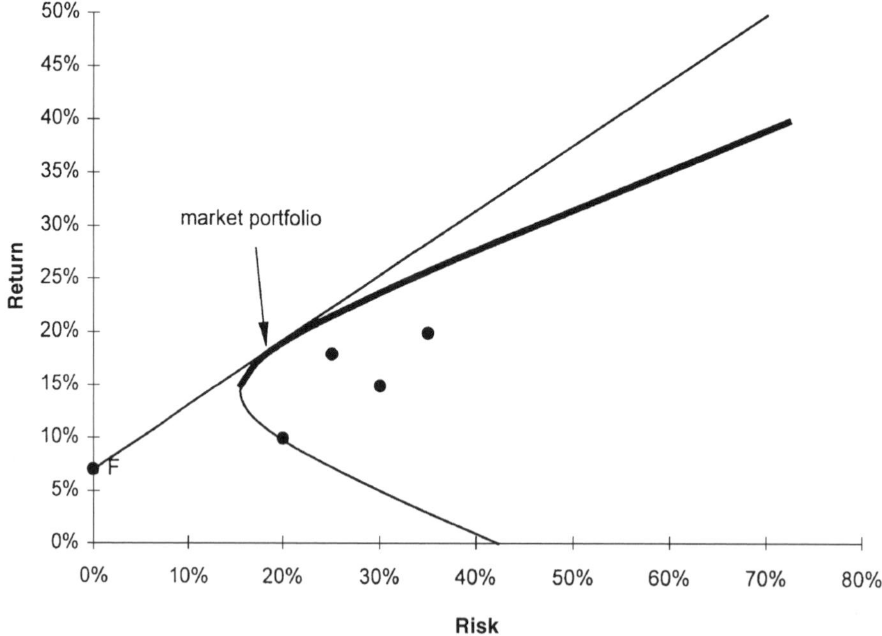

Figure 41.3 Portfolio possibilities and the efficient frontier.

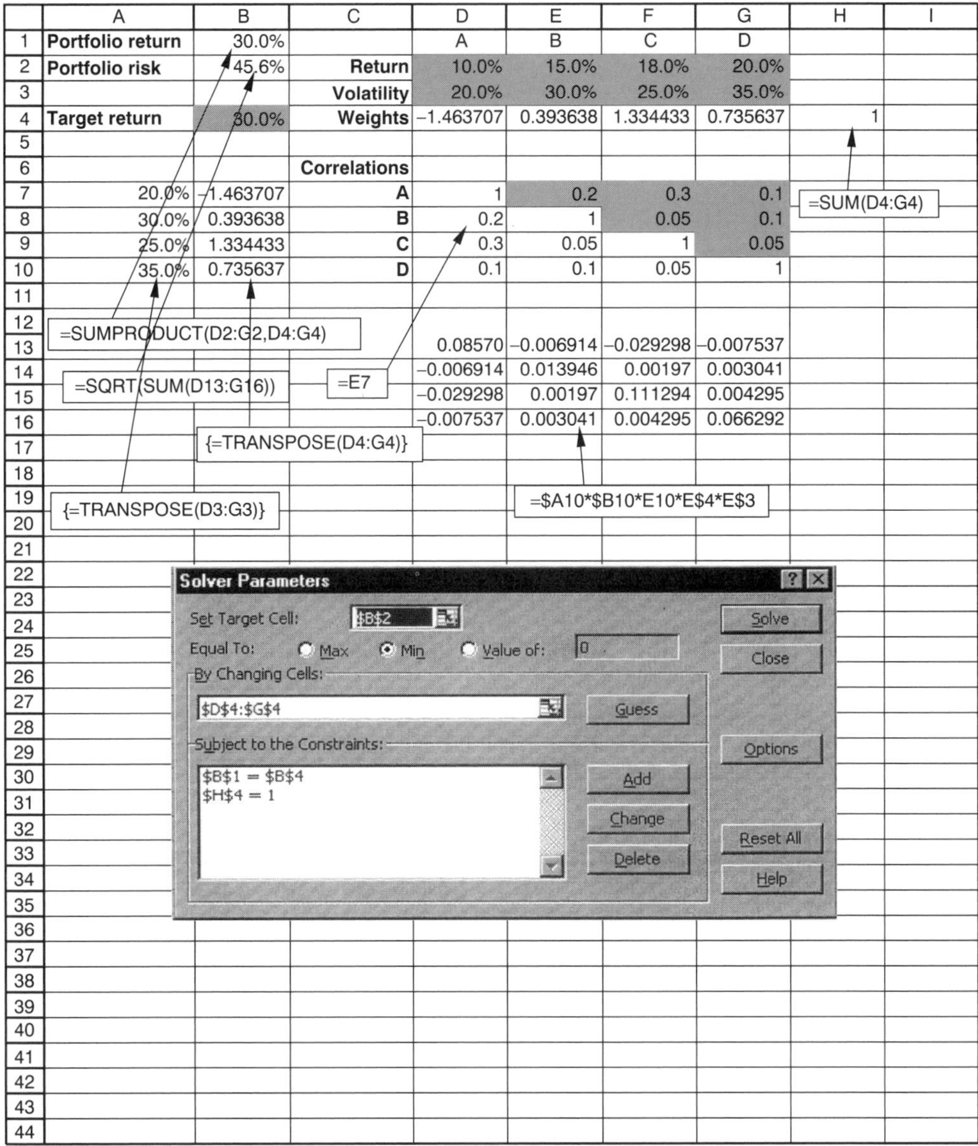

Figure 41.4 Spreadsheet for calculating one point on the efficient frontier.

The calculation of the risk for a given return is demonstrated in the spreadsheet in Figure 41.4. This spreadsheet can be used to find the efficient frontier if it is used many times for different target returns.

41.4.1 Including a Risk-free Investment

A risk-free investment earning a guaranteed rate of return r would be the point F in Figure 41.3. If we are allowed to hold this asset in our portfolio, then since the volatility of this asset is zero, we get the new efficient frontier which is the straight line in the figure. The portfolio for which the straight line touches the original efficient frontier is called the **market portfolio**. The straight line itself is called the **capital market line**.

41.5 WHERE DO I WANT TO BE ON THE EFFICIENT FRONTIER?

Having found the efficient frontier we want to know whereabouts on it we should be. This is a personal choice; the efficient frontier is objective, given the data, but the 'best' position on it is subjective.

The following is a way of interpreting the risk/reward diagram that may be useful in choosing the best portfolio.

The return on portfolio Π is Normally distributed because it is comprised of assets which are themselves Normally distributed. It has mean μ_Π and standard deviation σ_Π (I have ignored the dependence on the horizon T).

The slope of the line joining the portfolio Π to the risk-free asset is

$$s = \frac{\mu_\Pi - r}{\sigma_\Pi}.$$

This is an important quantity, it is a measure of the likelihood of Π having a return that exceeds r. If $C(\cdot)$ is the cumulative distribution function for the standardized Normal distribution then $C(s)$ is the probability that the return on Π is at least r. More generally

$$C\left(\frac{\mu_\Pi - r^*}{\sigma_\Pi}\right)$$

is the probability that the return exceeds r^*. This suggests that if we want to minimize the chance of a return of less than r^* we should choose the portfolio from the efficient frontier set Π_{eff} with the largest value of the slope

$$\frac{\mu_{\Pi_{\text{eff}}} - r^*}{\sigma_{\Pi_{\text{eff}}}}.$$

Conversely, if we keep the slope of this line fixed at s then we can say that with a confidence of $C(s)$ we will lose no more than

$$\mu_{\Pi_{\text{eff}}} - s\sigma_{\Pi_{\text{eff}}}.$$

Our portfolio choice could be determined by maximizing this quantity. These two strategies are shown schematically in Figure 41.5.

Neither of these methods give satisfactory results when there is a risk-free investment among the assets and there are unrestricted short sales, since they result in infinite borrowing.

Another way of choosing the optimal portfolio is with the aid of a **utility function**. This approach is popular with economists. In Figure 41.6 I show **indifference curves** and the efficient frontier. The curves are called by this name because they are meant to represent lines along which the investor is indifferent to the risk/reward trade off. An investor wants high return, and low risk. Faced with portfolios A and B in the figure, he sees A with low return and low risk, but B has a better reward at the cost of greater risk. The investor is indifferent between these two. However, C is better than both of them, being on a preferred curve.

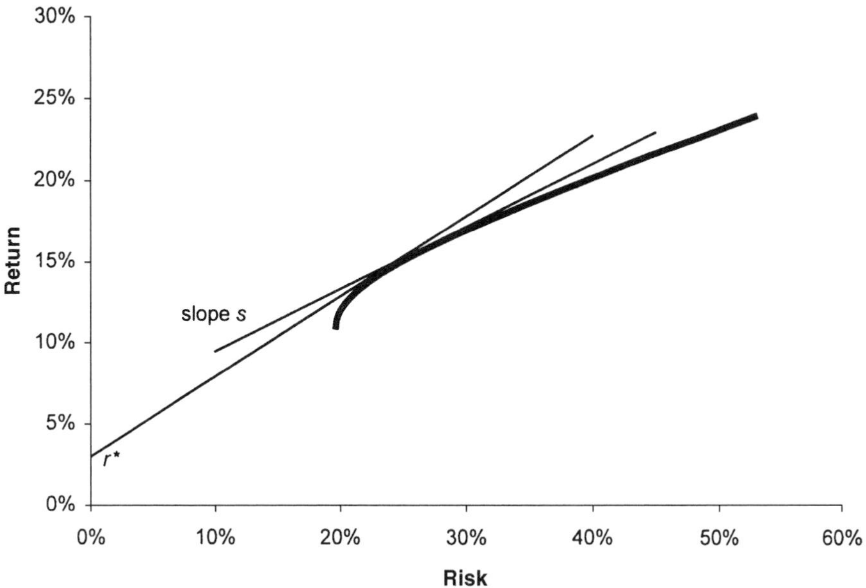

Figure 41.5 Two simple ways for choosing the best efficient portfolio.

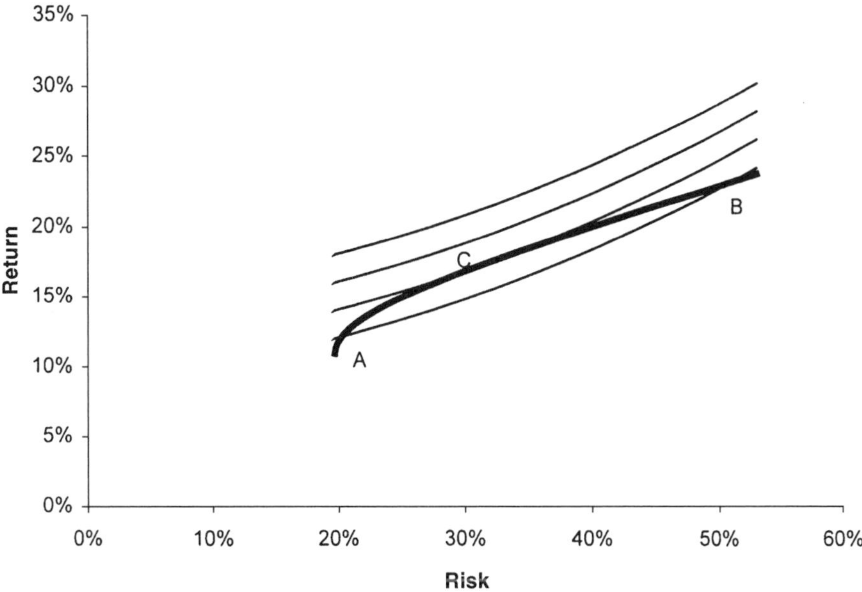

Figure 41.6 The efficient frontier and indifference curves.

41.6 MARKOWITZ IN PRACTICE

The inputs to the Markowitz model are expected returns, volatilities and correlations. With N assets this means $N + N + N(N - 1)/2$ parameters. Most of these cannot be known accurately (do they even exist?), only the volatilities are at all reliable. Having input these parameters, we must optimize over all weights of assets in the portfolio: choose a portfolio risk and find the weights that make the return on the portfolio a maximum subject to this volatility. This is a very time-consuming process computationally unless one only has a small number of assets.

The problem with the practical implementation of this model was one of the reasons for development of the simpler model of the next section.

41.7 CAPITAL ASSET PRICING MODEL AND ARBITRAGE PRICING THEORY

Before discussing the **Capital Asset Pricing Model** or **CAPM** we must introduce the idea of a security's beta. The beta, β_i, of an asset relative to a portfolio M is the ratio of the covariance between the return on the security and the return on the portfolio to the variance of the portfolio. Thus

$$\beta_i = \frac{\mathrm{Cov}[R_i R_M]}{\mathrm{Var}[R_M]}.$$

41.7.1 The Single-index Model

I will now build up a **single-index model** and describe extensions later. I will relate the return on all assets to the return on a representative index, M. This index is usually taken to be a wide-ranging stock market index in the single-index model. We write the return on the ith asset as

$$R_i = \alpha_i + \beta_i R_M + \varepsilon_i.$$

Using this representation we can see that the return on an asset can be decomposed into three parts: a constant drift, a random part common with the index M and a random part uncorrelated with the index, ε_i. The random part ε_i is unique to the ith asset, and has mean zero. Notice how all the assets are related to the index M but are otherwise completely uncorrelated. In Figure 41.7 is shown a plot of returns on Walt Disney stock against returns on the S&P500; α and β can be determined from a linear regression analysis. The data used in this plot ran from January 1985 until almost the end of 1997.

The expected return on the index will be denoted by μ_M and its standard deviation by σ_M. The expected return on the ith asset is then

$$\mu_i = \alpha_i + \beta_i \mu_i$$

and the standard deviation

$$\sigma_i = \sqrt{\beta_i^2 \sigma_M^2 + e_i^2}$$

where e_i is the standard deviation of ε_i.

If we have a portfolio of such assets then the return is given by

$$\frac{\delta\Pi}{\Pi} = \sum_{i=1}^{N} W_i R_i = \left(\sum_{i=1}^{N} W_i \alpha_i\right) + R_M \left(\sum_{i=1}^{N} W_i \beta_i\right) + \sum_{i=1}^{N} W_i \varepsilon_i.$$

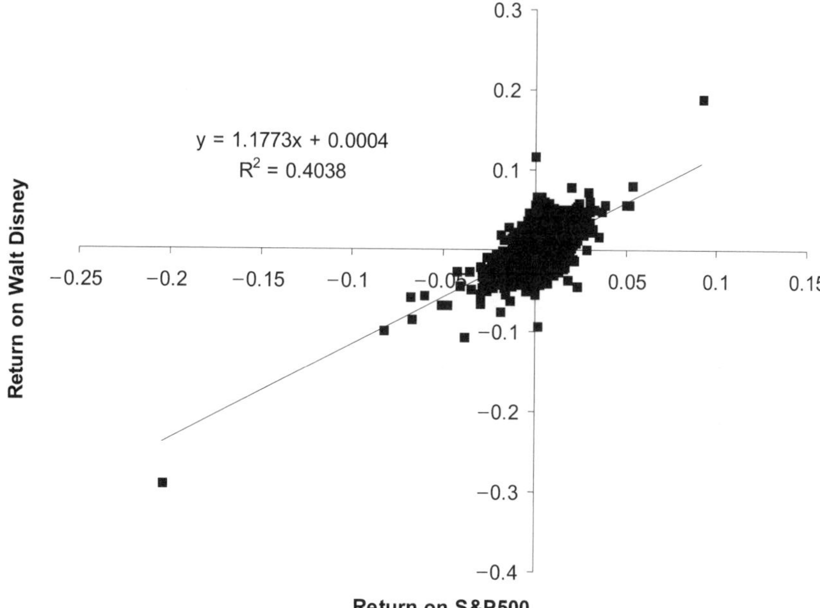

Figure 41.7 Returns on Walt Disney stock against returns on the S&P500.

From this it follows that

$$\mu_\Pi = \left(\sum_{i=1}^{N} W_i \alpha_i\right) + E[R_M]\left(\sum_{i=1}^{N} W_i \beta_i\right).$$

Let us write

$$\alpha_\Pi = \sum_{i=1}^{N} W_i \alpha_i \quad \text{and} \quad \beta_\Pi = \sum_{i=1}^{N} W_i \beta_i,$$

so that

$$\mu_\Pi = \alpha_\Pi + \beta_\Pi E[R_M] = \alpha_\Pi + \beta_\Pi \mu_M.$$

Similarly the risk in Π is measured by

$$\sigma_\Pi = \sqrt{\sum_{i=1}^{N}\sum_{j=1}^{N} W_i W_j \beta_i \beta_j \sigma_M^2 + \sum_{i=1}^{N} W_i^2 e_i^2}.$$

If the weights are all about the same, N^{-1}, then the final terms inside the square root are also $O(N^{-1})$. Thus this expression is, to leading order as $N \to \infty$,

$$\sigma_\Pi = \left|\sum_{i=1}^{N} W_i \beta_i\right| \sigma_M = |\beta_\Pi| \sigma_M.$$

Observe that the contribution from the uncorrelated εs to the portfolio vanishes as we increase the number of assets in the portfolio: the risk associated with the εs is called **diversifiable risk**. The remaining risk, which is correlated with the index, is called **systematic risk**.

41.7.2 Choosing the Optimal Portfolio

The principal is the same as the Markowitz model for optimal portfolio choice. The only difference is that there are a lot fewer parameters to be input, and the computation is a lot faster.

The procedure is as follows. Choose a value for the portfolio return μ_Π. Subject to this constraint, minimize σ_Π. Repeat this minimization for different portfolio returns to obtain efficient frontier. The position on this curve is then a subjective choice.

41.8 THE MULTI-INDEX MODEL

The model presented above is a single-index model. The idea can be extended to include further representative indices. For example, as well as an index representing the stock market one might include an index representing bond markets, an index representing currency markets or even an economic index if it is believed to be relevant in linking assets. In the multi-index model we write each asset's return as

$$R_i = \alpha_i + \sum_{j=1}^{n} \beta_{ji} R_j + \varepsilon_i,$$

where there are n indices with return R_j. The indices can be correlated to each other. Similar results to the single-index model follow.

It is usually not worth having more than three or four indices. The fewer the parameters, the more robust will be the model. At the other extreme is the Markowitz model with one index per asset.

41.9 COINTEGRATION

Whether you use MPT or CAPM you will always worry about the accuracy of your parameters. Both of these methods are only as accurate as the input data, CAPM being more reliable than MPT generally speaking, because it has fewer parameters.

There is another method which is gaining popularity, and which I will describe here briefly. It is unfortunately a complex technique requiring sophisticated statistical analysis (to do it properly) but which at its core makes a lot of sense. Instead of asking whether two series are correlated we ask whether they are **cointegrated**.

Two stocks may be perfectly correlated over short timescales yet diverge in the long run, with one growing and the other decaying. Conversely, two stocks may follow each other, never being more than a certain distance apart, but with any correlation, positive, negative or varying. If we are delta hedging then maybe the short timescale correlation matters, but not if we are holding stocks for a long time in an unhedged portfolio. To see whether two stocks stay close together we need a definition of **stationarity**. A time series is stationary if it has finite and constant mean, standard deviation and autocorrelation function. Stocks, which tend to grow, are not stationary. In a sense, stationary series do not wander too far from their mean.

We can see the difference between stationary and non-stationary with our first coin tossing experiment. The time series given by 1 every time we throw a head and -1 every time we throw a tail is stationary. It has a mean of zero, a standard deviation of 1 and an autocorrelation function that is zero for any non-zero lag. But what if we add up the results, as we might do if we are betting on each toss? This time series is non-stationary. This is because the standard deviation of the sum grows like the square root of the number of throws. The mean may be zero but the sum is wandering further and further away from that mean.

Testing for the stationarity of a time series X_t involves a linear regression to find the coefficients a, b and c in

$$X_t = aX_{t-1} + b + ct.$$

If it is found that $|a| > 1$ then the series is unstable. If $-1 \leq a < 1$ then the series is stationary. If $a = 1$ then the series is non-stationary. As with all things statistical, we can only say that our value for a is accurate with a certain degree of confidence. To decide whether we have got a stationary or non-stationary series requires us to look at the Dickey–Fuller statistic to estimate the degree of confidence in our result. From this point on the subject of cointegration gets complicated.

How is this useful in finance? Even though individual stock prices might be non-stationary it is possible for a linear combination (i.e. a portfolio) to be stationary. Can we find λ_i, with $\sum_{i=1}^{N} \lambda_i = 1$, such that

$$\sum_{i=1}^{N} \lambda_i S_i$$

is stationary? If we can, then we say that the stocks are cointegrated.

For example, suppose we find that the S&P500 is cointegrated with a portfolio of 15 stocks. We can then use these fifteen stocks to **track the index**. The error in this tracking portfolio will have constant mean and standard deviation, so should not wander too far from its average. This is clearly easier than using all 500 stocks for the tracking (when, of course, the tracking error would be zero).

We don't have to track the index, we could track anything we want, such as $e^{0.2t}$ to choose a portfolio that gets a 20% return. Clearly there are similarities with MPT and CAPM in concepts such as means and standard deviations. The important difference is that cointegration assumes far fewer properties for the individual time series. Most importantly, volatility and correlation do not appear explicitly.

41.10 PERFORMANCE MEASUREMENT

If one has followed one of the asset allocation strategies outlined above, or just traded on gut instinct, can one tell how well one has done? Were the outstanding results because of an uncanny natural instinct, or were the awful results simply bad luck?

The ideal performance would be one for which returns outperformed the risk-free rate, but *in a consistent* fashion. Not only is it important to get a high return from portfolio management, but one must achieve this with as little randomness as possible.

The two commonest measures of 'return per unit risk' are the **Sharpe ratio** of 'reward to variability' and the **Treynor ratio** of 'reward to volatility'. These are defined as follows:

$$\text{Sharpe ratio} = \frac{\mu_\Pi - r}{\sigma_\Pi}$$

and

$$\text{Treynor ratio} = \frac{\mu_\Pi - r}{\beta_\Pi}.$$

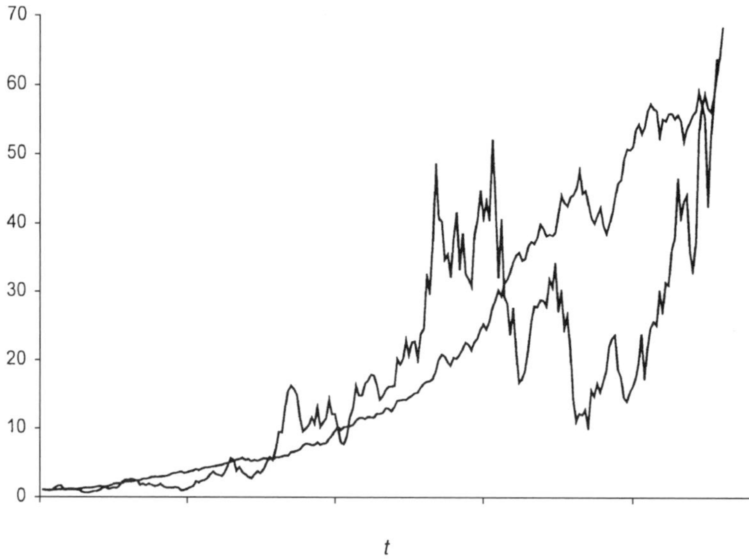

Figure 41.8 A good and a bad manager; same returns, different variablity.

In these μ_Π and σ_Π are the *realized* return and standard deviation for the portfolio over the period. The β_Π is a measure of the portfolio's volatility. The Sharpe ratio is usually used when the portfolio is the whole of one's investment and the Treynor ratio when one is examining the performance of one component of the whole firm's portfolio, say. When the portfolio under examination is highly diversified the two measures are the same (up to a factor of the market standard deviation).

In Figure 41.8 we see the portfolio value against time for a good manager and a bad manager.

41.11 SUMMARY

Portfolio management and asset allocation are about taking risks in return for a reward. The questions are how to decide how much risk to take, and how to get the best return. But derivatives theory is based on not taking any risk at all, and so I have spent little time on portfolio management in the book. On the other hand, as I have stressed, there is so much uncertainty in the subject of finance that elimination of risk is well-nigh impossible and the ideas behind portfolio management should be appreciated by anyone involved in derivatives theory or practice. I have tried to give the flavor of the subject with only the easiest-to-explain mathematics; the following sources will prove useful to anyone wanting to pursue the subject further.

FURTHER READING

- The classic reference texts on Blackjack are by Thorp (1962) and Wong (1981).
- See Markowitz's original book for all the details of MPT, Markowitz (1959).

- One of the best texts on investments, including chapters on portfolio management, is Sharpe (1985).
- For a description of cointegration and other techniques in econometrics see Hamilton (1994) and Hendry (1995).
- See Farrell (1997) for further discussion of portfolio performance.
- I have not discussed the subject of continuous-time asset allocation here, but the elegant subject is explained nicely in the collection of Robert Merton's papers, Merton (1992).
- Transaction costs can have a big effect on portfolios that are supposed to be continuously rebalanced. See Morton & Pliska (1995) for a model with costs, and Atkinson & Wilmott (1995), Atkinson, Pliska & Wilmott (1997) and Atkinson & Al–Ali (1997) for asymptotic results.
- For a description of chaos-based methods in finance, and how they won the First International Nonlinear Financial Forecasting Competition, see Alexander & Giblin (1997).
- For a review of current thinking in risk management see Alexander (1998).

EXERCISES

1. Work out the efficient frontier for the following set of assets:

Asset	μ	σ
A	0.08	0.12
B	0.10	0.12
C	0.10	0.15
D	0.14	0.20

   The correlation coefficients between the four assets are given by

$$\rho = \begin{pmatrix} 1 & 0.2 & 0.5 & 0.3 \\ 0.2 & 1 & 0.7 & 0.4 \\ 0.5 & 0.7 & 1 & 0.9 \\ 0.3 & 0.4 & 0.9 & 1 \end{pmatrix}.$$

2. Find the efficient frontier for the assets in the table above, when asset D is replaced by a risk-free asset, E, which has a mean of 0.10 over our time horizon of two years. Asset E is uncorrelated with the other assets.
3. Where should we be on the efficient frontier in Question 1 if we wish to minimize the chance of a return less than 0.05?
4. What are the economic significances of α and β in the Capital Asset Pricing Model and how are they measured or estimated in practice?

CHAPTER 42
value at risk

In this Chapter...

- the meaning of VaR
- how VaR is calculated in practice
- some of the difficulties associated with VaR for portfolios containing derivatives

42.1 INTRODUCTION

It is the mark of a prudent investor, be they a major bank with billions of dollars' worth of assets or a pensioner with just a few hundred, that they have some idea of the possible losses that may result from the typical movements of the financial markets. Having said that, there have been well-publicized examples where the institution had no idea what might result from some of their more exotic transactions, often involving derivatives.

As part of the search for more transparency in investments, there has grown up the concept of Value at Risk as a measure of the possible downside from an investment or portfolio.

42.2 DEFINITION OF VALUE AT RISK

One of the definitions of **Value at Risk** (VaR), and the definition now commonly intended, is the following.

> Value at Risk is an estimate, with a given degree of confidence, of how much one can lose from one's portfolio over a given time horizon.

The portfolio can be that of a single trader, with VaR measuring the risk that he is taking with the firm's money, or it can be the portfolio of the entire firm. The former measure will be of interest in calculating the trader's efficiency and the latter will be of interest to the owners of the firm who will want to know the likely effect of stock market movements on the bottom line.

The degree of confidence is typically set at 95%, 97.5%, 99% etc. The time horizon of interest may be one day, say, for trading activities or months for portfolio management. It is supposed to be the timescale associated with the orderly liquidation of the portfolio, meaning the sale of assets at a sufficiently low rate for the sale to have little effect on the market. Thus the VaR is an estimate of a loss that can be realized, not just a 'paper' loss.

As an example of VaR, we may calculate (by the methods to be described here) that over the next week there is a 95% probability that we will lose no more than \$10m. We can write this as

$$\text{Prob}\,\{\delta V \le -\$10\text{m}\} = 0.05,$$

where δV is the change in the portfolio's value. (I use $\delta\cdot$ for 'the change in' to emphasize that we are considering changes over a finite time.) In symbols,

$$\text{Prob}\,\{\delta V \le -\text{VaR}\} = 1 - c,$$

where the degree of confidence is c, 95% in the above example.

VaR is calculated assuming normal market circumstances, meaning that extreme market conditions such as crashes are not considered, or are examined separately. Thus, effectively, VaR measures what can be expected to happen during the day-to-day operation of an institution.

The calculation of VaR requires at least having the following data: the current prices of all assets in the portfolio and their volatilities and the correlations between them. If the assets are traded we can take the prices from the market (**marking to market**). For OTC contracts we must use some 'approved' model for the prices, such as a Black–Scholes-type model, this is then **marking to model**. Usually, one assumes that the movement of the components of the portfolio are random and drawn from Normal distributions. I make that assumption here, but make a few general comments later on.

For more information about VaR and data sets for volatilities and correlations see www.jpmorgan.com and links therein.

42.3 VaR FOR A SINGLE ASSET

Let us begin by estimating the VaR for a portfolio consisting of a single asset.

We hold a quantity Δ of a stock with price S and volatility σ. We want to know with 99% certainty what is the maximum we can lose over the next week. I am deliberately using notation similar to that from the derivatives world, but there Δ would be the number held *short* in a hedged portfolio. Here Δ is the number held long.

In Figure 42.1 is the distribution of possible returns over the time horizon of one week. How do we calculate the VaR? First of all we are assuming that the distribution is Normal. Since the time horizon is so small, we can reasonably assume that the mean is zero. The standard deviation of the stock price over this time horizon is

$$\sigma S \left(\frac{1}{52}\right)^{1/2},$$

since the timestep is 1/52 of a year. Finally, we must calculate the position of the extreme left-hand tail of this distribution corresponding to $1\% = (100 - 99)\%$ of the events. We only need do this for the standardized Normal distribution because we can get to any other Normal distribution by scaling. Referring to Table 42.1, we see that the 99% confidence interval corresponds to 2.33 standard deviations from the mean. Since we hold a number Δ of the stock, the VaR is given by $2.33\sigma\Delta S(1/52)^{1/2}$.

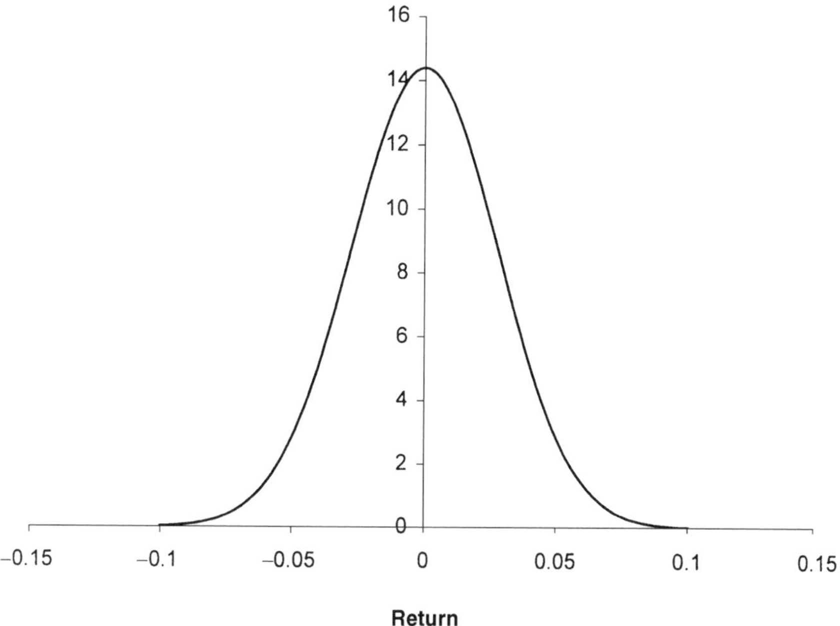

Figure 42.1 The distribution of future stock returns.

Table 42.1 Degree of confidence and the relationship with deviation from the mean.

Degree of confidence	Number of standard deviations from the mean
99%	2.326342
98%	2.053748
97%	1.88079
96%	1.750686
95%	1.644853
90%	1.281551

More generally, if the time horizon is δt and the required degree of confidence is c, we have

$$\mathrm{VaR} = -\sigma\Delta S(\delta t)^{1/2}\alpha(1-c), \tag{42.1}$$

where is $\alpha(\cdot)$ is the inverse cumulative distribution function for the standardized Normal distribution, shown in Figure 42.2.

In (42.1) we have assumed that the return on the asset is Normally distributed *with a mean of zero*. The assumption of zero mean is valid for short time horizons: the standard deviation of the return scales with the square root of time but the mean scales with time itself. For longer time horizons, the return is shifted to the right (one hopes) by an amount proportional to the

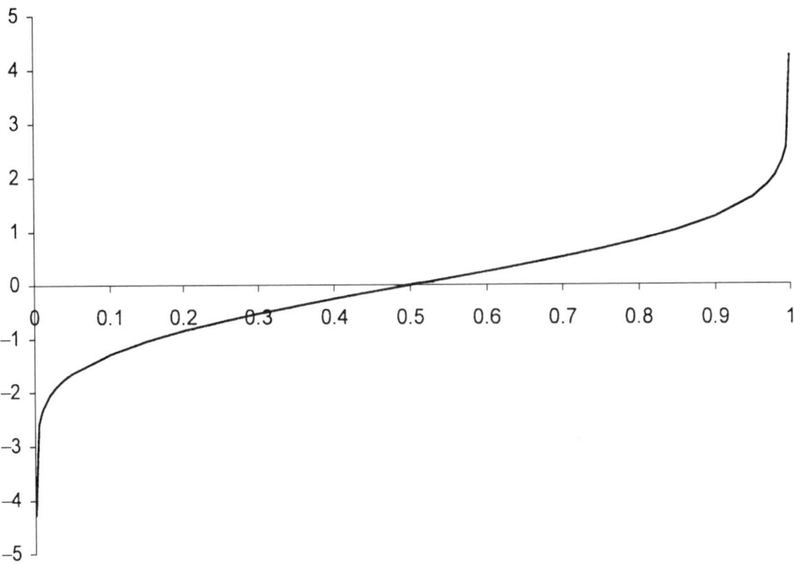

Figure 42.2 The inverse cumulative distribution function for the standardized Normal distribution.

time horizon. Thus for longer timescales, expression (42.1) should be modified to account for the drift of the asset value. If the rate of this drift is μ then (42.1) becomes

$$\mathrm{VaR} = \Delta S(\mu\,\delta t - \sigma\,\delta t^{1/2}\alpha(1-c)).$$

Note that I use the *real* drift rate and not the *risk-neutral*. I shall not worry about this adjustment for the rest of this chapter.

42.4 VaR FOR A PORTFOLIO

If we know the volatilities of all the assets in our portfolio and the correlations between them then we can calculate the VaR for the whole portfolio.

If the volatility of the ith asset is σ_i and the correlation between the ith and jth assets is ρ_{ij} (with $\rho_{ii} = 1$), then the VaR for the portfolio consisting of M assets with a holding of Δ_i of the ith asset is

$$-\alpha(1-c)\delta t^{1/2}\sqrt{\sum_{j=1}^{M}\sum_{i=1}^{M}\Delta_i\Delta_j\sigma_i\sigma_j\rho_{ij}}.$$

Several obvious criticisms can be made of this definition of VaR: returns are not Normal, volatilities and correlations are notoriously difficult to measure, and it does not allow for derivatives in the portfolio. We discuss the first criticism later; I now describe in some detail ways of incorporating derivatives into the calculation.

42.5 VaR FOR DERIVATIVES

The key point about estimating VaR for a portfolio containing derivatives is that, even if the change in the underlying *is* Normal, the essential nonlinearity in derivatives means that the change in the derivative can be far from Normal. Nevertheless, if we are concerned with very small movements in the underlying, for example over a very short time horizon, we may be able to approximate for the sensitivity of the portfolio to changes in the underlying by the option's delta. For larger movements we may need to take a higher order approximation. We see these approaches and pitfalls next.

42.5.1 The Delta Approximation

Consider for a moment a portfolio of derivatives with a single underlying, S. The sensitivity of an option, or a portfolio of options, to the underlying is the delta, Δ. If the standard deviation of the distribution of the underlying is $\sigma S \delta t^{1/2}$ then the standard deviation of the distribution of the option position is

$$\sigma S \delta t^{1/2} \Delta.$$

Δ must here be the delta of the whole position, the sensitivity of all of the relevant options to the particular underlying, i.e. the sum of the deltas of all the option positions on the same underlying.

It is but a small, and obvious, step to the following estimate for the VaR of a portfolio containing options:

$$-\alpha(1-c)\delta t^{1/2} \sqrt{\sum_{j=1}^{M} \sum_{i=1}^{M} \Delta_i \Delta_j \sigma_i \sigma_j \rho_{ij}}.$$

Here Δ_i is the rate of change of the *portfolio* with respect to the ith asset.

42.5.2 The Delta-Gamma Approximation

The delta approximation is satisfactory for small movements in the underlying. A better approximation may be achieved by going to higher order and incorporating the gamma or convexity effect.

I demonstrate this by example. Suppose that our portfolio consists of an option on a stock. The relationship between the change in the underlying, δS, and the change in the value of the option, δV, is

$$\delta V = \frac{\partial V}{\partial S}\delta S + \frac{1}{2}\frac{\partial^2 V}{\partial S^2}(\delta S)^2 + \frac{\partial V}{\partial t}\delta t + \cdots.$$

Since we are assuming that

$$\delta S = \mu S\, \delta t + \sigma S\, \delta t^{1/2} \phi,$$

where ϕ is drawn from a standardized Normal distribution, we can write

$$\delta V = \frac{\partial V}{\partial S}\sigma S\, \delta t^{1/2}\phi + \delta t \left(\frac{\partial V}{\partial S}\mu S + \frac{1}{2}\frac{\partial^2 V}{\partial S^2}\sigma^2 S^2 \phi^2 + \frac{\partial V}{\partial t} \right) + \cdots.$$

This can be rewritten as

$$\delta V = \Delta \sigma S\, \delta t^{1/2} \phi + \delta t \left(\Delta \mu S + \tfrac{1}{2}\Gamma \sigma^2 S^2 \phi^2 + \Theta \right) + \cdots. \tag{42.2}$$

To leading order, the randomness in the option value is simply proportional to that in the underlying. To the next order there is a deterministic shift in δV due to the deterministic drift of S and the theta of the option. More importantly, however, the effect of the gamma is to introduce a term that is nonlinear in the random component of δS.

In Figure 42.3 are shown three pictures. First, there is the assumed distribution for the change in the underlying. This is a Normal distribution with standard deviation $\sigma S\,\delta t^{1/2}$, drawn in bold in the figure. Second, is shown the distribution for the change in the option assuming the delta approximation only. This is a Normal distribution with standard deviation $\Delta\sigma S\,\delta t^{1/2}$. Finally, there is the distribution for the change in the underlying assuming the delta/gamma approximation.

From this figure we can see that the distribution for the delta/gamma approximation is far from Normal. In fact, because expression (42.2) is quadratic in ϕ, δV must satisfy the following constraint

$$\delta V \geq -\frac{\Delta^2}{2\Gamma} \quad \text{if} \quad \Gamma > 0$$

or

$$\delta V \leq -\frac{\Delta^2}{2\Gamma} \quad \text{if} \quad \Gamma < 0.$$

The extreme value is attained when

$$\phi = -\frac{\Delta}{\sigma S\Gamma\,\delta t^{1/2}}.$$

The question to ask is then 'Is this critical value for ϕ in the part of the tail in which we are interested?' If it is not then the delta approximation may be satisfactory, otherwise it will not be. If we cannot use an approximation we may have to run simulations using valuation formulae.

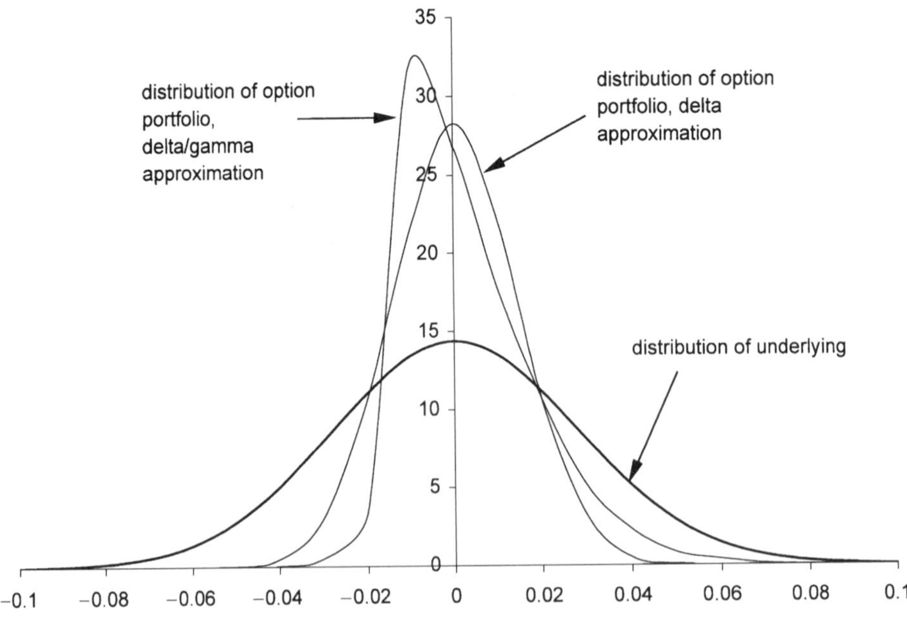

Figure 42.3 A Normal distribution for the change in the underlying (bold), the distribution for the change in the option assuming the delta approximation (another Normal distribution) and the distribution for the change in the option assuming the delta/gamma approximation (definitely not a Normal distribution).

One obvious conclusion to be drawn is that positive gamma is good for a portfolio and negative gamma is bad. With a positive gamma the downside is limited, but with a negative gamma it is the upside that is limited.

42.5.3 Use of Valuation Models

The obvious way around the problems associated with nonlinear instruments is to use a simulation for the random behavior of the underlyings and then use valuation formulae or algorithms to deduce the distribution of the changes in the whole portfolio. This is the ultimate solution to the problem but has the disadvantage that it can be very slow. After all, we may want to run tens of thousands of simulations but if we must solve a multifactor partial differential equation each time then we find that it will take far too long to calculate the VaR.

42.5.4 Fixed-income Portfolios

When the asset or portfolio has interest rate dependence then it is usual to treat the yield to maturity on each instrument as the Normally distributed variable. Yields on different instruments are then suitably correlated. The relationship of price to change in yield is via duration (and convexity at higher order). So our fixed-income asset can be thought of as a derivative of the yield. The VaR is then estimated using duration in place of delta (and convexity in place of gamma) in the obvious way.

42.6 SIMULATIONS

The two simulation methods described in this book are **Monte Carlo**, based on the generation of Normally distributed random numbers, and **bootstrapping** using actual asset price movements taken from historical data.

Within these two simulation methods, there are two ways to generate future scenarios, depending on the timescale of interest and the timescale for one's model or data. If one is interested in a horizon of one year and one has a model or data for returns with this same horizon, then this is easily used to generate a distribution of future scenarios. On the other hand, if the model or data is for a shorter timescale, a stochastic differential equation or daily data, say, and the horizon is one year, then the model must be used to build up a one-year distribution by generating whole year-long paths of the asset. This is more time consuming but is important for path-dependent contracts when the whole path taken must obviously be modeled.

Remember, the simulation must use *real* returns and not *risk-neutral*.

42.6.1 Monte Carlo

Monte Carlo simulation is the generation of a distribution of returns and/or asset price paths by the use of random numbers. This subject is discussed in great depth in Chapter 49. The technique can be applied to VaR: using numbers, ϕ, drawn from a Normal distribution, to build up a distribution of future scenarios. For each of these scenarios use some pricing methodology to calculate the value of a portfolio (of the underlying asset and its options) and thus directly estimate its VaR.

42.6.2 Bootstrapping

Another method for generating a series of random movements in assets is to use historical data. Again, there are two possible ways of generating future scenarios: a one-step procedure if you have a model for the distribution of returns over the required time horizon, or a multi-step procedure if you only have data/model for short periods and want to model a longer time horizon.

The data that we use will consist of daily returns, say, for all underlying assets going back several years. The data for each day is recorded as a vector, with one entry per asset.

Suppose we have real time-series data for N assets and that our data is daily data stretching back four years, resulting in approximately 1000 daily *returns* for each asset. We are going to use these returns for simulation purposes. This is done as follows.

Assign an 'index' to each daily change. That is, we assign 1000 numbers, one for each vector of returns. To visualize this, imagine writing the returns for all of the N assets on the blank pages of a notebook. On page 1 we write the changes in asset values that occurred from 8th July 1998 to 9th July 1998. On page 2 we do the same, but for the changes from 9th July to 10th July 1998. On page 3... from 10th to 11th July etc. We will fill 1000 pages if we have 1000 data sets. Now, draw a number from 1 to 1000, uniformly distributed; it is 534. Go to page 534 in the notebook. Change all assets from today's value by the vector of returns given on the page. Now draw another number between 1 and 1000 at random and repeat the process. Increment this new value again using one of the vectors. Continue this process until the required time horizon has been reached. This is one realization of the path of the assets. Repeat this simulation to generate many, many possible realizations to get an accurate distribution of all future prices.

By this method we generate a distribution of possible future scenarios based on historical data.

Note how we keep together all asset changes that happen on a certain date. By doing this we ensure that we capture any correlation that there may be between assets.

This method of bootstrapping is very simple to implement. The advantages of this method are that it naturally incorporates any correlation between assets, and any non-Normality in asset price changes. It does not capture any autocorrelation in the data, but then neither does a Monte Carlo simulation in its basic form. The main disadvantage is that it requires a lot of historical data that may correspond to completely different economic circumstances than those that currently apply.

In Figure 42.4 is shown the daily historical returns for several stocks and the 'index' used in the random choice.

42.7 USE OF VaR AS A PERFORMANCE MEASURE

One of the uses of VaR is in the measurement of performance of banks, desks or individual traders. In the past, 'trading talent' has been measured purely in terms of profit; a trader's bonus is related to that profit. This encourages traders to take risks. Think of tossing a coin with you receiving a percentage of the profit, but without the downside (which is taken by the bank), how much would you bet? A better measure of trading talent might take into account the risk in such a bet, and reward a good return-to-risk ratio. The ratio

$$\frac{\text{Return in excess of risk-free}}{\text{volatility}} = \frac{\mu - r}{\sigma},$$

	A	B	C	D	E	F	G	H	I	J	K	L	M
1	Index	Prob.	TELEBRAS	ELETROBRA	PETROBRAS	CVDR	USIMINAS	YPF	TAR	TEO	TGS	PEREZ	TELMEX
2	1	0.001	−0.0152210	0.0180185	0.0118345	−0.0240975	−0.0111733	0.0355909	0.0185764	0.0071943	0.0121214	−0.0182190	−0.0235305
3	2	0.001	0.0091604	0.0072214	−0.0046130	0.0001039	−0.0226244	0.0207620	0.0121953	0.0106953	0.0000000	−0.0026393	0.0327898
4	3	0.001	−0.0498546	−0.0397883	−0.0324353	−0.0246926	−0.0115608	0.0068260	−0.0121953	−0.0106953	0.0119762	−0.0067506	−0.0139213
5	4	0.001	−0.0357762	−0.0494712	−0.0358569	−0.1001323	−0.0602100	−0.0068260	−0.0123458	−0.0254097	0.0000000	−0.0144520	−0.0284379
6	5	0.001	0.0033058	−0.0204013	0.0112413	0.0264184	0.0114388	−0.0068729	0.0061920	0.0036697	−0.0240976	0.0096238	0.0000000
7	6	0.001	0.0424306	0.0260111	−0.0255043	−0.0022909	0.0004155	0.0067340	0.0452054	0.0438519	0.0115608	0.0140863	0.0421608
8	7	0.001	0.0279317	0.0006216	0.0006216	0.0006216	−0.0234759	0.0040080	−0.0208341	0.0000000	−0.0114287	0.0000000	0.0123205
9	8	0.001	−0.0139801	−0.0383626	−0.0346393	0.0161040	0.0122250	0.0000000	0.0259755	0.0176996	0.0114287	−0.0020299	0.0439192
10	9	0.001	−0.0052219	−0.0036563	0.0403377	0.0142520	0.0229896	0.0063898	0.0101524	0.0085349	0.0114287	−0.0019638	0.0000000
11	10	0.001	−0.0130693	0.0000000	−0.0116961	−0.0047282	0.0112996	0.0000000	0.0100503	0.0112677	0.0112996	0.0081304	−0.0267702
12	11	0.001	−0.0106656	−0.0148639	0.0069306	−0.0048541	−0.0114030	0.0000000	−0.0100503	−0.0169496	−0.0112996	−0.0166294	−0.0116960
13	12	0.001	0.0079035	0.0184167	−0.0023392	−0.0240975	0.0112996	0.0000000	−0.0050633	−0.0085837	0.0335227	−0.0170073	0.0039139
14	13	0.001	0.0000000	−0.0072225	−0.0284021	0.0001035	−0.0226248	0.0000000	−0.0257084	−0.0380719	−0.0110498	−0.0063762	0.0000000
15	14	0.001	0.0000000	−0.0042230	0.0242792	−0.0004134	−0.0126835	−0.0061920	0.0100001	0.0057471	0.0109291	0.0144183	0.0411581
16	15	0.001	−0.0475377	−0.0138620	−0.0251059	−0.0444106	−0.0254146	−0.0062305	−0.0150379	−0.0057471	0.0000000	0.0300138	−0.0080972
17	16	0.001	0.0297428	0.0102652	0.0114445	0.0714950	−0.0008256	0.0415490	0.0277796	0.0309303	0.0408220	−0.0035537	0.0419109
18	17	0.001	−0.0037045	−0.0192060	−0.0248187	0.0078541	−0.0129914	−0.0116280	−0.0045977	0.0052771	0.0000000	0.0007187	−0.0075758
19	18	0.001	−0.0208341	−0.0205823	−0.0264421	−0.0021947	−0.0267507	0.0231224	0.0091744	−0.0052771	−0.0304592	0.0152095	−0.0269766
20	19	0.001	0.0568874	0.0828276	0.1052577	0.0477150	0.0612661	0.0271019	0.0753494	0.0746435	0.0388398	0.0599762	0.0498324
21	20	0.001	0.0655911	0.0209154	0.0209922	0.0420456	0.0224756	−0.0173917	0.0165293	0.0223058	0.0000000	0.0232360	0.0036036
22	21	0.001	−0.0091109	0.0309987	0.0615672	−0.0428678	0.0221646	0.0058309	0.0122201	0.0145988	0.0392207	0.0139353	−0.0592766
23	22	0.001	0.0231470	−0.0036810	−0.0003084	0.0158210	0.0099482	0.0342891	0.0160646	0.0264121	0.0204089	0.0208262	0.0679507
24	23	0.001	0.0157998	−0.0014713	−0.0122804	−0.0094697	−0.0014375	0.0277026	0.0504962	0.0440396	0.0492710	0.0285456	−0.0073260
25	24	0.001	−0.0045147	−0.0054003	−0.0008614	−0.0020500	0.0379553	−0.0054795	−0.0191210	−0.0136988	0.0000000	0.0101176	−0.0073801
26	25	0.001	0.0270287	0.0275012	0.0583711	0.0001022	0.0361421	0.0280130	−0.0038536	0.0069849	0.0000000	0.0034104	−0.0109690
27	26	0.001	−0.0089286	0.0068362	0.0038686	0.0248968	−0.0087868	0.0000000	−0.0116506	−0.0093241	0.0000000	0.0110554	−0.0036832
28	27	0.001	0.0133632	0.0232183	0.0512933	0.0202027	0.0436750	−0.0167135	−0.0117880	−0.0285055	−0.0099503	−0.0080555	0.0000000
29	28	0.001	−0.0110341	0.0417395	0.0176995	0.0506932	0.0085108	0.0000000	−0.0240012	−0.0268636	0.0000000	0.0005324	0.0000000
30	29	0.001	−0.0044544	−0.0289144	0.0069770	−0.0002423	−0.0002043	−0.0056023	0.0000000	0.0024907	0.0000000	−0.0037901	0.0000000
31	30	0.001	0.0044544	0.0001022	−0.0344781	−0.0075315	0.0086859	0.0056023	0.0202027	0.0049628	0.0204089	0.0147792	0.0038241
32	31	0.001	−0.0044544	−0.0065956	−0.0225751	0.0151071	−0.0173439	0.0111112	−0.0040080	0.0024722	0.0396091	0.0090663	−0.0115164
33	32	0.001	0.0088685	−0.0067409	0.0284793	0.0204063	0.0261791	0.0096270	0.0043197	−0.0052632	0.0000000	0.0184492	−0.0076923
34	33	0.001	−0.0178163	−0.0084174	0.0036982	0.0183391	−0.0186661	−0.0242436	−0.0350913	−0.0240332	−0.0202027	−0.0280518	−0.0234386
35	34	0.001	−0.0205219	−0.0174839	−0.0199091	−0.0849882	−0.0120831	−0.0061539	−0.0134834	−0.0108697	0.0000000	−0.0075047	0.0039448
36	35	0.001	−0.0092167	0.0172806	0.0323986	0.0769500	−0.0145534	−0.0313505	−0.0368705	−0.0221003	0.0202027	−0.0096608	−0.0320027
37	36	0.001	−0.0256977	−0.0470936	−0.0464976	−0.0325785	−0.0460766	−0.0128207	−0.0189579	−0.0340942	−0.0100503	−0.0547012	−0.0081633

Figure 42.4 Spreadsheet showing bootstrap data.

the **Sharpe ratio**, is such a measure. Alternatively, use VaR as the measure of risk and profit/loss as the measure of return:

$$\frac{\text{daily P\&L}}{\text{daily VaR}}.$$

42.8 SUMMARY

The estimation of downside potential in any portfolio is clearly very important. Not having an idea of this could lead to the disappearance of a bank, and has. In practice, it is more important to the managers in banks, and not the traders. What do they care if their bank collapses as long as they can walk into a new job?

I have shown the simplest ways of estimating Value at Risk, but the subject gets much more complicated. 'Complicated' is not the right word, 'messy' and 'time-consuming' are better. And currently there are many software vendors, banks and academics touting their own versions in the hope of becoming the market standard. In Chapter 45 we'll see a few of these in more detail.

FURTHER READING

- See Lawrence (1996) for the application of the Value at Risk methodology to derivatives.
- See Chew (1996) for a wide ranging discussion of risk management issues and details of important real-life VaR 'crises.'
- See Jorion (1997) for further information about the mathematics of Value at Risk.
- The allocation of bank capital is addressed in Matten (1996).
- Alexander & Leigh (1997) and Alexander (1997 a) discuss the estimation of covariance matrices for VaR.
- Artzner, Delbaen, Eber & Heath (1997) discuss the properties that a sensible VaR model must possess.

EXERCISES

1. Assuming a Normal distribution, what percentage of returns are outside the negative two standard deviations from the mean? What is the mean of returns falling in this tail? (This is called the **censored mean**.)
2. What criticisms of Value at Risk as described here can you think of? Consider distributions other than Normal, discontinuous paths and nonlinear instruments.

CHAPTER 43
credit risk

In this Chapter...

- models for default based on the 'value of the firm'
- modeling the value of a firm based on measurable parameters and variables
- models for instantaneous and exogenous risk of default
- stochastic risk of default and implied risk of default
- credit ratings
- how to model change of rating
- how to model risk of default in convertible bonds

43.1 INTRODUCTION

So far, the products on which we have concentrated have all had cash flows that are *guaranteed*. We have assumed that these cashflows, coupons, payoffs and redemption values, are from a completely creditworthy source or underwritten in such a way that the income is certain. Options bought through an exchange are usually considered free of the risk of default because of the way that exchanges are underwritten, and partly because of the requirement for a margin to be deposited.

In practice, many bonds have no such guarantee. Perhaps they are issued by a company as a form of borrowing for expansion. In this case, the issuing company may declare bankruptcy before all of the cashflows have been paid. Alternatively, they may be issued by a government with a record for irregular payment of debt. Over the counter (OTC) options can have significant counterparty risks. For this reason there has grown up over the past decade a considerable body of rules and regulations governing **capital adequacy**, to ensure that banks are covered in the event of extreme market movements that might otherwise lead to collapse (see Chapter 42 on Value at Risk).

In this chapter we discuss the subject of modeling when there is **risk of default** or **credit risk**. There are two main approaches to the modeling of default. One revolves around modeling the value of the issuing firm (or country). The other models an exogenous risk of default. Later I describe the rating service provided by Standard & Poor's and Moody's, for example. These ratings provide a published estimate of the relative creditworthiness of firms.

43.2 RISKY BONDS

If you are a company wanting to expand, but without the necessary capital, you could borrow the capital, intending to pay it back with interest at some time in the future. There is a chance,

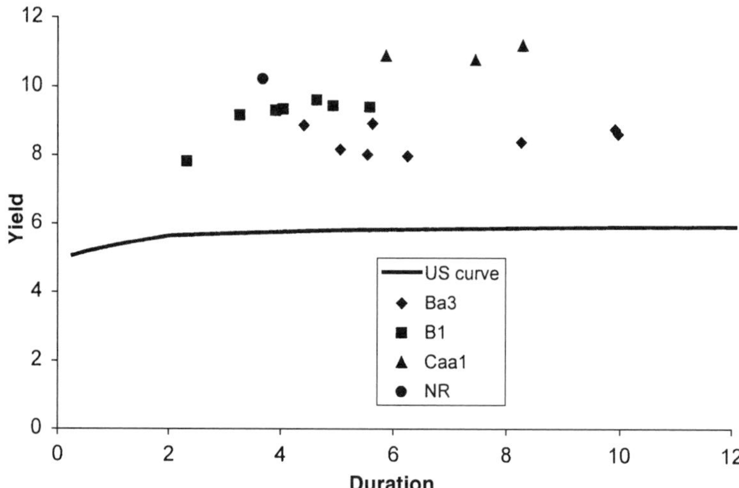

Figure 43.1 Yield *versus* duration for some risky bonds.

however, that before you pay off the debt the company may have got into financial difficulties or even gone bankrupt. If this happens, the debt may never be paid off. Because of this risk of default, the lender will require a significantly higher interest rate than if he were lending to a very reliable borrower such as the US government.

The real situation is, of course, more complicated than this. In practice it is not just a case of all or nothing. This brings us to the ideas of the seniority of debt and the partial payment of debt.

Firms typically issue bonds with a legal ranking, determining which of the bonds take priority in the event of bankruptcy or inability to repay. The higher the priority, the more likely the debt is to be repaid, the higher the bond value and the lower its yield. In the event of bankruptcy there is typically a long, drawn out battle over which creditors get paid. It is usual, even after many years, for creditors to get *some* of their money back. Then the question is how much and how soon? It is also possible for the repayment to be another risky bond, this would correspond to a refinancing of the debt. For example, the debt could not be paid off at the planned time so instead a new bond gets issued entitling the holder to an amount further in the future.

In Figure 43.1 is shown the yield *versus* duration, calculated by the methods of Chapter 31, for some risky bonds. In this figure the bonds have been ranked according to their estimated riskiness. We will discuss this later; for the moment you just need to know that Ba3 is considered to be less risky than Caa1 and this is reflected in its smaller yield spread over the risk-free curve.

The problem that we examine in this chapter is the modeling of the risk of default and thus the fair value of risky bonds. Conversely, if we know the value of a bond, does this tell us anything about the likelihood of default?

43.3 MODELING DEFAULT

The models that I describe here fall into two categories, those for which the likelihood of default depends on the behavior of the issuing firm and those for which the likelihood of default is exogenous. The former is appealing because it is clearly closer to reality. The downside is that these models are usually more complicated to solve, with parameters that are difficult to measure. I describe the most popular such model and then describe a similar model, one with more easily-measured parameters.

The instantaneous risk of default models are simpler to use and are therefore the most popular type of credit risk models. In its simplest form the time at which default occurs is completely exogenous. For example, we could roll a die once a month, and when a 1 is thrown the company defaults. This illustrates the exogeneity of the default and also its randomness. A Poisson process is a typical choice for the time of default. We will see that when the intensity of the Poisson process is constant (as in the die example), the pricing of risky bonds amounts to the addition of a time-independent spread to the bond yield. We will also see models for which the intensity is itself a random variable.

A refinement of the modeling that we also consider is the regrading of bonds. There are agents, such as Standard & Poor's and Moody's, who classify bonds according to their estimate of their risk of default. A bond may start life with a high rating, for example, but may find itself regraded due to the performance of the issuing firm. Such a regrading will have a major effect on the perceived risk of default and on the price of the bond. I will describe a simple model for the rerating of risky bonds.

43.4 THE VALUE OF THE FIRM AS A RANDOM VARIABLE

The starting point for pricing risk using the value of the firm is often choosing a model for this value (we see another starting point later). This value is taken to be stochastic so as to model the randomness in bond prices that is due to default risk. The original idea behind firm valuation goes back to Black, Scholes and Merton in the original option pricing work. The following is a version of the Longstaff & Schwartz model.

Suppose for instance that the company issuing the debt has a value A which is random and follows the stochastic differential equation

$$dA = \mu A\,dt + \sigma A\,dX.$$

This A will be one of our independent variables. Default is modeled via the idea of bankruptcy. We will assume that the firm will declare bankruptcy if its value ever goes below some critical level A_b. Already we can criticize this model. How do we measure the parameters μ, σ and A_b? What is the value of A today?

Let us consider the simplest example: this firm has a debt of D to pay back at time T. However, it will not pay back the debt if it has meanwhile gone bankrupt. To keep things as simple as possible to begin, assume that the interest rate is known.

43.4.1 Known Interest Rate

How can we give a fair value to something as risky as the debt issued by this business? We would like to use a hedging argument, as we have so often before. However, if the company has no traded shares then the risk associated with the debt of this firm cannot easily be hedged away. Stand back from the problem for a moment and ask how could we value a simple bet on the toss of a coin: heads you win one dollar, tails you get nothing. The easiest choice for the value of this bet is simply the expected value, 50 cents. This will be our approach initially; we will look at the *expected* value of the risky debt. This is not completely satisfactory since we would ideally like to put some value to the risk we are taking. However, we can think of this as being a starting point for more complicated models.

Consider what happens to the value of the bond during a small timestep:

$$dV = \left(\frac{\partial V}{\partial t} + \tfrac{1}{2}\sigma^2 A^2 \frac{\partial^2 V}{\partial A^2}\right) dt + \frac{\partial V}{\partial A}\, dA.$$

Now take *expectations* and set the expected instantaneous return on V equal to $rV\,dt$ to arrive at

$$\frac{\partial V}{\partial t} + \tfrac{1}{2}\sigma^2 A^2 \frac{\partial^2 V}{\partial A^2} + \mu A \frac{\partial V}{\partial A} - rV = 0,$$

The final condition for this equation is

$$V(A, T) = D,$$

representing the payment of the debt at maturity. Since the issuing company defaults when its value reaches A_b we have

$$V(A_b, t) = 0.$$

Compare this boundary condition with that for knockout barrier options. This completes the model. It is unrealistic for there to be no recovery of the debt on 'bankruptcy,' and this would obviously affect the boundary condition. I am not going to worry about this issue for the moment. It is of obvious practical importance, and not too difficult to model.

It is very important to note that we have taken real expectations in arriving at the above equation. For this reason, there is no market price of risk term associated with A; it could be included but I will not pursue this here.

43.4.2 Stochastic Interest Rates

We can make the model more realistic by introducing an interest rate model into the problem—after all, if there is no credit risk we would like to return to the simpler world of pricing non-risky debt. I will be vague about the choice of interest rate model and just write

$$dr = u(r, t)\, dt + w(r, t)\, dX_1.$$

Still we will assume that

$$dA = \mu A\, dt + \sigma A\, dX_2.$$

There will be a correlation of ρ between the two random walks.

Now the value of the debt V, say, is a function of three variables, we have $V(A, r, t)$. We have seen in earlier chapters how to derive the equation for a bond value in the absence of default risk. The result is a diffusion equation in r and t. The equation for V will be similar but now there will be some A dependence and derivatives with respect to A.

To find the equation satisfied by V we construct a portfolio of our risky bond, and hedge it with a riskless zero-coupon bond with price $Z(r, t)$:

$$\Pi = V(A, r, t) - \Delta Z(r, t).$$

From this, we calculate $d\Pi$,

$$d\Pi = \left(\frac{\partial V}{\partial t} + \tfrac{1}{2}w^2 \frac{\partial^2 V}{\partial r^2} + \rho\sigma w A \frac{\partial^2 V}{\partial r \partial A} + \tfrac{1}{2}\sigma^2 A^2 \frac{\partial^2 V}{\partial A^2} \right) dt$$
$$+ \frac{\partial V}{\partial A} dA + \left(\frac{\partial V}{\partial r} - \Delta \frac{\partial Z}{\partial r} \right) dr - \Delta \left(\frac{\partial Z}{\partial t} + \tfrac{1}{2}w^2 \frac{\partial^2 Z}{\partial r^2} \right) dt.$$

Choose Δ to eliminate dr terms, then take *expectations*. Many of the terms simplify because Z satisfies the basic bond pricing equation in the absence of risk of default. Finally, set the expected instantaneous return on Π equal to $r\Pi\, dt$ to arrive at

$$\frac{\partial V}{\partial t} + \tfrac{1}{2}w^2 \frac{\partial^2 V}{\partial r^2} + \rho\sigma w A \frac{\partial^2 V}{\partial r \partial A} + \tfrac{1}{2}\sigma^2 A^2 \frac{\partial^2 V}{\partial A^2} + (u - \lambda w)\frac{\partial V}{\partial r} + \mu A \frac{\partial V}{\partial A} - rV = 0,$$

where λ is again the price of interest rate risk. This is not a perfect hedge, we have only hedged the diffusive component due to the interest rate. The risk due to the firm's value is unhedged, we have assumed that it has no traded shares.

The final condition for this equation is

$$V(A, r, T) = D,$$

representing the payment of the debt at maturity. Since the issuing company defaults when its value reaches A_b we have

$$V(A_b, r, t) = 0.$$

In the special case when the correlation between the firm's value and the interest rate is zero, the solution can be written as

$$V(A, r, t) = Z(r, t; T)H(A, t),$$

for some function H, where $Z(r, t; T)$ is a riskless zero-coupon bond of the same maturity as the debt. $H(A, t)$ satisfies

$$\frac{\partial H}{\partial t} + \tfrac{1}{2}\sigma^2 A^2 \frac{\partial^2 H}{\partial A^2} + \mu A \frac{\partial H}{\partial A} = 0,$$

with

$$H(A_b, t) = 0 \quad \text{and} \quad H(A, T) = 1, \quad A > A_b.$$

All of the default modeling has gone into this problem for H.

The main criticism of this model is, as I have said, that it is very difficult to measure variables and parameters. Nevertheless, it can be useful as a phenomenological model, perhaps for estimating the *relative* value of different types of debt issued by the same business, or businesses with the same credit rating.

43.5 MODELING WITH MEASURABLE PARAMETERS AND VARIABLES

In this section I describe a model that takes easily measurable inputs. We will concentrate on valuing the debt when interest rates are deterministic; the model could easily be extended to stochastic interest rates at the cost of additional complexity and computing time.

We will value the debt of a company having a very simple operating procedure: they sell their product, they pay their costs and they put any profit into the bank. The key quantity we will model is the earnings of the company. Think of these earnings as being the gross income from the sale of the product. The net earnings or profit will be the gross earnings less the costs. Assume that the gross annualized earnings E of the company are random:

$$dE = \mu E\,dt + \sigma E\,dX.$$

(Of course, we need not choose a lognormal model, but it is the traditional starting point.)

We assume that the company has fixed costs of E^* p.a. and floating costs of kE. The profit of $E - E^* - kE = (1-k)E - E^*$ is put into a bank earning a fixed rate of interest r. If we denote by C the cash in this bank account then this is given by

$$C = \int_0^t ((1-k)E(\tau) - E^*)e^{r(t-\tau)}\,d\tau.$$

This expression represents the accumulation of income together with any bank interest. Differentiating this gives the stochastic differential equation satisfied by C:

$$dC = ((1-k)E - E^* + rC)\,dt.$$

I have chosen to model the earnings of the business rather than the firm's value since the former are far easier to measure, requiring only an examination of the firm's accounts perhaps. We shall see how the value of the firm is then an *output* of the model.

The well-being of the company is determined by its earnings and bank account balance at any time, i.e. by E and C. The owners of the company hope that $(1-k)E > E^*$, but even if it is not (at the start of trading, say), then perhaps the growth in earnings will eventually take the company into profit.

Suppose that the company owes D which must be repaid at time T. We make the simple assumption that if the company has D in the bank at time T then it will repay the debt, if it has less than D in the bank it will repay everything that it has, if there is a negative amount in the bank then they repay nothing. This gives a repayment of

$$\max(\min(C, D), 0). \tag{43.1}$$

Again, this would be more complicated if we were to incorporate partial repayment or refinancing.

The value of the debt will be a function of E, C and t. Introduce the quantity $V(E, C, t)$ as the present value of the *expected* amount in (43.1). This function satisfies the differential equation

$$\frac{\partial V}{\partial t} + \tfrac{1}{2}\sigma^2 E^2 \frac{\partial^2 V}{\partial E^2} + \mu E \frac{\partial V}{\partial E} + ((1-k)E - E^* + rC)\frac{\partial V}{\partial C} - rV = 0,$$

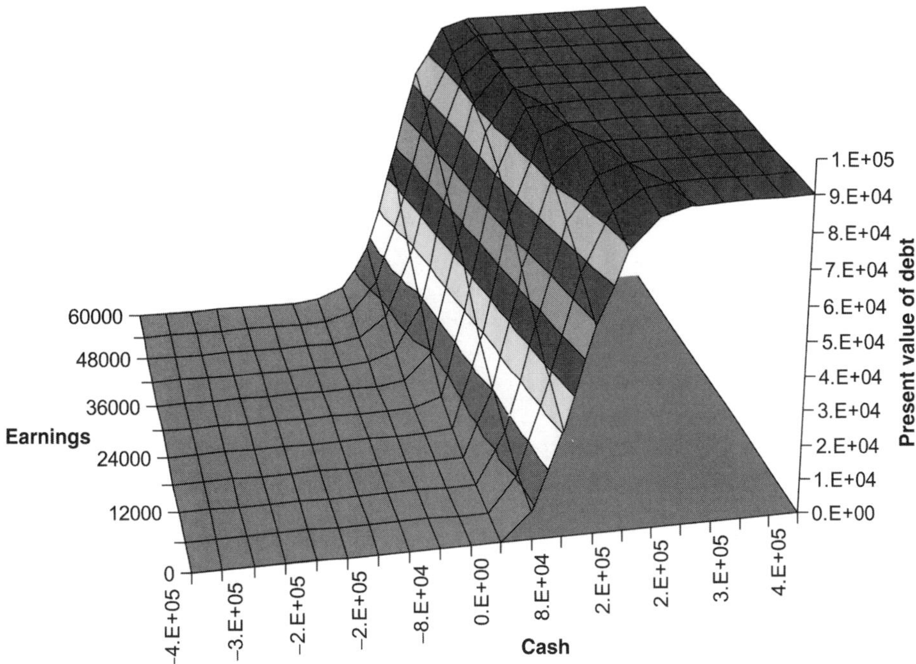

Figure 43.2 Value of debt issued by a limited liability company as a function of annual earnings and retained cash.

with final condition

$$V(E, C, T) = \max(\min(C, D), 0).$$

In Figure 43.2 we see a plot of the value of the debt according to this model when there is an amount \$100,000 to be repaid in two years, with a risk-free interest rate of 5%. The firm has fixed costs of \$30,000 p.a. and variable costs of 7%. The drift of the earnings is 10% and the volatility 25%. Observe that for both large C and E the value approaches the value of a risk-free zero-coupon bond.

As it stands this problem can be usefully used to value risky debt: the value of the debt is simply $V(E, C, t)$ with today's values for E, C and t. However, it can be modified quite simply to accommodate more sophisticated operating procedures for the company. One possibility is to say that the company closes down immediately that it goes into the red. This could be modeled by the boundary condition

$$V(E, 0, t) = 0.$$

43.5.1 Calculating the Value of the Firm

By changing final and boundary conditions it is a very simple matter to use the above model to value the firm, and to examine the effects of various business strategies on that value. For example, suppose that we take the value of the business to be the present value of the expected cash in the bank at some time T_0 in the future. Such a finite time horizon is a common assumption when we are estimating the present value of a potentially infinite sum of cashflows which are (one hopes) growing faster than the interest rate. In this case, the firm value $V(E, C, t)$

satisfies

$$\frac{\partial V}{\partial t} + \tfrac{1}{2}\sigma^2 E^2 \frac{\partial^2 V}{\partial E^2} + \mu E \frac{\partial V}{\partial E} + ((1-k)E - E^* + rC)\frac{\partial V}{\partial C} - rV = 0.$$

As an example of the flexibility of this approach, consider the different final conditions applying to the two different problems valuing a limited liability company and valuing an unlimited liability partnership.

Limited Liability

If the business has no liability when it has a negative amount in the bank at time T_0, then

$$V(E, C, T_0) = \max(C, 0).$$

Partnership

If the owners of the business are liable for the debts of the business then

$$V(E, C, T_0) = C.$$

In the former case, if the business expires in the red then the company directors declare bankruptcy and walk away from the debt (assuming that they have not acted negligently).

Not only can we use this model to examine the legal standing of the company, but also to study the effects of various operating procedures on its value. Here is an example.

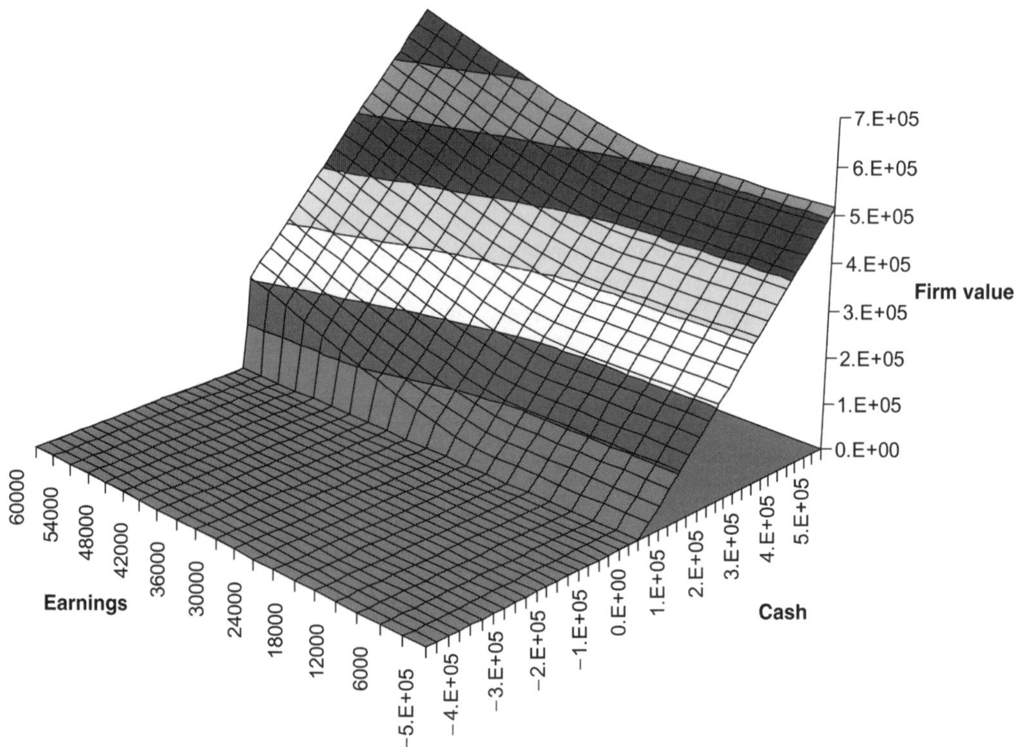

Figure 43.3 Company valuation with optimal close-down. Parameter values are the same as in the previous picture.

Optimal Close-Down

If the model gives a value of \$3,000,000 to your company but you currently have \$5,000,000 in the bank then the model is trying to tell you something: bad times are just around the corner. In such a situation it is not wise to keep trading, you will be better off closing down the business. The decision to close down the business can be optimized by a constraint of the form

$$V(E, C, t) \geq C$$

with continuity of the first derivatives. This is just like an American option problem and the justification is similar. An example of the company valuation problem with this constraint is shown in Figure 43.3.

43.6 THE POISSON PROCESS AND THE INSTANTANEOUS RISK OF DEFAULT

Another approach to the modeling of credit risk is via the **instantaneous risk of default**, p. If at time t the company has not defaulted and the instantaneous risk of default is p then the probability of default between times t and $t + dt$ is $p\,dt$. This is an example of a Poisson process, as described in Chapter 26; nothing happens for a while, then there is a *sudden* change of state. This is a continuous-time version of our earlier model of throwing a die.

IMPORTANT

The simplest example to start with is to take p constant. In this case we can easily determine the risk of default before time T. We do this as follows.

Let $P(t; T)$ be the probability that the company does not default before time T given that it has not defaulted at time t. The probability of default between later times t' and $t' + dt'$ is the product of $p\,dt$ and the probability that the company has not defaulted up until time t'. Thus, the rate of change of the required probability is

$$\frac{\partial P}{\partial t'} = pP(t'; T).$$

If the company starts out not in default then $P(T; T) = 1$. The solution of this problem is

$$e^{-p(T-t)}.$$

The value of a zero-coupon bond paying \$1 at time T could therefore be modeled by taking the present value of the *expected* cashflow. This results in a value of

$$e^{-p(T-t)}Z, \tag{43.2}$$

where Z is the value of a riskless zero-coupon bond of the same maturity as the risky bond. Again, note that this does not put any value on the risk taken. The yield to maturity on this bond is now given by

$$-\frac{\log(e^{-p(T-t)}Z)}{T-t} = -\frac{\log Z}{T-t} + p.$$

Thus the effect of the risk of default on the yield is to add a spread of p. In this simple model, the spread will be constant across all maturities.

Now we apply this to derivatives, including risky bonds. We will assume that the spot interest rate is stochastic. For simplicity we will assume that there is no correlation between the diffusive change in the spot interest rate and the Poisson process.

Construct a 'hedged' portfolio:

$$\Pi = V(r, p, t) - \Delta Z(r, t).$$

Consider how this changes in a timestep. See Figure 43.4 for a diagram illustrating the following analysis.

There is a probability of $(1 - p\,dt)$ that the bond does not default. In this case the change in the value of the portfolio during a timestep is

$$d\Pi = \left(\frac{\partial V}{\partial t} + \tfrac{1}{2}w^2\frac{\partial^2 V}{\partial r^2}\right)dt + \frac{\partial V}{\partial r}dr - \Delta\left(\left(\frac{\partial Z}{\partial t} + \tfrac{1}{2}w^2\frac{\partial^2 Z}{\partial r^2}\right)dt + \frac{\partial Z}{\partial r}dr\right). \tag{43.3}$$

Choose Δ to eliminate the risky dr term.

On the other hand, if the bond defaults, with a probability of $p\,dt$, then the change in the value of the portfolio is

$$d\Pi = -V + O(dt^{1/2}). \tag{43.4}$$

This is due to the sudden loss of the risky bond, the other terms are small in comparison.

Taking expectations and using the bond-pricing equation for the riskless bond, we find that the value of the risky bond satisfies

$$\frac{\partial V}{\partial t} + \tfrac{1}{2}w^2\frac{\partial^2 V}{\partial r^2} + (u - \lambda w)\frac{\partial V}{\partial r} - (r + p)V = 0. \tag{43.5}$$

Observe that the spread has been added to the discounting term.

This model is the most basic for the instantaneous risk of default. It gives a very simple relationship between a risk-free and a risky bond. There is only one new parameter to estimate, p.

To see whether this is a realistic model for the expectations of the market we take a quick look at the valuation of Brady bonds. In particular we examine the market price of Latin American Par bonds, described in full later in this chapter. For the moment, we just need to know that these bonds have interest payments and final return of principal denominated in US dollars. If

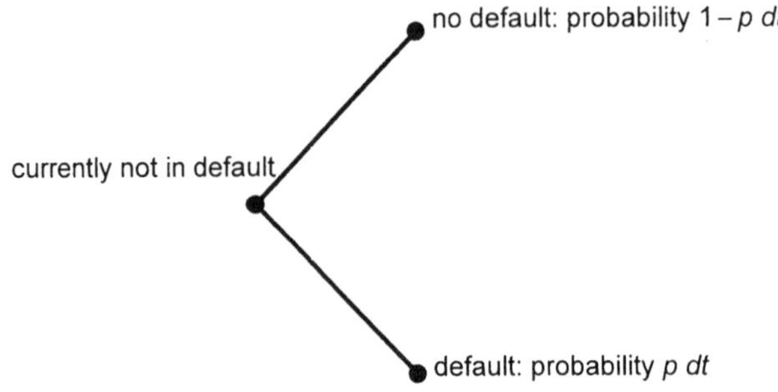

Figure 43.4 A schematic diagram showing the two possible situations: default and no default.

the above is a good model of market expectations with constant p then we would find a very simple relationship between interest rates in the US and the value of Brady bonds. To find the Brady bond value perform the following:

1. Find the risk-free yield for the maturity of each cashflow in the risky bond;
2. Add a constant spread, p, to each of these yields;
3. Use this new yield to calculate the present value of each cashflow;
4. Sum all the present values.

Conversely, the same procedure can be used to determine the value of p from the market price of the Brady bond: this would be the **implied risk of default**. In Figure 43.5 are shown the implied risks of default for the Par bonds of Argentina, Brazil, Mexico and Venezuela using the above procedure and assuming a constant p.

In this simple model we have assumed that the instantaneous risk of default is constant (different for each country) through time. However, from Figure 43.5 we can see that, if we believe the market prices of the Brady bonds, this assumption is incorrect: the market prices are inconsistent with a constant p. This will be our motivation for the stochastic risk of default model which we will see in a moment. Nevertheless, supposing that the figure represents, in some sense, the views of the market (and this constant p model *is* used in practice) we draw a few conclusions from this figure before moving on.

The first point to notice in the graph is the perceived risk of Venezuela, which is consistently greater than the three other countries. Venezuela's risk peaked in July 1994, nine months before the rest of South America, but this had absolutely no effect on the other countries.

The next, and most important, thing to notice is the 'Tequila effect' in all the Latin markets. The Tequila crisis began with a 50% devaluation of the Mexican peso in December 1994. Markets followed suit by plunging. Before December 1994 we can see a constant spread between Mexico and Argentina and a contracting spread between Brazil and Argentina. The consequences of Tequila were felt through all the first quarter of 1995 and had a knock-on effect thoughout South America. In April 1995 the default risks peaked in all the countries apart from Venezuela, but by late 1996 the default risk had almost returned to pre-Tequila levels in all four countries. By this time, Venezuela's risk had fallen to the same order as the other countries.

43.7 TIME-DEPENDENT INTENSITY AND THE TERM STRUCTURE OF DEFAULT

Suppose that a company issues risky bonds of different maturities. We can deduce from the market's prices of these bonds how the risk of default is perceived to depend on time. To make things as simple as possible let's assume that the company issues zero-coupon bonds and that in the event of default in one bond, all other outstanding bonds also default with no recovery rate.

If the risk of default is time dependent, $p(t)$, and uncorrelated with the spot interest rate, then the real expected value of a risky bond paying \$1 at time T is just

$$Ze^{-\int_t^T p(\tau)\,d\tau}.$$

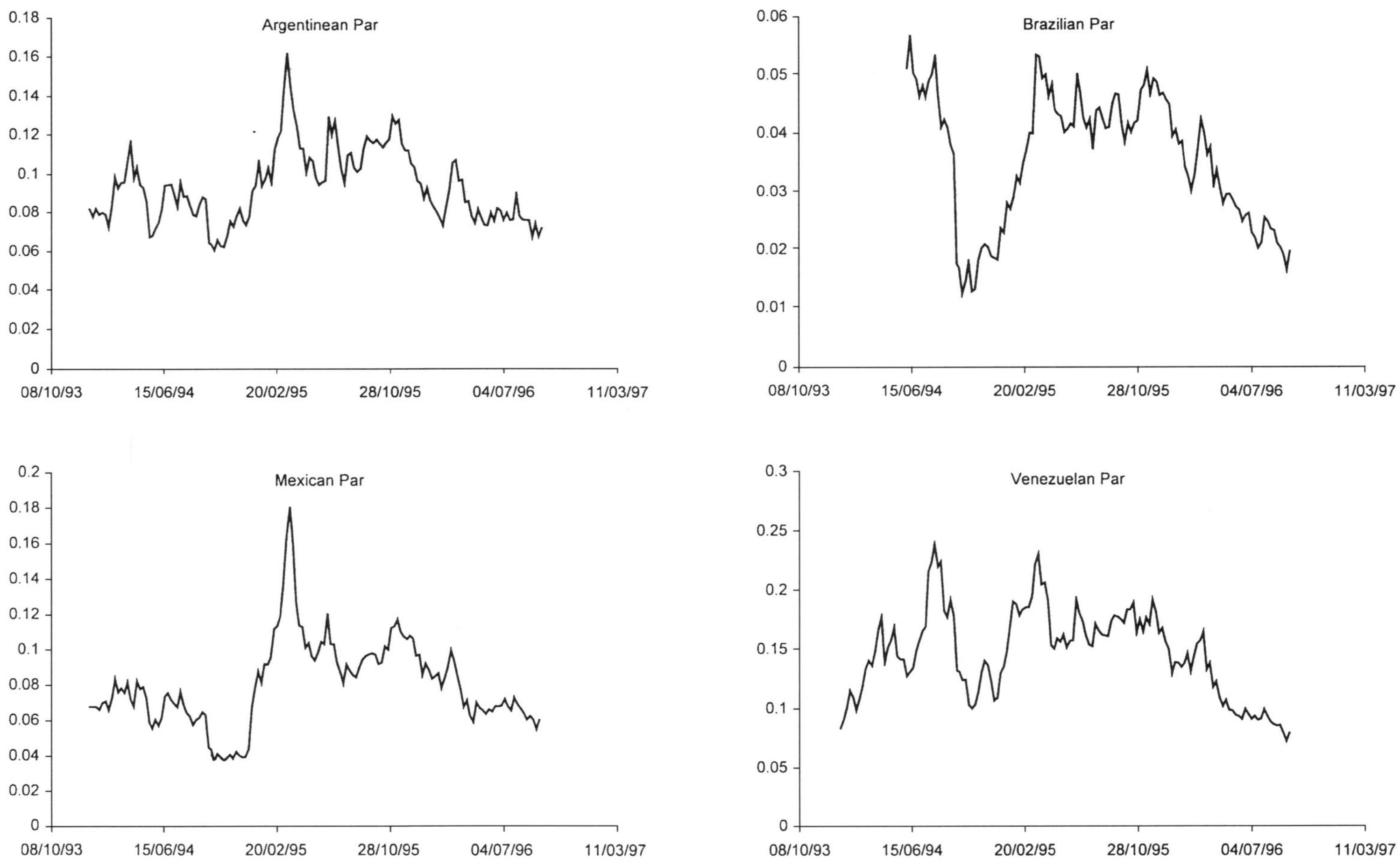

Figure 43.5 The implied risk of default for the Par bonds of Argentina, Brazil, Mexico and Venezuela assuming constant p.

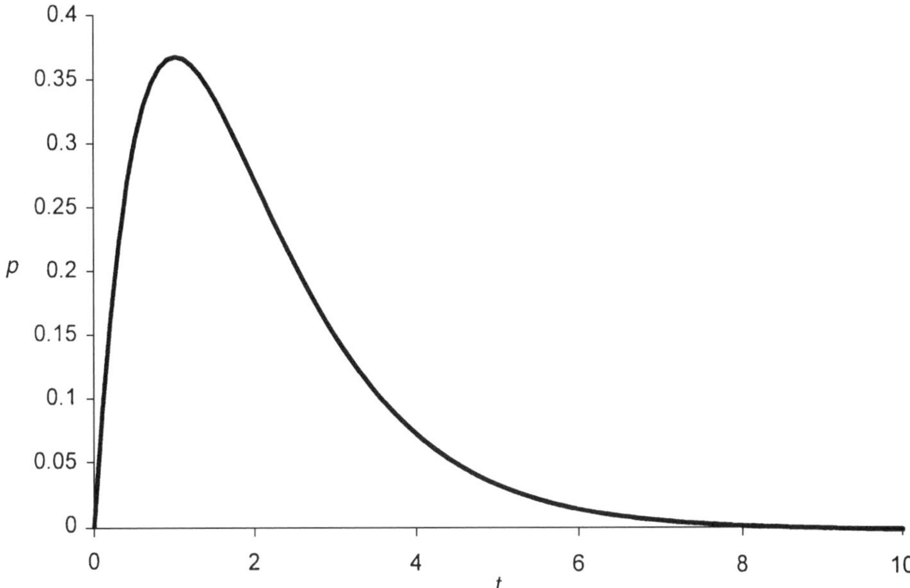

Figure 43.6 A plausible structure for a time-dependent hazard rate.

If the market value of the risky bond is Z^* then we can write

$$\int_t^T p(\tau)\,d\tau = \log\left(\frac{Z}{Z^*}\right).$$

Differentiating this with respect to T gives the market's view at the current time t of the **hazard rate** or risk of default at time T. A plausible structure for such a hazard rate is given in Figure 43.6. This figure shows a very small chance of default initially, rising to a maximum before falling off. The company is clearly expected to be around for at least a little while longer, and in the long term it will either have already expired or become very successful. If the area under the curve is finite then there is a finite probability of the company never going bankrupt.

43.8 STOCHASTIC RISK OF DEFAULT

To 'improve' the model, and make it consistent with market prices, we now consider a model in which the instantaneous probability of default is itself random. We assume that it follows a random walk given by

$$dp = \gamma(r, p, t)\,dt + \delta(r, p, t)\,dX_1,$$

with interest rates still given by

$$dr = u(r, t)\,dt + w(r, t)\,dX_2.$$

It is reasonable to expect some interest rate dependence in the risk of default, but not the other way around.

To value our risky zero-coupon bond we construct a portfolio with one of the risky bond, with value $V(r, p, t)$ (to be determined), and short Δ of a riskless bond, with value $Z(r, t)$

(satisfying our earlier bond pricing equation):

$$\Pi = V(r, p, t) - \Delta Z(r, t).$$

In the next timestep either the bond is defaulted or it is not. There is a probability of default of $p\,dt$. We must consider the two cases: default and no default in the next timestep. As in the two models above, we take expectations to arrive at an equation for the value of the risky bond.

First, suppose that the bond does not default; this has a probability of $(1 - p\,dt)$. In this case the change in the value of the portfolio during a timestep is

$$d\Pi = \left(\frac{\partial V}{\partial t} + \tfrac{1}{2}w^2\frac{\partial^2 V}{\partial r^2} + \rho w\delta\frac{\partial^2 V}{\partial r\partial p} + \tfrac{1}{2}\delta^2\frac{\partial^2 V}{\partial p^2}\right)dt + \frac{\partial V}{\partial r}dr + \frac{\partial V}{\partial p}dp$$
$$- \Delta\left(\left(\frac{\partial Z}{\partial t} + \tfrac{1}{2}w^2\frac{\partial^2 Z}{\partial r^2}\right)dt + \frac{\partial Z}{\partial r}dr\right),$$

where ρ is the correlation between dX_1 and dX_2. Choose Δ to eliminate the risky dr term.

On the other hand, if the bond defaults, with a probability of $p\,dt$, then the change in the value of the portfolio is

$$d\Pi = -V + O(dt^{1/2}).$$

This is due to the sudden loss of the risky bond; the other terms are small in comparison. It is at this point that we could put in a recovery rate, discussed in the next section. As it stands here default means no return whatsoever.

Taking expectations and using the bond-pricing equation for the riskless bond, we find that the value of the risky bond satisfies

$$\frac{\partial V}{\partial t}+\tfrac{1}{2}w^2\frac{\partial^2 V}{\partial r^2}+\rho w\delta\frac{\partial^2 V}{\partial r\partial p}+\tfrac{1}{2}\delta^2\frac{\partial^2 V}{\partial p^2}+(u-\lambda w)\frac{\partial V}{\partial r}+\gamma\frac{\partial V}{\partial p}-(r+p)V=0. \qquad (43.6)$$

This equation has final condition

$$V(r, p, T) = 1,$$

if the bond is zero coupon with a principal repayment of \$1.

Equation (43.6) again shows the similarity between the spot interest rate, r, and the hazard rate, p. The equation is remarkably symmetrical in these two variables, the only difference is in the choice of the model for each. In particular, the final term includes a discounting at rate r and also at rate p. These two variables play similar roles in credit risk equations.

As a check on this result, return to the simple case of constant p. In the new framework this case is equivalent to $\gamma = \delta = 0$. The solution of (43.6) is easily seen to be

$$e^{-p(T-t)}Z(r, t),$$

as derived earlier.

If γ and δ are independent of r and the correlation coefficient ρ is zero then we can write

$$V(r, p, t) = Z(r, t)H(p, t),$$

where H satisfies

$$\frac{\partial H}{\partial t} + \tfrac{1}{2}\delta^2 \frac{\partial^2 H}{\partial p^2} + \gamma \frac{\partial H}{\partial p} - pH = 0,$$

with

$$H(p, T) = 1.$$

In this special, but important case, the default risk decouples from the bond pricing.

43.9 POSITIVE RECOVERY

In default there is usually *some* payment; not all of the money is lost. In Table 43.1, produced by Moody's from historical data, is shown the mean and standard deviations for recovery according to the seniority of the debt. These numbers emphasize the fact that the rate of recovery is itself very uncertain. How can we model a positive recovery?

Suppose that on default we know that we will get an amount Q. This will change the partial differential equation. To see this we return to the derivation of Equation (43.5). If there is no default we still have Equation (43.3). However, on default Equation (43.4) becomes instead

$$d\Pi = -V + Q + O(dt^{1/2});$$

we lose the bond but get Q. Taking expectations results in

$$\frac{\partial V}{\partial t} + \tfrac{1}{2}w^2 \frac{\partial^2 V}{\partial r^2} + \rho w \delta \frac{\partial^2 V}{\partial r \partial p} + \tfrac{1}{2}\delta^2 \frac{\partial^2 V}{\partial p^2} + (u - \lambda w)\frac{\partial V}{\partial r} + \gamma \frac{\partial V}{\partial p} - (r + p)V + pQ = 0.$$

Now you are faced with the difficult task of estimating Q, or modeling it as another random variable.

43.10 SPECIAL CASES AND YIELD CURVE FITTING

We saw in Chapter 33 that some spot interest rate models lead to explicit solutions for bond prices, for example the Vasicek model, the CIR model and in general the affine model with four time-dependent parameters. We can find simpler equations than the two-factor diffusion equation for the value of a risky bond in the above framework if we choose the functions $u - \lambda w$, w, γ, δ and ρ carefully. Obviously, from the analysis of Chapter 33, we must choose $u - \lambda w$ and w^2 to be linear in r. For simplifications of (43.6) to exist we also require γ and δ^2 to be linear in r and p. The form of the correlation coefficient is more complicated so we shall choose it to be zero.

Table 43.1 Rate of recovery. Source: Moody's.

Class	Mean (%)	Std Dev. (%)
Senior secured	53.80	26.86
Senior unsecured	51.13	25.45
Senior subordinated	38.52	23.81
Subordinated	32.74	20.18
Junior subordinated	17.09	10.90

With these choices for the functions in the two stochastic differential equations we find that the solution of (43.6) with $V(r, p, T) = 1$ is

$$V = \exp(A(t, T) - B(t, T)r - C(t, T)p)$$

where A, B and C satisfy nonlinear first-order ordinary differential equations. I leave it as an exercise for the reader to derive them. In some cases these equations can be solved explicitly, usually in terms of special functions, but in others they must be solved numerically. Such a solution will of course be much quicker than the numerical solution of the two-factor diffusion equation.

If we allow the spot interest rate model to have some simple time dependence then we have the freedom to fit the yield curve. This concept is discussed in detail in Chapter 34 and the principle is the same here. In practice this may mean that we would restrict our attention to the extended Vasicek model with constant spot rate volatility. Similarly, if there is time dependence in the model for the hazard rate, and the model is sufficiently tractable, then you can also fit a hazard rate term structure.

43.11 A CASE STUDY: THE ARGENTINE PAR BOND

The Brady Plan was conceived in 1989 by former US Treasury Secretary Nicholas Brady. The plan consists of the repackaging of commercial bank debt into tradable fixed-income securities. Creditor banks either lower their interest on the debt or reduce the principal. Debtor countries, in exchange, are committed to make macroeconomic adjustments. Most Brady bonds are dollar denominated with maturities of longer than ten years and either fixed or floating coupon payments. At the time of writing many countries were beginning to buy back their Brady bonds. For up-to-date information see www.bradynet.com.

The US dollar-denominated Argentine Par bond has the specifications shown in Figure 43.7.

From time-series data for real risky bond prices and a suitable model, such as described above, we can calculate the value of the instantaneous risk of default for each data point that is needed for the model to give a theoretical value equal to the market value of the bond. This number is the implied instantaneous risk of default and plays a role in default risk analysis that is similar to that played by implied volatility for options: it is used as a trading indicator or as a measure of relative value.

In the analysis of the Argentine Par bond the risk of default was assumed to satisfy

$$dp = (f - hp)\,dt + jp^{1/2}\,dX_2, \tag{43.7}$$

and to be uncorrelated with the spot interest rate. In this model the risk of default is mean reverting. I have not included any interest rate dependence in this because, provided $f > j^2/2$, this precludes the possibility of negative risk of default. It also makes the yield-curve fitting very simple because of the decomposition of the present value of each cashflow into the product of risk-free bond value and a function of just p and t. In other words, an interest rate model is not needed if a risk-free yield curve is given. The speed of reversion is determined by h. The parameters were chosen to be $h = 0.5$, $f = 0.045$ and $j = 0.03$. This choice was made partly so that the resulting time series for the implied p had the right theoretical properties (deduced from (43.7)) and partly using common sense.

Republic of Argentina Par Bond	
Step-up coupon due 31 March 2023	
Obligor	Republic of Argentina
Guarantor	None
Form	Registered bonds
Amount issued	\$12.7 billion
Denomination	\$250,000
Currency	US dollar, Deutsche Mark
Date issued	31 March 1993
Maturity date	31 March 2023
Coupon	Semiannual coupon, 30/360 day count. 1^{st}year: 4% 2^{nd}year: 4.25% 3^{rd}year: 5% 4^{th}year: 5.25% 5^{th}year: 5.5% 6^{th}year: 5.75% 7-30^{th}year: 6% DMK bonds: 5.87%
Amortization	Bullet
Options	None
Enhancements	Us Treasury zero-coupon bonds to collateralize the principal and 12-months of rolling interest guarantees

Figure 43.7 Specifications of the Argentinean Par bond.

Finally, the value for p was chosen daily so that the market price of the bonds and their theoretical price coincided.

The period chosen (end December 1993 to end September 1996) is a particularly exciting one because of the 'Tequila Effect' and it could easily be argued that there was a dramatic change of market conditions (and hence model parameters) at that time. However, I have kept the same parameters for the whole of this period since it was risk of default causing the Tequila effect and should therefore be accounted for in these parameters.

The Tequila effect took place in December 1994 but its consequences lasted much longer, in some countries up to three and four months. In the case of Argentina, we can observe in Figure 43.8 the minimum price of the Par bond at the end of March 1995, dipping below \$35. Since then a steady recovery can be seen.

In Figure 43.9 we can observe that the Tequila effect was accompanied by a sharp increase in long rates in the US, which knocked Brady bond prices even further. The highest long rate over this period was 8% and it occurred in March 1995.

In Figure 43.10 is shown the implied instantaneous risk of default for Argentinean Par bonds over the period end December 1993 to end September 1996. As expected, the highest probability of default took place at the end of March 1995 when the Tequila Effect was at its worst. Since then there has been a steady, but obviously not monotonic, decrease in the risk of default implied by this model.

Figure 43.8 Market price of the Argentinean Par bond from end December 1993 to end September 1996.

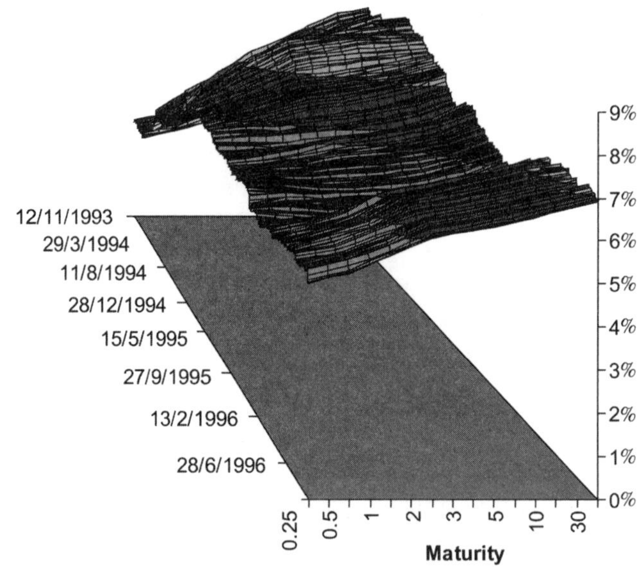

Figure 43.9 US yield curve from end December 1993 to end September 1996.

43.12 HEDGING THE DEFAULT

In the above we used riskless bonds to hedge the random movements in the spot interest rate. Can we introduce another risky bond or bonds into the portfolio to help with hedging the default risk? To do this we must assume that default in one bond automatically means default in the other.

Assuming that the risk of default p is constant for simplicity, consider the portfolio

$$\Pi = V - \Delta Z - \Delta_1 V_1,$$

where both V and V_1 are risky.

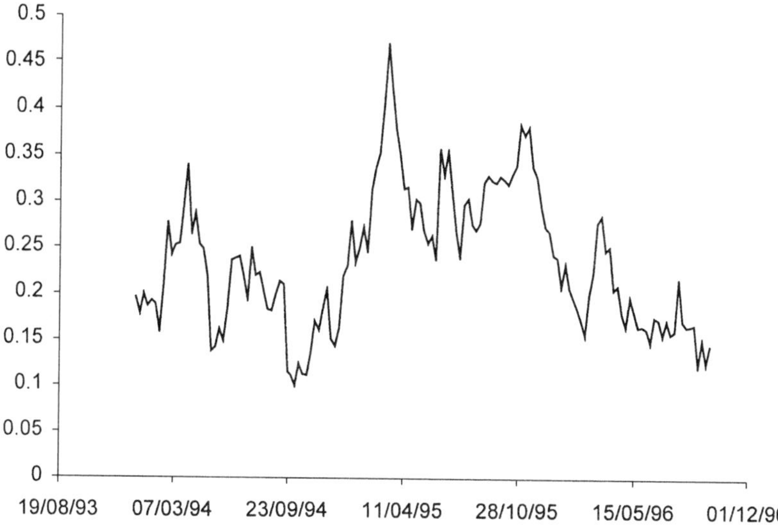

Figure 43.10 The implied risk of default for the Argentinean Par, see text for description of the stochastic model.

The choices

$$\Delta_1 = \frac{V}{V_1} \quad \text{and} \quad \Delta = \frac{V_1 \dfrac{\partial V}{\partial r} - V \dfrac{\partial V_1}{\partial r}}{V_1 \dfrac{\partial Z}{\partial r}}$$

eliminate both default risk and spot rate risk. The analysis results in

$$\frac{\partial V}{\partial t} + \tfrac{1}{2} w^2 \frac{\partial^2 V}{\partial r^2} + (u - \lambda w) \frac{\partial V}{\partial r} - (r + \lambda_1(r, t)p)V = 0.$$

Observe that the 'market price of default risk' λ_1 is now where the probability of default appeared before, thus we have a risk-neutral probability of default.

Can you imagine what happens if the risk of default is stochastic? There are actually three sources of randomness, the spot rate, the risk of default and the event of default. This means that we must hedge with *three* bonds, two other risky bonds and a risk-free bond, say. Where will you find market prices of risk?

43.13 CREDIT RATING

There are many **Credit Rating Agencies** who compile data on individual companies or countries and estimate the likelihood of default. The most famous of these are **Standard & Poor's** and **Moody's**. These agencies assign a **credit rating** or **grade** to firms as an estimate of their creditworthiness. Standard & Poor's rate businesses as one of AAA, AA, A, BBB, BB, B, CCC or Default. Moody's use Aaa, Aa, A, Baa, Ba, B, Caa, Ca, C. Both of these companies also have finer grades within each of these main categories. The Moody grades are described in the following Table 43.2.

In Figure 43.11 is shown the percentage of defaults over the past eighty years, sorted according to their Moody's credit rating.

Table 43.2 The meaning of Moody's ratings.

Aaa	Bonds of best quality. Smallest degree of risk. Interest payments protected by a large or stable margin.
Aa	High quality. Margin of protection lower than Aaa.
A	Many favorable investment attributes. Adequate security of principal and interest. May be susceptible to impairment in the future.
Baa	Neither highly protected nor poorly secured. Adequate security for the present. Lacking outstanding investment characteristics. Speculative features.
Ba	Speculative elements. Future not well assured.
B	Lack characteristics of a desirable investment.
Caa	Poor standing. May be in default or danger with respect to principal or interest.
Ca	High degree of speculation. Often in default.
C	Lowest-rated class. Extremely poor chance of ever attaining any real investment standing.

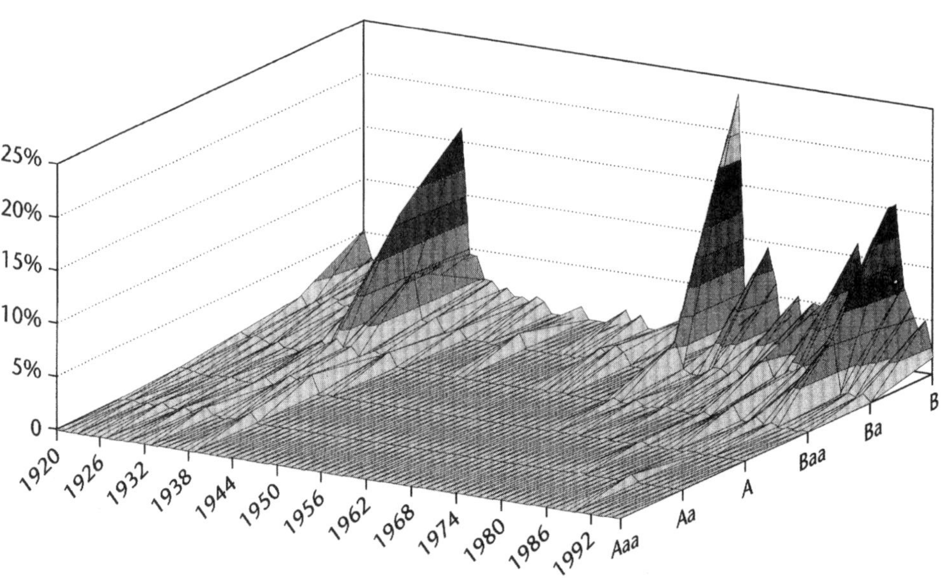

Figure 43.11 Percentage of defaults according to rating. Source: Moody's. Reproduced by permission *Moody's Investors Services*.

The credit rating agencies continually gather data on individual firms and will, depending on the information, grade/regrade a company according to well-specified criteria. A change of rating is called a **migration** and has an important effect on the price of bonds issued by the company. Migration to a higher rating will increase the value of a bond and decrease its yield, since it is seen as being less likely to default.

Clearly there are two stages to modeling risky bonds under the credit-rating scenario. First we must model the migration of the company from one grade to another and second we must price bonds taking this migration into account.

43.14 A MODEL FOR CHANGE OF CREDIT RATING

Company XYZ is currently rated A by Standard & Poor's. What is the probability that in one year's time it will still be rated A? Suppose that it is 91.305%. Now what is the probability that it will be rated AA or even AAA, or in default? We can represent these probabilities over the one year time horizon by a **transition matrix**. An example is shown in Table 43.3.

This table is read as follows. Today the company is rated A. The probability that in one year's time it will be at another rating can be seen by reading across the A row in the table. Thus the probability of being rated AAA is 0.092%, AA 2.42%, A 91.305%, etc. The highest probability is of no migration. By reading down the rows, this table can be interpreted as either a representation of the probabilities of migration of *all* companies from one grade to another, or of company XYZ had it started out at other than A. Whatever the grade today, the company must have some rating at the end of the year even if that rating is default. Therefore the probabilities reading across each row must sum to one. And once a company is in default, it cannot leave that state, therefore the bottom row must be all zeros except for the last number which represents the probability of going from default to default, i.e. 1.

This table or matrix represents probabilities over a finite horizon. But during that time a bond may have gone from A to BBB to BB, how can we model this sequence of migrations? This is done by introducing a transition matrix over an infinitesimal time period. We can model continuous-time transitions between states via **Markov chains**.

We will model migrations over the short time period from t to $t + dt$. Since this time period is very short, the chance of any migration at all is small. The most likely event is that there is no migration. I am going to scale the probability of a change of state with the size of the timestep dt, any other scaling will lead to a meaningless or trivial model. If the transition matrix over the timestep is $\mathbf{P}_{dt}$ then I can write

$$\mathbf{P}_{dt} = \mathbf{I} + dt\,\mathbf{Q},$$

for some matrix $\mathbf{Q}$ and where $\mathbf{I}$ is the identity matrix. The sum of the entries in each row of $\mathbf{Q}$ must sum to zero, and the bottom row must only contain zeros since default is an

Table 43.3 An example of a transition matrix.

	AAA	AA	A	BBB	BB	B	CCC	Default
AAA	0.90829	0.08272	0.00736	0.00065	0.00066	0.00014	0.00006	0.00012
AA	0.00665	0.90890	0.07692	0.00583	0.00064	0.00066	0.00029	0.00011
A	0.00092	0.02420	0.91305	0.05228	0.00678	0.00227	0.00009	0.00041
BBB	0.00042	0.00320	0.05878	0.87459	0.04964	0.01078	0.00110	0.00149
BB	0.00039	0.00126	0.00644	0.07710	0.81159	0.08397	0.00970	0.00955
B	0.00044	0.00211	0.00361	0.00718	0.07961	0.80767	0.04992	0.04946
CCC	0.00127	0.00122	0.00423	0.01195	0.02690	0.11711	0.64479	0.19253
Default	0	0	0	0	0	0	0	1

absorbing state. I will use $\mathbf{P}(t, t')$ to denote the transition matrix over a *finite* time interval from t until t'.

43.14.1 The Forward Equation

By considering how one can change from state to state during the timestep dt and the relevant probabilities we find that the relationship between $\mathbf{P}(t, t')$ and $\mathbf{P}_{dt}$ is simply

$$\mathbf{P}(t, t' + dt) = \mathbf{P}(t, t')\mathbf{P}_{dt}.$$

In terms of $\mathbf{Q}$ this is

$$\mathbf{P}(t, t' + dt) = \mathbf{P}(t, t')(\mathbf{I} + dt\mathbf{Q}).$$

Subtracting $\mathbf{P}(t, t')$ from both sides and dividing by dt we get

$$\frac{\partial \mathbf{P}(t, t')}{\partial t'} = \mathbf{P}(t, t')\mathbf{Q}.$$

This ordinary differential equation is the **forward equation** and must be solved with

$$\mathbf{P}(t, t) = \mathbf{I}.$$

The solution of this *matrix* equation for constant $\mathbf{Q}$ is

$$\mathbf{P}(t, t') = e^{(t'-t)\mathbf{Q}}. \tag{43.8}$$

The exponential of a matrix is defined via an infinite sum so that

$$e^{(t'-t)\mathbf{Q}} = \sum_{i=0}^{\infty} \frac{1}{i!}(t' - t)^i \mathbf{Q}^i.$$

We can use Equation (43.8) in several ways. First, suppose that at time $t = 0$ company XYZ is rated A. Supposing that we know $\mathbf{Q}$, how can we find the probability of being in any particular state at the future time T? This is simple. We just need to find the third row down in the matrix $\mathbf{P}(0, T)$. With $\mathbf{e}_i$ to denote the row vector with zeros everywhere except in the ith column, corresponding to the initial state. In our case $i = 3$. The answer to the question is

$$\mathbf{e}_i\mathbf{P}(0, T) = \mathbf{e}_i e^{T\mathbf{Q}}.$$

Another way to use the solution of the forward equation is to deduce the matrix $\mathbf{Q}$ from the transition matrix over a finite time horizon. In other words, we can solve

$$e^{T\mathbf{Q}} = \mathbf{P}(0, T)$$

for $\mathbf{Q}$. Why might we want to do this? One reason is that some rating agencies, and other firms, publish the transition matrix for a time horizon of one year, for example Table 43.3. If you want to know what might happen for shorter timescales than that (and you believe the one-year matrix) then you should find $\mathbf{Q}$.

Suppose that we can **diagonalize** the matrix $\mathbf{Q}$ in the form

$$\mathbf{Q} = \mathbf{M}\mathbf{D}\mathbf{M}^{-1},$$

where $\mathbf{D}$ is a diagonal matrix. If we can do this then the entries of $\mathbf{D}$ are the eigenvalues of $\mathbf{Q}$. We can then write

$$\begin{aligned}\mathbf{P}(0,T) = e^{T\mathbf{Q}} &= \sum_{i=0}^{\infty} \frac{1}{i!} T^i \mathbf{Q}^i \\ &= \sum_{i=0}^{\infty} \frac{1}{i!} T^i (\mathbf{MDM}^{-1})^i \\ &= \sum_{i=0}^{\infty} \frac{1}{i!} T^i \underbrace{(\mathbf{MDM}^{-1})\dots(\mathbf{MDM}^{-1})}_{i} \\ &= \mathbf{M} \sum_{i=0}^{\infty} \frac{1}{i!} T^i \mathbf{D}^i \mathbf{M}^{-1}.\end{aligned}$$

But since $\mathbf{D}$ is diagonal, when it is raised to the ith power the result is another diagonal matrix with each diagonal element raised to the ith power:

$$\mathbf{D}^i = \begin{pmatrix} d_1 & 0 & 0 & 0 & 0 \\ 0 & d_2 & 0 & 0 & 0 \\ 0 & 0 & d_3 & 0 & 0 \\ 0 & 0 & 0 & d_4 & 0 \\ 0 & 0 & 0 & 0 & d_5 \end{pmatrix}^i = \begin{pmatrix} d_1^i & 0 & 0 & 0 & 0 \\ 0 & d_2^i & 0 & 0 & 0 \\ 0 & 0 & d_3^i & 0 & 0 \\ 0 & 0 & 0 & d_4^i & 0 \\ 0 & 0 & 0 & 0 & d_5^i \end{pmatrix}.$$

From this it follows that

$$\mathbf{P}(0,T) = \mathbf{M}e^{T\mathbf{D}}\mathbf{M}^{-1},$$

where $e^{T\mathbf{D}}$ is the matrix with diagonal elements e^{Td_i}. The eigenvalues of the two matrices $\mathbf{P}(0,T)$ and $\mathbf{Q}$ are closely related. The strategy for finding $\mathbf{Q}$ is to first diagonalize $\mathbf{P}(0,T)$ to find $\mathbf{M}\,e^{T\mathbf{D}}$, from which it is a simple matter to determine the matrix $\mathbf{Q}$.

43.14.2 The Backward Equation

The **backward equation** which has a similar meaning to the backward equation for diffusion problems, can be derived in a similar manner. The equation is

$$\frac{\partial \mathbf{P}(t,t')}{\partial t} = -\mathbf{QP}(t,t'). \tag{43.9}$$

43.15 THE PRICING EQUATION

Having built up a model for rating migration, let's look at how to price risky bonds. We will concentrate on zero-coupon bonds. In the previous section we derived forward and backward equations for the transition matrix. The link between the backward equation and contract prices in the Brownian motion world is retained in the Markov chain world, so I will skip most of the details.

43.15.1 Constant Interest Rates

The price of the risky bond depends on the credit rating of the company. We will therefore need one value per rating. The column vector $\mathbf{V}$ will have as its entries the bond value for each of the credit states. Assuming for the moment that interest rates are constant, this vector will be a function of t only. In the same way that the value of an option is related to the backward equation for the transition density function, we now have the following equation for the bond value:

$$\frac{d\mathbf{V}}{dt} + (\mathbf{Q} - r\mathbf{I})\mathbf{V} = 0,$$

This is just the backward equation (43.9) with an extra discounting term. The final condition for this equation is

$$\mathbf{V}(T) = \mathbf{1},$$

where $\mathbf{1}$ is the column vector consisting of 1s in all the rows. How does the equation change if there is a recovery on default?

43.15.2 Stochastic Interest Rates

The extension to stochastic interest rate is quite straightforward. The governing equation is

$$\frac{\partial \mathbf{V}}{\partial t} + \tfrac{1}{2}\beta^2 \frac{\partial^2 \mathbf{V}}{\partial r^2} + (\alpha - \lambda\beta)\frac{\partial \mathbf{V}}{\partial r} + (\mathbf{Q} - r\mathbf{I})\mathbf{V} = 0,$$

43.16 CREDIT RISK IN CBS

The risk of default can be very important for the convertible bond (CB), discussed in some depth in Chapter 36 but with little reference to credit issues. The CB is like a bond in that it pays its owner coupons during its life and a principal at maturity. However, the holder may convert the bond at specified times into a number of the underlying stock. This feature makes the CB very like an option. The reader is referred to Chapter 36 for all the details and the notation.

We can combine the ideas in the present chapter with those from Chapter 36 to derive a model for CBs with risk of default priced in. I will present two possible approaches.

43.16.1 Bankruptcy When Stock Reaches a Critical Level

We can model the default of the issuing company by saying that should its stock fall to a level S_b then it will default. Such a model is similar in spirit to that described in Section 43.4. We only need to add the condition

$$V(S_b, t) = 0,$$

to our favorite (no credit risk) CB model.

43.16.2 Incorporating the Instantaneous Risk of Default

Another possibility, in line with the instantaneous risk of default model described above, is to have an exogenous default triggered by a Poisson process, as in Section 43.6. In a two-factor CB setting we arrive at

$$\frac{\partial V}{\partial t} + \tfrac{1}{2}\sigma^2 S^2 \frac{\partial^2 V}{\partial S^2} + \rho\sigma S w \frac{\partial^2 V}{\partial S \partial r} + \tfrac{1}{2} w^2 \frac{\partial^2 V}{\partial r^2}$$
$$+ rS\frac{\partial V}{\partial S} + (u - \lambda w)\frac{\partial V}{\partial r} - (r + p)V = 0.$$

In this model we have stochastic r and stochastic S. We can have p a constant, a known function of time, or even a known function of r and S.

This approach has the advantage that it reduces to common market pricing practice in the absence of any stock dependence. This allows us to price instruments in a consistent fashion.

When the stock price is very small the above model will yield a CB price that is close to the price of a non-convertible bond. It is market experience, however, that in such a situation the price of the CB falls dramatically. The market sees the low stock price as an indicator of a very sick company. This can be modeled by having the instantaneous risk of default being dependent on the stock price, $p(S)$. If p goes to infinity sufficiently rapidly as $S \to 0$ we find that the CB value goes to zero. Note that there is no more effort involved, computationally, in solving such a problem since we must anyway solve for the CB value as a function of S. In Figure 43.12 is shown the value of a CB with and without credit risk taken into account in a one-factor model, with deterministic interest rates.

In Figure 43.13 is shown the output of a two-factor model for the CB with risk of default. The interest rate model was Vasicek, fitted to a flat 7% yield curve.

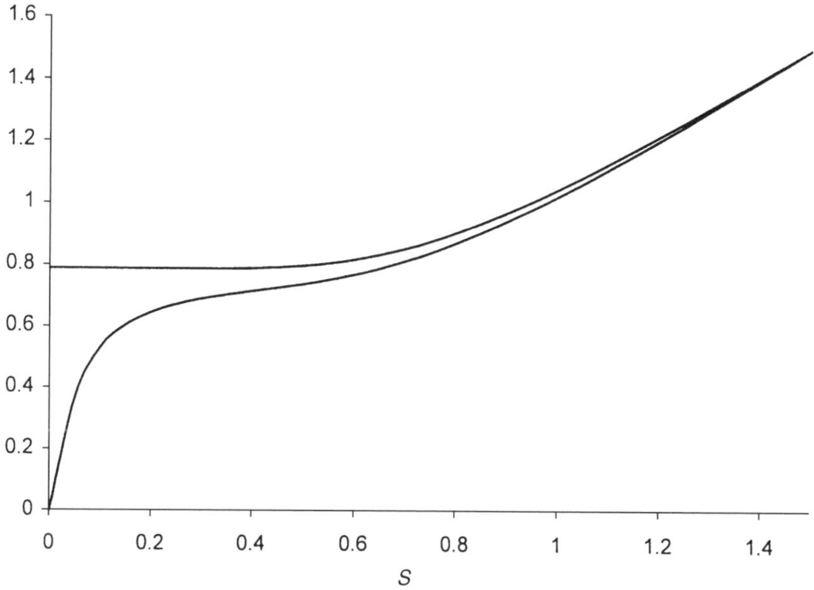

Figure 43.12 Value of a CB against underlying with (lower curve) and without (upper curve) risk of default.

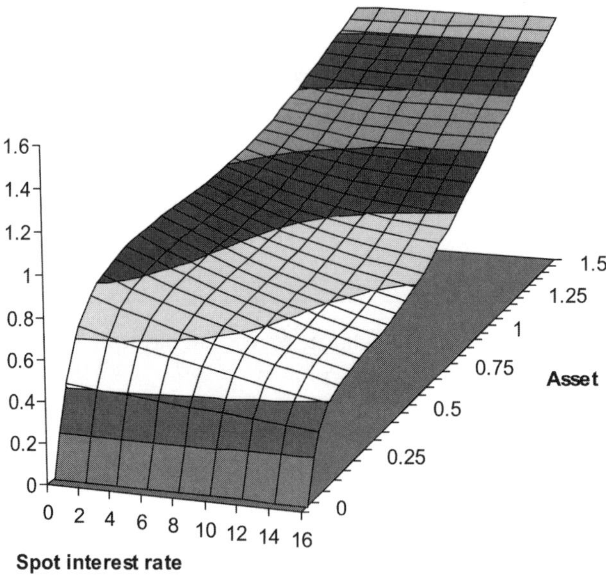

Figure 43.13 Value of a CB against underlying and interest rate with risk of default taken into account.

43.17 SUMMARY

As can be seen from this chapter, credit risk modeling is a very big subject. I have shown some of the popular approaches, but they are by no means the only possibilites. To aid with the assessment of credit risk, the bank JP Morgan have created CreditMetrics, a methodology for assessing the impact of default events on a portfolio. This is described in Chapter 45.

As a final thought for this chapter, suppose that a company issues just the one risky bond so that there is no way of hedging the default. If you believe that the market is underpricing the bond because it overestimates the risk of default then you might decide to buy it. If you intend holding it until expiry, then the market price in the future is only relevant in so far as you may change your mind. But you really do care about the likelihood of default and will pay very close attention to news about the company. On the other hand, if you buy the bond with the intention of only holding it for a short time your main concern should be for how the market is behaving and the real risk of default is irrelevant. You may still watch out for news about the company, but now your concern will be for how the market reacts to the news, not the news itself.

FURTHER READING

- See Black & Scholes (1973), Merton (1974), Black & Cox (1976), Geske (1977) and Chance (1990) for a treatment of the debt of a firm as an option on the assets of that firm. See Longstaff & Schwartz (1994) for more recent work in this area.
- The articles by Cooper & Martin (1996) and Schönbucher (1998) are general reviews of the state of credit risk modeling.

- See Apabhai, Georgikopoulos, Hasnip, Jamie, Kim & Wilmott (1998) for more details of the company and debt valuation model, especially for final and boundary conditions for various business strategies. Epstein, Mayor, Schönbucher, Whalley & Wilmott (1977 a, b) describe the firm valuation models in detail, including the effects of advertising and market research.
- The classic reference, and a very good read, for firm-valuation modeling is Dixit & Pindyck (1994). For a non-technical POV see Copeland, Koller & Murrin (1990).
- See Kim (1995) for the application of the company valuation model to the question of company mergers and some suggestions for how it can be applied to problems in company relocation and tax status.
- Important work on the instantaneous risk of default model is by Jarrow & Turnbull (1990, 1995), Litterman & Iben (1991), Madan & Unal (1994), Lando (1994 a), Duffie & Singleton (1994 a, b) and Schönbucher (1996).
- See Blauer & Wilmott (1998) for the instantaneous risk of default model and an application to Latin American Brady bonds.
- See Duffee (1995) for other work on the estimation of the instantaneous risk of default in practice.
- The original work on change of credit rating was due to Lando (1994 b), Jarrow, Lando & Turnbull (1997) and Das & Tufano (1994). Cox & Miller (1965) describes Markov chains in a very accessible manner.
- See Ahn, Khadem & Wilmott (1998) for the rather sensible use of utility theory in credit risk modeling.
- Current market conditions and prices for Brady bonds can be found at www.bradynet.com.
- See www.emgmkts.com for financial news from emerging markets.

EXERCISES

1. Show that we can reduce the equation for the value of a firm as a random variable to

$$\frac{\partial H}{\partial t} + \tfrac{1}{2}\sigma^2 A^2 \frac{\partial^2 H}{\partial A^2} + \mu A \frac{\partial H}{\partial A} = 0,$$

   in the case where

$$V(A, r, t) = Z(r, t; T)H(A, t).$$

2. When we value our firm as a function of earnings, how are the boundary conditions affected by the various business conditions and strategies that we can model?
3. Construct the intermediate steps in the derivation of the equation for the value of a risky bond (when default is governed by a Poisson process):

$$\frac{\partial V}{\partial t} + \tfrac{1}{2}w^2 \frac{\partial^2 V}{\partial r^2} + (u - \lambda w)\frac{\partial V}{\partial r} - (r + p)V = 0.$$

4. Adjust the two-factor model for the convertible bond price to accommodate a risk of default of the form

$$a + bS^{-\alpha}.$$

CHAPTER 44
credit derivatives

In this Chapter...

- credit derivatives triggered by default
- derivatives of the yield spread
- payment on change of rating
- pricing credit derivatives using different models

44.1 INTRODUCTION

In this chapter I continue with the theme of pricing risky contracts. Here 'risky' means that there is some exposure to default risk. With credit derivatives that risk of default is explicitly acknowledged, and in many cases the owner of the credit derivative will benefit in the case of default. Thus a credit derivative may be thought of as insurance for another risky contract such as a simple bond; the holder of a bond always loses out on default.

There are many different types of credit derivative and the business is currently growing very rapidly. I will only discuss the main issues in the pricing of these contracts, giving examples as much as space will allow.

44.2 DERIVATIVES TRIGGERED BY DEFAULT

The most basic form of credit derivatives are those that pay off in the event of default by the issuing company or country. Technically, the definition of default is any non-compliance with the exact specifications of a contract, so that a coupon paid just one day late would count as a default event.

44.2.1 Default Swap

In the **default swap** counterparty A pays interest to counterparty B for a prescribed time until default of the underlying instrument. In the event of default B pays A the principal. This is the simplest example of a credit derivative and can be thought of as insurance on the underlying instrument, bought by A from B.

44.2.2 Credit Default Swap

Very similar to the above is the **credit default swap** in which counterparty A pays LIBOR plus a fixed premium until default of the underlying instrument, and B pays A LIBOR for the whole life of the underlying instrument. In this case there is no exchange of principal. But again A is simply buying insurance against default.

44.2.3 Limited Recourse Note

The **limited recourse note** has a lesser exposure to default than the above contracts. Typically, there is an exposure to two underlying instruments. Interest is paid at a rate of r_1 while neither of the instruments has defaulted. When/if the first instrument is defaulted the interest is reduced to r_2, and reduced again to r_3 on the default of the second instrument.

44.2.4 Asset Swap

Counterparty A owns a risky bond, but wants to swap the credit risk. He gives the bond to counterparty B in return for interest payments of LIBOR plus some suitable fixed spread. B will pay this interest until maturity life of the bond, even after default. The risk of default has passed from A to B. This is an **asset swap**. This contract can be made more complicated by including call or put provisions.

44.3 DERIVATIVES OF THE YIELD SPREAD

Other derivatives do not require default for there to be a payoff. These can be thought of as derivatives of the spread in the risky yield above the yield for an equivalent risk-free contract with the same, but guaranteed, cashflows.

44.3.1 Default Calls and Puts

Defaults calls and **puts** are respectively the rights to buy and sell the underlying instrument. Clearly much of the theory that we have seen is relevant here, but crucially the risk of default must be included in some way.

Similar to the basic default options are the options giving you the right to exchange one bond for another. For example, the option may give you the right to give back the risky bond in exchange for a smaller quantity of the riskless bond. The ratio of riskless to risky bonds would be set at the start of the contract. With an asterisk denoting the risky bond, if the bonds are both zero coupon then the payoff for this exchange option would take the form

$$\max(qZ - Z^*, 0),$$

where q is the prearranged ratio.

44.3.2 Credit Spread Options

Calculate the yield to maturity of a risky bond using the methods of Chapter 31, call this Y^*, and similarly calculate the yield to maturity of the equivalent riskless bond, call this Y. The difference between these two yields, $Y^* - Y$, is the spread. Except in rather unusual circumstances this quantity would be positive. A contract having a payoff that depends on this spread would be a credit spread option.

The payoff could be the spread between two risky bonds, perhaps from the same issuer and perhaps not, in which case the spread could change sign. Typically the payoff would then take the form

$$\max(Y_1^* - Y_2^*, 0).$$

44.4 PAYMENT ON CHANGE OF RATING

The final kind of default derivative that I want to discuss are the derivatives that have a dependence on the rating of the issuer. The issuer begins with a certain rating and during the life of the contract the rating changes, possibly triggering some payment to the holder of the derivative.

In Figure 44.1 are the contract specifications for a puttable floating rate note issued by the Korea Development Bank in June 1997. This is a US dollar-denominated note that pays US three-month LIBOR plus 18.75 basis points every quarter. The contract was to mature in 2002. The 18.75 basis points excess over LIBOR is compensation for the risk of default; the Korea Development Bank is not thought to be as creditworthy as the US government. The interesting feature in this contract is that it can be sold back to the Korea Development Bank at par, i.e. for the amount of the principal, should the rating of the bank fall below A− (S&P) or A3 (Moody's).

Moody's rating was cut from A3 to Baa2 on 10th December 1997, as can be seen in this output from Bloomberg's on 11th December 1997. The S&P rating was also dropped from A− to BBB−. This triggered the put feature, and indeed most of the bonds were sold back at par, at a cost to the Korea Development Bank of $300m. Although this put even more pressure on South Korea at a time when it was facing a dramatic liquidity crisis, the bank did

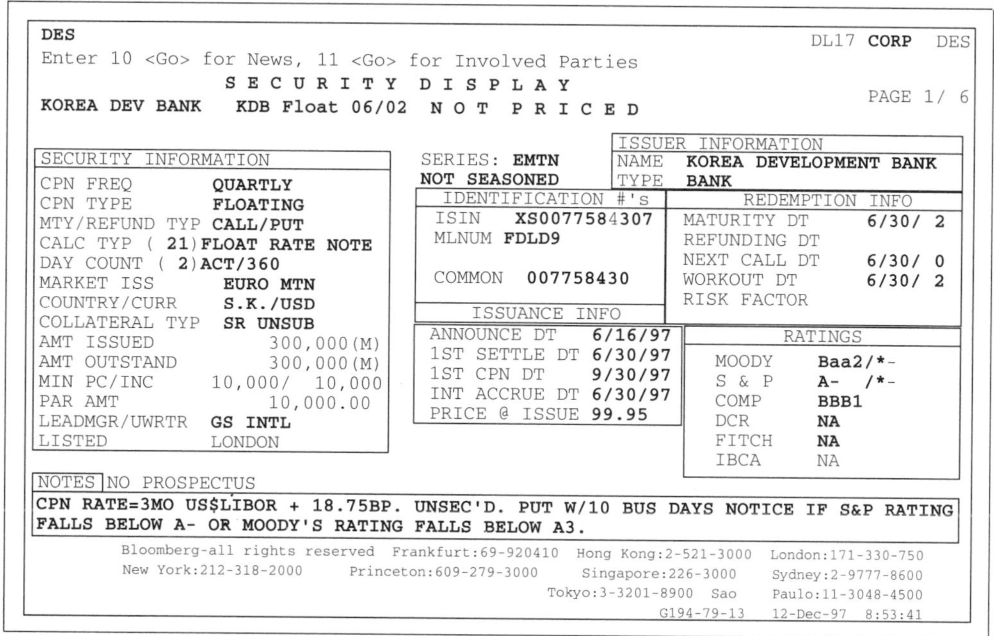

DES DL17 CORP DES
Enter 10 <Go> for News, 11 <Go> for Involved Parties
S E C U R I T Y D I S P L A Y
KOREA DEV BANK KDB Float 06/02 N O T P R I C E D PAGE 1/ 6

SECURITY INFORMATION
CPN FREQ QUARTLY
CPN TYPE FLOATING
MTY/REFUND TYP CALL/PUT
CALC TYP (21)FLOAT RATE NOTE
DAY COUNT (2)ACT/360
MARKET ISS EURO MTN
COUNTRY/CURR S.K./USD
COLLATERAL TYP SR UNSUB
AMT ISSUED 300,000(M)
AMT OUTSTAND 300,000(M)
MIN PC/INC 10,000/ 10,000
PAR AMT 10,000.00
LEADMGR/UWRTR GS INTL
LISTED LONDON

SERIES: EMTN
NOT SEASONED

ISSUER INFORMATION
NAME KOREA DEVELOPMENT BANK
TYPE BANK

IDENTIFICATION #'s
ISIN XS0077584307
MLNUM FDLD9
COMMON 007758430

REDEMPTION INFO
MATURITY DT 6/30/ 2
REFUNDING DT
NEXT CALL DT 6/30/ 0
WORKOUT DT 6/30/ 2
RISK FACTOR

ISSUANCE INFO
ANNOUNCE DT 6/16/97
1ST SETTLE DT 6/30/97
1ST CPN DT 9/30/97
INT ACCRUE DT 6/30/97
PRICE @ ISSUE 99.95

RATINGS
MOODY Baa2/*-
S & P A- /*-
COMP BBB1
DCR NA
FITCH NA
IBCA NA

NOTES NO PROSPECTUS
CPN RATE=3MO US$LIBOR + 18.75BP. UNSEC'D. PUT W/10 BUS DAYS NOTICE IF S&P RATING FALLS BELOW A- OR MOODY'S RATING FALLS BELOW A3.

Bloomberg-all rights reserved Frankfurt:69-920410 Hong Kong:2-521-3000 London:171-330-750
New York:212-318-2000 Princeton:609-279-3000 Singapore:226-3000 Sydney:2-9777-8600
Tokyo:3-3201-8900 Sao Paulo:11-3048-4500
G194-79-13 12-Dec-97 8:53:41

Figure 44.1 Contract specifications for a puttable floating rate note issued by the Korea Development Bank. Data provided by Bloomberg Financial Markets. ©1998 Bloomberg FP. All rights reserved.

not default. Later the KDB ratings fell even further; Korea was demoted to **junk bond** status, BB/Ba or less.

There are many other types of derivatives that depend on the rating of the issuer. The payoff, or new feature, as in the above example, might be triggered as soon as the rerating occurs. Alternatively, the payment may depend on the rating at a specific time, so that a downgrade followed by an upgrade to the initial level will result in no action. One can imagine subtle path dependency in the contract or a contract that pays off if there is a downgrade of two notches, without the intermediate notch being realized. One example of this is the contract that pays off in the event of default, without there having been any prior rerating.

44.5 **PRICING CREDIT DERIVATIVES**

We are going to examine two credit derivatives in detail to see possible approaches to the modeling. The first example is of an option to exchange a risky bond for a quantity of the equivalent riskless bond. To model this contract we will use a stochastic hazard rate model. The second example is a contract that pays off in the event of a rerating. For this we must obviously use a model that explicitly captures the possible change of rating.

44.5.1 An Exchange Option

An option to exchange a risky zero-coupon bond for a riskless zero-coupon bond at time T has a payoff

$$\max(qZ - Z^*, 0),$$

for some fixed q.

There are various levels of sophistication on which we can address the pricing of this bond.

The first level is to assume that risk-free rates and hazard rate are deterministic. We then arrive at a completely deterministic price for both the risk-free and the risky bonds. This is unsatisfactory because randomness is very important in the pricing of any nonlinear payoff such as the one we have here.

The second level of sophistication is to assume that one, but not both, of the interest rate and the risk of default is stochastic. For example, assume that interest rates are random but that the risk of default is constant. This is a common approach, resulting often in the simple addition of a fixed spread to yields as seen in Chapter 43. Let's see how this approach works with the exchange option.

The first stage is to price the risk-free bond. If this matures at time T_B when it receives the principal of \$1, then it will satisfy

$$\frac{\partial Z}{\partial t} + \tfrac{1}{2}w^2\frac{\partial^2 Z}{\partial r^2} + (u - \lambda w)\frac{\partial Z}{\partial r} - rZ = 0$$

with

$$Z(r, T_B) = 1$$

and where $u - \lambda w$ and w are the risk-adjusted drift and the volatility of the spot rate respectively.

The risky bond will similarly satisfy

$$\frac{\partial Z^*}{\partial t} + \tfrac{1}{2}w^2\frac{\partial^2 Z^*}{\partial r^2} + (u - \lambda w)\frac{\partial Z^*}{\partial r} - (r + p)Z^* = 0$$

with

$$Z^*(r, T_B) = 1.$$

The solution of this equation is simply

$$Z^*(r, t) = e^{-p(T_B-t)}Z(r, t).$$

This completely deterministic relationship between the two bonds, which is a result of the assumption of constant hazard rate, clearly scuppers the pricing of the exchange option. The subtlety in the pricing of this contract is due to the *randomness in the risk of default*. Usually, as in this example, the assumption of constant hazard rate is not appropriate for credit derivatives.

Still on the second level of complexity, a better assumption would be that interest rates are given by the forward rates and that the hazard rate, p, satisfies some stochastic differential equation. This approach should make more sense than the above for our contract.

Assuming that

$$dp = \gamma\, dt + \delta\, dX$$

and, for simplicity that interest rates are constant, we have

$$Z = e^{-r(T_B-t)}$$

and

$$\frac{\partial Z^*}{\partial t} + \tfrac{1}{2}\delta^2 \frac{\partial^2 Z^*}{\partial p^2} + \gamma \frac{\partial Z^*}{\partial p} - (r + p)Z^* = 0 \tag{44.1}$$

with

$$Z^*(p, T_B) = 1.$$

This problem for $Z^*(p, t)$ is mathematically identical to the earlier problem for $Z^*(r, t)$ when rates were stochastic but probability constant. Again we see the similarity between risk of default and the rate of interest. But now the payoff for our exchange option, having value $V(p, t)$, is

$$\max(qe^{-r(T_B-T)} - Z^*(p, T), 0).$$

The first term inside the parentheses is a constant and so this problem looks exactly like a put option on a zero-coupon bond, as discussed in Chapter 35. We could even go so far as to take the factor $e^{-r(T_B-t)}$ out from Z^* so losing it completely from Equation (44.1). The only difference then would be that you see a p instead of the usual r in the partial differential equation. Of course, there still remains the choice of functions γ and δ, but these are often chosen in practice so that we can find explicit solutions; again we are in territory familiar from Chapter 33.

The next level of sophistication is to have both stochastic interest rates and stochastic hazard rate. Both Z and Z^* satisfy the equation

$$\frac{\partial V}{\partial t} + \tfrac{1}{2}w^2 \frac{\partial^2 V}{\partial r^2} + \rho w \delta \frac{\partial^2 V}{\partial r \partial p} + \tfrac{1}{2}\delta^2 \frac{\partial^2 V}{\partial p^2} + (u - \lambda w)\frac{\partial V}{\partial r} + \gamma \frac{\partial V}{\partial p} - (r + p)V = 0. \tag{44.2}$$

However, the risk-free bond is independent of the risk of default so that we have $Z(r, t)$, with no p dependence. The risky bond does depend on the risk of default and is therefore a function of three variables, $Z^*(r, p, t)$.

We must first solve for the underlying bonds using

$$Z(r, T_B) = Z^*(r, p, T_B) = 1.$$

And then solve for the exchange option $V(r, p, t)$ which again satisfies (44.2) with

$$V(r, p, T) = \max(qZ(r, T) - Z^*(r, p, T), 0).$$

Because this exchange option is a second-order contract the price may be quite sensitive to the model.

44.5.2 Payoff on Change of Rating

More subtle than a simple payoff in default is payoff on change of rating, for example the Korea Development Bank note described above. I will describe the pricing of two distinct styles of such a contract. In the first example there will be a payment if the rating takes certain values at expiry and in the second there will be a payoff if certain ratings are realized at any time before expiry.

Suppose that an issuer is currently rated AAA and a contract specifies that a fixed amount will be paid to the owner of the contract if the issuer is rated only AA on a certain date. Clearly, to price this contract we need a model that explicitly allows for rating migration. Let us take the Markov chain model of Chapter 43 and assume that interest rates are constant. The equation to be solved is

$$\frac{d\mathbf{V}}{dt} + (\mathbf{Q} - r\mathbf{I})\mathbf{V} = 0.$$

The contract specification of payment if the grade is AA must be incorporated into the final condition. Since there is no payment unless the issuer is rated AA the final condition is simply

$$\mathbf{V}(T) = \mathbf{e}_{\mathrm{AA}},$$

where $\mathbf{e}_{\mathrm{AA}}$ is the column vector with a zero in all the rows, except for the row corresponding to the rating AA where there is a 1.

The contract that is triggered by a downgrade to AA at *any time* is more interesting, and not much harder to price.

It might help if you think of this contract as being like an 'in' barrier option. In this option the payment is triggered by the underlying hitting a given level. We have a similar situation with the present credit derivative, with the level of the credit rating playing the role of the underlying.

Again we must solve

$$\frac{d\mathbf{V}}{dt} + (\mathbf{Q} - r\mathbf{I})\mathbf{V} = 0.$$

with the final condition

$$\mathbf{V}(T) = \mathbf{e}_{\mathrm{AA}}.$$

But now we have an extra condition, corresponding to the barrier boundary condition in the knock-in:

$$\mathbf{V}_{\mathrm{AA}} = 1 \quad \text{for all} \quad t < T,$$

where $\mathbf{V}_{\mathrm{AA}}$ is the entry in the vector $\mathbf{V}$ corresponding to the AA rating.

In other words, the minute that the level AA is reached we receive a payment of 1. In such a contract it is common to limit the times when the trigger is active. In such a contract the condition on $\mathbf{V}_{\text{AA}}$ is only switched on when the trigger is active.

Finally, let's take a look at the Korea Development Bank note again. This is very similar to the last problem above. The difference is that instead of getting a fixed amount on a downgrade we are allowed to put the note back to the issuer. This results in the constraint

$$\mathbf{V}_i \geq 1 \quad \text{for all} \quad i \leq i^*,$$

where i^* is the index for the grade triggering the put option. (When the interest rate is non-diffusive the continuity of derivatives of the option price, as seen in American options, is no longer necessary.)

44.6 SUMMARY

The current state of default-risk modeling is, in my opinion, far from satisfactory. The problems associated with modeling and parameter estimation are enormous. In earlier chapters we saw how to get round uncertainty in parameters in the options world. These elegant methods, such as worst-case scenario analysis, are unlikely to be of much use here because of the extreme nature of the worst case. For once I don't have any remedy.[1] A possible direction for further work would be to distinguish between one's own estimation and pricing of default risk and the market's.

It is very difficult to assess the risk of default, by either analysis of time series data or fundamental analysis. And the results of your effort may not even be relevant to the matter of pricing. Suppose, for example, that you buy a risky bond, intending to hold it for only one year during which time you think there is no risk of default. When you come to sell it, hopefully at a profit after including any cashflows, how much is it then worth? The answer to this depends on the market's subjective view of the likelihood and timing of default and not on any objective risk of default. On the other hand, if you buy a bond intending to hold it to maturity then the risk of default is all that matters; who cares what the market thinks? This example illustrates the importance of distinguishing between the market's 'model' and your own model of reality. Some of the consequences of this have been discussed in Chapter 28.

FURTHER READING

- Very little has yet been written on credit derivatives. But see the papers by Das (1995), Schönbucher (1996, 1997 a, b, 1998) and Schönbucher & Schlögl (1996) for the pricing and, importantly, the hedging of credit derivatives.

EXERCISES

1. Invent some new credit derivative products that depend on the price of a risky bond. Experiment with pricing these contracts in a variety of settings, depending on whether

[1] Note added in proof: *Now* I do have the solution, but there isn't the space to include it here. Wait for the second edition.

interest rates and/or risk of default are stochastic. For what contracts will you need stochastic interest rate? For what contracts will you need stochastic hazard rate?

2. Invent some new credit derivative products that depend on the credit rating of an issuer. Experiment with pricing these contracts in a variety of settings, depending on whether interest rates are stochastic. Can you accommodate early exercise in you contracts?
3. How would you approach the modeling of a contract that pays off if a company defaults before it is downgraded?

CHAPTER 45

RiskMetrics, CreditMetrics and CrashMetrics

In this Chapter...

- the methodology of RiskMetrics for measuring value at risk
- the methodology of CreditMetrics for measuring a portfolio's exposure to default events
- the methodology of CrashMetrics for measuring a portfolio's exposure to sudden, unhedgeable market movements

45.1 INTRODUCTION

In Chapter 42 I described the concept of the 'Value at Risk' (VaR) of a portfolio. I repeat the definition of VaR here: VaR is 'an estimate, with a given degree of confidence, of how much one can lose from one's portfolio over a given time horizon.' In that chapter I showed ways of calculating VaR (and some of the pitfalls of such calculations). Typically the data required for the calculations are parameters for the 'underlyings' and measures of a portfolio's current exposure to these underlyings. The parameters include volatilities and correlations of the assets, and, for longer time horizons, drift rates. The exposure of the portfolio is measured by the deltas, and, if necessary, the gammas (including cross derivatives) and the theta of the portfolio. The sensitivities of the portfolio are obviously best calculated by the owner of the portfolio, the bank. However, the asset parameters can be estimated by anyone with the right data. In October 1994 the American bank JP Morgan introduced the system **RiskMetrics** as a service for the estimation of VaR parameters. Some of this service is free, the data sets are available at www.reuters.com (or follow links from www.jpmorgan.com), but the accompanying risk management software is not.

JP Morgan has also proposed a similar approach, together with a data service, for the estimation of risks associated with risk of default: **CreditMetrics**. CreditMetrics has several aims, two of which are the creation of a benchmark for measuring credit risk and the increase in market liquidity. If the former aim is successful then it will become possible to measure risks systematically across instruments and, at the very least, to make relative value judgments. From this follows the second aim. Once instruments, and in particular the risks associated with them, are better understood they will become less frightening to investors, promoting liquidity.

The final piece of the jigsaw for estimating risk in a portfolio is **CrashMetrics**. If Value at Risk is about normal market conditions then Crashmetrics is the opposite side of the coin, it is about 'fire sale' conditions and the far-from-orderly liquidation of assets in far-from-normal conditions. CrashMetrics is a dataset and methodolgy for estimating the exposure of a portfolio to extreme market movements or crashes. It assumes that the crash is unhedgeable and then finds the worst outcome for the value of the portfolio. The method then shows how to mitigate the effects of the crash by the purchase or sales of derivatives in an optimal fashion, so-called Platinum Hedging. Derivatives have sometimes been thought of as being a dangerous component in a portfolio; in the CrashMetrics methodology they are put to a benign use.

45.2 THE RISKMETRICS DATASETS

The RiskMetrics datasets are extremely broad and comprehensive. They are distributed over the internet. They consist of three types of data: one used for estimating risk over the time horizon of one day, the second having a one-month time horizon, and the third has been designed to satisfy the requirements in the latest proposals from the Bank for International Settlements on the use of internal models to estimate market risk. The datasets contain estimates of volatilities and correlations for over 400 instruments, covering foreign exchange, bonds, swaps, commodities and equity indices. Term-structure information is available for many currencies.

45.3 CALCULATING THE PARAMETERS THE RISKMETRICS WAY

A detailed technical description of the method for estimating financial parameters can be found at the JP Morgan web site. Here I only give a brief outline of major points.

45.3.1 Estimating Volatility

The volatility of an asset is measured as the annualized standard deviation of returns. There are many ways of taking this measurement. The simplest is to take data going back a set period, three months, say, calculate the return for each day (or over the typical timescale at which you will be rehedging) and calculate the sample standard deviation of this data. This will result in a time series of three-month volatility.[1] This approach gives equal weight to all of the observations over the previous three months. This estimate of volatility on day i is calculated as

$$\sigma_i = \sqrt{\frac{1}{\delta t(M-1)} \sum_{j=i-M+1}^{i} (R_j - \overline{R})^2},$$

where δt is the timestep (typically one day), M is the number of days in the estimate (approximately sixty three in three months), R_j is the return on day j and $\overline{R}$ is the average return over the previous M days. If δt is small then we can in practice neglect $\overline{R}$.

This measurement of volatility has two major drawbacks. First, it is not clear how many days, data we should use; what happened three months ago may not be relevant to today. But the more data we have the smaller will be the sampling error if the volatility really has not changed in that period. Second, a large positive or negative return on one day will be felt in

[1] Which may or may not bear any resemblance to three-month implied volatility.

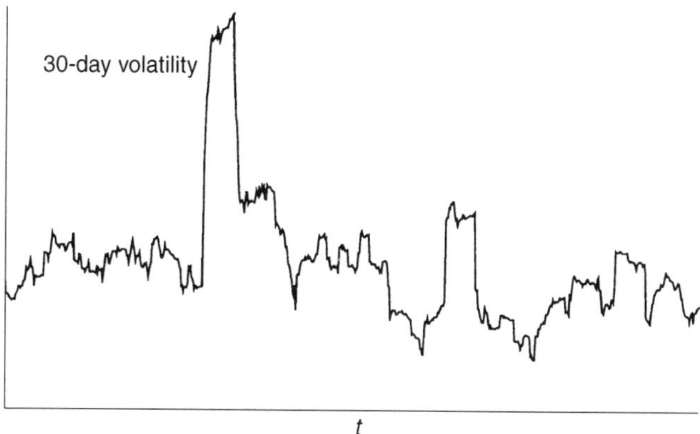

Figure 45.1 Thirty-day volatility.

this historical volatility for the next three months. At the end of this period the volatility will apparently drop suddenly, yet there will have been no underlying change in market conditions; the drop will be completely spurious. Thus, the volatility measured in this way will show 'plateauing.' A typical thirty-day volatility plot, with plateauing, is shown in Figure 45.1.

In RiskMetrics the volatility is measured as the square root of a variance that is an exponential moving average of the square of price returns. This ensures that any individual return has a gradually decreasing effect on the estimated volatility, and plateauing does not occur. This volatility is estimated according to

$$\sigma_i = \sqrt{\frac{1-\lambda}{\delta t}\sum_{j=-\infty}^{i} \lambda^{i-j} R_j^2},$$

where λ represents the weighting attached to the past volatility versus the present return (and we have neglected the mean of R, assuming that the time horizon is sufficiently small). This difference in weighting is more easily seen if we write the above as

$$\sigma_i^2 = \lambda\sigma_{i-1}^2 + (1-\lambda)\frac{R_i^2}{\delta t}.$$

The parameter λ has been chosen by JP Morgan as either 0.94 for a horizon of one day and 0.97 for a horizon of one month. Another possibility is to choose λ to minimize the difference between the squares of the historical volatility and an implied volatility.

The spreadsheet in Figure 45.2 shows how to calculate such an exponentially-weighted volatility. As can be seen from the plot, it is much 'better behaved' than the uniformly weighted version.

45.3.2 Correlation

The estimation of correlation is similar to that of volatility. To calculate the covariance σ_{12} between assets 1 and 2 we can take an equal weighting of returns from the two assets over the

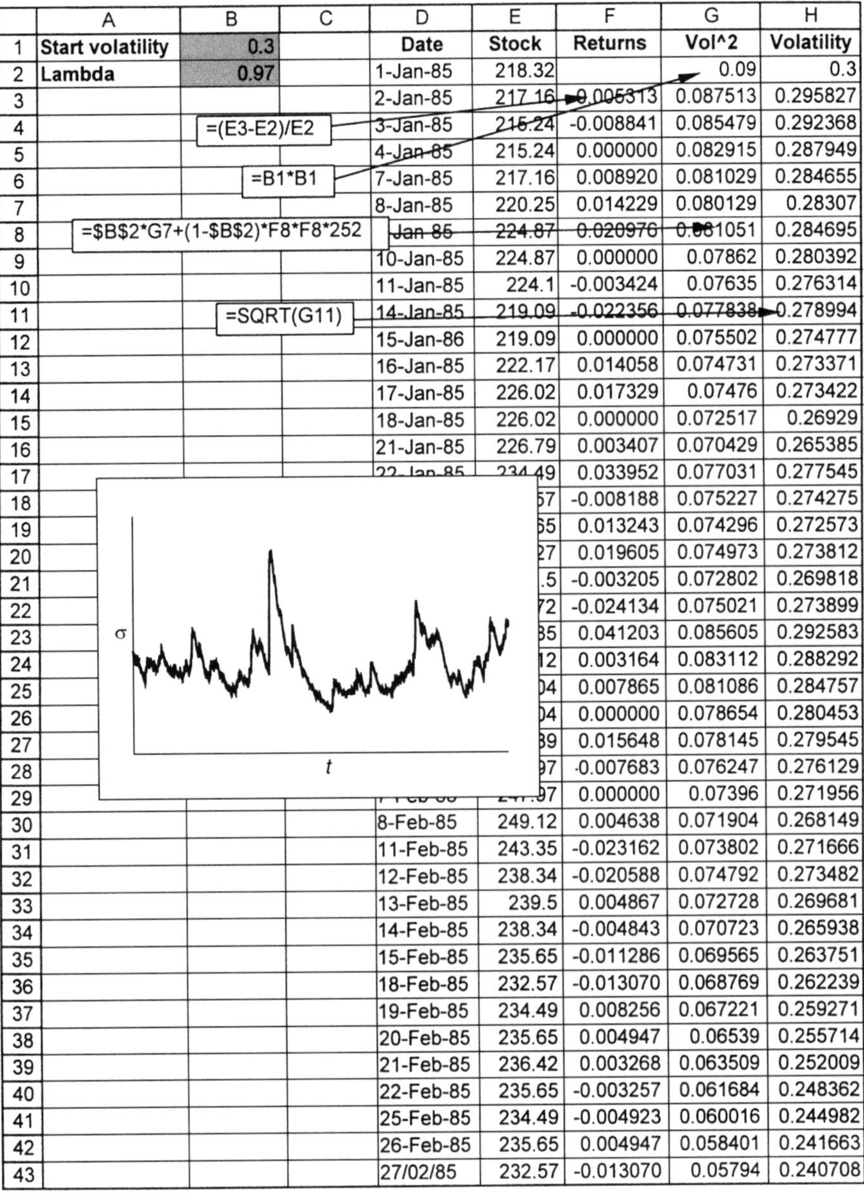

	A	B	C	D	E	F	G	H
1	Start volatility	0.3		Date	Stock	Returns	Vol^2	Volatility
2	Lambda	0.97		1-Jan-85	218.32		0.09	0.3
3				2-Jan-85	217.16	-0.005313	0.087513	0.295827
4				3-Jan-85	215.24	-0.008841	0.085479	0.292368
5				4-Jan-85	215.24	0.000000	0.082915	0.287949
6				7-Jan-85	217.16	0.008920	0.081029	0.284655
7				8-Jan-85	220.25	0.014229	0.080129	0.28307
8				Jan-85	224.87	0.020976	0.081051	0.284695
9				10-Jan-85	224.87	0.000000	0.07862	0.280392
10				11-Jan-85	224.1	-0.003424	0.07635	0.276314
11				14-Jan-85	219.09	-0.022356	0.077838	0.278994
12				15-Jan-86	219.09	0.000000	0.075502	0.274777
13				16-Jan-85	222.17	0.014058	0.074731	0.273371
14				17-Jan-85	226.02	0.017329	0.07476	0.273422
15				18-Jan-85	226.02	0.000000	0.072517	0.26929
16				21-Jan-85	226.79	0.003407	0.070429	0.265385
17					234.49	0.033952	0.077031	0.277545
18					57	-0.008188	0.075227	0.274275
19					55	0.013243	0.074296	0.272573
20					27	0.019605	0.074973	0.273812
21					.5	-0.003205	0.072802	0.269818
22					72	-0.024134	0.075021	0.273899
23					35	0.041203	0.085605	0.292583
24					12	0.003164	0.083112	0.288292
25					04	0.007865	0.081086	0.284757
26					04	0.000000	0.078654	0.280453
27					39	0.015648	0.078145	0.279545
28					97	-0.007683	0.076247	0.276129
29					.97	0.000000	0.07396	0.271956
30				8-Feb-85	249.12	0.004638	0.071904	0.268149
31				11-Feb-85	243.35	-0.023162	0.073802	0.271666
32				12-Feb-85	238.34	-0.020588	0.074792	0.273482
33				13-Feb-85	239.5	0.004867	0.072728	0.269681
34				14-Feb-85	238.34	-0.004843	0.070723	0.265938
35				15-Feb-85	235.65	-0.011286	0.069565	0.263751
36				18-Feb-85	232.57	-0.013070	0.068769	0.262239
37				19-Feb-85	234.49	0.008256	0.067221	0.259271
38				20-Feb-85	235.65	0.004947	0.06539	0.255714
39				21-Feb-85	236.42	0.003268	0.063509	0.252009
40				22-Feb-85	235.65	-0.003257	0.061684	0.248362
41				25-Feb-85	234.49	-0.004923	0.060016	0.244982
42				26-Feb-85	235.65	0.004947	0.058401	0.241663
43				27/02/85	232.57	-0.013070	0.05794	0.240708

Figure 45.2 Spreadsheet to calculate an exponentially-weighted volatility.

last M days:

$$\sigma_{12_i} = \sqrt{\frac{1}{\delta t(M-1)} \sum_{j=i-M+1}^{i} (R_{1_j} - \overline{R}_1)(R_{2_i} - \overline{R}_2)}.$$

Again, this measure shows spurious sudden rises and falls because of the equal weighting of all the returns.

Alternatively, we can use an exponentially weighted estimate

$$\sigma_{12_i}^2 = \lambda\sigma_{12_{i-1}}^2 + (1-\lambda)\frac{R_{1_i}R_{2_i}}{\delta t}.$$

There are problems with the estimation of covariance due to the synchronicity of asset movements and measurement. Two assets may be perfectly correlated but because of their measurement at different times they may appear to be completely uncorrelated. This is a problem when using data from markets in different time zones. Moreover, there is no guarantee that the exponentially-weighted covariances give a positive-definite matrix.

45.4 THE CREDITMETRICS DATASET

The CreditMetrics dataset is available free of charge from www.jpmorgan.com. The CreditMetrics methodology is also described in great detail at that site. The dataset consists of four data types: yield curves, spreads, transition matrices and correlations. Before reading the following sections the reader should be comfortable with the concept of credit rating, see Chapter 43.

45.4.1 Yield Curves

The CreditMetrics yield curve dataset consists of the *risk-free* yield to maturity for major currencies. In Figure 45.3 is shown an example of these risk-free yields. The dataset contains yields for maturities of one, two, three, five, seven, 10 and 30 years. For example, from the yield curve dataset we have information such as the yield to maturity for a three-year US dollar bond is 6.12%.

45.4.2 Spreads

For each credit rating, the dataset gives the spread above the riskless yield for each maturity. In Figure 45.3 is shown a typical riskless US yield curve, and the yield on AA and BBB bonds. For example, we may be given that the spread for an AA bond is 0.54% above the riskless

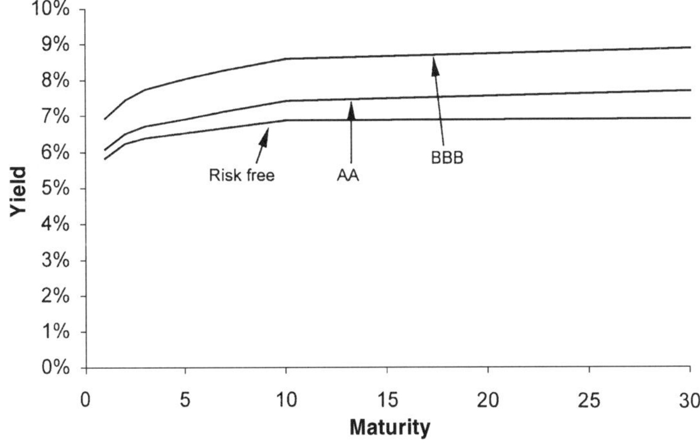

Figure 45.3 Risk-free and two risky yield curves.

yield for a three-year bond. Observe that the riskier the bond the higher the yield; the yield on the BBB bond is everywhere higher than that on the AA bond which is in turn higher than the risk-free yield. This higher yield for risky bonds is compensation for the possibility of not receiving future coupons or the principal.

45.4.3 Transition Matrices

The concept of the transition matrix has been discussed in Chapter 43. In the CreditMetrics framework, the transition matrix has as its entries the probability of a change of credit rating at the end of a given time horizon; for example, the probability of an upgrade from AA to AAA might be 5.5%. The time horizon for the CreditMetrics dataset is one year. Unless the time horizon is very long, the largest probability is typically for the bond to remain at its initial rating; let's say that the probability of staying at AA is 87% in this example. We discussed transition matrices in depth in Chapter 43.

45.4.4 Correlations

In the risk-free yield, the spreads and the transition matrix, there is sufficient information for the CreditMetrics method to derive distributions for the possible future values of a single bond. I show how this is done in the next section. However, when we come to examine the behavior of a portfolio of risky bonds, we must consider whether there is any relationship between the rerating or default of one bond and the rerating or default of another. In other words, are bonds issued by different companies or governments in some sense correlated? This is where the CreditMetrics correlation dataset comes in. This dataset gives the correlations between major indices in many countries.

Each company issuing bonds has the return on its stock decomposed into parts correlated with these indices and a part which is specific to the company. By relating all bond issuers to these indices we can determine correlations between the companies in our portfolio. We will see how this is used in practice later in this chapter.

45.5 THE CREDITMETRICS METHODOLOGY

The CreditMetrics methodology is about calculating the possible values of a risky portfolio at some time in the future (the time horizon) and estimating the probability of such values occuring. Let us consider just a single risky bond currently rated AA. Suppose that the bond is zero-coupon, with a maturity of three years and we want to know the possible state of this investment in one year's time. The yield to maturity on this instrument might be 6.12%, for a three-year riskless bond, plus 0.54% for the spread for a three-year AA-rated bond. The total yield is therefore 6.66%, giving a price of 0.819.

The value of the bond will fluctuate between now and one year's time for each of three reasons: the passage of time, the evolution of interest rates and the possible regrading of the bond. Let us take these three points in turn.

First, because of the passage of time our three-year bond will be a two-year bond in one year. But what will be the yield on a two-year bond in one year's time? This is the second point. The assumption that is made in CreditMetrics is that the forward rates do not change between today and the time horizon ('rolling down the curve'). From the yields that we have today we can calculate the forward rates that apply between now and one year, between one and two years, between two and three years, etc. This calculation is described in Chapter 31. We can

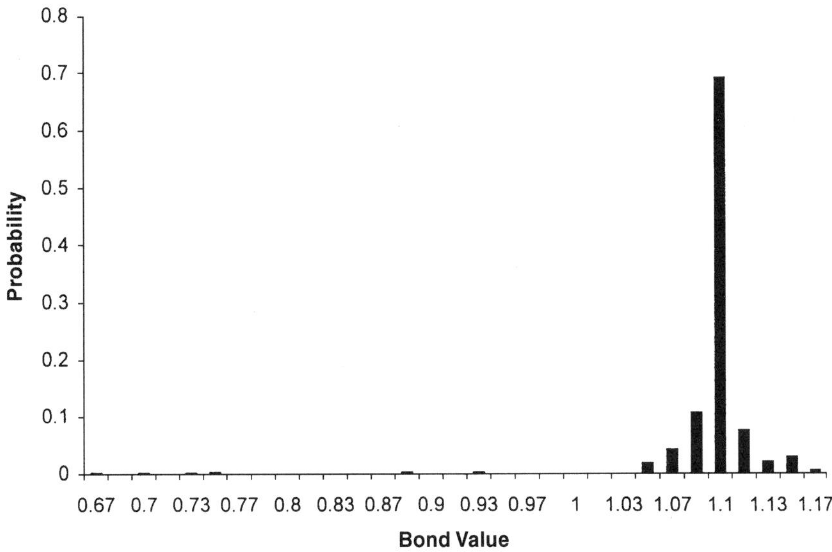

Figure 45.4 The probability distribution for the bond's value after one year.

calculate the value of the bond after one year, suppose it is 0.882. But why should the bond still be rated AA at that time? This is the third point. From our transition matrix we see that the probability of the bond's rating staying AA is 87%. So, there is an 87% chance that the bond's value will be 0.882. We can similarly work out the value of the bond in one year if it is rated AAA, A, BBB, etc. using the relevant forward rates and spreads that we assume will apply in one year's time. And each of these has a probability of occuring that is given in the transition matrix. A probability distribution of the possible bond values is shown in Figure 45.4.

This, highly skewed, distribution tells us all we need to know to determine the risk in this particular bond. We can, for example, calculate the expected value of the bond.

45.6 A PORTFOLIO OF RISKY BONDS

We have seen how to apply the CreditMetrics methodology to a single risky bond; to apply the ideas to a portfolio of risky bonds is significantly harder since it requires the knowledge of any relationship between the different bonds. This is most easily measured by some sort of correlation.

Suppose that we have a portfolio of two bonds. One, issued by ABC, is currently rated AA and the other, issued by XYZ, is BBB. We can calculate, using the method above, the value of each of these bonds at our time horizon for each of the possible states of the two bonds. If we assume that each bond can be in one of eight states (AAA, AA, ..., CCC, Default) there are $8^2 = 64$ possible joint states at the time horizon. To calculate the expected value of our portfolio and standard deviation we need to know the probability of each of these joint states occuring. This is where the correlation comes in.

There are two stages to determining the probability of any particular future joint state:

1. Calculation of correlations between bonds;
2. Calculate the probability of any joint state.

Stage 1 is accomplished by decomposing the return on the stock of each issuing company into parts correlated with the major indices.

45.7 CREDITMETRICS MODEL OUTPUTS

CreditMetrics is, above all, a way of measuring risk associated with default issues. From the CreditMetrics methodology one can calculate the risk, measured by standard deviation, of the risky portfolio over the required time horizon. Because of the risk of default the distribution of returns from a portfolio exposed to credit risk is highly skewed, as in Figure 45.4. The distribution is far from being Normal. Thus ideas from simple portfolio theory must be used with care. Although, it may not be a good absolute measure of risk in the classical sense, the standard deviation is a good indicator of relative risk between instruments or portfolios.

45.8 CRASHMETRICS

CrashMetrics is a methodology for evaluating portfolio performance in the event of extreme movements in financial markets. It is not part of the JP Morgan family of performance measures. In its most complex and sophisticated form, the concept and mathematics were explained in full in Chapter 27. There we saw how the portfolio of financial instruments is valued under a worst-case scenario with few assumptions about the size of the market move or its timing. The only assumptions made are that the market move, the 'crash' is limited in size and that the number of such crashes are limited in some way. There are no assumptions about the probability distribution of the size of the crash or its timing.

The simpler method, used for day-to-day portfolio protection, is concerned with the extreme market movements that may occur when we are not watching, or that cannot be hedged away. These are the fire sale conditions. This is the method I will explain for the rest of this chapter. There are many nice things about the method such as its simplicity and ease of generalization, and no explicit dependence on the annoying parameters volatility and correlation.

45.9 CRASHMETRICS FOR ONE STOCK

To introduce the ideas, let's consider a portfolio of options on a single underlying asset. For the moment think in terms of a stock, although we could equally well talk about currencies, commodities or interest rate products.

The change in the value of this portfolio can be approximated by a Taylor series in the change in the underlying asset:

$$\delta\Pi = \Delta\,\delta S + \tfrac{1}{2}\Gamma\,\delta S^2. \tag{45.1}$$

This approximation is good provided we are not too close to expiry and strike of an option.

What is the worst that could happen to the portfolio overnight say? In Figure 45.5 we see a plot of the change in the portfolio against δS. Note that it is zero at $\delta S = 0$. If the gamma is positive the portfolio change (45.1) has a minimum at

$$\delta S = -\frac{\Delta}{\Gamma}.$$

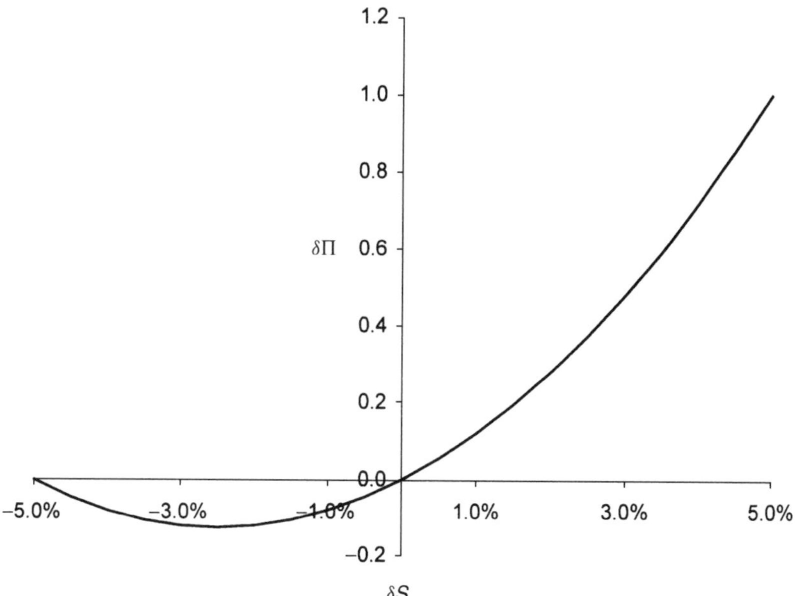

Figure 45.5 Size of portfolio change against change in the underlying.

The portfolio change in this worst-case scenario is

$$\delta\Pi_{\text{worst}} = -\frac{\Delta^2}{2\Gamma}.$$

This is the worst case given an arbitrary move in the underlying. If the gamma is small or negative the worst case will be a fall to zero or a rise to infinity, both far too unrealistic. For this reason we may want to constrain the move in the underlying by

$$-\delta S^- < \delta S < \delta S^+.$$

Now the portfolio fall is restricted.

45.9.1 Portfolio Optimization and the Platinum Hedge

Having found a technique for finding out what could happen in the worst case, it is natural to ask how to make that worst case not so bad. This can be done by optimal static hedging. Suppose that there is a contract available with which to hedge our portfolio. This contract has a bid-offer spread, a delta and a gamma. I will call the delta of the hedging contract Δ^*, meaning the sensitivity of the hedging contract to the underlying asset. The gamma is similarly Γ^*. Denote the bid-offer spread by $C > 0$, meaning that if we buy (sell) the contract and immediately sell (buy) it back we lose this amount.

Imagine that we add a number λ of the hedging contract to our original position. Our portfolio now has a first-order exposure to the crash of

$$\delta S(\Delta + \lambda\Delta^*)$$

and a second-order exposure of

$$\tfrac{1}{2}\delta S^2(\Gamma + \lambda\Gamma^*).$$

Not only does the portfolio change by these amounts for a crash of size δS but also it loses a *guaranteed* amount

$$|\lambda|C$$

just because we cannot close our new position without losing out on the bid-offer spread.

The total change in the portfolio with the static hedge in place is now

$$\delta\Pi = \delta S(\Delta + \lambda\Delta^*) + \tfrac{1}{2}\delta S^2(\Gamma + \lambda\Gamma^*) - |\lambda|C.$$

In general, the optimal choice of λ is such that the worst value of this expression for $-\delta S^- \leq \delta S \leq \delta S^+$ is as high as possible. Thus we are exchanging a guaranteed loss (due to bid-offer spread) for a reduced worst-case loss. This is simply insurance and the optimal choice gives the **Platinum Hedge**, named for the plastic card that comes after green and gold. For the optimal choice of the λ Figure 45.6 shows the change in the portfolio value as a function of δS. Note that it no longer goes through (0,0).

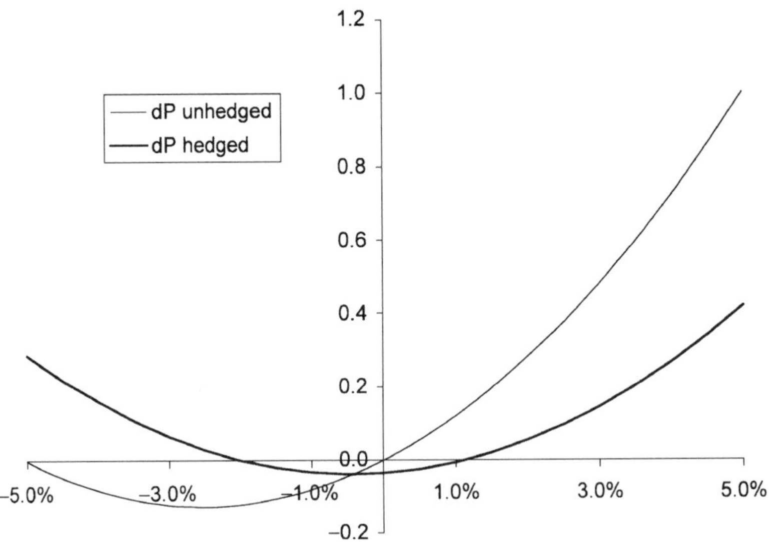

Figure 45.6 Size of portfolio change against δS after optimal hedging.

In Figure 45.7 is shown a simple spreadsheet for finding the worst-case scenario and the Platinum Hedge when there is a single asset.

45.10 THE MULTI-ASSET/SINGLE-INDEX MODEL

A bank's portfolio has many underlyings, not just the one. How does CrashMetrics handle them? This is done via an index or benchmark.

We can measure the performance of a portfolio of assets and options on these assets by relating the magnitude of extreme movements in any one asset to one or more **benchmarks** such as the S&P500. The relative magnitude of these movements is measured by the **crash**

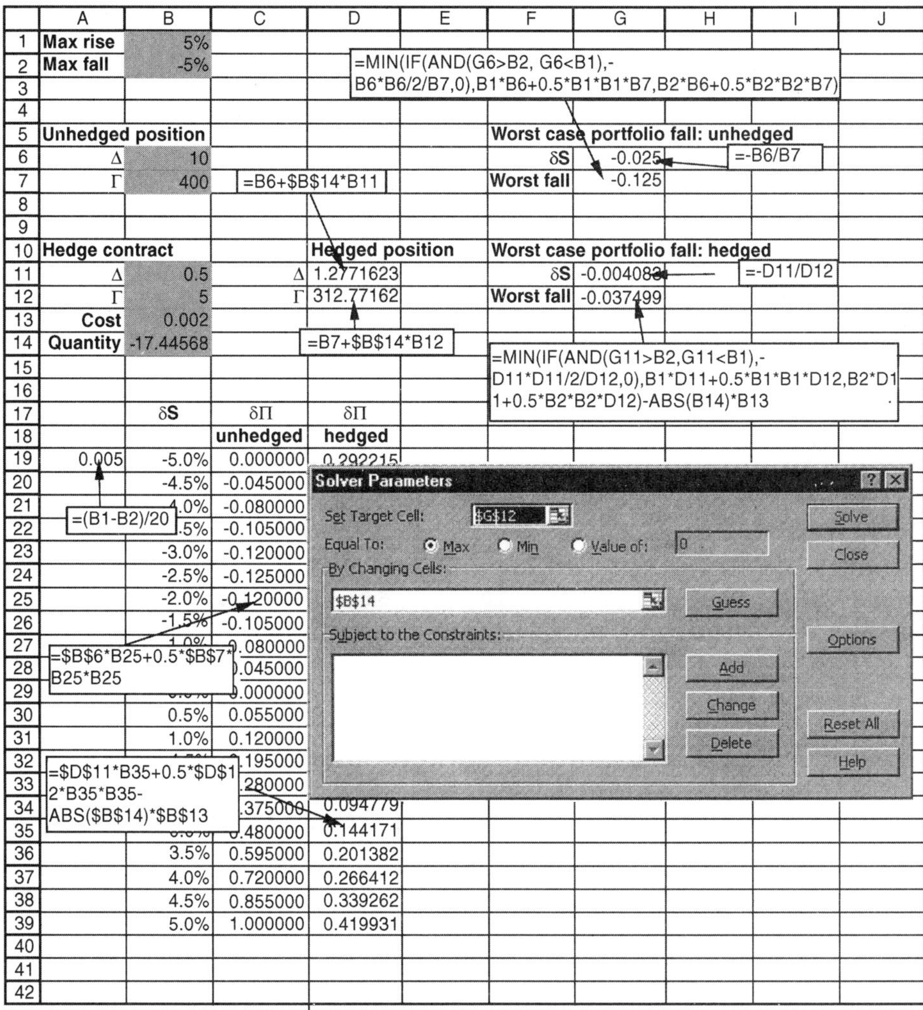

Figure 45.7 Spreadsheet for implementing basic CrashMetrics in one asset.

coefficient for each asset relative to the benchmark. If the benchmark moves by $x\%$ then the ith asset moves by $\kappa_i x\%$. Estimates of the κ_i for the constituents of the S&P500, with that index as the benchmark, may be downloaded free of charge from www.wilmott.com. Note that the benchmark need not be an index containing the assets, but can be any representative quantity. Unlike the RiskMetrics and CreditMetrics datasets, the CrashMetrics dataset does not have to be updated frequently because of the rarity of extreme market movements.

The following tables give the crash coefficients for a few constituents of major indices in several countries. The crash coefficients have been estimated using the tails of the daily return distributions from the beginning of 1985 until the end of 1997, and so include the Black Monday crash of October 1987 and the rice/dragon/sake effect starting in October 1997. For example, in Table 45.1 we see the 10 largest positive and negative daily returns in the S&P500 during that period. In this table are also shown the returns on the same days for several constituents of the index.

Table 45.1 The 10 largest positive and negative moves in several constituents of the S&P500 against the moves in the S&P500 on the same days.

Date	S&P500	% change	ABBOTT LABS.	ADOBE SYS.	ADVD.MICR. DEVC.	AEROQUIP-VICKERS	AETNA	AHMAN-SON (H.F.)
19-Oct-87	225	−20.4	−10.5	−22.2	−36.1	−36.6	−15.3	−20.8
26-Oct-87	228	−8.3	−7.3	−20.0	−14.3	−15.2	−4.5	−4.3
27-Oct-97	877	−6.9	−5.3	−6.1	−19.8	−6.7	−8.5	−6.5
08-Jan-88	243	−6.8	−3.8	−14.3	−6.8	−13.5	−7.1	−6.2
13-Oct-89	334	−6.1	−8.2	−12.5	−5.8	−9.3	−5.5	−3.7
16-Oct-87	283	−5.2	−4.6	0.0	−5.3	−6.4	−1.5	−1.3
11-Sep-86	235	−4.8	−5.2	−50.0	−4.7	−5.3	−3.3	−2.9
14-Apr-88	260	−4.4	−4.0	−12.5	−5.6	−2.6	−4.4	−4.8
30-Nov-87	230	−4.2	−6.7	−16.7	−1.4	−9.8	−2.7	−6.1
22-Oct-87	248	−3.9	−4.6	0.0	−5.9	−6.5	−1.9	−1.4
21-Oct-87	258	9.1	4.3	0.0	4.1	11.5	8.0	9.5
20-Oct-87	236	5.3	−0.6	−14.3	6.5	14.3	−3.7	3.3
28-Oct-97	921	5.1	5.2	4.3	19.0	−0.6	4.3	7.4
29-Oct-87	244	4.9	2.4	33.3	10.3	15.5	−1.9	3.2
17-Jan-91	327	3.7	4.3	0.0	4.6	8.0	2.8	3.0
04-Jan-88	255	3.6	0.8	0.0	7.6	−0.4	1.9	−0.7
31-May-88	262	3.4	2.7	0.0	5.3	0.9	3.9	2.5
27-Aug-90	321	3.2	5.4	8.3	4.5	2.2	1.4	3.1
02-Sep-97	927	3.1	3.8	2.6	3.3	0.1	2.5	2.3
21-Aug-91	391	2.9	3.1	4.2	3.5	0.0	−3.3	2.6

Table 45.2 The 10 largest positive and negative moves in several constituents of the FTSE100 against the moves in the FTSE100 on the same days.

Date	FTSE100	% change	ALLIED DOMECQ	ASDA FOODS	ASSD.BRIT.	BAA	BANK OF SCOTLAND	BARCLAYS
20-Oct-87	1802	−12.2	−7.1	−9.0	−10.1	−7.1	−12.7	−13.2
19-Oct-87	2052	−10.8	−11.5	−9.6	−3.1	−3.7	−3.8	−11.4
26-Oct-87	1684	−6.2	−7.6	−2.4	−3.0	−3.1	−9.0	−7.5
22-Oct-87	1833	−5.7	−4.0	−7.7	−4.7	−2.6	−1.8	−1.0
30-Nov-87	1580	−4.3	−3.0	−4.3	−2.3	−3.8	−2.1	−6.3
05-Oct-92	2446	−4.1	−2.0	−2.9	2.3	−3.4	−6.8	−4.6
03-Nov-87	1653	−4.0	−3.0	−1.7	−2.0	−0.8	−2.0	−7.8
09-Nov-87	1565	−3.4	−3.9	−5.5	−1.0	−4.5	−1.6	−2.2
29-Dec-87	1730	−3.4	−2.3	−1.8	−2.3	−2.1	−0.6	−2.6
16-Oct-89	2163	−3.2	−3.2	−5.0	−3.4	−3.3	0.0	−2.2
21-Oct-87	1943	7.9	7.7	4.9	2.6	2.7	1.5	8.7
10-Apr-92	2572	5.6	8.2	3.3	3.5	7.1	13.1	7.6
17-Sep-92	2483	4.4	3.5	3.6	2.4	2.5	9.6	15.5
11-Nov-87	1639	4.2	2.3	1.8	4.4	2.1	1.0	3.4
30-Oct-87	1749	4.0	1.5	5.0	6.9	3.2	4.6	2.1
12-Nov-87	1702	3.9	1.8	−0.6	−1.0	4.1	0.8	2.2
05-Oct-90	2143	3.6	5.9	0.0	−1.0	3.2	9.3	9.8
18-Sep-92	2567	3.3	6.7	3.4	4.9	3.0	4.2	3.0
26-Sep-97	5226	3.2	1.8	−0.3	1.9	3.2	9.5	8.9
31-Dec-91	2493	3.0	4.0	7.8	1.7	1.3	4.5	2.7

Table 45.3 The 10 largest positive and negative moves in several constituents of the Hang Seng against the moves in the Hang Seng on the same days.

Date	Hang Seng	% change	AMOY PROPS	BANK OF E. ASIA	CHEUNG KONG.	CHINA LT. & POW.	FIRST PACIFIC	GREAT EAGLE
26-Oct-87	2241	−33.3	−37.4	−37.0	−29.2	−32.2	−28.3	−57.3
05-Jun-89	2093	−21.7	−36.4	−22.9	−27.0	−16.6	−28.6	−41.3
28-Oct-97	9059	−13.7	−4.8	−12.7	−9.8	−10.8	−14.7	−19.3
19-Oct-87	3362	−11.1	−18.9	0.0	−9.6	−10.5	−10.7	−20.2
22-May-89	2806	−10.8	−18.6	−8.2	−10.7	−6.2	−14.9	−15.4
23-Oct-97	10426	−10.4	−14.0	−8.9	−13.4	−7.4	−26.9	−6.3
25-May-89	2752	−8.5	−16.6	−7.6	−10.8	−5.0	−9.5	−14.9
19-Aug-91	3722	−8.4	−11.6	−4.7	−6.8	−6.8	−10.2	−9.4
03-Dec-92	4978	−8.0	−2.4	−13.4	−4.8	−9.9	−7.5	−11.3
06-Aug-90	3107	−7.4	−10.3	−6.1	−6.1	−8.2	−6.9	−6.0
29-Oct-97	10765	18.8	9.2	4.9	17.8	20.2	17.3	18.0
23-May-89	3067	9.3	11.4	7.5	9.9	5.2	11.4	14.3
06-Nov-87	2113	7.8	8.5	1.2	12.2	5.4	2.2	9.7
12-Jun-89	2440	7.6	11.7	8.7	10.5	7.0	7.0	16.9
03-Sep-97	14713	7.1	6.0	6.2	5.3	11.9	11.2	5.0
24-Oct-97	11144	6.9	4.1	2.0	9.5	5.9	12.6	7.1
27-Oct-87	2395	6.9	20.1	−2.0	3.8	9.0	−11.4	1.8
03-Nov-97	11255	5.9	5.3	7.8	7.4	−2.9	13.7	6.8
14-Jan-94	10774	5.9	6.1	3.7	6.6	3.6	3.9	4.9
19-Jun-85	1510	5.8	0.0	6.1	6.1	6.2	0.0	13.2

Table 45.4 The 10 largest positive and negative moves in several constituents of the Nikkei against the moves in the Nikkei on the same days.

Date	Nikkei	% change	AJINOMOTO	ALL NIPPON AIRWAYS	AOKI	ASAHI BREW.	ASAHI CHEM.	ASAHI DENKA KOGYO
20-Oct-87	21910	−14.9	−14.4	−17.9	−18.9	−18.1	−15.7	−10.8
02-Apr-90	28002	−6.6	−3.2	−6.3	−13.7	−5.0	−1.2	−5.8
19-Aug-91	21456	−6.0	−12.1	−7.9	−8.4	−1.6	−5.5	−4.7
23-Aug-90	23737	−5.8	−7.6	−12.0	−9.6	−5.4	−8.4	−7.3
23-Jan-95	17785	−5.6	−8.0	−7.2	−4.9	−1.9	−5.3	−5.2
19-Nov-97	15842	−5.3	−9.0	−3.5	−16.3	−3.4	−3.2	−5.6
24-Jan-94	18353	−4.9	−4.3	−6.0	−6.8	−1.6	−4.1	−7.6
23-Oct-87	23201	−4.9	−4.0	−6.8	−0.9	−4.1	−6.8	−3.4
26-Sep-90	22250	−4.7	−5.2	−2.4	−5.4	−1.6	−2.7	−0.6
03-Apr-95	15381	−4.7	−2.2	−4.1	−2.3	−2.0	−8.4	−6.6
02-Oct-90	22898	13.2	16.0	14.7	9.8	11.4	10.0	15.8
21-Oct-87	23947	9.3	13.5	16.3	11.6	14.7	9.3	5.2
17-Nov-97	16283	8.0	7.3	6.1	0.0	7.4	11.8	9.9
31-Jan-94	20229	7.8	8.5	3.6	13.6	4.2	4.6	9.6
10-Apr-92	17850	7.5	10.5	3.9	13.3	0.0	6.1	3.5
07-Jul-95	16213	6.3	9.8	6.3	9.2	3.0	5.0	1.2
21-Aug-92	16216	6.2	7.9	3.3	21.2	5.6	2.9	2.5
27-Aug-92	17555	6.1	5.6	−1.0	9.4	10.1	5.8	1.8
06-Jan-88	22790	5.6	5.0	6.3	6.4	2.7	6.6	2.4
15-Aug-90	28112	5.4	2.2	6.9	5.4	3.2	3.8	3.8

Table 45.5 The 10 largest positive and negative moves in several constituents of the Dax against the moves in the Dax on the same days.

Date	Dax	% change	ALLIANZ HLDG.	BASF	BAYER	BAYER HYPBK.	BAYERISCHE VBK.	BMW
16-Oct-89	1385	−12.8	−11.3	−10.0	−7.0	−16.1	−13.8	−13.1
19-Aug-91	1497	−9.4	−9.9	−4.8	−5.8	−11.2	−11.2	−10.0
19-Oct-87	1321	−9.4	−10.4	−9.4	−8.5	−7.0	−3.6	−8.2
28-Oct-97	3567	−8.0	−4.7	−8.3	−9.6	−8.6	−7.8	−14.8
26-Oct-87	1193	−7.7	−10.2	−4.0	−5.3	−9.0	−5.5	−6.4
28-Oct-87	1142	−6.8	−7.1	−2.6	−3.2	−8.9	−5.7	−7.5
22-Oct-87	1287	−6.7	−4.2	−4.6	−6.9	−4.6	−5.8	−7.5
10-Nov-87	945	−6.5	−8.9	−4.8	−4.1	−7.4	−6.6	−7.8
04-Jan-88	943	−5.6	−9.9	−6.9	−5.7	−2.1	−5.6	−3.3
06-Aug-90	1740	−5.4	−3.4	−4.3	−6.1	−5.5	−5.2	−6.4
17-Jan-91	1422	7.6	7.8	5.3	6.9	5.8	9.6	9.3
12-Nov-87	1061	7.4	16.6	4.7	7.6	7.6	10.8	6.4
30-Oct-87	1177	6.6	10.2	3.6	8.1	7.8	2.7	7.4
17-Oct-89	1475	6.5	5.8	3.7	2.5	5.9	9.2	5.9
01-Oct-90	1420	6.4	7.8	7.4	9.0	6.0	9.5	7.0
05-Jan-88	1004	6.4	8.6	5.1	4.7	1.7	4.6	4.4
29-Oct-97	3791	6.3	3.5	8.4	8.2	5.9	6.8	12.0
27-Aug-90	1654	6.1	3.9	8.7	5.7	5.0	2.5	6.1
21-Oct-87	1379	5.9	10.9	1.5	8.8	8.7	4.1	4.2
08-Oct-90	1465	5.3	9.1	5.0	5.2	5.1	1.8	3.7

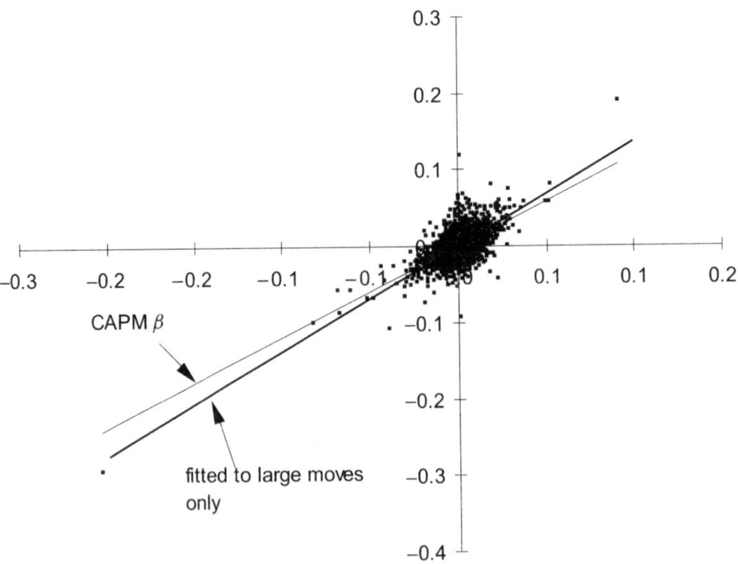

Figure 45.8 The returns on Disney versus returns returns on the S&P500. Also shown are the line with slope beta, fitted to all points, and the line with slope κ fitted to the 40 extreme moves and having zero intercept.

Figure 45.8 uses the same data as used in Chapter 41 for the calculation of the beta for Disney. The fine line in this figure has slope beta. On the figure is shown the line with zero intercept that fits the largest 20 rises and falls in the S&P500; this is the bold line.

In Figure 45.9 are the returns on the Hong Kong and Shanghai Hotel group versus returns returns on the Hang Seng and in Figure 45.10 are the 40 extreme moves in Daimler–Benz versus returns returns on the Dax. It is important to note at this stage that the crash coefficient is not the same as the asset's beta with respect to the index. Not only is the number different, but preliminary results suggest that the crash coefficient is more stable than the beta. Moreover, for large moves in the index the stock and the index are far more closely correlated than under normal market conditions. In other words, when there is a crash all stocks move together.

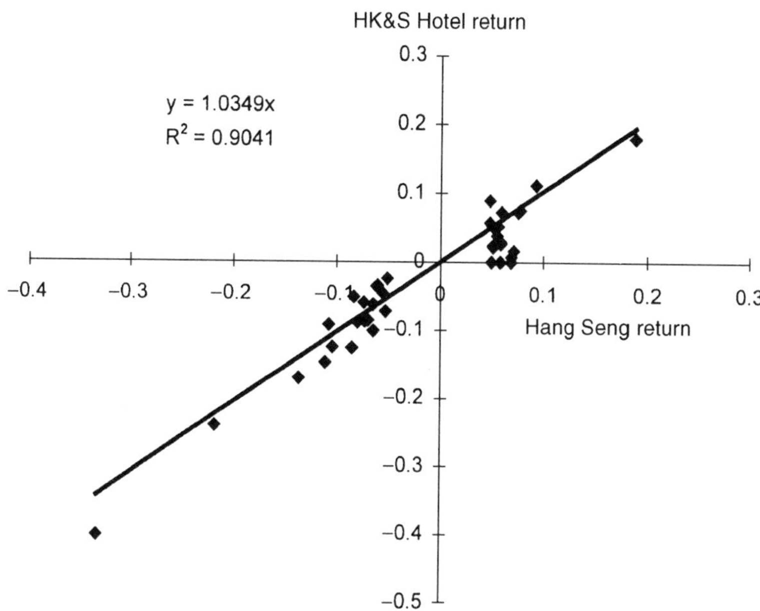

Figure 45.9 The returns on the Hong Kong and Shanghai Hotel group versus returns returns on the Hang Seng. Also shown is the line with slope κ fitted to the 40 extreme moves and having zero intercept.

In the single-index, multi-asset model we can write the change in the value of the portfolio as

$$\delta\Pi = \sum_{i=1}^{N} \Delta_i \delta S_i + \tfrac{1}{2} \sum_{i=1}^{N} \sum_{j=1}^{N} \Gamma_{ij} \delta S_i \delta S_j \tag{45.2}$$

with the obvious notation. (In particular, observe the cross gammas.) We assume that the percentage change in each asset can be related to the percentage change in the benchmark, x, when there is an extreme move:

$$\delta S_i = \kappa_i x S_i.$$

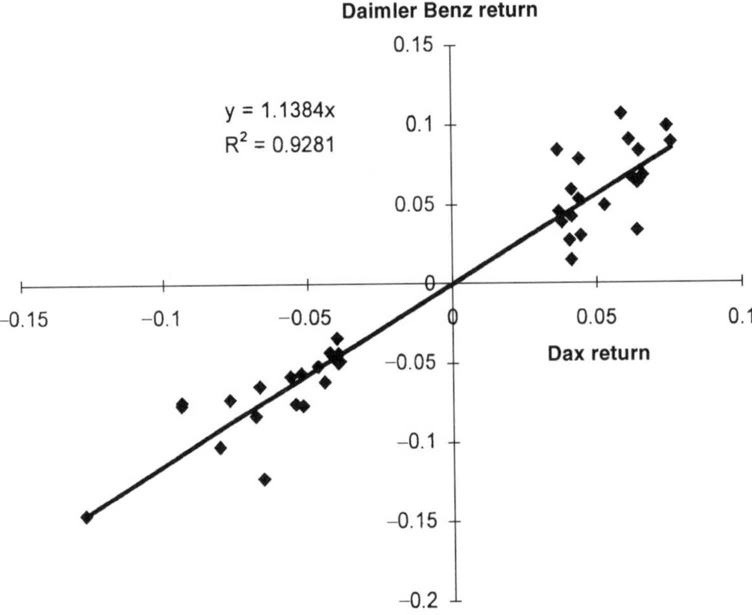

Figure 45.10 The returns on Daimler–Benz versus returns returns on the Dax. Also shown is the line with slope κ fitted to the 40 extreme moves and having zero intercept.

This simplifies (45.2) to

$$\begin{aligned}\delta\Pi &= x\sum_{i=1}^{N}\Delta_i\kappa_i S_i + \tfrac{1}{2}x^2\sum_{i=1}^{N}\sum_{j=1}^{N}\Gamma_{ij}\kappa_i S_i\kappa_j S_j \\ &= xD + \tfrac{1}{2}x^2 G.\end{aligned}$$

Observe how this contains a first- and a second-order exposure to the crash. The first-order coefficient D is the **crash delta** and the second-order coefficient G is the **crash gamma**.

Now we constrain the change in the benchmark by

$$-x^- \le x \le x^+.$$

The worst-case portfolio change occurs at one of the end points of this range or at the internal point

$$x = -\frac{D}{G}.$$

In this last case the extreme portfolio change is

$$\delta\Pi_{\text{worst}} = -\frac{D^2}{2G}.$$

We can also calculate the crash delta and gamma at this worst point.

All of the ideas contained in the single-asset model described above carry over to the multi-asset model, we just use x instead of δS to determine the worst that can happen to our portfolio.

45.10.1 Portfolio Optimization and the Platinum Hedge in the Multi-asset Model

Suppose that there are M contracts available with which to hedge our portfolio. Let us call the deltas of the kth hedging contract Δ_i^k, meaning the sensitivity of the contract to the ith asset, $k = 1, \dots, M$. The gammas are similarly Γ_{ij}^k. Denote the bid-offer spread by $C_k > 0$, meaning that if we buy (sell) the contract and immediately sell (buy) it back we lose this amount.

Imagine that we add a number λ_k of each of the available hedging contracts to our original position. Our portfolio now has a first-order exposure to the crash of

$$x\left(D + \sum_{k=1}^{M} \lambda_k \sum_{i=1}^{N} \Delta_i^k \kappa_i S_i\right)$$

and a second-order exposure of

$$\tfrac{1}{2}x^2\left(G + \sum_{k=1}^{M} \lambda_k \sum_{i=1}^{N} \sum_{j=1}^{N} \Gamma_{ij}^k \kappa_i S_i \kappa_j S_j\right).$$

Not only does the portfolio change by these amounts for a crash of size x but also it loses a guaranteed amount

$$\sum_{k=1}^{M} |\lambda_k|\, C_k$$

just because we cannot close our new positions without losing out on the bid-offer spread.

The total change in the portfolio with the static hedge in place is now

$$\delta\Pi = x\left(D + \sum_{k=1}^{M} \lambda_k \sum_{i=1}^{N} \Delta_i^k \kappa_i S_i\right) + \tfrac{1}{2}x^2\left(G + \sum_{k=1}^{M} \lambda_k \sum_{i=1}^{N} \sum_{j=1}^{N} \Gamma_{ij}^k \kappa_i S_i \kappa_j S_j\right) - \sum_{k=1}^{M} |\lambda_k| C_k.$$

45.10.2 The Marginal Effect of an Asset

We can separate the contribution to the portfolio movement in the worst case into components due to each of the underlying:

$$\delta\Pi_i = x^* \Delta_i \delta S_i + \tfrac{1}{2}x^{*^2} \sum_{j=1}^{N} \Gamma_{ij} \delta S_i \delta S_j,$$

where x^* is the value of x in the worst case. This has, rather arbitrarily, divided up the parts with exposure to two assets (when the cross gamma is non-zero) equally between those assets. The ratio

$$\frac{\delta\Pi_i}{\delta\Pi_{\text{worst}}}$$

measures the contribution to the crash from the ith asset.

45.11 THE MULTI-INDEX MODEL

In the same way that the CAPM model can accommodate multiple indices, so we can have a multiple index CrashMetrics model. I will skip most of the details, the implementation is simple.

We fit the extreme returns in each asset to the extreme returns in the indices according to

$$\delta S_i = \sum_{j=1}^{n} \kappa_i^j x_j,$$

where the n indices are denoted by the j sub/superscript.

The change in value of our portfolio of stocks and options is now quadratic in all of the x_js. At this point we must decide over what range of index returns do we look for the worst case. Consider just the two-index case, because it is easy to draw the pictures. One possibility is to allow x_1 and x_2 to be independent, to take any values in a given range. This would correspond to looking for the minimum of the quadratic function over the rectangle in Figure 45.11. Note that there is no correlation in this between the two indices; fortunately this difficult-to-measure parameter is irrelevant. Alternatively if you believe that there is some relationship between the size of the crash in one index and the size of the crash in the other you may want to narrow down the area that you explore for the worst case. An example is given in the figure.

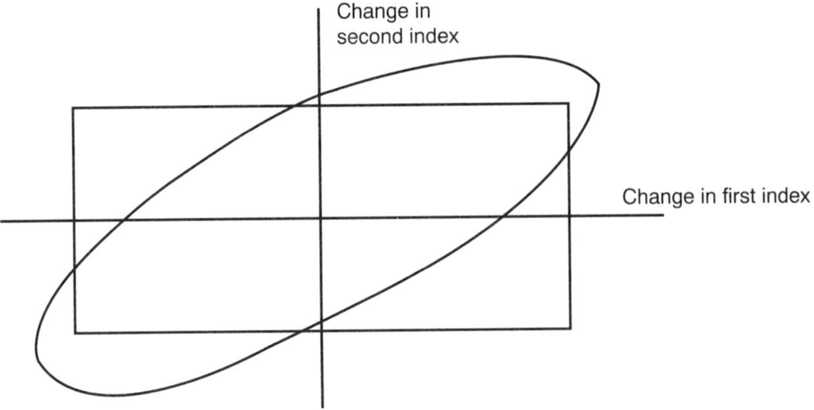

Figure 45.11 Regions of interest in the two-index model.

45.12 SIMPLE EXTENSIONS TO CRASHMETRICS

In this section I want to briefly outline ways in which CrashMetrics has been extended to other situations and to capture other market effects. Because of the simplicity of the basic form of CrashMetrics, many additional features can be incorporated quite straightforwardly.

First of all, I haven't described how the CrashMetrics methodology can be applied to interest rate products. This is not difficult, simply use a yield (or several) as the benchmark and relate changes in the values of products to changes in the yield via durations and convexities. The reader can imagine the rest.

A particularly interesting topic is what happens to parameter values after a crash. After a crash there is usually a rise in volatility and an increase in bid-offer spread. The rise in volatility can be incorporated into the methodology by including vega terms, dependent also on the size of the crash. This is conceptually straightforward, but requires analysis of option price data around the times of crashes. If you are long vanilla options during a crash, you will benefit from this rise in volatility. Similarly, crash-dependent bid-offer spread can be incorporated but again requires historical data analysis to model the relationship between the size of a crash and the increase in the spread.

Finally, it is common experience that shortly after a crash stocks bounce back, so that the real fall in price is not as bad as it seems. Typically 20% of the sudden loss is recovered shortly afterwards, but this is by no means a hard and fast rule. You can see this in the earlier data tables, a date on which there is a very large fall is followed by a date on which there is a large rise. To incorporate such a dynamic effect into the relatively static CrashMetrics is an interesting task. (Buying a down-and-in call in anticipation of the crash and bounce back is very effective.)

45.13 SUMMARY

This chapter has outlined some of the methodologies for competing and complementary Value at Risk measures. With something as important as Value at Risk there is an obvious case to be made for exploring all of the possible VaR measures to build up as accurate a profile as possible of the dangers lurking in your portfolio.

FURTHER READING

- Download the datasets and very detailed descriptions of both the RiskMetrics and CreditMetrics methodologies from www.jpmorgan.com.
- Download the CrashMetrics technical document, data set and demonstration software for CrashMetrics from www.wilmott.com. The document explains how to incorporate time decay.
- Alexander (1996 a) is a critique of RiskMetrics as a risk measurement tool.
- Shore (1997) describes and implements the CreditMetrics methodology.

EXERCISES

1. Extend the example CrashMetrics spreadsheet to incorporate many underlyings, all related via an index. How would interest rate products be incorporated?
2. Sudden, large movements in a stock are usually accompanied by an increase in implied volatilities. Incorporate a vega term into the one-asset CrashMetrics model. What is the role of actual volatility in CrashMetrics?

PART SIX
numerical methods

The sixth and final part of the book concerns the numerical methods needed for implementing the models described in the rest of the book. Many of the techniques have grown up in other branches of applied mathematics or physics and are now seeing successful use in financial problems. This part is necessarily just an overview, albeit quite detailed and self-contained, of possible techniques. The reader is encouraged to read widely on this subject.

Chapter 46: Finite-difference Methods for One-factor Models Most of the models we have seen in the book have led to some form of partial differential equation, usually, but not always, parabolic. The parabolic partial different equation is a very easy differential equation to solve numerically. This first chapter in this part describes the very basics of finite-difference meshes and the approximation of derivatives. It ends with a description of the explicit method.

Chapter 47: Further Finite-difference Methods for One-factor Models More sophisticated than the explicit method are the implicit methods. These are harder to program but this effort usually pays off in faster and more accurate results. Other techniques are explored. The methods are applied to American and path-dependent options.

Chapter 48: Finite-difference Methods for Two-factor Models When we have two stochastic factors we end up with a partial different equation with second derivatives in two variables. We can still use the explicit method, which is described, but for speed we may want to employ one of the available implicit methods.

Chapter 49: Monte Carlo Simulation and Related Methods For some path-dependent problems, or when we have a high-dimensional problem, we may want to use simulation methods for pricing. Related to these methods are the quasi-Monte-Carlo methods for numerical integration that are very useful but only in very special circumstances.

Chapter 50: Finite-difference Programs The book concludes with several Visual Basic programs demonstrating many of the numerical techniques that have been described.

CHAPTER 46
finite-difference methods for one-factor models

In this Chapter...

- finite-difference grids
- how to approximate derivatives of a function
- how to go from the Black–Scholes partial differential equation to a *difference* equation
- the explicit finite-difference method, a generalization of the binomial method

46.1 INTRODUCTION

Rarely can we find closed-form solutions for the values of options. Unless the problem is very simple indeed we are going to have to solve a partial differential equation numerically. In an earlier chapter I described the binomial method for pricing options. This used the idea of a finite tree structure branching out from the current asset price and the current time right up to the expiry date. One way of thinking of the binomial method is as a method for solving a partial differential equation. Finite-difference methods are no more than a generalization of this concept, although we tend to talk about **grids** and **meshes** rather than 'trees.' Once we have found an equation to solve numerically then it is much easier to use a finite-difference grid than a binomial tree, simply because the transformation from a differential equation (Black–Scholes) to a difference equation is easier when the grid/mesh/tree is nice and regular. Moreover, there are many, many ways the finite-difference method can be improved upon, making it faster and more accurate. The binomial method is not so flexible. And finally, there is a great deal in the mathematical/numerical analysis literature on these and other methods, it would be such a shame to ignore this. The main difference between the binomial method and the finite-difference methods is that the former contains the diffusion, the volatility, in the tree structure. In the finite-difference methods the 'tree' is fixed but parameters change to reflect a changing diffusion.

To those of you who are new to numerical methods let me start by saying that you will find the parabolic partial differential equation very easy to solve numerically. If you are not new to these ideas, but have been brought up on binomial methods, now is the time to wean yourself off them. On a personal note, for solving problems in practice I would say that I use finite-difference methods about 75% of the time, Monte Carlo simulations 20%, and the rest would be explicit formulae. Those explicit formulae are almost always just the regular Black–Scholes formulae for calls and puts, never for barriers for which it is highly dangerous to use constant volatility. Only once have I ever seriously used a binomial method, and that was more to help with modeling than with the numerical analysis.

In this chapter I'm going to show how to approximate derivatives using a grid and then how to write the Black–Scholes equation as a difference equation using this grid. I'll show how this can be done in many ways, discussing the relative merits of each. In the next chapter I'll also show how to extend the ideas to price contracts with early exercise and to price exotic options.

When I describe the numerical methods I often use the Black–Scholes equation as the example. *But the methods are all applicable to other problems, such as stochastic interest rates.* I am therefore assuming a certain level of intelligence from my reader, that once you have learned the methods as applied to the equity, currency, commodity worlds you can use them in the fixed-income world. I am sure you won't let me down.

46.2 PROGRAM OF STUDY

We are in the home straight now: only numerical methods separate us from the bibliography. If you are new to numerics and you really want to study them to implement the models I have described then you need a program of study. Here I make some suggestions for how you should approach the numerical methods I describe.

- **Explicit method/European calls, puts and binaries**: To get started you should learn the explicit method as applied to the Black–Scholes equation for a European option. This is very easy to program and you won't make many mistakes.
- **European option/American calls, puts and binaries**: Not much harder is the application of the explicit method to American options.
- **Crank–Nicolson/European calls, puts and binaries**: Once you've got the explicit method under your belt you should learn the Crank–Nicolson implicit method. This is harder to program, but you will get a better accuracy.
- **Crank–Nicolson/American calls, puts and binaries**: There's not much more effort involved in pricing American-style options than in the pricing of European-style options.
- **Explicit method/path-dependent options**: By now you'll be quite sophisticated and it's time to price a path-dependent contract. Start with an Asian option with discrete sampling, and then try a continuously-sampled Asian. Finally, try your hand at lookbacks.
- **Interest rate products**: Repeat the above program for non-path-dependent and then path-dependent interest rate products. First price caps and floors and then go on to the index amortizing rate swap.
- **Two-factor explicit**: To get started on two-factor problems price a convertible bond using an explicit method, with both the stock and the spot interest rate being stochastic.
- **Two-factor implicit**: The final stage, using methods described in this book, is to implement the implicit two-factor method as applied to the convertible bond.

If you get to the end of this program successfully then you will have reached a very high level of sophistication.

46.3 GRIDS

Figure 46.1 is the binomial tree figure from Chapter 12. This is the structure commonly used for pricing simple non-path-dependent contracts. The idea was explained in Chapter 12. In the world of finite differences we use the grid or mesh shown in Figure 46.2. In the former figure the **nodes** are spaced at equal time intervals and at equal intervals in $\log S$. The finite-difference grid usually has equal **timesteps**, the time between nodes, and either equal S steps or equal $\log S$ steps. If we wanted, we could make the grid any shape we wanted.

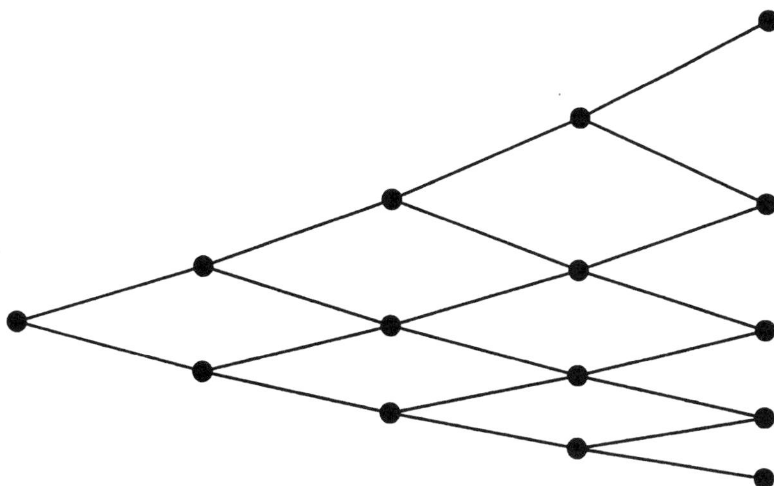

Figure 46.1 The binomial tree.

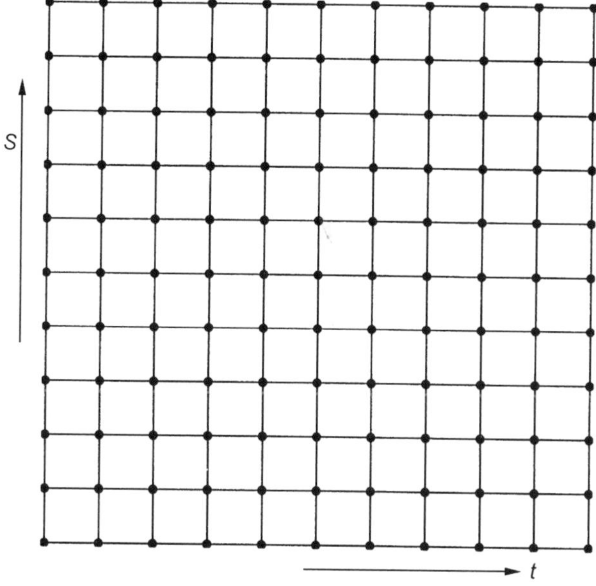

Figure 46.2 The finite-difference grid.

I am only going to describe finite-difference methods with constant time and asset step. There are advantages and disadvantages in this. If we are solving the Black–Scholes equation there is something appealing in having a grid with constant $\log S$ steps, after all, the underlying is following a lognormal random walk. But if you want to use constant $\log S$ steps then it is conceptually simpler to change variables, to write the Black–Scholes equation in terms of the new variable $x = \log S$. Once you have done this then constant $\log S$ step size is equivalent to constant x step size. You could even go so far as to transform to the much neater heat equation as in Chapter 6. One downside to such a transformation is that equal spacing in $\log S$ means that a lot of grid points are spread around small values of S where there is usually not very much happening. The main reason that I rarely do any transforming of the equation when I am solving it numerically is that I like to solve in terms of the real financial variables since terms of the contract are specified using these real variables: transforming to the heat equation could cause problems for contracts such as barrier options. For other problems such a transformation to something nicer is not even possible. Examples would be an underlying with asset- and time-dependent volatility, or an interest rate product.

I'm also going to concentrate on backward parabolic equations. Every partial differential equation or numerical analysis book explains methods with reference to the forward equation. But of course, the difference between forward and backward is no more than a change of the sign of the time (but make sure you apply initial conditions to forward equations and final conditions to backward).

46.4 DIFFERENTIATION USING THE GRID

Let's introduce some notation. The timestep will be δt and the asset step δS, both of which are constant. Thus the grid is made up of the points at asset values

$$S = i\,\delta S$$

and times

$$t = T - k\,\delta t$$

where $0 \le i \le I$ and $0 \le k \le K$. This means that we will be solving for the asset value going from zero up to the asset value $I\,\delta S$. Remembering that the Black–Scholes equation is to be solved for $0 \le S < \infty$ then $I\,\delta S$ is our approximation to infinity. In practice, this upper bound does not have to be too large. Typically it should be three or four times the value of the exercise price, or more generally, three or four times the value of the asset at which there is some important behavior. In a sense barrier options are easier to solve numerically because you don't need to solve over all values of S; for an up-and-out option there is no need to make the grid extend beyond the barrier.

I will write the option value at each of these grid points as

$$V_i^k = V(i\,\delta S, T - k\,\delta t),$$

so that the superscript is the time variable and the subscript the asset variable. Notice how I've changed the direction of time, as k increases so real time decreases.

Suppose that we know the option value at each of the grid points, can we use this information to find the derivatives of the option value with respect to S and t? That is, can we find the terms that go into the Black–Scholes equation?

46.5 APPROXIMATING θ

The definition of the first time-derivative of V is simply

$$\frac{\partial V}{\partial t} = \lim_{h \to 0} \frac{V(S, t+h) - V(S, t)}{h}.$$

It follows naturally that we can approximate the time derivative from our grid of values using

$$\frac{\partial V}{\partial t}(S, t) \approx \frac{V_i^k - V_i^{k+1}}{\delta t}. \tag{46.1}$$

This is our approximation to the option's theta. It uses the option value at the two points marked in Figure 46.3.

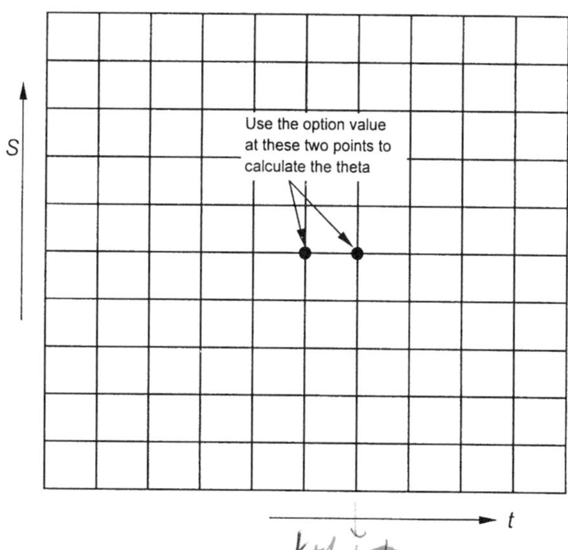

Figure 46.3 An approximation to the theta.

How accurate is this approximation? We can expand the option value at asset value S and time $t - \delta t$ in a Taylor series about the point S, t as follows.

$$V(S, t - \delta t) = V(S, t) - \delta t \frac{\partial V}{\partial t}(S, t) + O(\delta t^2).$$

In terms of values at grid points this is just

$$V_i^k = V_i^{k+1} + \delta t \frac{\partial V}{\partial t}(S, t) + O(\delta t^2).$$

Which, upon rearranging, is

$$\frac{\partial V}{\partial t}(S, t) = \frac{V_i^k - V_i^{k+1}}{\delta t} + O(\delta t).$$

Our question is answered, the error is $O(\delta t)$. It is possible to be more precise than this, the error depends on the magnitude of the second t derivative. But I won't pursue the details here.

There are other ways of approximating the time derivative of the option value, but this one will do for now.

46.6 APPROXIMATING Δ

The same idea can be used for approximating the first S derivative, the delta. But now I *am* going to present some choices.

Let's examine a cross section of our grid at one of the timesteps. In Figure 46.4 is shown this cross section. The figure shows three things: the function we are approximating (the curve), the values of the function at the grid points (the dots) and three possible approximations to the first derivative (the three straight lines). These three approximations are

$$\frac{V_{i+1}^k - V_i^k}{\delta S}, \quad \frac{V_i^k - V_{i-1}^k}{\delta S} \quad \text{and} \quad \frac{V_{i+1}^k - V_{i-1}^k}{2\,\delta S}.$$

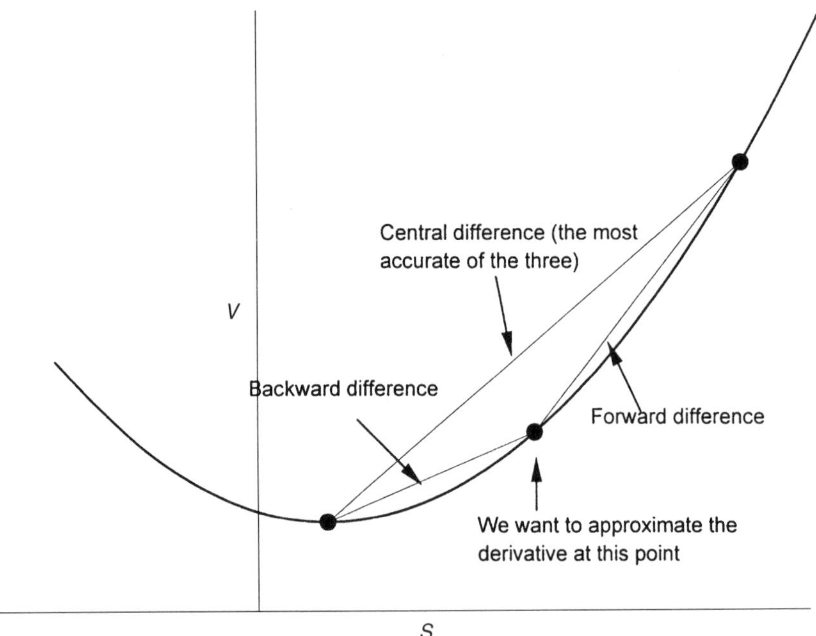

Figure 46.4 Approximations to the delta.

These are called a **forward difference**, a **backward difference** and a **central difference** respectively.

One of these approximations is better than the others, and it is obvious from the diagram which it is. From a Taylor series expansion of the option value about the point $S + \delta S, t$ we have

$$V(S + \delta S, t) = V(S, t) + \delta S \frac{\partial V}{\partial S}(S, t) + \tfrac{1}{2}\delta S^2 \frac{\partial^2 V}{\partial S^2}(S, t) + O(\delta S^3).$$

Similarly,

$$V(S - \delta S, t) = V(S, t) - \delta S \frac{\partial V}{\partial S}(S, t) + \tfrac{1}{2}\delta S^2 \frac{\partial^2 V}{\partial S^2}(S, t) + O(\delta S^3).$$

Subtracting one from the other, dividing by $2\,\delta S$ and rearranging gives

$$\frac{\partial V}{\partial S}(S, t) = \frac{V_{i+1}^k - V_{i-1}^k}{2\,\delta S} + O(\delta S^2).$$

The central difference has an error of $O(\delta S^2)$ whereas the error in the forward and backward differences are both much larger, $O(\delta S)$. The central difference is that much more accurate because of the fortunate cancellation of terms, due to the symmetry about S in the definition of the difference.

The central difference calculated at S requires knowledge of the option value at $S + \delta S$ and $S - \delta S$. However, there will be occasions when we do not know one of these values, for example if we are at the extremes of our region, i.e. at $i = 0$ or $i = I$. Then there are times when it may be beneficial to use a one-sided derivative for reasons of stability, an important point which I will come back to. If we do need to use a one-sided derivative, must we use the simple forward or backward difference or is there something better?

The simple forward and backward differences use only two points to calculate the derivative; if we use three points we can get a better order of accuracy. To find the best approximations using three points we need to use Taylor series again.

Suppose I want to use the points S, $S + \delta S$ and $S + 2\,\delta S$ to calculate the option's delta, how can I do this as accurately as possible? First, expand the option value at the points $S + \delta S$ and $S + 2\,\delta S$ in a Taylor series:

$$V(S + \delta S, t) = V(S, t) + \delta S \frac{\partial V}{\partial S}(S, t) + \tfrac{1}{2}\delta S^2 \frac{\partial^2 V}{\partial S^2}(S, t) + O(\delta S^3)$$

and

$$V(S + 2\,\delta S, t) = V(S, t) + 2\,\delta S \frac{\partial V}{\partial S}(S, t) + 2\,\delta S^2 \frac{\partial^2 V}{\partial S^2}(S, t) + O(\delta S^3).$$

If I take the combination

$$-4V(S + \delta S, t) + V(S + 2\,\delta S, t)$$

I get

$$-3V(S, t) - 2\,\delta S \frac{\partial V}{\partial S}(S, t) + O(\delta S^3),$$

since the second derivative, $O(\delta S^2)$, terms both cancel. Thus

$$\frac{\partial V}{\partial S}(S, t) = \frac{-3V(S, t) + 4V(S + \delta S, t) - V(S + 2\,\delta S, t)}{2\,\delta S} + O(\delta S^2).$$

This approximation is of the same order of accuracy as the central difference, but of better accuracy than the simple forward difference. It uses no information about V for values below S.

If we want to calculate the delta using a better *backward* difference then we would choose

$$\frac{\partial V}{\partial S}(S, t) = \frac{3V(S, t) - 4V(S - \delta S, t) + V(S - 2\,\delta S, t)}{2\,\delta S} + O(\delta S^2).$$

For most of the time I will use the central difference as the approximation to the delta, but there will be times when I need to use one of the one-sided approximations.

46.7 APPROXIMATING Γ

The gamma of an option is the second derivative of the option with respect to the underlying. The natural approximation for this is

$$\frac{\partial^2 V}{\partial S^2}(S,t) \approx \frac{V_{i+1}^k - 2V_i^k + V_{i-1}^k}{\delta S^2}.$$

Again, this comes from a Taylor series expansion. The error in this approximation is also $O(\delta S^2)$. I'll leave the demonstration of this as an exercise for the reader.

46.8 BILINEAR INTERPOLATION

Suppose that we have an estimate for the option value, or its derivatives, on the mesh points, how can we estimate the value at points in between? The simplest way to do this is to use a two-dimensional interpolation method called **bilinear interpolation**. This method is most easily explained via the following schematic diagram, Figure 46.5.

We want to estimate the value of the option, say, at the interior point in the figure. The values of the option at the four nearest neighbours are called V_1, V_2, V_3 and V_4, simplifying earlier notation just for this brief section. The areas of the rectangles made by the four corners

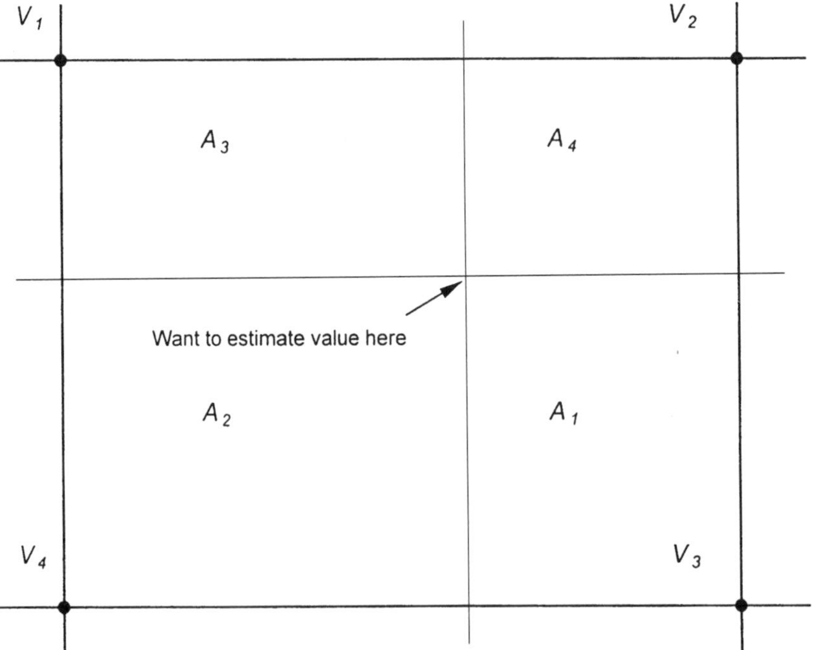

Figure 46.5 Bilinear interpolation.

and the interior point, are labelled A_1, A_2, A_3 and A_4. But note that the subscripts for the areas correspond to the subscripts of the option values at the corners *opposite*. The approximation for the option value at the interior point is then

$$\frac{\sum_{i=1}^{4} A_i V_i}{\sum_{i=1}^{4} A_i}.$$

46.9 FINAL CONDITIONS AND PAYOFFS

We know that at expiry the option value is just the payoff function. This means that we don't have to solve anything for time T. At expiry we have

$$V(S, T) = \text{Payoff}(S)$$

or, in our finite-difference notation,

$$V_i^0 = \text{Payoff}(i\,\delta S).$$

The right-hand side is a known function. For example, if we are pricing a call option we put

$$V_i^0 = \max(i\,\delta S - E, 0).$$

This final condition will get our finite-difference scheme started. It will be just like working down the tree in the binomial method.

46.10 BOUNDARY CONDITIONS

When we come to solving the Black–Scholes equation numerically in the next section, we will see that we must specify the option value at the extremes of the region. That is, we must prescribe the option value at $S = 0$ and at $S = I\,\delta S$. What we specify will depend on the type of option we are solving. I will give some examples.

Example 1

Suppose we want to price a call option. At $S = 0$ we know that the value is always zero, therefore we have

$$V_0^k = 0.$$

Example 2

For large S the call value asymptotes to $S - E^{-r(T-t)}$ (plus exponentially small terms). Thus our upper boundary condition could be

$$V_I^k = I\,\delta S - Ee^{-rk\,\delta t}.$$

This would be slightly different if we had a dividend.

Example 3

For a put option we have the condition at $S = 0$ that $V = Ee^{-r(T-t)}$. This becomes

$$V_0^k = Ee^{-rk\,\delta t}.$$

Example 4

The put option becomes worthless for large S and so

$$V_I^k = 0.$$

Example 5

A useful boundary condition to apply at $S = 0$ for most contracts (including calls and puts) is that the diffusion and drift terms 'switch off.' This means that on $S = 0$ the payoff is guaranteed, resulting in the condition

$$\frac{\partial V}{\partial t}(0, t) - rV(0, t) = 0.$$

Numerically, this becomes

$$V_0^k = (1 - r\delta t)V_0^{k-1}.$$

Example 6

When the option has a payoff that is at most linear in the underlying for large values of S then you can use the upper boundary condition

$$\frac{\partial^2 V}{\partial S^2}(S, t) \to 0 \quad \text{as } S \to \infty.$$

Almost all common contracts have this property. The finite-difference representation is

$$V_I^k = 2V_{I-1}^k - V_{I-2}^k.$$

This is particularly useful because it is independent of the contract being valued meaning that your finite-difference program does not have to be too intelligent.[1]

Often there are natural boundaries at finite, non-zero values of the underlying, which means that the domain in which we are solving either does not extend down to zero or up to infinity. Barrier options are the most common form of such contracts.

By way of example, suppose that we want to price an up-and-out call option. This option will be worthless if the underlying ever reaches the value S_u. Clearly,

$$V(S_u, t) = 0.$$

If we are solving this problem numerically how do we incorporate this boundary condition?

The ideal thing to do first of all is to choose an asset step size such that the barrier $S = S_u$ is a grid point, i.e $S_u/\delta S$ should be an integer. This is to ensure that the boundary condition

$$V_I^k = 0$$

[1] Sometimes I even use this condition for small values of S, not taking the grid down to $S = 0$.

is an accurate representation of the correct boundary condition. Note that we are no longer solving over an asset price range that extends to large S. The upper boundary at $S = S_u$ may be close to the current asset level. In a sense this makes barrier problems easier to solve; the solution region is always smaller than the region over which you would solve a non-barrier problem.

Sometimes it is not possible to make your grid match up with the barrier. This would be the case if the barrier were moving, for example. If this is the case then you are going to have to find an approximation to the boundary condition. There is something that you must not do, and that is to set V equal to zero at the nearest grid point to the barrier. Such an approximation is very inaccurate, of $O(\delta S)$, and will ruin your numerical solution. The trick that we can use to overcome such problems is to introduce a **fictitious point**. This is illustrated in Figure 46.6.

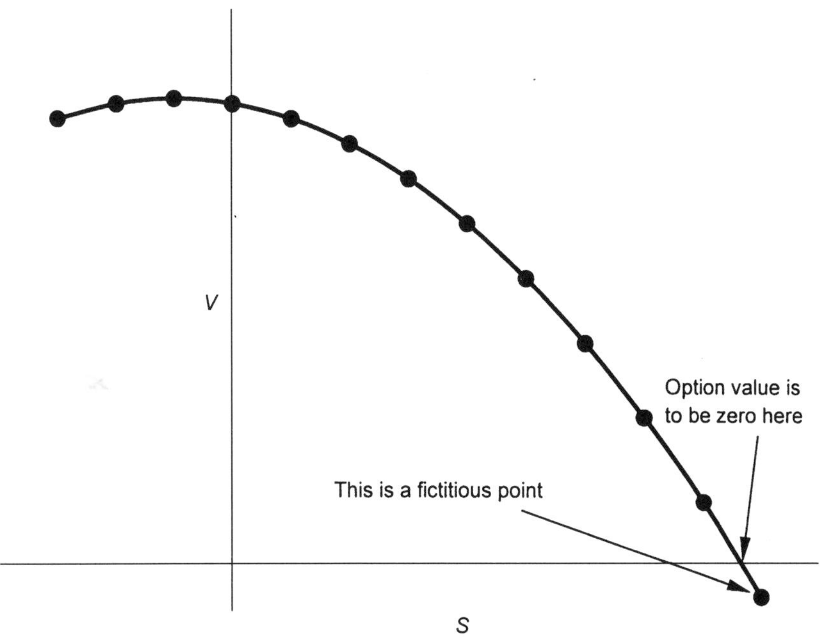

Figure 46.6 A fictitious point, introduced to ensure accuracy in a barrier option boundary condition.

The point $i = I - 1$ is a real point, within the solution region. The point $i = I$ is just beyond the barrier.

Example 7

Suppose that we have the condition that

$$V(S_u, t) = f(t).$$

If we have an 'out' option then f would be either zero or the value of the rebate. If we have an 'in' option then f is the value of the option into which the barrier option converts.

This condition can be approximated by ensuring that the straight line connecting the option values at the two grid points straddling the barrier has the value f at the barrier. Then a good discrete version of this boundary condition is

$$V_I^k = \frac{1}{\alpha}(f - (1 - \alpha)V_{I-1}^k)$$

where

$$\alpha = \frac{S_u - (I - 1)\delta S}{\delta S}.$$

This is accurate to $O(\delta S^2)$, the same order of accuracy as in the approximation of the S derivatives.

I have set up all the foundations for us to begin solving some equations. Remember, there has been nothing difficult in what we have done so far, everything is a simple application of Taylor series.

46.11 THE EXPLICIT FINITE-DIFFERENCE METHOD

The Black–Scholes equation is

$$\frac{\partial V}{\partial t} + \tfrac{1}{2}\sigma^2 S^2 \frac{\partial^2 V}{\partial S^2} + rS\frac{\partial V}{\partial S} - rV = 0.$$

I'm going to write this as

$$\frac{\partial V}{\partial t} + a(S,t)\frac{\partial^2 V}{\partial S^2} + b(S,t)\frac{\partial V}{\partial S} + c(S,t)V = 0$$

to emphasize the wide applicability of the finite-difference methods. The only constraint we must pose on the coefficients is that if we are solving a backward equation, i.e. imposing final conditions, we must have $a > 0$.

I'm going to take the approximations to the derivatives, explained above, and put them into this equation:

$$\begin{aligned} &\frac{V_i^k - V_i^{k+1}}{\delta t} \\ &+ a_i^k \left(\frac{V_{i+1}^k - 2V_i^k + V_{i-1}^k}{\delta S^2} \right) \\ &+ b_i^k \left(\frac{V_{i+1}^k - V_{i-1}^k}{2\delta S} \right) \\ &+ c_i^k V_i^k = O(\delta t, \delta S^2). \end{aligned}$$

I have used a different line for each of the terms in the original equation.

Points to note:

- The time derivative uses the option values at 'times' k and $k+1$, whereas the other terms all use values at k.

- The gamma term is a central difference; in practice one never uses anything else.
- The delta term uses a central difference. There are often times when a one-sided derivative is better. We'll see examples later.
- The asset- and time-dependent functions a, b and c have been valued at $S_i = i\,\delta S$ and $t = T - k\,\delta t$ with the obvious notation.
- The error in the equation is $O(\delta t, \delta S^2)$.

I am going to rearrange this **difference equation** to put all of the $k+1$ terms on the left-hand side:

$$V_i^{k+1} = A_i^k V_{i-1}^k + (1 + B_i^k)V_i^k + C_i^k V_{i+1}^k \tag{46.2}$$

where

$$A_i^k = \nu_1 a_i^k + \tfrac{1}{2}\nu_2 b_i^k,$$
$$B_i^k = -2\nu_1 a_i^k + \delta t\, c_i^k$$

and

$$C_i^k = \nu_1 a_i^k - \tfrac{1}{2}\nu_2 b_i^k$$

where

$$\nu_1 = \frac{\delta t}{\delta S^2} \quad \text{and} \quad \nu_2 = \frac{\delta t}{\delta S}.$$

The error in this is $O(\delta t^2, \delta t\,\delta S^2)$. I will come back to this in a moment. The error in the approximation of the differential equation is called the **local truncation error**.

Equation (46.2) only holds for $i = 1, \ldots I - 1$, i.e. for interior points, since V_{-1}^k and V_{I+1}^k are not defined. Thus there are $I - 1$ equations for the $I + 1$ unknowns, the V_i^k. The remaining two equations come from the two boundary conditions on $i = 0$ and $i = I$. The two end points are treated separately.

If we know V_i^k for all i then Equation (46.2) tells us V_i^{k+1}. Since we know V_i^0, the payoff function, we can easily calculate V_i^1, which is the option value one timestep before expiry. Using these values we can work step by step back down the grid as far as we want. Because the relationship between the option values at timestep $k+1$ is a simple function of the option values at timestep k this method is called the **explicit finite-difference method**. The relationship between the option values in Equation (46.2) is shown in Figure 46.7.

Equation (46.2) is only used to calculate the option value for $1 \le i \le I - 1$ since the equation requires knowledge of the option values at $i - 1$ and $i + 1$. This is where the boundary conditions come in. Typically we either have a V_i^k being prescribed at $i = 0$ and $i = I$ or, as suggested above, we might prescribe a relationship between the option value at an end point and interior values. This idea is illustrated in the following Visual Basic code fragment. This code fragment does not have all the declarations etc. at the top, nor the return of any answers. I will give a full function shortly, for the moment I want you to concentrate on setting up the final condition and the finite-difference time loop.

The array `V(i, k)` holds the option values. Unless we wanted to store all option values for all timesteps this would not be the most efficient way of writing the program. I will describe a better way in a moment.

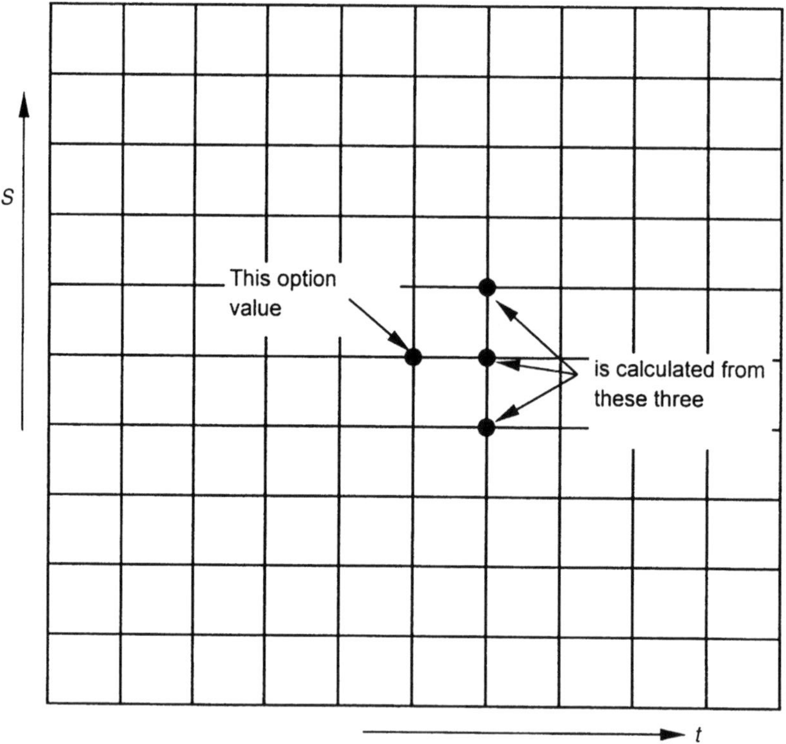

Figure 46.7 The relationship between option values in the explicit method.

First set up the final condition, the payoff.

```
For i = 0 To NoAssetSteps
    S(i) = i * AssetStep
    V(i, 0) = CallPayoff(S(i)) ' Set up final condition
Next i
```

Now we can work backwards in time using the following time loop.

```
' Time loop
For k = 0 To NoTimesteps
    RealTime = Expiry - k * Timestep
    For i = 1 To NoAssetSteps - 1
        V(i, k + 1) = A(S(i), RealTime) * V(i - 1, k) + _
                      B(S(i), RealTime) * V(i, k) + C(S(i), _
                      RealTime) * V(i + 1, k)
    Next i
' BC at S=0
    V(0, k + 1) = 0
' BC at "infinity"
    V(NoAssetSteps, k + 1) = 2 * V(NoAssetSteps - 1, k + 1) _
                      - V(NoAssetSteps - 2, k + 1)
Next k
```

The explicit finite-difference algorithm is simple, the functions `A(S(i), RealTime)`, `B(S(i), RealTime)` and `C(S(i), RealTime)` are defined elsewhere and are in terms of the asset price `S(i)` and the time `RealTime`. Since I am valuing a call option here the boundary condition at $S = 0$ is simply `V(0, k + 1) = 0` but the boundary condition I have used at the upper boundary `i = NoAssetSteps` is that the gamma is zero.

46.11.1 The Black–Scholes Equation

For the Black–Scholes equation with dividends the coefficients above simplify to

$$A_i^k = \tfrac{1}{2}\left(\sigma^2 i^2 - (r - D)i\right)\delta t,$$
$$B_i^k = -\left(\sigma^2 i^2 + r\right)\delta t$$

and

$$C_i^k = \tfrac{1}{2}\left(\sigma^2 i^2 + (r - D)i\right)\delta t.$$

This uses $S = i\,\delta S$. If the volatility, interest rate and dividend are constant then there is no time or k dependence in these coefficients.

46.11.2 Convergence of the Explicit Method

I can write the value of the option at any i point at the final timestep K as

$$V_i^K = V_i^0 + \sum_{k=0}^{K-1}(V_i^{k+1} - V_i^k).$$

Each of the terms in this summation is in error by $O(\delta t^2, \delta t\,\delta S^2)$. This means that the error in the final option value is

$$O(K\delta t^2, K\delta t\,\delta S^2)$$

since there are K terms in the summation. If we value the option at a finite value of T then $K = O(\delta t^{-1})$ so that the error in the final option value is $O(\delta t, \delta S^2)$.

Although the explicit method is simple to implement it does not always converge. Convergence of the method depends on the size on the timestep, the size of the asset step and the size of the coefficients a, b and c.

The technique often used to demonstrate convergence is quite fun, so I'll show you how it is done. The method, as I describe it, is not rigorous but it can be made so.

Ask the question, 'If a small error is introduced into the solution, is it magnified by the numerical method or does it decay away?' If a small error, introduced by rounding errors for example, becomes a large error then the method is useless. The usual way to analyze such stability is to look for a solution of the equation, Equation (46.2), of the form[2]

$$V_i^k = \alpha^k e^{2\pi i\sqrt{-1}/\lambda}. \tag{46.3}$$

In other words, I'm going to look for an oscillatory solution with a wavelength of λ. If I find that $|\alpha| > 1$ then there is instability. Note that I am not worried about how the oscillation gets started, I could interpret this special solution as part of a Fourier series analysis.

[2] This is the only place in the book that I use $\sqrt{-1}$. Normally I'd write this as i but I need i for other quantities.

Substituting (46.3) into (46.2) I get

$$\alpha = \left(1 + c_i^k\,\delta t + 2a_i^k\nu_1(\cos(2\pi/\lambda) - 1)\right) + \sqrt{-1}\,b_i^k\nu_2\sin(2\pi/\lambda).$$

It turns out that to have $|\alpha| < 1$, for stability, we require

$$c_i^k \le 0,$$

$$2\nu_1 a_i^k - \delta t\, c_i^k \le 1$$

and

$$\tfrac{1}{2}\nu_2|b_i^k| \le \nu_1 a_i^k.$$

To get this result, I have assumed that all the coefficients are slowly varying over the δS lengthscales.

In financial problems we almost always have a negative c, often it is simply $-r$ where r is the risk-free interest rate. The other two constraints are what really limit the applicability of the explicit method.

Typically we choose ν_1 to be $O(1)$ in which case the second constraint is approximately

$$\nu_1 \le \frac{1}{2a}$$

(ignoring sub- and superscripts on a). This is a serious limitation on the size of the timestep,

$$\delta t \le \frac{\delta S^2}{2a}.$$

If we want to improve accuracy by halving the asset step, say, we must reduce the timestep by a factor of four. The computation time then goes up by a factor of *eight*. The improvement in accuracy we would get from such a reduction in step sizes is a factor of four since the explicit finite-difference method is accurate to $O(\delta t, \delta S^2)$.

If the timestep constraint is not satisfied, if it is too large, then the instability is obvious from the results. The instability is so serious, and so oscillatory, that it is easily noticed. It is unlikely that you will get a false but believable result if you use the explicit method.

The final constraint can also be a serious restriction. It can be written as

$$\delta S \le \frac{2a}{|b|}. \tag{46.4}$$

If we are solving the Black–Scholes equation this restriction does not make much difference in practice unless the volatility is very small. It can be important in other problems though and I will show how to get past this restriction after the next Visual Basic program.

```
Function OptionValue(Asset As Double, Strike As Double, Expiry As_
                     Double, Volatility As Double, IntRate As_
                     Double, param As Integer, NoAssetSteps)
Dim VOld(0 To 100) As Double
```

```
Dim VNew(0 To 100) As Double
Dim Delta(0 To 100) As Double
Dim Gamma(0 To 100) As Double
Dim Theta(0 To 100) As Double
Dim S(0 To 100) As Double
Dim Ssqd(0 To 100) As Double
halfvolsqd = 0.5 * Volatility * Volatility
AssetStep = 2 * Strike / NoAssetSteps
NearestGridPt = Int(Asset / AssetStep)
dummy = (Asset - NearestGridPt * AssetStep) / AssetStep
Timestep = AssetStep * AssetStep / Volatility / Volatility /_
          (4 * Strike * Strike)
NoTimesteps = Int(Expiry / Timestep) + 1
Timestep = Expiry / NoTimesteps
For i = 0 To NoAssetSteps
    S(i) = i * AssetStep
    Ssqd(i) = S(i) * S(i)
    VOld(i) = max(S(i) - Strike, 0)
Next i
For j = 1 To NoTimesteps
    For i = 1 To NoAssetSteps - 1
        Delta(i) = (VOld(i + 1) - VOld(i - 1)) / (2 * AssetStep)
        Gamma(i) = (VOld(i + 1) - 2 * VOld(i) + VOld(i - 1)) /_
                   (AssetStep * AssetStep)
        VNew(i) = VOld(i) + Timestep * (halfvolsqd * Ssqd(i) *_
                  Gamma(i) + IntRate * S(i) * Delta(i) - IntRate_
                  * VOld(i))
    Next i
        VNew(0) = 0
        VNew(NoAssetSteps) = 2 * VNew(NoAssetSteps - 1) -_
                             VNew(NoAssetSteps - 2)
For i = 0 To NoAssetSteps
    Theta(i) = (VOld(i) - VNew(i)) / Timestep
    VOld(i) = VNew(i)
Next i
Next j
For i = 1 To NoAssetSteps - 1
    Delta(i) = (VOld(i + 1) - VOld(i - 1)) / (2 * AssetStep)
    Gamma(i) = (VOld(i + 1) - 2 * VOld(i) + VOld(i - 1)) /_
               (AssetStep * AssetStep)
Next i
If param = 0 Then OptionValue = (1 - dummy) * VOld(NearestGridPt) + _
                          dummy * VOld(NearestGridPt + 1)
If param = 1 Then OptionValue = (1 - dummy) * Delta(NearestGridPt) + _
                          dummy * Delta(NearestGridPt + 1)
If param = 2 Then OptionValue = (1 - dummy) * Gamma(NearestGridPt) + _
                          dummy * Gamma(NearestGridPt + 1)
If param = 3 Then OptionValue = (1 - dummy) * Theta(NearestGridPt) + _
                          dummy * Theta(NearestGridPt + 1)
End Function
```

This program will output the value of a call option, its delta, gamma or theta depending on whether the parameter `param` is 0, 1, 2 or 3. The program is fairly self-explanatory, the only points I want to comment on are the use of `VOld(i)` and `VNew(i)`, the size of the timestep and the interpolation to give the final answer.

If we wanted to keep values of the option at all values of the asset for all times up to expiry we would need a two-dimensional array. If we just want the option value today we only need two one-dimensional arrays. One of these is to store the values used on the right-hand side of (46.2) (`VOld(i)`) and one for the left-hand side (`VNew(i)`). After finding the new values for the option value at the new timestep we update the old values, setting them equal to the new. This is the line `VOld(i) = VNew(i)`. If we choose to do this then we save a great deal of storage space.

The timestep has been chosen so that it just about satisfies the constraint on ν_1.

Finally, the asset grid has been set up so that the strike price is a grid point. This means in general the current level of the asset `Asset` will not lie on a grid point. To find the option value at the asset value I have used a simple linear interpolation between the two option values either side of the current asset level. The nearest grid point on the left-hand side is `NearestGridPt` and the ratio of the distance of the current asset value from that point to the size of the asset step is `dummy`.

The error between the results of this explicit finite-difference program and the exact Black–Scholes formula as a function of the underlying is shown in Figure 46.8 for 50 asset points, a volatility of 20%, and interest rate of 10% an expiry of one year and a strike of 100.

The logarithm of the absolute error as a function of the logarithm of the square of the asset step size is shown in Figure 46.9. The $O(\delta S^2)$ behavior is very obvious. In these calculations I have kept ν_1 constant.

In Figure 46.10 is shown the error as a function of calculation time, time units will depend on your machine.

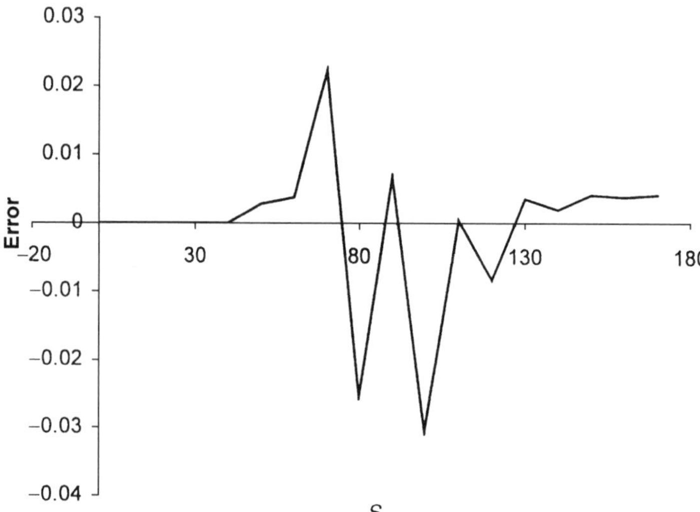

Figure 46.8 Error as a function of the underlying using the finite-difference scheme.

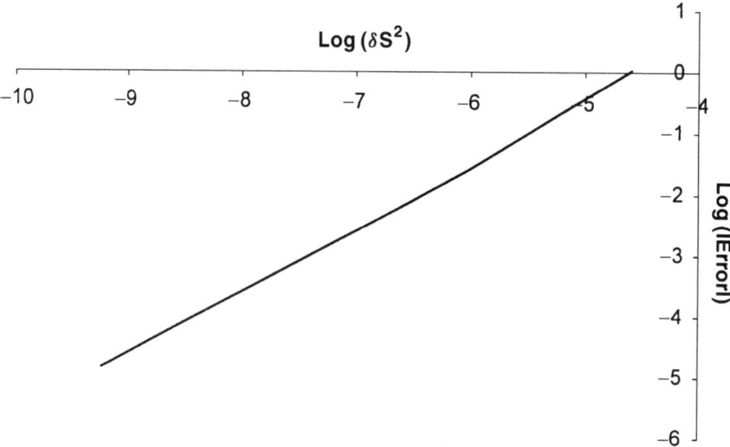

Figure 46.9 Log(Error) as a function of log(δS^2) using the finite-difference scheme.

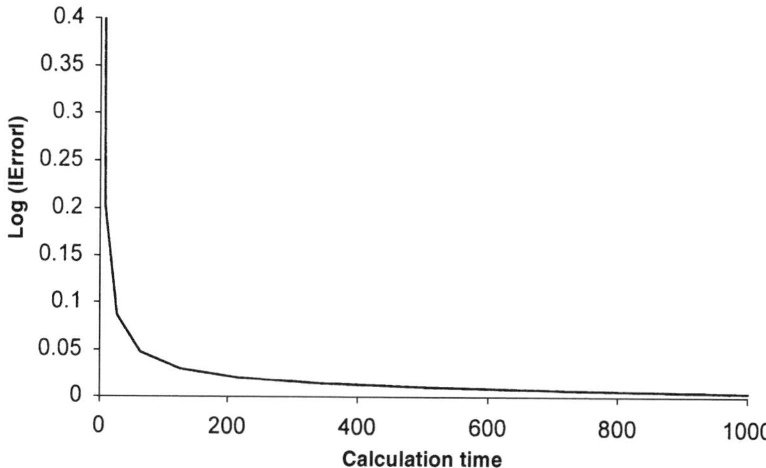

Figure 46.10 Absolute error as a function of the calculation time using the finite-difference scheme.

46.12 UPWIND DIFFERENCING

The constraint (46.4) can be avoided if we use a one-sided difference instead of a central difference for the first derivative of the option value with respect to the asset. As I said in Chapter 6 the first S derivative represents a drift term. This drift has a direction associated with it, as t decreases, moving away from expiry, so the drift is towards smaller S. In a sense, this makes the forward price of the asset a better variable to use. Anyway, the numerical scheme can make use of this by using a one-sided difference. That is the situation for the Black–Scholes equation. More generally, the approximation that we use for delta in the equation could depend on the sign of

b. For example, use the following

$$\text{if } b(S,t) \geq 0 \quad \text{then} \quad \frac{\partial V}{\partial S}(S,t) = \frac{V_{i+1}^k - V_i^k}{\delta S}$$

but if

$$b(S,t) < 0 \quad \text{then} \quad \frac{\partial V}{\partial S}(S,t) = \frac{V_i^k - V_{i-1}^k}{\delta S}.$$

This removes the limitation (46.4) on the asset step size, improving stability. However, since these one-sided differences are only accurate to $O(\delta S)$ the numerical method is less accurate.

The use of one-sided differences that depend on the sign of the coefficient b is called **upwind differencing**.[3] There is a small refinement of the technique in the choice of the value chosen for the function b:

$$\text{if } b(S,t) \geq 0 \quad \text{then} \quad b(S,t)\frac{\partial V}{\partial S}(S,t) = b_{i+1/2}^k \frac{V_{i+1}^k - V_i^k}{\delta S}$$

but if

$$b(S,t) < 0 \quad \text{then} \quad b(S,t)\frac{\partial V}{\partial S}(S,t) = b_{i-1/2}^k \frac{V_i^k - V_{i-1}^k}{\delta S}.$$

Notice how I have used the mid point value for b.[4]

Below is a Visual Basic code fragment that uses a one-sided difference, which one depending on the sign of the drift term. This code fragment can be used for interest rate products, since it is solving

$$\frac{\partial V}{\partial t} + \tfrac{1}{2}\sigma(r)^2 \frac{\partial^2 V}{\partial r^2} + (\mu(r) - \lambda(r)\sigma(r))\frac{\partial V}{\partial r} - rV = 0.$$

Note the arbitrary $\sigma(r)$=`Volatility(IntRate(i))` and $\mu(r)-\lambda(r)\sigma(r)$=`RiskNeutralDrift(IntRate(i))`.

This fragment of code is just the timestepping, above it would go declarations and setting up the payoff. Below it would go the outputting. It does not implement any boundary conditions at `i = 1` or at `i = NoIntRateSteps`, these would depend on the contract being valued.

```
For i = 1 To NoIntRateSteps - 1
    If RiskNeutralDrift(IntRate(i)) > 0 Then
         Delta(i) = (VOld(i + 1) - VOld(i)) / dr
         RNDrift = RiskNeutralDrift(IntRate(i)
                   + 0.5 * dr)
    Else
         Delta(i) = (VOld(i) - VOld(i - 1)) / dr
         RNDrift = RiskNeutralDrift(IntRate(i) - 0.5 * dr)
    End If
```

[3] That's 'wind' as in breeze, not as in to wrap or coil.

[4] This choice won't make much difference to the result but it does help to make the numerical method 'conservative,' meaning that certain properties of the partial differential equation are retained by the solution of the difference equation. Having a conservative scheme is important in computational fluid dynamics applications, otherwise the scheme will exhibit mass 'leakage.'

```
    Gamma(i) = (VOld(i + 1) -  2 * VOld(i) + VOld(i - 1)) /_
               (dr * dr)
    VNew(i) = VOld(i) + Timestep * (0.5 * Volatility(IntRate(i))_
              * Volatility(IntRate(i)) * Gamma(i) + RNDrift *_
              Delta(i) - IntRate(i) * VOld(i))
Next i
```

To get back the $O(\delta S^2)$ accuracy of the central difference with a one-sided difference you can use the approximations described in Section 46.6.

We have seen that the explicit finite-difference method suffers from restrictions in the size of the grid steps. The explicit method is similar in principle to the binomial tree method, and the restrictions can be interpreted in terms of risk-neutral probabilities. The terms A, B and C are related to the risk-neutral probabilities of reaching the points $i-1$, i and $i+1$. Instability is equivalent to one of these being a negative quantity, and we can't allow negative probabilities. More sophisticated numerical methods exist that do not suffer from such restrictions, and I will describe these next.

The advantages of the explicit method

- It is very easy to program and hard to make mistakes
- When it does go unstable it is usually obvious
- It copes well with coefficients that are asset and/or time dependent
- It is easy to incorporate accurate one-sided differences

The disadvantage of the explicit method

- There are restrictions on the timestep so the method can be slower than other schemes

46.13 SUMMARY

The diffusion equation has been around for a *long* time. Numerical schemes for the solution of the diffusion equation have been around quite a while too, not as long as the equation itself but certainly a lot longer than the Black–Scholes equation and the binomial method. This means that there is a great deal of academic literature on the efficient solution of parabolic equations in general. I've introduced you to the subject with the explicit method; in the next chapter I'll show you how the numerical methods can get more sophisticated.

FURTHER READING

- For general numerical methods see Johnson & Riess (1982) and Gerald & Wheatley (1992).
- The first use of finite-difference methods in finance was due to Brennan & Schwartz (1978). For its application in interest rate modeling see Hull & White (1990b).

EXERCISES

1. Write a program to value European call and put options by solving Black–Scholes equation with suitable final and boundary conditions. Include a constant, continuous dividend yield on the underlying share.
2. Adjust your program to value call options with the forward price as underlying.
3. Write a program to value a down-and-out call option, with barrier below the strike price.
4. Write a program to value compound options of the following form:
   (a) Call on a call,
   (b) Call on a put,
   (c) Put on a call,
   (d) Put on a put.
5. Alter your compound option program to value a chooser option which allows you to buy a call or a put at expiry.
6. Adjust your Black–Scholes pricer for calls and puts to price the options in a worst-case scenario, when we assume that volatility is uncertain, but

$$\sigma^- \leq \sigma \leq \sigma^+.$$

7. Adjust your Black–Scholes pricer to calculate the Greeks for a call option.

CHAPTER 47

further finite-difference methods for one-factor models

In this Chapter...

- implicit finite-difference methods including Crank–Nicolson
- Douglas schemes
- Richardson extrapolation
- American-style exercise
- exotic options

47.1 INTRODUCTION

We continue with one-factor numerical methods, discussing the more difficult to program implicit methods. The extra complexity of the methods is outweighed, though, by their superior stability properties. I also show how to extend the finite-difference method to cope with early exercise and path-dependent contracts.

47.2 IMPLICIT FINITE-DIFFERENCE METHODS

The **fully implicit method** uses the points as shown in Figure 47.1 to calculate the option value. The scheme is superficially just like the explicit method using finite-difference estimates of the option value, its delta and gamma but now at the timestep $k+1$. The relationship between the option values on the mesh is simply

$$\frac{V_i^k - V_i^{k+1}}{\delta t} + a_i^{k+1}\left(\frac{V_{i+1}^{k+1} - 2V_i^{k+1} + V_{i-1}^{k+1}}{\delta S^2}\right) + b_i^{k+1}\left(\frac{V_{i+1}^{k+1} - V_{i-1}^{k+1}}{2\,\delta S}\right) + c_i^{k+1}V_i^{k+1} = 0.$$

(It doesn't matter much whether the coefficients a, b and c are evaluated at the timestep $k+1$ or k.) The method is still accurate to $O(\delta t, \delta S^2)$.

This can be written as

$$A_i^{k+1}V_{i-1}^{k+1} + (1 + B_i^{k+1})V_i^{k+1} + C_i^{k+1}V_{i+1}^{k+1} = V_i^k \tag{47.1}$$

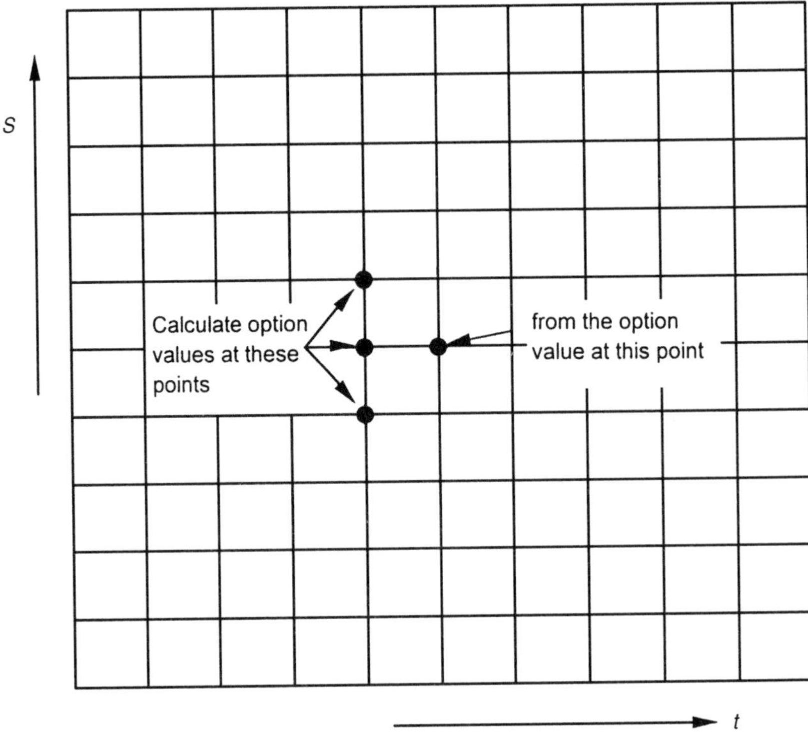

Figure 47.1 The relationship between option values in the fully implicit method.

where

$$A_i^{k+1} = -\nu_1 a_i^{k+1} - \tfrac{1}{2}\nu_2 b_i^{k+1},$$

$$B_i^{k+1} = 2\nu_1 a_i^{k+1} - \delta t\, c_i^{k+1}$$

and

$$C_i^{k+1} = -\nu_1 a_i^{k+1} + \tfrac{1}{2}\nu_2 b_i^{k+1}$$

where

$$\nu_1 = \frac{\delta t}{\delta S^2} \quad \text{and} \quad \nu_2 = \frac{\delta t}{\delta S}.$$

Again, Equation (47.1) does not hold for $i = 0$ or $i = I$, the boundary conditions supply the two remaining equations.

There is a world of difference between this scheme and the explicit finite-difference scheme. The two main differences concern the stability of the method and the solution procedure.

The method no longer suffers from the restriction on the timestep. The asset step can be small and the timestep large without the method running into stability problems.

The solution of the difference equation is no longer so straightforward. To get V_i^{k+1} from V_i^k means solving a set of linear equations, each V_i^{k+1} is directly linked to its two neighbours and thus indirectly linked to every option value at the same timestep.

I am not going to pursue the fully implicit method any further since the method can be significantly improved upon with little extra computational effort.

47.3 THE CRANK–NICOLSON METHOD

The **Crank–Nicolson method** can be thought of as an average of the explicit method and the fully implicit method. It uses the six points shown in 47.2.

The Crank–Nicolson scheme is

$$\frac{V_i^k - V_i^{k+1}}{\delta t} + \frac{a_i^{k+1}}{2}\left(\frac{V_{i+1}^{k+1} - 2V_i^{k+1} + V_{i-1}^{k+1}}{\delta S^2}\right) + \frac{a_i^k}{2}\left(\frac{V_{i+1}^k - 2V_i^k + V_{i-1}^k}{\delta S^2}\right)$$
$$+ \frac{b_i^{k+1}}{2}\left(\frac{V_{i+1}^{k+1} - V_{i-1}^{k+1}}{2\,\delta S}\right) + \frac{b_i^k}{2}\left(\frac{V_{i+1}^k - V_{i-1}^k}{2\,\delta S}\right)$$
$$+ \tfrac{1}{2}c_i^{k+1}V_i^{k+1} + \tfrac{1}{2}c_i^k V_i^k = O(\delta t^2, \delta S^2).$$

This can be written as

$$-A_i^{k+1}V_{i-1}^{k+1} + (1 - B_i^{k+1})V_i^{k+1} - C_i^{k+1}V_{i+1}^{k+1} = A_i^k V_{i-1}^k + (1 + B_i^k)V_i^k + C_i^k V_{i+1}^k, \qquad (47.2)$$

where

$$A_i^k = \tfrac{1}{2}\nu_1 a_i^k + \tfrac{1}{4}\nu_2 b_i^k,$$
$$B_i^k = -\nu_1 a_i^k + \tfrac{1}{2}\delta t\, c_i^k,$$

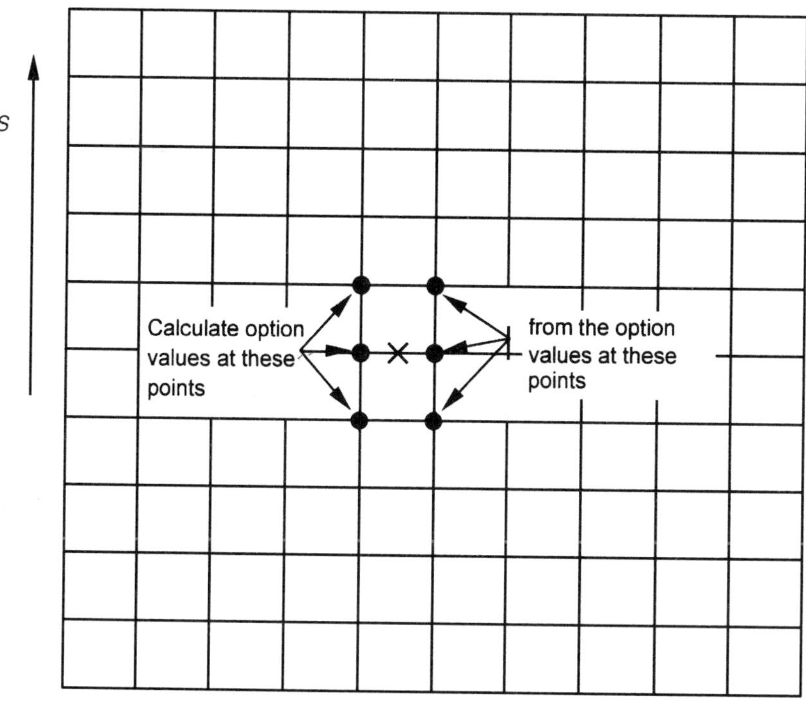

Figure 47.2 The relationship between option values in the Crank–Nicolson method.

and

$$C_i^k = \tfrac{1}{2}\nu_1 a_i^k - \tfrac{1}{4}\nu_2 b_i^k.$$

These equations only hold for $1 \le i \le I - 1$. The boundary conditions again supply the two missing equations. They are harder to handle than in the explicit method and I will discuss them in depth shortly.

Although this looks a bit messy, and it is harder to solve, the beauty of this method lies in its stability and accuracy. As with the fully implicit method there is no relevant limitation on the size of the timestep for the method to converge. Better yet, the method is more accurate than the two considered so far. The error in the method is $O(\delta t^2, \delta S^2)$. So now we can use larger timesteps, and still get an accurate solution. To see that the error due to the size of the timestep is now $O(\delta t^2)$ expand Equation (47.2) about the point S, $t - \left(\frac{1}{2}\right)\delta t$ (this is the point 'x' in Figure 47.2).

The Crank–Nicolson method can be written in the matrix form

$$\begin{pmatrix} A_1^{k+1} & 1+B_1^{k+1} & C_1^{k+1} & 0 & \cdot & \cdot & \cdot \\ 0 & A_2^{k+1} & 1+B_2^{k+1} & \cdot & \cdot & \cdot & \cdot \\ \cdot & 0 & \cdot & \cdot & \cdot & 0 & \cdot \\ \cdot & \cdot & \cdot & \cdot & 1+B_{I-2}^{k+1} & C_{I-2}^{k+1} & 0 \\ \cdot & \cdot & \cdot & 0 & A_{I-1}^{k+1} & 1+B_{I-1}^{k+1} & C_{I-1}^{k+1} \end{pmatrix} \begin{pmatrix} V_0^{k+1} \\ V_1^{k+1} \\ \cdot \\ \cdot \\ \cdot \\ \cdot \\ \cdot \\ V_{I-1}^{k+1} \\ V_I^{k+1} \end{pmatrix}$$

$$= \begin{pmatrix} -A_1^k & 1-B_1^k & -C_1^k & 0 & \cdot & \cdot & \cdot \\ 0 & -A_2^k & 1-B_2^k & \cdot & \cdot & \cdot & \cdot \\ \cdot & 0 & \cdot & \cdot & \cdot & 0 & \cdot \\ \cdot & \cdot & \cdot & \cdot & 1-B_{I-2}^k & -C_{I-2}^k & 0 \\ \cdot & \cdot & \cdot & 0 & -A_{I-1}^k & 1-B_{I-1}^k & -C_{I-1}^k \end{pmatrix} \begin{pmatrix} V_0^k \\ V_1^k \\ \cdot \\ \cdot \\ \cdot \\ \cdot \\ \cdot \\ V_{I-1}^k \\ V_i^k \end{pmatrix} \qquad (47.3)$$

The two matrices have $I - 1$ rows and $I + 1$ columns. This is a representation of $I - 1$ equations in $I + 1$ unknowns.

The two equations that we are missing come from the boundary conditions. Using these conditions, I am going to convert this system of equations, (47.3), into a system of equations involving a square matrix. The aim is to write the system of equations in the form

$$\mathbf{M}_L^{k+1}\mathbf{v}^{k+1} + \mathbf{r}^k = \mathbf{M}_R^k\mathbf{v}^k,$$

for known *square* matrices $\mathbf{M}_L^{k+1}$ and $\mathbf{M}_R^k$, and a known vector $\mathbf{r}^k$ and where details of the boundary conditions have been fully incorporated.

I will consider three cases separately, depending on the form of the boundary condition that is to be implemented. I will also only deal with a boundary condition at $i = 0$, obviously boundary conditions at $i = I$ are treated similarly.

47.3.1 Boundary Condition Type I: V_0^{k+1} Given

Sometimes we know that our option has a particular value on the boundary $i = 0$, or on $i = I$. For example, if we have a European put we know that $V(0, t) = Ee^{-r(T-t)}$. This translates to knowing that $V_0^{k+1} = Ee^{-r(k+1)\delta t}$. We can write

$$\begin{pmatrix} A_1^{k+1} & 1+B_1^{k+1} & C_1^{k+1} & 0 & \cdot & \cdot & \cdot \\ 0 & A_2^{k+1} & 1+B_2^{k+1} & \cdot & \cdot & \cdot & \cdot \\ \cdot & 0 & \cdot & \cdot & \cdot & 0 & \cdot \\ \cdot & \cdot & \cdot & \cdot & 1+B_{I-2}^{k+1} & C_{I-2}^{k+1} & 0 \\ \cdot & \cdot & \cdot & 0 & A_{I-1}^{k+1} & 1+B_{I-1}^{k+1} & C_{I-1}^{k+1} \end{pmatrix} \begin{pmatrix} V_0^{k+1} \\ V_1^{k+1} \\ \cdot \\ \cdot \\ \cdot \\ \cdot \\ \cdot \\ V_{I-1}^{k+1} \\ V_I^{k+1} \end{pmatrix}$$

as

$$\begin{pmatrix} 1+B_1^{k+1} & C_1^{k+1} & 0 & \cdot & \cdot & & \\ A_2^{k+1} & 1+B_2^{k+1} & \cdot & \cdot & \cdot & & \\ & 0 & \cdot & \cdot & \cdot & 0 & \\ & \cdot & \cdot & \cdot & 1+B_{I-2}^{k+1} & C_{I-2}^{k+1} & \\ & \cdot & \cdot & 0 & A_{I-1}^{k+1} & 1+B_{I-1}^{k+1} & \end{pmatrix} \begin{pmatrix} V_1^{k+1} \\ \cdot \\ \cdot \\ \cdot \\ \cdot \\ \cdot \\ V_{I-1}^{k+1} \end{pmatrix} + \begin{pmatrix} A_1^{k+1} V_0^{k+1} \\ 0 \\ 0 \\ \cdot \\ \cdot \\ 0 \\ \cdot \end{pmatrix} = \mathbf{M}_L^{k+1}\mathbf{v}^{k+1} + \mathbf{r}^k.$$

All I have done here is to multiply out the top and bottom rows of the matrix. The matrix $\mathbf{M}_L$ is square and of size $I - 1$. The vector $\mathbf{r}^k$, which is of length $I - 1$ only has non-zero elements at the top (and bottom) *and is completely known because it only depends on the function A and the prescribed value of V at the boundary.*

47.3.2 Boundary Condition Type II: Relationship Between V_0^{k+1} and V_1^{k+1}

If we have a barrier option for which a grid point does not coincide with the barrier we must use the approximation explained in Section 46.10:

$$V_0^{k+1} = \frac{1}{\alpha}(f - (1-\alpha)V_1^{k+1}).$$

This relationship between V_0^{k+1} and V_1^{k+1} for a 'down' barrier or between V_I^{k+1} and V_{I-1}^{k+1} for an 'up' barrier is seen in other contexts. Perhaps we know the slope of the option value for large or small S; this gives us a gradient boundary condition, which is also of this form. If we use a one-sided difference for the derivative then the boundary condition can also be written as a relationship between the last grid point and the last but one. More generally, suppose we have

$$V_0^{k+1} = a + bV_1^{k+1}.$$

This time the left-hand side of (47.3) can be written as

$$\begin{pmatrix} 1+B_1^{k+1} & C_1^{k+1} & 0 & \cdot & & \cdot & \\ A_2^{k+1} & 1+B_2^{k+1} & \cdot & \cdot & & \cdot & \\ & 0 & \cdot & \cdot & & \cdot & 0 \\ & \cdot & & \cdot & \cdot & 1+B_{I-2}^{k+1} & C_{I-2}^{k+1} \\ & \cdot & & \cdot & 0 & A_{I-1}^{k+1} & 1+B_{I-1}^{k+1} \end{pmatrix} \begin{pmatrix} V_1^{k+1} \\ \cdot \\ \cdot \\ \cdot \\ \cdot \\ \cdot \\ V_{I-1}^{k+1} \end{pmatrix} + \begin{pmatrix} A_1^{k+1}(a+bV_1^{k+1}) \\ 0 \\ 0 \\ \cdot \\ \cdot \\ 0 \\ \cdot \end{pmatrix}.$$

Again, this comes from multiplying out the top row of the matrix. By absorbing the V_1^{k+1} term into the matrix we can write this as

$$\begin{pmatrix} 1+B_1^{k+1}+bA_1^{k+1} & C_1^{k+1} & 0 & \cdot & & \cdot & \\ A_2^{k+1} & 1+B_2^{k+1} & \cdot & \cdot & & \cdot & \\ & 0 & \cdot & \cdot & & \cdot & 0 \\ & \cdot & & \cdot & \cdot & 1+B_{I-2}^{k+1} & C_{I-2}^{k+1} \\ & \cdot & & \cdot & 0 & A_{I-1}^{k+1} & 1+B_{I-1}^{k+1} \end{pmatrix} \begin{pmatrix} V_1^{k+1} \\ \cdot \\ \cdot \\ \cdot \\ \cdot \\ \cdot \\ V_{I-1}^{k+1} \end{pmatrix} + \begin{pmatrix} aA_1^{k+1} \\ 0 \\ 0 \\ \cdot \\ \cdot \\ 0 \\ \cdot \end{pmatrix}.$$

Again this is of the form

$$\mathbf{M}_L^{k+1}\mathbf{v}^{k+1} + \mathbf{r}^k$$

but for different $\mathbf{M}_L^{k+1}$ and $\mathbf{r}^k$ from before. This matrix and this vector are both known.

47.3.3 Boundary Condition Type III: $\dfrac{\partial^2 V}{\partial S^2} = 0$

More complicated, but still perfectly manageable, is the boundary condition

$$\frac{\partial^2 V}{\partial S^2} = 0.$$

This condition is particularly useful since it is independent of the type of contract, as long as the contract has a payoff that is at most linear in the underlying. This condition is, in central difference form,

$$V_0^{k+1} = 2V_1^{k+1} - V_2^{k+1}.$$

Thus, this time we can write the left-hand side of (47.3) as

$$\begin{pmatrix} 1+B_1^{k+1}+2A_1^{k+1} & C_1^{k+1}-A_1^{k+1} & 0 & \cdot & & \cdot & \\ A_2^{k+1} & 1+B_2^{k+1} & \cdot & \cdot & & \cdot & \\ & 0 & \cdot & \cdot & & \cdot & 0 \\ & \cdot & & \cdot & \cdot & 1+B_{I-2}^{k+1} & C_{I-2}^{k+1} \\ & \cdot & & \cdot & 0 & A_{I-1}^{k+1} & 1+B_{I-1}^{k+1} \end{pmatrix} \begin{pmatrix} V_1^{k+1} \\ \cdot \\ \cdot \\ \cdot \\ \cdot \\ \cdot \\ V_{I-1}^{k+1} \end{pmatrix}.$$

In this case there is no need to include an extra known vector $\mathbf{r}^k$. The left-hand side of our matrix equation is again

$$\mathbf{M}_L^{k+1}\mathbf{v}^{k+1} + \mathbf{r}^k$$

but again for different $\mathbf{M}_L^{k+1}$ and this time $\mathbf{r}^k$ is zero.

It will be instructive for the reader to absorb other boundary conditions into the matrix equation.

47.3.4 The Matrix Equation

Whichever of the boundary conditions we have, the Crank–Nicolson scheme, with boundary conditions incorporated, is

$$\mathbf{M}_L^{k+1}\mathbf{v}^{k+1} = \mathbf{M}_R^k\mathbf{v}^k - \mathbf{r}^k \tag{47.4}$$

where $\mathbf{v}^k$ is the column vector with $I-1$ entries V_i^k ($i = 1$ at the top) and $\mathbf{M}_L^{k+1}$ and $\mathbf{M}_R^k$ are square matrices of size $I-1$.

Remembering that we know $\mathbf{v}^k$, the matrix multiplication and vector addition on the right-hand side of (47.4) is simple enough to do. But how do we then find $\mathbf{v}^{k+1}$? This vector equation amounts to $I-1$ equations in $I-1$ unknowns, a set of linear simultaneous equations. In principle, the matrix $\mathbf{M}_L^{k+1}$ could be inverted to give

$$\mathbf{v}^{k+1} = (\mathbf{M}_L^{k+1})^{-1}(\mathbf{M}_R^k\mathbf{v}^k - \mathbf{r}^k),$$

except that matrix inversion is very time consuming, and from a computational point of view extremely inefficient. There are two much better ways for solving (47.4) called 'LU decomposition' and 'successive over-relaxation'.

47.3.5 LU Decomposition

The matrix $\mathbf{M}_L^{k+1}$ is special in that it is **tridiagonal**, the only non-zero elements lie along the diagonal and the sub- and superdiagonals. This means that it is not too hard to decompose the matrix into the product of two other matrices, one having non-zero elements along the diagonal and the subdiagonal and the other having non-zero elements along the diagonal and the superdiagonal. I will call these two matrices **L** and **U** respectively. For the rest of this section I will drop all unimportant sub- and superscripts. Thus we can write

$$\mathbf{M} = \mathbf{LU}. \tag{47.5}$$

I will first show how this **LU decomposition** is achieved and then show how it is used in the solution of (47.4). LU decomposition is an example of a 'direct method,' the aim being to find the exact solution of the equations in one go. The only error will be due to rounding.

Equation (47.5) is

$$\begin{pmatrix} 1+B_1 & C_1 & 0 & \cdot & \cdot & \cdot & 0 \\ A_2 & 1+B_2 & C_2 & 0 & \cdot & \cdot & \cdot \\ 0 & A_3 & 1+B_3 & \cdot & \cdot & \cdot & \cdot \\ \cdot & 0 & \cdot & \cdot & \cdot & 0 & \cdot \\ \cdot & \cdot & \cdot & \cdot & 1+B_{I-3} & C_{I-3} & 0 \\ \cdot & \cdot & \cdot & 0 & A_{I-2} & 1+B_{I-2} & C_{I-2} \\ \cdot & \cdot & \cdot & \cdot & 0 & A_{I-1} & 1+B_{I-1} \end{pmatrix}$$

$$= \begin{pmatrix} 1 & 0 & 0 & \cdot & \cdot & \cdot & 0 \\ l_2 & 1 & 0 & 0 & \cdot & \cdot & \cdot \\ 0 & l_3 & 1 & \cdot & \cdot & \cdot & \cdot \\ \cdot & 0 & \cdot & \cdot & \cdot & 0 & \cdot \\ \cdot & \cdot & \cdot & \cdot & 1 & 0 & 0 \\ \cdot & \cdot & \cdot & 0 & l_{I-2} & 1 & 0 \\ \cdot & \cdot & \cdot & \cdot & 0 & l_{I-1} & 1 \end{pmatrix} \begin{pmatrix} d_1 & u_1 & 0 & \cdot & \cdot & \cdot & 0 \\ 0 & d_2 & u_2 & 0 & \cdot & \cdot & \cdot \\ 0 & 0 & d_3 & \cdot & \cdot & \cdot & \cdot \\ \cdot & 0 & \cdot & \cdot & \cdot & 0 & \cdot \\ \cdot & \cdot & \cdot & \cdot & d_{I-3} & u_{I-3} & 0 \\ \cdot & \cdot & \cdot & 0 & 0 & d_{I-2} & u_{I-2} \\ \cdot & \cdot & \cdot & \cdot & 0 & 0 & d_{I-1} \end{pmatrix}$$

Where, without loss of generality, I have chosen the diagonal elements of **L** to be one. I will leave it to the reader to show that

$$d_1 = 1 + B_1$$

and then

$$l_i d_{i-1} = A_i, \quad u_{i-1} = C_{i-1} \quad \text{and} \quad d_i = 1 + B_i - l_i u_{i-1} \quad \text{for} \quad 2 \le i \le I - 1. \tag{47.6}$$

Notice how we work from $i = 1$ to $i = I$.

Here is a Visual Basic code fragment that takes in the diagonal, the superdiagonal and the subdiagonal of the matrix **M** in the arrays `Diag()`, `SuperDiag()` and `SubDiag()` each of length `NoElements`, and calculates d, u and l.

```
Dim d(1 To NoElements) As Double
Dim u(1 To NoElements) As Double
Dim l(1 To NoElements) As Double
      d(1)  =  Diag(1)
      For i  =  2 To NoElements
          u(i - 1)  =  SuperDiag(i - 1)
          l(i)  =  SubDiag(i) / d(i - 1)
          d(i)  =  Diag(i) - l(i) * SuperDiag(i - 1)
      Next i
```

So that's the first step, the decomposition of the matrix. Now we exploit the decomposition to solve (47.4).

Assuming that we have done the multiplication on the right-hand side of (47.4) to give

$$\mathbf{Mv} = \mathbf{q}$$

(where all sub- and superscripts have been dropped), we can write

$$\mathbf{LUv} = \mathbf{q}. \tag{47.7}$$

The vector **q** contains both the old option value array, at timestep k, and details of the boundary conditions.

I am going to solve Equation (47.7) in two steps. First find **w** such that

$$\mathbf{Lw} = \mathbf{q}$$

and then **v** such that

$$\mathbf{Uv} = \mathbf{w}.$$

And then we are done.

The first step gives

$$w_1 = q_1$$

and

$$w_i = q_i - l_i w_{i-1} \quad \text{for} \quad 2 \leq i \leq I - 1.$$

Again we must work from $i = 2$ to $i = I - 1$ sequentially. The second step involves working *backwards* from $i = I - 2$ to $i = 1$:

$$v_{I-1} = \frac{w_{I-1}}{d_{I-1}}$$

and

$$v_i = \frac{w_i - u_i v_{i+1}}{d_i} \quad \text{for} \quad I - 2 \geq i \geq 1.$$

Here is a Visual Basic code fragment that takes the just-calculated `l` and `d`, and the right-hand side `q` and calculates the `v`.

```
Dim v(1 To NoElements) As Double
Dim w(1 To NoElements) As Double

    w(1)  =  q(1)
    For i  =  2 To NoElements
        w(i)  =  q(i) - l(i) * w(i - 1)
    Next i

    v(NoElements)  =  w(NoElements) / d(NoElements)
    For i  =  NoElements - 1 To 1 Step -1
        v(i)  =  (w(i) - u(i) * v(i  +  1)) / d(i)
    Next i
```

If our matrix equation is time homogeneous then the LU decomposition need only be done the once. That is, if a, b and c are functions of S only then do we do the decomposition once and store the necessary results. The method therefore works well for the classic Black–Scholes equation where the coefficients are only functions of S. These days it is common to have time dependency in the coefficients. The drift and volatility terms, whether in equity or fixed-income problems, usually have some term structure. This means that there is important time dependence in the coefficients. This time dependency means that the LU decomposition must be done afresh at each timestep, significantly slowing down the computational time.

The advantages of the LU decomposition method

- It is quick
- The decomposition need only be done once if the matrix **M** is independent of time

> **The disadvantages of the LU decomposition method**
> - It is not immediately applicable to American options
> - The decomposition must be done each timestep if the matrix **M** is time dependent

47.3.6 Successive Over-relaxation, SOR

We now come to an example of an 'indirect method.' With this we solve the equations iteratively. Although the resulting 'solution' will never be exact we can find the solution to whatever accuracy we want, and as long as this can be done fast then it will be good enough. Indirect methods are applicable to a wider range of problems, our left-hand matrix need not be triadiagonal for example, so I will describe the ideas in generality. This means I am going to drop all sub- and superscripts and change notation slightly.

Suppose that the matrix **M** in the matrix equation

$$\mathbf{Mv} = \mathbf{q}$$

has entries M_{ij} then the system of equations can be written as

$$M_{11}v_1 + M_{12}v_2 + \cdots + M_{1N}v_N = q_1$$
$$M_{21}v_1 + M_{22}v_2 + \cdots + M_{2N}v_N = q_2$$
$$\ldots$$
$$M_{N1}v_1 + M_{N2}v_2 + \cdots + M_{NN}v_N = q_N$$

where now N is the number of equations, the size of the matrix.

Rewrite this as

$$M_{11}v_1 = q_1 - (M_{12}v_2 + \cdots + M_{1N}v_N)$$
$$M_{22}v_2 = q_2 - (M_{21}v_1 + \cdots + M_{2N}v_N)$$
$$\ldots$$
$$M_{NN}v_N = q_N - (M_{N1}v_1 + \cdots)$$

This system is easily solved *iteratively* using

$$v_1^{n+1} = \frac{1}{M_{11}}\left(q_1 - (M_{12}v_2^n + \cdots + M_{1N}v_N^n)\right)$$
$$v_2^{n+1} = \frac{1}{M_{22}}\left(q_2 - (M_{21}v_1^n + \cdots + M_{2N}v_N^n)\right)$$
$$\ldots$$
$$v_N^{n+1} = \frac{1}{M_{NN}}\left(q_N - (M_{N1}v_1^n + \cdots)\right)$$

where the superscript n denotes the level of the iteration *and not the timestep*. This iteration is started from some initial guess $\mathbf{v}^0$. (When solving our finite-difference problem it is usual to *start with the value of the option at the previous timestep as the initial guess for the next timestep.*) This iterative method is called the **Jacobi method**.

I can write the matrix **M** as the sum of a diagonal matrix **D**, an upper triangular matrix **U** with zeros on the diagonal and a lower triangular matrix **L** also with zeros on the diagonal:

$$\mathbf{M} = \mathbf{D} + \mathbf{U} + \mathbf{L}.$$

I can use this representation to write the Jacobi and other methods quite elegantly. The Jacobi method is then

$$\mathbf{v}^{n+1} = \mathbf{D}^{-1}(\mathbf{q} - (\mathbf{U} + \mathbf{L})\mathbf{v}^n).$$

When we implement the Jacobi method in practice we find some of the values of v_i^{n+1} before others. In the **Gauss–Seidel** method we use the updated values as soon as they are calculated. This method can be written as

$$v_i^{n+1} = \frac{1}{M_{ii}}\left(q_i - \sum_{j=1}^{i-1} M_{ij}v_j^{n+1} - \sum_{j=i}^{N} M_{ij}v_j^n\right).$$

Observe that there are some terms on the right-hand side with the superscript $n+1$. These are values of v that were calculated earlier but at the same level of iteration. This method can be written more compactly as

$$\mathbf{v}^{n+1} = \mathbf{D} + \mathbf{L}^{-1}\left(\mathbf{q} - \mathbf{U}\mathbf{v}^n\right).$$

When the matrix **M** has come from a finite-difference discretization of a parabolic equation (and that includes almost all finance problems) the above iterative methods usually converge to the correct solution *from one side*. This means that the corrections $v_i^{n+1} - v_i^n$ stay of the same sign as n increases, whether positive or negative depends on which side of the true solution was the initial guess. This is exploited in the **successive over-relaxation** or **SOR** method to speed up convergence.

The method can be written as

$$v_i^{n+1} = v_i^n + \frac{\omega}{M_{ii}}\left(q_i - \sum_{j=1}^{i-1} M_{ij}v_j^{n+1} - \sum_{j=i}^{N} M_{ij}v_j^n\right).$$

Again, the new values for v_i are used as soon as they are obtained. But now the factor ω, called the **acceleration** or **over-relaxation parameter** is included. This parameter, which must lie between 1 and 2, speeds up the converegence to the true solution.[1]

In matrix form we can write

$$\mathbf{v}^{n+1} = (\mathbf{I} + \omega\mathbf{D}^{-1}\mathbf{L})^{-1}(((1-\omega)\mathbf{I} - \omega\mathbf{D}^{-1}\mathbf{U})\mathbf{v}^n) + \omega\mathbf{D}^{-1}\mathbf{q})$$

where **I** is the identity matrix.

Following is a Visual Basic code fragment that calculates `v` given the matrix **M** and the right-hand side **q**. The code assumes that our matrix **M** is tridiagonal with diagonal `Diag(i)`, superdiagonal `SuperDiag(i)` and subdiagonal `SubDiag(i)`. The algorithm iterates until

[1] In iteration problems where successive results oscillate about the true solution the parameter ω would be chosen to be less than one, this would then be called **under-relaxation**.

the mean square error `Err` is less than some pre-specified tolerance `tol`. Notice that I keep track of how many iterations were needed; this is `NoIts`.

```
Dim q(1 To N) As Double
Dim v(0 To N + 1) As Double
Dim temp(1 To N) As Double
Dim Diag(1 To N) As Double
Dim SuperDiag(1 To N + 1) As Double
Dim SubDiag(0 To N) As Double

SuperDiag(N + 1) = 0
SubDiag(0) = 0
NoIts = 0
While Err > tol
   Err = 0
   For i = 1 To N
       temp(i) = v(i) + omega * (q(i) - SuperDiag(i) _
                 * v(i + 1) _
                 - Diag(i) * v(i) - SubDiag(i) * v(i - 1)) _
                 / Diag(i)
       Err = Err + (temp(i) - v(i)) * (temp(i) - v(i))
       v(i) = temp(i) ' use as soon as calculated
   Next i
   NoIts = NoIts + 1
Wend
```

47.3.7 Optimal Choice of ω

The error $\mathbf{e}^n = \mathbf{v}^n - \mathbf{v}$, where $\mathbf{v}$ is the exact solution, satisfies

$$\mathbf{e}^{n+1} = (\mathbf{I} + \omega\mathbf{D}^{-1}\mathbf{L})^{-1}((1-\omega)\mathbf{I} - \omega\mathbf{D}^{-1}\mathbf{U})\mathbf{e}^n.$$

The SOR method will converge provided that the largest of the moduli of the eigenvalues, a.k.a. the **spectral radius**, of the SOR matrix

$$(\mathbf{I} + \omega\mathbf{D}^{-1}\mathbf{L})^{-1}((1-\omega)\mathbf{I} - \omega\mathbf{D}^{-1}\mathbf{U})$$

is less than one. There is a theoretical optimal value for the acceleration parameter ω, and that is when the spectral radius is a minimum. This value for ω maximizes the rate of convergence of the SOR method. How to find the optimal value of ω is discussed in depth in Smith (1985). In practice it is very simple to iterate on ω to find the optimal value. This is done as follows.

Start with $\omega = 1$. After the first timestep is completed to the required accuracy, record the number of iterations taken to convergence. This is the quantity `Noits` in the Visual Basic code. For the next timestep increase ω by a small amount, say 0.05. Again record the number of iterations needed to get the required accuracy. If the number of iterations is fewer than for the first timestep then, for the third timestep, increase ω by another 0.05. Keep increasing ω at each timestep until the number of iterations begins to increase again. Choose ω to be the value that minimizes the number of iterations. If the SOR matrix is time homogeneous then you won't need to modify the parameter again. If there is a very strong time dependence in the matrix then you may want to experiment with retesting for the optimal ω.

The advantages of the SOR method

- It is easier to program than LU decomposition
- It is easily applied to American options

The disadvantage of the SOR method

- It is slightly slower than LU decomposition for European options

47.4 COMPARISON OF FINITE-DIFFERENCE METHODS

Now that we can have seen the explicit, the fully implicit and the Crank–Nicolson methods we can take a look at real, rather than theoretical errors in the methods. In the next two figures are shown the errors for the three schemes in the solution of an at-the-money European call option, with strike 20, three months to expiry, a volatility of 20% and an interest rate of 5%. In Figure 47.3 I show the logarithm of the error against the logarithm of the asset step size. As expected the slope of all three lines is about two. The error in the three methods decreases like δS^2. In Figure 47.4 I show the logarithm of the error against the logarithm of the timestep. Now we can see the difference between the three methods. Both the explicit and the fully implicit have an error that decreases like δt but the Crank–Nicolson method is much better, having an error that decreases like δt^2.

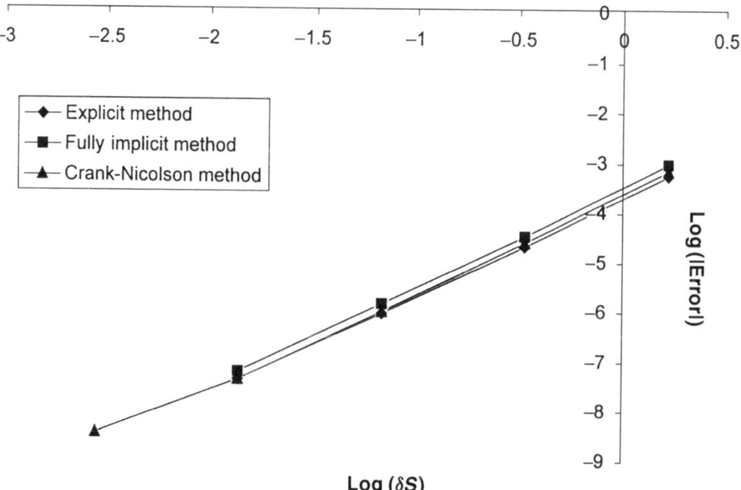

Figure 47.3 Log(Error) as a function of log(δS) for the three finite-difference schemes.

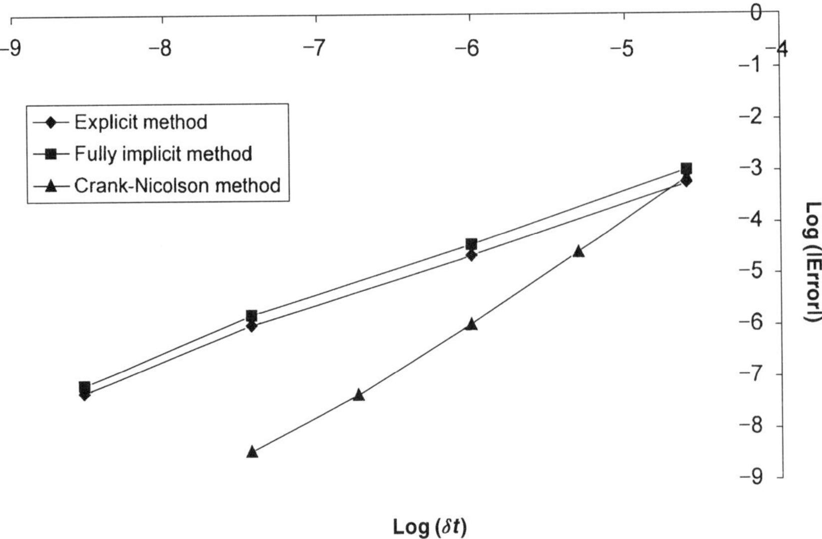

Figure 47.4 Log(Error) as a function of log(δt) for the three finite-difference schemes.

47.5 OTHER METHODS

The methods described above are just three of many schemes that have been tried out over the years in computational fluid dynamics for example. Other schemes are possible using more than three asset points, more than two time points etc. The questions that arise in any method are:

- What is the error in the method in terms of δt and δS?
- What are the restrictions on the timestep and/or asset step?
- Can I solve the resulting difference equations quickly?

We need answers to these three questions to decide which is the best method for our particular problem. Another question that arises, which may or may not be important, depending on how much effort you want to put into your programming:

- Is the method flexible enough to cope with changes in coefficients, boundary conditions, etc.?

That is, do you have to begin again from scratch if the contract changes slightly, or can you simply change a subroutine to cope with the new contract? One important example of this is early exercise; can the methods explained above handle American options? I will discuss this in a moment. But first, I want to describe a few more extensions of the finite difference ideas, ending up with a very, very simple technique that may speed up convergence. It doesn't always work, but it is definitely worth trying out because it involves no extra programming.

47.6 DOUGLAS SCHEMES

A method that has recently been rediscovered by financial researchers is the **Douglas scheme**. This is a method that manages to have a local truncation error of $O(\delta S^4, \delta t^2)$ for the same computational effort as the Crank–Nicolson scheme. It might be expected that to get a higher order of accuracy than Crank–Nicolson would require the use of more points in the S direction; this is not so.

I will describe the method using the basic diffusion equation. See the reading list at the end of this chapter for details of how to extend the method to convection-diffusion equations and equations with non-constant coefficients.

The basic diffusion equation is

$$\frac{\partial V}{\partial t} + \frac{\partial^2 V}{\partial S^2} = 0.$$

This is not quite how it is usually written, but I want to keep the equation as close as possible to what we have got used to.

The explicit method applied to this equation is just

$$\frac{V_i^{k+1} - V_i^k}{\delta t} = \frac{V_{i+1}^k - 2V_i^k + V_{i-1}^k}{\delta S^2}.$$

and the fully implicit is similarly

$$\frac{V_i^{k+1} - V_i^k}{\delta t} = \frac{V_{i+1}^{k+1} - 2V_i^{k+1} + V_{i-1}^{k+1}}{\delta S^2}.$$

The Crank–Nicolson scheme is just an average of these two methods. But is there any advantage in taking a *weighted* average? This leads to the idea of a θ method. Take a weighted average of the explicit and implicit methods to get

$$\frac{V_i^{k+1} - V_i^k}{\delta t} = \theta\left(\frac{V_{i+1}^{k+1} - 2V_i^{k+1} + V_{i-1}^{k+1}}{\delta S^2}\right) + (1-\theta)\left(\frac{V_{i+1}^k - 2V_i^k + V_{i-1}^k}{\delta S^2}\right).$$

When $\theta = \frac{1}{2}$ we are back to the Crank–Nicolson method. For a general value of θ the local truncation error is

$$O\left(\tfrac{1}{2}\delta t + \tfrac{1}{12}\delta S^2 - \theta\delta t, \delta S^4, \delta t^2\right).$$

When $\theta = 0$, $\frac{1}{2}$ or 1 we get the results we have seen so far. But if

$$\theta = \tfrac{1}{2} - \frac{\delta S^2}{12\,\delta t}$$

then the local truncation error is improved. The implementation of the method is no harder than the Crank–Nicolson scheme.

47.7 THREE TIME-LEVEL METHODS

Numerical schemes are not restricted to the use of just two time levels. We can construct many algorithms using three or more time levels. Again, we would do this if it gave us a better local truncation error or had better convergence properties. For simplicity, I shall still concentrate on the basic diffusion equation.

The obvious first method to try uses a central difference for the time derivative in an explicit scheme, after all, this is more accurate than the time derivative used in our earlier explicit scheme. With this approximation to the time derivative we get

$$\frac{V_i^{k+1} - V_i^{k-1}}{2\,\delta t} = \frac{V_{i+1}^k - 2V_i^k + V_{i-1}^k}{\delta S^2}.$$

Although this uses a more accurate approximation it is unstable for any timestep. This serves as a warning about the possible pitfalls in the search for good difference schemes.

An explicit scheme that is stable for all timesteps is

$$\frac{V_i^{k+1} - V_i^{k-1}}{2\,\delta t} = \frac{V_{i+1}^k - V_i^{k+1} - V_i^{k-1} + V_{i-1}^k}{\delta S^2}$$

leading to

$$(1 + 2\nu_1)\,V_i^{k+1} = 2\nu_1\left(V_{i+1}^k + V_{i-1}^k\right) + (1 - 2\nu_1)V_i^{k-1}.$$

To get this, or any three time-level method started requires an initial condition and data at the first time level. The latter must be found by some two time-level method, of the same accuracy as the three-level method that is to be used.

An implicit method with the same order of accuracy as the Crank–Nicolson method, but better for discontinuous initial data, is

$$-2\nu_1(V_{i+1}^{k+1} + V_{i-1}^{k+1}) + (3 + 2\nu_1)V_i^{k+1} = 4V_i^k - V_i^{k-1}.$$

And, of course, it is possible to improve the accuracy further in a three-level Douglas method:

$$\begin{aligned}(3 - 24\nu_1)V_{i+1}^{k+1} &+ (30 + 48\nu_1)V_i^{k+1} + (3 - 24\nu_1)V_{i-1}^{k+1}\\ &= 4V_{i-1}^k + 40V_i^k + 4V_{i+1}^k - V_{i+1}^{k-1} - 10V_i^{k-1} - V_{i-1}^{k-1}.\end{aligned}$$

47.8 RICHARDSON EXTRAPOLATION

In the explicit method the error is $O(\delta t, \delta S^2)$. If we assume that the approach to the correct solution as the timestep and asset step tend to zero is in a sense 'regular' then we could postulate that[2]

$$\text{approximate solution} = \text{exact solution} + \varepsilon_1\,\delta t + \varepsilon_2\,\delta S^2 + \varepsilon_3\,\delta t^2 + \cdots$$

for some coefficients ε_i. Suppose that we have *two* approximate solution V_1 and V_2 using different grid sizes, we can write

$$\begin{aligned}V_1 &= \text{exact solution} + \varepsilon_1\,\delta t_1 + \varepsilon_2\,\delta S_1^2 + \varepsilon_3\,\delta t_1^2 + \cdots\\ &= \text{exact solution} + \delta S_1^2\left(\varepsilon_1\frac{\delta t_1}{\delta S_1^2} + \varepsilon_2\right) + \cdots\end{aligned}$$

and

$$\begin{aligned}V_2 &= \text{exact solution} + \varepsilon_1\,\delta t_2 + \varepsilon_2\,\delta S_2^2 + \varepsilon_3\,\delta t_2^2 + \cdots\\ &= \text{exact solution} + \delta S_2^2\left(\varepsilon_1\frac{\delta t_2}{\delta S_2^2} + \varepsilon_2\right) + \cdots.\end{aligned}$$

[2] This is like a Taylor series. Think of $V(S, t; \delta S, \delta t)$ as the solution of the finite-difference equations, so that $V(S, t; 0, 0)$ is the exact solution. Now expand for small δt and δS.

If we choose

$$\frac{\delta t_1}{\delta S_1^2} = \frac{\delta t_2}{\delta S_2^2},$$

i.e. ν_1 constant, where the subscripts denote the step sizes used in finding the solutions V_1 and V_2, then we can find a *better* solution than both V_1 and V_2 by eliminating the leading-order error terms in the above two equations. This better approximation is given by

$$\frac{\delta S_2^2 V_1 - \delta S_1^2 V_2}{\delta S_2^2 - \delta S_1^2}.$$

The accuracy of the method is now $O(\delta t^2, \delta S^3)$.[3]

Now refer back to Figures 47.3 and 47.4. In those figures you can see just how well the error is approximated by the timestep and the square of the asset step size. Richardson extrapolation would work well in this case.

To give an example, use the Visual Basic function given in the previous chapter for the explicit scheme applied to the call option. For a strike of 100, maturity of one year, underlying asset at 100 with a volatility of 20% and an interest rate of 10% the exact Black–Scholes value is 13.269. Using the program and 20 points gives a result of 13.067. Because the number of calculations is proportional to $\delta t^{-1}\delta S^{-1}$ the time taken would be 8,000 in some units. With 30 points the value improves becoming 13.183, but the time taken is 27,000. Using Richardson extrapolation on these two values gives value of 13.275. The total time taken is $8,000 + 27,000 = 35,000$. But the error is just 0.006. To get such an accuracy using the explicit method directly would require 100 asset steps, a time of 1,000,000, and hence 30 times as long.

The same extrapolation principal can be applied to any of the methods described in this chapter. The method should be used with care. There is no guarantee that we can write the solution in a meaningful Taylor series expansion so the method could make matters worse. Also, the extrapolation method can increase rounding errors.

47.9 FREE BOUNDARY PROBLEMS AND AMERICAN OPTIONS

There is a great deal of theory behind what I am going to show you in the next couple of sections. This theory is obviously important, since it makes what I am going to do 'valid.' But the theory obscures the simplicity of the final result, so I am going to cut straight to the chase.

IMPORTANT

The value of American options must always be greater than the payoff, otherwise there will be an arbitrage opportunity

$$V(S,t) \geq \text{Payoff}(S).$$

The payoff function may also be time dependent. For example, if the option is Bermudan, i.e. exercise is only allowed on certain dates, then the payoff function is zero except on the special dates, when it is some prescribed function of the underlying. So I am going to write Payoff(S, t) and I need never mention Bermudan options again.

[3] The accuracy with respect to the asset step may be even better than this because of symmetry in the central differences for the derivatives.

American options are examples of 'free boundary problems.' We must solve a partial differential equation with an unknown boundary, the position of which is determined by having one more boundary condition than if the boundary were prescribed. In the American option problem we know that both the option value and its delta are continuous with the payoff function, the so called **smooth pasting condition**. Solving a problem where the boundary (or boundaries) are unknown is surely very complex. Wrong. If we approach the problem in the right way, the implementation could not be simpler.

The first point to note is that I am going to solve over a *fixed* range of S that I am sure contains the free boundary, and I am not going to try to find the boundary by any direct method.

47.9.1 Early Exercise and the Explicit Method

Let me tell you how to incorporate the early-exercise constraint into the explicit finite-difference scheme and then I will explain why it is clever.

Suppose that we have found V_i^k for all i at the timestep k (e.g. at the expiry date), timestep to find the option value at $k+1$ using the finite-difference scheme

$$V_i^{k+1} = A_i^k V_{i-1}^k + (1 + B_i^k) V_i^k + C_i^k V_{i+1}^k.$$

Don't worry about whether or not you have violated the American option constraint until you have found the option values V_i^{k+1} for all i. Now let's check whether the new option values are greater or less than the payoff. If they are less than the payoff then we have arbitrage. We can't allow that to happen so at every value of i for which the option value has allowed arbitrage, replace that value by the payoff at that asset value. That's all there is to it.

As far as the code is concerned, just put the following line of code instead of the line that updates the `VOld(i)`.

```
VOld(i) = max(VNew(i), Payoff(S(i), RealTime))
```

It is clear that this finite-difference solution will converge to something that has a value continuous with the payoff. What is not so clear is that the gradient constraint of continuous delta is also satisfied. But it is. The explicit method is just a fancy form of the binomial method and this simple replacement with the payoff is exactly what is done in the binomial method. The accuracy of the solution is still $O(\delta t, \delta S^2)$.

The early exercise boundary is somewhere between the asset values where to one side the option value is the payoff and to the other side the value is strictly greater than the payoff. It is perfectly possible for there to be more than one such boundary, and the method will find all of them with no extra effort.

47.9.2 Early Exercise and Crank–Nicolson

Implementing the American constraint in the Crank–Nicolson method is a bit harder than in the explicit method, but the rewards come in the accuracy. The method is still accurate to $O(\delta t^2, \delta S^2)$ with no limit on the timestep.

The only complication arises because the Crank–Nicolson method is implicit, and every value of the option at the $k+1$ timestep is linked to every other value at that timestep. It is therefore not good enough to just replace the option value with the payoff after the values have all been calculated,[4] the replacement must be done at the same time as the values are found:

$$v_i^{n+1} = \max\left(v_i^n + \frac{\omega}{M_{ii}}\left(q_i - \sum_{j=1}^{i-1} M_{ij}v_j^{n+1} - \sum_{j=i}^{N} M_{ij}v_j^n\right), \quad \text{Payoff}\right).$$

The payoff is evaluated at i and $k+1$ in the obvious manner. This method is called **projected SOR**.

Below is a Visual Basic code fragment that is identical to the SOR code with the exception of one line of code that checks whether the option value is greater than the `Payoff`. If it is not, then the payoff is used as the value.

```
Dim q(1 To N) As Double
Dim v(1 To N) As Double
Dim temp(1 To N) As Double
Dim MDiag(1 To N) As Double
Dim MSuperDiag(1 To N + 1) As Double
Dim MSubDiag(0 To N) As Double

MSuperDiag(N + 1) = 0
MSubDiag(0) = 0
NoIts = 0
While Error < tol
    Error = 0
    For i = 1 To N
        temp(i) = v(i) + omega * (q(i) - MSuperdiag(i + 1) _
                  * v(i + 1) - MDiag(i) * v(i) - MSubDiag(i - 1) _
                  * v(i - 1)) / MDiag(i)
        temp(i) = max(temp(i), Payoff(S(i)))
        Error = Error + (temp(i) - v(i)) * (temp(i) - v(i))
        v(i) = temp(i) ' use as soon as calculated
    Next i
    NoIts = NoIts + 1
Wend
```

47.10 JUMP CONDITIONS

As well as having final conditions (the payoff), boundary conditions (at zero, infinity or at a barrier) and the partial differential equation to satisfy we often have jump conditions. These can be due to a jump in the underlying on a dividend date, the payment of some coupon, or because of the jump in a discretely-sampled path-dependent quantity. One of these is very simple and the other two are basically the same as each other in their implementation.

47.10.1 A Discrete Cashflow

If our contract enititles us to a discretely-paid sum on a specified date (a coupon on a bond for example), then the contract value must jump by the amount of the cashflow. In continuous

[4] This can be done but the accuracy is then reduced to $O(\delta t)$.

time we have

$$V(S, t_d^-) = V(S, t_d^+) + C. \tag{47.8}$$

The cashflow C may be a function of the underlying, or even of the option value, and as always you can read r for S if you are valuing an interest rate product.

From a numerical point of view we would ideally like the date t_d on which there is a cashflow to lie exactly on a grid point, i.e. we would like the date to be exactly an integer number of timesteps before expiry. If that is the case then the implementation of (47.8) is straightforward. Simply calculate the option value up to and including the date t_d using whichever numerical method you prefer, then before moving on to the timestep after[5] the payment just add C to every option value.

Complications arise if the date does not coincide with grid points. The simplest implementation is to just add C at the first timestep after the date. This is accurate to $O(\delta t)$ and so is consistent for the explicit method. If you are using a more accurate numerical method such as Crank–Nicolson you should use a more accurate implementation of (47.8). If you are solving the basic Black–Scholes equation and the cashflow is a constant, independent of the underlying or option value, then it is simple to just present value C to make an equivalent cashflow that coincides with a timestep. If the cashflow is proportional to the underlying then (in the absence of dividends) it doesn't matter if you apply the jump condition at the nearest timestep since the underlying itself satisfies the Black–Scholes equation. There are many simple examples like

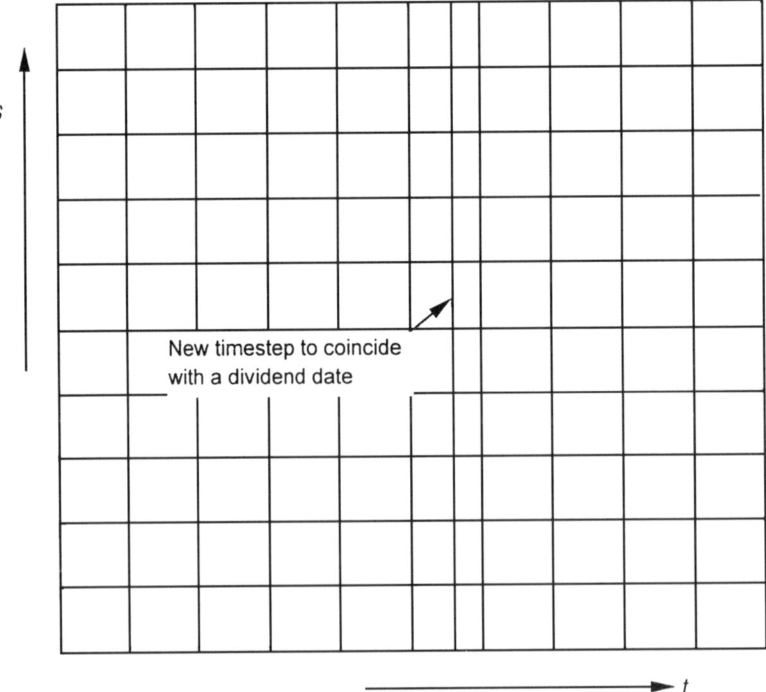

Figure 47.5 The grid near a discrete cashflow or a dividend date.

[5] In 'real' time *before*.

these where there is an obvious, sometimes tedious, way of accurately incorporating the cashflow. But if the cashflow is more complicated or you are solving for an interest rate product then the best thing to do is to make the timestep just after the cashflow (in real time) of the correct size to match up the grid with the cashflow date (see Figure 47.5). That way the cashflow is guaranteed to be incorporated at the same order of accuracy as the numerical method itself.

47.10.2 Discretely-paid Dividend

More interesting jump conditions arise when there is a finite jump in one of the independent variables. If there is a jump in the underlying asset we must implement a more complicated condition. I am going to restrict my explanation of the implementation to the one case; all others are dealt with in the same fashion.

Suppose that a dividend of $D(S)$ is paid on date t_d. Across this dividend date the asset value drops by an amount $D(S)$ (this is no arbitrage) but the option value does not change. This is explained fully in Chapter 8. Mathematically we write

$$V(S, t_d^-) = V(S - D(S), t_d^+). \tag{47.9}$$

When we are solving numerically we will find the right-hand side of this equation having timestepped from expiry. Before continuing with the timestepping backwards in time we want to implement (47.9). I will assume that either t_d lies on a timestep or a timestep has been adjusted to ensure this. This means that in implementing (47.9) we are only concerned with accuracy due to the finiteness of the asset step size.

I will show how to use linear interpolation to implement the jump condition. This method is accurate to $O(\delta S^2)$ and is therefore of the same accuracy as the other methods described above.

From the finite-difference scheme we know V_i^{k+1} for all i; this is the option value just after the dividend date, that is, at time t_d^+. To implement the jump condition we must first find the grid points between which lies the point $S - D$. Then we interpolate between these two grid points to find an accurate value for the option value before the dividend is paid.

Here is the Visual Basic code fragment that implements the jump condition. The dividend payment is `Div(S(i))`, a function of the underlying. The option values just after the dividend date are stored in `VOld(i)` and the values just before are stored in `VNew(i)`. `dummy` is the ratio of the distance between the point `S(i) - Div(S(i))` and the nearest grid point to the step size `AssetStep`.

```
For i = 0 To NoAssetSteps
    inew = Int((S(i) - Div(S(i))) / AssetStep)
    dummy = (S(i) - Div(S(i)) - inew _
            * AssetStep) / AssetStep
    VNew(i) = (1 - dummy) _
             * VOld(inew) + dummy * VOld(inew + 1)
Next i
```

There is slight complication. I have assumed that $0 \leq$ `inew` $\leq$ `NoAssetSteps`. If this is not the case then `S(i) - Div(S(i))` lies outside the original grid. To deal with this it is usual to make some assumption about the behavior of V beyond the grid, usually that it is constant or linear in the underlying depending on the problem. The modification is simple to incorporate.

47.11 PATH-DEPENDENT OPTIONS

Many of the path-dependent contracts that I described in Part Two have simple partial differential equation representations. Often the problem is in three dimensions, the usual underlying (asset, interest rate, etc.), time and the path-dependent quantity. These three-dimensional problems for exotic options come in two forms: in one there are no new terms in the equation because the path-dependent quantity is measured discretely, in the other there is an extra first derivative with respect to the new continuously-sampled variable.[6]

Clearly the most important aspect of the path-dependent problem is the extra dimension, we must solve in three dimensions and must therefore introduce the option value as

$$V_{i,j}^k.$$

The superscript k still refers to time, the subscript i to the asset but now j refers to the new variable.

There is sufficient information for the reader to be able to work out ways in which to solve these new problems. I will simply point the way and give a couple of concrete examples.

47.11.1 Discretely-sampled Quantities

When the path-dependent quantity is sampled discretely there are no new terms in the partial differential equation and thus no new terms in any difference equation approximation. This makes the finite-difference solution not too difficult. Any of the methods described can be used. Remember, though, that you will have a three-dimensional grid and that you must solve for each value of j, the grid value for the path-dependent quantity. In this way you timestep backwards until you reach one of the sampling dates.

A jump condition must be applied across the sampling date and the implementation is exactly as for the discretely paid dividend. Suppose that the jump condition is

$$V(S, I, t_d^-) = V(S, F(S, I), t_d^+).$$

This is again implemented by linear interpolation and is accurate to $O(\delta I^2)$ where δI is the step size for the path-dependent quantity I.

In the following Visual Basic code fragment the path dependent quantity is called `P` and its step size is `PDQStep`. If `jnew` lies outside the range zero to `NoPDQSteps` then some extrapolation will be required. Note that I have interpolated the jump condition between grid points.

```
For j = 0 To NoPDQSteps
    For i = 0 To NoAssetSteps
        jnew = Int(F(S(i), P(j)) / PDQStep)
        dummy = (F(S(i), P(j)) - jnew _
                * PDQStep) / PDQStep
        VNew(i, j) = (1 - dummy)  * VNld(i, jnew)_
                   + dummy * VOld (i, jnew + 1)
    Next i
Next j
```

[6] Lookbacks are special in that even if the maximum is measured continuously there is no new term.

47.11.2 Continuously-sampled Quantities

When the path-dependent quantity is sampled continuously there is usually a new term in the partial differential equation and thus new terms in a difference equation approximation:

$$\frac{\partial V}{\partial t} + a(S, I, t)\frac{\partial^2 V}{\partial S^2} + b(S, I, t)\frac{\partial V}{\partial S} + f(S, I, t)\frac{\partial V}{\partial I} + c(S, I, t) = 0.$$

(In practice the coefficients rarely depend on I.)

The implementation of anything but the explicit finite-difference method is more complicated so I shall concentrate on that here.

The updating of the scheme, the implementation of the boundary and final conditions are all very straightforward. The only point that I need comment on is the choice of the discrete version of the derivative

$$\frac{\partial V}{\partial I}.$$

Because there is no diffusion in the I direction (there is no second derivative of the option value with respect to I) the choice of difference is important. The derivative with respect to I represents convection in the I direction and the numerical scheme must be consistent with this. For this reason a one-sided difference must be used. If the coefficient $f(S, I, t)$ changes sign then the choice of difference must reflect this, upwind differencing *must* be used. Here is a possible choice for the difference:

$$\text{if } f(S, I, t) \geq 0 \quad \text{then} \quad f(S, I, t)\frac{\partial V}{\partial I}(S, I, t) = f^k_{i,j+\left(\frac{1}{2}\right)}\frac{V^k_{i,j+1} - V^k_{i,j}}{\delta I}$$

but if

$$f(S, I, t) < 0 \quad \text{then} \quad f(S, I, t)\frac{\partial V}{\partial I}(S, I, t) = f^k_{i,j-\left(\frac{1}{2}\right)}\frac{V^k_{i,j} - V^k_{i,j-1}}{\delta I}.$$

Alternatively, one of the three-point one-sided differences could be used for better accuracy.

One final point about the numerical solution of three-dimensional exotic option problems. If there is a similarity reduction taking the problem down from three to two dimensions then it should be exploited. Not only will the solution be much faster, but the choice of scheme will be greater and the implementation easier.

47.12 SUMMARY

If you have worked your way successfully through the methods in this chapter then you have reached a level of sophistication that is far higher than the binomial method... but there is still higher to go.

FURTHER READING

- Excellent books on the numerical solution of partial differential equations are Morton & Mayers (1994) and Smith (1985). Richtmyer & Morton (1976) and Mitchell & Griffiths

(1980) are very good on partial differential equations with non-constant coefficients, which is what we usually have in finance.

- Roache (1982) is a very interesting description of numerical methods as used in Computational Fluid Dynamics.
- See the original paper by Crank & Nicolson (1947).

EXERCISES

1. Adjust your Black–Scholes pricer for calls and puts to value options when the underlying asset pays a discrete dividend yield.
2. Write a program to price a continuously-sampled arithmetic Asian average-strike call option.
3. Write a program to price a discretely-sampled arithmetic Asian average-strike put option.
4. Write a program to value a European call option using an implicit method.

CHAPTER 48

finite-difference methods for two-factor models

In this Chapter...

- about the explicit finite-difference method for two-factor models
- about the ADI and Hopscotch methods

48.1 INTRODUCTION

Many currently popular financial models have two random factors. Convertible bonds are usually priced with both random underlying and random interest rate. Exotic equity derivatives are often priced with stochastic volatility; this is especially true of barrier options. Finite-difference methods are quite suited to such problems.

Once you get to three factors, three sources of randomness, then finite-difference methods start to become slow and cumbersome. When there are four random factors then, if possible, you should use a Monte Carlo approach for pricing. These are discussed in Chapter 49. Monte Carlo works well in high dimensions.

Finite-difference methods work well in low dimensions, and handle early exercise very efficiently. Some path dependency is also easy to cope with.

In this chapter I will describe the simplest forms of finite-difference methods used with two or more factors.

48.2 TWO-FACTOR MODELS

I am going to refer throughout this chapter to the two-factor equation

$$\frac{\partial V}{\partial t} + a(S, r, t)\frac{\partial^2 V}{\partial S^2} + b(S, r, t)\frac{\partial V}{\partial S} + c(S, r, t)V$$
$$+ d(S, r, t)\frac{\partial^2 V}{\partial r^2} + e(S, r, t)\frac{\partial^2 V}{\partial S \partial r} + f(S, r, t)\frac{\partial V}{\partial r} = 0. \qquad (48.1)$$

As I wrote in the previous chapter, everything will be perfectly applicable to any problem, whatever the underlying variables. I write the problem to be solved as (48.1) assuming that my readers prefer the concrete 'asset' S and 'interest rate' r to the more abstract x and y. Actually, it will be quite helpful if we think of solving the two-factor convertible bond problem of Chapter 36. This is because that problem contains many important features such as choice of interest rate model and how it is discretized, and early exercise. For the general two-factor problem (48.1) to be parabolic we need

$$e(S, r, t)^2 < 4a(S, r, t)\, d(S, r, t).$$

As in the one-factor world, the variables must be discretized. That is, we solve on a three-dimensional grid with

$$S = i\ \delta S, \quad r = j\ \delta r, \quad \text{and} \quad t = T - k\ \delta t.$$

Expiry is $t = T$ or $k = 0$. The indices range from zero to I and J for i and j respectively. I have assumed that the interest rate model is only specified on $r \geq 0$. This may not be the case; some simple interest rate models such as Vasicek, are defined over negative r as well. If we have such a model we would redefine r. All the comments that I made in the last chapters about interest rate models and boundary conditions apply in the two-factor world.

The contract value is written as

$$V(S, r, t) = V_{ij}^k.$$

Whatever the problem to be solved, we must impose certain conditions on the solution. First of all, we must specify the final condition. This is the payoff function, telling us the value of the contract at the expiration of the contract.

Suppose that we are pricing a long-dated warrant with a call payoff. This is a good candidate for a two-factor model; we may want to incorporate a stochastic interest rate since we do not think that the assumption of constant interest rates is a good one over such a long period. The final condition for this problem is then

$$V(S, r, T) = V_{ij}^0 = \max(S - E, 0).$$

As well as a final condition, we must impose boundary conditions around our domain. The S, r domain is shown in Figure 48.1. Boundary conditions must be imposed at all the grid

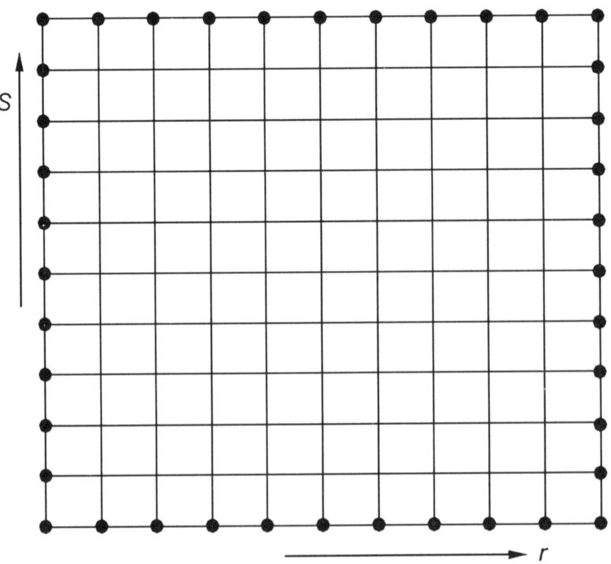

Figure 48.1 The S, r domain and boundary conditions.

points marked with a dot. The boundary conditions will depend on the contract. Remember that there is also a time axis coming out of the page, and not drawn in this figure.

48.3 THE EXPLICIT METHOD

The one-factor explicit method can be extended to two-factors with very little effort. In fact, the ease of programming make it a very good method for those new to the subject. I am going to use symmetric central differences for all derivatives in (48.1). This is the best way to approximate the second derivatives but may not be the best for the first derivatives. I will discuss this later.

We have seen how to use central differences for all of the terms with the exception of the second derivative with respect to both S and r,

$$\frac{\partial^2 V}{\partial S \partial r}.$$

I can approximate this by

$$\frac{\partial\left(\dfrac{\partial V}{\partial r}\right)}{\partial S} \approx \frac{\dfrac{\partial V}{\partial r}(S+\delta S, r, t) - \dfrac{\partial V}{\partial r}(S-\delta S, r, t)}{2\,\delta S}.$$

But

$$\frac{\partial V}{\partial r}(S+\delta S, r, t) \approx \frac{V^k_{i+1,j+1} - V^k_{i+1,j-1}}{2\,\delta r}.$$

This suggests that a suitable discretization might be

$$\frac{\dfrac{V^k_{i+1,j+1} - V^k_{i+1,j-1}}{2\,\delta r} - \dfrac{V^k_{i-1,j+1} - V^k_{i-1,j-1}}{2\,\delta r}}{2\,\delta S}$$
$$= \frac{V^k_{i+1,j+1} - V^k_{i+1,j-1} - V^k_{i-1,j+1} + V^k_{i-1,j-1}}{4\,\delta S\,\delta r}.$$

This is particularly good since, not only is the error of the same error as in the other derivative approximations but also it preserves the property that

$$\frac{\partial^2 V}{\partial S \partial r} = \frac{\partial^2 V}{\partial r \partial S}.$$

The resulting explicit difference scheme is

$$\frac{V^k_{ij} - V^{k+1}_{ij}}{\delta t} + a^k_{ij}\left(\frac{V^k_{i+1,j} - 2V^k_{ij} + V^k_{i-1,j}}{\delta S^2}\right) + b^k_{ij}\left(\frac{V^k_{i+1,j} - V^k_{i-1,j}}{2\,\delta S}\right) + c^k_{ij}V^k_{ij}$$
$$+ d^k_{ij}\left(\frac{V^k_{i,j+1} - 2V^k_{ij} + V^k_{i,j-1}}{\delta r^2}\right) e^k_{ij}\left(\frac{V^k_{i+1,j+1} - V^k_{i+1,j-1} - V^k_{i-1,j+1} + V^k_{i-1,j-1}}{4\,\delta S\,\delta r}\right)$$
$$+ f^k_{ij}\left(\frac{V^k_{i,j+1} - V^k_{i,j-1}}{2\,\delta r}\right) = O(\delta t, \delta S^2, \delta r^2).$$

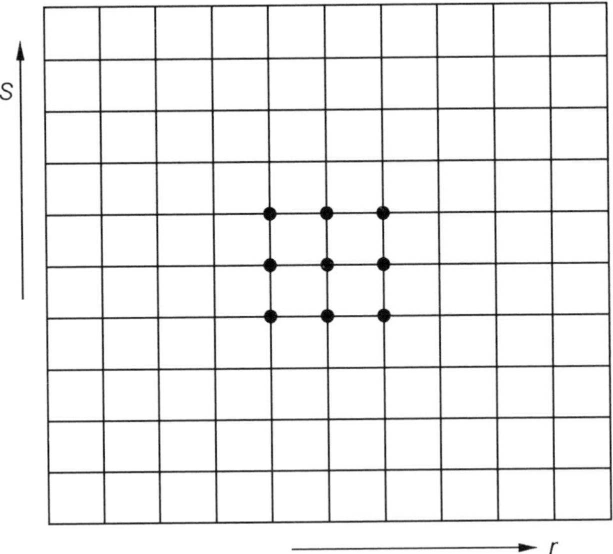

Figure 48.2 The nine option values used timestep in the explicit method.

I could rewrite this in the form

$$V_{ij}^{k+1} = \dots,$$

where the right-hand side is a linear function of the nine option values shown schematically in Figure 48.2. The coefficients of these nine values at timestep k are related to a, b, etc. It would not be very helpful to write the difference equation in this form, since the actual implementation is usually more transparent than this. Note that in general all nine points (ij), $(i \pm 1, j)$, $(i, j \pm 1)$, $(i \pm 1, j \pm 1)$ are used in the scheme. If there is no cross derivative term then only the five points (ij), $(i \pm 1, j \pm 1)$ are used. This simplifies some of the methods.

I will give an example now. The following is a Visual Basic code fragment for the pricing of a convertible bond. The underlying asset is `S(i)` and the interest rate is `r(j)`.

```
For j = 1 To MR - 1
For i = 0 To MS - 1
    VS = (VOld(i + 1, j) - VOld(i - 1, j)) /
         (2 * dS)
    Vrp = (VOld(i, j + 1) - VOld(i, j)) / dr
    Vrm = (VOld(i, j) - VOld(i, j - 1)) / dr
    Vr = Vrm
    If RDdrift(r(j), RealTime) > 0 Then Vr = Vrp
    VSS = (VOld(i + 1, j) - 2 * VOld(i, j) + VOld(i - 1, j)) /
          (dS * dS)
    Vrr = (VOld(i, j + 1) - 2 * VOld(i, j) + VOld(i, j - 1)) /
          (dr * dr)
    VSr = (VOld(i + 1, j + 1) - VOld(i - 1, j + 1) - _
                VOld(i + 1, j - 1) + VOld(i - 1, j - 1)) /
                (4 * dS * dr)
```

```
        VNew(i, j) = VOld(i, j) + dt * _
                     (0.5 * S(i) * S(i) * vol * vol * VSS _
                     + 0.5 * ratevol * ratevol * Vrr _
                     + rho * vol * ratevol * S(i) * VSr _
                         + r(j) * (S(i) * VS - VOld(i, j)) _
                         - div * S(i) * VS _
                         + RNDrift(r(j), RealTime) * Vr)
    Next i
    Next j
```

Notice how the derivatives of the option value `VOld(i, j)` are defined in turn. I have used a central difference for every derivative except the delta with respect to the interest rate. This is defined as a one-sided difference, using upwind differencing. I have used an inaccurate (error $O(\delta r)$) one-sided difference but this could be improved upon as suggested in Chapter 46. The reason for the use of upwind differencing for the interest rate first derivative is that the volatility of interest rates is usually quite small. The diffusion which makes the numerical solution easy is not very effective for the interest rate, making the problem almost hyperbolic rather than parabolic.

The volatility of the underlying is `vol` and the volatility of the interest rate is `ratevol`. The correlation is `rho`. The volatilities and correlation are constant.

The interest rate model that I have used is

$$dr = \texttt{RNDrift}(r, t)\,dt + \texttt{ratevol}\,dX.$$

I have allowed the risk-neutral drift `RNDrift` to be a function of both the interest rate and time, `RealTime`. The time dependence means that this code fragment could be used for a yield curve-fitted model.

The only other points I want to mention about this code fragment concern the boundary conditions. The interest rate index `j` ranges from `0` to `MR`. A boundary condition must be applied on `j = 0` and `j = MR` for all `i`. The same applies to the asset, with index `i` ranging from `0` to `MS`. In this code fragment you will notice that I have applied the timestepping algorithm at `i = 0`, i.e. at some boundary points. This is rather unusual. I can do this in some special cases because, as long as I allow `VOld(i, j)` to range from `i = -1` the application of the equation at `i = 0`, i.e. at $S = 0$, is still valid since the diffusion switches off at $S = 0$. This is another way of saying that the point $S = 0$ is singular.

After applying the relevant boundary conditions and before moving on to the next timestep, the convertibility feature must be incorporated. This is easily done in the explicit method. Here is the code fragment that ensures that there are no arbitrage opportunities.

```
For i = 0 To MS
For j = 0 To MR
    VOld(i, j) = max(VNew(i, j), ConvertRate * S(i))
Next j
Next i
```

This code simultaneously updates the old values to the new values `VNew(i, j)` and makes the bond values greater than the payoff from conversion `convertrate * S(i)`. Often conversion is only allowed on or between certain dates. In that case, the constraint is only applied at the timesteps on which conversion is permitted.

48.3.1 Stability of the Explicit Method

One of the advantages of the explicit method is again that it is easy to program. The main disadvantage comes in stability and speed. The method is only stable for sufficiently small timesteps. Having an upper bound on the timestep size seriously limits the speed of calculation.

We can again analyze the stability of the method by looking for solutions of the difference equation that are oscillatory in both the S and r directions. This means looking for a solution of the form

$$V_{ij}^k = \alpha^k e^{2\pi\sqrt{-1}\left(\frac{i}{\lambda_S}+\frac{j}{\lambda_r}\right)}$$

and assuming that all the coefficients A, b, c, etc. are slowly varying over the δS, δr lengthscales. I will skip the details, and simply state the result in one special and important case. If we have a pure diffusion problem with no convection or decay terms, and no correlation between the variables, then only a and d are non-zero. In this case, the stability requirement becomes

$$a\frac{\delta t}{\delta S^2} + d\frac{\delta t}{\delta r^2} \leq \tfrac{1}{2}.$$

This is an even more severe constraint than in the explicit method applied to one-factor problems.

To overcome this timestep constraint we can try an implicit scheme.

48.4 ALTERNATING DIRECTION IMPLICIT

There are many implicit methods used for one-factor problems. There are even more implicit methods for two-factor problems. Good numerical methods will be fast and require as little storage as possible. I am only going to describe two of the implicit finite-difference methods used for two factors; they are both intuitively appealing and use the same ideas that we saw in the previous chapter. The first method is called **Alternating Direction Implicit** or **ADI**.

We could try a two-factor extension of Crank–Nicolson to solve $(I-1)(J-1)$ equations in the same number of unknowns. This suffers from the problem that the resulting matrix does not have a nice form, and the solution is complicated and time consuming. If we want to keep the stability advantage of the implicit method and the ease of solution of the explicit method we could try to solve implicitly in one factor but explicitly in the other. This is the idea behind ADI. I will first explain the idea in words.

As well as V_{ij}^k, introduce an 'intermediate' value $V_{ij}^{k+(1/2)}$. Solve from timestep k to the intermediate step $k+\left(\frac{1}{2}\right)$ using explicit differences in S and implicit differences in r. Since only one direction is implicit, the solution by LU decomposition or SOR is no harder than in one factor. Having found the intermediate value $V_{ij}^{k+(1/2)}$ step forward to timestep $k+1$ using implicit differences in S and explicit differences in r. For this half timestep I have changed around explicit and implicit from the previous half timestep. Again the matrix equations are straightforward. The method is stable for all timesteps and the error is $O(\delta t^2, \delta S^2, \delta r^2)$.

Now let us see how this is done in practice. I will demonstrate the idea with the simpler equation

$$\frac{\partial V}{\partial t} + a(S,r,t)\frac{\partial^2 V}{\partial S^2} + d(S,r,t)\frac{\partial^2 V}{\partial r^2} = 0. \tag{48.2}$$

It is no harder to use the ADI method on the full equation, with first derivatives etc. provided that the differences can be decomposed into either S or r derivatives. The cross derivative term causes some problems in the basic implementation of ADI. This can be got around but is tedious.

The explicit S, implicit r discretization looks like this

$$\frac{V_{ij}^{k}-V_{ij}^{k+(1/2)}}{\frac{1}{2}\delta t}+a_{ij}^{k}\left(\frac{V_{i+1,j}^{k}-2V_{ij}^{k}+V_{i-1,j}^{k}}{\delta S^2}\right)$$
$$+\,d_{ij}^{k+(1/2)}\left(\frac{V_{i,j+1}^{k+(1/2)}-2V_{ij}^{k+(1/2)}+V_{i,j-1}^{k+(1/2)}}{\delta r^2}\right)=0.$$

Putting all of the $k+\left(\frac{1}{2}\right)$ timestep terms on the left and all k timestep terms on the right I get

$$V_{ij}^{k+(1/2)}-\tfrac{1}{2}d_{ij}^{k+(1/2)}\left(\frac{V_{i,j+1}^{k+(1/2)}-2V_{ij}^{k+(1/2)}+V_{i,j-1}^{k+(1/2)}}{\delta r^2}\right)\delta t=V_{ij}^{k}$$
$$+\,\tfrac{1}{2}a_{ij}^{k}\left(\frac{V_{i+1,j}^{k}-2V_{ij}^{k}+V_{i-1,j}^{k}}{\delta S^2}\right)\delta t.$$

If we know all of the k timestep terms we can find the $V_{ij}^{k+(1/2)}$ by solving a set of simultaneous equations. *This is the same as the fully implicit scheme mentioned in Chapter 47.* The only difference in this two-dimensional version is that the system must be solved for all i. Each set of equations, for each i, is of the same complexity as in one dimension, it is just that there are a lot more systems. The implicit scheme can be written as a matrix equation with a tridiagonal matrix on the left-hand side. The solution is found by LU decomposition or SOR.

Having found $V_{ij}^{k+(1/2)}$ we step forward to find V_{ij}^{k+1} by reversing the implicit and explicit roles:

$$\frac{V_{ij}^{k+1}-V_{ij}^{k+(1/2)}}{\frac{1}{2}\delta t}+a_{ij}^{k+1}\left(\frac{V_{i+1,j}^{k+1}-2V_{ij}^{k+1}+V_{i-1,j}^{k+1}}{\delta S^2}\right)$$
$$+\,d_{ij}^{k+(1/2)}\left(\frac{V_{i,j+1}^{k+(1/2)}-2V_{ij}^{k+(1/2)}+V_{i,j-1}^{k+(1/2)}}{\delta r^2}\right)=0.$$

This can be rewritten as

$$V_{ij}^{k+1}+\tfrac{1}{2}a_{ij}^{k+1}\left(\frac{V_{i+1,j}^{k+1}-2V_{ij}^{k+1}+V_{i-1,j}^{k+1}}{\delta S^2}\right)\delta t=V_{ij}^{k+(1/2)}$$
$$-\,\tfrac{1}{2}d_{ij}^{k+(1/2)}\left(\frac{V_{i,j+1}^{k+(1/2)}-2V_{ij}^{k+(1/2)}+V_{i,j-1}^{k+(1/2)}}{\delta r^2}\right)\delta t.$$

Again, this is a fully explicit scheme for finding V_{ij}^{k+1} from $V_{ij}^{k+(1/2)}$.

48.5 THE HOPSCOTCH METHOD

The final method I want to describe is the **Hopscotch method**. This is so called because of the way that grid points are used during the timestepping. Refer to Figure 48.3. I will again, for ease of exposition, assume that we are solving the equation (48.2).

At each timestep we perform two 'sweeps.' For $k = 1$ and all future odd values, we find V_{ij}^{k+1} for all of the grid points marked with a circle in Figure 48.3. The points marked with circles are defined by $i + j$ being odd. This is done explicitly using

$$V_{ij}^{k+1} = V_{ij}^k + a_{ij}^k \left(\frac{V_{i+1,j}^k - 2V_{ij}^k + V_{i-1,j}^k}{\delta S^2} \right) \delta t + d_{ij}^k \left(\frac{V_{i,j+1}^k - 2V_{ij}^k + V_{i,j-1}^k}{\delta r^2} \right) \delta t.$$

Now we perform a second sweep, at the same time level, using the same scheme *but now at the grid points marked with squares, and using the just-calculated values* of V_{ij}^{k+1}:

$$V_{ij}^{k+1} = V_{ij}^{k+1} + a_{ij}^{k+1} \left(\frac{V_{i+1,j}^{k+1} - 2V_{ij}^{k+1} + V_{i-1,j}^{k+1}}{\delta S^2} \right) \delta t + d_{ij}^{k+1} \left(\frac{V_{i,j+1}^{k+1} - 2V_{ij}^{k+1} + V_{i,j-1}^{k+1}}{\delta r^2} \right) \delta t.$$

Although technically implicit, the scheme has not required the solution of any simultaneous equations. The error in the method is $O(\delta t, \delta S^2, \delta r^2)$.

When we come to the next timestep, and all even numbered timesteps, the roles of the grid points marked with circles and squares is reversed.

When there is a cross derivative term in the partial differential equation the explicitness of the scheme is lost.

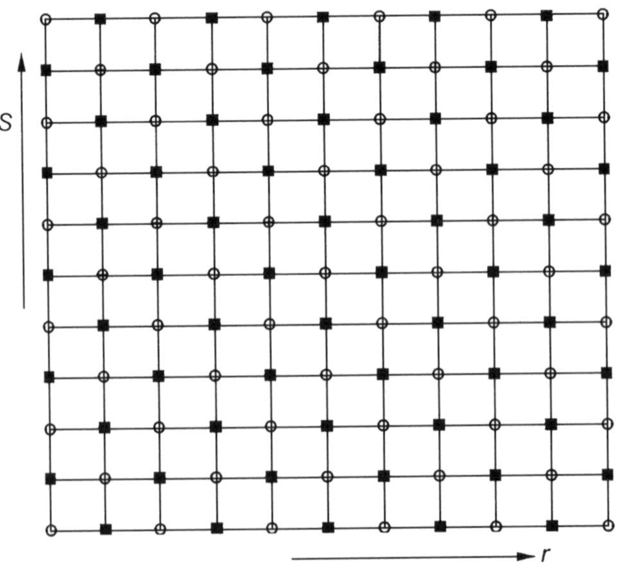

Figure 48.3 The use of grid points in the Hopscotch method.

48.6 SUMMARY

Finite-difference methods are suitable for solving financial problems with two or three random factors. Any more than that and Monte Carlo may be a better method. Finite-difference methods are particularly suited to contracts with early exercise features, or which are callable or puttable. Convertible bonds or American options with stochastic volatility (see Chapter 23) are the two obvious examples. Because simple explicit finite differences are similar to binomial trees, the methods in this chapter can do no worse than the binomial method. Some finite-difference methods can do a lot better though. The ADI and Hopscotch methods, although harder to code, are worth trying out as substitutes for the simpler but slower methods.

FURTHER READING

- See the books on the numerical solution of partial differential equations by Morton & Mayers (1994) and Mitchell & Griffiths (1980).
- Roache (1982) describes many more numerical methods with two or more factors.

EXERCISES

1. Write an explicit finite-difference program to price a convertible bond using a lognormal random walk for the asset price, and a Vasicek (unfitted) model for the interest rate, i.e.

$$V = V(S, r, t),$$

where

$$dS = \mu S\,dt + \sigma S\,dX_1,$$

and

$$dr = (a - br)\,dt + c\,dX_2,$$

with a, b and c constant. What range does r cover? What boundary conditions should you impose? How do you incorporate conversion, call and put constraints?

2. Write an explicit finite-difference program for pricing simple interest rate products such as bonds, caps and floors, for a two-factor Brennan and Schwartz model. Modify the code to make all of these contracts callable for a prescribed amount.

CHAPTER 49

Monte Carlo simulation and related methods

In this Chapter...

- the relationship between option values and expectations for equities, currencies, commodities and indices
- the relationship between derivative products and expectations when interest rates are stochastic
- how to do Monte Carlo simulations to calculate derivative prices and to see the results of speculating with derivatives
- how to do simulations in many dimensions using Cholesky factorization
- how to do numerical integration in high dimensions to calculate the price of options on baskets

49.1 INTRODUCTION

The foundation of the theory of derivative pricing is the random walk of asset prices, interest rates, etc. We have seen this foundation in Chapter 3 for equities, currencies and commodities, and the resulting option pricing theory from Chapter 5 onwards. This is the Black–Scholes theory leading to the Black–Scholes parabolic partial differential equation. We have also seen in Chapter 10 how the stochastic differential equation model for a random variable leads to a similar equation for the probability density function for the random variable. In that chapter I showed the relationship between option prices and the transition probability density. In this chapter we exploit this relationship, and see how derivative prices can be found from special simulations of the asset price, or interest rate, random walks. Briefly, the value of an option is the expected present value of the payoff. The catch in this is the precise definition of 'expected.'

I am going to distinguish between the valuation of options having equities, indices, currencies, or commodities as their underlying with interest rates assumed to be deterministic and those products for which it is assumed that interest rates are stochastic. First, I show the relationship between derivative values and expectations with deterministic interest rates.

49.2 RELATIONSHIP BETWEEN DERIVATIVE VALUES AND SIMULATIONS: EQUITIES, INDICES, CURRENCIES, COMMODITIES

Recall from Chapter 10 that the fair value of an option in the Black–Scholes world is the present value of the expected payoff at expiry under a *risk-neutral* random walk for the underlying.

The risk-neutral random walk for S is

$$dS = rS\,dt + \sigma S\,dX.$$

We can therefore write

$$\text{option value} = e^{-r(T-t)}E\left[\text{payoff}\,(S)\right]$$

provided that the expectation is with respect to the risk-neutral random walk, not the *real* one.

This result leads to an estimate for the value of an option by following these simple steps:

1. Simulate the risk-neutral random walk as discussed below, starting at today's value of the asset S_0, over the required time horizon. This time period starts today and continues until the expiry of the option. This gives one realization of the underlying price path.
2. For this realization calculate the option payoff.
3. Perform many more such realizations over the time horizon.
4. Calculate the average payoff over all realizations.
5. Take the present value of this average; this is the option value.

The initial part of this algorithm requires first of all the generation of random numbers from a standardized Normal distribution (or some suitable approximation). We discuss this issue below, but for the moment assume that we can generate such a series in sufficient quantities. Then one has to update the asset price at each timestep using these random increments. Here we have a choice how to update S.

An obvious choice is to use

$$\delta S = rS\,\delta t + \sigma S\sqrt{\delta t}\,\phi,$$

where ϕ is drawn from a standardized Normal distribution. This discrete way of simulating the time series for S is called the **Euler method**. Simply put the latest value for S into the right-hand side to calculate δS and hence the next value for S. This method is easy to apply to any stochastic differential equation. This discretization method has an error of $O(\delta t)$.[1]

For the lognormal random walk, however, we are lucky that we can find a simple, and exact, timestepping algorithm. We can write the risk-neutral stochastic differential equation for S in the form

$$d(\log S) = \left(r - \tfrac{1}{2}\sigma^2\right)dt + \sigma\,dX.$$

This can be integrated exactly to give

$$S(t) = S(0)\exp\left(\left(r - \tfrac{1}{2}\sigma^2\right)t + \sigma\int_0^t dX\right).$$

[1] There are better approximations, for example the **Milstein method** which has an error of $O(\delta t^2)$.

Or, over a timestep δt,

$$S(t+\delta t) = S(t) + \delta S = S(t) \exp\left(\left(r - \tfrac{1}{2}\sigma^2\right)\delta t + \sigma\sqrt{\delta t}\,\phi\right). \tag{49.1}$$

Note that δt need not be small, since the expression is exact. Because this expression is exact and simple it is the best timestepping algorithm to use. Because it is exact, if we have a payoff that only depends on the final asset value, i.e. is European and path independent, then we can simulate the final asset price in one giant leap, using a timestep of T.

The above algorithm is illustrated in the following spreadsheet. The stock begins at time $t = 0$ with a value of 100, it has a volatility of 20%. The spreadsheet simultaneously calculates the values of a call and a put option. They both have an expiry of one year and a strike of 105. The interest rate is 5%. In this spreadsheet we see a small selection of a large number of Monte Carlo simulations of the random walk for S, *using a drift rate of 5%*. The timestep was chosen to be 0.01. For each realization the final stock price is shown in row 102 (rows 13–93 have been hidden). The option payoffs are shown in rows 104 and 107. The mean of all these payoffs, over all the simulations, is shown in row 105 and 108. In rows 106 and 109 we see the present values of the means; these are the option values. For serious option valuation you

	A	B	C	D	E	F	G	H	I
1	**Asset**	100		**Time**	**Sim 1**	**Sim 2**	**Sim 3**	**Sim 4**	**Sim 5**
2	**Drift**	5%		0	100.00	100.00	100.00	100.00	100.00
3	**Volatility**	20%		0.01	100.30	102.34	97.50	98.38	96.14
4	**Timestep**	0.01		0.02	103.52	103.38	99.31	98.55	90.84
5	**Int.rate**	5%		0.03	106.01	101.98	101.44	96.12	92.94
6				0.04	101.85	106.67	103.02	94.69	93.17
7				0.05	104.75	107.17	105.05	93.25	91.23
8				0.06	106.57	110.24	109.55	94.50	89.97
9				0.07	101.15	107.73	110.77	93.83	81.08
10				[illegible]	[illegible]	[illegible]	[illegible]	[illegible]	[illegible].21
11				0.09	101.06	111.06	107.49	93.86	93.23
12				0.1	103.35	108.60	109.52	92.84	93.82
94				0.92	109.27	87.76	118.48	69.38	116.43
95				0.93	110.22	87.59	118.13	72.19	118.66
96				0.94	105.56	88.18	117.37	73.40	117.15
97				0.95	106.53	86.81	118.27	70.86	115.82
98				0.96	103.14	85.72	116.85	69.36	115.81
99				0.97	102.20	85.85	112.89	70.24	119.18
100				[illegible]	[illegible]	[illegible]	[illegible]	[illegible]	[illegible]75
101				0.99	101.91	87.83	[illegible]	[illegible]	[illegible]11
102				1	105.99	87.60	111.45	70.67	116.72
103									
104	**Strike**	105	**CALL**	**Payoff**	0.99	0.00	6.45	0.00	11.72
105			**Mean**	8.43					
106			**PV**	8.02					
107			**PUT**	**Payoff**	0.00	17.40	0.00	34.33	0.00
108			**Mean**	8.31					
109			**PV**	7.9					
110									
111									

= D3+$B$4

=E3*EXP(($B$5-0.5*$B$3*$B$3)*$B$4+$B$3*SQRT($B$4)*NORMSINV(RAND()))

= MAX($B$104-F102,0)

= MAX(G102-$B$104,0)

= AVERAGE(E104:IV104)

=D105*EXP(-$B$5*$D$102)

Figure 49.1 Spreadsheet showing a Monte Carlo simulation to value a call and a put option.

	A	B	C	D	E	F	G	H	I
1	**Asset**	100		**Time**	**Sim 1**	**Sim 2**	**Sim 3**	**Sim 4**	**Sim 5**
2	**Drift**	5%		0	100.00	100.00	100.00	100.00	100.00
3	**Volatility**	20%		0.01	100.52	100.35	98.46	98.55	102.11
4	**Timestep**	0.01		0.02	98.64	100.69	98.33	99.00	101.04
5	**Int. rate**	5%		0.03	100.82	103.25	96.91	95.31	102.61
6				0.04	98.01	105.38	96.20	98.92	102.74
7				0.05	96.74	101.44	93.65	100.90	104.26
8				0.06	100.11	101.38	94.17	102.83	101.12
9				[illegible]	[illegible]	[illegible]	[illegible]	[illegible]	[illegible]
10				[illegible]	[illegible]	[illegible]	[illegible]	[illegible]	[illegible]
11				0.09	103.22	105.43	92.58	99.95	96.21
12				0.1	100.27	104.74	95.78	100.26	96.07
13				0.11	105.30	107.28	95.63	100.63	95.31
93				0.91	122.57	130.32	96.94	89.13	76.70
94				0.92	120.91	129.89	95.93	90.42	78.30
95				0.93	120.79	132.15	93.64	96.30	77.16
96				0.94	123.17	129.20	94.64	98.06	78.16
97				0.95	123.06	130.71	97.95	97.76	80.39
98				[illegible]	[illegible]	132.16	101.34	98.88	80.95
99				0.97	122.10	129.39	98.71	101.35	82.83
100				0.98	123.00	125.35	[illegible]	[illegible]	[illegible]
101				[illegible]	126.74	121.66	[illegible]	[illegible]	[illegible]
102				[illegible]	127.27	124.60	95.50	101.52	85.99
103									
104				**Average**	113.43	113.62	93.61	102.48	88.96
105									
106	**Strike**	105	**ASIAN**	**Payoff**	22.27	19.60	0.00	0.00	0.00
107			**Mean**	8.28					
108			**PV**	7.88					
109									
110									
111									

Figure 49.2 Spreadsheet showing a Monte Carlo simulation to value an Asian option.

would not do such calculations on a spreadsheet. For the present example I took a relatively small number of sample paths.

The method is particularly suitable for path-dependent options. In the spreadsheet in Figure 49.2 I show how to value an Asian option. This contract pays of an amount $\max(A - 105, 0)$ where A is the average of the asset price over the one-year life of the contract. The remaining details of the underlying are as in the previous example. How would the spreadsheet be modified if the average were only taken of the last six months of the contract's life?

49.3 ADVANTAGES OF MONTE CARLO SIMULATION

Now that we have some idea of how Monte Carlo simulations are related to the pricing of options, I'll give you some of the benefits of using such simulations:

- The mathematics that you need to perform a Monte Carlo simulation can be very basic.
- Correlations can be easily modeled.

- There is plenty of software available, at the least there are spreadsheet functions that will suffice for most of the time.
- To get a better accuracy, just run more simulations.
- The effort in getting *some* answer is very low.
- The models can often be changed without much work.
- Complex path dependency can often be easily incorporated.
- People accept the technique, and will believe your answers.

49.4 USING RANDOM NUMBERS

The Black–Scholes theory as we have seen it, has been built on the assumption of either a simple up-or-down move in the asset price, the binomial model, or a Normally distributed return. When it comes to simulating a random walk for the asset price it doesn't matter very much what distribution we use for the random increments as long as the timestep is small and thus that we have a large number of steps from the start to the finish of the asset price path. All we need are that the variance of the distribution must be finite and constant. (The constant must be such that the *annualized* volatility, i.e. the annualized standard deviation of returns, is the correct value. In particular, this means that it must scale with $\delta t^{1/2}$.) In the limit as the size of the timestep goes to zero the simulations have the same probabilistic properties over a finite timescale regardless of the nature of the distribution over the infinitesimal timescale. This is a result of the central limit theorem.

Nevertheless, the most accurate model is the lognormal model with Normal returns. Since one has to worry about simulating sufficient paths to get an accurate option price one would ideally like not to have to worry about the size of the timestep too much. As I said above, it is best to use the exact expression (49.1) and then the choice of timestep does not affect the accuracy of the random walk. In some cases we can take a single timestep since the timestepping algorithm is exact. If we do use such a large timestep then we must generate Normally-distributed random variables. I will discuss this below, where I describe the Box–Muller method.

If the size of the timestep is δt then, for more complicated products, such as path-dependent ones, we may still introduce errors of $O(\delta t)$ by virtue of the discrete approximation to continuous events. An example would be of a continuous barrier. If we have a finite timestep we miss the possibility of the barrier being triggered between steps. Generally speaking, the error due to the finiteness of the timestep is $O(\delta t)$.

Because we are only simulating a finite number of an infinite number of possible paths, the error due to using N, say, realizations of the asset price paths is $O(N^{-1/2})$.

The total number of calculations required in the estimation of a derivative price is then $O(N/\delta t)$. This is then also a measure of the time taken in the calculation of the price. The error in the price is

$$O\left(\max\left(\delta t, \frac{1}{\sqrt{N}}\right)\right),$$

i.e. the worst out of either the error due to the discreteness of the timestep or the error in having only a finite number of realizations. To minimize this quantity, while keeping the total computing time fixed such that $O(N/\delta t) = K$, we must choose

$$N = O(K^{2/3}) \quad \text{and} \quad \delta t = O(K^{-1/3}).$$

49.5 GENERATING NORMAL VARIABLES

Some random number generators are good, others are bad, repeating themselves after a finite number of samples, or showing serial autocorrelation. Then they can be fast or slow. A particularly useful distribution that is easy to implement on a spreadsheet, and is fast, is the following approximation to the Normal distribution:

$$\left(\sum_{i=1}^{12} \psi_i\right) - 6,$$

where the ψ_i are independent random variables, drawn from a uniform distribution over zero to one. This distribution is close to Normal, having a mean of zero, a standard deviation of one, and a third moment of zero. It is in the fourth and higher moments that the distribution differs from Normal. I would use this in a spreadsheet when generating asset price paths with smallish timesteps.

If you need to generate decent Normally-distributed random numbers then the simplest technique is the **Box–Muller method**. This method takes uniformly-distributed variables and turns them into Normal. The basic uniform numbers can be generated by any number of methods, (see Press et al (1992) for some algorithms). The Box–Muller method takes two uniform random numbers x_1 and x_2 between zero and one and combines them to give two numbers y_1 and y_2 that are both Normally distributed:

$$y_1 = \sqrt{-2\ln x_1}\cos(2\pi x_2) \quad \text{and} \quad y_2 = \sqrt{-2\ln x_1}\sin(2\pi x_2).$$

Here is a Visual Basic function that outputs a Normally-distributed variable.

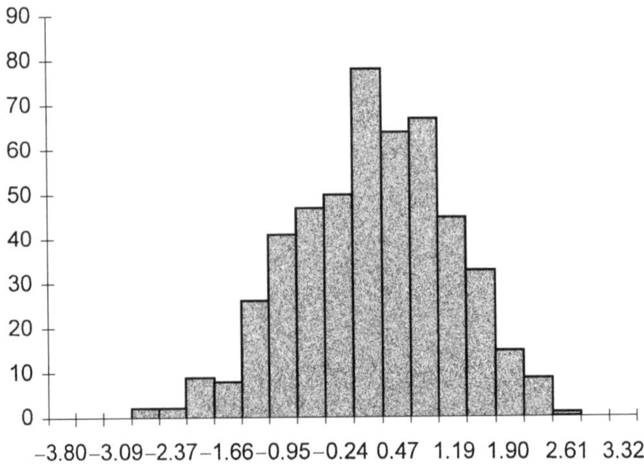

Figure 49.3 The approximation to the Normal distribution using 500 uniformly distributed points and the Box–Muller method.

```
Function BoxMuller()
Randomize
Do
        x = 2 * Rnd() - 1
        y = 2 * Rnd() - 1
        dist = x * x + y * y
Loop Until dist < 1
BoxMuller = x * Sqr(-2 * Log(dist) / dist)
End Function
```

In Figure 49.3 is the approximation to the Normal distribution using 500 points from the uniform distribution and the Box–Muller method.

49.6 REAL VERSUS RISK NEUTRAL, SPECULATION VERSUS HEDGING

In Figure 49.4 are shown several realizations of a risk-neutral asset price random walk with 5% interest rate and 20% volatility. These are the thin lines. The bold lines in this figure are the corresponding *real* random walks using the same random numbers but here with a drift of 20% instead of the 5% interest rate drift. Although I am here emphasizing the use of Monte Carlo simulations in valuing options we can of course use them to estimate the payoff distribution from holding an *unhedged* option position. In this situation we are interested in the whole distribution of payoffs (and their present values) and not just the average or expected value. This is because in holding an unhedged position we cannot guarantee the return that we (theoretically) get from a hedged position. It is therefore valid and important to have the real drift as one of the parameters; it would be incorrect to estimate the probability density function for the return from an unhedged position using the risk-neutral drift.

In Figure 49.5 I show the estimated probability density function and cumulative distribution function for a call with expiry one year and strike 105 using Monte Carlo simulations with

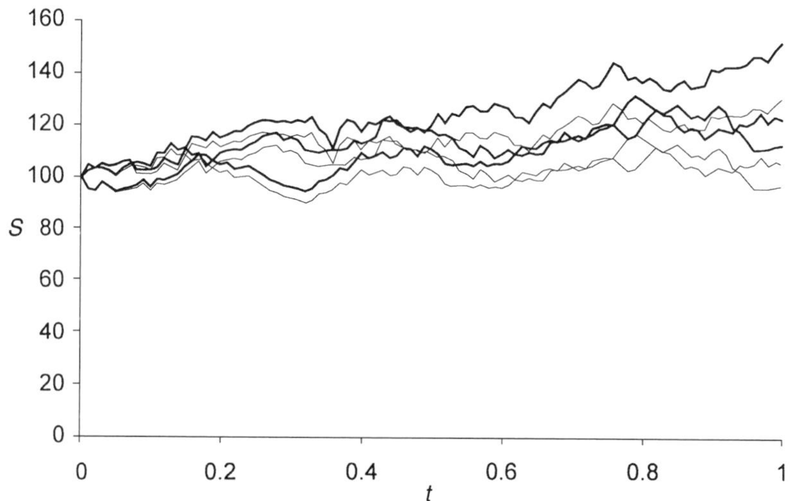

Figure 49.4 Several realizations of an asset price random walk.

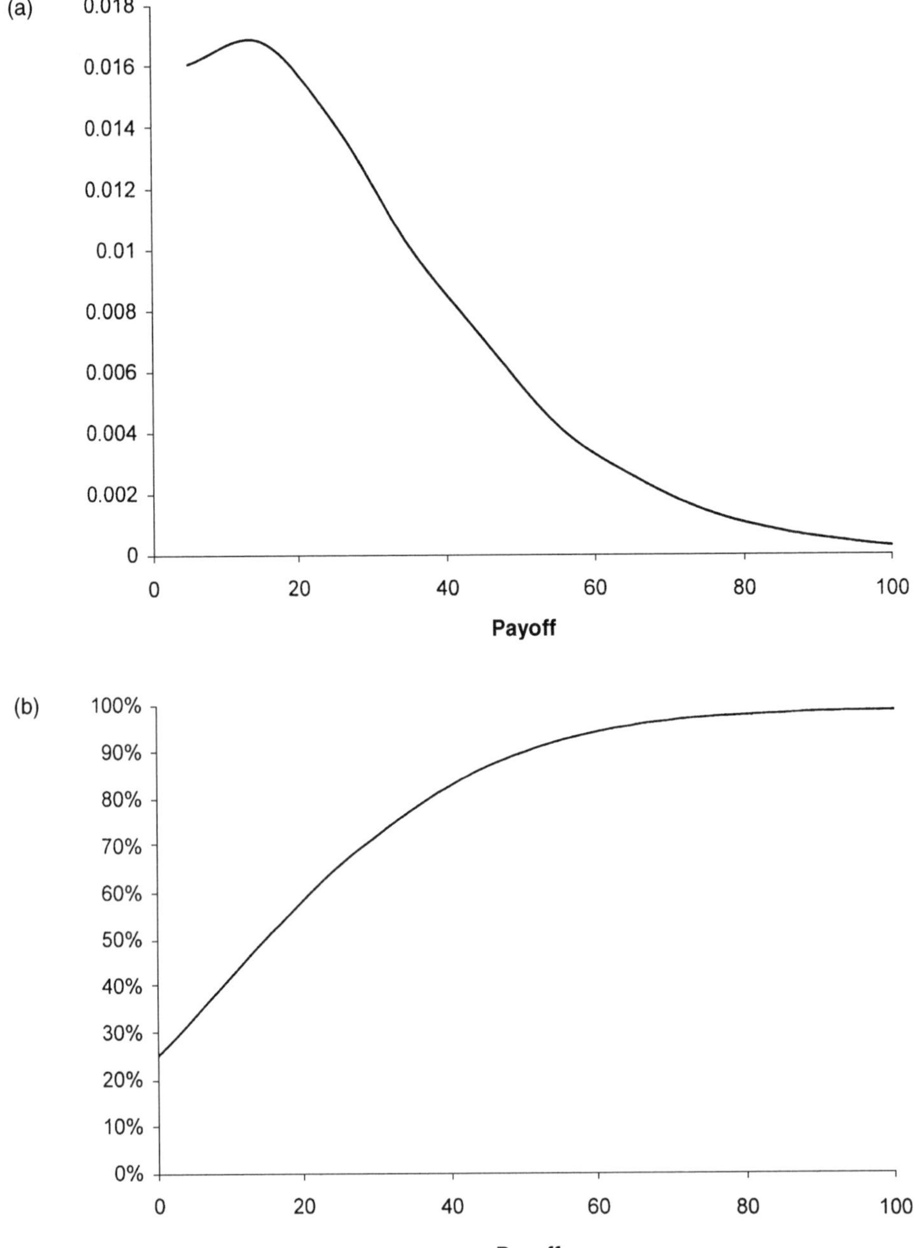

Figure 49.5 Real probability density function (top) and cumulative distribution function (bottom) for the payoff for a call.

$\mu = 20\%$ and $\sigma = 20\%$. The probability density function curve does not show the zero payoffs. The probability of expiring out-of-the money and receiving no payoff is approximately 25%.

In Figure 49.6 I show the estimated probability density function and cumulative distribution function for a put with the same expiry and strike, again using Monte Carlo simulations with $\mu = 20\%$ and $\sigma = 20\%$. The probability density function curve does not show the zero payoffs. The probability of expiring out-of-the money and receiving no payoff is approximately 75%.

Valuing options for speculation is the subject of Chapter 28.

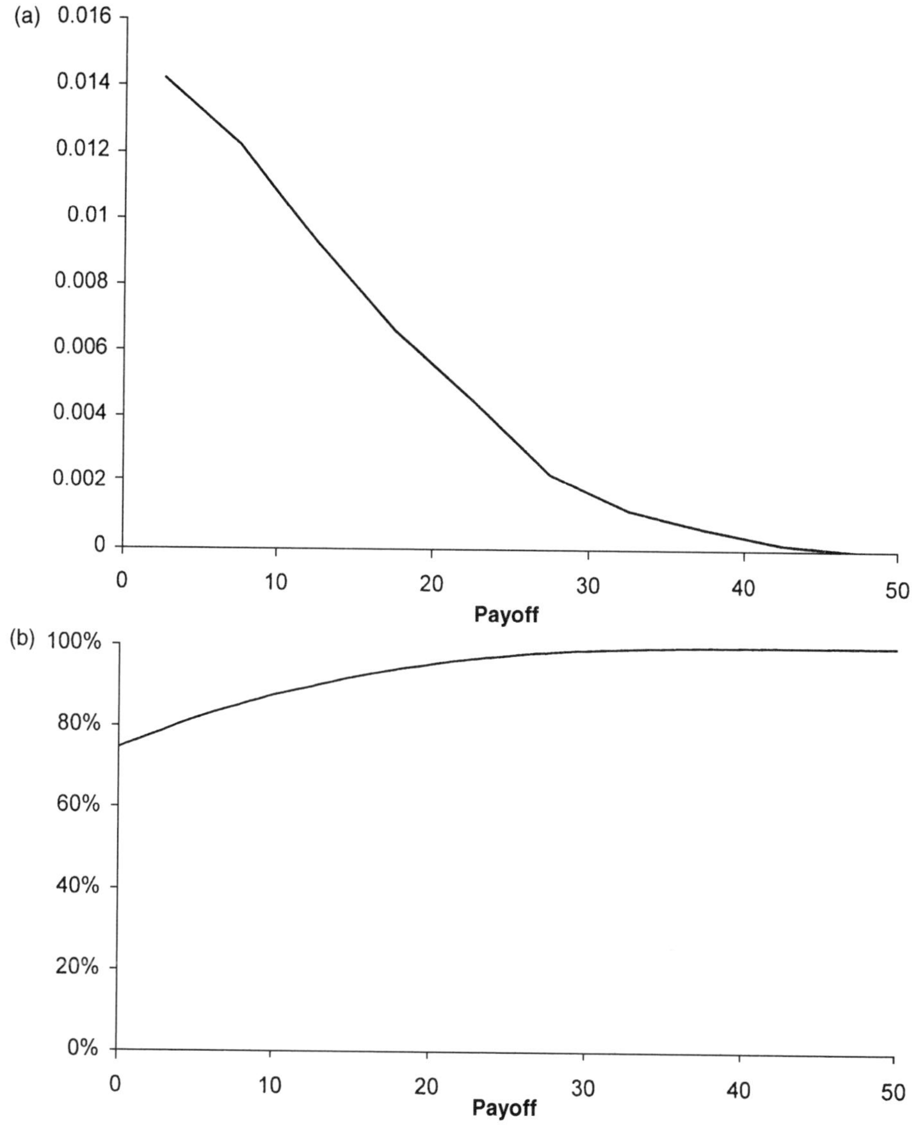

Figure 49.6 Real probability density function (top) and cumulative distribution function (bottom) for the payoff for a put.

49.7 INTEREST RATE PRODUCTS

The relationship between expected payoffs and option values when the short-term interest rate is stochastic is slightly more complicated because there is the question of what rate to use for discounting.

The correct way to estimate option value with stochastic interest rates is as follows:

1. Simulate the random walk for the risk-adjusted spot interest rate r, as discussed over, starting at today's value of the spot rate, over the required time horizon. This time period starts today and continues until the expiry of the option. This gives one realization of the spot rate path.
2. For this realization calculate two quantities, the payoff and the *average* interest rate realized up until the payoff is received.
3. Perform many more such realizations.
4. For each realization of the r random walk calculate the present value of the payoff for this realization discounting at the average rate for this realization.

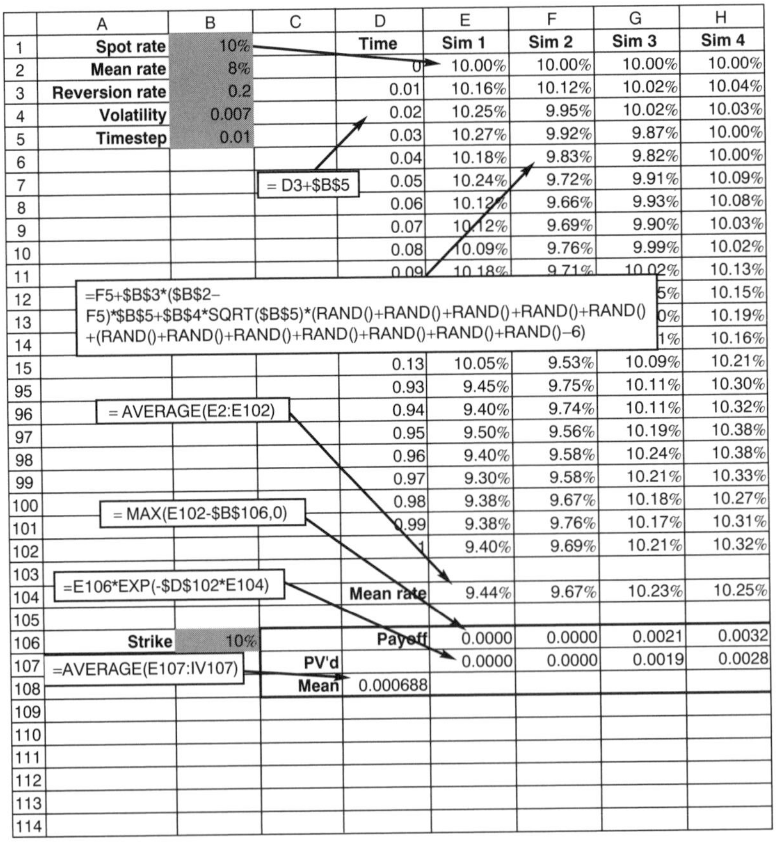

	A	B	C	D	E	F	G	H
1	Spot rate	10%		Time	Sim 1	Sim 2	Sim 3	Sim 4
2	Mean rate	8%		0	10.00%	10.00%	10.00%	10.00%
3	Reversion rate	0.2		0.01	10.16%	10.12%	10.02%	10.04%
4	Volatility	0.007		0.02	10.25%	9.95%	10.02%	10.03%
5	Timestep	0.01		0.03	10.27%	9.92%	9.87%	10.00%
6				0.04	10.18%	9.83%	9.82%	10.00%
7			= D3+$B$5	0.05	10.24%	9.72%	9.91%	10.09%
8				0.06	10.12%	9.66%	9.93%	10.08%
9				0.07	10.12%	9.69%	9.90%	10.03%
10				0.08	10.09%	9.76%	9.99%	10.02%
11				0.09	10.18%	9.71%	10.02%	10.13%
12							5%	10.15%
13							0%	10.19%
14							1%	10.16%
15				0.13	10.05%	9.53%	10.09%	10.21%
95				0.93	9.45%	9.75%	10.11%	10.30%
96	= AVERAGE(E2:E102)			0.94	9.40%	9.74%	10.11%	10.32%
97				0.95	9.50%	9.56%	10.19%	10.38%
98				0.96	9.40%	9.58%	10.24%	10.38%
99				0.97	9.30%	9.58%	10.21%	10.33%
100	= MAX(E102-$B$106,0)			0.98	9.38%	9.67%	10.18%	10.27%
101				0.99	9.38%	9.76%	10.17%	10.31%
102				1	9.40%	9.69%	10.21%	10.32%
103	=E106*EXP(-$D$102*E104)							
104				Mean rate	9.44%	9.67%	10.23%	10.25%
105								
106	Strike	10%		Payoff	0.0000	0.0000	0.0021	0.0032
107	=AVERAGE(E107:IV107)		PV'd		0.0000	0.0000	0.0019	0.0028
108			Mean	0.000688				
109								
110								
111								
112								
113								
114								

=F5+$B$3*($B$2–F5)*$B$5+$B$4*SQRT($B$5)*(RAND()+RAND()+RAND()+RAND()+RAND()+(RAND()+RAND()+RAND()+RAND()+RAND()+RAND()+RAND()–6)

Figure 49.7 Spreadsheet showing a Monte Carlo simulation to value a contract with a payoff max(r – 10%, 0).

5. Calculate the average present value of the payoffs over all realizations; this is the option value.

In other words,

$$\text{option value} = E\left[e^{-\int_t^T r(\tau)d\tau}\text{payoff}(r)\right].$$

Why is this different from the deterministic interest rate case? Why discount at the average interest rate? We discount all cashflows at the average rate because this is the interest rate received by a money market account, and in the risk-neutral world all assets have the same risk-free growth rate. Recall that cash in the bank grows according to

$$\frac{dM}{dt} = r(t)M.$$

The solution of which is

$$M(t) = M(T)e^{-\int_t^T r(\tau)d\tau}.$$

This contains the same discount factor as in the option value.

The choice of discretization of spot rate models is usually limited to the Euler method

$$\delta r = (u(r,t) - \lambda(r,t)w(r,t))\,dt + w(r,t)\sqrt{\delta t}\,\phi.$$

Rarely can the spot rate equations be exactly integrated.

In the next spreadsheet I demonstrate the Monte Carlo method for a contract with payoff $\max(r - 10\%, 0)$. Maturity is in one year. The model used to perform the simulations is Vasicek with constant parameters. The spot interest rate begins at 6%. The option value is the average present value in the last row.

49.8 CALCULATING THE GREEKS

The simplest way to calculate the delta of an option using Monte Carlo simulation is to estimate the option's value twice. The delta of the option is the derivative of the option with respect to the underlying

$$\Delta = \lim_{h\to 0}\frac{V(S+h,t) - V(S-h,t)}{2h}.$$

This is a central difference, discussed in Chapter 46. This is an accurate estimate of the first derivative, with an error of $O(h^2)$. However, the error in the measurement of the two option values at $S+h$ and $S-h$ can be much larger than this for the Monte Carlo simulation. These Monte Carlo errors are then magnified when divided by h, resulting in an error of $O(1/hN^{1/2})$. To overcome this problem, estimate the value of the option at $S+h$ and $S-h$ *using the same values for the random numbers*. In this way the errors in the Monte Carlo simulation will cancel each other out. The same principal is used to calculate the gamma and the theta of the option.

Another way to calculate the delta (and gamma) is to exploit the differential equation satisfied by the delta. Differentiate the Black–Scholes equation with respect to S. This gives

$$\frac{\partial\Delta}{\partial t} + \tfrac{1}{2}\sigma^2S^2\frac{\partial^2\Delta}{\partial S^2} + (r+\sigma^2)S\frac{\partial\Delta}{\partial S} = 0.$$

For a vanilla call option the delta at expiry is

$$\Delta(S, T) = \mathcal{H}(S - E),$$

the Heaviside function. We can estimate the value of the delta today by a Monte Carlo simulation in which we calculate the expected value of the final delta using the following random walk for S:

$$dS = (r + \sigma^2)S\,dt + \sigma S\,dX.$$

Since there is no discounting term in the partial differential equation there is no need to take the present value.

49.9 HIGHER DIMENSIONS: CHOLESKY FACTORIZATION

Monte Carlo simulation is a natural method for the pricing of European-style contracts that depend on many underlying assets. Supposing that we have an option paying off some function of S_1, S_2, ..., S_d then we could, in theory, write down a partial differential equation in $d + 1$ variables. Such a problem would be horrendously time consuming to compute. The simulation methods discussed can easily be extended to cover such a problem. All we need to do is to simulate

$$S_i(t + \delta t) = S_i(t) \exp\left(\left(r - \tfrac{1}{2}\sigma_i^2\right)\delta t + \sigma_i \sqrt{\delta t}\,\phi_i\right).$$

The catch is that the ϕ_i are correlated,

$$E[\phi_i \phi_j] = \rho_{ij}.$$

How can we generate *correlated* random variables? This is where **Cholesky factorization** comes in.

Let us suppose that we can generate d *uncorrelated* Normally distributed variables ε_1, $\varepsilon_2, \ldots, \varepsilon_d$. We can use these variables to get correlated variables with the transformation

$$\phi = \mathbf{M}\varepsilon \qquad (49.2)$$

where $\boldsymbol{\phi}$ and $\boldsymbol{\varepsilon}$ are the column vectors with ϕ_i and ε_i in the ith rows. The matrix $\mathbf{M}$ is special and must satisfy

$$\mathbf{M}\mathbf{M}^T = \boldsymbol{\Sigma}$$

with $\boldsymbol{\Sigma}$ being the correlation matrix.

It is easy to show that this transformation will work. From (49.2) we have

$$\boldsymbol{\phi}\boldsymbol{\phi}^T = \mathbf{M}\boldsymbol{\varepsilon}\boldsymbol{\varepsilon}^T\mathbf{M}^T. \qquad (49.3)$$

Taking expectations of each entry in this matrix equation gives

$$E[\boldsymbol{\phi}\boldsymbol{\phi}^T] = \mathbf{M}E[\boldsymbol{\varepsilon}\boldsymbol{\varepsilon}^T]\mathbf{M}^T = \mathbf{M}\mathbf{M}^T = \boldsymbol{\Sigma}.$$

We can take expectations through the matrix multiplication in this because the right-hand side of (49.3) is linear in the terms $\varepsilon_i \varepsilon_j$.

This decomposition of the correlation matrix into the product of two matrices is not unique. The **Cholesky factorization** gives one way of choosing this decomposition. It results in a matrix **M** that is lower triangular. Here is an algorithm for the factorization.

The matrix `Sigma` contains the correlation matrix with dimension `n`. The output matrix is contained in `M`.

```
Function cholesky(Sigma As Object)
Dim n As Integer
Dim k As Integer
Dim i As Integer
Dim j As Integer
Dim x As Double
Dim a() As Double
Dim M() As Double
n = Sigma.Columns.Count
ReDim a(1 To n, 1 To n)
ReDim m(1 To n, 1 To n)
For i = 1 To n
    For j = 1 To n
        a(i, j) = Sigma.Cells(i, j).Value
        M(i, j) = 0
     Next j
Next i
For i = 1 To n
    For j = i To n
    x = a(i, j)
    For k = 1 To (i - 1)
        x = x - M(i, k) * M(j, k)
    Next k
    If j = i Then
        M(i, i) = Sqr(x)
    Else
        M(j, i) = x / M(i, i)
    End If
    Next j
Next i
cholesky = M
End Function
```

49.10 SPEEDING UP CONVERGENCE

Monte Carlo simulation is inefficient, compared with finite-difference methods, in dimensions less than about three. It is natural, therefore, to ask how can one speed up the convergence. There are several methods in common use, two of which I now describe.

49.10.1 Antithetic Variables

In this technique one calculates two estimates for an option value using the one set of random numbers. We do this by using our Normal random numbers to generate one realization of the asset price path, an option payoff and its present value. Now take the same set of random numbers but change their signs, thus replace ϕ with $-\phi$. Again simulate a realization, and calculate the option payoff and its present value. Our estimate for the option value is the average of these two values. Perform this operation many times to get an accurate estimate for the option value.

This technique works because of the symmetry in the Normal distribution. This symmetry is guaranteed by the use of the antithetic variable.

49.10.2 Control Variate Technique

Suppose we have two similar derivatives: the former is the one we want to value by simulations and the second has a similar (but 'nicer') structure such that we have an explicit formula for its value. Use the *one* set of realizations to value *both* options. Call the values estimated by the Monte Carlo simulation V_1' and V_2'. If the accurate value of the second option is V_2 then a better estimate than V_1' for the value of the first option is

$$V_1' - V_2' + V_2.$$

The argument behind this method is that the error in V_1' will be the same as the error in V_2', and the latter is known.

A refinement of this technique is **Martingale variance reduction**. In this method, one simulates one or more new dependent variables at the same time as the path of the underlying. This new stochastic variable is chosen so as to have an *expected value of zero* after each time step. This new variable, the 'variate,' is then added on to the value of the option. Since it has an expected value of zero it cannot make the estimate any worse, but if the variate is chosen carefully it can reduce the variance of the error significantly.

Let's see how this is done in practice using a single variate. Suppose we simulate

$$\delta S = \mu S\,\delta t + \sigma S\sqrt{\delta t}\,\phi$$

to price our contract. Now introduce the variate y, satisfying

$$\delta y = f(S,t)(\delta S - E[\delta S]),$$

with zero initial value. Note that this has zero expectation. The choice of $f(S,t)$ will be discussed in a moment. The new estimate for the option value is simply

$$\overline{V} - \alpha e^{-r(T-t)}\overline{y},$$

where $\overline{V}$ is our usual Monte Carlo estimate and $\overline{y}$ is the average over all the realizations of the new variate at expiry. The choice of α is simple; choose it to minimize the variance of the error, i.e. to minimize

$$E[(V - \alpha e^{-r(T-t)}y)^2].$$

I leave the details to the reader.

And the function $f(S,t)$? The natural choice is the delta of an option that is closely related to the option in question, one for which there is a closed-form solution. Such a choice corresponds to an approximate form of delta hedging, and thus reduces the fluctuation in the contract value along each path.

49.11 PROS AND CONS OF MONTE CARLO SIMULATIONS

The Monte Carlo technique is clearly very powerful and general. The concept readily carries over to exotic and path-dependent contracts; just simulate the random walk and the corresponding cash flows, estimate the average payoff and take its present value.

The main disadvantages are twofold. First, the method is slow when compared with the finite-difference solution of a partial differential equation. Generally speaking this is true for problems up to three or four dimensions. When there are four or more stochastic or path-dependent variables the Monte Carlo method becomes relatively more efficient. Second, the application to American options is far from straightforward. The reason for the problem with American options is to do with the optimality of early exercise. To know when it is optimal to exercise the option one must calculate the option price *for all values of S and t up to expiry* in order to check that at no time is there any arbitrage opportunity. However, the Monte Carlo method in its basic form is only used to estimate the option price at one point in S, t-space, now and at today's value.

Because Monte Carlo simulation is based on the generation of a finite number of realizations using series of random numbers, the value of an option derived in this way will vary each time the simulations are run. Roughly speaking, the error between the Monte Carlo estimate and the correct option price is of the order of the inverse square root of the number of simulations. More precisely, if the standard deviation in the option value using a single simulation is ε then the standard deviation of the error after N simulations is $\varepsilon/\sqrt{N}$. To improve our accuracy by a factor of 10 we must perform 100 times as many simulations.

49.12 AMERICAN OPTIONS

Applying Monte Carlo methods to the valuation of European contracts is simple, but applying them to American options is very, very hard. The problem is to do with the time direction in which we are solving. We have seen how it is natural in the partial differential equation framework to work backwards from expiry to the present. If we do this numerically then we find the value of a contract at every mesh point between now and expiry. This means that along the way we can ensure that there is no arbitrage, and in particular ensure that the early-exercise constraint is satisfied.

When we use the Monte Carlo method in its basic form for valuing a European option we only ever find the option's value at the one point, the current asset level and the current time. We have no information about the option value at any other asset level or time. So if our contract is American we have no way of knowing whether or not we violated the early-exercise constraint somewhere in the future.

In principle, we could find the option value at each point in asset-time space using Monte Carlo. For every asset value and time that we require knowledge of the option value we start a new simulation. But when we have early exercise we have to do this at a large number of points in asset-time space, keeping track of whether the constraint is violated. If we find a value for the option that is below the payoff then we mark this point in asset-time space as one where we must exercise the option. And then for every other path that goes through this point we must exercise at this point, if not before. Such a procedure is possible, but the time taken grows exponentially with the number of points at which we value the option. At the time of writing there were few totally convincing ways around this problem.

49.13 NUMERICAL INTEGRATION

Often the fair value of an option can be written down analytically as an integral. This is certainly the case for non-path-dependent European options contingent upon d lognormal underlyings, for which we have

$$V = e^{-r(T-t)}(2\pi(T-t))^{-d/2}(\mathrm{Det}\boldsymbol{\Sigma})^{-1/2}(\sigma_1\ldots\sigma_d)^{-1}$$
$$\int_0^\infty \cdots \int_0^\infty \frac{\mathrm{Payoff}\,(S'_1\ldots S'_d)}{S'_1\ldots S'_d}\exp\left(-\tfrac{1}{2}\boldsymbol{\alpha}^T\boldsymbol{\Sigma}^{-1}\boldsymbol{\alpha}\right)dS'_1\ldots dS'_d$$

where

$$\alpha_i = \frac{1}{\sigma_i(T-t)^{1/2}}\left(\log\left(\frac{S_i}{S'_i}\right)+\left(r-D_i-\frac{\sigma_i^2}{2}\right)(T-t)\right)$$

and $\boldsymbol{\Sigma}$ is the correlation matrix for the d assets and Payoff$(\cdots)$ is the payoff function. Sometimes the value of path-dependent contracts can also be written as a multiple integral. American options, however, can rarely be expressed so simply.

If we do have such a representation of an option's value then all we need do to value it is to estimate the value of the multiple integral. Let us see how this can be done.

49.14 REGULAR GRID

We can do the multiple integration by evaluating the function on a uniform grid in the d-dimensional space of assets. There would thus be $N^{1/d}$ grid points in each direction where N is the total number of points used. Supposing we use the trapezium or mid-point rule, the error in the estimation of the integral will be $O(N^{-2/d})$ and the time taken approximately $O(N)$ since there are N function evaluations. As the dimension d increases this method becomes prohibitively slow. Note that because the integrand is generally not smooth there is little point in using a higher order method than a mid-point rule unless one goes to the trouble of finding out the whereabouts of the discontinuities in the derivatives. To overcome this 'curse of dimensionality' we can use Monte Carlo integration or low-discrepancy sequences.

49.15 BASIC MONTE CARLO INTEGRATION

Suppose that we want to evaluate the integral

$$\int\cdots\int f(x_1,\ldots,x_d)\,dX_1\ldots dX_d,$$

over some volume. We can very easily estimate the value of this by Monte Carlo simulation. The idea behind this is that the integral can be rewritten as

$$\int\cdots\int f(x_1,\ldots,x_d)\,dX_1\ldots dX_d = \text{volume of region of integration} \times \text{average } f,$$

where the average of f is taken over the whole of the region of integration. To make life simple we can rescale the region of integration to make it the unit hypercube. Assuming that we have done this

$$\int_0^1\cdots\int_0^1 f(x_1,\ldots,x_d)\,dX_1\ldots dX_d = \text{average } f$$

because the volume is one. Such a scaling will obviously be necessary in our financial problems because the range of integration is typically from zero to infinity. I will return to this point later.

We can sample the average of f by Monte Carlo sampling using uniformly distributed random numbers in the d-dimensional space. After N samples we have

$$\text{average } f \approx \frac{1}{N}\sum_{i=1}^{N} f(x_i) \tag{49.4}$$

where x_i is the vector of values of $x_1, \ldots, x_d$ at the ith sampling. As N increases, so the approximation improves. Expression (49.4) is only an approximation. The size of the error can be measured by the standard deviation of the correct average about the sampled average; this is

$$\sqrt{\frac{1}{N}\left(\overline{f^2} - \overline{f}^2\right)}$$

(which must be multiplied by the volume of the region), where

$$\overline{f} = \frac{1}{N}\sum_{i=1}^{N} f(x_i)$$

and

$$\overline{f^2} = \frac{1}{N}\sum_{i=1}^{N} f^2(x_i).$$

Thus the error in the estimation of the value of an integral using a Monte Carlo simulation is $O(N^{-1/2})$ where N is the number of points used, and is independent of the number of dimensions. Again there are N function evaluations and so the computational time is $O(N)$. The accuracy is much higher than that for a uniform grid if we have five or more dimensions.

I have explained Monte Carlo integration in terms of integrating over a d-dimensional unit hypercube. In financial problems we often have integrals over the range zero to infinity. The choice of transformation from zero-one to zero-infinity should be suggested by the problem under consideration. Let us suppose that we have d assets following correlated random walks. The risk-neutral value of these assets at a time t can be written as

$$S_i(T) = S_i(t)e^{\left(r-D_i-(1/2)\sigma_i^2\right)(T-t)+\sigma_i\phi_i\sqrt{T-t}},$$

in terms of their initial values at time t. The random variables ϕ_i are Normally distributed and correlated. We can now write the value of our European option as

$$e^{-r(T-t)}\int_{-\infty}^{\infty}\cdots\int_{-\infty}^{\infty} \text{Payoff}\,(S_1(T), \ldots, S_d(T))\,p(\phi_1, \ldots, \phi_d)\,d\phi_1 \ldots d\phi_d,$$

where $p(\phi_1, \ldots, \phi_d)$ is the probability density function for d correlated Normal variables with zero mean and unit standard deviation. I'm not going to write down p explicitly since we won't need to know its functional form *as long as we generate numbers from this distribution.* In effect, all that I have done here is to transform from lognormally distributed values of the assets to Normally distributed returns on the assets.

Now to value the option we must generate suitable Normal variables. The first step is to generate uncorrelated variables and then transform them into correlated variables. Both of these steps have been explained above; use Box–Muller and then Cholesky. The option value is then estimated by the average of the payoff over all the randomly generated numbers.

Here is a very simple code fragment for calculating the value of a European option in `NDim` assets using `NoPts` points. The interest rate is `IntRate`, the dividend yields are `Div(i)`, the volatilities are `Vol(i)`, time to expiry `Expiry`. The initial values of the assets are `Asset(i)`. The Normally-distributed variables are the `x(i)` and the `S(i)` are the lognormally distributed future asset values.

```
a = Exp(-IntRate * Expiry) / NoPts
suma = 0
For k = 1 To NoPts
For i = 1 To NDim
If test = 0 Then
    Do
        y = 2 * Rnd() - 1
        z = 2 * Rnd() - 1
        dist = y * y + z * z
    Loop Until dist < 1
x(i) = y * Sqr(-2 * Log(dist) / dist)
test = 1
Else
x(i) = z * Sqr(-2 * Log(dist) / dist)
test = 0
End If
Next i
For i = 1 To NDim
    S(i) = Asset(i) * Exp((IntRate - Div(i) - _
              0.5 * Vol(i) * Vol(i)) * Expiry + _
              Vol(i) * x(i) * Sqr(Expiry))
Next i
term = Payoff(S(1), S(2), S(3), S(4), S(5))
suma = suma + term
Next k
Value = suma * a
```

This code fragment is Monte Carlo in its most elementary form, and does not use any of the tricks described over. Some of these tricks are trivial to implement, especially those that are independent of the particular option being valued.

49.16 LOW-DISCREPANCY SEQUENCES

An obvious disadvantage of the basic Monte Carlo method for estimating integrals is that we cannot be certain that the generated points in the d-dimensional space are 'nicely' distributed. Indeed, there is inevitably a good deal of clumping. One way around this is to use a non-random series of points with better distributional properties.

Let us motivate the low-discrepancy sequence method by a Monte Carlo example. Suppose that we want to calculate the value of an integral in two dimensions and we use a Monte Carlo simulation to generate a large number of points in two dimensions at which to sample the integrand. The choice of points may look something like Figure 49.8. Notice how the points are not spread out evenly.

Now suppose we want to add a few hundred more points to improve the accuracy. Where should we put the new points? If we put the new points in the gaps between others then we increase the accuracy of the integral. If we put the points close to where there are already many points then we could make matters worse.

The above shows that we want a way of choosing points such that they are not too bunched, but nicely spread out. At the same time we want to be able to add more points later without spoiling our distribution. Clearly Monte Carlo is bad for evenness of distribution, but a uniform grid does not stay uniform if we add an arbitrary number of extra points. **Low discrepancy sequences** or **quasi-random sequences** have the properties we require.[2]

There are two types of low discrepancy sequences, open and closed. The open sequences are constructed on the assumption that we may want to add more points later. The closed sequences are optimized for a given size of sample, to give the best estimate of the integral for the number of points. The regular grid is an example of a closed low-discrepancy sequence. I will describe the open sequences here.

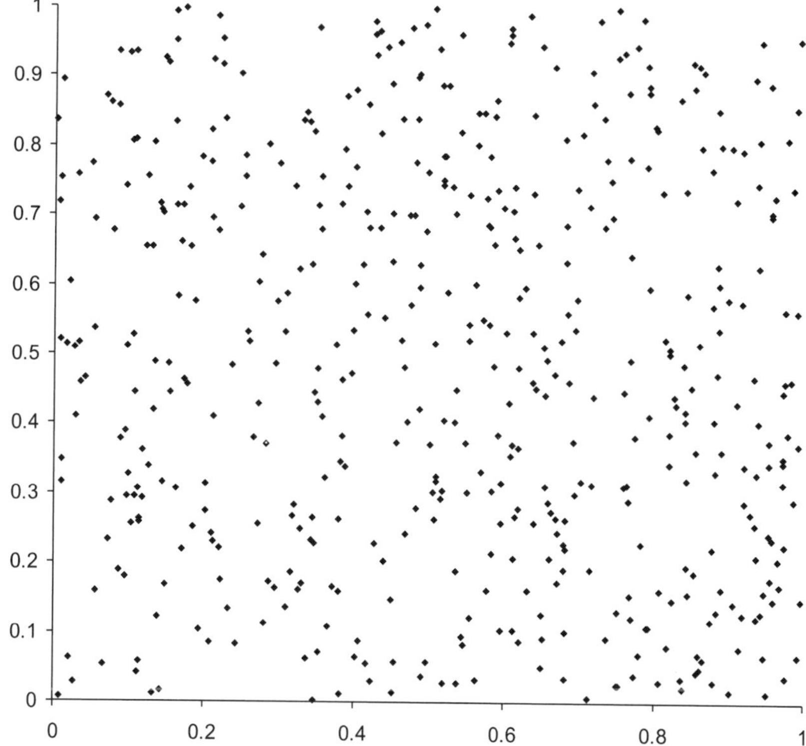

Figure 49.8 A Monte Carlo sample in two dimensions.

[2] There is actually nothing random about quasi-random sequences.

The first application of these techniques in finance was by Barrett, Moore & Wilmott (1992).[3] There are many such sequences with names such as **Sobol'**, **Faure**, **Haselgrove** and **Halton**. I shall describe the Halton sequence here; it is by far the easiest to describe.

The Halton sequence is a sequence of numbers $h(i; b)$ for $i = 1, 2, \ldots$. The integer b is the base. The numbers all lie between zero and one.[4] The numbers are constructed as follows. First choose your base. Let us choose 2. Now write the positive integers in ascending order in base 2, i.e. 1, 10, 11, 100, 101, 110, 111, etc. The Halton sequence base 2 is the reflection of the positive integers in the decimal point, i.e.

Integers base 10	Integers base 2	Halton sequence base 2	Halton number base 10
1	1	$1 \times \frac{1}{2}$	0.5
2	10	$0 \times \frac{1}{2} + 1 \times \frac{1}{4}$	0.25
3	11	$1 \times \frac{1}{2} + 1 \times \frac{1}{4}$	0.75
4	100	$0 \times \frac{1}{2} + 0 \times \frac{1}{4} + 1 \times \frac{1}{8}$	0.125
...	...	...	...

This has been called reflecting the numbers about the decimal point. If you plot the Halton points succesively you will see that the next number in the sequence is always as far as possible from the previous point. Generally, the integer n can be written as

$$i = \sum_{j=1}^{m} a_j b^j$$

in base b, where $0 \le a_j < b$. The Halton numbers are then given by

$$h(i; b) = \sum_{j=1}^{m} a_j b^{-j-1}.$$

Here is an algorithm for calculating Halton numbers of arbitrary base; the `n`th term in a Halton sequence of base `b` is given by `Halton(n, b)`.

```
Function Halton(n, b)
Dim n0, n1, r As Integer
Dim h As Double
Dim f As Double
    n0 = n
    h = 0
    f = 1 / b
While (n0 > 0)
    n1 = Int(n0 / b)
    r = n0 - n1 * b
    h = h + f * r
```

[3] Andy Morton says that this has been my best piece of work, knowing full well that the numerical analysts John Barrett and Gerald Moore should have all the credit.

[4] So we must map our integrand onto the unit hypercube.

```
    f = f / b
    n0 = n1
Wend
Halton = h
End Function
```

The resulting sequence is nice because as we add more and more numbers, more and more 'dots,' we fill in the range zero to one at finer and finer levels.

In Figure 49.9 is the approximation to the Normal distribution using 500 points from a Halton sequence and the Box–Muller method. Compare this distribution with that in Figure 49.3.

When distributing numbers in two dimensions choose, for example, Halton sequence of bases 2 and 3 so that the integrand is calculated at the points $(h(i, 2), h(i, 3))$ for $i = 1, \dots, N$. The bases in the two sequences should be prime numbers. The distribution of these points is shown in Figure 49.10. Compare the distribution with that in the previous figure.

The estimate of the d-dimensional integral

$$\int_0^1 \cdots \int_0^1 f(x_1, \dots, x_d)\, dX_1, \dots, dX_d$$

is then

$$\frac{1}{N}\sum_{i=1}^{N} f(h(i, b_1), \dots, h(i, b_n)),$$

where b_j are distinct prime numbers.

The error in these quasi-random methods is

$$O((\log N)^d N^{-1})$$

and is even better than Monte Carlo at all dimensions. The coefficient in the error depends on the particular low-discrepancy series being used. Sobol' is generally considered to be about the best sequence to use... but it's much harder to explain. See Press et al. (1992) for code to generate Sobol' points or download code from www.netlib.org/toms. In three or more dimensions the method beats the uniform grid. The time taken is $O(N)$.

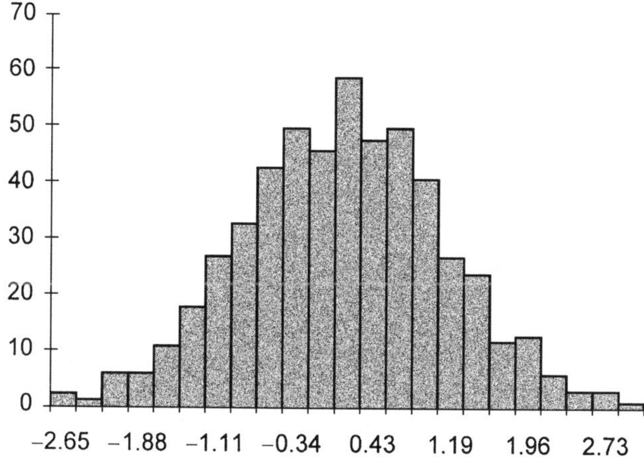

Figure 49.9 The approximation to the Normal distribution using 500 points from a Halton sequence and the Box–Muller method.

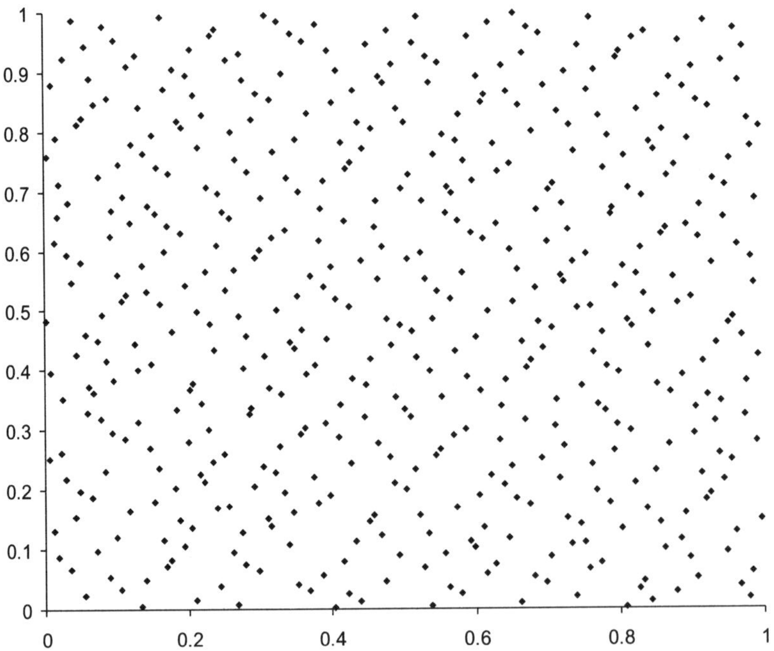

Figure 49.10 Halton points in two dimensions.

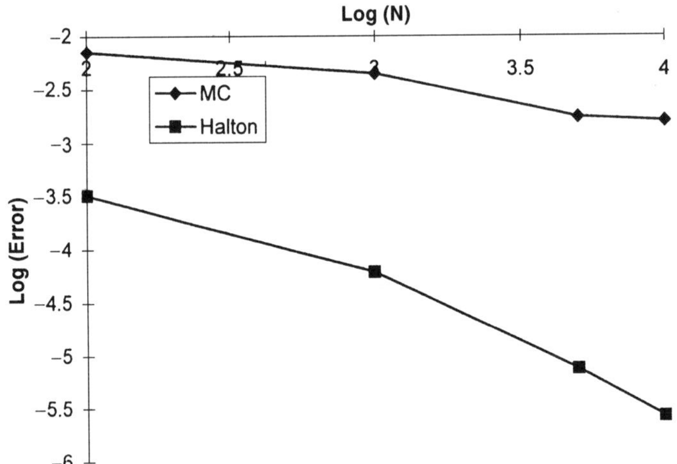

Figure 49.11 Estimate of the error in the value of a five-dimensional contract using basic Monte Carlo and a low-discrepancy sequence.

The error is clearly sensitive to the number of dimensions d. To fully appreciate the inverse relationship to N can require an awful lot of points. However, even with fewer points, in practice the method at its worst has the same error as Monte Carlo.

In Figure 49.11 is shown the relative error in the estimate of value of a five-dimensional contract as a function of the number of points used. The inverse relationship with the Halton sequence is obvious.

49.17 ADVANCED TECHNIQUES

There are several sophisticated techniques that can be used to improve convergence of Monte Carlo and related numerical integration methods. They can be generally classified as techniques for the **reduction of variance**, and hence for the increase in accuracy. None of these methods improve the speed of convergence with respect to N (for example, the error remains $O(N^{-1/2})$ for Monte Carlo) but they can significantly reduce the coefficient in the error term.

The method of **antithetic variables** described previously is *very* easily applied to numerical integration. It should always be used since it can do no harm and is completely independent of the product being valued.

Control variates can also be used in exactly the same way as described above. As with the pathwise simulation for pricing, the method depends on there being a good approximation to the product having an analytic formula.

The idea behind **importance sampling** is to change variables so that the resulting integrand is as close as possible to being constant. In the extreme case, when the integrand becomes exactly constant, the 'answer' is simply the volume of the region in the new variables. Usually, it is not possible to do so well. But the closer one gets to having a constant integrand, then the better the accuracy of the result. The method is rarely used in finance.

Stratified sampling involves dividing the region of integration into smaller subregions. The number of sampling points can then be allocated to the subregions in an optimal fashion, depending on the variance of the integral in each subregion. In more than one dimension it is not always obvious how to bisect the region, and can amount to laying down a grid, so defeating the purpose of Monte Carlo methods. The method can be improved upon by **recursive stratified sampling** in which a decision is made whether to bisect a region, based on the variance in the regions. Stratified sampling is rarely used in finance.

49.18 SUMMARY

Simulations are at the very heart of finance. With simulations you can explore the unknown future, and act accordingly. Simulations can also be used to price options. Although the future is uncertain, the result of hedging an option is theoretically guaranteed.

In this chapter I have tried to give a flavor of the potential of Monte Carlo and related methods. The reader should now be in a position to begin to use these methods in practice. The subject is a large, and growing one, and the reader is referred to the section below for more information.

FURTHER READING

- See Boyle (1977) for the original application of Monte Carlo simulations to pricing derivatives.
- Duffie (1992) describes the important theory behind the validity of Monte Carlo simulations and also gives some clues about how to make the method efficient.
- The subject of Monte Carlo simulations is described straightforwardly and in detail by Vose (1997).
- For a review of Monte Carlo methods applied to American options see Boyle, Broadie & Glasserman (1995).
- See Sloan & Walsh (1990) and Stetson, Marshall & Loeball (1995) for details of how to optimize a grid.

- See Barrett, Moore & Wilmott (1992) for details of the Haselgrove method applied to options. And see Haselgrove (1961) for more details of the method in abstract.
- For a practical example of pricing Mortgage Backed Securities see Ninomiya & Tezuka (1996)
- For more financial examples see Paskov & Traub (1995), Paskov (1996) and Traub & Wozniakowski (1994).
- See Niederreiter (1992) for an in-depth discussion of low-discrepancy sequences.
- See the amazing Press et al. (1992) for samples of code for random number generation and numerical integration. Make sure you use the latest edition, the random number generators in the first edition are not so good. They also describe more advanced integration techniques.

EXERCISES

1. Simulate the risk-neutral random walk for an asset using a spreadsheet package, or otherwise. Use this data to calculate the value of a European call option.
2. Why is it difficult to use Monte Carlo simulations to value American options?
3. Value a European call option using a Monte Carlo simulation. Use the simulation to estimate the value of an integral, as opposed to simulating the random walk for the asset.
4. Calculate Halton sequences for bases 2, 3 and 4. Compare the results (you may wish to plot one base against another). What do you notice? How should this affect the bases you choose for a multi-factor problem?

CHAPTER 50
finite-difference programs

In this Chapter...

- Examples of code for many of the models and numerical methods described

50.1 INTRODUCTION

Finite-difference methods can be a bit daunting when you first start out, so here are a collection of programs that demonstrate some of the ideas in the book.

50.2 EXPLICIT ONE-FACTOR MODEL FOR A CONVERTIBLE BOND

This Visual Basic code fragment shows an explicit finite difference solution of Equation (36.1) for a CB with intermittent conversion. The code allows many conversion periods. The timesteps on which conversion starts and ends for each period are stored in the arrays `ConvertDateStart` and `ConvertDateEnd`; between these timesteps conversion is into `ConvertRate` of the underlying. As the timestep passes over the `ConvertDateStart` value the integer `itest` is increased by one so that we start to look at the next conversion period. In real time this period with be earlier since we are timestepping backwards.

The bond values are kept in `VOld` and updated in `VNew`. Note that we have used the boundary condition

$$\frac{\partial^2 V}{\partial S^2} = 0,$$

at the top of the asset range. This is represented by `VNew(M) = 2 * VNew(M - 1) - VNew(M - 2)`. At $S = 0$ we have

$$\frac{\partial V}{\partial t} = rV,$$

i.e. `VNew(0) = VOld(0) - dt * IntRate * VOld(0)`.

All you have to do to this to make it a fully-fledged function is to top and tail it with variable declarations etc. Make sure that you choose the timestep `dt` sufficiently small to satisfy the stability constraint.

```
For j = 1 To N
        If (test = 0) Then
            itest = itest + 1
            test = 1
        End If

        For i = 1 To M - 1
            gamma = (VOld(i + 1) - 2 * VOld(i) + VOld(i - 1)) / _
                    dS / dS
            sdelta = S(i) * (VOld(i + 1) - VOld(i - 1)) / 2 / dS
            cash = sdelta - VOld(i)
            VNew(i) = VOld(i) + dt * (0.5 * S(i) * S(i) * sig * _
                      sig * gamma + IntRate * cash - div * _
                      sdelta)
        Next i
            VNew(0) = VOld(0) - dt * IntRate * VOld(0)
            VNew(M) = 2 * VNew(M - 1) - VNew(M - 2)

        For i1 = 0 To M
            VOld(i1) = VNew(i1)
            If j >= ConvertDateEnd(itest) And j _
                <= ConvertDateStart(itest) Then
                VOld(i1) = max(VOld(i1), ConvertRate(itest) *
                S(i1))
                If j = ConvertDateStart(itest) Then test = 0
            End If
    Next i1
Next j
```

50.3 AMERICAN CALL, IMPLICIT

This code values an American call via an implicit scheme with successive over relaxation. The current asset value is `Asset`, volatility is `Sigma`, the spot interest rate is `IntRate`, dividend yield is `Div`. The option expiry is `ExpTime`, and the exercise price is `Strike`. The code also takes in the number of asset steps and the timestep, `NoAssetSteps` and `Timestep`. Experiment with these. The solution range extends from $S = 0$ to $S = 3$ `Asset`, note the boundary conditions applied at the extremes of the range.

```
Function ImplicitUSCall(Asset, ExpTime, Sigma, IntRate, Div, _
Strike, NoAssetSteps, Timestep)
  Dim VNew(0 To 1000), VOld(0 To 1000), g(0 To 1000), _
    a(0 To 1000), b(0 To 1000), c(0 To 1000) As Double
  M = NoAssetSteps
  dS = Strike / M                      ' asset step
  frac = (Asset - M * dS) / dS
  M = 3 * M
  dt = Timestep
  kmax = Int(ExpTime / dt + 0.5)
  dt * = ExpTime / kmax
```

```
  w = 1.5                          ' relaxation parameter
' set initial conditions for call payoff
  For i = 0 To M
    temp = i * ds
    VOld(i) = 0
    If (temp > Strike) Then VOld(i) = temp - Strike
    g(i) = VOld(i)
  Next i
' preset the triagonal elements for constant Sigma, IntRate, _
    Div, dt.
  For i = 1 To M - 1
    a(i) = dt * 0.5 * i * (Sigma * Sigma * i + IntRate - Div)
    b(i) = 1 + dt * (Sigma * Sigma * i * i + IntRate)
    c(i) = dt * 0.5 * i * (Sigma * Sigma * i - IntRate + Div)
  Next i

' Start the time stepping.
  For j = 1 To kmax - 1
    t = j * dt
    For i = 1 To M - 1  ' set initial guess for time m+1.
      VNew(i) = VOld(i)
    Next i
    k = 0                   ' iteration count initialized
' set boundary conditions
    VNew(0) = 0
    VNew(M) = dS * M * Exp(-Div * t) - Strike * Exp(-IntRate * t)
10  norm = 0        ' set 12 norm to 0.
    For i = 1 To M - 1
        y = (VOld(i) + a(i) * VNew(i + 1) +  c(i) * VNew(i - 1)) / _
            b(i)
        temp = y - VNew(i)
        norm = norm + temp * temp
        VNew(i) = VNew(i) + w * temp
        If VNew(i) < g(i) Then VNew(i) = g(i)
      Next i
      k = k + 1
    If (norm > 0.0001) And (k < 50) Then GoTo 10
    For i = 1 To M - 1
      VOld(i) = VNew(i)
    Next i
  Next j

    ImplicitUSCall = frac * VNew(M / 3 + 1) + _
                     (1 - frac) * VNew(M / 3)
End Function
```

50.4 EXPLICIT PARISIAN OPTION

This code is the explicit method applied to a path-dependent contract, a Parisian option. Note that we need a two-dimensional array to keep track of the option value as a function of the underlying asset and the path-dependent quantity. All of the inputs to the function are obvious except for `BarTime`; this is the length of time the asset must be beyond the barrier for it to be triggered. What kind of Parisian option is this, up/down, in/out?

```
Function ParisianPut(Asset, ExpTime, Sigma, IntRate, Div, _
BarTime, Barrier, Strike, NoAssetSteps)
  Dim VNew(0 To 300, 0 To 500), VOld(0 To 300, 0 To 500), _
    q(0 To 300, 0 To 500) As Double
  dS = Strike / NoAssetSteps                ' asset step
  x = Int(Barrier / dS + 0.5)
  y = Int(Strike / dS + 0.5)
  z = Int(Asset / dS)
  l = 2 * y + 10                          ' number of asset points
  dt = 0.9 / (l * l * Sigma * Sigma)
  kmax = Int(ExpTime / dt + 1#)
  kmin = Int(BarTime / dt + 0.5)
  start1 = x
  end1 = l - 1
  start2 = 0
  end2 = x
' set initial conditions for put payoff
  For k = 0 To kmax
    For i = 0 To l
      temp = i * dS
      VOld(i, k) = 0#
      If (k <= kmin) And (temp < Strike) Then VOld(i, k) = Strike _
        temp
      q(i, k) = 0#
    Next i
  Next k
' reset boundary data at line tau=kmin
  For i = start2 To end2
    VOld(i, kmin) = 0#
  Next i
' Start the time stepping
  For j = 1 To kmax - 1
    t = j * dt
    ' solve BS equation in 1-d domain
    For i = start1 To end1
      VNew(i, 0) = VOld(i, 0) + dt * (0.5 * i * i * Sigma * _
                   Sigma * (VOld(i + 1, 0) -  2 * VOld(i, 0) + _
                   VOld(i - 1, 0)) + 0.5 * (IntRate - Div) * _
                   i * (VOld(i + 1, 0) - VOld(i - 1, 0)) -  _
                   IntRate * VOld(i, 0))
    Next i
    ' solve modified BS equation in 2-d domain
    For k = 0 To kmin - 1
      For i = start2 + 1 To end2 - 1
        VNew(i, k) = VOld(i, k + 1) + dt * (0.5 * i * i * Sigma _
                     * Sigma * (VOld(i + 1, k + 1) - 2 *  _
                     VOld(i, k + 1) + VOld(i - 1, k + 1))  _
                     + 0.5 * (IntRate - Div) * i *  _
                     (VOld(i + 1, k + 1) - VOld(i - 1, k + 1)) _
                     - IntRate * VOld(i, k + 1))
```

```
      Next i
    Next k
    ' put data in q array on line k=kmin
    For i = 0 To 1
      VNew(i, kmin) = q(i, j)
    Next i
    ' put boundary data in for tau>0, s=x.
    For k = 1 To kmin - 1
      VNew(x, k) = VNew(x, 0)
    Next k
    ' put boundary data in for tau>0, s=x.
    For k = 0 To kmin
      For i = 0 To 1
        VOld(i, k) = VNew(i, k)
      Next i
      VOld(1, k) = 0#
      If (k <= kmin) Then VOld(0, k) = Strike * Exp(-IntRate * t)
    Next k
  Next j

  ParisianPut = VNew(z, 0)
End Function
```

50.5 CRASH MODELING

Below is a fragment of Visual Basic code that could be used for the crash model of Chapter 27. Here `S(i)` is the asset array, *lognormally* distributed about the current stock level, i.e. `S(i) = Exp(Log(Asset) + i * step)`. This is different from our usual, equally-spaced asset price grid. It's easier to use a logarithmically-spaced grid because we are assuming a percentage fall during the crash. `BSOld` is the array of Black–Scholes values calculated by another finite-difference scheme (or coming from a formula). `ik` is the number of grid points that the asset falls during a crash, i.e. `ik = Int(-Log(1 - Crash) / Step)` where `Crash` is the percentage crash allowed. Then `kstar = 1 - Exp(-ik * Step)`. `testing` is used to see whether a crash is beneficial. `VOld` and `VNew` are the arrays holding the old and new values of the option. `Delta` is the optimal hedge ratio, either the 'Black–Scholes' delta or the crash delta.

```
For i = -N + ik To N

testing = VOld(i + 1) + (S(i) - S(i + 1) - kstar * S(i)) * _
          (VOld(i + 1) - VOld(i - 1)) / (S(i + 1) - S(i - 1))

If BSOld(i - ik) > testing Then
' **************** delta hedge
        Delta(i) = (VOld(i + 1) - VOld(i - 1)) / (S(i + 1) _
                   - S(i - 1))
        VNew(i) = (VOld(i + 1) + (S(i) - S(i + 1) + IntRate * _
                  S(i) * dt) * (VOld(i + 1) - VOld(i - 1)) / _
                  (S(i + 1) - S(i - 1))) / (1 + IntRate * dt)
Else
```

```
' **************** crash hedge
        Delta(i) = (BSOld(i - ik) - VOld(i + 1)) / (S(i) - _
                   S(i + 1) - kstar * S(i))
        VNew(i) = (BSOld(i - ik) + S(i) * (kstar + IntRate * dt) _
                  * (BSOld(i - ik) -  VOld(i + 1)) / (S(i) - _
                  S(i + 1) - kstar * S(i))) / (1 + IntRate * dt)
End If

Next i
```

This program needs to be topped and tailed.

How would you modify the code to allow for a range for the size of the crash?

50.6 EXPLICIT EPSTEIN–WILMOTT SOLUTION

This code solves the nonlinear first-order Epstein–Wilmott model for uncertain interest rate. The coupon dates go in `input1` and the coupon amounts go in `input2`. The current spot interest rate is `rNow` with `rMin` and `rMax` being the minimum and maximum allowed rates. The rates are allowed to grow or decay at a rate of at most `growth`. How would you change this program to value the bond in the best case?

```
Function EpsteinWilmott(input1, input2, rNow, rMin, rMax, growth)
Dim VNew(500), VOld(500), CouponVal(20), CouponDate(20) As Double
numcoup = input1.Rows.Count
tMin = 0
tMax = 0
      For i = 0 To numcoup - 1
            CouponDate(i) = input1(numcoup - i)
            CouponVal(i) = input2(numcoup - i)
            tMax = Application.Max(CouponDate(i), tMax)
      Next i

    m = 1

' set up variable data
dr = 1 / 100
dt = dr / growth
rSteps = Int((rMax - rMin) / dr)
tSteps = Int((tMax - tMin) / dt)
rateinteger = (rNow - rMin) / dr
frac = (rNow - rateinteger * dr + rMin) / dr

' initial data for arrays
For i = 0 To rSteps
    VOld(i) = CouponVal(0)
Next i

' solve the equation

For j = 1 To tSteps

    ' boundary values
    If VOld(0) * (1 - rMin * dt) < VOld(1) * (1 - _
      (rMin + 0.5 * dr) * dt) Then VNew(0) = VOld(0) * _
      (1 - rMin * dt)
```

```
        Else: VNew(0) = VOld(1) * (1 - (rMin + 0.5 * dr) * dt)
        End If

        If VOld(rSteps) * (1 - rMax * dt) < VOld(rSteps - 1) * (1 - _
          (rMax - 0.5 * dr) * dt) Then VNew(rSteps) = VOld(rSteps) * _
          (1 - rMax * dt)
        Else: VNew(rSteps) = VOld(rSteps - 1) * (1 - (rMax - 0.5 * _
                             dr) * dt)
        End If

        ' interior points
        Space = rMin + dr
        For i = 1 To rSteps - 1
            If VOld(i) * (1 - Space * dt) < VOld(i - 1) * (1 - (Space _
              - 0.5 * dr) * dt) And VOld(i) * (1 - Space * dt) < _
              VOld(i + 1) * (1 -  (Space + 0.5 * dr) * dt) Then  _
              VNew(i) = VOld(i) * (1 - Space * dt)
            ElseIf VOld(i - 1) * (1 - (Space - 0.5 * dr) * dt) < _
              VOld(i) * (1 - Space * dt) And VOld(i - 1) * (1 -  _
              (Space - 0.5 * dr) * dt) < VOld(i + 1) * _
              (1 - (Space + 0.5 * dr) * dt)
              VNew(i) = VOld(i - 1) * (1 - (Space - 0.5 * dr) * dt)
            Else: VNew(i) = VOld(i + 1) * (1 - (Space + 0.5 * dr) *
                            dt)
            End If

            Space = Space + dr
        Next i

    ' coupon dates
    If j = Int((tMax - CouponDate(m)) / dt) Then
        For i = 0 To rSteps
            VNew(i) = VNew(i) + CouponVal(m)
        Next i
        m = m + 1
    End If

    ' reset old values
    For i = 0 To rSteps
            VOld(i) = VNew(i)
        Next i

    Next j

    EpsteinWilmott = (1 - frac) * VOld(rateinteger) + frac * _
    VOld(rateinteger + 1)

    End Function
```

EXERCISES

1. Write an explicit finite-difference program to value an interest rate cap using the Vasicek model. Experiment with Richardson extrapolation to improve accuracy.
2. Write an implicit finite-difference program to price an interest rate floor. Experiment with Richardson extrapolation to improve accuracy.

3. Write an explicit finite-difference program to value a portfolio of European options, all with the same expiry and on the same underlying. Modify the code to allow arbitrary expiry dates, treating the whole portfolio as one contract.
4. Modify the code in the previous program to allow a range in volatility, dividend yield and interest rate. Value the portfolio in the best and worst cases.
5. Write a program to value a Black–Scholes call in the worst-case scenario when one crash is allowed before expiry. During a crash, the asset price changes from S to $(1-k)S$ where

$$k^- \le k \le k^+.$$

The worst-case option value is then given by

$$V_1 = \min_{k^- \le k \le k^+} \left(\frac{1}{1+r\delta t} \left(V_0 + S(k + r\delta t) \frac{V_0 - V_1^u}{S - S^u - kS} \right) \right),$$

when a crash occurs, and otherwise by

$$V_1 = \frac{1}{1+r\delta t} \left(V_1^u + (S - S^u + rS\delta t) \frac{V_1^u - V_1^d}{S^u - S^d} \right).$$

6. Write explicit two-factor convertible bond programs, allowing for conversion, call and put. For your first code have the underlying stochastic and the spot rate satisfying the Vasicek model. For your second code have constant interest rate but a stochastic risk of default.
7. Write a program to solve the Epstein–Wilmott model for a cap and a floor. Value the contract in best and worst cases. Modify the code so that it 'fits' the current yield curve.
8. Which of the above codes solve a nonlinear problem? For those problems apply the ideas of static hedging, together with an optimization code to find the optimal static hedges.

epilog

I hope you have had as much fun reading this book as I had writing it. I hope also that I have conveyed some of my enthusiasm for the subject of math finance, as well as some of my doubts. One thing I don't doubt is that this subject is much more exciting than fluid mechanics.

I have worked increasingly intensely and manically on this book over the last few months. My wife, Ingrid Blauer, has had to put up with a great deal. On the whole, she coped quite well. Whenever I needed data at short notice, or some obscure contract explained, she didn't let me down. I would like to thank her for her support in this, and other, hare-brained schemes. As I promised her, I will now enrol in Workaholics Anonymous, for detox.

Paul Wilmott
Surrey
19th January 1998

bibliography

Essential Books for Your Derivatives Library

Some of these books are for daily reference, others are insightful, and others are simply 'classics.' Some are pure finance, some mathematics and some in between. They are my own favorites.

Cox, DR & Miller, HD 1965 *The Theory of Stochastic Processes*. Chapman & Hall

Cox, J & Rubinstein, M 1985 *Options Markets*. Prentice–Hall

Crank, JC 1989 *Mathematics of Diffusion*. Oxford

Dixit, AK & Pindyck, RS 1994 *Investment Under Uncertainty*. Princeton

Elton, EJ & Gruber, MJ 1995 *Modern Portfolio Theory and Investment Analysis*. John Wiley www.wiley.com

Haug, EG 1997 *The Complete Guide to Option Pricing Formulas*. McGraw–Hill

Hull, J 1997 *Options, Futures and Other Derivative Securities*. Prentice Hall

Ingersoll, JE Jr 1987 *Theory of Financial Decision Making*. Rowman & Littlefield

Malkiel, BG 1990 *A Random Walk Down Wall Street*. Norton

Markowitz, H 1959 *Portfolio Selection: efficient diversification of investment*. John Wiley www.wiley.com

Merton, RC 1992 *Continuous-time Finance*. Blackwell

Miller, M 1997 *Merton Miller on Derivatives*. John Wiley www.wiley.com

Morton, KW & Mayers, DF 1994 *Numerical Solution of Partial Differential Equations*. Cambridge

Neftci, S 1996 *An Introduction to the Mathematics of Financial Derivatives*. Academic Press

Øksendal, B 1992 *Stochastic Differential Equations*. Springer–Verlag

Press, WH, Teutolsky, SA, Vetterling, WT & Flannery, BP 1992 *Numerical Recipes in C*. Cambridge

Schuss, Z 1980 *Theory and Applications of Stochastic Differential Equations*. John Wiley www.wiley.com

Schwager, JD 1990 *Market Wizards*. HarperCollins

Schwager, JD 1992 *New Market Wizards*. HarperCollins

Sharpe, WF 1985 *Investments*. Prentice–Hall

Smith, GD 1985 *Numerical Solution of Partial Differential Equations: Finite Difference Methods*. Oxford

Soros, G 1987 *The Alchemy of Finance*. John Wiley www.wiley.com

Taleb, N 1997 *Dynamic Hedging*. John Wiley www.wiley.com

Thorp, EO 1962 *Beat the Dealer*. Vintage

Wilmott, P, Dewynne, J & Howison, SD 1993 *Option Pricing: mathematical models and computation*.

Oxford Financial Press www.oxfordfinancial.co.uk

Wong, S 1981 *Professional Blackjack*. Pi Yee Press www.bj21.com

Other Books and Key Research Articles

Ahn, H, Arkell, R, Choe, K, Holstad, E & Wilmott, P 1998 Value at risk and optimal static hedging under stochastic volatility. MFG Working Paper, Oxford University

Ahn, H, Dayal, M, Grannan, E & Swindle, G 1998 Option replication with transaction costs: general diffusion limits. To appear in Annals of Applied Probability

Ahn, H, Khadem, V & Wilmott, P 1998 On the utility of risky bonds. MFG Working Paper, Oxford University

Ahn, H, Muni, A & Swindle, G 1996 Misspecified asset price models and robust hedging strategies. To appear in Applied Mathematical Finance

Ahn, H, Muni, A, Swindle, G 1998 Optimal hedging strategies for misspecified asset price models. To appear in Applied Mathematical Finance

Ahn, H, Penaud, A, & Wilmott, P 1998 Various passport options and their valuation. MFG Working Paper, Oxford University

Ahn, H, Wilmott, P 1998 On trading American options. MFG Working Paper, Oxford University

Alexander, CO 1994 History Debunked. Risk magazine **7** (12) 59–63

Alexander, CO 1995 Volatility and correlation forecasts. Derivatives Week (August)

Alexander, CO 1996 a Evaluating the use of Riskmetrics as a risk measurement tool for your operation. Derivatives: Use Trading and Regulation **2** (3) 277–285

Alexander, CO 1996 b Estimating and forecasting volatility and correlation: methods and applications. Financial Derivatives and Risk Management **7** (September) 64–72

Alexander, CO 1996 c Volatility and Correlation forecasting. In the *Handbook of Risk Management and Analysis* (C.Alexander, Ed) John Wiley 233–260

Alexander, CO 1997 a Splicing methods for generating large covariance matrices. Derivatives Week (June)

Alexander, CO 1997 b Estimating and forecasting volatility and correlation: methods and applications. In *Risk Management and Financial Derivatives: A Guide to the Mathematics* (S. Das, Ed) 337–354

Alexander, CO 1998 *The Handbook of Risk Management and Analysis*. John Wiley

Alexander, CO & Chibuma, A 1997 Orthogonal GARCH: An empirical validation in equities, foreign exchange and interest rates. Working Paper, Sussex University

Alexander, CO & Giblin, I 1997 Multivariate embedding methods: Forecasting high-frequency data in the first INFFC. Proceedings of the First International Nonlinear Financial Forecasting Competition, Finance and Technology Publishing

Alexander, CO & Leigh, C 1997 On the covariance matrices used in VAR models. Journal of Derivatives **4** (3) 50–62

Alexander, CO & Johnson, A 1992 Are foreign exchange markets really efficient? Economics Letters **40** 449–453

Alexander, CO & Johnson, A 1994 Dynamic Links. Risk magazine **7** (2) 56–61

Alexander, CO & Riyait, N 1992 The world according to GARCH. Risk magazine **5** (8) 120–125

Alexander, CO & Thillainathan, R 1996 The Asian Connections. Emerging Markets Investor **2** (6) 42–47

Alexander, CO & Williams, P 1997 Modelling the term structure of kurtosis: A comparison of neural network and GARCH methods. Working Paper, Sussex University

Apabhai, MZ 1995 Term structure modelling and the valuation of yield curve derivative securities. D.Phil. thesis, Oxford University

Apabhai, MZ, Choe, K, Khennach, F & Wilmott, P 1995 Spot-on modelling. Risk magazine, December **8** (11) 59–63

Apabhai, MZ, Georgikopoulos, NI, Hasnip, D, Jamie, RKD, Kim, M & Wilmott, P 1998 A model for the value of a business, some optimisation problems in its operating procedures and the valuation of its debt. IMA Journal of Applied Mathematics **60** 1–13

Artzner, P, Delbaen, F, Eber, J-M & Heath, D 1997 Thinking coherently. Risk magazine **10** (11) 68–72 (November)

Atkinson, C & Al-Ali, B 1997 On an investment-consumption model with transaction costs: an asymptotic analysis. Applied Mathematical Finance **4** 109–133

Atkinson, C & Wilmott, P 1993 Properties of moving averages of asset prices. IMA Journal of Mathematics in Business and Industry **4** 331–341

Atkinson, C & Wilmott, P 1995 Portfolio management with transaction costs: an asymptotic analysis. Mathematical Finance **5** 357–367

Atkinson, C, Pliska, S & Wilmott, P 1997 Portfolio management with transaction costs. Proceedings of the Royal Society A

Avellaneda, M, Friedman, C, Holmes, R & Samperi D, 1997 calibrating vol surfaces via relative-entropy minimization. Applied Mathematical Finance **4** 37–64

Avellaneda, M, Levy, A & Parás, A 1995 Pricing and hedging derivative securities in markets with uncertain volatilities. Applied Mathematical Finance **2** 73–88

Avellaneda, M & Parás, A 1994 Dynamic hedging portfolios for derivative securities in the presence of large transaction costs. Applied Mathematical Finance **1** 165–194

Avellaneda, M & Parás, A 1996 Managing the volatility risk of derivative securities: the Lagrangian volatility model. Applied Mathematical Finance **3** 21–53

Avellaneda, M & Buff, R 1997 Combinatorial implications of nonlinear uncertain volatility models: the case of barrier options. Courant Institute, NYU

Babbs, S 1992 Binomial valuation of lookback options. Midland Montagu Working Paper

Baker, CTH 1977 *The Numerical Treatment of Integral Equations*. Oxford, Oxford University Press

Barles, G, Burdeau, J, Romano, M & Samsen, N 1995 Critical stock price near expiration. Mathematical Finance **5** 77–95

Barone-Adesi, G & Whaley, RE 1987 Efficient analytic approximation of American option values. Journal of Finance **41** 301–320

Barrett, JW, Moore, G & Wilmott, P 1992 Inelegant efficiency. Risk magazine **5** (9) 82–84

Bergman, YZ, 1985 Pricing path contingent claims. Research in Finance **5** 229–241

Bergman, YZ, 1995 Option pricing with differential interest rates. Review of Financial Studies **8** 475–500

Black F 1976 The pricing of commodity contracts. Journal of Financial Economics **3** 167–79

Black, F & Cox, J 1976 Valuing corporate securities: some effects of bond indenture provisions. Journal of Finance **31** 351–367

Black, F, Derman, E & Toy, W 1990 A one-factor model of interest rates and its application to Treasury bond options. Financial Analysts Journal **46** 33–9

Black, F & Scholes, M 1973 The pricing of options and corporate liabilities. Journal of Political Economy **81** 637–59

Blauer, I & Wilmott, P 1998 Risk of default in Latin American Brady bonds. Net Exposure **5** www.netexposure.co.uk

Bloch, D 1995 One-factor inflation rate modelling. M.Phil. dissertation, Oxford University

Bollerslev, T 1986 Generalized Autoregressive Conditional Heteroskedasticity. Journal of Econometrics **31** 307–27

Bowie, J & Carr, P 1994 Static Simplicity. Risk magazine **7** 45–49

Boyle, P 1977 Options: a Monte Carlo approach. Journal of Financial Economics **4** 323–338

Boyle, P 1991 Mulit-asset path-dependent options. FORC conference, Warwick

Boyle, P, Broadie, M & Glasserman, P 1995 Monte Carlo methods for security pricing. Working Paper, University of Waterloo

Boyle, P & Emanuel, D 1980 Discretely adjusted option hedges. Journal of Financial Economics **8** 259–282

Boyle, P, Evnine, J & Gibbs, S 1989 Numerical evaluation of multivariate contingent claims. Review of Financial Studies **2** 241–50

Boyle, P & Tse, Y 1990 An algorithm for computing values of options on the maximum or minimum of several assets. Journal of Financial and Quantitative Analysis **25** 215–27

Boyle, P & Vorst, T 1992 Option replication in discrete time with transaction costs. Journal of Finance **47** 271

Brace, A, Gatarek, D & Musiela, M 1997 The market model of interest rate dynamics. Mathematical Finance **7** 127–154

Brennan, M & Schwartz, E 1977 Convertible bonds: valuation and optimal strategies for call and conversion. Journal of Finance **32** 1699–1715

Brennan, M & Schwartz, E 1978 Finite-difference methods and jump processes arising in the pricing of contingent claims: a synthesis. Journal of Financial and Quantitative Analysts **13** 462–474

Brennan, M & Schwartz, E 1982 An equilibrium model of bond pricing and a test of market efficiency. Journal of Financial and Quantitative Analysis **17** 301–329

Brennan, M & Schwartz, E 1983 Alternative methods for valuing debt options. Finance **4** 119–138

Brenner, M & Subrahmanyam, MG 1994 A simple approach to option valuation and hedging in the Black–Scholes model. Financial Analysts Journal 25–28

Brooks, M 1967 *The Producers.* MGM

Briys, EL, Mai, HM, Bellalah, MB & de Varenne, F 1998 *Options, Futures and Exotic Derivatives.* John Wiley

Carr, P 1994 European put–call symmetry. Cornell University Working Paper

Carr, P 1995 Two extensions to barrier option pricing. Applied Mathematical Finance **2** 173–209

Carr, P & Chou, A 1997 Breaking Barriers. Risk magazine **10** 139–144

Carr, P, Ellis, K & Gupta, V 1998 Static Hedging of Exotic Options. To appear in Journal of Finance

Carslaw, HS & Jaeger, JC 1989 *Conduction of Heat in Solids.* Oxford

Chan, K, Karolyi, A, Longstaff, F & Sanders, A 1992 An empirical comparison of alternative models of the short-term interest rate. Journal of Finance **47** 1209–1227

Chance, D 1990 Default risk and the duration of zero-coupon bonds. Journal of Finance **45** (1) 265–274

Chesney, M, Cornwall, J, Jeanblanc-Picqué, M, Kentwell, G & Yor, M 1997 Parisian pricing. Risk magazine **1** (1) 77–80

Chew, L 1996 *Managing Derivative Risk: the use and abuse of leverage.* John Wiley

Connolly, KB 1997 *Buying and Selling Volatility.* John Wiley

Conze, A & Viswanathan 1991 Path-dependent options—the case of lookback options. Journal of Finance **46** 1893–1907

Cooper, I & Martin, M 1996 Default risk and derivative products. Applied Mathematical Finance **3** 53–74

Copeland, T, Koller, T & Murrin, J 1990 *Valuation: measuring and managing the value of companies.* John Wiley

Cox, J, Ingersoll, J & Ross, S 1980 An analysis of variable loan contracts. Journal of Finance **35** 389–403

Cox, J, Ingersoll, J & Ross, S 1981 The relationship between forward prices and futures prices. Journal of Financial Economics **9** 321–346

Cox, J, Ingersoll, J & Ross, S 1985 A theory of the term structure of interest rates. Econometrica **53** 385–467

Cox, JC, Ross, S & Rubinstein M 1979 Option pricing: a simplified approach. Journal of Financial Economics **7** 229–263

Crank, J & Nicolson, P 1947 A practical method for numerical evaluation of solutions of partial differencial equations of the heat conduction type. Proceedings of the Cambridge Philosophical Society **43** 50–67

Das, S 1994 *Swaps and Financial Derivatives.* IFR

Das, S & Tufano, P 1994 Pricing credit-sensitive debt when interest rates, credit ratings and credit spreads are stochastic. Working Paper, Harvard Business School

Das, S 1995 Credit risk derivatives. Journal of Derivatives **2** 7–23

Davis, MHA & Norman, AR 1990 Portfolio selection with transaction costs. Mathematics of Operations Research **15** 676–713

Davis, MHA, Panas, VG & Zariphopoulou, T 1993 European option pricing with transaction costs. SIAM Journal of Controand & Optimization **31** 470–93

Derman, E, Ergener, D & Kani, I 1997 Static options replication. In *Frontiers in Derivatives*. (Ed. Konishi, A & Dattatreya, RE) Irwin

Derman, E & Kani, I 1994 Riding on a smile. Risk magazine **7** (2) 32–39 (February)

Derman, E & Kani, I 1997 Stochastic implied trees: arbitrage pricing with stochastic term and strike structure of volatility. Goldman Sachs Quantitative Strategies Technical Notes April 1997.

Derman, E & Zou, J 1997 Predicting the response of implied volatility to large index moves. Goldman Sachs Quantitative Strategies Technical Notes November 1997.

Dewynne, JN, Whalley, AE & Wilmott, P 1994 Path-dependent options and transaction costs. Philosophical Transactions of the Royal Society A. **347** 517–529

Dewynne, JN, Whalley, AE & Wilmott, P 1995 Mathematical models and partial differential equations in finance. In *Quantitative methods, super computers and AI in finance* (ed. S.Zenios) 95–124

Dewynne, JN & Wilmott, P 1993 Partial to the exotic. Risk magazine **6** (3) 38–46

Dewynne, JN & Wilmott, P 1994 a Exotic financial options. Proceedings of the 7th European Conference on Mathematics in Industry 389–397

Dewynne, JN & Wilmott, P 1994 b Modelling and numerical valuation of lookback options. MFG Working Paper, Oxford University

Dewynne, JN & Wilmott, P 1994 c Untitled. MFG Working Paper, Oxford University

Dewynne, JN & Wilmott, P 1995 a A note on American options with varying exercise price. Journal of the Australian Mathematical Society **37** 45–57

Dewynne, JN & Wilmott, P 1995 b A note on average-rate options with discrete sampling. SIAM Journal of Applied Mathematics **55** 267–276

Dewynne, JN & Wilmott, P 1995 c Asian options as linear complementarity problems: analysis and finite-difference solutions. Advances in Futures and Options Research **8** 145–177

Dewynne, JN & Wilmott, P 1996 Exotic options: mathematical models and computation. In *Frontiers in Derivatives* (Ed. Konishi and Dattatreya.) 145–182

Dothan, MU 1978 On the term structure of interest rates. Journal of Financial Economics **6** 59–69

Duffee, G 1995 The variation of default risk with treasury yields. Working Paper, Federal Reserve Board, Washington

Duffie, D 1992 *Dynamic Asset Pricing Theory*. Princeton

Duffie, D & Harrison, JM 1992 Arbitrage pricing of Russian options and perpetual lookback options. Working Paper

Duffie, D, Ma, J, Yong, J 1994 Black's consol rate conjecture. Working Paper, Stanford

Duffie, D & Singleton, K 1994 a Modeling Term Structures of Defaultable Bonds. Working Paper, Stanford

Duffie, D & Singleton, K 1994 b An econometric model of the term structure of interest rate swap yields. Working Paper, Stanford

Dupire, B 1993 Pricing and hedging with smiles. Proc AFFI Conf, La Baule June 1993

Dupire, B 1994 Pricing with a smile. Risk magazine **7** (1) 18–20 (January)

Eberlain, E & Keller, U 1995 Hyperbolic distributions in finance. Bernoulli **1** 281–299

El Karoui, Jeanblanc-Picqué, & Viswanathan 1991 Bounds for options. Lecture notes in Control and Information Sciences **117** 224–237, Springer-Verlag

Embrechts, P, Klüppelberg, C & Mikosch, T 1997 *Modelling Extremal Events*. Springer–Verlag

Engle, R 1982 Autoregressive conditional heteroscedasticity, with estimates of the variance of United Kingdom inflation. Econometrica **50** 987–1007

Engle, R & Bollerslev, T 1987 Modelling the persistance of conditional variances. Econometric Reviews **5** 1–50

Engle, R & Granger, C 1987 Cointegration and error correction: representation, estimation and testing. Econometrica **55** 251–276

Engle, R 1995 (ed.) *ARCH: Selected Readings*. Oxford

Engle, R & Mezrich, J 1996 GARCH for groups. Risk magazine **9** (8) 36–40

Epstein, D & Wilmott, P 1997 Yield envelopes. Net Exposure **2** August www.netexposure.co.uk

Epstein, D & Wilmott, P 1998 A new model for interest rates. International Journal of Theoretical and Applied Finance, **1** 195–226

Epstein, D, Mayor, N, Schönbucher, PJ, Whalley, AE & Wilmott, P 1997 a The valuation of a firm advertising optimally. MFG Working Paper, Oxford University

Epstein, D, Mayor, N, Schönbucher, PJ, Whalley, AE & Wilmott, P 1997 b The value of market research when a firm is learning: option pricing and optimal filtering. MFG Working Paper, Oxford University

Fabozzi, FJ 1996 *Bond Markets, Analysis and Strategies*. Prentice–Hall

Fama, E 1965 The behaviour of stock prices. Journal of Business **38** 34–105

Farrell, JL Jr 1997 *Portfolio Management*. McGraw–Hill

Fitt, AD, Dewynne, JN & Wilmott, P 1994 An integral equation for the value of a stop-loss option. Proceedings of the 7th European Conference on Mathematics in Industry 399–405

Frey, R & Stremme, A 1995 Market volatility and feedback effects from dynamic hedging. Working Paper, Bonn

Garman, MB & Kohlhagen, SW 1983 Foreign currency option values. Journal of International Money and Finance **2** 231–37

Geman, H & Yor, M 1993 Bessel processes, Asian options and perpetuities. Mathematical Finance **3** 349–375

Gemmill, G 1992 *Options Pricing*. McGraw–Hill

Gerald, CF & Wheatley, PO 1992 *Applied Numerical Analysis*. Addison Wesley

Geske, R 1977 The Valuation of corporate liabilities as compound options. Journal of Financial and Quantitative Analysis **12** 541–552

Geske, R 1978 Pricing of options with stochastic dividend yield. Journal of Finance **33** 617–25

Geske, R 1979 The valuation of compound options. Journal of Financial Economics **7** 63–81

Goldman, MB, Sosin, H & Gatto, M 1979 Path dependent options: buy at the low, sell at the high. Journal of Finance **34** 1111–1128

Grindrod, P 1991 *Patterns and Waves: The theory and applications of reaction-diffusion equations.* Oxford

Haber, R, Schönbucher, PJ & Wilmott, P 1997 Parisian options. MFG Working Paper, Oxford University

Hamilton, JD 1994 *Time Series Analysis*. Princeton

Harrison, JM & Kreps, D 1979 Martingales and arbitrage in multiperiod securities markets. Journal of Economic Theory **20** 381–408

Harrison, JM & Pliska, SR 1981 Martingales and stochastic integrals in the theory of continuous trading. Stochastic Processes and their Applications **11** 215–260

Haselgrove, CB 1961 A method for numerical integration. Mathematics of Computation **15** 323–337

Heath, D, Jarrow, R & Morton, A 1992 Bond pricing and the term structure of interest rates: a new methodology. Econometrica **60** 77–105

Hendry, DF 1995 *Dynamic Econometrics*. Oxford

Henrotte, P 1993 Transaction costs and duplication strategies. Working Paper, Stanford University

Heston, S 1993 A closed-form solution for options with stochastic volatility with application to bond and currency options. Review of Financial Studies **6** 327–343

Heynen, RC & Kat, HM 1995 Lookback options with discrete and partial monitoring of the underlying price. Applied Mathematical Finance **2** 273–284

Ho, T & Lee, S 1986 Term structure movements and pricing interest rate contingent claims. Journal of Finance **42** 1129–1142

Hodges, SD & Neuberger, A 1989 Optimal replication of contingent claims under transaction costs. The Review of Futures Markets **8** 222–239

Hogan, M 1993 Problems in certain two-factor term structure models. Annals of Applied probability **3** 576

Hoggard, T, Whalley, AE & Wilmott, P 1994 Hedging option portfolios in the presence of transaction costs. Advances in Futures and Options Research **7** 21–35

Hua, P 1997 Modelling stock market crashes. Dissertation, Imperial College, London

Hua, P & Wilmott, P 1997 Crash courses. Risk magazine **10** (6) 64–67 (June)

Hull, JC & White, A 1987 The pricing of options on assets with stochastic volatilities. Journal of Finance **42** 281–300

Hull, JC & White, A 1990 Pricing interest rate derivative securities. Review of Financial Studies **3** 573–592

Hull, JC & White, A 1990 Valuing derivative securities using the finite difference method. Journal of Financial and Quantitative Analysis **25** 87–100

Hull, JC & White, A 1996 Finding the keys. In *Over the Rainbow* (Ed. R Jarrow) Risk magazine

Hyer, T, Lipton–Lifschitz, A & Pugachevsky, D 1997 Passport to success. Risk magazine **10** (9) 127–132

Jackwerth, JC & Rubinstein, M 1996 Recovering probability distributions from contemporaneous security prices. Journal of Finance **51** 1611–31

Jamshidian, F 1989 An exact bond option formula. Journal of Finance **44** 205–9

Jamshidian, F 1990 Bond and option evaluation in the gaussian interest rate model. Working Paper, Merrill Lynch Capital Markets

Jamshidian, F 1991 Forward induction and construction of yield curve diffusion models. Journal of Fixed Income, June 62–74

Jamshidian, F 1994 Hedging, quantos, differential swaps and ratios. Applied Mathematical Finance **1** 1–20

Jamshidian, F 1995 A simple class of square-root interest-rate models. Applied Mathematical Finance **2** 61–72

Jamshidian, F 1996 a Sorting out swaptions. Risk magazine **9**

Jamshidian, F 1996 b Bonds, futures and options evaluation in the quadratic interest rate model. Applied Mathematical Finance **3** 93–115

Jamshidian, F 1997 LIBOR and swap market models and measures. In Finance and Stochastics

Jarrow, R, Lando, D & Turnbull, S 1997 A Markov model for the term structure of credit spreads. Review of Financial Studies **10** 481–523

Jarrow, R & Turnbull, S 1990 Pricing options on financial securities subject to credit risk. Working paper, Cornell University, Ithaca, NY.

Jarrow, R & Turnbull, S 1995 Pricing derivatives on securities subject to credit risk. Journal of Finance **50** 53–85

Johnson, HE 1983 An analytical approximation to the American put price. Journal of Financial and Quantitative Analysis **18** 141–148

Johnson, HE 1987 Options on the maximum or minimum of several assets. Journal of Financial and Quantitative Analysis **22** 277–283

Johnson, LW & Riess, RD 1982 *Numerical Analysis.* Addison–Wesley

Jordan, DW & Smith, P 1977 *Nonlinear Ordinary Differential Equations.* Oxford

Jorion, P 1997 *Value at Risk.* Irwin

Kelly, FP, Howison, SD & Wilmott, P (Eds) 1995 *Mathematical Models in Finance.* Chapman and Hall

Kemna, AGZ & Vorst, ACF 1990 A pricing method for options based upon average asset values. Journal of Banking and Finance (March) **14** 113–129

Kim, M 1995 Modelling company mergers and takeovers. MSc thesis, Imperial College, London

Klugman, R 1992 Pricing interest rate derivative securities. M.Phil. thesis, Oxford University

Klugman, R & Wilmott, P 1994 A class of one-factor interest rate models. Proceedings of the 7th European Conference on Mathematics in Industry 419–426

Korn, R & Wilmott, P 1996 a Option prices and subjective beliefs. To appear in International Journal of Theoretical and Applied Finance.

Korn, R & Wilmott, P 1996 b Room for a view. MFG Working Paper, Oxford University

Kruske, RA & Keller, JB 1998 Optimal exercise boundary for an American put option. To appear in Applied Mathematical Finance

Lacoste, V 1996 Wiener chaos: a new approach to option pricing. Mathematical Finance **6** 197–213

Lando, D 1994 a Three essays on contingent claims pricing. Ph.D. thesis, Graduate School of Management, Cornell University

Lando, D 1994 b On Cox processes and credit risky bonds. Working Paper, Institute of Mathematical Statistics, University of Copenhagen

Lawrence, D 1996 *Measuring and Managing Derivative Market Risk.* International Thompson Business Press

Leland, HE 1985 Option pricing and replication with transaction costs. Journal of Finance **40** 1283–1301

Levy, E 1990 Asian arithmetic. Risk magazine **3** (5) (May) 7–8

Lewicki, P & Avellaneda, M 1996 Pricing interest rate contingent claims in markets with uncertain volatilities. CIMS Preprint

Litterman, R & Iben, T 1991 Corporate bond valuation and the term structure of credit spreads. Financial Analysts Journal (Spring) 52–64

Longstaff, FA & Schwartz, ES 1992 A two-factor interest rate model and contingent claims valuation. Journal of Fixed Income **3** 16–23

Longstaff, FA & Schwartz, ES 1994 A simple approach to valuing risky fixed and floating rate debt. Working Paper, Anderson Graduate School of Management, University of California, Los Angeles

Lyons, TJ 1995 Uncertain volatility and the risk-free synthesis of derivatives. Applied Mathematical Finance **2** 117–133

Madan, DB & Unal, H 1994 Pricing the risks of default. Working Paper, College of Business and Management, University of Maryland

Mandelbrot, B 1963 The variation of certain speculative prices. Journal of Business **36** 394–419

Margrabe, 1978 The value of an option to exchange one asset for another. Journal of Finance **33** 177–186

Matten, C 1996 *Managing Bank Capital.* John Wiley

McMillan, LG 1996 *McMillan on Options.* John Wiley

Mercurio, F & Vorst, TCF 1996 Option pricing with hedging at fixed trading dates. Applied Mathematical Finance **3** 135–158

Merton, RC 1973 Theory of rational option pricing. Bell Journal of Econonomics and Management Science **4** 141–83

Merton, RC 1974 On the pricing of corporate debt: the risk structure of interest rates. Journal of Finance **29** 449–470

Merton, RC 1976 Option pricing when underlying stock returns are discontinuous. Journal of Financial Econonomics **3** 125–44

Miron, P & Swannell, P 1991 *Pricing and Hedging Swaps*. Euromoney Publications

Mitchell, AR & Griffiths, DF 1980 *The Finite Difference Method in Partial Differential Equations*. John Wiley

Mohamed, B 1994 Simulation of transaction costs and optimal rehedging. Applied Mathematical Finance **1** 49–62

Morton, A & Pliska, SR 1995 Optimal portfolio management with fixed transaction costs. Mathematical Finance **5** 337–356

Murphy, G 1995 Generalised methods of moments estimation of the short process in the UK. Bank of England Working Paper

Murray, J 1989 *Mathematical Biology*. Springer–Verlag

Naik, V 1993 Option valuation and hedging strategies with jumps in the volatility of asset returns. Journal of Finance **48** 1969–1984

Nelson, D 1990 Arch models as diffusion approximations. Journal of Econometrics **45** 7–38

Neuberger, A 1994 Option replication with transaction costs: an exact solution for the pure jump process. Advances in Futures and options Research **7** 1–20

Niederreiter, H 1992 *Random Number Generation and Quasi-Monte Carlo Methods*. SIAM

Nielson, JA & Sandmann, K 1996 The pricing of Asian options under stochastic interest rates. Applied Mathematical Finance **3** 209–236

Ninomiya, S & Tezuka, S 1996 Toward real-time pricing of complex financial derivatives. Applied Mathematical Finance **3** 1–20

Nyborg, KG 1996 The use and pricing of convertible bonds. Applied Mathematical Finance **3** 167–190

O'Hara, M 1995 *Market Microstructure Theory*. Blackwell

Options Institute 1995 *Options: Essential Concepts and Trading Strategies*. Irwin

Oztukel, A 1996 Uncertain parameter models. M.Sc. dissertation, Oxford University

Oztukel, A & Wilmott, P 1998 Uncertain parameters, an empirical stochastic volatility model and confidence limits. International Journal of Theoretical and Applied Finance **1** 175–189

Paskov 1996 New methodologies for valuing derivatives. In *Mathematics of Derivative Securities* (Eds Pliska and Dempster)

Paskov, SH & Traub, JF 1995 Faster valuation of financial derivatives. Journal of Portfolio Managament. Fall 113–120

Pearson, N & Sun, T–S 1989 A test of the Cox, Ingersoll, Ross model of the term structure of interest rates using the method of moments. Sloan School of Management, MIT

Penaud, A, Wilmott, P & Ahn, H 1998 Exotic passport options. MFG Working Paper, Oxford University

Peters, EE 1991 *Chaos and Order in the Capital Markets*. John Wiley

Peters, EE 1994 *Fractal Market Analysis*. John Wiley

Porter, DP & Smith, VL 1994 Stock market bubbles in the laboratory. Applied Mathematical Finance **1** 111–128

Ramamurtie, S, Prezas, A & Ulman, S 1993 Consistency and identification problems in models of term structure of interest rates. Working Paper, Georgia State University

Rebonato, R 1996 *Interest-rate Option Models.* John Wiley

Rich, D & Chance, D 1993 An alternative approach to the pricing of options on multiple assets. Journal of Financial Engineering **2** 271–85

Richtmyer, RD & Morton, KW 1976 *Difference Methods for Initial-value Problems.* John Wiley

Roache PJ 1982 *Computational Fluid Dynamics.* Hermosa, Albuquerque, NM

Roll, R 1977 An analytical formula for unprotected American call options on stocks with known dividends. Journal of Financial Economics **5** 251–258

Rubinstein, M 1991 Somewhere over the rainbow. Risk magazine **4** 10

Rubinstein, M 1994 Implied binomial trees. Journal of Finance **69** 771–818

Rupf, I, Dewynne, JN, Howison, SD & Wilmott, P 1993 Some mathematical results in the pricing of American options. European Journal of Applied Mathematics **4** 381–398

Sandmann, K & Sondermann, D 1994 On the stability of lognormal interest rate models. Working Paper, University of Bonn, Department of Economics

Schönbucher, PJ 1994 The feedback effect of hedging in illiquid markets. M.Sc. thesis, Oxford University

Schönbucher, PJ 1996 The term structure of defaultable bond prices. Discussion Paper B–384, University of Bonn

Schönbucher, PJ 1997 a Modelling defaultable bond prices. Working Paper, London School of Economics, Financial Markets Group

Schönbucher, PJ 1997 b Pricing credit risk derivatives. Working Paper, London School of Economics, Financial Markets Group

Schönbucher, PJ 1998 A review of credit risk and credit derivative modelling. To appear in Applied Mathematical Finance **5**

Schönbucher, PJ & Wilmott, P 1995 a Hedging in illiquid markets: nonlinear effects. Proceedings of the 8th European Conference on Mathematics in Industry

Schönbucher, PJ & Wilmott, P 1995 b The feedback effect of hedging in illiquid markets. MFG Working Paper, Oxford University

Schönbucher, PJ & Schlögl, E 1996 Credit derivatives and competition in the loan market. Working Paper, University of Bonn, Department of Statistics

Shore, S 1997 The modelling of credit risk and its applications to credit derivatives. M.Sc. dissertation, Oxford University

Sircar, KR & Papanicolaou, G 1996 General Black–Scholes models accounting for increased market volatility from hedging strategies. Stanford University, Working Paper

Sloan, IH & Walsh, L 1990 A computer search of rank two lattice rules for multidimensional quadrature. Mathematics of Computation **54** 281–302

Sneddon, I 1957 *Elements of Partial Differential Equations*. McGraw–Hill

Stetson, C, Marshall, S & Loeball, D 1995 Laudable lattices. Risk magazine **8** (12) 60–63 (December)

Strang, G 1986 *Introduction to Applied Mathematics*. Wellesley–Cambridge

Stulz, RM 1982 Options on the minimum or maximum of two risky assets. Journal of Financial Economics **10** 161–185

Swift, J 1726 *Travels into Several Remote Nations of the World... by Lemuel Gulliver* B. Motte, London.

Thorp, EO & Kassouf, S 1967 *Beat the Market*. Random House

Traub, JF & Wozniakowski, H 1994 Breaking intractability. Scientific American Jan 102–107

Ungar, E 1996 *Swap Literacy*. Bloomberg

Vasicek, OA 1977 An equilibrium characterization of the term structure. Journal of Financial Economics **5** 177–188

Vose, D 1997 *Quantitative Risk Analysis: A guide to Monte Carlo simulation modelling*. John Wiley

Whaley, RE 1981 On the valuation of American call options on stocks with known dividends. Journal of Financial Economics **9** 207–211

Whaley, RE 1993 Derivatives on market volatility: hedging tools long overdue. Journal of Derivatives **1** 71–84

Whalley, AE & Wilmott, P 1993 a Counting the costs. Risk magazine **6** (10) 59–66 (October)

Whalley, AE & Wilmott, P 1993 b Option pricing with transaction costs. MFG Working Paper, Oxford

Whalley, AE & Wilmott, P 1994 a Hedge with an edge. Risk magazine **7** (10) 82–85 (October)

Whalley, AE & Wilmott, P 1994 b A comparison of hedging strategies. Proceedings of the 7th European Conference on Mathematics in Industry 427–434

Whalley, AE & Wilmott, P 1995 An asymptotic analysis of the Davis, Panas and Zariphopoulou model for option pricing with transaction costs. MFG Working Paper, Oxford University

Whalley, AE & Wilmott, P 1996 Key results in discrete hedging and transaction costs. In *Frontiers in Derivatives* (Ed. Konishi and Dattatreya.) 183–196

Whalley, AE & Wilmott, P 1997 An asymptotic analysis of an optimal hedging model for option pricing with transaction costs. Mathematical Finance **7** 307–324

Wilmott, P 1994 Discrete charms. Risk magazine **7** (3) 48–51 (March)

Wilmott, P 1995 Volatility smiles revisited. Derivatives Week **4** (38) 8

Wilmott, P & Wilmott, S 1990 Dispersion of pollutant along a river, an asymptotic analysis. OCIAM Working Paper

Zhang, PG 1997 *Exotic Options*. World Scientific

Index

THE ACCOMPANYING CD

There's something to interest everyone on the CD which accompanies my book. There are demos of commercial software, spreadsheets and code illustrating models and methods from the book, cutting-edge research articles from famous names in derivatives, and data, document and demo from CrashMetrics, the Value at Risk methodology (there's even a jpeg of me to which you can add a moustache if you like).

For a more detailed description of the contents and information on installing the software take a look at the 'Hello' document. This also contains links to websites of particular interest. Updates and corrections will be found on www.wilmott.com.

The directory structure of the CD is as follows:

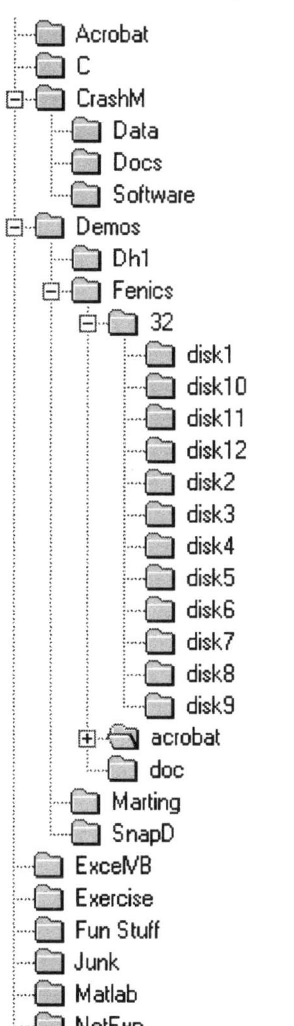

Adobe Acrobat Acrobat Reader 3 for reading pdf files; there are several such documents on the CD.

C Programs written in C by my postdoc Hyungsok Ahn.

CrashMetrics Data, documentation and software for the CrashMetrics methodology.

Demos Demonstration software from several vendors: DH1 Software Ltd, Inventure (developers of FENICS), Martingale Systems Inc. and SnapDragon.

ExcelVB Excel spreadsheets and Visual Basic code demonstrating various models.

Exercises Pdf and LaTeX files of all the Exercises that appear in the book.

Fun Stuff Demonstration Blackjack software.

Junk Miscellaneous html documents for hello.htm.

Matlab Programs written in Matlab by my student Varqa Khadem.

NetExp Articles from the electronic financial journal.

...ok, so a tiny proportion of the CD concerns my own commercial ventures but, heck, I've been restrained.

If you require any further assistance please do not hesitate to contact:

Wiley Customer Service
Technical Support Group
Tel: +44 (0) 1243 843 312
Fax: +44 (0) 1243 843 315
Email: cs-electronic@wiley.co.uk

WILEY COPYRIGHT INFORMATION AND TERMS OF USE

CD supplement to Derivatives: The theory and practice of financial engineering